THE OXFORD HANDBOOK OF

CENTRAL AMERICAN HISTORY

THE OXFORD HANDBOOK OF

CENTRAL AMERICAN HISTORY

Edited by
ROBERT H. HOLDEN

Oxford University Press is a department of the University of Oxford. It furthers
the University's objective of excellence in research, scholarship, and education
by publishing worldwide. Oxford is a registered trade mark of Oxford University
Press in the UK and certain other countries.

Published in the United States of America by Oxford University Press
198 Madison Avenue, New York, NY 10016, United States of America.

© Oxford University Press 2022

All rights reserved. No part of this publication may be reproduced, stored in
a retrieval system, or transmitted, in any form or by any means, without the
prior permission in writing of Oxford University Press, or as expressly permitted
by law, by license, or under terms agreed with the appropriate reproduction
rights organization. Inquiries concerning reproduction outside the scope of the
above should be sent to the Rights Department, Oxford University Press, at the
address above.

You must not circulate this work in any other form
and you must impose this same condition on any acquirer.

Library of Congress Control Number: 2022012628
ISBN 978–0–19–092836–0

DOI: 10.1093/oxfordhb/9780190928360.001.0001

1 3 5 7 9 8 6 4 2

Printed by Marquis, Canada

About the Editor

ROBERT H. Holden is a professor of Latin American history at Old Dominion University. He is the author of *Armies Without Nations: Public Violence and State Formation in Central America, 1821–1960*; the coauthor, with Rina Villars, of *Contemporary Latin America: 1970 to the Present*; and contributed the essay on modern Latin America to volume four of *The Cambridge World History of Violence*.

Contents

Contributors	xi
Note about the Cover Image	xiii

Introduction: Interpreting the History of a Region in Crisis   1
    Robert H. Holden

PART I: HUMAN AND TERRITORIAL CONTEXTS

1 Land and Climate: Natural Constraints and Socio-Environmental
   Transformations   27
   Anthony Goebel McDermott

2 Regaining Ground: Indigenous Populations and Territories   57
   Peter H. Herlihy, Matthew L. Fahrenbruch,
   and Taylor A. Tappan

3 The Ancient Civilizations   81
   William R. Fowler

4 Marginalization, Assimilation, and Resurgence: The Indigenous
   Peoples since Independence   107
   Wolfgang Gabbert

PART II: CONQUEST, COLONIALIZATION, AND THE PATH TO SELF-RULE

5 The Spanish Conquest?   141
   Laura E. Matthew

6 Central America under Spanish Colonial Rule   167
   Stephen Webre

7 The Kingdom of Guatemala as a Cultural Crossroads   191
   Brianna Leavitt-Alcántara

viii CONTENTS

8 From Kingdom to Republics, 1808–1840   219
   AARON POLLACK

PART III: CHALLENGES OF MODERNITY SINCE C. 1840: THE REGIONAL FRAME

9 The Political Economy   253
   ROBERT G. WILLIAMS

10 State-Making and Nation-Building   285
    DAVID DÍAZ ARIAS

11 Central America and the United States   309
    MICHEL GOBAT

12 The Cold War: Authoritarianism, Empire, and Social Revolution   335
    JOAQUÍN M. CHÁVEZ

13 Central America since the 1990s: Crime, Violence, and
    the Pursuit of Democracy   359
    CHRISTINE J. WADE

14 The Rise and Retreat of the Armed Forces   379
    ORLANDO J. PÉREZ AND RANDY PESTANA

15 Religion, Politics, and the State   403
    BONAR L. HERNÁNDEZ SANDOVAL

16 Women in Central America since Independence   431
    EUGENIA RODRÍGUEZ SÁENZ

17 Literature, Society, and Politics   455
    WERNER MACKENBACH

PART IV: CHALLENGES OF MODERNITY SINCE C. 1840: THE NATIONAL FRAME

18 Guatemala   485
    DAVID CAREY JR.

19 Honduras   519
    DARIO A. EURAQUE

20	El Salvador ERIK CHING	545
21	Nicaragua JULIE A. CHARLIP	567
22	Costa Rica IVÁN MOLINA	591
23	Panama MICHAEL E. DONOGHUE	615
24	Belize MARK MOBERG	637

Index   659

Contributors

David Carey Jr., Doehler Chair in History, Loyola University

Julie A. Charlip, Professor of History, Whitman College

Joaquín M. Chávez, Associate Professor of History, University of Illinois at Chicago

Erik Ching, Professor of History, Furman University

David Díaz Arias, Director of the Centro de Investigaciones Historicas de America Central, Universidad de Costa Rica

Michael E. Donoghue, Associate Professor of History, Marquette University

Dario A. Euraque, Professor of History & International Studies, Trinity College, Hartford, CT

Matthew L. Fahrenbruch, PhD Candidate, Department of Geography and Atmospheric Science, University of Kansas

William R. Fowler, Associate Professor of Mesoamerican archaeology and ethnohistory, Vanderbilt University

Wolfgang Gabbert, Professor of Development Sociology and Cultural Anthropology, Leibniz University Hannover

Michel Gobat, Professor of History, University of Pittsburgh

Anthony Goebel McDermott, Professor of the Department of History, Researcher of the Center for Central American Historical Studies (CIHAC), and Director of the Postgraduate Program in History, University of Costa Rica

Peter H. Herlihy, Professor of Geography, University of Kansas

Bonar L. Hernández Sandoval, Associate Professor, Department of History, Iowa State University

Robert H. Holden, Professor of Latin American History, Old Dominion University

Brianna Leavitt-Alcántara, Associate Professor of History, University of Cincinati

Werner Mackenbach, Researcher and Professor, Centro de Investigaciones Históricas de América Central (CIHAC)

Laura E. Matthew, Associate Professor of southern Mesoamerica and Central America, Marquette University

Mark Moberg, Professor of Anthropology, University of South Alabama

Iván Molina, Professor of History, University of Costa Rica

Orlando J. Pérez, Dean and Professor of Political Science, University of North Texas at Dallas

Randy Pestana, Assistant Director, Jack D. Gordon Institute for Public Policy, Florida International University

Aaron Pollack, Professor and Researcher, Centro de Investigaciones y Estudios Superiores en Antropología Social (CIESAS)–Sureste

Eugenia Rodríguez Sáenz, Professor of History, University of Costa Rica

Taylor A. Tappan, PhD Candidate, Department of Geography and Atmospheric Science, University of Kansas

Christine J. Wade, Professor of Political Science and International Studies, Washington College

Stephen Webre, Professor Emeritus of History, Louisiana Tech University

Robert G. Williams, Voehringer Professor of Economics, Guilford College, Greensboro, NC

COVER IMAGE

PAINTED limestone relief, La Pasadita, Guatemala, ca. 770 AD, signed by the court artist Chakalte'. Designed to decorate the dome of a Mayan palace entryway, this one-yard-square sculpture commemorates the visit of Tiloom (middle figure), the local ruler of La Pasadita, to Shield Jaguar IV (seated), the god-king of Yaxchilan (today, Chiapas, Mexico). Tiloom is paying homage to Shield Jaguar IV by presenting him a headdress with his left hand and what might be packets of incense or a plate of tamales in his right hand. The hat worn by the figure behind Tiloom was associated with traders. Political rivalry between Yaxchilan and the Guatemalan kingdom of Piedras Negras forced smaller polities like La Pasadita to choose between them. Entitled "Relief with Enthroned Ruler," the sculpture is part of the Michael C. Rockefeller Memorial Collection, Bequest of Nelson A. Rockefeller, 1979, the Metropolitan Museum of Art, New York.

INTRODUCTION

INTERPRETING THE HISTORY
OF A REGION IN CRISIS

ROBERT H. HOLDEN

THE seven countries of Central America (Belize, Costa Rica, El Salvador, Guatemala, Honduras, Nicaragua, and Panama) comprise Latin America's most cohesive region. Defined above all by its geographical unity as the isthmus separating the world's two great oceans, to a lesser but still sufficiently homogeneous extent, their regional identity also springs from the persistence of socioeconomic and political patterns that have consistently inspired recourse to the word "crisis" among its own peoples, as well as among scholars of the region's past and present. Indeed, if there is one idea of Central America that the historiography has converged upon across the decades, it is that of a region afflicted by a sequence of grave emergencies since 1821, the year of its self-declared and largely nonviolent exit from three centuries of comparatively equable rule by the Spanish monarchy. Disparate in character and origin, the crises have yielded up a grim *histoire événementielle* of violence, instability, and lawlessness. As the most durable, visible, and moving signs of continuity in the region's post-independence history, together they pose the problem of a region gripped by a secular crisis of order.

In broad terms, the historiography of the region since independence can fairly be said to locate the foundational motif of the crisis of order in cycles of putatively progressive ascent, challenged in turn by an array of long-standing internal norms, interests, and structures on the one hand and by hostile entities anchored outside the region on the other. According to this view, the justifications for reform or revolution in any of their diverse and protean liberalistic, democratic, or socialistic versions of what counts as enlightened change, and the reactionary counterrevolt they inevitably inspire, generate the crisis of order and keep it going. By the mid-twentieth century, "revolution" had come to signify a broadly popular quest (violent or nonviolent) for some combination of long-denied, liberal-democratic institutions, plus more or less radical, state-directed redistributions of wealth. Central America, in a phrase popularized by a historian in the 1980s, had thus become the land of "inevitable revolutions," an admirably synoptic expression of the apparent wellspring inside the region's secular crisis of order.[1]

Indeed, the 1980s seemed to gather up a century and half of strife in a single inescapable juncture by uniting reformers and revolutionaries in a final assault on military-oligarchic despotism and entrenched social inequities across Central America. Occupying regional center stage was the new, and authentically revolutionary, government of Nicaragua. Having seized power in 1979 against all odds, it owed its legitimacy to its success as the leading force in a popular uprising against a long-standing dictatorship. At almost the very moment of its triumph, civil war broke out in El Salvador between the united guerrilla armies of a coalition of reformers and revolutionaries and the Salvadoran armed forces, which had owned and operated the Salvadoran government for decades. On Nicaragua's northern and southern flanks, Honduras and Costa Rica, encouraged and compensated by the United States, lent their borders to guerrilla armies intent on replacing Nicaragua's revolutionary government with the liberal-democratic reformers whose alliance with the revolutionaries in power had soured and turned them into counterrevolutionaries. Farther north and west, the guerrilla warriors of a prospective Guatemalan revolution persisted in their two-decade battle against yet another military dictatorship, which by the early 1980s sought victory by massively targeting civilians suspected of revolutionary sympathies.

The 1980s ended ignominiously, in disappointment for the revolutionaries and a Pyrrhic victory for their nominally victorious opponents. The one unmistakable sign of success for the revolutionaries and their allies was the withdrawal of the armed forces from formal control of government and their replacement by elected civilians. Yet neither elections nor demilitarization resolved the crisis of order, whose persistence in the wake of the bloodiest decade in the region's history revealed not the inevitability of revolution (now decisively extinguished) after all but continuity in the reign of lawless violence. By all accounts, criminal violence exploded after the 1990s and reached world-record levels, abetted by states so systematically corrupt, feeble, and inept that analysts began referring to the phenomenon of "state capture" and of corruption as an "operating system."[2] In 2020, the El Salvador branch of the Facultad Latinoamericana de Ciencias Sociales (FLACSO), long the privileged rendezvous of Latin America's progressive intelligentsia, acknowledged the failure in Central America of both the "revolution as a solution" and the "neoliberal paradigm" of economic development that followed the 1980s. Today, FLACSO continued, Central America confronts

> a dangerous democratic retreat whose most obvious manifestations are the return in some countries of dictatorial, authoritarian and repressive regimes, the return of the military to politics, the deterioration of democratic institutions and the appearance of populist and authoritarian views and positions that threaten to violate the rule of law and the rules of the democratic game. This situation, added to the corruption scandals and the crisis of the traditional political parties and their leaderships, has led to ungovernability in some countries and further weakened the nation-states, some of which have been penetrated by drug trafficking and criminal groups. Added to this discouraging political panorama has been the increase in citizen insecurity

generated by the increase in violence and crime registered in the last decade in the region, particularly in El Salvador, Guatemala and Honduras, which in turn are the main countries of origin of migration to the United States. The decline in democracy and the increase in insecurity have been accompanied by stagnation in some economic and social indicators that had previously improved and, in some cases, by an increase in poverty and inequality.

As a result, the statement called variously for a "new narrative" and for the formulation of a new "general interpretative framework" sufficiently robust to both (a) explain the deep sources of the isthmus's multiple afflictions, and (b) to point the way toward a program of action capable of rectifying them.[3]

Well before the FLACSO initiative of 2020, some of those who had found hope in revolution had already adopted a "new narrative" affirming or implying that the inevitable may have turned out to be impossible after all. An attentive reader of Greg Grandin's widely cited 2004 study of post-World War II Guatemala would be hard pressed to find a ray of hope that it, or indeed any Latin American country, might ever reverse the legacies of the counterrevolutionary wave of violence, state terror, and genocide unleashed by the United States during the Cold War, which destroyed democracy and condemned the continent to poverty, inequality, racism, and sexual exploitation.[4] In 2018, Central America's leading historian, Héctor Pérez-Brignoli, detected the foundational motif of the crisis of order in the region's chronic propensity for violence—"recurrent," "multi-dimensional," and "structural," forever falling disproportionately on the poor, at least outside Costa Rica.[5] Not a trace remained of the summary interpretation of the region's woes that Pérez-Brignoli had proffered in the closing pages of the same book's 1985 edition. Then, he attributed the source of the general crisis to "the failures of the dominant classes," people whose "domination . . . rested exclusively on exploitation, violence and terror." While the Costa Rican model of gradual reform might work for Honduras, revolution and socialism on the Nicaraguan model were apposite elsewhere in the isthmus.[6]

Among the intellectuals most explicitly dispirited by the results of the revolutionary option was the Guatemalan historical sociologist Edelberto Torres-Rivas, secretary-general of FLACSO from 1985 to 1993 and perhaps the most erudite and influential of the vanguard of researchers who broke open the field of Central American studies in the 1970s. Like most of his cohort, as well as the generation of investigators who immediately followed, he was a scholar-activist for whom the region's main hope for advancement lay in radical reform if not social revolution, the scientific rationale for which he spent a lifetime documenting. Yet seven years before his death in 2018 at the age of 88, Torres-Rivas seemed overtaken by despair at the region's cyclical fate. Its contemporary history, he wrote in 2011, told of an "anguished and tormented region, full of rebellions and failures, and with a history of perseverance in making society less unjust. We haven't achieved it." The experience of the late twentieth century taught both "the necessity of revolution and the impossibility of attaining it." The self-negating character of the latter phrase—for what is impossible cannot be necessary, and to choose an impossible option is necessarily to choose failure—captured the essence of Central America's long crisis of order and the despair that now accompanied it. Heeding a "self-critical, *ex-post* impulse," Torres-Rivas asked himself whether the path of guerrilla warfare, with its aim of defeating the bourgeoisie and erecting a "radical" state, was ever even possible. "Of course it wasn't," he answered. The correct option in the 1970s would have been to cooperate with the democratic reformers among the hated bourgeoisie. Hence, futility and perhaps a sense of regret or even guilt, as suggested by the searing question that closed an essay he had written in 1997: "¿Valió la pena, para dejar en el camino 300.000 muertos, un millón de refugiados, 100.000 huérfanos?" (Was it worth leaving behind 300,000 dead, a million refugees, 100,000 orphans?)"[7] A courageous question, it failed to elicit even a tentative, exploratory response from its author.

About the same time, Rev. Próspero Penados del Barrio, archbishop-primate of Guatemala, was pondering the same question. In 1998, he posed and answered it. "Who was the victor in this war? We all lost. I do not believe that anyone is cynical enough to raise the flag of victory over the remains of thousands of Guatemalans—fathers, mothers, brothers and sisters, and young children—innocent of the inferno that consumed them." All who participated in the war, either directly or indirectly, must acknowledge their guilt and seek forgiveness:

> But they are not the only ones; society as a whole must engage in a process of reflection that reaches into the far corners of the collective conscience in order to enter into a period of transformation in the aftermath of the horrors that are only beginning to come to light. For this transformation to be genuine, however, we all—each sector of society—must acknowledge our faults, by commission or omission, and radically change our attitude towards our fellow human beings.[8]

According to the view of Penados del Barrio, hope for change—the advent of "a period of transformation"—depended not on contriving a "new narrative," much less yet another "general interpretative framework," but rather on a repudiation and an affirmation, the political implications of which were hard to miss: (a) that Guatemalans reject the conventional politics of class, party, and ethnic enmity as well as the mutually hostile ideologies that have stoked them over the decades; (b) that they would make not a revolution but a nation, a community of citizens whose loyalty to the good of the whole might effectively interrupt the violence and break the historic cycle of revolt and counterrevolt. In appealing to society as a whole to examine its "collective conscience" with a view toward a transformation in attitudes and the forging of a consensus on fundamental values strong enough to hold power holders and power seekers to account, Penados del Barrio implicitly posed what I argue below in the section "Authority and Power" is the historical problem at the heart of Central America's long crisis of order: The separation of power from a socially recognized, legitimacy-defining authority to which power remains accountable. As an unintended consequence of the rupture with the Spanish monarchy that commenced abruptly in 1808, power's separation from an authority capable of constraining it only deepened over the decades, in ways that continually thwarted the search for legitimacy and therefore order.

HISTORIOGRAPHICAL CONTINUITIES

Before introducing that topic, however, I would first like to briefly develop the theme I introduced at the outset: that of the two-century preeminence in the historiography of a society perpetually subject to a standoff between impractical aspirations and unbending resistance. When the liberal publicist and prolific historian Lorenzo Montúfar (1823–1898) looked back on the first six decades of independence, which coincided almost exactly with his own life span, he observed: "In all our history, what dominates is the incessant struggle between the present and the past, between the men who are dragging us back to the Middle Ages and the men who are pushing us forward."[9] In this, Montúfar—perhaps that century's activist-scholar counterpart of Torres-Rivas—prefigured the late-life conversions of both Torres-Rivas and Pérez-Brignoli from linear progressivism to cyclical inevitability. Between the age of Montúfar and the age of Torres-Rivas was that of the Nicaraguan Salvador Mendieta (1882–1958), perhaps the shrewdest analyst of Central America's history. In *La enfermedad de Centro-América* (*The Sickness of Central America*), Mendieta recapitulated Montúfar:

> Neither those in power nor those in opposition tolerate one another. The one in power does not recognize the justice of any opposition and therefore denies it all means of serene and reasoned discourse. The opponent never thinks the government is well intentioned and fights it with systematic tenacity. Unable to operate in the light of day, it is necessary to seek out the shadows; not being permitted to take a step on the surface, it is necessary to take subterranean action. That is why armed revolution is always latent in Central America.... The governments say that they oppress to avoid revolutions, and the revolutionaries say they rise up in order to free the people from the oppression of the governments.[10]

By the second half of the twentieth century, many historians, with Torres-Rivas and Pérez-Brignoli in the vanguard, softened the Sisyphian overtones of the Montúfar-Mendieta consensus by locating the multiple expressions of the aspirations for change, and the resistance they provoked, somewhere within the spacious confines of the concept of social revolution. Fortified by the historicist premises of the inevitability of class conflict and its redemptive dénouement, progressive ascent, social revolution was a narrative sufficiently flexible to be shared by liberals and Marxists alike. The older, grimmer assessment never faded entirely, however. In 1982, Torres-Rivas himself even reiterated, in a distinctly cyclical voice, Mendieta's equation of intolerance with sickness, observing that since the nineteenth century, political intolerance had turned politics into warfare, "a sickness . . . that is contagious and endemic."[11]

Despite, then, their mutual distance in time and ideology, the interpretations of Pérez-Brignoli and Torres-Rivas and Montúfar and Mendieta converge on the postulate of a region in torment, casting about for an exit in the form of one or another overarching program of betterment or "development" whose diverse advocates—whether incumbents or insurgents—can be counted on to scorn appeals to incremental or negotiated change while denying legitimate standing to their opponents. Hence, the ubiquity and inevitability of "revolutionary" attempts to rearrange institutions and structures in defiance of law and constitution. Hence too the inevitable summoning of enemies, external and internal. Calls to arms, accompanied by a rhetoric of demonization and appeals to mutual extermination, typically follow.[12]

THE GREAT RUPTURE OF 1808–1821

The interpretative continuity across the work of Montúfar, Mendieta, Torres-Rivas, and Pérez-Brignoli as encapsulated here, and as ratified by the tidal wave of research published over the last half-century, uncloaks the travails of a region possessed by a secular crisis of order whose proximate origin is not difficult to pinpoint. The great rupture of 1808–1821, when the Kingdom of Guatemala separated from the monarchy of Spain, remains the most transformative moment in Central America's history, second only to its violent incorporation into the monarchy in the sixteenth century. But to a degree unsurpassed across Spanish America, the French-imposed abdications of May 6, 1808, and their dramatic sequelae of peninsular invasion, occupation, resistance, and political reform stimulated only the slightest popular interest in independence in the Kingdom of Guatemala. Encompassing the entire territory of modern Central America minus Panama, plus today's Mexican state of Chiapas, the kingdom numbered about 1 million souls of whom 65 percent were Indigenous, some 30 percent mestizo, and no more than 4 percent White. Only within the latter group, divided between *criollos* (American-born Spaniards) and *peninsulares* (Spanish-born Spaniards), could be found the handful of men who directed the political and economic affairs of the kingdom. Unlike neighboring New Spain, the richest jewel in the crown of Spain, in Guatemala the momentous events of the decade and a half that followed the abdications and terminated in full independence would unfold without the involvement of the general populace, and with almost no violence.

To most creoles and peninsulares in Guatemala, the priority was the maintenance of order and solidarity with the local officials who continued to govern in the name of the deposed sovereign, Ferdinand VII. Among political activists, those who favored autonomy within a reformed Spanish constitutional monarchy, as opposed to full independence, outnumbered the latter until about 1820, after which any dependent status inferior to independence increasingly fell out of reach as a practical alternative. The constitutional monarchy at stake in this debate was not a theoretical one. It was erected in 1812 by the Spanish and American delegates (among whom were Guatemala's six) to the Cortes Extraordinarias that began meeting in Cádiz, Spain in 1810. Its constitution declared that sovereignty resided in the nation and defined the Spanish nation as the body of all free men born in the dominions of Spain. The constitution earned the exuberant endorsement of the colonial governing class, even including the archbishop of

Guatemala City, Ramón Casaus, for whom it was the constitution that was "the wisest and most equitable, the most worthy of the admiration of the world and of immortality."[13] But by 1821, owing above all to the increasing volatility and instability of the Spanish regime itself, independence had displaced autonomy as the preferred option within the ranks of the politically active elite, here as elsewhere in Spanish America.[14]

AUTHORITY AND POWER: THE COORDINATES OF POLITICAL LIFE

As a result, the great challenge awaiting the peoples of the kingdom in 1821 was not solely the design and construction of new political institutions suitable for self-governing republics. In order to deepen and, I hope, illuminate further the origins and persistence of Central America's long crisis of order, I propose as a tool of analysis the venerable distinction between power (*potestas*) and authority (*auctoritas*) as two fundamental but radically independent coordinates of political life. Power invariably acts in response to authority, its transcendent and therefore hierarchically superior epistemic complement.[15] Itself powerless and dependent on social recognition, authority dictates the criteria of legitimacy and thus the fitness to rule of the claimants to power. Authority cannot impede or execute; limited in expression to the word, it can only endorse or condemn. A socially recognized authority before which power kneels is thus essential to order. Sovereignty, as one of its preeminent theorists, Daniel Philpott, observed, is in fact always "accountable to something larger than itself."[16] Central America's extended crisis of order was therefore not owing solely to the destruction of the institutions of political power but even more to power's sudden separation from a socially recognized authority. The conditions under which such an authority would have had to be reasserted were particularly inauspicious, not only in the Kingdom of Guatemala but across the Hispanic American world, given the brutal abruptness with which a stable arrangement of power (Crown) and legitimacy-bestowing authority (Church) had been terminated. The collapse of the Spanish monarchy separated the Americans from a governing entity in which the *potestas* of monarchy and the *auctoritas* of religion, though overlapping rather than strictly separated, had together managed to generate and sustain order for more than three centuries.

Before 1808, what Edward Norman called the "Christendom" model still prevailed in the Hispanic world, in that the political and religious fields of action were still largely coextensive.[17] For William Taylor, Hispanic life until the late eighteenth century was governed by the "two majesties" of "the crown as father and the church as mother of the Hispanic family. Or the two together as the collective head of the social body."[18] The Enlightenment, in the words of Fernández Sebastian, did nothing to dislodge the Catholic worldview from its status as "the very center" of the system of beliefs that framed Hispanic life; that, in turn, made it difficult even to conceive of religion and politics as separate entities, long after such a possibility had become thinkable elsewhere in Europe. For a time even after 1808, it remained "virtually impossible to conceive of a totally secular sovereignty" anywhere in the Hispanic world.[19] "A public morality completely soaked in religious values," according to Guerra and Lempérière, left no space for contrary behavior and yet contributed to the maintenance of a juridical order that was widely shared and respected across social groupings. Independence therefore entailed a struggle to reconstruct that "lost consensus" with new values.[20] In a synthesis of the recent historiography of the question, Portillo Valdés argued that even the late Bourbon monarchy was thoroughly Catholic in an essential and constitutional sense. The Hispanic world was understood to be "una república de católicos" to such an extent that the framers of the 1812 Constitution famously (but vainly) posited religion as the very foundation of national identity, an attempt to "give continuity to the Catholic monarchy as a nation, where the moral ideal of the Catholic citizens of the Hispanic Enlightenment might find their means of development."[21]

In the Kingdom of Guatemala, relations between throne and altar adhered to the pattern just characterized for Spanish America as a whole. If the Church was "the bedrock of Hapsburg rule" in Guatemala, it remained so well into the Bourbon eighteenth century.[22] The surprising stability of Spanish rule in Guatemala was owed neither to military power nor to a notably "weak and underdeveloped" civil administrative apparatus but, rather, in Oss's estimate, to the Catholic clergy, "who provided the nerves and sinews guaranteeing continued colonial presence," particularly in their role as the guardian of the basic unit of Spanish society, the family. Spain prevailed because, in obedience to the Medieval and theocentric worldview still shared by few other colonizing powers, it "presented a single faith and a single order."[23] More recently, Belaubre has posited a degree of symbiosis between throne and altar in Guatemala that never flagged even during the last decades of Bourbon anticlericalism. As the "almost natural auxiliaries" of royal officeholders, the clergy "were consulted on all questions of social and economic life." Contrary to the conventional interpretation of the Bourbon reforms' impact on the Church in Guatemala, the monarchy largely failed to diminish the latter's "economic, social and political power" right up to the crisis of 1808.[24]

LIBERALISM WITHOUT MORAL AUTONOMY

Another distinctive and reciprocally related attribute of the Hispanic world had been its capacity to dodge the early modern shift toward a general culture of moral autonomy, away from obedience to God-given authority, and toward the eventual triumph of the relativization of authority. Much of that capacity lay in the success of the Iberian monarchies in fencing out Protestantism, a movement that had greatly accelerated the trend toward moral autonomy elsewhere. At the very moment of the great rupture between Spain and its American realms, political institutions in much of Europe, and of course in North America, were already surrendering to the prescriptions of moral autonomy. One result was the broadly liberal constitutions that emerged as templates of democratic rule; liberal institutions required a culture of moral autonomy for their proper functioning.[25] They have not performed well in Latin America, where the culture of moral autonomy had not taken root. Resistance to moral autonomy was bolstered by the persistence in the Hispanic world of a view of society not as a collection of individual wills but as an ordered mosaic of corporate bodies, in the form of estates and other collectivities.[26] Here, the long-standing "morality of the good" persisted even as the "morality of rights" took over elsewhere.[27] Comellas speculated that had Spain managed to forge a "Christian Enlightenment," synthesizing a limited-sense rationalism with the long-standing tenets of the faith, it might have avoided (in a phrase that seemed to ratify Archbishop Penados's judgment) the two-century "unbundling of the Hispanic conscience" (disociación de la conciencia hispana), which in turn gave rise to so much violence and instability. To the range of contemporary modernities there might have been added that of a Hispanic and theocentric version, alongside the dominant anthropic ones.[28]

Under different conditions, therefore, Central America might have deflected the crisis of order. But in the decades after 1821, institutions designed by Britons, Frenchmen, and North Americans were posited that had been contrived to function under the gaze of an authority principle—namely, the imaginary sovereignty of a popular electorate acting through representatives—that was radically incompatible with the long-standing Hispanic worldview, for which the only socially recognized authority fit to oversee power had been *given* by and through the Catholic Church, and secondarily by and through corporate bodies whose pacts with the monarchy similarly drew on the authority of religion.[29] The modern idea of a *state* endowed with an absolute sovereignty flowing upward from the people was never fully shared by Spanish society, not even by the most avid late-Bourbon absolutists. It seems likely that some of them would even have classified "state sovereignty" as one of those claims by governments that Michael Oakeshott dismissed as among the "implausible and gimcrack beliefs which few can find convincing for more than five minutes together."[30] Operating in a culture that was thoroughly "juridical and Catholic" (in the words of Guerra and Lempérière) and that never fell for modernity's fallacious distinction between public and private, the monarchy consisted of a diversity of powers throughout the Americas, where localisms, particularities, and exceptions to general rules prevailed despite the presence of a quasi-absolutist discourse. In 1808, the king's subjects still considered themselves vassals united to their lord by ties of reciprocity, such that at the moment of the monarchy's greatest crisis, the king's prerogatives were seen to be limited by divine law, natural law, and the rights of corporate bodies.[31] This and other distinctive features of Hispanic society would inhibit the adoption of a socially recognized authority compatible with the liberalism that dictated the architecture (including, most decisively, the criteria of legitimacy) of the institutions of power after independence. Just because loyalty to the Crown had for so long depended on the socially recognized authority of religion, no post-1821 institution of power could come close to replacing the monarchy.

Hence, a crisis of order brought on not simply by the collapse of traditional institutions, as is typically argued, but by a relativization of authority (and thus legitimacy) more sudden and profound than that experienced anywhere else in the West. Under the monarchy, authority had been organic and integral, not only in the sense of having been given by long tradition but because of the nonexistence of that pet binary of the liberal imaginary, "temporal versus spiritual" or "state versus church." The temporal world was understood to be ontologically Christian in the sense that, having been created for man and not made by him, it was naturally subject to the ends defined by Christian doctrine. It was a worldview in which the *auctoritas* of the Church, though not entirely external to the *potestas* of the monarchy, could act as a genuine constraint on the prerogatives of power. With the collapse of the Catholic monarchy and the declaration of independence, an authority capable in theory of constraining power would be constituted ideologically by power itself. In the naturalistic worldview of the state-makers who undertook that project, public order could only be understood in positivistic and utilitarian terms, making it answerable exclusively to power and the *faux* authority of its preferred ideology.

A restoration of the old order founded on the *potestas* of kingship and the *auctoritas* of religion, natural law, corporate rights, and the Church was now largely beyond reach. The leadership of the newly self-declared republics freely copied liberal institutions but could not liberate their subjects from the long-standing ethos of moral realism in favor of an ethos of individual moral autonomy, with its associated recalibration of older notions of equality, representation, and personal freedom. Hispanic societies divided deeply over the most important values, igniting an epoch of continuing crisis characterized above all by the deficit of socially recognized authority. Religion and liberalism made constant war on each other. "Epochs of crisis," García Pelayo noted, "are characterized by the absence of *auctoritas,* precisely because discord and the lack of commonality in values do not permit the establishment of unity in recognizing what is valuable." As putative authorities eliminate one another in the struggle for power, "everything tends to dissolve itself in power relations."[32]

In the decades of self-rule that have followed independence, it was precisely García-Pelayo's "establishment of unity in recognizing what is valuable"—a long-lasting invigoration, perhaps, of Archbishop Penados's "collective conscience"—that failed to occur, first under the auspices of the Central American Federation (July 1, 1823–ca. 1840) and subsequently under those of the five little republics that succeeded the defunct federation. Claimants to power alleged that they themselves embodied authority as an attribute of power itself. Or they appealed to one or another among a mélange of rival authorities—many associated with mutually incompatible criteria for evaluating the legitimacy of a power holder—as the source of their legitimacy.[33] Most of them found inspiration in the continuous arrival of European-derived mutations of liberalism, conservatism, and socialism, not one of which could remotely approach the level of social recognition enjoyed by the Catholic religion. Rather, they spawned a range of ideologies whose followers issued anathemas that regularly evoked mutual declarations of extermination. Real authority relativizes power. But under the conditions prevailing in the isthmus after 1821, incentives to ignore or manipulate authority, or simply assimilate it to power itself, gained the upper hand over commitments to adhere to the only authority with a credible claim to social recognition.

In motion against the liberalistic and anticlerical core of political modernity, or at least as a kind of leavening agent, there persisted a broad adherence to the belief in the traditional role of the Catholic religion in government. The depth of popular adherence to religion as the true *auctoritas* to power in public life was revealed above all in the triumph and rule of Rafael Carrera in Guatemala from 1839 to 1865. His revolution, "a religious crusade" in the estimate of Woodward, restored the Catholic Church to a level of authority in relation to power that was commensurate with that of the colonial era. Along with his collaborators in the legislature, Carrera professed the obedience of the state to the Catholic religion as well as its deference to the Church as the moral regulator of public life and the ultimate guarantor of order and prosperity. "Nearly every facet of Guatemalan life" became subject to the influence of the Church. The concordat of 1852 ensured that all educational institutions would once again teach in conformity to Church doctrine; it authorized Church censorship of certain publications and turned over collection of the tithe to the state, which also received the right to nominate bishops. Woodward attributed Carrera's popular appeal above all to his defense of "the rural masses," including the Indigenous communities, "from the economic exploitation of the creole elite." To the question, then, of why liberals so passionately opposed the influence of the Church (and thus Carrera), Woodward correctly joins other historians in arguing that to the hustlers and impresarios who had embraced liberal ideas, an unimpeded Church hindered their freedom. In fact, after liberals rode back into power for good in 1871 they wiped out the protective legislation and correlative religious measures in both Guatemala and cognate regimes elsewhere on the isthmus.[34]

By then, a diversity of rival legitimacies, bestowed inchoately upon a diversity of both aspiring and *pro tempore* power holders, and exteriorized in pacts subject only to coercive enforcement, led to the emergence in Central America of what I have elsewhere called "the improvisational state."[35] In summarizing the outcome, by the 1960s, of "the crisis of the old liberal order" implanted in the late nineteenth century, Pérez-Brignoli (writing in 2018) evoked the historiographical consensus epitomized by Montúfar, Mendieta, and Torres-Rivas: "Any protest, no matter how timid, put the system to the question and was seen as part of a subversive conspiracy. That interminable chain of exclusions—which extended inevitably to the political opposition—had over time another equally implacable consequence: the permanent questioning of the established order by social forces as broad-based as they were varied." Pérez-Brignoli attributed the crisis to the absence of institutions capable of channeling dissent.[36] But that causal argument, more descriptive than analytical, begged the question. More fundamentally still, in the absence of a single, socially recognized principle of authority, it was the very legitimacy of the state that was ceaselessly put to the question.

Socially recognized authority endows more than a concordant idea of the state. When coherently articulated, it conveys an idea of the nation, or "a commonality in values" (as García-Pelayo put it in the section "Liberalism without Moral Autonomy" above) to which citizens owe their loyalty. The widely acknowledged lack of such an idea gave rise to what most historians recognize as a yet another, but permanent, crisis in the region's history: that of national identity.[37] It was a crisis whose appearance naturally coincided with the shattering (owing to the collapse of the monarchy) of "a common culture forged above all in the forms and symbols of religious belief," in Eastman's estimate. That culture linked "the Americas to the metropole and elites to peasants and Indigenous actors, providing a shared language through which emerging collective identities could be constructed and articulated." Attempts to yoke this long-standing multiclass and multiethnic religious identity to the premises of liberal nationalism under the auspices of the Cádiz Constitution had proved unavailing.[38] Ironically, the failure was due in no small measure to the determination of liberal politicians to sacralize the state while crippling the Church, the one institution capable of feeding and sustaining an authentic sense of social solidarity across class and ethnicity. Perhaps unsurprisingly, Carol Smith argued that Guatemala under Carrera was more unified than *any* isthmian country until Nicaragua's revolutionary government took power in 1979.[39] Hence the descent into contested legitimacy and violence, which continued after the collapse of the Federation around 1840 as each "estadito" (statelet), in Mendieta's sarcastic account, faced off its rivals and "marked its historic feats according to the number of revolutions, factions, riots, and failed *coups,* pushing themselves ever downward and away from the concept of a civilized people."[40]

In the absence of a widely shared idea of the nation anchored in a socially recognized authority, personalistic political commitments turned the act of governing into the administration of a system of patrimonial exchange relationships intrinsically subject to violence. In addition to making every political opponent an enemy of the nation, patrimonialism infused the tendency, in Mendieta's words, to "extract personal advantage from any function of government, and not to look after the interests and rights of the collectivity," while encouraging the firm belief that "politics represents nothing more than the desire to live comfortably, without working."[41] The authoritarian habits inspired by the patrimonial ethos extended well beyond the many military figures who became the public faces of dictatorship. "The authoritarians are not only the military men," observed Torres-Rivas, guardedly anticipating the subsequent judgment of Penados del Barrio, "but the numerous social forces of society who call on and utilize them."[42]

A patrimonial ethos may have been organically compatible with traditional monarchy and its criteria of legitimacy. But patrimonialism metastasized under the liberal dispensation, contradicting the latter's foundational premise of legal equality, and gravely corrupting the rule of law. "With the exception of the schoolteacher," Mendieta wrote,

> I do not believe that there exists in the bureaucratic hierarchy of the four States of the north a man more unhappy than the judge; he is obligated to administer justice and needs to blindly obey the [local military] commander and the [local] administrator (who are often rivals), the president, the ministers and local political bosses. Imagine the situation of this poor devil and the justice imparted![43]

When separated from a socially recognized authority and thus from the rule of law, the web of mutual rights and duties ordained by citizenship collapses, and with it the very possibility of justice and therefore of self-government. As a result, in Central America indifference to the law became the fountainhead of every crisis, traceable ultimately to a political culture devoid of an authority capable of seeding, regulating, and sustaining a communitarian or national ethos. To Bravo Lira, what made independence "the greatest institutional catastrophe in the history" of Latin America was the subsequent collision between two constitutional regimes. The first was the lived, three-century experience of a stable, pluralistic "jurisdictional" constitution of fundamental law in which monarchy and Church shared supreme power in a mutually limiting way. The second governed according to an endless profileration of merely "written" and thus conveniently "disposable" constitutions; having replaced the rule of law with the rule of act, they propagated "distrust, opposition and resistance."[44]

THE FAILURE OF LIBERALISM

Until about 1990, a single premise and its correlates practically controlled scholarly discourse about public violence in Central America. Violence of all kinds—from military intervention to guerrilla war to more routine political violence—was an artifact of social inequities and political oppression. For those scholars writing in the liberal tradition, the solution was democracy; for those writing from a Marxist perspective, the solution was socialism. Although socialism has largely but not entirely receded as a credible political program, the liberal democracy-consolidation "narrative" has been well underway for more than two decades. But now, instead of the kind of violence once associated with military rule and popular rebellion, the region suffers from violence of a political and criminal kind nourished not by the state or the enemies of the state but by society itself—the very arena once assumed to encompass the victims of public violence, who would one day emerge, if sufficiently mobilized, as the revolutionary subjects of peace and democracy. Before, demilitarizing the state and subjugating it to the sovereignty of the people was the strategy of both Marxists and liberals. Today, the state remains at the center of discussion, but less as the powerful instrument of specialized agents of violence, or the beleaguered target of ideological enemies. Now it appears more and more as a desolated relic, hollowed out by corruption and incompetence, ungovernable and disbelieved.

As a result, in the study of state formation, the conventional focus on regime type now seems to be less relevant than the character of the relationship between state and society, a perspective that can no longer avoid, I argue here, confronting the authority/power binomial. *Pace* Jürgen Habermas, Central America's history suggests that the democratic process itself cannot produce the social solidarity required to sustain democracy. No political constitution can sustain itself without what John E. Finn calls "background principles" or "preconstitutional principles" that themselves embody "the activity of constitution making properly understood," binding the framers of the constitution and making their enterprise intelligible.[45] Such, I argue here, is the so-far neglected principle of authority, upon whose formation and effective enforcement depends the very existence of the "collective conscience" to which Penados del Barrios appealed.

Liberalism, adopted at independence as the first of the region's many doctrines of salvation, achieved a sort of hegemony in the late nineteenth century that it has never relinquished. By the time Torres-Rivas had begun writing in the early 1970s, it was an unmitigated failure in the eyes of almost everyone. The question then was whether liberalism could be reformed and redeemed. After two savage decades of death and destruction, the old liberalism emerged intact in the 1990s and persists today, fundamentally unchanged, still the reigning ideology, still an ignoble failure.[46] The fundamental social realities so authoritatively documented by Torres-Rivas in a series of books beginning in 1969—the gross inequalities of wealth, income, and status; the poverty; the racism; the everyday norm of lawlessness and its inescapable consort, everyday violence; and the thoroughly corrupted and inept institutions of government—have continued, in his own words of 2011 as quoted above, to make Central America an "anguished and tormented region" today.[47] The perennial albeit partial exception to these dismal qualifiers continues to be Costa Rica, which accounts for 10 percent of the region's population and area. The occasional recourse to military supremacy, dictatorial government, and political violence that marked its first century was gradually and for the most part overcome in the second. Explaining Costa Rica's relative success in this aspect of state formation remains a major challenge for historians. An early and continuing disposition to be bound by preconstitutional religious principles of authority, sharply limiting the range of rival criteria of legitimacy, stands out as a promising hypothesis.[48]

THIS HANDBOOK

If the historiography can be said to reduce the past to waves of radical revision and hardy resistance, it clearly rejects an analogous reduction of the aims, guiding ideas, and composition of the forces of ascent, or those of their enemies and allies, external and internal. Thus, at the level of the events that comprise the secular crisis of order, the picture is considerably more complex, as the chapters in this collection readily confirm. Central America has long attracted scholars who specialize in the study of its history and society, a trend that intensified notably after the 1960s. The rising volume, variety, and quality of specialized work on Central America's past—from regional, national, and subnational perspectives—therefore suggested the need for a guide to the scholarship, which this volume seeks to provide. The handful of such guides that first appeared around the early 1990s, as the post-1970s research boom was still gathering momentum, are now out of date.[49]

The chapters in Part I, "Human and Territorial Contexts," furnish panoramic assessments of five broad regional themes that cross all the major historical periods.

They aim to provide the essential contextual physical and social referents for the more monographic topics that follow in Parts II and III. Anthony Goebel McDermott's opening chapter synthesizes the extraordinary variety and complexity of the region's natural environment, shaped fundamentally by the contrasting combination of volcanic mountains and tropical lowlands. He highlights the myriad ways in which the natural world directed, and was in turn directed by, human action, from the beginnings of human settlement to the present day. The next chapter's analysis of human settlement and its changing quantity and distribution over time, by Peter H. Herlihy, Matthew L. Fahrenbruch, and Taylor A. Tappan, focuses on the Indigenous peoples of Central America. Drawing on a rich diversity of field and archival research as well as government survey data, the authors document a remarkable pattern of demographic collapse and territorial decline, followed in the twentieth century by population growth and growing recognition of Indigenous territorial claims. William R. Fowler synthesizes the present state of knowledge of the development of civilization or complex societies before European contact. Highlighting diverse interpretations of the archaeological data, his chapter traces the history of Indigenous civilization in the isthmus from the arrival of hunter-gatherers about 10,000–12,000 years ago, to the postclassic city-states encountered by the Europeans after 1500. The fate of the Indigenous peoples after the collapse of the Spanish monarchy in 1808, and the rise of Central America's self-governing republics, is the subject of Wolfgang Gabbert's chapter. It begins by highlighting the complexities, beginning in the period of colonial rule and continuing until today, of the very term "Indian." The exploitation and displacement of the Indigenous peoples did not end with Spanish rule but took new forms in obedience to modern ideas and the requirements of export-dependent economies. In recent decades, Indigenous movements favoring civil, cultural, and land rights have accumulated a mixed record of setbacks and success across the isthmus.

Part II reviews the progress of scholarship regarding the period of Spanish rule, from the conquest and the founding of the Kingdom of Guatemala to its gradual collapse after 1808, and the disintegration of the kingdom's successor state, the Central American Federation, about 1840. Laura E. Matthew's analysis of the conquest argues that it was actually not one event "but a centuries-long process that continued throughout the colonial period." Her chapter complicates the very identities of conquerors as well as conquered, while noting that the Indigenous peoples not only resisted but survived and recovered demographically under colonial rule. Stephen Webre breaks down the political, social, and economic institutions of Central America under Spanish rule. Beginning with the administrative consolidation of the isthmus as a single jurisdiction from 1543 onward, Spain sought to centralize control over land tenure, mining, agriculture, commerce, and relations with the Indigenous population, which included a regime of forced labor and Christianization. The exceptionally diverse cultural history of the Kingdom of Guatemala is the subject of Brianna Leavitt-Alcántara's chapter. Neglected by historians in comparison to the larger and more influential viceroyalties of Peru and New Spain, the kingdom gave rise to beliefs and practices that changed its society and economy, as well as areas beyond its borders, in important ways. She illustrates her argument by drawing on a rich new vein of historical research in the areas of religion, ethnicity, sexuality and technology. The path to national self-rule began not in Central America itself but in Spain as a result of the crisis of 1808. Aaron Pollack shows how the relative political tranquility of the old Kingdom of Guatemala gave way, with formal independence in 1821, to two decades of intense strife within the kingdom's successor, the chronically impotent Federal Republic of Central America. His chapter emphasizes the continuing influence, after independence, of some of the ideas and practices that defined the policies of the late Bourbon monarchy.

The subject of Part III is the ample scholarship on the period since the formation of national states around 1840, separated under two rubrics: regional themes that cut across national borders and national histories of the seven countries that comprise the region today. The changing structure of the political economy, beginning with the rise of coffee cultivation after the breakup of the Federation, is the subject of Robert G. Williams's contribution. Highlighting the rising prominence of US influence in economic affairs after about 1900, his chapter analyzes the class-based violence that accompanied economic diversification by the middle years of the century and contributed in no small part to the insurgencies of the 1970s and 1980s. Since those massively destructive decades, Williams goes on to show, the market-oriented ("neoliberal") policies that have broadly defined the region's economies have had diverse consequences for the working population from country to country. David Díaz Arias contrasts the relative richness of the historiography of the region's economy to the considerably less developed knowledge of state-making and nation-building across the region's five countries since independence. Both processes reveal an intense unevenness in the rise of ruling institutions and the formation of national identity, despite the shared dominance of liberalism as the controlling ideology at least until the civil wars of the 1970s and 1980s. Since then, the hopes raised for stable, peaceful, and democratic polities have been largely frustrated outside Costa Rica.

The inescapable presence of the United States as the defining foreign influence on the region over the last century and a quarter is the subject of Michel Gobat's analysis. He attributes Central America's record as the target of more US interventions than any other world region to two factors. The first is its isthmian nature, and therefore its allure to the United States and its rivals as a canal site. The second stems from the expansionist tendencies inherent in the United States since its founding, eventually finding in Central America "a prime testing ground for the US pursuit of global power." While Gobat focuses mainly on the bilateral aspects of the US-Central American relationship, Joaquín M. Chávez's treatment of the Cold War (ca. 1947–1992) presents the region and the United States in a global context. Asserting that "empire, authoritarianism, and social revolution in the Cold War constituted a single and closely interrelated process," Chávez shows how the myriad international interests at stake, in a war that was anything but "cold" across much of the Southern Hemisphere, deeply marked the recent histories of the isthmian countries. Christine J. Wade's study of the two and one-half decades (i.e., the mid-1990s to ca. 2020) that have elapsed since the formal end of the civil wars analyzes the widely anticipated transition to democracy. She places the region's postconflict governments "in the murky waters somewhere between authoritarianism and democracy," as they struggle with "low political participation, weak, corrupt state institutions and the persistence of militarized public security," as well as an unprecedented wave of criminal violence. Among the historic obstacles to democratic self-rule, the armed forces have been exceptionally prominent. Orlando J. Pérez and Randy Pestana survey the rise of national military forces from their origins in the *caudillo*-led bands of the nineteenth century. By the mid-twentieth century, politics had become thoroughly militarized. Despite their formal withdrawal from the political arena after the 1980s, their continuing influence on the course of civilian affairs remains an impediment to democratic consolidation.

Bonar L. Hernández Sandoval's survey of religion and politics points out that the once-reigning assumption among scholars that modernity would make religious belief irrelevant has been dramatically disproved, and that Central America's history is no exception. "Religion, both in its institutional and 'popular' manifestations, never ceased to shape the social and political landscape of Central America." Its diverse impacts have been further heightened by the extraordinary growth of Protestantism in the late twentieth century, which abolished Catholicism's long-standing monopoly on Christian worship. Among the most prominent themes in the historiography of the region since the 1970s is the experience of women. Eugenia Rodríguez Sáenz shows how it both matched and departed from that of women elsewhere in Latin America, as those of Central America first sought to attain the status of subjects of rights on a par with men and then, from the mid-twentieth century, extended their participation across the political and economic life of the region. In her analysis, Rodríguez Sáenz emphasizes the diverse experiences of women according to age, geography, ethnicity, and class. Another important, but often overlooked, aspect of social change is literature. Werner Mackenbach documents the close but ever-changing relationship between literature and society over time, while calling for renewed attention to the multiple ways in which "literary events are implicated in historical events and historical events in literary events."

This volume closes with critical surveys of each country that seek to highlight distinctive national experiences, in contrast to the regional approaches summarized above. A variety of approaches distinguishes the seven chapters. David Carey Jr.'s interpretation of Guatemalan history as a process of identity formation discloses the complex interactions over time among the country's many ethnic and racial groups, and how those relationships have shaped Guatemalan society. At the heart of Dario A. Euraque's perspective on Honduras is its two-century struggle to build state institutions capable of throwing off the corruption, exclusiveness, unaccountability, and indifference to the welfare of the populace that have characterized them since independence. The survey of El Salvador by Erik Ching highlights, as a decisive shaping force in the country's history, its racial and ethnic divisions. The impact of those divisions was multiplied over time as they evolved into ethnically homogeneous economic classes. One result was to turn political competition into a deadly struggle for survival that has largely been won by "authoritarian conservatives." Julie A. Charlip sees Nicaraguan history as defined above all by two long-term tendencies: (a) an endless competition for the offices of state among elite groups driven less by ideology than an elemental hunger for power and wealth; and (b) owing above all to the country's canal-friendly geography, an overbearing readiness by the US government to intervene in the country's turbulent politics, putting its weight behind the most compliant band. This self-defeating pattern often led to dictatorship until the 1980s, when Nicaragua's first victory over its historic frailties turned to dust as the result of yet another US military intervention. Iván Molina finds the core explanation for Costa Rica's exceptional record of tranquility and popular support for its governing institutions in the self-assertiveness of the middling and poorer classes. As a result of their corresponding capacity for "resistance," Costa Rica has managed, uniquely in Central America and almost uniquely in Latin America, to combine "capitalist modernization with broad processes of upward social mobility and unprecedented reduction of poverty."

Belize, known as British Honduras until it achieved independence from Britain in 1981, shared in few of the region's defining trends, except the dependence on commodity exports and the class-based economic inequities that have characterized so much of the isthmus, according to Mark Moberg's study of its colonial and postcolonial history. Owing in part to its solid record of political stability, Belize may be better prepared to face the economic and environmental challenges that also confront its Hispanic neighbors. The second-last country to achieve formal independence (though as a US protectorate) was Panama, a jurisdiction of Colombia until it was forcibly separated by the combined efforts of Panamanian nationalists and the US Navy and Marines in 1903. The canal that the United States proceeded to build across Panama remained the country's principal *raison d'etre* as well as the main obstacle to its government's exercise of full sovereignty over Panama. As Michael E. Donoghue notes in his study of Panama, the country's true independence had to await the transfer of the canal from the United States to Panama in 1999.

The critical syntheses of the historical questions treated here were shaped with three ends in mind. The first aim is to introduce the key problems that have framed the historiography of Central America for the last half-century. As introductions, they are intended to be both synthetic, in the sense of offering a rounded summary of the main directions in the particular historiography of the selected theme, but also critical. Their authors were encouraged to evaluate the historiography as well as to report it, probing the quality, breadth, and depth of the scholarship, while proposing new directions. The authors thus sought to reach out to both the neophyte seeking basic orientation and context, and to scholars already immersed in the question at hand.

The second aim is to illuminate, by means of a compact collection of essays by specialists, both Central America's distinctiveness as a region and the attributes it shares with the rest of Latin America. In many respects, its regional coherence stems not from any absolutely unique historical experience but from the particular character and intensity of patterns familiar across Latin America. Illustrations can be found in every chapter; exemplary instances include Goebel McDermott's on land and climate, Gobat's on relations with the United States, Mackenbach's on literature, and Matthew's on the conquest. In this sense, one may hope that this collection will encourage more explicitly comparative study of regions and nations across Latin America.

This volume is also meant to encourage more comparative study of distinctive national, cross-national, and subnational historical experiences across Central America itself, a place whose diversity is all the more notable given the history of its remarkable political geography. The region's long period of unity or quasi-unity (ca. 1530s–1840) was followed by the current era of fragmentation, which has nevertheless seen at least twenty-five formal but futile attempts to reconstitute the old union. In few other regions of the world, therefore, does a regional identity compete more ardently and multifariously with the national identities of its component states.[50] While the thematic chapters invariably convey aspects of that diversity across countries, the seven country-level chapters highlight some of the more prominent, as well as the less obvious, affinities and disparities among them. Central America is indeed "a nation divided," in the phrase made famous by Ralph Lee Woodward, Jr.'s survey of its history.[51] While the aspirational content of the phrase now seems more fanciful than ever, its pertinence for historical analysis remains indisputable, as these chapters suggest. Finally, this Introduction would be incomplete without an expression of my gratitude to all the scholars who accepted my invitation to contribute to this work. Without exception, their collaborative spirit and commitment to excellence made editing the book a joy and a privilege. I also wish to thank Louis Gulino, the ever-gracious Oxford editor who oversaw the production of this book from an early stage, for his unfailing support, flexibility and, perhaps most of all, his indomitable good humor.

NOTES

1. Walter LaFeber, *Inevitable Revolutions: The United States in Central America* (New York: W. W. Norton (1983).
2. Central America's "crime situation" stood out among other world regions in both its exceptional exposure to the flow of illegal drugs and in "the level of violence in its societies" where one finds "some of the highest recorded intentional homicide rates among all countries for which reliable data are available." United Nations Office of Drugs and Crime, *Crime and Development in Central America: Caught in the Crossfire* (New York: United Nations, 2007), 11, 12, 14, 15. See also Sarah Chayes, *When Corruption Is the Operating System: The Case of Honduras* (Washington, DC: Carnegie Endowment for International Peace, 2017) and Luis Jorge Garay Salamanca and Eduardo Salcedo-Albarán, "Captura del estado y reconfiguración cooptada del estado," in *Narcotráfico, corrupción y estados: Cómo las redes ilícitas han reconfigurado las instituciones en Colombia, Guatemala y México*, ed. Luis Jorge Garay Salamanca and Eduardo Salcedo-Albarán (México, D.F.: Debate, 2012), 33–48. For moving accounts of the human costs of contemporary violence, see Óscar Martínez, *A History of Violence: Living and Dying in Central America* (London: Verso, 2016).
3. FLACSO El Salvador, "Nueva narrativa y nueva agenda para la transformación social de El Salvador y Centroamérica" (San Salvador, El Salvador: September 2020), prepared statement circulated to participants, including the author, for a meeting convoked on December 4, 2020, to discuss the drafting of the new "framework."

4. Greg Grandin, *The Last Colonial Massacre: Latin America in the Cold War* (Chicago: University of Chicago Press, 2004), passim, 191.
5. Héctor Pérez-Brignoli, *Breve historia de Centroamérica*, 3rd ed. "ampliada" (Madrid: Alianza Editorial, 2018), 305, 308.
6. Héctor Pérez-Brignoli, *Breve historia de Centroamérica* (Madrid: Alianza Editorial, 1985), 147, 152.
7. Edelberto Torres-Rivas, *Revoluciones sin cambios revolucionarios: Ensayos sobre la crisis en Centroamérica*, 2nd ed. (Guatemala City, Guatemala: F&G Editores, 2013), 2, 7, 250–252; Edelberto Torres-Rivas, "Centroamérica: Revoluciones sin cambio revolucionario," *Nueva Sociedad*, no. 150 (1997): 89.
8. Próspero Penados del Barrio, "Palabras Preliminares," *in* Informe Proyecto Interdiocesano de Recuperación de la Memoria Histórica, *Guatemala, nunca más*, 4 vols., vol. 1: Impactos de la violencia (Guatemala City, Guatemala: ODHAG, 1998), x–xi.
9. Lorenzo Montúfar, *Reseña histórica de Centro-América* (Guatemala City, Guatemala: Tip. de "El Progreso," 1878), I: xii.
10. Salvador Mendieta, *La enfermedad de Centro-América*, 3 vols. (Barcelona: Tip. Maucci, 1934), I: 270–271.
11. Edelberto Torres-Rivas, *El tamaño de nuestra democracia* (San Salvador: Istmo Editores, 1982), 29.
12. Robert H. Holden, *Armies without Nations: Public Violence and State Formation in Central America, 1821–1960* (New York: Oxford University Press, 2004), 31–33.
13. Ramón Casaus, *Oración funebre predicada por* [. . .] *Ramón Casaus y Torres*, [. . .] *Arzobispo electo de Guatemala* [. . .] *en el aniversario por las víctimas del 2. de mayo* (Guatemala City, Guatemala: Don Manuel de Arevalo, 1812), 31.
14. An interpretation of the separation process as one of "liberalism vs. absolutism" or as the inevitable unfolding of some sort of progressive teleology would fit none of the American jurisdictions of Spain, least of all that of the Kingdom of Guatemala. The Americans largely did not seek independence. It was thrust on them by a Spanish government so inept it left them little choice; Roberto Breña, *El primer liberalismo español y los procesos de emancipación de América, 1808–1824: Una revisión historiográfica del liberalismo hispánico* (Mexico City: El Colegio de México, 2006), 41–44.
15. Here we set aside the conventional usage of "authority" as political (i.e., the authority of act or of the one giving commands) and revert to its classical usage as the knowledge that authorizes the act. The understanding of *auctoritas* and *potestas* presented here draws mainly on theses proposed or extensively commented by a group of largely Hispanic, late-twentieth-century thinkers in the history and philosophy of jurisprudence and politics, above all Alvaro D'Ors but also Jesús Fueyo Alvarez, Manuel García-Pelayo, Rafael Domingo, and María Alejandra Vanney. Some aspects of their ideas have been usefully elaborated, for the most part independently, by a limited group of political philosophers to whom I am also indebted: Augusto Del Noce, Michael Oakeshott, Christian Smith, Frederick D. Wilhelmsen, Jean Bethke Elshtain, Hannah Arendt, and David J. Levy.
16. Daniel Philpott, "Sovereignty," in *The Oxford Handbook of the History of Political Philosophy*, ed. George Klosko (Oxford: Oxford University Press, 2011), 571. See also Stephen R.L. Clark, *Civil Peace and Sacred Order* (Oxford: Clarendon Press, 1989), 85.
17. Edward Norman, *Christianity in the Southern Hemisphere: The Churches in Latin America and South Africa* (Oxford: Oxford University Press, 1981), 19.

18. William B. Taylor, *Magistrates of the Sacred: Priests and Parishioners in Eighteenth-Century Mexico* (Stanford, CA: Stanford University Press, 1996), 13.

19. Javier Fernández Sebastián, "Toleration and Freedom of Expression in the Hispanic World between Enlightenment and Liberalism," *Past & Present* 211, no. 1 (2011): 159, 164–165, 187.

20. François Xavier Guerra and Annick Lempérière, "Introducción," in *Los espacios públicos en Iberoamérica: Ambigüedades y problemas, siglos XVIII–XIX*, ed. François Xavier Guerra and Annick Lempérière (Mexico City, Mexico: Fondo de Cultura Económica, 1998), 11–14.

21. José M. Portillo Valdés, *Crisis atlántica: Autonomía e independencia en la crisis de la monarquía hispana* (Madrid: Fundación Carolina, Marcial Pons, 2006), 18–21.

22. Miles L. Wortman, *Government and Society in Central America, 1680–1840* (New York: Columbia University Press, 1982), 41.

23. A. C. van Oss, *Catholic Colonialism: A Parish History of Guatemala, 1524–1821* (Cambridge: Cambridge University Press, 1986), 153–154, 184.

24. Christophe Belaubre, *Élus de Dieu et élus du monde dans le royaume du Guatemala (1753–1808): Église, familles de pouvoir et réformateurs bourbons* (Paris: L'Harmattan, 2012), 178–180; 13, 417–418.

25. Brad S. Gregory, *The Unintended Reformation: How a Religious Revolution Secularized Society* (Cambridge, MA: Belknap Press of Harvard University Press, 2012), 212, 214, 217; Jeffrey Stout, *The Flight from Authority: Religion, Morality, and the Quest for Autonomy* (Notre Dame, IN: University of Notre Dame Press, 1981), 234–244.

26. Miguel Artola, *Los orígenes de la España contemporánea*, 3. ed., 2 vols. (Madrid: Centro de Estudios Políticos y Constitucionales, 2000), v. 1, 14–16; François Xavier Guerra, *Modernidad e independencias: Ensayos sobre las revoluciones hispánicas* (Madrid: Editorial MAPFRE, 1992), 72–79.

27. For "morality of the good" versus "morality of rights," see Gregory, *Unintended Reformation*, 185.

28. José Luis Comellas, *Historia de España moderna y contemporánea* (Madrid: Ediciones Rialp, 2003), 173.

29. Guerra, *Modernidad*, 72–79; Frederick D. Wilhelmsen, *Christianity and Political Philosophy* (Athens: University of Georgia Press, 1978), ch. 5.

30. Michael Oakeshott, *On Human Conduct* (Oxford: Clarendon Press, 1975), 191.

31. François Xavier Guerra, "De la política antigua a la política moderna: La revolución de la soberanía," in *Los espacios públicos en Iberoamérica: Ambigüedades y problemas, siglos XVIII–XIX*, ed. François Xavier Guerra and Annick Lempérière (Mexico City, Mexico: Fondo de Cultura Económica, 1998), 124–130; and Guerra and Lempérière, "Introducción," 11–14, in the same work. For the regime's "jurisdictional" rather than statist mode of exercising political power, and the latter's dependence on a religious worldview, see the magisterial work by Carlos Garriga, "Orden jurídico y poder político en el antiguo régimen," *ISTOR* 4, no. 16 (Spring 2004).

32. Manuel García-Pelayo, *Auctoritas* (Caracas, Venezuela: Fundación Manuel García-Pelayo, 1998), 31–32.

33. In attributing Latin America's two-century-old struggle with instability and civil war to the diffusion across national territories of "a multitude of sovereignties," Adelman correctly acknowledged the need for a shared sense of nationhood or a shared belief in "a fictional indivisibility of sovereignty and statehood." But without a theory of authority operating independently of power, and absent any acknowledgment of its relevance to the stability of the monarchy, the exclusive focus on sovereignty omits a key explanatory

variable. Jeremy Adelman, *Sovereignty and Revolution in the Iberian Atlantic* (Princeton, NJ: Princeton University Press, 2006), 396–397.

34. Ralph Lee Woodward, Jr., *Rafael Carrera and the Emergence of the Republic of Guatemala, 1821–1871* (Athens: University of Georgia Press, 1993). 68, 104, 134, 258, 260–261, 469; also see Héctor Lindo-Fuentes, *Weak Foundations: The Economy of El Salvador in the Nineteenth Century* (Berkeley: University of California Press, 1990), 134; Wayne M. Clegern, *Origins of Liberal Dictatorship in Central America: Guatemala, 1865–1873* (Niwot: University Press of Colorado, 1994), 133. For the devastating consequences to the Church of the liberal "reforms," see Ricardo Bendaña Perdomo, *La Iglesia en Guatemala: Síntesis Histórica del Catolicismo* (Guatemala City, Guatemala: Librerías Artemis-Edinter, 1996), 506.

35. Holden, *Armies without Nations,* 25–28.

36. Pérez-Brignoli, *Breve historia* (2018), 202, 210.

37. See Pérez-Brignoli, *Breve historia* (2018), 42. Barahona's explication of the "national question" in Central American and Honduran history documents the many obstacles to nationhood in the region. Marvin Barahona, *Evolución Histórica de la identidad nacional* (Tegucigalpa, Honduras: Editorial Guaymuras, 1991). The essays in Frances Kinloch Tijerino, ed., *Nicaragua en busca de su identidad* (Managua: Instituto de Historia de Nicaragua, Universidad Centroamericana, 1995) highlight the costs of identity fragmentation and the value of a common idea of citizenship. In its cruder forms, isthmian nationalism was rooted in "resentment, fear, frustration, and a sense of inferiority," and "frequently angry and violent"; Ralph Lee Woodward, Jr., *Central America: A Nation Divided*, 3rd ed. (New York: Oxford University Press, 1999), 211.

38. Scott Eastman, *Preaching Spanish Nationalism across the Hispanic Atlantic, 1759–1823* (Baton Rouge: Louisiana State University Press, 2012), 10, 180.

39. Although Smith didn't mention it, among the exceptional attributes of the Nicaraguan revolutionaries was their openness, as Marxists, to Catholic thought. Carol A. Smith, "Origins of the National Question in Guatemala: A Hypothesis," in *Guatemalan Indians and the State: 1540 to 1988*, ed. Carol A. Smith (Austin: University of Texas Press, 1990), 92. For a piercing analysis of the superiority of "the Catholic imaginary" over the hypocritcal oratory of the nineteenth-century liberal "religion" of science and progress, see Lowell Gudmundson, "Sociedad y política (1840–1870)," in *De la Ilustración al liberalismo (1750–1870)*, ed. Héctor Pérez Brignoli, v. 3 of *Historia General de Centroamérica*, 203–254 (Madrid: Sociedad Estatal Quinto Centenario, 1993), 235, 253.

40. Mendieta, *Enfermedad de Centro-América* II:243.

41. Ibid., I:398–399.

42. Torres-Rivas, *Tamaño de Nuestra Democracia*, 45.

43. Mendieta, *Enfermedad de Centro-América*, I:218.

44. Bernardino Bravo Lira, *Constitución y reconstitución: Historia del Estado en Iberoamerica (Siglos XVI al XXI)* (Santiago, Chile: Abeledo Perrot Legal Publishing, 2010), 48, 18, 50.

45. See Jürgen Habermas, "Pre-Political Foundations of the Democratic Constitutional State?," in *Dialectics of Secularization: On Reason and Religion*, ed. Florian Schuller (San Francisco, CA: Ignatius Press, 2006), 31–32, 27–28; John E. Finn, *Constitutions in Crisis: Political Violence and the Rule of Law* (New York: Oxford University Press, 1991), 22–24, 27. For an argument compatible with Finn's, see Ernst Wolfgang Böckenförde, *State, Society, and Liberty: Studies in Political Theory and Constitutional Law* (New York: Berg and St. Martin's Press, 1991), ch. 2.

46. For the claim that the mutant strains of liberalism that seized Central America in the late nineteenth and early twentieth century "profoundly influenced future political development in the region," see James Mahoney, *The Legacies of Liberalism: Path Dependence and Political Regimes in Central America* (Baltimore, MD: Johns Hopkins University Press, 2001), xi.

47. Torres-Rivas's first and perhaps most influential account of the region's agony was published in Chile in 1969 but received its widest reception as Edelberto Torres-Rivas, *Interpretación del desarrollo social centroamericano: Procesos y estructuras de una sociedad dependiente* (San José, Costa Rica: Editorial Universitaria Centroamericana, 1971). Subsequently reprinted several times, it was translated as *History and Society in Central America* (Austin: University of Texas Press, 1993).

48. Campos Salas concluded that ecclesiastical influence over the formation of the Costa Rican state in the five decades following the rupture with Spain was so strong that religion effectively legitimized the state. Owing in part to a strong clerical presence in the national legislature, 90 percent of the 416 legal dispositions approved by the legislature between 1824 and 1900 favored the Church; Dagoberto Campos Salas, *Relaciones Iglesia-Estado en Costa Rica (Estudio Histórico-Jurídico)* (San José, Costa Rica: Editorial Guayacán Centroamericana, 2000), 32. See also José Luis Vega Carballo, *Orden y progreso: La formación del estado nacional en Costa Rica* (San José, Costa Rica: Instituto Centroamericano de Administración Pública, 1981), especially 127–131, 134–135. For an analysis of religious influence that emphasizes continuity, see María Carmela Velásquez Bonilla, "Los cambios político-administrativos en la diócesis de Nicaragua y Costa Rica de las reformas borbónicas a la independencia," *Hispania Sacra* 63, no. 128 (julio-diciembre 2011). As she points out, Costa Rica today remains a confessional state—the only one left in Latin America besides Argentina.

49. The most complete in English is the compilation of eight review essays, with their respective bibliographical essays, in Leslie Bethell, ed. *Central America since Independence* (Cambridge: Cambridge University Press, 1991); the essays had already been published in various volumes of *The Cambridge History of Latin America*. Two years later, the six-volume *Historia General de Centroamérica* was published in Madrid under the general editorship of Edelberto Torres-Rivas by the Sociedad Estatal Quinto Centenario and the Facultad Latinoamericana de Ciencias Sociales. The venerable survey history of the region in English, Ralph Lee Woodward, Jr.'s *Central America: A Nation Divided* (Oxford: Oxford University Press, 1999), which includes a seventy-five-page bibliographical essay, was last revised in 1999. The encyclopedic Carolyn Hall and Héctor Pérez-Brignoli, *Historical Atlas of Central America* (Norman: University of Oklahoma Press, 2003), surveys the history (but not the historiography) of the isthmus with illustrated short articles that summarize basic information on a variety of themes.

50. For a study of Central America's borderlands as historic zones of violent and nonviolent forms of interaction that constitute both legacies of unity and obstacles to its revival, see Robert H. Holden, "Borderlands and Public Violence in a Shadow Polity: Costa Ricans, Nicaraguans and the Legacy of the Central American Federation," in *Politics and History of Violence and Crime in Central America*, ed. Sebastian Huhn and Hannes Warnecke-Berger (New York: Palgrave Macmillan, 2017), 207–240.

51. Woodward, *Central America*, ix, 307.

PART I

HUMAN AND TERRITORIAL CONTEXTS

CHAPTER 1

LAND AND CLIMATE

Natural Constraints and Socio-Environmental Transformations

ANTHONY GOEBEL MCDERMOTT

INTRODUCTION

The ultimate goal of environmental history is to consider the interactions between human societies and the natural world present in all historical processes experienced by humanity and the planet. These interactions tend to be made invisible or extremely minimized by Western historiography, since they are linked to modernity and the notion of "progress" that values nature only in terms of human labor invested to satisfy the social needs of diverse groups. The scarce capacity granted to nature as an historical agent that has interacted with the human being by either promoting or hampering its material development can be explained by this alleged dissociation between the natural world and human societies. It is against this trend that environmental history emerges and develops, seeking to recover the "lost" relations between nature and humanity in other fields of historiography.

Parting from the above premises, this chapter is developed along two key analytical axes: the first consists of natural constraints, understood as the main obstacles and restrictions imposed by the biophysical means of what is today Central America for the material development of its past and present inhabitants. Climate and climate variability, natural disasters—generated by the combination of specific geological and hydrometereological events, and the social construction of risk and vulnerability—and the recurrence of a wide array of tropical diseases will be the gateways for this first approach to analyzing the natural constraints in Central American history.

The second axis encompasses the socioenvironmental transformations, conceived as the ecological consequences of the productive and extractive activities, set forth hypothetically, which pushed the greatest changes not only at the ecosystem and landscape levels but also in the human societies that populated the Isthmus throughout its history.

The origin and background of the agrarian systems, mining activity, forest exploitation, and livestock farming were studied as a way for gaining access to some of the distinctive features of the region's socioenvironmental transformations, from the beginning of human occupation to the present.

Based on this two-pronged analysis (constraints/transformations), we seek to develop an approach to the socioenvironmental profiles that have characterized the region to date, their changes and continuities throughout time, as well as the differences and similarities with other geographical spaces.

BIOPHYSICAL CONSTRAINTS: NATURE'S AGENCY IN THE MATERIAL DEVELOPMENT OF CENTRAL AMERICA

Climate, Climate Variability, and Material Development

As has been properly analyzed by Héctor Pérez Brignoli, Central America is a land of contrasts characterized by a remarkable environmental and cultural diversity.[1] It is framed by the central highlands and the gentle and exuberant languor of its coastlines.[2] It was in this geographical space that human societies settled from pre-Hispanic times in the Central-Pacific axis.

The settlement of the Central American highlands is long-standing, characterized by a high population density. These lands were settled by pre-Columbian civilizations as well as by the first Hispanic colonial societies. The independent republics were born in these rugged mountains, as can be clearly noted in the iconography of the Central American national emblems.[3] The rich volcanic soil that fills the mountain valleys and a predominant subtropical climate which evokes an endless springtime turned these spaces into the territorial base of civilization and the economic hubs of what is today Central America.[4]

In contrast, the Central American coasts are low, warm, jungle areas.[5] They are known for their luxuriant growth and biological wealth, due to its biota and particular climate and hydrometeorological features that conditioned the development of human settlements even before the arrival of the Europeans.

Thus, we must first point out that Central America may be considered a prototypical case of the agency of climate features in cultural development by constraining or promoting a diversity of productive activities, conditioning the development and characteristics of human settlements. The variations in the rainfall regimes had a deep impact on the development of seasonal crops, which not only affected agriculture but entailed social and demographic consequences as well.

The Central American Isthmus is a small portion of land geographically located from the northwest to the southeast, somewhat like a bridge connecting North and South America, with the Caribbean Sea to the east and the eastern tropical Pacific Ocean to the west. The Guatemalan and Honduran mountain ranges that run south as far as Nicaragua characterize the northernmost part of the Isthmus. Plains prevail in the northern part of Costa Rica, delimiting an important gap in the mountain range that goes from the lowlands of Mosquitia (Nicaragua) and Tortuguero (Costa Rica) on the Caribbean side to the Gulf of Papagayo (Costa Rican Pacific).[6] These geographic and geomorphological features have a profound effect on the Central American climate.

In this sense, the Intertropical Convergence Zone (ITCZ), which is the area encircling the Earth where the northeast and southeast trade winds converge, is mainly concentrated in the eastern tropical Pacific and appears in the continental part of the region in October.[7] Solar radiation is relevant in the daytime rainfall pattern, as the precipitations of the ITCZ are characterized by high evaporation which gives way to abundant rains that reach their peak during the afternoon and last only a few hours.

From a climate perspective, Central America is part of the Intra-American Sea, a region conformed by the Gulf of Mexico, the Caribbean Sea, and the Eastern Tropical Pacific Ocean adjacent to southern Mexico, Central America, and the northwestern part of South America. The lands to the west of the Gulf of Mexico and to the east of the Eastern Tropical Pacific are influenced by regional oceanic characteristics, such as sea surface temperature patterns, and intense tropical storms and hurricane activity.[8] The region is also known for the presence of a great intraseasonal rainfall variability and climatic phenomena such as El Niño Southern Oscillation (ENSO) and the North Pacific Oscillation, also known as PDO (Pacific Decadal Oscillation).[9]

Characteristics such as latitude, altitude, and position with relation to the mountain ranges have an effect on the climate of the individual regions.[10] The precipitation regimes in the Caribbean, moving southward, show a greater abundance of rainfall and little annual variability, whereas the central highlands are characterized by less rainfall and greater variability.

There are few studies on the socioenvironmental effects of climate variability in Central America from a historical perspective. Due to geographic proximity, the Mexican case could well be a basic starting point. In Mexico, severe climate variability on a scale not experienced for at least five hundred years and maybe many millennia "occurred simultaneously with colonial-induced ecological change."[11] A severe drought occurred during the Conquest era followed by one of the most frigid and humid periods of the Holocene. From 1540 to around 1620, a period of high precipitations took place. Subsequent anomalies both in temperature as in precipitation levels occurred in the decades of 1640 and 1650, as well as from the decade of 1690 to approximately 1705. These climate anomalies, an effect of the global phenomenon known as the Little Ice Age, generated agricultural transitions, floods, prolonged droughts, epidemics, epizootic diseases, and recurrent agricultural crises that disrupted human health and stimulated high mortality rates. As pointed out by Skopyk and Melville, the peak of the Little Ice Age was a global event of millennial-scale importance in Mexico, and thus, presumably, in Central America, as posed in this chapter in a hypothetical manner.[12]

Between the middle and the end of the nineteenth century, in the context of the institutionalization of meteorology in the region, both the dominant features of climate and the influence of different phenomena and climate anomalies were documented for the first time.

In the case of Costa Rica, for example, temperature anomalies during the period of 1866–1899 have been documented. These show a rise in temperature associated with the El Niño events including the 1876–1878 event, considered the most intense episode of that century with a warming record of more than 2 °C. Furthermore, records show a drop in temperature in the Central Valley probably associated with the Krakatoa volcano eruption in 1883, whose effects were felt at a global level. Its ashes and dust were expelled into the upper troposphere affecting the incoming solar radiation and altering the Earth's climate for years.[13]

One of the biggest challenges and, at the same time, part of the wide range of opportunities of Central American environmental history is to expand to other countries of the region the historical studies on climate, and to associate such events with the social, economic, and political processes and junctures.

Natural Disasters, Cultural Change, and Institutional Responses

The Central American geomorphological and climatic characteristics gave way to a series of natural hazards that, together with the human actions in the ecosystems, generated numerous disasters that severely affected the societies of the Isthmus, impairing their own material and cultural development. Although we will not enter into the debates or theoretical developments generated particularly as of the social sciences regarding the natural or socially constructed character of disasters, the fact is that for the purpose of this chapter we do consider these as the confluence of natural phenomena—particularly hydrometeorological and geological—and the risk and vulnerability as social and historical constructions.[14] As Virginia García points out, disasters are "the processes resulting from pre-existing critical conditions in which the accumulated vulnerability and the social construction of risk play decisive roles in their association with a particular natural hazard."[15]

In Central America, volcanic eruptions and earthquakes have caused countless loss of human lives and an immeasurable material destruction. Just to mention a few of the most noteworthy cases, we have the Managua earthquake in 1972, with 6,000 deaths recorded, and the series of nineteen earthquakes in San Salvador, El Salvador from 1524 to date, twelve of which were severe enough to destroy most of the city's buildings, and the totality of them on one occasion.[16]

Other cases that stand out for their human, socioeconomic, and political consequences are those known as the Santa Marta earthquakes, a series of strong quakes that destroyed the city of Santiago de los Caballeros, currently Antigua, Guatemala, in 1773. In 1776, the constant earthquakes forced the final relocation of the Kingdom's capital to a new settlement called Nueva Guatemala de la Asunción, now Guatemala's capital city.[17] This tragedy brings to light the concatenation between the geological event and diseases. After the earthquakes, particularly due to sanitary effects on the people, a typhus epidemic broke out, causing more deaths among the mestizo and Indigenous population than the earthquakes themselves.[18]

In Costa Rica, the Cartago earthquake on May 4, 1910 is considered as the most destructive in the country's history. With an estimated grade 8 magnitude on the Richter scale, this earthquake completely devastated the city and surrounding towns, causing at least seven hundred deaths. The city's destruction and the human tragedy it entailed had a broad photographical coverage (Figure 1.1), thus generating a significant impact on the people's awareness as to the extent of the tragedy.

| Hurricanes and other hydrometereological events have also taken a heavy toll on human lives. One of the most devastating was Hurricane Mitch in 1998, which caused the death of 18,000 people in all Central America, as well as major property losses, to the extent that some people believe that Honduras receded some fifty years in terms of

FIGURE 1.1. The Church of San Nicolás and the Plaza del Cuartel in Cartago, Costa Rica, after the earthquake of May 4, 1910.

Source: Archivo Nacional de Costa Rica, NP-002514 (1–3), Fotografías 1910.

infrastructure and economic development. The destruction of 50 percent of that year's crops, 70,000 houses, and 70 percent of road infrastructure, including fifty-two bridges, and the water distribution system that left 4.5 million people without access to safe and reliable water sources, leaves no doubt as to the dimension of the tragedy associated with such an event.[19]

Historically, floods are perhaps one of the effects that has caused more damages due to the occurrence of localized and specific natural events in the Central American region. Such was the case of the already mentioned city of Cartago in Costa Rica, which in 1891—only nineteen years before it was hit by the strongest earthquake in the country's history—it was almost totally flooded by the overflowing of the Reventado River. Recent studies indicate that the most probable cause for the rains that led to the flooding was a "temporal" in the Caribbean, that is, a several-day period of continuous moderate to intense rains associated with a high-pressure system over the Gulf of Mexico, and the convergence of a low-level flow of moisture over part of Central America that reached the Cartago Valley.[20]

Thus, floods and other consequences generated by hydrometeorological events of different magnitudes have left a wake of death and destruction that cannot be dissociated from the social construction of vulnerability and risk to natural phenomena. The materials, constructive systems, and characteristics of institutional response to natural hazards certainly in both the loss of human lives and the damage to infrastructure, key for economic and social development.[21]

On the other hand, despite the human drama generated by disasters, these too have created cohesion and unity among the survivors, through a common and shared memory not only of the destruction but of the altruism and heroic deeds of thousands of people as well. They also create a necessary learning process for the reconstruction and construction of new cities and settlements, as well as the search for ways of coexisting with the phenomena that originate the disasters.[22]

Diseases and Their Human and Social Effects

Tropical diseases affected the Indigenous peoples before the arrival of the Spanish. But the introduction of pathogens for which the native populations had no resistance became one of the most serious consequences of the Spanish invasion of the American territories. Smallpox, measles, flu, whooping cough, typhus, typhoid fever, malaria, yellow fever, and others were devastating for the Indigenous populations, becoming a major factor in the American demographic collapse after the arrival of the Europeans.[23]

The Indigenous peoples were susceptible to these diseases which became epidemics due to the spread of the infections, their virulence, and the resulting mortality rates. Such epidemics are often known as "virgin soil" epidemics. This means that a disease introduced in populations that have never experienced it, or have been free from it for a period of time long enough to lose any acquired immunity, will produce a massive strike against such populations.[24]

Estimates show that during the period of the Spanish conquest, the territories that currently conform Honduras and Nicaragua had close to 800,000 Indigenous persons each.[25] By the end of the colonial period, the native population in both provinces had decreased by almost 90 percent. In Honduras it was reduced to nearly 70,000 Indigenous people, while in Nicaragua only little more than 80,000 remained.[26] Similar trends were observed in the rest of the region, despite the significant intraregional demographic differences existing before the arrival of the Europeans.

Documentary evidence shows that the greatest epidemics of smallpox (1520), plague (1531), measles (1533), and plague or typhus (1545) occurred during the first thirty years of the conquest in Central America. These diseases continued to ravage at intervals the native population throughout the colonial period, and toward the end, it took a major toll of victims among the Indigenous recently gathered in missions.

While an intense debate continues regarding the specific weight of tropical diseases in the dramatic decline in Central American Indigenous populations during the colonial period, there is a relative consensus as to their importance in the demographic recovery rate. This rate revealed significant intraregional variations linked to the environmental conditions that constrained or facilitated the spread of diseases, the size and characteristics of the settlements, and their impact on the reproductive capacity of the population.[27]

The infectious diseases not only affected the Indigenous population but, especially before the so-called bacteriological revolution, their incidence was overly frequent and, on many occasions, devastating for the entire population.[28] It was not until well into the twentieth century, when the miasmatic theory (based on the *miasms*, which were the foul-smelling vapors that arose from the ground and contaminated water and were the cause of the majority of infectious diseases) was substituted by the germ theory of disease, which proposes that microorganisms are responsible for a wide range of illnesses. This was critical, since the incorrect identification of the diseases' origin had an impact on its spread and recurrence.[29]

In this scientific–medical and social context, diseases and their epidemiological nature were overly recurring in the region. In Costa Rica, outbreaks of smallpox, yellow fever, malaria, and dysentery were quite frequent throughout the nineteenth century. Other infectious diseases, such as whooping cough, measles, influenza, chickenpox, mumps, typhoid, and infant cholera, were common among the childhood population.[30]

The population's greatest enemy was invariably the contagious diseases, mainly affecting children, caused by water contamination, absence of sanitary infrastructure, and lack of knowledge of hygiene standards,[31] all this in the context of an emerging urban development associated with an increasing social differentiation. These diseases that resulted from internal conditions were responsible for wreaking havoc among the population, up to the first half of the twentieth century.

Cholera deserves a special mention due to its worldwide impact. From the beginning of the nineteenth century to the end of the twentieth, seven pandemics of this disease developed in the region. Between 1836 and 1837, cholera hit Mexico, Guatemala, Nicaragua, and Panama.[32] The disease appeared again in Nicaragua between 1854 and 1855. Although its inhabitants appeared to have developed certain immunity, its neighbors to the south did not meet the same fate. The soldiers returning to Costa Rica after the Battle of Rivas in 1856 in the context of the war against William Walker's filibusters rapidly disseminated the disease,[33] which caused havoc in that country. It is estimated to have caused the death of between 8 percent and 10 percent of the Costa Rican population, the majority from the popular sectors located in the Central Valley, affecting mainly adults, and in a greater number, women.[34]

Thus, contagious diseases have been present in the Central American societies throughout history. This is explained by the combination of the endemic nature of some of these diseases, structural factors such as poverty, inequality, unequal access to health services added to a poor institutionalism, and other specific circumstances such as wars and natural phenomena.[35] This has led to the fact that even in in the twenty-first century, despite significant medical advances aimed at fighting a wide range of contagious diseases, such diseases continue to strike the Central American populations, while they slowly advance in the epidemiological transition—which is the shift from contagious diseases to chronic nontransmissible diseases as the leading cause of death—with sharp differences between and within the countries.[36]

Socioenvironmental Changes: The Human Footprint in Central America

Agrarian Systems: From Longstanding Agrobiodiversity to Modern Radical Simplification

The Central American territory was populated more than 10,000 years ago. Its first inhabitants would group in small bands of hunters and gatherers that moved in search of animals and wild plants, at the end of the Ice Age.[37] Toward 9.000–8.000 BC, "a climate change took place with extremely important results for ancient history. The new ecological conditions inherent to the Holocene period enabled the first experiments conducive to agriculture. Bit by bit, human societies became more numerous and complex, and the differences between them more distinct."[38] The Mayan Civilization settled in the northern part of Central America, in the Central-Pacific axis, toward the fourth millennium BC Owing to the growing development of agriculture and the consequent population growth, the Mayans reached their splendor as one of America's principal tributary empires between 300 and 600 BC, achieving a high degree of complexity.[39]

The intensification of agricultural production was carried out using various techniques: flooding, building terraces and planting that contoured the steepest hillsides, planting trees, and growing vegetable gardens. Some of the most important crops were maize (the indisputable base of the Indigenous people's diet), beans, peppers, pumpkins, tomatoes, and cocoa. Hunting and fishing complemented their diet, which prevailed despite the agricultural predominance.[40]

These characteristics were present in the Central and Southern regions. The importance of agriculture and the characteristics of the production techniques varied according to the degree of complexity of the different Indigenous groups and the ecological constraints of the spaces they inhabited. Even in the southern region, characterized by a clear dominance of Chibcha languages introduced from South America and the endogenous development of their cultures, maize production associated with other crops such as beans and squash enjoyed a significant importance.[41]

The predominant cultivation technique was known as "slash and burn," which consisted in cutting down the trees at the beginning of the dry season and then burning the timber and brush just before the rainy season started. The ashes and charcoal contributed to soil fertilization. Next, the seeds were planted, making sure that planting coincided with the first seasonal rains. The cornfield or "milpa" would be used for a couple of years, and then the land would be left fallow for a long period, from four to seven years.[42]

Despite the undeniable ecological originality and energy efficiency of the American agrarian systems, it is evident that in some cases the load on the ecospaces was exceeded, particularly in the large power centers.[43] The latter shows that the material complexity of human societies played a major role in the transformation of the ecosystems throughout time.

Such seems to be the case of the Mayan Civilization. Although a univocal interpretation is nonexistent as to their disappearance before the Spanish arrival, major explanatory hypotheses suggest that despite this group's adaptability to the tropical jungle and the ecological originality of their agrarian system, this was an extremely fragile one. The system could have been dismantled due to apparently minor alterations which began building up until it reached a deep subsistence crisis.[44]

In this context of ecological originality and biocultural diversity of the pre-Hispanic agrarian systems, and despite apparently having exceeded several limits, the arrival of the Spanish to the Isthmus takes place. The conquest had an unparalleled impact in the demographic, social, political, cultural, and environmental fields in the Central American region.[45] One of their key manifestations was precisely the radical transformation in land use and landscape. Central America and its natural resources were abruptly introduced into the European world economy by way of the Spanish monarchy's needs and demands, and later by the final insertion of the region into the world market.

The ecoregions were disarticulated and reorganized, thus triggering serious ecological imbalances due to the loss of biodiversity and subsequent vulnerability of the ecosystems. Suddenly, it was not about trying to imitate nature but to transform it into a productive instrument.[46] Land clearing by the Spanish aimed at expanding the cultivation of cash crops, in particular sugar cane and wheat, along with plowing the land in preparation for planting resulted in the erosion of the volcanic soil.[47] In Guatemala, where the Indigenous population continued to live in the highlands, the natives were forced to plant on hillside areas where the soil was thinner and erosion prone.[48]

According to Díaz and Viales, by the beginning of the 1750s, the institutional change implemented by the Bourbon reforms was accompanied by a far-reaching economic change.[49] Indigo was the product that exerted a greater weight on the Central American economic dynamism toward the end of the colonial period, whose earnings were reinvested in highly profitable activities of the moment such as livestock farming. Indigo flourished thanks to the strong demand in the European dye markets in the first stages of industrialization. During the following decades the dye business thrived, and it was not until 1799 that it began to decline.[50]

Indigo was planted in the Central American Pacific region, from the Guatemalan southeast to the Rivas Isthmus. Still, El Salvador was the indigo land par excellence. There, indigo was planted both in small and large farms. This generated a significant impact in land ownership, by allowing the consolidation and expansion of the haciendas, with negative consequences for the Indigenous communities. The high demand of dye also caused the banning of restrictions on Indigenous labor at the dye works (*obrajes de añil*), previously forbidden for their unhealthy conditions.[51]

The environmental impact of the dyeing activity was directly related to the productive transformation process. Reports from the sixteenth and seventeenth centuries evidenced the problems caused by plant residues once the dye was extracted.[52] Recent research shows the impact of indigo production on the vegetation associated with rivers and other water sources. Apart from the contamination and its effects on human and animal health, the blue-tinged water affected the ecosystems' trophic networks. Certain microalgae reduce their growth rate as the concentration of the indigo dye effluent increases.[53]

The main socioenvironmental transformations generated by the indigo boom in Central America, however, were indirect. The increase in indigo production as a driving force of the economy of the *Reino de Guatemala* stimulated the productive specialization at the inter- and intraregional levels. As mentioned above, indigo production was concentrated mainly in El Salvador. This brought about an increasing displacement of other agricultural and manufactured products required to feed and clothe the growing labor force of the indigo production. As a result, several Guatemalan regions specialized in *ropa de tierra*, maize, and wheat.[54] Livestock farming gained momentum in Honduras, Nicaragua, and Costa Rica stimulated not only by the demand for foodstuffs in the dyeing areas but for leather as well, which was used for manufacturing the bags or pouches used for packing the dye. Furthermore, due to the expansion of the intraregional trade networks, Costa Rica experienced a short but dynamic cycle of tobacco production which was marketed in Nicaragua and Panama.[55]

After the downfall of the indigo trade and the subsequent disarticulation of the productive chains associated with its production and export, the young Central American republics sought relentlessly to enter the world market in a stable and continuous way.[56] One of the strategies carried out for this purpose was the introduction of new crops, and in this context the one with the greatest impact in all fields of regional history begins to excel: coffee.

Although coffee was first introduced in Panama at the end of the eighteenth century, Costa Rica was first in experimenting successfully with coffee for commercial purposes, followed later by El Salvador and Guatemala.[57] Nicaragua had a late coffee expansion, while in Honduras the coffee-growing areas were rather small, producing only enough to meet local demand (see Figure 1.2).[58]

Toward the end of the nineteenth century and the beginning of the twentieth, two predominantly coffee-growing agrarian systems coexisted in Central America. These were the industrialized farming, clearly monoculture, and the organic-based agriculture, characterized by polyculture for self-consumption and surplus marketing. In the latter case, whether coffee was the main product or not, it necessarily coexisted with other crops.[59]

In this context, the predominantly coffee-growing agroecosystems had lost part of their energy and nutrient self-sufficiency, noted by the initial import of external inputs to the agroecosystem. Some of these external inputs were organic-based such as leguminous trees planted not only for regulating sunlight but for fixing nitrogen and organic matter in the soil as well.[60] Another of these inputs was guano, imported to fill the lack of

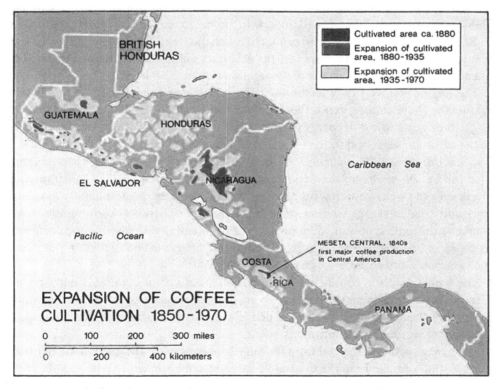

FIGURE 1.2. Coffee cultivation and expansion, c. 1850–1970.
Source: Map by John V. Cotter, in *Historical Atlas of Central America* by Carolyn Hall and Héctor Pérez Brignoli. © 2003 University of Oklahoma Press. Reprinted by permission of the publisher.

cattle manure due to the displacement of livestock resulting from the high specialization of the coffee-growing activity.[61] In sum, guano had to be imported for replacing the energy and nutrients the agroecosystem no longer provided.[62]

It is noted that by the end of the nineteenth century, the transition to coffee specialization was overwhelming. This modernization, however, was not total: the agrarian systems still depended largely on the reutilized biomass which derived from the agroecosystem itself. For example, maize was used as animal feed, pastures turned into cattle manure for fertilizing purposes, beans and other legumes helped replace soil nutrients, and trees, in addition to providing shade for coffee and nutrients to the soil, also supplied timber and building materials for the farmers. In short, organic-based traditional agroecosystems were still numerous, despite the prevalent coffee monoculture in the Central American rural landscape.

As of the second half of the twentieth century, coffee cultivation witnessed an important production intensification process, closely bound to the shift toward smaller size and higher-yielding coffee varieties. This brought along an increase in plant density per cultivated area, together with a growing dependence on external energy inputs to the agroecosystem, particularly agrochemicals (for nutrient replenishment in detriment of the shade system) and fungicides (for fighting diseases such as rust which expanded globally, though with differentiated impacts in the various coffee regions of the world).[63]

Hence, the dramatic increase in productivity, characteristic of the Green Revolution boom, resulted in a growing loss of energy efficiency of the ecosystems, and the consequent increase in unsustainability of the agrarian system as a whole.

The loss of biodiversity (and the reduction of its associated ecological functions) due to the monoculture trend, the drastic transformation of the agricultural landscape, the dramatic loss of energy efficiency due to the dependence on external inputs to the agroecosystem, and the territorial disarticulation can be considered as the main socioenvironmental consequences of the Central American coffee industrialization. These add to others already existing since the nineteenth century, such as contaminated rivers with the water resulting from the wet-milling process, predominantly in Costa Rica and Guatemala, generating protests and conflicts between communities surrounding the milling sites and their owners.[64] An increasing shortage of wood occurred in the areas where an accelerated specialization and intensification of coffee production took place, as was the case of Costa Cuca in Guatemala.[65]

The banana crop is considered as the other spearhead of agrarian capitalism in Central America. Bananas became the driving product of the Honduran economy, while in other Central American countries such as Guatemala, Costa Rica, and Nicaragua bananas are regarded as complementary.

The banana activity emerged from the huge land concessions granted to the railroad construction companies in the Central American Caribbean, which later found in banana cropping a highly profitable business.[66]

Toward the end of the nineteenth century, banana production began in the hands of small-scale farmers, but it soon passed on to large capitalist firms. The most important was by far the United Fruit Company (UFCo), founded in New Jersey in 1899 after a merger of several companies. Other companies such as Cuyamel Fruit Co. and Standard Fruit Co. also stood out in the region.[67] The majority of banana plantations occupied barely transformed lands, located in the flood plains of the valleys of rivers that flow into the Caribbean, and by the end of the 1930s, the companies also established business operations in the Guatemalan and Costa Rican Pacific regions (see Figure 1.3).[68]

The banana activity shares the majority of the environmental consequences that result from the coffee modernization process, such as the degradation of the ecosystems, the loss of energy efficiency, and the contamination of water sources, among others.[69]

Even so, banana cropping has several socioenvironmental specificities that deserve to be highlighted. One of these is that banana is a typical cash crop and has never formed part of traditional polycultures. It was a railside crop that developed along with the railroads built to connect the economic and political centers of the Central American countries with the Caribbean. As plantations expanded, the fruit companies constructed a market for its produce particularly in the United States. In banana cropping, the economic exchange took precedence over ecological exchange right from the planting process. It was preceded by the rainforest destruction and lacked a clear

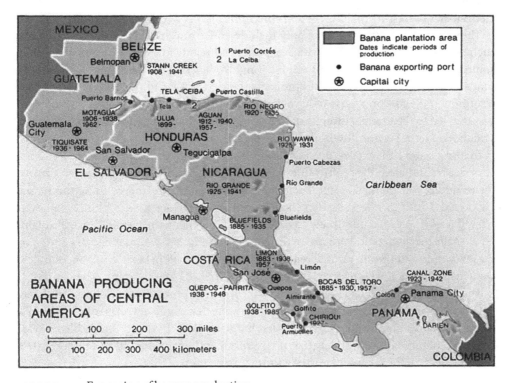

FIGURE 1.3. Expansion of banana production.

Source: Map by John V. Cotter, in *Historical Atlas of Central America* by Carolyn Hall and Héctor Pérez Brignoli. © 2003 University of Oklahoma Press. Reprinted by permission of the publisher.

socioecological transition—as in the previously mentioned coffee case—where the traditional agroecosystems stood as a sort of cultural resistance to commercial crops and the global mass consumption that went along with it.[70]

The evident monoculture trend of banana production, and the loss of complexity of the ecosystems associated with it, brought along other ecological transformations, both in human and social terms as in the productive field. In 1903, in the UFCo banana plantations in Bocas del Toro (Panama), the Panama disease (*Fusarium cubense*) appeared, a fungus that attacks the stem and roots of the plant causing its death.[71] For decades, the infested lands were abandoned, turning the banana activity into one of the most predatory in territorial terms within the export crops. In the 1940s the UFCo discovered that the fungus dissappeared by flooding the land for a three- to six-month period.[72] This method led to drastic ecosystem transformations.

Yet another disease, the Sigatoka, caused by an anaerobic fungus, developed in the 1940s. In an attempt to control it, a solution of copper sulfate and lime in water was used to spray the crops. This compound called Bordeaux Mixture had to be applied intensively, later causing severe health problems to the workers who performed this task.[73]

Chemical fertilization was relatively widespread toward 1950, which clearly contrasts with the gradual manner in which agrochemicals were introduced in other crops such as coffee.[74] Companies would prepare their own formulas and compounds at their laboratories for testing in different divisions or farms.

The agroexport supply did not only include coffee and bananas. Other cash crops, such as cocoa and sugar cane, which experienced relatively short economic cycles in some cases, carried significant economic weight.[75] Sugar cane underwent a productive modernization and intensification process regarded similar to that of coffee, with the irruption and widespread use of agrochemicals and an important mechanization process that led to the gradual disappearance of *trapiches* (small sugar mills) and to the construction of large sugar mills or *ingenios*, especially after 1950.[76]

In the context of export diversification and postwar developmentalism, Central America stimulated the cultivation of new agricultural export products. Cotton, for example, was planted in the Pacific plains, mainly in Nicaragua, El Salvador, and Guatemala, and, to a lesser extent, in Honduras and Costa Rica.[77] The Pacific zone offered important soil and climate advantages. Among them, the terrain, since the plains favored the mechanization process of the crops, in addition to well-defined dry and rainy seasons, and an optimum rainfall regime.[78] The major problem these crops encountered were insect plagues, which forced the producers to invest large sums in pesticides.[79]

The relation between DDT and the cotton crop development in the Central American Pacific deserves special mention. DDT was only one of a whole new class of organochlorine insecticides that resulted from research during World War II. They killed a wide spectrum of insects so effectively that their promoters began advocating a total eradication of insects at the farms, instead of a simple "pest control."

The first Latin American countries to systematically use pesticides soon found themselves trapped in the despicable "pesticides treadmill": a form of technological lock-in in which farmers, attracted by the financing by local banks and international organizations, and encouraged by extension services, were forced to purchase a variety of insecticides, herbicides, fungicides, and nematicides in increasingly large amounts, aimed at maintaining productivity in the face of a growing pesticide resistance and proliferation of a diversity of pest species. The intensive use of pesticides brought about a cotton cultivation boom along the Central American Pacific coast with an elevated social cost resulting from pesticide poisoning.[80]

Moreover, cotton cultivation, intensive in external energy inputs (agrochemicals, tractors, and agricultural machinery, among others) exacerbated social inequalities instead of reducing them, by playing a signature role in making Central America one of the hot spots of political conflicts at the end of the 1970s and 1980s.[81]

Further on, in the rising liberalization and deregulation of the agricultural activity in general, typical of the neoliberal policies' impact on the Central American agricultural sector, the Caribbean Basin Iniciative (1982) permitted the entrance of diverse products to the United States in clearly favorable conditions.[82] This consolidated the United States as the prime destination of Central American export goods. Other tropical fruits (pineapple, melon, watermelon), flowers, and foliage were added to the exports, but again, these required an intensive use of fertilizers and pesticides.[83]

Extractivism in Central America: Mining, Forests, and Livestock Farming

The major mining operations in Central America took place in Honduras, becoming the main economic activity throughout the entire colonial period.[84] First, the gold "placeres" were exploited, which are mineral deposits of alluvial origin, interspersed with gravel, sand, and rocks. Then, c. 1560, important silver deposits were discovered. From the very beginning, silver mining faced severe problems, in particular, labor shortages, lack of capital, and primitive exploitation and processing techniques.[85] The fire technique to soften the minerals was used from the sixteenth century up to the middle of the eighteenth, when the use of gunpowder for this purpose became widespread. The Honduran mining operations used hydraulic energy for processing the minerals containing silver, using the water courses that flowed toward the valleys. Yet it should be noted that in times of water shortage, the mining sites remained closed.

In the smelting process, both wood charcoal and mercury amalgamation were used. In the case of smelting with firewood, the pressure this activity exerted on the forests was unquestionable. Calculations show that to melt 46 kilos of the ore, 12 kilos of firewood were needed.[86]

In the context of this economic boom that took place between the middle and the end of the eighteenth century, silver mining in Honduras was intensified, boosted by a series of incentives granted by the authorities, such as the reduction from 20 percent to 10 percent in a tax imposed by the Crown, a decrease in the price of mercury, the creation of a bank for financing the miners' activities, and the reinstatement of the Indigenous *repartimiento* in the mines.[87]

With the advent of the liberal regimes in Central America between the end of the nineteenth century and the first decades of the twentieth, in the midst of the agroexport boom, mining became an integral part of foreign investment, especially by the United States. The strong capital injection allowed for solving the chronic problems of the silver mines, such as technical limitations and capital shortage. In that same period, a similar situation happened in Nicaragua and Costa Rica during the gold mining boom.[88]

As for the Costa Rican case, the predominance of foreign companies in the mining industry at this time, such as the Abangares Gold Mining, associated with the UFCo which controlled maritime and railway transport in the Costa Rican Caribbean, may explain why the minerals extracted in Guanacaste (Pacific coast) were transported to Port Limon on the Atlantic/Caribbean, instead of to the Pacific port of Puntarenas.

As Reinaldo Funes well analyzed for the Great Caribbean, from the 1990s to the present, a new mining boom has taken place in countries such as the Dominican Republic (gold and nickel), Cuba (nickel), and particularly in some Central American countries like Honduras, Nicaragua, and Guatemala. In this new context, dominated, moreover, by open-pit mining megaprojects, Canadian and US companies prevail, in addition to the demand of emerging powers such as China.[89]

The socially excluding and environmentally predatory character of this new type of mining has caused many social conflicts.[90] These are due to both the environmental impact arising from the production processes and its effect on human health as by the unequal appropriation of environmental services and natural resources, such as water and minerals. Open-pit mining also generates a strong competition over land use and water availability for agricultural production.[91]

Forest exploitation for commercial purposes in Central America is long-standing. Already in the early colonial period, during relatively short economic cycles of forest products such as balsam, which abounded in the coast of El Salvador, and the sarsaparilla root were gathered in what is currently Honduran territory and transported by ship from the country's northern ports.[92] From the pine forests in the Nicaraguan central mountain region, tar was obtained for medicinal purposes as well as for pitch. These products were exported from the Nicaraguan port of Realejo and destined for Peru.[93]

The revitalization of the Central American economy and trade due to the indigo boom in the second half of the eighteenth century decisively influenced the creation of vast and unprecedented global trade networks which anticipated the formal insertion of the region into the global market, in which wood held a prominent place.[94]

Toward the mid-nineteenth century, logging activity was a well-articulated business. Travelers such as E. G. Squier highlighted the extensive mahogany reserves found in Honduras, and the well-organized and systematic cutting and transport processes.[95] Central American woods were in high demand for making fine handicrafts (for consumption by the new industrial European bourgeoisie) in mahogany, *genizaro*, cedar, and other precious woods.

This luxury wood consumption obtained from the extractive exploitation of the tropical forests included the manufacture of furniture, handicrafts, sports articles (chess pieces), tool handles, musical and scientific instruments, piano boxes, veneers, and plywood, among others.[96] Other lumber uses were related to a strategic nature, such as shipbuilding, construction of military fortifications, and the manufacture of diverse military supplies, blatantly increasing the pressure on forest ecosystems.[97]

The exploitation of dye woods gave way to traditional clothing manufacture, expanding later to industrial textile production. Despite their minor importance in the world dye market, the Central American dye woods paraded through the European dyeing plants for industrial textile dyeing, between the eighteenth and mid-nineteenth centuries.

Toward the end of the nineteenth century and the beginning of the twentieth, while still in full agroexport boom, the trade of woods of extractive origin continued to be a dynamic and highly profitable business in Central America. Toward the mid-twentieth century, the commercial exploitation of timber in the region took on a new dimension, and an evidently different territorial and mercantile dynamics. Though extractive wood exploitation persisted, forest trade was led by a combination between the sale of "cheap" woods (once lacking trade value) and timber obtained from forest crops or tree "plantations" (a new and lucrative forest exploitation modality).

In the case of tree plantations, balsa wood stood out, employed in building a variety of military supplies, which explains why during World War II and in a war economy context, the US State Department encouraged the development of balsa plantations in countries such as Ecuador and Costa Rica.[98] In Costa Rica, balsa wood stood in first place in timber exports during the war years (see Figure 1.4).

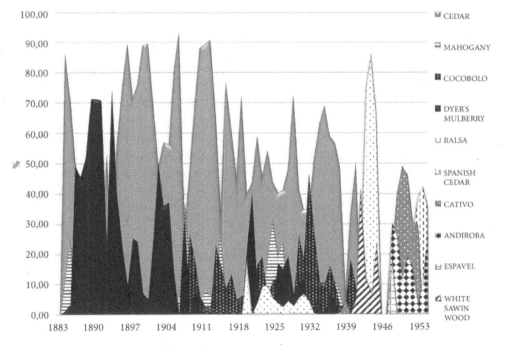

FIGURE 1.4. Wood exports of Costa Rica, 1883–1955, by species.

Source: Dirección General de Estadística y Censos (DGEC). Anuarios Estadísticos, 1883–1955 and Resúmenes Estadísticos, 1883–1910.

The publishing market, in particular the written press, became one of the economic sectors whose growth spurred the aggregate demand for forest products in the United States (the main consumer of Central American forestry products).[99]

Beginning in the 1940s, the United States started importing low-cost logged and sawn wood, associated with the housing construction and war supplies manufacturing boom, as well as plywood for industrial and domestic use. The latter was linked to the creation and expansion of the typical middle-class suburbs of the 1950s, when wood continued to be the construction material par excellence.

The extractive exploitation of precious woods from the Central American forests brought along profound ecological aftereffects. Both the destruction of the forest and the expansion of the agricultural and livestock farming activities associated with the changes in land use had a critical impact on the irreversible alteration of the trophic networks and the hydrological cycle, the intensification of erosion processes, and forest fragmentation, which entailed area reduction and connectivity between fragments.[100]

Regarding "tree plantations," the deforestation of biodiverse forests for planting uniform single-species trees generated the loss of many of the forest's ecological functions, as well as its essential productions for human life and its livelihood.[101] The massification of forestry products, together with the region's development and intensification of productive and extractive activities, contributed to the depletion of two thirds of the Central American forests between 1940 and 1990, to the extent that the destruction of the forest cover that occurred between 1950 and 1990 was greater than that of the last five hundred years.[102]

As in other Latin American countries, livestock development and its socioenvironmental consequences in Central America are long-standing. In the Isthmus, livestock easily multiplied in a first stage due to abundant natural pastures. The main products obtained from cattle were tallow and hides and, in a smaller measure, meat. During the second half of the sixteenth century, great quantities of hides were exported to Spain from the northern ports of Honduras.[103]

Between the mid-eighteenth century and the end of the colonial period, in light of the already mentioned indigo specialization, a greater demand for other products grew, among them, cattle. This laid the foundations for huge estates in Costa Rica's North Pacific, and along the Pacific coast of Nicaragua and Honduras. In the years following the political independence, livestock farming provided considerable fortunes in Honduras and Nicaragua,[104] while in Costa Rica's North Pacific it became a prevalent economic activity (see Figure 1.5).[105]

Although the debate persists on the environmental impact caused by traditional or precapitalized livestock farming in Latin America regarding deforestation and the creation of anthropogenic savannahs, the fact is that the nomadic cattle that once roamed in extensive natural grasslands do not seem to have been too numerous in relation to the local resource base. Documentary evidence suggests that during the colonial period, the environmental impact of livestock and other animals was limited.[106] Central America does not seem to be the exception.[107]

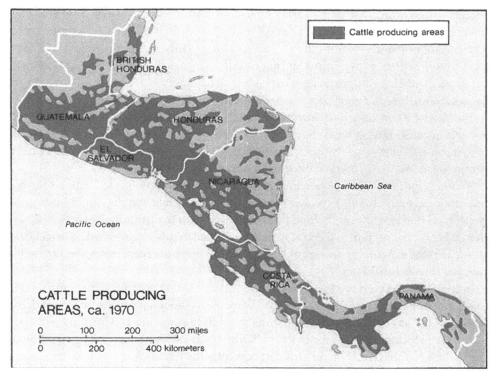

FIGURE 1.5. Cattle-producing areas, c. 1970.
Source: Map by John V. Cotter, in *Historical Atlas of Central America* by Carolyn Hall and Héctor Pérez Brignoli. © 2003 University of Oklahoma Press. Reprinted by permission of the publisher.

Between the middle and the end of the nineteenth century, however, livestock farming became a driving force of landscape transformation. In the Isthmus, cattle raising turned into an increasingly capitalized and liberalized activity, endowed with a larger productive investment underpinned by livestock sales (for meat consumption), in both the domestic and the international markets, thus encouraging the consolidation of large livestock estates. Between 1850 and 1950, livestock advanced over the deciduous forest, especially in the Central American Pacific, favored by the widespread introduction of African grasses such as pará, guinea, and yaraguá.[108]

Other major innovations that helped set the stage for the modernization-capitalization of the Central American livestock activity were the introduction of improved livestock breeds, especially Indian or Brahman, such as Nelore, and the widespread use of barbed-wire fences in cattle-raising regions.[109] Toward the 1950s, in the context of the livestock boom throughout Latin America, the Central American case was a prototypical example of how beef exports stimulated livestock expansion.[110] In the 1950s, the increase in meat consumption and the nascent fast food industry in the United States prompted the search for new sources of inexpensive livestock. When a serious outbreak of foot-and-mouth disease affected South American beef, the US Department of Agriculture urged the certification of meat packing plants in Central America in 1957, triggering livestock expansion at an unprecedented pace.[111] Part of this development occurred through the appropriation of peasant farms, and pasture expansion in existing estates. Nevertheless, a great part of it occurred at the expense of the regions' forests.[112]

The activity's productive intensification was overwhelming in some Central American cattle-raising areas. Such was the case of Guanacaste, Costa Rica, when in 1950 it showed an average livestock density per person comparable to that of Uruguay, a prototypical country of marked livestock specialization in Latin America.[113]

Between 1961 and 1981, 38 percent of the regional production was destined for the international market. This gave way for Norman Myers's talk about a "hamburger connection" as the driving force behind forest destruction in the Isthmus. Nevertheless, domestic beef consumption in Central America doubled in this same period, which clearly shows that the economic pressure of livestock farming on the ecosystems was not exclusively of external character.[114]

In the Central American livestock boom context, another environmental impact due to the modernization process was the load of excessive stocking density on the methane levels, as well as carbon dioxide emissions through the clearing and burning of forests and savannahs to make way for pastures.[115] The Food and Agriculture Organization of the United Nations (FAO) estimates that currently the livestock sector generates more greenhouse gases—18 percent, as measured in CO_2 equivalent—than transport.[116]

From the 1980s, livestock lost ground in Central America. The reduction in the external and internal demand for meat due to economic (subsidy removal), institutional (US restrictions on livestock exports), and even cultural factors (changes in food consumption patterns) slowed down livestock production.[117] This loss in dynamism brought about positive effects in some Latin American countries, though in an uneven manner. Precisely in Central America, the total pasture area has been reduced by 2 percent since 1990, although this has not necessarily meant the substitution of livestock for more sustainable or socially inclusive activities.[118]

THE CENTRAL AMERICAN ENVIRONMENT
BETWEEN PESSIMISM AND HOPE

Central America is certainly a land of contrasts, visible in its geomorphological, biological, and climatic characteristics as a whole. This has unquestionably influenced the differentiated character of the human–environmental relations that prevailed in the region throughout its history. Even so, apart from intraregional differences and contrasts, the Isthmus's environmental history reveals common and shared features, some of which we attempted to shed light on in this chapter, based on the analysis of the major natural conditioning factors of culture and sociocultural transformations of nature.

Therefore, nature as a determining factor of human material and cultural development has played a decisive role—which went easily unnoticed—in the configuration of the human societies that inhabited the region from the first settlements to the present. The geological and climatic features that spurred the development of a vast agricultural and livestock production, allowing the region to meet its food requirements and later those of the resources world market, also had an impact on the destruction of settlements and infrastructure and an enormous loss of human lives, situations with which Central Americans have learned to cope. Nonetheless, the undeniable agency of the natural world seems insufficient to justify the socioeconomic problems or the human tragedies. In the Central American case, it seems clear that human action—or the lack of it—has exacerbated the role of nature as a cultural conditioning factor. The unsustainable ways of relating with the natural world, the institutional weakness, and many other distinctly human and specifically social factors have come together and changed the direction and consequences of diverse historical processes in which—as in those mentioned herein—the main conditioning factor has been nature.

In regard to the socioenvironmental transformations on the ecosystems generated by human action, Central American environmental history may be considered convulsive, a result of the structural mark of extractive and productive activities that witnessed important modernization processes. In addition, the inherent characteristics of more recently developed productive activities had a significant impact on ecological change and landscape transformation, as was the case of industrialized farming in all its forms. Thus, environmental transformation in Central America was an integral part of a lengthy, complex, and unfinished civilizing process, such as present-day global society seems to face, a sort of change of skin of a region in constant tension due to changes in both the Global North and the Global South. This complex regional socioecological transition generated a considerable dilapidation—although certainly not an absolute one—of the greatest wealth that this geographical space has possessed since the beginning of human occupation: its biological and cultural diversity. This appears to justify the tremendous efforts realized by individuals, communities, organizations, and institutions of diverse nature to no longer *preserve* or *protect* a pristine nature but rather to rethink the relationship between Central Americans and the environment, and act accordingly.

In this brief attempt to determine the dimensions of change and permanence of the human–environmental relationship in Central America, many areas were excluded from the analysis. The impact of urban development and the distinctive mark of industrial metabolism, as well as the changes in the marine and fluvial ecosystems and their conditioning factors, are only a few of the unexplored areas in this study which, for an overall view of the region's environmental history, may be deemed fundamental. Even so, the extractive and productive activities examined in this study deserve a deeper analysis in future works of research.

NOTES

1. Héctor Pérez Brignoli, *El laberinto centroamericano: los hilos de la historia* (San José, Costa Rica: Vicerrectoría de Investigación/Centro de Investigaciones Históricas de América Central, 2017), 3.
2. Ibid.
3. Ibid.
4. Ibid., 14–16.
5. Ibid., 3.
6. Jorge A. Amador, María J. Anderson, Blanca Calderón, and Kathleen Pribyl, "The October 1891 Cartago (Costa Rica) Floods from Documentary Sources and 20CR Data," *International Journal of Climatology* 38 (2018): 4831.
7. Ibid.
8. Ibid., 4832.
9. Ibid.
10. Bradley Skopyk and Elinor G. K. Melville, "Disease, Ecology, and the Environment in Colonial Mexico," *Oxford Research Encyclopedia of Latin American History* Oxford: Oxford University Press), 2018, https://oxfordre.com/latinamericanhistory/view/10.1093/acref ore/9780199366439.001.0001/acrefore-9780199366439-e-496.
11. Ibid., n.p.
12. Ibid.
13. Jorge A. Amador, "Some Aspects of Climate in Costa Rica Using Historial Data from the XIX Century," *Tópicos Meteorológicos y Oceanográficos* 9, no. 2 (2002): 71.
14. Virginia García, "La perspectiva histórica en la antropología del riesgo y del desastre. Acercaminetos metodológicos" *Relaciones* XXV 97 (2004): 124–142.
15. Ibid., 129.
16. Shawn William Miller, *An Environmental History of Latin America* (New York: Cambridge University Press, 2007), 119.
17. Felipe Cadena, *Breve descripción de la noble ciudad de Santiago de los Caballeros de Guatemala y puntual noticia de su lamentable ruina ocasionada de un violento terremoto el día veintinueve de julio de 1773* (Guatemala City: Imprenta La Luna, 1774), https://comm ons.wikimedia.org/w/index.php?title=File:Breve_Descripci%C3%B3n_de_la_Noble_ Ciudad_de_Santiago_de_los_Caballeros_de_Guatemala.pdf.
18. Carlos Martínez, *Las ciencias médicas en Guatemala: Origen y evolución* (Guatemala City: Editorial Universitaria, 1964).
19. Miller, *Environmental History*, 119.
20. Amador et al., "October 1891 Cartago (Costa Rica) Floods," 4831.
21. Anthony Goebel McDermott and Ronny J. Viales, "Blaming It on the Weather: The Role of 'Inclement' Rainfall in Society-Nature Relations in Liberal Costa Rica (1860–1940)," *Global Environment* 6 (2011): 8–67; Ana Yolanda Zúñiga, ed., *Perspectivas Interdisciplinarias: Riesgo y vulnerabilidad ante fenómenos hidrometeorológico*s (Heredia, Costa Rica: EUNA, 2015); Sherry Johnson, "The History and Science of Hurricanes in the Greater Caribbean," *Oxford Research Encyclopedia of Latin American History*, Oxford University Press, September 2015, https://oxfordre.com/latinamericanhistory/view/10.1093/acrefore/9780199366439.001.0001/acrefore-9780199366439-e-57.
22. Miller, *Environmental History*, 125.

23. Skopyk and Melville, "Disease, Ecology, and the Environment," 7. See also Linda A. Newson, "Indian Population Patterns in Colonial Spanish America," *Latin American Research Review* 20, no. 3 (1985): 41–47.

24. Woodrow Borah, "Introducción," in *Juicios secretos de Dios: Epidemias y despoblación indígena en Hispanoamérica colonial*, edited by W. George Lovell and Noble David Cook, 21 (Quito, Ecuador: Ediciones Abya-Yala, 1999).

25. Linda A. Newson, "Variaciones regionales en el impacto del dominio colonial español en las poblaciones indígenas de Honduras y Nicaragua," *Mesoamérica* 13, no. 24 (1992): 298; Linda A. Newson, *The Cost of Conquest: Indian Decline in Honduras Under Spanish Rule* (Boulder, CO: Westview Press, 1986), 330.

26. Newson, "Variaciones regionales," 298.

27. Ibid., 302–304.

28. Luis Urteaga, "Miseria, miasmas y microbios. Las topografías médicas y el estudio del medio ambiente en el siglo XIX," *Geocrítica: Cuadernos críticos de geografía humana* 29 (1980), http://www.ub.edu/geocrit/geo29.htm.

29. W. George Lovell and Noble David Cook, "Desenredando la madeja de la enfermedad," in *Juicios secretos de Dios: Epidemias y despoblación indígena en Hispanoamérica colonial*, edited by W. George Lovell and Noble David Cook (Quito, Ecuador: Ediciones Abya-Yala, 1999), 247.

30. Ana María Botey, *Los orígenes del Estado de Bienestar en Costa Rica: Salud y protección social (1850-1940)* (San José, Costa Rica: Editorial de la Universidad de Costa Rica, 2019), 63–70.

31. Ibid., 72–75.

32. Ibid., 72.

33. Ibid., 81–84.

34. Ibid., 87.

35. Organización Panamericana de la Salud, "Principales enfermedades infecciosas en Centroamérica durante 1998, antes y después de Mitch," *Revista Panamericana de Salud Publica/Pan American Jouranl of Public Health* 6, no. 6 (1999): 440–443, https://scielosp.org/article/ssm/content/raw/?resource_ssm_path=/media/assets/rpsp/v6n6/0973.pdf.

36. Mariachiara Di Cesare, *El perfil epidemiológico de América Latina y el Caribe: desafíos, límites y acciones* (Santiago, Chile: Comisión Económica para América Latina y el Caribe, 2011), https://repositorio.cepal.org/bitstream/handle/11362/3852/1/S2011938.pdf.

37. Programa de las Naciones Unidas para el Medio Ambiente (PNUMA) and Comisión Centroamericana de Ambiente y Desarrollo (CCAD), *GEO Centroamérica: Perspectivas del medio ambiente 2004* (Mexico City: PNUMA and CCAD, 2006), 12, http://www.pnuma.org/deat1/pdf/GEO%20Centroamerica%202004.pdf.

38. Ibid.

39. Ibid., 13.

40. Ibid.

41. Ibid., 14–15.

42. Ibid., 13.

43. Miller, *An Environmental History*, 8–48.

44. Antonio Brailovsky, *Historia ecológica de Iberoamérica: De los mayas al Quijote* (Buenos Aires: Capital Intelectual, 2006), 89.

45. Guillermo Castro, *Naturaleza y sociedad en la historia de América Latina* (Panama City: Centro de Estudios Latinoamericanos (CELA), 1996), 113–224. See also Guillermo Castro H., "The Environmental Crisis in Latin America," *Oxford Research Encyclopedia of Latin American History*, Oxford University Press, July 2015, https://oxfordre.com/latin americanhistory/view/10.1093/acrefore/9780199366439.001.0001/acrefore-9780199366 439-e-60.
46. Ibid., 164–165.
47. PNUMA and CCAD, *GEO Centroamérica*, 17.
48. Ibid.
49. David Díaz and Ronny Viales, *El impacto económico de la independencia en Centroamérica, (1760–1840): Una interpretación desde la historia global* (San José, Costa Rica: Editorial de la Universidad de Costa Rica, 2016), xi.
50. Ibid., xii; José Fernández, *Pintando el mundo de azul: El auge añilero y el mercado centroamericano, 1750–1810* (San Salvador, El Salvador: CONCULTURA, 2003); DavidMcCreery, "Las cadenas de la materia prima índigo en los Imperios español y británico, de 1560 a 1850," in *De la plata a la cocaína: Cinco siglos de historia económica de América Latina, 1500–2000*, edited by Carlos Marichal, Steven Topik, and Frank Zephyr, 76–107 (Mexico City: Fondo de Cultura Económica/El Colegio de México, 2017).
51. PNUMA and CCAD, *GEO* Centroamérica, 19.
52. Adrianna Catena, "Indigo in the Atlantic World," *Oxford Research Encyclopedia of Latin American History*, Oxford University Press, February 2018, https://oxfordre.com/latin americanhistory/view/10.1093/acrefore/9780199366439.001.0001/acrefore-9780199366 439-e-494.
53. Mathias A. Chia and Rilwan I. Musa, "Effect of Indigo Dye Effluent on the Growth, Biomass Production and Phenotypic Plasticity of Scenedesmus quadricauda (Chlorococcales)" *Anais da Academia Brasileira de Ciências* 86, no. 1 (2014): 419–428.
54. They were rectangular blocks of woven cloth made of cotton and wool elaborated by skilled artisans in Indigenous communities. In regions without direct access to gold and silver mines, the commercialization of this type of goods generated considerable profits for Spaniards. See Karen B. Graubart, *With Our Labor and Sweat: Indigenous Women and the Formation of Colonial Society in Peru, 1550–1700* (Standford, CA: Stanford University Press, 2007), 29.
55. Díaz and Viales, *El impacto económico de la independencia*, xiii-xiv.
56. Miles Wortman, "Government Revenue and Economic Trends in Central America, 1787–1819," *The Hispanic American Historical Review* 55, no. 2 (May 1975): 251–286.
57. PNUMA and CCAD, *GEO Centroamérica*, 20; Héctor Pérez Brignoli, "Economía política del café en Costa Rica (1850–1950)," in *Tierra, café y sociedad: Ensayos sobre la historia agraria centroamericana*, edited by Héctor Pérez Brignoli and Mario Samper (San José, Costa Rica: FLACSO, 1994), 83–116; Lowell Gudmundson, "*Costa Rica Before Coffee: Society and Economy on the Eve of the Export Boom* (Baton Rouge: Louisiana State University Press, 1986); David McCreery, "El impacto del café en las tierras de las comunidades indígenas: Guatemala, 1870–1930," in Pérez Brignoli and Samper, *Tierra, café y sociedad*, 227–278; Héctor Lindo-Fuentes, "La introducción del café en El Salvador," in Pérez Brignoli and Samper, *Tierra, café y sociedad*, 55–82.
58. PNUMA and CCAD, *GEO* Centroamérica, 22; Elizabeth Dore, "La producción cafetalera nicaragüense, 1860–1930: Transformaciones estructurales," in Pérez Brignoli and Samper, *Tierra, café y sociedad*, 377–436; Eduardo Baumeister, "El café en Honduras," in

Pérez Brignoli and Samper, *Tierra, café y sociedad*, 437–493; Mario Samper, *Producción Cafetalera y Poder Político en Centroamérica* (San José, Costa Rica: EDUCA, 1998).

59. Andrea Montero, "Una aproximación a los cambios en el paisaje en el Valle Central de Costa Rica (1820–1900)," *HALAC* 3, no. 2 (2014): 276–309.

60. Mario Samper, "Tierra, trabajo y tecnología en el desarrollo del capitalismo agrario en Costa Rica," *Historia Agraria* 29 (2003): 81–104.

61. Iván Molina, *Costa Rica (1800–1850): El legado colonial y la génesis del capitalismo* (San José, Costa Rica: Editorial de la Universidad de Costa Rica, 2002), 248.

62. Carlos Naranjo, "Abonad vuestros cafetales: La recuperación de la fertilidad de los suelos del Valle Central de Costa Rica (1870–1915)," *Revista de Historia* (Costa Rica) 65–66 (2012): 53–67. For a global vision of the process of exploitation of guano in the context of nineteenth-century scientific plant breeding and its socioenvironmental consequences, see Gregory T. Cushman, *Guano and the Opening of the Pacific World: A Global Ecological History* (Cambridge, UK: Cambridge University Press, 2013); Gregory T. Cushman, "Guano, Intensive Agriculture, and Environmental Change in Latin America and the Caribbean," *Oxford Research Encyclopedia of Latin American History*, Oxford University Press, September 2017, https://oxfordre.com/latinamericanhistory/view/10.1093/acrefore/9780199366439.001.0001/acrefore-9780199366439-e-113.

63. On agrochemicals: Juan Infante-Amate and Wilson Picado, "La transición socio-ecológica en el café costarricense: Flujos de energía, materiales y uso del tiempo (1935–2010)," *Old and New Worlds: The Global Challenges of Rural History International Conference* (Lisbon: ISCTE-IUL, 2016), 9. See also Juan Infante-Amate and Wilson Picado, "Energy Flows in the Coffee Plantations of Costa Rica: From Traditional to Modern Systems (1935–2010)," *Regional Environmental Change* 18, no. 4 (2018): 1059–1071, https://doi.org/10.1007/s10113-017-1263-9. On fungicides: Stuart McCook, "The Global Rust Belt: *Hemileia vastatrix* and the Ecological Integration of World Coffee Production since 1850," *Journal of Global History* 1, no. 2 (2006): 177–195; Stuart McCook, "La roya del café en Costa Rica: Epidemias, innovación, y medio ambiente, 1950–1995," *Revista de Historia* (Costa Rica) 59–60 (2009): 99–117, https://www.revistas.una.ac.cr/index.php/historia/article/view/3471.

64. Gladys Rojas, *Café, ambiente y sociedad en la cuenca del Río Virilla, Costa Rica (1840–1955)* (San José: Editorial de la Universidad de Costa Rica, 2000); Andrea Montero and José Aurelio Sandí, "La contaminación de las aguas mieles en Costa Rica: un conflicto de contenido ambiental (1840–1910)," *Diálogos, Revista electrónica de historia* 10, no. 1 (2009): 4–15, http://www.redalyc.org/articulo.oa?id=43913137001; Mario Ramírez, "Problemas, Protestas y Conflictos Ambientales en la Cuenca Del Río Virilla: 1850–1900," *Diálogos, Revista Electrónica de Historia* 4, no. 2 (2004): 1–62, https://revistas.ucr.ac.cr/index.php/dialogos/article/view/6279.

65. Stefania Gallini, *Una historia ambiental del café en Guatemala. La Costa Cuca entre 1830 y 1902* (Guatemala City: AVANCSO, 2008), 262–268.

66. PNUMA and CCAD, *GEO Centroamérica*, 22.

67. Ibid.

68. Ibid., 23.

69. Ronny Viales and Andrea Montero, "Una aproximación al impacto ambiental del cultivo del banano en el Atlántico/Caribe de Costa Rica (1870–1930)," in *Costa Rica: Cuatro ensayos de historia ambiental*, edited by Ronny Viales and Anthony Goebel McDermott (San José, Costa Rica: Sociedad Editora Alquimia 2000, 2011), 83–124.

70. For a detailed analysis of the relationship between the socioenvironmental transformations associated with banana cultivation and the massive consumption of bananas in the US market, see John Soluri, *Banana Cultures. Agriculture, Consumption and Environmental change in Honduras and the United States* (Austin: University of Texas Press, 2005).

71. PNUMA and CCAD, *GEO Centroamérica*, 23; John Soluri, "Consumo de masas, biodiversidad y fitomejoramiento del banano de exportación, 1920–1980," *Revista de Historia* (Costa Rica) 44 (2001): 50.

72. PNUMA and CCAD, *GEO Centroamérica*, 23.

73. Ibid.

74. Maximiliano López and Wilson Picado, "Plantas, fertilizantes y transición energética en la caficultura contemporánea de Costa Rica: Bases para una discusión," *Revista de Historia* (Costa Rica) 65–66 (2012): 37.

75. Juan Rafael Quesada, "Comercialización y Movimiento Coyuntural del cacao," *Revista de Historia* (Costa Rica) 3, no. 6 (January–July 1978): 69–110; Juan Rafael Quesada, "Algunos aspectos de la historia económica del cacao en Costa Rica (1880–1930)," *Revista de Historia* (Costa Rica) 3, no. 5 (July–December 1977): 65–100.

76. Jorge León y Nelson Arroyo, *Desarrollo histórico del sector agroindustrial de la caña de azúcar en el siglo XX: Aspectos económicos, institucionales y tecnológicos* (San José, Costa Rica: Instituto de Investigaciones en Ciencias Económicas, Universidad de Costa Rica, 2012).

77. PNUMA and CCAD, *GEO Centroamérica*, 25.

78. Ibid.

79. Ibid.

80. Cushman, "Guano, Intensive Agriculture, and Environmental Change," 19.

81. Ibid., 20.

82. Ronny Viales, "Desarrollo rural y pobreza en Centroamérica en la década de 1990: Las políticas y algunos límites del modelo 'neoliberal,'" *Anuario de Estudios Centroamericanos* 25, no. 2 (2000): 139–157.

83. PNUMA and CCAD, *GEO Centroamérica*, 26.

84. The decision was made to include livestock farming as an extractive activity based on Marc Edelman's conceptualization for the case of the Costa Rican North Pacific, the country's cattle raising region par excellence. According to the author, stockbreeding went from being just another extractive activity, with low capital investment, low productivity, and specialization in bovine tallow and hides, to an expanding capitalized and liberalized activity, endowed with a greater productive investment supported by cattle sales for beef consumption. See Marc Edelman, *La lógica del latifundio: Las grandes propiedades del noroeste de Costa Rica desde finales del siglo XIX* (San José: Editorial de la Universidad de Costa Rica, 1998). On mining: PNUMA y CCAD, *GEO* Centroamérica, 17.

85. Ibid., 17.

86. Ibid.

87. Díaz and Viales, *El impacto económico de la independencia*, xiii–xiv; PNUMA and CCAD, *GEO Centroamérica*, 19.

88. Ibid., 23; Carlos Araya Pochet, "El segundo ciclo minero en Costa Rica (1890–1930)," in *Avances de Investigación* (San José: Escuela de Historia y Geografía, Universidad de Costa Rica, 1976); Guillermo García, *Las minas de Abangares: Historia de una doble explotación* (San José: Escuela de Estudios Generales, Universidad de Costa Rica, 1977). See also Ronny Viales, "La colonización agrícola de la Región Atlántica (Caribe) costarricense entre 1870

y 1930: El peso de la política agraria liberal y de las diversas formas de apropiación territorial," *Anuario de Estudios Centroamericanos* 27, no. 2 (2001): 57–100. A suggestive critical analysis on the concept of "mining enclave" exposed by Pochet, coming from the concept developed by Cardoso and Faletto among others, together with a remarkable documentary contribution to this topic, can be seen in Lowell Gudmunson, "Documentos para la historia del distrito minero de Guanacaste: ¿Enclave minero?," *Revista de Historia* (Costa Rica) 3, no. 6 (1978): 129–162.

89. Reinaldo Funes, "The Greater Caribbean and the Transformation of Tropicality," in *A Living Past: Environmental Histories of Modern Latin America*, edited by John Soluri, Claudia Leal, and José Augusto Pádua, 56–57 (New York: Berghahn Books, 2018).

90. Ibid., 57.

91. The socioenvironmental impact of mining megaprojects as part of the economy of dispossession that dominates many of the Latin American countries in a neoliberal context, has been analyzed in depth in other cases such as the state of Zacatecas, Mexico, with which the Central American case has remarkable parallels especially in the initial stadiums of this type of mining development. See Federico Guzmán López, "Impactos ambientales causados por megaproyectos de minería a cielo abierto en el estado de Zacatecas, México," *Revista de Geografía Agrícola* 57 (2016): 7–26.

92. PNUMA and CCAD, *GEO Centroamérica*, 17.

93. Ibid.

94. Juan Carlos Solórzano, "Las Relaciones comerciales de Costa Rica en el Pacífico (1575–1821)," *Revista de Historia* (Costa Rica) 43 (2001): 129–131.

95. Ephraim George Squier, *Notes on Central America, Particularly the States of Honduras and San Salvador: Their Geography, Topography, Climate, Population, Resources, Productions, etc., etc., and the Proposed Honduras Inter-oceanic Railway* (New York: Harper & Bros., 1855), 173. Available from the Kislak Collection (Library of Congress), https://upload.wikimedia.org/wikipedia/commons/4/4e/Notes_on_Central_America_-_particularly_the_states_of_Honduras_and_San_Salvador_-_their_geography%2C_topography%2C_climate%2C_population%2C_resources%2C_productions%2C_etc.%2C_etc.%2C_and_the_proposed_Honduras_%2814586698670%29.jpg; see also Elizet Payne, *El puerto de Truxillo: Un viaje hacia su melancólico abandono* (Tegucigalpa, Honduras: Guaymuras, 2007), 231–232.

96. Quírico Jiménez, *Árboles Maderables en peligro de extinción en Costa Rica* (Heredia, Costa Rica: Instituto Nacional de Biodiversidad, 1998), 78–81 and 137–143.

97. Miguel Roldán, *Cartilla de construcción y manejo de los buques para instrucción de los guardias marinas*, edited by Francisco Chacón y Orta (Cádiz, Spain: Imprenta de la Revista Médica, [1831] 1864), 45. https://books.google.co.cr/books?hl=es&lr=&id=zBBFAAAAYAAJ; PNUMA and CCAD, *GEO Centroamérica*, 17; J. R. McNeill, "Woods and Warfare in World History," *Environmental History* 9, no. 3 (2004): 388–410.

98. Anthony Goebel McDermott, *Los bosques del "progreso": Explotación forestal y régimen ambiental en Costa Rica: 1883–1955* (San José, Costa Rica: Editorial Nuevas Perspectivas, 2013), 78–118; Richard P. Tucker, *Insatiable Appetite: The United States and the Ecological Degradation of the Tropical World* (Berkeley: University of California Press, 2000). For an overview of global deforestation, its drivers, and its conditions, see Michael Williams, *Deforesting the Earth: From Prehistory to Global Crisis: An Abridgment* (Chicago: University of Chicago Press, 2006).

99. Don D. Humphrey, *American Imports* (New York: Twentieth Century Fund, 1955), 286–290.

100. Luis Cayuela, "Deforestación y fragmentación de bosques tropicales montanos en los altos de Chiapas. Efectos sobre la diversidad de árboles" (PhD qualifying exam, University of Alcalá, Spain, 2006), 135–136. http://hdl.handle.net/10017/475.
101. Joan Martínez Alier, *El ecologismo de los pobres. Conflictos ambientales y lenguajes de valoración* (Barcelona: Icaria Antrazyt-Flacso, 2004), 150–152.
102. PNUMA and CCAD, *GEO Centroamérica*, 35–36.
103. Ibid., 16.
104. Ibid., 20.
105. Edelman, *Lógica del Latifundio*; Lowell Gudmundson, "Apuntes para una Historia de la Ganadería en Costa Rica, 1850–1950," *Revista de Ciencias Sociales*, 17–18 (1979): 61–111. Lowell Gudmundson, *Hacendados, Políticos y Precaristas: La ganadería y el latifundio Guanacasteco. 1800–1950* (San José: Editorial Costa Rica, 1983); Wilder Sequeira, *La hacienda ganadera en Guanacaste: Aspectos económicos y sociales* (San José, Costa Rica: Editorial de la Universidad Estatal a Distancia, 1985); Roberto Cabrera, *Tierra y Ganadería en Guanacaste* (Cartago: Editorial Tecnológica de Costa Rica, 2007); Julián Guerrero and Lola Soriano de Guerrero, *Historia de la ganadería de Nicaragua* (Managua, Nicaragua: Editorial Unión Cardoza y Cía, 1992).
106. Shawn Van Ausdal and Robert W. Wilcox, "Hoofprints: Cattle Ranching and Landscape Transformation," in *A Living Past: Environmental Histories of Modern Latin America*, edited by John Soluri, Claudia Leal, and José Augusto Pádua (New York: Berghahn Books, 2018), 184.
107. Patricia Clare, "Cambios en los paisajes y sistemas productivos del Pacífico norte de la actual Costa Rica (1750–1892)," in *De colonia a República: economía, política e iglesia en Costa Rica (siglos XVIII–XIX)*, edited by Alejandra Boza, Manuel B. Chacón, Esteban Corella, David Díaz, Verónica Jerez, Elizet Payne, and Carmela Velásquez (San José: Fundación Museos Banco Central de Costa Rica, 2017), 90.
108. Van Ausdal and Wilcox, "Hoofprints," 185–187; Edelman, *Lógica del Latifundio*, 84.
109. Edelman, *Lógica del Latifundio*, 88–90, 94.
110. Van Ausdal and Wilcox, "Hoofprints," 190.
111. Ibid.
112. Ibid.
113. Dirección General de Estadística y Censos (DGEC), *Censo Agropecuario de 1950* (San José, Costa Rica 1953), 92–93; DGEC, *Anuario Estadístico, 1950*, 41; FAO/CEPAL, *Livestock in America Latina: Status, Problems and Prospects*, vol. 1, *Colombia, Mexico, Uruguay and Venezuela* (New York, 1962), 49.
114. Van Ausdal and Wilcox, "Hoofprints," 190–191.
115. Ibid., 197.
116. Henning Steinfeld, Pierre Gerber, Tom Wassenaar, Vincent Castel, Mauricio Rosales, Cees de Haan, *Livestock's Long Shadow: Environmental Issues and Options* (Roma: Food and Agriculture Organization of the United Nations (FAO)/Livestock, Environment and Development Initiative (LEAD), 2006).
117. Van Ausdal and Wilcox, "Hoofprints," 196.
118. Ibid.; Edgar Blanco, "¿Testimonios de un despojo? Desarrollo turístico en Guanacaste y sus impactos a nivel social y ambiental, 1990–2016," *Revista de Ciencias Sociales* 155 (2017): 13–27.

FURTHER READING

Amador, Jorge A. "Some Aspects of Climate in Costa Rica Using Historical Data From the XIX Century." *Tópicos Meteorológicos y Oceanográficos* 9, no. 2 (2002): 64–74

Botey, Ana María. *Los orígenes del Estado de Bienestar en Costa Rica: Salud y protección social (1850–1940)*. San José: Editorial de la Universidad de Costa Rica, 2019.

Castro, Guillermo. *Naturaleza y Sociedad en la Historia de América Latina*. Panamá City: Centro de Estudios Latinoamericanos, 1996.

Díaz, David, and Ronny Viales. *El impacto económico de la independencia en Centroamérica, (1760–1840): Una interpretación desde la historia global*. San José: Editorial de la Universidad de Costa Rica, Serie Cuadernos de Historia de Centroamérica, 2016.

Edelman, Marc. *La lógica del latifundio: Las grandes propiedades del noroeste de Costa Rica desde finales del siglo XIX*. San José: Editorial de la Universidad de Costa Rica, 1998.

Gallini, Stefania. *Una historia ambiental del café en Guatemala: La Costa Cuca entre 1830 y 1902*. Guatemala City: AVANCSO, 2008.

Goebel McDermott, Anthony. *Los bosques del "progreso": Explotación forestal y régimen ambiental en Costa Rica: 1883–1955*. San José, Costa Rica: Editorial Nuevas Perspectivas, 2013.

Infante-Amate, Juan, and Wilson Picado. "Energy Flows in the Coffee Plantations of Costa Rica: From Traditional to Modern Systems (1935–2010)." *Regional Environmental Change* 18, no. 4 (2018): 1059–1071

Lovell, W. George, and Noble David Cook. "Desenredando la madeja de la enfermedad." In *Juicios Secretos de Dios: Epidemias y despoblación indígena en Hispanoamérica colonial*, edited by W. George Lovell and Noble David Cook, 227–250. Quito, Ecuador: Ediciones Abya-Yala, 1999.

McCook, Stuart. "La roya del café en Costa Rica: Epidemias, innovación, y medio ambiente, 1950–1995." *Revista de Historia* (Costa Rica) 59–60 (2009): 99–117. https://www.revistas.una. ac.cr/index.php/historia/article/view/3471.

Miller, Shawn William. *An Environmental History of Latin America*. New York: Cambridge University Press, 2007.

Montero, Andrea. "Una aproximación a los cambios en el paisaje en el Valle Central de Costa Rica (1820–1900)." *HALAC* 3, no. 2 (2014): 276–309.

Newson, Linda A. "Variaciones regionales en el impacto del dominio colonial español en las poblaciones indígenas de Honduras y Nicaragua." *Mesoamérica* 13, no. 24 (1992): 298.

Pérez Brignoli, Héctor. *El laberinto centroamericano: Los hilos de la historia*. San José, Costa Rica: Vicerrectoría de Investigación/Centro de Investigaciones Históricas de América Central, 2017.

Programa de las Naciones Unidas para el Medio Ambiente (PNUMA) and Comisión Centroamericana de Ambiente y Desarrollo (CCAD). *GEO Centroamérica: Perspectivas del medio ambiente 2004*. Mexico City: PNUMA y CCAD, 2006. http://www.pnuma.org/deat1/pdf/GEO%20Centroamerica%202004.pdf.

Rojas, Gladys. *Café, ambiente y sociedad en la cuenca del Río Virilla, Costa Rica (1840–1955)*. San José: Editorial de la Universidad de Costa Rica, 2000.

Soluri, John. *Banana Cultures. Agriculture, Consumption and Environmental Change in Honduras and the United States*. Austin: University of Texas Press, 2005.

Van Ausdal, Shawn, and Robert W. Wilcox. "Hoofprints: Cattle Ranching and Landscape Transformation." In *A Living Past: Environmental Histories of Modern Latin America*, edited by John Soluri, Claudia Leal, and José Augusto Pádua, 183–204. New York: Berghahn Books, 2018.

Viales, Ronny, and Andrea Montero. "Una aproximación al impacto ambiental del cultivo del banano en el Atlántico/Caribe de Costa Rica (1870–1930)." In *Costa Rica: Cuatro Ensayos de Historia Ambiental*, edited by Ronny Viales and Anthony Goebel McDermott, 83–124. San José, Costa Rica: Sociedad Editora Alquimia 2000.

CHAPTER 2

REGAINING GROUND
Indigenous Populations and Territories

PETER H. HERLIHY,
MATTHEW L. FAHRENBRUCH,
AND TAYLOR A. TAPPAN

INDIGENOUS POPULATIONS

Indigenous peoples represent significant minority populations in Central America. But defining who is Indigenous is no easy task. And while dozens of Indigenous languages remain widely spoken in Central America, many disappeared as processes of assimilation have brought Indigenous peoples in ever closer proximity to Spanish-speaking majorities. Likewise, Indigenous peoples' precolonial spiritual traditions, settlement patterns, and subsistence activities have undergone dramatic changes through missionizing, land dispossession, and the growing importance of cash-based economies. These changes complicate how states and international organizations define who is and who is not Indigenous.

Indeed, no universal definition exists for indigeneity, but states, multilateral organizations (the United Nations, International Labour Organization, World Bank, European Union, and Inter-American Development Bank), and academics alike recognize "Indigenous peoples" as those who descended from colonized populations, who maintain an attachment to ancestral lands, who self-identify as a distinct people, and who practice customary activities. In recent decades, national-level censuses have often elected for simplicity by requesting participants to self-identify as Indigenous, and indeed, this may be the most reasonable solution. But even this method is problematic and has underrepresented Indigenous peoples in the past. In Guatemala, for instance, a person of mixed Maya-Ch'orti' and Castilian heritage might self-identify as *mestizo* or white (but not Indigenous) when surveyed by a census taker. However, the same individual might claim her Maya-Ch'orti' identity in conversation to illustrate that she isn't Maya-Tz'utujil or Maya Poqomam. We recognize that no approach is flawless, and our discussion here borrows from national censuses and archives where Indigenous population data were typically recorded based on self-identification and/or use of an Amerindian language.[1]

What is clear to historical demographers is that Indigenous settlements covered the Central American Isthmus when the Spanish conquistadors arrived in the early 1500s. In the decades and centuries that followed, diseases, warfare, miscegenation, and assimilation caused the decimation of Indigenous populations, the loss of countless languages, and the dispossession of their ancestral lands. In the last century, however, Indigenous peoples in Central America have witnessed a demographic resurgence despite expanding agricultural fronts, encroachment of cattle ranchers, extractive mining and logging, and narco-trafficking that threaten their remaining territories. In 2020, forty-six distinct Indigenous groups survive in the region (Figure 2.1).

The twentieth-century demographic resurgence of Indigenous peoples in Central America coincides with an expansion of territorial rights. In the 1970s–1980s, Indigenous visionaries mobilized to counteract territorial threats by demanding that land rights and governance authority be restored to their communities. Central American states responded (slowly, at first) to these demands through initiatives offering varying degrees of legal land recognition or title, governance authority, and natural resource use rights. This movement is part of a burgeoning "territorial turn" in Latin America, in which

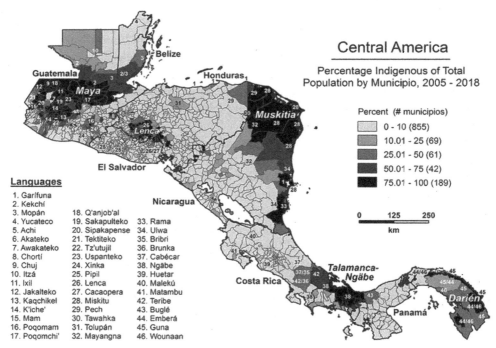

FIGURE 2.1. Central America: percentage self-identified Indigenous people of total population by *municipio*, 2005–2018. Based on boundary data from national geographic or statistic institutes; population data are from the national censuses (see note 1).

millions of hectares of land have been returned to Indigenous peoples in collective tenure through a variety of "Indigenous territorial jurisdictions" (ITJs)—a term describing sovereignty regimes with functional and legal expressions providing for Indigenous territoriality within the context of the modern states.[2]

Here we present a geographic portrait of Central America's native communities from past to present. The region's population and settlement distribution in the centuries leading up to the colonial era provides a baseline to measure the demographic collapse and territorial dispossession resulting from colonialism and the birth of modern states. We rely on first-hand field and archival research, land use and cadastral mapping, and geographic information systems (GIS)-based analysis to inform our narrative recounting the parallel histories of demographic collapse and territorial decline that have given way to population growth and heightened territorial recognition in recent decades for Indigenous peoples of Central America.[3]

PRE-COLUMBIAN PAST: FROM ANTIQUITY TO CONQUEST

The chronology and routes by which Paleoindians from Asia first crossed the Bering Strait to settle in North America are still debated. Indeed, there is no consensus for precisely when the first colonists arrived or whether they came in one or more migration waves. Genetic studies now imply that migrants from Siberia crossed the Bering Land Bridge between 30,000 BP and 15,000 BP, after the last glacial maximum at ~22,000 BP. Intersecting current genetic, archaeological, and environmental data points to a conservative estimates of ~15,000 BP for the peopling of the Americas—a time that coincides with the deglaciation of the Pacific coastal corridor. Numerous archaeological sites appear throughout the Americas at about the same time, ranging from the well-known Monte Verde site in southern Chile to Meadowcroft Rockshelter site in Pennsylvania and parts in between.[4]

The diffusion of people from North America to South America seems to have happened relatively quickly. This migration would have been funneled almost inevitably through the Central American isthmus and bottlenecked in present-day Panamá, but archaeological data are virtually nonexistent there earlier than 11,500 BP. Archaeologist Richard Cooke and colleagues attributes the dearth of evidence, among other factors, to rising sea levels. For instance, he explains how the lowland Pacific littoral of Panamá—a likely conduit for prehistoric human migration—has been inundated by a 50-meter rise in sea level since 11,500 BP, thus eliminating a previously available swath of land 40–50 kilometers wide, and with it, any sites dating back to the first human settlers. Some archaeological and paleoecological records show early human presence elsewhere in Panamá and Central America. At Vampiros-1 rock shelter near Panamá's Pacific shoreline, both North American Clovis and South

American fishtail fluted projectile points were discovered in a radiocarbon-dated deposit of 11,050 BP. Similar blades and scrapers were also found in Costa Rica, Honduras, and Guatemala and pollen and particulate carbon records indicate human occupation throughout the Isthmus at this time.[5]

While some scholars have suggested that the pre-Columbian communities of southern Central America were part of an ancient immigrant population from South America, Cooke and colleagues say archival documents, historical linguistics, and recent work on mitochondrial DNA all suggest that the twelve ethnic groups that still speak languages belonging to the Misumalpan (Miskitu, Sumu, and Matagalpa), Paya-Chibchan, and Chocoan families represent only the latest stage of a protracted sociopolitical fragmentation of ancestral populations that have lived in their present-day locations for as long as 10,000 years.

Archaeological plant remains show early Central Americans populations began to cultivate arrowroot, squash, and bottle gourds in forest openings around 8,500 BP. Maize, squash, and root crop cultivation appeared a thousand years later. By 4,000 BP, hunting, fishing, and gathering transitioned into supplementary activities as cultivation provided a stable source of calories, with the earliest agricultural villages dating to 3,700 BP.

Strong cultural differences between the societies living in northern and southern Central America emerged around 4,000 BP to mark the onset of the Pre-Classic Period. The region's first great civilization—the Olmec in Mexico's Veracruz and Tabasco lowlands—reached its zenith between 3,200 and 2,800 BP. The Olmec lived in planned settlements with advanced architecture, art, math, calendars, and written language. Their influence spread from Mexico south into Guatemala and El Salvador, where major trading cities of Kaminaljuyú and Chalchuapa, respectively, flourished on the exchange of obsidian tools and pottery.

Mayan urban centers with towering pyramids developed at Tikal, El Mirador, and Uaxactún in the Petén after 0 CE, linking to towns, production sites, and trade networks in neighboring Belize, the Yucatán, western Honduras, and the Guatemalan highlands. The pinnacle of Mayan civilization in the Classic Period (250 CE to 900 CE) was marked by a boom in Mesoamerican social complexity, urban centers, agricultural production, writing traditions, mathematics, monumental architecture, and arts. Mayan territory covered a vast and topographically variegated landscape. Beyond *milpa* farming (slash–burn, rotational forest-fallow), the Maya developed intensive agricultural methods of ditching, draining, mounding, terracing, and fertilizing. These technological advances provided food surpluses that allowed for economic specialization. The Maya communities constructed ball courts; recorded detailed histories of kinship and warfare on stone stelae, bark, wood, and deerskin; and used remarkably accurate *solar* and *ritual* calendars. The lowland Mayan societies reached their zenith between 250 and 900 CE, when Tikal had 80,000 inhabitants, before mysteriously falling into decline in the tenth century.

After the fall of Teotihuacan and later Tula, some Nahua peoples left central Mexico for northern Central America. About 700 CE, Pipil families began colonizing the rich volcanic soils of southeast Guatemala and adjacent El Salvador, while the Nicarao settled farther south along coastal Nicaragua. The Mangue (also known as the Chorotega or Matambú of Guanacaste) and Subtiaba peoples migrated even farther south to settle the coastal lowlands between the Gulfs of Fonseca and Nicoya. This area marked an important cultural divide between peoples of Mesoamerican heritage (especially those belonging to Mayan linguistic groups) and the Misumalpan- and Paya-Chibchan peoples of southeastern Central America and Colombia. Trade emerged in this transitional area and gave rise to multicultural towns that were populated by an amalgamation of Pipil, Nicarao, Mangue, Maya, Misumalpan, and Paya (Pech).

Precolonial peoples of southern Central America—encompassing the Caribbean lowlands of Honduras and Nicaragua and trans-isthmian Costa Rica and Panamá—never lived in urban centers rivaling the majestic architectural wonders of the Maya. Nor did they practice intensive agriculture, but instead they planted milpas with root crops of South American origin. The Coclé of south-central Panamá and the Huetar, spanning Costa Rica from the Caribbean to Pacific, were significant cultural areas. While these societies were less literate (or nonliterate) and more egalitarian in class structure than their Mesoamerican counterparts, they had a more personalized form of art and religion evidenced by exquisitely fashioned gold jewelry and ceramics decorated with highly sophisticated polychrome motifs. Another lesser-known area existed in the uplands of Muskitia in eastern Honduras and Nicaragua, where a complex of archaeological sites has been recently documented.[6]

Historical demographers and geographers conservatively estimated an aboriginal population of 5.6 million inhabitants lived in Central America at the time of European contact (roughly 10 percent of the hemispheric total of 53.9 million). The population was distributed roughly as follows: 2,000,000 in Guatemala; 800,000 in Nicaragua; 750,000 in El Salvador; 800,000 in Honduras; 400,000 in Costa Rica; 800,000 in Panamá; and 50,000 in Belize. Upon the arrival of Spanish explorers, roughly 60 percent of the regional population inhabited the northern isthmus, where Mesoamerican influence was greater; the other 40 percent lived in the southern isthmus where Misumalpan and Paya-Chibcha influences were strongest.[7]

DEMOGRAPHIC DEMISE

The first permanent Spanish settlement and seat of Spanish authority in Central America was at the southeasternmost point of the Isthmus in present-day Colombia. Vasco Núñez de Balboa and his men founded Santa María la Antigua del Darién on a site overlooking the mouth of the Río Atrato in the Gulf of Urabá, whose western hinterlands were settled by non-Carib peoples (possibly Cuevan or Guna speakers). From here, Balboa set out for discovery of the Pacific, thereafter ceding authority to 70-year-old Pedrarias Dávila who ruled ruthlessly as the new governor of Castilla de Oro and who had Balboa beheaded for unjust accusations of treason in 1519. At the time, Darién had a church, a Franciscan convent, government buildings, and well-constructed residences where conquistadors like Pizarro, Almagro, Pascual de Andagoya, and Hernando de Soto lived. From here the spread of Old World disease and forced labor gold-panning in rivers quickly decimated native peoples, upon whom the Spaniards depended. Dávila subsequently moved to the Pacific side of the Isthmus to establish the new administrative center of Panamá in 1519, much closer to the gold-rich Coclé peoples, whose communities the Spaniards mercilessly ransacked for gold and slaves.[8]

From Panamá, the Spaniards sent ships to scout the Pacific coast of Central America. In 1524, Francisco Hernández de Córdoba conquered the densely settled Chorotega (Mangue), Nicarao, and Subtiaba peoples of Nicaragua and founded the cities of Granada and León. Like Dávila, Córdoba looted communities for their gold, then sent captives to wash gold in the Nicaraguan highlands or to provide hard labor in Panamá or Perú.

The Spaniards ambushed the native peoples from both the north and south. As Córdoba looted and ransacked communities from Panamá to Nicaragua, Hernán Cortés—fresh off his conquest of the Aztec—turned his attention southward, sending the ruthless Pedro de Alvarado to conquer Soconusco and the Guatemalan highlands. Alvarado waged a violent campaign against the Maya K'iche' and Maya Kaqchikel and then founded Santiago de los Caballeros de Guatemala (present-day Antigua) in 1524. With new administrative centers in Guatemala and Panamá, colonial towns, missions, mines, and haciendas developed quickly along the Pacific coastal plains and temperate valleys of the Central American Isthmus.

This initial conquest and colonization had a devastating impact. Native populations dropped by 80 or 90 percent in many parts and disappeared altogether in others, particularly in the newly settled Pacific lowlands. Among those most affected in Central America were the Cueva, Coclé, Dorasque, Chorotega (Mangue), Nicarao, Matagalpa, and Pipil populations which were decimated by Old World diseases and subjected to warfare and slavery. In 1524, the collective population of these groups numbered more than one million; by 1549, only a few thousand remained. A similar fate befell the Huetar and Talamancan groups of Costa Rica's Meseta Central. By 1562, when Cartago was established, they had had already been devastated. The few who survived were assimilated into the dominant Spanish and *mestizo* society, thus suffering the dispossession of their lands and cultural heritages.

Spanish settlement did not develop as rapidly on the Caribbean Coast. The earliest Spanish accounts portray it as a wild and sparsely inhabited place. Unlike the Pacific lowlands, it lacked gold and a large native labor pool; and the hot, humid, rainforests were not attractive for most Spaniards. Cortés sent Spaniards to settle the well-occupied Indigenous areas of the Ulúa Valley at Puerto Caballos and the Aguán Valley at Trujillo, but native populations died off quickly and the settlements did not flourish. Although the Caribbean coast of Central America was eventually incorporated into British control, Indigenous populations there attracted little attention from Spanish conquistadors or early settlers, and as a result, these remote areas remain bastions of indigeneity into the 21st century.

Rising Indigenous Populations

Estimating the size and distribution of the Indigenous population of Central America has always been a difficult task. Notwithstanding the logistical challenges of census taking in remote, geographically isolated Indigenous communities, the sociocultural challenges pertaining to Indigenous identification obfuscate the process. Concomitant with the demographic collapse of Indigenous populations was the appearance of Afro-descendants, Spaniards, and mixed-race individuals. Although the Spanish Crown preached racial purity, miscegenation occurred from the onset and was so prominent that most Central Americans are now endowed with some degree of Indigenous heritage, resulting in the birth of a new racial category called *mestizo*, describing people of mixed Indigenous and European ancestry. Similarly, Afro-descendants were integrated into Central America's growing population, but they were not always singled out as a separate racial category, because they were neither fully Indigenous nor of European origin.[9]

In 1684, there was an estimated Indigenous population of half a million in Central America, while a century later the population had risen to nearly 600,000 (Table 2.1). These figures, however, were highly speculative. At independence in 1821, the Indigenous population had grown to about 750,000, with 80 percent concentrated in Guatemala, El Salvador, and western Honduras. By the end of the nineteenth century, censuses and vital statistics taken by the post-independence-but-still-fledgling Central American states made estimating the Indigenous population somewhat less speculative, but not all countries classified the population by ethnic affiliation, so much remained open to interpretation. Moreover, census takers working in remote and often inaccessible Indigenous areas have been notoriously unreliable. This has led to a persistent undercounting of Indigenous populations. Estimates show a growing population of perhaps 1.5 million Indigenous people by 1900.

Table 2.1. Indigenous Population of Central America, 1492–c. 2018*

Year	Indigenous population
1492	5,625,000
1684	546,079
1800	587,069
1900	1,557,000
1940	1,869,928
1990	3,961,168
2018	8,112,213

* Based on national census data and various estimates (see note 1).

Censuses that do collect data on ethnicity often rely on respondents to self-identify as Indigenous. After generations of violent assimilationist policies, as well as political marginalization and integration into capitalist systems, Indigenous peoples may not retain their Indigenous knowledge, or even consider themselves Indigenous. Among the Ch'orti' of Eastern Guatemala and western Honduras, this sort of discrimination manifests socially, economically, and politically and results in the rejection of indigeneity. This type of anti-Indigenous discrimination has been widespread since colonial times. But recent decades have witnessed a change in this trend through the growth of Indigenous rights movements and increasing recognition of ITJs. Government census offices now increasingly employ census takers from local Indigenous populations, as Indigenous leaders are acutely aware of the need to develop accurate census and cartographic information for their constituents and territories.

The Indigenous population of Central America doubled to 4 million between 1940 and 1990, accounting for 14 percent of the region's 29 million people. Now, the most recent censuses indicate the population has doubled again over the past three decades.[10] More than 8 million self-identified Indigenous people now live in Central America, accounting for nearly 20 percent of the region's population (see Table 2.2; Figure 2.1). Guatemala's Indigenous population of 6.5 million in 2018 accounts for 80 percent of this total. The other six Central America countries include twenty-five Indigenous groups with a total 1.6 million people, distributed mostly along the Caribbean lowlands and in Darién. Even though seemingly small numbers, they represent significant minority populations and percentages of the national population in most Central American states.

Table 2.2. Central America: Indigenous Population and Indigenous Territorial Jurisdictions, 2005–2018*

Country (census year)	Total population	# Ind. lang.	Total Indigenous population	% total pop.	Total area country (km²)	# ITJ	Area ITZ	% total area
Belize (2010)	322,453	4	56,149	17.41	21919	8	305	1.39
Costa Rica (2011)	4,301,714	8	104,143	2.42	51080	24	3484	6.82
El Salvador (2007)	5,744,013	3	13,093	0.23	20775	N/A	N/A	N/A
Guatemala (2018)	14,901,286	23	6,496,199	43.59	107541	1106	13584	12.63
Honduras (2013)	7,657,486	7	581,921	7.60	111402	16	16050	14.41
Nicaragua (2005)	5,142,098	6	443,166	8.62	118944	23	38854	32.67
Panama (2010)	3,405,813	7	417,542	12.26	74730	6	17089	22.87
Total in Central America	41,474,863		8,112,213	19.56	506391	1183	89366	17.65

* The total area of each country was calculated in GIS including islands; population data from national censuses (see note 1).

Population estimates show Central America's Indigenous communities have grown significantly since the mid-twentieth century. In particular, the number of people who self-identify as Indigenous is on the rise. No fewer than forty-six distinct Indigenous groups survive in Central America in 2020, although their territories are often bifurcated by international borders. Such geopolitical inconveniences require Indigenous communities to engage in politics at the local, provincial, state, and international levels.[11]

INDIGENOUS LANDS TODAY

To understand the distribution of Indigenous populations in Central America, we constructed a regional digital map in ArcGIS displaying the most recent census results by *municipios*, which is the Spanish word for municipality or county (Figure 2.1). Municipios are the most detailed disaggregated geographical unit of analysis that encompasses all Central America. Municipios are not, however, homelands or territorial jurisdictions designed to grant ownership and governance rights to Indigenous populations; instead, they are the geopolitical units for the administration of state government. Our analysis showed about 20 percent (231) of the total 1,216 *municipios* in Central America have a 50 percent or greater rate of indigeneity, as evidenced by self-identification in the most recent national censuses. The landscapes of these municipios have been shaped and reshaped by the subsistence and cash-cropping economies of the Indigenous communities for centuries. They cover 24 percent of the total land area of Central America.

Based on our analysis of these municipios, we identify four distinct core areas of Central America that have retained their Indigenous character since colonial times (see Figure 2.1): (1) the Maya area of central and western Guatemala; (2) the Miskitu Coast of eastern Honduras and Nicaragua; (3) the Talamanca-Ngäbe area of Costa Rica and Panamá; and (4) the Darién-San Blas-Bayano area of eastern Panamá. Except for the Maya area, these core Indigenous areas remained outside most influences of the dominant Spanish-speaking mestizos until mid-twentieth century. An additional Indigenous area of Lenca identity reemerges in western Honduras.

Maya Area

Guatemala's most recent population and housing census (2018) shows 6.2 million self-identified Indigenous people and twenty-one distinct Mayan languages. Of these, the Maya-K'iche' of the midwestern highlands is the largest Indigenous group in both Guatemala and Central America with 1.7 million speakers, followed by the Maya-Q'eqchi'/Kekchí with 1.4 million, Kaqchikel with 1 million, and Mam with 840,000. These four groups account for 80 percent of the Maya speakers. The remaining seventeen

Maya language groups are dispersed around these, accounting for about 20 percent of the country's Indigenous population.

Across western and central Guatemala, small Mayan hamlets and towns dot the pine-oak-forested uplands of the Sierra Madre, Cuchumatanes, and Sierra de las Minas ranges. Lower elevation settlements extend north and east into the rainforest areas of the southern Petén and Belize. Maya-Q'eqchi' settlements reach into southern Belize and the Maya Mountains where Maya-Mopan communities are found. Now apart from the contiguous Maya area, Xinka, Poqomamm, and Ch'orti' Maya settlements reach eastward, even into Honduras where the latter live on and farm the slopes around their ancient ceremonial site of Copán.

The upland municipios in central and western Guatemala formed mostly during colonial times and are comparatively small with the highest settlement densities for any Indigenous area in the region. Maya communities here—fallaciously portrayed as Marxist guerrillas by the Guatemalan state—suffered the brunt of the state-sponsored violence during the country's civil war (1962–1996). Guatemalan Special Forces, equipped with US financial assistance and military training, applied scorched-earth tactics that destroyed hundreds of villages and resulted in a genocide of 200,000 Mayan civilians and the displacement of hundreds of thousands more.[12] Nevertheless, Indigeneity and territorial control are strong in some areas such as in the municipios of the Department of Totonicapán where communities have had success managing their forests.

Muskitia Area

The Muskitia area of eastern Honduras and Nicaragua is the ancestral homeland of the Miskitu, Pech, Tawahka, Mayangna (Sumu), and Rama peoples. It is the largest Indigenous area in Central America, covering more territory than Belize. During the seventeenth and eighteenth centuries, the Miskitu obtained weapons through trade with the British and leveraged political backing to expand their territory along the Caribbean coastal lowlands from Honduras to Costa Rica. Still relatively isolated, Muskitia has stayed beyond the reach of the national highway systems; rivers remain avenues of communication and exchange. A north-to-south buffer of rainforest (in the Río Plátano and Tawahka Asangni Biosphere Reserves) still separates most Indigenous communities from the advancing colonization front that has overrun westernmost Miskitu, Pech, Garifuna subsistence lands. Illegal colonization along the Río Patuca in the Tawahka Asangni Biosphere is presently destroying both the reserve and the last Tawahka communities. The impact of this colonization is evidenced in census data that demonstrate a reduction between 2001 and 2013 in the percentage of Indigenous people living in these areas. Indeed, government-sponsored colonization programs have resulted in the loss of Indigenous territory, a process further exacerbated by an increase in collateral damage from drug trafficking in which rainforest is razed for landing strips and cattle pasture. These sad realities are not unique to Tawahka communities. In

Nicaragua, Miskitu, Rama, and Mayangna communities experience similar threats and land dispossession.[13]

In 2018, more than 125,000 Miskitu lived in three hundred communities in eastern Honduras—an area covering approximately 17,000 km^2. Just south, another 120,000 more Miskitu live in communities scattered along the shores and inland rivers of Nicaragua's Atlantic Coast. Although the Miskitu are the largest Indigenous population in the region, there are also several thousand Pech, Tawahka, Rama, Mayangna, and Garífuna inhabitants.

Talamanca-Ngäbe Area

The Talamanca Highlands and Ngäbe area (Figure 2.1) is the second most populous Indigenous expanse in Central America. Rainforest sits atop a topographically rugged landscape while Indigenous settlements are found near streams and rivers. Native communities here practice slash–burn and slash–mulch farming. Hunting, fishing, and collecting add variety to their diet, while selling surplus crops and working as wage laborers offer limited cash income.[14]

The 2010 and 2011 censuses from Panamá and Costa Rica reveal 350,000 Indigenous inhabitants in this Indigenous area. About 85 percent live in the Caribbean coastal lowlands, piedmonts, and uplands of tropical rainforests extending inland from Panamá's Laguna de Chiriquí south to the continental divide. A few scattered settlements cross south to the Pacific slopes. With a population of 250,000, the Ngäbe of Panamá are by far the largest group here. Just east of their settlements, another 20,000 identify as Buglé. In the Costa Rican part, the Bribri (pop. 16,000), Cabécar (12,000), and Teribe/Térraba (2,000) are the largest Indigenous populations whose communities occupy the Caribbean slopes and rugged Talamancan Highlands.

The Darién-San Blas-Bayano Area

The Darién region remains the most inaccessible Indigenous area in Central America. A road-less "gap" of more than 60 miles of tropical rainforest looms between the terminus of the Pan-American Highway in eastern Panamá and the closest road in Colombia. Despite the absence of a road network, more than 125,000 Indigenous people reside in the Darién-San Blas Area in dispersed communities. Like in Muskitia, rivers are the main thoroughfares upon which transportation, commerce, and communication depend.

These isthmian interiors were Guna territory until the eighteenth century when they abandoned their riverine settlements in the Chucunaque-Tuira and Bayano Basins. The Guna settled along the San Blas coast and near-shore islands where the 2010 census showed more than 80,000 living in about fifty village. Only two small enclaves of ancestral Guna settlements survive in the rainforests of Darién—one at Paya-Pucuro in a sacred and remote corner of Chucunaque-Tuira river basin and the other at Mortí at the opposite northwestern end. Just west from there, several Guna villages with a few thousand individuals are in the drainage Lago Bayano Basin.

Emberá families from the Colombian Chocó region migrated into Darién during the late 1700s. Most Guna had abandoned the area after Franciscan missionaries resettled them in communities, and they rebelled against Spanish invaders who demanded their labor for gold mines in the region. The Emberá allied with Spanish soldiers in attempts to pacify the Guna populations, thereafter moving in from the Colombian Chocó to settle the riverine areas the Guna abandoned. Emberá spread along the resource-rich riverine habitats of the Darién Province, including the Chucunaque-Tuira, Balsas, Sambu, and Jaque rivers and their tributaries. The 2010 census shows about one hundred communities with more than 18,000 Emberá and 4,000 Wounaan there. Other Emberá settlements extend into the drainage of the Lago Bayano, and several Wounaan villages with several thousand people are along the Maje and Hondo Rivers that drain into the Pacific Ocean.

A fifth re-emerging Indigenous zone consists of more than 100,000 self-identified Lenca living in about six hundred mostly small communities in southwestern Honduras. Peaceful resurgent Lenca leadership since the 1980s organized communities to revitalize their indigeneity; they lost their language and many cultural practices decades ago. Lenca community leaders formed a federation and developed stronger identity recognizing their heritage and their ancestral lands, where they continue to farm. Now more than in previous census reports, families proudly self-identify as Lenca.

Outside these predominantly rural areas, Indigenous populations have a growing presence in cities large and small throughout the region. There is greater resistance to cultural assimilation than in the past and native families now quite often maintain their languages and traditions, and they also tend to keep ties with their territorial homelands. All Central America's capital cities have Indigenous populations that often concentrate in neighborhoods (*barrios*) of families from the same ethnic group. The 2010 Panamanian census registered 10,000 Indigenous inhabitants in the capital city, composed of mostly Guna (>6,000), Emberá (>1,400), and Ngäbe (>1,000). They concentrate in the mainly Guna barrios of Pedregal and Juan Díaz, and in the Emberá/ Wounaan barrio of Curundú. Similarly, Tegucigalpa, the capital of Honduras, has a largely Indigenous Miskitu barrio called "Kennedy," where Miskitu is commonly spoken.

Threats to Indigenous Territories

By the mid-twentieth century, the Pan-American Highway crossed the poorly connected border areas, linking capital cities and economies up and down the western side of the Isthmus. State and international policies aimed to solve the problem of "demographic imbalance" in Central America caused by urban primacy and land shortages. New policies encouraged colonization of *baldíos* (remote, forested areas falsely represented as empty quarters or green spaces) by Spanish-speaking mestizos for exploitation and agricultural development. These baldíos—chronically under-represented by censuses and cartographic data—were in many cases the ancestral homelands of Indigenous populations whose subsistence livelihoods depended on extensive forest use, hunting, and fishing. Massive deforestation and environmental destruction ensued as penetration roads with both planned and impromptu colonization eventually pierced into the Darién of Panamá, the Muskitia of Honduras and Nicaragua, and Guatemala's Petén during the 1970s. A decade later, secondary roads cut deeper yet into the forests as colonists flocked to receding forest frontiers to carve out space for farms and pastures. In many cases, these colonists acquired legal land title for their individual parcels after demonstrating land *mejoras* (improvements) in having converted forest to agriculture.[15]

The establishment of national parks, biosphere reserves, forest reserves, and other categories of protected areas was a significant top-down response to the unfolding environmental crisis during the 1980s–1990s. Alarmed by the rapid deforestation caused by expanding agricultural fronts, conservationists lobbied for a Central American biological corridor that would connect plants, animals, and Indigenous communities in a contiguous chain of protected areas. Many of Central America's largest parks and reserves, such as Río Plátano and Tawahka-Asangni in Honduras, Bosawas in Nicaragua, Amistad Bi-National Park in Costa Rica and Panamá, and Darién National Park in Panamá, were born of this impetus. Although the establishment of these protected areas signified a major victory for Central American rainforests, most were drawn with boundaries that overlap Indigenous peoples' territories. In contrast to national parks, which do not permit subsistence land use activity within their boundaries, biosphere reserves were of consequence for Indigenous peoples. They offered varying degrees of land use rights and resource management authority to resident communities. Conservationists at the time considered the biosphere model a viable alternative for balancing environmental conservation with the recognition of Indigenous peoples' rights to manage their own land and natural resources.[16]

In 2020, the situation is far from resolved. Biosphere reserves, for the most part, have failed to stop deforestation. National agrarian and top-down conservation policies often have come into conflict with one another, resulting in inadequate protection of the biospheres. Colonists, cattle ranchers, and other squatters continue to settle deep into forests perceived as open, often encroaching upon Indigenous subsistence lands. Hydroelectric dam projects and the proliferation of drug trafficking activity has only intensified the struggle for control over Central America's remaining rainforests, including those encompassed by biospheres. Within this milieu of conflict, Indigenous leaders have criticized top-down approaches to conservation, including the biosphere and national park models, which have largely failed to curb deforestation and colonization of Indigenous territories. Instead, Indigenous leaders have mobilized local and international support in petitioning for governance authority over their lands and resources.

Indigenous Territorial Responses

Indigenous–state relations in Central America have been marred by a long history of assertive and passive assimilationist policies and the systematic appropriation of native peoples' labor, territories, natural resources, and even material cultures. Recent decades, however, have ushered in a wave of territorial changes as Indigenous leaders have worked with advocates at state and international levels to demand increased political participation.[17] This "quiet revolution" over Indigenous land rights began inauspiciously in Panamá in the mid-twentieth century with the emergence of the semiautonomous *comarca*—an ITJ setting aside land and collective resource use areas for Guna communities.[18] The comarca model was adopted by other Indigenous groups in Panamá, and it influenced Indigenous land rights movements elsewhere in Central America. Since the 1970s Indigenous leaders across the region have formed federations to represent their populations and to lobby state agencies for ownership and decentralized governance of their ancestral lands.

ITJs presently cover much of Central America's core Indigenous areas (Figure 2.2). Their establishment marks a "territorial turn" against patterns of land dispossession that began

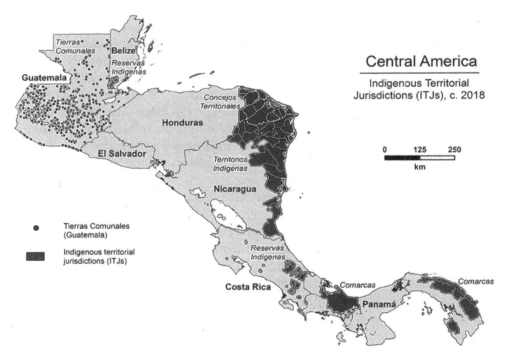

FIGURE 2.2. Central America: Indigenous territorial jurisdictions, 2005–2018. Boundary data from official sources: land registries, national geographic institutes, and Indigenous federations; population data from national censuses (see note 1).

during the colonial era and continued unabated until the end of colonization and agricultural development schemes in the twentieth century. Now a movement of repossession and ownership has taken hold among Central America's Indigenous and Afro-descendant populations, but it remains to be seen whether the proliferation of ITJs will succeed in balancing local peoples' land rights with sustainable environmental practices.[19]

De facto recognition of Indigenous peoples' territories is a phenomenon of the last few decades, but de jure support traces back to nineteenth-century Honduras and Nicaragua, when international treaties signed by Great Britain ceded extensive territories along the Caribbean lowlands to the postindependence governments. Such treaties (see the Wyke-Cruz Treaty of 1859, for instance) included nonspecific stipulations to respect Indigenous communities and their territories. All Central American countries affirm the rights of their resident Indigenous populations in their national constitutions, except Costa Rica, which does so in a separate Indigenous law. Broader recognition of Indigenous land rights comes from ratification of the 1989 International Labour Organization Convention on Indigenous and Tribal Peoples (ILO No. 169) by Costa Rica, Guatemala, Honduras, and Nicaragua. The ILO Convention details the rights of ownership and possession of the Indigenous populations over the lands which they traditionally occupy, following their own customs and land use practices. Moreover, environmental, forestry, agrarian, and protected areas legislation now routinely recognizes the responsibilities each state has toward its Indigenous peoples.

Since the 1970s, large areas of Central America have been awarded to Indigenous populations (Figure 2.2). Each country, except El Salvador, has its own ITJ to meet its distinct territorial obligations to its Indigenous peoples. The ITJs are sovereignty regimes with functional and legal expressions providing for Indigenous territoriality within the context of the modern states. Geographers recognize that different states have different "sovereignty regimes" with distinctive combinations of central state authority and decentralized political territoriality. ITJs represent the de facto internal functional geographic divisions of the ancestral Indigenous territories. They are organized to facilitate administration and governance of the population within, but they do not focus on or accommodate the broader distributions or territories of an Indigenous population. The ITJs are characterized by semiautonomy with different levels of governance authority at the local, regional, and federal levels. Generally, the ownership and titles of the ITJs are collectively shared by the communities and they are legally inalienable, nontransferable, imprescriptible, indefeasible, and indivisible.[20]

ITJs are distinct geopolitical strategies for accommodating Indigenous populations and their lifeways within the context of each state. They provide varying degrees of recognition for Indigenous peoples' property ownership and tenure control over communal lands, ancestral lands, natural resources, sites sacred to local worldview, and more. They recognize the overlapping nature of land and resource use among communities. ITJs were previously administered as "national" or "municipal" lands, or as biosphere reserves and other protected areas. They contain important forestry, agricultural, hydrological, maritime, and mineral resources beyond their inherent cultural patrimony.

The first ITJs in Central America were "reserves" that did not grant resident communities land ownership rights or governance autonomy over their own lands. In the early 1980s, a study by geographer William Davidson found just twenty such reserves set aside for Indigenous and Afro-descendent communities in the region; one-third of these had been created by the British in the late nineteenth century for the Maya-Mopan and Maya-Q'eqchi' of southern British Honduras (Belize). Others were established for Paya and Jicaque (Tol) communities in Honduras, for the Talamancan groups of southern Costa Rica, and for the Guaymí (Ngäbe), Guna, and Emberá of Panamá. These early reserves, however well-intended, covered small areas and were not well-defined or delimited in declaring documents, much less demarcated with on-the-ground enforcement.[21]

The lands owned or in possession of Indigenous (or campesino) communities in Guatemala are called *tierras comunales* (communal lands). The agrarian reforms initiated by Decree 900 in the 1950s focused on the development of these tierras comunales as areas where property rights, land ownership, and land tenure were shared collectively by the community, and where the "sale, embargo, or dissolution" of these tierras comunales is illegal. They are lands governed and administered at the community level through an assembly. While traditionally owned and held under communal tenure by both Indigenous and non-Indigenous campesino communities, tierras comunales typically are found on state or municipality lands. Indeed, one study of 213 tierras comunales (covering 92,240 hectares) showed 59 percent of them on municipal lands, 40 percent on lands already in possession or ownership of the communities, and barely one percent on state or national lands, meaning more than half are likely confronting unresolved tenure disputes over their communal lands. In 2018, the more than 1,100 tierras comunales covered 12 percent of Guatemala's extent.

The seventy-eight ITJs mapped outside Guatemala are based on official boundary data from Central America's national geographic institutes, land registries, and Indigenous federations. Guatemala's tierras comunales are represented above only as georeferenced point locations. Outside Guatemala, Figure 2.2 displays only legally declared lands—not showing others proposed or with unresolved land claims. As such, these data certainly underrepresent Central America's ITJs when accounting for future land titling and legalization campaigns.[22]

ITJs with land titles and shared governance structures have multiplied since the 1980s. The semiautonomous *comarca* homeland in Panamá opened the realm of possibilities for recognizing the land rights, semiautonomous governance, and territorial sovereignty of the Indigenous populations in Central America. The Guna comarca served as a model and hundreds of Indigenous leaders from other parts of Panamá and Central America participated in exchanges with Guna leaders to learn about their Comarca Guna Yala. These exchanges have helped shape the development of ITJs elsewhere, beginning with their involvement in the crusade to launch the Emberá-Wounaan Comarca in Darién in 1983, followed by their involvement forming four additional comarcas in the country. Since the 1990s, Guna leaders have been highlighted in South–South exchanges, recently contributing to the establishment of Concejos Territoriales in Honduras and Territorios Indígenas in Nicaragua.[23]

Our research shows that ITJs cover 18 percent of Central America in 2020. As expected, ITJs overlap with municipalities containing the highest Indigenous population densities. Outside Guatemala, the seventy-eight ITJs cover more than 75,000 km² or nearly 15 percent of Central America. The mean size of an ITJ exceeds 1,000 km² and many are much larger. In Panamá, the six comarcas cover nearly one-quarter of the country. The well-known Comarca Guna Yala—situated along the country's rugged northeastern coast—covers 2,306 km² of rainforest from atop precipitous slopes to narrow coastal plain and onto offshore Caribbean islands where most villages are found. The Comarca Ngäbe-Buglé is the largest ITJ in Central America spanning nearly 7,000 km² of coastal rainforest and lagoon systems in western Panamá. The 2010 census recorded more than 150,000 residents in Comarca Ngäbe-Bugle. Comarca Emberá-Wounaan in the country's easternmost Darién region is two-thirds the size of Ngäbe-Bugle (4,384 km²), but with only 10,000 residents, it enjoys a miniscule population density of less than one-half of one person per square kilometer, conserving expansive forested lands.

Nicaragua has the largest contiguous area under ITJs in the region, with twenty-three such "Indigenous territories" covering one-third of the country (38,853 km²) for Indigenous and Afro-descendent groups. In Honduras, of the 16 Indigenous "territorial councils" cover 14 percent of the county, with one called FINZMOS (its acronym in the Miskitu language) belonging to thirty Miskitu communities and encompassing nearly 4,000 km² of pine savannah and tropical rainforest. In Costa Rica—where barely 2 percent of the total population identifies as Indigenous—twenty-four semiautonomous reserves covering more than one-fifth of the country's areal extent have been set aside for eight different Indigenous groups.

A Hopeful but Uncertain Future

The colonial history of Indigenous peoples in Central America is one characterized by drastic population decline and territorial dispossession. The Spaniards ravaged the native communities whose inhabitants were decimated by warfare, slavery, and disease. Conquest and colonization resulted in territorial dispossession and population fragmentation up and down the Isthmus, ultimately molding the geographic distribution of Indigenous peoples into the five core areas discussed in this chapter.

Since the mid-twentieth century, though, Indigenous peoples have shown remarkable resilience such that there are more people who identify as Indigenous (over 8 million in 2020) in Central America than ever before. And while Indigenous peoples and their lands remain threatened by myriad factors, they are actively reclaiming their historical rights to lands and natural resources. These trends impart an optimism that tells of increasingly empowered Indigenous populations that are regaining ground and defining their rightful place in Central America.

Indigenous territoriality in Central America, if imagined like a statistical line of best fit describing periods of relatively high and low land rights, runs parallel to the Indigenous population curve through time—characterized by precipitous decline between the sixteenth and nineteenth centuries and then by a resurgence in the last one hundred years. Territory is no longer just about dispossession as Indigenous communities reclaim ancestral rights to lands and resources. Indigenous rights movements since the mid-twentieth century have ushered in (mostly) peaceful changes providing increased political participation and territorial recognition for constituent communities. ITJs with new governance structures have begun to accommodate the settlement patterns and subsistence lifeways of many Indigenous communities. Within the delimitations of the numerous ITJs are some of the region's largest expanses of rainforests with other valuable natural resources. These new sovereignty regimes provide for decentralized governance and community conservation—representing a fundamental change in the established power structures controlling access to and use of natural resources since the colonial era.

Yet the book on Indigenous peoples' population and territorial rights in Central America is far from closed. Here we conclude by asking: How will Central America's Indigenous population and territoriality correlate in the future? Will new ITJs continue to be recognized, mapped, and protected by Central American governments? Will ITJs succeed in guaranteeing Indigenous peoples' rights to territory and resources while ensuring sustainable use of the natural environments within their boundaries? Next-generation Indigenous leaders, scholars (especially geographers), and well-informed policymakers will best address these concerns working together.

Notes

1. William V. Davidson and Melanie A. Counce, "Mapping the Distribution of Indians in Central America," *Cultural Survival Quarterly* 13, no. 3 (1989): 37–40; Ronald Niezen, *The Origins of Indigenism: Human Rights and the Politics of Identity* (Berkeley: University of California Press, 2003).

    Our disaggregated census data are drawn from: Belize: Statistical Institute of Belize, *2010 Belize Population and Housing Census Dataset*. Online database, http://redatam.sib. org.bz:81/redbin/RpWebEngine.exe/Portal?BASE=BELIZECENSUS_2010&lang=eng; Costa Rica: Instituto Nacional de Estadísticas y Censos, *Censo 2011*. Online database, https://www.inec.cr/censos/censos-2011; El Salvador: Dirección General de Estadística y Censos, *VI Censo de Población y V de Vivienda 2007*. Online database, http://www.digestyc.gob.sv/servers/redatam/htdocs/CPV2007S/index.html; Guatemala: Instituto Nacional de Estadísticas Guatemala. *Resultados del Censo 2018*. Online database,https://www.censopoblacion.gt/explorador; Honduras: Instituto Nacional de Estadísticas, *XVII Censo de Población y VI de Vivienda 2013*. Online database, http://170.238.108.227/binhnd/RpWebEngine.exe/Portal; Nicaragua: El Instituto Nacional de Estadísticas y Censos (INEC), *2005 VIII Censo de Población y IV de Vivienda: Cifras Oficiales*.

PDF online, https://www.inide.gob.ni/censos2005/CifrasCompleto.pdf; Panamá: Instituto Nacional de Estadística y Censo, *XI Censo de Población y VII de Vivienda de Panamá: Año 2010*. Online database, https://www.inec.gob.pa/panbin/RpWebEngine.exe/Portal?BASE=LP2010.

Our disaggregated boundary data of municipios and Indigenous territorial jurisdictions are drawn from: Belize: Vector data for Districts acquired in ESRI shapefile (.shp) polygon format from DIVA-GIS, 2014. https://www.diva-gis.org/; Costa Rica: Vector data for *cantones* and Indigenous reserves acquired in ESRI shapefile (.shp) polygon format from Instituto Nacional de Estadística y Censo, 2014. Scale: 1:250,000. Projected coordinate system: CRTM05; El Salvador: Vector data for municipios acquired in ESRI shapefile (.shp) polygon format from Centro Nacional de Registros, 2014. https://www.cnr.gob.sv/geoportal-cnr/. Scale: 1:250,000. Projected coordinate system: Lambert Conformal Conic NAD27; Guatemala: Vector data for municipios acquired in ESRI shapefile (.shp) polygon format from Instituto Geográfico Nacional (IGN), 2014. Scale: 1:250,000. Projected coordinate system: NAD83 UTM Zone 15N. Vector data for tierras comunales acquired in ESRI shapefile (.shp) point format from Registro de Información Catastral, 2016. Geographic coordinate system: WGS84; Honduras: Vector data for municipios acquired in ESRI shapefile (.shp) polygon format from Dirección General de Catastro y Geografía, Instituto de la Propiedad, 2013. Scale: 1:250,000. Geographic coordinate system: WGS84. Vector data for concejos territoriales acquired in ESRI shapefile (.shp) polygon format from Programa de Administración de Tierras de Honduras (PATH II), 2013. Geographic coordinate system: WGS84. Additional vector data for concejos territoriales acquired in ESRI shapefile (.shp) polygon format from Instituto de Conservación Forestal, 2015. Scale: 1:250,000. Geographic coordinate system: WGS84;

Nicaragua: Vector data for municipios acquired through the digitization of the municipio boundaries on ESRI World Topographic Map. https://www.arcgis.com/home/item.html?id=6e850093c837475e8c23d905ac43b7d0.

Additional vector data for territorios indígenas acquired through the digitization of two maps from La Comisión Nacional de Demarcación y Titulación (CONADETI), 2012. Scale: 1:750,000. Geographic coordinate system: WGS84, and 2016. Scale: 1:2,600,000. Geographic coordinate system: WGS84; Panama: Vector data for distritos and comarcas acquired in ESRI Shapefile (.shp) polygon format from ARCGIS Online, 2014. Based on Censo Nacional de Población y Vivienda 2010 de Panamá. Instituto Nacional de Estadística y Censo, Controlaría General de la República de Panamá.

In addition, we have consulted population estimates from William M. Denevan, *The Native Population of the Americas in 1492* (Madison: University of Wisconsin Press, 1976), 2–7; W. George Lovell and Christopher H. Lutz, *Demography and Empire: A Guide to the Population History of Spanish Central America, 1500–1821* (London: Routledge, 1995), 4–14; Héctor Pérez Brignoli, "Estimaciones de la población indígena de América Central (del siglo XVI al siglo XX)," in *De los mayas a la planificación familiar: Demografía del istmo*, edited by Luis Rosero Bixby, Anne Pebley, and Alicia Bermúdez Méndez, 25–35 (San José: Editorial de la Universidad de Costa Rica, 1997); Ángel Rosenblat, *La población indígena y el mestizaje en América* (Buenos Aires: Editorial Nova, 1954).

2. Offen coined the term "territorial turn," see Karl H. Offen, "The Territorial Turn: Making Black Communities in Pacific Colombia," *Journal of Latin American Geography* 2, no. 1 (2003): 47. Herlihy and Tappan coined the term "Indigenous territorial jurisdictions," see

Peter H. Herlihy and Taylor A. Tappan, "Recognizing Indigenous Miskitu Territory in Honduras," *Geographical Review* 109, no. 1 (2019): 69.

3. This research was part of the University of Kansas–American Geographical Society Bowman Expedition called *Centroamérica Indígena* funded by a Minerva Initiative Grant for University-Led Research from the Office of the Secretary of the United States Department of Defense (supported by the US Army Research Laboratory and the U.S. Army Research Office under Contract/Grant W911NF1310281).

4. Ted Goebel, Michael R. Waters, and Dennis H. O'Rourke, "The Late Pleistocene Dispersal of Modern Humans in the Americas," *Science* 319, no. 5869 (2009): 1497–1502.

5. Richard Cooke. "The Native Peoples of Central America during pre-Columbian and Colonial Times," in *Central America: A Natural and Cultural History*, edited by Anthony G. Coates (New Haven, CT: Yale University Press, 1997), 137–163; Richard Cooke, Anthony Ranere, Georges Pearson, and Ruth Dickau, "Radiocarbon Chronology of Early Human Settlement on the Isthmus of Panamá (13,000–007,000 BP) With Comments on Cultural Affinities, Environments, Subsistence, and Technological Change," *Quaternary International* 301 (2013): 3–22; Richard G. Cooke, "Prehistory of Native Americans on the Central American Land Bridge: Colonization, Dispersal, and Divergence," *Journal of Archaeological Research* 70, no. 2 (2005): 129–187; Timothy E. Scheffler, Kenneth G. Hirth, and George Hasemann, "El Gigante Rockshelter: Preliminary Observations on an early to Late Holocene Occupation in Sothern Honduras," *Latin American Antiquity* 23, no. 4 (2012): 597–610; Robert C. West, "Pre-Conquest Mexico and Central America," in *Middle America: Its Lands and Peoples*, 3rd ed., edited by Robert C. West and John P. Augelli, 209–233 (Englewood Cliffs, NJ: Prentice-Hall, 1989).

6. For a popularized account of the new archaeological discoveries, see Douglas Preston, *The Lost City of the Monkey God* (New York: Grand Central, 2017).

7. Denevan, *Native Population of the Americas*, 2–7; Lovell and Lutz, *Demography and Empire*, 4–14.

8. James J. Parsons, "Urabá in the Sixteenth Century," in *Hispanic Lands and Peoples: Selected Writings of James L. Parsons*, edited by William M. Denevan, 81–91 (Boulder, CO: Westview Press, 1989); Robert C. West, "Conquest and Settlement of Mexico and Central America," in *Middle America: Its Lands and Peoples*, 3rd ed., edited by Robert C. West and John P. Augelli, 234–255 (Englewood Cliffs, NJ: Prentice-Hall, 1989); David R. Radell, "The Indian Slave Trade and Population of Nicaragua During the Sixteenth Century," in *The Native Population of the Americas in 1492*, edited by William M. Denevan, 67–76 (Madison: University of Wisconsin Press, 1976),.

9. Lovell and Lutz, 4–14; Héctor Pérez Brignoli, "Estimaciones de la población indígena de América Central (del siglo XVI al siglo XX)," in *De los mayas a la planificación familiar: demografía del istmo*, edited by Luis Rosero Bixby, Anne Pebley, and Alicia Bermúdez Méndez, 25–35 (San José: Editorial de la Universidad de Costa Rica, 1997); Angel Rosenblat, *La población indígena y el mestizaje en América*, 2 vols. (Buenos Aires: Editorial Nova, 1954).

10. Today's Indigenous population data are based on the most recent census presently available as follows: Statistical Institute of Belize, 2010; Instituto Nacional de Estadística y Censos de Costa Rica, 2011; El Salvador, Ministerio de Economía, Dirección General de Estadística y Censos, 2007; Guatemala, Instituto Nacional Geográfico, 2018, Tierras Comunales; Honduras, Instituto Nacional de Estadística, 2013; Nicaragua, Instituto Nacional de Información de Desarrollo, 2005; Panamá, Instituto Nacional de Estadística y Censo de Panamá, 2010. See note 1.

REGAINING GROUND   77

11. Peter H. Herlihy, "Central American Indian Peoples and Lands Today," in *Central America: A Natural and Cultural History*, edited by Anthony G. Coates, 215–240 (New Haven, CT: Yale University Press, 1997).

12. Geographer Lovell penned an extraordinary, compassionate, and reflective book telling the sad but compelling story: W. George Lovell, *A Beauty that Hurts: Life and Death in Guatemala*, revised ed. (Austin: University of Texas Press, 2000).

13. Peter H. Herlihy, "Indigenous Peoples and Biosphere Reserve Conservation in the Mosquitia Rainforest Corridor, Honduras," in *Conservation Through Cultural Survival: Indigenous Peoples and Protected Areas*, edited by Stan Stevens, 99–129 (Washington, DC: Island Press, 1997); Kendra McSweeney, Nazih Richani, Zoe Pearson, Jennifer Devine, and David J. Wrathall, "Why Do Narcos Invest in Rural Land?" *Journal of Latin American Geography* 16, no. 2 (2017): 3–29; Anne Larson, Fernanda Soto, Dennis Mairena, Edda Moreno, Eileen Mairena, and Jadder Mendoza-Lewis, "The Challenge of 'Territory': Weaving the Social Fabric of Indigenous Communities in Nicaragua's Northern Caribbean Autonomous Region," *Bulletin of Latin American Research* 35, no. 3 (2016): 322–337.

14. Burton L. Gordon, *A Panamá Forest and Shore: Natural History and Amerindian Culture in Bocas del Toro* (Pacific Grove, CA: Boxwood Press, 1982); Carlos Borge and Roberto Castillo, *Cultura y conservación en la Talamanca indígena* (San José, Costa Rica: Editorial Universidad Estatal a Distancia, 1997); D. A. Smith, M. B. Holland, A. Michon, A. Ibáñez, and F. Herrera, "The Hidden Layer of Indigenous Land Tenure: Informal Forest Ownership and its Implications for Forest Use and Conservation in Panamá's Largest Collective Territory," *International Forestry Review* 19, no. 4 (2017): 478–494.

15. Stanley Heckadon-Moreno, "Spanish Rule, Independence, and the Modern Colonization Frontiers," in *Central America: A Natural and Cultural History*, edited by Anthony G. Coates, 177–214 (New Haven, CT: Yale University Press, 1997); Herlihy, "Indigenous Peoples and Biosphere Reserve Conservation," 99–129; Peter H. Herlihy, "Opening Panamá's Darién Gap," *Journal of Cultural Geography* 9, no. 2 (1989):41–59; Anthony Stocks, John Benjamin McMahan, and Peter Taber, "Indigenous, Colonist, and Government Impacts on Nicaragua's Bosawas Reserve," *Conservation Biology* 21, no. 6 (2007), 1495–1505; Norman B. Schwartz, "Colonization of Northern Guatemala: the Petén," *Journal of Anthropological Research* 43, no. 2 (1987): 163–183; Avrum J. Shriar, "Theory and Context in Analyzing Livelihoods, Land Use, and Land Cover: Lessons from Petén, Guatemala," *Geoforum* 55 (2014), 152–163; Sarah M. Howard, "Land Conflict and Mayangna Territorial Rights in Nicaragua's Bosawás Reserve," *Bulletin of Latin American Research* 17, no. 1 (1998), 17–34.

16. Peter H. Herlihy, "Wildlands Conservation in Central America During the 1980s: A Geographical Perspective," *Yearbook for Conference of Latin Americanist Geographer* 17/18 (1992): 31–43; Herlihy "Indigenous Peoples and Biosphere Reserve Conservation," 215–240.

17. Roger Plant and Soren Hvalkof, *Land Titling and Indigenous Peoples* (Washington, DC: Inter-American Development Bank, 2001); Roque Roldán-Ortega, *Models for Recognizing Indigenous Land Rights in Latin America* (Washington, DC: World Bank Environment Department, 2004), 1–33; Charles Hale, "Neoliberal Multiculturalism: The Remaking of Cultural Rights and Racial Dominance in Central America," *Political and Legal Anthropology Review* 28, no. 1 (2005): 10–28.

18. Peter H. Herlihy, "Panamá's Quiet Revolution: Comarca Homelands and Indian Rights," *Cultural Survival Quarterly* 13, no. 3 (1989): 17–24; Peter H. Herlihy, "La revolución

silenciosa de Panamá: Las tierras de comarca y los derechos indígenas," *Mesoamerica* 29 (1995): 77–93.

19. Herlihy and Tappan, "Recognizing Indigenous Miskitu Territory"; Offen, "Territorial Turn"; Larson et al., "The Challenge of Territory"; Mary Finley-Brook, "Territorial 'Fix'? Tenure Insecurity in Titled Indigenous Territories," *Bulletin of Latin American Research* 35, no. 3 (2016): 338–354.

20. This study does not include community titles awarded to individual Indigenous communities, because they are not ITJs with tenure and governance protections; indeed, individual community titles such as those issued to the Tawahka and Garífuna communities in Honduras have led to land dispossession, causing individual communities to constrict their customary subsistence patterns into checkerboards of use and ownership.

21. William V. Davidson, "Geography of Minority Populations in Central America," in *Latin America Case Studies*, edited by Richard G. Boehm and Sent Visser, 31–37 (Dubuque, IA: Kendall/Hunt, 1984).

22. For example, similar GIS research in Panamá included both legally established ITJs and Indigenous "claimed lands" for a combined total of 23,470 km^2, covering 31.6 percent of Panamá. Our estimate is lower because it only included the legally established or titled ITJs covering a smaller area of 22.87 percent (17,089 km^2) of the country. See Gerardo Vergara-Asenjo and Catherine Potvin, "Forest Protection and Tenure Status: The Key Role of Indigenous People and Protected Areas in Panamá," *Global Environmental Change* 28 (2014): 205–215.

23. Roman Álvarez, Enrique Pantoja, Gerson Granados, and Alain Paz, "Strengthening Indigenous Peoples Land Rights in Honduras: The Miskitu People's Experience of Collective Land Titling, Lessons Learned, and Main Challenges for the Future," presented at the World Bank Conference on Land and Poverty, Washington, DC, 2017; Herlihy, "Panamá's Quiet Revolution"; Herlihy and Tappan, "Recognizing Indigenous Miskitu Territory," 74.

FURTHER READING

Barquero, Jaime I. "El cuarto viaje de Colón." In *Colón y la Costa Caribe de Centroamérica*. Edited by Jaime I. Barquero. Managua, Nicaragua: Fundación Vida, 2002.

Brignoli, Héctor Pérez. "Estimaciones de la población indígena de América Central del siglo XVI al siglo XX." In *De los mayas a la planificación familiar: Demografía del istmo*. Edited by Luis Rosero Bixby, Anne Pebley, and Alicia Bermúdez Méndez. San José: Editorial de la Universidad de Costa Rica, 1997.

Coates, Anthony G., ed. *Central America: A Natural and Cultural History*. New Haven, CT: Yale University Press, 1997.

Cooke, Richard, Anthony Ranere, Georges Pearson, and Ruth Dickau. 2013. "Radiocarbon Chronology of Early Human Settlement on the Isthmus of Panamá (13,000–7000 BP) with Comments on Cultural Affinities, Environments, Subsistence, and Technological Change." *Quaternary International* 301(2013): 3–22.

Davidson, William V., and Melaine A. Counce. "Mapping the Distribution of Indians in Central America," *Cultural Survival Quarterly* 13, no. 3 (1989): 37–40.

Denevan, William M., ed. *The Native Population of the Americas in 1492*. Madison: University of Wisconsin Press, 1976.

Dow, James W., and Robert van Kemper, eds. *Encyclopedia of World Cultures.* Volume VIII, *Middle America and the Caribbean.* New York: G. K. Hall, 1995.

Goebel, Ted, Michael R. Waters, and Dennis H. O'Rourke. "The Late Pleistocene Dispersal of Modern Humans in the Americas." *Science* 319, no. 5869 (2009): 1497–1502.

Hall, Carolyn, Héctor Pérez Brignoli, and John V. Cotter. *Historical Atlas of Central America.* Norman: University of Oklahoma Press, 2003.

Herlihy, Peter H. "Central American Indian Peoples and Lands Today." In *Central America: A Natural and Cultural History,* 215–240. Edited by Anthony G. Coates. New Haven, CT: Yale University Press, 1997.

Lovell, W. George, and Christopher H. Lutz. *Demography and Empire: A Guide to the Population History of Spanish Central America, 1500–1821.* Dellplain Latin American Studies 33. London: Routledge, 1995.

Rosenblat, Angel. 1954. *La población indígena y el mestizaje en América.* 2 vols. Buenos Aires: Nova, 1954.

West, Robert C., and John P. Augelli. *Middle America: Its Lands and Peoples.* 2nd ed. Englewood Cliffs, NJ: Prentice-Hall, 1976.

CHAPTER 3

THE ANCIENT CIVILIZATIONS

WILLIAM R. FOWLER

INTRODUCTION

CENTRAL America comprises seven modern nations: Guatemala, Belize, El Salvador, Honduras, Nicaragua, Costa Rica, and Panama. For geographical reasons and historical and cultural connections, it is convenient to include the Mexican state of Chiapas also as part of Central America. The total area encompasses 597,090 square kilometers and is home to an estimated population of more than 52 million, with an estimated population density of 88/square kilometer (2016).[1] With its relatively high population density, the area is highly susceptible to volcanic, seismic, and climatic natural disasters such as droughts, tropical storms, flooding, and landslides, and the same was true in the past.[2] A recurrent theme in the study of ancient Central American civilizations is the impact of natural disasters and societal responses to cataclysmic events.

The area may be subdivided into five main geographical zones: (1) the highlands of Chiapas, Guatemala, Honduras, and western El Salvador; (2) the Pacific coastal plain and lowlands running from Chiapas to Costa Rica; (3) the northern lowlands of the Department of Petén in Guatemala, Belize, and northwestern Honduras; (4) the eastern Caribbean coastal lowlands of northern and eastern Honduras and Nicaragua; and (5) the southern isthmus of Panama and Costa Rica.[3] These regions are highly diverse in terms of geography, environment, resources, adaptations, and cultural identity. In terms of external affinities, the first three, in northern Central America, formed the eastern and southeastern regions of the Mesoamerican culture area, whereas the final two, in lower Central America, formed the northern frontier of the Isthmo-Colombian or Intermediate Area. This chapter refers to northern Central America as "Mesoamerican" and lower Central America as "Isthmian."

This chapter presents a brief synthetic overview of the current state of knowledge of the development of civilization, or complex society, in Central America. It focuses mainly on interpretations of archaeological data rather than theoretical perspectives, although theory clearly guides and influences data and interpretations. The organization of the narrative reflects a broad underlying interest in ancient political economies and the development of social and political complexity. One final introductory note: the information available on the earlier and middle prehistoric periods is much greater than that for the final centuries before the arrival of Spanish invaders in the early sixteenth century, and this overview reflects that historiographic imbalance.

EARLIEST INHABITANTS, 10,000–8,000 BCE

The earliest Central Americans were hunter-gatherers whose ancestors entered North America from northeast Asia during the Late Pleistocene geological epoch. Many of these migrations probably occurred by land across the Bering Strait when sea levels dropped during the Wisconsin Glacial Episode, 23,000 to 11,000 years BCE, opening up an "ice-free corridor" from Beringia to Alberta, Montana, and points south. Shortly after the end of the Wisconsin glaciation, between 9,500 and 9,000 BCE, Clovis stone tool technology, characterized by thin, fluted, lanceolate projectile points and associated implements used for hunting large mammals, appeared in the Americas.[4]

These finds establish an early time frame, referred to as the "Clovis baseline," for human presence in the Americas, a hotly debated topic in American archaeology.[5] The corresponding "Clovis-first" argument maintains that Clovis people were the first inhabitants of the Americas. An alternative interpretation holds that earlier inhabitants arrived by watercraft following a coastal route originating along the North Pacific Rim and moving southward down the west coasts of North and South America. The coastal route model provides a parsimonious explanation for the presence and distribution of undisputed pre-Clovis sites in North and South America.[6] The most unambiguous Late Pleistocene, pre-Clovis site known in America is Monte Verde, in southern Chile, where charcoal from hearths yielded radiocarbon dates at about 31,000 BCE. The upper-level (Monte Verde II) occupation—composed of artifacts, faunal and floral remains, shelters, hearths, and living floors—provides clear evidence of "a human settlement practicing a generalized economy throughout the year" dated to 12,800–11,800 BCE, more than two thousand years earlier than the estimated time span for Clovis in North America.[7]

Questions abound concerning the timing and routes of entry of the earliest human migrants to Central America. The earliest Central American sites with unequivocal evidence of human occupation are few in number and date to the Late Pleistocene/Early Holocene transition.[8] All except Santa Marta cave, in the Mexican state of Chiapas, have yielded Clovis, Clovis-like, or related fishtail points and associated artifacts.[9] Located in the Ocozocuautla region of northwest Chiapas, Santa Marta's oldest levels date to more than 10,000 BCE. Simple flake tools found here indicate a broad-spectrum adaptation with expedient technology rather than a specialized hunting adaptation. This evidence suggests reduced mobility of the local population which allowed multiple successive generations to immerse themselves in their environment and experiment with useful plants. They probably also engaged in the cultivation of semidomesticated plant species or, in other words, horticulture.[10] Santa Marta and similar long-term, low-mobility occupations in Central America laid the pattern for future generations and gave rise to continuing developments in plant domestication and storage technologies in the Archaic period.

It is very significant to note that the earliest human societies in Central and South America, from Chiapas to southern Chile, appear to have had generalized subsistence economies in contrast to the specialized big-game hunting adaptations that prevailed in the Plains and the Great Basin of North America during this time after the end of the last great glaciation.

THE ARCHAIC PERIOD: ORIGINS OF AGRICULTURE AND PRELUDE TO SEDENTISM, 8000–2000 BCE

In the historiography of New World archaeology, the Archaic period is the time of the origins of agriculture and sedentary life. The period is defined by the absence of Pleistocene animals and ceramics and by the widespread use of cultigens. It was facilitated by a long period of global warming beginning in the Holocene after about 9,650 BCE. Rising temperatures and increasing rainfall provided a favorable climate in the Neotropics for the development of mixed economies based on hunting and trapping of medium-size or small game animals and horticulture.[11] The form of social structure in Central America at this time consisted of biologically related nuclear families living together as small, egalitarian, patrilineal bands. They inhabited caves, rockshelters, or small open-air camps with shelters of perishable structures. These seasonal camps shifted locations several times a year based on the availability of plant foods, the locations of game, and other natural resource factors. Small, semisedentary bands coalesced during times of resource abundance to form seasonal macrobands.[12] In richer environments, especially coastal regions, where fish and shellfish were always available in abundance, sedentism developed earlier. This form of socioeconomic organization and subsistence-settlement pattern continued from the time of earliest inhabitants into the Archaic period. The origins of Mesoamerican and Isthmian religious ceremonalism, shamanic ritual, and cosmological mythologies may also be traced to these earliest periods.[13]

The Archaic may be subdivided into three substages: Early Archaic, 8000–5000 BCE, Middle Archaic, 5000–3500 BCE, and Late Archaic, 3500–2000 BCE.[14] The Early Archaic in the Central American highlands is represented by the Late Pleistocene/Early Holocene levels of Santa Marta which show correspondences with early domestication in the Tehuacan Valley and in the Valley of Oaxaca.[15] Evidences for Middle and Late Archaic domesticated maize and other cultigens in Central America indicate the beginnings of maize agriculture from about 3000 to 2000 BCE. El Gigante Rockshelter, in the highlands of western Honduras, has produced remains of well-preserved cobs of fully domesticated maize dated to as early as 2390 BCE.[16] In the Maya lowlands, excavations and lake coring at several sites in northern Belize with Late Archaic occupation produced evidence of *Zea mays* pollen as early as 3360 BCE with maize cultivation becoming increasingly common in the lowlands beginning about 2400 BCE.

The earliest evidence for human occupation of the Pacific coastal plain occurs at a group of six sites consisting of large mounds of accumulated shells (discarded after human consumption) on the inland edge of the mangrove estuary (outer edge of the coastal plain) in the Soconusco region of Chiapas, dated to the Middle Archaic and Early Formative, 5550–1550 BCE.[17] The most important of these is Tlacuachero, a giant, truncated conical shellmound 175 meters in diameter and more than 7 meters in height, dated to as early as 4000 BCE. These tumuli served as platforms for drying fish and shellfish.[18]

Precocious early cultivators in Soconusco, the Gulf Coast of Mexico, and the Pacific coastal lowlands of Guatemala and El Salvador participated in what Robert M. Rosenswig has dubbed an "archipelago of complexity," derived from the evocative phrase "archipelago of towns" used by Fernand Braudel to describe the "handful of extraordinary cities" of the early capitalist world economy in Europe and their spatial context. The sophisticated cities of Medieval western Europe were islands of economic, political, and cultural power surrounded by a sea of backwardness, " 'black holes' outside *world* time."[19] The archipelago metaphor implies the value and significance of social network ties among the cities. Applied to Late Archaic Central America, the idea is that only a few important centers began to adopt all the trappings of Early Formative village life while still surrounded by a "wilderness" of Archaic foraging societies. Their linkages to each other formed a crucial element in the transition from the Archaic to the Formative way of life and the development of Formative culture in Central America.[20]

A somewhat similar pattern may be discerned for the Isthmo-Colombian coastal regions of lower Central America. Late Archaic societies of this area were farmers who also practiced fishing and shellfish collecting (or coastal collectors who also practiced horticulture). The southern isthmus area is also important for early ceramic technology. Monagrillo ware, the earliest known pottery in Central America, began to appear as early as 3520 BCE in central Panama, from Parita Bay on the Pacific coast to the Coclé drainage on the Caribbean side of the peninsula. The Monagrillo culture has been the subject of intensive archaeological and geoarchaeological research for the past sixty-five years.[21] A relatively poorly made ware with simple decoration, Monagrillo ware was probably the product of local invention rather than diffusion from the south where earlier ceramics occur. Concerning the function of the vessels, recent interpretations favor a role for Monagrillo vessels in social interaction and the expression of social identity in feasting or drinking rituals.[22]

In summary, the Archaic period represents the deep history of human-plant interaction and plant domestication. Traditional narratives depict the Archaic as a long, almost static period during which foragers and early horticulturalists experimented with plant domestication. Domestication was not a rapid or a homogeneous process. The spread of domesticated cultigens in Mexico and Central America involved a series of slow, complex processes, each occurring at a different rate of speed. Domestication resulted from everyday activities, occurring on the scale of individual time, but cumulative practices in the realm of agriculture over the course of thousands of years resulted in long-term structural changes not only in food production itself but also in the economic, social, political, and religious realms of the cultures that engaged in these experiments. These cumulative changes culminated in the Late Archaic period, possibly amplified by a global mid-latitude prolonged drought between 2300 and 2100 BCE (the "4.2 ka BP event"), followed by climatic amelioration.[23]

Initial Formative Period: Origins of Village Life and Social Inequality, 2000–1200 BCE

The secondary effects of sedentary farming that began in the Late Archaic included population growth, increased agricultural production based primarily on maize, the creation of an agricultural surplus, the appearance of new social institutions, incipient social ranking, fissioning of social units, differential access to basic resources, and an increase in social and economic exchange. These changes continued and intensified in the Formative period all over Central America.

An Early Formative ceramic complex appeared in northwestern Costa Rica a few centuries after Monagrillo ware made its initial appearance in central Panama. Known as the Tronadora complex, and dated to 2000–1800 BCE at the type site of Tronadora Vieja, located on the shore of Lake Arenal, eastern Guanacaste province, this is a sophisticated ceramic ware with jar, bowl, and bottle forms featuring a variety of decorative motifs. Fragments of ceramics were recovered from a domestic level consisting of a small, circular house floor with postholes, associated with grinding stones and chipped-stone tools. Evidence for *Zea mays* was recovered in the form of charred maize kernels, phytoliths, and pollen.[24] As with Monagrillo, Tronadora-complex ceramics represent a local elaboration of a ceramic tradition that became widespread in Central America at this time, and the impetus for making and using these vessels was likely social and political (social identity and competitive, ritual feasting) rather than utilitarian (food preparation and cooking).

Precocious Initial Formative villages developed in various locales of Mesoamerican Central America, from the Pacific coast of Chiapas to El Salvador, and into the Maya lowlands during the period from about 2000 to 1200 BCE. These early hot spots represent islands in Rosenswig's Braudelian archipelago of complexity, discussed above. They were considerably larger than most other coeval settlements in their respective regions.

They possessed elite residential architecture, substantial ritual structures (elevated temple platforms), or both. Some had public civic-ceremonial spaces such as plazas and ball courts. All had well-made ceramics used in commensal rituals, specialized stone tools, and botanical evidence for maize and other cultigens.

The material culture inventory of the Mazatan Initial Formative centers in Soconusco features an array of symbolic goods that indicate social inequality such as elaborate pottery used in ritual display and commensal feasts; ceramic figurines portraying obese males attired in ritual garb, wearing animal masks, and sporting round disks (representing iron-ore mirrors) on their chests or attached to a helmet or headdress, interpreted as depictions of shamanistic rulers; and elite residential architecture. The best-known example is Paso de la Amada, an ancient village dated to 1900–1450 BCE.[25] The earliest known pottery in southern Mesoamerica appears at Paso de la Amada and about thirty other Mazatan sites during the initial phase of occupation (1900–1700 BCE). This was a well-made, elaborately decorated ware. The predominant forms consist of the *tecomate* (neckless jar with rounded shoulders and restricted orifice) and a small to medium-size cuplike vessel imitating the shape of a natural gourd, suggesting use for storage, serving, and imbibing liquids, possibly maize-based *chicha*, chocolate, presumably on ritual occasions.

Paso de la Amada increased in size during the succeeding phase (1700–1550 BCE), and became the largest regional center of several two-tiered settlement systems in the Mazatan zone during the Initial Formative. The core of the site covered an area of approximately 37 hectares, and the entire settlement covered 140 hectares of dispersed construction, more than eight times the size of the next largest known center in the Mazatan zone. Construction of the settlement was planned and incorporated cosmolological symbolism. Based on the criteria of size, Paso de la Amada could be considered a small town rather than a small village, but the site's researchers do not make this claim.

The architectural sequence of a structure at one important site suggests a lineage of tribal rulers successfully consolidating power and passing their leadership to succeeding generations in their chiefly household.[26] Excavations of an elite residence at Paso de la Amada revealed a sequence of at least nine superimposed platform construction levels, sequential rebuilding episodes of an early palace for an elite household that increased in relative wealth and status over the course of multiple generations. A monumental civic-ceremonial structure, located a short distance north of the palace at Paso de la Amada, is the earliest known ball court and the largest construction for its time in Mesoamerica.[27] The location of the ball court near the palace suggests that members of this chiefly lineage were patrons of the ballgame. The court's construction and use were closely bound to the development of hereditary inequality and ascribed leadership in this community. The final residential level of the palace and the ball court at Paso de la Amada fell into disuse at about 1450 BCE. The site itself was abandoned about a century later and never reoccupied. It was eclipsed by the neighboring town of Cantón Corralito, a Gulf Coast Olmec ethnic enclave with direct ties to the great Early Formative Olmec center of San Lorenzo.[28]

EARLY TO MIDDLE FORMATIVE PERIOD: STRATIFIED SOCIETY AND ORIGINS OF THE STATE, 1200 BCE–300 BCE

The Early and Middle Formative periods represent a crucial time in Central American prehistory, marked by the appearance of complex, stratified societies and hierarchical political structures. Central to understanding this development is the Olmec civilization on the Gulf Coast, known at four major centers and dozens of secondary centers. Its antecedents may be traced to Isthmian precedents in the Initial Formative at early centers like Paso de la Amada.

The Early to Middle Formative Olmec phenomenon in Mexico and Central America refers both to a specific culture centered on the Gulf Coast region of the Mexican states of Veracruz and Tabasco and to the first widely distributed art style of pre-Columbian Mesoamerica. The term "Olmec" is derived from the Nahuatl *Olmecatl* ("People of Olman" or "People of the Land of Rubber"), the ethnonym employed by the Aztecs in late pre-Hispanic times for inhabitants of the Gulf Coast region. The language spoken by the earliest inhabitants of Olman was almost certainly an ancestral form of Mixe-Zoquean. In reality, the name "Olmec" is a misnomer that has nothing to do with the Early to Middle Formative inhabitants of Olman or the widely distributed art style of the Early to Middle Formative.[29]

This early civilization exerted a powerful stimulus on contemporary cultures all over Mexico and Central America. Olmec-inspired motifs are found in ceramics and rock carvings over an enormous area extending from Chalcatzingo, in the Mexican state of Morelos, in the west, to Chalchuapa, El Salvador, in the southeast. The distribution of Olmec-style carved greenstone objects is even greater, extending from the Mexican state of Guerrero to Honduras and Costa Rica. The widespread distribution of these objects and symbols can be seen as the product of long-distance exchange and interactions linking elites all over Mexico and northern Central America during the Early and Middle Formative and, perhaps more important, the materialization of pan-Mesoamerican religious and cosmological concepts.

The earliest major center in Olman was San Lorenzo Tenochtitlan. A veritable metropolis located in the middle reaches of the Coatzacoalcos River, San Lorenzo sits on a high plateau rising to a height of about 50 meters, appearing as an island looming over the surrounding floodplain. Its base is a natural geological formation, but the upper 7 meters consists of artificial fill deposited and was shaped by the immense labor force that built this ancient tropical city. It boasts about 200 mounds on its surface, mostly remains of temple platforms, residences, and palaces of shamanistic kings.[30]

The best-known artistic features of the San Lorenzo Olmecs are the colossal stone heads, which are actually portraits carved in the round of the Olmec kings (and possibly queens, in some cases) who ruled this city-state, and the so-called monumental altars, which served as royal thrones. The San Lorenzo colossal head corpus consists of only thirteen examples of varying sizes up to 3 meters high and weighing as much as 28 tons. They all depict rulers as ballplayers wearing helmets, each with distinctive insignia. Their faces are naturalistic with no obvious supernatural connotations. About 130 additional sculpted monuments depict ballplayers, animals, a supernatural being associated with rain, and other themes. The earliest occupation at San Lorenzo dates to about 1500 BCE. From 1200 to 900 BCE, it became the largest and most powerful center of Indigenous American civilization during the Early Formative period. Other Early Formative sites in the San Lorenzo region include Potrero Nuevo, El Azuzul, and El Manatí. The latter has extraordinary preservation of organic objects, including a variety of wooden objects and rubber balls designed for use in the ritual Mesoamerican ball game.

San Lorenzo was destroyed and largely abandoned at about 900 BCE. It was succeeded as the major Gulf Coast Olmec center during the Middle Formative period, from 900 to 400 BCE, by La Venta, Tabasco, east of San Lorenzo, located on a salt dome or "island" in a coastal marshland. Like San Lorenzo, the central ritual precinct of La Venta was carefully planned and constructed with massive amounts of human labor, but its architectural and sculptural programs are very different from those of its predecessor. A settlement survey of the region shows a large population in the riverine periphery of the central core of La Venta, contradicting models that assume that La Venta was an empty ceremonial center.[31]

The monumental architecture of La Venta was the first in Mesoamerica to combine a large pyramid flanked by low platform mounds forming a large, rectangular plaza. Generally regarded as an effigy volcano, the pyramid stands more than 30 meters high.[32] To the north of the pyramid, a plaza, dated to 900–700 BCE, featured two large, rectangular pits filled with massive offerings of large serpentine blocks capped by a mosaic pavement laid out as a cosmogram depicting the sacred landscape of La Venta and its relationship to the underworld. The enormous investment of labor required to construct these features underscores La Venta's role as a pilgrimage center during the Middle Formative. The practice of carving colossal royal head portraits continued but abated; only four examples have been recovered from La Venta.[33]

A number of large centers on the Pacific coastal plain of Chiapas and Guatemala and the piedmont and southern highlands of Guatemala and El Salvador were full participants in the Middle Formative southern Gulf-Pacific interaction sphere. These include Izapa, Chiapas, Soconusco, Mexico; Kaminaljuyu, Guatemala; and Chalchuapa, El Salvador. By 700 BCE, the Izapa kings had already established their regional center at the apex of a four-tiered administrative hierarchy, indicating stratified society and a redistributive economy.[34] Like Izapa in Soconusco, Kaminaljuyu, in the highlands on the western edge of present-day Guatemala City, and Chalchuapa in western El Salvador were major Middle Formative centers that peaked in the Late Formative. They all present a complex mix of monumental architecture, Middle Formative Olmec-style low-relief carvings, Late Formative Izapan-style narrative sculpture, and Lowland Maya-style low-relief stelae and altars.[35]

The Late Formative in the Maya Lowlands and Highlands: Early Cities and States, 300 BCE–CE 250

The Middle Formative in the Isthmus and the Pacific coast and piedmont served as a dress rehearsal for the dramatic, explosive development of stratified chiefdoms and states in the Maya lowlands and highlands during the Late Formative. This period is characterized by a population increase on the order of about 300 percent greater than Middle Formative levels. Urban centers appeared throughout the lowlands of the Yucatan Peninsula and the Peten jungle region of northern Guatemala, and cultural dominance shifted from the Gulf and Isthmus to these regions. Ritualists transmitted the distinctive Izapan sculptural style to the lowlands, evidence of a highland/lowland dialectic that served as a catalyst in the development of lowland civilization.

Monumental architecture of the period—the most visible expression of elite ruling ideology—consists of large temple platforms, spacious plazas, triadic complexes of temple-pyramids ("E- Groups"), architectural sculpture consisting of stucco masks flanking broad staircases, and polychrome murals adorning temple walls. Interpolity competition and conflict led to increasing violence and warfare. At the same time, the period sees increasing economic, social, political, and ideological interaction. Widespread uniformity in Lowland Maya ceramics during the Late Preclassic attests to a high degree of craft specialization and strong interregional economic and ideological ties throughout the area that transcended political hostilities. Highland and lowland centers maintained close cultural and ideological connections.

Sometime between 30 BCE and CE 80, San Antonio volcano, a component of the Tacaná volcanic complex in western Guatemala, erupted with disastrous force. Pyroclastic flows from this event filled local ravines with deposits more than 10 meters thick. The urban center of Izapa did not suffer a direct hit by the eruption, but thick debris from these deposits dammed nearby rivers. Heavy rains set in soon after the eruption, and swollen rivers choked with mud created an enormous lahar that flowed through the piedmont with catastrophic effects on crops, settlements, and human lives. Swirling waves of mud and water six meters in height engulfed the monuments and constructions at Izapa. The social, political, and economic impact of this major environmental disaster consisted of, at minimum, a hastening of the collapse of the Izapa kingdom of the Late Formative period.[36]

The Early Classic in the Maya Lowlands and Highlands, CE 250–600

The Early Classic period represents a great fluorescence throughout the Maya world with continued population expansion and advances in architecture, arts, sciences, and crafts.

Sophisticated concepts of time and calendrical reckoning became an integral part of the political, religious, and economic power of royalty and nobility. The stela cult, centered on the practice of erecting elaborately carved stelae and altars inscribed with hieroglyphic texts carrying historical information and a distinctive iconography, developed at the beginning of this period.[37] The earliest known lowland monument with a Long Count calendrical date is Stela 29 at Tikal (8.12.14.13.15, CE 292).[38] The inscriptions on the stelae record dates of royal births, deaths, marriages, accessions, conquests, and other significant personal and political events in the lives of Maya kings, queens, their dynasties, and their cities.

By far the most transcendent political event recorded in Early Classic Lowland Maya inscriptions is known simply as "the *entrada*" of CE 378 or, more explicitly, the Teotihuacan intrusion in the lowlands. The epigraphic evidence is known from three sites: El Perú/Waka, 8.17.1.4.4, 8 Jan. 378; Uaxactun, Stelae 5 and 22; and Tikal, Stelae 4 and 31; 8.17.1.4.12, 16 Jan. 378. In brief summation, the inscriptions recount the story of strangers who "arrived" from the west, led by General Siyaj K'ak' ("Fire Born"), representative of Spearthrower Owl, a king of Teotihuacan or possibly Kaminaljuyu, where he ruled from CE 374 to 439. Siyaj K'ak' killed the fourteenth king of Tikal, Chak Tok Ich'aak I ("Jaguar Paw"), who is said to have "slipped into the water," and the general seems to have served as regent for 5 years before installing Yax Nuun Ayiin I ("First Crocodile"), son of Spearthrower Owl, as king of Tikal, He ruled from CE 379 to 404 and was succeeded by his son (and grandson of Spearthower Owl), Sihyaj Chan K'awil II ("Stormy Sky"), who ruled Tikal from CE 411 to 456.[39] Supporting archaeological evidence consists of Teotihuacan ceramic styles and imagery at Tikal, Uaxactun, and several other Lowland Maya sites in the central Peten region, including the distinctive *talud-tablero* architectural decoration, thought to have originated in central highland Mexico in the Late Formative period.[40]

Another major event that impacted the Maya area in the late fifth or early sixth century was a natural disaster rather than a political event. Sometime between CE 440 and 550, according to radiocarbon assays, a massive, Surtseyan volcanic eruption spewed forth from Ilopango caldera, located immediately east of modern San Salvador, El Salvador, blanketing an area of at least 10,000 square kilometers with a layer of ash 2 to 3 meters in depth, in total more than 80 cubic kilometers of pyroclastic flows and ash. Areas immediately adjacent to the caldera were buried by 20 to 40 meters of ash. The immediate impact zone included all of El Salvador and adjacent portions of eastern Guatemala, western Honduras, and southwest Nicaragua, within a radius of about 100 km from Ilopango. The entire area impacted by the eruption was depopulated, and major centers such as Chalchuapa in the west and the Lenca city of Quelepa in eastern El Salvador were temporarily abandoned. Trade routes in the southern Pacific regions were disrupted. The tight-knit exchange networks that had existed between Chalchuapa and Kaminaljuyu were severed. Agricultural production was paralyzed for a century or more. The Ilopango eruption is currently the best candidate known for the cause of the enigmatic CE 536 world event that darkened the earth, brought on a fourteen-year cold spell in the northern hemisphere, and led to crop failures from China to the Mediterranean.[41] In Mesoamerica and Central America, effects of this catastrophe may have been felt from central Mexico to northern Colombia.

Ancient Chibchan societies of the Isthmo-Colombian area in lower Central America began to develop social inequality and multivillage chiefdom settlement systems at around CE 300. Research on a number of nucleated sites in Honduras, Nicaragua, Costa Rica, and Panama have provided evidence of a transition from egalitarian tribal social structure to incipient social ranking occurring from CE 300 to 600.[42] These sites were hot spots like those of the Soconusco Initial Formative, discussed earlier. They were primary centers of regional settlement hierarchies with elite architecture and plazas, causeways, and elite cemeteries, associated with elaborate sculpture, fancy ceramics, carved stone thrones, stone mace heads, and symbolic personal objects of greenstone and gold. Some probably served as cultic centers for charismatic shamanistic leaders. The overall pattern suggests a network of interacting elites in the process of acquiring centralized political power. These changes appear to have been mostly endogenous, although some heirloom Olmec objects and Early Classic Maya greenstones circulated in the Isthmo-Colombian area during this period, indicating awareness of northern neighbors and their politics. An external stimulus may have formed part of the process. The distant impact of the Ilopango eruption could have disrupted the availability of marine resources, forcing populations inland and creating an incentive for riskier agricultural subsistence which, in turn, would have strengthened the role of chiefs in rituals and the management of trade networks to assure security and sustenance.[43]

LATE CLASSIC MAYA CITY-STATES AND THE COLLAPSE, CE 600–900

The southern Maya lowlands in northern Central America encompassed the territories of as many as eighty city-states during the Late Classic period. About a dozen major Maya cities dominated the region during the Late Classic. Primary centers varied widely in area, complexity, scale, and population, but each one ruled over a large territory of secondary and tertiary centers that owed political allegiance and paid tribute to the kings of primary centers. Small to intermediate-size states such as Coba and Calakmul had estimated populations of about 50,000 with areas in the range of 65–70 square kilometers. At the other end of the spectrum was the jungle megalopolis of Caracol with an estimated population of about 150,000 in an area of some 170 square kilometers.[44]

Patron-client relationships were extremely important in the maintenance of the political economy which was heavily dependent on tribute and long-distance trade. The domestic economy was largely in the hands of nonelites, farmers and specialists in everyday crafts such as pottery making, weaving, obsidian and chert tool production, ground stone production, woodworking, fiber production, basket making, and salt production.[45] A uniquely complete view of the domestic economy of a Late Classic Maya provincial village has been provided by the investigations of Payson D. Sheets and his colleagues at Joya de Cerén, El Salvador, which was completely entombed by a volcanic eruption at about CE 650.[46]

Foreign affairs among the Lowland Maya city-states consisted of tribute exchanges, elite marriage exchange, interpolity participation in dynastic rites of passage, ceremonial gifting of high-status goods, interpolity exchange of royal scribes and artists, and other forms of mutually beneficial contact. Intense rivalries often interrupted peaceful relations, however, resulting in ruptured alliances and ritualized aggression between royal elites that often led to raids and the capture and sacrifice of an enemy king. The apprehension and dispatch of a foreign royal often meant not only humiliation but also loss of sovereignty. All these practices have their origins in the Late Formative, if not earlier. Large-scale interpolity violence gradually increased during the Late Classic period, as seen in explicit statements in historical texts, depictions of militarism in murals, iconography on ceramics and monuments, archaeological recovery of weaponry, and human skeletal evidence of traumatic injuries suffered in battle. By the Terminal Classic, interpolity violence had accelerated into full-scale, endemic warfare for territory and tribute that engulfed all the states of the Maya lowlands during the late eighth and ninth centuries CE.[47]

Endemic warfare was but one of many factors involved in the so-called Maya collapse of the ninth century, a reference to the failure of elite culture and withdrawal of support for divine kings. Possible causes of the collapse include climate change (droughts), environmental deterioration, incessant warfare, poor management by the ruling elite, and demographic pressure. Both urban and rural areas suffered massive depopulation within a period of only about fifty or sixty years. The geographic focus was in the oldest and most developed regions of the central and southern lowlands. The timing of the disaster is indicated by the sequence of final Long Count dates inscribed on stelae. A directional trend from west to east can be discerned in the latest Long Count dates at major lowland centers. Thus was the demise of one of the greatest civilizations of ancient America, one that during the course of more than a thousand years engineered a most successful exploitation of one of the most challenging environments in the world.[48]

The collapse did not affect the northern lowlands in Yucatan where northern Maya kingdoms flourished in the Río Bec and Chenes regions during the Late and Terminal Classic. In the Escuintla region of the Guatemalan Pacific piedmont, the unique Cotzumalhuapa culture developed, characterized by a distinctive sculptural style and writing system which show connections with central Mexico, the Mixteca-Puebla region of southern Mexico, and the Gulf Coast. Related sites are known in the central highlands of Guatemala and along the Pacific coast eastward as far as western El Salvador.[49]

TERMINAL CLASSIC AND EARLY POSTCLASSIC MAYA CITY-STATES IN THE NORTHERN LOWLANDS, CE 800–1200

During the Terminal Classic and Early Postclassic periods, the center of gravity of Maya civilization shifted to the Yucatan Peninsula, as overland and martitime trade became more significant. Major cities of the Puuc region, in northwest Yucatan, especially Kabah, Sayil, Labna, and Uxmal, developed a distinctive architectural style. The international city of Chichen Itza, with its northern port at Isla Cerritos, dominated central Yucatan. Chichen Itza was the center of a large tributary state from about CE 850 to 1224. Its architecture includes both Maya Puuc-style temples as well as the Central Mexican Toltec-style pyramid known as the Castillo and the Great Ballcourt.[50] It is worthy of note that Chichen Itza is one of the few Maya cities where gold objects from the Isthmo-Colombian area (Colombia, Panama, and Costa Rica) have been recovered.[51]

Nahua-speaking Pipil populations migrated during the Terminal Classic and Early Postclassic from central Mexico and the Mexican Gulf Coast to Guatemala, El Salvador, and Honduras. In El Salvador, they are known for the ruins of their cities with Central Mexican-style architecture and site plans, such as the Tazumal architectural group at Chalchuapa in the west and the major urban center of Cihuatan in the central portion of the country. The reasons for their migrations are associated with droughts in central Mexico in the ninth and twelfth centuries.[52] Quelepa, in eastern El Salvador, was reoccupied by a group with strong ties to the Gulf Coast region of Mexico from CE 625 until its abandonment at about CE 1000.[53]

Scholars consider the traditional migration accounts of Mangue-speaking Chorotegan groups from central Mexico to Nicaragua and Costa Rica to refer to population movements in the ninth century CE. Archaeological testing of these historical accounts indicates that the migrants who participated in these large-scale movements mixed readily with local populations. Archaeological research at the sites of Tepetate and El Rayo, near Granada, Nicaragua, on the shore of Lake Nicaragua, dated to a crucial transition between ceramic phases at CE 800, shows continuities between the two phases and evidence of contacts with central Honduras, rather than a sudden introduction of a new suite of cultural traits and practices. This evidence points to a hybridization process or ethnogenesis of Chorotega culture as an amalgam of earlier Chibchan societies and Chorotega migrant groups arriving in lower Central America from Mexico.[54]

Late Postclassic City-States, CE 1200–1500

The Mesoamerican regions of Central America participated in long-distance international trade with central and southern Mexico and received ongoing migrations from Mexico to Central America. In the Yucatan peninsula, the city-state of Mayapan overthrew Chichen hegemony in CE 1224. Ruling from this small, walled city, a confederation of three elite, Mexican-influenced lineages united the northern lowlands until CE 1441. After the breakup of Mayapan, an estimated sixteen to twenty-four small city-states competed for power and economic advantage.[55] One of these petty kingdoms was centered at Tulum, a major port and trading center on the Caribbean coast, noteworthy for being the first Maya city sighted by Spaniards in their first expedition from Cuba to Yucatan in 1517. Its temples were decorated with brightly painted polychrome murals in the Mixteca-Puebla art style, an international style that was widespread throughout Mesoamerica from central Mexico to Yucatan.

In highland Guatemala, the Maya cities of Zaculeu, Utatlan, Iximche, Mixco Viejo, and Chinautla Viejo served as the dynastic centers of elite lineages claiming Toltec heritage.[56] Pipil city-states, whose rulers also claimed epigonal Toltec descent, held territories in southeastern Guatemala, western and central El Salvador, and western Honduras. Their major centers included Escuintla in southeastern Guatemala, Izalcos in western El Salvador, and Cuscatlan in central El Salvador. These centers faced the violent Spanish invasion led by Pedro de Alvarado in 1524.

Farther to the south, in lower Central America, the complex chiefdoms of the Nahua-speaking Nicaraos in Nicaragua and the Mangue-speaking Chorotegas in Nicaragua and Costa Rica are well-known for their historically documented migration accounts and Central Mexican-style traits in ceramics.[57] Intriguingly, research at the site of Santa Isabel, in the Isthmus of Rivas on the western shore of Lake Nicaragua, often equated with the historical Nicarao town of Quauhcapolca, revealed traits and practices associated more with the Chorotegas than the Nicaraos.[58] This interpretation represents an important departure from uncritical acceptance of the traditional migration accounts pertaining to the period. Recent interpretations indicate that these accounts must be revised to account for the cultural hybridity revealed in the archaeological record.

NOTES

1. United Nations, Department of Economic and Social Affairs, Population Division. https://population.un.org/wpp.
2. Jochen Bundschuh, Manuel Winograd, Michael Day, and Guillermo E. Alvarado, "Geographical, Social, Economic, and Environmental Framework and Developments," in *Central America: Geology, Resources, Hazards*, vol. 1, ed. Jochen Bundschuh and Guillermo E. Alvarado, 1–52 (London: Taylor and Francis, 2007); Sheryl Luzzadder-Beach, Timothy Beach, Scott Hutson, and Samantha Krause, "Sky-Earth, Lake-Sea: Climate and Water in Maya History and Landscape," *Antiquity* 90 (2016): 426–432
3. Robert M. Carmack, *The Indigenous Peoples of Mesoamerica and Central America* (Lanham, MD: Lexington Books, 2017); Susan T. Evans, *Ancient Mexico and Central America: Archaeology and Culture History*, 3rd ed. (London: Thames and Hudson, 2013); John W. Hoopes and Oscar M. Fonseca Z., "Goldwork and Chibchan Identity: Endogenous Change and Diffuse Unity in the Isthmo-Colombian Area," in *Gold and Power in Ancient Costa Rica, Panama, and Colombia*, ed. Jeffrey Quilter and John W. Hoopes (Washington, DC: Dumbarton Oaks Research Library and Collection, 2003); Robert Rosenswig, "The Southern Pacific Coastal Region of Mesoamerica: A Corridor of Interaction from Olmec to Aztec Times," in *Oxford Handbook of Mesoamerican Archaeology*, ed. Deborah L. Nichols and Christopher A. Pool, 419–433 (Oxford: Oxford University Press, 2012); Thomas M. Whitmore and B. L. Turner II, *Cultivated Landscapes of Middle America on the Eve of the Conquest* (Oxford: Oxford University Press, 2001).

THE ANCIENT CIVILIZATIONS   95

4. John L. Cotter, "The Occurrence of Flint and Extinct Animals in Pluvial Deposits near Clovis, New Mexico," *Proceedings of the Philadelphia Academy of Natural Sciences* 89 (1937): 2–16; Frank H. H. Roberts, Jr., "The New World Paleo-Indian," *Annual Report of the Board of Regents of the Smithsonian Institution* (Washington, DC: Smithsonian Institution, 1944), 405; H. Marie Wormington, *Ancient Man in North America* (Denver, CO: Denver Museum of Natural History, 1957), 47–48.

5. Bruce Bradley and Dennis Stanford, "The North Atlantic Ice-Edge Corridor: A Possible Paleolithic Route to the New World," *World Archaeology* 36 (2004): 459–478; C. V. Haynes, Jr., "Clovis Origin Update," *Kiva: Journal of Southwestern Anthropology and History* 52 (1987): 83–93; D. Shane Miller, Vance T. Holliday, and Jordan Bright, "Clovis across the Continent," in *Paleoamerican Odyssey*, ed. Kelly E. Graf, Caroline V. Ketron, and Michael R. Waters, 207–220 (College Station: Texas A&M University Press, 2014). Michael R. Waters and Thomas W. Stafford, Jr., "Redefining the Age of Clovis: Implications for the Peopling of the Americas," *Science* 315, no. 5815 (2007):1122–1126, propose a revised time span for Clovis in North America of 11,050 to 10,800 BP (calibrated).

6. Guillermo Acosta Ochoa, "Ice Age Hunter-Gatherers and the Colonization of Mesoamerica," in *The Oxford Handbook of Mesoamerican Archaeology*, ed. Deborah L. Nichols and Christopher A. Pool, (Oxford: Oxford University Press, 2012). DOI: 10.1093/oxfordhb/9780195390933.013.0009; Thomas D. Dillehay, *The Settlement of the Americas: A New Prehistory* (New York: Basic Books, 2000).

7. Dillehay, *Settlement of the Americas*, 167; see also Tom D. Dillehay and Michael B. Collins, "Early Cultural Evidence from Monte Verde in Chile," *Nature* 332 (1988):150–152; Tom D. Dillehay and Cecilia Mañosa, *Un asentamiento humano del pleistoceno tardío en el sur de Chile* (Santiago, Chile: LOM Ediciones, 2004).

8. These are Santa Marta Rockshelter and Los Grifos, Chiapas; Los Tapiales and Piedra del Coyote, Guatemala; Finca Guardiría, Turrialba Valley, Costa Rica; and Cueva de los Vampiros 1 and La Mula-West, Panama. Diana Santamaría Estévez and Joaquín García-Bárcena, *Puntas de proyectil, cuchillos y otras herramientas de la Cueva de los Grifos, Chiapas* (Mexico City, Mexico: Instituto Nacional de Antropología e Historia, 1989); Michael J. Snarkis, "Turrialba: A Paleo-Indian Quarry and Workshop Site in Eastern Costa Rica," *American Antiquity* 44 (1979): 125–138; Anthony J. Ranere and Richard G. Cooke, "Stone Tools and Cultural Boundaries in Prehistoric Panama: An Initial Assessment," in *Paths to Central American Prehistory*, ed. Frederick W. Lange, 49–77 (Niwot: University Press of Colorado, 1986); Georges A. Pearson and Richard G. Cooke, "The Role of the Panamanian Land Bridge during the Initial Colonization of the Americas," *Antiquity* 76 (2002): 931–932; Richard Cooke, Anthony Ranere, Georges Pearson, and Ruth Dickau, "Radiocarbon Chronology of Early Human Settlement on the Isthmus of Panama," in "A Late Pleistocene/Early Holocene Archaeological 14C Database for Central and South America: Palaeoenvironmental Contexts and Demographic Interpretations," ed. Lucas Bueno, Gustavo Politis, Luciano Prates, and James Steele, *special issue, Quarternary International* 301 (2013): 3–22.

9. In addition, isolated surface finds of Clovis, Clovis-like, and fishtail points have been reported from Ladyville, Belize; Chajbal, Chivacabé, Chujuyub, Piedra Parada (or Canchón), San Rafael, and Nahualá, Guatemala; La Esperanza, Honduras; Arenal and Guanacaste, Costa Rica; and Macapalé Island, Madden (or Alajuela) Lake, Panama.

Complementing these discoveries are the finds from three submerged caves in the Mexican state of Quintana Roo, near Tulum, Yucatan, of eight human skeletons associated with hearths and remains of a diverse megafauna, dated to the Late Pleistocene/Early Holocene transition. Arturo H. González, Alejandro Terrazas, Wolfgang Stinnesbeck, Martha E. Benavente, Jerónimo Avilés, Carmen Rojas, José Manuel Padilla, Adriana Velásquez, Eugenio Acevez, and Eberhard Frey, "The First Human Settlers on the Yucatan Peninsula: Evidence from Drowned Caves in the State of Quintana Roo (South Mexico)," in Graf et al., eds., *Paleoamerican Odyssey*, 323–337.

10. Faunal remains include whitetail deer, peccary, armadillo, rabbit, tortoise, and a wide range of other small to medium-size animals. Macrobotanical remains feature Zea (maize or teosinte, the closest relative of maize) and Theobroma sp. (cacao) pollen as well as seeds of tomato, nance, and wild fig in Late Pleistocene levels, dated to about 10,050 BP. Crude grinding stones with microfossil remains (starch grains) from *Zea* occur in slightly later levels, at about 9800 BP. A number of superimposed living floors in the earliest levels indicate intermittent rainy-season occupations by small groups of hunter-gatherers with an intimate knowledge of their environment and its neotropical faunal and floral resources.

    Guillermo Acosta Ochoa, "Cronología cultural en cuevas y abrigos del área de Ocozocoautla, Chiapas," *Quaderni di Thule: Rivista italiana di studi americanistici* 5 (2005); "Ice Age Hunter-Gatherers and the Colonization of Mesoamerica" (2012); "El poblamiento temprano y variabilidad cultural en el sureste de México," in *Simposio Román Piña Chan, 10 años de memorias: Visiones de la arqueología en el Siglo XXI*, pp. 1203–1222 (Mexico City: Instituto Nacional de Antropología e Historia, 2013); "Late-Pleistocene/ Early-Holocene Tropical Foragers of Chiapas, Mexico: Recent Studies," *Current Research in the Pleistocene* 27:1–4 (2010); "Cazar y recolectar en la selva: Cotidianidad y paisaje en los cazadores-recolectores en la transición Pleistoceno Terminal-Holoceno Temprano en Chiapas, México," in *Arqueologías de la vida cotidiana: Espacios domésticos y áreas de actividad en el México antiguo y otras zonas culturales*, ed., Guillermo Acosta Ochoa, pp. 475–501. VII Coloquio Pedro Bosch Gimpera (Mexico City: Universidad Nacional Autónoma de México, Instituto de Investigaciones Antropológicas, 2012); Itzel Natgely Eudave Eusebio, *Subsistencia de los cazadores recolectores, un estudio de los restos faunísticos de la cueva de Santa Marta, Chiapas*. Licenciate thesis, Escuela Nacional de Antropología e Historia (Mexico City: Instituto Nacional de Antropología e Historia, 2008).

11. Neither putative absence is quite true. Some Pleistocene mammals lingered into the Early Holocene, and pottery was adopted in the Late Archaic. As the evidence from Santa Marta indicates, incipient horticulture had already begun during the Early Holocene (9000–7000 BCE), or in the cultural chronology, a thousand years before the Early Archaic period (8000–5500 BCE).

12. Richard S. MacNeish, "Ancient Mesoamerican Civilization," *Science* 143 (1964): 531–537; Kent V. Flannery, *Guila Naquitz: Archaic Foraging and Early Agriculture in Oaxaca, Mexico* (Orlando, FL: Academic Press, 1986).

13. Manuel Aguilar, Miguel Medina Jaen, Tim M. Tucker, and James E. Brady, "Constructing Mythic Space: The Significance of a Chicomoztoc Complex at Acatzingo Viejo," in *In the Maw of the Earth Monster: Mesoamerican Ritual Cave Use*, eds., James E. Brady and Keith M. Prufer, pp. 69–87 (Austin: University of Texas Press, 2005).

14. Richard S. MacNeish, "Archaic Period (c. 8000–2000)," in *Archaeology of Ancient Mexico and Central America*, ed. Susan T. Evans and David W. Webster, 30–33 (New York: Garland, 2001).

15. Plant domesticates during these times included the bottle gourd (*Lagenaria siceraria*), squash (*Cucurbita* spp.), chili pepper (*Capsicum annuum*), avocado (*Persea americana*), and

THE ANCIENT CIVILIZATIONS   97

cotton (*Gossypium hirsutum*). Richard S. MacNeish, "Tehuacán Region," in *Archaeology of Ancient Mexico and Central America*, ed. Susan T. Evans and David W. Webster, 705–710 (New York: Garland, 2001).

16. Douglas J. Kennett, Heather B. Thakar, Amber M. VanDerwarker, David L. Webster, Brendan J. Culleton, Thomas K. Harper, Logan Kistler, Timothy E. Scheffler, and Kenneth Hirth, "High-Precision Chronology for Central American Maize Diversification from El Gigante Rockshelter, Honduras," *Proceedings of the National Academy of Sciences* 114 (2017): 9026–9031.

17. Voorhies refers to the Soconusco Archaic archaeological culture as the "Chantuto people," complex foragers with a semisedentary way of life; *Coastal Collectors in the Holocene: The Chantuto People of Southwest Mexico* (Gainesville: University Press of Florida, 2004); Barbara Voorhies, "Soconusco—South Pacific Coast and Piedmont Region," in *Archaeology of Ancient Mexico and Central America: An Encyclopedia*, ed. Susan Toby Evans and David L. Webster, 667–671 (New York: Garland, 2001); Barbara Voorhies, Douglas J. Kennett, John G. Jones, and Thomas A. Wake, "A Middle Archaic Archaeological Site on the West Coast of Mexico," *Latin American Antiquity* 13 (2002):179–200; Douglas J. Kennett, "Archaic-Period Foragers and Farmers in Mesoamerica," in *The Oxford Handbook of Mesoamerican Archaeology*, ed. Deborah L. Nichols and Christopher A. Pool (Oxford: Oxford University Press, 2012). DOI: 10.1093/oxfordhb/9780195390933.013.0010.

18. Voorhies, *Coastal Collectors*, 397–417; Douglas J. Kennett, Dolores R. Piperno, John G. Jones, Hector Neff, Barbara Voorhies, Megan K. Walsh, and Brendan J. Culleton, "Pre-Pottery Farmers on the Pacific Coast of Southern Mexico," *Journal of Archaeological Sciences* 37 (2010): 3401–3411; Barbara Voorhies and Douglas J. Kennett, "A Gender-Based Model for Changes in Subsistence and Mobility during the Terminal Late Archaic on the Coast of Chiapas, Mexico, in *Early Mesoamerican Social Transformations: Archaic and Formative Lifeways in the Soconusco Region*, ed. Richard G. Lesure, pp. 27–46 (Berkeley: University of California Press, 2011); Robert M. Rosenswig, "Mesoamerica's Archaic Period," in *Encyclopedia of Global Archaeology*, ed. Claire Smith, 4823–4836 (New York: Springer, 2014); Hector Neff, Deborah M. Pearsall, John G. Jones, Bárbara Arroyo, Shawn K. Collins, and Dorothy E. Freidel, "Early Maya Adaptive Patterns: Mid-Late Holocene Paleoenvironmental Evidence from Pacific Guatemala," *Latin American Antiquity* 17 (2006): 287–315; Hector Neff, Deborah M. Pearsall, John G. Jones, Bárbara Arroyo de Pieters, and Dorothy E. Freidel, "Climate Change and Population History in the Pacific Lowlands of Southern Mesoamerica," *Quaternary Research* 65 (2006): 390–400.

19. Robert M. Rosenswig, *The Beginnings of Mesoamerican Civilization: Inter-Regional Interaction and the Olmec* (Cambridge: Cambridge University Press, 2010); Fernand Braudel, *Civilization and Capitalism, 15th-18th Century*, vol. 3: *The Perspective of the World*, trans. Siân Reynolds (Berkeley: University of California Press, 1992), 30, 42–43. Braudel attributed the "striking" phrase "archipelago of towns" to the German economic historian Rudolph Häpke, who wrote "apropos of Flanders, to describe how its cities were linked to each other, and particularly to Bruges, in the fifteenth century (later to Antwerp)." *Civilization and Capitalism, 15th-18th Century*, vol. 1: *The Structures of Everyday Life: The Limits of the Possible*, trans. Siân Reynolds (Berkeley: University of California Press, 1992), 504. Due to an error in the volume 3 citation, Häpke is identified there as "Richard" rather than Rudolph.

20. For more detailed insights on the transition from the Late Archaic to the Early Formative in the Mesoamerican portions of Central America, see Rosenswig, *Beginnings of Mesoamerican Civilization*; and Lesure, ed., *Early Mesoamerican Social Transformations*.

21. Gordon R. Willey and Charles R. McGimsey III, *The Monagrillo Culture of Panama*. Papers of the Peabody Museum of Archaeology and Ethnology 49(2) (Cambridge: Harvard University Press, 1954.); Richard G. Cooke and Anthony J. Ranere, "The Origin of Wealth and Hierarchy in the Central Region of Panama (12,000–2,000 BP), with Observations on Its Relevance to the History and Phylogeny of Chibchan-Speaking Polities in Panama and Elsewhere," in *Wealth and Hierarchy in the Intermediate Area*, ed. Frederick W. Lange, 243–316 (Washington, DC: Dumbarton Oaks Research Library and Collection, 1992); Richard Cooke, "Monagrillo, Panama's First Pottery: Summary of Research, with New Interpretations," in *The Emergence of Pottery: Technology and Innovation in Ancient Societies*, ed. William K. Barnett and John W. Hoopes, 169–184 (Washington, DC: Smithsonian Institution Press, 1995); Fumie Iizuka, "The Earliest Panamanian Pottery: Reconstructing Production and Distribution of Monagrillo Ceramics through Petrographic Provenance Analysis," *Geoarchaeology* 32 (2017): 575–595; Fumie Iizuka, Richard Cooke, Lesley Frame, and Pamela Vandiver, "Inferring Provenance, Manufacturing Technique, and Firing Temperatures of the Monagrillo Ware (3520–1300 BC), Panama's First Pottery," in *Craft and Science: International Perspectives on Archaeological Ceramics*, ed. Marcos Martinón-Torres, 19–29 (Doha: Bloomsbury Qatar Foundation, 2014).

22. John W. Hoopes, "Interaction in Hunting and Gathering Societies as a Context for the Emergence of Pottery in the Central American Isthmus," in Barnett and Hoopes, eds., *Emergence of Pottery*, 185–198.

23. Rosenswig, "Mesoamerica's Archaic Period," 4831–4832; Robert M. Rosenswig, "A Mosaic of Adaptation: The Archaeological Record for Mesoamerica's Archaic Period," *Journal of Archaeological Research* 23 (2015):115–162, esp. 147; "Olmec Globalization: A Mesoamerican Archipelago of Complexity," in *The Routledge Handbook of Globalization and Archaeology*, ed. Tamar Hodos, 177–193 (Abingdon, UK: Routledge, 2017); Robert K. Booth, Stephen T. Jackson, Steven L. Forman, John E. Kutzbach, E. A. Bettis, III, Joseph Kreigs, and David K. Wright, "A Severe Centennial-Scale Drought in Midcontinental North America 4200 Years Ago and Apparent Global Linkages, *The Holocene* 15 (2005): 321–328; Roberto Risch, Harald Meller, Helge Wolfgang Arz, and Reinhard Jung, "Preface of the Editors," in *2200 BC—A Climatic Breakdown as a Cause for the Collapse of the Old World?*, ed. Harald Meller, Helge Wolfgang Arz, Reinhard Jung, and Roberto Risch, 9–22 (Halle: Tagungen des Landesmuseums für Vorgeschichte, 2015).

24. John W. Hoopes, *The Isthmian Alternative: Reconstructing Patterns of Social Organization in Formative Costa Rica*, in *The Formation of Complex Society in Southeastern Mesoamerica*, ed. William R. Fowler, 171–192 (Boca Raton, FL: CRC Press, 1991); John W. Hoopes, "Early Formative Cultures in the Intermediate Area: A Background to the Emergence of Social Complexity," in Lange, ed., *Wealth and Hierarchy*, 43–83; John W. Hoopes, "The Tronadora Complex: Early Formative Ceramics in Northwestern Costa Rica," *Latin American Antiquity* 5 (1994): 3–30; John W. Hoopes, "Ceramic Analysis and Culture History in the Arenal Region," in *Archaeology, Volcanism, and Remote Sensing in the Arenal Region*, ed. Payson D. Sheets and Brian R. McKee, 158–210 (Austin: University of Texas Press, 1994). Dolores R. Piperno, "Phytolith Records from the Proyecto Prehistórico Arenal," in Sheets and McKee, eds., *Archaeology, Volcanism, and Remote Sensing*, 286–292;

THE ANCIENT CIVILIZATIONS   99

Karen H. Clary, "Pollen Evidence for Prehistoric Environment and Subsistence Activities," in Sheets and McKee, eds., *Archaeology, Volcanism, and Remote Sensing*, 293–302; Nancy Mahaney, Meredith H. Matthews, and Aida Blanco Vargas, "Macrobotanical Remains of the Proyecto Prehistórico Arenal," in Sheets and McKee, eds., *Archaeology, Volcanism, and Remote Sensing*, 303–311; Payson D. Sheets, "Summary and Conclusions," in Sheets and McKee, eds., *Archaeology, Volcanism, and Remote Sensing*, 312–325.

25. Michael E. Blake, "An Emerging Early Formative Chiefdom at Paso de la Amada, Chiapas, Mexico," in *The Formation of Complex Society in Southeastern Mesoamerica*, ed. William R. Fowler, 27–46 (1991); John E. Clark, "The Beginnings of Mesoamerica: Apologia for the Soconusco Early Formative," in Fowler, ed., *Formation of Complex Society in Southeastern Mesoamerica*, 13–26; John E. Clark, "Mesoamerica Goes Public: Early Ceremonial Centers, Leaders, and Communities," in *Mesoamerican Archaeology: Theory and Practice*, ed. Julia A. Hendon and Rosemary A. Joyce, 43–72 (Malden, MA: Blackwell, 2004); John E. Clark, "Surrounding the Sacred: Geometry and Design of Early Mound Groups as Meaning and Function," in *Signs of Power: The Rise of Cultural Complexity in the Southeast*, ed. Jon L. Gibson and Philip J. Carr, 162–213 (Tuscaloosa: University of Alabama Press, 2004). John E. Clark and Michael E. Blake, "The Power of Prestige: Competitive Generosity and the Emergence of Rank Societies in Lowland Mesoamerica," in *Factional Competition and Political Development in the New World*, ed. Elizabeth Brumfiel and John Fox, 17–30 (Cambridge: Cambridge University Press, 1994). John E. Clark and David Cheetham, "Mesoamerica's Tribal Foundations," in *The Archaeology of Tribal Societies*, ed. William A. Parkinson, 278–339 (Ann Arbor, MI: Berghahn Books, 2002); John E. Clark and Mary E. Pye, "The Pacific Coast and the Olmec Question," *Olmec Art and Archaeology in Mesoamerica*, ed. John E. Clark and Mary E. Pye, 17–251 (Washington, DC: National Gallery of Art, 2000);Warren D. Hill and John E. Clark, "Sports, Gambling, and Government: America's First Social Compact?," *American Anthropologist* 103 (2001): 331–345; Richard G. Lesure, "Early Formative Platforms at Paso de la Amada, Chiapas, Mexico," *Latin American Antiquity* 8 (1997): 217–235); "Refining an Early Formative Ceramic Sequence from the Chiapas Coast of Mexico," *Ancient Mesoamerica* 9 (1998): 67–81; Richard A. Diehl, *The Olmecs: America's First* Civilization (London: Thames and Hudson, 2004), 128–132; Christopher A. Pool, *Olmec Archaeology and Early Mesoamerica*, 183–189 (Cambridge: Cambridge University Press, 2007); William R. Fowler, "Mesoamerica: Complex Society Development," in *Encyclopedia of Global Archaeology*, ed. Claire Smith, 4802–4806 (New York: Springer, 2014).

26. Michael Blake, Richard G. Lesure, Warren D. Hill, Luis Barba, and John E. Clark, "The Residence of Power at Paso de la Amada," in *Palaces and Power in the Americas: From Peru to the Northwest Coast*, ed. Jessica Joyce Christie and Patricia Joan Sarro, 191–210 (Austin: University of Texas Press, 2006).

27. By comparison, the largest ball court in Mesoamerica, the Great Ball Court of Chichen Itza, dedicated in CE 864, measures 166 meters in length, 68 meters in width, and 12 meters in height, with a playing alley 146 meters in length and 36 meters in width. Robert J. Sharer and Loa P. Traxler, *The Ancient Maya*, 6th ed. (Stanford, CA: Stanford University Press, 2006), 565.

28. Clark and Pye, "Pacific Coast and the Olmec Question," 230–236; David Cheetham, "Early Olmec Figurines from Two Regons: Style as Cultural Imperative, in *Mesoamerican Figurines: Small-Scale Indices of Large-Scale Social Phenomena*, ed. Christina T. Halperin, Katherine A. Faust, Rhonda Taube, and Aurore Giguet, 149–179 (Gainesville: University

Press of Florida, 2009); David Cheetham, "Cultural Imperatives in Clay: Early Olmec Carved Pottery from San Lorenzo and Cantón Corralito," *Ancient Mesoamerica* 21, no. 1 (2010): 165–185; Diehl, *Olmecs*, 131–132; Pool, *Olmec Archaeology*, 191–193.

29. Ignacio Bernal, *The Olmec World* (Berkeley: University of California Press, 1969); Lyle Campbell and Terrence Kaufman, "A Linguistic Look at the Olmecs," *American Antiquity* 41 (1976): 80–89; Diehl, *Olmecs*, 11–23; Lilia Lizama Aranda, "Olmec: Geography and Culture," in *Encyclopedia of Global Archaeology*, ed. Claire Smith, 5579–5584 (New York: Springer, 2014); Pool, *Olmec*.

30. John E. Clark, "Mesoamerica's First State," in *The Political Economy of Ancient Mesoamerica: Transformations during the Formative and Classic Periods*, eds. Vernon L. Scarborough and John E. Clark, 11–46 (Albuquerque: University of New Mexico Press, 2007); John E. Clark and Mary E. Pye, eds., *Olmec Art and Archaeology in Mesoamerica* (Washington, DC: National Gallery of Art, 2000). Michael D. Coe, "Gift of the River: Ecology of the San Lorenzo Olmec," in *The Olmec and Their Neighbors*, ed. Elizabeth P. Benson, 15–19 (Washington, DC: Dumbarton Oaks Research Library and Collection, 1981); Michael D. Coe, "San Lorenzo Tenochtitlan." in *Handbook of Middle American Indians*, ed. Victoria R. Bricker, *Supplement 1: Archaeology*, ed. Jeremy A. Sabloff and Patricia A. Andrews, 117–146 (Austin: University of Texas Press, 1981). Ann Cyphers, "San Lorenzo Tenochtitlán (Veracruz, Mexico)," in *Archaeology of Ancient Mexico and Central America: An Encyclopedia*, ed. Susan Toby Evans and David L. Webster, 645–649 (London: Routledge, 2001); Ann Cyphers, "The Olmec, 1800–400 BCE," in *The Cambridge World Prehistory*, ed. Colin Renfrew and Paul Bahn. vol. 2, 1005–1025 (New York: Cambridge University Press, 2014);Diehl, *Olmecs*, 29–59; David C. Grove, "Public Monuments and Sacred Mountains: Observations on Three Formative Period Sacred Landscapes," in *Social Patterns in Pre-Classic Mesoamerica*, ed. David C. Grove and Rosemary A. Joyce, 255–299 (Washington, DC: Dumbarton Oaks Research Library and Collection, 1999). Ponciano Ortíz C. and María del Carmen Rodríguez, "Olmec Ritual Behavior at El Manatí: A Sacred Space," in Grove and Joyce, eds., *Social Patterns in Pre-Classic Mesoamerica*, 225–254; Stacey Symonds and Roberto Lunagómez, "El sistema de asentamientos y el desarrollo de poblaciones en San Lorenzo Tenochtitlán," in *Población, subsistencia y medio ambiente en San Lorenzo Tenochtitlán*, ed. Ann Cyphers, 119–152 (Mexico City: Universidad Nacional Autónoma de México, 1997); and Carl J. Wendt, "A San Lorenzo Phase Household Assemblage from El Remolino, Veracruz," *Ancient Mesoamerica* 21 (2010): 107–122.

31. William F. Rust, "A Settlement Survey of La Venta, Tabasco, Mexico" (Unpublished PhD diss., University of Pennsylvania, 2008); William F. Rust and Robert J. Sharer, "Olmec Settlement Data from La Venta, Tabasco, Mexico," *Science* 242 (1988): 102–104; Rosenswig, *Beginnings of Mesoamerican Civilization*, 72–73.

32. John E. Clark, "Gulf Lowlands: South Region," in *Archaeology of Ancient Mexico and Central America: An Encyclopedia*, eds., Susan Toby Evans and David L. Webster, pp. 340–344 (2001). Susan D. Gillespie, "Archaeological Drawings as Re-Presentations: The Maps of Complex A, La Venta, Mexico," *Latin American Antiquity* 22:3–36 (2011); David C. Grove, "Public Monuments and Sacred Mountains" (1999).

33. Diehl, *Olmecs*, 60–82; Pool, *Olmec Archaeology*, 156–165, 177. Kent Reilly has interpreted the massive offerings as effigy lakes. F. Kent Reilly, III, "Mountains of Creation and Underworld Portals: The Ritual Function of Olmec Architecture at La Venta, Tabasco," in *Mesoamerican Architecture as a Cultural* Symbol, ed. Jeff Karl Kowalski, 14–39

(New York: Oxford University Press, 1999); Carolyn E. Tate, "Patrons of Shamanic Power: La Venta's Supernatural Entities in Light of Mixe Beliefs," *Ancient Mesoamerica* 10 (1999): 169–188; Carolyn E. Tate, "Landscape and a Visual Narrative of Creation and Origin at the Olmec Ceremonial Center of La Venta Landscape and Narrative in Mesoamerica," in *Pre-Columbian Landscapes of Creation and Origin*, ed. John E. Staller, 31–65 (New York: Springer, 2008); Carolyn E. Tate, *Reconsidering Olmec Visual Culture: The Unborn, Women, and Creation*, 143–146, 178–179 (Austin: University of Texas Press, 2012).

34. Gareth W. Lowe, Thomas A. Lee, Jr., and Eduardo Martínez Espinosa, *Izapa: An Introduction to the Ruins and* Monuemnts, Papers of the New World Archaeological Foundation No. 31 (Provo, UT: New World Archaeological Foundation, 1982); Robert M. Rosenswig and Julia Guernsey, "Introducing Izapa," *Ancient Mesoamerica* 29, no. 2 (2018): 255–264; Robert M. Rosenswig, Brendan J. Culleton, Douglas J. Kennett, Rosemary Lieske, Rebecca R. Mendelsohn, and Yahaira Núñez-Cortés, "The Early Izapa Kingdom: Recent Excavations, New Dating, and Middle Formative Ceramic Analyses," *Ancient Mesoamerica* 29 (2018): 373–393.

35. Jonathan Kaplan and Federico Paredes Umaña, *Water, Cacao, and the Early Maya of Chocolá* (Gainesville: University Press of Florida, 2018);. Arnaud F. Lambert, *Olmec-Style Art, Rock Art, and Social Practice in the Complex Societies of Mesoamerica* (Unpublished PhD diss., Brandeis University, 2011); Michael W. Love, "Ideology, Material Culture, and Daily Practice," in *Preclassic Mesoamerica: A Pacific Coast Perspective. In Social Patterns in Pre-Classic Mesoamerica*, ed. David Grove and Rosemary Joyce (Washington, DC: Dumbarton Oaks Research Library and Collection, 1999), 136–139 Rosenswig, *Beginnings of Mesoamerican Civilization*, 69, 120–131; Christa Schieber de Lavarreda and Miguel Orrego Corzo, "Preclassic Olmec and Maya Monuments and Architecture at Takalik Abaj," in *The Place of Stone Monuments: Context, Use, and Meaning in Mesoamerica's Preclassic Transition*, ed. Julia Guernsey, John E. Clark, and Barbara Arroyo, 177–205 (Washington, DC: Dumbarton Oaks Research Library and Collection, 2010).

36. José Luis Macías, José Luis Arce, Lucia Capra, Ricardo Saucedo, and Juan Manuel Sánchez-Núñez, "Late Formative Flooding of Izapa after an Eruption of Tacaná Volcano," *Ancient Mesoamerica* 29 (2018): 361–371.

37. The breakthroughs in decipherment of the Maya script, which began in the 1960s, have made it possible—some would say mandatory—to combine textual interpretation with archaeological research. The result has been an avalanche of richly textured reconstructions reaching into every imaginable area of Maya history, thought, and culture. Michael D. Coe, *Breaking the Maya Code* (New York: Thames and Hudson, 1992); Stephen D. Houston, *Reading the Past: Maya Glyphs* (London: British Museum, 1989); David Humiston Kelley, *Deciphering the Maya Script* (Austin: University of Texas Press, 1976).

38. The Lowland Maya Long Count is a vigesimal calendar that counts forward from the mythical date of creation of 4 Ahau, 8 Cumku, 11 August 3114 BCE. The dates are expressed with five numerical positions. The first position is the count of 144,000-day cycles elapsed, the second is the number of *katuns* (7,200 days, or periods of 20 solar years), the third is the number of *tuns* or 360-day years, the fourth is the number of 20-day *winals* or lunar months, and the fifth position denotes the number of single days in the count. Thus, a date of 8.17.1.0.0 would denote: 8 X 144,000 days + 17 X 7,200 days + 1 year of 360 days = 1,164,241 days (3492 years) elapsed since 3114 BCE = CE 378. Sylvanus Griswold Morley, *An Introduction to the Study of the Maya Hieroglyphs*, 60–63 (Washington, DC: Smithsonian Institution, 1915).

39. Geoffrey E. Braswell, ed., *The Maya and Teotihuacan: Reinterpreting Early Classic Interaction* (Austin: University of Texas Press, 2003); Prudence M. Rice, *Maya Political Science: Time, Astronomy, and the Cosmos* (Austin: University of Texas Press, 2004), 102–106.; Robert J. Sharer and Loa B. Traxer, *Ancient Maya* (Stanford, CA: Stanford University Press, 2006), 311, 321–333; David Stuart, " 'The Arrival of Strangers': Teotihuacan and Tollan in Classic Maya History," in *Mesoamerica's Classic Heritage: From Teotihuacan to the Aztecs*, ed. David Carrasco, Lindsay Jones, and Scott Sessions, 465–513 (Boulder: University of Colorado Press, 2000).

40. Arthur A. Demarest, *Ancient Maya: The Rise and Fall of a Rainforest Civilization*, 218–222 (Cambridge: Cambridge University Press, 2004); Heather McKillop, *The Ancient Maya: New Perspectives* (Gaviota, CA: ABC-Clio, 2004), 182–186; Robert J. Sharer and Loa P. Traxler, *The Ancient Maya*, 6th ed., 341 Stanford: Stanford University Press, 2005); Kathryn Reese-Taylor and Debra S. Walker, "The Passage of the Late Preclassic into the Early Classic," in *Ancient Maya Political Economies*, ed. Marilyn A. Masson and David A. Freidel, 87–122 (Walnut Creek, CA: AltaMira Press, 2002).

41. Robert A. Dull, John R. Southon, and Payson D. Sheets, "Volcanism, Ecology, and Culture: A Reassessment of the Volcán Ilopango TBJ Eruption in the Southern Maya Realm," *Latin American Antiquity* 12 (2001): 25–44; Robert Dull, John Southon, Steffen Kutterolf, Armin Freundt, David Wahl, and Payson Sheets, "Did the Ilopango Eruption Cause the AD 536 Event?," Poster presented at American Geophysical Union, Fall Meeting 2010, abstract id. V13C-2370 (2010), http://adsabs.harvard.edu/abs/2010AG UFM.V13C2370D, accessed 11 June 2019. Payson D. Sheets, "People and Volcanoes in the Zapotitan Valley, El Salvador," in *Living Under the Shadow: The Cultural Impacts of Volcanic Eruptions*, ed. John Grattan and Robin Torrence, 67–89 (Walnut Creek, CA: Left Coast Press, 2007); Payson D. Sheets, "Responses to Explosive Volcanic Eruptions by Small to Complex Societies in Ancient Mexico and Central America," in *Surviving Sudden Environmental Change: Answers from Archaeology*, ed. Jago Cooper and Payson Sheets, 43–63 (Boulder: University Press of Colorado, 2012); Payson D. Sheets, ed., *Before the Volcano Erupted: The Ancient Cerén Village in Central America* (Austin: University of Texas Press, 2002); Joel D. Gunn, *The Years Without Summer: Tracing A.D. 536 and Its Aftermath*, BAR International Series 872 (Oxford: Archaeopress, 2000).

42. These sites include Altas de Subirana, La Floresta, and Talgua, in eastern Honduras; El Cascal de Flor de Pino, near Kukra Hill, and El Tamarindito, in eastern Nicaragua; Güiligüisca, Cacaulí I, and Las Tapias, in the Chinandega region of Greater Nicoya, north-central Nicaragua; Ayala, near Granada, and Playas Verdes, near Masaya, Nicaragua; Las Huacas, Río Naranjo, Sitio Bolivar, and Finca Linares, in Guanacaste province; Severo Ledesma, La Selva, and El Tres de Guácimo, in the Atlantic Watershed of the central highlands; and Las Brisas, in the Diquis Delta of Costa Rica; Barriles, in Chiriqui, Panama; and La Mula-Sarigua, in the Parita Bay region, near the Parita River of central Pacific Panama.

43. Geoffrey E. Braswell, "El intercambio comerial entre los pueblos prehispánicos de Mesoamérica y la Gran Nicoya," *Revista de la Universidad del Valle de Guatemala* 7 (1997): 17–29; Geoffrey E. Braswell, Silvia Salgado González, Laraine A. Fletcher, and Michael D. Glascock, "La antigua Nicaragua, la periferia sudeste de Mesoamérica y la región maya: Interacción interregional (1-1522 d.C.)," *Mayab* 15 (2002): 19–39; Carrie Lynd Dennett, "The Ceramic Economy of Pre-Columbian Pacific Nicaragua" (Unpublished PhD diss., University of Calgary, 2016), 331–337; Carlos M. Fitzgerald-Bernal, "Prestige Goods in the Archaeological Sequences of Costa Rican and Panamanian Chiefdoms," in

Chieftains, Power and Trade: Regional Interaction in the Intermediate Area of the Americas, ed. Carl H. Langebaek and Felipe Cádenas-Arroyo, 47–62 (Bogotá, Colombia: Universidad de los Andes, 1996); John W. Hoopes, "The Emergence of Social Complexity in the Chibchan World of Southern Central America and Northern Colombia, AD 300–600," *Journal of Archaeological Research* 13 (2005): 1–47; Patricia Hansell, "The Formative in Central Pacific Panama," in *Chiefdoms in the Americas*, ed. Robert D. Drennan and Carlos A. Uribe (Lanham, MD: University Press of America, 1987), 119; Michael J. Snarskis, "The Archaeological Evidence for Chiefdoms in Eastern and Central Costa Rica," in Drennan and Uribe, eds., *Chiefdoms in the Americas*, 105–117.

44. Nicholas P. Carter, "These Are Our Mountains Now: Statecraft and the Foundation of a Late Classic Maya Royal Court," *Ancient Mesoamerica* 27 (2016): 233–253; Arlen F. Chase and Diane Z. Chase, "More Than Kin and King: Centralized Political Organization among the Late Classic Maya," *Current Anthropology* 37 (1996): 803–810; Demarest, *Ancient Maya*, 214; McKillop, *Ancient Maya*, 175–181.

45. Nicholas P. Carter, "Sources and Scales of Classic Maya History," in *Thinking, Recording, and Writing History in the Ancient World*, ed. Kurt A. Raaflaub, 340–371 (New York: John Wiley and Sons, 2014); Oswaldo Chinchilla Mazariegos, "Classic Maya Culture, History, and Myth," in *Ancient Maya Art at Dumbarton Oaks*, ed. Joanne Pillsbury, Miriam Doutriaux, Reiko Ishihara-Brito, and Alexandre Tokovinine, 28–37 (Washington, DC: Dumbarton Oaks Research Library and Collection, 2012); Demarest, *Ancient Maya*, 113–174; Antonia E. Foias and Kitty F. Emery, eds., *Motul de San José: Politics, History, and Economy on a Classic Maya Polity* (Gainesville: University Press of Florida, 2012); Patricia A. McAnany, *Ancestral Maya Economies in Archaeological Perspective* (New York: Cambridge University Press, 2010); Sharer and Traxler, *Ancient Maya*, 632–664.

46. Payson D. Sheets, *Before the Volcano Erupted: The Ancient Cerén Village in Central America.* (Austin: University of Texas Press, 2002); Payson D. Sheets, *The Ceren Site: An Ancient Village Buried by Volcanic Ash in Central America*, 2nd ed. (Belmont, CA: Thomson Wadsworth, 2006). Sheets has also suggested that the Ilopango eruption may have been connected with the so-called Classic Maya hiatus which refers to a long pause in the practice of erecting dated monuments, accompanied by a decrease in ceremonial construction and ritual behavior, usually dated from 9.5.0.0.0 (CE 534) to 9.8.0.0.0 (CE 593) in the lowlands. Rice, *Maya Political Science*, 118.

47. Kazuo Aoyama, "Classic Maya Warfare and Weapons: Spear, Dart, and Arrow Points of Aguateca and Copan," *Ancient Mesoamerica* 16 (2005): 291–304; Diane Z. Chase and Arlen F. Chase, "Texts and Contexts in Maya Warfare: A Brief Consideration of Epigraphy and Archaeology at Calakmul," in *Ancient Mesoamerican Warfare*, ed. M. Kathryn Brown and Travis W. Stanton, 171–188 (Walnut Creek, CA: AltaMira Press, 2003); Arthur A. Demarest, "War, Peace, and the Collapse of a Native American Civilization: Lessons for Contemporary Systems of Conflict," in *A Natural History of Peace*, ed. Thomas Gregor, 249–272 (Nashville, TN: Vanderbilt University Press, 1996); Takeshi Inomata, "The Last Day of a Fortified Classic Maya Center: Archaeological Investigations at Aguateca, Guatemala," *Ancient Mesoamerica* 8 (1997): 337–351; Harri Kettunen, "Ancient Maya Warfare: An Interdisciplinary Approach," in *Socio-Political Strategies among the Maya from the Classic Period to the Present*, BAR International Series 2619, ed. Verónica A. Vásquez López, Rogelio Valencia Rivera, and Eugenia Gutiérrez González, 95–107 (Oxford: Archaeopress, 2014); Charles Golden and Andrew K. Scherer, "Territory, Trust, Growth, and Collapse in Classic Period Maya Kingdoms," *Current Anthropology*

54 (2013): 397–417; Charles Golden, Andrew K. Scherer, Melanie Kingsley, Stephen D. Houston, and Héctor Escobedo, "The Life and Afterlife of the Classic Period Piedras Negras Kingdom," in *Ritual, Violence, and the Fall of the Classic Maya Kings*, ed. Gyles Iannone, Brett A. Houk, and Sonja A. Schwake, 108–133 (Gainesville: University Press of Florida, 2016).

48. Mark Brenner, Michael F. Rosenmeier, David A. Hodell, and Jason H. Curtis, "Paleolimnology of the Maya Lowlands: Long-Term Perspectives on Interactions among Climate, Environment, and Humans," *Ancient Mesoamerica* 13 (2002): 141–157; T. Patrick Culbert, ed., *The Classic Maya Collapse* (Albuquerque: University of New Mexico Press, 1973); Arthur A. Demarest, *The Petexbatun Regional Project: A Multidisciplinary Study of the Maya Collapse*. Vanderbilt Institute of Mesoamerican Archaeology Series, vol. 1 (Nashville, TN: Vanderbilt University Press, 2006); Demarest, *Ancient* Maya, 246–249; David Webster, *The Fall of the Ancient Maya: Solving the Mystery of the Maya Collapse* (New York: Thames and Hudson, 2002); Richardson B. Gill and Jerome P. Keating, "Volcanism and Mesoamerican Archaeology," *Ancient Mesoamerica* 13 (2002): 125–140; Richardson B. Gill, Paul A. Mayewski, Johan Nyberg, Gerald H. Haug, and Larry C. Peterson, "Drought and the Maya Collapse," *Ancient Mesoamerica* 18 (2007): 283–302.

49. Oswaldo Chinchilla Mazariegos, "Settlement Organization and Monumental Art of a Major Pre-Columbian Polity: Cotzumalhuapa, Guatemala" (Unpublished PhD diss., Vanderbilt University, 1996); Oswaldo Chinchilla Mazariegos, "La ciudad clásica de Cotzumalguapa," in *Ciudades mesoamericanas*, ed. Horacio Cabezas Carache, 39–57 (Guatemala City, Guatemala: Universidad Mesoamericana, 2012).

50. Arthur A. Demarest, Prudence M. Rice, and Don S. Rice, eds., *The Terminal Classic in the Maya Lowlands: Collapse, Transition, and Transformation* (Boulder: University of Colorado Press, 2004); Arlen Chase and Prudence Rice, eds., *The Lowland Maya Postclassic* (Austin: University of Texas Press, 1985); Rafael Cobos, ed., *Arqueología en Chichén Itzá: Nuevas explicaciones* (Mérida: Universidad Autónoma de Yucatán, 2016).

51. Clemency Coggins, ed., *Cenote of Sacrifice: Maya Treasures from the Sacred Well at Chichén Itzá* (Minneapolis: Science Museum of Minnesota, 1984); John W. Hoopes, "Authority," in *Revealing Ancestral Central America*, ed. Rosemary A. Joyce, 45–57 (Washington, DC: Smithsonian Institution, 2013).

52. William R. Fowler, Jr., *The Evolution of Ancient Nahua Civilizations: The Pipil-Nicarao of Central America* (Norman: University of Oklahoma Press, 1989); William R. Fowler, Jr., "The Pipil Migrations in Mesoamerica: History, Identity, and Politics," in *Migrations in Late Mesoamerica*, ed. Christopher S. Beekman, 285–326 (Gainesville: University Press of Florida, 2019).

53. Andrews, *Archaeology of Quelepa*, 183–186.

54. Carrie L. Dennett, "The Ceramic Economy of Pre-Columbian Pacific Nicaragua" (Unpublished PhD diss., University of Calgary, 2016), 329–331; Geoffrey McCafferty, Silvia Salgado, and Carrie Dennett, "¿Cuándo llegaron los mexicanos?: La transición entre los períodos Bagaces y Sapoá en Granada, Nicaragua," *Actas del III Congreso Centroamericano de Arqueología en El Salvador* (San Salvador, El Salvador: Museo Nacional de Antropología "Dr. David J. Guzman," 2010).

55. Susan Kepecs and Marilyn Masson, "Political Organization in Yucatán and Belize," in *The Postclassic Mesoamerican World*, ed. Michael E. Smith and Frances F. Berdan, 40–44 (Salt Lake City: University of Utah Press, 2003); Marilyn A. Masson, *In the Realm of Nachan Kan: Postclassic Maya Archaeology at Laguna de On, Belize* (Boulder: University Press of Colorado, 2000).

56. Thomas F. Babcock, *The Constituted Community of the K'iche' Maya of Q'umarkaj* (Boulder: University Press of Colorado, 2012); Geoffrey E. Braswell, "Post-Classic Maya Courts of the Guatemalan Highlands: Archaeological and Ethnohistorical Approaches," in *Royal Courts of the Ancient Maya*, ed. Takeshi Inomata and Stephen D. Houston, vol. 2, 308–331 (Boulder, CO: Westview Press, 2001); "Highland Maya Polities," in *The Postclassic Mesoamerican World*, ed. Michael E. Smith and Frances F. Berdan, 45–49 (Salt Lake City: University of Utah Press, 2003); Robert M. Carmack, *The Quiché Mayas of Utatlán: The Evolution of a Highland Maya Kingdom* (Norman: University of Oklahoma Press, 1981); John W. Fox, *Quiche Conquest: Centralism and Regionalism in Highland Guatemalan State Development* (Albuquerque: University of New Mexico Press, 1978); John W. Fox, *Maya Postclassic State Formation* (Cambridge: Cambridge University Press, 1987); C. Roger Nance, Stephe L. Whittington, and Barbara E. Borg, *Archaeology and Ethnohistory of Iximché* (Gainesville: University Press of Florida, 2003).

57. Fowler, *Ancient Nahua Civilizations* (1989); Francisco Moscoso, *Los cacicazgos de Nicaragua antigua* (San Juan: Universidad de Puerto Rico, 1991); Karen Niemel, Manuel Román Lacayo, and Silvia Salgado González, "Las secuencias cerámicas de los periodos Sapoá (800-1350 DC) y Ometepe (1350-1522 DC) en el Pacífico Sur de Nicaragua," in *XI Simposio de Investigaciones Arqueológicas en Guatemala, 1997*, eds., Juan Pedro Laporte and Hector Escobedo, pp.790–798. Guatemala City: Museo Nacional de Arqueología y Etnología, 1998; Silvia Salgado González and Elisa Fernández León, "Elementos para el estudio de una migración antigua: El caso de los Chorotega-Mangue," *Cuadernos de Antropología* 21:1–30.

58. Paul F. Healy, *Archaeology of the Rivas Region, Nicaragua* (Waterloo, Canada: Wilfrid Laurier Press, 1980); Geoffrey G. McCafferty, "Domestic Practice in Postclassic Santa Isabel, Nicaragua," *Latin American Antiquity* 19, no. 1 (2008): 64–82; Geoffrey McCafferty, Larry Steinbrenner, and Deepika Fernández, "Reencuentro con Santa Isabel: Observaciones preliminares sobre un sito del período Sapoá en el suroeste de Nicaraga," *Vínculos* 29 (2006): 17–31.

FURTHER READING

Bundschuh, Jochen, and Guillermo E. Alvarado, eds. *Central America: Geology, Resources, Hazards.* 2 vols. London: Taylor and Francis, 2007.

Carmack, Robert M. *The Indigenous Peoples of Mesoamerica and Central America.* Lanham, MD: Lexington Books, 2017.

Demarest, Arthur A. *Ancient Maya: The Rise and Fall of a Rainforest Civilization.* Cambridge: Cambridge University Press, 2004.

Diehl, Richard A. *The Olmecs: America's First Civilization.* London: Thames and Hudson, 2004.

Dillehay, Thomas D. *The Settlement of the Americas: A New Prehistory.* New York: Basic Books, 2000.

Evans, Susan T. *Ancient Mexico and Central America: Archaeology and Culture History.* 3rd ed. London: Thames and Hudson, 2013.

Flannery, Kent V. *Guila Naquitz: Archaic Foraging and Early Agriculture in Oaxaca, Mexico.* Orlando, FL: Academic Press, 1986.

Fowler, William R. Jr. *The Evolution of Ancient Nahua Civilizations: The Pipil-Nicarao of Central America.* Norman: University of Oklahoma Press, 1989.

Martin, Simon, and Nikolai Grube. *The Chronicle of the Maya Kings and Queens: Deciphering the Dynasties of the Ancient Maya*. New York: Thames and Hudson, 2000.

Nichols, Deborah L., and Christopher A. Pool, eds. *The Oxford Handbook of Mesoamerican Archaeology*. Oxford: Oxford University Press, 2012.

Quilter, Jeffrey, and John W. Hoopes, eds. *Gold and Power in Ancient Costa Rica, Panama, and Colombia*. Washington, DC: Dumbarton Oaks Research Library and Collection, 2003.

Pool, Christopher A. *Olmec Archaeology and Early Mesoamerica*. Cambridge: Cambridge University Press, 2007.

Schele, Linda, and David Freidel. *A Forest of Kings: The Untold Story of the Ancient Maya*. New York: William Morrow, 1990.

Sharer, Robert J., and Loa P. Traxler. *The Ancient Maya*. 6th ed. Stanford, CA: Stanford University Press, 2005.

Whitmore, Thomas M., and B. L. Turner II. *Cultivated Landscapes of Middle America on the Eve of the Conquest*. Oxford: Oxford University Press, 2001.

CHAPTER 4

....

MARGINALIZATION, ASSIMILATION, AND RESURGENCE

The Indigenous Peoples since Independence

....

WOLFGANG GABBERT

INDIANS—THE INTRICACIES OF A COLONIAL CATEGORY

At first glance, Central America's colonial past might suggest a clear differentiation between the descendants of the Spanish conquerors (variously called mestizos, ladinos, creoles, or whites[1]) and the conquered Indians. However, the meaning of the categories "Spanish" and "Indian" (*indio* or *indígena*) cannot be taken for granted. Regarding the latter term, many studies part from the idea that a clearly identifiable Indigenous population once existed or still exists and that the continuity between present-day Indians and those of earlier periods would be unproblematic. Often, a kind of essence is assumed to account for "being" Indian.[2] However, as Edwin Ardener reminded us, continuities in populations "are only in part biological." Categories such as "Indian" are "created by definition as much as by procreation."[3]

The criteria employed to categorize someone as Indian (administrative status, descent, cultural traits such as language, and self-identification) changed over time indeed. They varied from place to place and differed among actors. Beyond this, ethnic categorization depends on who undertakes it (oneself or others) and on the social context.[4] This is particularly important in relation to such value-laden categories as "Indian," which has mostly been related to poverty, primitiveness, and backwardness by non-Indians. No wonder that people often avoided the term for self-identification, stressing their membership in a specific community instead.[5]

The fact that self-designations and categorizations by others do often not coincide makes ethnicity a particular tricky issue. While the local elite in the Nicaraguan municipality Diriomo considered themselves mestizos and therefore superior to the Indians in the early twentieth century, rich coffee planters from the neighboring city of Granada deemed everyone in Diriomo Indian.[6] Redfield reported a similar situation from Guatemala in the 1930s, where upper-class Spanish-speakers (ladinos) tended to identify lower-class ladinos as Indians.[7] More recently, self-defined *indígenas* with some wealth or who are culturally Hispanized are sometimes considered ladinos by their compatriots.[8] In some more urbanized and educated communities the term "mestizo" and sometimes "civilized" (*civilizado*) is adopted by people who do not want to deny their Indigenous origins but try to avoid being identified with illiterate Indigenous peasants (sometimes referred to as *naturales*).[9]

Analyses are likewise encumbered by a loose use of the slippery concept "identity," a bias toward an ethnic interpretation of events by prematurely accepting a dichotomic view juxtaposing Indians and non-Indians, and the confusion of distinct levels of categorization and identification (Indian, language group, local community). Speakers of Indigenous languages such as Nahua, Maya, or K'iche' are often referred to as "peoples" or "ethnies" with an overarching ethnic consciousness, social cohesion, and solidarity. However, these are mostly categories coined by linguists in the nineteenth century. An ethnic consciousness above the community level was absent and emerged only in recent decades in most cases (see "From Colonial Categories to Ethnic Communities" section).[10]

At least from an administrative point of view, things seemed relatively clear in colonial times. Colonial society was divided into two sets of partly self-governing bodies, the *repúblicas de indios* and the *repúblicas de españoles*. Indians were mostly those living in rural and urban Indigenous communities obliged to pay the tribute and perform forced labor. With independence the colonial system of legally defined administrative and social categories (*castas*) based on alleged descent was abolished and Indians became citizens.[11] The restrictions on voting rights present in most Central American constitutions well into the twentieth century were based on property and literacy qualifications but not on ethnic status.[12] However, municipal councils often included *alcaldes ladinos* and *alcaldes indígenas* even in the late nineteenth century.[13] Official documentation such as census and birth registries—not to speak of everyday language—often differentiated between Indians and non-Indians well into the twentieth century.[14] The category *indígena* lost relevance for self-identification as communal property, religious organization (*cofradías*), and typical community structures waned. However, it persisted as a term used to refer to others.[15]

Biological mixing and cultural Hispanization (*mestizaje*) of the Indigenous population has occurred in all Central American countries since independence. With the exception of the Atlantic lowlands and the Guatemalan western highlands ethnic markers such as the native language and a particular dress had been largely abandoned by the 1920s.[16] However, biological *mestizaje* and cultural ladinization varied considerably among regions and their dimensions and timing are still debated. In Nicaragua, save the Atlantic region, Indians had already merged into the national mestizo population in the late nineteenth and early twentieth centuries according to widely held views. Gould, in contrast, argues against this "myth of mestizaje" that many Indigenous groups "survived as ethnic communities" well into the twentieth century and that "many of their descendants today consider themselves 'indígenas.'"[17] Tilley contends in the same vein that Indians in El Salvador remained recognizable as such at least up to the mid-twentieth century. They did not suddenly "disappear" (giving up Indigenous dress, language, and self-identification) as a result of the massive repression campaign (*matanza* = massacre) after the uprising of 1932 against General Martínez, as has often been suggested.[18]

Nevertheless, the proportion of people considered Indian declined in all Central American countries due to Hispanization and assimilation for most of the twentieth century. An increase in the number of self-identified *indígenas* and a revitalization of Indigenous culture (e.g., language, dress, and handicrafts) can only be noted since the 1980s against the background of the rise of multiculturalism in international politics and the emergence of ethnic movements. Even some people hitherto considered mestizo or ladino began to claim an Indian identity.[19] In addition, the Indigenous population increases more rapidly than the non-Indians due to higher birth rates.[20]

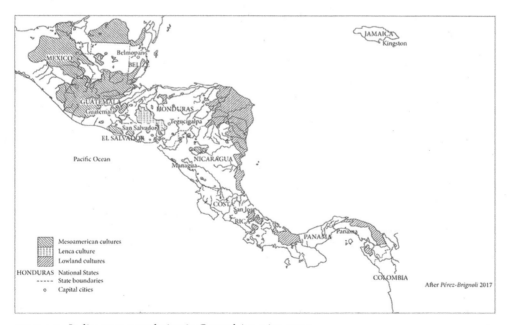

MAP 4.1. Indigenous population in Central America, 2000

In light of the mentioned conceptual problems, any attempt at quantification is problematic and results can differ tremendously according to the criteria employed (e.g., the use of native language and dress or self-identification), the historical context that may hamper or foster self-identification (e.g., the intensity of discrimination or aid programs dedicated to Indigenous populations), and the political or economic interests involved (e.g., inflating or minimizing numbers to foster or deny rights or resources). Thus, only about 30 percent of the population reported speaking a Maya language in the Guatemalan 1994 census, but 42 percent identified as *indigena*. While El Salvador's government assessed the proportion of Indians in the country at 2 percent in 1993, Indigenous organizations suggested between 10 and 12 percent in 2003.[21] Existing estimates provide at least a gross picture of the relative numerical weight of people considered Indian in different countries nonetheless. They agree that Indigenous people of the Mesoamerican tradition make up a substantial portion of the Guatemalan population. Much smaller populations of the same stock are left in El Salvador and the Pacific and central parts of Honduras and Nicaragua. Numerically important groups of lowland Indians remain in the Atlantic parts of Honduras, Nicaragua, and Panama and in remote areas in southern Costa Rica (see Table 4.1).[22]

Table 4.1. Percentages of the Indigenous Population in Central America

Country/Year	1800	1900	2010
Guatemala	82.3	65.0	41.0
El Salvador	34.7	20.0	0.2
Honduras	23.0	21.0	7.0
Nicaragua	27.6	34.5	8.9
Costa Rica	4.2	1.0	2.4
Panama	30.5	20.3	12.3

Note. Data for the years 1800 and 1900 are from Héctor Pérez Brignoli, *El laberinto centroamericano: Los hilos de la historia* (San José, C.R.: CIHAC, 2017), 39, Table 4.1. Numbers for 2010 are taken from ECLAC, *Guaranteeing Indigenous People's Rights in Latin America*, 37. The data are mostly based on official census figures. Criteria for counting Indigenous people vary somewhat among time periods and countries. While administrative criteria were paramount in the colonial period, cultural traits, especially language, gained importance after Independence. Self-identification has been employed only since the 1990s. Detailed discussions of population estimates can be found in Brignoli, *El laberinto centroamericano*, 42–58, and PNUD (Programa de las Naciones Unidas para el Desarrollo), *Segundo Informe sobre Desarrollo Humano en Centroamérica y Panamá* (San José, Costa Rica, 2003), 334–355.

INDIGENOUS PEOPLE AND THE ECONOMY IN CENTRAL AND WESTERN CENTRAL AMERICA

After Independence from Spain in 1821, Central America was integrated into the capitalist world economy as a provider of agricultural products and natural resources. An enclave economy of banana cultivation, logging, and gold mining mostly controlled by foreign capital emerged in the sparsely settled Atlantic lowlands in the second half of the nineteenth century (see "The Struggles for Autonomy in the Atlantic Lowlands" section). Coffee production became one of the most important economic endeavors in all countries except Panama in the mountainous Pacific and central parts of the region with their more fertile volcanic soils particularly from the 1870s to the 1930s.[23] It profoundly changed the living conditions of the Indigenous population. While temporalities and details vary, all Central American states opened up lands for commercial agriculture, mainly by the privatization of national (*tierras baldías*) as well as church or communal lands (either *ejidos* belonging to a municipality or areas belonging to an Indigenous community). Land privatization severely hit the peasant milpa swidden system of production that required large tracts of wooded or fallow areas.[24] While the plantation became the main organizational model for coffee production in Guatemala, El Salvador, and Nicaragua, the family farm emerged as the dominant form in Honduras and Costa Rica, which somewhat limited tendencies toward proletarianization in this economic sector.[25]

THE PRIVATIZATION OF COMMUNAL LANDS

The struggle between Liberals and Conservatives decisively shaped political conflicts in nineteenth-century Central America. They strongly disagreed about the Catholic Church's role in the independent republics. While the formers' policies of secularization were hotly contested, both factions shared liberal economic views, particularly the key role of private property in the hands of individuals as a precondition for "responsible" citizens and economic development. Indigenous communal land holding and community structures were considered obstacles to progress and therefore lost their official recognition in the course of the nineteenth and early twentieth century all over Central America.[26] This attack on community institutions has been often ascribed to the Liberal governments, which came to power in Costa Rica in 1870, in El Salvador in 1871, in Guatemala in 1873, in Honduras in 1876, and in Nicaragua in 1893. More recent studies have shown, however, that they merely continued and intensified policies already begun under their Conservative predecessors.[27] Measures to foster land privatization were initiated in Nicaragua with the Agricultural Law of 1877 by Conservative President Pedro Joaquín Chamorro, for example. Thus, the presidency of the Liberal José Santos Zelaya (1893–1909) merely intensified tendencies yet present.[28] Towns had already received the juridical status of municipalities in the Constitution of 1858. However, Indigenous communities were not mentioned and their legal status remained unspecified.[29] While Conservative and Liberal governments repeatedly decreed the abolition of Indian communities (1877, 1881, 1895, 1906, 1918), these measures were only partly successful since a number of communities continued to exist de facto.[30]

The privatization of Indigenous community lands in the central highlands (*Meseta Central*) of Costa Rica, well-apt for coffee cultivation and favorably located, began immediately after independence and was completed before 1870. Indians who lost access to land in the area were forced to hire out as day laborers or to colonize more remote zones of the country. Since the Indigenous population was too small to satisfy the labor demand on plantations, family farms, which could draw on kinship or friendship ties to cover the expanded needs for workers at harvest, dominated the commercial production of coffee. The elite, on their part, concentrated mostly on processing the produce of the farmers.[31]

El Salvador's Indigenous communities were particularly affected by the privatization of their lands of mostly volcanic highland soils perfectly suitable for coffee growing. In 1881 the Liberal government abolished all "communal lands" (*tierras comunales*). In the following decades, commercial coffee production increasingly displaced subsistence agriculture to steep mountain slopes and many landholding peasants became landless plantation workers (peons). Most Indian townships experienced social differentiation and cultural change implying the loss of the native language and distinctive community costume in the long run.[32]

Land privatization in Guatemala affected mostly Indigenous communities located at intermediate altitudes particularly attractive for coffee growers. While the Conservative government of Rafael Carrera (1838–1871) had encouraged the rental of community lands to entrepreneurs and the settlement of ladinos in Indigenous communities, it was only under the Liberal Rufino Barrios that land privatization was backed by law. However, to prevent unrest, Barrios granted communities lands adjacent to their holdings in the highland in exchange for renouncing lands they had used without formal title on lower elevations.[33] In contrast to the other Central American states, communities were not abolished. Many retained at least some of their lands and survived the liberal reforms as institutions. With the exception of Alta Verapaz, most Indians lived in areas too high for coffee production. In fact, they became an important source of cheap labor for the seasonal work in the coffee plantations at lower elevations.[34]

Coffee growing became prominent in Honduras decades later than in the other countries. Communal property in peasant hands persisted in mountain areas due to the state's weakness and the limited role of coffee production in the national economy. Three-fourths of the coffee fincas were located on lands rented from rural municipalities (*ejidos*) or Indigenous communities still in 1915. Most coffee was grown by Indigenous or ladino small producers on ejidal lands, "processed on dirt patios, and sold in village markets" before World War II.[35]

Several studies have questioned the claim of earlier interpretations that the introduction of coffee cultivation led to rapid and ample land loss of the peasantry already in the boom years (1870–1930). They argue that privatization of communal lands and proletarianization were much more protracted and complex than hitherto thought. Initially, Indigenous and ladino peasants participated in the privatization of communal lands since legal titles could be obtained at relatively low cost. Thus, many peasants retained access to at least some land for cultivation well into the twentieth century. Processes of social stratification did not result in a simple binary order of land barons and rural proletarians but implicated the emergence of a relative strong middle sector of non-Indigenous and Indigenous farmers dedicated to the artisanal cultivation of coffee, grains, or other commercial products.[36]

THE RECRUITMENT OF AGRICULTURAL LABOR

While access to land for coffee cultivation was often a problem and involved conflicts with Indigenous villages, labor was an even scarcer resource in the nineteenth century. This resulted from a number of factors:

1. Population density was relatively low in most of the Central American countries ranging from sixty-nine persons per square mile in El Salvador followed by Guatemala with twenty-nine persons per square mile down to seven persons per square mile in Honduras and Nicaragua in the late 1870s and early 1880s. 2. The agrarian export economy required not only numerous farmhands but also massive efforts in the construction of infrastructure such as roads, railroads, and ports. While the capital often came from foreign investors, particularly in the case of infrastructure, the labor force had to be locally recruited among the ladino and Indigenous peasantry in the central highlands. 3. The establishment of plantations and the cultivation of export crops required considerably more labor than subsistence agriculture. Coffee, for example, needed three times the labor per acre than corn. 4. Many Indigenous and non-Indigenous peasants had access to land for cultivation on their own privately or communally held lands well into the twentieth century. In addition, especially in Guatemala and Nicaragua peasants could find land on the agricultural frontier. Thus, they had little need to hire themselves out. 5. The peak demand for labor in coffee cultivation (picking of berries) coincided with harvest times in subsistence production.[37]

Where "the mute compulsion" of economic forces (Marx) was insufficient to compel country dwellers to sell their labor power, extra-economic means such as vagrancy laws, debt peonage, or forced labor had to be employed by the state and the landlords to induce peasants to work on plantations or in the building of infrastructure. While wage labor played a major role in El Salvador and Costa Rica, compulsory labor was widely used to recruit seasonal workers for the coffee plantations in Guatemala and, albeit to a lesser extent, in Nicaragua.[38] The use of coercion also kept the wages lower than in El Salvador and Costa Rica.[39] While forced labor was officially abolished in Guatemala in

1894 and in Nicaragua in 1905, it persisted informally at least up to the 1920s. In addition, debt peonage and vagrancy laws remained essential means to recruit laborers from the highland communities for the plantations.[40]

Indigenous people were commonly associated with rural indigence and agricultural work as poor peasant or peon and the terms "Indian" and "farmhand" were often used interchangeably in the nineteenth and early twentieth centuries.[41] Defining farmhands as Indians allowed landowners, politicians, and intellectuals to claim that not only income and wealth set them apart from the lower classes but fundamental cultural and physical differences as well. The authoritarian relations of production and the miserable living conditions on the haciendas and plantations were legitimized as necessary measures to counter the "natural idleness" of the allegedly Indian farmhands. Thus, exploitation and oppression could be embellished as civilizing acts.[42]

However, as long as labor was scarce, employers competed for workers, and the state institutions were often unable to enforce compliance with compulsory labor and debt. Workers often evaded their obligations and "moved about with apparent ease, disregarding their contracts and playing one *patrón* off another to gain the best outcome for themselves."[43] This situation did not last, however. The promotion of coffee cultivation led to a reduction of food production and thus to rising prices for nourishments which augmented the peasants' need for cash.[44] Massive proletarianization began in the mid-1920s when indebted peasants and farmers lost their mortgaged lands to capital owners. In addition, peasants could not obtain additional land after the privatization of national and communal lands was completed. Their parcels had to be bequeathed to just one son or divided among their offspring, reducing the area each heir could work. Both procedures led to an increase of the land poor and landless.[45] Access to land for cultivation by Indigenous and non-Indigenous peasants shrank even further in the mid-twentieth century when cotton-growing (since the 1950s) and cattle-breeding (since the 1960s) added to the effects of the increased commercial production of coffee.[46] Thus, economic need, aggravated by the effects of population growth in the communities, sufficed to make many peasants work for landlords.

INDIGENOUS PEOPLE, STRATIFICATION, AND CULTURAL CHANGE

Processes of social differentiation and stratification within the Indigenous population have received comparatively little attention in the scholarly literature on postcolonial Central America. As a matter of fact, stereotypes and discourses have often equated ethnicity and class. The contemporary Spanish-speaking elite increasingly lost sight of differences in wealth among Indians after independence. Social and economic inequalities were often conceived as peculiarities of different "races." Commerce and the possession of large estates appeared as a ladino or white prerogative. In El

Salvador, for example, people were often categorized as ladinos "simply because they farmed commercially."[47] "Literate, urban Indigenous leaders could not be Indians" in late nineteenth- and early twentieth-century Nicaragua, because "upon receiving an education the Indians, in the eyes of ladinos, ceased to be Indians, for they lost their defining characteristics of ignorance and dependence."[48] While contemporary observers, and much of the later academic literature, attributed to Indians a kind of "natural" inclination to subsistence agriculture, many participated actively and often voluntarily in the market economy and in the privatization of national and communal lands.[49] This led to an increasing stratification among Indians. As Gould puts it for Matagalpa in north-central Nicaragua, "The coffee industry and the Liberal Revolution did not destroy the comunidad indígena, but they did weaken its economic base and divide Indigenous society in ways that could not be reversed."[50]

Actually, no dichotomic view, juxtaposing Indian communities to non-Indians and the state, can do justice to the historical facts. Neither Indians nor ladinos were homogeneous actors. Economic differentiation among Indians shaped their political behavior decisively. Stratification fostered the cooperation of the Indigenous elite with the ladino authorities in Matagalpa in the decades after 1880, for example.[51] Indigenous middlemen played an important role in the recruitment of the seasonal labor force sent to the coffee plantations and Indigenous authorities "captured fellow Indians" who tried to evade forced labor or had fled from the plantations.[52] Beyond this, the expansion of the commercial production of coffee or other crops fostered land conflicts not only between Indians and non-Indians but also within the Indigenous communities. While some Indian agriculturalists welcomed the privatization of communal land in Sutiava (Nicaragua), for example, others preferred extending their already privileged access to these lands without formally changing the legal status of the property.[53] Even for some poorer Indians the liberal project of dividing common lands into private plots was attractive. In Cantel, a community in the environs of Quetzaltenango (Guatemala), for example, it freed them from control by the community elites who had hitherto controlled land use and denied the cultivation of woodlands to preserve the forest, which they used for lumbering themselves.[54]

Tendencies of social differentiation notwithstanding, most Indians were living in rural areas or smaller towns as peasants or farmworkers up to the middle of the twentieth century. At that time, *Acción Católica*, a movement of lay Catholics, and rapidly expanding Protestant groups began to fight against syncretic religious customs particularly in the Indigenous towns in Guatemala. Young Indigenous activists joined the organizations and participated in programs of education and agricultural modernization including the foundation of cooperatives. As a result of these and other development initiatives and improvements of schooling in the countryside, more and more Indians had access to formal education and began to enter the job market as professionals.[55] New economic opportunities in the small-scale production of flowers and vegetables for exportation to the United States emerged more recently for Indians with some capital in the highland communities of Guatemala. Other Indian entrepreneurs managed to strengthen their position in the local and regional commerce. All this led to a burgeoning concentration of wealth and land in the communities.[56] At the same time, the new Indigenous elite groups prominent by their relative prosperity and Western education began to question the local authority of the elders, who legitimized their status through their leading role in the system of civil and religious offices (*cargos*).[57]

Shortages of land for cultivation have further increased in recent decades due to dispossession or as the result of demographic growth. This and the devastation of the civil wars in Guatemala and El Salvador triggered important migratory movements. Indians from the western and central parts of the region moved to the agrarian frontier in the east and north (see Protected Areas and Neo-extractivism section), to the most important urban centers of their countries or, mostly since the 1990s, to the United States pursuing new kinds of occupation.

INDIGENOUS PEOPLE
AND NATIONAL POLITICS

Indigenous people have been often depicted as somewhat outside political party politics either succumbing to or resisting repression by the ladino-dominated state. If their participation in the wider political struggles was recognized at all, they were mainly seen as duped by ladino politicians and abused as gullible voters or forcibly recruited soldiers in the civil wars. Such interpretations have been widespread among the contemporary ladino elite and intellectuals.[58] Some more recent formulations seem not too far from such views.[59] The idea of the manipulated Indians implies that they did not act conforming to their own "real" interests and that some "objective" interests of the Indigenous community existed. I would argue instead that divisions among Indians including their attachment to different ladino patrons, factions, or political parties were the reflection of the communities' internal social and economic differentiation and the resulting conflicting interests rather than the outcome of elite manipulation.

That local conflicts and national politics were often related and that contending parties included Indians and non-Indians is no wonder considering the importance of patron-client relations and *caudillismo* in the entire nineteenth and far into the twentieth century. As Holden puts it: "Traditions of personalism and clientage were not discarded but maintained as the state in effect informally deputed subalterns to act on its behalf in return for protection and favours."[60] Political groupings displayed the characteristics of "factions"—that is, conflict groups that cross-cut strata and ethnic categories by integrating members of different social positions, such as landlords and peons, members of the elite and the urban poor, and ladinos and Indians. While clientelism is based on unequal power relations, it relies on some kind of reciprocity. Therefore, patrons and caudillos had to take the interests of their ladino and Indian followers into account.

Indigenous people often played an active part in the political and military struggles between ladino political factions at the national level or in interventions by neighboring states. Their backing as voters or soldiers was much desired by regional or national caudillos. At times, Indians related quite consciously to national debates and political ideologies and entered into alliances with ladino politicians regularly.[61] They supported liberal policies and politicians in some cases but were generally more attracted by Conservatives such as Rafael Carrera in Guatemala.[62] The military triumph of Carrera over the Liberals in 1837 and the establishment of a conservative regime for more than thirty years depended to an important degree on his support among the Indigenous population.[63] In the pursuit of their own political aims the Conservatives regularly supported Indian rebellions in El Salvador up to the last quarter of the nineteenth century.[64]

While these facts have been acknowledged by a number of authors, the Indians' motives are often reduced to the preservation of the Indigenous community structure, lands, and customs; individual reasons to participate in national politics are rarely discussed.[65] But Indians did not always struggle on the same side in conflicts and political groups and factions often included Indigenous people and ladinos.[66] The Indians revolting in Matagalpa in 1881, for example, had ladino allies and several Indigenous leaders and their henchmen even allied with the government troops in the suppression of the uprising.[67] At times national governments backed Indigenous groups in their struggles with local ladinos. Thus, the Nicaraguan Conservative regime supported the Indigenous population in their conflicts with the overwhelmingly Liberal local ladino elites in the central highlands of Nicaragua in the early twentieth century.[68] In 1934, President Ubico decreed the abolition of debt peonage and the replacement of locally elected *alcaldes* (mayors) by *intendentes* (administrators) appointed by the central government and sent from other parts of Guatemala. This weakened the economic and political power of local ladino elites who had controlled the ballots for municipal elections before.[69]

INDIGENOUS RESISTANCE

As James Scott convincingly argues, resistance does not need to be apparent and violent to induce wide-ranging effects. Everyday forms of resistance such as desertion, foot-dragging, playing dumb, and the like might be highly efficient and much less risky than open rebellion. They were doubtless common in peasant communities.[70] However, violent uprisings are a lot more visible and therefore much better documented.

The colonial division between colonialists and the colonized—Spaniards or ladinos against Indians—has deeply shaped interpretations of Central American history. Thus, struggle between both categories appeared as "natural" and a "caste war" imminent to many contemporary observers. However, important issues have seldom been addressed. What can be counted as "Indigenous" resistance? Who participated in the contention? Had Indians particular motives to participate in rebellions? These queries are often difficult to answer not the least for the lack of documentation, the tendency of contemporary elites to consider all peasants Indians, and the inclination to treat Indigenous communities as unified actors with a shared collective interest.

Numerous rebellions were recorded in the rural areas in Central America in the nineteenth century. Insurgents particularly targeted those considered immediate enemies such as repressive local officials or fraudulent moneylenders. Government response was generally bloody. But these movements were often not limited to the Indigenous population. There is ample evidence that both ladinos and Indians jointly participated in local uprisings against central states' attempts to curtail the relative autonomy of local communities in El Salvador and Nicaragua in the 1830s and 1840s, for example. Indian and non-Indian protest was also directed against anticlerical policies.[71]

While Indians shared most grievances with non-Indian peasants, such as taxes or military conscription, at times separate forms of community organization and specific types of land tenure gave their struggles a specific character. Assaults on community lands provoked several Indigenous uprisings in Nicaragua (1848 and 1849) and in El Salvador (1884, 1885, 1889), for example.[72] Very few rebellions occurred between 1900 and 1930. Discontent expressed itself in institutionalized forms, such as petitions, and small-scale or individual acts of violence.[73] This was a result of advances in statebuilding, particularly the creation of permanent and well-equipped armies that began to replace the militias or conscripted military units that had been the combat forces of contesting governments and political factions in the nineteenth century. As Lauria-Santiago puts it for El Salvador: "A professional military, the containment of conflicts and divisions among the civilian political elite, stability brought by land privatization, which in turn reduced the coherence of Indian communities, contributed to the decline of popular mobilizations after the 1890s."[74]

The Great Depression following 1929 had a devastating impact on the Central American lower classes and led to widespread social unrest.[75] While the participation of Indians in the 1932 uprising planned by the Communist Party (PCS) in El Salvador has often been neglected or downplayed, Tilley considers this event "the last major Indian uprising in American history." Between ten thousand and thirty thousand peasants were annihilated as supposed participants in the uprising or as communist sympathizers in the massacres that followed. While the killings were not directed against the Indigenous population as such, thousands of Indians in the core areas of the insurgency were slain.[76] Tilley argues that the PCS had no control over the rural mobilization of several thousand Indians in the countryside. In addition, she stresses the importance of the local Indigenous leadership and the specificity of the Indian peasant demands of "regaining private title to their subsistence plots"—instead of nationalization of private property—and installment of their own instead of ladino authorities. The insurgents killed mostly "prominent ladino individuals hated for debt or land swindles against Indians."[77] However, in her endeavor to highlight the particular Indigenous role in the uprising and its ethnic character Tilley seems to overstate her point by downplaying or neglecting the role of Communist organizers and ladino leaders.[78]

Indians also participated in leftist rebel movements in Guatemala where Indigenous organizations such as cooperatives and peasant leagues had formed in the western highlands in the 1960s and 1970s.[79] Maya began to join the guerrilla movements in substantial numbers mostly as a reaction to army repression in the late 1970s and early 1980s.[80] The ruthless counterinsurgency campaigns resulted in the death of about two hundred thousand people, mostly Indigenous, suspected to be members or sympathizers of the guerrillas, peasant organizations, or non-conformist political parties. In the scorched-earth campaigns of the military, hundreds of villages were destroyed and countless villagers displaced. The Historical Clarification Commission, which investigated human rights violations after the *Peace Accords* of 1996, qualified such campaigns as "acts of genocide" and identified racism as an important cause for the indiscriminate nature and brutality of the military's repression.[81]

DEFINING THE NATION—FROM *MESTIZAJE* TO MULTICULTURALISM

The Indigenous past played an important ideological role in the struggle for independence in most Latin American states. The rightfulness of the Spanish conquest had to be questioned, the dissolution of all bonds to the Spanish crown legitimized, and the creoles' quality as biological and cultural descendants of the conquerors downplayed or denied. This was an especially delicate affair since the leading groups of the independence movement, the creoles, and their main adversaries, the European Spaniards, shared the same culture and language. Thus, particularly the pre-Columbian past of the Mesoamerican tradition began to be claimed in Central America as part of the new nations' heritage albeit in varying degrees in the nineteenth century.[82]

Eulogies of the Indigenous heritage did not, however, include the wretched masses of contemporary Indian peasants. Central American elites considered the Spanish-speaking, "white" part of the population as the center of the newly independent nations. Indians were regarded as obstacles to progress for their alleged backwardness and inclination to idleness. Thus, the task of society was, in the Liberals' view, to "civilize" the Indians. Besides the generalization of private property, education and the creation of new wants were considered important civilizing factors. Some commentators were convinced that even living with the "civilized" section of the population, for example, in the cities, was a contribution in itself to the intellectual improvement of Indians by association.[83] Apart from these acculturation-oriented concepts, the idea that a biological "improvement" of the Indigenous population could be achieved by a "mixture of races" was not uncommon. However, in keeping with the then accepted theories of evolution, which were unable to differentiate between changes in the behavioral repertoire of populations based on learning and those founded on biological inheritance, the intended result of the "mingling of races" was not a mixed population and culture but the absorption of the Indians by the "prevailing mass of the white population."[84]

Ideas of Indigenism and Indohispanism became influential in Central America in the 1920s and 1930s not the least as a reaction to the growing US imperialism and European and Anglo-Saxon racism. The new ideology advocated *mestizaje* (racial and cultural mixing) and education as necessary conditions for progress and nation-building. It also stressed the importance of the Indigenous past for national culture. Indian warriors who fought against the Spanish conquerors such as Tecún-Umán in Guatemala, Atlacatl in El Salvador, Lempira in Honduras, or Nicarao in Nicaragua were claimed as national heroes. However, in contrast to the former elite views, the new ideology suggested the result of miscegenation to be the mestizo, who was considered the core of the nation. Contemporary Indians had to be assimilated to the Hispanic culture and thus dissolve into national society, although precious aspects of the Indigenous culture, such as handicrafts, should be preserved.[85]

After World War II, governments, international organizations, and the churches launched numerous projects dedicated to the development and assimilation of the Indigenous groups. According to the strategy of "community development," members of alleged "backward" communities were themselves expected to become the carriers of "modernization."[86] As already mentioned, this provided new opportunities for organization and upward social mobility, such as professional training and jobs for Indians.[37] However, it did not take long for these Indigenous teachers, cultural promoters, university students, and nurses to recognize that their possibilities for social mobility were extremely limited and that assimilation was not always possible. They were rarely able to compete successfully with whites or mestizos for the desired middle- or high-level positions. Not only was their training frequently of a lesser quality, but more significantly here, they met with the open contempt and discrimination of the national majority. This created a consciousness of the importance of their origin and they became one of the most vital forces in the Indigenous movements, which were growing in all countries—albeit to different extents—demanding cultural and political rights and an end to discrimination.[88]

International organizations such as the United Nations or the World Bank promoted democratization, decentralization, and respect for cultural diversity and established development programs particularly designed for "Indigenous people." Latin American governments tried to regain the legitimacy they had lost due to the civil wars, a severe economic crisis, and increasing poverty. This led to constitutional reforms in Guatemala (1985) and Nicaragua (1986) that acknowledged the multicultural and ethnically diverse character of the nation and recognized Indigenous legal and political practices (*usos y costumbres*, habits and customs) as valid.[89]

Under the conditions of generalized repression any act of non-conformist political activity had been life-threatening in the late 1970s and early 1980s in Guatemala. New political spaces opened for Maya organizations only after the formal end of military rule in 1985. In addition, the new government began to support Indigenous cultural activities. Maya activists concentrated on cultural issues which seemed less threatening to the dominant sector of society and thus less risky. Indigenous leaders also played an important role in the negotiations about a peace accord finally signed in 1996.[90] In the last decades, Indians could increase their political weight in many regions where they constitute the majority of the population at the local level. They began to assume offices in the municipalities and supply mayors in various towns, ousting many ladinos from their positions of power. Beyond this, a limited number of Indigenous people were also elected to congress and others began to gain positions in the government and state institutions.[91]

THE STRUGGLES FOR AUTONOMY IN THE ATLANTIC LOWLANDS

Most of the Atlantic lowlands remain isolated from the central and Pacific parts of the Central American countries up to the present. The Spaniards were unable to effectively dominate and settle these regions during colonial times due to the resistance of the local Indigenous groups. The latter often acted in accord with the British who disputed Spanish sovereignty. Even after independence, integration into the nation-states was more nominal than real. Elites considered the lowland Indians particularly primitive due to their economy of hunting, fishing, gathering, and the cultivation of root crops and their small and dispersed settlements. In contrast to the precolonial states and complex chiefdoms of the Mesoamerican tradition, political organization was limited to kin and tribal groups and to small chiefdoms. From the perspective of the post-independence governments, the lowlands appeared as vast, sparsely settled, and economically underused areas whose riches—natural resources such as minerals and lumber, and land free for colonization—had to be harnessed for national development.[92] As said before, concessions for the use of vast areas have been given to mostly foreign banana, logging, or mining companies since the middle of the nineteenth century. While many laborers were imported from the West Indies from the 1850s to the early 1930s, companies also recruited workers among the local Indigenous groups such as the Miskitu, Kuna, and Guaymi. While there were some conflicts over land with the foreign companies, no large-scale dispossession occurred. Wage labor and the cultivation of cash crops did not become the sole or even the most important means of livelihood. Most people engaged in migratory wage labor for a specific period only (a few months, a year), returning afterward to their villages, a pattern still found today.[93]

Although the Indigenous groups in the lowlands are only numerical minorities on the national scale, ladino elites considered their autonomy demands as threats to the national integrity. This is due to the geographical isolation, the weakness of state institutions in the region, and the conflictive history, particularly the involvement of external influences in former autonomy struggles of Indigenous groups. British negotiators backed the Kuna in the northern Darién when they revolted against the Spaniards in 1778, for example. The uprising was only defeated nine years later. In February 1925, a Kuna insurgency took place in Panama and the "Republic of Tule" was proclaimed on the island of Aligandí. At the same time, a request was made to the United States to take over the new "state" as a protectorate. However, this did not happen. After a short time, the uprising collapsed and the US government brokered a peace agreement. One result of the Kuna uprising was the preservation of their internal autonomy, recognized by the Panamanian state with the creation of the *Comarca de San Blas* (now *Guna Yala*) in 1938.[94]

The "Mosquito kingdom" claimed a large part of eastern Central America from Black River in what is today Honduras to Bocas del Toro in Panama with British support in the mid-nineteenth century. Great Britain recognized the sovereignty of the Central American states over most of this area only by the mid-nineteenth century (treaties of 1859 with Honduras and 1860 with Nicaragua). As a result, a semiautonomous *Mosquito reservation* was created for the Indigenous inhabitants, which ended only in 1894 after its occupation by Nicaraguan troops.[95] The enclave economy and the lack of a coherent development policy of the Somoza dictatorship (1936–1979) did nothing to overcome the division between the Pacific and Atlantic regions. Attempts to foster the region's integration into the national state by the left-wing Sandinistas after 1979 were doomed to failure against the background of the conflictual history. Confronted with strong opposition from the US government, which supported counterrevolutionary armed groups (Contras), the Sandinista government considered the far-reaching autonomy demands of Miskitu organizations as disguised separatism. Miskitu began to fight the government on their own or jointly with the Contras. The resulting war claimed numerous victims. The Sandinista government therefore sought to redirect the military conflict into political channels, announced several amnesties for Indian guerrilla fighters after 1983, and negotiated several times with representatives of militant Indian organizations. In this context, it developed a project of regional self-government that was to take up the demands of the Atlantic coasts' ethnic groups (Miskitu, Mayagna, Rama, and Afro-descendants). After a discussion phase lasting several years, the National Assembly finally adopted a Statute of Autonomy for the Atlantic region on September 2, 1987, which can be characterized as a project of far-reaching administrative decentralization. The statute provided for the creation of two autonomous regions (*Región Autónoma Atlántico Norte*, and *Región Autónoma Atlántico Sur*), each with its own regional assembly (*Consejos Regionales de Autonomía*).[96] Besides the *Comarca de San Blas*, the autonomy process for the Atlantic region represents the most extensive attempt to date to take into account the cultural and historical peculiarities of the inhabitants of the Caribbean rim of Central America while maintaining state unity.

From Colonial Categories
to Ethnic Communities

While the economic and political changes that began in the mid-nineteenth century (privatization of communal lands, proletarianization, the abolition of the institution of

Indigenous community, etc.) had fostered ladinization all over Central America, the timing, dimensions, and results were quite different. In principle, wealthy and educated Indians had the best chances to shed the stigma of being categorized as such and opt for assimilation. However, not all of them tried. While being categorized as Indian meant scorn and discrimination by non-Indians, it could help to maintain privileged access to resources and the manpower of poorer Indians in the villages, for example.[97] In any case, the scope of ethnic identification has mostly remained confined to relatively small collectivities such as towns, municipalities, or kin groups.[98] Tendencies toward the emergence of a more encompassing ethnic consciousness within Indigenous language groups are relatively recent.

Among the Miskitu of eastern Nicaragua and Honduras, for example, Protestant Moravian missionaries contributed to the linguistic unification of the different Miskitu dialects by making one of them a written language. The missionaries developed new means of communication, such as the monthly newsletter *Miskito Moravian* for evangelists and lay workers, and organizational structures (schools, community feasts, and evangelization meetings) connecting different residence groups. This allowed speakers of Miskitu to become aware of their common membership of this category. However, criteria for group membership changed profoundly in the second half of the twentieth century. Until then, mutual aid among kin and fellow villagers and the generous distribution of food (especially meat) was the principal mechanism used to integrate Miskitu communities. Villagers defined themselves as "the poor" and only those who participated in the system of generalized reciprocity were accepted as fellow Miskitu. Upward social mobility entailed a change of ethnic categorization. Thus, shop owners or traders of Miskitu descent, who began to favor their commercial interests at the expense of the generosity expected by kinsmen, were not considered in-group members but mestizos or Afro-descendants. The prominent role of descent as the chief determinant of individual identification is a more recent development and the result of missionary work and the growing social differentiation that weakened relations of reciprocity even *within* the villages in the 1960s and 1970s.[99]

In Guatemala, contacts beyond the single community, including exogamous marriages, have increased since the mid-twentieth century as a consequence of new educational facilities for Indians, particularly teacher training schools, the founding of radio stations broadcasting in native languages, movements to the agrarian frontier, and rural–urban as well as transnational migration. Forced resettlement during the civil war also resulted in the mixing of people from different villages and towns. All this fostered tendencies toward a broader identification as member of a certain language group or as *indígena*.[100] Consciousness-raising by Catholic priests in secondary and teacher training schools also strengthened the development of an encompassing pan-Maya identification among their Indigenous students.[101] The *Academia de las Lenguas Mayas*, founded in 1986, developed a unified alphabet for Maya languages, which became legally recognized in 1988.[102] Backed by nongovernmental organizations (NGOs) and international academics, Maya organizations began to adopt symbolic elements considered to have characterized the pre-Columbian Classic Maya elite culture such as hieroglyphic writing and the calendar.[103]

Protected Areas and Neo-extractivism

Since the early 1990s, we have witnessed contradictory developments. On the one hand, Central American countries have answered to recent international policies on climate change and biodiversity by establishing protected areas and biosphere reserves, largely in Indigenous territories in the Atlantic lowlands. Protected areas make up more than 25 percent of the national territory in Guatemala, Costa Rica, and Panama, for example.[104] Some progress has also been made in securing Indigenous land tenure by demarcation and land titling programs.[105] In the Atlantic region of Nicaragua, Indigenous and Afro-descendant communities had received titles over almost 37,813 square kilometers by 2017 which corresponds to 31.6 percent of the national territory. Panama had recognized five Indigenous territories covering 22 percent of the national territory up until 2010.[106] In Honduras a dozen Indigenous territorial jurisdictions have been created in the Mosquitia.[107] The Costa Rican government began to establish reserves mostly in the south and southeast of the country for the eight Indigenous groups already in the 1950s. At present there are twenty-four reserves comprising 5.9 percent of the national territory (more than three hundred thousand hectares) declared the exclusive and inalienable property of the Indigenous communities by the Indian law.[108]

On the other hand, Central American governments have followed a neo-extractivist development model since the 1980s that seriously threatens the land rights of Indigenous communities by activities such as mining, logging, oil exploitation, the construction of hydroelectric dams, and monoculture cultivation such as oil palm.[109] In the mid-1990s, the Panamanian government awarded mining concessions covering more than half of the *Comarca* area.[110] Foreign companies received concessions for the exploitation of ores and fish stocks, and in 1993 and 1996 also the rights of the timber exploitation for an area of 106,000 hectares, claimed for the most part by the Mayagna community Awas Tingni, in Nicaragua.[111] In addition, the Nicaraguan government granted the concession for the construction of an interoceanic canal to a Chinese company that would cause serious environmental damage and affect 240 rural (non-Indigenous and Indigenous) communities.[112] The Honduran state had issued about fifty concessions for the exploitation of energy sources to national and international firms in 2010. In Guatemala alone the government had granted almost 370 mining concessions in 2013, most of them in Indigenous territories.[113]

These more recent attacks on Indigenous land rights further exacerbate the effects of the colonization by large cattle breeders and peasants ousted from the Pacific and Central parts of their countries because of the expansion of agricultural export production since the mid-twentieth century. In Nicaragua, this process accelerated again after a short-term slowdown during the civil war in the early 1980s. In addition, Nicaraguan governments granted large extensions of land in areas claimed by Indigenous communities in the Atlantic region to former fighters of the anti-Sandinista Contras. In many parts of the Atlantic lowlands, mestizo settlers have already reached the retreats of lowland Indians (especially in Nicaragua, in Talamanca in the south of Costa Rica, and

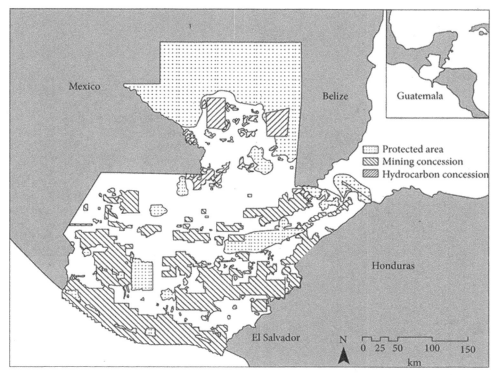

MAP 4.2. Protected areas and resource extraction in Guatemala, 2014. After Bebbington et al., "Resource Extraction," p. 6, and Laura Aileen Sauls and Herman Rosa "Impacts of Extractive Industry and Infrastructure on Forests: Central America," Climate and Land Use Alliance, 2018 (https://www.climateandlandusealliance.org/reports/impacts-of-extractive-industry-and-inf rastructure-on-forests/).

in Bocas del Toro and Darién in Panama). Land conflicts have therefore increased in recent decades.[114]

Perspectives

The current political perspectives and the legal situation of Indigenous people in Central America are quite diverse reflecting their different demographic weight and regional distribution. Accordingly, Maya organizations have struggled for the recognition of cultural and linguistic rights (e.g., education in Indigenous languages), including customary legal practices, affirmative action programs, and proportional representation in political bodies with some success in Guatemala.[115] Indigenous movements have been much less influential in the other countries. While important progress has been made in the recognition of language rights and cultural difference, discrimination is still present in everyday life and the key problems of poverty and the grossly unequal distribution of land and wealth have not even been tackled yet.[116] Neither the recognition of Indian

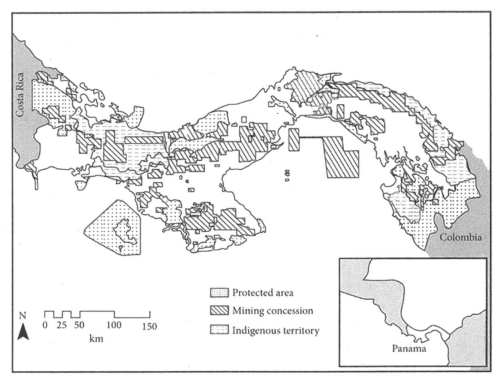

MAP 4.3. Protected areas, resource extraction and Indigenous territories in Panama, 2014. After Bebbington et al., "Resource Extraction," p. 6, and Laura Aileen Sauls and Herman Rosa "Impacts of Extractive Industry and Infrastructure on Forests: Central America," Climate and Land Use Alliance, 2018 (https://www.climateandlandusealliance.org/reports/impacts-of-extractive-industry-and-infrastructure-on-forests/).

land titles in Nicaragua and Honduras nor the establishment of reserves in Panama and Costa Rica resulted in the effective protection from exploitation by foreign companies or illegal land grabbing by cattle breeders or peasants. Even the Kuna *Comarca de San Blas* is threatened by colonization. Thus, securing land rights has, even today, remained a central problem of the rural Indigenous population not only in the lowlands.

Acknowledgments

Sincere thanks to Anthony Bebbington and Héctor Pérez-Brignoli for generously allowing me to use their maps as a basis for the illustrations included in this article.

Notes

1. For discussions of the history of and interrelation between these terms and regional variations in their use, see, for example, John M. Watanabe, "Racing to the Top: Descent

Ideologies and Why Ladinos Never Meant to Be Mestizos in Colonial Guatemala," *Latin American and Caribbean Ethnic Studies* 11, no. 3 (2016): 305–322; Julian Pitt-Rivers, "Ladino or Mestizo?," *Race & Class* 10, no. 4 (1969): 463–477; Arturo Taracena Arriola (n.d.), "Guatemala: Del mestizaje a la ladinización, 1524–1964," Centro de Investigaciones Regionales de Mesoamerica (CIRMA). http://lanic.utexas.edu/project/etext/llilas/vrp/arriola.pdf.

2. Wolfe, for example, recognizes that in rural Nicaragua the majority of Indians and ladinos "drew from the same well of cultural referents of rural, communal life" in the 1840s but then continues, "Ladinos, of course, were *not* Indians" without disclosing the basis for this differentiation. See Justin Wolfe, *The Everyday Nation-State: Community & Ethnicity in Nineteenth-Century Nicaragua* (Lincoln: University of Nebraska Press, 2007), 190–191.

3. Edwin Ardener, "Language, Ethnicity, and Population," *Journal of the Anthropological Society of Oxford* 3, no. 3 (1972): 131.

4. See, for example, Wolfgang Gabbert, "Social Categories, Ethnicity, and the State in Yucatán, México," *Journal of Latin American Studies* 33, no. 3 (2001): 459–484, esp. 461–464.

5. *Indígena* was often used as a synonym for *indio* but carries less derogatory connotations.

6. Elizabeth Dore, *Myths of Modernity. Peonage and Patriarchy in Nicaragua* (Durham, NC: Duke University Press, 2006), 136.

7. Robert Redfield, "The Relation between Indians and Ladinos in Agua Escondida, Guatemala," *América Indígena* 16, no. 4 (1956): 255; for similar in Yucatán, see Wolfgang Gabbert, *Becoming Maya: Ethnicity and Social Inequality in Yucatán since 1500* (Tucson, AZ: University of Arizona Press, 2004), 62–64, 75–78, 110–123.

8. Richard N. Adams and Santiago Bastos, *Las relaciones étnicas en Guatemala, 1944–2000* (Antigua: CIRMA, 2003), 504; Aldo Lauria-Santiago, "Land, Community, and Revolt in Late-Nineteenth-Century Indian Izalco, El Salvador," *Hispanic American Historical Review* 79, no. 3 (1999): 523–524.

9. Adams and Bastos, *Relaciones étnicas en Guatemala*, 516; Jeffrey L. Gould, " '¡Vana Ilusión!' The Highlands Indians and the Myth of Nicaragua Mestiza, 1880–1925," *Hispanic American Historical Review* 73, no. 3 (1993): 426; and *To Die in this Way. Nicaraguan Indians and the Myth of Mestizaje, 1880–1965* (Durham, NC: Duke University Press, 1998), 122.

10. On this argument see Wolfgang Gabbert, "Indigeneity, Culture and the State: Social Change and Legal Reforms in Latin America," in *Indigeneity on the Move. Varying Manifestations of a Contested Concept*, edited by Eva Gerharz, Nasir Uddin, and Pradeep Chakkarath, 240–269, esp. 242–249 (Oxford: Berghahn Books, 2018).

11. Indians were not mentioned in the constitutions of the Central American Federation (1824) and of Nicaragua (1826, 1838, 1854, 1858, and 1893), for example. Cf. texts in https://nicaragua.justia.com/nacionales/constituciones-politicas-de-nicaragua/.

12. Arturo Taracena Arriola, *Etnicidad, estado y nación en Guatemala, 1808–1944* (Guatemala: Nawal Wuj, 2002), 157, 175–177, 196, 392; Adams and Bastos, *Relaciones étnicas en Guatemala*, 151; Marvin Barahona, "Del mestizaje a la diversidad étnica y cultural: la contribución del movimiento indígena y negro de Honduras," in *Memorias de Mestizaje: Cultura política en Centroamérica de 1920 al presente*, edited by Darío A. Euraque, Jeffrey L. Gould, and Charles R. Hale, 219 (Guatemala: Centro de Investigaciones Regionales de Mesoamérica, 2004); and Marvin Barahona, *Pueblos indígenas, estado y memoria colectiva en Honduras*. Colección Códices: Ciencias sociales (El Progreso, Yoro, Honduras: Editorial Casa San Ignacio, 2009), 137–139.

13. See for Nicaragua, Gould, *To Die in This Way*, 84; Julie A. Charlip, *Cultivating Coffee: The Farmers of Carazo, Nicaragua, 1880–1930* (Athens, OH: Ohio University Press, 2003),

55; Dore, *Myths of Modernity*, 50. A separate K'iche' Indian town council (*cabildo*) was reestablished in Quetzaltenango when Rafael Carrera came to power in Guatemala in 1840. It was only abolished in 1895. See Greg Grandin, *The Blood of Guatemala: A History of Race and Nation* (Durham, NC: Duke University Press, 2000), 2. On El Salvador, see Virginia Q. Tilley, *Seeing Indians: A Study of Race, Nation and Power in El Salvador* (Albuquerque: University of New Mexico Press, 2005), 112.

14. See, for example, Dore, *Myths of Modernity*, 44; Tilley, *Seeing Indians*, 179–186; Aldo Lauria-Santiago, *An Agrarian Republic: Commercial Agriculture and the Politics of Peasant Communities in El Salvador, 1823–1914* (Pittsburgh: Pittsburgh University Press, 1999), 59–60; Barahona, *Pueblos indígenas, estado y memoria colectiva*, 140–141. Other "racial" categories such as white, black, mestizo, mulatto or zambo were also used. See, for example, Wolfe, *Everyday Nation-State*, 154–162.

15. For Nicaragua, see Dore, *Myths of Modernity*, 31; Charlip, *Cultivating Coffee*, 53. The relationship between participation in local communal organizations and Indigenous self-identification in El Salvador is discussed in Lauria-Santiago, *An Agrarian República*, 57.

16. Jeffrey L. Gould, "Dictadores indigenistas y los orígenes problemáticos de la democracia centroaméricana," in *Desencuentros y desafíos: Ensayos sobre la historia contemporánea centroamericana*, edited by Jeffrey L. Gould, 49–52 (San José, C.R.: CIHAC, 2016); and Gould, *To Die in This Way*, 17–18; Jeffrey L. Gould and Aldo Lauria-Santiago, *To Rise in Darkness: Revolution, Repression, and Memory in El Salvador, 1920–1932* (Durham, NC: Duke University Press, 2008), 102–105, 252–261; Tilley, *Seeing Indians*, 70–71.

17. Gould, " '¡Vana Ilusión!,' " 394–397, 427 (quote); Gould, *To Die in this Way*, 6–10.

18. Tilley, *Seeing Indians*, 71–74, 79, 164–168, 179–186.

19. Nicaragua's Pacific and central parts, for example, witnessed processes of ethnic recategorization in recent decades. Thus, more than one hundred thousand people identified themselves as Chorotega-Nahua-Mange, Nahoa-Nicarao, Xiu-Sutiava or Cacaopera-Matagalpa in the 2005 census. See INEC (Instituto Nacional de Estadística y Censos), *VIII Censo de Población y IV de Vivienda, 2005. Resumen Censal* (Managua: INEC, 2006), 40–41.

20. Adams and Bastos, *Relaciones étnicas en Guatemala*, 509; ECLAC (Economic Commission for Latin America and the Caribbean), *Guaranteeing Indigenous People's Rights in Latin America: Progress in the Past Decade and Remaining Challenges* (Santiago: United Nations Publications, 2014), 41.

21. Tilley, *Seeing Indians*, 78, 171. A thorough discussion of the size of El Salvador's Indian population can be found in Tilley, *Seeing Indians*, 170–188. See also World Bank, *El Perfil de los Pueblos Indígenas de El Salvador* (Washington, DC: World Bank, 2003), 13. http://documents.worldbank.org/curated/en/939901468234885618/El-Perfil-de-los-Pueblos-Ind-237-genas-de-El-Salvador.

22. Valuable information on the history and current situation of Indigenous people in Central America can be found in OACNUDH (Oficina Regional del Alto Comisionado de Naciones Unidas para los Derechos Humanos), *Diagnóstico sobre la situación de los derechos humanos de los pueblos indígenas en América Central* (Panama: OACNUDH, 2011). http://www.oacnudh.org/oacnudh-publica-diagnostico-sobre-la-situacion-de-los-derechos-humanos-de-los-pueblos-indigenas-en-america-central/.

23. For the regions of coffee production, see Mario K. Samper, "Café, trabajo y sociedad en Centroamérica (1870–1930): Una historia común y divergente," in *Historia General de*

Centroamérica, vol. 4, *Las repúblicas agroexportadoras, 1870–1945*, edited by Víctor Hugo Acuña Ortega, 40–42 (Madrid: FLACSO, 1993).

24. Samper, "Café, trabajo y sociedad," 11–12, 26–30, 67.

25. Robert G. Williams, *States and Social Evolution: Coffee and the Rise of National Governments in Central America* (Chapel Hill: University of North Carolina Press, 1994), 145–146, 226.

26. See, for example, Héctor Lindo-Fuentes, *Weak Foundations: The Economy of El Salvador in the Nineteenth Century* (Berkeley: University of California Press, 1990), 127–128, 135; Gould, " '¡Vana Ilusión!' " 413, 415–416; Dore, *Myths of Modernity*, 5, 78; Rene Reeves, *Ladinos with Ladinos, Indians with Indians: Land, Labor, and Regional Ethnic Conflict in the Making of Guatemala* (Stanford: Stanford University Press, 2006), 6, 8–9, 14, 171, 181–183. See also the contribution of David Díaz-Arias in this volume. For Liberal and conservative ideologies in Latin America in general, see Charles A. Hale, "Political and Social Ideas in Latin America, 1870–1930," in *The Cambridge History of Latin America*, vol. 4, edited by Charles Hale, 367–441 (Cambridge: Cambridge University Press, 1986).

27. Samper, "Café, trabajo y sociedad," 57–58; Reeves, *Ladinos with Ladinos*, 6, 13, 50–71. Indigenous communities were also forced to sell parts of their communal lands to settle debts they had incurred to pay lawyers, for example (Gould, " '¡Vana Ilusión!' " 424).

28. Williams, *States and Social Evolution*, 176–177; Gould, " '¡Vana Ilusión!' " 403.

29. Wolfe, *Everyday Nation-State*, 166–167.

30. Federico López Rivera, "Proyecto de Ley presentado por el Poder Ejecutivo al congreso Nacional sobre Comunidades Indígenas," *Nicaragua Indígena*, 2nd ser., 1 (1954): 7–9; Gould, " '¡Vana Ilusión!' " 397 n. 12.

31. Williams, *States and Social Evolution*, 227; Samper, "Café, trabajo y sociedad," 60.

32. Williams, *States and Social Evolution*, 74–76, 124, 228; Samper, "Café, trabajo y sociedad," 62; Gould, " '!Vana Ilusión!' " 397; Shelton H. Davis, "Agrarian Structure and Ethnic Resistance: The Indian in Guatemalan and Salvadoran National Politics," in *Ethnicities and Nations: Processes of Interethnic Relations in Latin America, Southeast Asia and the Pacific*, edited by Remo Guidieri et al., 86–88 (Houston, TX: Chapel, 1988); Aldo Lauria-Santiago, *An Agrarian Republic: Commercial Agriculture and the Politics of Peasant Communities in El Salvador, 1823–1914* (Pittsburgh: Pittsburgh University Press, 1999), particularly Chapter 8.

33. Williams, *States and Social Evolution*, 63, 228. For ladino encroachment under the Conservative governments, see also Julio Cambranes, *Coffee and Peasants: The Origins of the Modern Plantation Economy in Guatemala, 1853–1897* (Stockholm: Institute of Latin American Studies, 1985), 67–71, 77–85, 89; Reeves, *Ladinos with Ladinos*, 63–71.

34. Samper, "Café, trabajo y sociedad," 63–64, 85, 88.

35. Williams, *States and Social Evolution*, 192 (quote); Samper, "Café, trabajo y sociedad," 12, 22, 65.

36. See especially Samper, "Café, trabajo y sociedad," 63; Gould, " '¡Vana Ilusión!' " 409, 420–421; Gould, *To Die in This Way*, 114, 126; David McCreery, *Rural Guatemala, 1760–1940* (Stanford, CA: Stanford University Press, 1994), 242–243; Lauria-Santiago, *Agrarian Republic*, 51, 99, 157–159, 163–164; Grandin, *Blood of Guatemala*, 113, 116, 120–121; Charlip, *Cultivating Coffee*, 3, 38; Tilley, *Seeing Indians*, 129–130; Dore, *Myths of Modernity*, 77–96; Wolfe, *Everyday Nation-State*, 17, 81, 119–121. For the earlier view, see, for example, Jaime Wheelock, *Imperialismo y dictadura: Crisis de una formación social* (México, D.F: Siglo XXI, 1982), 69–83; E. Bradford Burns, *Patriarch and Folk: The Emergence of Nicaragua*,

1798–1858 (Cambridge, MA: Harvard University Press, 1991), 4. Privatization was often hampered by the resistance of affected communities, the need for them to pay surveying, the lack of surveyors and conflicts over property lines (Lindo-Fuentes, *Weak Foundations*, 147–150; Lauria-Santiago, *Agrarian Republic*, 174, 182, 196, 207–209).

37. Lindo-Fuentes, *Weak Foundations*, 83–85; Williams, *States and Social Evolution*, 78, 105–109, 126, 145; Dore, *Myths of Modernity*, 111.

38. Samper, "Café, trabajo y sociedad en Centroamérica," 104; Williams, *States and Social Evolution*, 145. A vagrancy law existed in the Central American Federation already in 1825. Further laws and police regulations addressing this issue followed in El Salvador in 1841, 1854, and 1855 (Lindo-Fuentes, *Weak Foundations*, 82, 205 n. 10; see also Lauria-Santiago, *Agrarian Republic*, 155–156). Forced labor was used in Guatemala for agricultural enterprise and the construction of infrastructure such as roads already in the late 1850s. The Guatemalan *Reglamento de jornaleros* (1877) combined forced labor and debt peonage. Reglamento de jornaleros, Guatemala, April 3, 1877, http://leygt.blogspot.de/2013/11/reglamento-de-jornaleros.html; Reeves, *Ladinos with Ladinos*, 14, 89–91, 155; McCreery, *Rural Guatemala*, 167, 218–228, 265–276; Cambranes, *Coffee and Peasants*, 98, 104–105, 172–228; Williams, *States and Social Evolution*, 113, 115–119. In Nicaragua, "vagrancy" was outlawed already in 1843. The Zelaya regime renewed the ban in 1894 and required workers to carry along a card showing their indebtedness and current employment. See Benjamin I. Teplitz, "The Political and Economic Foundations of Modernization in Nicaragua: The Administration of José Santos Zelaya 1893–1909" (PhD diss., Howard University, 1973), 196; Charlip, *Cultivating Coffee*, 148, 152.

39. Davis, "Agrarian Structure and Ethnic Resistance," 82; Samper, "Café, trabajo y sociedad," 88.

40. Cambranes, *Coffee and Peasants*, 228–239; Gould, "'¡Vana Ilusión!'" 417; Davis, "Agrarian Structure and Ethnic Resistance," 83–84; David McCreery, "'An Odious Feudalism': Mandamiento Labor and Commercial Agriculture in Guatemala, 1858–1920," *Latin American Perspectives* 13, no. 1 (1986): 114; McCreery, *Rural Guatemala*, 317–322; Grandin, *Blood of Guatemala*, 278 n. 31.

41. Cf., for example, "Memoria . . . Chenes," *La Discusión* (Campeche), May 29, 1874, 3; Alfonso Luis Velasco, *Geografia y estadística de la república mexicana*, bk. 16, *Geografia y estadística del estado de Campeche* (México: n.p., 1895), 112.

42. Gabbert, *Becoming Maya*, 70.

43. Reeves, *Ladinos with Ladinos*, 93 (emphasis in original), 96; Gould, "'¡Vana Ilusión!'" 419; Lindo-Fuentes, *Weak Foundations*, 84; Antonio Batres Jáuregui, *Los indios. Su historia y su civilización* (Guatemala: Tipografía la Unión, 1893), 159.

44. Davis, "Agrarian Structure and Ethnic Resistance," 88; Lindo-Fuentes, *Weak Foundations*, 40.

45. Lauria-Santiago, *Agrarian Republic*, 191–193, 229, 233–234.

46. Charlip, *Cultivating Coffee*, 219.

47. Lauria-Santiago, *Agrarian Republic*, 58. Cf., for example, John L. Stephens, *Incidents of Travel in Central America, Chiapas and Yucatan*, vol. 2 (New York: Dover, 1969, first published in 1841), 411; Emiliano Busto, *Estadística de la República Mexicana. Estado que guardan la agricultura, indústria, minería y comercio*, vol. 3 (México: Imprenta Ignacio Cumplido, 1880), 256.

48. Gould, *To Die in This Way*, 75–76.

49. See, for example, Gould, "'¡Vana Ilusión!'" 399.

MARGINALIZATION, ASSIMILATION, AND RESURGENCE 131

50. Gould, "'¡Vana Ilusión!,'" 399, 409. See also for Nicaragua, Wolfe, *Everyday Nation-State*, 17, 81; for El Salvador, Lindo-Fuentes, *Weak Foundations*, 90–91, 135, 145; for Guatemala, Grandin, *Blood of Guatemala*, 116.

51. Gould, "'¡Vana Ilusión!,'" 395; Gould, *To Die in This Way*, 291.

52. Gould, "'¡Vana Ilusión!,'" 420 (quote). See also Davis, "Agrarian Structure and Ethnic Resistance," 84; McCreery, *Rural Guatemala*, 228, 261; Grandin, *Blood of Guatemala*, 180.

53. Gould, "'¡Vana Ilusión!,'" 421; Gould, *To Die in This Way*, 114. For Guatemala, see Cambranes, *Coffee and Peasants*, 95–96; for El Salvador, see Lauria-Santiago, "Land, Community, and Revolt," 504–506.

54. Grandin, *Blood of Guatemala*, 114, 117–118, 157. Communal lands were also monopolized by Indian elites in other cases. See, for example, Lauria-Santiago, *Agrarian Republic*, 99.

55. Adams and Bastos, *Relaciones étnicas en Guatemala*, 140–142, 187–191, 493–498, 500, 502, 504; Betsy Konefal, *For Every Indio Who Falls: A History of Maya Activism in Guatemala, 1960–1990* (Albuquerque: University of New Mexico Press, 2010), 41–45, 49, 57; Gabbert, "Indigeneity, Culture and the State," 254.

56. See, for example, Ricardo Falla, *Quiché Rebelde: Estudio de un movimiento de conversión religiosa, rebelde a las creencias tradicionales, en San Antonio Ilotenango, Quiché (1948–1970)* (Guatemala: Editorial Universitaria de Guatemala, 1978), 126–131, 145–175, 241–259; Edward F. Fischer and Carol Hendrickson, eds., *Tecpán Guatemala. A Modern Maya Town in Global and Local Context* (Boulder, CO: Westview, 2003), 135–141.

57. Edgar Esquit and Iván García, *El derecho consuetudinario, la reforma judicial y la implementación de los acuerdos de paz* (Guatemala: FLACSO, 1998), 50–71; Adams and Bastos, *Relaciones étnicas en Guatemala*, 205–230, 501, 517. The hierarchy of religious and civil offices organized the rituals for the community-specific Catholic saint or saints and communal works, mediated internal conflicts, and, at least up to the 1950s, represented the Indigenous villagers or townspeople in their dealings with the state in Guatemala.

58. For an example from late nineteenth-century Nicaragua, see Gould, *To Die in This Way*, 75.

59. Cf., e.g., Gould, "'¡Vana Ilusión!,'" 422.

60. Robert H. Holden, "Constructing the Limits of State Violence in Central America: Towards a New Research Agenda," *Journal of Latin American Studies* 28, no. 2 (1996): 435–459 (quote from 446). See also Robert H. Holden, *Armies without Nations: Public Violence and State Formation in Central America, 1821–1960* (Oxford: Oxford University Press, 2004), 37–41. For an example from late nineteenth-century El Salvador, see Lauria-Santiago, "Land, Community, and Revolt," 524.

61. Jaime Wheelock, *Raíces indígenas de la lucha anticolonialista en Nicaragua* (México, D.F: Siglo XXI, 1974), 90–101; Lauria-Santiago, *Agrarian Republic*, 114–119, 123–127, 130; Lauria-Santiago, "Land, Community, and Revolt," 507, 519–527; Tilley, *Seeing Indians*, 120–122; Barahona, *Pueblos indígenas, estado y memoria colectiva*, 108–125; Holden, *Armies without Nations*, 37–39, 54–55, 61–63.

62. See, for example, Víctor Hugo Acuña Ortega, "Clases subalternas y movimientos sociales en Centroamérica (1870–1930)," in *Historia General de Centroamérica*, vol. 4, *Las repúblicas agroexportadoras (1870–1945)*, edited by Víctor Hugo Acuña Ortega, 310 (Madrid: FLACSO, 1993); Gould, "'¡Vana Ilusión!,'" 409–413; Gould, *To Die in This Way*, 118–127, 189–190; Lauria-Santiago, *Agrarian Republic*, 119, 123; Lauria-Santiago, "Land, Community, and Revolt," 507; Grandin, *Blood of Guatemala*, 20–22, 102–104, 108–109, 154–157.

63. For Carrera and his regime, see Hazel M. B. Ingersoll, *The War of the Mountain: A Study of Reactionary Peasant Insurgency in Guatemala, 1837–1873* (PhD diss., George Washington

132   WOLFGANG GABBERT

University, 1972); Keith L. Miceli, "Rafael Carrera: Defender and Promoter of Peasant Interests in Guatemala, 1837–1848," *The Americas* 31, no. 1 (1974): 72–95; Grandin, *Blood of Guatemala*, 18–24, 99–109.

64. Lindo-Fuentes, *Weak Foundations*, 131.

65. Cf., for example, E. Bradford Burns, "Cultures in Conflict: The Implication of Modernization in Nineteenth-Century Latin America," in *Elites, Masses, and Modernization in Latin America, 1850–1930*, edited by E. Bradford Burns and Thomas E. Skidmore, 46–50 (Austin: University of Texas Press, 1979); Lauria-Santiago, *Agrarian Republic*, 112.

66. Indians in Boaco and Sutiaba, Nicaragua, for example, were split between supporters of the Conservative and Liberal parties in the early decades of the twentieth century (Gould, *To Die in this Way*, 92–94, 120–121, 127).

67. Gould, "'¡Vana Ilusión!,'" 401 n. 24, 402.

68. Gould, *To Die in This Way*, 74, 89.

69. Gould, "Dictadores indigenistas," 60–64; for similar processes in El Salvador and Nicaragua in the 1930s, see ibid., 55, 57, 65–66 and Gould, *To Die in this Way*, 188–192. See also article by David Carey in this volume.

70. James C. Scott, *Weapons of the Weak: Everyday Forms of Peasant Resistance* (New Haven: Yale University Press, 1985). Consider, for example, the endless complaints of landlords about Indian idleness and desertion of workers.

71. Acuña Ortega, "Clases subalternas y movimientos sociales," 310–311; David McCreery, "State Power, Indigenous Communities and Land in Nineteenth-Century Guatemala, 1820–1920," in *Guatemalan Indians and the State: 1540 to 1988*, edited by Carol A. Smith, 97, 108–112 (Austin: University of Texas Press, 1990); Lindo-Fuentes, *Weak Foundations*, 136; Aldo Lauria-Santiago, "Los indígenas de Cojutepeque: La política faccional y el Estado nacional en El Salvador, 1830–1890," in *Identidades nacionales y Estado moderno en Centroamérica*, edited by Arturo Taracena Arriola and Jean Piel, 237–252 (San José, C.R.: Editorial de la Universidad de Costa Rica, 1995); Lauria-Santiago, *Agrarian Republic*, 105–114, 120–121, 123; Lauria-Santiago, "Land, Community, and Revolt," 495–496; Burns, *Patriarch and Folk*, 146–155; Dore, *Myths of Modernity*, 46–47, 49; Wolfe, *Everyday Nation-State*, 190–191.

72. Burns, *Patriarch and Folk*, 149–150; Acuña Ortega, "Clases subalternas y movimientos sociales," 310–311; Lauria-Santiago, *Agrarian Republic*, 122; Tilley, *Seeing Indians*, 115–119 and the table on Indigenous Revolts in El Salvador, 1771–1918 on 123–127. For Honduras, see Barahona, "Del mestizaje a la diversidad étnica y cultural," 220–221.

73. Acuña Ortega, "Clases subalternas y movimientos sociales," 311–312; Cambranes, *Coffee and Peasants*, 268–272.

74. Lauria-Santiago, *Agrarian Republic*, 127; see also 129; Lindo-Fuentes, *Weak Foundations*, 135; for Nicaragua, see Teplitz, *Political and Economic Foundations of Modernization*, 106–145; Burns, *Patriarch and Folk*, 68.

75. See, for example, Davis, "Agrarian Structure and Ethnic Resistance," 88–89; Gould, "Dictadores indigenistas," 45–48.

76. Tilley, *Seeing Indians*, 138; Erik Ching and Virginia Tilley, "Indians, the Military and the Rebellion of 1932 in El Salvador," *Journal of Latin American Studies* 30, no. 1 (1998): 121–156; Gould, "Dictadores indigenistas," 54; see also the article by Erik Ching in this volume.

77. Tilley, *Seeing Indians*, 138–165 (first quote is from 144, second quote from 152).

78. Pérez Brignoli also highlighted the ethnic aspects of the insurgence and its repression, however with less zeal. He also stressed the central role of Indigenous people in

the coffee-growing areas of Western El Salvador to the uprising, underlined the importance of *cofradías* (religious brotherhoods) in the mobilization and, as Tilley, that ladinos were the victims of the rebels. Héctor Pérez Brignoli, "Indians, Communists, and Peasants: The 1932 Rebellion in El Salvador," in *Coffee, Society and Power in Latin America*, edited by William Roseberry et al., 249–256 (Baltimore: Johns Hopkins University Press, 1995). For a nuanced and exhaustive discussion of these issues, see also Gould and Lauria-Santiago, *To Rise in Darkness*.

79. For the early organizing processes, see Konefal, *For Every Indio Who Falls*; Edward F. Fischer, "Beyond Victimization. Maya Movements in Post-War Guatemala," in *The Struggle for Indigenous Rights in Latin America*, edited by Nancy Postero and Leon Zamosc, 87 (Brighton: Sussex, 2004).

80. Arturo Arias, "Changing Indian Identity: Guatemala's Violent Transition to Modernity," *Guatemalan Indians and the State: 1540 to 1988*, edited by Carol A. Smith, 252–254 (Austin: University of Texas Press, 1990); Grandin, *The Blood of Guatemala*, 224; Konefal, *For Every Indio who Falls*, 40, 48, 134.

81. CEH (Comisión para el Esclarecimiento Histórico), *Guatemala, memoria del silencio* (Guatemala: UNOPS, 1999), 13, 314–423; Fischer, "Beyond Victimization," 81; and the article by David Carey in this volume.

82. On the construction of the national past in Central America, see, for example, Batres Jáuregui, *Indios*, 73–87; Taracena Arriola, *Etnicidad, estado y nación en Guatemala*, 50–66, 80–92; Teresa García Giráldez, "El pensamiento político liberal centroamericano del siglo XIX: José Cecilio del Valle y Antonio Batres Jáuregui," *Revista Complutense de Historia de América* 35 (2009): 23–45; Barahona, *Pueblos indígenas, estado y memoria colectiva*, 143–144, 161–164; Kevin Rubén Ávalos, "Hacia la definición de una política estatal de protección del patrimonio cultural en Honduras: El caso de la Arqueología (1845-1948)," *Yaxkin* 25, no. 2 (2009): 53–86.

83. A Guatemalan Liberal expressed this view particularly clearly: "Civilization is contagious. It spreads among the people and penetrates those who are nearest to the centers of culture and commerce." See Batres Jáuregui, *Indios*, 178, my translation.

84. José María Luis Mora, *México y sus revoluciones*, vol. 1 (México: Porrua, 1965, first published in 1836), 73–74. For discussions of the nationalist discourse in the nineteenth century and how elites argued not to put the contemporary Indigenous populations at the center of the new nations, see Rebecca Earle, *The Return of the Native: Indians and Myth-Making in Spanish America, 1810–1930* (Durham, NC: Duke University Press, 2007); Wolfgang Gabbert, "Imagining a Nation—Elite Discourse and the Native Past in Nineteenth-Century Mexico," in *Globalized Antiquity: Uses and Perceptions of the Past in South Asia, Mesoamerica, and Europe*, edited by Ute Schüren, Daniel Segesser, and Thomas Späth, 189–210 (Berlin: Reimer, 2015).

85. See, for example, Barahona, "Del mestizaje a la diversidad étnica y cultural," 222–226; Tilley, *Seeing Indians*, 84–85, 90–95, 190–208; Taracena Arriola, *Etnicidad, estado y nación en Guatemala*, 107–110; Gould, "Dictadores indigenistas," 48–50, 56–57.

86. See, for example, Gonzalo Aguirre Beltrán, "Community Development," *América Indígena* 26, no. 3 (1966): 219–228.

87. Arias, "Changing Indian Identity," 233–234; Kay B. Warren, "Indigenous Movements as a Challenge to the Unified Social Movement Paradigm for Guatemala," in *Cultures of Politics, Politics of Cultures: Re-visioning Latin American Social Movements*, edited by Sonia E. Alvarez, Evelina Dagnino, and Arturo Escobar, 181–183 (Boulder, CO:

Westview Press, 1998); Gould, *To Die in This Way*, 209; Konefal, *For Every Indio Who Falls*, 33–54.

88. See, for example, Fischer, "Beyond Victimization," 87, 96–102; Konefal, *For Every Indio Who Falls*, 48, 57–59, 65–67; John M. Watanabe, "Unimagining the Maya: Anthropologists, Others, and the Inescapable Hubris of Authorship," *Bulletin of Latin American Research* 14, no. 1 (1995): 31–32; Kay B. Warren, *Indigenous Movements and Their Critics: Pan-Maya Activism in Guatemala* (Princeton, NJ: Princeton University Press, 1998), 11, 22, 36–38, 46, 134, 201–202; Brent Metz, "Without Nation, without Community: The Growth of Maya Nationalism among Ch'orti's of Eastern Guatemala," *Journal of Anthropological Research* 54, no. 3 (1998): 337–338, 342–343. Many Indian activists in Guatemala are employed by the National Program of Bilingual Education PRONEBI (Edward F. Fischer, "Induced Culture Change as a Strategy for Socioeconomic Development: The Pan-Maya Movement in Guatemala," in *Maya Cultural Activism*, edited by Edward F. Fischer and R. McKenna Brown, 68, 70 (Austin: University of Texas Press, 1996).

89. See, for example, Willem Assies, Gemma van der Haar, and André Hoekema, eds., *El reto de la diversidad. Pueblos indígenas y reforma del Estado en América Latina* (Zamora: El Colegio de Michoacán, 1999); Donna Lee van Cott, *The Friendly Liquidation of the Past. The Politics of Diversity in Latin America* (Pittsburgh, PA: Pittsburgh University Press, 2000); Nancy Postero and Leon Zamosc, eds., *The Struggle for Indigenous Rights in Latin America* (Brighton, UK: Sussex Academic Press, 2004); Tilley, *Seeing Indians*, 37–41, 218–239; ECLAC, *Guaranteeing Indigenous People's Rights in Latin America*, 12–22; Gabbert, "Indigeneity, Culture and the State"; S. James Anaya, *Indigenous Peoples in International Law* (Oxford: Oxford University Press, 2004), 56–72.

90. Warren, "Indigenous Movements," 169; Fischer, "Beyond Victimization," 84.

91. Adams and Bastos, *Relaciones étnicas en Guatemala*, 497–498, 511; Fischer, "Beyond Victimization," 87–88, 92–93; Demetrio Cojti Cuxil, "Indigenous Nations in Guatemalan Democracy and the State," in *Indigenous Peoples, Civil Society, and the Neo-Liberal State in Latin America*, edited by Edward F. Fischer, 130–141 (New York: Berghahn Books, 2009); Konefal, *For Every Indio Who Falls*, 80; Miguel González, Vivian Jiménez Estrada, and Manuel del Cid, "Indigenous and Afro-descendant Social Movements in Central America," in *Handbook of Central American Governance*, edited by Diego Sánchez-Ancochea and Salvador Martí i Puig, 291 (London: Routledge, 2014).

92. Gerhard Sandner, *Zentralamerika und der ferne Karibische Westen: Konjunkturen, Krisen und Konflikte, 1503–1984* (Stuttgart: Steiner, 1985), is somewhat dated but provides a still valuable detailed overview of Central America's development since the conquest. A more recent overview enriched with numerous maps is Carolyn Hall, Héctor Pérez Brignoli, and John V. Cotter, *Historical Atlas of Central America* (Norman: University of Oklahoma Press, 2003). For the history of the Atlantic regions and their relation to the central and Pacific parts with a special focus on the Indigenous population, see Klaus Meschkat et al., eds., *Mosquitia—die andere Hälfte Nicaraguas: über Geschichte und Gegenwart der Atlantikküste* (Hamburg: Junius, 1987); Carlos M. Vilas, *State, Class, and Ethnicity in Nicaragua: Capitalist Modernization and Revolutionary Change on the Atlantic Coast* (Boulder, CO: Lynne Rienner, 1992); Wolfgang Gabbert, *Creoles. Afroamerikaner im karibischen Tiefland von Nicaragua* (Münster: Lit, 1992); Charles A. Hale, *Resistance and Contradiction. Miskitu Indians and the Nicaraguan State, 1894–1987* (Stanford, CA: Stanford University Press, 1994); Edmund T. Gordon, *Disparate Diaspora: Identity and Politics in an African-Nicaraguan Community* (Austin: University of Texas Press, 1998) and

the two volumes by Luciano Baracco, ed., *National Integration and Contested Autonomy: The Caribbean Coast of Nicaragua* (New York: Algora, 2011) and *Indigenous Struggles for Autonomy. The Caribbean Coast of Nicaragua* (Lanham, MD: Lexington Books, 2019). Eleonore von Oertzen, Lioba Rossbach, and Volker Wünderich, eds., *The Nicaraguan Mosquitia in Historical Documents, 1844–1927* (Berlin: Reimer 1990) provide a valuable collection of key documents from Moravian missionaries and British and US diplomats. For Honduras, see Águeda Gómez Suárez, *Movilización política indígena en las selvas latinoamericanas: los tawahka de la Mosquitia centroamericana* (México: Plaza y Valdés Editores, Universidad Autónoma de Tamaulipas, 2003). For the Atlantic and Pacific lowlands of Costa Rica, see Alejandra Boza Villarreal, *La Frontera Indígena de la Gran Talamanca, 1840–1930* (Cartago: Editoriales Universitarias Públicas Costarricenses, 2014). For Panama, see James Howe, *A People Who Would Not Kneel: Panama, the United States and the San Blas Kuna* (Washington, DC: Smithsonian Institution Press, 1998), and several contributions in *Mesoamérica* 29 (1995).

93. See, for example, Philippe Bourgois, *Ethnicity at Work: Divided Labor on a Central American Banana Plantation* (Baltimore: John Hopkins University Press, 1989); Wolfgang Gabbert, "Racism as Social Closure—Social Conflicts within the Working Class on Middle American Banana Plantations, 1880–1940," *Anales del Caribe* 19–20 (1999/2000): 117–132; Gabbert, *Creoles*, 253–255; Philip A. Dennis, *The Miskitu People of Awastara* (Austin: University of Texas Press, 2004), 107–164; Baron L. Pineda, *Shipwrecked Identitities. Navigating Race on Nicaragua's Mosquito Coast* (New Brunswick, NJ Rutgers University Press, 2006), 108–151; Eric Rodrigo Meringer, "The Company Times. Neocolonialism and Ethnic Relations on Nicaragua's Caribbean Coast in the Twentieth Century," in *Indigenous Struggles for Autonomy. The Caribbean Coast of Nicaragua*, edited by Luciano Baracco, 33–51 (Lanham, MD: Lexington Books, 2019).

94. See Sandner, *Zentralamerika und der ferne Karibische Westen*, 117, 186; Howe, *A People Who Would Not Kneel* and Holger M. Meding, *Panama. Staat und Nation im Wandel (1903–1941)* (Cologne: Böhlau, 2002), 303–325, for the Kuna uprising. For Kuna autonomy, see Miguel Bartolomé and Alicia Barabas, "Recursos culturales y autonomía étnica. La democracia participativa de los kuna de Panamá," *Alteridades* 8, no. 6 (1998), 159–174; Juan Pérez Archibold, "Autonomía kuna y estado panameño," in *Autonomías étnicas y Estados nacionales*, edited by Miguel Bartolomé and Alicia Barabas, 243–274 (México, D.F.: Consejo Nacional para la Cultura y las Artes, 1998).

95. For the history of the "Mosquito kingdom" and its aftermath, see Wolfgang Gabbert, "The Kingdom of Mosquitia and the Mosquito Reservation: Precursors of Indian Autonomy?," in *National Integration and Contested Autonomy: The Caribbean Coast of Nicaragua*, edited by Luciano Baracco, 11–43 (New York: Algora, 2011); and Wolfgang Gabbert, "'God Save the King of the Mosquito Nation!'—Indigenous Leaders on the Fringe of the Spanish Empire," *Ethnohistory* 63, no. 1 (2016): 71–93.

96. For the background and history of the conflict and the opposing views on nationalism and autonomy, see, e.g., Meschkat et al., *Mosquitia*; Gabbert, *Creoles*, 290–330; Vilas, *State, Class, and Ethnicity in Nicaragua*; Hale, *Resistance and Contradiction*, 141–165; Miguel González Pérez, *Gobiernos pluriétnicos: La constitución de regiones autónomas en Nicaragua* (México, D.F.: Plaza y Valdés, 1997).

97. See, for example, Grandin, *Blood of Guatemala*, 229.

98. See for Guatemala, Sol Tax, "The Municipios of the Western Highlands of Guatemala," *American Anthropologist* 39, no. 3 (1937): 423–444; Stener Ekern, "The Production of

Autonomy: Leadership and Community in Mayan Guatemala," *Journal of Latin American Studies* 43, no. 1 (2011): 109.

99. For a detailed discussion of these processes, see Wolfgang Gabbert, "Ethnicity and Social Change—Miskitu Ethno-Genesis in Eastern Nicaragua," in *New World Colors: Ethnicity, Belonging and Difference in the Americas*, edited by Josef Raab, 193–208 (Trier: Wissenschaftlicher Verlag, 2014); and Gabbert, *Creoles*, 228–230, 263–274, 302–303.

100. Adams and Bastos, *Relaciones étnicas en Guatemala*, 507, 513–514; Konefal, *For Every Indio Who Falls*, 41–54. For El Salvador, see Tilley, *Seeing Indians*, 62–63, 101.

101. Konefal, *For Every Indio Who Falls*, 41–42, 49–50. Cojti Cuxil, for example, considers the Maya to be a people consisting of different nations. See Cojti Cuxil, "Indigenous Nations in Guatemalan Democracy," 124–147. For pan-Maya cultural activism in Guatemala see, for instance, Richard A. Wilson, *Maya Resurgence in Guatemala. Q'eqchi' Experiences* (Norman: University of Oklahoma Press, 1995); Watanabe, "Unimagining the Maya," 31–33, 36–39; Warren, *Indigenous Movements and Their Critics*. Indigenous movements emerged at the same time in the other Central American countries. However, they are much less organized and influential than that of Guatemala. See, for example, Barahona, "Del mestizaje a la diversidad étnica y cultural," 231–248; Tilley, *Seeing Indians*, 218–231; Mneesha Gellman, *Democratization and Memories of Violence: Ethnic Minority Rights Movements in Mexico, Turkey, and El Salvador* (London: Routledge, 2016), 131–169.

102. Fischer, "Beyond Victimization," 89.

103. Ute Schüren, "Heirs of the Ancient Maya: Indigenous Organizations and the Appropriation of History in Yucatán, Mexico, and Guatemala," *Globalized Antiquity: Uses and Perceptions of the Past in South Asia, Mesoamerica, and Europe*, edited by Ute Schüren, Daniel Segesser, and Thomas Späth, 231–250 (Berlin: Reimer, 2015); Fischer, "Beyond Victimization," 93–95.

104. FAO (Food and Agriculture Organization of the United Nations), *Tenure of Indigenous Peoples Territories and REDD+ as a Forestry Management Incentive: The Case of Mesoamerican Countries* (Geneva: FAO, 2013), 24–26.

105. FAO, *Tenure of Indigenous Peoples Territories*, 21–24.

106. FAO, *Tenure of Indigenous Peoples Territories*, 12, 14; Miguel González, "Securing Rights in Tropical Lowlands: Community Land Property Ownership in the Nicaraguan Autonomous Regime," *Alternative* 8, no. 4 (2012): 426–446; Mary Finley-Brook, "Market Citizenship in Eastern Nicaraguan Indigenous Territories," *Alternative* 8, no. 4 (2012): 394–395; Francisco Sequeira Rankin et al., "A 30 años del estatuto de autonomía del caribe. Otra autonomía es posible," *Revista envio* 429 (2017): 1–4. http://www.envio.org.ni/artic ulo/5420.

107. Peter H. Herlihy and Taylor A. Tappan, "Recognizing Indigenous Miskitu Territory in Honduras," *Geographical Review* 109, no. 1 (2019): 67–86.

108. Luis A. Tenorio Alfaro, *Reservas indígenas de Costa Rica* (San José, C.R.: Imprenta Nacional, 1990); Elizabeth Solano Salazar, "La población indígena en Costa Rica según el censo del año 2000," *Notas de Población* 29, no. 75 (2002): 225–227; FAO, *Tenure of Indigenous Peoples Territories*, 15; Rubén Chacón Castro, María Cajiao Jiménez, and Marcos Guevara Berger, *El estado y la recuperación de tierras en las reservas indígenas de Costa Rica (1977–1995)* (San José, C. R.: Instituto de Investigaciones Jurídicas, Facultad de Derecho, Universidad de Costa Rica, 1999).

109. See, for example, Mary Finley-Brook, "El Tratado de Libre Comercio entre Centroamérica, República Dominicana y Estados Unidos (CAFTA-DR) y el desarrollo desigual," *Mesoamérica* 54 (2012): 54–93; Mary Finley-Brook and Curtis Thomas, "Renewable Energy and Human Rights Violations: Illustrative Cases from Indigenous Territories in Panama," *Annals of the Association of American Geographers* 101, no. 4 (2011): 863–872; Anthony J. Bebbington et al., "Resource Extraction and Infrastructure Threaten Forest Cover and Community Rights," *Proceedings of the National Academy of Sciences* 115, no. 52 (2018): 1–10; Santiago Bastos and Quimy de León, *Dinámicas de despojo y resistencia en Guatemala. Comunidades, Estado, empresas* (Guatemala: Diakonía, 2014). Many of these activities form part of the Mesoamerican Project, a huge regional program for capitalist development. See Wolfgang Gabbert, *Indigenous Rights, Natural Resources and the State—the Intricacies of Sustainable Development in Middle America*, ISH Working Paper (Hannover: Institute of Sociology, Leibniz University). https://www.ish.uni-hannover.de/fileadmin/soziologie/B.A._Sozialwissenschaften/Arbeitspapiere/ISH-WP_Gabbert_III-1.pdf.
110. Verena Sandner Le Gall, *Indigenes Management mariner Ressourcen in Zentralamerika* (Kiel: Geographisches Institut der Universität Kiel, 2007), 142.
111. González Pérez, *Gobiernos pluriétnicos*, 354–355, 358–359, 387; OACNUDH, *Diagnóstico sobre la situación de los derechos humanos*, vol. 2, 340–343. One of the concessions was canceled after significant protests in 1998. In 2001, the land claims of the Awas Tingni community were recognized by the OAS Inter-American Court of Human Rights and Nicaragua requested to title the respective lands. See María Luísa Acosta, "Awas Tingni versus Nicaragua, y el proceso de demarcación de tierras indígenas en la Costa Caribe Nicaragüense," *Wani*, no. 47 (2007): 6–15.
112. Michael González, "Leasing Communal Lands . . . in 'Perpetuity.' Post-Titling Scenarios on the Caribbean Coast of Nicaragua," in *Indigenous Struggles for Autonomy: The Caribbean Coast of Nicaragua*, edited by Luciano Baracco, 83 (Lanham, MD: Lexington Books, 2019).
113. González et al., "Indigenous and Afro-descendant Social Movements," 291.
114. Cornelio McLean and Esther Melba, "Report on the advances in territorial property rights of the Sumu-Mayangna community of Awas Tingni, Nicaragua," *Alternative* 8, no. 4 (2012): 476–477; González, "Leasing Communal Lands"; Alejandra Gaitán-Barrera and Govand Khalid Azeez, "Autonomy in the Caribbean Coast. Neoliberalism, Landless Peasants, and the Resurgence of Ethnic Conflict," in *Indigenous Struggles for Autonomy. The Caribbean Coast of Nicaragua*, edited by Luciano Baracco, 139–144 (Lanham, MD: Lexington Books, 2019); González Pérez, *Gobiernos pluriétnicos*, 373; Gabbert, *Creoles*, 262; PNUD, *Segundo Informe sobre Desarrollo Humano*, 359, 363; Sandner, *Zentralamerika*, 275, 301–303, 312. In Costa Rica, 38 percent of the lands in recognized Indigenous territories were still occupied by non-Indians in 2009. See OACNUDH, *Diagnóstico sobre la situación de los derechos humanos*, vol. 1, 80, and vol. 2, 418–424.
115. Fischer, "Beyond Victimization," 96–97. Demands for political autonomy for the different language groups have been put forth only rarely. In spite of certain advances in political participation, Cojti Cuxil, "Indigenous Nations in Guatemalan Democracy," strongly criticizes the absence of proportional representation, and continuing discrimination, among other things.

116. For a recent overview, see Germán Freire et al., *Indigenous Latin America in the Twenty-first Century: The First Decade* (Washington, DC: World Bank Group, 2015). http://documents.worldbank.org/curated/en/145891467991974540/Indigenous-Latin-America-in-the-twenty-first-century-the-first-decade.

FURTHER READING

Adams, Richard N., and Santiago Bastos. *Las relaciones étnicas en Guatemala, 1944–2000*. Antigua: CIRMA, 2003.

Barahona, Marvin. *Pueblos indígenas, estado y memoria colectiva en Honduras*. Colección Códices: Ciencias sociales. El Progreso, Yoro, Honduras: Editorial Casa San Ignacio, 2009.

Bastos, Santiago, Aura Cumes, and Leslie Lemus. *Mayanización y vida cotidiana. La ideología multicultural en la sociedad guatemalteca. Texto para debate*. Guatemala: FLACSO, CIRMA Cholsamaj, 2007.

Brockett, Charles D. *Political Movements and Violence in Central America*, Cambridge Studies in Contentious Politics. Cambridge: Cambridge University Press, 2005.

Casaús Arzú, Marta E. "El mito impensable del mestizaje en América Central. ¿una falacia o un deseo frustrado de las élites intelectuales?" *Anuario de Estudios Centroamericanos* 40 (2014): 77–113.

Earle, Rebecca. *The Return of the Native. Indians and Myth-Making in Spanish America, 1810–1930*. Durham, NC: Duke University Press, 2007.

Fischer, Edward F., ed. *Indigenous Peoples, Civil Society, and the Neo-Liberal State in Latin America*. New York: Berghahn Books, 2009.

Freire, Germán, et al. *Indigenous Latin America in the Twenty-first Century: The First Decade*. Washington, DC: World Bank Group, 2015. http://documents.worldbank.org/curated/en/145891467991974540/Indigenous-Latin-America-in-the-twenty-first-century-the-first-decade.

Hall, Carolyn, Héctor Pérez Brignoli, and John V. Cotter. *Historical Atlas of Central America*. Norman: University of Oklahoma Press, 2003.

Lovell, William George. *A Beauty that Hurt: Life and Death in Guatemala*. 2nd rev. ed. The Linda Schele Series in Maya and Pre-Columbian Studies. Austin: University of Texas Press, 2010.

Stocks, Anthony. "Too Much for Too Few: Problems of Indigenous Land Rights in Latin America." *Annual Review of Anthropology* 34, no. 1 (2005): 85–104.

Taracena Arriola, Arturo. *Etnicidad, estado y nación en Guatemala, 1808–1944*. Guatemala: Nawal Wuj, 2002.

Warren, Kay B., and Jean E. Jackson, eds. *Indigenous Movements, Self-representation, and the State in Latin America*. 2nd ed. Austin: University of Texas Press, 2004.

Watanabe, John M. *"Los que estamos aqui." Comunidad e identidad entre los Mayas de Santiago Chimaltenango, Huehuetenango, 1937–1990*. South Woodstock, VT: Plumsock Mesoamerican Studies, 2006.

Williams, Robert G. *States and Social Evolution. Coffee and the Rise of National Governments in Central America*. Chapel Hill: University of North Carolina Press, 1994.

PART II

CONQUEST, COLONIALIZATION, AND THE PATH TO SELF-RULE

CHAPTER 5

THE SPANISH CONQUEST?

LAURA E. MATTHEW

INTRODUCTION

The Spanish conquest is a historical moment of epic proportions, the consequences of which are difficult to overstate. It is also highly mythologized. For some, it represents the launching of a global Catholic empire—perhaps with lamentable violence, but ultimately as part of an inevitable march of Euro-Christian progress. For Indigenous populations, the meaning of the Spanish conquest is decidedly more somber: the invasion of their lands, the criminalization of their customs, the loss of sovereignty, the closest they have ever come to total extermination, and despite the fact that they survived, the beginnings of a deeply persistent lie that they did not. In between these two poles of interpretation, scholars have sought not only new sources and information beyond published Spanish works but also new perspectives from less famous actors. Central America features prominently in this recent scholarship, which has ended up questioning all three parts of the phrase "the Spanish conquest." Indigenous Central America's sixteenth-century experience of military invasion and colonization—made worse by legalized Indigenous slavery—was brutal, and more complex than the mythology usually admits. It was not a single sweeping event, it was not militarily won only by Spaniards or even Europeans, and ultimately, it was incomplete.[1]

THE SPANISH CONQUEST? PEDRO DE ALVARADO, 1524–1540

In popular culture, the demise of the Triple Aliance (Aztec) and the Inka empires commonly stands in for all eventual Native American encounters with Old World peoples, technologies, and diseases. Likewise, Pedro de Alvarado's iconic invasion in 1524–1525 of what is today Guatemalan territory is often *the* Spanish conquest of Central America that comes to mind. This oversimplification obscures a longer, more complicated process of confrontation, subjugation, and resistance throughout the region. Nevertheless, there are good reasons to dwell on Pedro de Alvarado, including his aggressiveness, his leadership of an influential network of Spanish conquistadors, and the extraordinary violence of the early conquest period in Central America sparked by his original campaigns.

Alvarado's expedition was an extension of both Mesoamerican and Spanish imperialism. After the fall of the Aztec capital city Tenochtitlan in 1521—the result of an alliance between the Spanish and the Aztecs' most powerful enemies, the Tlaxcalteca—the Indigenous leaders of central Mexico and the Spanish aimed to assert control over and beyond the vast expanses of Aztec tributary provinces. The Soconusco of Chiapas, an important trade corridor along the Pacific coast and a rich source of cacao, feathers, and other luxury items, was a major target. Control of this corridor would also open the way into the independent Maya kingdoms of Guatemala. Unsurprisingly, the Nahua allies of the Spanish pointed the Europeans in this direction in the wake of Tenochtitlan's defeat.[2] In 1522, Nahua and Spanish forces cleared the coastal route to the Soconusco by making a strategic alliance with the Tenochca ruler of the coastal Zapotec city of Tehuantepec, Xolotl, against the Mixtec confederation of Tututepec to the northwest. This Nahua-Spanish-Zapotec alliance then attacked the eastern land route to the Soconusco along the Coatzacoalcos River from the Gulf Coast to Chiapas, held by independent polities of mostly Mixe-Zoque and Popoluca speakers who had successfully held the Triple Alliance at bay.[3] By 1523–1524, the way was clear for military incursions through the Soconusco into the mountainous highlands of what is today Chiapas, Guatemala, and El Salvador.

The swift trajectory of Pedro de Alvarado's first invasion of Maya territory in 1524 is well known and deservedly so, although its success is sometimes exaggerated. Following the coastal plain from Tehuantepec, the invaders first engaged K'iche' warriors at Xetulul (Zapotitlán) and subsequently in the valley of Xelajuj (Quetzaltenango), where the K'iche' warrior Tekum was killed in the battle. Tekum's feathered costume, indicative of his powerful quetzal bird *nahual* or spirit animal, is widely understood to have given Quetzaltenango ("place of the feathered wall") its alternative, Nahuatl name which has endured ever since. The invading forces then entered the K'iche' city of Qumarkaj (Utatlán, near modern-day Santa Cruz del Quiché), preemptively torched it, and hanged its leaders Ajpop 3 Deer and Ajpop K'amaja 9 Dog.[4]

Xelajuj's and Qumarkaj's destruction sent a powerful signal to the K'iche' confederation's greatest rivals in the region, the Kaqchikel of Iximché with whom they had fought a series of bitter wars since the 1470s. We have few documents that indicate the Kaqchikel leaders' thinking at this moment. It was surely prudent to leverage Qumarkaj's defeat to their advantage, and to position themselves favorably as they ascertained a quickly changing situation. There is significant discrepancy regarding the numbers of warriors sent from Iximché to join the invading forces; the *Anales de los Kaqchikeles* says that four hundred Kaqchikel were sent to help subdue Qumarkaj, while Alvarado claimed there were thousands. In any case, the leaders of Iximché

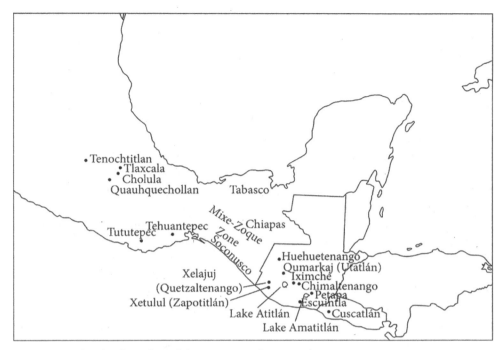

MAP 5.1. Pedro de Alvarado and the Conquest of Guatemala

subsequently welcomed the Nahua, Spaniards, and Zapoteca into their city. From there, new campaigns that now included both Kaqchikel and some K'iche' warriors were launched against other peoples against whom the Kaqchikel of Iximché had recently fought: the Tz'utujil of the Lake Atitlán region (who quickly capitulated) and the Nawat-speaking peoples of coastal Escuintla in modern Guatemala and Cuscatlán in modern El Salvador (who successfully resisted).[5]

Upon his return to Iximché, however, Pedro de Alvarado's demands on his hosts—especially for gold—became intolerable. The Kaqchikel abandoned their city, and the alliance. Suddenly surrounded by hostile locals intent on driving them out, and with many of their mostly Nahua allies dead or returned to Mexico, the remaining Spanish and Nahua split themselves between a small defensive force at Iximché and a separate military camp at Olintepeque in K'iche' territory. From there, they launched military campaigns into the Cuchumatán Mountains that although fleeting, caused significant destruction. Dozens of *probanzas* (notarized testimonies of service to the Crown made by the conquistadors, in expectation of compensation) and lawsuits left not only by various members of the extended Alvarado family (Pedro, Jorge, Gonzalo, Gómez, Diego) but also by less well-known Spaniards like Hernando de Chávez, Juan Durán, Andres de Rodas, Diego de Rojas, Cristóbal Lobo, Pedro González Nájera, and Gonzalo de Ovalle attest to multiple expeditions against the Mam near Huehuetenango and the Poqomam near Mixco, Petapa, and Lake Amatitlán, as well as continuing battles with the Kaqchikel, Nawat-Pipil, and Xinka, during this time period, periodically reinforced by Spanish-led forces from Mexico and Honduras.[6]

Relief came in the form of a major re-invasion from Mexico in March 1527 led by Pedro's brother Jorge de Alvarado. By November of that year, the first successful Spanish cities in Central America were established in the heart of restive Nawat-Pipil and Kaqchikel territory: San Salvador at the abandoned site of an earlier attempt at Spanish settlement in 1525, near Cuscatlán, and Santiago de Guatemala in the valley of Almolonga near Comalapa and Chimaltenango. Additional campaigns penetrated Honduras, Nicaragua, and the Guatemalan highlands of modern-day Huehuetenango, El Quiché, and the Verapaces. Slavery, mining, and tribute payments were violently established[7] By the mid-1530s, most of what is today El Salvador had also been at least nominally pacified. In 1540 the leaders of the Kaqchikel resistance at the time, Kaji' Imox and Kiyawit Kawoq, were imprisoned in Santiago and later hanged.[8] While Pedro de Alvarado held the position of lieutenant governor of Guatemala, during most of this period his time was spent traveling to Spain and Mexico to assert his position and preparing for costly and ultimately wasteful expeditions to far-flung places like Peru and the Spice (Maluku) Islands. As Wendy Kramer first noted in 1994, and Florine Asselbergs's analysis of the Nahua *Lienzo de Quauhquechollan* in 2004 plus the recent re-discovery of Santiago's city council books from 1530–1541 have confirmed, Jorge de Alvarado's role as both conquistador and acting governor in his brother's absence was decisive for establishing a permanent Spanish presence in what is today Guatemala, El Salvador, and Honduras.[9]

Nevertheless, it is Pedro de Alvarado who continues to personify the Spanish conquistador in Central America. In the nineteenth century he was heralded by the Guatemalan intelligentsia as a national if blemished hero: the ancestral, Hispanic father of Spanish-American independence and Guatemalan nationhood. As Adrian Recinos put it in his 1952 biography, while Alvarado's "faults have not been pardoned by history . . . in Mexico and Guatemala it cannot be forgotten that, with a soldier's roughness, he was one of the men who most helped to sow in this land the fields in which the ideas of Christianity and Western civilization flourished."[10]

Most academicians since the 1960s have viewed the Christian civilizing project as less celebratory and Alvarado as pure villain. He was "bloodthirsty" even by the standards of his own day, according to Severo Martínez Peláez in his classic work: described by Fr. Bartolomé de Las Casas as an "unhappy and unfortunate tyrant" and by Bernal Díaz del Castillo as an "impulsive warrior" whom Hernando Cortés had to restrain from the most "cruel blunders and abuses."[11] In the wake of Guatemala's brutal counterinsurgency civil war of the 1970s–1990s, many directly compared the Spanish conquest with the Guatemalan military's campaign against the Maya. The ladino-dominated state claims that "if we would only just say 'thank you' to Pedro de Alvarado, we would be at peace," wrote Luis Enrique Sam Colop on Guatemalan Independence Day in 2004, but "what must be recognized is that Alvarado's practices were continued by the Guatemalan military with scorched earth and genocide."[12] W. George Lovell and Christopher Lutz agree. Alvarado's "clout was heavy, his authority incontestable . . . [N]ever one to miss an opportunity for self-aggrandizement," he had "an explosive temperament," they write.

"Corruption, impunity, deceit and subterfuge, ruthless exploitation, intimidation by terror, and blatant disregard of the rule of law, hallmarks of Guatemala today, have in Pedro de Alvarado a fertile progenitor" who "set the parameters within which subjugation would unfold."[13]

For the Maya, Pedro de Alvarado also symbolizes the transition to a new historical era. The Dance of the Conquest, an annual dance-drama with local variations performed in Maya towns throughout the Guatemalan highlands since at least the nineteenth century, reenacts the confrontation between Alvarado and K'iche' warrior Tekum, or Tecum Umán. Tecum's death in battle after refusing to submit to Alvarado is understood in different and overlapping ways: as a personal sacrifice on behalf of his people, a misguided refusal to give up power in the face of inevitable change, and a necessity for the rising of a new "sun" personified by Pedro de Alvarado, who is called Tonatiuh (Nahuatl for "day" or "sun") in colonial-era Indigenous documents. But Tecum's transformation into a revered ancestor who resides in the sacred cave where he was buried, and the survival of his aid, diviner, and son Aj Itz—whose disorderly conduct during the play provides comic relief, and who acts as a messenger between Tecum and the Spanish and later guards Tecum's body—suggest that Alvarado's triumph was incomplete. At the end of the play the K'iche' leaders accept conversion to Catholicism and subordination to the Spanish in the name of peace, but Aj Itz escapes to the mountains to continue practicing divination and transmitting traditional knowledge to the living community. Like other Maya dance-dramas that emphasize the cyclical nature of history, the Dance of the Conquest holds forth the possibility of resistance in the present and the promise of Indigenous resurgence in the future.[14]

FROM PANAMA TO THE PETÉN

The weight of Pedro de Alvarado's legacy obscures the fact that his invasion was only one of many such expeditions, and not even the first. Rodrigo de Bastidas and Christopher Columbus landed on the eastern islands of the Gulf of Honduras in 1501 and 1502, respectively. Spanish ships explored the coastline of what is today Belize as early as 1508.[15] Santa María la Antigua, the first Spanish outpost along the Caribbean coast of what is today Panama, was founded in 1510, and Vasco Nuñez de Balboa (the first European to see the American Pacific), Pedrarias Dávila (governor of Castilla del Oro, the first Spanish territory on the American mainland), and others had gained a permanent foothold on the Panamanian isthmus by 1515.[16] Exploration of the Pacific coast of what is today Costa Rica and Nicaragua began in 1519. The Spanish settlements of Villa de Bruselas in modern-day Costa Rica, León and Granada in Nicaragua, and Trujillo in Honduras were all founded in 1524, the same year that Alvarado was entering Maya territory from Oaxaca.[17]

In the wake of Alvarado's 1524 invasion, Honduras in particular became a battleground of internecine warfare between Spaniards who entered Central America from all different directions: Hernando Cortés from Mexico versus Cristobal de Olid and Gil González de Ávila from the Caribbean in 1524, Francisco Hernández de Córdoba and Hernando de Saavedra from Mexico versus Pedrarias Dávila from Panama in 1526, a series of Crown-appointed governors of Panama, Nicaragua, and Honduras fighting against each other into the early 1530s, and Pedro de Alvarado in Guatemala versus the governor of the Yucatán Francisco de Montejo from 1533 until Alvarado's death in 1541.[18] At the same time, in 1526–1527, an alliance of hundreds of distinct Indigenous communities destroyed the mining settlement of Villa Hermosa near Trujillo, killing scores of Spaniards including the well-known explorer and conquistador Juan de Grijalva.[19] In the late 1530s significant resistance was coordinated by the Jicaque leader Cicimba in the northwestern Ulua Valley and the Lenca leader Lempira deep in the southwest at Cerquín, until both were killed. In the midst of it all, the Spanish were only able to penetrate as far as Gracias a Dios, Comayagua, and the Olancho valley in a west-to-east line through central Honduras (which nonetheless continued to experience significant uprisings) and to defend the vulnerable Atlantic port towns of Puerto de Caballos (now called Puerto Cortés after Hernando Cortés who founded it in 1525) and Trujillo.[20]

What made Central America worth fighting over? Control over important pre-Columbian trade, communication, and transportation routes allowed the invaders to insert themselves into well-established regional economies. Traditional products

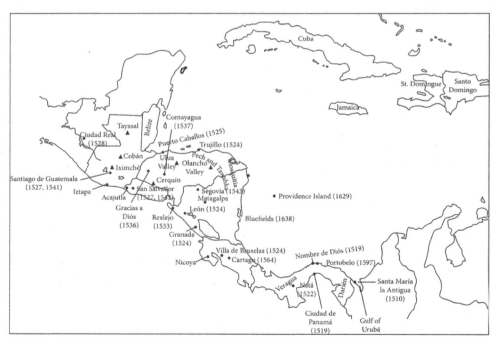

MAP 5.2. From Panamá to the Petén. (NOTE: Cities and Regions with a triangle instead of a dot are places with notable Indigenous resistance; European settlements have dates of foundation.)

THE SPANISH CONQUEST? 147

like cacao and resins as well as imports like cattle and indigo promised riches especially along the Pacific coast of Central America from the Soconusco to Lake Managua, placing increasingly onerous demands on local and migrant Indigenous workers and contributing significantly to their demographic collapse, discussed in "Biological Killers".[21] Areas of dense population promised significant tributary revenue, although this proved difficult to implement due to Indigenous resistance and, once again, the impact of epidemic disease.[22] The search for a trans-isthmian crossing engendered conflicts between conquistadors eager to cash in on the Crown's desire find a direct route to the Spice (Maluku) Islands, and placed significant burdens on thousands of Indigenous people forced to cut and haul enormous quantities of wood, in addition to cotton woven for sails, across Chiapas, Guatemala, and Honduras. By the mid-sixteenth century, however, central Panama was the only functioning transoceanic route south of the Veracruz-Mexico City-Acapulco corridor, and was the main passageway to Peru. Goods were transported by water and mule train along the Chagres River, or along the Camino Real from Nombre de Dios (abandoned in 1597) and later from Portobelo, both of which ended on the Pacific side at the fortified port of Panama City.[23]

True to stereotype, gold and silver mining ventures abounded. In Chiapas and Guatemala, a brief but intense blitz of mining activities drew attention from many quarters. References to the kidnapping and enslavement of Indigenous to form mining *cuadrillas* (gangs), as well as heavy tribute demands to supply mining camps, are littered throughout the early *residencias* (judicial reviews) and *probanzas* of the first generation of Spanish conquistadors. Three trunks of gold transported from Guatemala to Spain by Spanish conquistador Juan Rodríguez de Cabrillo in 1532, for instance, were recorded as a result of investigations into seven missing bars from the Crown's portion; Cabrillo's mining venture at Cobán was closed down five to six years later, due to local resistance.[24] In Honduras, alluvial deposits of gold and the discovery of silver near Comayagua in 1539 and gold in the Olancho valley in the 1540s kicked off a mining boom that lasted into the mid-1560s, powered by Indigenous labor. Thousands of Maya, Xinka, and Nawat-Pipil from Guatemala and El Salvador were compelled to work in the Honduran mines and transport precious metals to the coast, alongside a smaller but significant number of Lenca, Chorti' Maya, Jicaque, and other Indigenous people from the western and central regions of Honduras.[25] Some fled into unconquered Pech and Tawahka/Mayangna territory in eastern Honduras to escape this fate.[26]

In southern Central America, Spaniards exploited an already-existing trade in gold nuggets and objects that mediated political relationships throughout Panama, Costa Rica, and Nicaragua, as well as relations with peoples further north and south in Meso- and South America. Gold was traded for prisoners of war, salt, cacao, cotton, and shell beads. Finely worked gold objects were collected for ritual purposes and prestige value. Control of gold deposits and large collections of objects with important civic and sacred functions increased a group's political, economic, and cosmic power. The Spanish entered into this trade eagerly and immediately in the first decade of the 1500s. They bartered gold for cotton ropes and iron axes, stole gold from plundered villages, and demanded it as tribute when the situation allowed. By 1515 the Spanish had established a foundry at Santa María la Antigua in Darién and another was established at León in Nicaragua in 1527, where nuggets were smelted and finely worked pieces destroyed. As historian Eugenia Ibarra puts it, as they converted ritual items and markers of prestige into gold bars, "[t]he crucibles and furnaces of the Spaniards literally melted the "soul" of a society."[27]

Equally attractive, and devastating, was the business of capturing and enslaving Indigenous peoples for sale overseas. Thousands of Indigenous from Chiapas to Costa Rica were kidnapped, branded, and forcibly removed from Central America throughout the 1520s–1540s. Most were sent south to Peru, passing through newly established shipyards built along the Pacific coast at Itzapa (Guatemala), Acajutla (El Salvador), Realejo (Nicaragua), and Nicoya (Costa Rica). Others went east to the Caribbean islands, and even across the Atlantic to Europe.[28] To a great extent, the imperial New Laws of 1542 outlawing the enslavement of Indigenous people—shaped by the Dominican Fr. Bartolomé de Las Casas, who had most recently served as bishop of Chiapas and supervised a non-military evangelization project in the Guatemalan Verapaces—responded to this extreme violence of the extended conquest period in Central America. Despite its prohibition, slaving of Indigenous Central Americans in nominally Spanish territories continued into the eighteenth century, especially due to raids by Afro-Indigenous Miskitu who instigated conflicts in order to capture war prisoners and sell them into the mostly African slave trade of the Caribbean and North America.[29]

The interior of Costa Rica, the lowland Maya regions of Chiapas and Tabasco in Mexico, and the Petén in Guatemala were the last Central American provinces to be colonized by the Spanish. (The Atlantic coasts of Honduras and Nicaragua as well as parts of Panama and coastal Costa Rica were claimed by Spain but never successfully subjugated.) By the second half of the sixteenth century, Spanish-led forces faced fierce attacks from Indigenous people who now had significant prior knowledge of Spanish strategies and tactics. After their first contacts with Franciscan missionaries in 1604, the Tawahka of Honduras threw out the intruders in 1611–1612 and 1623, deterred further attempts until the 1670s, and again attacked and forced the abandonment of missions in 1724 and 1750.[30] The invasion and settlement of Costa Rica did not begin in earnest until the 1560s. Vásquez de Coronado founded the interior Spanish town of Cartago in 1563–1564 and Governor Alonso Anguiciano de Gamboa (1573–1577) managed to establish the first Spanish *encomiendas*, but only in the central valley. Military expeditions to pacify unconquered areas continued in Costa Rica into the eighteenth century.[31] Likewise, the Spanish did not manage to take control of the independent Maya kingdom of Tah Itzá (Tayasal) on Lake Petén Itzá—today, the city of Flores where thousands of tourists come to visit the nearby ancient Maya ruins of Tikal—until 1697, while the more dispersed and isolated groups that would come to be known as the Lacandon Maya of the lowland rainforest of the Petén and Chiapas were not truly threatened by outsiders until the nineteenth century.[32] Spanish conquest was not a single event but a centuries-long process that continued throughout the colonial period.

The *Spanish* Conquest? Allies, Auxiliaries, and Slaves

Ironically, the Alvarado expeditions have received outsized attention in recent years because of a historiographic turn since the 1990s seeking new and especially Indigenous perspectives on the Spanish conquest. Going beyond published sources like conquistador letters and Spanish historical chronicles, scholars have delved deep into the manuscript *probanzas* or affidavits of lesser-known conquistadors, have reconsidered Indigenous histories of the period, and have brought to light two unique documents: the painted *Lienzo de Quauhquechollan* depicting Jorge de Alvarado's 1527 invasion and the *probanza* of the Nahua and Zapotec allies who remained as colonists in Central America, both dating to the mid-sixteenth century.

The Central American subject matter of the *Lienzo de Quauhquechollan*, an enormous painted cloth measuring 2.35 by 3.25 meters currently on display at the Museo Regional de Cholula, Mexico, was identified in 2002 by Dutch scholar Florine Asselbergs. Quauhquechollan, a frontier city in the Basin of Puebla-Tlaxcala, was Jorge de Alvarado's *encomienda* and contributed hundreds if not thousands of warriors to his 1527 re-invasion of Guatemala. The *Lienzo de Quauhquechollan* depicts this campaign from the Quauhquecholteca perspective, for a Quauhquecholteca audience. It shows a warm embrace of alliance with Hernando de Cortés (Figure 5.1), and the Spanish led by Jorge de Alvarado as honored and noble companions. It also shows extraordinary moments of violence meted out by the Spanish, for instance, in setting mastiff dogs to attack Maya opponents (Figure 5.2). But the Quauhquecholteca are the main actors of the *Lienzo de Quauhquechollan*, filling every scene with their elaborate warrior costumes and brandishing Spanish swords against the Maya (Figure 5.3). The *Lienzo* depicts the spoils of conquest not as Christian churches, Spanish cities, or boats filled with gold and slaves bound for Europe but as new Nahua colonies and access to trade routes and natural resources like cotton and cacao. Like the Spanish conquistadors in their letters and chronicles, the Quauhquecholteca emphasized themselves.[33]

The same prideful tone is evident in an over eight-hundred-page *probanza* produced between 1564 and 1572 by the Nahua and Zapotec allies who remained in Central America as colonists—a group that included Tlaxcalteca, Cholulteca, Tenochca and Tlatelolca Mexica, Xochimilca, Huejotzinca, Acolhua, Quauhquecholteca, Zapoteca, and Otomí from Otumba. In this document held at the Archivo de Indias in Sevilla, Spain, the Indigenous allies from central Mexico and Oaxaca requested royal recognition and reward as equal allies—not subordinate subjects and certainly not slaves—of the Spanish conquistadors of Central America. Indeed, they presented themselves as *yndios conquistadores*, or "Indian conquistadors."[34] Spanish and Nahua conquistadors alike detailed the Indigenous allies' contributions to specific campaigns. Hundreds of "Indian conquistadors" and their sons now living in or near Santiago, San Salvador, and Valladolid (Honduras) were individually named. For seventy-five years, the leaders of

FIGURE 5.1. Embrace of Quauhquecholteca leaders and Hernando Cortés with translator Malintzin Detail of the *Lienzo de Quauhquechollan*. Digital restoration Universidad Francisco Marroquín/Banco G&T Continental.

Source: © 2007 Universidad Francisco Marroquín, Guatemala. Images are available under the Creative Commons license Attribution-Noncommercial-Share Alike.

FIGURE 5.2. Battle between Quauhquecholteca and Maya at Tecolotlán in the Cuchumatán mountains, Guatemala. Detail of the *Lienzo de Quauhquechollan*. Digital restoration Universidad Francisco Marroquín/Banco G&T Continental.

Source: © 2007 Universidad Francisco Marroquín, Guatemala. Images are available under the Creative Commons license Attribution-Noncommercial-Share Alike.

FIGURE 5.3. Spanish dogs attack Kaqchikel Maya at Pochutla while a Spaniard watches. Detail of the *Lienzo de Quauhquechollan*. Digital restoration Universidad Francisco Marroquín/Banco G&T Continental.

Source: © 2007 Universidad Francisco Marroquín, Guatemala. Images are available under the Creative Commons license Attribution-Noncommercial-Share Alike.

Ciudad Vieja, Guatemala, the largest Nahua and Zapotec colony in Central America, spearheaded the campaign insisting on legal recognition of the Indigenous allies' nobility and high status within Spanish colonial society. In the end, they were rewarded with partial exemption from tribute for them and for their descendants, a ruling that was respected for the entirety of the colonial period.[35]

These two sources, together with lesser-known Spanish *probanzas*, have sparked an academic conversation full of political and emotional sensitivity. Should scholars take the self-interested posturings of the Nahua and other allies at any more or less face value than those of the Spanish? Should we rethink partnerships that have traditionally been seen as either unequal (i.e., facing Spanish technology and violence, the Indigenous had no choice) or traitorous (i.e., in making self-interested alliance with the Spanish, the Indigenous betrayed their own people)? Given the consistent presence, guidance, and numerical superiority of the Indigenous allies, was the Spanish conquest of Central America really *Spanish*?

The questions deepen when we acknowledge the variety of Indigenous experiences in conquest expeditions over space and time. The central Mexican Nahua nobility and warrior class, including the defeated Tenochca Mexica, appear to have participated in the Central American conquests with considerable autonomy, authority, and Spanish favor well into the 1540s. Thousands of new allies from Oaxaca, Guatemala, Chiapas, Honduras, Tabasco, and elsewhere were also recruited with promises of recompense and an eye toward their future settlement as pacifying colonists. As conquest, slavery, and disease shattered communities throughout southern Meso- and Central America, however, to resist such recruitment surely became more difficult. Many thousands were violently forced to fight or carry supplies on long, dangerous expeditions as *encomienda* "Indians" or as slaves. Even the Quauhquecholteca, for all their self-fashioning as equal allies, were nonetheless part of Jorge de Alvarado's *encomienda*—and as former tributaries of the defeated Tenochca, doubly obligated to contribute to conquest campaigns. More vulnerable still were the Lenca and Jicaque from Honduras, the highland Maya of Chiapas, and the Chontal and other Indigenous of the Tabasco region who were all essentially harvested by the Francisco de Montejo clan (father and son) in the 1540s and forced to serve as slaves and porters in the Montejos's third and only successful military campaign against the Maya of the Yucatán peninsula.[36]

Similar questions of power and agency attend to another oft-neglected group of conquistadors in Central America: Africans, both free and slave. While Spanish conquistadors tend to be villainized, African participants in conquest expeditions are often heralded as part of the recovery of a forgotten history.[37] Africans rarely appear in *probanzas* or *lienzos*; the *Lienzo de Quauhquechollan* depicts what is surely an inaccurate count of one lone African among scores of Spaniards and hundreds if not thousands of Indigenous. Nevertheless, bureaucratic documents reveal a significant African presence from the earliest years of Spanish conquest and settlement in Central America.[38] In Santiago de Guatemala at Almolonga, for example, city council books from 1530 to 1541 identify enslaved and free Africans as owners of real estate, town criers, barbers, bakers, supervisors of Indigenous labor, and guardsmen. Africans in Santiago were repeatedly forbidden from carrying weapons independently or entering the Indigenous marketplace, and were threatened with mutilation and death if they attempted to escape slavery.[39] As colonial settlement spread, free Africans and even slaves often had significant possibilities for social mobility.[40] Like the wide range of Indigenous participants in the so-called Spanish conquest, these Africans cannot be adequately described by the either/or terminology of victors and vanquished.

The tendency to treat all conquistadors as Spanish, all Indigenous participants as subordinated auxiliaries fully under Spanish control, and all Africans as powerless slaves has thus given way to a more complex discussion. Not all conquistadors were Spanish. Not all slaves were African. Not all Africans were enslaved, some presumably fought in conquest battles, and from an Indigenous point of view they were unambiguously invaders. In Central America, so were many if not most of the Nahua or "Mexican" and other Mesoamerican warriors from central Mexico and Oaxaca who came from the highest military and social ranks of their societies, and who were treated with necessary if sometimes grudging respect by their Spanish allies. Other Indigenous, however, were forced to participate in conquest expeditions and violently removed from their homelands forever.

A proper discussion of the sixteenth-century invasions of Central America must admit and contextualize all these experiences through the lens not only of European expansion but also of Mesoamerican and African patterns of warfare, diplomacy, trade, and empire-building. Just as the Atlantic World cannot be understood without Africa, it is impossible to understand why thousands of central Mexican Nahua joined the Spanish and advised them to travel southwest toward Central America after the fall of Tenochtitlan, or why the Spanish turned toward the Nawat-Pipil Pacific coast after defeating the K'iche' and being welcomed by the Kaqchikel, without first understanding the geopolitics of the Triple Alliance, the importance of the Soconusco trade corridor, the competition between the Mixtec and Zapotec kingdoms of Oaxaca, the independence of the Mixe-Zoque, and the geographical directions of K'iche' and Kaqchikel expansion in the first quarter of the sixteenth century. This is not a matter of blaming the victims of European conquest for their own subjugation but of rejecting simplistic narratives that treat Indigenous actors as if they were primitive and easily dominated peoples who acted without any historical precedents or context of their own. The Spanish conquest of Central America was shaped by Mesoamerican politics and history, in ways that the initial waves of invading Europeans and Africans barely understood.

ENGLISH AND OTHER IMPERIALISMS

Nor were the Spanish the only "European conquistadors," though rarely is this term used to describe the British, Dutch, French, Scots, Swedish, Danish, and others who almost immediately sailed west to take over Spanish ships loaded with American exports, raid Indigenous territory for slaves and booty, and set up their own colonies.[41] French corsairs were the earliest new arrivals to Central America, sacking Nombre de Dios in Panama in 1537. The Dutch appeared as a major threat in the mid-sixteenth century and the English soon thereafter. While privateers such as Francis Drake, Thomas Cavendish, and Pieter Esaiasz also raided along the Pacific coast, Spanish Central America's biggest vulnerability during the sixteenth century was the Atlantic. Beginning in the 1630s, however, the range and intensity of attacks by other Europeans expanded considerably, affecting not only major ports cities like Portobelo (Panama), Nicoya (Costa Rica), and Realejo (Nicaragua) on both the Atlantic and the Pacific but also riverine towns deep in the interior such as Granada, Nueva Segovia, and Matagalpa in Nicaragua.[42]

These other European challengers needed Indigenous and Africans to help them establish a foothold on the mainland of Central America just as much as the Spanish did. Conversely, Indigenous and Africans leveraged competing European interests to their own advantage. When the short-lived English colony of Providence Island was sacked by the Spanish in 1641, hundreds of African slaves of the English escaped to the mainland. The result was the independent Afro-Indigenous society of Mosquitia, which controlled much of the Honduran and Nicaraguan Atlantic coastline throughout the colonial period. Alliance with the English allowed the Miskitu to launch inland attacks on Spanish-held territory. They also recruited the English to fight on various sides of their own disputes, often between Indigenous and Afro-descended factions. For their part, the English were happy to support the Miskitu's contraband and raids on Spanish territory from the Yucatán to Costa Rica in exchange for permission to colonize the mainland coast. As piracy diminished in the eighteenth century, the English navy and especially the Afro-descended "Zambo Mosquitos" constituted the main military threats to Spanish Central America. Mosquitia and England would maintain their close relationship until the territory's still contested incorporation into Nicaragua in 1894.[43]

Belize, too, became an English colony. Its shallow shores, complex mangrove ecology, and inhospitable climate discouraged most privateers and joint stock companies from venturing onto the coastline. But the cayes were a different matter. By the mid-seventeenth century, countless islands off the shores of Belize and Honduras bore names suggestive of the frequent though often ephemeral activities of French, Dutch, and especially English actors.[44] Such incursions opened the door to English logging on the mainland beginning in the second half of the seventeenth century, and intensified after the Spanish ejected the English from the Yucatán in the early eighteenth century. Unable to prevent English loggers from entering the lightly colonized and relatively unguarded territory of Belize, the Spanish resorted to frequent military attacks on "Baymen" camps, legalization and regulation of English logging through treaties, and, when all else failed, local participation in contraband. For Maya and Africans, the Yucatán-Belize frontier became a buffer zone. While inland Maya found refuge in Belize from Spanish colonization and missionization, African slaves of the Spanish and English sought freedom by escaping into the other's domain.[45]

Panama provides a final illustration of how conquest unfolded in areas not fully under Spanish control, and of the ways Indigenous and Africans simultaneously served, manipulated, and suffered because of European ambitions. The ill-fated Company of Scotland landed in the Darién in 1698, only to abandon its settlement Caledonia within two years after the vast majority of its colonists died due to poor planning, malnutrition, and disease. They had joined a crowded field of Europeans attempting to control this potentially valuable passage to the Pacific.[46] The Spanish held numerous port cities but controlled almost none of the interior. French buccaneers were attempting colonize the nearby Gulf of Urabá. English pirates attacked regularly. The Tule and other Indigenous in the area of Darién tended to bargain with each group of intruders separately, be they Spanish turtlers from Cartagena, French pirates looking to settle down, African escaped slaves, Catholic friars hoping to evangelize, or Crown bureaucrats. Many Indigenous in the interior interacted with these foreigners infrequently or never, relying on intermediaries—sometimes of mixed heritage—who consolidated their own power in the process.[47]

These intermediaries were full participants in the Atlantic world: for instance, a Tule named Corbette who engaged with the Scots. Corbette's leadership role as a "go-between" derived from his prior experience with Europeans. He had been taken as a young boy to English Jamaica presumably during a slaving expedition, was rescued (stolen?) from the English by the French, raised on the island of Petit-Goave west of Hispaniola's

French-held St. Domingue as a household servant, and later returned to the Darién. For Corbette, as for other Indigenous, contact with Europeans carried significant risks, as is also apparent from the interview with a European seaman who was summoned with him. A slave merchant, the European had met the Scots while searching the San Blas coastline for "Indians" to take back to the French governor of St. Domingue.[48] European imperial competition may have provided Indigenous Central Americans with opportunities for resistance, trade, and power, but never without danger.

BIOLOGICAL KILLERS

Spanish and other European conquest in Central America was pursued via invasion and warfare, advantageous alliances, and the violent imposition of long-term labor demands, forced resettlement, and militant Christianity. Ultimately, however, the single biggest killer of Indigenous Central Americans during the extended conquest period was epidemic disease brought over from Europe and Africa, exacerbated by the violence, hunger, and displacement of the era. This, too, can be seen as part of conquest, although the massive demographic collapse of the Indigenous population also frustrated Spanish goals.

Historical demographers have sought ways to accurately estimate the Indigenous population of the Americas and its precipitous drop as a result of early modern globalization since the late 1960s. Acrimonious debates between "high" and "low" counters that dominated into the 1990s have been replaced with a consensus, if not on exact numbers, then on the magnitude of the holocaust.[49] A great deal of detailed scholarship has confirmed that for Central America as elsewhere, the rate of decline of the Indigenous population in the first 150 years after contact was truly staggering—so much so that combined with losses across the Americas, it impacted the global climate.[50] Likewise, the false choice between mortality being driven primarily by lack of immunity versus European exploitation has been largely abandoned, in favor of an analysis that acknowledges both of these causes and adds other aggravating factors at the local and regional level such as locust plagues, drought, and crop failures.[51]

Reviewing a lifetime of scholarship, W. George Lovell and Christopher Lutz estimate that for the entirety of modern-day Guatemala, by the first quarter of the seventeenth century the population had fallen from around two million to 131,250 Indigenous, or by 93.4 percent.[52] Linda Newson calculates even more precipitous declines of 95 percent by 1550 in the densely populated areas of central and western parts of Honduras and the Pacific coast of Nicaragua, which suffered intense internecine warfare between the Spanish as well as slaving. The less dense populations of eastern Honduras and central and eastern Nicaragua suffered similar but more protracted loss, reaching their nadir in the late sixteenth and early seventeenth centuries.[53] Epidemic disease often traveled ahead of the Spanish. The Kaqchikel suffered a new and mortal "sore-sickness," likely smallpox, in 1520, four years before Pedro de Alvarado's initial invasion. Likewise, when the Spanish first entered central Costa Rica in 1561 they wrote of recently emptied villages and sparse populations especially in the regions bordering Nicaragua, where repeated waves of death had already been recorded.[54]

The seventeenth-century annals of the Kaqchikel Xajil lineage memorialize the emotional and political toll better than any academic prose:

> First, people got sick, coughing, then their noses bled, and yellow urine.
> The dying that happened long ago was truly frightening.
> That was when the lord Waqaqi' Ajmaq died.
> Little by little a great darkness, a long night befell our fathers, grandfathers,
> And us, you, my sons, when the sore-sickness came . . .
> There was no healer for it. Thus, the people were peeled.
> Two twenty-day months after the sickness began was when our fathers, our
> grandfathers died.
> On twelve Kamay died the lord Jun Iq', your great-grandfather.
> Two days later died our father, the rajpop achi B'alam, your grandfather, you, my sons!
> They died almost together, your grandfather and his father.
> Truly the people stank, were acrid, in death when our father, our grandfather died.
> Other people were thrown down the ravine.
> Just dogs, just buzzards ate the people.
> The death was frightening; your grandfathers were being killed.
> They were companions in death: the sons of the lords with their younger siblings, their
> elder siblings.
> Thus we were left in orphanhood,
> you, my sons!
> We were still little boys when all of us were abandoned.
> The pain of being born![55]

Historians dislike counterfactuals. But it is well worth contemplating how differently the Spanish conquest might have transpired had the Indigenous of Central America not simultaneously been experiencing the most destructive series of pandemics in recorded human history, made even deadlier by warfare, massacre, displacement, slavery, hunger, and despair.

THE SPANISH *CONQUEST?* ANTICOLONIALISM AND INDIGENOUS SURVIVAL

And there's the rub, for despite everything, the Indigenous of Central America almost everywhere resisted, survived, and began to demographically recover by the eighteenth century. At between six and eight million, today's Maya population spanning Chiapas, Guatemala, Belize, and also the Yucatán peninsula in Mexico—the highest concentration of Indigenous in Central America—approximates the pre-European contact population.

In Guatemala, organizations such as the Academia de las Lenguas Mayas de Guatemala, the Consejo de Organizaciones Mayas de Guatemala, and the Cholsamaj publishing house took root in the midst of the counterinsurgency war of the 1980s, developing institutionalized ways for Maya and other Indigenous to speak out against racism and exclusion and in defense Indigenous culture and lands.[56] In Chiapas, persistent poverty in the midst of state-sponsored modernization, cultural repression, and the corruption of the Mexican government led to the Zapatista uprising in 1994.[57] As migration to the United States has increased, vibrant transnational Maya associations have also developed.[58]

Although they have not yet gained significant political or economic power within the nation-state, at the turn of the over five-thousand-year *oxlanh b'aktun* cycle of 2012 the Maya are forging what Victor Montejo has called an intellectual renaissance in prophetic times. "Racism in Guatemala is best understood by examining the problems that originated in the inequality established by the Spanish conquest," he writes. "Current processes of self-representation are enabling the Maya to emerge from under centuries of denigrating images as 'Indians' and second-class citizens. The shared Maya base culture draws upon the values and creative knowledge of the ancestors, and the new and powerful pan-Maya identity arising from the ancient Maya culture can shatter the stereotypes imposed in 1524."[59]

The Maya are some of the most visible Indigenous of Central America today, but they are not alone. The Xinka and Afro-Indigenous Garífuna also survive in Guatemala and Belize, as do the Nawat-Pipil, Ch'orti' Maya, Lenca, and Kakawira in El Salvador; the Lenca, Ch'orti' Maya, Pech, Tawahka, Jicaque, Rama, Paya, Tolupán, Nahua, and Garífuna in Honduras; the Rama, Mayangna, and Miskitu in Nicaragua; the Cabécar, Bri Bri, Boruca, Ngöbe, Chorotega, Huetar, Maleku, and Teribe in Costa Rica; and the Kuna, Ngöbe, Buglé, Emberá, Wounaan, Bokota, and Naso Teribe in Panama, among others. In Honduras, Lenca leaders like Berta Cáceres, Nelson García, and Lesbía Yaneth Urquía—all of whom were assassinated in 2016—have been at the forefront of attempts to stop environmentally destructive dams and mines in Indigenous territories.[60] Plurinationality, respect for Indigenous law, and the common struggle of Indigenous people in the Americas and internationally have been cornerstones of new approaches to the nation-state.[61] Some groups have secured a degree of autonomy and official recognition of their own territories, for instance, in Panama where groups like the Kuna have been negotiating treaties with the Spanish, Colombian, and Panamanian governments since 1789.[62] Today, there exist five Indigenous territories in Panama for the Kuna, Embera, and Ngöbe, and similarly, though more weakly protected, twenty-four Indigenous territories in Costa Rica.[63]

At the same time, the liberal nation-state, industrialization, and global trade, as well as continued Christian missionization by both Catholics and Protestants, have all taken a heavy toll on Central America's Indigenous since 1824. National boundaries artificially divide Indigenous territories. National unity has hinged on assimilationist, state-sponsored programs that celebrate and privilege mixed Spanish and Indigenous *mestizo* culture. National economies have continued to exploit Indigenous land and labor for export-oriented agriculture and mining. In El Salvador, by the beginning of the twentieth century the Nawat-Pipil of El Salvador constituted a majority population only in the country's western highlands. After the government massacred thousands in reprisal for a regional peasant uprising in 1932, Nawat-Pipil culture went underground. For generations afterward, survivors avoided being identified by external ethnic markers such as language or dress and were subject to the Spanish-centric, monolingual policies of national education programs and prejudice against being too "Indian" in the workplace. As a result, today fewer than five hundred native speakers of Nawat-Pipil struggle to pass their language on to the youngest generations.[64] Likewise, in Nicaragua Indigenous communities faced extraordinary pressure from the coffee industry and the Hispanizing impulse of both the liberal and the revolutionary state. Despite significant Indigenous organizing into the mid-twentieth century, by the 1980s Indigenous survival beyond the Mayangna and Miskitu Atlantic coast was widely denied.[65] In 1992, the Federation of Indigenous Communities of Nicaragua declared:

> Not only have we lost our language, but we have also disintegrated as communities through the destruction of our values such as: communal unity, solidarity, respect for the elders as community authorities, the transcendental role of the woman . . . Because of our resistance we have not disappeared, they wanted to assimilate (absorb) us so that we would think like the colonizers . . . so that we would reject our culture and our Indigenous consciousness would be erased. At the beginning of this century, many Indigenous communities existed in the Pacific, Central, and Northern regions [of Nicaragua], many of which have disappeared, others have been assimilated into the rest of society. WE ARE HERE, HOLDING ONTO OUR ROOTS TO SURVIVE AGAINST THIS POLICY OF CULTURAL ETHNOCIDE.[66]

The term "conquest" is therefore controversial. On the one hand, it succinctly marks a critical moment in which everything changed for Central America's Indigenous peoples and captures a violence that was and remains ongoing. On the other hand, the mythification of the Spanish conquest has long implied Indigenous Central Americans' total and permanent subjugation, successful Christian conversion and Hispanization, and relegation to a distant past: death by many generations of Eurocentric history. Academic archaeologists, historians, and anthropologists—whose scholarship over the centuries has helped build the edifice, unwittingly or not—now face the difficulty of uprooting what Matthew Restall calls the "myth of Native desolation."[67] The notion that Indigenous Central Americans all died or "end[ed] their culture" is pervasive.[68] "Conquest" stands for defeat, and the persistent use of the term cannot help but reinforce this idea. "At an ideological level, colonialism is manifested through a discourse that idealizes the sixteenth-century invader and justifies his aggression, a discourse that rationalizes the extinction of Maya culture and languages," writes Luis Enrique Sam Colop. "1 B'aqtun, 5 K'atuns, and 7 Tuns (500 solar years) after the beginning of European expansion on this continent, colonialism continues in force. It is part of the dominant ideology: 'We are the conquistadors.'"[69] In a bid to change the discourse, Colop, Demetro Cojtí Cuxil, and other Indigenous academics have purposefully replaced the term "conquest" with "invasion."

Conclusion

Or perhaps we should speak of invasions in the plural. By stepping slightly to the side of the weighty myths of the Spanish conquest, the term "invasions" directs us away from the tendency, after hundreds of years of repetition, to oversimplify this important series of events. It invites us to speak of particular expeditions rather than collapsing many different military encounters into one. It does not imply success in every instance. It leaves more space for discussing the great complexity of actors that made Spanish efforts viable. It also avoids conflating the sixteenth century with the present. The earliest invasions of Central America brought the region's Indigenous people into contact with the rest of the globe for the first time, with truly dire consequences. The conquistadors' claims of success were often exaggerated, but the long-term effects were all too real. In order to understand how the past has led to the present, and also to build up the historiography of Central America without artificially dividing the pre- from the post-Columbian, we must first understand the many experiences of sixteenth-century invasion and encounter on their own terms. We also need to build up the historical record beyond the centers of colonial-administrative and academic power reflected in the Guatemalan, Maya-centric, and English-language bent of this article. There is still much to discover about the earliest global invasions of Indigenous Central America, in archival corners, local traditions and knowledge, and archaeological sites that have hardly been explored.

Notes

1. Throughout this article I use the names of modern nations that did not exist during the conquest period in order to orient the reader geographically. Similarly, I label groups of people using commonly accepted names that are often based on linguistics, but which mask a great deal of diversity and do not necessarily reflect the way that Indigenous people have organized their societies or thought about their identities, in either the past or the present.

2. Janine Gasco, "The Polities of Xoconochco," in *The Postclassic Mesoamerican World*, edited by Michael Ernest Smith and Frances Berdan, 50–54 (Salt Lake City: University of Utah Press, 2003); Carlos Navarrete, "Elementos arqueológicos de mexicanización en las tierras altas mayas," in *Temas mesoamericanas*, edited by Sonia Lombardo and Enrique Nalda, 347–348 (Mexico City: Instituto Nacional de Antropología e Historia, 1996); Michel Oudijk and Matthew Restall, "Mesoamerican Conquistadors in the Sixteenth Century," in *Indian Conquistadors: Mesoamerican Allies in the Conquest of Mesoamerica*, edited by Laura E. Matthew and Michel Oudijk, 28–64 (Norman: University of Oklahoma Press, 2007).

3. Joseph Whitecotton, *Zapotec Elite Ethnohistory: Pictorial Genealogies of Eastern Oaxaca* (Nashville, TN: Vanderbilt University Publications in Anthropology, 1990); Michel Oudijk, *Historiography of the Benizaa: The Postclassic and Early Colonial Periods (1000–1600 A.D.)* (Leiden, The Netherlands: Research School CNWS, 2000); Alonso Barros van Hövell tot Westerflier, "Cien años de guerras mixes: territorialidades prehispánicas,

expansión burocrática y zapotequización en el istmo de Tehuantepec durante el siglo xvi," *Historia Mexicana* 57, no. 2 (2016): 347.

4. Irma Otzoy, "Tekum Umam: From Nationalism to Maya Resistance" (PhD diss., University of California-Davis, 1999); Ruud van Akkeren, *La visión indígena de la conquista* (Guatemala: Serviprensa, 2007), 55–74. Luis Enrique Sam Colop published a series of columns on Tekum in the Guatemalan newspaper *Prensa Libre,* available at the digital archive *Ucha'xik.* https://uchaxik.wordpress.com/?s=tekum.

5. Jorge Luján Muñoz and Horacio Cabezas Carcache, "La conquista," in *Historia General de Guatemala*, Vol. II (Guatemala City: Asociación de Amigos del País/Fundación para la Cultura y el Desarrollo, 1994), 50–55; Judith Maxwell and Robert M. Hill, eds., *Kaqchikel Chronicles: The Definitive Edition* (Austin: University of Texas Press, 2006), 258–269.

6. Wendy Kramer, *Encomienda Politics in Early Colonial Guatemala, 1524-1544: Dividing the Spoils* (Boulder, CO: Westview Press, 1994), ch. 2; Adrian Recinos, *Pedro de Alvarado, Conquistador de México y Guatemala* (México, D.F.: Fondo de Cultura Económica, 1952), 107–127.

7. Wendy Kramer and Jorge Luján Munoz, eds., *Libro Segundo del Cabildo de la çibdad de Santiago de la provinçia de Guatemala començado a XXVII de mayo de MDXXX años* (Ciudad de Guatemala: Centro de Investigaciones Regionales de Mesoamérica, 2018); W. George Lovell and Christopher Lutz, *Strange Lands and Different Peoples: Spaniards and Indians in Colonial Guatemala* (Norman: University of Oklahoma Press, 2013), provide an excellent overview of the earliest campaigns throughout Guatemala, including the intentional burning of Mam settlements near Huehuetenango in 1530. One of these settlements, Chiantla Viejo, was briefly reoccupied and has been a significant site of religious ritual into the present day; see Victor Castillo, *Informe Proyecto Chiantla Viejo* (Ciudad de Guatemala: 2018). https://www.academia.edu/36846374/Informe_Proyecto_Chiantla_Viejo.

8. Francis Polo Sifontes, *Los Cakchiqueles en la conquista de Guatemala* (Ciudad de Guatemala: Editorial Plus Ultra, 1986).

9. Kramer, *Encomienda Politics,* 63-68; Florine Asselbergs, *Conquered Conquistadors: The Lienzo de Quauhquechollan: A Nahua Vision of the Conquest of Guatemala* (Boulder: University Press of Colorado, 2008).

10. Recinos, *Pedro de Alvarado,* 238.

11. Severo Martínez Peláez, *La patria del criollo: Ensayo de interpretación de la realidad colonial guatemalteca* (México, D.F.: Fondo de Cultura Económica, 2011), 43–45.

12. Luis Enrique Sam Colop, "La patria de ellos," *Prensa Libre,* September 15, 2004, archived at https://uchaxik.wordpress.com/2004/09/15/la-patria-de-ellos/.

13. Lovell and Lutz, *Strange Lands,* 251; W. George Lovell and Christopher Lutz, "Unsung Heroes: Cahí Ymox, Belehé Qat, and Kaqchikel Resistance to the Spanish Invasion of Guatemala, 1524–1540," in *Faces of Resistance: Maya Heroes, Power, and Identity*, edited by S. Ashley Kistler, 37, 43 (Tuscaloosa: University of Alabama Press, 2018).

14. Kay Warren, "Reading History as Resistance: Maya Public Intellectuals in Guatemala," in *Maya Cultural Activism in Guatemala*, Edward Fischer and R. McKenna Brown, 96–98 (Austin: University of Texas Press, 1996); Garrett W. Cook, *Renewing the World: Expressive Culture in a Highland Town* (Austin: University of Texas Press, 2000), 118–141; Matthew Krystal, *Indigenous Dance and Dancing Indian: Contested Representation in the Global Era* (Boulder: University Press of Colorado, 2012), 73–81; Irma Otzoy, "Tecún Uman and the Conquest Dance," in *The Guatemala Reader*, edited by Greg Grandin, Deborah Levenson, and Elizabeth Oglesby, 51–61 (Durham, NC: Duke University Press, 2011);

Oswaldo Chinchilla Mazariegos, "Tecum, the Fallen Sun: Mesoamerican Cosmogony and the Conquest of Guatemala," *Ethnohistory* 60, no. 4: 693–719; Victoria Bricker, *The Indian Christ, The Indian King: The Historical Substrate of Maya Myth and Ritual* (Austin: University of Texas Press, 1981); Robert Hill, *Colonial Cakchikeles: Highland Maya Adaptations to Spanish Rule, 1600–1700* (Fort Worth, TX: Harcourt Brace Jovanovich, 1992), 1–9.

15. Elizabeth Graham, *Maya Christians and Their Churches in Sixteenth-Century Belize* (Gainesville: University Press of Florida, 2011), 122; Victor Bulmer-Thomas and Barbara Bulmer-Thomas, "The Origins of the Belize Settlement," *TEMPUS Revista en Historia General* 4 (2016): 137–160; Matthew Restall, "Creating 'Belize': The Mapping and Naming History of a Liminal Locale," *Terrae Incognitae* 51 (2018): 5–35.

16. María del Carmen Mena García, *El oro de Darién: Entradas y cabalgadas en la conquista de Tierra Firme (1509–1526)* (Madrid: Consejo superior de Investigaciones Científicas, 2011).

17. Linda Newson, *The Cost of Conquest: Indian Decline in Honduras Under Spanish Rule* (Boulder, CO: Westview Press, 1986); Jorge Díaz Ceballos, "New World Civitas, Contested Jurisdictions, and Inter-Cultural Conversation in the Contruction of the Spanish Monarchy," *Colonial Latin American Review* 27, no. 1 (2018): 30–51.

18. Robert S. Chamberlain, *The Conquest and Colonization of Honduras, 1502–1550* (New York: Octagon Books, 1966)

19. Antonio Herrera de Tordesillas, *Descripción de las Islas y Tierra Firme de el Mar Occeano que llaman Indias Occidentales* (Madrid: Nicolás Rodríguez Franco, 1730), 27; Rodolfo Pastor, *Historia mínima de centroamérica* (México, D.F.: El Colegio de México, 2011), 81.

20. Newson, *Cost of Conquest*, 96–97.

21. Murdo MacLeod, *Spanish Central America: A Socioeconomic History, 1520–1720* (Berkeley: University of California Press, 1973); Noa Corcoran-Tadd and Guido Pezzarossi, "Between the South Sea and the Mountainous Ridges: Biopolitical Assemblages in the Spanish Colonial Americas," in *Post-medieval Archaeology* 52, no. 1 (2018): 86–89.

22. For example, in Chiapas: see Tadashi Obara-Saeki and Juan Pedro Viqueira Alban, *El arte de contar tributos: Provincia de Chiapas, 1560–1821* (México, D.F.: El Colegio de México, 2017), 42–48.

23. Gudrun Lenkersdorf, *Genésis Histórica de Chiapas, 1522–1523: El conflicto entre Portocarerro y Mazariegos* (México, D.F.: Universidad Nacional Autónoma de México, 1993), esp. 144–148; Kris Lane, *Colour of Paradise: The Emerald in the Age of Gunpowder Empires* (New Haven, CT: Yale University Press, 2010); John W. Hopes and Oscar M. Fonseca Z., "Goldwork and Chibchan Identity: Endogenous Change and Diffuse Unity in the Isthmo-Colombian Area," in *Gold and Power in Ancient Costa Rica, Panama, and Colombia*, edited by Jeffrey Quilter and John Hoopes (Washington, DC: Dumbarton Oaks, 2003); Hall and Pérez Brignoli, *Historial Atlas of Central America*, 124–125.

24. Wendy Kramer, *El español que exploró California: Juan Rodríguez Cabrillo (c. 1497–1543), De Palma del Río a Guatemala* (Córdoba, Spain: Diputación de Córdoba, 2018), 47–48, 89–94; Kramer, *Encomienda Politics*, 217–220; Barros, "Cien años de guerras mixes."

25. Newson, *Cost of Conquest*, 111–114.

26. The Pech and Mayangna speak Misulmapan languages and represent the northern limits of a genetic-linguistic group of peoples (also including speakers of Chibchan languages) that extends into South America. See Jane Hill, "The Historical Linguistics of Maize Cultivation in Mesoamerica and North America," in *Histories of Maize in Mesoamerica: Multidisciplinary Approaches*, edited by John E. Staller et al., 235–249

(New York: Routledge, 2010); and Atanasio Herranz, *Estado, sociedad y lenguage: La política lingüística en Honduras* (Tegucigalpa, Honduras: Editorial Guaymuras, 1996).

27. Eugenia Ibarra Rojas, "Gold and the Daily Lives of Indigenous Peoples," in *Gold and Power in Ancient Costa Rica, Panama, and Colombia*, edited by Jeffrey Quilter and John Hoopes, 413 (Washington, DC: Dumbarton Oaks, 2003).

28. Newson, *Cost of Conquest*, 101–106; Nancy E. Van Deusen, *Global Indios: The Indigenous Struggle for Justice in Sixteenth-Century Spain* (Durham, NC: Duke University Press, 2015); William Sherman, *Forced Native Labor in Sixteenth-Century Central America* (Lincoln: University of Nebraska Press, 1979), 216; Juan Carlos Solórzano and Claudia Quirós Vargas, *Costa Rica en el siglo xvi: descubrimiento, exploración y conquista* (San José: Editorial Universidad de Costa Rica, 2006); Juan Carlos Solórzano, *Los indígenas en la frontera de la colonización, Costa Rica 1502–1930: Cuatuso, Orosi, Tucurrique, Tuis, Chirripó, Talamanca, y el Pacífico Sur* (San José, Costa Rica: Editorial Universidad Estatal a Distancia, 2013).

29. Eugenia Ibarra Rojas, *Pueblos que capturan: Esclavitud indígena al sur de América central del siglo xvi a xix* (San José: Editorial Universidad de Costa Rica, 2012), ch. 4; Mary Helms, "Miskito Slaving and Culture Contact: Ethnicity and Opportunity in an Expanding Population," *Journal of Anthropological Research* 39, no. 2 (1983): 179–197.

30. William Davidson and Fernando Cruz S., "Delimitación de la región habitada por los sumos taguacas de Honduras en el período de 1600 a 1990," *Mesoamérica* 29 (1995): 159–165.

31. Carolyn Hall and Héctor Pérez Brignoli, with John V. Cotter, *Historical Atlas of Central America*, (Norman: University of Oklahoma Press, 2003), 138–139; Wendy Kramer, W. George Lovell, and Christopher Lutz, "La conquista española de Centroamérica," in *Historia General de Centroamérica*, Vol. II, edited by Julio Pinto Soria, 36–40 (Madrid: Sociedad Estatal Quinto Centenario/FLACSO, 1993); and Elizabeth Fonseca Corrales, "Economía y Sociedad en Centroamérica (1540-1680)," in *Historia General de Centroamérica*, Vol. II, edited by Julio Pinto Soria, 69–70 (Madrid: Sociedad Estatal Quinto Centenario/FLACSO, 1993).

32. Grant Jones, *The Conquest of the Last Maya Kingdom* (Stanford, CA: Stanford University Press, 1998); Jan de Vos, *La Paz de Dios y del Rey: La conquista de la Selva Lacandona: 1525–1821* (México, D.F.: Fondo de Cultura Económica, Mexico City, 1988); and Jan de Vos, *Oro verde: La conquista de la Selva Lacandona por los madereros tabasqueños, 1822–1949* (México, D.F.: Fondo de Cultura Económica, Mexico City, 1988); Joel Palka, *Unconquered Lacandon Maya: Ethnohistory and Archaeology of Indigenous Culture Change* (Gainesville: University of Florida Press, 2005).

33. Florine Asselbergs, *Conquered Conquistadors: The Lienzo de Quauhquechollan, A Nahua Vision of the Conquest of Guatemala*, (Boulder: University Press of Colorado, 2008).

34. Laura E. Matthew and Michel Oudijk, eds., *Indian Conquistadors: Mesoamerican Allies in the Conquest of Mesoamerica* (Norman: University of Oklahoma Press, 2007); Pedro Escalante Arce, *Los tlaxcaltecas de Centro América* (San Salvador, El Salvador: Consejo Nacional para la Cultura y el Arte, 2001).

35. Laura E. Matthew, *Memories of Conquest: Becoming Mexicano in Colonial Guatemala* (Chapel Hill: University of North Carolina Press, 2012).

36. John Chuchiak, "Forgotten Allies: The Origins and Roles of Native Mesoamerican Auxiliaries and Indios Conquistadores in the Conquest of Yucatán, 1526–1550," in *Indian Conquistadors: Mesoamerican Allies in the Conquest of Mesoamerica*, edited by Laura E. Matthew and Michel Oudijk, 175–226 (Norman: University of Oklahoma Press, 2007).

37. Matthew Restall, "Black Conquistadors: Armed Africans in Early Spanish America," *The Americas* 57, no. 2 (October 2000): 171–205; Matthew Restall and Ben Vinson, "Black Soldiers, Native Soldiers: Meanings of Military Service in the Spanish American Colonies," in *Beyond Black and Red: African-Native Relations in Colonial Latin America*, edited by Matthew Restall, 15–52 (Albuquerque: University of New Mexico Press, 2005).

38. Robinson Herrera, *Natives, Europeans, and Africans in Sixteenth-Century Santiago de Guatemala* (Austin: University of Texas Press, 2003); Christopher Lutz, *Santiago de Guatemala, 1541–1773: City, Caste, and the Colonial Experience* (Norman: University of Oklahoma Press, 1994).

39. Wendy Kramer and Jorge Luján Muñoz, *Libro Segundo de Cabildo de la çibdad de Santiago de la provincia de Guatemala començando a xxxvii de mayo de MDXXX años* (Wellfleet, MA: Plumsock Mesoamerican Studies, 2018), 62, 162, 189, 197, 207, 216, 218, 243, 311, 280.

40. Paul Lokken, "Angolans in Amatitlán: Sugar, African Migrants, and Gente Ladina in Colonial Guatemala," in *Blacks and Blackness in Central America: Between Race and Place*, edited by Lowell Gudmundson and Justin Wolfe, 42–45 (Durham, NC: Duke University Press, 2010).

41. Jorge Cañizares Esguerra, *Puritan Conquistadors: Iberianizing the Atlantic, 1550–1700* (Stanford, CA: Stanford University Press, 2006), points out the similarities between Spanish conquistadors and English and other pirates, including their common goal to plunder, their entrepreneurial spirit loosely linked to monarchical loyalty, and the eschatalogical language they shared.

42. Hall and Pérez Brignoli, *Historical Atlas of Central America*, 134–141.

43. Karl Offen, "Puritan Bioprospecting in Central America and the West Indies," *Itinerario* 35, no. 1 (2011): 15–47; and Karl Offen, "The Sambo and Tawira Miskitu: The Colonial Origins and Geography of Intra-Miskitu Differentiation in Eastern Nicaragua and Honduras," *Ethnohistory* 49, no. 2 (2002): 319–372; Bernard Nietschmann, "Conservación, autodeterminación y el Area Protegida Costa Miskita, Nicaragua," *Mesamérica* 29 (1995): 1–55; Newson, *Cost of Conquest*, 276–284.

44. Bulmer-Thomas and Bulmer-Thomas, "Origins of the Belize Settlement," 154–155.

45. Matthew Restall, "Crossing to Safety? Frontier Flight in Eighteenth-Century Belize and Yucatan," *Hispanic American Historical Review* 94, no. 3 (2014).

46. J. R. McNeill, *Mosquito Empires: Ecology and War in the Greater Caribbean, 1620–1914* (Cambridge, UK: Cambridge University Press, 2010): 106–123; Julie Orr, *Scotland, Darien and the Atlantic World, 1698–1700* (Edinburgh: University of Edinburgh Press, 2018).

47. Ignacio Gallup-Díaz, *The Door of the Seas and Key of the Universe: Indian Politics and Imperial Rivalry in the Darién, 1640–1750* (New York: Columbia University Press, 2008); Mónica Martínez Mauri, *La autonomía indígena en Panamá: La experiencia del pueblo kuna (siglos xvi-xxi)* (Quito, Ecuador: Ediciones Abya-Yala, 2011); Neil Whitehead, "Tribes Make States and States Make Tribes: Warfare and the Creation of Colonial Tribes and States in Northeastern South America," in *War in the Tribal Zone: Expanding States and Indigenous Warfare*, edited by R. Brian Ferguson and Neil L. Whitehead, 127–150 (Santa Fe, NM: School for Advanced Research, 2000).

48. Gallup-Díaz, *Door of the Seas*, 122–125.

49. Noble David Cook and W. George Lovell, *Secret Judgments of God: Old World Disease in Colonial Spanish America* (Norman: University of Oklahoma Press, 1992); Susanna Alchón, *A Pest in the Land: New World Epidemics in a Global Perspective* (Albuquerque: University of New Mexico Press, 2003); Lourdes Márquez Morfán and Rebecca Storey, "Population

History in Pre-Columbian and Colonial Times," in *Oxford Handbook of the Aztecs*, edited by Deborah L. Nichols and Enrique Rodríguez-Alegría, 189–200 (Oxford: Oxford University Press, 20); Thomas H. Charlton, Cynthia L. Otis Charlton, and Patricia Fournier García, "The Basin of Mexico A.D. 1450–1620: Archaeological Dimensions," in *The Postclassic to Spanish-Era Transition in Mesoamerica: Archaeological Perspectives*, edited by Susan Kepecs and Rani T. Alexander, 49–64 (Albuquerque: University of New Mexico Press, 2005).

50. Simon Lewis and Mark Andrew Maslin, "Defining the Anthropocene," *Nature* 519, no. 7542 (2015): 171–180; Ji-Hyung Cho, "The Little Ice Age and the Coming of the Anthropocene," *Asian Review of World Histories* 2, no. 1 (2014): 1–16.

51. Massimo Livi-Bacci, "The Depopulation of Hispanic America after the Conquest," *Population and Development Review* 32, no. 2 (2006): 199–232; Julie Hoggarth, Matthew Restall, James Wood, and Douglas Kennett, "Drought and Its Demographic Effects in the Maya Lowlands," *Current Anthropology* 58, no. 1 (2017): 82–113.

52. Lovell and Lutz, *Strange Lands*, 252.

53. Newson, *Cost of Conquest*, ch. 17; Linda Newson, *Indian Survival in Colonial Nicaragua* (Norman: University of Oklahoma Press, 1987).

54. Eugenia Ibarra Rojas, "Las epidemias del Viejo Mundo entre los indígenas de Costa Rica antes de la conquista española: ¿mito o realidad? (1502-1561)," *Mesoamérica* 19, no. 36 (1998): 593–618; Juan Carlos Solórzano, "La población indígena de Costa Rica en el siglo xvi al momento del contacto con los europeos," *Anuario de Estudios Centroamericanos* 43 (2017): 313–345.

55. Maxwell and Hill, *Kaqchikel Chronicles*, 245–248.

56. Victor Montejo, *Maya Intellectual Renaissance: Identity, Representation, and Leadership* (Austin: University of Texas Press, 2005), 31–32 and ch. 7. See also Arturo Arias, *Recovering Lost Footprints: Contemporary Maya Narratives*, Vol. 1 (Buffalo: State University of New York Press, 2017), 64–73; Edward Fischer and R. McKenna Brown, eds., *Maya Cultural Activism in Guatemala* (Austin: University of Texas Press, 1996); Kay Warren, *Indigenous Movements and Their Critics: Pan-Maya Activism in Guatemala* (Princeton, NJ: Princeton University Press, 1998); Betsy Konefal, *For Every Indio Who Falls: A History of Maya Activism in Guatemala, 1960–1990* (Albuquerque: University of New Mexico Press, 2010).

57. Marco Estrada Saavedra and Juan Pedro Viqueira, eds. *Los indígenas de Chiapas y la rebelión zapatista: microhistorias políticas* (México, D.F.: El Colegio de México, 2010); Shannan Mattiace, *To See With New Eyes: Political Identity and Indian Autonomy in Chiapas, Mexico* (Albuquerque: University of New Mexico Press, 2003); Rosalva Aída Castillo, *Histories and Stories from Chiapas: Border Identities in Southern Mexico* (Austin: University of Texas Press, 2001).

58. Allan Burns, *Maya in Exile: Guatemalans in Florida* (Philadelphia: Temple University Press, 1993); James Louky and Marlyn M. Moors, *The Maya Diaspora: Guatemalan Roots, New American Lives* (Philadelphia: Temple University Press, 2000). A similar literature has developed around the Garífuna diaspora in the United States; see Nancie L. González, *Sojourners of the Caribbean: Ethnogenesis and Ethnohistory of the Garífuna* (Urbana: University of Illinois Press, 1988); and Sara England, *Afro-Central Americans in New York City: Garífuna Tales of Transnational Movements in Racialized Space* (Gainesville: University Press of Florida, 2006).

59. Victor Montejo, *Maya Intellectural Renaissance*, xx, 1, 118.

60. India Rakusen with Nina Lakhani, "Honduras, a dam and the murder of Berta Cáceres," *The Guardian*, December 2, 2018. https://www.theguardian.com/news/audio/2018/dec/03/honduras-a-dam-and-the-of-berta-caceres

61. For instance, Arrellys Barbeyto and Edda Moreno Blanco, *Rescate de normas tradicionales de administración de justicia de acuerdo al derecho indígena del pueblo Miskitu en las diez comunidades indígena, municipio de Puerto Cabezas* (Managua, Nicaragua: URACCAN, Instituto de Estudios y Promoción de la Autonomía, 2008); Demetrio Cojtí Cuxil, "The Politics of Maya Revindication," in *Maya Cultural Activism in Guatemala*, edited by Edward Fischer and R. McKenna Brown, 19–50 (Austin: University of Texas Press, 1996); *Principios de derecho indígena maya k'iche': sobre el uso del agua, del bosque, y la vida silvestre: el caso de San Vicente Buenabaj, Momostenango, Totonicapán, Guatemala* (Ciudad de Guatemala: Centro de Acción Legal-Ambiental y Social de Guatemala, 2008).

62. Martínez, *Autonomía indígena en Panamá*.

63. "Diagnóstico de la Población Indígena en Panamá con base en los Censos de Población y Vivienda de 2010," Instituto Nacional de Estadística y Censo, 2010, http://www.contralo ria.gob.pa/inec/archivos/P6571INDIGENA_FINAL_FINAL.pdf; "X Censo de Población y VI de Vivienda 2011, Territorios indígenas: Principales indicadores demográficos y socioeconómicos" (San José, Costa Rica: Instituto Nacional de Estadistica y Censos, 2011), https://www.uned.ac.cr/extension/images/ifcmdl/02._Censo_2011._Territorios_ Indigenas.pdf;

64. Aldo Lauria-Santiago and Jeffrey Gould, *To Rise in Darkness: Revolution, Repression, and Memory in El Salvador* (Durham, NC: Duke University Press, 2008); Jorge Lemus, "Un modelo de revitalización lingüística: el caso de náhuat/pipil de El Salvador," *Identità delle Comunità Indigene del Centro America, Messico e Caraibi: aspetti culturali e antropologici*, edited by Antonio Luigi Palmisano, 127–149 (Rome: IILA, 2010).

65. Jeffrey Gould, *To Die in This Way: Nicaraguan Indians and the Myth of Mestizaje, 1880–1965* (Durham, NC: Duke University Press, 1998).

66. Jeffrey Gould, *El mito de "la Nicaragua mestiza" y la resistencia indígena, 1880–1980* (San José: Editorial de la Universidad de Costa Rica, 1997), 17. Capitalized section in the original: "No sólo hemos perdido nuestra lengua, sino que nos hemos desintegrado como comunidades a través de la destrucción de nuestros valores, tales como: la unidad comunical, la solidaridad, el respeto a los ancianos como autordades comunales, el transcendental papel de la mujer . . . Debido a nuestra resistencia no hemos desaparecido, nos quisieron asimilar (absorber) para que pensáramos igual que los colonizadores . . . para que rechazáramos nuestra cultura y se borrara nuestra conciencia indígena. A comienzos del presente siglo, existía en la Región Pacífico, Central y Norte una cantidad de comunidades indígenas, muchas de ellas han desaparecido, otras se han asimilado al resto de la sociedad. NOSOTROS ESTAMOS AQUI AFERRANDONOS A NUESTRAS RAICES PARA SOBREVIVIR CONTRA TODA ESA POLITICA DE ETNOCIDIO CULTURAL."

67. Matthew Restall, *Seven Myths of the Spanish Conquest* (Oxford: Oxford University Press, 2003), ch. 6.

68. Nancy J. Wellmeier, *Ritual, Identity, and the Mayan Diaspora* (New York: Garland Press, 1998), 17. The Maya must additionally contend with the romantic myth of the so-called Maya collapse of the ninth century, in reference to the abandonment of a cluster of large cities in the Maya lowlands of the Petén (Guatemala) and Belize. See Avexnim Cojti Ren, "Maya archaeology and the political and cultural identity of contemporary Maya in Guatemala," *Archaeologies* 2, no. 1 (2006): 8–19; and Patricia A. McAnany and Sarah Rowe,

Maya Cultural Heritage: How Archaeologists and Indigenous Communities Engage the Past (Lanham, MD: Rowman & Littlefield, 2016).

69. Luis Enrique Sam Colop, "The Discourse of Concealment and 1992," in *Maya Cultural Activism in Guatemala*, edited by Edward Fischer and R. McKenna Brown, 105, 112 (Austin: University of Texas Press, 1996).

FURTHER READING

Asselbergs, Florine. *Conquered Conquistadors: The Lienzo de Quauhquechollan: A Nahua Vision of the Conquest of Guatemala*. Boulder: University Press of Colorado, 2008.

Escalante Arce, Pedro. *Los tlaxcaltecas en Centro América*. San Salvador, El Salvador: Consejo Nacional para la Cultura y el Arte, 2001.

Jones, Grant. *The Conquest of the Last Maya Kingdom*. Stanford, CA: Stanford University Press, 1998.

Kramer, Wendy. *El español que exploró California: Juan Rodríguez Cabrillo (c. 1497–1543): de Palma del Río a Guatemala*. Córdoba, Spain: Diputación de Córdoba, 2018.

Lenkersdorf, Gudrun. *Genésis Histórica de Chiapas, 1522–1523: El conflicto entre Portocarerro y Mazariegos*. México City: Universidad Nacional Autónoma de México, 1993.

Lovell, W. George, and Christopher Lutz. *Strange Lands and Different Peoples: Spaniards and Indians in Colonial Guatemala*. Norman: University of Oklahoma Press, 2013.

Luján Muñoz, Jorge, and Horacio Cabezas Carcache. "El descubrimiento y la conquista." In *Historia General de Guatemala*, Vol. II, edited by Jorge Luján Muñoz and Ernesto Chinchilla Aguilar, 31–38. Guatemala: Asociación de Amigos del País/Fundación para la Cultura y el Desarrollo, 1994.

Mena García, María del Carmen. *El oro de Darién: Entradas y cabalgadas en la conquista de Tierra Firme (1509–1526)*. Seville, Spain: Consejo Superior de Investigaciones Científicas/Centro de Estudios Andaluces, 2011.

Montejo, Victor. *Maya Intellectual Renaissance: Identity, Representation, and Leadership*. Austin: University of Texas Press, 2005.

Newson, Linda. *The Cost of Conquest: Indian Decline in Honduras under Spanish Rule*. Boulder, CO: Westview Press, 1986.

Sherman, William. *Forced Native Labor in Sixteenth-Century Central America*. Lincoln: University of Nebraska Press, 1979.

Solórzano, Juan Carlos, and Claudia Quirós Vargas. *Costa Rica en el siglo XVI: descubrimiento, exploración y conquista*. San José: Editorial Universidad de Costa Rica, 2006.

CHAPTER 6

CENTRAL AMERICA UNDER SPANISH COLONIAL RULE

STEPHEN WEBRE

ON a scale without precedent in its day, the Spanish Empire sought to unify under its rule a widely scattered assortment of Iberian settlements and native communities. Separated by forbidding terrain and vast expanses of ocean, these outposts of colonial rule were held together by a precarious web of legal traditions, ideological assumptions, and primitive technologies of communication and transportation. Reliance upon sailing vessels and handwritten correspondence made it difficult for colonial authorities to maintain effective supervision over their new possessions.[1] Over time an administrative structure emerged that adjusted adequately, if not brilliantly, to the demands of a worldwide empire. This institutional construct exhibited many characteristics of the modern nation-state then taking form in contemporary Europe. Like its metropolitan counterpart, its ability to acquire and defend territorial control, extract revenue, and secure monopolies over the administration of justice and exercise of violence was limited. It may not be far-fetched to apply the term "state" to the improvised collection of institutions and practices by which Spain sought to exercise domination in its global holdings, but, given the distance that separated its agents from the ultimate center of authority and the exploitative nature of the enterprise as a whole, "colonial state" may be more appropriate.

Early studies of Spanish colonial administration tended to focus on legal precepts and formal institutions.[2] In what might be called the "sociological" approach, more recent efforts have sought to examine actual human behavior in specific historical contexts. Considering the merits of both traditional and innovative approaches, historian John Lynch has suggested that the gap between the two may not be as great as it seems, arguing that "it may be that the term 'colonial state' sounds more impressive than 'colonial institutions', and we are simply studying the same thing under a different name."[3] This chapter acknowledges the pertinence of Lynch's suggestion. Although it opts to employ the more current terminology, it is heavily indebted to the work of scholars laboring in both traditions.[4]

The traditional chronological frame of reference for discussions of the colonial era in Central America is the period between 1502 and 1821, that is, between the initial contact of European and Native American and the date conventionally cited to mark national independence from Spain. In geographical terms, colonial Central America typically refers to the area occupied by the modern republics of Guatemala, El Salvador, Honduras, Nicaragua, and Costa Rica, plus the Mexican state of Chiapas. Despite proximity and some similarity in historical experience, it is not generally understood to include Panama, which in the colonial era was more closely tied to Peru than to its northern neighbors. In studies of colonial Central America, Panama typically enters only when directly relevant to a larger issue, as does Belize, a former British colony sometimes thought of as Central American and sometimes as West Indian.[5]

During the Spanish regime the area now called Central America was known as Guatemala and might be referred to as the "audiencia of Guatemala," the "captaincy-general of Guatemala," or the "kingdom of Guatemala." Whatever the formal meaning of these terms may have been in the colonial era, writers since then have treated them as synonymous and interchangeable. The term "Guatemala" applied as well to the smaller territory that corresponded roughly to the modern republics of Guatemala and El Salvador combined. Guatemala was also the name applied to the largest and most important city in the region. The most populous and most culturally complex of the Central American provinces, Guatemala was also the richest in surviving historical documentation.[6] For that reason, it has been the most frequently studied by historians, anthropologists, geographers, and other specialists and it figures more prominently than its isthmian neighbors in the narrative and analysis that follow.

THE PEOPLE

To begin, one might ask who the subjects of the colonial state in Central America were. In 1502, when his fourth voyage carried him along the isthmus's sparsely settled Caribbean coast, the land that Christopher Columbus touched upon was already a cultural frontier. To the west and north, its Mesoamerican inhabitants were largely Mayas, but they included some Nahua-speakers as well. To the east and south were peoples of South American heritage. Whatever its origin, at the time of contact most of the region's population dwelt in the interior highlands and along the ample Pacific coastal plain, a pattern that continued for much time to come. Estimates of the number of native inhabitants living in Central America at the moment of initial contact with Europeans are numerous and wide-ranging. Counts collected and analyzed by W. George Lovell and Christopher H. Lutz range from a high of perhaps 13,500,000, to a low of approximately 800,000. For their part Lovell and Lutz prefer a number in the vicinity of 5,000,000.[7] Such figures remain controversial, as seen, for example, in Juan Carlos Solórzano Fonseca's defense of century-old estimates for Costa Rica in preference to more recent and higher numbers.[8]

In terms of human resources (from the colonial state's point of view, i.e., tax base and labor supply) the size of the region's population is important to know, but also important are the rate and direction of demographic change and the social realities that lie behind the numbers. As in other Spanish American overseas possessions, the initial encounter was followed closely by a massive population decline with notable impact on the formation of colonial societies. Once again, precise data are difficult to come by. Lovell and Lutz propose a native population loss between contact and the mid-seventeenth century of as much as 80 to 90 percent, a figure consistent with estimates reported for other Spanish overseas possessions.[9] Most authorities attribute this hecatomb to the introduction of previously unknown Old World diseases, but frequently mentioned as contributing factors also are losses due to warfare, forced migration, and the impact of coerced labor. Some scholars report that as many as 500,000 Indians may have perished from Nicaragua alone as a result of capture and shipment to slave markets in Panama and Peru. This figure is widely contested, among others by Patrick S. Werner and Frederick W. Lange, who demonstrate convincingly that such a total would far exceed the transport capacity of the ships available in Pacific ports to carry human cargos of the size suggested.[10]

The rapid decline of the native population during the first century of Spanish rule had economic and social effects. For one thing, it caused the abandonment of large expanses of previously productive agricultural land, which became available for grants to Spanish settlers. It also reduced the labor supply, prompting colonial authorities to promote measures for stricter control of remaining Indigenous communities. Meanwhile, Spanish landowners dedicated their new properties to labor-extensive activities, such as stock-raising and large-scale production of marketable commodities. These shifts accompanied what might be called a "biological revolution," which among other things brought the introduction of new crops, such as wheat and sugar cane, and new domesticated animals, such as cattle, sheep, horses, mules, and chickens.[11] They also involved a complex scrambling of human bloodlines.

As the native population of Central America shrank, the nonnative population expanded, due to both natural increase and immigration by Spaniards and enslaved Africans. Mostly young unaccompanied males, Spanish newcomers sought companionship among Indigenous and Afro-descendant women. Children born of unions between Spaniards and Indians were known as *mestizos,* and the offspring of Spaniards and Africans were called *mulatos.* Spanish colonial authorities saw racially discriminatory policies as both appropriate and desirable, but, in a world in which miscegenation was normalized and widely practiced, the task of identifying individuals by race became more complicated with each passing generation. At one point imperial policymakers recognized and documented as many as sixty-four specific degrees of race mixture, but for practical purposes colonial speakers collapsed all these categories into a few general labels, such as *casta* and *pardo.* An ethnic label with a history peculiar to Central America is *ladino.* Like casta and pardo, ladino was and remains more a cultural designation than a biological one. In the early colonial era it meant simply an Indian who spoke Spanish, but over time it came to apply to any Westernized person—that is, to any person not unambiguously identifiable as either Spanish or Indigenous.[12]

It is generally thought that native population reached its nadir and began to recover in the early seventeenth century, at which time demographic patterns familiar to later observers of Central America began to take definitive shape. Allowing for reporting errors remarked by Lovell and Lutz, a count dating from 1778 may offer a general glimpse of the isthmian population as it stood near the close of the colonial period. Of a total population for Central America of possibly 892,652, persons classified as Indians numbered 479,273, or about 54 percent. Although by far the largest component of the colonial population, the monarchy's Indigenous subjects had evidently recovered only a fraction of the losses they had experienced in the more than two centuries since the conquest. The next most numerous category in the report was ladinos, who numbered 297,400, or about 31 percent, followed by Spaniards, whose numbers totaled 133,979, or 15 percent.[13]

As informative as these numbers may appear, the reader should be aware that there are significant reporting gaps. For example, it would be good to know how many of the "Spaniards" appearing on the roll were peninsulars (Spaniards born in Spain), and how many were creoles (Spaniards born in the Americas). More interesting yet would be to know how many creoles were, in fact, not pure-blooded Europeans at all, but rather ladinos, who exploited possession of certain outward markers of elite status, such as light skin, education, or material wealth, to mask their humbler origins.[14] The absence of a separate count for enslaved persons, or for persons of African descent in general, may be evidence of the effectiveness of similar "whitening" strategies employed by those particular subaltern groups. Long marginalized, denied, or simply ignored in national historiographies, colonial Central America's significant Afro-descendant population began to receive serious scholarly attention only in the late twentieth century. Since what might be called the "discovery" of African influence, important work has been done on all the Central American countries.[15] Even for Costa Rica, a country with a strong reputation for historical scholarship but also a deeply rooted national myth of "Whiteness," scholars such as genealogist Mauricio Meléndez Obando and historian K. Russell Lohse have documented the extent to which even the most prominent of elite families numbered enslaved Africans among their ancestors.[16] Considering the 1778 census data in light of increased knowledge and understanding of the African experience in colonial Central America, it seems reasonable to imagine that by the final decades of the colonial period the isthmus's Black and mulato population had been largely absorbed into the ladino category, or possibly even that of creole Spaniards. As to the Afro-descendant inhabitants of the Caribbean coast, it is unlikely that imperial authorities took them into account at all.

Colonial Cities

Among other things, instituting Spanish rule in Central America meant founding cities, which if successful became platforms for defense, administration, production, exchange, and distribution, activities essential to the formation and maintenance of the colonial state. Among the earliest cities to be founded were Panama City (1519); Granada and León, Nicaragua (both 1524); San Salvador and San Miguel, El Salvador (1525 and 1530); San Pedro Sula and Comayagua, Honduras (1536 and 1537); and Ciudad Real, Chiapas (1538), later known as San Cristóbal de Las Casas. Due to warfare, earthquakes, and other hazards, many of these newly established cities did not remain in their original locations. This was conspicuously the case of Santiago de Guatemala, which, despite repeated misfortunes, over time became Central America's largest and most important urban center.

The conqueror Pedro de Alvarado established Santiago in 1524, choosing for a site Iximché, the principal city of his Kaqchikel Maya allies. The first Spanish inhabitants promptly abandoned the site, however, when their disillusioned hosts rose up against them.[17] In 1527, after roaming for three years throughout the central and western highlands, Alvarado's followers finally resettled in the valley of Almolonga, located on the lower slopes of Agua Volcano near the Indigenous settlement later known as Ciudad Vieja. Disaster soon struck again, however. In 1541, torrential rains loosened rocks and earth on the volcano's slopes, producing a massive landslide that destroyed Santiago de Guatemala, left many of its inhabitants dead or homeless, and induced the survivors to relocate themselves once again. This time the move was to a valley called Panchoy, where the new Santiago was constructed and where it remained, grew, and prospered until 1773, when a series of earthquakes left it so badly damaged that royal authorities ordered yet another removal, this time to the valley of La Ermita, approximately 45 kilometers from the remains of Santiago.[18] Named Nueva Guatemala de la Asunción, the new establishment eventually became the national capital known as Guatemala City. Many of Santiago's inhabitants joined the exodus to the new city, but others sought opportunity elsewhere, especially in Quetzaltenango, a K'iche' Maya town located in the western highlands.[19] Those who chose not to move stayed in place among the ruins of once-impressive baroque structures and worked to rebuild their lives and properties.[20] By the mid-twentieth century the old city gained new importance as the tourism center called Antigua Guatemala, formally recognized by the United Nations Educational, Scientific, and Cultural Organization (UNESCO) as a World Heritage Site.[21]

When it came to building a city, Renaissance-era Spaniards had a clear mental image of what one should look like.[22] Except in ports and mining centers, which tended to grow organically, streets in Spanish American cities were laid out perpendicularly, creating rectangular spaces to be distributed to settlers as *solares* (house sites) for residential use and the tending of household gardens and domestic animals. At the center of the grid was the *plaza mayor* (main square), an ample public arena for ceremonies, celebrations, markets, and recreational activities.[23] Encircling the plaza were the parish church, the *casas reales* (government house), and the *cabildo* (town hall), facilities whose presence emphasized the central space's importance to colonial life. Nonetheless, studies of colonial Santiago residential patterns by David L. Jickling challenge the common assertion that elite householders gathered purposely around the plaza and its immediate vicinity.[24]

If there was an accepted model for laying out a city, there was also a recognized scheme for governing one, and, as Helen Nader points out, any adult Castilian male would have been familiar with it.[25] With historic roots running back to the Middle Ages and perhaps even to the Roman era, the Spanish municipal council was known variously as the *concejo* or the *ayuntamiento*, but perhaps most often as the *cabildo*, a term that might refer to the body itself, to the building in which it met, or to any formal assembly of its members. As traditionally organized, a cabildo had two components, the *justicia* and the *regimiento*. Depending upon the size and importance of the municipality, the justicia consisted of either one or two *alcaldes ordinarios* (municipal magistrates) and was a court of first instance for civil and criminal matters arising within its jurisdiction. Once again varying with the size and importance of the municipality, the regimiento was made up of from four to twenty or more aldermen known as *regidores*, who were responsible for routine matters of municipal governance, such as public order; street maintenance; water supply; and oversight of prices, weights, and measures in local markets.[26]

Alcaldes ordinarios were elected by the regimiento for one-year terms, but the process for choosing regidores varied by time and place. In smaller places, they might be elected, also for one-year terms, either by the outgoing aldermen or by the body of Spanish settlers. In some cities that over time grew in population, wealth, and importance, methods of filling vacant positions might change. In Santiago de Guatemala, for example, a major urban center for which archival records survive in abundance, by the middle of the sixteenth century the Spanish monarchy began to grant petitions for direct appointments for life. By the 1590s, municipal offices were being sold at public auction, again for the life of the purchaser. These innovations had the effect of consolidating a powerful and influential municipal aristocracy, but, as studies by Stephen Webre and José Manuel Santos Pérez have revealed, the closed, hereditary, creole landowning oligarchies described in established historiography did not exist, at least not everywhere. In Santiago throughout the city's history, the municipal council was dominated by peninsula-born Spaniards, whose fortunes originated not in landholding but in trade, finance, transport, and similar activities.[27]

RURAL LIFE

Regardless of their specific ethnic origins, the native peoples of Central America had much in common. For example, they were all agriculturalists, dependent for their livelihoods on the production of domesticated plants and animals for both market and subsistence. For this reason, they tended to live not in densely nucleated settlements, as the Spanish did, but spread out through the countryside in proximity to their *milpas* (cultivated fields). Although rational from the Indigenous point of view, this preference poorly served the needs of imperial agents, whose task was to impose social control, tribute payment, and Christian belief on the monarchy's newest subjects. Promoted by religious leaders such as Francisco Marroquín and Bartolomé de Las Casas, beginning in the 1540s the solution adopted was to relocate the rural population to permanent towns, known as *congregaciones* or *reducciones*. In implementing the new policy, Roman Catholic missionaries were assisted by royal magistrates and native community leaders.[28] Many of the inhabitants of the newly created towns adapted well to their environments, and their towns survived as majority Indigenous communities, while others either disappeared or transformed into centers of ladino population.[29]

If urbanization promoted imperial rule by shaping Spanish settlement patterns, the congregation campaign did much the same for the native landscape. Like their Spanish and ladino counterparts, native towns were established as semiautonomous municipalities governed by cabildos composed of alcaldes ordinarios and regidores. Due to a paucity of records, these important bodies are little studied, but Kaqchikel historian Héctor Concohá has obtained valuable insight by probing the internal politics of his native town of San Juan Sacatepéquez.[30]

The formation of reductions represented a major alteration in the traditional Indigenous way of life, one that, along with other major changes, native peoples did not always accept easily. Forms of resistance observed throughout the colonial period ranged from violent uprisings to such passive responses as flight to neighboring unsettled areas or clandestine preservation of precontact religious beliefs, rituals, and lines of community authority. Although significant episodes of armed resistance were not as frequent as one might imagine, historian Severo Martínez Peláez has convincingly challenged the commonly held misconception that in general Central American Indians accepted colonial domination peaceably.[31] On the other hand, colonial-era resistance movements cannot generally be described as revolutionary. Rebellions with religious content tended to fuse together elements of both European and native belief systems, and even those uprisings that occurred in the context of the independence movements of the early nineteenth century focused more on the pursuit of localized objectives than on sweeping social or political change.[32]

Land and Labor

As in any agrarian society, land and labor were major issues in colonial Central America.

Due in part to native population decline during the sixteenth century, land was a relatively abundant resource throughout Central America, although some provinces offered more ready access to persons of modest means than did others. Easy availability of land in Costa Rica's central valley, for example, has been advanced in support of that country's myth of smallholding agrarian democracy, an argument critiqued by such scholars as Elizabeth Fonseca and Lowell Gudmundson.[33]

Given the matter's fundamental importance, the colonial state took an active interest in questions of land distribution.[34] To ensure that the people in the recently established Indigenous towns were able to feed themselves and meet their tribute obligations, new reduction villages, once they were formed, were assigned lands to be held in common. As part of Spanish settlement policy, non-Indian towns were granted lands as well. Some such grants were intended as *ejidos,* property held in common for use as pasturage and other collective needs. Other holdings served as *propios* (i.e., as sources of revenue for municipal governments). Both natives and Europeans had traditions of communal property holding, but Spaniards' interest lay more in entrepreneurial ventures than in mere subsistence, so they sought private property as well. Individual title to land could be acquired by *merced,* an outright royal concession, or by *composición,* a transaction that involved payment of a fee to regularize a title that might otherwise be questionable. After the 1590s, as the Spanish monarchy experienced increasing financial difficulties, composition became the favored method of conveying title to significant tracts of land.

Some private ownership of land occurred in Indian pueblos also, but communal possession was by far more common. A good deal of land was held by lay religious brotherhoods known as *cofradías,* or confraternities, which employed much of it in stock-raising. Confraternity wealth served to finance cult activities associated with the organization's patron saint and also for relief of members and their families in the event of illness, death, or other mishap. Indigenous patterns of land use seemed irrational to many Spaniards, who reported uncultivated tracts as abandoned in an effort to acquire them through composition. During the seventeenth century when the native population bottomed out, land may have seemed a surplus commodity, but later as Central America's Indian communities began to experience a demographic revival, pressure on available resources grew as well, leading to frequent litigation over boundaries, titles, and other issues associated with land ownership. Records of such disputes can be valuable documentation for students of social history.[35]

Historian Severo Martínez Peláez and other scholars have sought the origins of Central America's characteristic patterns of unequal land distribution in the colonial period. Although extensive landed estates did exist, especially in the western highlands and along the Pacific coast, the typical pattern appears to have been less reminiscent of the giant haciendas of northern New Spain described by François Chevalier and better represented by the mixture of private and common, small, medium, and large holdings identified by William B. Taylor in colonial Oaxaca.[36] The so-called mestizo agrarian blockade proposed by Severo Martínez Peláez as one of the factors favoring the emergence of latifundia in colonial Central America appears to have little support in the documentary record.[37]

In colonial Central America, land was of little use without the hands to work it. Spanish elites sought constantly for ways to access Indian labor at the lowest cost possible.[38] Even before the first European invaders entered the isthmian provinces, the Spanish monarchy had outlawed native slavery. Nonetheless, conquerors and settlers found pretexts to continue the practice, which remained common in the early years. A contemporary institution was the *encomienda,* under which specific Indigenous communities were assigned to favored Spaniards, who profited from their tribute payments and coerced labor. More than a labor institution, the encomienda was also a means for officials in Spain to reward loyal service and to establish the king's authority, all at minimal expense to the royal treasury. In return for the material benefits received, *encomenderos*, as the beneficiaries of encomienda grants were called, were expected to provide military service, administer justice, and promote the Christianization of their charges. Technically, encomienda Indians were not slaves but rather free vassals of the monarch. On a daily basis, however, the difference between these two conditions may have been difficult for their objects to appreciate. Abuses were common and well documented.

Promoted by the influential Dominican friar and defender of native rights Bartolomé de Las Casas, the New Laws issued at Barcelona in 1542 intended a major reform of native labor systems in the Spanish American Empire. Indian slavery was definitively forbidden and all remaining enslaved Indigenous persons were ordered freed. Also, the labor obligations of encomienda Indians were terminated. To meet the continued demand for native labor, the colonial state instituted a system known as *repartimiento* (distribution), under which native communities were each required to provide a certain number of workers on a rotating basis. Public functionaries would then apportion labor to Spanish petitioners, presumably according to need. Repartimiento differed from encomienda in that it took work assignments out of private hands and also ended the ecomenderos' monopoly claim to the available workforce. Also, the new system contained measures for the good treatment of draft laborers and required payment for work performed. In some colonies, such as New Spain, by the middle of the seventeenth century the repartimiento system gave way to free wage labor at least in agriculture, but in Central America it endured until the end of the colonial period, and in one form or another even beyond that.

Whenever issues concerning Indian labor were debated, Spanish settlers were quick to make the argument that Indians were "lazy," and that they would not plant crops even for their own subsistence except under coercion. Allegedly to prevent widespread starvation, royal authorities in Guatemala instituted a new office known as the *juez de milpas* (overseer of planting), whose task it was to conduct inspections of Indigenous communities to ensure that maize production quotas were being met.[39] Apparently unique in Spanish America, the *jueces de milpas* were the objects of repeated controversy. Citing the burden placed on Indigenous leaders to fulfill quotas while providing hospitality to visiting officials and their entourages, critics denounced the post as abusive. The monarchy outlawed the practice at least ten times between 1581 and 1681. In the end, however, as a source of public employment for needy Spaniards it was too beneficial to be given up.[40]

INSTITUTIONS OF COLONIAL RULE

The encomienda, congregation, and municipal institutions in general promoted the implantation of Spanish rule on a local level, but institutions with more extensive jurisdictions were needed as well. The outlines of the later territorial organization of Central America began to emerge as leaders of the conquest asserted claims to govern provinces that largely prefigured the modern republics. The first governor of Guatemala, for example, was the conqueror Pedro de Alvarado (1527–1541). In Nicaragua, Pedrarias Dávila (1527–1531) held command, and after him his son-in-law Rodrigo de Contreras (1534–1544). Possessed of gold and silver deposits considered significant at the time, Honduras was governed briefly by a royal appointee, Diego López de Salcedo (1525–1530), but soon found itself the object of competing Spanish ambitions. In 1539, Pedro de Alvarado surrendered his claim to Honduras to Francisco de Montejo, conqueror of Yucatan, in exchange for the latter's interest in Chiapas. Meanwhile, Costa Rica was late to come under Spanish rule. When it finally did so in the 1560s, Juan Vázquez de Coronado asserted his family's claim to the *adelantazgo* (hereditary governorship). Although more in form than in substance, the monarchy continued to recognize the Coronados' right to the title for generations to come.[41]

Early governors possessed ample powers, including the authority to make land grants and award encomiendas. The latter were particularly important in the political calculations of the early colony.[42] The provision of certain public services by individual encomenderos at Indigenous rather than royal expense helped to compensate for the colonial state's inability to maintain an autonomous bureaucracy of adequate size, training, and material resources. Aware of the role their cooperation played in sustaining colonial rule, the conquest veterans, first settlers, and other Spaniards who made up early Central America's dominant families repeatedly petitioned the monarchy for rewards and favors, including supplementary grants of income, appointments to remunerative public offices, and especially perpetual inheritance of encomiendas, an appeal that royal authorities consistently rejected. Wary of colonial ambition, the Castilian monarchy sought every opportunity to limit the political influence of local elites. During the sixteenth century, the monarchy implemented significant policy changes, but the fact is that the colonial state never possessed the human or material resources needed to establish unquestioned hegemony. Throughout the colonial period, for the state to perform its essential functions it remained dependent upon the voluntary collaboration of elites.[43]

A major step in the effort to strengthen the monarchy's grip on the new territories was the creation of royal tribunals known as *audiencias*. These bodies possessed executive, legislative, and judicial powers and were the supreme authorities in the districts they governed. Each audiencia consisted of a president and a varying number of *oidores* (judges). In order to insulate against excessive local elite influence, the monarchy drew audiencia personnel from the ranks of career civil servants, holders of university degrees, and only rarely of colonial birth. Like other officeholders in the Spanish Indies, presidents and oidores were all subject to both regular and extraordinary performance reviews, known, respectively, as *residencias* and *visitas*.

The first audiencia to be established in Spain's overseas possessions was at Santo Domingo in 1511, followed by Mexico in 1528, and Panama in 1538. In 1542, a provision of the New Laws authorized two additional tribunals, one at Lima and one to govern Central America. Originally to be called the audiencia of Los Confines, the new Central American high court initially convened at Gracias a Dios, a mining center in western

Honduras.[44] That location proved inconvenient, and in 1549 the audiencia moved its seat to Santiago de Guatemala, after which it became known as the audiencia of Guatemala. The body remained at Santiago until the earthquakes of 1773, when the colonial capital relocated to Guatemala City.

The Spanish monarchy recognized the growing importance of the audiencia presidency by assigning its occupant additional titles. In 1560, designation as governor-general of Guatemala acknowledged the president's sweeping executive authority throughout the Central American provinces, and 1609 saw the addition of the military grade of captain-general. Therefore, by the early seventeenth century the chief colonial magistrate of Central America bore three lofty titles simultaneously and might be referred to by any or all of them. Despite the multiple honorifics, it was not possible for the audiencia president to attend personally to every matter that arose in Spanish Central America. To address that need, beginning in the 1540s the monarchy introduced a corps of district magistrates, known variously as governors, *alcaldes mayores,* or *corregidores.*[45]

According to an administrative handbook compiled in the 1640s, at that time the audiencia of Guatemala was divided into four governorships, eight alcaldías mayores, and sixteen corregimientos.[46] In general, governors and alcaldes mayores received much higher salaries than corregidores, were appointed by the monarch, and were more likely to govern districts with significant resources, substantial non-Indian populations, or other distinguishing characteristics. By contrast, corregidores were usually assigned to heavily Indigenous areas. They were poorly paid, but, because they were named by the audiencia presidents rather than by authorities in Spain, their positions were more accessible to employment-seeking local elites, who pursued them energetically. Differences in pay and modes of appointment suggest a hierarchical relationship more apparent than real. In fact, there was no difference in the authority, responsibilities, or place in the chain of command of governors, alcaldes mayores, or corregidores.

A notable exception to the system described here was the jurisdiction known as the Corregimiento del Valle de Guatemala, which included the region immediately surrounding the city of Santiago. Governed on a rotating basis by the cabildo's two alcaldes ordinarios, the Valle de Guatemala was in reality a complex of seven smaller districts, all called "valleys" as well. With approximately eighty Indigenous communities, when the city of Santiago itself was included the Valle was home in the late seventeenth century to perhaps as many as 100,000 residents of all social levels. The district was a major source of income and the municipality's claim to it was frequently contested. On several occasions, colonial officials recommended that the arrangement be terminated, which was ultimately done in 1753.[47]

Church and State

Intimately involved in constructing the colonial state was the Roman Catholic Church, whose institutional presence was felt from the beginning. Ecclesiastical authorities maintained their own bureaucracy parallel to, and frequently entangled with, that of civil government. During the sixteenth and seventeenth centuries, the Spanish monarchy treated the Church as an ally essential to its imperial project, but by the closing decades of the colonial period royal officials came to see it more as rival than as partner.[48]

The basic unit of church administration was the parish, known in missionary areas by the term *doctrina*. Parishes in turn were organized into dioceses, and each diocese was presided over by a bishop. Under a long-standing traditional arrangement known as the *patronato real* (royal patronage), bishops and other senior ecclesiastical personnel were nominated by the king and submitted for papal approval, which was rarely withheld. During the colonial period there were four dioceses in Central America. Beginning with León, Nicaragua (1531), these included Trujillo, Honduras (1531, transferred to Comayagua in 1571); Santiago de Guatemala (1534); and Ciudad Real, Chiapas (1538). Similar to what occurred in colonial civil government, these divisions foreshadowed modern national boundaries, although what eventually became the republic of El Salvador did not have its own bishop until 1842 and Costa Rica not until 1850, in both cases well after independence from Spain. Initially, all the Central American dioceses were suffragan to the archbishop of Mexico, a subordinate relationship that lasted until 1743, when the diocese of Guatemala was itself elevated to metropolitan (archdiocesan) status.

Parishes were administered by *curas* (pastors), who, depending upon circumstances, might be *seculares* (diocesan clergy) or *religiosos* (members of religious orders). The latter was more likely to be so in mission doctrinas, where authorities tended to favor the assignment of members of religious orders, whom they perceived to be more learned, better disciplined, and more devout than their secular counterparts. Although a number of religious orders were present in colonial Central America, only three were heavily involved in evangelization efforts. Most numerous were the Franciscans, who maintained mission settlements in the central Guatemalan highlands, Honduras, Nicaragua, and what is now El Salvador. Franciscan friars were the only missionaries active in Costa Rica. For their part, Dominican friars dominated the missions in Chiapas and northern Guatemala, especially in Verapaz, subject of a notable experiment in "peaceful" conquest conceived by Bartolomé de Las Casas.[49] Finally, the Order of Mercy controlled the western highlands of Guatemala and also maintained a significant presence in Honduras and Nicaragua.[50]

Pastoral work was a departure for the order clergy, who in Europe were more accustomed to the contemplative routine of monastic life. Royal authorities anticipated that, once active evangelization was completed, the friars would be reassigned and their doctrinas secularized (i.e., transferred to diocesan control). Because order clergy operated under the direction of their own superiors outside episcopal supervision, both civil and ecclesiastical authorities considered successful completion of the secularization process to be vital to strengthening the colonial state. As was to be expected, missionary clergy resisted secularization, but at the same time secular priests had little interest in pastoral service in poor rural communities far from the comforts of city life and for which, in addition, they lacked the needed skills in Indigenous languages. As a consequence, the religious orders remained dominant in many areas until after independence, when they were suppressed by anticlerical Liberal regimes.

Apart from missionary work, the Church fulfilled many other purposes of the colonial state, providing divine reassurance in times of personal misfortune as well as times of epidemics, earthquakes, and other calamities. Clergy also drew upon the Church's moral authority to urge proper behavior and reinforce ideological conformity. Such tasks may be associated in popular imagination with the Holy Office of the Inquisition, but that body had no tribunal in Central America and local agents typically concerned themselves with such routine matters as complaints of sexual misconduct by clergymen and inspections of arriving vessels for contraband reading material.[51] Prosecutions for witchcraft did occur, and historian Martha Few has made good use of Mexico City tribunal records to study Central American women's involvement in illicit ritual activities.[52]

The Church's substantial material wealth reflected its lofty status in colonial society. Sources of ecclesiastical revenue included tithes, fees collected for the administration of certain sacraments, pious bequests and donations, and income from rental property and moneylending. These assets helped to finance ostentatious public display in the form of churches and other ecclesiastical buildings, elaborate altarpieces, paintings, sculptures, and other church furnishings.[53] Not everyone was impressed. For example, in his travel account published in London in 1648, the English-born Dominican friar Thomas Gage, who resided in Central America for several years during the 1620s and 1630s, wrote disdainfully of what he called "fat friars" and nuns who led lives of great luxury in the convents surrounded by private servants and even slaves.[54] Having converted to Protestantism following his return to England, Gage was scarcely an impartial observer, but in years to come, Spanish reformers would echo some of his concerns, citing as obstacles to economic expansion the so-called dead hand of the Church, the number of priests and nuns maintained without productive employment, and the frequency in the liturgical calendar of designated feast days, on which work was not performed and business not transacted. Agents of a financially pressed monarchy, Spanish officials coveted what they perceived as copious assets held or administered in one way or another by the Church. These included the *cajas de comunidad* (community chests) maintained by Indian pueblos, the rents due on funds invested by cofradías, and the principal represented by *capellanías* (private trust funds established for the long-term support of family members who chose to pursue clerical careers) invested with monasteries, convents, and other ecclesiastical institutions. When toward the close of the colonial period, the monarchy attempted to liquidate and take control of these assets, the result was resentment, resistance, and evasion.[55]

It was one thing to appraise ecclesiastical wealth in terms of its supposed impact on the colonial economy or its potential to close gaps in the imperial budget but quite another to appreciate the implications of the Church's connectedness to colonial subjects at all levels of society. For example, prosopographical research by historian Christophe Belaubre has shown in detail the ties binding elite creole families to the Roman Catholic clergy in Central America and the pecuniary interests involved.[56] Linkages existed to humbler sectors as well. The fact is that Church wealth was not employed solely in ostentatious display but also in a number of socially beneficial ways that might be seen to serve the ends of the colonial state as well. These included mortgage lending and other financial services, education at all levels, hospitals, and assistance to the poor. Because access to these benefits was concentrated in the most important urban centers, there were serious inequities in their distribution, but the Church nonetheless maintained a crucial presence even in the most remote parishes. According to Adriaan Cornelis van Oss, "in the colonial period no policy could be executed, no census carried out, no tax collected, without the intervention of the parish priest. To the Spanish colonial mind, the rural clergy provided the difference between order and anarchy in the countryside."[57]

COLONIAL SPACE AND IMPERIAL SPACE

Referring to colonial Argentina and Chile, historian Margarita Gascón has proposed a useful distinction between "colonial space" and "imperial space." Events that occurred in colonial space would be known to local residents and possibly to local authorities, but rarely more than that. By contrast, when something happened in imperial space, it was likely to draw the attention of important regional interests and even of royal officials in Spain itself.[58] Occurrences in such an environment were most likely to attract metropolitan scrutiny if they appeared to threaten a colony's production of wealth or its role in strategic imperial defense.

A peripheral possession without the massive mineral endowments of New Spain or Peru, Central America might seem to belong permanently to colonial space. Even so, there were some places whose location or other circumstances situated them for better or worse in the realm of imperial concern. Among these, trans-isthmian transit routes and their terminal ports ranked highly. For example, the Lake Nicaragua–San Juan River corridor provided European rivals to Spanish dominion with a possible alternative to Panama as a passage for crossing from the Atlantic to the Pacific coast. Situated on the lake itself, Granada was ideally placed to link a Pacific-slope hinterland to the Atlantic world via connections to Caribbean ports, such as Matina, Portobelo, or Cartagena de Indias.[59] Other important and potentially vulnerable ports on the Atlantic side were Trujillo, Puerto Caballos, and Santo Tomás de Castilla, and on the Pacific coast Caldera, El Realejo, and Sonsonate.[60] Sensitive locations other than ports included the Honduran silver-mining district surrounding Tegucigalpa, whose modest output nonetheless played an important role in providing specie to buoy the local economy and help the colonial state cover its obligations.[61] Finally, there were the still-unconquered territories of Itzá and Lacandón in the Guatemalan Petén, Taguzgalpa and Tologralpa (known collectively as the Mosquito Coast) on the Caribbean littorals of Honduras and Nicaragua, and Talamanca in Costa Rica.[62]

From the beginning, Spanish settlers sought ways to insert themselves into imperial space, which offered greater prospects of influence and reward. Multiple efforts to find what Murdo J. MacLeod, following historians of Atlantic commerce Pierre and Huguette Chaunu, calls a *produit moteur*, that is, a product able to link profitably to external markets, foreshadowed the emergence in Central America of a monocultural export economy. Characterized by cycles of boom and bust and extremely sensitive to outside forces, such an economy would dominate Central America until at least the late twentieth century, when stronger tendencies toward diversification came to prevail.

In a now-classic work first published in 1973, MacLeod outlines a series of alternating cycles of prosperity and economic collapse. According to this scheme, Spanish economic activity during the first half century of the colonial experience (1520s to 1570s) amounted essentially to pillage. Easily extracted by exploiting plentiful Indigenous labor, marketable commodities such as gold, slaves, and cacao promised healthy returns with little investment. By the 1570s, the pillage economy reached its limits, due among other causes to severe epidemics, which accelerated the process of native population decline. During the recessionary cycle that followed (1580s–1630s), government officials promoted efforts to revive the economy, including experimentation with new products and construction of port facilities. Such activities yielded little benefit, however, and by the 1630s the colony was sinking into a prolonged depression, which, according to MacLeod endured for the next five decades (1630s–1680s). Among the outcomes of this economic contraction was the abandonment of urban centers by impoverished Spaniards and ladinos, an increase in the countryside of non-Indigenous small holding, and a more pronounced ethnic bifurcation, in which the region west of Santiago de Guatemala became more firmly identified as Indian, while that stretch of Central American territory lying to the east experienced an increased loosening of native cultural identity. Finally, a weakening of regional unity occurred, as shifts in market demand redirected economic activity toward new opportunities. For example, Costa Rica found itself drawn to Panama, while Chiapas's production found more profitable opportunities in markets in New Spain.[63]

MacLeod's secular depression represents an important intervention in the lengthy debate over a "general crisis of the seventeenth century."[64] Although colonial Central America has not attracted as much scholarly attention as European examples, or even such major Spanish American centers as Mexico or Peru, the depression thesis has been challenged in particular by historians Miles L. Wortman, who sees greater signs of intercolonial trade and circulation of metal money than MacLeod does, and Jorge Luján Muñoz, who stresses the documentary evidence for the robust local economy of the Valle de Guatemala. Although Wortman accepts the existence of a Central American crisis, he dates it much later in the century than MacLeod and presents it more in political than economic terms.[65]

Whatever conclusion scholars may ultimately reach about the existence, precise nature, and chronological and geographic dimensions of a "general crisis," it should not be difficult to agree that a crisis and a depression are not necessarily the same thing. On the other hand, the documentary record does offer abundant evidence that in the late seventeenth and early eighteenth centuries, the colonial state in Central America was experiencing at least a "crisis of authority."[66] As noted previously, the colonial state depended for what effectiveness it possessed upon the collaboration of local elites, who provided necessary personnel for the discharge of public responsibilities and also contributed financially to sustain essential state functions for which there was no room in the royal budget.[67] As necessary as this partnership may have been, it had its disadvantages from the monarchy's point of view. Colonial elites expected something in return for their services and what royal authorities were most able to offer were abundant opportunities for graft, whether through the abuse of public office or of more general practices that incentivized disregard for the law.[68] The result was that Central America was notoriously difficult to govern and that royal authorities were frequently the objects of disrespect, as evidenced among other things by the 1688 assassination attempt against an unpopular oidor. In an effort to exert greater control, between 1671 and 1702 officials in Spain ordered four *visitas generales* to investigate allegations of public corruption. None of these inquiries yielded useful results and the last one ended when the *visitador* was driven from the province.

BOURBON CENTRAL AMERICA

A serious attempt to reorganize the colonial state began in 1700. In that year, King Charles II died without issue and was replaced on the throne by his cousin, Philip V. The change marked the end of the Spanish Habsburg line and the arrival in power of the French Bourbons. Like his grandfather, King Louis XIV of France, the new Spanish monarch was an advocate of royal absolutism, and he saw much need for improvement in a state apparatus that he and his imported ministers considered corrupt and inefficient. In response, Philip launched an ambitious series of policy changes that continued under his successors, especially King Charles III (1759–1788). Known as the Bourbon Reforms, these measures sought to promote economic expansion, professionalize the bureaucracy, and strengthen imperial defenses. More than anything, however, they aimed to increase revenue and consolidate royal authority. In Central America, this meant the abandonment of familiar practices in favor of new impositions by a reinvigorated colonial state.[69]

A thorough redesign of imperial administration would have been beyond the means of the Habsburg monarchy. Throughout the eighteenth century, however, the Bourbons enjoyed a booming colonial economy, due primarily to indigo, for which demand was growing in England and other North Atlantic textile-production centers. The newfound prosperity was welcome, but it had its drawbacks. For example, it depended heavily on trade with Great Britain, with which Spain was frequently at war and with which, in any case, Spanish commercial regulations prohibited commerce. Not only did the indigo trade appear to promote smuggling, but also it encouraged regional and social resentments. Salvadoran producers complained of exploitation by Guatemalan merchants, who controlled credit, marketing, and transport, and the latter feared displacement by a new wave of peninsular immigrants, among them the powerful Aycinena family.[70]

In addition to their financial good fortune, Bourbon administrators proved to be resourceful and demanding as they identified new sources of revenue and appropriated old ones. One early target was the Roman Catholic Church, whose wealth and power modernizing bureaucrats saw as obstacles to the consolidation of an absolutist state. Measures adopted to assert civil control of Church assets brought in additional income, but they also inspired disaffection, as did reforms adopted to impose order, accountability, and equity on the collection of taxes. One unpopular innovation was the establishment of *estancos* (state monopolies) over certain commodities, among them tobacco and *aguardiente* (an inexpensive intoxicating beverage).[71] Under this system, the monopoly determined where, by whom, and at what price these items of general consumption could be produced or sold. Such restrictions were offensive to interests at all levels of colonial society, including to creole elites, who resented the award of lucrative monopoly concessions to peninsulars in preference to American-born Spaniards. Rejection of the estancos could even turn violent, as happened in 1786 when opposition to the aguardiente monopoly provoked a riot in Quetzaltenango.[72]

Although raised at some political cost, new revenues served to fund the expansion of the colony's administrative infrastructure. Major new positions included the intendancies, introduced in Central America in 1786. Modeled on a French institution that dated to the previous century, intendants possessed broad authority at the provincial level, were generously compensated, and, to the annoyance of job-seeking creoles, tended to be recruited from peninsular ranks. With the exception of Guatemala, which continued to be governed by the captain-general, the reform divided Central America into four intendancy districts: Chiapas; El Salvador, separated from Guatemala for the first time; Honduras; and Nicaragua, which now included the formerly separate Costa Rica. The intendancy system was introduced too late in the colonial period to evaluate its effectiveness. Salvadoran elites were likely pleased by the new dispensation, which recognized them as a separate jurisdiction for the first time, but Costa Ricans, who found their province now subordinated to Nicaragua, may well have felt otherwise.[73]

Most of the new revenue went to an expensive reform of provincial defenses. This project called for construction of fortifications at strategic locations, notably Omoa on the Caribbean cost of Honduras, and also for a reorganization of the colonial militia. Existing companies were increased in strength, issued quality weapons, and taught proper military discipline, and experienced peninsular officers were brought into staff command and training positions. Creole elites may have grumbled at their initial exclusion from the higher ranks, but when authorities in Spain failed to rotate in new peninsular personnel on a regular basis, American-born Spaniards came to dominate senior positions anyway. In any case, the reformed militia appeared to demonstrate its worth in 1782 when it drove the British from their positions on the Mosquito Coast, thus eliminating the single greatest threat to colonial Central America's territorial integrity.[74]

Historians differ in their assessments of the Bourbon Reforms. In terms of the monarchy's specific objectives, the changes may have been successful, at least temporarily, and the unlikely triumph of Spanish arms over the British might seem to prove the point. But the reforms also altered colonial life in ways obnoxious not only to creole elites but also to Indian and ladino masses. The true test would come in 1808 with the imperial crisis precipitated by Napoleon Bonaparte's invasion of Spain. As historian Miles L. Wortman summarizes what happened next, "When Spain itself came under attack in the nineteenth century, the fissure became a fracture, the center gave out, the colony became independent localities, and order was destroyed."[75]

Notes

1. Sylvia Sellers-García, *Distance and Documents at the Spanish Empire's Periphery* (Stanford, CA: Stanford University Press, 2014), is an admirable history of the production, distribution, and storage of written records in colonial Central America.
2. For example, C. H. Haring, *The Spanish Empire in America* (New York: Oxford University Press, 1947); Mario Góngora, *El estado en el derecho indiano: época de fundación, 1492–1570* (Santiago de Chile: Universidad de Chile, 1951).
3. John Lynch, "The Institutional Framework of Colonial Spanish America," *Journal of Latin American Studies* 24 (1992).
4. Murdo J. MacLeod's suggested label "primitive nation state" seems to pass over the "colonial" nature of the phenomenon, but his little-known essay, "The Primitive Nation State, Delegation of Functions, and Results: Some Examples from Early Colonial Central America," in *Essays in the Political, Economic and Social History of Colonial Latin America*, ed. Karen Spalding, 53–68 (Newark: University of Delaware, Latin American Studies Program, 1982), is a thorough and insightful analysis of the colonial state in the specific case of Central America, what it was, and how it functioned.
5. Belize's Spanish-colonial experience has only recently received serious scholarly attention. See Mavis C. Campbell, *Becoming Belize: A History of an Outpost of Empire Searching for Identity, 1528–1823* (Kingston: University of West Indies Press, 2011. On colonial Panama, see Christopher Ward, *Imperial Panama: Commerce and Conflict in Isthmian America, 1550–1800* (Albuquerque: University of New Mexico Press, 1993).
6. The principal documentary repositories for studying colonial Central America are the Archivo General de Centroamérica, Guatemala City, and the Archivo General de Indias, Seville.
7. W. George Lovell and Christopher H. Lutz, *Demography and Empire: A Guide to the Population History of Spanish Central America, 1500–1821*, Dellplain Latin American Studies, no. 33 (Boulder, CO: Westview Press, 1995), 5.
8. Juan Carlos Solórzano Fonseca, "La población indígena de Costa Rica en el siglo XVI al momento del contacto con los europeos," *Anuario de Estudios Centroamericanos* 43 (2017): 313–345.
9. Lovell and Lutz, *Demography and Empire*, 6.
10. Patrick S. Werner and Frederick W. Lange, "Un nuevo punto de vista de la exportación de esclavos en Nicaragua durante el siglo XVI," *Cuadernos de Antropología* 30, no. 1 (2020): 1–22.
11. For Central America, this process is described in detail by Iraís Alquicira Escartín, "Redes de abasto y sociedad en el reino de Guatemala durante el siglo XVII" (PhD diss.,

Centro de Investigaciones y Estudios Superiores, Unidad Peninsular, Mérida, Yucatán, México, 2017).

12. "Ladino" is often treated as synonymous with "mestizo," but the matter is more complex than that. See, e.g., Julian Pitt-Rivers, "Mestizo or Ladino?" *Race: The Journal of the Institute of Race Relations* 10, no. 4 (April 1969): 463–477; and John M. Watanabe, "Racing to the Top: Descent Ideologies and Why Ladinos Never Meant to be Mestizos in Colonial Guatemala," *Latin American and Caribbean Ethnic Studies* 11, no. 3 (November 2016): 305–322.

13. Lovell and Lutz, *Demography and Empire*, 105–106.

14. A provocative study argues that ethnic reassignment could function downward as well, as creole families that settled in rural areas came to live as, and be considered to be, ladinos. See Isabel Rodas Núñez, *De españoles a ladinos: Cambio social y relaciones de parentesco en el altiplano central colonial guatemalteco* (Guatemala City, Guatemala: Ediciones ICAPI, 2004).

15. For a useful guide to some of the most important contributions, see the essays in Lowell K. Gudmundson and Justin Wolfe, eds., *Blacks and Blackness in Central America: Between Race and Place* (Durham, NC: Duke University Press, 2010. Particularly strong on shifting identities is Paul Lokken, "From Black to Ladino: People of African Descent, Mestizaje, and Racial Hierarchy in Rural Colonial Guatemala, 1600–1730" (PhD diss., University of Florida, 2000).

16. Tatiana Lobo and Mauricio Meléndez Obando, *Negros y blancos, todo mezclado* (San José: Editorial Universidad de Costa Rica, 1997); K. Russell Lohse, *Africans into Creoles: Slavery, Ethnicity, and Identity in Colonial Costa Rica* (Albuquerque: University of New Mexico Press, 2014).

17. The standard account of the early history of Guatemala City is Christopher H. Lutz, *Santiago de Guatemala, 1541–1773: City, Caste, and the Colonial Experience* (Norman: University of Oklahoma Press, 1994).

18. The most comprehensive treatment of the destruction and relocation of the colonial capital is Christophe Belaubre, "El traslado de la capital del reino de Guatemala, 1773–1779: conflictos de poder y juegos sociales," *Revista de Historia* (Heredia, Costa Rica) no. 57–58 (Jan.–Dec.2008): 23–61. See also María Cristina Zilbermann de Luján, *Aspectos socioeconómicos del traslado de la ciudad de Guatemala, 1773–1783* (Guatemala City: Academia de Geografía e Historia de Guatemala, 1987).

19. On the emergence of Quetzaltenango from K'iche' pueblo to Guatemala's western metropolis, see especially Jorge González Alzate, *La experiencia colonial y transición a la independencia en el occidente de Guatemala: Quetzaltenango: de pueblo indígena a ciudad multiétnica, 1520–1825* (Mérida: Universidad Nacional Autónoma de México, 2015).

20. Mario René Johnston Aguilar, "De Santiago de Guatemala a la Villa de La Antigua Guatemala: Transformación y vida social ante una crisis" (licenciatura thesis, Universidad del Valle de Guatemala, 1997).

21. Other colonial Central American cities recognized by UNESCO are Panamá Viejo and León Viejo, Nicaragua.

22. Dan Stanislawsky, "Early Spanish Town Planning in the New World," *Geographical Review* 37, no. 1 (Jan. 1947): 94–107.

23. For a vivid account of daily life at colonial Santiago's central market, see Alquicira Escartín, "Redes de abasto," 152–198. Also, Luis Luján Muñoz, *La plaza mayor de Santiago de Guatemala hacia 1678*, Publicación Especial, no. 3 (Guatemala City, Guatemala: Instituto de Antropología e Historia, 1969.

24. David L. Jickling, "Los vecinos de Santiago de Guatemala en 1604," *Mesoamérica* 3, no. 3 (1982): 145–231.

25. Nader, *Liberty in Absolutist Spain: The Habsburg Sale of Towns, 1516–1700* (Baltimore: Johns Hopkins University Press, 1990), 38–45.

26. Ernesto Chinchilla Aguilar, *El ayuntamiento colonial de la ciudad de Guatemala* (Guatemala City, Guatemala: Editorial Universitaria, 1960); Stephen Webre, "The Social and Economic Bases of Cabildo Membership in Seventeenth-Century Santiago de Guatemala" (PhD diss., Tulane University, 1980).

27. Webre, "Social and Economic Bases"; José Manuel Santos Pérez, *Elites, poder local y regimen colonial: el cabildo y los regidores de Santiago de Guatemala, 1700–1787* (Cádiz, Spain: Servicio de Publicaciones, Universidad de Cádiz, 1999).

28. Carmelo Sáenz de Santa María, "La reducción a poblados en el siglo XVI en Guatemala," *Anuario de Estudios Americanos* 29 (1972): 187–228.

29. Sidney D. Markman, "Extinción, fosilización y transformación de los 'pueblos de indios' del reino de Guatemala," *Mesoamérica* 8, no. 14 (December 1987): 407–427. According to Patrick S. Werner, "Un bosquejo de la dinámica de la población de Nicaragua, 1548–1685," *Nicaraguan Academic Journal* 5, no. 1 (July 2011): 81–101, of 115 native villages counted in Nicaragua in 1581 only 64 still existed a century later.

30. Héctor Aurelio Concohá Chet, "El concepto de montañés entre los kaqchikeles de San Juan Sacatepéquez, 1524–1700," in *La época colonial en Guatemala: Estudios de historia cultural y social*, ed. Robinson A. Herrera and Stephen Webre, 19–41 (Guatemala City, Guatemala: Editorial Universitaria, 2013).

31. Martínez Peláez, *Motines de indios: La violencia colonial en Centroamérica y Chiapas* (Puebla, Mexico: Universidad Autónoma, Centro de Investigaciones Históricas y Sociales, 1983).

32. See, for example, Kevin Gosner, *Soldiers of the Virgin: The Moral Economy of a Colonial Maya Rebellion* (Tucson: University of Arizona Press, 1992); Aaron Pollack, *Levantamiento k'iche' en Totonicapán, 1820: Los lugares de las políticas subalternas* (Guatemala City: Asociación para el Avance de las Ciencias Sociales en Guatemala, 2008).

33. Elizabeth Fonseca, *Costa Rica colonial: La tierra y el hombre*, 2nd ed. (San José, Costa Rica: Editorial Universitaria Centroamericana, 1984); Lowell Gudmundson, *Costa Rica before Coffee: Society and Economy on the Eve of the Export Boom* (Baton Rouge: Louisiana State University Press, 1986).

34. Despite the issue's importance, there is no solid general history of land tenure for colonial Central America as a whole. A good body of work exists for Guatemala, including Francisco de Solano, *Tierra y sociedad en el reino de Guatemala* (Guatemala City, Guatemala: Editorial Universitaria, 1977); David McCreery, *Rural Guatemala, 1760–1940* (Stanford: Stanford University Press, 1994); and J. C. Cambranes, *Ruch'ojinem qalewal: 500 años de lucha por la tierra: Estudios sobre propiedad rural y reforma agraria en Guatemala* (Guatemala: Editorial Cholsamaj, 2004). Also useful are various contributions to the country's rich tradition of community studies, such as Michele Bertrand, *Terre et société coloniale: Les communautés maya-quichés de la region de Rabinal du XVIe au XIXe siècle* (Mexico City: Centre d'Etudes Mexicaines et Centraméricaines, 1987); W. George Lovell, *Conquest and Survival in Colonial Guatemala: A Historical Geography of the Cuchumatán Highlands, 1500–1821*, 3rd ed. (Montreal and Kingston: McGill-Queen's University Press, 2005); and Daniele Pompejano, *Popoyá-Petapa: historia de un poblado maya, siglos XVI–XIX* (Guatemala: Editorial Universitaria, 2009). Nothing comparable exists for other Central American countries, but two essential studies are Fonseca, *Costa Rica*

colonial, and Germán Romero Vargas, *Las estructuras sociales de Nicaragua en el siglo XVIII* (Managua: Editorial Vanguardia, 1987).

35. A valuable guide to land records surviving for colonial Guatemala is Gustavo Palma Murga, ed., *Indice general del Archivo del Extinguido Juzgado Privativo de Tierras depositado en la Escribanía de Cámara del Supremo Gobierno de la República de Guatemala* (Mexico City, Mexico: Ediciones de la Casa Chata, 1991).

36. François Chevalier, *Land and Society in Colonial Mexico: The Great Haciendas*, ed., trans. Alvis Eustin (Berkeley: University of California Press, 1963); William B. Taylor, *Landlord and Peasant in Colonial Oaxaca* (Stanford, CA: Stanford UniversityPress, 1972).

37. Severo Martínez Peláez, *La patria del criollo: An Interpretation of Colonial Guatemala*, ed. W. George Lovell and Christopher Lutz, trans. Susan M. Neve, 92–96 (Durham, NC: Duke University Press, 2009).

38. William L. Sherman, *Forced Native Labor in Sixteenth-Century Central America* (Lincoln: University of Nebraska Press, 1979).

39. Manuel Rubio Sánchez, *Los jueces reformadores de milpas en Centroamérica* (Guatemala City: Academia de Geografía e Historia de Guatemala, 1982).

40. Stephen Webre, "El trabajo forzoso de indígenas en la política colonial guatemalteca (siglo XVII)," *Anuario de Estudios Centroamericanos* 13, no. 2 (1987): 49–61.

41. D. L. Molinari, "Los distritos institucionales en Centro América, 1522–1563", in *Contribuciones para el estudio de la historia de América: homenaje al doctor Emilio Ravignani* (Buenos Aires, Argentina: Peuser, 1941), 571–604.

42. Wendy Kramer, *Encomienda Politics in Early Colonial Guatemala,1524–1544: Dividing the Spoils*, Dellplain Latin American Studies, no. 31 (Boulder, CO: Westview Press, 1994).

43. MacLeod, "Primitive Nation State," emphasizes the extent to which the Habsburg monarchy relied upon elite collaboration to ensure performance of essential state functions.

44. The name signified that the new audiencia lay between and included Chiapas and Nicaragua; in other words, it was too far removed from the audiencias of Mexico City and Panama to be adequately served by either of those courts.

45. Carlos Molina Argüello, "Gobernaciones, alcaldías mayores y corregimientos en el reino de Guatemala," *Anuario de Estudios Americanos* 17 (1960): 105–132.

46. Juan Diez de la Calle, *Memorial, y noticias sacras, y reales del imperio de las Indias occidentales* (Madrid: 1646).

47. Beatriz Suñe Blanco, "El Corregimiento del Valle de Guatemala: una institución española para el control de la población indígena," *Revista de la Universidad Complutense* 28, no. 117 (1979): 153–168; Jorge Luján Muñoz, *Agricultura, mercado y sociedad en el corregimiento del Valle de Guatemala, 1670–80* (Guatemala City: Dirección de Investigación, Universidad de San Carlos de Guatemala, 1988), 20–23.

48. Studies on church topics are plentiful. Representative of some of the best work in the field are Adriaan C. van Oss," Catholic Colonialism: A Parish History of Guatemala, 1524–1821" (PhD diss., University of Texas, 1982); José María Tojeira, *Panorama histórico de la iglesia en Honduras* (Tegucigalpa: Centro de Documentación de Honduras, 1986); Carmela Velásquez Bonilla, *El mundo de la piedad colonial: Ritos y mentalidad religiosa en la diócesis de Nicaragua y Costa Rica, siglos XVII y XVIII* (San José, Costa Rica: Editorial Universidad Estatal a Distancia, 2016).

49. For a detailed account of early Dominican activities in Verapaz, see André Saint-Lu, *La Vera Paz: Esprit évangélique et colonisation* (Paris: Centre des Recherches Hispaniques, Institut des Études Hispaniques, 1968).

50. Anne C. Collins, "La misión mercedaria y la conquista espiritual del occidente de Guatemala," in *La sociedad colonial en Guatemala: Estudios locales y regionales*, ed. Stephen Webre, 1–31 (Antigua Guatemala: Centro de Investigaciones Regionales de Mesoamérica, 1989); Víctor C. Cruz Reyes, *El convento mercedario de las minas de Tegucigalpa, 1650–1830* (Tegucigalpa: Instituto Hondureño de Antropología e Historia, 1989); Nancy J. Black, *The Frontier Mission and Social Transformation in Western Honduras: The Order of Our Lady of Mercy, 1525–1773* (Leiden, The Netherlands: E. J. Brill, 1995).

51. Ernesto Chinchilla Aguilar, *La Inquisición en Guatemala* (Guatemala City, Guatemala: Editorial Universitaria, 1953).

52. Martha Few, *Women Who Live Evil Lives: Gender, Religion, and the Politics of Power in Colonial Guatemala, 1650–1750* (Austin: University of Texas Press, 2003).

53. An innovative study by Brianna Leavitt-Alcántara, *Alone at the Altar: Single Women and Devotion in Guatemala, 1670–1870* (Stanford, CA: Stanford University Press, 2018), reveals the role played by widows and spinsters of all social levels in financing Church activities.

54. Thomas Gage, *Thomas Gage's Travels in the New World*, ed. J. Eric S. Thompson, 188–191 (Norman: University of Oklahoma Press, 1958).

55. For a detailed account of one ecclesiastical institution's financial activities, see Christophe Belaubre, "Lugar del poder y poder del lugar: el convento de la Concepción en la capital del reino de Guatemala, siglo XVIII," in *La época colonial en Guatemala: Estudios de historia cultural y social*, ed. Robinson A. Herrra and Stephen Webre, 133–168 (Guatemala City, Guatemala: Editoria Universitaria, 2013).

56. Christophe Belaubre, *Élus de Dieu et élus de monde dans le royaume de Guatemala, 1753–1808: Église, familles de pouvoir et réformateurs bourbons* (Paris: Harmattan, 2012).

57. Van Oss, "Catholic Colonialism," 99.

58. Margarita Gascón, *Periferias imperiales y fronteras coloniales en Hispanoamérica* (Buenos Aires, Argentina: Editorial Dunken, 2011), 9–10.

59. Carlos Meléndez Chaverri, "Historia más antigua de la ciudad de Granada en Nicaragua y de su fase de desarrollo como puerto del Caribe, 1524–1685," *Revista del Archivo Nacional* (San José) 63 (1994): 111–137; David Radell, "Exploration and Commerce on Lake Nicaragua and the Río San Juan, 1524–1800," *Journal of Inter-American Studies and World Affairs* 12 (1970): 107–125.

60. Taylor E. Mack, "Ephemeral Hinterlands and the Historical Geography of Trujillo, Honduras, 1525–1950" (PhD diss., Louisiana State University, 1997); Elizet Payne Iglesias, *El puerto de Trujillo, un viaje hacia su melancólico abandono* (Tegucigalpa, Honduras: Editorial Guaymuras, 2007); David R. Radell and James J. Parsons, "Realejo: A Forgotten Colonial Port and Shipbuilding Center in Nicaragua," *Hispanic American Historical Review* 52, no. 2 (May 1971): 295–312.

61. Linda A. Newson, "Silver Mining in Colonial Honduras, *Revista de Historia de América* no. 97 (January–June 1984): 45–76.

62. Grant D. Jones, *Maya Resistance to Spanish Rule: Time and History on a Colonial Frontier* (Albuquerque: University of New Mexico Press, 1990); Jan de Vos, *La paz de Dios y del rey: La conquista de la selva lacandona, 1525–1821*, 2nd ed. (Mexico City, Mexico: Fondo de Cultura Económica, 1988); Lawrence H. Feldman, trans., ed., *Lost Shores and Forgotten Peoples: Spanish Explorations in the South East Maya Lowlands* (Durham, NC: Duke University Press, 2000); Troy S. Floyd, *The Anglo-Spanish Struggle for Mosquitia* (Albuquerque: University of New Mexico Press,1967).

63. Murdo J. MacLeod, *Spanish Central America: A Socioeconomic History, 1520–1720* (Berkeley: University of California Press, 1973). For a thoughtful critique of the east–west

CENTRAL AMERICA UNDER SPANISH COLONIAL RULE   189

division thesis, see Christopher H. Lutz and W. George Lovell, "Core and Periphery in Colonial Guatemala," in *Guatemalan Indians and the State, 1540–1988*, ed. Carol A. Smith, 35–51 (Austin: University of Texas Press, 1990).

64. Essential early arguments may be found in Trevor Aston, ed., *Crisis in Europe, 1560–1660* (Garden City, NY: Doubleday, 1967). *American Historical Review* 113, no. 4 (2008) devoted an entire number to more recent contributions to the debate. Among other places, Latin America receives attention in John Lynch, *Spain Under the Habsburgs*, 2 vols. (Oxford: Basil Blackwell, 1965–1969); Herbert S. Klein and John J. TePaske, "The Seventeenth-Century Crisis in New Spain: Myth or Reality," *Past and Present* 90, no.1 (1981): 116–135; and Ruggiero Romano, *Coyunturas opuestas: La crisis del siglo XVII en Europa e Hispanoamérica* (Mexico City, Mexico: Fondo de Cultura Económica, 1993). Woodrow Borah, *New Spain's Century of Depression*, IberoAmericana, no. 35 (Berkeley: University of California Press, 1951) antedates the discussion but is clearly relevant to it.

65. Miles L. Wortman, *Government and Society in Central America,1680–1840* (New York: Columbia University Press, 1982), esp. 91–107; Luján Muñoz, *Agricultura, mercado y sociedad*.

66. Stephen Webre, "La crisis de autoridad en el siglo XVII tardío: Centroamérica bajo la presidencia de don Jacinto de Barrios Leal, 1688–1695," *Revista de Historia* (Heredia, C.R.) no. 27 (January–June, 1993): 9–28.

67. Stephen Webre, "Defense, Economy, and Politics in Seventeenth-Century Nicaragua: Don Fernando Francisco de Escobedo and the Fortification of the San Juan River, 1672–1673," *Jahrbuch für Geschichte Lateinamerikas* 44 (2007): 93–110, describes a personal tour of Honduras and Nicaragua undertaken by a captain-general in an effort to convince local elites to contribute to the cost of a fort to defend the city of Granada from a repeat of the pirate attacks of 1665 and 1670.

68. On the payment of *indultos* (fines or bribes, depending upon one's point of view) to excuse criminal conduct, see MacLeod, "Primitive Nation State," 57–58.

69. For good overviews of the Bourbon Reforms, see Wilbur Eugene Meneray, "The Kingdom of Guatemala during the Reign of Charles III, 1759–1788" (PhD diss., University of North Carolina, 1975); Wortman, *Government and Society*, esp. 129–156; and the essays collected in Jordana Dym and Christophe Belaubre, eds., *Politics, Economy, and Society in Bourbon Central America, 1759–1821* (Boulder: University Press of Colorado, 2006).

70. José Antonio Fernández Molina, "Colouring the World in Blue: The Indigo Boom and the Central American Market, 1750–1810" (PhD diss., University of Texas, 1992). On late colonial Central America's elite family networks, see Richmond F. Brown, *Juan Fermín de Aycinena: Central American Colonial Entrepreneur, 1729–1796* (Norman: University of Oklahoma Press, 1997); Marta Elena Casaus Arzú, *Guatemala: Linaje y racismo* (San José, Costa Rica: FLACSO, 1992); Diana Balmori, Stuart F. Voss, and Miles L. Wortman, *Notable Family Networks in Latin America* (Chicago: University of Chicago Press, 1984).

71. Jorge Luján Muñoz, "El establecimiento del estanco del tabaco en el reino de Guatemala," *Mesoamérica* 22, no. 41 (June 2001): 99–136; Jesús Rico Aldave, *La renta del tabaco en Costa Rica, 1766–1860* (San José, Costa Rica: Editorial Universidad Estatal a Distancia, 2014).

72. Alvis E. Dunn, "Aguardiente and Identity: The Holy Week Riot of 1786 in Quezaltenango, Guatemala" (PhD diss., University of North Carolina, 1999).

73. Héctor Humberto Samayoa Guevara, *Implantación del régimen de intendencias en el reino de Guatemala* (Guatemala City, Guatemala: Editorial del Ministerio de Educación Pública "José de Pineda Ibarra," 1960).

74. Ana Margarita Gómez, "'Al servicio de las armas': The Bourbon Army of Late Colonial Guatemala, 1762–1821" (PhD diss., University of Minnesota); Aarón Arguedas, "The

Kingdom of Guatemala Under the Military Reform, 1755–1808" (PhD diss., Texas Christian University, 2006); Manuel Claro Delgado, *Ejército y sociedad en Centroamérica en el siglo XVIII* (Madrid, Spain: Ministerio de Defensa, 2010).

75. Wortman, *Government and Society*, 156.

FURTHER READING

Brown, Richmond F. *Juan Fermín de Aycinena: Central American Colonial Entrepreneur, 1729–1796*. Norman: University of Oklahoma Press, 1997.

Dym, Jordana, and Christophe Belaubre, eds. *Politics, Economy, and Society in Bourbon Central America, 1759–1821*. Boulder: University Press of Colorado, 2006.

Feldman, Lawrence H., trans. and ed. *Lost Shores and Forgotten Peoples: Spanish Explorations in the South East Maya Lowlands*. Durham, NC: Duke University Press, 2000.

Few, Martha. *Women Who Live Evil Lives: Gender, Religion, and the Politics of Power in Colonial Guatemala, 1650–1750*. Austin: University of Texas Press, 2003.

Floyd, Troy S. *The Anglo-Spanish Struggle for Mosquitia*. Albuquerque: University of New Mexico Press, 1967.

Gage, Thomas. *Thomas Gage's Travels in the New World*. Edited by J. Eric Thompson. Norman: University of Oklahoma Press, 1958. (Originally published in 1648.)

Gudmundson, Lowell K., and Justin Wolfe, eds. *Blacks and Blackness in Central America: Between Race and Place*. Durham, NC: Duke University Press, 2010.

Lohse, K. Russell. *Africans into Creoles: Slavery, Ethnicity, and Identity in Colonial Costa Rica*. Albuquerque: University of New Mexico Press, 2014.

Lovell, W. George. *Conquest and Survival in Colonial Guatemala: A Historical Geography of the Cuchumatán Highlands, 1500–1821*. 3rd ed. Montreal: McGill-Queen's University Press, 2005.

Lutz, Christopher H. *Santiago de Guatemala, 1541–1773: City, Caste, and the Colonial Experience*. Norman: University of Oklahoma Press, 1994.

MacLeod, Murdo J. *Spanish Central America: A Socioeconomic History, 1520–1720*. Berkeley: University of California Press, 1973.

Martínez Peláez, Severo. *La patria del criollo: An Interpretation of Colonial Guatemala*. Edited by W. George Lovell and Christopher H. Lutz. Translated by Susan M. Neve. Durham, NC: Duke University Press, 2009.

Sellers-García, Sylvia. *Distance and Documents at the Spanish Empire's Periphery*. Stanford, CA: Stanford University Press, 2014.

Sherman, William L. *Forced Native Labor in Sixteenth-Century Central America*. Lincoln: University of Nebraska Press, 1979.

Wortman, Miles L. *Government and Society in Central America, 1680–1840*. New York: Columbia University Press, 1982.

CHAPTER 7

THE KINGDOM OF GUATEMALA AS A CULTURAL CROSSROADS

BRIANNA LEAVITT-ALCÁNTARA

APPROACHING A BORDERLANDS: CULTURAL HISTORIES IN COLONIAL CENTRAL AMERICA

COLONIAL Central America was a relatively compact geographical region, constituted by the modern-day Mexican state of Chiapas and the countries of Guatemala, Belize, El Salvador, Honduras, Nicaragua, and Costa Rica. One might expect to find cultural homogeneity in a region this size, and yet the narrow isthmus produced diverse regional cultures and identities during the colonial period. Central America's history of cultural diversity was already well established during the pre-Columbian era. A borderlands region for millennia, the northern half of colonial Central America belongs to Mesoamerica, a term used to describe the Indigenous region stretching from central Mexico through Guatemala and parts of El Salvador and Honduras which shared urban settlement patterns; cultural and religious beliefs and ritual practices; and social, economic, and political systems. Within Central America's Mesoamerican territories, most Indigenous peoples were Maya, a broad cultural umbrella encompassing over thirty distinct linguistic groups, many of them mutually unintelligible despite their shared Proto-Mayan ancestry.[1] Indigenous populations in the southern half of colonial Central America had more in common with other semisedentary circum-Caribbean and South American societies than with their neighbors across the Mesoamerican border.

Spanish colonial officials attempted to unite this diverse territory, the Kingdom of Guatemala, under the immediate political jurisdiction of the *audiencia* (high court) capital of Santiago de Guatemala, the city known today as Antigua. Yet, for much of the colonial period, many Central American regional cultures and societies developed quite autonomously from one another and from the distant provincial capital and dictates of Church and Crown. As Sylvia Sellers-García points out, in the sixteenth century, most official roads, trade, and communication were oriented toward Mexico City, the vice-regal capital, and Spain via the port cities of Veracruz and Trujillo. Far less developed were the internal networks between Central American regions. The most extreme example was Costa Rica. Due to road conditions, it took a full fifty days to traverse the 500 miles separating Costa Rica from the provincial capital in Guatemala.[2] The coastlines of Nicaragua and southern Honduras largely evaded Spanish rule entirely and became a violently contested border between British and Spanish empires and home to the independent Afro-Amerindian Mosquito Kingdom. Even within Guatemala, rocky roads over rough terrain including dense forests, steep ravines, and rushing rivers, made travel challenging between many towns and between towns and the provincial capital. Over the course of the seventeenth and eighteenth centuries, stronger regional networks formed as a result of the indigo economy, the rise of pilgrimage sites, and official investments in better roads and improved communication.[3] Still, regional cultural diversity and local autonomy remained defining features of Central America through the end of the colonial period and underlay the post-independence conflicts and division into distinct nation-states.

Colonial Central American history, and particularly its cultural history, remains in a nascent stage of development compared to other parts of colonial Spanish America such as Mexico and Peru. This partly reflects historical study's "center–periphery paradigm," which has tended to concentrate scholarly attention on powerful political and economic centers while neglecting places like Central America, deemed as peripheral.[4] Twentieth-century civil wars and political violence impeded archival research and also directed research agendas to modern historical topics, particularly politics and economics. The destruction of documents, whether by accident, negligence, or intent, and the underfunding of archives pose other significant challenges for researchers interested in the colonial period. Nevertheless, a small but lively field in colonial cultural history has expanded in exciting directions over the last thirty years. Cultural history generally refers to the study of beliefs, ideas, values, racial ideologies, gender roles and norms, kinship and family formation, religion, ritual, and daily practices. Cultural beliefs and practices significantly shaped the formation of colonial Central American societies and economies and the broader Spanish empire. There are four key themes of recent research: colonial religious encounters and the emergence of diverse Maya Christianities; Afro-Central American society and culture; women, sexuality, and gender in urban society; and the images, ideas, and innovations that brought Central Americans closer together over the eighteenth century, but also sparked controversies and conflicts.

Religious Encounters and Maya Christianities

Evangelization efforts in Central America began in earnest in the second half of the sixteenth century, with the Dominican order dominating most of the Maya highland region.[5] Much as tales of "complete" military conquest were long taken for granted, scholars also believed missionary accounts of a rapid "spiritual conquest" of native peoples. This view has largely been overturned in recent decades by historical studies of native-language sources and expansive interrogations of Spanish-language sources alongside the work of anthropologists, archaeologists, and religious studies scholars.[6] While vibrant dialogue and debate continues about the nature of religious encounters, scholars largely agree that the Christianization of native peoples in Spanish America was not simply a "one-way transfer" but rather a dynamic, interactive, and ongoing process of exchanges and negotiations out of which emerged diverse local Catholicisms.[7]

The Maya were no strangers to conquest. In addition to long-standing competitive rivalries among Maya city-states and kingdoms, Maya communities also endured invasions from central Mexican empires like Teotihuacan, Toltecs, and Itza. In the face of Spanish colonization, the Maya thus drew on a long history of religious pluralism and engagement with the religions of "distant kings" while assiduously maintaining local traditions.[8] For their part, Spanish missionaries mostly ignored private and domestic ritual life, which they saw as a "low" form of superstition rather than "high" idolatry.[9] In this context, Maya beliefs and rituals related to birth, illness, and death continued strongly, as did *nagualismo*, the belief in a mystical–physical connection between every human and a designated animal.[10] Also continuing to thrive were ritual-healing beliefs and techniques involving plants, herbs, incense, animals, bloodletting, mineral hot springs, *temascales* (ritual steam baths), offerings, and divination. Indeed, elite Spaniards and priests frequently recognized the efficacy of Mesoamerican medical cultures and eagerly appropriated Indigenous knowledge about the curative properties of specific hot springs, medicinal value of plants and trees, and more effective medical techniques.[11]

At the same time, Maya communities and leaders were curious about the potential power of alphabetic script and certain aspects of Christianity including the Christian God. As William Hanks put it, "far from attempting to exclude Christianity, the way the Spanish tried to exclude 'idolatry,' the Maya appear to have followed the opposite strategy. They absorbed the new religion and its language, encompassed it, and appropriated it."[12] Missionaries facilitated this process by working closely with native scholars to translate Christian texts and messages into Mesoamerican languages.[13] Rather than a uniform finished product, translated Christianity, or more precisely *Christianties*, emerged as dynamic and diverse. In Central America, this process is best documented for Guatemala's highland K'iche' Maya. Some K'iche' Maya leaders utilized the alphabetic script developed with missionaries to create a new kind of record of oral and hieroglyphic sacred mythohistories, such as the extensively studied Popol Vuh. Although often treated as a "freestanding" Maya sacred text, the Popol Vuh actually played a critical role in missionary efforts.[14] Early Dominican missionaries and Maya scholars drew upon K'iche' ceremonial rhythms and rhetorical devices found in the Popol Vuh, using similar repetitions and parallelisms, couplets and triplets that echoed the chants and incantations of K'iche' priests in doctrinal texts.[15] Dominicans and Maya leaders also mapped central Christian concepts onto preexisting K'iche' concepts which made Christianity more intelligible but also provided a means for continuity of K'iche' beliefs.[16] For example, translated texts described the Christian god as Tz'aqol B'itol, the name of the K'iche' dual-gendered creator god.[17] Divine Glory became "yellowness and greenness," a K'iche' metaphor that linked divinity to the earthy abundance of ripe corn, while "faith" became "kojo" meaning ritual offerings or ceremonial activities.[18]

Maya K'iche' local leaders continued the dynamic "K'iche'anization" of Christianity by manipulating and transforming Christian theology to develop new K'iche' mythohistories and identities and a "hybrid colonial reality."[19] Néstor Quiroa found evidence of this process in K'iche' *Títulos*, documents produced in the mid- to late sixteenth century to settle land disputes. These *Títulos* also incorporated local mythohistories and origin stories. The *Título de Totonicapán*, for example, described the Garden of Eden like "Tullan," the K'iche' place of origin. Instead of one tree, there were two, the tree of life and the tree of knowledge, and both were zapote trees, a Mesoamerican fruit tree that played an important role in K'iche' myths of human creation. The *Título* described Adam and Eve as "our father and mother," echoing descriptions of K'iche' mythical ancestors, the divine couple Xpiacoc and Xmucane who birthed the first K'iche' people, while Moses and Aaron became Hero Twins, key figures in Maya creation stories.[20] The *Título de Totonicapan* helped lay the foundation for new kinds of K'iche' Christian pride and the strategic alliance with Christianity to gain political power. At the same time, other communities utilized alphabetic language to resist colonization and Christianization. The *Título de C'oyoi* from the Quetzaltenango area recounted the terrible suffering wrought by Spanish and Nahua conquerors and rejected any alliance with Spanish Christianity, assuring readers that "you can defeat the visitor, as if he was your son."[21]

The degree to which Christian and Maya's worldviews were ultimately incommensurable remains a point of debate among scholars. Clearer are the ways in which colonial Maya communities actively rejected and appropriated aspects of Catholicism on their own terms. For all the missionary efforts, the Maya seem mostly unmoved by concerns about salvation. Many approached confession as a means to cure illness and achieve a good life rather than to cleanse sins.[22] Communities also never fully accepted narrow Christian sexual morality, and many avoided marriage due to the costs associated with both the ceremony and higher tribute requirements for married couples.[23] Nor did Maya accept a Catholic "monopoly" on communication with the divine.[24] Like other Indigenous societies across Spanish America, Maya "often reached for direct communication with divine power and will in traditional ways laden with their own meanings."[25] Mesoamerican deities remained a powerful presence among those divine powers for centuries. As late as the 1790s, Spanish officials continued to discover shrines dedicated to Maya deities, which received regular offerings from local political officials and elders to ensure abundant agricultural cycles and the community's overall health and well-being.[26] Local priests in highland communities often turned a blind eye or quietly tolerated these devotions, aware of their own isolation and the real prospect of violence if they pressed the issue.[27]

At the same time, Maya communities found some aspects of Christianity appealing. Christian eschatology and apocalyptic narratives of destruction and world renewal were especially popular given the centrality of time and the cycles of creation and destruction within Maya and Mesoamerican worldviews more generally.[28] Christian material culture including candles and fireworks was also of interest. Maya communities long appreciated the power of monumental architecture, and in the Guatemalan highlands and elsewhere, "church structures became important in Mayan thinking since they were considered the dwelling places of the saints."[29] Maya towns also enthusiastically appropriated the teeming universe of Catholic saints. Like Maya pre-Hispanic deities, Catholic saints had diverse personalities and histories and acted in the world as protectors of communities. Maya communities created new mythohistories of origin with patron saints as founders and heroes and sometimes fused with pre-Hispanic gods.[30]

Maya communities in colonial Central America also embraced lay religious brotherhoods known as *cofradías* as an institutional mechanism for devotion to saints. In addition to funding and coordinating the ritual life of given saints, *cofradías* served as mutual aid associations ensuring proper feasts and vigils when members died and ongoing ritual links to the souls of the dead.[31] They also provided opportunities for elected leadership positions, collective religious organizing, and community defense.[32] Some Indigenous *cofradías* elected female officers, reworking the Spanish institution in accordance with Mesoamerican notions of gender complementarity and female religious authority.[33] Although often hidden in colonial records, anthropological and ethnographic studies in the Maya highlands indicate that women have also frequently exercised informal leadership positions, as elected male officers usually work in tandem with their wives to fulfill ritual duties.[34]

Although *cofradías* played a critical role in the religious life of Indigenous communities in colonial Central America, they could also reflect and exacerbate internal town divisions and identities. In some towns, *cofradías* replaced or overlapped with pre-Hispanic kin-based *calpolli* (wards).[35] *Cofradías* also reinforced divisions between Indigenous nobles and commoners. Noble native men and women highlighted their status through membership in and leadership of the wealthiest and most prestigious *cofradías*, an elite status put on explicit display through ritual dress, positioning in processions, and burial location.[36] *Cofradías* also funneled wealth toward church officials and local native elites. Missionaries and church officials relied heavily upon *cofradías* for basic revenue. This was especially true in colonial Central America, a more modest province that lacked the wealth of Mexico. *Cofradías* that laid extra burdens upon Maya commoners or transferred wealth to local elites or church officials stoked resentments and discord.[37]

At times, Maya saints and *cofradías* extended well beyond the reaches of Catholic orthodoxy. In 1677, the bishop of Chiapas discovered a Tzeltal Maya *cofradía* whose members claimed to be the incarnated Holy Trinity.[38] A more famous and enduring example is Maximón, or Saint Simon, a Maya deity that emerged in colonial Maya towns in the western highlands of Guatemala and has spread through parts of Central America, Mexico, and beyond. Like some pre-Columbian Mesoamerican deities, Maximón is a trickster and dual gendered, shape shifting back and forth between male and female identities.[39] Ritual devotion to Maximón reflects his transsexual and hypersexual nature. During Holy Week festivities in the Guatemalan town of Santiago Atitlan, the community continues to believe that Maximón symbolically copulates with and inseminates fruits that symbolize Christ. These acts help renew the world and initiate the rainy season and also bring about Christ's maturity and resurrection or "rebirth" as maize on Easter Sunday.[40] David Carrasco describes devotees of Maximón as "Jaguar Christians" as a way to capture the creative religious formations that emerged in colonial contact zones.[41]

At times, Maya saints channeled radical millenarian movements that threatened to overturn Spanish colonialism entirely. In 1712, a Tzeltal Maya thirteen-year-old girl, María de Candelaria, saw an apparition of the Virgin Mary who requested a chapel built in her honor. After Chiapas church officials violently attempted to suppress the devotion, María de Candelaria relayed a radicalized divine message that the time had come to "unite in order to kill the Spaniards" so that native communities could be left in their "ancient freedom," liberated from tribute and the Spanish king, priests, and all colonial officials.[42] Not long after, a Tzotzil Maya man from the nearby town of Chenalo arrived proclaiming that he had ascended to heaven and Saint Peter had granted him divine authority to ordain Maya men as priests and bishops.[43] The community began ordaining Maya priests as thousands of Maya "soldiers of the Virgin," from thirty-two towns representing three distinct Mayan ethnolinguistic groups, Tzeltal, Tzotzil, and Ch'ol, joined the cause, destroying churches and Spanish property and executing Spanish and mixed-race colonists over a series of months. Over the course of the rebellion, leaders conceptually turned Spanish colonialism upside down calling Spaniards "demons" and "Jews," while newly ordained Maya priests officiated mass with María de Candelaria standing by their sides wearing priestly vestments herself.[44] Only after officials deployed six thousand troops, was the colonial government able to declare victory over the rebels. The Spanish secured a military victory, but the dynamic process of transculturation and formation of Maya Christianities continued through the colonial period and indeed up to the present day.

BLURRING LINES: AFRO-CENTRAL AMERICAN MOBILITY AND NETWORKS

The prominent social and cultural role played by Africans and their descendants in colonial Central America barely registers in much of the region's popular historical memory today. This selective amnesia reflects the explicit efforts of modern Central American nations to claim mestizo (Indigenous and Spanish) ancestry while denying African influences.[45] Until recently, historians did little to challenge that view as studies of African slavery focused mostly on Brazil and the Caribbean.[46] And yet tens of thousands of enslaved Africans arrived to colonial Central America. By the seventeenth and eighteenth centuries, Afro-Central Americans outnumbered Indigenous and Spanish populations in many regions. Through their personal, religious, and labor-based networks, Afro-Central Americans pursued freedom and social mobility, crossed ethnoracial lines, and played a predominant role in the formation of the "ladino" mixed-race population and Central American cultures.

Like most of Spanish America, the first Black slaves in Central America came as conquistadors. In the early 1520s, Black conquistadors participated in campaigns to conquer Costa Rica and Nicaragua while Pedro de Alvarado brought dozens, perhaps more than a hundred Black slaves as "armed auxiliaries," alongside Spaniards and native allies to conquer highland Guatemala.[47] Many of these Black conquistadors were already culturally Hispanicized to varying degrees, having spent years in Iberia or the Caribbean. A minority were already Afro-Iberian by birth, perhaps second or third generation, and some of these may have arrived as already free men. Most who came as slaves gained their freedom as a reward for military service on behalf of the Crown, making free Black men an important segment of early settler populations.[48]

As the initial conquest phase gave way to the construction of a colonial society, the nature of African slavery in the region shifted. Across Spanish America, the African slave trade increased steadily from the second half of the sixteenth century through the mid-seventeenth century with ships carrying enslaved Africans directly from West Central Africa to the Spanish American mainland. West Central Africans, who made up the vast majority of Central America's enslaved population, were more culturally and linguistically homogeneous compared to other parts of Africa and exerted an outsized influence on Central American culture. West Central Africa also had long historical links to Europe, and many West Central Africans were already familiar with Iberian languages and Catholicism before arriving in the Americas, which facilitated linguistic, cultural, and social mobility.[49] By 1640, the African slave trade to Central America slowed dramatically, never to return to the levels of the early seventeenth century.[50] Over the late seventeenth century, Central America's enslaved population became *criollo* (American born) and increasingly mixed race. The free Black population steadily grew and worked for wages in a wide variety of occupations across the region.

Like Mexico, Peru, and other parts of mainland Spanish America, Central America was always a "society with slaves" rather than a "slave society." Slavery was one form of labor among others including tributary, draft, and free wage labor systems. Enslaved Africans in Central America concentrated in economic "niches" not covered by native labor, especially silver mining, sugar mills, and wheat farms, cacao and indigo plantations, ranching, construction, transportation, domestic service, militias, and urban artisan labors.[51] While the Spanish colonial ideal envisioned clear separations between Africans and Indians, in reality, Spanish colonialism routinely brought enslaved

Africans and native peoples into close proximity.[52] This context facilitated diverse relations and networks between enslaved and free, Black, and Indigenous populations and opportunities for slaves to pursue social mobility and freedom. For example, as Spaniards established cattle ranches, wheat farms, and sugar mills in the Maya regions of Guatemala, they brought large numbers of enslaved Africans as a permanent labor force.[53] Because slaves were permanent and often skilled laborers, Africans frequently served as supervisors of temporary Maya workers, fulfilling draft labor duties. Indeed, widespread Spanish preferences for urban life led many to leave their rural estates under enslaved African oversight for long periods.[54]

Similar patterns emerged throughout colonial Central America, so that although native peoples technically occupied a superior position to Africans in the Spanish colonial caste system, in day-to-day practice, enslaved Africans often exercised authority over Indigenous laborers due to language, skills, occupation, and permanency.[55] In this context, Black–Indigenous relations were often marked by violence and conflict.[56] But the close proximity between African and Indigenous populations also fostered other kinds of interactions, including friendship, patronage, kinship ties, informal sexual unions, and marriage.[57] For example, given the low numbers of enslaved African women on Guatemalan agricultural estates, many enslaved African men sought unions with Indigenous women, whose free status would also be transmitted to their children.[58] Black–Maya marriages and informal unions fueled the growth of a sizable free "mulatto" population by the late seventeenth century, which over time became identified as "ladinos."[59]

Black slaves in colonial Central America also frequently enjoyed significant levels of autonomy, which further facilitated relationships with free populations and routes to freedom. In Costa Rica, Spanish colonists eschewed the hot and humid climate of the cacao-producing region, particularly given the risks of disease and added dangers posed by frequent pirate raids. As a result, Spaniards left enslaved African men largely in charge of day-to-day operations for cacao production, processing, and sale.[60] Because cacao production required less intensive labor, enslaved men were able to develop their own plots of cacao and participate in the thriving black market of British goods. Not only did the sale of cacao provide access to funds, but cacao beans also served as legal tender in Costa Rica.[61] Access to independent housing, autonomy, and money blurred the lines between enslaved and free status on Costa Rica's cacao haciendas. To an even larger degree than Guatemala's sugar and wheat farms, enslaved Africans in Costa Rica's cacao regions established marital and informal unions with free women, giving rise to a large free Afro–mestizo population. Access to money and marriages with free women also paved the way for enslaved men to gain their own freedom and establish themselves as small cacao farmers in the area.[62]

As in other parts of Spanish America, colonial Central American cities also exhibited a high demand for enslaved African labor for domestic service, skilled artisan fields, metalworking, construction, and more.[63] Throughout the world, urban slavery tended to offer greater flexibility, independence, and paths to freedom compared with rural or plantation-based slavery. Skilled African slaves often hired themselves out in their free time and saved their wages or proceeds, and some masters periodically or permanently rented out skilled slaves, collecting part of their salaries and leaving them the rest. In this context, slaves could both save money and perhaps live independently of their masters, facilitating opportunities to form relationships within the free Black community and across ethnoracial lines.[64] By the mid-seventeenth century, the free Black and mulatto population in Central America's capital of Santiago de Guatemala outnumbered the enslaved population and continued to grow at far faster rates than the slave population for the next century.[65] Not only did the free Black population outnumber the enslaved population, but the free Black and mulatto population became a dominant demographic in the city, constituting the largest ethnoracial group in Santiago during most of the eighteenth century.[66] As Catherine Komisaruk put it, "In the capital city at least, the free population was increasingly African in ancestry, and the population of African ancestry was increasingly free."[67] In fact, this phenomenon extended well beyond the capital city. Those of African descent also outnumbered Spaniards and Indians in every major city of late colonial Nicaragua.[68] Indeed, the "mixed-casta" category, which generally reflected African and Indigenous ancestry, represented between 70 percent and 90 percent of late colonial urban populations in Guatemala, El Salvador, Nicaragua, Honduras, and Costa Rica.[69]

Colonial Central American cities, mines, ports, and key agricultural regions were thus prime meeting grounds for the cultural and racial mixture. Central Americanists have yet to fully explore the region's relationship to the Black Atlantic and how African cultures shaped Central American values and mores; food, dress, and music; medicinal practices; gender and family relations; and religious worldviews and practices.[70] Most nascent explorations of this topic focus on the Mosquito Kingdom, an independent Afro-Amerindian confederation that governed along the Caribbean coasts of Honduras and Nicaragua in the borderlands where Spanish and British empires vied for control.[71] During the seventeenth century, hundreds of Africans arrived at the largely autonomous Mosquito Indigenous coastline as runaways and shipwrecked slaves. Eugenia Ibarra argues that "cultural complementarity" between West Central Africans and Mosquito Amerindians, particularly related to the organization of agricultural labor and funerary practices, facilitated alliances and group cohesion.[72] John Thornton emphasizes the importance of West Central African military culture, contending that a significant population of soldiers from Mbwila, a kingdom in Angola, arrived on the Mosquito Coast and played a key role in the aggressive seventeenth-century growth of the Mosquito Kingdom through warfare and by taking Indigenous captives, particularly women and children.[73] By the late seventeenth century, the racial and cultural mixture with Amerindians had produced a population of Afro-Mosquito "Zambos" who mostly concentrated in northern territories and eventually rose to political power within the Mosquito Kingdom and "interacted with British and Spanish as equals."[74]

In Central America, as in other parts of Spanish America, African slaves actively used legal strategies to defend their rights and pursue freedom. Spanish law provided certain minimal legal protections to enslaved Africans, including freedom from excessive abuse, rights to self-purchase and a fixed purchase price, owning personal property, making contracts, and marrying persons of their choice.[75] For example, Guatemalan slaves on a Dominican hacienda repeatedly filed legal complaints about working conditions and abuses and also sought to legally restrict the Dominicans' right to sell them. The negotiated settlements significantly altered the nature of slavery on the estate as the Dominicans agreed to pay slaves the same wages paid to free and tribute laborers, reduce workloads, and allow access to personal livestock. As Komisaruk notes, "the slaves' litigation had amounted to a conscious, collective renegotiation of the terms of their labor."[76] Through legal strategies such as these, slaves accessed better living conditions, heightened the flexibility of slave systems, and actively blurred the lines between slave and free labor.

Studies from other parts of Spanish America suggest that Black and mulatto men utilized *cofradías*, Black militias, and professional success to cultivate positive Black identity, gain social mobility, and access corporate privileges and vassal status.[77] Nascent scholarship suggests similar patterns in colonial Central America. Although Black male participation in Central American *cofradías* has yet to be explored, Brianna Leavitt-Alcántara finds that Black and mulatto women were active participants and elected officers in *cofradías* in the colonial capital of Santiago de Guatemala. Through their devotional networks and pious personas, these women challenged racialized discourses and "forms of rule."[78] And Paul Lokken finds that Black and mulatto men in seventeenth- and eighteenth-century El Salvador invoked their militia membership in order to secure freedom from bondage and inferior tributary status.[79] By the late eighteenth century, participation in militias alongside petitions and lawsuits led to universal relief from tribute requirements for Afro-Central Americans.[80] Free Black and mulatto men also achieved social mobility through professional opportunities. When the capital relocated after the 1773 earthquakes, the new city's chief architect was Bernardo Ramírez, a mulatto man.[81] Ramírez joined other socially mobile Central American mulattos in the 1780s and 1790s who attempted to take advantage of the royal sale of certificates of whiteness, which allowed people of African ancestry the opportunity to access all privileges of whiteness such as university entrance, professions, and honors.[82] Although not always successful, these efforts spurred Guatemala's provincial Franciscan head to lobby the Crown to remove caste restrictions on people of African descent, arguing that the restrictions were irrational given the "admirable qualities and virtuous customs" of the large mulatto population.[83] Afro-Central Americans' personal and collective struggles gradually eroded many colonial caste restrictions and laid the foundation for the post-independence abolition of the colonial caste system and declaration of legal equality for all American-born males.

Sex and the City: Gender, Sexuality, and Race in the Central American Capital

Santiago de Guatemala was the political capital of Central America from 1541 until 1775, when officials initiated a forced relocation following the devastating 1773 earthquakes.

After 1775, the relocated capital was renamed Nueva (New) Guatemala or Guatemala City, while Santiago became "Antigua" or Old City. With almost forty thousand residents by the late seventeenth century, Santiago was one of the largest and most important cities in Spanish America after Mexico City and Lima.[84] In 1660, Santiago opened its first printing press and around 1680 the city founded the University of San Carlos.[85] The late seventeenth century also witnessed opulent reconstructions of churches, and between 1670 and 1725, the number of female convents in the city also more than doubled, from two to five.[86] For Spanish American cities, female convents served as coveted symbols of pious identity and cultural prestige.[87] The only other city in all of Central America that could claim a female convent during the colonial period was Ciudad Real in Chiapas. The turn of the eighteenth century proved to be the pinnacle of monastic institutions in Santiago, as upward of 10 percent of Spanish women professed as nuns, and hundreds of more women were housed in convents as students, servants, and slaves.[88] The rich topic of female monastic life, so deeply explored for Mexico and Peru, remains wide open for discovery in colonial Guatemala.

Like most cities, Central America's capital was also a study in contrast. A thriving contraband trade in alcohol from Peru alongside local bootlegged production and underground taverns supplied a high demand for alcohol consumption. As one scholar put it, "Santiago in the 1740s and 50s seems to have become a relatively unmanageable haven for the drunk, the rowdy, and the slovenly."[89] The town council in 1749 bemoaned the frequency of robberies, violence, and homicides linked to alcohol consumption.[90] Criminal records reinforce the town council's perception. A recent study of 3,500 criminal cases in the colonial capital finds that alcohol was a primary factor in assaults and homicides.[91] Many sources suggest an increase in poverty, unemployment, and violence in the decades following the capital's relocation to Guatemala City, despite late-colonial policing tactics that were "energetic in the extreme."[92]

Assessing levels of violence against women, domestic or otherwise, is challenging as the record is sparse. Guatemala's judges were generally unmoved by female complaints of domestic violence in part because husbands and fathers had the legal right to physically "correct" wives and children. Even in cases where abuse ended in homicide, officials frequently declined to prosecute male offenders.[93] The record of sexual violence is even more limited because rape in the modern sense did not exist as a legal criminal category in colonial Central America. The only legally viable charge was *estupro*, that is deflowering of a virgin, an expansive legal category that encompassed both violent rape by a stranger and consensual sex with a fiancée.[94] Of course, social status also shaped outcomes. Courts assumed that nonelite women were sexually promiscuous by nature and generally refused to believe their rape allegations. By contrast, Sellers-García found a case of an elite young widow in Guatemala City who successfully brought charges against the illustrious local doctor, Narciso Esparragosa, for stalking, forced entry, and sexual assault.[95] Still, the elite woman in question endured the harassment for eight long years before finally involving the authorities. While elite women enjoyed greater benefit of the doubt, they also risked their valuable reputations and honor by taking these cases public.

Contrary to Spanish Catholic ideals, illegitimacy rates were especially pronounced in the Central American capital, even compared to the relatively high rates found throughout Spanish America. Among the nonelite population, a striking 77 percent of births in the 1640s were illegitimate. That figure gradually dropped over several decades, but it never fell below 43 percent.[96] One key factor was the particularly acute gender imbalances within the nonelite young adult population. The heavy demand for Indigenous and African female labor in domestic service and marketing made Santiago a "city of women" by the eighteenth century if not well before.[97] This gendered urban phenomenon reflected broader trends throughout Spanish America, where most cities had female majorities due to high urban demand for female labor, while male laborers left cities to work in mining and agriculture.[98] For reasons not entirely clear, this trend was even more pronounced in Guatemala than in other parts of Spanish America. A census taker in the mid-eighteenth century pointedly remarked that among the capital's nonelite population "the feminine sex abounds in total profusion."[99] Gender imbalances continued in the "New" capital of Guatemala City. In citywide censuses taken in 1796, 1805, and 1825, women accounted for 60 percent of the total population. In some neighborhoods, that figure rose to 64 percent.[100] And in the late colonial period, it appears women represented half of all household heads in the city.[101]

Other social, economic, and cultural factors shaped this urban society marked by fluid and impermanent sexual relationships and a remarkably high number of single mothers and female-headed households. Slightly more than half of all female laborers in the city worked as domestic servants and the nature of domestic service prohibited many workers from forming independent households.[102] Marriage was also expensive and could be out of reach for the urban poor. Catherine Komisaruk argued that the capital city's "cash and credit economy" meant that urban households did not depend upon a gendered combination of complementary male and female labor as was the case for rural households, thus allowing for more flexible sexual and conjugal relations.[103] Women in the capital supported their households in a variety of ways, dominating the informal economy in petty marketing, laundering, alcohol brewing, and sales and also finding ample opportunities to work in formal stores, bakeries, weaving, and more.[104] Cultural values also clearly played a role and some argue that nonelite societies in both Spain and Spanish America were simply apathetic or resistant to Catholic sexual mores.[105] In Santiago, even among the Spanish population, illegitimacy rates were 40 percent in the 1640s and dropped only as low as 26 percent, still a remarkably high figure.[106] These figures are striking given that Spanish culture was honor-based, Spanish female honor was directly tied to sexual virtue, and the ideal states for women were either the convent or marriage. Given Santiago's economically diverse Spanish population, it is difficult to determine illegitimacy rates for the small elite population, but studies indicate that even elite Spanish American women found loopholes in order to circumvent strict feminine ideals of sexual virtue and honor.[107]

Evidence certainly indicates a surprising degree of social and legal tolerance in colonial Central America toward female independence and sexual activity outside marriage. For example, prior sexual activity did not automatically restrict nonelite women's marital prospects.[108] In the capital, official concern about sexual morality was also muted, even among local priests and the ecclesiastical court, perhaps because the city lacked the infrastructure required to systematically prosecute and incarcerate women who engaged in informal unions.[109] Local courts also adapted to gendered realities of informal sexual unions and marital separations. Courts frequently sided with single women seeking child support, upheld property rights of women separated from their husbands, recognized women as primary breadwinners for households, and rarely asked for spousal consent when married women bought or sold properties.[110]

Nonelites were clearly more tolerant of sex outside the bounds of marriage; however, evidence also suggests active religious, cultural, and social engagement with marital ideals. As noted previously, the illegitimacy rate among nonelites did drop by a precipitous 30 percent over the late seventeenth century.[111] Within the complex internal hierarchies of nonelite communities, legitimacy, sexual morality, marriage, and behavior mattered and shaped social status as well as vital access to credit and mutual aid.[112] Leavitt-Alcántara argued that some single nonelite women in the capital navigated these tensions by invoking "alternative" ideals of female conduct other than chastity and enclosure.[113] In their wills, nonelite women frequently highlighted their hard work and resourcefulness, their "labor and sweat," as well as their participation in *cofradías* and active devotional networks. *Cofradía* records from Guatemala's capital confirm that nonelite women often comprised a majority of members, a trend also found in colonial Mexico.[114] As eighteenth-century economic growth and social mobility allowed some laboring women to gain assets and humble houses, many stepped into the role of pious benefactors, actively investing in local religious life through donations and modest endowments.[115] Leavitt-Alcántara concludes that as "much as scholars recognize that race in colonial Latin America was a flexible category and individuals might claim multiple racial identities simultaneously, gender ideals were malleable and multifaceted in colonial Central America, and poor single women could sometimes claim more than one moral status."[116]

Through their devotional practices and relationships, Indigenous, African, and mixed-race women also shaped the local religion of Central America's capital as well as other towns and cities. Although Spanish *cofradías* traditionally elected only male officers, female leadership became a common feature of Santiago's *cofradías* in accordance with Indigenous and African gender norms and traditions. Far more research is necessary to understand this phenomenon in depth, but early studies show by the 1630s that the Indigenous *cofradía* of San Joseph in Santiago de Guatemala was electing both male and female officers. Records described the women as "tenantzines," a reverential term for mothers in Nahuatl, and stipulated that they would be responsible for cleaning the church, collecting alms, visiting sick members, preparing members' bodies for their funerals, consoling widows, and caring for orphans. More generally, the *cofradía* explicitly charged the female officers to act as moral guardians of the community.[117] By the eighteenth century, even mixed-race and predominantly Spanish *cofradías* were electing female officers as *capitanas* (captains), *madres mayores* (senior mothers), and *diputadas* (representatives), a pattern replicated in Chiapas as well.[118] And unlike Mexico, where female leadership in Indigenous and Black *cofradías* dwindled and even disappeared over the eighteenth century, opportunities continued into the nineteenth century in the capital as well as in Chiapas.[119]

Indigenous, Black, and mixed-race female healers and magic-ritual practitioners, often labeled "witches" by authorities, also played a key role in the urban capital's cross-cultural exchanges. The practitioners drew upon overlapping and competing Mesoamerican, African, and Spanish medical knowledge about herbs, roots, and foods as well as rituals and beliefs regarding the natural/supernatural nature of illnesses and cures for all manner of personal ailments from sickness to abusive partners. Martha Few argues that these women cultivated informal networks which fueled transculturation through the movement of "people, ideas, and ritual goods," across the "ethnic, status, and rural/urban boundaries of colonial society."[120] For example, women in Santiago, from elite Spaniards to poor women of color, sought out female specialists for love magic which often involved female sexual body parts and fluids.[121] Modern readers might be tempted to scoff at love magic as trivial; however, in colonial Central América, women's welfare, honor, status, social mobility, and even basic safety and survival often depended upon the nature of their sexual and marital relations. As noted earlier, there was often little official recourse for abandonment, chronic domestic abuse, or sexual violence. And most men and women in this time and place believed that love magic or sexual witchcraft had the power to attract desired mates, ensure marriage promises were kept, end extramarital affairs, and tame violent spouses.

MOVEMENT, MIRACLES, AND MEDICINE: INTEGRATION AND CONFLICT IN THE LONG EIGHTEENTH CENTURY

Over the long eighteenth century, here defined roughly as 1670 to 1820, colonial officials, seeking more efficient administration and extraction, invested in better roads and improved communication, which strengthened internal Central American networks as well as external links with Mexico and the Atlantic world. But as Sellers-García argues, "the contours of this network were neither perceived nor determined by the urban centers alone."[122] The growing devotion and pilgrimages to the miraculous Black Christ of Esquipulas and other shrines offer a prime example of how rural Indigenous and mixed-race communities shaped the movement of people, goods, and cultural values. Esquipulas's Ch'orti' Indigenous population first recognized the image as miraculous at some point in the seventeenth century. During the eighteenth century, a time of surging devotion to miraculous shrines across New Spain, the Black Christ of Esquipulas began to draw tens of thousands of pilgrims each year from as far as Oaxaca and Costa Rica.[123] Unlike Mexico's Virgin of Guadalupe and other regional shrines located in major cities and towns on key highways, the Black Christ of Esquipulas was far off the beaten trail.

Esquipulas's pilgrims highlight Sellers-García's point that rural Central Americans often viewed the landscape through a different lens than colonial and Church officials.[124] Esquipulas was not on any major route of commerce; however, it was literally at the very center of Central America, the meeting point of Guatemala, El Salvador, and Honduras. For Indigenous populations, it may have been propitiously linked to the nearby pre-Columbian religious center of Copán.[125] And many rural pilgrims were accustomed to traveling by foot and had the strength and familiarity to traverse difficult terrain more easily than elite officials on mule or horseback.[126] The rising popularity of the Black Christ of Esquipulas and other regional shrines like Our Lady of Peace of San Miguel, in modern-day El Salvador, ultimately shaped the dynamic eighteenth-century indigo trade, which was carried out through a network of fairs celebrated in conjunction with religious holidays of local patron saints and miraculous images. These religious celebrations/fairs became points of dynamic cultural interaction as traders, travelers, and pilgrims converged from different parts of Central America to mingle, enjoy music and food, participate in religious activities, and buy and sell indigo, artisan goods, and devotional memorabilia.[127]

Improved regional and trans-Atlantic transportation and communication also fed a thriving local intellectual climate in Central America's relocated capital of Guatemala City. The University of San Carlos became an important hub of Enlightenment-era intellectual, medical, and philosophical exchange during the late eighteenth century. Other contributors to the local and global exchange of ideas were Catholic clergy, doctors, local printing presses, the serial newspaper *Gazeta de Guatemala*, and the Royal Economic Society whose mission was to "excite the zeal of all good citizens to come together with their discoveries, their work, and their intellects to promote the good of the Guatemalan patria."[128] Ordinary men and women including nonelite, Indigenous, and mixed-race peoples also actively developed and promoted innovative ideas and initiatives. Between the 1760s and 1790s, for example, Guatemalan priests and laypeople pioneered new educational models, opening "free" or "public" schools for poor boys and girls of all racial backgrounds in and around the capital before many Mexican cities did the same.[129] The innovative design, organization, and curriculum within these schools reflected creative engagement with Bourbon reforms, Enlightenment ideas, and progressive Catholicism. The 1792 foundation of a "Teacher's College" for native women in Guatemala City's Beaterio de Indias, possibly the first of its kind in Spanish America, put Guatemala at the forefront of challenges to entrenched racial ideologies and a new acknowledgment of native women's capacity to serve as teachers and spiritual leaders.[130]

Guatemala was also in the vanguard of global public health initiatives and vaccination campaigns in the late eighteenth and early nineteenth centuries. Martha Few finds a lively Guatemalan medical culture or, more precisely "multiple medical cultures in play," which engaged with European ideas to be sure but also reflected Indigenous Mesoamerican "medical knowledges and practices" and local experimentation, innovation, and adaptation.[131] In this context, José Flores, Guatemalan physician and chair of medicine at the University of San Carlos, became an early public health pioneer, coordinating an extensive inoculation campaign with human smallpox matter in 1780, one of the first in Spanish America before both Mexico and Peru.[132] Flores relied upon cross-cultural knowledge exchanges in order to successfully adapt the inoculation campaign to the local Guatemalan and Maya cultural context. Noting that lancets provoked fear in Maya communities, Flores developed a "local method" involving poultices made from a beetle that raised blisters which could then easily be opened for inoculation.[133] If beetles could not be found, then Maya tools used for medical bloodletting were used instead of lancets. Working alongside local priests, Flores turned vaccination into a kind of religious ceremony or rite like baptism or marriage complete with a priest, altar boy, godparents, candles, and prayers. Records would be kept by priests in parish vaccine books and the inoculation fluid would be treated as a sacred substance like holy oil.[134] Flores's celebrated successes in the 1780s and again in the 1790s led to his prominent role in the development of the Spanish smallpox vaccine campaign throughout its colonies, a massive, pioneering, and unprecedented global public health campaign.

Although the late colonial period was a time of greater regional integration and cross-cultural exchanges, it was also a time of cultural conflicts, frequently gendered, over beliefs and practices related to the body, illness, sexuality, and death. In Guatemala City, many residents were offended by the use of cadavers for the study of anatomy. Many also refused to send their sick loved ones to the hospital, preferring that female family members care for them at home.[135] As in other parts of the world, formally educated medical professionals attempted to delegitimize midwives and folk ritual healers, many of them female. Results were decidedly mixed in Central America, as many people continued to believe in supernatural causes and cures for diseases and seek out trusted folk practitioners through the colonial period and indeed up to the present day.[136] At the same time, Spanish Bourbon reformers and Church officials attempted to exert more control over female bodies, sexual morality, and racial mixture.[137] Martha Few finds that in the late colonial period, leading Guatemalan intellectuals and medical figures advocated for postmortem caesareans as a way for Guatemala to compete as a "modern nation" on the global stage. Accordingly, in the 1780s, Guatemalan governing officials declared unborn fetuses to be colonial subjects and further required cesarean operations when pregnant women died.[138] The religious, medical, and political arguments in favor of the new law "dissolved the autonomy of women over matters of birth and reimagined the pregnant woman as a vessel carrying the uterus, a space that became of public interest and possible intervention."[139] The legal implications for women were complex. On the one hand, they became legally obligated to inform their parish priest of their pregnancy. On the other hand, some women were able to strategically invoke the new legal status accorded to fetuses in order to protect themselves from domestic or social violence.[140]

Throughout Spanish America, many people also sharply opposed "enlightened" efforts to reform funerary practices and bury the dead in cemeteries outside town rather than under church floors where they could receive the spiritual benefits of prayers and Masses.[141] Cemetery burials also posed a direct challenge to long-standing Mesoamerican, African, and Spanish Catholic understandings of the intimate bonds between the living and the dead.[142] During a typhus outbreak in the Maya Cuchumatan highlands in 1798, a Guatemalan professor of medicine arrived at the Ixil-Maya town of Nebaj and ordered residents to bury their dead in the cemetery. Furthermore, residents were prohibited from holding customary vigils to mourn the dead and instead were required to bury the bodies immediately upon death.[143] The community violently rejected these regulations, with women taking the lead as mothers, caretakers, and guardians of the community. Over seventy women backed by hundreds of armed villagers confronted the medical official and declared an effective end to the regulations.[144] Highland communities continued to reject cemetery burials well into the nineteenth century. It was not only public health officials taking aim at funerary practices. On his pastoral visit through Guatemala and El Salvador in the 1770s, Archbishop Pedro Cortés y Larraz vigorously opposed what he viewed as raucous and scandalous vigils for the dead, particularly those for infants and small children, which included dancing, card playing, and drinking.[145] His efforts to reform public mourning rituals similarly met a staunch wall of resistance.

Tensions also emerged as Guatemala's enlightened "humanitarianism" intertwined with growing colonial efforts to control and Hispanicize Indigenous and rural populations.[146] In the late colonial period, public health and colonial officials attempted to intervene in many intimate aspects of Indigenous daily life, including language, diet, and ritual-healing practices. In the eighteenth century, the Bourbon Spanish Crown turned away from the earlier Hapsburg model, which had accepted Indigenous communities as semiautonomous kingdoms with distinctive languages, clothing, and customs. In 1753, King Ferdinand declared that all native peoples should learn to speak Spanish.[147] Amid Indigenous resistance, this effort largely failed, as did efforts to force the Hispanicization of Indigenous dress. Meanwhile, medical professionals blamed Indigenous diets for high death rates and attempted to prohibit the eating of spicy foods.[148] And in the 1790s, the *audiencia* went so far as to prohibit the use of *temascales* (ritual steam baths), which were a central feature of Maya healing practices.[149] Public health visits also became an opportunity to investigate and repress the ongoing worship of Maya deities. In the late 1790s, officials destroyed or blocked the entrance to several shrines dedicated to Mesoamerican deities.[150] Some communities responded with force, as noted earlier, but more commonly residents simply abandoned towns and hid in mountains or forests where they found freedom to continue rituals of healing and mourning. To a large extent, Indigenous active and passive resistance effectively limited the impact of colonial and medical reform efforts.

Conclusion: At the Crossroads of Cultural Exchange and Conflict

The trend toward denser networks and regional integration in the eighteenth century came to a dramatic halt after independence. Exactly how and why remains open for further exploration, as do most topics of study for Central America in the first decades after independence.[151] Certainly the process of integration bore its own seeds of discord. Regions long accustomed to greater autonomy bristled at efforts to further centralize political and economic authority in Guatemala. And although the flourishing indigo economy intensified regional exchanges, it also heightened tensions between Salvadoran producers and Guatemalan merchants.[152] In the politically divisive aftermath of independence, the fierce political factionalism between "Liberals" and "Conservatives" converged with the long history of distinct regional histories and identities. Rivalries and tensions erupted into open warfare through the 1820s and 1830s, severely impeding travel and communication between regions. By the early 1840s, the Federal Republic of Central America dissolved into five nation-states.

The fierce sense of local autonomy carved into modern national borders also reflects Central America's long history as a cultural borderland. More than three centuries of colonial rule and the formation of modern nation-states never erased the pre-Columbian border between Mesoamerica and the culturally distinct southern half of Central America. In 1850, Central America remained a meeting point of a "densely settled Indigenous majority in the north and a mestizo equivalent in the underpopulated south."[153] The ensuing rise of Atlantic, and later Pacific, trade networks shifted roads and infrastructure toward ports, while the interior artery connecting Central American countries suffered from neglect.[154] And yet, annual fairs and pilgrimages continued to draw Central Americans from far and wide through the nineteenth century. The histories of those ongoing exchanges largely remain to be written.

Cultural histories of colonial Central America illuminate key points of encounter, negotiation, and conflict in this "complicated and sometimes violent crossroads" where Mesoamerica and the circum-Caribbean, Spanish and British empires met.[155] Contrary to the assumptions of Spanish crowns and missionaries (not to mention modern historians), there was no "spiritual conquest" of Central America. Spiritual beliefs and practices, from Catholicism to Indigenous medical-ritual practices became meeting grounds for native, Spanish, and African peoples marked by exchange and collaborations as well as tensions, repression, and resistance. Rather than a crystallized spiritual synthesis, we find diverse and dynamic processes of transculturation which continue to this day. Enslaved Africans and free Black individuals and communities cultivated relationships and networks that blurred the lines between slavery and freedom and between ethnoracial categories, helping to transform the forced labor system into a free wage labor system and dismantle the caste hierarchy after independence. In Central America's colonial capital, a "city of women" emerged as Indigenous, Black, and mixed-race laboring women became the urban majority; expanded the flexibility of gender and sexual ideals; established female leadership in Catholic lay associations as a local norm; and cultivated cross-cultural magical-religious healing practices and beliefs. Eighteenth-century trends facilitated greater cultural and intellectual exchanges across Central America and between the isthmus and the broader Spanish Empire and Atlantic world. These exchanges put Central America at the forefront of global efforts in education and public health. The growing field of cultural history in colonial Central America feels much like a frontier, with the exciting paths of research explored here only just begun, and many others yet to be charted. Current and future explorations promise not just to shed light on this culturally diverse borderlands region but also to reframe our understanding of colonial centers and broader Spanish America.[156]

NOTES

1. Michael Coe and Stephen Houston, *The Maya*, 9th ed. (New York: Thames and Hudson, 2015), 26. On the complexities of Maya ethnic identity from pre-Columbian times to the present, see European Maya Conference, and Frauke Sachse, *Maya Ethnicity: The Construction of Ethnic Identity From Preclassic to Modern Times: Proceedings from the 9th European Maya Conference, Bonn, December 10–12, 2004* (Markt Schwaben, Germany: A. Saurwein, 2006).
2. Sylvia Sellers-García, *Distance and Documents at the Spanish Empire's Periphery* (Stanford, CA: Stanford University Press, 2014), 9–14.
3. Ibid., 14.
4. Martha Few, *For All Humanity: Mesoamerican and Colonial Medicine in Enlightenment Guatemala* (Tucson: University of Arizona Press, 2015), 7. One senior scholar told me that her advisor refused to allow her to pursue a dissertation on a Central American topic, believing it would undermine her job prospects.
5. Adriaan Van Oss, *Catholic Colonialism: A Parish History of Guatemala*, 1524–1821 (Cambridge: Cambridge University Press, 2002), 7.
6. William Taylor, "Foreword," in *Words and Worlds Turned around: Indigenous Christianities in Colonial Latin America*, ed. David Tavárez (Boulder: University Press of Colorado, 2017), xi.
7. Louise Burkhart, "Introduction," in Tavárez, ed., *Words and Worlds*, 4–5.
8. Gary Gossen and Richard Leventhal, "The Topography of Ancient Maya Religious Pluralism: A Dialogue with the Present," in *Lowland Maya Civilization in the Eighth Century A.D.: A Symposium at Dumbarton Oaks*, ed. Jeremy Sabloff and John S. Henderson (Washington, DC: Dumbarton Oaks Research Library and Collection, 1993), 185–186.
9. Nancy Farriss, *Maya Society under Colonial Rule: The Collective Enterprise of Survival* (Princeton, NJ: Princeton University Press, 1984), 289.
10. Daniele Dupiech-Cavaleri and Mario Ruz, "La deidad fingida: Antonio Margil y la religiosidad Quiche del 1704," *Estudios de Cultura Maya* 17 (1988): 232, 235.
11. Ibid., 14–15, 69.
12. William Hanks, *Converting Words: Maya in the Age of the Cross* (Berkeley: University of California Press, 2010), 345.
13. Sergio Romero, "Language, Catechisms, and Mesoamerican Lords in Highland Guatemala: Addressing 'God' after the Spanish Conquest," *Ethnohistory* 62, no. 3 (July 2015): 623.
14. See Néstor Quiroa, "Friar Francisco Ximenez and the Popol Vuh: From Religious Treatise to a Digital Sacred Book," *Ethnohistory* 64, no. 2 (April 2017).
15. Romero, "Language, Catechisms," 628.
16. Frauke Sachse, "The Expression of Christian Concepts in Colonial K'iche' Missionary Texts," in *La transmision de conceptos cristianos a las lenguas amerindias: Estudios sobre textos y contextos de la época colonial*, ed. Sabine Dedenbach-Salazar Sáenz (Sankt Augustin, Germany: Academia Verlag, 2016), 105.

17. Néstor Quiroa, "Revisiting the Highland Guatemalan Títulos: How the Maya-K'iche' Lived and Outlived the Colonial Experience," *Ethnohistory* 58, no. 2 (Spring 2011): 306.
18. Sachse, "Expression of Christian Concepts," 105–107.
19. Quiroa, "Revisiting the Highland Guatemalan Títulos," 302, 316.
20. Ibid., 306–307.
21. Ibid., 312–314
22. Mario Humberto Ruz, "Amarrando juntos: La religiosidad Maya en la época colonial," in *Religión Maya*, ed. Mercedes de Garza Camino and Martha Ilia Nájera Coronado (Madrid: Editorial Trotta, 2002), 259; Juan Pedro Viqueira, "Éxitos y fracasos de la evangelización en Chiapas (1545–1859)," in *La Iglesia Católica en México*, ed. Nelly Sigaut (Michoacán, Mexico: El Colegio de Michoacán, 1995), 89.
23. Ruz, "Amarrando juntos," 257. See also Juan Pedro Viqueira, "Matrimonio y sexualidad en los confesionarios en lenguas indígenas," *Cuicuilco: Revista de la Escuela Nacional de Antropología e Historia*, no. 12 (January 1984).
24. Viqueira, "Éxitos y fracasos de la evangelización," 88.
25. Taylor, "Foreword," xiv.
26. Few, *For All Humanity*, 79.
27. Ibid., 82.
28. Mark Christensen, "Predictions and Portents of Doomsday in European, Nahuatl, and Maya Texts," in Tavárez, ed., *Words and Worlds*, 258.
29. John D. Early, "Some Ethnographic Implications of an Ethnohistorical Perspective of the Civil-Religious Hierarchy among the Highland Maya," *Ethnohistory* 30, no. 4 (Autumn 1983): 190. See also Elizabeth Graham, *Maya Christians and Their Churches in Sixteenth-Century Belize* (Gainesville: University Press of Florida, 2011).
30. Mario Humberto Ruz, "La Familia divina: Imaginario hagiografico en el mundo Maya," in Sigaut, ed., *Iglesia Católica en México*, 382–383.
31. Mario Humberto Ruz, "Una muerte auxiliada: Cofradías y hermandades en el mundo Maya colonial," *Relaciones. Estudios de historia y sociedad* 24, no. 94 (Spring 2003): 19.
32. Murdo MacLeod, "Papel social y económico de las cofradías indígenas de la colonial en Chiapas," *Mesoamérica* 4, no. 5 (1983): 85
33. Ruz, "Muerte auxiliada," 37. Mexicanists have examined this phenomenon in more depth. See Edward Osowski, *Indigenous Miracles: Nahua Authority in Colonial Mexico* (Tucson: University of Arizona Press, 2010); James Lockhart, *The Nahuas after the Conquest: A Social and Cultural History of the Indians of Central Mexico, Sixteenth through Eighteenth Centuries* (Stanford, CA: Stanford University Press, 1992), 226–28;
34. Alvis Dunn, "A Cry at Daybreak: Death, Disease, and Defense of Community in a Highland Ixil-Mayan Village," *Ethnohistory* 42, no. 4 (Fall 1995): 601. See also Leslie Devereaux, "Gender Difference and the Relations of Inequality in Zinacantan," in *Dealing with Inequality: Analysing Gender Relations in Melanesia and Beyond*, ed. Marilyn Stathern and Frank Cancian, *Economics and Prestige in a Maya Community: The Religious Cargo System in Zinacantán* (Stanford, CA: Stanford University Press, 1965).
35. Amos Megged, "The Religious Context of an 'Unholy Marriage': Elite Alienation and Popular Unrest in the Indigenous Communities of Chiapa, 1570–1680," *Ethnohistory* 46, no. 1 (Winter 1999): 149.
36. Greg Grandin, *The Blood of Guatemala: A History of Race and Nation* (Durham, NC: Duke University Press, 2000), 45.
37. Megged, "Religious Context," 155–157.

THE KINGDOM OF GUATEMALA AS A CULTURAL CROSSROADS 211

38. Ruz, "Amarrando juntos," 274.
39. Cecilia Klein, "None of the Above: Gender Ambiguity in Nahua Ideology," in *Gender in Pre-Hispanic America: A Symposium at Dumbarton Oaks*, ed. Cecilia Klein (Washington, DC: Dumbarton Oaks, 2001), 216–217.
40. Ibid.
41. David Carrasco, "Jaguar Christians in the Contact Zone: Concealed Narratives in the Histories of Religion in the Americas," in *Beyond Primitivism: Indigenous Religious Traditions and Modernity*, ed. Jacob Olupona (New York: Routledge, 2004), 130, 138.
42. "Testimonio de los autos hechos sobre la sublevación de treinta y dos pueblos del partido de los Zendales, Coronas, Chinampas, y Guardianía de Gueitiupa en la provincial de Chiapa," 1712, Signatura: Guatemala 295, 135f, Archivo de las Indias (AGI). See also Juan Pedro Viqueira, *Indios rebeldes e idólatras: Dos ensayos históricos sobre la rebelión india de Cancuc, Chiapas, acaecida en el año de 1712* (Mexico City: Centro de Investigaciones y Estudios Superiores en Antropología Social, 1997); Kevin Gosner, *Soldiers of the Virgin: The Moral Economy of a Colonial Maya Rebellion* (Tucson: University of Arizona Press, 1992).
43. Gosner, *Soldiers of the Virgin*, 125.
44. Ibid., 143. On María de Candelaria wearing priestly vestments, see "Testimonio de autos sobre la administración de los sacramentos por algunos aindios durante la sublevación de los zendales," 1712, Signatura: Guatemala, 294, 49f, AGI.
45. Lowell Gudmundson and Justin Wolfe, eds., *Blacks and Blackness in Central America: Between Race and Place* (Durham, NC: Duke University Press, 2010), 1
46. For an overview of recent scholarship that expands the view of the African diaspora in Latin America, see Rachel Sarah O'Toole, "As Historical Subjects: The African Diaspora in Colonial Latin American History," *History Compass* 11/12 (2013); Sherwin K. Bryant, Rachel Sarah O'Toole, and Ben Vinson III, eds. *Africans to Spanish America: Expanding the Diaspora* (Urbana: University of Illinois Press, 2012); Ben Vinson III, "Introduction: African (Black) Diaspora History, Latin American History," *The Americas* 63, no. 1 (July 2006).
47. Matthew Restall, "Black Conquistadors: Armed Africans in Early Spanish America," *The Americas* 57, no. 2 (October 2000), 173, 182–183. See also Leo Garofalo, "The Shape of a Diaspora: The Movement of Afro-Iberians to Colonial Spanish America," in Bryant et al., eds., *Africans to Spanish America*, 32, 38.
48. Restall, "Black Conquistadors," 189.
49. John Thornton, "Central Africa in the Era of the Slave Trade," in *Slaves, Subjects, and Subversives: Blacks in Colonial Latin America*, ed. Jane Landers and Barry Robinson (Albuquerque: University of New Mexico Press, 2006), 84.
50. Paul Lokken, "Angolans in Amatitlán: Sugar, African Migrants, and Gente Ladina in Colonial Guatemala," in Gudmundson and Wolfe, eds., *Blacks and Blackness*, 35.
51. On Africans filling economic "niches" see Herbert Klein and Ben Vinson III, *African Slavery in Latin America and the Caribbean*, 2nd ed. (Oxford: Oxford University Press, 2007), 33. For Central American context, see Gudmundson and Wolfe, *Blacks and Blackness*, 11.
52. This pattern was established from the start on the earliest sugar plantations in Hispaniola. See Lynne Guitar, "Boiling It Down: Slavery on the First Commercial Sugarcane Ingenios in the Americas (Hispaniola, 1530–45)," in Landers and Robinson, eds., *Slaves, Subjects, and Subversives*, 48.
53. Christopher Lutz and Matthew Restall, "Wolves and Sheep? Black–Maya Relations in Colonial Guatemala and Yucatan," in *Beyond Black and Red: African-Native Relations in Colonial Latin America*, ed. Matthew Restall (Albuquerque: University of New Mexico, 2005), 195.

54. Ibid., 194, 197.
55. Paul Lokken, "Mulatos, negros y el mestizaje en las Alcaldías mayores de San Salvador y Sonsonate (siglo XVII)," in *Mestizaje, poder, y Sociedad*, ed. Ana Margarita Gómez and Sajid Alfredo Herrera (San Salvador: FLACSO Programa El Salvador, 2003), 18.
56. Lutz and Restall, "Wolves and Sheep," 197.
57. Catherine Komisaruk, *Labor and Love in Guatemala: The Eve of Independence* (Stanford, CA: Stanford University Press, 2013), 80.
58. Lokken, "Angolans in Amatitlán," 32.
59. Ibid., 35.
60. Russel Lohse, "Cacao and Slavery in Matina, Costa Rica, 1650–1750," in Gudmundson and Lowell, eds., *Blacks and Blackness*, 57.
61. Ibid., 74–77.
62. Ibid., 80–81.
63. Klein and Vinson, *African Slavery*, 25.
64. Ibid., 27; Lutz and Restall, "Wolves and Sheep," 204–206.
65. Catherine Komisaruk, "Becoming Free, Becoming Ladino: Slave Emancipation and *Mestizaje* in Colonial Guatemala," in Gudmundson and Lowell, eds., *Blacks and Blackness*, 150.
66. Christopher Lutz, *Santiago de Guatemala, 1541–1773: City, Caste, and the Colonial Experience* (Norman: University of Oklahoma Press, 1994), 92.
67. Komisaruk, "Becoming Free," 150.
68. Gudmundson and Lowell, *Blacks and Blackness*, 11.
69. Lutz, *Santiago de Guatemala*, 167.
70. For an early exploration of this theme, see Leonardo Hernández, "La Ilustración ante la sociedad de 'magicos' y 'monstruos': cultura urbana y rural de la provincia de San Salvador según el arzobispo Cortés y Larraz (siglo XVIII)" in *Mestizaje, poder, y sociedad*, ed. Ana Margarita Gómez and Sajid Alfredo Herrera (San Salvador: FLACSO Programa El Salvador, 2003), 36–38.
71. For an overview of scholarship on the Mosquito Kingdom, see Daniel Mendiola, "The Rise of the Mosquito Kingdom in Central America's Caribbean borderlands: Sources, Questions, and Enduring Myths," *History Compass* 16 (2018): 1–10.
72. Eugenia Ibarra, "La complementariedad cultural en el surgimiento de los grupos Zambos del Cabo Gracias a Dios, en la Mosquitia, durante los siglos XVII y XVIII," *Revista de Estudios Sociales* 26 (April 2007): 105–115.
73. John Thornton, "The Zambos and the Transformation of the Miskitu Kingdom, 1636–1740," *Hispanic American Historical Review* 97, no. 1 (2017): 10–11. On the centrality of female captivity to the Mosquito Kingdom, see Karl Offen, "Mapping Amerindian Captivity in Colonial Mosquitia," *Journal of Latin American Geography* 14, no. 3 (2015): 35–65.
74. Karl Offen, "Race and Place in Colonial Mosquitia, 1600–1787," in Gudmundson and Wolfe, eds., *Blacks and Blackness*, 121.
75. Klein and Vinson, *African Slavery*, 165–66.
76. Komisaruk, *Labor and Love*, 74.
77. See Ann Twinam, *Purchasing Whiteness: Pardos, Mulattos, and the Quest for Social Mobility in the Spanish* Indies (Stanford, CA: Stanford University Press, 2015); Ben Vinson III, *Bearing Arms for His Majesty: The Free-Colored Militia in Colonial Mexico* (Stanford, CA: Stanford University Press, 2001); Nicole von Germeten, *Black Blood Brothers: Confraternities and Social Mobility for Afro-Mexicans* (Gainesville: University Press of Florida, 2006).

78. Leavitt-Alcántara cites here Ann Stoler, "Tense and Tender Ties: The Politics of Comparison in North American History and (Post) Colonial Studies," *The Journal of American History* 88, no. 3 (2001); and Brianna Leavitt-Alcántara, "Single Women and Spiritual Capital: Sexuality and Devotion in Colonial Guatemala," in *The Routledge Companion to Sexuality and Colonialism*, ed. Dagmar Herzog and Chelsea Schields (forthcoming).

79. Lokken, "Mulatos, negros, y el mestizaje," 20.

80. Twinam, *Purchasing Whiteness*, 113.

81. Komisaruk, *Labor and Love*, 157.

82. Ibid.; Twinam, *Purchasing Whiteness*, 35

83. Laura E. Matthew, "'Por que el color decide aquí en la mayor parte la nobleza': Una carta de Fr. José Antonio Goicoechea, Guatemala, siglo XIX," *Mesoamérica* 55 (December–January 2013): 162.

84. Alvis Dunn, "A Sponge Soaking up All the Money: Alcohol, Taverns, Vinaterías, and the Bourbon Reforms in Mid-Eighteenth-Century Santiago de los Caballeros, Guatemala," in *Distilling the Influence of Alcohol: Aguardiente in Guatemalan History*, ed. David Carey (Gainesville: University Press of Florida, 2012), 71.

85. Miles Wortman, *Government and Society in Central America, 1680 to 1840* (New York: Columbia University Press, 1982), 92–93. Wortman cited Guatemalan chronicler Francisco Fuentes y Guzman's assertion that Santiago's fountain and plaza were "second only to Lima." See Francisco Antonio de Fuentes y Guzmán, *Recordación Florida: Discurso Historial Y Demostración Natural, Material, Militar Y Política Del Reyno De Guatemala*, 2nd ed., 3 vols. (Guatemala: Sociedad de Geografía e Historia, 1932–1933), 1:215.

86. Verle Lincoln Annis, *The Architecture of Antigua Guatemala, 1543–1773* (Guatemala City: Universidad de San Carlos, 1968), 80–97, 166–172; Domingo Juarros, *Compendio De La Historia De La Ciudad De Guatemala* (Guatemala City: Academia de Geografía e Historia de Guatemala, 2000), 155–159.

87. Margaret Chowning, *Rebellious Nuns: The Troubled History of a Mexican Convent, 1752–1863* (Oxford: Oxford University Press, 2006), 9.

88. Brianna Leavitt-Alcántara, *Alone at the Altar: Single Women and Devotion in Guatemala, 1670–1870* (Stanford, CA: Stanford University Press, 2018), 24; Annis, *Architecture*, 165–66; Lutz, *Santiago de Guatemala*, 110. Archivo Histórico Arquidiocesano de Guatemala. Fondo Diocesano, Secretaria de Gobierno, Visitas de los Monasterios de esta ciudad desde 1659 hasta 1780.

89. Dunn, "'Sponge Soaking up All the Money,'" 79.

90. Ibid., 78.

91. Sylvia Sellers-García, *The Woman on the Windowsill: A Tale of Mystery in Several Parts* (New Haven, CT: Yale University Press, 2020), 37–38.

92. Ibid., 44.

93. Ibid., 8.

94. Ibid., 47; Catherine Komisaruk, "Rape Narratives, Rape Silences: Sexual Violence and Judicial Testimony in Colonial Guatemala," *Biography* 31, no. 3 (Summer 2008): 373.

95. Sellers-García, *Woman on the Windowsill*, 97.

96. Lutz, *Santiago de Guatemala*, 234.

97. Komisaruk, *Labor and Love*, 61, 117.

98. Jay Kinsbruner, *The Colonial Spanish-American City: Urban Life in the Age of Atlantic Capitalism* (Austin: University of Texas Press, 2005), 113.

99. Cited in Komisaruk, *Labor and Love*, 61.
100. Padrón echo en fines de Diciembre de 1796 por el Alcalde de Barrio don Pedro José de Gorriz, correspondiente al Quartel de Santo Domingo y Barrio de las Capuchinas, 1796, Sig. A1, Leg. 5344, Exp. 45056, Archivo General de Centroamérica (AGCA); Padrones formados por los Alcaldes de Barrio de Orden del Superior Gobierno, 1805, Sig. A1, Leg. 2190, Exp. 15738, AGCA. Padrón general del Barrio de San José, en el Quartel de la Merced de Guatemala, formado por el Regidor José Echeverría y el comicionado por la hacienda Publica Ciudadano Cleto Córdova, 1825, Sig. B84, Leg. 1131, Exp. 25989, AGCA. See also Komisaruk, *Labor and Love*, 9.
101. Beatriz Palomo de Lewin, "'Por ser una pobre viuda': La viudez en la Guatemala de fines del siglo XVIII y principios del siglo XIX," *Dialogos. Revista electronica de historia* 5, nos. 1–2 (Mar. 2004–Feb. 2005); Komisaruk, *Labor and Love*, 247.
102. Lutz, *Santiago de Guatemala*, 83, 234.
103. Komisaruk, *Labor and Love*, 191.
104. Ibid., 116, 120.
105. Allyson Poska, "Elusive Virtue: Rethinking the Role of Female Chastity in Early Modern Spain," *Journal of Early Modern History* 8, nos. 1–2 (2004): 135.
106. Lutz, *Santiago de Guatemala*, 234.
107. See Ann Twinam, *Public Lives, Private Secrets: Gender, Honor, Sexuality, and Illegitimacy in Colonial Spanish America* (Stanford, CA: Stanford University Press, 1999)
108. Komisaruk, *Labor and Love*, 224.
109. Leavitt-Alcántara, *Alone at the Altar*, 52.
110. Komisaruk, *Labor and Love*, 173, 186, 193, 233.
111. Lutz, *Santiago de Guatemala*, 234.
112. Richard Boyer, "Honor among Plebeians: Mala Sangre and Social Reputation," in *Faces of Honor: Sex, Shame, and Violence in Colonial Latin America*, ed. Lyman Johnson and Sonya Lipsett-Rivera (Albuquerque: University of New Mexico Press, 1998), 156.
113. For an anthropological model of "alternative" feminine ideals, see Heidi Kelley, "Unwed Mothers and Household Reputation in a Spanish Galician Community," *American Ethnologist* 18, no. 3 (1991): 565.
114. Leavitt-Alcántara, *Alone at the Altar*, 78–80; von Germeten, *Black Blood Brothers*, 46; Margaret Chowning, "La feminización de la piedad en México: Género y piedad en las cofradías de españoles. Tendencias coloniales y pos-coloniales en los arzobispados de Michoacán y Guadalajara," in *Religión, política, e identidad en la independencia de México*, ed. Brian Connaughton (Mexico City: Universidad Autónoma Metropolitana, 2010), 481, 83.
115. Ibid., 86–90.
116. Ibid., 7.
117. Ruz, "Muerte auxiliada," 37.
118. Leavitt-Alcántara, *Alone at the Altar*, 80. For Chiapas, see María Dolores Palomo Infant, *Juntos y congregados: Historia de las cofradías en los pueblos de indios tzotziles y tzeltales de Chiapas (siglos XVI a XIX)* (Mexico City: CIESAS, 2009), 87.
119. Leavitt-Alcántara, *Alone at the Altar*, 81.
120. Martha Few, *Women Who Live Evil Lives: Gender, Religion, and the Politics of Power in Colonial Guatemala* (Austin: University of Texas Press, 2002), 3, 7.
121. Ibid., 44.
122. Ibid.

123. Douglass Sullivan-González, *The Black Christ of Esquipulas: Religion and Identity in Guatemala* (Lincoln: University of Nebraska Press, 2016), 42, 47. On growing popularity of miraculous shrines in broader eighteenth-century New Spain, see William B. Taylor, *Theater of a Thousand Wonders: A History of Miraculous Images and Shrines in New Spain* (Cambridge: Cambridge University Press, 2016).

124. Sellers-García, *Distance and Documents*, 63.

125. Ibid., 45.

126. Ibid., 63.

127. Lindo-Fuentes, "Economy of Central America," 67.

128. Few, *For All Humanity*, 9; See also Elisa Luque Alcaie, *La Sociedad Economica de Amigos del Pais de Guatemala* (Seville, Spain: Escuela de Estudios Hispano-Americanos de Seville, 1962).

129. Andrés Lira González, "Las escuelas de primeras letras en la Municipalidad de Guatemala hacía 1824 (un intent para organizer la educación elemental)," *Latino América* 3 (1970): 117–140.

130. Leavitt-Alcántara, *Alone at the Altar*, 104.

131. Few, *For All Humanity*, 17.

132. Martha Few, "Circulating Smallpox Knowledge: Guatemalan Doctors, Maya Indians and Designing Spain's Smallpox Vaccination Expedition, 1780–1803," *The British Society for the History of Science* 43, no. 4 (Dec 2010): 520.

133. Ibid., 525.

134. Ibid., 534.

135. Sellers-García, *Woman on the Windowsill*, 117.

136. Martha Few, "That Monster of Nature: Gender, Sexuality, and the Medicalization of a 'Hermaphrodite' in Late Colonial Guatemala," *Ethnohistory* 54, no. 1 (Winter 2007): 162–163. On continuity of folk-healing practices in modern Costa Rica, see Ana Paulina Malavassi Aguilar, *Entre la marginalidad social y los orígenes de la salud pública: Leprosos, curanderos y facultativos en el Valle Central de Costa Rica (1784–1845)* (San José, Costa Rica: Editorial de la Universidad de Costa Rica, 2003); Ana Paulina Malavassi Aguilar, "De parteras a obstétricas: La profesionalización de una practica tradicional en Costa Rica (1900–1940)," in *Mujeres, genero, e historia en América Central durante los siglos XVIII, XIX, y XX* (San José, Costa Rica: UNIFEM, 2002).

137. Eugenia Rodríguez-Sáenz, "Relaciones Ilícitas y Matrimonios Desiguales: Bourbon Reforms and the Regulation of Sexual Mores in Eighteenth-Century Costa Rica," in *Politics, Economy, and Society in Bourbon Central America, 1759–1821*, ed. Jordana Dym and Christopher Belaubre (Boulder: University Press of Colorado, 2007), 186–187, 195.

138. Few, *For All Humanity*, 99–100.

139. Ibid., 114.

140. Ibid., 130.

141. For an in-depth analysis of cemetery debates in Mexico, see Pamela Voekel, *Alone before God: The Religious Origins of Modernity in Mexico* (Durham, NC: Duke University Press, 2002).

142. On early modern Spanish Catholic beliefs and practices related to dying, see Carlos Eire, *From Madrid to Purgatory: The Art and Craft of Dying in Sixteenth-Century Spain* (Cambridge: Cambridge University Press, 1995).

143. Alvis Dunn, "A Cry at Daybreak: Death, Disease, and Defense of Community in a Highland Ixil-Maya Village," *Ethnohistory* 42, no. 4 (Fall 1995): 595–797.

144. Ibid., 599, 603.
145. Hernández, "Ilustración," 38.
146. Few, *For All Humanity*, 10, 100.
147. Sajid Alfredo Herrera, "Primary Education in Bourbon San Salvador and Sonsonate, 1750–1808," in Dym and Belaubre, eds., *Politics, Economy, and Society*, 21.
148. Few, *For All Humanity*, 52.
149. Ibid., 71.
150. Ibid., 80–82.
151. Lowell Gudmundson, "Society and Politics in Central America, 1821–1871," in *Central America, 1821–1871: Liberalism before Liberal Reform*, ed. Lowell Gudmundson and Héctor Lindo-Fuentes (Tuscaloosa: University of Alabama Press, 1995), 79.
152. Héctor Lindo-Fuentes, "The Economy of Central America: From Bourbon Reforms to Liberal Reforms," in Gudmundson and Lindo-Fuentes, eds., *Central America, 1821–1871*, 19.
153. Gudmundson, "Society and Politics," 111.
154. Lindo-Fuentes, "Economy of Central America," 31.
155. Few, *For All Humanity*, 7.
156. Sellers-García, *Distance and Documents*, 3, 5.

FURTHER READING

Dunn, Alvis. "A Cry at Daybreak: Death, Disease, and Defense of Community in a Highland Ixil-Mayan Village." *Ethnohistory* 42, no. 4 (Fall 1995): 595–606.

Dunn, Alvis. "'A Sponge Soaking up All the Money': Alcohol, Taverns, Vinaterías, and the Bourbon Reforms in Mid-Eighteenth-Century Santiago de los Caballeros, Guatemala." In *Distilling the Influence of Alcohol: Aguardiente in Guatemalan History*. Edited by David Carey, 71–95. Gainesville: University Press of Florida, 2012.

Few, Martha. *Women Who Live Evil Lives: Gender, Religion, and the Politics of Power in Colonial Guatemala*. Austin: University of Texas Press, 2002.

Few, Martha. *For All Humanity: Mesoamerican and Colonial Medicine in Enlightenment Guatemala*. Tucson: University of Arizona Press, 2015.

Gómez, Ana Margarita, and Sajid Alfredo Herrera, eds. *Mestizaje, poder, y sociedad*. San Salvador: FLACSO Programa El Salvador, 2003.

Gosner, Kevin. *Soldiers of the Virgin: The Moral Economy of a Colonial Maya Rebellion*. Tucson: University of Arizona Press, 1992

Gudmundson, Lowell, and Justin Wolfe, eds. *Blacks and Blackness in Central America: Between Race and Place*. Durham, NC: Duke University Press, 2010.

Komisaruk, Catherine. *Labor and Love in Guatemala: The Eve of Independence*. Stanford, CA: Stanford University Press, 2013.

Leavitt-Alcántara, Brianna. *Alone at the Altar: Single Women and Devotion in Guatemala, 1670–1870*. Stanford, CA: Stanford University Press, 2018.

Lutz, Christopher. *Santiago de Guatemala: 1541–1773: City, Caste, and the Colonial Experience*. Norman: University of Oklahoma Press, 1994.

Megged, Amos. *Exporting the Catholic Reformation: Local Religion in Early-Colonial Mexico*. Leiden, The Netherlands: E.J. Brill, 1996.

Quiroa, Néstor. "Revisiting the Highland Guatemalan Títulos: How the Maya-K'iche' Lived and Outlived the Colonial Experience." *Ethnohistory* 58, no. 2 (Spring 2011): 293–321.

Romero, Sergio. "Language, Catechisms, and Mesoamerican Lords in Highland Guatemala: Addressing 'God' after the Spanish Conquest." *Ethnohistory* 62, no. 3 (July 2015): 623–649.

Ruz, Mario Humberto. "Amarrando juntos: La religiosidad Maya en la época colonial." In *Religión Maya*, ed. Mercedes de Garza Camino and Martha Ilia Nájera Coronado, 247–281. Madrid: Editorial Trotta, 2002.

Sellers-García, Sylvia. *Distance and Documents at the Spanish Empire's Periphery*. Stanford, CA: Stanford University Press, 2014.

Sellers-García, Sylvia. *The Woman on the Windowsill: A Tale of Mystery in Several Parts*. New Haven, CT: Yale University Press, 2020.

Sullivan-Gonzalez, Douglass. *The Black Christ of Esquipulas: Religion and Identity in Guatemala*. Lincoln: University of Nebraska Press, 2016.

Tavárez, David, ed. *Words and Worlds Turned around: Indigenous Christianities in Colonial Latin America*. Boulder: University Press of Colorado, 2017.

Viqueira, Juan Pedro. *Indios rebeldes e idólatras: Dos ensayos históricos sobre la rebelión india de Cancuc, Chiapas, acaecida en el año de 1712*. Mexico City: Centro de Investigaciones y Estudios Superiores en Antropología Social, 1997.

CHAPTER 8

FROM KINGDOM TO REPUBLICS, 1808–1840

AARON POLLACK

THE crisis of the Spanish monarchy in 1808 added a set of political complications to a Central American society in flux and slogging through an economic crisis.[1] The political, fiscal, social, religious, and territorial changes begun in the middle years of the eighteenth century under the earlier Bourbons and more fully developed under Charles III throughout Spanish America would continue under his successors and the independent American political entities through the following decades. Between 1808 and 1840, turmoil engulfed the territories of the Kingdom of Guatemala that would become the five independent Central American countries and the Mexican state of Chiapas, turning much more violent after independence in 1821. The political and social upheavals tend to overshadow the ongoing societal changes and policy reforms that accompanied and at times promoted them. Nonetheless, the ideas that had spawned the eighteenth-century reforms continued to thrive and many of the processes that had begun in that period continued well into the nineteenth, even while economic shifts, social unrest, and political violence played their part in modifying them. With that premise in mind, this article describes the novelties of this period of obvious political transition, and how they fit into larger processes that began much earlier and continued long after it ended.[2]

A BOURBON KINGDOM IN THE CRISIS OF THE SPANISH MONARCHY

The later Bourbons sought to strengthen the Spanish position vis-à-vis France and England, their principal imperial rivals, implementing changes that would finance military improvements. Influenced by the rationalist thinking of the eighteenth century, the Bourbon policies were intended to improve the manner in which their territories were governed and move toward the creation of a modern state (one step in a process that would continue after independence) that could act as lone arbiter in aspects of social and political life previously under the jurisdiction of corporations which were ultimately subservient to the Crown. Territorial reorganization, with the creation of intendancies in many parts of Spanish America, accompanied fiscal changes and efforts to place the Catholic Church firmly under Crown control, improve agricultural production, and regain military control in areas threatened by European rivals. These policies did not necessarily bring about the planned results, but they nevertheless did provoke changes throughout American societies.[3]

In the Kingdom of Guatemala, the Crown established intendancies in the 1780s which would maintain into the early nineteenth century: Ciudad Real (Chiapas), Comayagua (Honduras), León (Nicaragua), and San Salvador (El Salvador). Anomalously, the territory of present-day Guatemala, along with Sonsonate, continued to be administrated through *alcaldías mayores* and *corregimientos*. The governor, captain general, and president of the *audiencia* supervised fiscal concerns in these territories that also formed a single jurisdiction for questions of land tenancy.[4] Costa Rica formed part of the intendancy of León, managing its economic, political, and judicial affairs independently. Belize, controlled by the British had become the primary point of entry for contraband English textiles by the end of the colonial period. Notwithstanding the spread of contraband, augmented by the difficulties posed to legal trade by wars and British control of the seas, *alcabala* (including customs duties and a sort of sales tax), the collection of which had passed from municipal to Crown officials in the latter half of the eighteenth century, would continue to be, along with tribute and tobacco, one of the principal sources of royal income at the time of independence. The establishment of a tobacco monopoly proved to be the most important fiscal innovation of the late eighteenth century, bringing in nearly a third of royal income in the Kingdom by the end of the independence period. The liquor monopoly, while less successful in fiscal terms, demonstrated the Crown's willingness to intervene more directly in local livelihoods, while reforms to tribute payments by Indians (and others, to a lesser extent) increased royal income in the latter part of the eighteenth century.[5]

Municipal reform would, for the most part, strengthen the position of the few *ayuntamientos* active in the Kingdom prior to the Cádiz reforms, even as these bodies now negotiated with the newly established intendancies, providing a precedent for the relationships that would develop in the decades after independence.[6] Royal efforts to reduce public and affective forms of religious celebration, promoting instead more rational and private forms of worship, received support from enlightened prelates and clergymen, creating tensions that would come to a head with the more radical anticlerical policies of the 1830s. Pious foundations and *capellanías* in the Kingdom of Guatemala, it should be remembered, acted as creditors to many merchants and landholders, giving an inordinate amount of power to those individuals, often well connected to the merchants themselves, who controlled access to loans.[7] The power of the Guatemala City merchants over indigo growers in El Salvador, miners in Honduras, as well as cattlemen in Nicaragua and Honduras created constant tensions that played an increasingly important role from the moment of independence until the fall of the Central American Federation. Conflicts between capital cities and the towns and regions within the intendancies, and later states, would form a basic part of the dynamics of the period.[8]

By the time Carlos IV and Ferdinand VII had renounced the Spanish throne in favor of Napoleon in 1808, the inhabitants of the Kingdom of Guatemala were struggling through an economic depression brought on by a crisis in indigo production and trade, which had been the lifeblood of the Central American formal economy.[9] Accompanying this economic downturn were increasing demands by a Spanish Crown in grave fiscal difficulties and in need of funds to finance its wars. Forced and voluntary loans along with special taxes (*contribuciones extraordinarias*) charged to individuals became common in the last decades of the eighteenth century and would continue after independence. In 1804 the Crown applied in its American colonies a 1798 decree initially used in peninsular Spain through which it alienated property and capital owned by "pious works" (cathedrals, convents, parishes, religious brotherhoods, chantries, etc.), in the form of forced loans, monies that permitted the payment of interest owed on government bonds. Given that some of these institutions offered much of the credit available in the Kingdom of Guatemala, the decree (known as the *consolidación de los vales reales*) decapitalized the territory.[10]

Unlike what occurred in many other parts of the Spanish monarchy, both on the Peninsula and in America, the political crisis provoked by Napoleon did not result in the creation of a local governing junta in the Kingdom of Guatemala during 1808 and 1809, though unrest would follow not long after.[11] In the capital, the merchant class, through their participation in the Guatemala City *ayuntamiento*, would seem to have entered into some sort of unstated agreement with Captain General González Saravia, by virtue of which it would continue, and extend, the political and economic power it had long enjoyed in the isthmus, in return for not pressing demands for autonomy.[12] In Ciudad Real, capital of the Chiapas intendancy, the *ayuntamiento* ousted the acting intendant José Mariano Valero in 1809, accusing him of sympathizing with the French. The conflict between the municipal government and the crown official had been public since 1805, and the city authorities used the French invasion as an excuse to rid themselves of a thorn in their side.[13] Minor street protests in Guatemala City in 1808 did not produce any broader political developments nor did it create especially significant concerns among Spanish authorities, though repressive measures were applied.

During the *vacatio regis*, that would last until the return of Fernando VII in 1814, wars, revolts, and general social unrest wracked Spanish America as the colonies looked first for autonomy and later for Independence, even as liberal ideas and policies would spread throughout the Spanish territories, most notably with the debates surrounding, and later enactment of, the Cádiz constitution of 1812.[14] José Bonaparte had been named king, but his authority was questioned by the peninsular juntas, later unified under the Supreme Central Junta, a body whose power was severely limited in the peninsula, though it retained authority over those territories in America that remained under royal control, the Kingdom of Guatemala among them.

With limited suffrage and indirect voting, the elections for Cortes convoked by the Supreme Central Junta in 1809 set an important precedent for electoral processes in Spanish America. After the recognition by the Junta that American territories should not be considered colonies but rather part of the Spanish nation, a new political path opened for what were, or would become, independence- or autonomy-minded Americans. The decision by the Supreme Central Junta to dissolve itself and transfer its power to a Regency Council in January 1810 provoked criticism by many American *ayuntamientos* that argued from a pactist perspective that they should have been consulted previously, creating a specific point of rupture with the acting Spanish authorities, though not, for the most part, with the monarchy.[15] The *ayuntamientos* in the Kingdom of Guatemala recognized the Regency Council, though Comayagua questioned the legitimacy of such a decision, and in Guatemala City five municipal council members opposed the measure, sustaining their position with the same pactist argument.[16]

The enormous popular revolt in neighboring New Spain that erupted in September 1810 would provoke response in the Kingdom of Guatemala and a proposal by the *ayuntamiento* of Guatemala to mediate in the conflict. The violent and, at times, brutal anti-Spaniard sentiment expressed by the primarily Indian and mestizo peasants who followed parish priest Miguel Hidalgo provoked fear in certain sectors of the population in the captaincy general, as it did in Mexico. In part as a response to this crisis, Dominican Friar Ramón Casaús y Torres, whose declared antipathy for the insurgents had been shown in his written censures of Hidalgo, arrived from Oaxaca to take charge of the Guatemalan Archdiocese in 1811, on the heels of new captain general, José de Bustamante. These two men successfully worked to limit insurgent activity in the Kingdom of Guatemala during the tense years that followed, in which most of Spanish America suffered through independence wars, though they would be sorely tried in the process.[17]

The lack of an armed movement in favor of autonomy or independence in the captaincy general sets the region apart from the remainder of continental Spanish American territories.[18] It would seem that the *ayuntamiento* of Guatemala City, the body that could most easily have created a governing junta in the Kingdom, preferred to expand its powers within the Spanish monarchy, creating a certain amount of "autonomy," not terribly unlike what other American territories struggled for and often obtained, at times through the use of violence, in the second decade of the nineteenth century.[19] The efforts at creating regional juntas in San Salvador and León did not find purchase, facing resistance from dominant groups in those cities and from other regions in their respective intendancies. Given the desires of the provinces to escape the control of the Guatemala City merchants, it is unlikely that any formal attempt at declaring autonomy or independence by that group would have met a positive response elsewhere. Through his counterinsurgency policies, Captain General Bustamante effectively weakened attempts at creating insurgent movements, though Hawkins has recently argued that this cannot be seen as a sufficient explanation for the lack of organized armed efforts to gain independence in the Kingdom.[20]

During the final months of 1811, the tranquility that seemed to reign on the isthmus came to an end, with an uprising in the city of San Salvador in November and a set of violent protests in Indian towns in the Guatemalan highlands. The uprising in the city of San Salvador provoked similar actions in towns in the intendancy that it governed, preceding rebellions in León, Granada, a number of towns in the Intendancy of León, Tegucigalpa in the Intendancy of Comayagua, and San José in Costa Rica. These events were quite complex, and their virulence and duration varied greatly, but in each of them local realities, in part constructed by the policies of Charles III and Charles IV, developed in a Spanish American context defined by war, the *vacatio regis*, and liberal policies.[21]

Alliances, coordination, and conflicts between subaltern actors and local elites were a common aspect of nearly all the urban conflicts mentioned, and the analysis of these relationships and of the underlying causes for the revolts continues to provoke discussion among historians. Fiscal concerns, anti-peninsular Spaniard sentiment, the desire of previously excluded groups to participate in municipal government, and resentment resulting from repression became entangled with local intra-elite conflicts and desires for regional autonomy in different forms, including the above-mentioned attempts to create regional governmental juntas.[22] Many of these concerns can be traced to policies implemented in the preceding decades, but the mobilizations also drew on the new political situation provoked by the *vacation regis*: changes implemented in Cádiz (including popular sovereignty, elections, the elimination of tribute, and the denial of the vote to men of African ancestry) and the news of rebellion in other parts of Spanish America.[23]

The changing notions of sovereignty, which recent historiography has underlined, must be emphasized here. If the *vacatio regis* had thrown open the question of where sovereignty lay and what doctrines would be used to justify it, calls for clear breaks with the Spanish monarchy in other American territories only emphasized the uncertainty around who in fact was sovereign. In the pactist tradition, sovereignty belonged to the people and had been delegated to the king. Without the king, sovereignty reverted to the people. But what exactly did "the people" mean? Did it refer to elected regional bodies such as those that would soon be established by the Cádiz constitution, or to the *ayuntamientos*? While these last had traditionally expressed the concerns of dominant groups in urban centers, the Cádiz constitutions brought other classes into previously existing *ayuntamientos*, leaving open a window for new voices to be heard. The constitution also created new *ayuntamientos* and, at least on the formal and symbolic level, brought Indian and Ladino town councils onto equal footing with those dominated by Spaniards.[24] According to the new liberal political doctrines as well, sovereignty resided with the people, or, in the case the Cádiz constitution, the nation.[25] The point is not so much whether or not popular sovereignty can be considered to be effective but rather the fact that it did become the commonly accepted form of political legitimacy, and remains so.

The competition between dominant groups in different regions within the intendancies, shown in the rejected calls for governmental juntas, repeated the experience in many parts of South America, and the dynamic would recur during the discussions around annexation to the Mexican Empire and later during the years of the Federation. Dominant regional groups did not necessarily feel that following the lead of intendancy capitals would benefit them and they often found themselves in conflict with one another, commonly expressed via the *ayuntamientos*. In the suddenly politically uncertain context of these years, conflicts over economic dominance turned into political and later military confrontations. An example of this sort of tension can be found in Honduras, where the creation of the intendancy of Comayagua in 1786 meant a loss of power for the dominant groups in the city of Tegucigalpa that no longer controlled the hinterland that had formed a part of the *alcaldía mayor* of the same name. After years of legal maneuvering, the long-standing conflict between elites in the cities of Tegucigalpa and Comayagua ended with an 1812 declaration by the Junta Superior reestablishing the *alcaldía mayor* of Tegucigalpa.[26]

By early 1812, the situation was anything but under control and though a negotiated settlement in Granada seemed to have put an end to the unrest by April of that year, the mobilization of royal troops to bring it about, and the exchange of fire between them and the local population, provoked a change in the manner that Captain General Bustamante would manage rebellious acts in the *audiencia*.[27] The forced march of the Granadan rebels, many of whom were creole elites, to Guatemala City where they would be imprisoned and tried, stoked the ire of other creoles in the isthmus, as can most readily be appreciated in the failed Belén Conspiracy, planned between September and December 1813, seemingly intended to overthrow Bustamante.[28] Discovered and brought to an end just before military action would have been taken, the Belén conspirators included at least one member of the Guatemala City *ayuntamiento*, José Francisco Barrundia, who would play a leading role in the "Jacobin" government in the state of Guatemala after independence and continue as a political force in the following decades.[29]

CONSTITUTION AND UNREST

Input from both peninsular Spain and the Americas informed the creation of the Cádiz Constitution of 1812, in many senses a revolutionary document. In addition to sending representatives to the Cortes, ideas from the Kingdom of Guatemala flowed across the Atlantic through instructions sent by several isthmian *ayuntamientos*.[30] The members of the *ayuntamiento* of Guatemala City, unable to agree on a single document, sent two different proposals, widely discussed since, to the courts for consideration.[31] The constitution recognized all people living in the Spanish territories as members of the Spanish nation but denied citizenship to those of African heritage, a rather inelegant means of reducing the American representation in the Cortes. It also established the separation of powers, freedom of the press, the basis for a system of proportional taxes on income, and three popularly elected levels of government: the national *cortes*, including representatives from all territories that formed part of the Spanish monarchy, the *diputaciones provinciales* (provincial councils), and the *ayuntamientos*. The constitution also resolved the problem of sovereignty that had become of paramount concern in the King's absence, by placing it in the nation.[32] The Cádiz Constitution would remain in effect in Central America until the Federal Constitution of 1825 supplanted it, and it would continue to influence constitutional thought in the isthmus and in the remainder of Spanish America.

The liberal constitution and laws were in part intended to weaken autonomous sentiment in America, and in the *audiencia* of Guatemala, like other American territories where Spanish authorities managed to maintain control, they offered a political opening for many who wished to continue forward as part of the Spanish monarchy, but under a different set of rules and with greater local autonomy. It offered the isthmian population, and the *ayuntamientos* in particular, legal means to question policies implemented by Bustamante, who in turn slowed the application of the Cádiz reforms as much as possible, especially to the degree that they weakened the harsh counterinsurgency policies that he had begun to implement in 1812.[33]

Unrest continued between 1812 and 1814 in the Indian towns of the Guatemalan highlands. A second (January 1814) uprising in the city of San Salvador, shortly after the Belén Conspiracy was brought to an end, marked the last of the urban rebellions in the isthmus, just prior to the return of King Ferdinand VII in March 1814. Ferdinand abolished the Cádiz Constitution, disavowing the actions of the Regency Council and the elected Courts of Cádiz in his absence. With Ferdinand back on the throne, and the Restoration blooming in Europe, Bustamante, whose actions had been severely questioned by the Guatemala City *ayuntamiento*, sought to weaken his most outspoken critics, including the politically and economically powerful house of Aycinena and its allies.[34] Among other things, this meant a more severe treatment of contraband, which had been steadily increasing, thanks in great measure to the Aycinenas, since the beginning of the century. By 1818, however, the Crown had softened its stance and moved closer to Guatemalan merchants, replacing Bustamante with new Captain General Carlos Urrutia. This shift put the merchants into a stronger position, allowing them a very significant role in the debate around independence from Spain and annexation to Mexico that followed. Prior to the spring of 1820, when news arrived that Spanish general Rafael Riego had refused to lead a military expedition to South America and insisted on the reestablishment of the Cádiz Constitution, Spanish control of the *audiencia* faced few obstacles. An Indian rebellion in the western highlands of Guatemala in opposition to tribute payment had been slowly building for years and was gaining strength just as the restored constitution came into force. The rebels, centered in Totonicapán, celebrated the reestablishment of the constitution as they assumed that tribute would be newly eliminated, as it had been between 1812 and 1815.[35]

The reestablishment of the constitution marked a return to the political, territorial, and judicial structures established in 1812, and also to the freedom of the press, which began to be used immediately and powerfully. Carlos Urrutia, ex-Captain General (transformed into Superior Political Chief by the constitution) demonstrated less resistance to the liberal reforms associated with the constitution than his predecessor

Bustamante, but the provincial council in Guatemala City struggled against him in order to gain what power it could in the new political context. Nevertheless, the León and Guatemala City provincial councils gained power during this period, and their work was facilitated when Urrutia "temporarily" resigned in favor of a more sympathetic Gabino Gaínza.[36]

INDEPENDENCE

With the "army of the three guarantees" (*ejército trigarante*) led by Agustín de Iturbide in neighboring New Spain proposing a politically very moderate form of independence, including a Bourbon on the Mexican throne, elites in many isthmian cities began to consider joining the Mexican Empire. Though *ayuntamientos* in Chiapas would be the first to declare adherence to Iturbide's project, the merchants of the Kingdom capital, under the leadership of the house of Aycinena, had been in contact with Iturbide for months, and had developed an alliance with the radical liberals present in Guatemala City.[37] These two groups, in a meeting that included representatives from the *diputacion provincial* of Guatemala as well religious and political leaders in the capital, managed to push through a declaration of independence from Spain on September 15, 1821, against the wishes of Archbishop Casaus y Torres and moderates led by Cecilio del Valle. Those present could not come to an agreement on whether to join the Mexican Empire, considering that such a decision should be decided in a general congress that they convened for March of the following year. In the meantime, the Spanish constitution would be respected, as it was in Mexico. Over the following weeks, the isthmian *ayuntamientos* and provincial councils voiced different positions regarding independence from Spain, possible adherence to Mexico, and future political relationships with Guatemala City. Many Central American leaders questioned the viability of the territory as an independent political entity, citing the paucity of individuals with adequate preparation to govern and administer the country, along with concerns regarding the territorial ambitions of neighboring Mexico and Colombia as well as those of Great Britain, whose presence on the Caribbean Coast continued.

The declarations by the *ayuntamientos* surrounding possible adherence to the Mexican Empire showed the differences among the dominant groups in different provinces and cities, but also how positions relative to Guatemala City reflected their particular contexts. The provincial council of Comayagua opted to join Mexico, rejecting continued rule from Guatemala City, declaring independence from Spain as well; León, which while still under Spanish rule had already proposed political autonomy from Guatemala, chose Mexico, separating itself from its erstwhile capital and, tentatively, from Spain. Tegucigalpa and Granada, traditional rivals to their respective intendancy capitals of Comayagua and León, preferred to continue under the aegis of the old capital of the Kingdom. The *ayuntamiento* of Quetzaltenango, which in 1813 had petitioned to become the capital of an Intendancy in western Guatemala and wanted to create a similar situation under the Mexican Empire, rejected Guatemala City. San Salvador declared itself in favor of a Central American republic while in Costa Rica, a meeting with representatives from the principal *ayuntamientos* declared independence from Spain, refusing union with Nicaragua or Guatemala.[38] These different pronouncements reflected deep-seated conflicts among cities within the different provinces, and they would be a basic element in the conflicts involving the structuring and control of the states, as well as the wars, during the federal period. Chiapas would maintain its initial adhesion to Iturbide, and though with the fall of the Mexican Empire it declared itself independent of both Mexico and Central America in 1823, the following year, it—excepting Soconusco—rejoined Mexico.

CENTRAL AMERICA AND THE MEXICAN EMPIRE

In this moment of political uncertainty, agents of Iturbide worked to promote Central American adherence to the Mexican Empire in Chiapas, the Guatemalan western highlands, and Guatemala City. A letter sent by Iturbide to the ex-political chief of the Kingdom of Guatemala, Gabino Gaínza, who continued in that position in the now independent territory, warned that he had sent troops toward Central America. In an order sent to the *ayuntamientos* of the ex-Kingdom of Guatemala, calling on each of them to hold a public meeting in which a decision about Central America's eventual adherence to Mexican Empire should be made, Gaínza included a copy of Iturbide's threatening letter. Though not all of the *ayuntamientos* responded to this consultation, the results clearly showed a preference for annexation to Mexico over the formation of a Central American republic.

With the majority of votes in hand, the Provisional Consultative Junta that had been formed on September 15, 1821, declared, with discordant views present, union with Mexico in early January 1822. San Salvador rejected this union, provoking a military intervention ordered by Gaínza later that year, and eventually fell to Mexican troops under the command of General Vicente Filisola in February 1823, even as the Mexican Empire crumbled. The depleted treasury, the difficulties that the existing (Cádiz) constitution provoked, the costs associated with the war in San Salvador, and the lack of interest in the region shown by the Mexican authorities left most Central American leaders unenthused with the experience of annexation to Mexico.[39] With the fall of the empire, Vicente Filisola, the governor of Central America appointed by Emperor Iturbide, convoked a congress for July 1823 with representatives from the territories that had formed the Kingdom of Guatemala, the meeting initially proposed on September 15, 1821, at the moment that independence had been declared. The congress pronounced the creation of the United Provinces of the Center of America, independent from Mexico, Spain, and any other power. Dominated by more radical liberals who had gained influence after the negative imperial experience, the newly created National Constituent Assembly began the most difficult process of creating a Central American Federation, one that, after a period of initial hopefulness, would show few signs of possible success.

A WEAK FEDERATION

Moderates, led by the Guatemala City elite, who had preferred the centralist polices of Iturbide, fell out of favor after the collapse of the Mexican Empire and the federalists, who promoted more radically liberal polices, came to power in the National Constituent Assembly. Their views are reflected in the 1825 Constitution of the Federal Republic of Central America.[40] Fear of territorial expansion by Colombia (a regional power that Costa Rica briefly considered joining), Mexico, and Great Britain pushed the different provinces of what had been the Kingdom of Guatemala toward unification, as a means to assure their capacity for self-defense. Exactly what sort of political entity should be created would remain a concern throughout the life of the Federation and the constitution did little to resolve the issue. Assemblymen created a federalist constitution that reflected their priorities: assuring that the states would retain power relative to that of the Federation and that the interests of Guatemala City elites would not predominate. The federalist position received criticism from those wanting a strong central authority, led by the merchants of Guatemala City who, in part, felt that this would facilitate their continued dominance of the isthmus. The centralists found some backing in other provinces and supported their position arguing the difficulties posed by existing institutional weaknesses, a lack of trained officials in the territory, and a largely illiterate population.[41] In an attempt to assure that Guatemala, with by far the largest population among the states, would not dominate the Federation through its power in congress, the constitution provided for a Senate, considered to be separate from the legislative branch of government, with two members from each of the states. The extensive prerogatives assigned to the senate effectively weakened the executive and legislative branches of government. Additionally, the constitution provided the Federation with limited revenue relative to that apportioned to the states. Customs duties, along with monies from the tobacco monopoly, managed by the states, could offer significant income to the Federation, unlike the other revenues assigned to it: the gunpowder monopoly, the postal system, and amounts that each state government would provide upon request. Conflicts regarding the relative power allotted to the Federation and to the states produced the First Federal War (1826–1829), and criticism of the constitution and calls for its reform proliferated during the following decade, largely focused on attempting to resolve these issues, from both more centralist and more federalist positions.[42] Yet one has the sense that the moment for the Federation had already passed: without the support of the centralists, the principal players in the isthmian economy, who opposed the type of loose federation that, generally speaking, the states preferred, real possibilities for success had become quite limited.[43] The final reform to the constitution, approved in May 1838 allowed each state to organize itself as it saw fit, effectively recognizing that the Federation had ceased to exist.

The Central American Republic had been imagined by many, probably most, of its founders as a very loose federation, in which each state would retain a great deal of autonomy and sovereignty. The weak fiscal structure reflected that reality, and the reticence of the states to transfer what they owed to the federal government confirmed their lack of interest in maintaining it. Federal leaders, under Arce and then Morazán, attempted to maintain a more robust union through military action but, particularly after the First Federal War, the importance of the Federation would steadily weaken.

Territory

With some exceptions, the territorial division of the new Federation into five states corresponded to that put into place with the intendancy system in the 1780s (and later largely reproduced by the provincial councils of the Cádiz Constitution), with the intendancies of León, Comayagua, and San Salvador becoming the states of Nicaragua, Honduras, and (El) Salvador. Costa Rica, which had formed part of the intendancy of León, became a state. Nicoya, whose relationship with Costa Rica and Nicaragua had varied in previous epochs, would become part of the former, at least in part due to the fears of the Nicoyans regarding the violence and wars of the 1820s in the latter.[44] The state of Guatemala would include what had been the *alcaldías mayores* of Escuintla, Sacatepéquez, Suchitepéquez, Sololá, Sonsonate, Totonicapán, and Verapaz along with the *corregimientos* of Chiquimula and Quetzaltenango. What had been the *alcaldía mayor* of Sonsonate, an important site of indigo production that had previously been administered with the other *alcaldías mayores* and *corregimientos*, joined (El) Salvador—not without controversy—almost immediately after the Federation was formed. Conflicts regarding the border between Nicaragua and Costa Rica began in this period, and in the following years Colombia would assume control of the Bocas del Toro region, which had been governed by Costa Rica prior to independence. Great Britain maintained control over the extremely important entrepôt of Belize and would continue to preserve important footholds on the Caribbean coast, particularly in Mosquitia.

Beginning in 1830, there were concerns about eastern portions of the state of Guatemala joining El Salvador, at that moment due primarily to tensions between municipal and state governments, and this possibility would reappear a few years later. As the Federation was collapsing, several towns still loyal to it in southern Honduras declared themselves part of El Salvador, at that point the last remaining state still in the union, while others proclaimed themselves part of Nicaragua.[45] The historic interest of elite groups in western Guatemala, led by the city of Quetzaltenango, for some sort of self-rule, would manifest itself in the creation of the sixth state of the Federation (now in its terminal phase), Los Altos (1838–1840).[46] Between 1824 and 1842, Soconusco, on the Pacific Coast, once a *gobierno* and later part of the intendancy of Chiapas, maintained a neutral condition, both Mexican and Central American, part of the states of both Chiapas and Guatemala.[47]

The 1825 Constitution provided for the eventual creation of a federal district, yet it would only be established in 1835, in a large region that ran from the city of San Salvador in the northwest to the Pacific Coast and eastward to the Lempa River.[48] The Federation established this district to weaken what was perceived to be an overly close relationship between the federal government and the state of Guatemala, and also to maintain control over what had become the very tumultuous territory of El Salvador. The establishment of the federal district in the region surrounding San Salvador occurred largely against the will of the Salvadorans, who understood that it could weaken their control over a large portion of the state.

In the early years of the Federation, the congress of El Salvador erected a bishopric in its territory, citing the *patronato real* which had given the Spanish monarchy the power to name church officials, a power that had been passed to the intendants in the late eighteenth century. El Salvador had always formed part of the bishopric and later archbishopric of Guatemala, a situation that left the tithes created by the agriculturally wealthy region in the hands of the church officials in the Kingdom capital, another example of Guatemalan economic influence that Salvadorans sought to eliminate.[49]

The Impact of War

During the life of the Central American Federation, war had a nearly permanent impact, though it varied widely both geographically and temporally, and its importance must be analyzed as part of a broader whole in which many other aspects play important roles. Nonetheless, the First Federal War (1826–1829), engaged just as state and federal governments began to structure themselves, threw a long shadow.[50]

José Cecilio del Valle gained a relative majority in the first federal elections, but without an absolute majority, the choice of who would be named president fell to the federal congress, dominated by moderates, who surprisingly chose Manuel José Arce, a Salvadoran considered to be more closely aligned with federalist positions. A conflict soon developed between the Federation and the more radically liberal government of Guatemala, in some sense related to the support that Arce received from the moderates, but also, on both symbolic and material planes, with what the relationship between state and federal governments should be. The tensions would eventually result in the arrest of Guatemalan Governor (*jefe de estado*) Juan Barrundia, and Arce calling for new state elections in which moderate centralists led by Aycinena took over the government of Guatemala.[51] The first Federal War followed. At that point, both the Federation and Guatemala were controlled by moderates, the political and economic elite of Guatemala City who had dominated the Kingdom prior to independence. This situation, and the overtly centralist tendencies of these governments, motivated the recently named Governor of El Salvador Mariano Prado to invade Guatemalan territory in 1827 and to lead the other states in what would become a coordinated military effort to defeat the centralists.[52]

Prior to the First Federal War, Central Americans had little experience with military conflict, beyond the attacks (1822 and 1823) that brought El Salvador ephemerally into the Mexican Empire, the Ochomogo War (1823) in Costa Rica, and the Nicaraguan conflict (1822–1825) that had joined inter-elite rivalries with popular struggle.[53] Beginning in 1826 and, after something of a hiatus between 1829 and 1832, continuing through 1839 (and later), the region experienced the types of violent confrontation that had been present in many parts of Spanish America beginning in 1810, reconfiguring relationships between popular sectors and dominant groups that had been present in the urban uprisings between 1811 and 1814.[54]

El Salvador suffered the greatest number of military actions in the First Federal War, but Nicaragua, Honduras, and Guatemala were not spared. Those regions where battles occurred and troops mobilized suffered greater damage to agricultural production and trade, impoverishing the people. A significant portion of the population, very significant in some regions, was drafted into the war effort as soldiers and carriers, and mobilization implied the presence of women who accompanied the troops. Many of those who did not form part of the armed groups, or deserted from them, fled from their home communities to avoid those responsibilities.[55] Even Costa Rica and the western highlands of Guatemala felt the effects of military recruitment and requisitions.

The First Federal War ended when the Ejercito Aliado Protector de la Ley, made up of Salvadoran, Honduran, and Nicaraguan troops (and some federalist Guatemalans) led by the state of El Salvador, took the Federation capital, Guatemala City, in April 1829 under the military leadership of Honduran General Francisco Morazán. This victory brought federalists into power, who would, most notably in Guatemala, apply more radically liberal policies that continued and accentuated reforms that had begun in the late eighteenth century.

The Second Federal War (1832–1839) involved different but related actions undertaken in opposition to Morazán and the policies implemented under his watch. A coordinated effort in 1832 brought an invasion by ex-President Arce from Soconusco, an assault on the Honduran port of Omoa that received support from Spanish Cuba, and an uprising in the city of San Miguel in opposition to federal army conscription. These were put down by President Morazán in 1833. Over the following years, relative peace reigned in Honduras, Nicaragua, and Guatemala as family members and close associates of Morazán ruled the former two while Mariano Gálvez pushed through reforms in the latter, and largely financed the Federation.

In El Salvador, however, war and rebellion would continue and in Costa Rica the Guerra de la Liga was fought in 1835. The causes of the 1835 civil war in Costa Rica ostensibly revolved around the location of the state capital: either rotating between the four principal cities of Alajuela, Heredia, Cartago, and San José or permanently fixed in the latter. With the victory by the troops of Braulio Carrillo, the capital remained in San José, a result that helped to consolidate the Costa Rican state government.

New taxes and changes in the judicial system, along with expropriations by governments in El Salvador, and the presence of federal troops in the state, brought resistance between 1833 and 1834 led by the same dominant groups in San Miguel that had participated in the 1832 uprising. Scattered rebellions included that led by the Indian Anastasio Aquino in Nonualco in the central part of the state in 1833. Salvadoran Governor (*jefe de estado*) Nicolás Espinoza, having gained the support of Indians by invoking the defense of communal lands, procured munitions and began organization for an attack on federal troops in El Salvador in 1835. As underlined by Lauria-Santiago, the type of relationship that Espinoza developed with the Indians can be seen as an important precursor to the 1837 Rebelión de la Montaña in the department of Chiquimula, Guatemala. The similarities between western El Salvador and eastern Guatemala make it possible to view that territory as a single region and an 1835 proposal by Espinoza that Chiquimula become part of El Salvador serves to underline that fact. This proposal, which seems to have never been seriously considered, received support from authorities in Chiquimula, and drew on a discourse that called for unity among the Indians in Honduras, Guatemala, and El Salvador.[56]

El Salvador, eastern Guatemala, and southern Honduras would bear the brunt of the damages caused by the Second Federal War, but, again, they were not the only regions affected.[57] By the end of 1836, the tensions in El Salvador had spread to Honduras and in 1837, in the midst of a cholera epidemic in eastern Guatemala, El Salvador, and Honduras, the Rebelión de la Montaña took root in eastern Guatemala, leading to the overthrow of Chief of State Mariano Gálvez, and in 1839 to the defeat of Morazán by Rafael Carrera in Guatemala City, effectively putting an end to the Federation.

The locally centered politics of the colonial and early republican eras brought regionally dominant actors into the war as military commanders who could take advantage of access to capital and clientelist relationships with workers cum soldiers, Indians among them, to further their interests.[58] War implied the need for resources, human and otherwise, that put pressure on all sectors of society: the ever-present relationship between fiscal systems and the military often drew on forced loans and, when necessary, simple appropriation of goods and sacking.[59] War provoked dire social and economic consequences for many of the poor peasants who sought to survive this period, often by deserting the military forces that they had become part of and, at times, taking advantage of experience gained in war to use violence as a means to enrich themselves.[60] Recent research points to the need to understand how a society heavily marked by, but not reduced to, war and political violence functioned during this period, looking at the experiences of men and women who continued to carry on with the daily routines of urban and rural life, including work, public celebrations, spiritual and religious practices, and domestic activities. How did these routines affect politics and new governmental policies? How did politics and policies affect these routines?[61]

Most notably in Honduras and El Salvador, military actions had coupled regional leaders with peasants (at times through recruitment by hacienda owners) and Indian towns in military actions. The above-mentioned case involving Espinoza and the 1838 Indian uprising in Santa Ana and Texiguat— coordinated with Coronel José

Bustillo—in southeastern Honduras are two examples. After the initial success of the 1833 Nonualco Indian rebellion in El Salvador, sparked by land issues, poor treatment by local landowners, and military recruitment, opponents of the state government provided the movement with arms. Violence in the predominantly Indian town of San Juan Ostuncalco in the western highlands of Guatemala, however, was more similar to colonial era protests, which looked to resolve a specific problem without involving the rebels in broader political concerns. A poorly thought out decision to use a communally owned plot of land for the construction of a new courthouse ostensibly provoked the protest in Ostuncalco, but its resolution had as much to do with the legal struggle undertaken by neighboring San Martín Sacatepéquez to retain control over its very extensive communal lands in the Pacific piedmont. The *Rebelión de la Montaña* can be seen as a continuation of the types of alliances between Indian peasants and regional or state-level leaders present in the Honduran and Salvadoran cases mentioned.[62] This form of political action resonates with the argument of Fradkin who claims that the independence struggles in Río de la Plata opened a period in which popular sectors became mobilized, often as allies with dominant social groups which in the process effectively lost control over them and would only regain it in the latter part of the nineteenth century.[63]

Revenue, Debts, and the Economy

The need for funds to fill their coffers and continue payments on wartime and other debts pushed state government to find funds wherever they could. Many states mined church resources, and the Salvadoran state appropriated monies from the Montepio de Añileros, a late colonial institution designed to provide indigo growers with credit and to thereby free them from dependence on merchant capital in Guatemala City.[64] The states took capital from the religious brotherhoods and pious foundations, and out of the hands of the men who managed it, many of whom, most especially in Guatemala City, formed part of the moderate, centralist camp and were some of the most wealthy and powerful men in the isthmus.[65] These policies provided much needed funds to the state governments, as did the confiscation of properties owned by the vanquished centralists, weakening their power, even as their leaders were exiled after the 1829 victory of the *Ejercito Aliado*.

State and federal financial systems depended heavily on loans from merchants, which were usually repaid through *libranzas*, a form of state-backed security, that merchants presented as payment for customs duties or the purchase of state-owned property, much of which had often been recently confiscated from religious institutions. Merchants and others traded these securities freely, along with *vales* (promissory notes used by governments in partial payment of salaries), and their value steadily decreased, though governments were forced to accept these documents, that had become a sort of paper money, at face value. This situation weakened the still young fiscal systems, and created dependence on merchant capital, but governments continued to use securities and promissory notes in the absence of other alternatives. Some principal cities in Costa

Rica sold off their communal lands to private owners, and the state government offered up state-owned properties for sale, permitting the acquisition of land for incipient coffee production there.[66]

The state and federal fiscal systems largely reproduced those used prior to independence: state monopolies (most importantly tobacco and liquor), import and export duties, and capitation taxes, the latter provoking rural unrest in El Salvador, Honduras, and Guatemala during the federal period.[67] Municipal governments took on the responsibility for much tax collection, and for many other duties that the understaffed states delegated to them, thereby strengthening local power.

As mentioned, the constitution provided the federal government with very limited funding and the state governments rarely fulfilled their obligations, except for Guatemala, whose support became necessary for the Federation to operate. Attempting to gain something from a situation beyond its control, in 1833 the federal government declared that all tobacco revenues and 5 percent of the maritime customs duties would pass to the states, under the condition that they pay the salaries of their senate and congressional representatives in the capital. A £1,428,571 loan from London bankers in 1825, unfortunately negotiated just before a major financial crisis rocked England, did little to promote the economic development that early leaders of the Federation had desired, eventually leaving the debt with the five national governments that formed after the Federation disbanded.

Indigo continued to be at the center of export production in El Salvador in the decades after independence, while cochineal, particularly in the region around Antigua Guatemala, became the most important export crop in Guatemala, and by the 1830s, coffee—the cash crop par excellence in late-nineteenth- and early-twentieth-century Central America—had become a profitable venture in Costa Rica, thanks in part to European immigrants.[68] War significantly affected agricultural production, most notably in El Salvador, though other regions also suffered as potential workers became soldiers or made themselves scarce to avoid conscription, reducing available hands. English textiles, flooding many Latin American markets at this time, continued to pour into Central America, primarily, though certainly not only, through Belize, putting an end to what had been a vibrant center of textile production in Antigua, though Los Altos of Guatemala continued to sell woolen goods that would travel as far as Costa Rica even into the late 1840s.[69]

Since 1825, liberal policies in Guatemala had promoted state expropriation of untitled (*baldío*) lands for resale on the market, insisting that landowners, including Indian towns, show proof of ownership to avoid expropriation. This type of policy had been initially proposed as a means of redistributing land into able hands in the eighteenth century, but early efforts by the Spaniards during the Cádiz period had been weak, as were the initial attempts by the state government after independence, that effectively excluded communal lands from any risk of expropriation. As time passed, Guatemalan state authorities insisted ever more vehemently that community land must be titled, such that by 1835 tensions had increased notably. The 1836 law that permitted the sale of communally owned *ejido* lands and the redemption of lands held in *censo enfiteútico* provoked greater unrest in Indian towns, and would be effectively rescinded in 1837 as a result.[70] Attempts at similar legislation in El Salvador during the 1820s met with limited success, though in the following decade the appropriation of Indian lands by Ladinos created tensions.[71]

The International Context

The Federation maintained strained relations with Mexico over the uncertain status of Soconusco, the use of that territory as a staging ground for the 1832 invasion by Arce and the possibilities that the shared border offered to potential revolutionaries from both countries. Concerns about the territorial ambitions of Colombia continued, particularly as it later appropriated the region of Bocas del Toro in Costa Rica. Great Britain maintained a very significant presence in Central America, using the weight of the London bank loan as a negotiating piece, while promoting its interests—trade, logging, the possibility of a Nicaraguan canal—and preserving its positions on the Atlantic Coast, most notably in Belize and Mosquitia. The canal project, which at the advent of the Federation had been seen by some as a mechanism that could propel Central America forward economically, continued to be a central issue, rightly so, as the mid-century California gold rush brought a Nicaraguan cross-isthmian transport route into being. The Netherlands and the United States both showed interest in a canal and the latter became an important player in the regional international context as it sought to promote its commercial interests in the region.[72]

Constructing the States and Abandoning the Federation

The newly created states drew on their historical experiences, notably the intendancy system and the period of Cádiz constitutionalism, to organize themselves territorially and administratively, a slow process that at times involved dominant local actors looking to further their interests at the state level rather than through municipal governments, the institutions through which they had traditionally exerted power. This was by no means a linear or homogenous process.[73] Early in the federal period it became clear that local powerbrokers involved themselves with, and sought to exercise power in, the state governments, rather than engage with the Federation, a practice that became more accentuated after the First Federal War.[74]

From the time of the Cádiz Constitution, when popular suffrage began, elections, if indirect and often censitary, had become one part of the evolving relationship between newly minted citizens and their rulers. The indirect electoral systems tended to reinforce the power of dominant local and regional leaders, who would almost inevitably be chosen as electors. Even in the many cases where control of the state depended on military power, victors used elections to legitimize themselves.[75] Liberal institutions, military power, and the weight of history, expressed in local and regional power relationships as well as in the pactist tradition, all formed part of the scenario of the times. Small Ladino and Indian towns took advantage of the new electoral, political, and judicial systems as they could, using, among other things, the new constitutional *ayuntamientos*, at times in the ways that they had used the colonial Indian and Ladino *cabildos*.[76] In many towns, considered Indian republics prior to the reforms, the constitutional *ayuntamientos* created tensions as Ladinos could come to dominate and use them to their favor, notably to facilitate access to communal lands.[77]

Continuing Reforms

The appropriation of church funds by state governments, as mentioned above, had as much to do with fiscal necessity as it did with an anticlerical agenda, as did the elimination of the tithe, which would guide fiscal resources to civil, rather than religious, authorities. In fact, these policies appear to repeat the logic of the *consolidación de los vales reales* that the Spanish Crown had applied shortly before the monarchal crisis. After their victory in 1829, the radical liberals exiled the Archbishop of Guatemala and sent most of the religious orders packing, confiscating much of their property.

During the 1830s, Guatemalan Governor (*jefe de estado*) Mariano Gálvez legalized secular marriage and divorce, while also, for sanitary reasons, prohibited burial in churches, calling for cemeteries to be constructed outside town centers. The Church continued to have an important public role notwithstanding these actions, though its power and public presence decreased.[78] Nonetheless, the impact of secularizing and anticlerical policies cannot be underestimated, in part as a motivator for parish priests who supported the Carrera revolt in 1837. Daniele Pompejano has argued that these policies could have been perceived by many, Carrera's supporters among others, as one more step in the slow process, begun in Europe and Iberian America after the Council of Trent, and pushed forward by the late Bourbon reforms, through which religious and civil authority were being separated from one another.[79] By limiting Church strength, Guatemalan policies had gone beyond the later Bourbon interest in promoting private and interior forms of worship over more affective and public religious manifestations, yet another issue that may have unsettled Indian and Ladino peasants.[80]

Collapse

The Rebelión de la Montaña, which began in 1837 and led to the downfall of Gálvez and the radical liberals of Guatemala, and to the formal demise of an already weak federation, has been thoroughly studied. Myriad reasons help to explain the motivation for the movement and its success, many of them related to the policies implemented by Gálvez, including land reform, the capitation tax, and the efforts to weaken Church power and influence. In addition to those policies, applied throughout the state of Guatemala,

FROM KINGDOM TO REPUBLICS, 1808–1840 · 237

dominant groups in eastern Guatemala, particularly in Chiquimula, resented the fact that their interests had been ignored when lands on the Atlantic Coast had been given to European colonists. Another contributing factor were the poor men and women who participated in criminal activities along important roads between Guatemala City and the Atlantic ports who resented the excessive punishment they often received. Some of these people may well have participated in the wars, since Chiquimula had sent an inordinate number of men to battle, creating not only economic disruption but veterans with military experience. A cholera epidemic in 1837 that entered Guatemala via Belize created unease in an already tried population. Government measures to weaken the impacts of the disease met resistance, particularly as some parish priests spread rumors that these were actually intended to promote cholera rather than combat it. Dominant groups in the region, many of whom were of African heritage, offered economic support and legitimacy to the rebels, whose reach had spread to El Salvador. The brutal repression of the uprising only served to strengthen it.[81]

Many of the reforms Gálvez pushed through in Guatemala were not applied in other states, in the Salvadoran case probably because resistance had, or would have, prohibited it.[82] In eastern Guatemala, as in El Salvador, people rejected the radical changes pushed forward not only because of their economic and social impacts but also due to the lack of a "series of images, an identity, a discourse capable of galvanizing mass support," as Lowell Gudmundson's much cited phrase would have it. It has been argued that the lack of symbolic domination in Spanish America during the period after independence made necessary the use of violence as a means to assert control.[83]

Leadership of the rebellion passed to Rafael Carrera, an uneducated mestizo with military experience, who had married into an important family in the region. Galvez's support waned even among stalwart allies like José Francisco Barrundia who opposed the repressive measures used to stop the uprising and the autocratic behavior of the government. Gálvez began to backpedal on some of the more radical reforms and brought moderates, many of whom had been permitted reentry into Guatemala in previous years, into the state government with the hope of consolidating power and somehow staving off the rebellion. Concern among the elite of Guatemala City about the military power of the insurgents would lead to a short-lived alliance between Gálvez and the moderates. Fear would impel the latter, archrivals of Morazán, to call on him to defend, albeit unsuccessfully, Guatemala City from Carrera's army. The existence of the Federation had become untenable, and after Nicaragua declared itself sovereign and independent in April 1838, and the following month the federal constitution was modified, allowing for each state to govern itself as it saw fit, the already moribund union came to an end. The instability of Guatemala would allow for the creation, only after that last constitutional reform, of the state of Los Altos in December 1838, in the densely populated and largely Indigenous, western part of the state. This situation could have changed the balance of power in the Federation, if the collapse of the union had not prevented it. Carrera defeated Morazán in April 1839 and shortly thereafter, with the support of Indian towns in Los Altos, reincorporated the short-lived sixth state in 1840.[84] Based in El Salvador,

Morazán and his followers fought against the states of Honduras and Nicaragua who, with support from Carrera in Guatemala, won victory in 1841.

By this time, the states of Guatemala and El Salvador had developed governing apparatuses with some capacity to exercise power in their territories and in Costa Rica, where the impact of the wars had been much less dramatic, these structures were even more consolidated, notably due to the efforts of Governor (*jefe de estado*) Braulio Carrillo. In Honduras and Nicaragua, where internal conflict continued, much less had been achieved along these lines. Notwithstanding their de facto autonomy, the states waited some years before declaring themselves as independent republics: Guatemala and Costa Rica in 1847, El Salvador and Nicaragua in 1854, and finally Honduras in 1862.

In the 1840s, Carrera would surround himself with a collection of men from both the more moderate and more radical camps, attempting to balance them, just as he sought to strengthen his power through alliances with Indian and peasant towns throughout the state. After 1850, with a more consolidated government under Carrera, Guatemala became decidedly more conservative, developing close ties to the Church and willing to intervene, as the federal government under Morazán had done, in other parts of Central America.[85] In the decades immediately following the end of the Federation, the slow construction of state apparatuses continued, in the midst of wars that commonly implied state-sponsored military interventions in neighboring territories. Though initially some of these attacks were directed toward reestablishing the Federation—a position related to Morazán's followers, identified as liberals—, these and other military confrontations reproduced many of the local and regional dynamics present during the wars of the federal period. The end of the Central American union did not mean the end of the ties among the newly independent territories, as can be observed in the 1857 war against William Walker in Nicaragua and the many, albeit generally weak, attempts to reconstruct some sort of union, a siren call of later liberals.

WHAT WE KNOW, AND WHAT ELSE WE COULD KNOW: SUGGESTIONS FOR FURTHER STUDY

From their final years as colonies of the Spanish monarchy through the demise of the Central American Federation, the people of what had been the Kingdom of Guatemala passed through experiences similar to those in other regions of Spanish America, though marked by regional specificities. The pull of eighteenth-century ideas associated with the Enlightenment dominated the political thinkers of the era on both sides of the Atlantic, pushing forward politically and economically liberal policies, whose radical application, more notably in Guatemala, did not create economic conditions that might have made them more acceptable to men and women who experienced them, at least in part, as attacks on their livelihoods and ways of life. The negative social and economic impacts of war did not facilitate the application of new policies, particularly in a context where their experience as soldiers had made Indian and Ladino peasants more politically active.

The Spanish Constitution of 1812 implanted a new political organization, and legitimation, of government that would be the foundation for the independent territories after independence, yet this would be implemented in a context of powerful municipal governments that would only slowly relinquish their power to state authorities. Attempts at ordering state institutions after independence drew on the structures and policies of the intendancies, the provincial councils, and local experience, all the while struggling against the realities of war and the social and economic impacts that it implied, enormous foreign and domestic debts not least among them.

Historic tensions between the dominant merchant class of Guatemala City and the provinces of the Kingdom of Guatemala made themselves visible throughout this period. While the provinces, later states, looked to form a loose confederation, the centralist Guatemala City elites looked first to Mexico and then to a centralized state as means to maintain their dominant position. Nonetheless, upon retaking power in 1829, the erstwhile federalists had no qualms about intervening in other states in order to promote their policies.

The interplay among dominant and subaltern groups (acting at times outside the formal institutional structure), and the municipal, state, and federal governments made for a complex panorama that rigorous local and regional studies help to understand. More of this sort of work should be promoted, including studies that consider regions that include parts of more than one province/state. In the past few decades, researchers have successfully bridged the gap between late colonial and early republican Central America, clearly demonstrating the historical continuities and novelties present in this period. Most recently, efforts are once again being made to reconsider economic conditions and the power dynamics they promote, an approach that has been somewhat marginalized in recent decades by more purely political histories. This work begins to look not only at the institutions but more specifically the people and social groups that conform and use them, showing a great deal of promise for future studies of this period. The next steps would involve connecting that research to work on changes in political culture, in whatever parts of society they occur, and to how those relate to political imaginaries, evidently in a process of modification. That said, it is also necessary to develop studies on promising but less fully developed fields of study, such as religion, work, daily life (particularly in rural areas), and gender relations, whose careful consideration could not only provide greater general knowledge about the deeper social transformations at work but also help to more fully understand the economic and political realities that tend to dominate studies of the epoch.

NOTES

1. Much of what is presented here owes a great deal to conversation and communication with many colleagues, among them Juan Carlos Sarazúa Pérez, Luis Pedro Taracena, Brian Connaughton, Mario Vázquez Olivera, and Clara Pérez Fabregat.

2. For general overviews that focus on Central America as a whole in this period, see Miles Wortman, *Government and Society in Central America, 1680–1840* (New York: Columbia University Press, 1982); Julio César Pinto Soria, *Centroamérica, de la colonia al Estado nacional (1800–1840)*, 2nd ed. (Guatemala: Editorial Universitaria, 1989); Jordana Dym, *From Sovereign Villages to Nation States: City, States and Federation in Central America* (Albuquerque: University of New Mexico Press, 2006).

3. On the late eighteenth-century reforms in the Kingdom of Guatemala, see Wortman, *Government and Society*; Jordana Dym and Christophe Belaubre, eds., *Politics, Economy and Society in Bourbon Central America, 1759–1821* (Boulder: University of Colorado Press, 2006). Lynch has called these reforms a "second conquest" and Brading has argued that they alienated criollo elites, creating tensions with peninsular Spaniards, and laid the groundwork for independence movements, but this does not seem to have been the case in the Kingdom of Guatemala, where the two groups tended to share interests. David Brading, "La España de los Borbones y su imperio americano," in *Historia de América Latina*, edited by Leslie Bethell, vol. 2, 85–126 (Barcelona: Editorial Crítica, 1990); John Lynch, *Las revoluciones hispanoamericanas, 1818–1826* (Barcelona: Editorial Ariel, 2001); Gustavo Palma, "Núcleos de poder local y relaciones familiares en Guatemala a finales del siglo XVIII," *Mesoamérica* 12 (1986): 241–308.

4. The territory of the Captaincy General of Guatemala was also an *audiencia* (a judicial district) and was often called the Kingdom of Guatemala. Very early on (1609 in the Kingdom of Guatemala) the Crown created captaincies general in regions that required greater military presence, and while technically part of larger viceroyalties, they operated with total or nearly total autonomy relative to them. The Captain General functioned as the president of the *audiencia* and was also referred to as its governor.

5. Miles Wortman, "Government Revenue and Economic Trends in Central America, 1787–1819," *Hispanic American Historical Review* 55, no. 2 (May 1975): 251–286.

6. Dym, *From Sovereign Villages*.

7. Christophe Belaubre, *Élus de Dieu et Élus du Monde dans le Royaume du Guatemala (1753–1808)* (Paris: L'Harmattan, 2012), 333–356.

8. In-depth regional studies into these dynamics have been extremely fruitful. Arturo Taracena, *Invención criolla, sueño ladino, pesadilla indígena. Los Altos de Guatemala: de región a Estado, 1740–1871* (Antigua Guatemala: Editorial El Porvenir/CIRMA, 1999); Clara Pérez Fabregat, *San Miguel y el oriente salvadoreño. La construcción del Estado de El Salvador, 1780–1865* (San Salvador: Universidad Centroamericana "José Simeón Cañas"), 2018.

9. Perhaps as a result of the economic downturn, in Guatemala City at least, daily life had become quite violent. In that city, like many others in Latin America, women made up a significant majority of the population, which continued to live and work notwithstanding the economic downturn and the violence. Leonardo Fabricio Hernández, "Implicated Spaces, Daily Struggles: Home and Street Life in Late Colonial Guatemala City, 1750–1824" (PhD diss., Brown University, 1999); Tania Sagastume Paiz, *Trabajo urbano y tiempo libre en la ciudad de Guatemala, 1776–1840* (Guatemala: Universidad de Guatemala, 2008);

Catherine Komisaruk, *Love and Labor in Guatemala: The Eve of Independence* (Stanford, CA: Stanford University Press, 2013).

10. Geoffrey E. Cabat, "The Consolidation of 1804 in Guatemala," *The Americas* 29, no. 1 (1971): 20–38; Juan Carlos Solórzano Fonseca, "Los años finales de la dominación española," in *Historia general de Centroamérica* (vol. 3, *De la Ilustración al Liberalismo*, vol. ed. Héctor Pérez Brignoli), edited by Edilberto Torres-Rivas, 13–71 (San José: FLACSO, 1994); Héctor Lindo Fuentes, "The Economy of Central America: From Bourbon Reforms to Liberal Reforms," in *Central America, 1821–1871: Liberalism before Liberal Reforms*, edited by Lowell Gudmundson and Héctor Lindo-Fuentes, 13–78 (Tuscaloosa: University of Alabama Press, 1995); José Antonio Fernández Molina, *Pintando el Mundo Azul* (San Salvador: Consejo Nacional para la Cultura y el Arte [CONCULTURA], 2003); Wortman, *Government and Society*.

11. To compare with other Spanish American experiences, see Roberto Breña, *En el umbral de las revoluciones hispánics: el bienio 1808–1810* (Mexico City: El Colegio de México, 2010).

12. Late eighteenth-century Bourbon attempts failed to limit the power wielded by this group, though Captain General José de Bustamante (1811–1818) had some success in similar efforts; the victors of the First Federal War exiled many of its members in 1829. On the Bourbon attempts, see Christophe Belaubre, "'Elus du Monde' et 'Elus de Dieu', Familles de pouvoir et haut clergé en Amérique centrale, 1753–1829," in *Ecrits et peintures indigènes*, edited by Bernard Grunberg, 201-231 (Paris: L'Harmattan, 2006), 16.

13. Amanda Úrsula Torres Freyermuth and Aquiles Omar Ávila Quijas, "El ayuntamiento de Ciudad Real y el asesor letrado José Mariano Valero. Conflicto político en vísperas de la independencia, 1804–1809," *Signos Históricos* 19, no. 38 (2017): 88–137.

14. Philip F. Flemion, "States' Rights and Partisan Politics: Manuel José Arce and the Struggle for Central American Union," *The Hispanic American Historical Review* 53, no. 4, 600-619 (Nov. 1973): 601 n. 3; Lowell Gudmundson and Héctor Lindo-Fuentes, *Central America, 1821 -1871 : Liberalism before Liberal Reform* (Tuscaloosa, The University of Alabama Press, 1995); Adolfo Bonilla Bonilla, *Ideas económicas en la Centroamérica ilustrada, 1793–1838* (San Salvador: FLACSO San Salvador, 1999); Víctor Hugo Acuña "El liberalismo en Centroamérica en tiempos de la independencia (1810–1850)," in *La aurora de la libertad. Los primeros liberalismos en el mundo iberamericano*, edited by Javier Fernández Sebastián, 117-145 (Madrid: Marcial Pons, 2012); Olga Vásquez Monzón, "Liberal/Liberalismo," in *Centroamérica durante las revoluciones atlánticas. El vocabulario político, 1750–1850*, edited by Jordana Dym and Sajid Alfredo Herrera Mena (San Salvador: IEESFORD Editores, 2014); Arturo Taracena Arriola, "La mirada de tres actores guatemaltecos sobre la Guerra Federal de 1826 a 1829: Montúfar y Coronado, Córdova y García Granados. Reflexiones metodológicas sobre un conflicto armado," in *La primera Guerra Federal centroamericana, 1826–1829: nación y estados*, edited by Arturo Taracena Arriola, 87-117 (Guatemala: Universidad Rafael Landívar/Universidad Autónoma Metropolitana-Iztapalapa/Centro Peninsular en Humanidades y en Ciencias Sociales [CEPHCIS]-UNAM, 2015).

For an early, relative to the many works undertaken regarding related themes sparked by François-Xavier Guerra, and important, account of the impact of the Cádiz experience on Central America, see Mario Rodríguez, *The Cadiz Experiment in Central America, 1808–1826* (Berkeley: University of California Press, 1978); François-Xavier Guerra, *Modernidad e independencies. Ensayos sobre las revoluciones hispánicas* (Madrid: Fundación MAPFRE, 1992).

For the purposes of this article, it is assumed that all, or nearly all, of the Central American political leadership during the period discussed did not question political liberalism and that, at least after independence, favored economic liberalism, in the form of free trade, as well. The common historiographic division between "liberals" and "conservatives" in terms of political ideology often clouds shifting political alliances, forcing categories on individuals whose positions were more nuanced, and changing. This is not to say that differences did not exist between moderate (described at the time as *servil* and by later historiography as conservative) and more radical positions on the role of the Catholic Church, the type of electorate that would control political institutions, what sorts of reforms should be implemented, and the speed at which they should be applied.

15. Jaime E. Rodríguez O., *La independencia de la América española* (2nd ed.) (Mexico City: El Colegio de México/Fondo de Cultura Económica, 2005), 197–297.

16. Jordana Dym, "Soberanía transitiva y adhesión condicional: lealtad e insurrección en el reino de Guatemala, 1808–1811," in *1808: La eclosión juntera en el mundo hispano*, edited by Miguel Chust, 105-136 (Mexico City: Fondo de Cultura Económica/El Colegio de México, 2007).

17. Regarding the efforts of Bustamante in particular, see Timothy Hawkins, *José de Bustamante and Central American Independence: Colonial Administration in an Age of Crisis* (Tuscaloosa: University of Alabama Press, 2004).

18. On the period of Central American independence, see Rodríguez, *The Cádiz Experiment*; Pinto Soria, *Centroamérica*; Dym, *From Sovereign Villages*; Hawkins, *José de Bustamante*; Horacio Cabezas Carcache, *Independencia centroamericana. Gestión y ocaso del "Plan Pacífico"* (Guatemala City: Editorial Universitaria, Universidad San Carlos de Guatemala, 2010); Coralia Gutiérrez Álvarez, "La historiografía contemporánea sobre la independencia en Centroamérica," in *Jaque a la corona: la cuestión política en las independencias iberoamericanas*, edited by Juan Ortiz Escamilla and Ivana Frasquet, 313-341 (Castelló de la Plana: Universitat Jaume I, 2010); Aaron Pollack, ed., *Independence in Central America and Chiapas, 1770–1823* (Norman: University of Oklahoma Press, 2019).

19. Aaron Pollack, "By way of Introduction to Central American Independence: A Historical and Historiographical Overview," in *Independence in Central America and Chiapas, 1770–1823*, edited by Aaron Pollack,1-34 (Norman: University of Oklahoma Press, 2019), 7-8.

20. Hawkins, *José de Bustamante*.

21. Francisco Peccorini Letona, *La voluntad del pueblo en la emancipación de El Salvador. Un estudio sobre las relaciones del pueblo con los próceres en la independencia y en la anexión a México* (San Salvador: Ministerio de Educación, 1972); Pinto Soria, *Centroamérica*; Xiomara Avendaño Rojas and Norma Hernández Sánchez, *¿Independencia o autogobierno? El Salvador y Nicaragua, 1786–1811* (Managua: LEA Grupo Editorial, 2014); Elizet Payne Iglesias, "Local Powers and Popular Resistance in Nicaragua, 1808–1813," in *Independence in Central America and Chiapas, 1770–1823*, edited by Aaron Pollack, 133-157 (Norman: University of Oklahoma Press, 2019).

22. In most of Spanish America, the creation of local governing juntas and the appearance of rebellions in the first years after 1808 did not seek to sever ties with the Spanish Monarchy but rather to acquire greater autonomy within it. With the passage of time, in a situation of great fluidity, some groups called for complete independence while others sought autonomy. Rodríguez O., *Independencia*. Though there are indications that some individuals

FROM KINGDOM TO REPUBLICS, 1808–1840   243

favored independence, there is very little indication that any organized group was working toward it in the Kingdom of Guatemala prior to 1813, and even at that time, evidence for a desire for a full break with Spain is minimal.

23. Peccorini Letona, *La voluntad del pueblo*; Pinto Soria, *Centroamérica*; Edgar Soriano Ortiz, "Una aproximación a las experiencias del juramento de la Constitución de Cádiz en el contexto de Tegucigalpa (1812–1820)," in *Bicentenario de la constitución de Cádiz en Honduras*, 89–106 (Tegucigalpa: Agencia Española de Cooperación Internacional para el Desarrollo, 2012); Avendaño Rojas and Hernández Sánchez, *¿Independencia o autogobierno?*; and Payne Iglesias, "Local Powers."

24. Dym, *Sovereign*, 128–138.

25. For discussion of the political terminology used during the epoch, see Javier Fernández Sebastián, ed., *Diccionario político y social del mundo iberoamericano. La era de las revoluciones, 1750–1850 [Iberconceptos-I]* (Madrid: Fundación Carolina/Sociedad Estatal de Conmemoraciones Culturales/Centro de Estudios Políticos y Constitucionales, 2009) and Jordana Dym and Sajid Herrera, eds., *Centroamérica durante las revoluciones atlánticas: el vocabulario político, 1750–1850* (San Salvador: IEESFORD Editores, 2014).

26. Marta Lorente Sarañina, "El fracaso de la intendencia en Honduras: La alcaldía mayor de Tegucigalpa (1799–1819)," in *Pacis Artes. Obra homenaje al profesor Julio D. González Campos*, vol. II, 2017-2044 (Madrid: Edifer, 2005), 2031.

27. Hawkins, *José de Bustamante*, 125–126.

28. Several meetings were held in the Belén convent, hence the name given to the conspiracy. For the most recent treatment, see Christophe Belaubre, "Al cruce de la historia social y política: un acercamiento crítico a la 'conjuración de Belén', Guatemala (1813), in *Conspiración, guerras y revoluciones políticas en la América hispano-portuguesa, 1808-1824*, coordinated by Sajid Alfredo Hererra Mena, 9-29 (San Salvador: UCA Editores, 2013).

29. Using the term "Jacobin" to describe these governments, Daniele Pompejano, though perhaps overstating the case, gives some measure of the radicality in their thinking, policies, and, at times, actions. Daniele Pompejano, *Il Dio nero degli uomini bianchi* (Rome: Carocci, 2015). As occurred elsewhere in independent Spanish America, some radical liberals referred to "year one of our independence," following the French revolutionary tradition. Yolanda Dachner T., "Centroamérica: una nación antigua en la modernidad republicana," *Anuario de Estudios Centroamericanos* 24, nos. 1/2, 7-20 (1998): 8.

30. Dym, *Sovereign*, 106.

31. Bonilla Bonilla, *Ideas económicas*, 160–199; Jordana Dym, "Central America and Cádiz: A Complex Relationship," in *The Rise of Constitutional Government in the Iberian Atlantic World: The Impact of the Cádiz Constitution of 1812*, edited by Scott Eastman and Natalia Sobrevilla Perea, 63-90 (Tuscaloosa: University of Alabama Press, 2015).

32. On the neoscholastic, yet non-Thomist, origins of the idea of popular sovereignty, see Mónica Quijada, "La *potestas populi*: una revisión del pensamiento político hispánico y la modernidad," in *Entre la Colonia y la República. Insurgencias, rebeliones y cultura política en América del Sur*, edited by Beatriz Bragoni and Sara E. Mata, 29-50 (Buenos Aires: Prometio Libros, 2008).

33. Hawkins, *José de Bustamante*, 115–147.

34. For an interesting and nuanced account of the importance of spirituality, for politics and other realms of social reality, and more specifically the role of the mystic Sister María Teresa Aycinena in the conflicts between the *ayuntamiento* of Guatemala City and Bustamante during the often understudied period between 1814 and 1820, see Brianna

Leavitt-Alcántara, *Alone at the Altar: Single Women and Devotion in Guatemala 1670–1870* (Stanford, CA: Stanford University Press, 2018), 134–172.

35. Aaron Pollack, *Levantamiento K'iche' in Totonicapán, 1820. Los lugares de la política subalterna* (Guatemala City: AVANCSO, 2009).

36. In the first constitutional period the Cortes established only two provincial councils, in Guatemala City and León. Intendant José Tinoco and local authorities in Comayagua failed in their attempts to create a provincial council without royal approval in Comayagua in late 1820, but after the Crown agreed to create councils in each of the intendancies, one was established there shortly before independence. Chiapas and San Salvador began the process of creating those bodies just before independence and they began to function shortly after it was declared. In their final condition, the territorial division of the provincial councils reproduced that put in place by the intendancies. Wortman, *Government*, 221, 324 n. 9; Dym, *Sovereign*, 148–154.

37. Cabezas Carcache, *Independencia centroamericana*.

38. Dym, *Sovereign*, 177–193; Mario Vázquez Olivera, *El Imperio Mexicano y el reino de Guatemala. Proyecto político y campaña militar* (Mexico City: Fondo de Cultura Económica/Centro de Investigaciones sobre América Latina y el Caribe (CIALC)–UNAM, 2009), 64.

39. The relationship between Central America and the Mexican Empire has been thoroughly discussed in Vázquez Olivera, *Imperio*.

40. A more detailed recent discussion of the Federation can be found in Luis Pedro Taracena Arriola, "The Federal Republic of Central America, 1824–1840."

41. For a sympathetic view of the centralist position as it developed from the Cádiz period onward, see Adolfo Bonilla Bonilla, "Triunfos y fracasos de la política ilustrada centroamericana (1774–1838)," in *Repensando Guatemala en la época de Rafael Carrera*, edited by Brian Connaughton, 41–110 (Mexico City: UAM-Iztapalapa/Editorial Gedisa S.A., 2015).

42. Three separate essays published in the United States by Juan José Aycinena between 1832 and 1834, called the *Toro Amarillo*, emphasized a comparison between the federal systems in the US and Central America and called for the Federation to disband and begin anew from scratch. Juan José de Aycinena, *El toro amarillo* (Guatemala: Editorial José de Pineda Ibarra, 1980). On other reform proposals, see Xiomara Avendaño Rojas, *Centroamérica entre lo antiguo y lo moderno. Institucionalidad, ciudadanía y representación política, 1810–1838* (Castello de la Plana: Universitat Jaume I, 2009), 197–202.

43. Arturo Taracena, "Nación y República en Centroamérica (1821–1865)," in *Identidades nacionales y Estado moderno en* Centroamérica, edited by Arturo Taracena Arriola and Jean Piel, 50–51 (Mexico City: Centro de Estudios Mexicanos y Centroamericanos/FLACSO Guatemala/Universidad de Costa Rica 1995).

44. Clotilde Obregón Quesada, *El Río San Juan en la lucha de las potencias (1821–1860)* (San José: Editorial Universidad Estatal a Distancia, 1993), 41–48.

45. Ethel García Buchard, *Política y Estado en la sociedad hondureña del siglo XIX (1838–1872)* (Tegucigalpa: Instituto Hondureño de Antropología e Historia, 2008), 61–64; Pompejano, *Dio nero*, 130–134; Avendaño, *Centroamérica*, 203.

46. Taracena, *Invención criolla*.

47. After Central America separated from Mexico in 1823, and the rest of Chiapas rejoined it in 1824, the two federal governments did not sign a formal agreement regarding Soconusco, though an 1825 informal pact prohibited both from sending troops into Soconusco until

borders were defined. Individuals, groups, and towns in Soconusco used the legal systems of both governments according to their interests: rule had effectively fallen to dominant groups in the region. Mario Vázquez, *Chiapas mexicana. La gestación de la frontera entre México y Guatemala durante la primera mitad del siglo XIX* (Mexico City: Centro de Investigaciones sobre América Latina y el Caribe (CIALC)-UNAM/Centro de Investigaciones Multicisciplinarias sobre Chiapas y la Frontera Sur (CIMSUR)-UNAM, 2018), 143–149.

48. Carolyn Hall and Hector Pérez Brignoli, *Historical Atlas of Central America* (Norman: University of Oklahoma Press, 2003), 174.

49. The issue created one more point of stress dividing Guatemala and El Salvador, and it also brings into focus a question that may have had bearing on the weakness of the Federation: prior to the creation of the Archbishopric of Guatemala in 1743, the four bishoprics of the Kingdom of Guatemala were suffragan to three different archbishoprics, perhaps limiting certain types of relationships among the provinces. Hall and Pérez Brignoli, *Historical Atlas*, 110. The Salvadoran dioceses would only be officially formed with Vatican approval in 1842.

50. As Juan Pro Ruiz puts it, it is necessary to see "war as the framework in which the construction of states was produced and which, as a result, conditioned that process at all times" (translation by the author). Juan Pro Ruiz, "Guerra y Estado en tiempos de construcción nacional: comentarios sobre América Latina en el siglo XIX," in *Las fuerzas de guerra en la contrucción del Estado: América Latina, siglo XIX*, edited by Juan Carlos Garavaglia, Juan Pro Ruiz, and Eduardo Zimmermann, 17-32 (Rosario, Argentina: Prohistoria ediciones, 2012), 17.

51. Early on, the Government of the state of Guatemala argued that in a federation, the state governments should be recognized as holding a stature equal to that of federal government, and this equality should be demonstrated in how authorities from each government should be seated during public celebrations. Shortly thereafter, a conflict arose regarding a proposal, not to the liking of President Arce, that the federal military forces should depend on the state militias. Flemion, "States' Rights," 612; Taracena Arriola, "Mirada de tres actores guatemaltecos," 60. Tensions mounted and the possibility of military conflict appeared, which led to the arrest of Barrundia and the displacement of the Guatemalan state congress westward, eventually leading to battles in Los Altos, won by Arce and the moderates.

52. Arturo Taracena, ed., *La primera guerra federal centroamericana, 1826-1829. Nación y estados, republicanismo y violencia* (Mexico City: UAM-Iztapalapa/UNAM/Cara Parens/ Unversidad Rafael Landívar, 2015). Though limited in number, Costa Rica did in fact send troops to fight with the federal forces. Pablo Augusto Rodríguez Solano, "'Aislada y en absoluta orfandad'. Costa Rica y la Guerra Civil centroamericana (1826–1829)," in *La primera guerra federal centroamericana, 1826-1829. Nación y estados, republicanismo y violencia*, edited by Arturo Taracena Arriola, 165-197 Mexico City: UAM-Iztapalapa/ UNAM/Cara Parens/Universidad Rafael Landívar, 2015); Esteban Corella Ovares, "Al servicio de la Federación: El Batallón ligero de Costa Rica en la Guerra Civil Federal, 1826-1827," in *La primera guerra federal centroamericana, 1826-1829. Nación y estados, republicanismo y violencia*, edited by Arturo Taracena Arriola, 199-230 (Mexico City: UAM-Iztapalapa/UNAM/Cara Parens/Universidad Rafael Landívar, 2015).

53. Frances Kinloch Tijerino, *Nicaragua: identidad y cultura política (1821-1858)* (Managua: Banco Central de Nicaragua, 1999), 66-68.

54. Latin American historiography of the period, which had once focused on dominant political groups or individuals and later on economic concerns, and more recently has

emphasized the importance of the political thinking of the epoch, institutional development, and the role of popular or subaltern actors, has most recently shown signs of a move toward an understanding of how these aspects meshed. How did the relations between popular sectors and dominant groups play out, both inside and outside institutions, and what role did transformations in the (dominant and subaltern) political cultures and political imaginaries play? One recent work that works *toward* this sort of synthesis is Hilda Sabato, *Republics of the New World: The Revolutionary Political Experiment in 19th-Century Latin America* (Princeton, NJ: Princeton University Press, 2018).

55. Luis Pedro Taracena, "Mujeres, guerra y política (1826–1829)," *Revista de Historia* 9 (1999): 5-30; Lizet Jiménez Chacón, "Mujeres y vida cotidiana en tiempos de guerra (1837–1840)," in *Repensando Guatemala en la época de Rafael Carrera. El país, el hombre y las coordenadas de su tiempo*, edited by Brian Connaughton, 365-388 (Mexico City: UAM-Iztapalapa/Editorial Gedisa S.A., 2015).

56. Lauria-Santiago, *República agraria*, 176–180; Pérez Fabregat, *San Miguel*, 274–275.

57. García Buchard, *Políticas y Estado*, 57–58; Kinloch Tijerino, *Nicaragua*, 68; Pérez Fabregat, *San Miguel*, 188–190.

58. Clientelist relationships were one of the most basic forms of social organization in this period. Juan Pro Ruiz, "Considering the State from the Perspective of Bureaucracy: Lessons from the Latin American *Sattelzeit*," in *Latin American Bureaucracy and the State Building Process (1780–1860)* edited by Juan Carlos Garavaglia and Juan Pro Ruiz, translated by Tiffany Carter and Edward W. Krasny 1-23 (Newcastle upon Tyne: Cambridge Scholars Publishing, 2013), 10–11.

59. On the notion of the fiscal military state in Europe see John Brewer, *The Sinews of War: War and the English State, 1688–1783* (London: Unwin Hyman, 1989); Charles Tilly, *Coercion, Capital, and European States, AD 990–1992* (Oxford: Blackwell, 1994); and Richard Bonney, *Economic Systems and State Finance* (Oxford: Oxford University Press, 1995). Miguel Angel Centeno questioned the adequacy of the European model for nineteenth-century Latin America, noting that even in Europe, war helped states to develop only when some bureaucracy already existed. Miguel Angel Centeno, *Blood and Debt: War and the Nation-State in Latin America* (University Park: Pennsylvania State University Press, 2002). For further discussion on critiques of the model developed by Tilly, Brewer, and Bonney, see Wolfgang Knöbl, "State Building in Western Europe and the Americas in the Long Nineteenth Century," in *State and Nation Making in Latin America and Spain. Republics of the Possible*, edited by Miguel A. Centeno and Agustín E. Ferraro, 56-76 (New York: Cambridge University Press, 2013). The work by Juan Carlos Garavaglia, Juan Pro Ruiz, and their collaborators has brought a more specifically historical focus to the question, looking at the development of states in Latin America in terms of bureaucracy and war, as a process, eschewing a predefined notion of the state. Juan Carlos Garavaglia, Juan Pro Ruiz, and Eduardo Zimmermann, eds., *Las fuerzas de guerra en la construcción del Estado: América Latina, siglo XIX* (Rosario, Argentina: Prohistoria ediciones, 2012); Juan Carlos Garavaglia and Juan Pro Ruiz, eds., *Latin American Bureaucracy and the State Building Process (1780–1860)*, translated by Tiffany Carter and Edward W. Krasny (Newcastle upon Tyne: Cambridge Scholars, 2013).

60. Tania Sagastume Paiz, "La vida a la vera del camino. Cuatreros y asaltantes en Guatemala," *Revista Estudios* 64 (2018).

61. Eugenia Rodríguez Sáenz, "Civilizando la vida doméstica en el Valle Central de Costa Rica (1750–1850)," in *Entre silencios y voces: género e historia en América Central, 1750–1990*,

edited by Eugenia Rodríguez Sáenz, 41-77 (San José: Universidad de Costa Rica, 2000); Sagastume Paiz, *Trabajo urbano*; Jiménez Chacón, "Mujeres y vida cotidiana."

62. Aldo Antonio Lauria-Santiago, *Una república agraria. Los campesinos en la economía y la política de El Salvador en el siglo XIX*, trans. Márgara Zablah de Sumán (San Salvador: Consejo Nacional para la Cultura y el Arte [CONCULTURA], 2003), 173-182; René Reeves, *Ladinos with Ladinos Indians with Indians: Land, Labor and Regional Ethnic Conflict in the Making of Guatemala* (Stanford, CA: Stanford University Press, 2006), 45-46; Marvin Barahona, *Pueblos indígenas, Estado y memoria colectiva en Honduras* (Tegucigalpa: Guaymuras, 2009), 109-114; Pérez Fabregat, *San Miguel*, 311. The events in San Juan Ostuncalco may also be related to Indian rejection of the Livingston Codes that moved judicial proceeding out of the hands of town governments and into the hands of juries. Sonia Alda Mejías, *La participación indígena en la construcción de la República de Guatemala, S. XIX* (Madrid: Universidad Autónoma de Madrid, 2000), 261.

63. *Raúl O. Fradkin*, "Paradigmas en discusión. Independencia y revolución en Hispanoamérica y en el Río de La Plata," in *Las revoluciones en el largo siglo XIX latinoamericano*, edited by Rogelio Altez and Manuel Chust, 87-107 (Madrid: Vervuert/Iberoamericana, 2015), 102. In some cases, the ubiquity of violence can be related to its legitimation by the notion of the "citizen in arms," whose duty it was to prevent tyranny. Hilda Sabato, "Horizontes republicanos en Iberoamérica. Una perspectiva de largo plazo," in *Entre la Colonia y la República. Insurgencias, rebeliones y cultura política en América del Sur*, edited by Beatriz Bragoni and Sara E. Mata, 311-325 (Buenos Aires: Prometio Libros, 2008), 321.

64. Clara Pérez Fabregat has underlined the pragmatic nature of the anticlerical actions in El Salvador during the 1830s. Pérez Fabregat, *San Miguel*, 272.

65. Belaubre, "'Elus du monde.'"

66. This was common enough in Spanish America during this period. Juan Carlos Garavaglia, "State Building in Latin America: The Preceding Steps," in *Latin American Bureaucracy and the State Building Process (1780–1860)*, edited by Juan Carlos Garavaglia and Juan Pro Ruiz, translated by Tiffany Carter and Edward W. Krasny, 24-48 (Newcastle upon Tyne: Cambridge Scholars, 2013), 37-38; Juan Carlos Sarazúa Pérez, "Recolectar, administrar y defender: la construcción del estado y las resistencias regionales en Guatemala, 1800-1871" (PhD diss., Universitat Pompeu Fabra, 2013), 62-63, 164-167; Pérez Fabregat, *San Miguel*, 171-173, 188-190. Rodríguez Solano, *La cuestión fiscal*, 82-83, 99; Daniele Pompejano, *La crisis del antiguo régimen en Guatemala (1839–1871)*, translated by Diana Jalul (Guatemala: Editorial Universitaria, 1997).

67. Guatemala attempted more progressive fiscal measures, albeit with very limited success. Juan Carlos Sarazúa Pérez, "Finanzas estatales en Guatemala, 1823-1850," in *Independencias. Estado y política(s) en la Centroamérica del siglo XIX. Las huellas históricas del bicentenario*, edited by David Díaz Arias and Ronny Viales Hurtado, 65-87 (San José: Universidad de Costa Rica, 2012).

68. Víctor Hugo Acuña Ortega and Iván Molina Jiménez, *Historia económica y social de Costa Rica, 1750–1850* (San José: Editorial Porvenir, 1991), 69-90.

69. Lowell Gudmundson, "Society and Politics in Central America, 1821-1871," in *Central America, 1821–1871: Liberalism before Liberal Reform*, edited by Lowell Gudmundson and Héctor Lindo-Fuentes, 79-130 (Tuscaloosa: University of Alabama Press, 1995), 112.

70. Through *censo enfitéutico*, communally held lands could be rented out for years at a time. The 1836 law allowed renters to purchase those lands. Michael F. Fry, "Política agraria y reacción campesina en Guatemala: la región de la Montaña, 1821–1838," *Mesoamérica*

248   AARON POLLACK

9, no. 15 (1988), 25-46; Ralph Lee Woodward, *Rafael Carrera and the Emergence of the Republic of Guatemala, 1821-1871* (Athens: University of Georgia, 1993); David McCreery, *Rural Guatemala, 1760-1940* (Stanford, CA: Stanford University Press, 1994), 55-56; Tania Sagastume Paiz, "La política agraria del primer liberalismo en Guatemala, 1823-1837," *Anuario Estudios* 4, no. 1 (2016). 93-130.

71. Pérez Fabregat, *San Miguel*, 108, 115.

72. Mario Vázquez Olivera, *La República Federal de Centro-América. Territorio, nación y diplomacía, 1823-1838* (Antiguo Cuscatlán: Universidad Dr. José Matías Delgado, 2012).

73. García Buchard, *Política y Estado*, 75-134; Xiomara Avendaño Rojas, "Estado y corporaciones en la Nicaragua del siglo XIX," in *Independencias, estados y política(s) en la Centroamérica del siglo XIX*, edited by David Díaz Arias and Ronny Viales Hurtado, 121-152 (San José: Universidad de Costa Rica, 2012); Hugo Vargas González, "La formación del Estado en Nicaragua: entre el sufragio y la violencia (1821-1854)," in *Independencias, estado y política(s) en la Centroamérica del siglo XIX*, edited by David Díaz Arias and Ronny Viales Hurtado, 153-195 (San José: Universidad de Costa Rica, 2012); Sarazúa, "Recolectar, administrar"; Rodríguez Solano, *Cuestión fiscal*; Pérez Fabregat, *San Miguel*.

74. Arturo Taracena Arriola, "Nación y República en Centroamérica (1821-1865)," in *Identidades nacionales y Estado moderno en Centroamérica*, edited by Arturo Taracena Arriola and Jean Piel, 45-61 (Mexico City: Centro de Estudios Mexicanos y Centroamericanos/FLACSO Guatemala/Universidad de Costa Rica, 1995); Rodríguez Solano, *Cuestión fiscal*.

75. Sajid Alfredo Herrera Mena, *El ejercicio de gobernar. Del cabildo borbónico al ayuntamiento liberal: El Salvador colonial, 1750-1821* (Castello de la Plana: Universitat Jaume I, 2010); Sajid Alfredo Herrera Mena, "La práctica electoral en la provincia/estado de El Salvador, 1821-1839," in *Jaque a la Corona: La cuestión política en las Independencias Iberoamericanas*, edited by Juan Ortiz Escamilla and Ivana Frasquet, 251-272 (Castelló de la Plana: Universitat Jaume I, 2010); Vargas González, "Formación."

76. Alda Mejías, *Participación indígena*.

77. Lina Barrios, *Tras las huellas del poder local: La Alcaldía Indígena en Guatemala, del siglo XVI al siglo XX* (Guatemala: Universidad Rafael Landívar, 2001), 145-155.

78. Douglass Sullivan-González, "'A Chosen People': Religious Discourse and the Making of the Republic of Guatemala, 1821-1871," *The Americas* 54, no. 1 (July 1997), 17-38.

79. Daniele Pompejano, *Il Dio nero*, 150-155.

80. Douglass Sullivan-González, *Piety, Power, and Politics: Religion and Nation Formation in Guatemala, 1821-1871* (Pittsburgh: University of Pittsburgh, 1998). On the strength of popular devotion, see also Leavitt-Alcántara, *Alone at the Altar*.

81. William Joyce Griffith, *Empires in the Wilderness: Foreign Colonization and Development in Guatemala, 1834-1844* (Chapel Hill: University of North Carolina Press, 1965); Juan Carlos Solórzano Fonseca, "Rafael Carrera, ¿Reacción conservadora o revolución campesina? Guatemala 1837-1873," *Anuario de Estudios Centroamericanos* 13, no. 2 (1987), 5-35; Fry, "Política agraria"; Woodward, *Rafael Carrera*; Ann Jefferson, "'Nuestra América': la visión de la gente parda del distrito de Mita, 1837," in *Repensando Guatemala en la época de Rafael Carrera. El país, el hombre y las coordenadas de su tiempo*, edited by Brian Connaughton, 113-149 (Mexico City: Universidad Autónoma Metropolitana-Iztapalapa, 2015); Juan Carlos Sarazúa, "Santa Rosa y Chiquimula, participación fiscal y militar, 1839-1870," in *Repensando Guatemala en la época de Rafael Carrera. El país, el hombre y las coordenadas de su tiempo*, edited by Brian Connaughton, 209-248 (Mexico

FROM KINGDOM TO REPUBLICS, 1808–1840   249

City: Universidad Autónoma Metropolitana–Iztapalapa, 2015). For El Salvador, see Lauria-Santiago, *República agraria*, 181–182. Rumors about governments spreading disease, though the sources make no reference to their diffusion by priests, also arrived in Honduras and El Salvador. Lauria-Santiago, *República agraria*, 181; García Buchard, *Política y Estado*, 60.

82. A regional study encompassing eastern Guatemala, western El Salvador, and western Honduras during this period could be very fruitful.
83. Gudmundson, "Society and Politics.", 108 ; Pro Ruiz, "Considering the State," 14–15.
84. Taracena, *Invención criolla*.
85. Woodward, *Rafael Carrera*.

FURTHER READING

Dym, Jordana. *From Sovereign Villages to Nation States: City, States, and Federation in Central America, 1759–1839*. Albuquerque: University of New Mexico Press, 2006.

García Buchard, Ethel. *Política y Estado en la sociedad hondureña del siglo XIX (1838–1872)*. Tegucigalpa: Instituto Hondureño de Antropología e Historia, 2008.

Gudmundson, Lowell, and Héctor Lindo-Fuentes. *Central America, 1821–1871: Liberalism before Liberal Reform*. Tuscaloosa: University of Alabama Press, 1995.

Hawkins, Timothy. *Jose de Bustamante and Central American Independence: Colonial Administration in an Age of Imperial Crisis*. Tuscaloosa: University of Alabama Press, 2004.

Herrera Mena, Sajid Alfredo. *El ejercicio de gobernar. Del cabildo borbónico al ayuntamiento liberal: El Salvador colonial, 1750–1821*. Castelló de la Plana: Universitat Jaume I, 2013.

Kinloch Tijerino, Frances. *Nicaragua: identidad y cultura política (1821–1858)*. Managua: Banco Central de Nicaragua, 1999.

Molina Jiménez, Iván. *Costa Rica (1800–1850): el legado colonial y la génesis del capitalism*. San José: Universidad de Costa Rica, 1991.

Pérez Fabregat, Clara. *San Miguel y el oriente salvadoreño. La construcción del Estado de El Salvador, 1780–1865*. San Salvador: Universidad Centroamericana José Simeón Cañas (UCA), 2018.

Pinto Soria, Julio César. *Centroamérica, de la colonia al Estado nacional (1800–1840)*. 2nd ed. Guatemala: Editorial Universitaria, 1989.

Rodríguez, Mario. *The Cádiz Experiment in Central America, 1808 to 1826*. Berkeley: University of California Press, 1978.

Rodríguez Solano, Pablo Augusto. *La cuestión fiscal y la formación del Estado en Costa Rica. 1821–1859*. San José: Universidad de Costa Rica, 2017.

Taracena Arriola, Arturo. *Invención criolla, sueño ladino, pesadilla indígena. Los Altos de Guatemala: de región a Estado, 1740–1871*. Antigua Guatemala: Editorial El Porvenir/Centro de Investigaciones Regionales de Mesoamérica (CIRMA), 1999.

Vázquez Olivera, Mario. *El imperio mexicano y el reino de Guatemala. Proyecto político y campaña militar*. Mexico City: Fondo de Cultura Económica/Centro de Investigaciones sobre América Latina y el Caribe (CIALC)–UNAM, 2009.

Woodward, Ralph Lee Jr. *Rafael Carrera and the Emergence of the Republic of Guatemala, 1821–1871*. Athens: University of Georgia, 1993.

Wortman, Miles L. *Government and Society in Central America, 1680–1840*. New York: Columbia University Press, 1982.

PART III

CHALLENGES OF MODERNITY SINCE C. 1840: THE REGIONAL FRAME

CHAPTER 9

....

THE POLITICAL ECONOMY

....

ROBERT G. WILLIAMS

WHEN Spain retreated from Central America in the 1820s, age-old rivalries that smoldered under Spanish imperial rule broke into flame. When the union of five former provinces broke down in the late 1830s, provinces declared themselves independent nations. But elite factions continued to fight each other from power bases in colonial-era administrative townships in each province. For several decades, elites fought over which township would become the capital and the role of government in directing the economy. Conservatives were cautious about opening up to international forces of change and honored traditional rights of commercial townships, *haciendas*, and Indigenous communities, upholding the role of the Church as protector of communities against excessive commercial encroachment. Liberals embraced the modernizing forces of the industrial revolution and favored policies that would speed integration into the world system; they viewed the Church and Indigenous communities as backward, superstitious, and impediments to private wealth accumulation. By 1900, coherent national institutions had formed with some of the basic features that survive to this day. From 1840 to 1900, commercial and landed elites built national institutions to expand their fortunes, especially in the production of coffee for a booming world market. In Guatemala, El Salvador, and Nicaragua, where Indigenous communities occupied prime coffee lands, elites built armies to overpower communities resisting takeover of their lands. Once ancestral lands were seized for coffee plantations, armed force was essential in harnessing labor and protecting plantations from peasant sabotage. By 1900, elites in Guatemala, El Salvador, and Nicaragua had built states with large militaries to support large plantations. In Costa Rica and Honduras, small farmers participated in commercial development and militaries were not built for the purpose of displacing peasants from their lands or taking their labor, thus creating business models with less conflict between elites and peasant communities.

1840 TO 1900: COFFEE AND THE CONSTRUCTION OF NATIONAL STATES

Farthest removed from the colonial center of power, Costa Rica was the first to settle on a permanent capital, the first to enter the coffee trade, and the first to build coherent national state institutions.[1] Costa Rican elites in the Central Valley took a go-slow approach, granting small and medium-sized farmers private titles to lands surrounding commercial townships if a portion of that land was put into coffee cultivation. Elites came to own some larger coffee properties, but they concentrated their investments in export/import houses and in modern wet processing mills, which bought ripe coffee berries from growers and used controlled techniques to wash, de-pulp, dry, and sort the beans. The wet method required more capital but less labor than the traditional dry method, and it yielded a superior grade of coffee that fetched a premium on world markets. With access to international credit at low interest rates, processing mills extended short-term credit at higher rates to small and medium-sized growers in return for delivery of ripe coffee berries at harvest time. Elites collected profits more from coffee processing, trade, and finance than from growing coffee, and the government did not seize properties from peasant communities but encouraged small farmers' access to land. The pace of coffee exports was slow and steady as family farms with coffee groves also grew food crops. A prosperous class of small and medium-sized producers emerged that had some voice in governance. By 1900, Costa Rican elites relied on the military more to prevent foreign incursions than to seize land from small farmers and force them to work, allowing a greater share of government budgets to be spent on public education than was true of neighbors to the north.[2]

Under the presidency of peasant leader Rafael Carrera, Conservatives in Guatemala restored church property and protected traditional peasant communities from 1838 to 1871, when a faction of coffee-growing Liberals from Quetzaltenango took over the national government and introduced sweeping reforms that turned Guatemala into an export powerhouse.[3] In 1873, the government of General Justo Rufino Barrios seized some two hundred thousand acres in the Pacific piedmont and began auctioning off large blocks to wealthy investors, including the general himself, his in-laws, and foreign investors. That same year, Barrios expropriated Church properties, auctioned them, and used the proceeds to start Guatemala's first mortgage bank, which lent to coffee investors. To supply harvest labor, the government instituted labor drafts on Maya villages in the western highlands, where it was too cold to grow coffee. Villages that delivered harvest labor were allowed to keep ancestral lands surrounding their highland communities and were sometimes awarded larger holdings in exchange for lands seized in the piedmont. For disloyal highland villages that resisted labor drafts, Barrios ordered neighboring ladino (non-Indian) militias to crush rebellions and awarded militia leaders private titles to those villages' ancestral lands. To pay the rent, villagers were sent to work on piedmont plantations.[4] Debt servitude later replaced labor drafts from highland villages. Agents for coffee plantations advanced credit to poorer villagers at times of duress in return for several months of contracted harvest labor. In less than a decade of Liberal reforms, more than a hundred thousand Maya villagers were forced to migrate to piedmont plantations at harvest time, and Guatemala surpassed Costa Rica as the largest exporter of coffee. As early as 1875, the essential features of Guatemala's present-day wealth engine were in place (see Figure 9.1). With 60 percent of the

FIGURE 9.1. Birth of a Nation: Guatemala's wealth engine on display for foreign investors in 1875. Redesigned in 1871 by Guatemala's first Liberal government, the national flag flies over headquarters of Quezaltenango Department. From this building, Governor Juan Aparicio dispatches reinforcements for local *ladino* militias to crush Mayan community resistance to land takeovers and labor drafts that the governor's son-in-law, General Justo Rufino Barrios, initiated in 1873. The land office registers private titles to properties auctioned to domestic and foreign investors at lower altitudes in the department's coffee belt beginning fifteen miles south of this plaza. Several years after this photograph was taken, Quezaltenango had become the largest coffee-producing department in Guatemala, which had become the largest coffee producer in Central America. In an 1890 coffee census, Juan Aparicio and Sons is listed with holdings of 400,000 coffee trees, General Barrios's mother's family has holdings of 300,000 trees, General Barrios's widow has sold the general's properties to a German consortium, President Manuel Barillas has the largest holdings in the country with 1.3 million coffee trees, and numerous foreign firms, especially from Germany, have holdings from 100,000 to more than one million trees. The Pacific Mail Steamship Company, which transported coffee along the Pacific coast, commissioned photographer Eadweard Muybridge to spend six months in Guatemala and two months in Panama in 1875–1876 capturing images of the region's commercial potential for foreign investors. Credit: Eadweard Muybridge, "Reception of the Artist in Quetzaltenango, 1875," from *The Pacific Coast of Central America and Mexico; the Isthmus of Panama; Guatemala; and the Cultivation and Shipment of Coffee*. Courtesy of Department of Special Collections, Stanford University Libraries.

government budget, the military could carry out the wishes of the nation's business elite, which had a direct channel to the military high command.[5]

Guatemala's wealth engine became the envy of Salvadoran and Nicaraguan elites, but their militaries were weak and resistance from Indigenous communities was strong. Lands belonging to commercial townships were privatized and coffee growing got a peaceful start. But in 1875, when Salvadoran coffee growers attempted to purchase village lands from Indian communities in the western part of the country, villagers resisted. In 1881, the Salvadoran government legally abolished all communal rights to land, but Indigenous communities ignored the privatization decree and sabotaged growers' attempts to take land. In 1889, the national government funded a mounted police force to crush the resistance. By 1890, 60 percent of Salvadoran government revenue went to the military, and coffee barons regularly participated in running the government. El Salvador's wealth engine was finally up and running, and Salvadoran coffee exports caught up with Costa Rica, which had a three-decade head start.[6]

Between 1871 and 1890, Nicaraguan coffee production expanded tenfold. At first, the coffee boom took place peacefully around existing commercial townships. When coffee investors moved into north central Nicaragua in the early 1880s, they met stiff resistance from the Indigenous community of Matagalpa, where some 30,000 to 35,000 Indigenous people cultivated food crops on approximately 175,000 acres of land. In March 1881, one thousand armed peasants attacked departmental government headquarters of Matagalpa demanding an end to forced labor drafts, and in August 1881 five to seven thousand Indigenous people with ladino allies attacked government headquarters again. Government officials in Managua sent in the army and killed one to two thousand peasant farmers over a three-month period, but Indigenous communities continued to resist labor drafts and encroachments on ancestral lands. It was not until Liberal General José Santos Zelaya (1893–1909) took power that the national government made more serious inroads in the Matagalpa region. In 1895, the largest coffee grower in Matagalpa was assassinated and a popular mobilization followed. By 1898, General Zelaya had crushed the rebellion and large coffee plantations finally got military assistance securing harvest labor and protection from peasant sabotage.[7]

Peasant communities in Honduras largely escaped the ravages of capitalist coffee development suffered by neighbors in Guatemala, El Salvador, and Nicaragua, but Honduran economic growth was more subdued. Liberals connected with General Barrios of Guatemala took power in Honduras in 1876, and in 1880, the capital was permanently moved to Tegucigalpa. Liberal governments enacted decrees encouraging commercial development, but the Honduran state did not enact land laws or use military force to pressure townships to privatize municipal and communal lands. This allowed peasant communities to participate in coffee cultivation for local markets as a cash sideline to diversified food production. Honduran capital investment was concentrated in silver mines around Tegucigalpa and in the burgeoning banana zone on the North Coast around San Pedro Sula, where Honduran capitalist farmers hiring wage labor sold bananas to US fruit companies, whose steamships transported the product to US markets.[8]

1900 TO 1929: RAILROADS, BANANA ENCLAVES, AND US STRATEGIC MIGHT

By 1900, fundamental political economic structures of the five nations had formed on their own without armed intervention by imperial powers. In Guatemala, El Salvador, and Nicaragua, national militaries were constructed to protect owners of large plantations. In Costa Rica and Honduras, smaller militaries allowed more room for small farmers and peasant communities to flourish. During the first three decades of the twentieth century the United States asserted increasing military and economic influence, but imperial policies worked through national institutions and social formations already in place. From 1904 to the present, whenever US security interests have perceived an outside power gaining a foothold in the region, the US security state has intervened. Fear of foreign powers building a canal through Nicaragua provoked a US Marine invasion and overthrow of President Zelaya in 1909, and direct US military presence reinforced Nicaragua's large plantation business model until 1933, when General Anastasio Somoza García (1896–1956) was left in charge of the US-created National Guard, a strategic partnership passed on to his sons that lasted until 1979. US strategic relations with Central American governments enabled greater economic integration with the booming US economy. Regional coffee exports increased from less than two million bags in 1904 to more than three million bags in 1930, with trade shifting toward the US market during and after World War I. And during this period, US-based fruit companies used a railroads-for-concessions model developed earlier in Costa Rica to take over vast territories, especially in Guatemala and Honduras.

In 1884, the Costa Rican government made a deal with US engineer Minor Keith to complete a treacherous fifty-two-mile stretch of railroad to link the Central Valley with the Atlantic Coast. Keith assumed Costa Rica's outstanding debt to the British and promised to complete the railroad in return for control over railroad profits for ninety-nine years. The deal included a package of tax exemptions and rights to some eight hundred thousand acres of land. Keith's Costa Rican enterprise increased banana exports from one million stems in 1890 to three million stems in 1899, when Keith merged his enterprise with Boston Fruit Company to form United Fruit Company.[9]

In 1904, United Fruit Company made a similar contract by assuming Guatemala's outstanding debt on a railroad project abandoned in 1885. The company agreed to complete a difficult sixty-mile stretch between Guatemala City and Puerto Barrios in return for control over the docks, tax exemptions on imports and exports, 168,000 acres of land with enclave privileges, and exclusive rights to acquire and develop Guatemala's railroad network.

Avoiding a United Fruit Company monopoly, the Honduran government contracted with three US fruit companies, granting rights to more than four hundred thousand acres of land in designated zones of the North Coast in return for building railroads with links to the capital of Tegucigalpa. The companies built the railroads to service their banana plantations, but they never completed the links to Tegucigalpa.

By 1913, bananas had become Central America's second most important export after coffee, and the investment boom continued through the 1920s. By 1930, United Fruit Company was the largest employer in Central America and controlled most of the rail lines in Guatemala, Costa Rica, and Honduras including a link to El Salvador. Railroad building and banana plantations attracted workers to fertile river valleys and altered labor relations, coastal ecologies, and national politics, especially in Guatemala, Costa Rica, and Honduras.

1929 TO 1941: THE GREAT DEPRESSION TO WORLD WAR II

The boom from rising coffee prices and abundant credit during the 1920s collapsed when global financial crisis struck. From 1929 to 1932 world coffee prices dropped from twenty-two cents to nine cents per pound. International credit through trading houses and banks seized up, shutting down short-term crop loans which coffee growers depended on to hire harvest workers. Especially hard hit were Guatemala, El Salvador, and Nicaragua, where large capitalist plantations, heavily reliant on credit, dominated the coffee sector. Export volumes in those three countries dropped by more than 30 percent during the early 1930s, and militaries intervened to protect large plantation owners.

In Guatemala, General Jorge Ubico (1931–1944) counteracted the credit crunch on growers by prohibiting cash advances to secure harvest labor. To harness seasonal workers, Ubico reinstalled nineteenth-century labor drafts on highland Indian communities, requiring those without adequate property or income to work 100 to 150 days a year on the plantations or face forced labor on road construction crews. Only after the work requirements were completed were employers permitted to pay workers' wages.[10]

In El Salvador, coffee growers responded to the 1929–1932 crisis by cutting wages from fifty centavos per day to twenty and by evicting permanent workers from their estates. Already shaken economically, Salvadoran elites were shocked in 1931, when a civilian promising land reform won the presidential election. When campaign promises were not delivered, the Salvadoran Communist Party under the leadership of Farabundo Martí National Liberation Front (FMLN) mobilized students, workers, and peasant groups. In the western districts of El Salvador, Indigenous groups occupied coffee estates and town halls, demanding a return of communal lands. The Salvadoran coffee elite engineered a military coup in December 1931, installing General Maximiliano Hernández Martínez (1931–1944), who arrested communist leaders and in January 1932 sent reinforcements to the western district to assist large plantation owners and their ladino militias. Security forces assassinated Indigenous leaders and slaughtered suspected sympathizers. The genocide lasted several months, taking ten thousand to twenty-five thousand lives, many times the number involved in the uprising. The 1932 *matanza* (slaughter) etched in public memory the extremes Salvadoran elites would go to protect their wealth engine.[11]

Nicaraguan coffee growers responded to the crisis by suspending cash advances for harvest labor and abandoning plantations in remote areas. In Matagalpa and Jinotega, where Indigenous lands were seized for coffee in the 1880s and 1890s, peasants invaded idle properties. When the National Guard entered the area to evict them, Augusto Cesar Sandino's guerrilla army, which had been attacking US mines and marine outposts to the north, repelled the guard units. General Anastasio Somoza García ordered guardsmen to assassinate Sandino and two of his generals in 1934. National Guard troops swept through Matagalpa and Jinotega, killing suspected supporters of Sandino, evicting peasants, and claiming idle coffee farms for Somoza and his officers. In 1937, Somoza maneuvered to become president of the country, giving him a virtual monopoly on diplomatic, military, and economic relations with the United States that was passed down to his sons and lasted until the dynasty was toppled in 1979.[12]

In Costa Rica, the coffee crisis manifested itself as a struggle between wealthy coffee mill owners and small coffee growers who supplied the mills with ripe berries. In 1929, Costa Rican coffee mill owners suspended cash advances to small growers and demanded payment of outstanding debts. As world coffee prices continued to drop, mill owners reduced at a faster rate the prices paid for ripe berries, thereby shifting the brunt of the crisis onto small growers. Large growers, processors, and exporters formed their own national organization, while small growers formed theirs. The Costa Rican government mediated the conflicts without attacking the small growers, so violence did not erupt, and the collapse of coffee production was less severe than in Guatemala, El Salvador, and Nicaragua, where the large plantation model was dominant.[13]

US fruit companies responded to declining markets by laying off workers, cutting wages, slashing prices paid to independent banana growers, and shutting down plantation areas infected with fungal diseases. In Guatemala, General Ubico used military force to project a united front with fruit companies against organized labor and land invasions, supporting a relatively orderly transition as the company abandoned plantations infected by Panama Disease on the Atlantic and shifted production to new concessions at Tiquisate (1936) on the Pacific Coastal Plain. In Nicaragua, Standard Fruit Company suffered from the spread of Panama Disease and from work stoppages when Sandino's Army passed through. Nicaraguan banana exports dropped from four million bunches in 1929 to two million in 1936.

In 1929, Honduras exported some twenty-nine million bunches of bananas, making it the largest producer in Central America. When the international crisis hit, Honduran workers went on strike against wage cuts, culminating in a major strike in 1932. With support from US fruit companies, Tiburcio Carías Andino (1933–1949) took control in 1933, placing loyal appointees to the North Coast to keep a lid on organized labor. The Aguán River Valley was so devastated by Panama Disease that in 1935, United Fruit Company shut down the railroad and plantations in this valley. Unemployed workers survived by squatting on abandoned plantations and raising food crops.

In Costa Rica, United Fruit Company had already abandoned Atlantic Coast plantations, selling or leasing lands infected by Panama Disease to independent banana growers, who absorbed the crop risk, or to West Indian workers, who planted food crops and cacao.[14] In the Costa Rican strike of 1934, United Fruit Company played off ethnic divisions and attributed the strike to the work of the Communist Party. In 1934, Costa Rican officials granted United Fruit Company concessions to uncontaminated land on the Pacific Coast, but in 1938 Sigatoka Disease, an air-borne fungus, spread to the Pacific plantations.[15] The company invested heavily in hydraulic pipe systems allowing workers to spray the leaves with a toxic mixture containing copper sulfate. Spraying allowed longer life of banana plantations but destroyed workers' lungs and ultimately poisoned the earth so banana roots could no longer absorb nutrients.[16]

Despite violence inflicted on workers and peasants during the depression, the collapse of international trade and abandoned plantations created opportunities for peasant economies to increase production for local markets, absorbing some of the shocks from the global economy.[17]

1941 TO 1954: SHIFTING US POLICY— ANTIFASCISM DURING WORLD WAR II TO ANTICOMMUNISM OF THE COLD WAR

Shortly after entering World War II (December 1941), the US government pressured Central American leaders to cut ties with Axis Powers, expropriate enemy nationals' assets, and deport those involved in pro-fascist organizations. This unsettled Depression-era dictators who had fascist leanings and close ties with German-owned businesses, creating openings for civil society groups to challenge their power.

In 1944, General Ubico reluctantly expropriated properties owned by German nationals, including some seventy-five large coffee estates, representing one-fifth of Guatemalan production. Farmworkers went on strike in Tiquisate, further weakening the dictatorship. Emboldened by a brief democratic opening in El Salvador, civil society groups mobilized in Guatemala City, and disaffected junior officers ousted Ubico.[18] Juan José Arévalo (1945–1951), Guatemala's first elected president, responded to organized farmworkers' demands and abolished forced labor drafts.[19] Peasants invaded abandoned banana company lands and idle portions of expropriated German coffee plantations. Facing frequent coup attempts, President Arévalo tried to tame the agrarian movement, but his democratically elected successor, Jacobo Arbenz (1951–1954) validated land invasions of idle properties with the land reform law of 1952, placing Communist Party leaders in charge of implementing it. By 1954, peasant communities were legally positioned to reclaim 1.7 million acres, including half the territory of United Fruit Company, whose former lawyer, John Foster Dulles, was US Secretary of State, whose brother, Allen Dulles, was head of the CIA. In 1954, a CIA-engineered coup replaced President Arbenz with General Carlos Castillo Armas, who dismantled revolutionary advances of the previous decade and was restoring Guatemala's badly damaged wealth engine when he was assassinated in 1957.[20] Alarmed, the Guatemalan business community united forming the Coordinating Committee of the Agricultural, Commercial, Industrial and Financial Associations of Guatemala (CACIF), so that business elites could speak with one voice to military, civilian, and US officials. Since 1957, US officials have worked on matters of economic policy with Guatemala through CACIF, which has direct channels to Guatemala's military. From 1957 to the present, CACIF has held the business community together to fight land reform and labor unions, sometimes at odds with US democratic policies toward Guatemala.[21]

Expropriation of Axis properties was not so disruptive in El Salvador, where German and Italian investors had intermarried with other elites, so property titles could be switched into names of relatives not on the State Department's expropriation list. General Martínez ruled El Salvador on behalf of large landowners until 1944, when a student-led strike gained widespread support of professionals and workers, forcing Martínez to resign. The democratic opening lasted only six months when military officers squelched it in a coup, removing a potential threat to El Salvador's wealth engine.

Expropriated properties in Honduras were easily sold with little disruption. When a democratic opening appeared in 1944 and San Pedro Sula business and civilian groups protested the dictatorship, President Carías called on his local security forces, who crushed the protests and massacred some fifty people, allowing the dictator to continue suppressing organized labor on behalf of US fruit companies until 1949. Labor unions in 1954 organized a strike, but CIA operatives helped steer the 1954 movement, lobbying the strike committee to purge itself of communists in favor of delegates affiliated with the US anticommunist labor confederation, the AFL-CIO. This divided the movement but created political space in the Cold War environment for Honduran workers to pressure for change without government repression. In 1955, a national labor code legalized existing unions and established bargaining rights for organized labor. By the late 1960s and early 1970s, Honduras had the most organized labor force and peasant movement in Central America, capable of influencing national elections and the military without provoking US intervention. And Honduran business elites remained divided on ethnic and regional lines, giving sometimes conflicting policy directives to officials.[22]

When the Nicaraguan government expropriated German properties, members of the Somoza family and close associates acquired them and kept them working with little disruption. Anastasio Somoza García's father had owned a sizable coffee plantation, but by 1944 the son had used his political and military power to become the largest coffee grower in Nicaragua with forty-six plantations.[23] With the onset of the Cold War, the Somoza regime pushed through an anticommunist and anti-labor constitution that benefited big business groups in Nicaragua for years to come. The US strategic partnership with Nicaragua through a single family dynasty enabled the Somoza family to use the National Guard and government institutions to build their private fortunes and hand out favors to loyal associates (the Somoza Group), sometimes at the expense of other big business groups.

In Costa Rica, organized labor supported the 1940 landslide victory of Rafael Calderón Guardia, who ushered in social security, a progressive labor code, and the public university system. Instead of being sold off to wealthy businesses, some of the largest German properties were turned into producer cooperatives. The onset of the Cold War and complex political maneuvering brought a civil war in 1948 and the rise to power of José Figueres, whose staunch anticommunist stance provided Costa Rican leaders space to carry out social democratic programs without provoking US intervention. President Figueres purged communists from government but retained Calderón's progressive labor code, social security, and support for public education. Figueres even nationalized the banks and the electric company and abolished the Costa Rican Army, and his political party won national elections for more than three decades. Costa Rica's social democratic brand of anticommunism allowed Costa Rican workers and peasants room to organize and register their grievances at a national level, without setting off alarms at the pentagon.[24]

Economic Boom of the 1950s and 1960s, Economic Shocks and Unrest in the 1970s

Cold War strategic partnerships between the United States and Central American militaries were already in place by 1954, but after the Cuban Revolution in 1959, Washington pumped massive resources through military, business, and government channels to prevent the spread of revolution. In 1961, John F. Kennedy's Alliance for Progress was a ten-year multi-billion-dollar economic development program for Latin America. To sustain funding from Congress, democracy and social justice reforms were promised alongside military aid and economic packages to expand and diversify private enterprise. Washington promoted industrial growth in the region through the Central American Common Market (CACM) and stimulated modern agribusiness by opening US markets, funding roads, and providing subsidized credit. With special programs targeting nontraditional exports, cotton export volumes expanded fivefold between 1961 and 1973; beef export volumes rose sevenfold; and a host of other products diversified the export mix. Each new activity brought increased prosperity for investors but placed stress on peasant communities and the environment. Export-led growth continued in the 1970s, but world system shocks in 1973–1975 and 1977–1983 simultaneously squeezed business profits and livelihoods of the poor, triggering waves of unrest and repression, which culminated in the overthrow of the Somoza regime in Nicaragua (1979) and revolutionary insurrections in El Salvador and Guatemala.

During the 1950s, business elites pushed for protective tariffs on imported goods that increased manufacturing, especially in the two countries with the largest markets, Guatemala and El Salvador. Without US backing, the United Nations Economic Commission for Latin America (ECLA) promoted a five-country trade zone based on principles of balanced development and managed trade.[25] After the Cuban Revolution, US policymakers finally embraced industrialization through a common market but scrapped the balanced growth plans of the ECLA treaties, preferring a free market approach. During the 1960s trade between common market partners expanded dramatically, industrial manufacturing flourished, and the CACM was widely recognized as the most successful case of economic integration in the developing world. But trade imbalances and uneven development created tensions as Guatemala and El Salvador racked up massive trade surpluses while others suffered trade deficits, especially Honduras, where Tegucigalpa's petty producers suffered a depression from the flood of manufactured imports from Guatemala and Salvador.[26] Tegucigalpa's business community finally pressured the Honduran government to drop out of the CACM in December 1970, despite protests from North Coast manufacturers, who had competed well in the common market.[27]

Cotton brought a new dynamism to Central America's Pacific Coastal Plain, which has some of best soil and climate conditions in the world for growing cotton were it not for insect infestations, which traditionally made the crop unprofitable. Applying modern insecticides, Central American cotton growers enjoyed increased yields per acre in the 1950s and by the 1960s, they consistently achieved yields 20 to 25 percent higher than growers in the Mississippi Delta. Because of an abundant supply of inexpensive seasonal labor, Central American growers could continue to have the crop handpicked, which fetched a price premium over machine-picked US cotton.

With funding from the World Bank and US Agency for International Development (USAID), a coastal highway with feeder roads opened up the Pacific Coastal Plain for mechanized agriculture, and government development banks channeled credit into cotton, allowing growers to rent land from absentee landowners and buy inputs from agribusiness supply houses. Before cotton, peasant families lived year-round on coastal haciendas, plowing the land with oxen to raise food crops, delivering half the crop to the landlord at harvest time. As the coastal plain was opened up for cotton during the 1950s and 1960s, landlords evicted entire peasant communities as owners switched to tractors. Mechanization reduced the holding capacity for peasants on the coastal plain of Nicaragua, El Salvador, and Guatemala where cotton development was strongest. Families expelled from coastal haciendas lost food security. Many migrated to urban slums, where they found marginal work in the informal sector while they waited for seasonal harvest jobs. Other families sought food security by migrating to remote areas on the agricultural frontier, where they continued the tradition of carving out patches from the forest to raise food crops.[28]

The US Alliance for Progress shifted sugar and beef quota allocations from Cuba to Central America as a way to award loyal allies and diversify the region's exports. The Somoza government bestowed Nicaragua's beef quota on Somoza's packing plant, which was the first in Central America to collect profits from selling beef at high prices in the protected US market. The US State Department handed out beef quotas to the four other countries, while the US Department of Agriculture (USDA) approved modern packing plants. USAID, the World Bank, and the Inter-American Development Bank (IADB) financed roads into potential cattle zones and provided credit and technical support to ranchers. In 1959, three USDA-approved packing plants shipped 17 million pounds of beef to the United States. In 1968, fourteen packing plants exported 109 million pounds of beef to the United States, and by 1978, twenty-eight packing plants in the five Central American countries shipped 220 million pounds of beef to US fast-food businesses.

While the beef export boom supported faster GDP growth, it permanently destroyed vast areas of tropical forest and displaced hundreds of thousands of peasant families living on the edge of the forest as cattle ranchers drove out corn producers. One ranch of a thousand acres owned by a single family could displace from 70 to 140 peasant families. Every country with a beef quota and a modern packing plant experienced rural violence as peasants resisted takeover of lands by cattle ranchers.

In 1965, Honduras experienced its first publicized massacre of peasants at the hands of ranchers in Olancho Department, a major cattle expansion zone. In the late 1960s, Honduran ranchers pressured their government to serve eviction notices on Salvadoran peasants, leading to forced deportation of one hundred thousand Salvadorans from Honduras, resulting in a war between the two countries in 1969.[29]

In the mid-1960s, peasants resisted cattle rancher intrusions in eastern Matagalpa province, Nicaragua's largest corn-producing area and a strong attractor of population at the time. A small band of Sandinista National Liberation Front (FSLN) guerrillas began supporting the peasants of the area. In 1967 the Somoza regime declared eastern Matagalpa a counterinsurgency zone and obtained US funding to construct military roads for the National Guard to clear the area. Thousands of peasant families, most of which were not connected with the Sandinistas, were forced to flee, and eastern Matagalpa became a net expulsion zone for population as meat production displaced basic grains. Some forty National Guard officers were awarded ranches of 1,700 acres each, and 1,300 peasant collaborators received land grants of 7 acres each.[30]

In the late 1960s, a similar counterinsurgency drive cleared an area of northeastern Guatemala for cattle ranching. Using techniques developed in Vietnam, US Special Forces and US intelligence operatives assisted the Guatemalan army in "pacifying" the zone, where a band of guerrillas had been organizing villagers to resist takeover of lands by ranchers. Between 1966 and 1968, the sweep killed six to eight thousand mostly ladino peasants, forcing many thousands more to flee. Security personnel received land grants of different sizes depending on rank. General Carlos Arana, who commanded the operation, received a large cattle ranch for services rendered.[31] In the 1970s the Guatemalan military's attention turned to the Northern Transversal Strip, a vast area with only eight miles of paved roads, where Maya settlers from the overcrowded western highlands had formed food production cooperatives. After oil was discovered in the zone, a nickel concession granted, and a hydroelectric project approved, a Washington-funded road project made cattle ranching profitable. Army units evicted Maya settlers and officers were awarded ranches.[32] In 1978, a highly publicized massacre of Maya civilians at the hands of ranchers and an army unit triggered the mass participation of Guatemala's Indian population in the Committee for Peasant Unity (CUC).

Peasant resistance was concentrated in Central America's cattle expansion zones, but when global economic shock waves hit the region, first in 1973–1975 and then 1977–1982, social unrest broke out in the cities and the countryside. Spikes in costs of fuel, fertilizer, pesticides, and credit squeezed profits, and consumer prices soared. Workers struck for higher wages, urban poor protested transportation price hikes, and peasants invaded idle properties. In Nicaragua, El Salvador, and Guatemala, governments used brute force against protestors and peasants. Instead of dividing the opposition, repression stimulated coalitions of groups that had never worked together before. Even Catholic action groups began dialogue and coordination with groups calling for armed insurgency.

Nicaragua, the most successful case of export-led economic growth, was the first country to break out in revolution. Despite brutal repression that took the lives of some fifty thousand people, revolutionary forces toppled the Somoza dictatorship in 1979, emboldening revolutionary movements in El Salvador and Guatemala, where big business groups and their militaries formed a united front to crush the insurgencies. In contrast, governments of Costa Rica and Honduras refrained from wholesale repression of protests and in some cases responded with upward adjustments to minimum wages and food or transportation subsidies. Through land occupations and national mobilizations for land reform, peasant organizations in Honduras reclaimed approximately 210,000 acres of land between 1973 and 1976, and no revolutionary movement developed there. In Costa Rica by 1975, peasant groups had successfully pressured the national agrarian agency for some 178,000 acres of land, and no armed insurrection took place there.[33]

REVOLUTION, CIVIL WARS, AND US INTERVENTION, 1979 TO THE 1990S PEACE ACCORDS

Nicaragua's wealth engine was more vulnerable than El Salvador's and Guatemala's, because it channeled capital almost exclusively into Somoza properties at the expense of other wealthy Nicaraguans. As the popular uprising against Somoza grew, disgruntled business elites helped the FSLN oust Somoza and in 1979 formed the Superior Council of Private Enterprise (COSEP), which had representatives in a provisional government before the Sandinistas took full control. National guardsmen and others associated with Somoza took their livestock and whatever capital was movable and fled to other countries, especially to Honduras. During the 1980s, COSEP remained in Nicaragua as the organized voice of private enterprise, which continued to control approximately 80 percent of large scale business activity. The FSLN commanded the former Somoza properties, including one-fifth of Nicaragua's land area in farms. Sandinista leaders kept expropriated properties intact as state-owned enterprises or state-managed cooperatives with some fifty thousand farmworkers under FSLN management. But by the mid-1980s, peasant groups pressured the Sandinista government to allow settlement on idle portions of large estates. This second wave of land reform solidified allegiance of some three hundred thousand peasants to the FSLN, but it angered members of COSEP, who were permitted to keep only the actively cultivated portions of their estates.[34]

Shortly after Somoza fell, Honduras became military headquarters for US intervention in the region. Military aid skyrocketed as Honduran officials conceded territory for US military bases, air strips, and strategic roads. With a core base recruited from Somoza's National Guard, the CIA organized the Counter-revolutionary Army (Contras) of approximately twenty-two thousand troops, which used clandestine bases in Honduras to invade Nicaragua. Between 1980 and 1989, the Contras destroyed basic infrastructure, attacked FSLN-controlled farms, and displaced five hundred thousand people, killing some thirty thousand Nicaraguans. In 1982 the US Congress cut off funding for the Contras, so the Reagan Administration bypassed Congress, setting up covert enterprises with offshore bank accounts and private contractors to traffic illegal arms to fund the Contra Army. US intervention promoted the most hardline anticommunist, anti-labor, anti-peasant officers in the Honduran military.[35] Honduran peasant communities lost territory to military bases, and Honduran military commanders learned from their US mentors how to create off-balance-sheet enterprises to accumulate private wealth while doing covert operations and construction jobs for the US military.[36]

In 1984, a bipartisan panel headed by Henry Kissinger persuaded reluctant members of Congress to fund a Marshall Plan for Central America. Arguing how successful Kennedy's Alliance for Progress was, the Kissinger Report called for an identical mix of military aid, export promotion, private investment incentives, democratic elections, and centrally controlled social reforms that were used during the 1960s.[37] The Kissinger Report went so far as to recommend increasing US beef quota allocations to friendly governments in Central America, despite evidence from the 1960s and 1970s that military aid plus beef export promotion equals mass displacement of populations, food insecurity, deforestation, and armed resistance.

In Guatemala's Northern Transversal Strip, the army massacred whole villages of Maya settlers and occupied highland villages where settlers had come from.[38] The military forced the Maya to resettle in USAID-funded "model villages," drafted them into civil patrols, and provided them food in return for road work. In 1982–1983 General Efraím Ríos Montt oversaw some 105 massacres of Maya Ixil civilians, but his talk of land reform angered business leaders in CACIF, and army officers deposed him in 1983 for disrupting the tradition of awarding them ranches for counterinsurgency services. Between 1980 and the Peace Accords in 1996,[39] counterinsurgency drives and road building opened up the Northern Transversal Strip for oil drilling, nickel mining, hydroelectric power, logging, and cattle ranching, and promoted a generation of army officers into the ranks of Guatemala's landed elite.[40]

US air strikes from bases in Honduras hit peasant strongholds in northern El Salvador, where the land was too poor to raise export crops but where peasants, with the help of FMLN guerrillas, had regained territory from cattle ranchers. USAID used land reform as an instrument of counterinsurgency to draw peasants away from the FMLN. But land reform hit large estates in the Pacific Coastal Plain, enraging El Salvador's large landholders, who sabotaged the reform by contracting death squads to intimidate peasant applicants of the US-funded reform.[41] Between 1979 and 1992, when UN-shepherded Peace Accords were signed by the government and the FMLN, some seventy-five thousand civilians were killed or disappeared in El Salvador, 85 percent at the hands of government security forces or death squads attached to them.[42] Some one million Salvadorans fled the country during the civil war, with more than six hundred thousand making their way to the United States.

US support of the Contras ground to a halt in 1988 after a congressional investigation exposed the Iran-Contra Affair. FSLN commanders and Contra leaders signed a ceasefire agreement in March 1988. With the Nicaraguan economy suffering from hyperinflation and shortages, Sandinista officials agreed to schedule elections for 1990 in which Contra leaders would be allowed to compete. In 1989, the Soviet Union and Cuba withdrew military presence from Nicaragua, while the United States supported opposition candidates in the elections. In January 1990, opposition candidate Violeta Chamorro, who campaigned to end the war, abolish the draft, and reduce the armed forces, won against FSLN candidate Daniel Ortega. Congress reduced military funding for Guatemala, El Salvador, and Honduras (Northern Triangle), and UN delegations brokered Peace Accords in El Salvador in 1992 and finally in Guatemala in 1996. In Nicaragua, El Salvador, and Guatemala, military commanders agreed to large staff reductions and reforms to respect human rights, while rebel groups agreed to lay down their arms in return for rights to participate in elections. In addition to loss of human life, wars dragged the economies of the region down, with El Salvador and Nicaragua suffering the greatest economic losses.[43]

1990S TO 2019: POST-PEACE ACCORD NEOLIBERAL POLICIES AND ECONOMIC DEVELOPMENT OUTCOMES

The peace process ended the wars, reduced the size of militaries, and set up all five countries of Central America for postwar economic recoveries (see Tables 1 and 2).[44] Postwar governments needed debt relief, infrastructure loans, and aid to get their economies going. During the 1990s, the US government, the International Monetary Fund (IMF), and the World Bank offered financial support conditioned upon governments adopting

Table 9.1. Average Annual Growth Rates of Real GDP, Selected Periods

	War	Transition		CAFTA	
	1978–1989	1990–2000	2000–2017	2006–2017	1990–2017
Guatemala	1.27%	4.03%	3.38%	3.39%	3.62%
El Salvador	-2.31%	3.29%	1.98%	1.99%	2.47%
Honduras	2.84%	3.12%	3.90%	3.38%	3.61%
Nicaragua	-3.62%	3.33%	3.79%	4.08%	3.62%
Costa Rica	2.36%	4.73%	3.99%	3.81%	4.26%

Source: World Bank, *Word Development Indicators*, "Real GDP, Constant 2010 $US," https://databank.worldbank.org/source/world-development-indicators.

Table 9.2. Real GDP Per Capita, Constant 2010 $US

	1960	1978	1989	1995	2000	2005	2017
Guatemala	$1,462	$2,420	$2,131	$2,356	$2,555	$2,638	$3,124
El Salvador	n/a	$3,157	$2,086	$2,548	$2,686	$2,820	$3,464
Honduras	$1,096	$1,652	$1,587	$1,594	$1,620	$1,799	$2,211
Nicaragua	$1,528	$2,294	$1,164	$1,117	$1,310	$1,429	$2,016
Costa Rica	$2,857	$4,952	$4,484	$5,652	$6,230	$2,954	$9,792

Source: World Bank, *World Development Indicators*, "Real GDP per capita, Constant 2010 $US," https://databank.worldbank.org/source/world-development-indicators.

neoliberal policies designed to shrink the size of governments, remove social subsidies, sell off state-owned assets, reduce regulations on business, promote free trade, and provide incentives for foreign direct investment. Neoliberal policies gained region-wide traction in 2002 when the Bush Administration initiated negotiations on the Central American Free Trade Agreement with the United States and the Dominican Republic (CAFTA-DR), which entered into force in 2006 for all countries except Costa Rica, where social resistance delayed its introduction until 2009.[45] From 2001 before CAFTA negotiations began and 2018, the value of Central American exports to the United States quadrupled. As businesses took advantage of trade opportunities, exports of apparel, tropical fruits, nuts and melons, electrical parts, scientific equipment, sugar, and African palm oil surged. But peasant economies suffered from land loss to agribusiness and the sudden influx of subsidized corn and basic grains from the United States.[46] Business groups in all five countries embraced neoliberal policies including CAFTA, while civil society organizations resisted the policies, which they perceived as benefiting big business at the expense of the poor and the environment. Political space for civil society groups to cushion the blow of neoliberal policies differed in the five countries, leading to contrasting development outcomes. In the Northern Triangle the military/big business model led to violence and massive displacements of populations as businesses used security forces to respond to investment opportunities. In Costa Rica and Nicaragua, big business did not have full capture of security forces, and economic growth occurred in a more sustainable, non-violent manner without the mass exodus of civilians experienced in the Northern Triangle.

Costa Rica was poised to reap the largest peace dividend. Austerity measures and neoliberal structural adjustment programs whittled away at redistributive aspects of Costa Rica's social democratic state and increased crime rates, but civil society groups resisted wholesale privatization and environmental deregulation, allowing more sustainable development than elsewhere.[47] During the early 1990s, Costa Rica attracted low-paying jobs in apparel manufacturing. But by the late 1990s Costa Rican presidents engaged with business leaders to attract information technology firms, and Costa Rica's Central Valley became known as "Silicon Valley South."[48] By picking strategic sectors, Costa Rica continued to climb the international value chain attracting high-technology firms to free trade zones clustered around research and educational centers in the Central Valley.[49] Lower-paying agricultural jobs increased in the coastal regions as multinational fruit companies expanded banana production and began exporting pineapples, mangoes, and other tropical fruits. Tourism revenues exceeded coffee export earnings by the mid-1990s. By 2018, 2.5 million tourists were bringing in ten times the foreign exchange earnings of coffee, and eco-tourism and environmentalist groups had joined forces to protect forests, rivers, wetlands, and seashore.[50] Costa Rica's "green trademark" became an issue of national pride, and Costa Rica is the only country in Central America whose neoliberal policies were accompanied by reforestation, not massive deforestation.[51] Of the five governments, Costa Rica's has faced the most effective popular resistance to neoliberal policies, but Costa Rica's economy has been the star performer in the region with the fastest overall economic growth since the 1990s, coupled with low rates of outmigration, low crime rates, the lowest poverty rates, the lowest income dependency on foreign remittances, the most effective environmental regulations, and the star attractor of foreign investors, especially in relatively high-skilled, high-paying jobs.

Nicaragua suffered the greatest destruction of infrastructure and collapse of the capitalist sector during the war years, and during the early 1990s implemented severe austerity measures to dampen inflation. Members of Nicaragua's wealthy business class who had remained in the country in the 1980s beat FSLN candidate Daniel Ortega in presidential elections in 1990, 1996, and 2001.[52] They privatized state-owned properties and applied other neoliberal economic policies with zeal, but a significant share of state-owned assets were already taken as private property by Sandinista leaders in the two months leading up to transfer of power in 1990.[53] With this starting capital, Sandinista commanders owned large capitalist enterprises that have competed with businesses owned by members of COSEP, creating a deep ideological rift in Nicaragua's big business class. The remainder of former Somoza properties were privatized, but workers bargained for a 30 percent stake and some enterprises have remained as worker-owned cooperatives. Former Contras returned in the early 1990s, resettling in areas they acquired in the Somoza period or on the agricultural frontier. Former Contras were allowed to participate in elections, but the disarmament pact left Sandinista commanders in charge of reducing the Nicaraguan military from eighty-six thousand in 1990 to fourteen thousand in 1994. This angered career Sandinista soldiers who were laid off, but many received lands in compensation. Nicaragua's remaining transition military were veteran Sandinista soldiers who considered peasants, workers, and urban poor as allies, not suspected enemies as Northern Triangle militaries were trained to view these groups. Sandinista neighborhood watch committees morphed into crime watch networks in the 1990s and 2000s, preventing takeover of communities by gangs in the transition period.[54] Nicaragua's security state transition made a safer environment for the informal economy to flourish, unlike the Northern Triangle countries where security forces and gangs extort wage earners, self-employed, and small businesses in poor urban neighborhoods and public markets. Peasant families that received idle lands from large estates during the second wave of Sandinista land reform kept their holdings during the transition, giving them food security along with former Contras and laid off Sandinista soldiers who received land as part of the disarmament pact.[55] Daniel Ortega ran as FSLN candidate for a fourth time in 2006, pledging to continue neoliberal policies and CAFTA, despite criticism from some of his revolutionary Sandinista colleagues of the 1980s.[56] President Ortega, who maneuvered to remain in office for three terms as of 2019, delivered on his campaign promises of 2006. An economic boom already under way intensified under Ortega's administrations, with significant increases in agribusiness exports, mining concessions, and generous tax incentives that have attracted apparel manufacturers and other low-wage employers to Nicaragua's free trade zones.[57] From 2006, when CAFTA went into effect, until 2017, Nicaragua experienced the fastest economic growth in the region, though per capita income as measured by real GDP/population remains the lowest in the region and has not recovered to 1978 levels (see Tables 9.1 and 9.2). In contrast to the Northern Triangle, Nicaragua's growth was accompanied by much lower homicide rates (see Table 9.3), a smaller number of

Table 9.3. Intentional Homicides per 100,000 People

	1995	2000	2005	2011	2016
Guatemala	32.5	24.9	40.8	38.0	27.3
El Salvador	139.1	60.5	64.4	70.6	82.8
Honduras	n/a	48.7	43.6	85.1	56.5
Nicaragua	15.2	9.5	13.6	12.7	7.4
Costa Rica	5.3	6.3	7.9	10.3	11.9
United States	8.1	5.5	5.7	4.7	5.4

Source: World Bank, *World Development Indicators*, "Intentional Homicides (per 100,000 people)," https://data.worldbank.org/indicator/.

citizens living abroad, much lower income dependency on remittances from workers abroad (see Table 9.4), and a healthier environment for peasant and urban informal economies.[58] However, conditions deteriorated in 2018 and 2019. Opposition groups organized protests in 2018, and the US president ordered financial sanctions against FSLN officials similar to sanctions applied in Venezuela. The Ortega regime cracked down on protests and raided opposition media headquarters. As of 2019, US sanctions and support for regime change have not brought down the Ortega regime, but tourism, foreign investment, and economic growth have stagnated.[59]

In the Northern Triangle during the 1990s, tens of thousands of security personnel lost their jobs as military budgets were cut. Reorganized militaries shifted from counterinsurgency sweeps back to the traditional model of supporting big business. Laid-off military took jobs at private security companies or as freelance security guards for businesses and wealthy individuals. The violence did not stop; it just shifted from "mass killings of civilians at the hands of government troops working cohesively in large groups" to "intentional homicides."[60] Northern Triangle public/private security systems target human rights activists, leaders of peasant and worker organizations, lawyers representing the poor, environmentalist activists, international observers, and journalists investigating the inner workings of the business model. During the civil wars, the military repressed and dismantled poor community social organizations, leaving those communities defenseless when gang members incarcerated in US prisons were deported back to Central America after the Peace Accords.[61] Gangs represent a small fraction of the urban poor, but they have excellent surveillance and enforcement networks to extort "war taxes" from workers, small businesses, the self-employed, and those receiving remittances from relatives abroad. Police forces protect wealthy, not poor communities, and sometimes gangs pay a portion of their tribute to police. Studies of the Northern Triangle reveal that gangs form the lowest rung of the public/private security system, which hires gang members not as peers but as subcontractors for hit jobs on sensitive targets. National security officials publicize gang violence to increase budgets, get support from the United States, stimulate demand for private security companies, and divert attention from their own acts of violence.[62] With CAFTA's export opportunities, the Northern Triangle business model has taken more territory from peasant economies and increased repression of labor organizations. After CAFTA, the situation for the poor deteriorated, and caravans of women, children, and unaccompanied minors began fleeing north seeking asylum in the United States. By 2013, 75 percent of all unaccompanied minors arriving at the US border were from the Northern Triangle countries of Central America.[63]

Big business groups have had to compete with civil society organizations, which engage in electoral politics with the help of international observers and non-governmental organizations (NGOs). El Salvador's big business community adapted well to the post-Peace Accord environment by supporting Nationalist Republican Alliance Party (ARENA) candidates who won presidential elections from 1989 to 2009. Privatization of state-owned sugar complexes, cement factories, power plants, hotels, and free trade zones proceeded quickly as capital parked abroad during the civil war flowed back in. Salvadoran business leaders formed joint ventures with military officers who oversaw these enterprises during the war, reinvigorating the traditional fusion of big business and the military. When mass demonstrations blocked highways, sprayed graffiti on US businesses, and occupied legislative chambers to stop ratification of CAFTA, El Salvador's most powerful business organization, the National Association of Private Enterprise (ANEP), prompted ARENA representatives to sneak the bill through at three o'clock in the morning, making El Salvador the first country to ratify CAFTA in December 2004.[64] With ANEP as a driving force, El Salvador's government has been recognized as the star reformer in the region at applying neoliberal policies, but the Salvadoran economy in the 2000s has been the poorest performer with the slowest economic growth rates, record-setting crime rates, the largest number of citizens living abroad, and the greatest dependency on remittances of any economy in the region (see Table 9.4).[65]

Guatemala's military was cut by 30 percent, but the traditional connection between the military and CACIF, the most powerful business group, continued to run the economy despite candidates representing civil society groups winning some presidential elections. Mass protests against CAFTA prompted the Guatemalan business community to follow El Salvador's lead and rush ratification through the legislature in 2005. Agribusiness flourished with CAFTA, and free trade zone real estate complexes with heavy security presence collected rent from apparel manufacturers and other foreign investors. Guatemalan civil society groups have achieved significant gains that documented wartime atrocities and exposed ongoing government corruption. And a renaissance among the Maya has reasserted their peoples' cultural and political rights.[66] In 2007, the UN-backed International Commission against Impunity in Guatemala (CICIG) began assisting investigations of government corruption and connections with organized crime.[67] In 2014, the Guatemalan government agreed to a reparations plan for thirty-three Maya communities that were displaced by the Chixoy hydroelectric project four decades earlier, and NGOs and Indigenous communities in Northern Guatemala successfully lobbied for Maya communities to manage protection of forest reserves in

Table 9.4. Personal Remittances Received as % of GDP

	1978	1989	1995	2000	2017
Guatemala	0.36	1.01	2.44	3.09	11.17
El Salvador	2.17	5.44	11.92	14.97	20.04
Honduras	0.04	0.89	2.32	6.68	19.94
Nicaragua	0.19	n/a	1.81	6.27	10.07
Costa Rica	0.08	0.19	1.07	0.91	0.96

Source: World Bank, *World Development Indicators*, "Personal Remittances Received as % of GDP," http://databank.worldbank.org/source/world-development-indicators.

sections of the Maya Biosphere. These and other hard-won successes give signs of hope, but civil society groups have but a tiny fraction of the funding and enforcement capacity of Guatemala's big business/military establishment, which has expanded territory in response to trade incentives.[68]

Knowing the nineteenth century roots of their business model, that Guatemala and El Salvador's export growth came at the expense of peasants and workers should not be a surprise. However, Honduran peasant communities' loss of political space to aggressive business interests, who have fully captured the security forces, is a relatively recent development of the past three or four decades. Honduras has become an intolerable place for workers, the urban poor, and peasant communities with homicide rates that rival El Salvador. From 1990 to 2015, Honduras experienced the highest rate of outmigration in the region and transitioned from having the lowest reliance on income from workers' remittances in 1978 to the second highest in the region in 2017. (see Tables 3 and 4).

When the US government made Honduras its regional military headquarters in the 1980s, it greatly strengthened the powers of the most anti-peasant elements in the Honduran security forces, who invested directly in major industries. It was not until 1992, however, that Honduran business elites created a law to accomplish what their Salvadoran counterparts achieved a century earlier. The 1992 Honduran Agricultural Modernization Act outlawed collective forms of land tenure in favor of private titling. Corporations have used fraudulent means and intimidation to secure private titles to land occupied by peasant communities and have employed private security forces to evict peasants. When peasants move in to reclaim land, Honduran military units back up the corporations.

Particularly hard hit are peasant African palm cooperatives in the Bajo Aguán Valley that had claimed abandoned fruit company lands in the 1970s under the 1974 Agrarian Reform Act. After passage of the 1992 law, peasant cooperatives lost some sixty thousand acres to agribusiness food giant Dinant Corporation, which had received funding from the World Bank to expand its biofuel and cooking oil exports. Peasant communities had no success with court appeals until the election of President Manuel Zelaya (2006–2009) who agreed in 2006 to investigate the legality of the land transfers in the Bajo Aguán region. Responding to other peasant communities' protests in mineral rich areas, President Zelaya declared a moratorium on new mining concessions. Zelaya broadened his appeal to peasant and worker groups in 2008 by joining Venezuela's and Cuba's Bolivarian Alternative for the Americas. In January 2009, Zelaya raised the minimum wage 60 percent, provoking Honduras's most powerful business organization, the Honduran Private Enterprise Council. President Zelaya was planning a national referendum to allow him to run for a consecutive term when the military, with support from big business groups, ousted him.[69]

After the 2009 coup, a revival of mining and timber concessions led to forced evictions of Tolupanes Indigenous peoples from ancestral lands in northeastern Honduras, violence that continues in 2019. Between the coup in 2009 and 2012, more than ninety peasants in the Bajo Aguán Valley and their lawyer were assassinated. Investigations implicated corporate security forces, which receive assistance from US

Special Forces-trained Fifteenth Battalion.[70] Despite widespread knowledge of its role in the violence, Dinant Corporation continues to receive loan disbursements from Washington-based lending institutions.[71]

In November 2018, the Honduran National Criminal Court convicted seven men for the March 2016 murder of Berta Cáceres, a founder of the Civil Council of Popular Indigenous Organizations. Since 1993, Berta Cáceres's coalition fought illegal logging and mining company intrusions on Indigenous peoples' land, and since 2006 has brought international attention to takeover of ancestral Lenca lands for a hydroelectric project, leading to the cancellation of international funding for Energy Developments, SA (DESA)'s dam. The court charged DESA's president, a former national intelligence officer, of hiring the death squad, which included a former DESA security chief with US training, a former Honduran Special Forces sergeant, a former Honduran Special Forces major with US training, the DESA environmental manager, and three other individuals.[72]

Honduras's big business/military wealth engine had a late start, but its current features closely resemble Guatemala's 1875 model.

Conclusion: Policy Lessons from History

Unlike Honduras's recent (1980s–2000s) transformation, the US government had practically nothing to do with the creation of Central American state institutions in the late nineteenth century. After 1900, the United States increased its military presence to protect US investors and prevent foreign powers from gaining a strategic foothold in the region. It was not until 1954 when a CIA-assisted coup restored Guatemala's traditional wealth engine that the United States began subsidizing private sector development, a policy Washington applied to the entire region with the Alliance for Progress in the 1960s and has continued to apply to the present day. Whether it was cotton in the 1950s and 1960s, beef in the 1960s and 1970s, or melons, pineapples, and African palm in the 2000s, these promotional efforts carved out territory for mono-crops without respect for the environment or the shock-absorbing qualities of diversified peasant economies. Like banana expansion in 1900–1929, modern corporations clear thousands of contiguous acres to maximize production of a single species, leaving no forests to protect water and air quality and no room for peasant food producers. When wealthy investors have captured the military to serve their private interests and more US aid has been pumped through this type of structure, the results have been devastating for peasant communities. Resistance to this model erupted in the 1970s, leading to the overthrow of the Somoza regime (1979) and revolutionary insurrections in El Salvador and Guatemala. US neoliberal policies in the 1990s and 2000s fed the military/big business model in Guatemala, El Salvador, and Honduras, producing growth at the expense of peasant economies, while in Nicaragua and Costa Rica, economic growth was not so harsh on peasants and workers, because the security forces were not the right arm of big business in those countries. Democratic and human rights reforms have been positive, because they have allowed openings for members of civil society to engage the state and shape some outcomes. However, military aid and corporate stimulus in Northern Triangle countries enabled big business to use force to hold down wages, take over more territory from peasant communities, and target human rights activists. Washington policies fueled the Northern Triangle business model, which stimulated GDP growth and dispossessed hundreds of thousands of people who fled the violence, many seeking asylum in the US.

NOTES

1. Material from this section is largely derived from Robert G. Williams, *States and Social Evolution: Coffee and the Rise of National Governments in Central America* (Chapel Hill: University of North Carolina Press, 1994).
2. Carolyn Hall, *El café y el desarrollo histórico-geográfico de Costa Rica* (San José: Editorial Costa Rica y Universidad Nacional, 1978); Lowell Gudmundson, *Costa Rica Before Coffee* (New Orleans: Louisiana State University Press, 1987).
3. Ralph Lee Woodward Jr., *Rafael Carrera and the Emergence of the Republic of Guatemala, 1821–1871* (Athens, GA: University of Georgia Press, 1993).
4. Some of the largest piedmont plantations, including ones owned by German corporations, acquired the titles to highland village lands from militia leaders and managed them as private labor reserves, *fincas de mozos*, which were kept intact until the Guatemalan Revolution of the 1940s. Most of the private labor farms were located in the northwestern highlands of Huehuetenango and Quiche, which in the early 1980s became the scene of massacres of Maya civilians at the hands of the military. David McCreery, "Land, Labor, and Violence in Highland Guatemala: San Juan Ixcoy (Huehuetenango), 1893–1945," *The Americas* 45, no. 2 (Oct. 1988): 237–249.
5. David McCreery, "An Odious Feudalism: Mandamiento Labor and Commercial Agriculture in Guatemala, 1858–1920," *Latin American Perspectives* 48 (Winter 1986): 99–117; Julio Castellanos Cambranes, *Coffee and Peasants: The Origins of the Modern Plantation Economy in Guatemala, 1853–1897* (Stockholm: Tryckop, 1985).
6. David Browning, *El Salvador: Landscape and Society* (Oxford: Clarendon Press, 1971); Héctor Lindo-Fuentes, *Weak Foundations* (Berkeley: University of California Press, 1991).
7. In 1892, before Zelaya, military patrols could only protect coffee plantations along a narrow strip of road between Matagalpa and Jinotega. Jeffrey Gould, "El trabajo forzoso y las comunidades indígenas Nicaragüenses," in *El café en la historia de Centroamérica*, edited by Héctor Pérez Brignoli and Mario Samper (San José, Costa Rica: FLACSO, 1993).
8. Darío Euraque, *Reinterpreting the Banana Republic: Region and State in Honduras, 1870–1972* (Chapel Hill: University of North Carolina Press, 1996), 5–12, 24–30.
9. Clarence F. Jones & Paul C. Morrison, "Evolution of the Banana Industry of Costa Rica," *Economic Geography* 28, no. 1 (January 1952): 1–19. https://www.jstor.org/stable/141616.
10. McCreery, "Odious Feudalism," 110.

11. A. Douglas Kincaid, "Peasants into Rebels: Community and Class in Rural El Salvador," *Comparative Studies in Society and History* 29, no. 3 (July 1987): 474–480, https//www.jstor.org/stable/179034; Thomas P. Anderson, *Matanza: El Salvador's Communist Revolt of 1932* (Lincoln: University of Nebraska Press, 1971).

12. Knut Walter, *The Regime of Anastasio Somoza, 1936–1956* (Chapel Hill: University of North Carolina Press, 1993).

13. Víctor Hugo Acuña-Ortega, "Clases sociales y conflicto social en la economía cafetalera Costarricense: productores contra beneficiadores (1932–36)," *Serie de Avances de Investigación del Centro de Investigaciones Históricas*, No. 10 (San José: Universidad de Costa Rica, 1984.)

14. Avi Chomsky, "Afro-Jamaican Traditions and Labor Organizing on United Fruit Company Plantations in Costa Rica, 1910, *Journal of Social History* 28, no. 4 (Summer 1995): 837–855; Phillippe Bourgois, "The Black Diaspora in Costa Rica: Upward Mobility and Ethnic Discrimination," *New West Indian Guide* 60, no. 3/4 (1986): 149–165.

15. Ronald N. Harpelle, "Racism and Nationalism in the Creation of Costa Rica's Pacific Coast Banana Enclave," *The Americas* 56, no. 3 (Jan., 2000): 29–51. https://www.jstor.org/stable/1007587.

16. Independent farmers who bought copper-contaminated plantations discovered the soil could not support shallow-rooted food crops, but agronomists later discovered that African Palm could thrive on the poisoned earth. Former banana zones of Costa Rica, Guatemala, and Honduras contaminated by copper sulfate are now African palm plantations. Steven Marquadt, "Pesticides, Parakeets, and Unions in the Costa Rican Banana Industry, 1938–1962," *Latin America Research Review* 37, no. 2 (2002): 3–36. https://www.jstor.org/stable/2692147.

17. Edelberto Torres-Rivas, "Central America Since 1930," in *Cambridge History of Latin America*, Vol. 7 (Cambridge, U.K.: University of Cambridge Press, 1990), 166; Victor Bulmer-Thomas, *The Political Economy of Central America Since 1920* (Cambridge, U.K.: Cambridge University Press, 1987), ch. 4, and Tables A.5, A.6, A.8, A.10, A.11, A.18.

18. Williams, *States and Social Evolution*, 170–172, 257–259.

19. Cindy Forster, *The Time of Freedom: Campesino Workers in Guatemala's October Revolution* (Pittsburgh, PA: University of Pittsburgh Press, 2001), 117–137. Forster emphasizes the strong *campesino* identity of the banana workers at Tiquisate, a hotbed of labor organizing with a national presence between 1944 and 1954.

20. Jim Handy, *Revolution in the Countryside: Rural Conflict and Agrarian Reform in Guatemala, 1944–54* (Chapel Hill: University of North Carolina Press, 1994).

21. Comité Coordinador de Asociaciones Agrícolas, Comerciales, Industriales y Financieras (CACIF), "Nuestra Historia." https://www.cacif.org.gt/nuestra-historia.

22. Euraque, *Reinterpreting the Banana Republic*, 34–39, 95–103. Ciro F. S. Cardoso, "Central America in the Liberal Era, c. 1870–1930," in Leslie Bethel, *Cambridge History of Latin America*, Vol. 5, (Cambridge: Cambridge University Press, 1936), 210–215.

23. Williams, *States and Social Evolution*, 180–181.

24. Iván Molina, "The Polarization of Politics, 1932–1948," in *The Costa Rica Reader*, edited by Steven Palmer and Iván Molina, 162–169 (Durham, NC: Duke University Press, 2004); Edelberto Torres-Rivas, "Central America since 1930," in *Cambridge History of Latin America*, Vol. 7 (Cambridge, UK.: University of Cambridge Press, 1990), 174–176.

25. Enrique Delgado, "Institutional Evolution of the Central American Common Market and the Principle of Balanced Development," in *Economic Integration in Central America*,

edited by William R. Cline and Enrique Delgado, 17–58 (Washington, DC: The Brookings Institution, 1978).

26. Guatemala and El Salvador captured two-thirds of the industrial growth due to the common market and 60 percent of new foreign investment in manufacturing. At the other extreme, Honduras captured only 8 percent of common market-induced industrialization, and practically all of that was concentrated on the North Coast, where industrial profitability was high and the business community ready to compete. Robert G. Williams, "The Central American Common Market: A Case Study of the State and Peripheral Capitalism," *Secolas Annals* 13 (March 1982): 71–82.

27. Robert G. Williams, "The Central American Common Market: Unequal Benefits and Uneven Development" (PhD diss., Stanford University, 1978), 213–242; Meldon E. Levine, *El Sector Privado y El Mercado Común: Relaciones de la Iniciativa Privada de Honduras, Nicaragua, y El Salvador* (Guatemala City: Instituto Nacional de Administración para el Desarrollo, 1968).

28. Material in this section on cotton and beef exports is largely taken from Robert G. Williams, *Export Agriculture and the Crisis in Central America* (Chapel Hill: University of North Carolina Press, 1986).

29. William Durham, *Scarcity and Survival in Central America: The Ecological Origins of the Soccer War* (Stanford, CA: Stanford University Press, 1979).

30. Williams, *Export Agriculture,* 129–134.

31. Williams, *Export Agriculture,* 134–139.

32. In 1975, thirty-seven members of a Maya settlement cooperative were abducted and carried off in a helicopter, never to be seen again. In 1976, an army unit arrived at another settlement and ordered the settlers to "plant grass seed and move." Father Bill Woods, a priest who was making the eviction case known in Guatemala City, was killed in a mysterious plane crash.

33. Williams, *Export Agriculture,* 166–189.

34. José Luis Rocha, "The Contradictory Legacy of the Sandinista Agrarian Reform," *Envio* no. 348 (July 2010). http://www.envio.org.ni/articulo/4212.

35. Trevor Paglen, *Blank Spots on the Map: The Dark Geography of the Pentagon's Secret World,* (New York: Penguin, 2009), chs. 13 and 14.

36. Williams, *Export Agriculture,* Introduction and ch.8.

37. Henry Kissinger et al., *Report of the President's National Bipartisan Commission on Central America* (New York: Macmillan, 1984), 41, 52–53, 63–67.

38. Some of the same highland villages that had resisted the labor drafts during the coffee export boom of the late nineteenth century became subject to military occupation during the 1980s.

39. Human Rights Watch World Report, "Events in Guatemala 2018." https://www.hrw.org/world-report/2019/country-chapters/guatemala. The total Guatemalan death toll from military repression from 1954 to 1996 is estimated at two hundred thousand people with forty-five thousand disappeared.

40. General Lucas García (1978–1982), who got in on the ground floor of the counterinsurgency project, ended up owning more than eighty thousand acres in the Northern Transversal strip.

41. A USAID study reported that one-third of the sixty-three thousand peasant applicants to receive land were not farming because they "had been threatened, evicted or had disappeared." Williams, *Export Agriculture,* 173.

42. UN Security Council, *From Madness to Hope: The 12-Year War in El Salvador: Report of the Commission on the Truth for El Salvador*, S/25500 (New York: United Nations, 1993).

43. Gross domestic product (GDP) attempts to account for all income generated by production of goods and services inside a country, but for Central America a sizable portion of peasant economy production, especially for home use and local markets, is off the radar screen along with urban informal economy small-scale production and provision of petty services. The increasing portion of peasant production organized in cooperatives or sold to capitalist vendors is accounted for in GDP, though the conversion of production from home use and local markets is not subtracted. With these caveats in mind, GDP is a reasonable indicator of production passing through enterprises that report value added (supply) and final sales (demand), the two angles for measuring GDP. Average annual growth rates in real GDP indicate the performance of the capitalist sector for the various periods in Table 9.1, and real GDP per capita is an indicator of the incomes (wages and gross profits) generated by that sector divided by the total population Table 9.2. The two indicators interpreted together show how bad the damage was to the capitalist sector of Nicaragua and El Salvador during the 1980s and that while GDP grew during the war years in the other countries, it was not fast enough to keep up with population growth, so every country experienced declining per capita incomes by this measure (Table 9.2).

44. For the overall period 1990–2017, Guatemala, Honduras, and Nicaragua experienced practically identical capitalist performance as measured by average annual growth rates of real GDP of 3.6 percent, but paradoxically, the poor populations of Guatemala and Honduras suffered more from this growth as indicated by mass outmigration of population.

45. Hereinafter CAFTA will be used to refer to CAFTA-DR. From the beginning of CAFTA negotiations in 2002, representatives from the most important national business coalitions and local chapters of the American Chamber of Commerce provided technical expertise and political muscle power in the planning phase without broader consultation with civil society organizations. The business group coalitions consulted were representatives from Coordinating Committee of the Agricultural, Commercial, Industrial and Financial Associations of Guatemala (CACIF) in Guatemala, National Association of Private Enterprise (ANEP) in El Salvador, Honduran Private Enterprise Council (COHEP) in Honduras, Superior Council of Private Enterprise (COSEP) in Nicaragua, and the Costa Rican Investment Promotion Agency (CINDE), Promoter of Foreign Commerce (PROCOMER), Costa Rican Union of Chambers and Associations of the Private Sector (UCCAEP) in Costa Rica.

46. There were neoliberal promotional efforts to integrate peasant economies into the capitalist sector through production, marketing, and credit cooperatives, and through direct small farmer sales to agribusiness firms. It would be an interesting future study to compare results across the five-country region to determine how surrounding political economic structures might have influenced success or failure of these efforts. Coffee cooperatives have been very successful in Costa Rica (e.g., La Victoria, one of the oldest coffee and sugar cooperatives) and Nicaragua (e.g., AGROCAFE, a worker-owned cooperative kept intact by organized struggle when former Somoza properties were expropriated; this organization has a processing mill and nine coffee estates representing 7 percent of Nicaragua's coffee production). Rocha, "Contradictory Legacy."

Northern Triangle countries have numerous coffee cooperatives of small producers. One study of the integration of peasant producers in coffee production in Honduras in 2011 showed pessimistic outcomes for communities there. Daniel R. Reichman, *The Broken*

Village: Coffee, Migration, and Globalization in Honduras (Ithaca, NY: Cornell University Press, 2011). A five-country study of integration of peasant economies into coffee production could be extended to examine niche products in individual countries (e.g., cardamom production in Alta Verapaz, Guatemala, is reported to have integrated 350,000 small producers in this industry). Susana M. Sánchez, Kinnon Scott, and J. Humberto López, *Guatemala: Closing Gaps to Generate More Inclusive Growth*, Systematic Country Diagnostic (Washington, DC: World Bank Group, 2016), 100.

47. Richard Sandbrook, Marc Edelman, Patrick Heller, and Judith Teichman, "Costa Rica: Resilience of a Classic Social Democracy," in *Social Democracy in the Global Periphery*, (Cambridge, U.K.: Cambridge University Press, 2007).

48. Robert G. Williams, "The Legacies of Coffee: Costa Rica and Guatemala 1840–1900" (paper presented at the Oxford Coffee Conference, St. Antony's College, Oxford University, September 10–12, 1998).

49. Attraction of foreign direct investment in strategic sectors has been promoted through the Costa Rican Investment Promotion Agency (CINDE), a nonprofit enterprise set up by USAID in the early 1980s. CINDE has organized big business and government official coordination to attract foreign direct investment in sectors with the greatest economic potential. See https://www.cinde.org/en.

50. High-technology business parks in the Central Valley have been largely compliant with strict environmental zoning and regulatory constraints, and some of the most visible foreign corporations like Boston Scientific, Intel, and IBM have constructed LEED-certified labs and office buildings. Medaglia Monge and Erick Mora Álvarez, *Balance de Zonas Francas: beneficio neto del régimen para Costa Rica 2011–2015* (San José, Costa Rica: Procomer, 2016), 50–66.

51. In 1983, forests covered only 26 percent of Costa Rica's land area, but environmental activists pushed for the acquisition of national forest areas, highly regulated conservation zones, environmentally strict development zoning laws, and laws that compensate large landowners for planting trees and maintaining existing forest cover. By 2014, 52 percent of Costa Rica's land area was covered in forest, approximately the area in forests in 1950 before the beef export boom. Costa Rican civil society groups also pushed the Costa Rican government in 2007 to set the ambitious goal of becoming 100 percent carbon-neutral by 2021. Ana María Oviedo, Susana M. Sánchez, Kathy A. Lindert, and J. Humberto López, *Costa Rica's Development: From Good to Better*, Systematic Country Diagnostic (Washington, DC: World Bank Group, 2015), 19–20.

52. President Violeta Barrios de Chamorro (1990–1997) is from a large landholding family from southern Nicaragua (Rivas) with major investments in beef cattle ranching. She was married to Pedro Joaquín Chamorro Cardenal, assassinated in 1978, owner of *La Prensa*, the opposition newspaper to the Somoza regime; he descended from landed/commercial wealth stretching back to the colonial period. President José Arnoldo Alemán Lacayo (1997–2002) is from a large landholding family with major coffee investments outside Managua; he had been a lawyer for the Somoza regime, was thrown in jail for nine months by the Sandinistas in 1980, and suffered expropriation of properties, but he remained in Nicaragua in the 1980s as a leader of the private coffee industry and also a member of COSEP. He was mayor of Managua in the early 1990s before becoming president. President Enrique Bolaños Geyer (2002–2007) is from a wealthy landed family who expanded the family fortune by investing in cotton beginning in 1952; he was president of COSEP (1983–1988), an ardent promoter of free enterprise, and an opponent to the Sandinistas.

53. Joaquín Ibarz, "Piñata Theology: the Sandinista's Preferential Option for the Rich," *Crisis Magazine*, September 1, 1991. https://www.crisismagazine.com/1991/pinata-theology-the-sandinistas-preferential-option-for-the-rich.

54. Sandinista neighborhood watch groups were reinforced in the 1990s by the National Police adopting a "community-based policing system."

55. Farmworkers on state-owned properties were able to bargain for rights to 30 percent of the valuation of the former Somoza properties that were not taken by FSLN officials in the piñata. It is estimated that the transition policies of the 1990s resulted in a net loss of one million acres from the peak gains of the Sandinista land reforms, but during the post-Peace Accord period, the Nicaraguan peasant economy retained a land base 2.5 million acres larger than it had at the end of the Somoza regime in 1979. Of 22,000 demobilized Contras, some 11,385 received an average of fifty acres apiece by 1992, though some of this land was in remote areas in eastern Nicaragua, where Indigenous groups contested the grants. Rocha, "Contradictory Legacy."

56. Mónica Baltodano, "What Mutations Have Turned the FSLN into What It Is Today?" *Envio*, no. 390 (January 2014). http://www.envio.org.ni/articulo/4804.

57. "Zonas Francas Nicaragua," *Reporte Anual Estadístico*, Asociación de Zonas Francas de Latín América, January 2017; Jackson Chen, "B2Gold sells Nicaraguan mines to Calibre for $100 million," *MiningDotCom*, July 2, 2019. https://www.mining.com/b2gold-sells-nicaraguan-mines-to-calibre-for-100m/.

58. World Bank Group, *Nicaragua: Paving the Way for Faster Growth and Inclusion* (Systematic Country Diagnostic) (Washington, DC: IBRD, 2017), 23, 96.

59. Human Rights Watch, "Nicaragua: Events in 2018," *World Report 2019*. https://www.hrw.org/world-report/2019/country-chapters/nicaragua.

60. "Intentional homicides" include purposeful acts resulting from "domestic disputes, interpersonal violence, violent conflict over land resources, intergang violence over turf or control, and predatory violence and killing by armed groups." UN Office on Drugs and Crime's International Homicide Statistics, "Long Definition: Intentional Homicides per 100,000 population." https://dataunodc.un.org/crime/intentional-homicide-victims.

61. Between 1999 and 2014, 97 percent of Central American prisoners deported from the United States were from the Northern Triangle countries, many from large cities like Los Angeles, where they had served in gangs. Only 2.8 percent were Nicaraguans. World Bank, "Nicaragua: Paving the Way," 41.

62. Robert Brenneman and Adriana García, *Youth Gangs in Latin America* (Oxford: Oxford University Press, 2014) (online); Jon Carter, "Gothic Sovereignty: Gangs and Criminal Community in a Honduran Prison," *South Atlantic Quarterly* 113, no. 3; Alberto Arce, *Blood Barrios: Dispatches From the World's Deadliest Street* (London: Zed Books, 2018). Ellen Moodie, *El Salvador in the Aftermath of Peace* (Philadelphia: University of Pennsylvania Press, 2010).

63. Ana González-Barerra, Jens Manuel Krogstad, and Mark Hugo López, "DHS: Violence, Poverty are Driving Children to Flee Central America to U.S.," *FactTank* (Pew Research Center), July 1, 2014, https://www.pewresearch.org/fact-tank/2014/07/01/dhs-violence-poverty-is-driving-children-to-flee-central-america-to-u-s/; D'Vera Cohn, Jeffrey S. Passel, and Ana González-Barerra, "Rise in US Immigrants from El Salvador, Guatemala, and Honduras Outpaces Growth from elsewhere" (Washington, DC: Pew Research Center), December 2017.

64. Rose J. Spalding, "Civil Society Engagement in Trade Negotiations: CAFTA Opposition Movements in El Salvador," *Latin American Politics and Society* 49, no. 4 (Winter

2007): 85–114, https://www.jstor.org/stable/30130825. The siphoning of funds from the state was perfected by ARENA presidents, but did not go away when an FMLN candidate won. In 2018 a court found two administrations guilty of embezzling more than $300 million each: ARENA's Antonio Saca (2004–2009), who was a former director of ANEP, and the FMLN's Mauricio Funes (2009–2014), the first FMLN candidate to win the presidency. Human Rights Watch, "El Salvador: Events in 2018," *World Report 2019*. https://www.hrw.org/world-report/2019/country-chapters/el-salvador.

65. Oscar Calvo-González and J. Humberto López, *El Salvador: Building on Strengths for a New Generation*, Systematic Country Diagnostic (Washington, DC: World Bank, 2015).

66. Recuperación de la Memoria Histórica (REMHI), *Nunca Más* (Guatemala City, Guatemala: Human Rights Office of the Archbishop of Guatemala, 1998); Commission for Historical Clarification (CEH), Guatemala: Memory of Silence (Guatemala City, Guatemala: CEH, 1999); Nikolai Grube, "Maya Today—From Indios Deprived of Rights to the Maya Movement," in Maya: Divine Kings of the Rain Forest, edited by Nikolai Grube et al., 417–425 (Potsdam, Germany: H.F. Ullmann, 2012).

67. Between 2007 and 2019, when Guatemala's president suspended CICIG for investigating his involvement in election fraud, CICIG and the Attorney General's office exposed more than sixty corruption schemes, one leading to the resignation and arrest of a president and his vice president for pocketing money from customs officials. CICIG also assisted the attorney general's office to convict former President Efraín Ríos Montt for genocide and crimes against humanity for the massacres of 1,771 Maya Ixil civilians when he was president in 1982 and 1983. Human Rights Watch, "Guatemala: Events in 2018," *World Report 2019*. https://www.hrw.org/world-report/2019/country-chapters/guatemala.

68. Sánchez et al., *Guatemala: Closing* Gaps, 128–134.

69. There were accusations that Miguel Facussé, founder of Dinant Corporation, and a group of very wealthy Honduran investors of Middle Eastern descent, funded the 2009 military coup against Zelaya. For the ethno-historical context of this accusation and the rise of this group of investors from economic power in the 1940s to national political power in the 1990s culminating in the election of Miguel Facussé's nephew, Carlos Roberto Flores Facussé (1998–2002), as president of Honduras, see Darío Euraque, "La configuración histórica de las élites de Honduras ante el golpe de Estado del 2009," *Anuario de Estudios Centroamericanos*, Vol.45: 19–48 (San José: University of Costa Rica, 2019.) Also on the coup against Zelaya see, Reichman, *Broken Village*, 170–173.

70. Annie Bird, "Human Rights Violations Attributed to Military Forces in the Bajo Aguán Valley of Honduras," *Washington: Rights Action*, February 20, 2013, www.rightsaction.org; Human Rights Watch, "There Are No Investigations Here: Impunity for Killings and Other Abuses in Bajo Aguán, Honduras," February 12, 2014, https://www.hrw.org/report/2014/02/12/there-are-no-investigations-here/impunity-killings-and-other-abuses-bajo-aguan; US Embassy in Honduras, "Land Rights Conflicts: Bajo Aguán," July 27, 2014, https://hn.usembassy.gov/our-relationship/policy-history/current-issues/lrc-bajo-aguan/.

71. Dinant Corporation continued to receive loan disbursements from the World Bank, but the bank responded to human rights complaints by having the company change its security protocols and by sponsoring company and community workshops on nonviolent conflict resolution. Marco Antonio Hernández Ore, Liliana D. Sousa, and J. Humberto López, *Honduras: Unlocking Economic Potential for Greater Opportunities*, Systematic Country Diagnostic (Washington, DC: World Bank, 2017), 97–98.

72. Front Line Defenders, "Case History: Berta Cáceres," December 2018, https://www.frontli
nedefenders.org/en/case/case-history-berta-c%C3%A1ceres; Goldman Environmental Prize,
"Berta Cáceres: 2015 Goldman Prize Recipient Central and South America," https://www.
goldmanprize.org/recipient/berta-caceres/.

Further Reading

Central America

Bulmer-Thomas, Victor. *The Political Economy of Central America since 1920*. Cambridge, U.K.: Cambridge University Press, 1987.

Holden, Robert H. *Armies without Nations: Public Violence and State Formation in Central America, 1821–1960*. Oxford: Oxford University Press, 2004.

Pérez-Brignoli, Héctor. *A Brief History of Central America*. Berkeley: University of California Press, 1989.

Woodward, Ralph Lee, Jr. *Central America: A Nation Divided*. Oxford: Oxford University Press, 1985.

Costa Rica

Gudmundson, Lowell. *Costa Rica before Coffee: Society and Economy on the Eve of the Export Boom*. Baton Rouge: Louisiana State University Press, 1987.

Palmer, Steven, and Iván Molina, eds. *The Costa Rica Reader: History, Culture, Politics*. Durham, NC: Duke University Press, 2004.

El Salvador

Browning, David. *El Salvador: Landscape and Society*. Oxford: Clarendon Press, 1971.

Lauria-Santiago, Aldo. *An Agrarian Republic: Commercial Agriculture and the Politics of Peasant Communities in El Salvador, 1823–1914*. Pittsburgh, PA: University of Pittsburgh Press, 1999.

Guatemala

Castellanos Cambranes, Julio. *Coffee and Peasants: The Origins of the Modern Plantation Economy in Guatemala, 1853–1897*. Stockholm: Tryckop, 1985.

McCreery, David J. "An Odious Feudalism: Mandamiento Labor and Commercial Agriculture in Guatemala, 1858–1920." *Latin American Perspectives* 13, no. 1 (1986): 99–117.

Smith, Carol A., ed. *Guatemalan Indians and the State, 1540–1988*. Austin: University of Texas Press, 1990.

Honduras

Boyer, Jefferson. "Food Security, Food Sovereignty, and Local Challenges for Transnational Agrarian Movements: the Honduras Case." *The Journal of Peasant Studies* 37, no. 2 (2010): 319–351.

Euraque, Darío A. *Reinterpreting the Banana Republic: Region and State in Honduras, 1870–1972*. Chapel Hill: University of North Carolina Press, 1996.

Nicaragua

Gould, Jeffrey L. *To Lead as Equals: Rural Protest and Political Consciousness in Chinandega, Nicaragua, 1912–1979*. Chapel Hill: University of North Carolina Press, 1991.

Spalding, Rose J. *Capitalists and Revolution in Nicaragua: Opposition and Accommodation, 1979–1993*. Chapel Hill: University of North Carolina Press, 1994.

CHAPTER 10

STATE-MAKING AND NATION-BUILDING

DAVID DÍAZ ARIAS

CENTRAL America is a region composed of weak democratic states with the single exception of Costa Rica. In 2017, the independent researchers of the State of the Region, an organization composed of researchers who have analyzed Central America since 1999, reported that the democratization process of the period between 1990 and 2010 failed to consolidate due to the persistence of chronic obstacles in the states' ability to provide for basic public services. Chronic weaknesses included abuse of power, militarization, shortcomings in the administration of justice, new and serious cases of political corruption, and the absence of truly electoral competition which in some cases has been limited by political pacts. According to the report:

> Falling rates of support for democracy in recent years suggest that Central American political systems are not able to provide satisfactory responses to demands for representation, participation, transparency, and justice, and, in general, to public expectations of well-being and development. Persistent social protest reflects that dissatisfaction. The states still exhibit a chronic inability to exert their presence and fully control their territories, limiting their maneuvering room to tackle the drug trafficking and organized crime manifested in differing ways within the countries.[1]

Is this current situation part of an historical legacy in Central America? How did state-building take place in this region and did states evolve in time? This article analyzes state-making and nation-building processes in Central America from independence in 1821 to the present. It explores the main historical statehood projects put into place in the region and how national identities appeared as a product of these historical processes. I conceptualize Central America as the five republics that formed the Central American Federation from 1824 to 1839: Guatemala, Honduras, El Salvador, Nicaragua, and Costa Rica.

First, this article explores the main political transformations experienced in Central America before independence. Second, it surveys the Central American Federation Project (1824–1839) and the political discussions through an in-depth analysis of identity and the Federation's regional nationhood project. Third, it studies the liberal nation-states between the years 1840 and 1954 with an emphasis on the constitution of discourses about institutions and race. Fourth, it traces ideas about nation, revolution, and political crisis in Central America from 1954 until 1996, when the peace accords to put an end to civil wars occurred. The final part of this article discusses the problems of democracy in Central America and describes social problems like migration, identity issues, and corruption in contemporary Central America.

Political Identity in Central America after Independence, 1821–1839

By the end of the eighteenth century, Central America was better known as the Kingdom of Guatemala, politically administered as a captaincy general as part of the viceroyalty of New Spain (Mexico). This kingdom was divided into provinces: Guatemala, Honduras, El Salvador, Nicaragua, and Costa Rica—Chiapas (today part of Mexico) also belonged to Guatemala until independence. When the house of Bourbon rose to power in Spain in 1710, the new Crown brought about transformations in its Latin American colonies. The Kingdom of Guatemala was important for the Bourbon state because it could produce new agricultural products and because the Crown wanted to solve the lack of control over the Mosquito Shore—a territory from Caribbean Nicaragua to Caribbean Honduras ruled by Indigenous peoples who were allied to the British empire.[2] The Bourbon's policies, known as the Bourbon reforms, sought to create direct relations with the Iberian Peninsula in order to develop communication and trade media, limit ecclesiastical power, support producers to free them from the control of the merchants of Santiago de Guatemala, reform the administrative structure to replace "corrupt officials," change the tax system to collect higher tax revenue, and enhance military defense to contain the commercial and military activities of the English in the Central American coasts.[3] These reforms eventually propelled two important moves toward independence: (1) a significant need in the provinces of El Salvador, Nicaragua, and Costa Rica to break up their political and economic ties to Guatemala and (2) the foundational economy products and labor relationships that marked differences in the first stage of the construction of states in Central America.

Indigo was the product that best bolstered the Central American economy at the end of the colonial period. The rise of indigo production was a result of high demand in Europe at a time when the indigo produced in the Kingdom of Guatemala was reputed as the highest-quality dye in the international market.[4] The increase in indigo production allowed the development of local labor and trade market that stimulated economic relations in Central America. But indigo also allowed elites in the provinces to see the Guatemalan elite as a corrupted group that did nothing and received all the economic benefits. The demand for workers in indigo plantations in El Salvador, even in 1757, led to the *cabildos* of San Salvador, San Vicente, and San Miguel to request an equitable distribution of the labor force in order to prevent concentration in "a few of the most powerful families."[5] As a result, indigo production began to dominate farmland in El Salvador, replacing maize and beans in certain areas. In turn, the plantation workers' need for food and "leather pouches" required for bundling dye powder boosted livestock farming in Honduras and Nicaragua. Cattle were transported from Nicaragua and Honduras to Cerro Redondo in Escuintla, where 50,000 heads of livestock were sold annually.[6]

Spatiality and specialization of regional domestic production were even more diverse. In the central area of Honduras, major mines were developed, which also encouraged the Choluteca region to specialize in the production of mules, intended not only for the mines but also to export to Panama, although this export activity began to decline after 1750. Tegucigalpa continued with mining activities. In the 1960s, Troy S. Floyd estimated that during the second half of the eighteenth century, mines in Central America produced about 230,000 silver pesos per year, although a similar quantity also went through unofficial channels to avoid the collection of the King's Fifth (*Quinto Real*).[7] In Guatemala, the western region specialized in the production of clothing for land workers, while the eastern region focused on developing cattle grazing farms. The western region also produced wheat and maize, and the farms functioned as a true pantry for the urban zones of Guatemala. Along with that, eight sugar mills were developed in the village of Valle. In Costa Rica, the rise in tobacco production, which was soon sold to Nicaragua and Panama, started during the second half of the eighteenth century. The establishment of the Royal Tobacco Monopoly (*Real Renta del Tabaco*) in 1766 tried to monopolize production and commercialization. Tobacco production allowed for some capital accumulation, and it especially facilitated the development of San José. The splendor of Costa Rican tobacco exports took place during a short period between 1789 and 1791.[8]

As mentioned, the Guatemalan economic elites benefited the most from this economic transformation in late colonial Central America. In three hundred years of colonial ruling, this was probably the first time the region flourished as a result of intense trade with the world, division of production, and intense business connections. The colonial elite, united by marriage and trade ties, monopolized the income generated by the commercial upturn of the second half of the eighteenth century. The merchant elite's privileged position in the trade between the Kingdom of Guatemala and Cadiz—where they also developed family ties—further increased their dominance. Guatemalan merchants were also key players in the regional market, as they bought various products generated within the Central American regional economy and were, at the same time, the source of currency and credit of the kingdom.[9] This arrangement resulted in a marked uneasiness among *provincianos*, which eventually generated an interest for independence, but not from the Spanish Crown but rather from Guatemala. By the late eighteenth century, the tensions among farmers in the provinces of Honduras, Nicaragua, Costa Rica, and Guatemala intensified even more when Guatemalan merchants attempted to control livestock trade and ban the sale of livestock outside the Chalchuapa Fair. These tensions encouraged the separatism that took place in those provinces during the independence process.[10]

The economic boom at the end of the eighteenth century motivated the elites from provinces to demand political and administrative transformations in Central America because they believed they could receive more economic benefits if they were independent from Guatemala. Moreover, the Bourbon Reforms created four intendances in Central America—Chiapas, San Salvador, Nicaragua, and Comayua—that consolidated by 1786. The cabildos of those intendances experienced increasing power.[11] Along with the economic boom the juridical independence of the intendances gave evidence for provincial elites that they needed more independence from Guatemala. In the context of the Cádiz Constitution discussions (1812) after Napoleon Bonaparte's invasion of Spain, the deputies of Costa Rica and Nicaragua demanded political independence.[12] Thus, along with the corporate colonial identities based on ethnicity and labor, some municipalities began developing political identities.

Although some anti-tax movements took place in El Salvador in 1811 and even though some individuals discussed the need to rebel for independence, Central America remained loyal to the Spanish Crown until September 1821. In early September, the General Captain in Guatemala, Gabino Gaínza, and the Guatemalan elite received news from Mexico announcing its independence and recommending Guatemala to do the same. Worried about a possible Mexican invasion and fearing a popular revolution, the Guatemalan elite declared independence on September 15, 1821. Gaínza sent instructions to the *ayuntamientos* in all Central America to join Guatemala's independence and to send deputies to a political meeting in Guatemala to decide what to do. Between 1821 and 1823 Central Americans had to make political decisions pressured by Mexico, by Colombia, and by the fear of being conquered by other European countries. They discussed which political path they could take according to their regional situation: (1) they could create a regional federation which would maintain the ancient colonial provinces as a single republic; (2) individually, they could decide to forge separate independent states; or (3) they could accept Augustin de Iturbide's invitation to join his Mexican empire. Central American elites sided with annexation to Mexico but when Iturbide fell, they focused on creating a Federal Republic.[13]

In 1824, deputies from all Central America met in Guatemala to discuss the project of a Federal Republic. Initially, some deputies doubted the ability to make a federation in a region they characterized as heterogeneous, divided up by "*castas*," and with a scattered population.[14] Yet, representatives also believed the Federal Republic plan to be the only way to survive piracy and possible external attacks. Liberal deputies also thought that pushing for a good government would help the integration of *castas* and forge equality among new citizens.[15] This is why they drafted the 1824 Political Constitution of the Federal Republic of Central America as a tool to promote happiness, to secure freedom, equality, security, and property, and to establish order and a "perfect federation."[16]

The Federal Constitution defined only men older than eighteen years or married men born or naturalized in Central America as citizens.[17] Women did not have political rights. The first liberal politicians did not consider race to be a requisite for citizenship and all individuals living in this region were conceived as national inhabitants.[18] The Constitution also defined Guatemala, Honduras, El Salvador, Nicaragua, and Costa Rica as single states and part of a Federal Republic. The member states believed this political project would last, but they were wrong. In 1841, when John L. Stephens traveled across Central America, he interviewed people who were against the federation project.[19] Although there were many attempts to rebuild the Central American Federation, none succeeded. In 1910, US historian Dana Gardner Munro pointed out that the Federation was still a dream for some Central American politicians and intellectuals without any chance to make it real.[20]

The Central American Federation existed from 1824 to 1839, but it did not work as expected. Instead, it generated great animosity among the northern Central American states (Guatemala, El Salvador, Honduras, and Nicaragua) that ended up producing a civil war between 1826 and 1829 which had a big impact on the economic development—thousands of men died because of the war, crops were burnt or robbed, and haciendas were abandoned. Moreover, federal authorities were not able to create an independent and competitive standing army, which could confront local armies. Having copied the US Constitution was a mistake since the Central American situation was very different from that of the United States. In economic terms, the Federation was born underfunded and doomed to have more expenses than revenues.[21] In brief, the federal government was extremely weak, poor, and disorganized.[22]

Between 1838 and 1841, the five states claimed, one after another, their sovereignty to govern themselves. First of all, they had to create institutions to politically control their populations and to confront municipal governments. In 1822 Costa Rica, where the Central American civil war did not alter the political life, politicians organized a Junta with the purpose of keeping the territory in peace and avoiding a political vacuum for anarchy.[23] From 1823 to 1835 Costa Rican elites bolstered an image of the country as a peaceful land guided by legal instruments and organized institutions. They also presented Costa Rica as a society composed of small property owners.[24] Even though localism was still a powerful political identity in 1830s and 1840s Costa Rica, some discourses about a Costa Rican identity were under construction, particularly that of a peaceful land compared to other Latin American countries. After its separation from the Federation, Costa Rica experienced a tumultuous period between 1842 and 1848; in 1848, Costa Rica became an independent republic. During the 1830s and 1840s, the coffee boom introduced the country to the international market, allowing the elite to reinforce their interests in becoming an internationally recognized country under reformist liberalism—that is, a liberal state that implemented political reforms one after another.[25] Between 1856 and 1857, Costa Rica consolidated its capacity to become a republic by confronting William Walker and the threat posed by the filibusters' army in Nicaragua. Walker (1824–1860), a Tennessee-born physician, took power in Nicaragua in 1855 leading that country into a war against the other Central American nations that finished in May 1856 when Walker surrendered. This war allowed politicians to believe Costa Rica could become a modern nation-state as they were able to mobilize soldiers into another country to defend their "patria" and because Costa Ricans claimed victory with this war.[26]

Costa Rica's remoteness from the federation's war problems was pivotal for the fortification of its political institutions and for reaching an early consensus among the elites on the state-making project. Two brief civil wars in 1823 and 1835 did not impact that process. By this time, Guatemala, El Salvador, Honduras, and Nicaragua were living a different experience. In Nicaragua, for instance, civil war combined with foreign pressure limited Nicaragua's state-making process. After independence, two main cities, León and Granada, competed to be the capital city and this eventually started a civil war. Many doubts surrounded Nicaragua's real chances to become a nation; E. Bradford Burns noted: "fragility characterized a nation that seemed to exist more in theory than in reality."[27] This strong confrontation lasted until the 1840s and involved Great Britain's interests to build a transisthmian canal in Nicaragua's territory. Politicians used a patriotic language to face British Consul Frederick Chatfield's pressure to recognize the Miskito kingdom's protectorate; however, this did not imply that there existed an actual consensus on how Nicaragua would become a nation-state. Nicaragua's politicians dreamed of building a fluvial canal using the San Juan River and the Nicaraguan Lake to connect the Caribbean to the Pacific Ocean. This canal became an image of progress which would place Nicaragua at the center of the world's economy.[28] But this dream was not enough to stop confrontations; starting in 1844 an administrative-territorial conflict between León and Granada created another civil war in which the British representative favored Granada's elite. The tensions experienced between Granada and León reached the international sphere when León's liberal politicians invited US filibuster William Walker to help combat Granada's conservatives. Many Nicaraguans believed Walker would bring progress and civilization to their country.[29] This is why Granada's mulattoes and Indigenous population from Masatepe initially saw Walker and his filibusters as the leaders who would reform Nicaragua.[30] Instead, Walker decided to go to war against the other Central American countries between 1856 and 1857. At the end of the war, Nicaragua was able to reconstruct itself and give birth to a conservative republic that would conduct the country in peace and as a constitutional nation-state.[31] Coffee production also helped Nicaragua's economy to grow.[32]

The Federation disappeared in the early 1840s, but in Guatemala and El Salvador its image continued to be a necessary political project moving forward. In El Salvador, the champion of the Federation, Francisco Morazán, played a significant role as a national hero during the administrations of Gerardo Barrios, Francisco Dueñas, and Rafael Zaldívar in the 1860s.[33] In Guatemala, the sentiment in favor of the Federation was also present; however, liberal politicians had to face two issues, first, to decide whether Indigenous communities would be part of the nation-state project and to confront the secessionist plan of Los Altos from 1838 to 1849.[34] In Honduras, between 1839 and 1876 the central government did not have enough power to control political rebellions, social disobedience, and even secessionist attempts in Texíguat during 1843–1844 and Olancho in the 1860s.[35]

In northern Central America political instability and the failure to create republican institutions was the consequence of the liberal politicians' inability to convince Indigenous communities to be part of a political community in formation. In 1832, Guatemalan intellectual and politician Manuel Montúfar y Coronado considered Central America's route after independence a total fiasco.[36] In Guatemala, Indigenous communities believed that the "liberal law," that is, the new republican codes and constitution, was only a plan to destroy Indian *cabildos* and *caciques'* power.

In 1837, the emergence of Rafael Carrera in eastern Guatemala kept the liberals' political project in check after he conducted an Indigenous rebellion to abolish most of the Guatemalan liberal laws. Carrera's demands included the abolition of the Livingston Codes, the protection of life and property, the return of the archbishop, and the restoration of the religious orders, among others.[37] After a long campaign against Morazán's forces, Carrera entered Guatemala City in April 1839. By 1841 he was in control of Guatemala, but it was not until 1844 that he formally took the presidency.[38] In October, 1851 the Constitutional Assembly promulgated a new constitution, which enabled Carrera to rule the country with an iron fist until his death in 1865.[39] Then, with the exception of Costa Rica, political *conservadores* ruled everywhere which meant that priests and the Catholic Church retained power while colonial laws reappeared. However, liberals would not wait for too long. In the 1870s liberals proclaimed themselves as those who restored the republican order and law.[40]

LIBERAL NATIONS, 1870–1954

By 1870, the five Central American republics had begun their state-building process. Certainly, there were significant differences among them, especially on issues relating to economic development, social integration, political stability, and politicians' ability to integrate different social classes into the notion of national identity that they were defining.

Costa Rica was at the forefront in the nation-building process because, from 1821 to 1870, the country was able to stabilize its economy, create republican institutions, organize elections, to be internationally recognized as a sovereign state, and to integrate its population. In September, 1871 a governmental newspaper affirmed that Costa Rica was a society composed of a white homogeneous race, with continuous progress, without social divisions, no pro-slavery sentiments, and very peaceful, all of these ideas were combined with modern concepts like freedom, equality, and fraternity.[41] This narrative evidences the presence of fundamental ideas related to an ongoing national discourse which highlighted cultural differentiations in ethnicity (a country of "white" people), politics (democracy and social peace), and history. This process was accelerated after 1882, when Tomás Guardia dies and a group of young professionals take power and start a series of reforms based on new ideas about the role of state and rooted in the commitment of transforming Costa Rican society.[42] The most important events associated with this group were the 1884 Liberal Reforms which attempted to reduce the Catholic Church's influence on the popular classes and to expand scientific and secular visions of life and nature among them.

During this period, Costa Rican intellectuals produced an important body of national literature that was deeply rooted in liberal ideas. This in turn reinforced the politicians' national discourse still under construction. Therefore, most of the intellectuals' work posed solutions to social conflicts by emphasizing the need to reach a middle ground that could balance "tradition" and capitalist "progress."[43] The state considered public education to be another realm to control. Steven Palmer and Gladys Rojas state that after 1885, Costa Rican politicians sought to keep the public schools under the control of the central government as a way to confront the municipalities' administrative power and that of the Catholic Church. At the same time, by controlling schools, liberal politicians could "more directly oversee the 'civilizing' of the popular sectors and the forging of a homogeneous national culture."[44] Furthermore, liberal Costa Rican politicians increased investments in education, health, and public infrastructure in order to materialize a national discourse of social equality and racial homogeneity. National identity in Costa Rica also involved the historical recuperation of the war against Walker's filibusters held in 1856–1857 as the most important part of Costa Rican history and also the transformation of one of its participants—soldier Juan Santamaría—into Costa Rica's most important national hero.[45] In the 1920s, Costa Rican society identified itself as a strong nation.[46] By the 1940s, when President Rafael Angel Calderón Guardia produced the most important social reform in the history of the country, Costa Ricans were strongly integrated as an imagined community. This circumstance, yet, did not stop the political violence the country experienced during the 1940s up to the Civil War of 1948.

The war against Walker was also pivotal in the construction of the Nicaraguan national identity. After 1870, the commemoration of the San Jacinto battle and its main figure, José Dolores Estrada, became an invented tradition to officially celebrate Nicaragua's rise against Walker and his men. This tradition was a useful tool to combat political and local division inside Nicaragua that still remained as a heritage from the independence days.[47] Yet, Nicaraguan politicians strengthened pro-American feelings while US President Ulysses S. Grant's scientific missions in Nicaragua worked to find the best place to build the transatlantic canal. Nicaraguan attraction for the American way of life became very important after 1909, when conservative politicians celebrated the increasing adoption of US customs and fashion among young Nicaraguans.[48]

Indigenous identity certainly was not among the conservative and liberal Nicaraguan politicians' interests. Since 1881, conservative intellectuals asserted the country to be composed of a homogeneous "mestizo" race. According to Jeffrey L. Gould, the José Santos Zelaya's liberal revolution of 1893 continued representing Indigenous people as primitive savages and stooges of unscrupulous conservative politicians.[49] Zelaya's government fortified notions of heroic and romantic patriotism among its followers while it repressed Indians, took their land, and tried to transform them into mestizos. In 1894, when Zelaya unified the country by annexing the Miskito Caribbean Coast, liberals characterized the Indigenous communities living in that coast as miserable tribes incapable of forming a government by themselves.[50] In the following years, the Nicaraguan state made numerous but unsuccessful attempts to exert sovereign control over the Miskito region by renaming it Departamento Zelaya. Charles R. Hale described how "state officials imposed taxes, usurped Indian lands, established local structures of political rule, and imposed strict prohibitions on education in languages other than Spanish."[51] Something similar had occurred to the Indians in the Pacific coast of Nicaragua. Since their rebellion against local government in 1881, liberal and conservative politicians repressed Matagalpa Indians attempting to dissolve their communities and portraying Nicaragua as a homogeneous mestizo nation. In 1906, for the third time in twenty-five years, the state decreed the abolition of the Indigenous communities and all forms of communal land; in 1914 the Conservative government rescinded this decree and communities were legalized in an attempt to earn the Indians' support of the new government imposed in 1909.[52] However, during 1910–1924 Indigenous communities led their social struggle against the state using a nationalist discourse that emphasized Nicaragua as an Indo-Hispanic nation. This way Indians took advantage of a national identity that made them Nicaraguans.[53] By the end of the 1920s, some of those Indigenous communities joined Augusto César Sandino's *Ejército Defensor de la Soberanía Nacional*, a standing army that confronted US marines' presence in Nicaragua.[54] Even after Sandino's death in February 1934 and despite the National Guard's strong repression, Indians kept fighting until they were able to get some protective laws during the 1930s. However, during the 1940s and 1950s Indigenous communities had to confront new violence, several attempts to dissolve their ethnic identity, and efforts to destroy their languages, ethnic dress, and forms of societal organization.[55]

In late-nineteenth-century El Salvador, liberals also labeled Indians as barbarians, therefore legitimizing violence against their communities.[56] During the 1910s and 1920s, the *Federación Regional de Trabajadores Salvadoreños* started an intensive campaign in urban and rural towns against labor exploitation. The *Federación* sought to affirm class identity among workers. Therefore, Salvadoran politicians and Liberal intellectuals focused on trying to integrate Indigenous people into national identity. In that context, they resurrected Atlacatl, an Indian rebel who was a protagonist in the struggle against the Spaniard Conquistadors in the sixteenth century, as the first national hero of El Salvador. In 1926, on Independence Day commemoration, a monument to Atlacatl was built in San Salvador, the capital city. In the 1920s, various intellectuals affirmed that El Salvador had a great Indian past and that this heritage should be commemorated. In 1919, Miguel Ángel Espino published *Mitología de Cuzcatlán*, an anthology of short stories for children based on Cuzcatleco Indians' mythology. In 1930, María de Baratta was officially rewarded for her book *Cuzcatlán Típico* in which she presented El Salvadoran Indians as the purest and more vernacular representatives of costumes, legends, and music.[57] Yet, Indigenous communities suffered proletarianization, land displacement, and lack of work.[58] After the 1932 slaughter, a massacre of Indians who rebelled against mestizos' power, the El Salvadoran elites invented the Day of the Indian as a way to earn some acceptance among Indigenous communities, even though Indians remained marginalized.[59] Cultural transformations did not stop and Indians kept losing their identity through the following decades.[60]

In Honduras, the state claimed sovereignty over the Miskito Coast in 1859—earlier than Nicaragua—by signing an international treaty with Great Britain. At that moment, the national government and municipal authorities produced reports about Caribbean lands describing Miskito and Garifuna communities as "the laziest people made by nature" and highlighting the need to bring civilization to those lands. In a report written in 1882, a Special Commission recommended the construction of public schools and churches in the region in order to force Indians to dress properly and be moralized. The report stated that Indians would not deserve constitutional rights like the other Honduras citizens because they were "imperfect people."[61] In sum, during the 1870s and 1880s the annexation of the Caribbean coast in Honduras allowed the renovation of racist images about the Indians. In other parts of the country, liberal politicians applied the same politics as their Nicaraguan counterparts by identifying Honduras as a homogenous nation composed of mestizo population. In 1887, the national census instructed that every "mixed race" should be categorized under the label mestizo in clear opposition to the Caribbean Indians.[62] According to Darío Euraque, this *ladinización* of Honduras matured during the 1920s and 1930s. At the same time, Honduras experienced a "mayanization."[63] By the end of the 1940s, Monsignor Federico Lunaldi, an Italian papal nuncio set in Honduras, wrote his book *Honduras maya: etnología y arqueología de Honduras* arguing that ancient Honduras' Indians were all Mayas even though he knew this affirmation to be false. Like in El Salvador, in Honduras the *mestizaje* discourse brought back the figure of an Indian as a national hero, Lempira, who combated Conquistadors.[64] In 1926, Honduras's national currency was named after Lempira; in 1935 the government declared a National Day—July 20—for Lempira, and in 1943 Department Gracias a Dios—the old Mosquitia—was named Department of Lempira.[65]

The aforementioned experiences reveal at least two patterns that the Central American Liberal states followed in regard to the Indigenous communities. On the one hand, in Costa Rica, politicians and intellectuals denied any Indian heritage by asserting Costa Ricans were direct descendants of Spaniard Conquistadors. On the other hand, in Nicaragua, El Salvador, and Honduras, politicians and intellectuals referred to *mestizaje* in order to portray their societies while the Miskito Indians were rejected as part of their nations. A third trend is that of Guatemala, the most populated among the five countries with a population of 70 percent of Indians by the 1870s. Since independence, Conservatives and Liberals clashed over the role Indigenous people would have in the new country. Liberals believed Indians should be integrated to the nation-state project, but after Carrera's triumph they shifted their position and began thinking Indians did not deserve to be treated as civilized citizens.[66] With Carrera's help, conservatives implanted a republican political system that discarded liberal principles and based on the *Leyes de Indias*—the Spanish colonial law—and its institutions, on the consuetudinary laws, on the Canon Law Provisions to assert the Catholic Church's power, and on the very image of Rafael Carrera as a caudillo.[67] When Liberals seized power in 1871, they produced new legislation on labor, land, education, citizenry, population, and nationality which deeply affected Indigenous communities.[68] Liberal Ladinos controlled the state and the coffee economy during the following decades; their plan was whitening the Criollo and Ladino population in order to present Guatemala as a white society. Liberal historiography contributed a great deal to this goal by asserting the Indian race was scientifically considered a degenerate race. Basically, those politics homogenized the non-Indian population while Indigenous people remained out of the nation-state as well as their rights—this way they segregated Indigenous communities and their culture.[69] According to Arturo Taracena, the so-called *Generación del 20* with intellectuals like Miguel Ángel Asturias, Jorge García Granados, Jorge del Valle Matéu, Carlos Wyld Ospina, Carlos Samayoa Chinchilla, David Vela, and Jorge Luis Arriola also succumbed to the state's segregationist policies during the 1930s even though they had denounced the social and economic conditions of the Indigenous communities and had identified them like the "*alma nacional.*"[70] In 1944, a popular uprising overthrew dictator Jorge Ubico and started a period of democratization in Guatemala. This Revolution of 1944 promoted public discussions about Guatemala's Indians giving some hope for a better society by bringing social justice to those communities.[71] However, the 1954 coup d'état against President Jacobo Arbenz stopped the new politics and transformed Indians into communists to whom the state should combat with no mercy.[72]

NATION, REVOLUTION, AND CRISES, 1954–1996

The fall of Arbenz was planned and produced by the Central Intelligence Agency—CIA—which argued that he was part of an international communist effort to make all Latin America part of the Soviet Union. These allegations became more common in newspapers and political addresses after 1959, when the Cuban Revolution triumphed and established a socialist government in the Caribbean basin. In that context, Central America became very important for US national security geopolitics. Governments in the region happily received promises of US economic help through the Alliance for Progress. In early March 1963, when President John F. Kennedy visited San José, Costa Rica, the Central American presidents announced strong collaboration with the United States against Cuba and the Soviet Union involvements in the Caribbean.[73] Unfortunately, in Guatemala and Nicaragua most of US assistance resulted in military aid, the introduction of the National Security Doctrine, and the concept of "internal enemy" to name the groups that opposed dictatorial and authoritarian governments.[74] During the 1960s and 1970s, military and repressive administrations took over in Guatemala and El Salvador.[75]

In Nicaragua, Anastasio Somoza García, who had been in power since the 1930s, reorganized political institutions, centralized power, controlled organized workers, and, using an iron fist, assured peace and security for economic business.[76] When Somoza was shot on September 21, 1956, his sons Luis and Anastasio Somoza Debayle consolidated family power along with state power during the following years. US presidents supported Somoza's dynasty power as Somoza and the United States became best allies in confronting communism and endorsing US foreign policies and economic demands. To the extent that he became the regime's main man, Anastasio Somoza Debayle ruled on the basis of repression, brutal violence, and corruption using the National Guard as his personal army.[77]

In Honduras, in October 1963, a military group led by Colonel Osvaldo López Arellano overthrew Ramón Villeda Morales's government and inaugurated a time of military intervention. During his presidency, Villeda Morales confronted the most important peasant mobilization in the twentieth century in Honduras by issuing in 1967 a land reform program. This land reform affected numerous Salvadoran families living in southern Honduras where more than 100,000 people were expelled in a short period of time. The Salvadoran army invaded Honduras for three days. The mediation of the Organization of American States (OAS) solved this international affair but Honduras and El Salvador relations remained tense for some time. Although Arellano lost the presidential elections in 1971, he overthrew the government again in 1972, showing how easily military men could disrupt democracy attempts in Honduras.[78]

After the civil war of 1948, the so-called Junta Fundadora de la Segunda República ruled Costa Rica for eighteen months. Among its decisions, the Junta discarded taxes on flour, increased the legal wages to workers in coffee plantations and sugar mills, transformed the *Instituto del Café*, imposed a tax to the United Fruit Company, strengthened the Consejo Nacional de Producción, created the Instituto Costarricense de Electricidad and the Servicio Civil, abolished the national army, decreed female suffrage, and granted citizenship to Afro-Costa Ricans of the Caribbean region. On July 17, the Junta issued a decree prohibiting the participation of communist parties in political and electoral activities in Costa Rica—this decree was not abolished until the 1970s.[79] In 1949, a National Constitutional Assembly approved a new constitution; during the following years, Costa Rica consolidated an electoral democracy. The Partido Liberación Nacional (PLN), founded in 1951 by winners of the war, concentrated power by winning most of the elections between 1953 and 1978. PLN Presidents José Figueres, Francisco J. Orlich, and Daniel Oduber defended an orientation of the state based on social democracy policies. This meant the construction of state monopolies on fundamental economic places: electricity generation and public banks. The number of public employees grew during this period and so did state enterprises, particularly during the period between 1970 and 1978 when the PLN ruled the country for eight years consecutively. State expenditure and international loans increased Costa Rica's foreign debt. The PLN opposition reorganized several times but did not have political power enough to confront the PLN state style. In 1978 a political coalition brought Rodrigo Carazo into power as a solution to the PLN corruption. Yet, a strong economic crisis exploded in 1980–1981 and the country rushed to stagnation and high levels of poverty and unemployment. This crisis, however, did not allow leftist political parties to get more electoral power, nor did it motivate a social revolution even though some small groups of youths planned to rise against the bourgeois state.[80] In several ways, democratic institutions and social inclusion kept Costa Rica out of the revolution attempts that were taking place in the other Central American countries during the 1980s.

During the 1970s, Nicaragua, El Salvador, and Guatemala entered into a revolutionary cycle produced by guerrilla warriors who wanted to overthrow dictatorships and bring social and economic equality to their societies. In Nicaragua, in 1961, Tomás Borge, Silvio Mayor, and Carlos Fonseca Amador founded the Frente Sandinista para la Liberación Nacional (FSLN); their main goal was to overthrow Somoza. After gaining support among peasants and international help, the FSLN became an inter-classist movement during early 1970s. On July 19, 1979, the Sandinistas won the Revolution. After a brief period of class collaboration, the FSLN members concentrated power and proclaimed themselves as Marxist-Leninists. Sandinistas wanted to transform Nicaragua into a different society; many collaborators undertook a national alphabetization campaign and the government attempted an agrarian reform. Yet, when Ronald Reagan took office in 1981, the Sandinista Revolution was considered dangerous for the United States. An economic embargo and a civil war financed by the US State Department limited Sandinistas' possibilities. As a result, the Nicaraguan state transformation was aborted.[81]

In El Salvador, revolutionary leaders founded the Fuerzas Populares de Liberación "Farabundo Martí" (FPL), the Ejército Revolucionario del Pueblo, and the Fuerzas Armadas de Resistencia Nacional. All those guerrilla groups merged to form the Frente Farabundo Martí para la Liberación Nacional (FMLN) which began a social revolution in rural areas in El Salvador in early 1981.[82] In Guatemala, the rebellion began in the 1960s, when reformist army officers formed a guerrilla group which disappeared in the early 1970s. However, thanks to the 1979 Sandinistas' triumph, new social revolution attempts began to flourish. In Honduras, two guerrilla groups emerged in 1979: the Frente Morazanista para la Liberación de Honduras (FMLH) and the Movimiento Popular de Liberación Cinchonero; these two groups organized attacks against US presence in Honduras during the 1980s.[83] Marxism, Leninism, and Liberation Theology ideas were combined within these guerrilla movements that sought agrarian reform and social justice. From their political point of view, these guerilla groups considered Central American states to be repressive, deeply unequal, with malfunctioning institutions, and focused solely on the elites' interests. Indigenous communities were part of and supported the guerrilla movements. As a consequence, Indigenous communities suffered repression in Guatemala and El Salvador, and in Nicaragua, Sandinistas failed to understand the Miskito communities' demands and their ethnic identity.[84]

The Central American civil wars produced thousands of civilian casualties: 70,000 casualties in El Salvador, 200,000 in Guatemala, and 90,000 in Nicaragua. Refugees of this region reached about five million people.[85] Terrorism was a common practice to confront guerrilla warriors' and peasants' collaboration with rebels in Guatemala and El Salvador.[86] Essentially, the civil war impeded any step forward to the consolidation of strong democratic institutions—on the contrary, human rights violations and increased violence gave way to more social exclusion, racism, and distrust in government representatives.

Besides the political and social crises experienced throughout the 1980s, state institutions also experienced some changes. In Honduras, due to its geopolitical position bordering Nicaragua and due to US presence in the region, the military junta was forced to turn power over to a Constitutional Assembly and call for free presidential elections. This was the first time after years of military rule that Hondurans were able to freely vote for a non-military candidate, as they elected liberal Roberto Suazo Córdoba as president. In El Salvador, elections took place in 1982, 1984, and 1985 bringing some opportunities for democracy to appear as a possible solution to confrontation. In 1988, new legislative and municipal elections took place preceding the presidential elections of 1989—all these electoral events provided an opportunity for democratic institutions to compete against weapons and repression. In November 1989, when the FMLN launched a major offensive to control San Salvador but was not able to impose itself over national army, many people were convinced rebellion was not a way out anymore for transformations in El Salvador. In September 1991 the FMLN and the Salvadoran Government signed the peace agreement in New York City. In Guatemala, elections opened the door for some political changes when Vinicio Cerezo won the presidential electoral race in 1986. Although Cerezo was not able to put an end to the internal social conflict or to limit military power, his successor, Jorge Serrano, did advance in consolidating political parties' competition, establishing relatively free elections and the constitution of new institutions such as the Corte de Constitucionalidad, the Procuraduría de los Derechos Humanos, and the Tribunal Supremo Electoral. Consequently, when Serrano self-perpetrated a coup in 1993 by suspending the Constitution, dissolving the National Congress, and fragmenting the Supreme Court, huge civilian demonstrations and fast action by the OAS Secretary General hindered Serrano's intentions and forced him into exile. In 1996 the government and the guerrillas agreed to sign a peace accord to end the civil war. In Nicaragua, elections also took place in 1984 but the strong US economic embargo and its support to the Contra war forced Sandinistas to negotiate peace in 1988. Free presidential elections took place in 1990 and people voted for peace against war and embargo by electing Violeta Barrios de Chamorro as President.[87] The peace agreements gave hope to Central American countries; by 1996 many political analysts believed a better future was possible for this region while recent elections and the army's retreat from government administration offered the opportunity to finally create modern states.[88]

Nation-States in Contemporary Central America

By the end of the twentieth century, none of the authoritarian regimes that existed before 1979 persisted in Central America. Hope was everywhere in this region. Analysts believed democracy would be consolidated and military men would restrain themselves from intervening in matters that belong to the civil society. Nonetheless, the main political problem of the region was the persistence of what Guillermo O'Donnell called a low intensity citizenship, that is to say that citizens of the Central American countries have little or no interest to get involved in politics.[89] By the beginning of the 2000s, researchers had doubts about the consolidation of democracy in Central America mainly because of the region's uneven economic development, the prevalence of poor people, the increasing social inequality, and the lack of public education. Moreover, drug trafficking, corruption, and security problems led Central America to be classified as the most violent and insecure region in Latin America.[90] In sum, even though the end of civil wars gave hope for the region, most Central American states did not experience the consolidation of democracy.

At the beginning of the twenty-first century, political stability remained weak in Central America. In 2009, Honduras President Manuel Zelaya scheduled a non-binding poll on holding a referendum on convening a constituent assembly to rewrite the constitution. The Honduran Supreme Court ordered Zelaya to cease and he refused; then, the Supreme Court ordered the National Army to overthrow President Manuel Zelaya and send him into exile. This event led the country to a rise in political violence, abuse of power, and electoral fraud. In September 2015 after massive social mobilizations and the congressional vote in favor of stripping Otto Pérez Molina's immunity from prosecution, he resigned from the Guatemalan presidency. In 2007 Daniel Ortega, who competed for the presidential election four times between 1990 and 2007, attained the presidency in Nicaragua and shortly after began concentrating power and eroding democratic institutions after a period when the Independent Liberal Party (Partido Liberal Independiente) had dominated politics. In April 2018, hundreds of college students began protesting in Managua against Ortega's attempt to tax retired people's pensions. National police repressed students who continued protesting during the following weeks while other groups joined demonstrations demanding Ortega's resignation.

A new politically significant group in Central America appeared in this context— political parties guided by religious leaders who opposed abortion, gay marriage, and sexual education in public schools and condemned feminism. Many Central American citizens were supporting this conservative agenda and some political leaders found help in those religious leaders to confront their political challengers. In Guatemala, in October 2015 comedian Jimmy Morales won the presidential election, but he allied with the conservative politicians when he was accused of corruption by Guatemalan mass media. In Costa Rica, the 2018 presidential elections were almost won by conservative Partido Restauración Nacional whose leader openly was against same-sex marriage and abortion.

Today's Central America is the result of the failure in the construction of the liberal state projects of the nineteenth century. Liberalism did not fulfill its promises in this region—deep social injustices gave rise to social unrest, but various forms of political mobilization that resulted were not able to transform these societies either. In countries like Guatemala, El Salvador, and Nicaragua the modern state only partially consolidated by the 1990s–2000s but dictatorships dominated politics during most of the twentieth century. By the 1990s, the peace accords gave some hope for a transition from corrupt and violent states to democracies. Yet, the consolidation of electoral institutions, and the realization of ethnic and gender equality and social justice remained only a promise. During the 1980s, thousands of Central Americans escaped from their home countries to secure themselves and their families from the civil wars. Again, by 2019 poor people were leaving Honduras, El Salvador, and Guatemala to search for a better life in Mexico or the United States because their states cannot guarantee security and protection or labor opportunities.

After 1821, Central American societies confronted a difficult political scenario: they gained independence from Spain but had to decide where to go from there. Political and economic leaders attempted to build states based on the modern experiences that they saw at the time: the brief case of republican France and the example of the United States. Just as in the other countries of Latin America, Central America lacked the political experience and the institutions and had only a blurred vision of what its republics should be like. Between 1825 and 1840, Central American politicians formed a Federal Republic to keep the region integrated as a single country. The problem was that even though representatives wrote a federal constitution that politically legitimated the existence—at least in words—of the five new states (Guatemala, El Salvador, Honduras, Nicaragua, and Costa Rica), they failed to create an army powerful enough to control the federal territory. Nor were they able to build an integrated regional economy or centralize political activity in a federal capital. Guatemalan and the El Salvadoran elites exploited political differences between their two countries, leading them, along with Honduras, into a bloody civil war.

Only Costa Rica remained relatively peaceful during the first decades after independence. That situation allowed for the consolidation of republican institutions, the separation of powers, and the establishment of a supreme court and local courts. Internal confrontations between local elites did not interrupt the centralization of power in an Executive Branch. Meanwhile, the production of coffee since the 1840s helped to unify economic interests in the country. During the second half of the nineteenth century, Costa Rican politicians and intellectuals created representations of their new nation as prosperous, white, and united.

During much of the nineteenth century, the other four countries confronted the problem of how to achieve political centralization. But local *caudillos*, the confrontations between elites, internal civil wars, economic weakness, and imperial interventions limited their plans. In Nicaragua, the disputes between elites led to a confrontation between the country's two main cities: León and Granada. Because elites in those cities could not arrive at political agreements, state institutions remained weak—that is, until the arrival of William Walker and his filibusters in 1855. The war against Walker's dominion of Nicaragua helped to unify the Nicaraguan elites. But it was not until the 1870s that coffee haciendas appeared as the solution to connect the country to the international economy.

In Honduras, the state remained weak in terms of territorial occupation: the elites were divided and the Caribbean coast was under British dominion. The banana economy contributed the division of the elite: the North Coast came to develop an industrial bourgeoisie led by Palestinian-Syrian-Lebanese Christian immigrants who were much more liberal than the traditional landowning elite of the interior and connected to the federal government in Tegucigalpa and Comayagua. At that time political power was subjected to the economic power of the US banana producers in the country. In El Salvador, the coffee economy also helped to unite the local elite, but most of Indigenous communities remained outside the focus of the state institutions. It was only after the massacre of 1932 that the mestizo elite began incorporating a much-invigorated discourse on El Salvador as a mestizo society. In Guatemala, the liberal elite lost the battle against Rafael Carrera in the beginning of the 1840s, which meant the recuperation of colonial laws by Carrera and friends to impose their rule. After the 1870s, when liberal politicians returned to power, they decided not to incorporate the Indian communities into any state project. In Guatemala and El Salvador, where most people were not effectively subjected to the nation-state, standing armies were pivotal to keep the population under control. In Nicaragua, the US intervention during the 1910s and 1920s permitted the creation of the Guardia Nacional, which transformed itself into the personal army of the Somoza dynasty, enabling the family to remain in power until the Sandinista Revolution of 1979.

After the 1940s, a brief period of democratization allowed social and economic reforms in Guatemala. But the CIA-supported coup d'état of 1954 put an abrupt stop to those reforms. In Guatemala and El Salvador, dictatorships returned during the 1950s and 1960s. The social revolutions commanded by guerrilla groups with the support of Indigenous communities during the 1980s were a consequence of illegitimate states, a weak popular identification with national identities, and the legacy of decades of social exclusion, state violence, and inequality. In Nicaragua, the Sandinistas tried to give birth to a new state. A campaign of popular literacy and land reform appeared as part of that effort. But the US-funded Contras waged war on the country, together with a US embargo, and the Sandinistas' authoritarian style served ultimately to undermine any revolutionary political project. By the end of the 1980s, local elites, political authorities, and guerrilla warriors in Guatemala, El Salvador, and Nicaragua attempted to negotiate peace. During the 1990s, access to power was decided through elections throughout Central America, and state institutions, such as supreme courts, legislative assemblies, ministers, and press, had the opportunity to bloom.

In Costa Rica, the civil war of 1948 offered the opportunity for some state transformations. The Partido Liberación Nacional (PLN, founded in 1951) created a model of social democracy that the Costa Rican Right was not able to defeat: between 1953 and 1990 the PLN won six of a total of nine elections. Yet, the economic crisis of 1980–1981 forced the country to bring about state reforms in order to obtain financial help from the World Bank and the International Monetary Fund. The PLN began to renounce its center-left ideals and embraced the neoliberal dogma and the "Washington Consensus" of economic policies prescribing financial liberalization and deregulation, producing a reform that was designed to decimate state control in economics and society. Owing to social mobilizations between 1986 and 2001, however, the neoliberals were not able to transform the Costa Rican state totally. People, especially peasants and middle-class urban groups, rejected the attempt to decimate the welfare state. In 2007, the negotiation of the Dominican Republic-Central American Free Trade Agreement (CAFTA-DR, also comprising Costa Rica, El Salvador, Guatemala, Honduras, and Nicaragua) with the United States offered the opportunity for local elites to finally approve most of the neoliberal reforms.

By 2019 Central America was experiencing, again, the legacy of weak states. In Honduras, a conservative elite took power after the coup d'état against Zelaya (in 2009) and have since used state institutions to prosecute political opponents. In Guatemala, political corruption appears to be the norm. In El Salvador, the FMLN governments did not transform the structures that produce inequality, nor did they solve the most difficult social problems; as a result, a new populist government came to power in 2019. In Nicaragua, Ortega was able to disperse his opposition and dominate state institutions and mass media using state institutions for his personal interests. Costa Rica's democracy was experiencing new inquiries while state institutions were undergoing new neoliberal reforms.

Even though we have a good understanding of Central American history, most researchers have focused on the history of the coffee and banana economies and their relationships to the state formation while others have gone deeper in the analysis of Indigenous participation in politics, the study of armies during the nineteenth century, and how national identities were built.[91] New historical research about Central America should pay attention to how state institutions have evolved, like the division of political powers, elections, political legitimacy, and local municipal governments. We have extensive knowledge of some periods, like the emergence of the liberal state (1870–1930s), but we also have many lacunae about others: we know very little about the 1920s–1930s and the 1950s–1970s, while the neoliberal reforms (1980s–present) have been much more thoroughly analyzed in economic terms rather than on how neoliberalism impacted state institutions, political legitimacy, and national identities.

ACKNOWLEDGMENTS

I want to acknowledge comments and revisions by Robert Holden, Kevin Coleman, Isabel Álvarez, and Krysta Beam.

NOTES

1. Programa Estado de la Nación, *Summary: Fifth State of the Region Report on Sustainable Human Development 2016* (San José: PEN, 2017), 49.
2. Craig L. Dozier, *Nicaragua's Mosquito Shore: The Years of British and American Presence* (Tuscaloosa: University of Alabama Press, 2002).
3. Miles Wortman, *Government and Society in Central America, 1680–1840* (New York: Columbia University Press, 1982), 130.

4. José Antonio Fernández Molina, *Pintando el mundo de azul. El auge añilero y el mercado centroamericano, 1750–1810* (San Salvador: Dirección de Publicaciones e Impresos, 2003), 49.
5. Wortman, *Government and Society*, 126.
6. Troy S. Floyd, "The Indigo Merchant: Promoter of Central Economic Development, 1750–1808," *Business History Review* 39, no. 4 (Winter 1965): 466–488, esp. 473.
7. Troy S. Floyd, "Bourbon Palliatives and the Central American Mining Industry, 1765–1800," *The Americas* 18, no. 2 (October 1961): 103–125, esp. 108.
8. Víctor Hugo Acuña Ortega, "Historia económica del tabaco en Costa Rica: época colonial," *Anuario de Estudios Centroamericanos* 4, no. 1 (1978): 279–392.
9. Troy S. Floyd, "The Guatemalan Merchants, the Government, and the Provincianos, 1750–1800," *The Hispanic American Historical Review* 41, no. 1 (February 1961): 90–110, esp. 99.
10. Floyd, "Guatemalan Merchants."
11. Jordana Dym, *From Sovereign Villages to National States: City, State, and Federation in Central America, 1759–1839* (Albuquerque: University of New Mexico Press, 2006), 50–59.
12. David Díaz Arias, "Ensayo y conceptos políticos en Centroamérica, 1770–1870," in *Historia Global y Circulación de Saberes en Iberoamérica. Siglos XVI–XXI*, edited by David Díaz Arias and Ronny Viales Hurtado, 75–109 (San José: CIHAC, 2018).
13. Ralph Lee Woodward Jr., *Central America: A Nation Divided* (New York: Oxford University Press, 1999), 92–119.
14. José Cecilio del Valle, *El Amigo de la Patria*, November 30, 1821, 139.
15. Arturo Taracena, *Etnicidad, Estado y Nación en Guatemala 1808–1944* (Guatemala: CIRMA, 2002), 55–58.
16. *Constitución de la República Federal de Centro-América* (Guatemala: Imprenta a cargo de J. J. de Arév, 1824), 1.
17. *Constitución*, 2.
18. Jordana Dym, "Citizen of which Republic? Foreigners and the Construction of National Citizenship in Central America, 1823–1845," *The Americas* 4, no. 64 (April 2008): 477–510.
19. John L. Stephens, *Incidents of Travel in Central America, Chiapas, and Yucatan* (New York: Harper & Bros., 1841), 201.
20. Dana Gardner Munro, *The Five Republics of Central America* (New York: Oxford University Press, 1918), 164–184.
21. Reinhard Liehr, "La deuda interna y externa de la República Federal de Centroamérica, 1823–1839," *Estudios. Revista de Antropología, Arqueología e Historia* (Guatemala) 4, no. 1 (July 2003): 1–29, esp. 12. See also Robert S. Smith, "Financing the Central American Federation, 1821–1838," *The Hispanic American Historical Review* 43, no. 4 (November 1963): 483–510.
22. Thomas L. Karnes, *The Failure of Union; Central America, 1824–1960* (Chapel Hill: University of North Carolina Press, 1961). More on the Federation in Jordana Dym, *From Sovereign Villages to National States: City, State, and Federation in Central America, 1759–1839* (Albuquerque: University of New Mexico Press, 2006).
23. Víctor Hugo Acuña Ortega, "La invención de la diferencia costarricense, 1810–1870," *Revista de Historia*, no. 45 (January–June 2002): 191–228.
24. Acuña Ortega, "Invención," 204.
25. Lowell Gudmundson, *Costa Rica before Coffee: Society and Economy on the Eve of the Export Boom* (Baton Rouge: Louisiana State University Press, 1986); James Mahoney, *The Legacies of Liberalism: Path Dependence and Political Regimes in Central America* (Baltimore, MD: Johns Hopkins University Press, 2001), 142–164.

26. Víctor Hugo Acuña Ortega, *Centroamérica: filibusteros, estados, imperios y memorias* (San José: ECR, 2016).

27. E. Bradford Burns, *Patriarch and Folk: The Emergence of Nicaragua, 1798–1858* (Cambridge, MA: Harvard University Press, 1991), 19.

28. Frances Kinloch, *El imaginario del canal y la nación cosmopolita: Nicaragua, siglo XIX* (Managua: IHNCA-UCA, 2015), 179–292.

29. Michel Gobat, *Confronting the American Dream: Nicaragua under U.S. Imperial Rule* (Durham, NC: Duke University Press, 2005), 34–37.

30. Justin Wolfe, *The Everyday Nation-State: Community and Ethnicity in Nineteenth-Century Nicaragua* (Lincoln: University of Nebraska Press, 2007), 37–38.

31. Arturo J. Cruz, Jr., *Nicaragua's Conservative Republic, 1858–93* (New York: Palgrave, 2002), 46–121.

32. Julie A. Charlip, *Cultivating Coffee: The Farmers of Carazo, Nicaragua, 1880–1930* (Athens: Ohio University Press, 2003), 87–215.

33. Catherine Lacaze, *Francisco Morazán: Le Bolívar de l'Amérique Centrale?* (Rennes, France: Presses Universitaires de Rennes, 2018), 85–160.

34. Arturo Taracena, *Invención criolla, sueño ladino, pesadilla indígena. Los Altos de Guatemala: de región a estado 1740–1850* (Guatemala: Fundación Soros, 2011), 139–214.

35. Ethel García Buchard, *Política y estado en la sociedad hondureña del siglo XIX (1838–1872)* (Tegucigalpa, Honduras: Instituto Hondureño de Antropología e Historia, 2008), 231–302.

36. Manuel Montúfar y Coronado, *Memorias para la historia de la revolución de Centro-América* (Guatemala, Tipografía Sánchez y de Guise, 1934), 248–253.

37. Ralph Lee Woodward Jr., *Rafael Carrera and the Emergence of the Republic of Guatemala 1821–1871* (Athens: University of Georgia Press, 1993), 65.

38. Woodward, *Carrera*, 65–127.

39. About Carrera and his relations with the Catholic Church, see Douglass Sullivan-González, *Piety, Power, and Politics: Religion and Nation Formation in Guatemala, 1821–1871* (Pittsburgh: University of Pittsburgh Press, 2007), 81–119.

40. Sonia Alda Mejías, "Las revoluciones liberales y su legitimidad. La restauración del orden republicano. El caso centroamericano. 1870–1876," *Revista de Historia*, no. 45 (January–June 2002): 229–263.

41. *La Gaceta*, September 16, 1871, 3–4.

42. Mahoney, *Legacies of Liberalism*, 142–163.

43. Alvaro Quesada Soto, *Uno y los otros. Identidad y literatura en Costa Rica, 1890–1940* (San José: EUCR, 1998), 34–54.

44. Steven Palmer and Gladys Rojas, "Educating Señorita: Teacher Training, Social Mobility, and the Birth of Costa Rican Feminism, 1885–1925," *Hispanic American Historical Review* 78, no. 1 (February 1998): 45–82.

45. Steven Palmer, "Getting to Know the Unknown Soldier: Official Nationalism in Liberal Costa Rica, 1880–1900," *Journal of Latin American Studies* 25, no. 1 (February 1993): 45–72.

46. Iván Molina Jiménez, *Costarricense por dicha. Identidad nacional y cambio cultural en Costa Rica durante los siglos XIX y XX* (San José: Editorial de la Universidad de Costa Rica, 2002), 43–78.

47. Patricia Fumero, "De la iniciativa individual a la cultura oficial. El caso del general José Dolores Estrada," in *La Sonora Libertad del Viento. Sociedad y Cultura en Costa Rica y Nicaragua (1821–1914)*, edited by Iván Molina and Patricia Fumero, 13–41 (México: Instituto Panamericano de Geografía e Historia, 1997).

48. Michel Gobat, "Contra el espíritu burgués: la élite nicaragüense ante la amenaza de la modernidad, 1918–1929," *Revista de Historia*, no. 13 (1999): 17–34.

49. Jeffrey L. Gould, *To Die in this Way: Nicaraguan Indians and the Myth of Mestizaje, 1880–1965* (Durham, NC: Duke University Press, 1998), 49.

50. Volker Wünderich, "La unificación nacional que dejó una nación dividida. El gobierno del presidente Zelaya y la 'reincorporación' de la Mosquitia a Nicaragua en 1894," *Revista de Historia*, no. 34 (July–December 1996): 9–44.

51. Charles R. Hale, *Resistance and Contradiction. Miskitu Indians and the Nicaraguan State, 1894–1987* (Stanford, CA: Stanford University Press, 1994), 45–46.

52. Gould, *To Die in this Way*, 81.

53. Jeffrey L. Gould, *El Mito de la "Nicaragua Mestiza" y la Resistencia Indígena 1880–1980* (San José: Editorial de la Universidad de Costa Rica, 1997), 124.

54. Volker Wünderich, "'Dios hablará por el indio de las Segovias.' Las bases sociales de la lucha de Sandino por la liberación nacional en Nicaragua. 1927–1934," *Revista de Historia*, no. 17 (January–June 1988): 13–32.

55. Gould, *Mito de la "Nicaragua Mestiza,"* 167–185.

56. Patricia Alvarenga, *Cultura y Ética de la Violencia. El Salvador 1880–1932* (San José: EDUCA, 1996), 275–322.

57. Carlos Gregorio López Bernal, "Identidad nacional, historia e invención de tradiciones en El Salvador de la década de 1920," *Revista de Historia*, no. 45 (January–June 2002): 35–71.

58. Jeffrey Gould and Aldo Lauria Santiago, "'They Call Us Thieves and Steal Our Wages': Toward a Reinterpretation of the Salvadoran Rural Mobilization, 1929–1931," *Hispanic American Historical Review* 84, no. 2 (2004): 191–237.

59. Jeffrey L. Gould, "Revolutionary Nationalism and Local Memories in El Salvador," in *Reclaiming the Political in Latin American History: Essays from the North*, edited by Gilbert M. Joseph, 138–173 (Durham, NC: Duke University Press, 2001).

60. Jeffrey L. Gould and Aldo Lauria-Santiago, *To Rise in Darkness: Revolution, Repression, and Memory in El Salvador, 1920–1932* (Durham, NC: Duke University Press, 2008), 240–274.

61. Marvin Barahona, "Imagen y percepción de los pueblos indígenas en Honduras," in *Rompiendo el espejo. Visiones sobre los pueblos indígenas y negros en Honduras*, edited by Marvin Barahona and Ramón Rivas, 17–33 (Tegucigalpa: Editorial Guaymuras, 1998).

62. Darío A. Euraque, *Estado, poder, nacionalidad y raza en la historia de Honduras: ensayos* (Tegucigalpa: Ediciones Subirana, 1996), 78–79.

63. Darío A. Euraque, "Antropólogos, arqueólogos, imperialismo y la mayanización de Honduras: 1890–1940," *Revista de Historia*, no. 45 (January–June 2002): 73–103.

64. Darío A. Euraque, "La creación de la moneda y el enclave bananero en la costa caribeña de Honduras: ¿en busca de una identidad étnico-racial?," *Yaxkin* 14, nos. 1–2 (October 1996): 138–150.

65. Elizet Payne Iglesias, "Identidad y nación: el caso de la Costa Norte e Islas de la Bahía en Honduras," *Mesoamérica* 22, no. 42 (December 2001): 75–103.

66. Teresa García Giráldez, "Nación cívica, nación étnica en el pensamiento político centroamericano del siglo XIX," in *Historia Intelectual de Guatemala*, edited by Marta Elena Casaus Arzú and Oscar Peláez Almengor, 51–118 (Guatemala: CEUR.UAM, 2001).

67. Taracena, *Etnicidad, Estado y Nación*, 70–78.

68. David McCreery, *Rural Guatemala, 1760–1940* (Stanford, CA: Stanford University Press, 1994), 161–294.

69. Taracena, *Etnicidad, Estado y Nación*, 411–412. See also Greg Grandin, *The Blood of Guatemala: a History of Race and Nation* (Durham, NC: Duke University Press, 2000), 130–156.
70. Taracena, *Etnicidad, Estado y Nación*, 412.
71. Richard N. Adams, "Ethnic Images and Strategies in 1944," in *Guatemalan Indians and the State: 1540–1988*, edited by Carol Ann Smith, 141–162 (Austin: University of Texas Press, 1990).
72. Grandin, *Blood of Guatemala*, 159–233; Greg Grandin, *The Last Colonial Massacre: Latin America in the Cold War* (Chicago: University of Chicago Press, 2011), 73–168.
73. David Díaz Arias, "A los pies del águila: la visita de John F. Kennedy a Costa Rica en 1963," in *El verdadero anticomunismo. Política, género y Guerra Fría en Costa Rica (1948–1973)*, edited by Iván Molina Jiménez and David Díaz Arias, 179–2014 (San José: EUNED, 2017).
74. Edelberto Torres-Rivas, "Central America since 1930: An Overview," in *The Cambridge History of Latin America*, vol. 7, edited by Leslie Bethell, 159–210 (Cambridge, UK: Cambridge University Press, 1990).
75. V. Sanford, *Buried Secrets: Truth and Human Rights in Guatemala* (New York: Palgrave Macmillan, 2016), 147–179; Héctor Lindo-Fuentes and Erik Ching, *Modernizing Minds in El Salvador: Education Reform and the Cold War, 1960–1980* (Albuquerque: University of New Mexico Press, 2012), 71–102.
76. Knut Walter, *The Regime of Anastasio Somoza 1936–1956* (Chapel Hill: University of North Carolina Press, 1993), 236–248.
77. Morris H. Morley, *Washington, Somoza, and the Sandinistas: State and Regime in U.S. Policy toward Nicaragua, 1969–1981* (Cambridge, UK: Cambridge University Press, 1994), 62–171.
78. Torres-Rivas, "Central America since 1930," 195–197; J. Mark Ruhl, "Honduras: Militarism and Democratization in Troubled Waters," in *Repression, Resistance, and Democratic in Central America*, edited by Thomas W. Walker and Ariel C. Armony, 47–66 (Wilmington, DE: SR Books, 2000).
79. David Díaz Arias, *Crisis social y memorias en lucha: guerra civil en Costa Rica, 1940–1948* (San José: Editorial de la Universidad de Costa Rica, 2015), 284–296.
80. Anthony Winson, *Coffee and Democracy in Modern Costa Rica* (New York: Palgrave Macmillan, 1989), 50–76; Lowell Gudmundson, *Costa Rica después del café. La era cooperativa en la historia y la memoria* (San José: EUNED, 2018); Jorge Rovira Mas, *Estado y política económica en Costa Rica, 1948–1970* (San José: Editorial de la Universidad de Costa Rica, 2000); Mary A. Clark, *Gradual Economic Reform in Latin America: The Costa Rican Experience* (New York: State University of New York Press, 2001), 43–68; David Díaz Arias, "El crimen de Viviana Gallardo," in *Ahí me van a matar. Cultura, violencia y Guerra Fría en Costa Rica (1979–1990)*, edited by Iván Molina Jiménez and David Díaz Arias, 79–126 (San José, Editorial Universidad Estatal a Distancia, 2018).
81. Matilde Zimmermann, *Carlos Fonseca and the Nicaraguan Revolution* (Durham, NC: Duke University Press, 2000), 69–221; Rose J. Spalding, *Capitalists and Revolution in Nicaragua: Opposition and Accommodation, 1979–1993* (Chapel Hill: University of North Carolina Press, 1994); Jeff Goodwin, *No Other Way Out: States and Revolutionary Movements: 1945–1991* (Cambridge, UK: Cambridge University Press, 2001), 142–213.
82. Erik Ching, *Stories of Civil War in El Salvador: a Battle over Memory* (Chapel Hill: University of North Carolina Press, 2017), 162–202; Jeffrey L. Gould, *Solidarity under Siege: The Salvadoran Labor Movement, 1970–1990* (Cambridge, UK: Cambridge University Press, 2019), 88–225.

83. Clara Nieto, *Masters of War: Latin America and United States Aggression from the Cuban Revolution to the Clinton Years* (New York: Seven Stories Press, 2003), 115.
84. Dirk Kruijt, *Guerrillas: War and Peace in Central America* (London: Zed Books, 2008).
85. David Garibay, "De la guerra civil a la violencia cotidiana. El difícil arraigo de las democracias centroamericanas," in *Violencia y transiciones violentas a finales del siglo XX*, edited by Sophie Baby, Olivier Compagnon, and Eduardo González Calleja, 213-224 (Madrid: Casa de Velásquez, 2006).
86. Leigh Binford, *The El Mozote Massacre* (Tucson: University of Arizona Press, 1996), 90-115.
87. Carlos Figueroa Ibarra, "Centroamérica: entre la crisis y la esperanza (1978-1990)," in *Historia General de Centroamérica*, vol. 6, edited by Edelberto Torres-Rivas, 35-83 (Madrid: Ediciones Siruela S.A., 1993); Charles A. Reilly, *Peace-Building and Development in Guatemala and Northern Ireland* (New York: Palgrave, 2009), 17-40; Robert Kagan, *A Twilight Struggle: American Power and Nicaragua 1977-1990* (New York: Free Press, 1996), 633-720; Charles T. Call, "Assessing El Salvador's Transition from Civil War to Peace," in *Ending Civil Wars: The Implementation of Peace Agreements*, edited by Stephen John Stedman, Donald Rodchild, and Elizabeth M. Cousens, 383-420 (Boulder, CO: Lynne Rienner, 2002).
88. Jorge Rovira, "Transición a la democracia y su consolidación en Centroamérica: un enfoque para su análisis," *Anuario de Estudios Centroamericanos* 28, nos. 1/2 (2002): 9-56; Dirk Kruijt, "Guatemala's Political Transitions, 1960's-1990's," *International Journal of Political Economy* 30, no. 1 (Spring, 2000): 9-35; Óscar Catalán Aravena, "A Decade of Structural Adjustment in Nicaragua," *International Journal of Political Economy* 30, no. 1 (Spring, 2000): 55-71; Chris Van Der Borgh, "The Politics of Neoliberalism in Postwar El Salvador," *International Journal of Political Economy* 30, no. 1 (Spring, 2000): 36-54; Susanne Jonas, "Democratization through Peace: The Difficult Case of Guatemala," *Journal of Interamerican Studies and World Affairs* 42, no. 4 (2008): 9-38.
89. Guillermo O'Donnell, "On the State, Democratization, and Some Conceptual Problems (A Latin American View with Glances at Some Post-Communist Countries)," Working Papers, No. 192, Kellogg Institute (April 1993). Available online at https://kellogg.nd.edu/sites/default/files/old_files/documents/192_0.pdf.
90. Proyecto Estado de la Nación, *Estado de la Región* (San José: Editorama S.A., 1999-2016). All the reports are available online at https://estadonacion.or.cr/informes/
91. Robert H. Holden, *Armies without Nations: Public Violence and State Formation in Central America, 1821-1960* (London: Oxford University Press, 2004), 25-49; Víctor H. Acuña Ortega et al., *Formación de los Estados Centroamericanos* (San José: Estado de la Región, 2014).

Further Reading

Burns, E. Bradford. *Patriarch and Folk: The Emergence of Nicaragua, 1798-1858*. Cambridge, MA: Harvard University Press, 1991.
Euraque, Darío A. *Reinterpreting the Banana Republic: Region and State in Honduras, 1870-1972*. Chapel Hill: University of North Carolina Press, 1997.
Gobat, Michel. *Empire by Invitation William Walker and Manifest Destiny in Central America*. Cambridge, MA: Harvard University Press, 2018.

Gould, Jeffrey L. *To Die in this Way: Nicaraguan Indians and the Myth of Mestizaje, 1880–1965.* Durham, NC: Duke University Press, 1998.

Grandin, Greg. *The Blood of Guatemala: A History of Race and Nation.* Durham, NC: Duke University Press, 2000.

Holden, Robert H. *Armies without Nations: Public Violence and State Formation in Central America, 1821–1960.* London: Oxford University Press, 2004.

Kagan, Robert. *A Twilight Struggle: American Power and Nicaragua 1977–1990.* New York: Free Press, 1996.

Kruijt, Dirk. *Guerrillas: War and Peace in Central America.* London: Zed Books, 2008.

Lindo-Fuentes, Héctor. *Weak Foundations: The Economy of El Salvador in the Nineteenth Century.* Berkeley: University of California Press, 1991.

Mahoney, James. *The Legacies of Liberalism: Path Dependence and Political Regimes in Central America.* Baltimore, MD: Johns Hopkins University Press, 2001.

McCreery, David. *Rural Guatemala, 1760–1940.* Stanford, CA: Stanford University Press, 1994.

Sullivan-González, Douglass. *Piety, Power, and Politics: Religion and Nation Formation in Guatemala, 1821–1871.* Pittsburgh: University of Pittsburgh Press, 2007.

Walter, Knut. *The Regime of Anastasio Somoza 1936–1956.* Chapel Hill: University of North Carolina Press, 1993.

Williams, Robert G. *States and Social Evolution: Coffee and the Rise of National Governments in Central America.* Chapel Hill: University of North Carolina Press, 1994.

Woodward, Ralph Lee Jr. *Central America: A Nation Divided.* New York: Oxford University Press, 1999.

Wortman, Miles. *Government and Society in Central America, 1680–1840.* New York: Columbia University Press, 1982.

CHAPTER 11

··

CENTRAL AMERICA AND THE UNITED STATES

··

MICHEL GOBAT

CENTRAL America has endured more US interventions than any other region in the world. This history reflects the long-standing belief of US officials that their country's global aspirations hinged on its control of a Central American canal that linked the Atlantic and Pacific oceans. Already in 1788, Thomas Jefferson maintained that such a waterway was critical to the destiny of the fledgling United States.[1] Yet geography alone does not explain the centuries-long fixation with the isthmus. Often called "America's backyard," Central America has also been a prime testing ground for the US pursuit of global power. This was especially true in the 1980s, when revolutionary turmoil turned the region into a well-known laboratory for counterinsurgency strategies that Washington would subsequently deploy elsewhere in the world. Yet Central America had become an "empire's workshop" for the United States much earlier: in the mid-nineteenth century, when agents of Manifest Destiny made it the first major site of US settler colonialism by sea.[2] Despite the experiment's disastrous outcome, the isthmus remained a proving ground for new forms of US power until recent times.

Central America's lengthy encounter with the United States has traditionally been viewed by scholars in dichotomous terms: Central Americans either abetted US impositions or bravely rejected them.[3] These Manichean images of accommodation and resistance have also served as powerful political weapons for Central Americans and foreigners alike. But, as the newer scholarship underscores, such images obscure the ambiguities that define the region's history with the northern "colossus"—and best capture the limits of US power.

MANIFEST DESTINY

··

The shared dream of an interoceanic canal ensured that the destinies of the United States and Central America would be closely entwined after the latter's independence from

Spain in 1821. Plans for such a waterway go back to the early sixteenth century, when Spain sought to conquer the region. But only with the post-1830s expansion in global trade and the steamship revolution did North Atlantic powers truly consider building a canal across the isthmus, with none expressing greater interest than the United States. If the canal promised the United States easy access to the fabled Asian market, Central American nations hoped it would lead to the massive influx of investment and "civilized" immigrants from Europe and the United States. Most US canal projects sought to exploit Panama's narrow isthmus or Nicaragua's transisthmian waterways (the San Juan River and Lake Nicaragua). Such efforts intensified during the antebellum era of Manifest Destiny expansion. Especially crucial was the US annexation of California in 1848, which made a Central American pathway indispensable to the transformation of the United States into a continental nation.

Central America's first major encounter with the United States occurred during the California Gold Rush of 1849–1855. Although US citizens had previously visited the isthmus and Central Americans had been to *El Norte*, such contacts remained limited. The slim historiography of this era stresses haphazard US efforts to curb Great Britain's growing hegemony in the region following the collapse of Spanish colonial rule.[4] Yet recent studies have shown how these decades also deepened Central Americans' dream of a US-built canal and their valorization of the United States as a model state.[5] Not by chance did Central Americans readily welcome the gold rushers. The isthmus became a popular transit for the northern adventurers because the sea routes cutting through it were the fastest and safest ways to navigate between both US coasts—and would remain so until the 1869 opening of the US transcontinental railroad. While most gold rushers passed through Nicaragua or Panama, many visited the other Central American nations as well, with some making the isthmus their new home.

Because the Gold Rush has long been studied within the confines of US domestic history, we are only beginning to grasp its impact on Central America. Focusing on Nicaragua and Panama, recent studies have shown how the US visitors impressed the local populace with their entrepreneurialism, technological innovation, goods, modern pastimes—and big spending.[6] The Gold Rush triggered what contemporaries called the Americanization of the region. Better studied are the anti-US sentiments resulting from this global event: if alcohol and racial prejudices led many gold rushers to commit violent acts, US businesses ruined local entrepreneurs catering to the transients. This emerging tension between Americanization and anti-Americanism would mark Central American–US relations well into the twentieth century.

Another scholarly trend is to situate Central America's encounter with Manifest Destiny in the history of US imperialism.[7] Such a framing has allowed scholars to show how the isthmus became the center of the first overseas US commercial empire.[8] Forged by New York–based shipping companies, this empire hinged on the transformation of the Nicaraguan and Panamanian transits into Latin America's earliest US-dominated economic enclaves. The corporate takeover of these highly profitable transits was hardly seamless, as evident in the local resentments underpinning the US Navy's razing of the Nicaraguan port of San Juan del Norte in 1854 and Panama's Watermelon Slice Riot of

1856. By surviving such challenges, the enclaves demonstrated that overseas US expansion did not have to entail outright conquest of foreign territories.

At first, however, the transit enclaves appeared to promote the US annexation of Central America. This expansionist impulse came not from Washington but from the so-called filibusters (Spanish for freebooters) who violated US law by invading Latin American nations under the banner of Manifest Destiny, a racist ideology that justified Anglo-American conquests of supposedly backward societies.[9] The Nicaraguan and Panamanian transits ensured that Central America became a prime target of this private form of expansion, as they made it easy for filibusters to reach the isthmus. In addition, the transits' popularity with the gold rushers led the US press to depict Central America as a propitious site for Anglo-American settler colonialism.

All filibuster expeditions failed except for that led by William Walker, who seized control of Nicaragua in 1855 and then sought to subjugate the rest of Central America. The US public celebrated his triumph as a testimony to Anglo-American racial superiority when in fact he succeeded only thanks to local support. Indeed, Walker's men had been invited by Nicaraguan Liberals to overthrow the ruling Conservatives and then "Americanize" their country. Thanks to the transit, Walker's realm received up to twelve thousand US settler colonists, including women and children. This exodus abruptly ended in 1857, when Central American armies expelled Walker's group after a war that killed thousands on the Nicaraguan battlefields and many more in Costa Rica, El Salvador, and Guatemala due to cholera brought by returning troops.[10]

The Walker episode was the moment when Central America came the closest to being absorbed by the United States. What kind of Americanized polity Walker's group sought to forge remains a matter of scholarly dispute. While much of the US public believed that Walker's conquest would lead to their country's annexation of the entire isthmus, his regime preferred to create its own independent "American empire." Scholars have generally believed that it would be a proslavery entity. Buttressing this view is Walker's infamous decree re-legalizing slavery and his 1860 book that equated his Central American venture with the expansion of slavery. Recent studies downplay the role of slavery in Walker's enterprise by stressing how his regime's policies were shaped by the antislavery doctrine of free-soilism and how most of his followers were antislavery colonists hailing from the US North, including utopian socialists and European veterans of the 1848 revolutions.[11] With good reason did Walker enjoy strong support from Nicaraguan leaders of peasant-based movements fighting for a more democratic and equitable society. Only when his regime began to unravel did Walker issue his slavery decree. Since he never implemented it, his antislavery supporters believed it was just a ploy to obtain financial support from wealthy US southerners.

The latest scholarship thus sees Walker's enterprise not as the last gasp of proslavery expansion but as an early moment of US liberal imperialism with its promises of democracy, open trade, and progress. Such a reframing helps us better understand Central American support for a US-led empire. It also points to the little-known connections between Manifest Destiny in Central America and European liberal imperialism in Africa and Asia. But if Central Americans played a greater role in the global rise of liberal imperialism than commonly thought, they were also among the first to highlight its perils.

Central Americans still celebrate the victory over the filibusters as their main war of independence. In the United States, by contrast, memory of the Walker fiasco faded quickly and latter-day historians have tended to view it through the eyes of the filibuster.[12] Drawing mainly on his 1860 memoir, they typically claim that Walker's defeat was brought about by his main US enemy (the shipping tycoon Cornelius Vanderbilt) when in fact it was due to Central American resistance.[13] A few scholars have flipped the script by showing how the Central American triumph impacted the United States, both in the coming of the Civil War and in ending US overseas settler colonialism.[14] Central America's encounter with Manifest Destiny thus led to the demise of a US imperial strategy. But it also engendered another one—enclave imperialism[15]—which would help shape the post-1898 rise of the United States as a global power.

"Banana Republics"

Following the Walker fiasco, Central America remained free from major US impositions until the latter's victory over Spain in the War of 1898. With its takeover of Spain's Caribbean and Pacific colonies, the United States became a major overseas empire and deemed a Central American canal ever more crucial to its global ambitions. It initially sought to build the waterway in Nicaragua, only to opt for Panama. Construction on the canal started shortly after US gunboat diplomacy secured Panama's independence from Colombia in 1903.[16] Thus began a three-decade-long era of US military incursions, with the northern colossus acting, to cite the Roosevelt Corollary of 1904, as an "international police power."[17] Of the sixteen invasions that Central America suffered between 1903 and 1933, some sought to protect US business interests.[18] Most, however, aimed to ensure US control over the Panama Canal and its access routes, while blocking European powers from constructing a rival canal elsewhere in the region.

Gunboat diplomacy did not just turn the isthmus into a US sphere of influence. It also consolidated Central America's infamy as the home of "banana republics" that were run by oligarchic despots in the pocket of US companies seeking to exploit the region's natural resources. The banana republics of Central America have often been dismissed, to quote the famous Chilean poet Pablo Neruda, as "comic opera" offerings.[19] In reality, they were laboratories for US imperial policies based on new forms of private-public cooperation.[20]

When the term "banana republic" was coined at the turn of the century by the US writer O. Henry, it referred to Honduras, where US companies were establishing what would soon become the world's largest banana industry. Eventually, it also applied to the other Central American states whose export economies were not dominated by the banana industry but appeared to have fallen under the thumb of exploitative US companies.[21] While the derogatory term framed US views of Central America, it also entered the local lexicon.[22] A good example is Costa Rican President José Figueres, who stated in 1953: "I am a citizen of a 'banana republic.' I know how it feels to have a state within a state; to play host to a privileged business that does not abide by the law of the land, but by the terms of its own 'concession,' by the terms of economic occupation."[23]

And US banana, logging, and mining companies did exploit generous land, railroad, and tax concessions to forge enclave economies—mainly in the Caribbean lowlands—that exacerbated underdevelopment, poverty, inequality, and authoritarian rule.[24] No company was more powerful than the Boston-based United Fruit Company, whose reach was so great that it was locally known as *el pulpo* (the octopus). These companies blocked the local populace from reaping its fair share of their huge profits. They also undermined Central American sovereignty by functioning as " 'national enclaves' that assumed the presence of a dominant political class at the local level," albeit a class that readily called on US troops to intervene on its behalf.[25] Small wonder that the likes of United Fruit fanned anti-US sentiments, with some Central Americans equating the corporate threat to their nationality with that previously posed by Walker's filibusters.[26]

Newer scholarship has revealed that the power of the US companies was more limited than typically imagined. While the companies may have claimed to have built enclave economies from scratch, they in fact benefited from the preexisting infrastructure created by native planters, miners, and other entrepreneurs.[27] Because these independent actors persisted, the companies had to constantly contend with them. They also had to negotiate with their employees to a greater extent than previously thought.[28] Even brutally repressed labor protests could produce major changes in corporate rule, as when the massive strikes of 1909–1910 led by United Fruit's West Indian plantation workers in Costa Rica and Guatemala pushed the company to recruit Spanish-speaking natives in order to forge a more divided—and pliable—workforce.[29] This strategy backfired as it produced a labor force that enjoyed strong support from national politicians, thus enhancing the bargaining power of workers vis-à-vis "the octopus."

Recent studies have further chipped away at the companies' omnipotent image by highlighting the enclave's porous borders. Rather than deeming the enclave an Americanized "state within a state," they stress its manifold ties with local society. Such an approach has uncovered the critical role of previously hidden actors, especially small-time women entrepreneurs.[30] Among its most surprising findings are that United Fruit's much-vaunted "civilizing mission" was ineffective and that the enclaves unintentionally created local political cultures that stood out for their democratic-reformist bent.[31] At the same time, the power of US companies was undermined by transnational processes beyond their control, as when West Indian migrant networks shaped United Fruit's labor force in the isthmus.[32] And if local peoples are no longer seen as passive actors acted upon by the companies in seemingly isolated enclaves, the same holds for the natural environment.[33] Indeed, few local actors more undercut the power of United Fruit than the Panama disease that wreaked havoc on its banana plantations in the 1910s and 1920s.

The banana republics nevertheless helped secure US dominance over Central America. These entities reflected the post-1898 US strategy of eschewing formal colonial rule. For a long time, scholars have asserted that companies like United Fruit exploited US gunboat diplomacy to forge a corporate "empire" that spanned the entire isthmus, from British Honduras to Panama.[34] In reality, this private-public partnership was more equitable: while Washington certainly pressured Central American governments to enact polices favorable to the companies, it also forced the latter to do its bidding against their will.[35] And in managing their enclaves, United Fruit and its kind drew on policies implemented by US government officials in charge of the Panama Canal Zone.[36] Their collaboration with the Canal Zone government went beyond the simple transfer of ideas, as both exchanged workers and managerial personnel.

Dollar diplomacy was another novel form of private-public cooperation that buttressed US hegemony in Central America—and eventually shaped US policy elsewhere in the world.[37] Although dollar diplomacy originated in the Dominican Republic in 1905, it flourished in the isthmus, especially in US-occupied Nicaragua (1912–1933). It typically entailed the extension of US private bank loans to Central American governments in exchange for Wall Street's supervision of state finances and state-owned enterprises (mainly railways). While such exchanges were sought by local governments, many were imposed through US gunboat diplomacy. By the 1920s, dollar diplomacy had turned all Central American nations (except Costa Rica) into US financial protectorates, with Wall Street banks exercising extensive control over their internal affairs.

Contemporary critics claimed that dollar diplomacy served to prop up US business interests.[38] And many US companies did profit from the Wall Street-fueled loan frenzy of the 1920s, which financed the massive expansion of public works in Central America.[39] Few better articulated the popular belief that dollar diplomacy was a corporate-run "racket" than US Marine General Smedley Butler, who publicly admitted to having "helped in the raping of half a dozen Central American republics for the benefit of Wall Street."[40]

Newer research, however, suggests that dollars helped diplomacy more than the other way around. This was largely because Washington used dollar diplomacy to implement a new diplomacy of modernization based in the US Progressive movement.[41] Although dollar diplomats rarely used the term "modernization," they invoked key aspects of the modernization paradigm that came to prevail within the US foreign policy establishment after World War II. Dollar diplomats sought to secure US hegemony over Central America by ensuring that state institutions would be run by the principles of professionalism and bureaucracy. For its architects, dollar diplomacy was a universal project that could be applied anywhere. In reality, it not only promoted a US vision of progress but was a form of imperial control and thus inherently disruptive. Little wonder that political instability marked its reign in Central America.

Because dollar diplomacy has usually been explored from a US-centered perspective, its impact on Central America remains unclear. The few existing studies focus on its Nicaraguan showcase.[42] They reveal that dollar diplomats not only failed to modernize state institutions but actually undermined a preexisting modern state.[43] Hence, Nicaraguans denounced dollar diplomacy as a form of "feudal banker imperialism."[44]

Perhaps most surprisingly, dollar diplomacy in Nicaragua unintentionally engendered a financial environment more conducive to peasant than estate production; this outcome challenges widespread views that US intervention inherently widens the gap between the rich and the poor.[45]

When the Great Depression broke out in 1929, Central America confronted three interrelated forms of US domination: dollar diplomacy, gunboat diplomacy, and the enclaves overseen by United Fruit and its kind.[46] Of the many movements resisting the region's transformation into "America's backyard," none was stronger than the Nicaraguan guerrilla force that between 1927 and 1933 fought a bloody war against US troops occupying their country.[47] So greatly did this peasant-based insurgency grab international attention that its leader Augusto Sandino became arguably the era's most famous anti-imperial icon, with his cause celebrated throughout Latin America as well as in Asia, Europe, and the United States itself.[48] While the Sandino Rebellion was mainly rooted in Nicaragua's long subjection to US military and economic intervention, the rebels also opposed the Americanization of local culture, with Sandino blaming his compatriots' embrace of US lifestyles on "the corrupting influence of the dollar" introduced by Wall Street.[49]

Dollar diplomacy's reign indeed dovetailed with the dramatic spread of US cultural practices to the isthmus.[50] During the 1920s, Central Americans witnessed the influx of US Protestant missionaries bent on Americanizing local customs. Even greater agents of Americanization were US film, magazine, and radio industries, whose overseas expansion allowed Central Americans to enjoy mass exposure to the newest US cultural trends. No figure better symbolized US-style modernity than the "modern woman" who embodied *yanqui* consumption and leisure habits, such as daring new fashions, bobbed haircuts, sensual dance forms like the foxtrot, and sports (especially basketball), which had hitherto been the exclusive domain of men. How this Americanization affected the isthmus remains little studied. It could certainly have reinforced US hegemony, as Sandino lamented. But it also had the opposite effect, as when opposition to Americanization pushed Nicaragua's most oligarchic elites to seek an alliance with Sandino and his peasant rebels. Ironically, these elites had until recently been such staunch supporters of dollar diplomacy that they were among Central America's most-vilified *vendepatrias* (sellouts). Their overture to Sandino, even if unsuccessful, highlights the instability of pro- and anti-Americanism in Central America.

With the Sandino Rebellion culminating in the end of Latin America's lengthiest US occupation, the era of banana republics seemed to come to a close in the early 1930s. Not only had Washington renounced dollar diplomacy and radically scaled back gunboat diplomacy, but companies like United Fruit saw their power much reduced in the isthmus. This shift was embodied in President Franklin Roosevelt's 1933 proclamation of the Good Neighbor policy, which disavowed US intervention in Latin America. The new doctrine responded to the Great Depression, which drastically diminished Washington's ability to maintain a military presence abroad. But it mainly resulted from local opposition to US impositions. Such pressure also forced United Fruit to enact its own Good Neighbor policy, as when in the mid-1930s it was able to establish new plantations in the isthmus (to replace those ravaged by the Panama Disease) only after succumbing to nationalist demands that it better treat native-born planters and exclude West Indian immigrants from its workforce.[51] Similar concessions were wrested by Panamanian nationalists from the Canal Zone government.[52]

Still, the extent to which Roosevelt's Good Neighbor policy ended the era of banana republics remains unclear. Scholars have long maintained that the policy represented just a superficial shift, for it not only "carried on interventionism in Central America" but actually "tightened" it.[53] Indeed, US power during the Good Neighbor years (1933–1945) rested on authoritarian regimes that had swept the region following the mild democratic opening of the 1920s and that did good business with United Fruit and its kind.[54] For some scholars, these regimes proved to be "better guarantors of a *Pax Americana* than the US Marines," as their main pillars were local military establishments that, via training and arms sales, had become thoroughly Americanized—a strategy the United States extended to the global level during the Cold War.[55] Yet recent studies reveal that these regimes were more independent of Washington and had greater populist underpinnings than previously realized.[56] This was even true of the Nicaraguan dictator Anastasio Somoza García, who headed a US-created military (the *Guardia Nacional*) and was deemed Washington's favorite son in the isthmus.

The end of the banana republics likely had more to do with World War II.[57] After all, the Americanization of most Central American armies did not begin until the United States forged a hemispheric alliance against the Axis powers.[58] The war also triggered a "democratic spring" in the isthmus that was backed by Washington and targeted dictators in league with US companies such as United Fruit. Most importantly, World War II led the US government to become "the single most important purchaser, creditor and employer" in Central America.[59] The war thus ushered in the transition from the private-public partnership underpinning the banana republics to the state-centric mode of US domination that came to prevail during the Cold War.

COLD WAR

As much as Central American–US relations during the Cold War were rooted in earlier processes, they were greatly transformed by this novel global conflict. Above all, the Cold War gave ideological coherence to US policy toward the isthmus, with anticommunism its driving force. And it was in the name of anticommunism that Washington's chief local allies—military establishments—waged unprecedented terror campaigns against their people. Since the state violence targeted groups striving for democracy and social justice, it led the United States to be widely identified as a reactionary power. The worst violence occurred during the Central American revolutions of the 1980s, yet Washington had come to be deemed an obstacle to democratic reformism much earlier: in 1954 when the CIA orchestrated the overthrow of Guatemala's democratic government. The brutal end to Guatemala's "Ten Years of Spring" suggested to many Central Americans that a more just society could be achieved only via an armed revolution targeting US hegemony. Hence Walter LaFeber's influential argument about how revolution became "inevitable" in the world region most "tightly integrated into the United States political-economic system."[60] But if this system turned the isthmus into a revolutionary hotspot, key questions remain about its role in making Central America "the Cold War's final killing fields."[61]

The region's prominence in US foreign policy of the 1980s contrasts sharply with the minimal attention it received from Washington during the initial phase of the Cold War. US officials neglected post-1945 Central America mainly because they assumed it was safe from Soviet "penetration" and thus in no need of costly economic programs similar to the Marshall Plan for Western Europe. The famous exception proved the rule: fearing Guatemala had become a "Soviet beachhead," Washington contrived the 1954 coup against reformist President Jacobo Arbenz and then propped up brutal military regimes that stood out for their anticommunism.[62]

Yet the Guatemalan case was not as exceptional as often thought. US efforts to use the military to control Guatemala built on a strategy it had been implementing in the isthmus since World War II. Thanks to postwar US military aid, Central American security forces achieved "the greatest gains in capacity in their histories."[63] At the same time, the entire isthmus—like Latin America more generally—saw the rise of democratic movements that incorporated leftist parties and unions, while decolonization strengthened a type of economic nationalism in the nascent "Third World" that Washington equated with communism.[64] Both processes led the tightest of US spheres of influence to experience the earliest challenges to the global Pax Americana emerging in shadow of the Cold War.

The first challenge occurred in Costa Rica during the civil war of 1948. Claiming about four thousand lives, the conflict resulted in the overthrow of a democratically elected government of elite reformers and their Communist allies by pro-US rebels under the command of José Figueres, a virulently anticommunist Social Democrat. In justifying this regime change, Figueres and US officials maintained that Costa Rica had become Latin America's first battleground against "world communism." Costa Rican communists, too, viewed the conflict through a Cold War lens, insisting that anticommunism had driven the United States to secure the rebel victory.[65] In reality, local factors determined the war's outcome.[66] Future research could nonetheless clarify the extent to which US officials pressured the victorious rebels to repress the communist architects of Costa Rican social democracy. It could also elucidate how Figueres and his successors managed to defy Washington by pursuing both the "communistic" social reforms of their vanquished opponents and a state-led project of economic nationalism aimed at US companies, especially United Fruit.

If US involvement in the Costa Rican conflict signaled the end of the Good Neighbor era, its 1954 intervention in Guatemala led it to become identified with anti-reformism. The CIA-engineered operation began when a small exile force led by ex-Colonel Carlos Castillo Armas invaded Guatemala from Honduras. It quickly culminated in the military's overthrow of Arbenz's democratic government and the enthronement of Castillo Armas as president. With US support, Castillo Armas overturned the social reforms of the Guatemalan Spring (1944–1954). So egregious was this rollback that it led the United States to be viewed as a counterrevolutionary power around the world, including among its West European allies.[67] For Washington, however, the operation was a resounding success and served as a template for future interventions such as in Indonesia (1958), Cuba (1961), and the Dominican Republic (1965).[68]

Recent research suggests that the CIA greatly overestimated its role in one of the Cold War's most notorious episodes.[69] Traditionally, scholars also have attributed Arbenz's overthrow to US actors. Some claim that it was masterminded by United Fruit, which bitterly opposed Arbenz's agrarian reform.[70] Others stress Washington's fear of how Arbenz threatened US strategic interests, because he was spreading the "Communist virus" in its backyard, staked out an independent foreign policy that challenged US influence in international forums, or promoted a radical brand of economic nationalism that could be emulated throughout the Third World.[71] Newer scholarship has qualified the US role in the coup by highlighting the agency of local actors.[72] In particular, it suggests that the Guatemalan armed forces turned against the popular president not so much to preempt a full-scale US invasion, as they later claimed, than to block his agrarian reform from undermining their control of the all-important countryside.[73]

That the Guatemalan military acted more independently of the United States than commonly thought is revealed by the few studies of the coup's aftermath.[74] While US officials endorsed the military's repression of pro-Arbenz forces, they also expected that the military-dominated regimes of the post-1954 era would turn one of Latin America's most rigidly stratified and ethnically divided countries into a showcase of anticommunist reform. Washington granted much economic assistance so that these regimes could modernize the economy, improve the living conditions of the masses, expand the rural middle class, and establish a liberal democracy. To the dismay of US officials, Castillo Armas and his successors carried out policies that blocked democratization while exacerbating poverty and inequality. The challenges Washington faced in using Guatemala as a laboratory for combating communism presaged those plaguing its greatest effort to reform Latin America: the Alliance for Progress.

The Alliance for Progress was inaugurated in 1961 by President John Kennedy as a ten-year Marshall Plan for Latin America. Its impetus had less to do with the Cuban Revolution's recent embrace of communism than with Washington's fear that other Latin American nations would exit the "American system" by replicating Cuba's revolutionary path. If US officials had previously believed communism would be spread mainly by external forces, the 1959 triumph of the Cuban Revolution led them to focus on its internal sources. To curb communism's local appeal, the Kennedy administration enacted a massive aid and reform program that was to advance economic development, social welfare, and democracy. By 1970, the Alliance had helped block the triumph of a Cuban-inspired revolution. Yet it failed to achieve its main economic and social goals, while much of Latin America came under brutal military rule.[75] This failure was especially apparent in Central America. To be sure, the isthmus experienced high economic growth rates thanks to the agro-export boom of the 1960s. But the boom exacerbated inequality, with many peasant families losing their land and migrating to cities, thus leading to the explosion of shantytowns.[76]

Above all, the Alliance greatly militarized Central America by turning it into a US "counterinsurgency laboratory."[77] This well-studied transformation occurred under the banner of the National Security Doctrine, which stood out for viewing Latin American politics as "a kind of internal war, to be conducted with the same urgency (and the same methods) as traditional military conflict" and for defining subversion broadly so that it included left-leaning civic groups such as unions, student organizations, peasant movements, and Christian base communities (comunidades eclesiales de base).[78] Bolstered by US counterinsurgency aid and training, the region's security forces dramatically increased the level of political repression, with some initiating scorched-earth campaigns.[79] On the other hand, the Alliance also converted the Central American armed forces into leading agents of modernization by providing them with resources to implement "civic action" programs that were designed to build infrastructure for economic development, provide basic services to the rural poor, and strengthen the military's respect for civilian rule. Ultimately, these programs only reinforced the belief of Central American officers that they were more competent rulers than civilians. Moreover, many officers misused Alliance funds to amass estates and businesses, thus furthering their hold over local society. Little wonder that the Alliance's military side helped sow the seeds of the civil wars that would ravage the isthmus in the 1980s.

Less well understood is how these wars were also rooted in the polarizing effects of the Alliance's social reforms. US officials firmly believed that such reforms would strengthen the political center, yet the outcome was often the opposite. This was true of programs as different as the modest agrarian reform carried out by the Somoza dictatorship in Nicaragua, the Guatemalan rural community projects implemented by the US Agency for International Development (USAID) with the help of US priests, and USAID-sponsored education reforms pursued by Salvadoran military regimes.[80] If these social reforms typically radicalized their targeted beneficiaries, they pushed antireformist elites further to the right, leading many to support death squads that targeted "subversive" groups.

The escalating state terror compelled Washington to carry out its second major attempt to reform Central America during the Cold War: President Jimmy Carter's human rights crusade of 1977–1980. Like the Alliance for Progress, Carter's project had continental aspirations and sought to protect US power. While his human rights policy was long judged ineffective, recent studies suggest that it had a more positive impact.[81] This was truer for South America than for the isthmus, however, even though Washington deemed the latter region "a great testing ground for [its] human rights policy."[82] Nowhere were the limits of Carter's crusade more apparent than in Somoza's Nicaragua, where US officials failed in their efforts to reform the region's most Americanized—and depraved—dictatorship and thus stave off the 1979 triumph of a Cuban-inspired revolution led by the Sandinista National Liberation Front, which took its name from Sandino. In insisting on the reformability of Somocismo, Washington vastly underestimated Nicaraguans' desire for a revolutionary end to US predominance. But as is true for the

Alliance of Progress, we still know too little about how Central Americans responded to "perhaps the most altruistic uplifting activity in the history of US–Latin American relations."[83]

This US uplift quickly gave way to a murderous counterrevolutionary campaign that Washington waged in Central America following the consolidation of Nicaragua's Sandinista Revolution. The socialist-leaning Sandinistas struck such fear among US officials both because they were deemed to be forging a "second Cuba" and because their revolutionary triumph invigorated leftist guerrillas elsewhere in the isthmus, especially in El Salvador and Guatemala.

US efforts to regain control of its backyard are widely identified with the proxy wars initiated by President Ronald Reagan shortly after taking office in 1981.[84] Under Reagan, Washington once again viewed the spread of communism primarily in an international context, albeit with Cuba now as its main promoter. To squash Central America's burgeoning revolutions, Reagan officials rejected the reformism of the Alliance for Progress, dismantled Carter's human rights crusade, and pursued instead a militaristic strategy. This break in US policy was not as sharp as is often thought. Indeed, the Carter administration had paved the way for Reagan's proxy wars by propping up El Salvador's murderous military junta, helping remnants of Somoza's destroyed Guardia Nacional organize a counterrevolutionary force, and transforming Honduras into the US military's linchpin to contain "communist" expansion. Reagan's presidency was nonetheless essential to turning Central America into a "killing zone."[85] Above all, he and his advisers steadfastly insisted on a military solution to the region's civil wars—mainly so that they could eradicate the so-called Vietnam syndrome, which had soured the US public on an aggressive foreign policy. So obsessed were Reagan officials with the isthmus that they ended up devoting "more time, effort, and resources to Central America than any other administration in the history of the United States."[86]

The Reagan administration waged its militaristic campaign in Central America on two fronts. First, it sponsored the war that Nicaraguan counterrevolutionaries—the Contras—waged against the Sandinista regime from their bases in Costa Rica and Honduras. Contrary to conventional wisdom, the Contras were not US lackeys, for they evolved into a peasant-based army whose field commanders enjoyed much autonomy from their US handlers.[87] Although the Contras never managed to control Nicaraguan territory, their deadly attacks greatly undermined the Sandinista Revolution. Second, the Reagan administration provided massive aid to the other Central American countries to combat leftist insurgencies based mainly in El Salvador and Guatemala. In doing so, Reagan officials consistently whitewashed the gross human rights violations of their military allies. They also undercut regional peace efforts by reinforcing the belief of Guatemalan and Salvadoran officers that they could win their brutal counterinsurgency campaigns.[88] When the civil wars ended in the early 1990s, they had taken the lives of hundreds of thousands, with the vast majority killed by pro-US forces. While these bloody conflicts were rooted in local factors, they were intensified and prolonged by US policy.

Reagan's proxy wars in Central America had serious effects for the United States, too. Most palpably, they engendered one of the largest-ever grassroots movements to oppose US foreign policy: the Central American solidarity movement, which encompassed about two thousand local groups ranging from leftist and peace organizations to faith- and immigrant-based groups.[89] This decentralized movement was also unusually trans-national, with about one hundred thousand US citizens visiting Nicaragua to express their solidarity with the Sandinista Revolution. Although the movement failed to end Reagan's Central American crusade, it helped ensure that Congress limited the intensity of his proxy wars, especially by prohibiting military aid to the Contras.[90] And it was this ban that provoked the infamous Iran-Contra affair, which broke out in 1986 when the Reagan administration was found to have provided the Contras with illegal aid that was partly funded with the secret sale of US weapons to Iran. Although Reagan escaped impeachment, various administration officials were convicted and the scandal almost destroyed his presidency.[91]

The most enduring domestic outcome of Reagan's crusade was the arrival of about one million Central American war refugees to the United States. Although the vast majority were fleeing political violence, they were treated very differently by US authorities: if Nicaraguans tended to be considered bona fide refugees escaping "communist" repression and thus received political asylum, the others (mostly Salvadorans and Guatemalans) were deemed economic migrants fleeing poverty and were often deported.[92] To provide a safe haven for the latter, thousands of US citizens joined the Sanctuary movement. Despite facing government prosecution for violating immigration laws, the movement prevailed and the unofficial war refugees became a permanent population. The refugees, in turn, established strong migrant networks so that the influx of Central Americans continued unabated well after the civil wars had ended.[93] The dramatic growth of Central American immigrant communities in the United States was arguably the greatest blowback from Reagan's proxy wars.

Yet militarism alone did not define Reagan's crusade in Central America. From the start, his administration used the isthmus as a laboratory to develop new political strategies for restoring US hegemony. The most important was the "low-intensity conflict" doctrine that Washington inaugurated in El Salvador in order to defeat the region's strongest leftist guerrilla, the Farabundo Martí National Liberation Front (FMLN).[94] While this counterinsurgency doctrine built on the National Security Doctrine, it more explicitly promoted democratic reform. (It also drew heavily on the US conservative evangelicalism that had helped bring Reagan to power.)[95] In exchange for massive aid, US officials compelled the Salvadoran military to carry out relatively fair elections and the demilitarization of the state apparatus. Yet the new doctrine failed to curb the military's human rights abuses and to secure the FMLN's defeat. Its poor record notwithstanding, the low-intensity conflict doctrine was later applied by Washington to other parts of the world, especially to its "war on drugs" in the Andes and its occupation of Iraq.

Regime change via democratic means was another key strategy that the Reagan administration initiated in Central America. Its main target was revolutionary Nicaragua, where Washington combined the Contra war with the promotion of an unarmed civic opposition within the country. The strategy's linchpin was the National Endowment for Democracy (NED), a quasi-private institution funded largely by the US Congress.[96] After first supporting the anti-Sandinista media and trade unions, the NED focused its efforts on propping up the disparate political coalition that would oust the Sandinistas in the elections of 1990. While the NED's precise role in securing the revolution's electoral defeat remains unclear, its "democracy promotion" program was used by Washington as a blueprint to promote subsequent regime changes across the globe.[97]

For US officials, the unexpected collapse of the Nicaraguan Revolution vindicated Reagan's Central American crusade. In reality, the revolution's democratic end was part of a regional peace process that had been led by Costa Rican President Oscar Arias and that the Reagan administration had fiercely opposed. Launched in 1987, the Arias peace plan helped end the region's civil wars by the mid-1990s. Its Central American architects clearly benefited from the Iran-Contra scandal's crippling impact on US policy toward the isthmus. (A key exception was the 1989 US invasion of Panama that overthrow the dictatorship of General Manuel Noriega, who ended up in a Miami prison on narcotics-trafficking charges.)[98] But the Arias peace plan would have hardly succeeded had the leftist guerrillas not forced the Guatemalan and Salvadoran governments to the negotiation table. Just as important was the pressure exerted by Central American civic actors who are often overlooked, such as human rights activists, Indigenous movements, neighborhood associations, and women's organizations.[99] Their mobilization highlights the critical role that civil society played in promoting the region's democratization—a success that ultimately had far more to do with local efforts to make a revolutionary break with Central America's authoritarian past than with US democracy promotion.[100]

Postwar Integration

Washington's minimal role in the peace process led many observers to assume that the post-Cold War era would be marked by greater US detachment from the isthmus. In reality, both regions became more integrated than ever before.[101] This process reflected the efforts of US and Central American governments to better integrate their economies—endeavors that culminated in the controversial Central American Free Trade Agreement (CAFTA) of 2004.[102] It also built on the transregional solidarity movements of the 1980s and newer ones such as the Honduran Solidarity Network, which emerged in response to the 2009 coup that ousted democratically-elected President Manuel Zelaya.[103] Ultimately, however, the unprecedented integration of both regions was mainly driven by the unceasing migration of Central Americans to the United States and the transregional communities they forged in El Norte.

That the post-1990 peace settlement led Central American immigrants to become the fastest growing Latinx group had much to do with US policies implemented in the isthmus. Especially critical were the neoliberal economic reforms that Washington compelled war-torn Central America to adopt in exchange for financial aid. While these free-market policies produced an economic boom, poverty and inequality persisted. Making matters worse was the devastation wrought by natural disasters such as Hurricane Mitch of 1998. Not surprisingly, the precarious situation deterred most war refugees from returning home, while pushing ever more Central Americans to seek a better life in the north. Yet the case of Nicaragua—the region's poorest country—reveals that US-style neoliberalism was not the principal driver of the post-1990 emigration, for far fewer Nicaraguans left for the United States than those departing from the so-called Northern Triangle (El Salvador, Guatemala, and Honduras).

As in the 1980s, the migratory flow was fueled by violence. However, its chief perpetrators were no longer state forces but criminal organizations that made the Northern Triangle one of the world's deadliest regions of the post-Cold War era.[104] For long, this violence was firmly associated with two California-based gangs—Mara Salvatrucha and 18th Street—that were dominated by young Central American war refugees (mostly Salvadorans).[105] In the 1990s, both gangs expanded throughout the Northern Triangle due to Washington's new policy of massively deporting Central American immigrants who had violated US law.[106] Although most deportees were not criminal offenders but merely undocumented immigrants, they included many gang members who introduced California's exceptionally violent gang culture to the isthmus.[107] This violence was exacerbated when Northern Triangle governments, with Washington's support, implemented draconian anti-gang measures. Newer scholarship has relativized the role of gang-related violence in driving emigration by stressing the violence associated with drug trafficking, which boomed in the 1990s, when the isthmus became the main transit point for Andean cocaine bound for the United States.[108] Because of the drug trade's illicit nature, the extent to which it is responsible for the region's high murder rates remains unclear.

Once in El Norte, Central American immigrants promoted the integration of both regions by maintaining close relations with their home communities.[109] This is most noticeable in the high level of remittances they wire back home. Perhaps more important, many have pooled their resources by forming hometown associations that send money and goods to their communities of origin. Because these associations often work with local authorities to develop infrastructure and social projects, they enable migrants to remain politically active in their hometowns. Reinforcing such ties are the intense cultural exchanges between migrants and their communities of origins, especially in the form of visiting sport teams and musical groups.[110] This integration has also been promoted by governments and companies based in the isthmus: while Central American officials have formed joint partnerships with the hometown associations and created state agencies to support their compatriots in the United States, business groups have developed a vibrant transregional market for goods and services.[111] A transregionalism from below and above thus underpins Central America's unprecedented integration with the United States—one that is giving rise to the imagined community of "US Central Americans."[112]

CONCLUSION

Given that the fledgling community of US Central Americans is propelled by non-state actors, scholars might be inspired to reconceptualize the history of Central American–US relations, a field that in many ways remains beholden to state-centered frameworks of the Cold War era. The more important question is whether the ongoing integration of both regions will transform US policy toward Central America. As Reagan's proxy wars turned the isthmus into a killing zone, US scholars called on their country to be not only a "close neighbor" but also a "close friend to all the people of Central America."[113] Because of the lengthy history of US intervention, they believed their call could succeed only if the region's governments strengthened their position vis-à-vis Washington by promoting greater integration among their own nations and by exerting greater influence on the US political process.[114] Little did they imagine that the key to such success might instead lie in the hands of immigrant communities forged in the crucible of war.

ACKNOWLEDGMENTS

I am grateful to Robert Holden for his very helpful comments on a draft of this article.

NOTES

1. Gerstle Mack, *The Land Divided: A History of the Panama Canal and Other Isthmian Canal Projects* (New York: Alfred A. Knopf, 1944), 101.
2. The term comes from Greg Grandin, *Empire's Workshop: Latin America, the United States, and the Rise of the New Imperialism* (New York: Metropolitan Books, 2006). For a pioneering study of how Central America—together with the Caribbean—served as a US imperial laboratory from 1898 onward, see Louis Pérez, "Intervention, Hegemony, and Dependency: The United States in the Circum-Caribbean, 1898–1980," *Pacific Historical Review* 51, no. 2 (1982): 165–194.
3. For historical surveys of Central American–US relations, see John Coatsworth, *Central America and the United States: The Clients and the Colossus* (New York: Twayne, 1994); Walter LaFeber, *Inevitable Revolutions: The United States in Central America* (New York: W. W. Norton, 1984). For surveys of US relations with individual countries, see Karl Bermann, *Under the Big Stick: Nicaragua and the United States since 1848* (Boston: South End, 1986); Michael Conniff, *Panama and the United States: The Forced Alliance* (Athens, GA: University of Georgia Press, 2012).
4. For an overview, see Charles Stansifer, "United States-Central American Relations, 1824–1850," in *United States–Latin American Relations, 1800–1850: The Formative Generations*, edited by T. Ray Shurbutt (Tuscaloosa: University of Alabama Press, 1991).
5. Frances Kinloch Tijerino, *Nicaragua: Identidad y cultura política (1821–1858)* (Managua: Banco Central de Nicaragua, 1999).

CENTRAL AMERICA AND THE UNITED STATES   325

6. Aims McGuinness, *Path of Empire: Panama and the California Gold Rush* (Ithaca, NY: Cornell University Press, 2008); Miguel Angel Herrera C., *Bongos, bogas, vapores y marinos: Historia de los "marineros" del río San Juan, 1849–1855* (Managua: Centro Nicaragüense de Escritores, 1999); Michel Gobat, *Empire by Invitation: William Walker and Manifest Destiny in Central America* (Cambridge, MA: Harvard University Press, 2018).

7. Amy Greenberg, *Manifest Manhood and the Antebellum American Empire* (Cambridge, UK: Cambridge University Press, 2005); Víctor Hugo Acuña, *Centroamérica: Filibusteros, estados, imperios y memorias* (San José: Editorial Costa Rica, 2014).

8. See especially McGuinness, *Path of Empire*.

9. Robert May, *Manifest Destiny's Underworld: Filibustering in Antebellum America* (Chapel Hill: University of North Carolina Press, 2002); Víctor Hugo Acuña Ortega, ed., *Filibusterismo y Destino Manifiesto en las Américas* (Alajuela, Costa Rica: Museo Histórico Cultural Juan Santamaría, 2010).

10. For a historiographical overview of the war, see Iván Molina Jiménez, *La cicatriz gloriosa: Estudios y debates sobre la Campaña Nacional: Costa Rica (1856–1857)* (San José: Editorial Costa Rica, 2014).

11. The Free-Soil movement of the 1840s–1850s opposed the westward expansion of slavery into new US territories. It was not an antiracist movement, however, as Free Soilers typically advocated for the white settlement of these territories and thus sought to block free Blacks from emigrating to them. On Walker's Nicaraguan and non-Nicaraguan supporters, see Gobat, *Empire by Invitation*.

12. Victor Hugo Acuña Ortega, *Memorias comparadas: las versiones de la guerra contra los filibusteros en Nicaragua, Estados Unidos y Costa Rica (Siglos XIX–XXI)* (Alajuela, Costa Rica: Museo Histórico Santamaría, 2009); Brady Harrison, *Agent of Empire: William Walker and the Imperial Self in American Literature* (Athens, GA: University of Georgia Press, 2004).

13. William Walker, *The War in Nicaragua* (Mobile, AL: Goetzel, 1860); Acuña, *Centroamérica*, 98–136. On Vanderbilt's role in the Walker episode, see T. J. Stiles, *The First Tycoon: The Epic Life of Cornelius Vanderbilt* (New York: Knopf, 2009), 270–299.

14. Robert May, *Slavery, Race, and Conquest in the Tropics: Lincoln, Douglas, and the Future of Latin America* (Cambridge, UK: Cambridge University Press, 2013), 194–204; Gobat, *Empire by Invitation*, 280–290; Thomas Schoonover, "Misconstrued Mission: Expansionism and Black Colonization in Mexico and Central America during the Civil War," *Pacific Historical Review* 49, no. 4 (1980): 607–620.

15. The term comes from Jane Burbank and Fredrick Cooper, *Empires in World History: Power and the Politics of Difference* (Princeton, NJ: Princeton University Press, 2010), 437.

16. On how the canal construction helped shape the post-1898 US empire, see Julie Greene, *The Canal Builders: Making America's Empire at the Panama Canal* (New York: Penguin Press, 2009).

17. The corollary was proclaimed by President Theodore Roosevelt in a message to Congress; it declared that the United States, as a "civilized nation," had the duty to uphold order in the Western Hemisphere by intervening in the internal affairs of Latin American nations seemingly plagued by "chronic wrongdoing, or an impotence which results in a general loosening of the ties of civilized society." The corollary justified countless US interventions in the Caribbean basin until it was renounced by the Hoover administration (1929–1933).

18. Coatsworth, *Central America and the United States*, 34–35.

19. Pablo Neruda, *Canto General*, trans. Jack Schmitt (Berkeley: University of California Press, 1991), 179. Originally published 1950. See also Lester Langley and Thomas Schoonover, *The Banana Men: American Mercenaries and Entrepreneurs in Central America, 1880–1930* (Lexington: University Press of Kentucky, 1995).

20. For how these entities also served as a laboratory for the Rockefeller Foundation's quest to discover and test "the elements of a global health system for the twentieth century," see Steven Palmer, *Launching Global Health: The Caribbean Odyssey of the Rockefeller Foundation* (Ann Arbor: University of Michigan Press, 2010), 1.

21. On how the concept also applies to Belize, see Mark Moberg, "Crown Colony as Banana Republic: The United Fruit Company in British Honduras, 1900–1920," *Journal of Latin American Studies* 28, no. 2 (1996): 357–381.

22. Héctor Pérez-Brignoli, "El fonógrafo en los trópicos: sobre el concepto de *banana republic* en la obra de O. Henry," *Iberoamericana* 6, no. 3 (2006): 127–141.

23. As cited in Aviva Chomsky, *West Indian Workers and the United Fruit Company in Costa Rica, 1870–1940* (Baton Rouge: Louisiana State University Press, 1996), 255–256.

24. Mario Posas, "La plantación bananera en Centroamérica (1870–1929)," in *Historia general de Centroamérica*, edited by Víctor Hugo Acuña Ortega, 4:111–165 (Madrid: FLACSO, 1993); Carlos Araya Pochet, "El enclave minero en Centroamérica: 1880–1945, un estudio de los casos de Honduras, Nicaragua y Costa Rica," *Revista de Ciencias Sociales* 17/18 (1979): 13–59. For a pioneering case study, see Jeffery Casey Gaspar, *Limón: 1880–1940: Un estudio de la industria bananera en Costa Rica* (San José: Editorial Costa Rica, 1979).

25. Edelberto Torres Rivas, *History and Society in Central America*, translated by Douglass Sullivan-Gonález), 40 (Austin: University of Texas Press, 1993).

26. Chomsky, *West Indian Workers*, 213. See also Thomas O'Brien, *The Revolutionary Mission: American Enterprise in Latin America, 1900–1945* (Cambridge, UK: Cambridge University Press, 1996), 47–106.

27. John Soluri, *Banana Cultures: Agriculture, Consumption, and Environmental Change in Honduras and the United States* (Austin: University of Texas Press, 2005); Darío Euraque, *Reinterpreting the Banana Republic: Region and State in Honduras, 1870–1972* (Chapel Hill: University of North Carolina Press, 1996); Ronny Viales Hurtado, "La colonización agrícola de la region Atlántica (Caribe) costarricense entre 1870 y 1930: El peso de la política agraria liberal y de las diversas formas de apropiación territorial," *Anuario de Estudios Centroamericanos* 27, no. 2 (2001): 57–100.

28. On how the companies also had to negotiate with their white-collar employees who tended to be white US citizens, see James W. Martin, *Banana Cowboys: The United Fruit Company and the Culture of Corporate Colonialism* (Albuquerque: University of New Mexico Press, 2018).

29. Jason Colby, *The Business of Empire: United Fruit, Race, and U.S. Expansion in Central America* (Ithaca, NY: Cornell University Press, 2011). On the role of African American workers in these strikes, see Frederick Opie, *Black Labor Migration in Caribbean Guatemala, 1882–1923* (Gainesville: University Press of Florida, 2009).

30. Lara Putnam, *The Company They Kept: Migrants and the Politics of Gender in Caribbean Costa Rica, 1870–1960* (Chapel Hill: University of North Carolina Press, 2002).

31. Putnam, *Company They Kept*; Euraque, *Reinterpreting the Banana Republic*.

32. Colby, *Business of Empire*.

33. See especially Soluri, *Banana Cultures*.

34. For a foundational study, see Charles Kepner and Jay Soothill, *The Banana Empire: A Case Study of Economic Imperialism* (New York: Vanguard Press, 1935).

35. Paul Dosal, *Doing Business with the Dictators: A Political History of United Fruit in Guatemala, 1899–1944* (Wilmington, DE: Scholarly Resources, 1993), esp. 205–223.

36. Colby, *Business of Empire*, 82–117; Soluri, *Banana Cultures*, 152; Chomsky, *West Indian Workers*, 89, 111.

37. Emily Rosenberg, *Financial Missionaries to the World: The Politics and Culture of Dollar Diplomacy, 1900–1930* (Cambridge, MA: Harvard University Press, 1999).

38. Scott Nearing and Joseph Freeman, *Dollar Diplomacy: A Study in American Imperialism* (New York: B. W. Huebsch, 1925); Carlos Quijano, *Nicaragua: Ensayo sobre el imperialismo de los Estados Unidos (1909–1927)* (Managua, Nicaragua: Vanguardia, 1987). Originally published 1928.

39. Victor Bulmer-Thomas, *The Political Economy of Central America since 1920* (Cambridge, UK: Cambridge University Press, 1987), 33–38.

40. As cited in Hans Schmidt, *Maverick Marine: General Smedley D. Butler and the Contradictions of American Military History* (Lexington: University Press of Kentucky, 1987), 2.

41. Rosenberg, *Financial Missionaries to the World*.

42. Oscar René Vargas, *La intervención norteamericana y sus consecuencias: Nicaragua, 1910–1925* (Managua, Nicaragua: CIRA, 1989); Michel Gobat, *Confronting the American Dream: Nicaragua under U.S. Imperial Rule* (Durham, NC: Duke University Press, 2005).

43. On how a similar process occurred in Panama, where US canal builders razed entire towns in the name of modernity, thus turning into jungle what had been for centuries an urban and agricultural landscape, see Marixa Lasso, *Erased: The Untold Story of the Panama Canal* (Cambridge, MA: Harvard University Press, 2019).

44. Salvador Mendieta, *La enfermedad de Centro-América* (Barcelona: Maucci, 1934), 1:324.

45. Gobat, *Confronting the American Dream*, 150–174. For how US-occupied Puerto Rico experienced a similar outcome, see César Ayala and Laird Bergad, "Rural Puerto Rico in the Early Twentieth Century Reconsidered: Land and Society, 1899–1915," *Latin American Research Review* 37, no. 2 (2002): 65–97.

46. For an overview of Central American resistance to US domination, see Richard Salisbury, *Anti-Imperialism and International Competition in Central America, 1920–1929* (Wilmington, DE: Scholarly Resources, 1989). On how anti-imperial views even swept El Salvador, the only Central American nation yet to experience US gunboat diplomacy, see Héctor Lindo-Fuentes, *El alborotador de Centroamérica: El Salvador frente al imperio* (San Salvador, El Salvador: UCA Editores, 2019); Jeffrey Gould and Aldo Laura-Santiago, *To Rise in Darkness: Revolution, Repression, and Memory in El Salvador, 1920–1932* (Durham, NC: Duke University Press, 2008), 48–52. On how Central American cartoonists of the era depicted distinct forms of US domination, see Sofía Vindas Solano, "Cerdos que se alimentan con oro: El imperialismo Yankee en las caricaturas costarricenses, 1900–1930," *Istmica* 21 (2018): 95–148.

47. On the Sandino Rebellion, see Neill Macaulay, *The Sandino Affair* (Durham, NC: Duke University Press, 1967); Michael Schroeder, "The Sandino Rebellion Revisited: Civil War, Imperialism, Popular Nationalism, and State Formation Muddied Up Together in the Segovias of Nicaragua, 1926–1934," in *Close Encounters of Empire: Writing the Cultural History of U.S.–Latin American Relations*, edited by Gilbert Joseph, Catherine LeGrand, and Ricardo Salvatore (Durham, NC: Duke University Press, 1998); Michelle Dospital, *Siempre*

328   MICHEL GOBAT

más allá . . . : El movimiento Sandinista en Nicaragua, 1927–1934 (Managua: Instituto de Historia de Nicaragua, 1996); Richard Grossman, "The Nation Is Our Mother: Augusto Sandino and the Construction of a Peasant Nationalism in Nicaragua, 1927–1934," *Journal of Peasant Studies* 35, no. 1 (2008): 80–99. For biographies of Sandino, see Alejandro Bendaña, *Sandino: Patria y libertad* (Managua, Nicaragua: Anamá Ediciones, 2016); Volker Wünderich, *Sandino: una biografía política* (Managua: Editorial Nueva Nicaragua, 1995); Gregorio Selser, *Sandino: General of the Free* (New York: Monthly Review Press, 1981).

48. Alan McPherson, *The Invaded: How Latin Americans and their Allies Fought and Ended U.S. Occupations* (New York: Oxford University Press, 2014), 194–237; Barry Carr, "Pioneering Transnational Solidarity in the Americas: The Movement in Support of Sandino, 1927–1934," *Journal of Iberian and Latin American Research* 20, no. 2 (2014): 141–152.

49. Sandino as cited in Donald Hodges, *Intellectual Foundations of the Nicaraguan Revolution* (Austin: University of Texas Press, 1986), 117.

50. This paragraph is based on Gobat, *Confronting the American Dream*, 175–201.

51. Colby, *Business of Empire*, 181–197.

52. Conniff, *Panama and the United States*, 67–68.

53. LaFeber, *Inevitable Revolutions*, 81.

54. Dosal, *Doing Business with the Dictators*.

55. Héctor Pérez-Brignoli, *A Brief History of Central America*, translated by Ricardo Sawrey and Susana Stettri de Sawrey, 125 (Berkeley: University of California Press, 1989).

56. Jeffrey Gould, "Indigenista Dictators and the Problematic Origins of Democracy in Central America," in *The Great Depression in Latin America*, edited by Paulo Drinot and Alan Knight, 188–212 (Durham, NC: Duke University Press, 2014).

57. On how World War II had a greater impact on US–Central American relations than commonly thought, see Jorrit van den Berk, *Becoming a Good Neighbor among Dictators: The U.S. Foreign Service in Guatemala, El Salvador, and Honduras* (Cham, Switzerland: Palgrave Macmillan, 2018).

58. Robert Holden, *Armies without Nations: Public Violence and State Formation in Central America, 1821–1960* (New York: Oxford University Press, 2004), 119–124.

59. Colby, *Business of Empire*, 200.

60. LaFeber, *Inevitable Revolutions*, 5.

61. Gilbert Joseph, "What We Now Know and Should Know: Bringing Latin America More Meaningfully into Cold War Studies," in *In from the Cold: Latin America's New Encounter with the Cold War*, edited by Gilbert Joseph and Daniela Spenser, 15 (Durham, NC: Duke University Press, 2008).

62. On how President Eisenhower claimed that the 1954 intervention had "averted a Soviet beachhead in our hemisphere," see Stephen Rabe, *The Killing Zone: The United States Wages Cold War in Latin America* (New York: Oxford University Press, 2012), 51.

63. Holden, *Armies without Nations*, 229.

64. van den Berk, *Becoming a Good Neighbor among Dictators*, 241–282; Leslie Bethell and Ian Roxborough, eds., *Latin America Between the Second World War and the Cold War, 1944–1948* (Cambridge, UK: Cambridge University Press, 1992). On how Washington's fear of economic nationalism drove its postwar policy toward Central America, see Michael Krenn, *The Chains of Interdependence: U.S. Policy toward Central America, 1945–1954* (Armonk, NY: M. E. Sharpe, 1996), 46–57.

65. Steven Schwartzberg, *Democracy and U.S. Policy in Latin America during the Truman Years* (Gainesville: University Press of Florida, 2003), 179–181; Kirk Bowman, *Militarization,*

Democracy, and Development: *The Perils of Praetorianism in Latin America* (University Park: Pennsylvania University Press, 2002) 95–96; Silvia Elena Molina Vargas, "La violencia política contra los comunistas tras la guerra civil en Costa Rica (1948–1949)," *Cuadernos Interc.a.mbio sobre Centroamérica y el Caribe* 15, no. 1 (2018): 248.

66. David Díaz Arias, *Crisis social y memorias en lucha: Guerra civil en Costa Rica, 1940–1948* (San José, Costa Rica: Editorial UCR, 2015). For studies that stress the US role, see Schwartzberg, *Democracy and U.S. Policy*; Kyle Longley, *The Sparrow and the Hawk: Costa Rica and the United States during the Rise of José Figueres* (Tuscaloosa: University of Alabama Press, 1997); Jacobo Schifter, *Las alianzas conflictivas: Las relaciones de Estados Unidos y Costa Rica desde la Segunda Guerra Mundial a los inicios de la Guerra Civil* (San José, Costa Rica: Libro Libre, 1986); Marcia Olander, "Costa Rica in 1948: Cold War or Local War?," *The Americas* 52, no. 4 (1996): 465–493.

67. Max Paul Friedman, "Significados transnacionales del golpe de estado de 1954 en Guatemala: Un suceso de la Guerra Fría internacional," in *Guatemala y la Guerra Fría en América Latina, 1947–1977*, edited by Roberto Garcia Ferreira (Guatemala City, Guatemala: CEUR, USCA, 2010), 19–28; Michelle Getchell, "Revisiting the 1954 Coup in Guatemala: The Soviet Union, the United Nations, and 'Hemispheric Solidarity,'" *Journal of Cold War Studies* 17, no. 2 (2015): 73–102.

68. Lindsey O'Rourke, *Covert Regime Change: America's Secret Cold War* (Ithaca, NY: Cornell University Press, 2018), 120; James Callahan, "Eisenhower, the CIA, and Covert Action," in *A Companion to Dwight D. Eisenhower*, edited by Chester Patch, 360–361 (Malden, MA: Wiley-Blackwell, 2017).

69. On how the CIA also came to this conclusion four decades after the coup, see Nick Cullather, *Secret History: The CIA's Classified Account of its Operations in Guatemala, 1952–1954* (Stanford, CA: Stanford University Press), 1999.

70. Stephen Schlesinger and Stephen Kinzer, *Bitter Fruit: The Story of the American Coup in Guatemala* (Garden City, NY: Doubleday, 1982).

71. See, respectively, Richard Immerman, *The CIA in Guatemala: The Foreign Policy of Intervention* (Austin: University of Texas Press, 1982); Piero Gleijeses, *Shattered Hope: The Guatemalan Revolution and the United States, 1944–1954* (Princeton, NJ: Princeton University Press, 1992); James Siekmeier, *Aid, Nationalism, and Inter-American Relations: Guatemala, Bolivia, and the United States, 1945–1961* (Lewiston, NY: Edwin Mellen, 1999).

72. For an overview, see Timothy Smith, "Reflecting upon the Historical Impact of the Coup," in *After the Coup: An Ethnographic Reframing of Guatemala, 1954*, edited by Timothy Smith and Abigail Adams, 1–16 (Champaign: University of Illinois Press, 2011).

73. Jim Handy, *Revolution in the Countryside: Rural Conflict and Agrarian Reform in Guatemala, 1944–1954* (Chapel Hill: University of North Carolina Press, 1994), 169–190; Greg Grandin, *The Last Colonial Massacre: Latin America in the Cold War* (Chicago: University of Chicago Press, 2004), 62–65; Sergio Tischler Visquerra, "Guatemala, 1954: La síntesis reaccionaria del poder y la revolución inconclusa," in *Guatemala: Historia Reciente (1954–1996)*, edited by Virgilio Alvarez Aragón et al. (Guatemala City, Guatemala: FLACSO, 2012), 1: 54–55; Francisco Villagrán Kramer, *Biografía política de Guatemala: los pactos políticos de 1944 a 1970* (Guatemala City, Guatemala: FLACSO, 2009), 132–143.

74. This paragraph is based on Stephen Streeter, *Managing the Counterrevolution: The United States and Guatemala, 1954–1961* (Athens, OH: Ohio University Press, 2000).

75. Jeffrey Taffet, *Foreign Aid as Foreign Policy: The Alliance for Progress in Latin America* (New York: Routledge, 2007).

76. Robert Williams, *Export Agriculture and the Crisis in Central America* (Chapel Hill: University of North Carolina Press, 1986).

77. The term comes from Susanne Jonas, *The Battle for Guatemala: Rebels, Death Squads, and U.S. Power* (Boulder, CO: Westview Press, 1991). See also Grandin, *Last Colonial Massacre*; Michael McClintock, *The American Connection: State Terror and Popular Resistance in El Salvador* (London: Zed Books, 1985); Michael Gambone, *Capturing the Revolution: The United States, Central America, and Nicaragua, 1961–1972* (Westport, CT: Praeger, 2001).

78. Hal Brands, *Latin America's Cold War* (Cambridge, MA: Harvard University Press, 2010), 73. On how the National Security Doctrine was considerably more variegated than commonly thought, see David Pion-Berlin, "Latin American National Security Doctrines: Hard- and Softline Themes," *Armed Forces and Society* 15, no. 3 (1989): 411–429.

79. On how much of this US counterinsurgency training occurred at the School of the Americas in the Panama Canal Zone, see Lesley Gill, *The School of the Americas: Military Training and Political Violence in the Americas* (Durham, NC: Duke University Press, 2004). On how the Guatemalan army carried out its first scorched-earth campaign in October 1966 by killing some eight thousand people to vanquish a few hundred guerrillas, see Grandin, *Last Colonial Massacre*, 98.

80. Jeffrey Gould, *To Lead as Equals: Rural Protest and Political Consciousness in Chinandega, Nicaragua, 1912–1979* (Chapel Hill: University of North Carolina Press, 1990), 245–269; Stephen Streeter, "Nation-Building in the Land of Eternal Counter-Insurgency: Guatemala and the Contradictions of the Alliance for Progress," *Third World Quarterly* 27, no. 1 (2006), 57–68; Bonar Hernández Sandoval, *Guatemala's Catholic Revolution: A History of Religious and Social Reform, 1920–1968* (Notre Dame, IN: University of Notre Dame Press, 2019), 129–158; Héctor Lindo-Fuentes and Erik Ching, *Modernizing Minds in El Salvador: Education Reform and the Cold War, 1960–1980* (Albuquerque: University of New Mexico Press, 2012).

81. Kathryn Sikkink, *Mixed Signals: U.S. Human Rights Policy and Latin America* (Ithaca, NY: Cornell University Press, 2004), 121–147.

82. Carter's Director of Central American Affairs (Wade Matthews), as quoted in Morris Morley, *Washington, Somoza, and the Sandinistas: State and Regime in U.S. Policy toward Nicaragua, 1969–1981* (Cambridge, UK: Cambridge University Press, 1994), 96.

83. Lars Schoultz, *In Their Own Best Interest: A History of the U.S. Effort to Improve Latin Americans* (Cambridge, MA: Harvard University Press, 2018), 224.

84. For a historiographical overview, see Jason Colby, "Reagan and Central America," *A Companion to Ronald Reagan*, edited by Andrew Johns, 438–452 (Malden, MA: Wiley, 2015).

85. The term comes from Rabe, *Killing Zone*.

86. John Coatsworth, "Cold War in Central America, 1975–1991," in *The Cambridge History of the Cold War*, edited by Melvyn Leffler and Odd Arne Westad, 3:218 (Cambridge, UK: Cambridge University Press, 2010).

87. Lynn Horton, *Peasants in Arms: War and Peace in the Mountains of Nicaragua, 1979–1994* (Athens, OH: Ohio University Press, 1998).

88. Brian D'Haeseleer, *The Salvadoran Crucible: The Failure of U.S. Counterinsurgency in El Salvador, 1979–1992* (Lawrence: University Press of Kansas, 2017), 164.

89. Christian Smith, *Resisting Reagan: The U.S. Central American Peace Movement* (Chicago: University of Chicago Press, 1996); Donald Peace, *A Call to Conscience: The Anti-Contra War Campaign* (Amherst: University of Massachusetts Press, 2012); Molly Todd, "'We Were Part of the Revolutionary Movement There': Wisconsin Peace Progressives and Solidarity with El Salvador in the Reagan Era," *Journal of Civil and Human Rights* 3, no. 1 (2017): 1–56. On how this solidarity movement was also shaped by Central Americans, see Héctor Perla, *Sandinista Nicaragua's Resistance to US Coercion: Revolutionary Deterrence in Asymmetric Conflict* (Cambridge, UK: Cambridge University Press, 2016); Van Gosse, "'The North American Front': Central American Solidarity in the Reagan Era," in *Reshaping the US Left: Popular Struggles of the 1980s*, edited by Mike Davis and Michael Sprinker (London: Verso, 1988), 11–50.

90. Cynthia Arnson, *Crossroads: Congress, the President, and Central America, 1976–1993* (University Park, PA: Penn State University Press, 1993); William LeoGrande, *Our Own Backyard: The United States in Central America, 1977–1992* (Chapel Hill: University of North Carolina Press, 1998).

91. Kyle Longley, "An Obsession: The Central American Policy of the Reagan Administration," *Reagan and the World: Leadership and National Security, 1981–1989*, edited by Bradley Coleman and Kyle Longley, 227 (Lexington: University Press of Kentucky, 2017).

92. María Cristina García, *Seeking Refuge: Central American Migration to Mexico, the United States, and Canada* (Berkeley: University of California Press, 2006), 112–118.

93. Norma Stoltz Chinchilla and Nora Hamilton, "Central American Immigrants: Diverse Populations, Changing Communities," in *The Columbia History of Latinos in the United States Since 1960*, edited by David Gutiérrez, 197 (New York: Columbia University Press, 2006).

94. Benjamin Schwarz, *American Counterinsurgency Doctrine in El Salvador: The Frustrations of Reform and Illusions of Nation Building* (Santa Monica, CA: RAND, 1991); D'Haeseleer, *Salvadoran Crucible*.

95. Grandin, *Empire's Workshop*, 150–156. For the impact of US conservative evangelicalism on the Central American civil wars, see Virginia Garrard-Burnett, *Terror in the Land of the Holy Spirit: Guatemala under General Efraín Ríos Montt, 1982–1983* (New York: Oxford University Press, 2010); Lauren Turek, "Ambassadors for the Kingdom of God or for America? Christian Nationalism, the Christian Right, and the Contra War," *Religions* 7, no. 12 (2016).

96. Mara Sankey, "Promoting Democracy?: The Role of Transnational Non-State Actors in Inter-American Relations, 1980–1993" (PhD diss., University College London, 2016); Robert Pee, "The Rise of Political Aid: The National Endowment for Democracy and the Reagan Administration's Cold War Strategy," *The Reagan Administration, the Cold War, and the Transition to Democracy Promotion*, edited by Robert Pee and William Schmidli, 51–73 (Cham, Switzerland: Palgrave Macmillan, 2019).

97. For studies stressing the NED's role in shaping the outcome of the 1990 elections, see Schoultz, *In Their Own Best Interest*, 267–275; William Robinson, *Promoting Polyarchy: Globalization, US Intervention, and Hegemony* (Cambridge, UK: Cambridge University Press, 1996). For a contrary view, see Robert Kagan, *A Twilight Struggle: American Power and Nicaragua, 1977–1990* (New York: Free Press, 1996). For the critical role of local factors, see Vanessa Castro and Gary Prevost, eds., *The 1990 Elections in Nicaragua and Their Aftermath* (Lanham, MD: Rowman & Littlefield, 1992).

98. On how this intervention shaped the 2003 US invasion of Iraq, see Brian D'Haeseleer, "Paving the Way for Baghdad: The US Invasion of Panama, 1989," *International History Review* 41, no. 6 (2019): 1194–1215.

99. For an overview of the role that Central American governments, international organizations, and local citizen groups played in the peace process, see Thomas Walker and Ariel Armony, eds., *Repression, Resistance, and Democratic Transition in Central America* (Wilmington, DE: Scholarly Resources, 2000).

100. For how the Central American revolutions of the 1980s promoted the region's transition to democracy, see Jeffrey Paige, *Coffee and Power: Revolution and the Rise of Democracy in Central America* (Cambridge, MA: Harvard University Press, 1997).

101. Cristina Eguizábal, "The United States and Central America since 2000: Free Trade and Diaspora Diplomacy," *Contemporary U.S.–Latin American Relations: Cooperation or Conflict in the 21st Century?*, edited by Jorge Domínguez and Rafael Fernández de Castro, 79 (New York: Routledge, 2010).

102. On the fierce debate over CAFTA, see Rose Spalding, *Contesting Trade in Central America: Market Reform and Resistance* (Austin: University of Texas Press, 2014).

103. Dana Frank, *The Long Honduran Night: Resistance, Terror, and the United States in the Aftermath of the Coup* (Chicago: Haymarket Books, 2018).

104. Heidrun Zinecker, "How to Explain and How Not to Explain Contemporary Criminal Violence in Central America," *Politics and History of Violence and Crime in Central America*, edited by Sebastian Huhn and Hannes Warnecke-Berger, 23–63 (New York: Palgrave Macmillan, 2017).

105. Thomas Bruneau, Lucia Dammert, and Elizabeth Skinner, eds., *Maras: Gang Violence and Security in Central America* (Austin: University of Texas Press, 2011).

106. Especially critical was the Illegal Immigration Reform and Immigrant Responsibility Act of 1996.

107. Sonja Wolf, "Street Gangs of El Salvador," in *Maras: Gang Violence and Security in Central America,* edited by Thomas Bruneau, Lucia Dammert, and Elizabeth Skinner, 49 (Austin: University of Texas Press, 2011). For a case study centered on young Salvadoran-born deportees, see Susan Bibler Coutin, *Exiled Home: Salvadoran Transnational Youth in the Aftermath of Violence* (Durham, NC: Duke University Press, 2016).

108. Otto Argueta, "Drug-trafficking and governance in Central America," *Handbook of Central American Governance*, edited by Diego Sánchez-Anochea and Salvador Martí i Puig, 198–215 (London: Routledge, 2012).

109. Chinchilla and Hamilton, "Central American Immigrants," 216–225.

110. On the key role of US-based hometown associations in promoting such cultural exchanges, see Sarah Loose, "El Comité con Santa Marta: memoria histórica, testimonio y organización transnacional en El Salvador," in *Migraciones en América Central: Políticas, territorios y actores*, edited by Carlos Sandoval García, 365–388 (San José, Costa Rica: Editorial UCR, 2016).

111. Eguizábal, "United States and Central America since 2000," 73–75; Susan Bibler Coutin, *Nations of Emigrants: Shifting Boundaries of Citizenship in El Salvador and the United States* (Ithaca, NY: Cornell University Press, 2007), 73–99.

112. Karina Alvarado, Alicia Estrada, and Ester Hernández, eds., *U.S. Central Americans: Reconstructing Memories, Struggles, and Communities of Resistance* (Tucson: University of Arizona Press, 2017).

113. John Findling, *Close Neighbors, Distant Friends: United States–Central American Relations* (Westport, CT: Greenwood Press, 1987), 182.

114. Coatsworth, *Central America and the United States*, 14.

FURTHER READING

Alvarado, Karina, Alicia Estrada, and Ester Hernández, eds. *U.S. Central Americans: Reconstructing Memories, Struggles, and Communities of Resistance*. Tucson: University of Arizona Press, 2017.

Coatsworth, John. *Central America and the United States: The Clients and the Colossus*. New York: Twayne, 1994.

Colby, Jason. *The Business of Empire: United Fruit, Race, and U.S. Expansion in Central America*. Ithaca, NY: Cornell University Press, 2011.

Coutin, Susan Bibler. *Nations of Emigrants: Shifting Boundaries of Citizenship in El Salvador and the United States*. Ithaca, NY: Cornell University Press, 2007.

D'Haeseleer, Brian. *The Salvadoran Crucible: The Failure of U.S. Counterinsurgency in El Salvador, 1979–1992*. Lawrence: University Press of Kansas, 2017.

García, María Cristina. *Seeking Refuge: Central American Migration to Mexico, the United States, and Canada*. Berkeley: University of California Press, 2006.

Gleijeses, Piero. *Shattered Hope: The Guatemalan Revolution and the United States, 1944–1954*. Princeton, NJ: Princeton University Press, 1992.

Gobat, Michel. *Confronting the American Dream: Nicaragua under U.S. Imperial Rule*. Durham, NC: Duke University Press, 2005.

Grandin, Greg. *Empire's Workshop: Latin America, the United States, and the Rise of the New Imperialism*. New York: Metropolitan Books, 2006.

Greene, Julie. *The Canal Builders: Making America's Empire at the Panama Canal*. New York: Penguin Press, 2009.

LaFeber, Walter. *Inevitable Revolutions: The United States in Central America*. New York: W. W. Norton, 1984.

LeoGrande, William. *Our Own Backyard: The United States in Central America, 1977–1992*. Chapel Hill: University of North Carolina Press, 1998.

Lindo-Fuentes, Héctor, and Erik Ching. *Modernizing Minds in El Salvador: Education Reform and the Cold War, 1960–1980*. Albuquerque: University of New Mexico Press, 2012.

McGuinness, Aims. *Path of Empire: Panama and the California Gold Rush*. Ithaca, NY: Cornell University Press, 2008.

Perla, Héctor. *Sandinista Nicaragua's Resistance to US Coercion: Revolutionary Deterrence in Asymmetric Conflict*. Cambridge, UK: Cambridge University Press, 2016.

Schroeder, Michael. "The Sandino Rebellion Revisited: Civil War, Imperialism, Popular Nationalism, and State Formation Muddied Up Together in the Segovias of Nicaragua, 1926–1934." In *Close Encounters of Empire: Writing the Cultural History of U.S.–Latin American Relations*, edited by Gilbert Joseph, Catherine LeGrand, and Ricardo Salvatore, 208–268. Durham, NC: Duke University Press, 1998.

Soluri, John. *Banana Cultures: Agriculture, Consumption, and Environmental Change in Honduras and the United States*. Austin: University of Texas Press, 2005.

Streeter, Stephen. *Managing the Counterrevolution: The United States and Guatemala, 1954–1961*. Athens, OH: Ohio University Press, 2000.

van den Berk, Jorrit. *Becoming a Good Neighbor among Dictators: The U.S. Foreign Service in Guatemala, El Salvador, and Honduras*. Cham, Switzerland: Palgrave Macmillan, 2018.

CHAPTER 12

THE COLD WAR

Authoritarianism, Empire, and Social Revolution

JOAQUÍN M. CHÁVEZ

INTRODUCTION

Global and regional political and cultural trends shaped a set of interrelated and persistent conflicts between authoritarian regimes and democratic and revolutionary forces during the Cold War in Central America (1947–1992). US Cold War anticommunism, in particular, abetted obdurate authoritarian regimes that sparked major conflicts in Central America; it did so, paradoxically, in the name of democracy, security, and stability. The confrontations between authoritarian regimes and democratic forces in the post-World War II period (henceforth the postwar, 1945–1954) mutated into persistent revolutionary and counterrevolutionary politics in Guatemala, El Salvador, and Nicaragua. The failed attempts of democratization conducted by civic-military movements, that is, anti-dictatorial mobilizations led by military officers and civilians in Guatemala and El Salvador during the postwar, informed the radicalization of intellectuals, students, and labor leaders who played major roles in insurgent politics in the 1960s and 1970s. During the epochal transformations of the 1960s and 1970s new cohorts of intellectuals, students, peasant leaders, and labor activists created insurgent movements to confront authoritarian regimes in El Salvador, Guatemala, and Nicaragua. The 1959 Cuban Revolution, the Second Vatican Council (1962–1965), a major event in Catholic Church history that redefined the Church's social doctrine, and the 1979 Sandinista Revolution crucially shaped insurgent and counterinsurgent politics in Central America during the Cold War. In the aftermath of the Cuban Revolution, authoritarian governments sponsored by the United States formed potent counterinsurgent structures to fight what they deemed Cuban-sponsored subversion in the region. Only Costa Rica created a demilitarized democracy and a welfare state in the postwar. These historical conditions allowed Costa Rica to experience a high degree of political stability during the turbulent Cold War period.

Postwar Democratic Romanticism and Persistent Authoritarianism (1944–1954)

The democratic rhetoric and antifascism promoted by the Allies against Nazi Germany echoed the democratic aspirations of the urban working class, students, intellectuals, professionals, and military officers in Central America. It inspired a form of democratic romanticism, the idealistic notion that the end of World War II, the defeat of Nazi Germany, and "the democratic values represented by the United States" would enable the democratization of Central America.[1] The postwar period brought to the fore new political and social actors who advocated comprehensive notions of democracy and social citizenship.[2] In 1944, civic-military movements that sought democratization overthrew the authoritarian regimes that had prevailed in El Salvador and Guatemala since the early 1930s. These civic-military mobilizations had remarkably different outcomes. El Salvador quickly relapsed into authoritarianism. In contrast, a democratic revolution emerged in Guatemala.

In May 1944, a civic-military movement that gained widespread support among urban workers, students, and intellectuals in San Salvador and other cities ousted President Maximiliano Hernández Martínez, a tyrant who ruled El Salvador for twelve years. Martínez ordered one of the most atrocious mass killings in the history of Latin America. In the aftermath of a failed peasant rebellion, army units, security forces, and armed civilians massacred thousands of Indigenous peasants in western El Salvador in January 1932. A series of military governments between 1945 and 1948 curtailed the democratic impetus of the civic-military movement that ousted Martínez and consolidated oligarchic-military authoritarianism.

The democratic revolution in Guatemala (1944–1954) arguably constituted the most emblematic episode in the history of US Cold War policy and social revolution in postwar Latin America. It confronted emerging democratic forces with entrenched oligarchic authoritarianism and US-sponsored counterrevolution. The civic-military movement that overthrew the thirteen-year dictatorship of President Jorge Ubico in July 1944 led to a democratic revolution. Ubico, a dictator with Nazi proclivities, protected the interests of wealthy landholders, mostly coffee growers, and the United Fruit Company, a US corporation that owned important enclaves and public infrastructure in Guatemala.[3] A group of military officers and civilians led by Captain Jacobo Arbenz and Major Francisco Arana ousted General Federico Ponce Vaides, Ubico's successor, and organized the first democratic elections in the country's history. Juan José Arévalo, a professor of philosophy, became the first democratically elected president in the history of Guatemala in 1945. This event constituted the starting point of the ten-year democratic revolution in Guatemala.

Arévalo carried out comprehensive political and socioeconomic reforms that challenged oligarchic structures in Guatemala. Arévalo advocated "spiritual socialism," a radical liberal thought that emphasized individual freedom, ethics, and social justice. Freedom of speech, voting rights, and unrestricted access to books and newspapers were current in Guatemala during Arévalo's term. Arévalo also enforced the 1947 Labor Code, which granted labor rights to urban workers, created the Guatemalan Institute of Social Security, and implemented a modest education reform. The highly unequal agrarian structure in Guatemala remained practically unchanged during Arévalo's government.[4] However, the landed elites and the Catholic hierarchy repeatedly tried to overthrow Arévalo. The support of his Minister of Defense Jacobo Arbenz allowed Arévalo to complete his term.[5] In November 1950, Arbenz was elected president of Guatemala in a landslide victory.[6]

The Arbenz government (1951–1954) carried out an unprecedented agrarian reform. Like his predecessor, Arbenz also faced a powerful reaction led by the Catholic Church hierarchy, landowners, and middle-class students. But in the end, a CIA coup overthrew President Arbenz in 1954. The CIA coup against Arbenz led to the restoration of military dictatorship and heralded a new era of state terror in Guatemala that military regimes across Latin America replicated in the 1960s. The illegal ousting of Arbenz radicalized left intellectuals who embraced insurgent politics in Cuba and Central America.[7]

In 1944, civic mobilizations also challenged the dictator Tiburcio Carías Andino in Honduras. Carías, the leader of the National Party, was a prototypical strongman backed by the United Fruit Company who ruled Honduras from 1932 to 1949. Mobilizations against Carías took place in San Pedro Sula and Tegucigalpa. In San Pedro Sula, security forces opened fire on demonstrators killing several persons.[8] Carías also faced strikes in Tegucigalpa organized "by students, professionals, and the wives of prominent liberal dissidents" in May 1944. But unlike the dictators Martínez in El Salvador and Ubico in Guatemala, Carías transferred "power in an orderly manner to his chosen successor."[9] Under US pressures, Carías decided not to seek reelection and appointed Juan Manuel Gálvez Durón as the National Party candidate in the 1948 presidential elections. Gálvez became president of Honduras the following year.[10] Thus the departure of Carías enabled the continuity of authoritarianism in Honduras.

Costa Rica became the only demilitarized democracy and welfare state in Central America in the postwar. In other words, Costa Rica became the only Central American country able to guarantee basic social services (i.e., healthcare, education, and social security) to its citizens. The government of President Rafael Angel Calderón Guardia (1940–1944) and his successor Teodoro Picado Michalski (1944–1948) conducted major socioeconomic reforms with the support of Vanguardia Popular, a political party formed by Costa Rican communists, and trade unions, effectively transforming Costa Rica into a welfare state. Vanguardia Popular supported Calderón's and Picado's reforms, particularly the creation of the Caja Costarricense de Seguridad Social (a social security program) and a new labor code.[11] A potent reaction to Calderón's and Picado's reformism emerged between 1946 and 1948. Otilio Ulate Blanco, a conservative leader, challenged the reelection of President Calderón in the 1948 presidential election while José Figueres Ferrer, a charismatic liberal leader, formed a progressive but staunchly anticommunist party. Both Ulate and Figueres were deeply suspicious of the growing influence of communists in Costa Rican politics. Fear of communism apparently enabled Ulate's victory in the 1948 election. However, the Costa Rican Congress declared Ulate's election null due to alleged irregularities in the electoral process. In response to the Congress's decision, Figueres led an armed insurgency against the Picado government, a conflict known as the "1948 Costa Rican Revolution." During the brief but bloody conflict, which "claimed 2,000 lives," Figueres's forces prevailed over the Costa Rican army. This event led to the abolition of the army and the banning of the communist party in Costa Rica.[12]

Flouting the postwar wave of democratization, the dictator Anastasio Somoza García remained firmly in control of Nicaragua. Somoza rose to power in 1936 after he ordered the assassination of General Augusto César Sandino, a liberal leader who led a protracted resistance against the US Marines' occupation of Nicaragua. The US-supported Somoza dynasty ruled Nicaragua during four decades. Only in July 1979, a popular insurrection led by the Sandinista National Liberation Front (FSLN), a left-wing nationalist insurgency, ousted Anastasio Somoza Debayle, the last heir of the Somoza clan. The Sandinista Revolution had major reverberations in the 1980s Cold War in Central America.

The transformative post-World War II period in Central America featured the mobilization of labor movements, students, left and liberal intellectuals, and military officers who sought an end to authoritarianism. The postwar civic-military movements advocated comprehensive notions of democracy that included political and labor rights, free elections, and modernization. The Arbenz government constituted the pinnacle of the postwar wave of democratization in Central America. The failed attempts of democratization in the postwar shaped in fundamental ways societies, economies, and politics in Central America over the next three decades. The persistence of autocracy in Nicaragua and oligarchic-military rule in El Salvador and Honduras, the illegal ousting of Arbenz, and the subsequent restoration of military dictatorship in Guatemala further polarized Central American societies and politics and sparked the formation of powerful revolutionary movements in the 1960s and 1970s.

THE DEMOCRATIC REVOLUTION AND THE CIA COUP IN GUATEMALA (1951–1954)

President Jacobo Arbenz's program sought capitalist modernization, democratization, and the defense of national sovereignty. Arbenz declared his intention to transform Guatemala from a semifeudal agrarian society dominated by an oligarchy into a modern capitalist country with a diverse agricultural and industrial economy that benefited socially excluded Guatemalans. The Arbenz government welcomed foreign investors that respected the country's laws, including tax laws, and labor rights.[13] The Arbenz government was particularly keen on the defense of national sovereignty vis-à-vis the overwhelming influence that the United Fruit Company wielded over the country's economy and politics. The company owned 550,000 acres on the country's Pacific and Atlantic coasts and public infrastructure such as "railroads, telephone and electrical systems."[14]

An unparalleled democratic-revolutionary movement made up of Ladino (non-Indigenous) and Maya workers and intellectuals brought Arbenz to power. A coalition that comprised several revolutionary parties, including the recently formed Partido Guatemalteco del Trabajo (PGT, the communist party), and "the country's two labor confederations," the General Confederation of Workers of Guatemala (CGTG) and the National Peasant Confederation of Guatemala (CNCG), backed Arbenz.[15] The story of the cohort of communist intellectuals who formed Arbenz's kitchen cabinet, in particular, the close political relation between José Manuel Fortuny, the PGT's secretary general, and President Arbenz, is well known. PGT intellectuals drafted Arbenz's agrarian reform program.[16] Maya leaders also played important roles in the democratic revolution in Guatemala. Alfredo Cucul became an important figure in the agrarian reform program in Alta Verapaz. Efraín Reyes Maaz, a former United Fruit Company dockworker, joined the PGT and fought counterrevolutionary forces in Puerto Barrios in 1954. In the 1960s Reyes Maaz articulated a political discourse that drew on Maya cosmovision and Marxism to conduct clandestine activism in Alta Verapaz.[17] Cucul and Reyes Maaz incarnated a democratic ethos that challenged oligarchic structures through their daily engagements with "hierarchical, private, and steadfastly obdurate relations of domination and control" in rural Guatemala.[18]

Arbenz conducted an agrarian reform program unprecedented in Central America.[19] The Agrarian Reform Law (decree 900) sanctioned by the Guatemalan Congress on June 17, 1952, sought to eliminate semifeudal agrarian structures (i.e., semifeudal forms of property, production, and labor) and to create a capitalist agrarian economy to set the basis for the industrialization of Guatemala. In other words, the agrarian reform transferred large unproductive estates (latifundia) to landless peasant communities in an effort to modernize Guatemala's agrarian society and economy. The program featured proper forms of compensation for former owners and method of payment for beneficiaries alike. The declared tax value of the expropriated estates determined their estimated value.[20]

The agrarian reform program created a national structure that operated in parallel to local state structures (e.g., municipal governments), which were usually dominated by local landowners. The agrarian reform altered traditional power relations in the countryside and generated a virulent rural counterrevolution led by wealthy landowners.[21] Agrarian reform also expropriated unproductive tracts of land owned by the United Fruit Company at the Tiquisate and Bananera plantations. In accordance with the Agrarian Reform Law, the Guatemalan government compensated the United Fruit Company for the expropriated land with a payment based on the declared tax value of the properties. The company complained that the market value of the expropriated land tracts was in fact twenty times higher than its declared tax value. The State Department swiftly endorsed the United Fruit Company's position in this controversy.[22]

Despite the radical opposition to agrarian reform organized by landowners, the United Fruit Company, and the Catholic Church hierarchy, the program was largely successful. Between January and June 1954, the government expropriated 1,002 estates and 100,000 families received land in this period. Nearly a half million people out of a total population of three and half million benefited from the agrarian reform. The government also gave rural communities technical assistance, credit, and training to foment agricultural productivity.[23]

The CIA operation that forced Arbenz to resign as president of Guatemala on June 27, 1954, has been carefully studied. The CIA operation (PBSUCCESS) sought to generate an overwhelming psychological impact on President Arbenz and military officers loyal to his government through the mobilization of a ragtag mercenary army led by the Guatemalan Colonel Carlos Castillo Armas, sabotage, propaganda, and the "the implicit threat" of a US military intervention in Guatemala.[24] Castillo Armas ruled Guatemala as the president of a US-backed military junta from September 1, 1954, until July 26, 1957, when he was killed by a "palace guard."[25] A fierce repression against Arbenz supporters followed Arbenz's resignation.[26] Latin American intellectuals and activists who joined the democratic revolution in Guatemala entered the embassies of Argentina, Mexico, and El Salvador to escape the witchhunt conducted by counterrevolutionary forces at that time.[27]

US Cold War anticommunism and imperial hubris and not "economic imperialism" (i.e., the defense of the United Fruit Company's interests in Guatemala) constituted the fundamental impetus behind the CIA coup.[28] In the midst of McCarthyism and the increasing tensions between the United States, China, and the Soviet Union, the Eisenhower Administration feared the regional impact of a defiant President Arbenz. Arbenz openly challenged US power in Latin America, a region the United States considered its crucial sphere of influence (i.e., the proverbial "US backyard") during the Cold War. The growing influence of communist intellectuals in the Arbenz government and Guatemalan society and a potential communist infiltration of the Guatemalan army constituted major US concerns. Arbenz's agrarian reform was successful, popular support for the PGT was growing, and civil and political freedoms were being respected in Guatemala. This situation became "intolerable" for the United States.[29] The trajectory of the democratically elected President Arbenz and his PGT advisors contradicted the notion that communists were intrinsically anti-democratic. In Guatemala at least, communist intellectuals shaped in crucial ways the democratic and modernizing impetus of the fated "Guatemalan Spring."[30]

Anti-imperial sentiments against the United States grew significantly in Latin America in the aftermath of the 1954 CIA coup in Guatemala. In several Latin American capitals large crowds gathered to condemn the coup. Diego Rivera, the famed Mexican artist, produced a fresco that portrayed US and Guatemalan protagonists of the coup as henchmen of the Guatemalan people. The illegal and violent ousting of President Arbenz radicalized an emerging generation of militants who conducted armed struggle in subsequent revolutionary mobilizations in Cuba and Central America.[31] Famously, Ernesto "Che" Guevara, an Argentinean medical doctor who witnessed the fall of

Arbenz as a refugee at the Argentinean embassy in Guatemala City, and Fidel Castro, the leader of the Cuban Revolution, vowed that the experience of the CIA coup in Guatemala would not be repeated in Cuba.

THE GLOBAL SIXTIES AND THE RISE OF THE NEW LEFT IN CENTRAL AMERICA

The multiple political, ideological, and cultural impacts that the Cuban Revolution and progressive Catholicism had in Central American societies in the 1960s influenced revolutionary and counterrevolutionary politics in the next two decades. To new cohorts of left intellectuals (i.e., university students and faculty and working-class leaders) that emerged at that time, the Cuban Revolution proved that armed struggle was a feasible strategy to defeat authoritarian regimes and that socialism was indeed possible in Latin America. Authoritarian governments in Central America feared the reverberations of the Cuban Revolution among intellectuals, students, and workers and swiftly joined US efforts to isolate the Cuban Revolution in the Americas. The Alliance for Progress, a reformist program formulated by the Kennedy Administration, sought to demonstrate the superiority of capitalist modernization over Cuban socialism and the potent counterinsurgent apparatuses created in this period to coerce intellectuals and social movements sympathetic to the Cuban Revolution. The Alliance for Progress failed to produce economic modernization and social reforms in Central America in part due to the intransigence of the landed oligarchies. The most notable remnants of President Kennedy's carrot-and-stick policy at the end of the decade were the massive state security sectors that pitilessly repressed intellectuals, activists, and progressive Catholics in El Salvador, Guatemala, and Nicaragua. The failure of US-sponsored modernization in the 1960s heralded a revolutionary time in Central America.[32]

The transformation of the Catholic Church from a conservative institution allied with authoritarian regimes into a progressive institution that sided with the poor and the oppressed posed a major challenge to Central American elites. The Second Vatican Council (1962–1965), a major event in the Church's history that redefined the roles that Catholics played in modern societies, constituted a watershed in the trajectory of Catholicism in Central America. Key council documents like Gaudium et Spes unambiguously declared that the Church had the foremost responsibility to side with "the poor and the afflicted."[33] Progressive Catholicism formulated a critique of liberal capitalism, challenged "traditional Catholic anti-Marxist attitudes," and validated the use of violence as means of self-defense against tyranny.[34] University and high school students affiliated with Catholic organizations and influenced by the Church's reform played crucial roles in the formation of revolutionary movements in El Salvador, Nicaragua, and Guatemala in the 1970s. Rural and urban Catholic communities also became major actors of revolutionary politics in this period. The convergence between radicalized urban intellectuals and peasant communities in the context of pedagogical initiatives and institutions sponsored by the Catholic Church constituted a major feature of popular politics in El Salvador, Nicaragua, Honduras, and Guatemala.[35]

The first wave of revolution in Central America originated in Guatemala. On November 13, 1960, a military uprising against President Miguel Ydígoras took place at Fort Matamoros in the outskirts of Guatemala City.[36] Almost a third of the Guatemalan army supported the uprising against Ydígoras. The rebel military rejected Ydígoras's corruption and his decision to allow the use of Guatemalan territory to train anti-Castro Cubans in preparation for the Bay of Pigs invasion.[37] The military uprising against Ydígoras was quickly defeated "with the help of CIA B-26 bombers piloted by anti-Castro Cubans" but some rebel military officers relocated to the countryside and conducted guerrilla warfare in the aftermath of this episode.[38] With the tacit support from the PGT, which had adopted a resolution that supported "all forms of struggle" in 1960, Luis Augusto Turcios Lima and Marco Antonio Yon Sosa, two young military officers who participated in the uprising at Fort Matamoros, created the Revolutionary Movement of November 13 (MR-13) in 1961, the first guerrilla movement founded in Guatemala.[39] In late 1962, leaders of the PGT, members of the party's youth section, the Juventud Patriótica del Trabajo (JPT), and rebel military officers founded the Fuerzas Armadas Rebeldes (FAR, initially the armed wing of the PGT).[40] Turcios Lima became the FAR's main leader. These groups operated in El Petén in non-Indigenous areas. Guerrillas of the first wave of revolution in Guatemala were mostly young Ladino (non-Indigenous) males and few women with middle-class backgrounds. Most guerrillas were students, university intellectuals, professionals, and military officers. The participation of combatants of peasant and Indigenous backgrounds in the first guerrilla organizations in Guatemala was insignificant.[41]

The Cuban revolutionary experience heavily influenced the cohort of radicalized students who created the FSLN, a revolutionary movement that fought the Somoza dictatorship in Nicaragua. Carlos Fonseca Amador and other founders of the FSLN lived in Cuba in the early 1960s and witnessed the initial facets of the Cuban Revolution. The empowerment and mobilization of workers and peasants, the formation of the revolutionary state, the fight against counterrevolutionary groups, and the Cuban Missile crisis (1962) crucially informed the politics and ideology of Sandinista leaders.[42] Fonseca Amador bluntly asserted that left intellectuals in Nicaragua only started talking about socialism in the aftermath of the 1959 Cuban Revolution.[43]

In El Salvador a new generation of left intellectuals also emerged in the aftermath of the Cuban Revolution. The Salvadoran new left "blended multiple and often conflicting intellectual and political traditions."[44] Progressive Catholic thought, dependency theory, "a neo-Marxist interpretation of underdevelopment" formulated by Latin American sociologists and economists, the Cuban Revolution, and revolutionary traditions from Latin America, China, and Vietnam influenced this cohort.[45] Students, Catholic intellectuals, teachers, poets, and communist and Christian Democrat dissidents were key figures of the Salvadoran new left. These intellectuals formed several guerrilla groups between 1969 and 1975. They constituted a different cohort from "militants, academics, politicians, and working-class intellectuals associated with the Communist Party of El Salvador (PCS) founded in 1930."[46] While the PCS (i.e., the old left) embraced electoral politics until 1979, new left intellectuals waged war on the oligarchic-military regime from 1970 onward. The political and ideological antagonism between new and old left intellectuals constituted a fundamental feature of revolutionary politics in El Salvador in the 1970s and throughout the country's civil war.

Revolutionary politics in Nicaragua and Guatemala also featured a sharp antagonism between old and new left intellectuals. Carlos Fonseca Amador, the leader of the FSLN, was critical of the Socialist Party of Nicaragua (PSN, the communist party) on a number of strategic and programmatic issues, including the PSN's views on working-class internationalism, pacifism, and subordination to the Soviet Union.[47] In Guatemala, older PGT leaders and young members of the FAR (the armed wing of the PGT in the early 1960s) clashed over the party's recurrent interest in electoral politics despite its formal support for armed revolution.[48]

The Catholic Church reform had multiple reverberations in Central American societies and politics, particularly in El Salvador, Nicaragua, and Guatemala. In El Salvador, members of the student organization Salvadoran Catholic University Action (ACUS) became founders of the first guerrilla groups in the early 1970s. The Popular Liberation Forces—(FPL Farabundo Martí)—a guerrilla organization founded by former ACUS activists, university students, and dissidents of the PCS, invoked the Christian doctrine of the just war to emphasize the legitimacy of revolutionary violence to fight "the oligarchic-military regime and to create a humane and just society."[49] ACUS activists also played crucial roles as popular educators working in pedagogical initiatives sponsored by the Catholic Church among rural and urban communities.[50]

Liberation Theology, a school of Catholic theology that emerged in Latin America in the late 1960s, crucially influenced Catholic communities and intellectuals who played fundamental roles in revolutionary politics in Central America. Liberation Theology sought to interpret the "Christian faith" from the perspective of the poor. It constituted a radical critique of capitalist societies and ideologies.[51] Liberation Theology had important reverberations among bishops, priests, nuns, congregations, and laypeople in Nicaragua, El Salvador, and Guatemala. In Nicaragua, Liberation Theology influenced urban and rural communities, middle- and upper-class intellectuals, and students who joined or supported the Sandinista movement. Priests influenced by Liberation Theology founded Ecclesial Base Communities in neighborhoods that became Sandinista strongholds in Managua.[52] Ernesto Cardenal, a priest and poet, who later joined the FSLN, established a Christian community in the island of Solentiname in Lake Nicaragua in 1966. Members of the Solentiname community gathered to study and interpret biblical texts that informed their revolutionary activism.[53] Members of religious orders also played major roles in the history of Liberation Theology and Sandinismo in Nicaragua.[54]

In conclusion, a convergence between radicalized Catholic students, priests, and Marxist intellectuals took place in Nicaragua and El Salvador. Catholic students who became Sandinista leaders were part of Catholic communities or attended Catholic high schools and universities influenced by Liberation Theology. Ernesto Cardenal and Marxist Sandinista leaders conducted political and intellectual dialogues that led to the integration of Cardenal into the FSLN.[55] In El Salvador a convergence between Catholic and Marxist intellectuals took place at the University of El Salvador.[56] Catholic students also played a major role in the formation of a student movement at the University of El Salvador that became the "cradle of the Salvadoran guerrillas" in the late 1960s.[57] In contrast with anticlerical tendencies in the Russian, Mexican, and Cuban revolutions, Marxist revolutionaries in Nicaragua and El Salvador actively sought to establish strategic alliances with Catholic communities. The transclass urban-rural convergence between radicalized Catholic intellectuals, communities, and social movements became a crucial feature of revolutionary politics in Nicaragua and El Salvador. Catholic intellectuals turned into revolutionaries incarnated a Catholic anti-capitalist ethos that influenced social and revolutionary movements in El Salvador, Nicaragua, and to a lesser extent Guatemala.[58]

The Second Wave of Revolution and the Sandinista Paradigm (1970–1989)

The massive participation of peasant and Indigenous communities in revolutionary politics, the formation of alliances between peasant organizations and urban social movements, and the emergence of powerful guerrilla movements, which were deeply rooted in peasant and urban social movements, were major features of the second wave of revolution in Central America. From the early 1970s onward powerful peasant and Indigenous movements formed coalitions with student, teacher, and worker movements in Guatemala and El Salvador. Elites in both countries responded to these unprecedented urban-rural mobilizations with unabated state terror. In Guatemala a "new generation of social movements (labor, peasant, Indigenous, community)" demanded socioeconomic and democratic rights for socially excluded Indigenous and Ladino communities. Since 60 percent of the population in Guatemala is Indigenous the intersection between "ethnic identity and democratic rights" for Indigenous communities was paramount in that country. Guatemalan elites and the state responded to the social mobilizations in the 1970s with a level of repression often "unmatched anywhere in Latin America."[59] Between 1978 and 1985 death squads and military forces killed between 50,000 and 75,000 people in Guatemala.[60] In El Salvador, poverty and landlessness fueled the political mobilization of peasant communities that preceded the country's civil war.[61] The potent peasant organizations formed in the 1970s articulated the socioeconomic demands of landless rural workers and small landholders who worked at large coffee, cotton, and sugar plantations. These peasant organizations formed alliances with urban social movements made up of high school and university students, teachers, workers, and dwellers of marginalized communities in San Salvador.

These transclass urban-rural alliances posed a formidable challenge to oligarchic-military authoritarianism in El Salvador. Fiercely anticommunist and paternalistic economic elites considered any labor unrest as subversion and relied on the military and public security forces to repress labor or political mobilizations.[62] In the 1970s, state forces perpetrated summary executions and urban and rural massacres to contain the growing social mobilizations. Between 1978 and 1983 state forces killed 42,171 persons or "close to 1 percent of the population."[63] However, heightened repression proved counterproductive. State terror radicalized the massive social movements in the midst of a major political crisis in the late 1970s. Social activists massively joined or supported guerrilla movements, transforming the small insurgencies created at the beginning of that decade into formidable political and military forces.

Guerrilla movements were also major actors of revolutionary politics in the 1970s. In Guatemala, militants who survived the extermination of guerrilla groups in the 1960s formed a new generation of guerrilla organizations that achieved a much greater development than their predecessors in the previous decade. In the mid-1970s, four guerrilla groups existed in Guatemala: FAR, PGT, the Guerrilla Army of the Poor (EGP), and the Revolutionary Organization of the People in Arms (ORPA). "Peasants, rural and urban workers, artisans and students, and middle-class professionals" made up these organizations. The leaders of FAR, EGP, and ORPA were men of middle-class backgrounds. Artisans and middle-class professionals led the PGT.[64] The Guatemalan guerrillas in the 1980s had a national presence, particularly among Maya communities, and "competed furiously" to influence trade unions in Guatemala City. However, trade unions remained autonomous and did not submit to the leadership of the guerrillas.[65]

Guerrilla groups also emerged in El Salvador in the 1970s. Founders of these groups were university students, communist and Christian Democrat dissidents, Catholic intellectuals, teachers, and poets. Four guerrilla groups operated in El Salvador in the mid-1970s: the Popular Liberation Forces (FPL Farabundo Martí), the People's Revolutionary Army (ERP), the National Resistance (RN), and the Revolutionary Party of Central American Workers (PRTC). These guerrilla groups developed strong ties with the massive peasant and urban social movements formed in the 1970s. The FPL and the ERP combined constituted the backbone of the Salvadoran insurgency prior to and during the country's civil war.

On July 19, 1979, a popular insurrection led by the FSLN overthrew the US-sponsored dictator Anastasio Somoza Debayle in Nicaragua. The Sandinista Revolution had a major impact on Continental politics. The ousting of Somoza showed the weakness of US-abetted authoritarianism in Central America. The Carter Administration (1977–1981) articulated an ambiguous policy toward Somoza and grossly underestimated the popular support and political acumen of the FSLN. The Carter Administration initially struggled to sustain Somoza in power. Once the fall of Somoza was imminent, the Carter Administration attempted to preserve the basis of the old regime in Nicaragua (i.e., *Somocismo sin Somoza*). Ironically, on the eve of the Sandinista victory, the Carter Administration demanded moderation of the FSLN after the United States had sustained a brutal dictatorship in Nicaragua for nearly four decades.[66] This demand rang hollow since the Sandinistas had already formed a broad-based coalition with sectors of the Nicaraguan elites that opposed Somoza and solid international relations with social democratic governments and parties in Europe and Latin America.

The Sandinista Revolution became a revolutionary paradigm in Central America. Since the Sandinistas' political pragmatism, namely, their ability to form internal and international alliances and to outmaneuver Somoza, seemed to adequately fit the domestic and international conditions that revolutionary movements faced in Central America, guerrilla groups in Guatemala and El Salvador deemed the Sandinista experience archetypal.[67] More to the point, in the early 1980s, insurgencies in El Salvador and Guatemala emulated to a certain extent the revolutionary politics of the Terceristas, the hegemonic faction of the FSLN. The Terceristas became the dominant faction of the FSLN through a combination of political pragmatism, insurrectionary tactics, and a foreign policy that privileged relations with social democratic parties and governments in Europe and Latin America.[68] The Terceristas decisively shaped the Sandinistas' revolutionary model. Such model featured the unification of revolutionary factions, broad-based alliances with opposition parties and business sectors, a democratic-revolutionary program, and relations with social democratic parties and governments. In short, the Sandinista revolutionary model was apparently pluralistic, democratic, and inclusive. Following the Sandinista example, the factious guerrilla movements that operated in Guatemala and El Salvador created insurgent coalitions to unify the political and military commands of the revolutionary movements in both countries. Guerrilla organizations created the Farabundo Martí National Liberation Front (FMLN) in El Salvador and the Guatemalan National Revolutionary Unity (URNG) in Guatemala. Both movements replicated aspects of the Sandinista revolutionary model. However, both the FMLN and the URNG were autonomous revolutionary movements with their own particular histories, political and ideological identities, and strategies. Neither the FMLN nor the URNG was a subordinate actor of the FSLN or Cuba for that matter. Instead, these guerrilla movements fought revolutionary wars that mobilized vast social sectors in both countries. They were firmly rooted in the history of empire, dictatorship, and revolution in Central America.

The URNG was virtually defeated between 1982 and 1983 as a result of the military offensive and the mass killings conducted by the Guatemalan army against Maya communities in rural areas of the country. In contrast, the FMLN resisted the massive military offensives and scorched earth operations conducted by the Salvadoran military against peasant communities between 1981 and 1983. The FMLN became a remarkable political and military force, which effectively contested the state's sovereignty during El Salvador's twelve-year civil war.

The Sandinista Revolution had multiple reverberations in the political crisis in El Salvador. Oligarchic and military elites feared imminent revolution and demanded that President Carlos H. Romero (1977–1979) escalate repression against the potent social movements that emerged during that decade. The overthrow of Somoza in Nicaragua elevated the fighting morale of the revolutionary left and also motivated a group of young military officers to oust President Romero in October 1979 in a last-ditch effort to avert revolution in El Salvador.[69] In part as a result of their interactions with Sandinista leaders, FMLN leaders seriously considered political negotiations with the Salvadoran government as a key component of their revolutionary strategy since the early 1980s. They also became keenly interested in developing relations with the Socialist International, the international organization formed by social democratic parties from Europe, Latin America, and other regions. The exchanges between Salvadoran guerrilla commanders and social democratic leaders became a source of contention between pragmatic and orthodox insurgent leaders in the early 1980s.[70] As a result of these interactions, the development of the war on the ground, and the movement's political and diplomatic activism, FMLN leaders relinquished Marxism-Leninism as the movement's ideology and embraced socialist democratic politics during that decade. These political and ideological transformations also informed the FMLN's pragmatism during the peace negotiations with the Salvadoran government that ended the conflict.

President Ronald Reagan (1981–1989) deemed the Sandinista Revolution and the Salvadoran insurgency part of a Soviet and Cuban aggression in Central America. Throughout the 1980s Reagan implemented a "rollback policy" in Central America, which mainly consisted of an effort to defeat the Sandinista government and the FMLN insurgency in El Salvador. The Contra War in Nicaragua and US military, political, and diplomatic efforts to defeat the FMLN were key components of this policy.

The Contra War (1981–1989) was an armed conflict between counterrevolutionary forces sponsored by the United States and the Sandinista government. Former Somocista commanders based in Honduras and Miami led the Fuerza Democrática Nicaraguense (FDN), the main counterrevolutionary army. In the early 1980s, "the Contras" as the FDN and other counterrevolutionary groups were collectively known, became a major military force that operated in "a range of 34,000 square kilometers of Nicaragua's interior" and disrupted "agricultural production, road traffic, and services to the population."[71] The Contras mobilized disaffected peasant and Indigenous communities in Nicaragua. Some authors argue that the Contra War was fundamentally a domestic rebellion led by peasants from the Nicaraguan highlands.[72] In fact, peasants, including former Sandinista combatants, from northern Nicaragua formed the Milicias Populares Anti-Sandinistas (MILPAS), a regional counterrevolutionary force that eventually joined the FDN. Peasants from Quilalí, a municipality in the Nueva Segovia department of Nicaragua, who joined the Contras, rejected the Sandinista revolutionary ideology and considered the Sandinistas "outsiders responsible for deepening the militarization" in the region.[73] However, the Contras were first and foremost a military force created and funded by the United States with the goal of defeating the Sandinista government. The Contras were a crucial tool of US foreign policy in Central America. To the point that the Reagan Administration embarked in the notorious "Iran-Contra Scandal" (1985–1986), a clandestine operation that featured the sale of weapons to Iran to illegally fund the Contras.[74] By 1983 the Contra army had grown from several hundred men to nearly 8,500 troops operating in northern Nicaragua. Heightened Contra military activity forced the Sandinista government to sanction a military draft known as the Patriotic Military Service (SMP). This military draft required Nicaraguan males between the ages of seventeen and twenty-four to serve two years in the Popular Sandinista Army (EPS). As a result of the Contra War, the EPS became the largest military force in Central America. The Sandinista Army was able to mobilize 60,000 troops "at any given time" in an effort to combat and "eventually contain" the Contra army.[75] Contra forces constantly attacked civilian targets and the Sandinista army in Nicaragua.[76]

The Central American conflicts engulfed the entire region and produced a veritable social catastrophe. Seventy-five thousand Salvadorans lost their lives as a result of El Salvador's civil war.[77] Nearly one million Salvadorans were forcibly displaced during the civil war and settled in Honduras, Nicaragua, Costa Rica, Belize, Mexico, the United States, and elsewhere.[78] The UN-sponsored El Salvador's Truth Commission Report issued in 1993, attributed 95 percent of the human rights violations committed during the conflict, including massacres, summary executions, kidnappings, torture, sexual violence, and the forced disappearance of civilians, to members of the armed forces, security forces, paramilitaries, and death squads. It attributed 5 percent of human rights violations committed during the civil war to FMLN insurgents.[79] According to Guatemala's Comisión para el Esclarecimiento Histórico (CEH—the UN administered Guatemala's Truth Commission) report issued in 1999, during the conflict that confronted the state and the left-wing guerrillas, the military perpetrated 626 massacres that included "multiple acts of ferocity that preceded, matched or followed the death of the victims."[80] The CEH attributed 93 percent of the human rights violations committed during the conflict, including nearly 200,000 political murders to the military. The Commission held the guerrillas responsible for 3 percent of the human rights violations, including thirty-two massacres.[81] According to the CEH, in the context of "counterinsurgent operations carried out in the years 1981 and 1983," the Guatemalan army conducted "acts of genocide" against Maya communities in Guatemala.[82] The magnitude of the social and psychosocial damage produced by the conflicts in Guatemala, El Salvador, and Nicaragua among several generations of Central Americans remains to be fully understood.

The Political Settlement of the Central American Conflicts (1987–1996)

The political settlements of the conflicts in Nicaragua, El Salvador, and Guatemala were the result of sustained efforts conducted by domestic and international actors who advocated negotiated political solutions to the conflicts for more than a decade. Peace movements formed by churches, universities, and social movements emerged in Guatemala and El Salvador despite the widespread persecution against social activists in the 1980s. The Contadora Group, formed by the foreign ministers of Mexico, Venezuela, Colombia, and Panama in 1983, constituted a form of activist diplomacy that first promoted regional negotiations to end the Central American conflicts. Leaders of the Socialist International produced numerous declarations and conducted public and private initiatives in favor of political settlements in Nicaragua, El Salvador, and Guatemala.[83] Potent solidarity movements formed by religious leaders, students, workers, intellectuals, celebrities, artists, and citizens of different backgrounds in the United States, Europe, and Latin America also posed a considerable political and ethical challenge to President Reagan's militaristic policy in Central America throughout the 1980s. These solidarity movements pressured their respective governments to seek a political solution to the Central American crisis.

In this context, Costa Rican President Oscar Arias formulated a regional peace initiative in 1987 known as Esquipulas II, which became a template to conduct a regional political settlement of the Central American conflicts. The Nicaraguan government supported a negotiated settlement to the Contra War under the terms of Esquipulas II, which called for the unconditional demobilization of irregular armies like the Contras and left-wing guerrillas like the FMLN. Under the pressure of the US war against Nicaragua (i.e., "The Contra War"), which produced massive casualties among the Nicaraguan youth and tremendous damage to the country's economy, and the Soviet Union's decision to halt military aid to the Nicaraguan government, the Nicaraguan President Daniel Ortega negotiated an end to the Contra War that included the demobilization of the Contra forces in exchange for unrestricted elections in Nicaragua and the end of Sandinista support to the insurgent FMLN. Under these circumstances, the FMLN conducted an unprecedented military offensive in November 1989 in San Salvador, San Miguel, Santa Ana, Usulután, San Vicente, and other major cities and towns in an effort to open serious negotiations with the Salvadoran government.[84] The 1989 FMLN offensive shook the Salvadoran regime to its core. In retrospect, the FMLN offensive opened the door to the creation of a liberal democracy in El Salvador. The guerrilla offensive ultimately enabled the UN-mediated peace negotiations between the government of President Alfredo F. Cristiani (1989–1994) and the FMLN that ended the conflict in 1992 and set the basis for the only sustained democratic period in the country's history. In the aftermath of the 1989 guerrilla offensive, the FMLN leadership asked the UN Secretary General Javier Pérez de Cuellar to mediate a negotiated settlement of the Salvadoran conflict. President Cristiani accepted the UN mediation but tried to limit Pérez de Cuellar's role in the negotiation. Pérez de Cuellar drew on UN Security Council Resolution 637 issued in July 1989, which mandated the UN Secretary General to assume an active role in the Central American peace process, to serve as mediator in the Salvadoran conflict.[85] Thus the Salvadoran peace process unfolded under the terms of the UN Secretary General's mediation and not Esquipulas II. The FMLN rejected what it considered a bogus symmetry between the Contras and the FMLN implicit in Esquipulas II's 1989 San Isidro Coronado Declaration, which called for the unconditional demobilization of both the Contras, an irregular army created by the CIA, and the FMLN, a political-military movement deeply rooted in Salvadoran history, politics, and society. This false symmetry ignored the fundamentally different origins, legitimacy, and demands of those forces. During a meeting held in Malta in December 1989,

President George H. W. Bush (1989–1993) and the Soviet leader Mikhail Gorbachev (1985–1991) agreed to support a political settlement to the Central American conflicts and Pérez de Cuellar's mediation in El Salvador's peace negotiations. Ambassador Thomas Pickering, the US permanent representative to the UN also expressed support for UN mediation in the Salvadoran peace negotiations, omitting any reference to the parallelism between the Contras and the FMLN stated in Esquipulas II's San Isidro Coronado Declaration. FMLN negotiators deemed Pickering's statement key to the success of the peace talks with Cristiani.[86]

The domestic negotiation with broad international support that terminated the Salvadoran conflict influenced conflict resolution models in various regional settings over the next two decades. El Salvador's peace process was a crucial facet of the political transitions that took place in Latin America after the collapse of the Soviet Union and the East bloc.[87] The Salvadoran peace process also informed subsequent UN-mediated negotiations and peacekeeping missions in Guatemala, Haiti, Georgia, Western Sahara, and East Timor.[88]

The 1991 presidential election in Nicaragua brought to power President Violeta Chamorro, a conservative leader, and allowed the gradual and problematic demobilization of Contra and Sandinista forces and the transformation of the FSLN into an opposition party. The pacification of Nicaragua faced major domestic and international obstacles. Thousands of Contra fighters and nearly one thousand EPS veterans engaged in banditry in the postwar. On May 30, 1990, Antonio Lacayo, President Chamorro's minister of the presidency, signed "the Managua Protocol" with Contra commanders, which promised land and credit to nearly 18,000 Contra fighters. But still in 1993 Contra fighters and to a lesser extent EPS veterans engaged in banditry. President Chamorro, the head of a sector of the Nicaraguan elites known as "Las Palmas group," made an unofficial political agreement with FSLN leaders to ensure a democratic transition and the pacification of Nicaragua. The "concertación," as the accord between the Chamorro government and the Sandinista leaders was known, was vigorously rejected by rightwing extremists in Chamorro's own coalition, the Unión Nacional Opositora (UNO), the ultraconservative US Senator Jesse Helms, an ardent supporter of the Contras, and sectors of the FSLN who considered the deal between the Sandinista commanders and Las Palmas group a deviation of revolutionary politics. But despite the turbulent transition from war to peace that took place in Nicaragua in the early 1990s, the Chamorro government was able to demobilize some 100,000 soldiers effectively putting an end to the Contra War.[89]

The peace negotiations that put an end to the Guatemalan conflict in 1996 replicated to a certain extent the conflict resolution model in El Salvador, but it also featured other important components such as specific accords on Indigenous and women rights. El Salvador's Truth Commission report offered an ahistorical explanation on the origins of the civil war in El Salvador.[90] In contrast, Guatemala's CEH (i.e., Guatemala's Truth Commission) produced a comprehensive and historically grounded report on the atrocities overwhelmingly committed by state forces during the conflict. It traced the origins of the conflict to "the structure and the nature of the economic, cultural, and social relations in Guatemala" rooted in colonial history and the formation of an "authoritarian state" that excluded the majority of the population (i.e., Indigenous communities), which incarnated a racist ideology and practice "to protect the interests of privileged sectors." The Guatemalan army's perception of Maya communities as "natural allies of the guerrillas" contributed to "increase and aggravate human rights violations committed against Maya peoples." The Guatemalan army's conduct toward Maya communities evidenced "an aggressive racist [ideological] component" characterized by "extreme cruelty" that led to "the massive extermination" of "defenseless Maya communities," including "children, women, and elderly people using methods whose cruelty generates horror in the moral consciousness" of the international community.[91] In El Salvador the peace negotiations generated the demilitarization of state and society and a substantial political reform largely due to the FMLN's military might and political pragmatism. In contrast, the peace negotiation in Guatemala produced modest political and socioeconomic reforms due to the relative weakness of the URNG at the end of war. The FMLN mutated into a legally established political party that played a major role in the transition to democracy and ruled El Salvador during an entire decade (2009–2019). On February 3, 2019, Nayib Bukele, a young businessman, was elected president of El Salvador. The FMLN lost more than one million votes in that presidential election. Commentators attributed this result to both failures in the political party FMLN and the FMLN governments of President Mauricio Funes (2009–2014) and President Salvador Sánchez Cerén (2014–2019).[92] In sharp contrast, the URNG became a minor political force in postwar Guatemala. These dramatically different outcomes might be attributed to the insurgent FMLN's capacity to develop a massive social base despite the devastating impacts of US-sponsored counterinsurgency in El Salvador, its military power, broad international alliances, and political acumen. In contrast, the "acts of genocide" committed by the Guatemalan military against Maya communities in the context of counterinsurgent campaigns it carried out in 1981 and 1983 and the state terror inflicted on vast sectors of Guatemalan society during the civil war, devastated Guatemalan social movements, the country's intellectual community, and the URNG, and consequently diminished their capacity to transform politics and society in postwar Guatemala. State terror clearly undermined social and political forces and intellectuals who advocated comprehensive notions of social democracy in Guatemala.[93]

Overall, the peace negotiations that ended the conflicts in Nicaragua, El Salvador, and Guatemala produced neoliberal democracies, formal and fragile democracies that matched an economic restructuring promoted by multilateral financial institutions, which heightened social exclusion, poverty, social violence, crime, and environmental degradation in the region. The economic restructuring conducted in the late 1980s and the 1990s featured the deregulation of capital flows, reduction of tariffs, privatization of state assets, reprivatization of nationalized banks, massive layoffs, and cutback of social services. Discourses on economic liberalization articulated by domestic and international elites and institutions such as the Foundation for Social and Economic Development (FUSADES), a think tank funded by USAID, based in San Salvador, fomented "a consensus for the development of neoliberal social and economic policies" that matched US counterinsurgency during the civil war and heavily influenced postwar society and politics in El Salvador. President Cristiani fully implemented FUSADES's economic liberalization blueprint. Cristiani reprivatized the banking system, privatized state assets, and drastically reduced public spending on social services, especially healthcare and education.[94] Historically, the peace processes in El Salvador, Nicaragua, and Guatemala, constituted political reforms in line with the neoliberal restructuring in Central America. Neoliberal democracies enabled various degrees of pluralism and civil and political freedoms in those countries but were unable to adequately deal with the social devastation generated by the state terror, the politically motivated violence, and the armed conflicts that transpired in the Cold War period.

CONCLUSION

Interpretations on the roles that the United States played in the Cold War in Latin America are polemical. Hal Brands made the case that multiple international dynamics shaped Cold War conflicts in Latin America. Brands also deemphasized the role that the United States played in those conflicts. Brands maintained that "U.S. military aid certainly *enabled* state terror in various countries, but to hone in too narrowly on this variable as the *source* of such terror is to risk ignoring the importance of local circumstances [cursives in the original]."[95] Greg Grandin, on the other hand, argued that US-abetted state terror restricted the meaning of democracy and ushered neoliberalism in Latin America.[96] In his examination of the history of peace processes in Central America, James Dunkerley reasoned that Central American politics "cannot be properly understood as a simple reflection of U.S. power." Neither is it possible to correctly comprehend regional politics without a careful examination of "Washington policies, however secretly these may be formulated and however clumsy their implementation."[97] In Central America, the history of empire, authoritarianism, and social revolution in the Cold War constituted a closely interrelated process. Throughout the Cold War the United States consistently supported authoritarian regimes and forces in the name of anticommunism, security, stability, and democracy. This paradoxical policy undermined civic-military movements that advocated social democracy in the post-World War II period, particularly the Arbenz government in Guatemala. The tenacity of US-backed authoritarian regimes and the failure of subsequent attempts to conduct democratic reforms through electoral politics and political mobilizations, led to persistent insurgent and counterinsurgent politics in Nicaragua, El Salvador, and Guatemala in the 1960s, 1970s, and 1980s. The Central American conflicts in the 1980s constituted the apex of a revolutionary era that started with the democratic revolution in Guatemala and continued with the first wave of revolution. The era ended with the demilitarization of state and society (i.e., the dismantling of the US-sponsored counterinsurgent state) and a comprehensive democratic reform in El Salvador, the electoral defeat of the FSLN, the end of the Contra War, and the cooptation of the Sandinista Revolution in Nicaragua, and a modest democratic reform in Guatemala. The Reagan Administration was ultimately unable to achieve a clear-cut political and military victory over the Sandinistas or to annihilate the FMLN. At the end of the Cold War, the Bush Administration modified Reagan's initial goals in Central America and supported negotiated settlements to the conflicts in El Salvador and Nicaragua. The transitions from war to peace, the dismantling of long-standing oligarchic-military authoritarianism, and the emergence of neoliberal democracies matched the twilight of social revolution in Central America. The URNG became a minor political actor in postwar Guatemala. The political party FMLN (1992–present) relinquished the revolutionary ethos, critical thinking, and ideological pluralism that characterized the historical FMLN (1980–1992). Instead, leaders of the political party FMLN became a new political and economic elite that rejected ideological pluralism and fomented a dogmatic political culture and unconditional adherence to the centralized authority of the party leadership. They distanced themselves from the movement's historical social base and even expelled FMLN veterans from party politics. Along with the right-wing party the Alianza Republicana Nacionalista (ARENA), the FMLN formed a bipartisan political system that constituted the core of neoliberal democracy in El Salvador. The FSLN's alliance with sectors of the Nicaraguan elites (i.e., "la concertación") in the early 1990s clearly modified the Sandinistas' revolutionary politics. As a derivative of the concertación, Chamorro's minister of the presidency Lacayo and the Sandinista generals Humberto Ortega and Joaquín Cuadra signed a "Transition Protocol" on March 1990 that preserved the institutional integrity and leadership of the EPS. In exchange for these and other major concessions, the FSLN refrained from encouraging social mobilizations against the Chamorro government.[98] These negotiations between Sandinista leaders and traditional Nicaraguan elites anticipated the rise of a new political and economic elite in Nicaragua. In short, the end of the Cold War and the peace processes in El Salvador and Nicaragua marked the end of a revolutionary era in Central America.

ACKNOWLEDGMENTS

A sabbatical granted by the Department of History at the University of Illinois at Chicago (UIC) and a Research Fellowship for Experienced Researchers granted by the Alexander Von Humboldt Foundation (Germany) allowed me to complete this article. Many thanks to Chris Boyer, chair of the Department of History at UIC, Stefan Rinke and Debora Gerstenberger from the Latinamerika-Institut at the Freie Universität Berlin, Eduardo Rey Tristán from the University of Santiago de Compostela, and Dirk Kruijt from the University of Utrecht for their contributions to my research.

NOTES

1. Greg Grandin, *The Last Colonial Massacre: Latin America in the Cold War* (Chicago: University of Chicago Press, 2011), 9.

2. Leslie Bethell and Ian Roxborough, "The Impact of the Cold War on Latin America," in *The Origins of the Cold War: An International History*, edited by Melvyn Leffer and David Painter, 299–316 (New York: Routledge, 1992).

3. Roberto García Ferreira, "La revolución guatemalteca y el legado del Presidente Arbenz," *Anuario de Estudios Centroamericanos, Universidad de Costa Rica* 38 (2012): 41–78, esp. 43.

4. Piero Gleijeses, *Shattered Hope: The Guatemalan Revolution and the United States, 1944–1954* (Princeton, NJ: Princeton University Press, 1991), 41–45.

5. Gleijeses, *Shattered Hope*, 54; García Ferreira, "La revolución guatemalteca," 46.

6. Gleijeses, *Shattered Hope*, 28–29, and 83.

7. Grandin, *Last Colonial Massacre*, 5.

8. James A. Morris, *Honduras: Caudillo Politics and Military Rulers* (Boulder, CO: Westview Press, 1984), 9.

9. Dario Euraque, *Reinterpreting the Banana Republic: Region and State in Honduras, 1870-1972* (Chapel Hill: University of North Carolina Press, 1996), 68–69.

10. Morris, *Honduras*, 9–10.

11. Silvia Elena Molina Vargas, "Los Asesinatos del Codo del Diablo (1948-1951)," in *El verdadero anticomunismo: Política, género y Guerra Fría en Costa Rica (1948-1973)*, edited by Iván Molina Jiménez and David Díaz Arias, 5 (San José Costa Rica: Editorial Universidad Estatal a Distancia, 2017).

12. Thomas L. Pearcy, *The History of Central America* (Westport, CT: Greenwood Press, 2006), 126–127.

13. García Ferreira, "La revolución guatemalteca," 61.

14. Stephen G. Rabe, *The Killing Zone: The United States Wages Cold War in Latin America* (Oxford and New York: Oxford University Press, 2012), 38.

15. Gleijeses, *Shattered Hope*, 172.

16. Gleijeses, *Shattered Hope*, 182; Rabe, *Killing Zone*, 38; and Garcia Ferreira, "La revolución guatemalteca," 65.

17. Grandin, *Last Colonial Massacre*, 56–57, 105, 124–125.

18. Grandin, *Last Colonial Massacre*, 16.

19. García Ferreira, "La revolución guatemalteca," 66–67; Grandin, *Last Colonial Massacre*, 54; and Gleijeses, *Shattered Hope*, 150.

20. Gleijeses, *Shattered Hope*, 151.

21. Grandin, *Last Colonial Massacre*, 55; and García Ferreira, "La revolución guatemalteca," 67.

22. Gleijes, *Shattered Hope*, 164, 165; and García Ferreira, "La revolución guatemalteca," 68.

23. García Ferreira, "La revolución guatemalteca," 68.

24. Nick Cullather, *Secret History: The CIA's Classified Account of Its Operation in Guatemala 1952-1954* (Stanford, CA: Stanford University Press, 1999), 74, 101.

25. Rabe, *Killing Zone*, 50.

26. Cullather, *Secret History*, 106–110; Grandin, *Last Colonial Massacre*, 66–67.

27. Tula Alvarenga, interview by Joaquín M. Chávez (February 3, 2014).

28. Garcia Ferreira, "La revolución guatemalteca," 69; Gleijeses, *Shattered Hope*, 361–362.

29. Gleijeses, *Shattered Hope*, 365, 366.

30. Grandin, *Last Colonial Massacre*, 52.

31. Cullather, *Secret History*, 112–113.

32. LaFeber made this case for El Salvador. Walter LaFeber, *Inevitable Revolutions: The United States in Central America* (2nd ed.) (New York and London: W.W. Norton, 1993), 178.

THE COLD WAR   355

33. "Constitucion pastoral sobre la Iglesia en el mundo actual: Gaudium et Spes," in *Documentos Completos del Vaticano II* (4th ed.) (Bilbao: Mensajero, 1966), 125.
34. Joaquín M. Chávez, *Poets and Prophets of the Resistance: Intellectuals and the Origins of El Salvador's Civil War* (New York: Oxford University Press, 2017), 50.
35. Carlos R. Cabarrús, *Génesis de una revolución: Análisis del surgimiento y desarrollo de la organización campesina en El Salvador* (Mexico D.F.: Ediciones de la Casa Chata, 1983); Chávez, *Poets and Prophets*; Debra Sabia, *Contradiction and Conflict: The Popular Church in Nicaragua* (Tuscaloosa: University of Alabama Press, 1997); Anna L. Peterson, *Martyrdom and the Politics of Religion: Progressive Catholicism in El Salvador's Civil War* (Albany: State University of New York Press, 1996); Michael Löwy, *The War of Gods: Religion and Politics in Latin America* (London: Verso, 1996); and Juan Ramón Vega, *Las comunidades cristianas de base en América Central: Estudio sociológico* (San Salvador: Publicaciones del Arzobispado de San Salvador, 1994).
36. Sheldon B. Liss, *Radical Thought in Central America* (Boulder, CO: Westview Press, 1991), 32–33.
37. Grandin, *Last Colonial Massacre*, 91; Deborah Levenson-Estrada, *Trade Unionists against Terror: Guatemala City, 1954-1985* (Chapel Hill: University of North Carolina Press, 1994), 42.
38. Grandin, *Last Colonial Massacre*, 91; and Levenson-Estrada, *Trade Unionists against Terror*, 43.
39. Levenson-Estrada, *Trade Unionists against Terror*, 43.
40. Grandin, *Last Colonial Massacre*, 92.
41. Timothy P. Wickham-Crowley, *Guerrillas and Revolution in Latin America: A Comparative Study of Insurgents and Regimes since 1956* (Princeton, NJ: Princeton University Press, 1992), 19, 20, Table 2-1, 22, 23, 24, 25, Table 2-2, 27, 29.
42. Matilde Zimmermann, *Sandinista: Carlos Fonseca and the Nicaraguan Revolution* (Durham, NC: Duke University Press, 2001), 7.
43. Zimmerman, *Sandinista*, 67.
44. Chávez, *Poets and Prophets*, 6.
45. Chávez, *Poets and Prophets*, 7.
46. Chávez, *Poets and Prophets*, 6.
47. Zimmerman, *Sandinista*, 66.
48. Grandin, *Last Colonial Massacre*, 92–93.
49. Chávez, *Poets and Prophets*, 68–69.
50. Chávez, *Poets and Prophets*, 49–71.
51. Phillip Berryman, *Liberation Theology* (New York: Pantheon Books, 1986), 6.
52. Sabia, *Contradiction and Conflict*, 8.
53. Ernesto Cardenal, *The Gospel in Solentiname* (New York: Orbis Books, 2010).
54. Sabia, *Contradiction and Conflict*, 38–39.
55. Sabia, *Contradiction and Conflict*, 47, 59.
56. Chávez, *Poets and Prophets*, 59–60.
57. Chávez, *Poets and Prophets*, 63.
58. Berryman, *Liberation Theology*, 81; Löwy, *War of Gods*, 4–31.
59. Susanne Jones, *Of Centaurs and Doves: Guatemala's Peace Process* (Boulder, CO: Westview Press, 2000), 20.
60. William Stanley, *The Protection Racket State: Elite Politics, Military Extortion, and Civil War in El Salvador* (Philadelphia: Temple University Press, 1996), 3.
61. Elisabeth Jean Wood, *Insurgent Collective Action and Civil War in El Salvador* (Cambridge, UK: Cambridge University Press, 2003), 23–24.

62. Stanley, *Protection Racket State*, quoted in Wood, *Insurgent Collective Action*, 24.
63. Stanley, *Protection Racket State*, 3.
64. Levenson-Estrada, *Trade Unionists against Terror*, 132.
65. Levenson-Estrada, *Trade Unionists against Terror*, 135, 147.
66. James Dunkerley, *The Long War: Dictatorship and Revolution in El Salvador* (London: Verso, 1985), 120.
67. Dunkerley, *Long War*, 119.
68. Dunkerley, *Long War*, 122–123.
69. Adolfo A. Majano, *Una oportunidad perdida: 15 de Octubre 1979* (San Salvador: Índole Editores, 2009), 44–46.
70. Ana Guadalupe Martínez, interview by Joaquín M. Chávez (June 2, 2017).
71. Lynn Horton, *Peasant in Arms: War and Peace in the Mountains of Nicaragua, 1979–1994* (Athens: Ohio University for International Studies, 1998), 173.
72. Timothy C. Brown, *The Real Contra War: Highlander Peasant Resistance in Nicaragua* (Norman: University of Oklahoma Press, 2001), 199–203.
73. Horton, *Peasant in Arms*, 171.
74. James Dunkerley, *The Pacification of Central America* (London: Verso, 1994), 26–28.
75. Horton, *Peasant in Arms*, 172, 174.
76. Horton, *Peasant in Arms*; Orlando Nuñez, ed., *La guerra y el campesinado en Nicaragua* (2nd ed.) (Managua: Centro para la promoción, investigación y desarrollo rural y social, 1995); Brown, *Real Contra War*; and Salvador Martí I Puig, *The Origins of the Peasant-Contra Rebellion in Nicaragua, 1979-1987* (London: University of London, Institute of Latin American Studies, 2001).
77. Elisabeth Jean Wood, *Insurgent Collective Action and Civil War in El Salvador* (Cambridge, UK: Cambridge University Press, 2003), 8.
78. James Dunkerley, *The Pacification of Central America* (London: Verso, 1994), 47.
79. *De la locura a la esperanza la guerra de 12 años en El Salvador: Informe de la Comisión de la Verdad* (San Salvador and New York: Naciones Unidas, 1993), 41.
80. Comisión para el esclarecimiento histórico, *Guatemala memoria del silencio* (Guatemala: Oficina para el servicio de proyectos de las Naciones Unidas, 1999), 35.
81. *Guatemala memoria del silencio*, 34, 43; Greg Grandin, "The Instruction of Great Catastrophe: Truth Commissions, National History, and State Formation in Argentina, Chile, and Guatemala," *American Historical Review* 110, no. 1 (2005): 46–67, esp. 58.
82. *Guatemala memoria del silencio*, 42.
83. "Socialist International Communiqué on El Salvador (March 1981)," in *The Central American Crisis Reader*, edited by Robert S. Leiken and Barry Rubin, 395–400 (New York: Summit Books, 1987).
84. Martínez interview.
85. Joaquín M. Chávez, "How Did the Civil War in El Salvador End?," *American Historical Review* 120, no. 5 (2015): 1784–1797, esp. 1790.
86. Chávez, "How Did El Salvador Civil War End?," 1791.
87. Roberto Regalado, ed., *Insurgencias, Dialogos y Negociaciones: Centroamerica, Chiapas y Colombia* (Mexico: Ocean Sur, 2013).
88. Teresa Whitfield, *Friends Indeed? The United Nations, Group of Friends, and the Resolution of Conflict* (Washington, DC: United States Institute of Peace, 2007); and Riordan Roett and Frank Smyth, *Dialogue and Armed Conflict: Negotiating the Civil War in El Salvador* (Washington, DC: Foreign Policy Institute School of Advanced International Studies, Johns Hopkins University, 1988).

89. Dunkerley, *Pacification of Central America*, 57–60.
90. *De la locura a la esperanza la guerra de 12 años en El Salvador*, 1–7.
91. *Guatemala memoria del silencio*, 17, 35.
92. Ralph Sprenkels, "The FMLN's Electoral Implosion: A Fiasco Foretold," *PoLar, Political and Legal Anthropology Review, Journal of the Association for Political and Legal Anthropology* (April 15, 2019). https://polarjournal.org/2019/04/15/the-fmlns-electoral-implosion-in-el-salvador-a-fiasco-foretold/ Accessed on June 9, 2019; Alvaro Rivera Larios, "La Elite Nepotista," Contrapunto, June 6, 2019. http://www.contrapunto.com.sv/opinion/debatehoy/la-elite-nepotista/10045 accessed on June 9, 2019.
93. Grandin, *Last Colonial Massacre*, 196–197.
94. Ellen Moodie, *El Salvador in the Aftermath of Peace: Crime, Uncertainty, and the Transition to Democracy* (Philadelphia: University of Pennsylvania Press, 2010), 41–45.
95. Hal Brands, *Latin America's Cold War* (Cambridge, MA: Harvard University Press, 2010), 259.
96. Grandin, *Last Colonial Massacre*, 14.
97. Dunkerley, *Pacification of Central America*, 26.
98. Dunkerley, *Pacification of Central America*, 59–63.

FURTHER READING

Cardenal, Ernesto. *The Gospel in Solentiname*. New York: Orbis Books, 2010.

Chávez, Joaquín M. *Poets and Prophets of the Resistance: Intellectuals and the Origins of El Salvador's Civil War*. New York: Oxford University Press, 2017.

Dunkerley, James. *The Pacification of Central America*. London: Verso, 1994.

Euraque, Dario. *Reinterpreting the Banana Republic: Region and State in Honduras, 1870–1972*. Chapel Hill: University of North Carolina Press, 1996.

García Ferreira, Roberto. "La revolución guatemalteca y el legado del Presidente Arbenz," *Anuario de Estudios Centroamericanos, Universidad de Costa Rica 38* (2012): 41–78.

Gleijeses, Piero. *Shattered Hope: The Guatemalan Revolution and the United States, 1944–1954*. Princeton, NJ: Princeton University Press, 1991.

Grandin, Greg. *The Last Colonial Massacre: Latin America in the Cold War*. Chicago: University of Chicago Press, 2011.

Jones, Susanne. *Of Centaurs and Doves: Guatemala's Peace Process*. Boulder, CO: Westview Press, 2000.

Lowy, Michael. *The War of Gods: Religion and Politics in Latin America*. London: Verso, 1996.

Molina Jiménez, Iván, and David Díaz Arias, eds. *El verdadero anticomunismo: Política, género y Guerra Fría en Costa Rica (1948–1973)*. San José Costa Rica: Editorial Universidad Estatal a Distancia, 2017.

Peterson, Anna L. *Martyrdom and the Politics of Religion: Progressive Catholicism in El Salvador's Civil War*. Albany: State University of New York Press, 1996.

Rabe, Stephen G. *The Killing Zone: The United States Wages Cold War in Latin America*. New York: Oxford University Press, 2012.

Sprenkels, Ralph. *After Insurgency: Revolution and Electoral Politics in El Salvador*. South Bend, IN: Notre Dame University Press, 2018.

Wickham-Crowley, Timothy P. *Guerrillas and Revolution in Latin America: A Comparative Study of Insurgents and Regimes since 1956*. Princeton, NJ: Princeton University Press, 1992.

Zimmermann, Matilde. *Sandinista: Carlos Fonseca and the Nicaraguan Revolution*. Durham, NC: Duke University Press, 2001.

CHAPTER 13

··

CENTRAL AMERICA SINCE THE 1990S: CRIME, VIOLENCE, AND THE PURSUIT OF DEMOCRACY

··

CHRISTINE J. WADE

DURING the 1970s and 1980s much of the Central American isthmus was engulfed by conflict. The protracted civil wars in El Salvador, Guatemala, and Nicaragua and the military repression in Honduras were fueled by grievances at home and by the US Cold War agenda. More than 300,000 Central Americans were killed in the violence. A regional peace process led by Costa Rica and the end of the Cold War brought renewed prospects for peace as adversaries sought negotiated ends to the conflicts. The 1990s were a profound period for the region, from war to peace, from dictatorship to democracy. The end of civil wars in El Salvador and Guatemala, counterinsurgency in Nicaragua, and the transition to civilian control of the military in Honduras meant that Central America was, belatedly, joining Samuel Huntington's so-called third wave of democracy.[1]

Since the late 1990s, however, political violence has given way to social and economic violence. By the mid-2000s Central America had the highest homicide rates in the world, a distinction it continued to hold in 2019. While such increases in levels of social and economic crime are not uncommon in post-conflict societies, the crime wave in northern Central America has been particularly pronounced in terms of its duration and lethality. In some cases, the annual homicide rates in postwar Central American countries are higher than they were during the wars themselves. Even Costa Rica, which was largely immune to political violence during the 1980s, has experienced rising crime rates over the past two decades. This crime wave posed significant challenges to new democracies in the region, which frequently employed repressive policies to reduce violence and insecurity and revealed the fragility of state institutions.

This chapter begins with an overview of the dimensions of violence in the region, which are more complex and varied than headlines suggest. I then explore explanations for violence related to criminal activity with a focus on illicit networks and the state, followed by a discussion of anti-crime policies. Finally, I provide a brief overview of the effects of violence on citizen attitudes toward democratic norms and institutions.

DIMENSIONS OF VIOLENCE IN CENTRAL AMERICA

Central America has one of the highest rates of violence in the world. Most of that violence is concentrated in El Salvador, Guatemala, and Honduras, where transnational gangs, drug traffickers, and organized crime syndicates have taken advantage of weak institutions and porous borders. While countries in the region suffer from a range of violence and insecurity, including petty crime, assault, trafficking in illicit goods, sexual violence, and extortion, the most extreme manifestation of violence is homicide.

The regional experiences with violence and insecurity since the 1990s have not been uniform. As seen in Figure 13.1, homicide rates have been highest in El Salvador and Honduras and lowest in Costa Rica and Nicaragua. While El Salvador, Guatemala, and Honduras have experienced protracted homicide epidemics, homicides in Nicaragua, which now has the lowest rate in the region, have declined. However, Costa Rica's homicide rate has marginally increased in recent years, evidence of growing criminal networks in the country. While certainly lower than its neighbors' to the north, Costa Rica's homicide rate is higher than the rate in many South American states. Even the

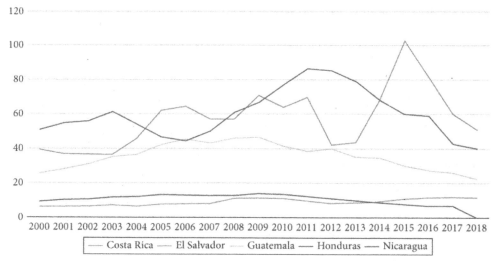

FIGURE 13.1. Central American homicide rates per 100,000 by country, 2000–2018. Courtesy of UNODC Homicide Statistics 2013 and official police sources from each country (https://www.unodc.org/gsh/en/data.html).

homicide rates in El Salvador, Guatemala, and Honduras have fluctuated over the years, declining in most recent years. And, of course, levels of violence and insecurity are not evenly distributed throughout any country. Much of the violence is concentrated in urban areas, though the countryside is not immune.

A 2014 study by the United Nations Office on Drugs and Crime (UNODC) classifies homicides according to those stemming from (a) other criminal activities, including gang violence and organized crime; (b) interpersonal conflict, including interpartner or familial violence; and (c) sociopolitical issues, including hate crimes related to identity issues, terror, extrajudicial killings by police, mob violence/vigilantism, and the killings of journalists and aid workers.[2] I would also argue that the murder of land and environmental activists should be included in this category, particularly in the Americas.

Homicides related to criminal activity are the main drivers of violence in El Salvador, Guatemala, and Honduras. In general, most of this violence can be attributed to two sources: transnational street gangs (*maras*) and drug trafficking organizations. Transnational gangs that originated in the United States took root in Central America in the 1990s. Formed in Los Angeles in the 1980s predominately by Salvadorans but also other Central Americans who had fled political violence in the isthmus, Mara Salvatrucha (MS-13) and the Eighteenth Street Gang have dominated the Central American gang scene since the mid- to late 1990s when deportations from the United States increased. Between 2000 and 2004, some twenty thousand Central Americans with criminal records were deported to their countries of origin.[3] Once back in their home countries, gang deportees were able to capitalize on conditions that draw youth to gangs: lack of educational opportunities and employment, abuse and neglect at home, societal marginalization, and familial disintegration.[4] Indeed, for many youth, gangs provided structure and security. According to the UNODC, there were as many as seventy thousand gang members in El Salvador, Guatemala, and Honduras.[5] Continuing migration and strong gang networks in the United States also aided the expansion and evolution of the *maras* over time. Gang members engage in numerous criminal activities, including extortion, kidnapping, drug trafficking, prostitution, murder, and possibly human trafficking.[6]

Central America's location between the producers and consumers of illegal drugs has made it a prime transshipment location. It's estimated that 90 percent of the cocaine from Colombia is trafficked through Central America and Mexico before reaching the United States.[7] According to the UNODC, homicide levels in Central America are largely the result of competition over drug-trafficking routes or turf wars between groups. While organized crime groups and gangs are just as present in other regions, they produce less violence because "violence is often linked to competition between involved parties, such as organized criminal groups, or between them and the State, with regard to control over territory or illicit activities, including trafficking."[8] This issue is explored in greater detail in Understanding Postwar Violence below.

Interpersonal and sociopolitical violence are often overlooked by policymakers and scholars. Doing so, however, obscures the scope and severity of violence in the region. Because few homicides are ever fully investigated, it is difficult to know how many are the result of interpersonal grievances as opposed to criminal activity, or how much overlap may exist between the two.[9] While most homicides in El Salvador, Guatemala, and Honduras appear to be related to criminal activities, in Costa Rica, 47 percent of homicides were related to interpersonal violence.[10]

Gender-based violence is a significant problem in all Central American countries, but particularly in El Salvador, Guatemala, and Honduras where femicide rates have been unusually high. In 2017, the femicide rate was 10.2/100,000 in El Salvador and 5.1/100,000 in Honduras, by far the highest in the hemisphere.[11] Nearly twelve hundred women were murdered in Guatemala from January 2002 to June 2004; many had been raped or tortured.[12] The highly publicized murders increased pressure on the region to address femicide, or the murder of a woman or girl because she is a woman. Despite laws against femicide, which define femicide as a specific crime, in Costa Rica (2007), Guatemala (2008), El Salvador (2010), Nicaragua (2012), and Honduras (2013), impunity rates for femicide remain above 95 percent in the region. The impunity rates speak to the normalization of violence against women, fed by a culture of machismo.[13] Even during El Salvador's gang truce (discussed in Anti-Crime Policies below), which dramatically reduced homicides among men, the level of femicides remained unchanged.

While the number of murders associated with sociopolitical issues has dramatically decreased since the end of the wars, politicized violence remains a serious problem. Dozens of political candidates and party supporters have been killed in Guatemalan elections. Guatemalan citizens also targeted criminals in acts of vigilante justice. Extrajudicial killings and death squads by state security forces have targeted alleged gang members in El Salvador. Between 1998 and 2002 more than fifteen hundred youths were murdered in Honduras, most of them males under the age of eighteen, killed by state and parastatal forces in what was described as "social cleansing."[14] In the aftermath of the 2009 coup in Honduras that removed elected president Manuel Zelaya from office, dozens were killed by state forces with impunity.[15] The truth commission categorized more than eighty forms of aggression by state agents, including the excessive use of force, rape, and the repression and criminalization of public protest.[16] Likewise, the Honduran state responded to protestors with repression following the 2017 elections and again in 2019. In Nicaragua, more than three hundred were killed in political violence in 2018 following anti-government protests. The Interdisciplinary Group of Independent Experts (GIEI) documented various forms of state violence, including extrajudicial killings, the disproportionate and indiscriminate use of violence against protestors and the use of parapolice, torture, sexual violence, arbitrary arrests, and denial of due process, among other offenses.[17]

The problem has been particularly acute for the region's environmental and land rights activists, who often clashed with private and criminal interests, as well as the state. More than 120 environmental activists have been killed in Honduras since 2010.[18] Nearly two hundred rights activists were killed in Guatemala between 2000 and 2016, and twenty-six Indigenous rights leaders were killed in 2018 alone.[19] In 2016 there were eleven environmental activists killed in Nicaragua, the highest per capita death rate for activists that year.[20] Although it has the highest homicide rate in the region, the killings of activists in El Salvador were relatively rare. One notable exception were the murders of five anti-mining activists in Cabanas between 2009 and 2011.

Journalists have also been targets of violence, particularly those who work on issues related to corruption and organized crime. In Honduras, more than sixty journalists have been murdered since the 2009 coup (seventy-seven since 2001). Nineteen journalists have been killed in Guatemala since 2007. The killings of journalists are rare in El Salvador (six since 2007, one of which was a case of domestic violence), Nicaragua (three since 2004, including one in 2018), and Costa Rica (only two in Costa Rica since 2001).[21]

It's difficult to know exactly how many hate crimes targeted members of the LGBTI community in Central America because governments don't track these numbers, but evidence from regional non-governmental organizations suggests high levels of targeted violence against the community. Between 2009 and 2017 there were 264 reported murders of LGBTI people in Honduras, 58 percent of whom were gay men and 32.5 percent were transpeople.[22] One study found that Honduras had the highest numbers of transgender murders per capita in the world, more than double the rate of the second highest country.[23] Using data collected by civil society groups, El Salvador's Ministry of Social Inclusion, some six hundred LGBTI persons were killed between 1993 and 2017.[24]

Thus, violence in Central America was far more complex than headlines about gangs and drug trafficking would seem to suggest. While violence related to criminal groups was the main driver of homicides in the region, interpersonal violence, particularly violence against women and girls, was widespread. And while sociopolitical violence has greatly diminished in the postwar era, the region was still home to some of the highest levels of targeted violence per capita against journalists, activists, and LGBTI persons in the world.

Understanding Violence in
Postwar Central America

Violence is not a new phenomenon in Central America. From conquest to US intervention to state-sponsored violence to revolutions and civil war, violence has shaped the region's politics and society for centuries. The region's history of violence has played an important role in creating conditions that have allowed current, chronic violence to take root.[25] While the focus of this article is specifically on those factors emerging in the aftermath of war, the context for those factors is part of a much more extensive history than readers can observe in articles on individual countries. El Salvador, Guatemala, and Honduras have all experienced prolonged crime waves that have accompanied their dual transitions to peace and democracy. These transitions, for as much as they changed the political landscape, did not resolve many underlying issues that contributed to violence, particularly those related to criminal activity and rule of law.

Epidemic violence in postwar Central America is a complex phenomenon. Although we often speak of violence in regional terms, there are unique circumstances in each country. This makes developing a uniform explanation of violence somewhat challenging, even among countries in the so-called northern triangle. For example, *maras* are much more organized and widespread in El Salvador than either in Guatemala or in Honduras. Drug-trafficking organizations, including Mexican cartels, are more present and powerful in Guatemala and Honduras than in the rest of the region. Crime by *maras* is typically more prevalent in urban areas whereas violence associated with illicit trafficking, vigilantism, and land issues are more common in rural areas. Nicaragua suffered a devastating civil war, like El Salvador and Guatemala, but experienced much lower levels of violence than other post-conflict countries in the region. In Costa Rica, generally the most peaceful country in the isthmus, recent increases in crime have challenged the country's police forces as criminal organizations have become increasingly sophisticated.[26] Thus, even the only country to enter and emerge from the 1980s as a democracy was not immune to rising insecurity.

Empirical evidence clearly demonstrates that social and economic violence are likely to increase in post-conflict societies. Explanations for this, while varying and complex, tend to focus on the vacuum left by the period between the demobilization of old police and military forces and the deployment of new forces.[27] The weakness of other institutions charged with the implementation of the rule of law, particularly the judiciary, also helps to create an environment for lawlessness. But for all the post-conflict countries in the world, northern Central American stands out for its unusual and sustained level of epidemic violence. Most post-conflict countries experience a security gap or challenges in rooting out old security networks in addition to weak institutions. In all of them, poverty, weak economies, and a surfeit of arms persist, while most confront the need to absorb returning populations. Why have northern Central America's transitions from war to peace, from dictatorship to democracy, been plagued by violence?

A few factors made northern Central America particularly vulnerable to organized crime syndicates, whether those be transnational gangs, drug traffickers, or other illicit organizations. However, two bodies of literature merit exploration here. First, transitions to democracy did not effectively eradicate illegal or clandestine groups within the security forces. Neither the peace processes in El Salvador or Guatemala nor the security reforms in Honduras during the 1990s were successful in disrupting historical patterns of violence. This is because violence, as a norm, was deeply embedded across institutions and within society as well. As Holden astutely noted, the "Central American . . . pattern of state-sponsored violence cannot be attributed to one institution but to the particular way in which violence was diffused across many kinds of social relationships and reconcentrated in particular ways within the organs of state power."[28]

Support for this argument can clearly be seen in the case of El Salvador, where there were issues with security reforms mandated by the 1992 Peace Accords between the government of El Salvador and the Farabundo Martí National Liberation Front (FMLN). One key provision of the accords was the creation of a new civilian police force, which was to be composed of vetted former police, members of the FMLN, and new recruits.

But the government continued funding old police forces at the expense of the new civilian police force. Additionally, entire divisions of the old police force, including those with ties to illicit organizations, were transferred into the new force in violation of the accords.[29] The delays also resulted in a security vacuum common in postwar countries that was accompanied by a crime wave.[30] Moreover, the demobilization of former soldiers and combatants, who received little compensation through the peace process, some with access to organized criminal networks, was cause for concern.[31] The United Nations Observer Mission in El Salvador (ONUSAL) expressed concern about organized crime and state institutions as early as 1994, as trafficking networks established during the war expanded.

El Salvador's postwar crime wave served as justification to retain most of Guatemala's former security agents, many of whom had ties to organized crime, in its new police force.[32] In many respects, Guatemala's 1996 Peace Accords were less transformative than those in El Salvador largely because significant parts of the agreement were never implemented, but also because of the failure to uncover and disrupt clandestine security networks. The links between organized crime and members of security forces resulted in the criminalization of the state through sophisticated clandestine networks.[33] The failure to demilitarize Guatemalan police enabled clandestine security groups to transform into organized criminal networks.[34] A 1998 United Nations Development Program (UNDP) study found that there were as many as six hundred gangs of organized crime comprised of twenty thousand members with the majority headed by ex-army officials.[35]

There was a similar pattern in Honduras. The Honduran government implemented a series of reforms in the 1990s to separate the police from the military and place both under civilian control. A Special Commission was created to reform the country's public security force (FUSEP), which had participated in drug trafficking and extrajudicial killings during the 1970s and 1980s, but abusive police remained within the new Honduran National Police.[36] The case of Nicaragua, which also suffered a protracted civil war, offers a striking contrast. Following the Sandinista revolution, Somoza's National Guard, which ran numerous illicit crime rings, was removed from power and a new police force was constructed. Nicaragua's new army was composed of the Sandinista forces and new recruits. Even following the loss of the Sandinista National Liberation Front (FSLN) in the 1990 elections, the police and army structures remained intact. There were issues with corruption and criminality in the early 1990s, but most of those were addressed relatively swiftly.[37] It is noteworthy that the three cases in northern Central America that suffered from post-conflict crime waves failed to dismantle or fully purge new security forces in the transitions while Nicaragua, now with the lowest levels of violence crime in the region, introduced entirely new security apparatuses following the revolution. That said, the growth of criminal networks in Costa Rica suggests that even countries with highly professionalized police forces are susceptible to illicit networks.

The second explanation regarding elevated levels of violence in the region deals with territorial competition among criminal actors in the region. Drug trafficking has also fostered corruption in the region.[38] Criminal organizations have found willing partners in public officials at all levels, undermining fragile institutions.[39] The problem has been particularly acute in Guatemala and Honduras. According to the UNODC, the dramatic increase in cocaine seizures in Mexican ports after 2006 resulted in a shift to trafficking through Central America.[40] Central America is, in many respects, geographically disadvantaged. Located between producers (South America) and consumers (United States), the isthmus became a prime transshipment location. But why did the increase in drug trafficking through the isthmus result in such high homicide rates? After all, there are illicit economies and trafficking networks that operate all over the world without such homicide rates. One answer is that new traffickers (or *transportistas*) collided with old territorial networks, which focus on control of territory and taxing activity.[41] This battle for control over territory has proved deadly for the region. This phenomenon has been most devastating for Guatemala and Honduras, which have the highest volume of cocaine trafficking in the region. Approximately 90 percent of the cocaine flow to Mexico moved through Guatemala.[42] In Costa Rica and Nicaragua, there are far fewer territorial groups and trafficking activity tends to be concentrated along the coast, which could explain their lower homicide rates.

Deborah Yashar reviews the arguments of four bodies of literature (political transitions, societal conflicts, economic grievances, and state formation) that have addressed elevated homicides in post-conflict countries.[43] While acknowledging the contributions made by these works, she argues for the need to understand how illicit economies and competition over territory for criminal activity have driven the region's homicide epidemic. Unlike the UNODC report, Yashar also includes gangs as territorial actors, which makes sense given their control over territory in the region. As gangs evolved over the past two decades, they increasingly sought to control territory for profit, namely, through extortion. Within that territory, gangs control transport routes, businesses, access to neighborhoods, and so on. As with other forms of organized crime, violence is greatest where there is competition for territory.[44] This explains varying patterns of violence within countries. Additionally, illicit economies, including gangs and drug-trafficking organizations, seek out spaces where state capacity is weak. Once rooted, these illicit economies can further weaken state capacity.

Anti-Crime Policies

Efforts to combat crime and insecurity in Central America have relied more on repression than prevention. They have also had a rather singular focus: gangs. If one were to look at any newspaper in El Salvador, Guatemala, or Honduras over the past two decades, one would easily get the impression that gangs were almost singularly responsible for the region's crime wave.

Comprised predominantly of young, poor, heavily tattooed men from urban environments, they were the menacing face of postwar violence. For the region's governments, they were the new "communist threat."[45] Anti-gang policy relied heavily on militarized policing, which was prohibited by the Salvadoran and Guatemalan Peace Accords, and the 1996 Honduran law that mandated the separation of police and military roles. Indeed, governments in the region, which had generally evidenced only modest support for demilitarization, used crime as a justification for violating the laws on the separation of military and policing. Other features of anti-gang policies have also included harsh penalties for gang members, mass arrests and incarcerations, long-term pretrial detentions, prison overcrowding, and limitations on due process. Human rights organizations have also documented extrajudicial killings associated with these policies in El Salvador and Honduras. While popular with the masses, human rights advocates and analysts have raised concerns about both the effectiveness and abuses that have accompanied these policies.

The region's anti-gang policies as we know them today originated in Honduras and were then copied by other countries in the region. Ricardo Maduro, whose own son was killed in a kidnapping, was elected president in 2001 on a zero-tolerance platform and pledge to crackdown on crime. Maduro sent ten thousand soldiers into the streets under *Operacion Guerra Contra la Delincuencia* and appointed a military official as the head of security.[46] Honduras's 2003 anti-gang law allowed police to arrest individuals for having tattoos and provided prison sentences of twelve years for gang leadership and four years for gang membership. New anti-gang laws passed in 2005 increased prison sentences for membership to twenty years and thirty years for leadership, prohibited bail for gang members, and automatically granted bail to anyone who killed a gang member in self-defense. While there was a decrease in homicides after the legislation was introduced, it was accompanied by reports of police death squads targeting youth.

El Salvador's president Francisco Flores announced a similar anti-gang plan in 2003. *Mano dura* authorized soldiers to work with the police to crack down on crime. The plan also included harsh penalties for merely being a member of a gang (or even appearing to be a gang member), which was grounds for arrest and punishable with a prison sentence of two to five years, and proposed to treat children as young as twelve as adults. As many as three thousand alleged gang members were arrested in the first three months of the plan, although most were released. Numerous judges also opposed the plan claiming it was unconstitutional to arrest someone for *being* a gang member, not committing an actual crime. Between July 2003 and August 2004, approximately twenty thousand gang members were arrested. Flores's successor Antonio Saca also campaigned heavily on gang violence in the 2004 elections. Shortly after assuming office, Saca proposed a heightened version of *mano dura*, known as *Supra Mano Dura*, which continued to rely on mass arrests and the deployment of military patrols.

While proposed anti-gang legislation was never enacted in Guatemala, President Oscar Berger also sent soldiers into the streets with police to combat crime in 2004 in *Plan Escoba* ("Clean Sweep"), his anti-gang offensive. In 2005, Guatemala's homicide rate was 42/100,000—the third highest murder rate in the world.[47] Following the killings of two dozen bus drivers by gangs in early 2006, Berger ordered some eleven thousand soldiers into the streets. Unlike in El Salvador and Honduras, Guatemalan public officials acknowledged that gangs weren't the only source of violence in the country, claiming that corruption within police and security forces was a serious problem and that criminal networks threatened to overrun the state. Vice President Eduardo Stein claimed that criminal networks controlled six of Guatemala's twenty-two departments.[48]

Perhaps unsurprisingly, *mano dura* policies were unsuccessful in reducing gang violence in the region. In many ways, they were a continuation of policies targeting political "subversives" in the 1980s.[49] By 2019, little had changed in security policy. Governments in El Salvador and Honduras continued to rely heavily on militarized policing and anti-gang laws even when presidents who campaigned for more preventative policies came to power. In Honduras, Manuel (Mel) Zelaya left the anti-gang law intact as did the Funes and Sánchez Cerén administrations in El Salvador. In fact, some of El Salvador's toughest anti-gang policies, including the expansion of the country's 2006 anti-terror law to gang members, occurred during the Sánchez Cerén administration. State security forces in El Salvador were linked to extrajudicial killings during his tenure.[50]

One brief exception to the *mano dura* policies occurred under the Funes administration in El Salvador. During the early years of his administration, Funes continued policies of prior administrations. He increased military deployments into high-crime neighborhoods and passed additional anti-gang penalties in 2010. He also appointed former generals David Munguía Payés and Francisco Salinas, respectively, as Minister of Justice and Public Security and as director of the National Civilian Police. Critics argued their appointments violated the 1992 Peace Accords, which separated the military from the civilian police. In March 2012 leaders of the MS-13 and Eighteenth Street gangs announced a truce in which gang leaders ordered a moratorium on killings in exchange for improvements in various prison conditions. There was also the promise of reintegration and vocational training, and the establishment of violence-free municipalities throughout the country. The truce was negotiated Bishop Fabio Colindres and former FMLN guerrilla and legislator Raul Mijango, though it was later revealed that security minister David Munguía Payés was the intellectual author of the truce and that it had been endorsed by Funes.[51]

Figure 13.1 shows that the truce resulted in a dramatic decline in homicides in 2012 and 2013, but it was not to last. In 2013, the Constitutional Chamber of the Supreme Court ruled Munguía Payés's and police director Francisco Salinas's appointments unconstitutional because they violated the law against military serving in civilian security positions. The truce, which had little political support, collapsed shortly thereafter due to Payés's removal. The truce was politically unpopular; nearly 90 percent of Salvadorans opposed negotiating with gangs and most believed, despite clear evidence to the contrary, that it had not reduced crime.[52] After the truce collapsed, the government aimed to prevent future negotiations with gangs. In 2016 the legislature passed new anti-gang measures, which prohibited negotiating with gangs and classified gangs as terrorists. Soon after, Attorney General Douglas Meléndez began prosecuting public officials and civilians who facilitated the truce.

Mark Ungar finds that most security policy has been ineffective and counterproductive due to the relationships between networks of security providers, policymakers (presidents, legislatures, foreign donors, political parties), the criminal justice sector (prosecutors, judges, penitentiary, community policing), and non-state networks (private security, vigilantes, rural militias, death squads).[53] This means that the state has selectively targeted some forms of violence while protecting others. In particular, the state doesn't address the underlying nature of criminality in the state. Indeed, the persistence of elevated violent crime in the region is deeply connected to rampant impunity and pervasive corruption. If state security agencies, members of the judiciary, and elected officials are known to be involved in illicit networks, merely jailing gang members and disrupting their extortion rings would only solve part of the region's violence epidemic.

While there have been some attempts to purge so-called bad apples from state security agencies, many efforts have been superficial at best. Honduras is a particularly compelling case in point. Between 2012 and 2016 there were three separate attempts to purge the Honduran police, yet widespread corruption and death squads persisted. In fact, in 2012, the police chief selected to be in charge of the purge was himself accused for forced disappearances and extrajudicial killings.[54] In 2016 it was revealed that there were hit squads operating within the Honduran police who were tasked with assassinating law enforcement officials.[55] Targets included the anti-drug chief and the former head of the anti-narcotics commission, who had accused the police of being infiltrated by criminal elements. In response, the government created the Special Commission for the Purging and Reform of the National Police in 2016. Though some five thousand members of the Honduran National Police (of approximately thirteen thousand) were removed from their posts, only a fraction have been referred for further investigation.[56] In 2018, in the midst of the commission's work, Jose David Aguilar Moran was appointed police chief. Within days of his appointment, it was revealed that Aguilar had personally facilitated the shipment of nearly a ton of cocaine while the director of national intelligence in 2013.[57] He was still in his post in 2019.

The case of Honduras illustrates the difficulty of pursuing effective security policy when police and security forces play a vital role in sustaining the government's kleptocratic networks or, as Sarah Chayes describes it, when "corruption is the operating system."[58] To succeed, security policy must root out crime and corruption from within the government as well as addressing other root causes of violence. Of course, addressing corruption requires the same actors who benefit from it to challenge it.

In 2006, the government of Guatemala and the United Nations agreed to the creation of the International Commission against Impunity in Guatemala (CICIG). The independent body was established to target the operations of armed criminal networks in the country. Its mandate permits it to recommend policy, carry out independent investigations, and act as an adjunct prosecutorial body. CICIG also helped with the implementation of a witness protection program, established rules for wiretaps, assisted with the development of ballistics and DNA forensics capabilities creating high-risk courts for dangerous defendants, conducted investigations, and worked to support and strengthen the prosecutor's office. The results of CICIG's work were impressive. From 2006 to 2013, the homicide conviction rate improved from 7 percent to 28 percent.[59] From 2006 to 2018, CICIG dismantled sixty criminal networks and more than three hundred individuals were convicted. Homicides decreased by more than 30 percent.[60] The International Crisis Group credits CICIG with the drop in Guatemala's homicide rate, estimating that Commission's work prevented more than 4,600 homicides from 2007 to 2017.[61] In addition to pursuing cases against security officials for extrajudicial killings and targeting officials and drug traffickers involved in illicit activities, CICIG uncovered a massive customs fraud scheme (called La Linea) involving nearly two dozen public officials, including President Otto Pérez Molina and Vice President Roxana Baldetti, who are currently in prison awaiting trial.

But schemes like CICIG threaten the interests of political and economic elites, as well as their criminal partners. In 2017, the son and brother of Guatemalan president Jimmy Morales, who campaigned on an anti-corruption agenda, were arrested and charged with money laundering and fraud. Months later Guatemala's attorney general announced that she was investigating campaign contributions to Morales, and requested his immunity be lifted. Days later, Morales declared CICIG's head *persona non grata* and later announced that he would not renew CICIG's mandate which expired in September 2019. In January 2019 he attempted to expel CICIG, though the Constitutional Court rejected this maneuver. In September 2019, CICIG's mandate was not renewed and the body was shut down.

IMPACT OF VIOLENCE ON POST-CONFLICT DEMOCRACIES

Post-conflict governments in the region exist in the murky waters somewhere between authoritarianism and democracy. In these "low intensity democracies" formal democratic procedures, such as elections, coexist alongside low political participation, weak, corrupt state institutions, and the persistence of militarized public security.[62] Crime and insecurity have created a "paradox of regimes that are electoral democracies but that live under a de facto state of siege."[63] In the Freedom House report, El Salvador was the only post-conflict state in the region classified as "free." Guatemala and Honduras were rated "partly free," while Nicaragua had been downgraded from "partly free" to "not free" as a result of government repression in 2018.[64]

While there have been varying levels of success in the region's transitions to democracy, the relationship between crime and democracy is unclear. Costa Rica has maintained its democratic status despite spillover violence during the 1980s and the growth of criminal networks in the 2000s and 2010s. El Salvador, despite having some of the highest levels of violence in the region, has held regular, free, and fair elections since 1994. Nicaragua's democracy, despite being largely free of violence since the end of the war in 1990, gradually backslid toward autocracy with President Daniel Ortega's consolidation of power over political institutions in the 2010s. Honduras's transition to democracy was interrupted by the 2009 coup, which greatly contributed to the growth of illicit networks. By 2019, the country had become a veritable narco-state. As in Nicaragua, deeply flawed elections in 2017 also revealed the autocratic tendencies of the Hernandez government. Guatemala, which has held regular elections since the 1990s, has also struggled to fully democratize. Like Honduras, illicit networks became deeply entrenched in the country's political institutions.[65]

One thing that is clear is that crime and insecurity have impacted voter attitudes and preferences regarding democratic norms. Several studies have shown that violence has eroded support for democratic regimes, increased support for extralegal violence, and increased support for coups.[66] Results from multiple Latin American Public Opinion Projects (LAPOP) surveys reveal that crime and violence have also impacted support for institutions. Crime victims were less likely to express confidence in state institutions and individuals who felt insecure were less tolerant, had lower levels of interpersonal trust, and were less likely to state that democracy was the best political system.

In the 2016 LAPOP surveys, slightly less than half of Guatemalans (48.4 percent) supported democracy as the best form of government, the lowest rate of support for democracy in Central America and its lowest level since 2004. Honduras had the second lowest level of support for democracy at 51 percent. In El Salvador, support for democracy in 2016 was 54.6 percent in 2016, down significantly from 67.8 percent in 2004. For comparison, 58 percent of Nicaraguans and 71.5 percent of Costa Ricans said democracy was the best form of government in 2016. Guatemalans also expressed the highest level of support for military coups under high-crime conditions (49.4 percent) and for military coups under conditions of high corruption (47.8 percent) in Central America. Support for military coups under high-crime conditions in Honduras (35.8 percent), El Salvador (34.1 percent), and Nicaragua (26.7 percent) were significantly lower. Support for military coups under high corruption was somewhat higher in Honduras (37.3 percent) and El Salvador (35.5 percent), but slightly lower in Nicaragua (25.7 percent).[67]

High levels of crime and violence played a significant role in undermining attitudes toward human rights and rule of law. Politicians and citizens alike criticize human rights in the fight against crime, arguing that the rights of criminals often take precedent over those of victims. This is something I heard frequently from Salvadorans over the years, who often complained that *mano dura* laws weren't tough enough. In fact, there is broad support in the region for harsher criminal punishment. Eighty-five percent of Hondurans, nearly 84 percent of Guatemalans, 83 percent of Nicaraguans, and nearly 80 percent of Salvadorans support harsher punishment.[68]

While most Salvadorans still expressed support for democracy, it was evident that violent crime had eroded respect for human rights norms. In El Salvador, less than half of respondents (47.4 percent) said that police should always uphold the law.[69] In another survey, 40 percent of Salvadorans said that they approved of torture as a crime-fighting technique while 35 percent said the same of extrajudicial killings.[70] By comparison, 61.6 percent of Guatemalans and approximately 54 percent of Hondurans and Nicaraguans said that authorities should always uphold the law.[71] While the drivers of these attitudes are too complex to unpack here, Malone finds that crime victimization and fear of crime explain some of this variance.

In general, trust in the police is middling to low in the region. At least some of this is due to citizen exposure to police corruption, such as bribery, while some of it is due to ineffectiveness in fighting crime. In the 2012 LAPOP surveys, majorities in Guatemala (61.9 percent) and Honduras (63.2 percent) said the police were involved in crime while less than half (45.3 percent) said the same in El Salvador. Strikingly, only 26.6 percent of Nicaraguans said police were involved in crime.[72] When asked whether the police protected citizens against crime, only 23 percent of Guatemalans, 24 percent of Hondurans, and 33.3 percent of Salvadorans agreed. In contrast, more than half of Nicaraguans (54.7 percent) said that the police protected citizens against crime. By 2016 the number of Salvadorans saying that police protected citizens had risen to 54 percent, as trust in the police reached its highest levels (44.5 percent) since the survey began in 2004. The percentage of those who believed police were involved in criminal activity remained the same. It is noteworthy then, given Guatemalans' pessimism about the police, that CICIG has the highest levels of public trust of any institution in the country. In 2017, 70.6 percent of the population expressed some degree of trust in the institution.[73]

Fear of crime also had a significant impact on behavior, curtailing social interactions that are essential to building interpersonal trust and social capital in democracies. Nearly 66 percent of Salvadorans and 70 percent of Guatemalans report they had prevented their children from playing outside. Majorities in both countries, 60 percent in El Salvador and 56 percent in Guatemala, reported limiting their recreational hours, particularly going out at night. Nearly half of Guatemalans and over 42 percent of Salvadorans reported avoiding the use of public transportation. Moreover, 21.1 percent of Salvadorans and nearly 10 percent of Guatemalans reported they felt the need to change neighborhoods to avoid violent crime.[74] More than 516,000 internally displaced Salvadorans were forced to flee their homes and communities in 2016 and 2017.

Violence was a significant driver of external migration. Between October 2013 and September 2014, 68,541 unaccompanied minors, three-quarters of whom were from El Salvador, Honduras, and Guatemala, were apprehended at the US–Mexico border. Most of the children said they were fleeing gang violence.[75] In a 2016 survey of Central American refugees in Mexico, nearly half of those surveyed said that crime and violence were their main reasons for fleeing. Forty percent of Salvadorans and Hondurans surveyed said that they left the country following an assault, extortion, or attempt at forced recruitment. Not surprisingly, 67 percent of Salvadorans and 57 percent of Hondurans reported that they never felt safe at home.[76] In 2018 and 2019, tens of thousands of Central Americans left the region in organized caravans, resulting in a humanitarian crisis at the US–Mexico border. It was estimated that in FY 2019 more than five hundred thousand citizens of El Salvador, Guatemala, and Honduras left the region for the United States. In addition to violence, those who joined the caravans increasingly cited poverty and a combination of factors for their departures.[77]

CONCLUSION

Central America's transitions to democracy have been deeply marred by a wave of criminal violence. During the past decade, more than 150,000 Salvadorans, Guatemalans, and Hondurans have been killed in this violence. In El Salvador, more people have died in the postwar era (1992–2019) than died during the war. Criminal networks, including gangs and drug traffickers, found that weak institutions, poor rule of law, and preexisting criminal networks created a ripe environment for their businesses. Citizens in El Salvador, Guatemala, and Honduras were caught in their battle for control of territory. Violence and corruption in the region drove Central Americans to leave their homes by the tens of thousands. It also impacted their attitudes toward democracy and trust in institutions. Attempts to reduce violence were often anchored in repressive policies that relied on the re-militarization of state security, reversing reforms intended to separate police and military functions. Not only were these policies ineffective, they resulted in abuses by the state reminiscent of past violence.

But there were also stark reminders that sociopolitical violence was not, in fact, a remnant of the past. The killings of journalists and Indigenous and environmental land rights activists in the region underscored the danger in defying powerful actors. While Nicaragua had largely been spared levels of criminal violence seen in other post-conflict countries, in 2018 the Ortega regime responded to protests with state-sponsored violence that killed more than three hundred people. More than two decades after the region's transitions to democracies Central America's present increasingly resembled its past.

NOTES

1. Samuel Huntington, *The Third Wave: Democratization in the Late Twentieth Century* (Tulsa: University of Oklahoma Press, 1991).
2. United Nations Office on Drugs and Crime (UNODC), *Global Study on Homicide 2013* (UNODC: Vienna, : UNODC, 2013). https://www.unodc.org/documents/gsh/pdfs/2014_G LOBAL_HOMICIDE_BOOK_web.pdf.
3. Ana Arana, "How the Street Gangs Took Central America," *Foreign Affairs* (May/June 2005): 100.
4. Maria Santacruz-Giralt et al., *Inside the Neighborhood: Salvadoran Street Gangs' Violent Solidarity* (San Salvador, El Salvador: Pan American Health Organization/Universidad Centroamericana, 2002).
5. United Nations Office on Drugs and Crime, *Crime and Development in Central America: Caught in the Crossfire* (New York: United Nations Publications, 2007).
6. Jose Miguel Cruz, "Central American *maras*: From Youth Street Gangs to Transnational Protection Rackets," *Global Crime* 11, no. 4 (November 2010): 379–398; Arana, "Street Gangs Took Central America," 98–110; Donna DeCesare, "Deporting America's Gang Culture," *Mother Jones* (July/August 1999): 44–51.

7. DEA Intelligence Brief, "Colombian Cocaine Production Expansion Contributes to Rise in Supply in the United States," DEA-DCI-DIB-014-17, August 2017. https://ndews.umd.edu/sites/ndews.umd.edu/files/dea-colombian-cocaine-production_expansion-contributes-to-rise-in-us-supply2.pdf.

8. UNODC, *Global Study on Homicide 2013*, 42–44.

9. An intensive study of Guatemalan homicides by Steven Dudley at InSight Crime for USAID revealed problems in police data collection and classification that led to an overestimation of drug-trafficking related homicides. Moreover, Dudley was unable to attribute responsibility for over 35 percent of homicides to any one criminal group. Steven Dudley, *Homicides in Guatemala: The Challenge and Lessons of Disaggregating Gang-Related and Drug Trafficking-Related Murders* (USAID, Washington, D.C., October 2016). https://www.insightcrime.org/images/PDFs/2017/Gang-and-DTO-Homicides-in-Guatemala-Final-Report_CARSI-USAID-InSight-Crime.pdf.

10. UNODC, *Global Study on Homicide 2013*, 15.

11. United Nations Economic Commission on Latin American and the Caribbean, "Gender Equality Observatory for Latin America and the Caribbean." https://oig.cepal.org/en/indicators/femicide-or-feminicide.

12. See the United Nations Economic and Social Council, "Integration of the Human Rights of Women and the Gender Perspective: Preliminary Note on the mission to El Salvador and Guatemala," submitted by Special Rapporteur on Violence against women, Yakin Erturk, United Nations doc. No. E/CN.4/2004/66/Add.2.

13. Cecilia Menjivar and Shannon Drysdale-Walsh, "The Architecture of Femicide: The State, Inequalities, and Everyday Violence in Honduras," *Latin American Research Review* 52, no. 2 (2017): 221–240.

14. United Nations Report of the Special Rapporteur, *Civil and Political Rights, Including the Question of Disappearances and Summary Executions*, United Nations doc. no E/CN.4/2003/3/Add.2 (New York: United Nations Economic and Social Council Commission on Human Rights, 2002).

15. Comision de Verdad y la Reconciliacion, *Hallazgos y recomendaciones para que los hechos no se repitan. Informe de la Comision de la Verdad y la Reconciliacion* (Editorama: San José, Costa Rica, 2011). https://www.oas.org/es/sap/docs/DSDME/2011/CVR/Honduras%20-%20Informe%20CVR%20-%20RECOMENDACIONES.pdf.

16. Comision de Verdad y la Reconciliacion, *Hallazgos y recomendaciones*.

17. Grupo Interdisciplinario de Expertos Indepentientes, *Nicaragua: Informe sobre los hechos de violencia ocurridos entre el 18 de abril y el 30 de mayo de 2018* (February 2019). https://gieinicaragua.org/giei-content/uploads/2019/02/GIEI_INFORME_DIGITAL_07_02_2019_VF.pdf.

18. Global Witness, "Honduras: The Deadliest Country in the World for Environmental Activism" (January 2017). https://www.globalwitness.org/fr/campaigns/environmental-activists/honduras-deadliest-country-world-environmental-activism/.

19. Simon Granovsky-Larsen, "Terror in Guatemala," *NACLA*, June 21, 2018. https://nacla.org/news/2018/06/21/terror-guatemala.

20. Global Witness, *Defenders of the Earth: Global killings of land and environmental defenders in 2016*. https://www.globalwitness.org/en/campaigns/environmental-activists/defenders-earth/.

21. UNESCO Observatory of Killed Journalists. https://en.unesco.org/themes/safety-journalists/observatory/country.

22. Amnesty International, "No Safe Place: LGBTI Salvadorans, Guatemalans, and Hondurans Seeking Asylum in Mexico," November 27, 2017. https://www.amnestyusa.org/reports/no-safe-place-lgbti-salvadorans-guatemalans-and-hondurans-seeking-asylum-in-mexico/.
23. TransGender Europe, *Trans Murder Monitoring 2015* (May 8, 2015). https://tgeu.org/tmm-idahot-update-2015/.
24. Andrea Fernández Aponté, *Left in the Dark: Violence Against Women and LGBTI Persons in Honduras and El Salvador.* Latin American Working Group (March 7, 2018). https://www.lawg.org/wp-content/uploads/storage/documents/Between_Dangers_Part_8.pdf.
25. In particular, see Robert Holden, "Constructing the Limits of State Violence in Central America: Towards a New Research Agenda," *Journal of Latin American Studies* 28 no. 3 (1996): 435–459; Sebastian Huhn and Hannes Warnecke-Berger, eds., *Politics and History of Violence and Crime in Central America* (New York: Palgrave, 2017).
26. Javier Villalba, "Los Moreco, Worrying new Type of Criminal Group for Costa Rica," *InSight Crime,* May 3, 2019. https://www.insightcrime.org/news/brief/los-moreco-worrying-type-criminal-group-costa-rica/.
27. See, in particular, Charles Call and William Stanley, "Civilian Security," in *Ending Civil Wars: The Implementation of Peace Agreements,* edited by Stephen John Stedman, Donald Rothchild, and Elizabeth M. Cousens, 303–326 (Boulder, CO: Lynne Rienner, 2002); and Roy Licklider, "Obstacles to Peace Settlements," in *Turbulent Peace: The Challenges of Managing International Conflict,* edited by Chester Crocker, Fen Olser Hampson, and Pamela Aall, 704–706 (Washington, DC: United States Institute of Peace, 2003).
28. Robert Holden, "Constructing the Limits of State Violence in Central America: Towards a New Research Agenda," *Journal of Latin American Studies* 28 no. 3 (1996): 452–453.
29. Wade, *Captured Peace: Elites and Peacebuilding in El Salvador.* (Athens, OH: Ohio University Press, 2016):47–51; Héctor Silva Àvalos, *Infiltrados: Crónica de la corrupción en la PNC* (1992-2013) (San Salvador, El Salvador: UCA Editores, 2014).
30. Charles T. Call, "Democratisation, War and State-Building: Constructing the Rule of Law in El Salvador," *Journal of Latin American Studies* 35, no. 4 (November 2003): 827–862.
31. William Stanley and Robert Loosle, "El Salvador: The Civilian Police Component of Peace Operations," in *Policing the New World Disorder,* edited by Robert B. Oakley, Eliot M. Goldberg, and Michale J. Dziedzic, 117 (Washington, DC: National Defense University Press, 1998).
32. William Stanley, "Building New Police Forces in El Salvador and Guatemala: Learning and Counter-Learning," *International Peacekeeping* 6, no. 4 (1999): 113–134.
33. Susan C. Peacock and Adriana Beltrán, *Hidden Powers in Post-conflict Guatemala* (Washington, DC: Washington Office on Latin America (WOLA), 2003); Washington Office on Latin America (WOLA) Special Report, *The Captive State: Organized Crime and Human Rights in Latin America* (Washington, DC: WOLA, October 2007).
34. WOLA, *Captive State,* 8–11.
35. United Nations Development Program, *Guatemala: los contrastes del desarollo humano 1998* (Guatemala City, Guatemala: UNDP), 1998.
36. David R. Dye, *Police Reform in Honduras: The Role of the Special Purge and the Transformation Commission* (Washington, DC: The Wilson Center, June 21, 2019), 5. https://www.wilsoncenter.org/publication/police-reform-honduras-the-role-the-special-purge-and-transformation-commission
37. Jose Miguel Cruz, "Criminal Violence and Democratization in Central America: The Survival of the Violent State," *Latin American Politics and Society* 54, no. 4 (2011): 19–20.

38. UNODC, *Crime and Development*, 17–18.
39. WOLA, *Captive State*, 2.
40. United Nations Office on Drugs and Crime, *Transnational Organized Crime in Central America and the Caribbean: A Threat Assessment* (Vienna: UNODC, 2012), 18–20.
41. UNODC, *Transnational Organized Crime*, 21–30.
42. UNODC, *Transnational Organized Crime*, 39.
43. Deborah Yashar, *Homicidal Ecologies: Illicit Economies and Complicit States in Latin America* (New York: Cambridge University Press, 2018), 24–60.
44. Yashar, *Homicidal Ecologies*, 95–97.
45. Mo Hume, "Mano Dura: El Salvador Responds to Gangs," *Development in Practice* 17, no. 6 (2007): 746.
46. S. J. Ismael Moreno, "A New President and Cracks in the Two-Party Structure," *Envio* (January–February 2002): 37–43.
47. "Murder Rate in Guatemala High and Still Rising," January 24, 2006, ACAN-EFE World News Connection.
48. Patrick Gavigan, "Organized Crime, Illicit Power Structures and Guatemala's Threatened Peace Process," *International Peacekeeping* 16, no. 1 (2009): 70.
49. Mark Ungar, "La Mano Dura: Current Dilemmas in Latin American Police Reform," in *Criminality, Public Security, and the Challenge to Democracy in Latin America*, edited by Marcelo Bergman and Laurence Whitehead, 95 (Notre Dame, IL: University of Notre Dame Press, 2009).
50. United Nations Human Rights Council, *Report of the Special Rapporteur on extrajudicial, summary or arbitrary executions on her mission to El Salvador* (December 7, 2018), A/HRC/38/44/Add.2. https://documents-dds-ny.un.org/doc/UNDOC/GEN/G18/359/05/PDF/G1835905.pdf?OpenElement.
51. Angelika Albaladejo, "El Salvador Gang Truce Was 'State Policy': Trial Testimony," *InSight Crime*, August 9, 2017. https://www.insightcrime.org/news/brief/el-salvador-gang-truce-state-policy-trial-testimony/.
52. IUDOP, "Los salvadoreños y salvadoreñas evalúan la situación del país a finales de 2012," *Boletín de prensa Año* 27, no.4 (December 12, 2012). http://www.uca.edu.sv/publica/iudop/archivos/boletin4_2012.pdf.
53. Mark Ungar, "Networks of Criminality: The State and Crime Policy in Contemporary Democracy," *Desafíos* 28, no. 2 (2016): 318.
54. Hannah Stone, "Honduras' New Top Cop Comes with Dark Past," *InSight Crime*, May 29, 2012. https://www.insightcrime.org/news/analysis/honduras-new-top-cop-comes-with-dark-past/.
55. Christine Wade, "Police Scandal in Honduras Could Lead to Even More Militarized Policing," *World Politics Review*, May 5, 2016. https://www.worldpoliticsreview.com/articles/18690/police-scandal-in-honduras-could-lead-to-even-more-militarized-policing.
56. United Nations Human Rights Council, *Annual Report of the United Nations High Commissioner for Human Rights on the Human Rights Situation in Honduras* (February 9, 2017).
57. Christopher Sherman, Martha Mendoza, and Garance Burke, "Secret Report: Honduras' new top cop helped move cocaine," Associated Press, January 26, 2018. https://www.apnews.com/0cc4031c058545fb9247ce5095c644c0.
58. Sarah Chayes, *When Corruption Is the Operating System: The Case of Honduras* (Washington, DC: Carnegie Endowment for International Peace, 2017).

CENTRAL AMERICA SINCE THE 1990S   377

59. Tristan Clavel and Parker Asmann, "Is Anti-Graft Body CICIG Behind Guatemala Homicide Drop?" *InSight Crime*, November 22, 2018. https://www.insightcrime.org/news/analysis/anti-graft-body-cicig-behind-guatemala-homicide-drop/.

60. Mark Schneider, *Democracy in Peril: Facts on CICIG in Guatemala* (Washington, DC: Center for Strategic and International Studies, April 11, 2019). https://www.csis.org/analysis/democracy-peril-facts-cicig-guatemala.

61. International Crisis Group, "Saving Guatemala's Fight against Crime and Impunity," October 24, 2018. https://d2071andvipowj.cloudfront.net/070-saving-guatemalas-fight-against-crime-and-impunity.pdf.

62. Dirk Kruit, "Low Intensity Democracies: Latin America in the Post-dictatorial Era," *Bulletin of Latin American Research* 20, no. 4 (2001): 409–430; Richard Stahler-Sholk, "El Salvador's Negotiated Transition." From Low-Intensity Conflict to Low-Intensity Democracy," *Journal of Interamerican Studies and World Affairs* 36, no. 4 (1994): 1–60.

63. Cruz, "Criminal Violence and Democratization in Central America," 1–2.

64. Freedom House, *Democracy in Retreat: Freedom in the World 2019*. (Freedom House: Washington, D.C.) https://freedomhouse.org/sites/default/files/Feb2019_FH_FITW_2019_Report_For Web-compressed.pdf.

65. John Booth, Christine J. Wade, and Thomas W. Walker, *Understanding Central America: Global Forces and Political Change* (New York: Routledge Press, 2020).

66. José Miguel Cruz, *Violence and Insecurity as Challenges for Democratic Political Culture in Latin America* (Nashville, TN: Latin American Public Opinion Project (LAPOP), 2008) http://sitemason.vanderbilt.edu/files/iicjwk/Cruz.pdf; Orlando J. Pérez, "Democratic Legitimacy and Public Insecurity: Crime and Democracy in El Salvador and Guatemala," *Political Science Quarterly* 118, no. 4 (Winter 2003–2004): 627–644.

67. Dinorah Azpuru, Mariana Rodriguez, and Elizabeth Zechmeister, *The Political Culture of Democracy in Guatemala and The Americas 2016/2017: A Comparative Study of Democracy and Governance* (Nashville, TN: LAPOP, February 2018), 5–6, 8.

68. Sophie Price, Stella Sechopoulos, and James Whitty, *Support for Harsher Criminal Punishments Is Greater among the Young, the Insecure, Victims, and Those with Low Trust in the Police* (Nashville, TN: LAPOP, 2019). https://www.vanderbilt.edu/lapop/insights/IO94 oen.pdf.

69. Mary Malone, *The Rule of Law in Central America* (New York: Bloomsbury, 2012), 108.

70. Azam Ahmed, "They Will Have to Answer to Us," *The New York Times Magazine*, November 29, 2017.

71. Malone, *Rule of Law*, 108.

72. Mary F. Malone and Christine Malone-Rowe, "Central America: Crime, Corruption, and the Police," in *Encyclopedia of Public Administration and Public Policy* (3rd ed.) (New York: Taylor & Francis, 2015), 5–6.

73. Elizabeth Zechmeister and Dinorah Azpuru, *What Does the Public Report on Corruption, the CICIG, the Public Ministry, and Constitutional Court in Guatemala?* (Nashville, TN: LAPOP, 2017). https://www.vanderbilt.edu/lapop/insights/ITB029en.pdf.

74. Dinorah Azpuru, Mariana Rodriguez, and Elizabeth Zechmeister, *The Political Culture of Democracy in Guatemala and The Americas 2016/2017: A Comparative Study of Democracy and Governance* (Nashville, TN: LAPOP, February 2018).

75. UNHCR, *Children on the Run, Unaccompanied Children Leaving Central American and Mexico and the Need for International Protection.* https://www.unhcr.org/56fc266f4.html.

76. Médecins Sans Frontières, "Forced to Flee Central America's Northern Triangle: A Neglected Humanitarian Crisis" (May 11, 2017). https://doctorswithoutborders.org/sites/default/files/2018-08/msf_forced-to-flee-central-americas-northern-triangle_E.pdf.

77. Congressional Research Service, "Central American Migration: Root Causes and U.S. Policy" (June 13, 2019). https://fas.org/sgp/crs/row/IF11151.pdf.

FURTHER READING

Arana, Ana. "How the Street Gangs Took Central America." *Foreign Affairs* 84, no. 3 (2005): 98–110.

Chayes, Sarah. *When Corruption Is the Operating System: The Case of Honduras*. Washington, DC: Carnegie Endowment for International Peace, 2017.

Cruz, José Miguel. "Criminal Violence and Democratization in Central America: The Survival of the Violent State." *Latin American Politics and Society* 53, no. 4 (2011): 1–33.

Huhn, Sebastian, and Hannes Warnecke-Berger, eds. *Politics and History of Violence and Crime in Central America*. New York: Palgrave Macmillan, 2017.

Hume, Mo. "Mano Dura: El Salvador Responds to Gangs." *Development in Practice* 17, no. 6 (2007): 739–751.

Malone, Mary F. *The Rule of Law in Central America: Citizens' Reactions to Crime and Punishment*. New York: Continuum, 2012.

Menjavir, Cecilia, and Shannon D. Walsh, "The Architecture of Feminicide: The State, Inequalities, and Everyday Gender Violence in Honduras." *Latin American Research Review* 52, no. 2 (2017): 221–240.

Peacock, Susan, and Adriana Beltrán. *Hidden Powers in Post-conflict Guatemala: Illegal Armed Groups and the Forces Behind Them*. Washington, DC: Washington Office on Latin America (WOLA), 2003.

Pérez, Orlando J. "Democratic Legitimacy and Public Insecurity: Crime and Democracy in El Salvador and Guatemala." *Political Science Quarterly* 118, no. 4 (2003): 627–644.

Santacruz-Giralt, Maria, Jose Miguel Cruz, Alberto Concha-Eastman. *Barrio adentro: la solidaridad violenta de las pandillas en El Salvador*. San Salvador, El Salvador: Universidad Centroamericana, 2001.

Silva Àvalos, Héctor. *Infiltrados: Crónica de la corrupción en la PNC (1992–2013)*. San Salvador, El Salvador: UCA Editores, 2014.

Ungar, Mark. "Networks of Criminality: The State and Crime Policy in Contemporary Democracy." *Desafios* 28, no. 2 (2016): 297–329.

United Nations Office on Drugs and Crime. *Transnational Organized Crime in Central America and the Caribbean: A Threat Assessment*. Vienna: UNODC, 2012.

Wade, Christine J. *Captured Peace: Elites and Peacebuilding in El Salvador*. Athens, OH: Ohio University Press, 2017.

Yashar, Deborah. *Homicidal Ecologies: Illicit Economies and Complicit States in Latin America*. New York: Cambridge University Press, 2018.

CHAPTER 14

....

THE RISE AND RETREAT OF
THE ARMED FORCES

....

ORLANDO J. PÉREZ AND RANDY PESTANA

FEW state actors have been more central to the development of state capacity and authority in Central America than the armed forces. The military as a source of social and political power dates to the Spanish conquest. Military power was central to the subordination of popular will in the context of weak institutions, economic underdevelopment, and social inequalities. From the colonial period through to the end of the twentieth century, with few exceptions, the armed forces were allied with local elites and transnational actors to enforce unequal and exploitative structures of economic development and authoritarianism.

The transitions to democracy in the late twentieth century were made possible by the military's exhaustion with exercising power and their struggle to maintain institutional autonomy vis-à-vis other state actors. In most cases, the depth of democratization was influenced by the extent to which the armed forces were able to secure their central role as guarantors of national sovereignty, and their ability to preserve quotas of institutional power even after inconclusive civil wars. The military's ability to maintain corporate autonomy over defense and security policies in post-conflict Central America limited democratic reforms, particularly in the areas of defense and security. While the armed forces today no longer rule directly in any of the countries of Central America, their political influence still frames the strength of civilian institutions to govern effectively.

Max Weber refers to the state as that political unit that exercises a monopoly on the legitimate use of force.[1] The armed forces are the principal—although not the only—institution that provides the state the ability to exercise legitimate force. The role of the military in Central America, and indeed in the rest of Latin America, was shaped by the weakness—or absence—of state institutions, particularly during the birth of Central America's independent nation-states. In most of Latin America, some form of military organization predated the development and consolidation of power of the nation-state. Under those circumstances, military men acting alone or as part of the armed forces exercised political power in many countries of Central America well into the twentieth century.

The formation of the Federal Republic of Central America (Guatemala, El Salvador, Honduras, Nicaragua, and Costa Rica) in 1823 maintained political divisions prevalent during Spanish rule. The Liberals who were unwilling to replace one form of colonial rule (Spanish) for that of Guatemalan imperialism clashed with Conservatives leading to a series of civil wars between 1826 and 1829.[2] Guatemala had been both the colonial administrative center and trade center in Central America during Spanish rule. This allowed a group of local elites to control large swathes of land and power, creating tensions between the newly independent Central American states.

The rise of *caudillo* politics occurred during this period of conflict that saw the genesis of the armed forces in Central America. Civil wars rarely involved more than one hundred men with factions closely tied to local politicians.[3] Many of the armies were instead disparate bands and militia groups fighting on behalf of charismatic *caudillos* and the Conservative/Liberal elite at large. Promotion was often limited to the Creole elite who associated themselves with the upper classes—this identification would continue through the breakup of the Federal Republic of Central America.[4]

Two figures who exemplified *caudillo* politics were Francisco Morazán and Jose Rafael Carrera. Morazán led an overmatched Liberal army against a Conservative army in a series of battles in 1829, propelling him to the presidency of the Federal Republic of Central America.[5] Liberal rule challenged the Guatemalan elite's hold on power over the subsequent eight years, leading to increased conflict. Conflict with the Church was particularly concerning for Conservatives who saw Morazán's tenure as an end to religion. The 1837 War of the Mountain was a turning point for Conservatives with the rise of Carrera, a young charismatic swine farmer supported by the Church and wealthy landowners.[6] The subsequent battles between Morazán's and Carrera's armies ultimately led to the dissolution of the Federal Republic of Central America, the death of Morazán in 1842, and the rise of Conservative rule in Central America. More importantly, this period cemented the Conservative-Liberal divide that remains today.

THE DEVELOPMENT OF THE ARMED FORCES: 1840–1929

The connection between the armed forces and the political elite increased following the disbanding of the Federal Republic of Central America. The decades that followed saw Central American elites utilize the armed forces for their personal gain, creating a symbiotic relationship between those who ruled and the groups responsible for protecting those states.[7] Most states developed laws that placed the armed forces above traditional prosecution and allowed greater leeway to utilize violence as a means of change. This

THE RISE AND RETREAT OF THE ARMED FORCES   381

"privileged caste [system] exempted [the military] from public liability and civil responsibility" further solidifying their role at the top of the state.[8]

Contrary to popular belief, the armed forces were not tied to specific parties. The ideological differences between the Conservative and Liberal parties were minuscule as most members of each ruling faction came from the upper class. The overriding interest of the military was power and not party. The inherent Conservative leaning of the military had more to do with age and rank, which resulted in younger, more ambitious officers seeking to advance through their affiliation with the liberal parties.[9] One anecdote from Honduras where "blue solders" (Liberals) would carry a red (Conservative) armband and vice versa in the event they needed to change affiliations demonstrates this point.[10] Thus, infighting among officers was common and led to numerous changes in military and political leadership. As Edwin Lieuwen pointed out, "in the first half-century of independence, nearly everywhere politics was little more than military convulsion and anarchy."[11]

Each country's military saw differing levels of political influence and infighting during their evolution. In Guatemala, Rafael Carrera governed in conjunction with the Conservative elite, reestablishing the political and military models implemented during Spanish rule.[12] The Guatemalan armed forces and militia groups were unique in that they had access to more resources than other Central American counterparts. Nevertheless, they were, as David McCreery stated, "no better than ad hoc, ragtag affairs based in the towns and commanded mostly by amateurs."[13] Liberals worked with German agrarian entrepreneurs who introduced them to modern military techniques—this was especially evident when Liberals militarized Guatemala's rural society beginning in 1871.[14] Justo Rufino Bárrios (1873–1885) ruled Guatemala with an iron fist, promoting foreign investment and modernization of the economy by favoring coffee production. Bárrios opened Indigenous communal lands to cultivation by large landowners and curtailed the economic power of the Catholic Church. Military force was used to displace Indigenous and poor peasants from their land. Rural residents were forced to work on government projects, and many migrated to cities and became poorly paid laborers.[15]

In El Salvador, military involvement in politics was commonplace for most of the nineteenth century. The officer corps was formed by *caudillos*, with and without military experience, creating a civil-military divide whereby officers took orders from the leaders of respective political factions. Military officers like elsewhere in the region rose through the ranks along with the local politicians they linked themselves with; it was typical for the military to be loyal to elected officials and not citizens. The formal Salvadoran army formed in the late 1850s with key influences from other countries. Colombians and, later, French and Spanish officers trained infantry, cavalry, and artillery units.[16] The Spanish played a substantive role in the development of the National Guard in 1912, who were responsible to answer the call of any landowner, especially those few elite families that controlled the majority of coffee fields throughout the country.[17]

Honduras lacked any real military institution following its independence in 1838. Honduras lacked the exports and political institutions of its Central American neighbors making it the poorest of the five republics, hindering its ability to invest in professional forces. The only remnants of a military establishment were the departmental militia groups linked to *caudillo* politicians.[18] Unlike its Central American counterparts, the Honduran military lacked any real influence on politics. Competing politicians used these militia groups to rise to power, creating a series of revolts.[19] Mobilizations often coincided with elections, making the military a largely unorganized, undisciplined, and partisan tool.[20] This became evident in the 1870s when the military was unable to fight off a British incursion in response to unpaid debt.[21] It would not be until the 1950s with the support of the United States that Honduras began to institutionalize and professionalize the armed forces.

Upon seceding from the Federation in 1838, Nicaragua was faced with a series of interventions by the United States that shaped the nation's ability to develop its own armed forces. Nicaragua saw eleven incursions beginning in 1853 following a street melee that left an American diplomat injured.[22] In 1856, an American mercenary named William Walker seized power with the support of Liberals against their Conservative adversaries.[23] However, efforts to further consolidate power led Conservatives and Liberals to come together in order to oust Walker from power.[24] The US Marines invaded again in 1912, occupying the country until 1933[25] and helping Nicaragua establish its first national constabulary force—the infamous Guardia Nacional de Nicaragua.

Ironically, given its history during the twentieth century, Costa Rica was the test case for military rule from the time of independence. From 1824 to 1899, the military ruled the country 44 percent of the time—nearly one in five governments ended by coup d'état.[26] Unlike its Central American neighbors, the influence of the Costa Rican military surpassed that of the landed elite. The military broke away and expanded following the 1857 Central American war and would see its Liberal military leader, Tomas Guardia, assume power in 1870.[27] Many of the traditional elites were exiled or had their property taken away during Guardia's rule. The last military regime led by General Federico Tinoco would take over in 1917 but would end in 1919 following the assassination of his brother and Secretary of War José Joaquín Tinoco—Federico would flee the country and live in exile in Paris.[28]

THE RISE OF DICTATORSHIPS AND CIVIL WARS: 1930–1980

In the aftermath of the Great Depression, Central America saw the transition from liberal leadership to the rise of national *caudillos* utilizing the military to consolidate their power. This period also saw the United States exercise increasing influence in the region as the East-West conflict with the USSR led the United States to promote stability over democracy and the status quo over reform. The latter half of this period saw social and political mobilizations in three of the five countries of the region led by leftist intellectuals, peasants, and middle-class reformers. The civil wars, and their conclusion, shaped the politics of the region in significant ways. The extent and limits to democracy in modern-day Guatemala, El Salvador, and Nicaragua are directly attributable to the legacy of the internal wars.

When General Jorge Ubico (1931–1944) assumed the presidency of Guatemala in 1931, he was the seventh army officer to assume the presidency since 1838. Ubico rose to prominence quickly, achieving the rank of colonel by the time he was twenty-eight years old. He would later rise to general and defense minister under General José Maria Orellana, where he developed the strategy of making the army visible in main population centers.[29] This served the dual purpose of emphasizing the military's role within the state and creating political inroads that would see him follow General Lázaro Chacón González as president in 1931.

During the Ubico regime military officers' participation in political and social life was pervasive. General officers held all of Guatemala's gubernatorial and ministerial posts.[30] By the mid-1940s, the geopolitical environment as well as the social conditions within Guatemala had changed sufficiently for Ubico's regime to come under intense pressures. On the one hand, Franklin Delano Roosevelt's Good Neighbor Policy limited the use of US military assets to prop up friendly governments in the region; World War II and the fight against Nazism led the United States to help develop an international system that, at the very least, paid lip service to democracy and basic human rights. On the other hand, inside Guatemala, peasants, laborers, and middle-class military officers all pushed for political, social, and economic reforms.

Political unrest, middle-class push for democratization, and a loss of US support caused Ubico to resign in 1944. The interim government of General Federico Ponce Vaides could not gain control of the situation. General Ponce, who belonged to the so-called old guard of the military, tried several political tactics such as allowing political dissent and the formation of political parties in order to gain legitimacy but to no avail. Modernization of the armed forces under General Ubico led to the development of an expanding corps of well-trained and professionalized junior officers who considered themselves better prepared than their commanders from the old guard who had begun their careers prior to the establishment of the military academy and had gained their rank through political maneuvering. The young officers, in coalition with the newly emergent middle class, argued the army had a duty not only to defend the nation's sovereignty but also to uphold the constitution against a corrupt government. In order to oust the old guard, the young officers felt it necessary to promote the notion that the military was the guarantor of constitutional order, and had a duty to oust corrupt, unrepresentative, and unconstitutional regimes. Claiming the right to be the guarantors of constitutional order was not new for the military, having exercised such authority since before the birth of the modern state; what was new was the makeup and ideological outlook of the officers who were now using such claims to mobilize against the extant regime.

On October 20, 1944, a group of junior army officers revolted against the old military elite. The new military-led government pledged to install a civilian as president after free and fair elections. Thus, in 1945, Juan José Arévalo Bermejo became Guatemala's first civilian elected president. The military's support for Arévalo came with a price. The leaders of the uprising received promotions and held the highest positions within the military structure. In addition, the new constitution made the armed forces for the first time virtually independent of the government. Colonel Juan Jacobo Árbenz Guzmán was elected president in 1950. He enjoyed overwhelming support from the military in part because he had graduated from the military academy. However, Árbenz's agenda—agrarian reform and his alleged relationship with communists—would eventually result in the government's distancing from the military. Árbenz sought to reduce the power of the United Fruit Company, a US-owned banana exporter, which controlled the banana industry not only in Guatemala but throughout Central America.

At the height of the Cold War, Árbenz's reforms and connections to members of the Guatemalan Communist Party alarmed the United States.[31] As a result, the United States launched a relentless political and psychological campaign against the Guatemalan government. In June 1954, the CIA-supported National Liberation Army, led by Colonel Carlos Castillo Armas, invaded Guatemala.[32] Colonel Castillo Armas dismantled the labor and peasant movements, killed and jailed thousands, repressed political parties, and returned confiscated lands to their former owners.[33] By the early 1960s, armed rebellions—some led by disgruntled army officers—challenged the authority of the military-led government. These early armed insurgents morphed into guerrilla fighters who led a thirty-six-year-long civil war against the military-dominated political system.[34] During the 1970s, while the military solidified its control over the political process, new insurgency groups sprang up in the highlands. In 1980, a second generation of guerrillas came together to form a unified front against the government after the original guerrilla groups were nearly destroyed by government forces. This unified guerrilla front was called the Guatemalan National Revolutionary Unity (URNG). The URNG was made up of four different guerrilla groups: the Guerrilla Army of the Poor (EGP), the Organization of People in Arms (ORPA), the Rebel Armed Forces (FAR), and the Guatemalan Labor Party (PGT).

The beginning of the 1980s witnessed an intensification of counterinsurgency activity, including massive levels of violence directed at the Indigenous Maya communities in the highlands, as part of a strategy to starve the guerrilla movements of support. According to the Historical Clarification Commission, recorded cases of extrajudicial killings rose from one hundred in 1978 to over ten thousand in 1981.[35] The period 1982–1983, under the leadership of General Efraín Ríos Montt, saw the greatest level of violence. The Historical Clarification Commission, which examined Ríos Montt's years, detailed the annihilation of almost six hundred villages, including the massacres of Plan de Sánchez in July 1982 and Dos Erres in December of the same year, which together killed more than 450 people.[36] General Ríos Montt was deposed on August 8, 1983, and was succeeded by General Óscar Humberto Mejía Victores. By the time General Mejía came to power the counterinsurgency war had terrorized the countryside and separated the insurgents from the population. Terror had worked to intimidate the population but had not completely defeated the guerrillas. By 1984, international pressures moved the regime to begin a process of liberalization which turned power over to a civilian president, Venicio Cerezo, in 1985. The war continued, however, through the rest of the 1980s and early 1990s.

Military involvement in politics was commonplace in El Salvador throughout the nineteenth and most of the twentieth century. By the end of the nineteenth century El Salvador's economic and political system was characterized by concentration of wealth and power in the hands of a few elite families supported by a strong military. The Great Depression of the 1930s undermined the export basis of the economy and induced economic and political crisis for the regime. Economic elites and the military moved to brutally put down an uprising by rural peasants led by Agustín Farabundo Martí. The peasant revolt was crushed by security forces, which in a few weeks killed between ten thousand and forty thousand people. This event, referred to as *La Matanza*, strongly shaped El Salvador's politics throughout the twentieth century.[37] Beginning with General Maximiliano Hernández Martínez in 1932 an almost unbroken succession of military governments ruled for five decades. From the suppression of the peasant rebellion in 1932 until the civil war (with brief exceptions), military officers ruled, usually through a facade of tightly controlled elections won by the official party, the Partido de Conciliación Nacional (PCN), while the economic elites controlled economic policy.[38]

Resistance to military domination of the political system and oligarchic control over the economy emerged in the form of five revolutionary groups that banded together to form the Farabundo Martí National Liberation Front (FMLN). The response of the government and its allies within the economic elite was to step up counterinsurgency operations, which extended to political activists who were seeking to organize urban and rural workers. As a result, civil war engulfed El Salvador for two decades beginning in the 1970s. The war, the reaction of the economic elites, and the support of the United States in the context of the Cold War empowered the armed forces and led to a series of military regimes.

The emergence of the modern Honduran military was closely tied to the rise to power of the National Party and to the protection of US economic interests in the country. General Tiburcio Carías Andino (1933–1949) sought to create a military that could guarantee political and economic stability conducive to maintaining National Party rule and the safety of US investments. Unlike his predecessors, who failed to quell disputes within the officer corps, Carías took advantage of close ties to US banana investors to siphon funds to his military project.[39] The weakness of political parties and civilian institutions, plus the influence of US economic interests following the Carías presidency limited the ability of the government to counter internal conflicts, leaving the newly trained military as the main political power in Honduras.[40]

This process of modernization of the armed forces was institutionalized in 1954 through a new law which provided for the professionalization of the military, the signing of bilateral aid agreements with the United States, and the creation of the first infantry battalion. In 1957, the armed forces obtained institutional autonomy with the creation of the Chief of the Armed Forces. The 1957 Constitution gave direct command over the troops to the Chief of the Armed Forces and not to the President of the Republic.

For the next thirty years, the military maintained control over the political system and a monopoly on the defense and security apparatus. The sole challenge to the military came in 1963 with the expected election of Modesto Rodas Alvarado—a "radical" Liberal candidate who organized protests against the military.[41] Air Force Colonel Oswaldo Lopez Arrellano would lead a military coup ten days prior to the election and maintained power off and on through 1975. Arellano monopolized power for the military and faced little challenge from the dominant political parties.[42] The largest challenge came from neighboring El Salvador which launched an attack following the expulsion of thousands of Salvadorans living in Honduras in what would be known as the 1969 "Soccer War."[43]

Unlike most Latin American nations, Nicaragua never had a truly autonomous military institution before the 1990s. The military was the instrument of the traditional political parties (prior to the 1920s, the Liberals and Conservatives), then the creation and supporter of a foreign intervention (the United States from 1926 through 1932), then the instrument of a single family (the Somozas until 1979), and finally the bulwark of a revolutionary regime (the Frente Sandinista de Liberación Nacional from 1979 until the mid-1990s). While each institution was different in form and political orientation, they all shared the characteristic that military command was determined by political loyalties, and every effort was made to suppress institutional autonomy.

When the US Marines left Nicaragua in 1933, they left behind a constabulary force, the National Guard, with the hope that the institution would maintain political stability and protect US economic interests in the country. The US anointed Anastasio "Tacho" Somoza García as head of the Guard.[44] Somoza soon consolidated power and killed or exiled most of his political rivals, including Augusto Cesar Sandino, a Liberal leader who had fought against US military occupation since the 1920s. Between 1934 and 1979, the Somoza family ruled the country as their private plantation. The military institution became subordinate to the personal interests of the Somoza family. As such, the armed forces became more of a praetorian guard than a national institution. The military became a weak and highly corrupt institution incapable of maintaining order or national security. By the 1970s, guerrillas under the umbrella of the Frente Sandinista de Liberación Nacional (FSLN) led a rebellion, which toppled the Somoza regime in 1979. The FSLN replaced the National Guard with a new military structure—the Sandinista People's Army (Ejército Popular Sandinista, EPS). From 1979 until 1990, it was impossible to separate the state, the army, and the party.

Following the collapse of the Tinoco regime in Costa Rica, the control the military gained during the nineteenth century quickly vanished. The army dropped from five thousand members in 1918 to five hundred in 1921—a decrease of over 90 percent.[45] Despite this, the newly depleted army continued to get involved in politics. They attempted to manipulate a series of electoral contests, which resulted in declining confidence in the Costa Rican political system.[46] This continued until the civil war in 1948.

The 1948 Civil War lasted six weeks under the leadership of Social Democrat José "Pepe" Figueres Ferrer. Figueres along with his National Liberation Army attacked President Rafael Calderón Guardia who was defeated in his reelection bid in 1948.[47]

Following Calderón's defeat at the hands of Figueres's rebels, the government negotiated favorable terms protecting members from political retaliation. Figueres and his National Liberation junta would rule by decree for the subsequent eighteen months, creating the conditions that would lead to a democratic transition and would ultimately abolish the army.

At the suggestion of Minister of Security Edgar Cardona, Figueres announced the abolition of the armed forces on December 1, 1948. In what would later be known as the *Cardinazo*, the military plotted to overthrow Figueres when, on April 2, 1949, the military took control of the Bella Vista Fort and demanded the removal of key members of the ruling government.[48] After the coup attempt, the military would dissolve rather quickly with the country remaining without a traditional uniformed armed force until today.[49]

The United States and the Cold War in Central America

United States power and influence is intimately connected to the emergence of the modern militaries of Central America. As we have observed, interest in the region emerged in the nineteenth century as US investors, adventurers, and ex-Southern slave owners sought to control parts of the region. By the beginning of the twentieth century, building, controlling, and protecting an interoceanic canal became of paramount importance to the United States. In the second half of the twentieth century, fighting communism became the overriding interest that justified support for military dictatorships and counterinsurgency activities.[50] Nicaragua in particular was the subject of intense US interest: beginning in 1853 with the first military incursion, continuing with the invasions by William Walker in the 1850s, and the Marine Corps intervention in 1912 that lasted, with the exception of a short period in 1925, until 1933. Nicaragua's first national constabulary force was established under US supervision in 1925. A force that as we have seen already developed into the National Guard which sustained the brutal Somoza regime from 1936 to 1979.

From the late 1940s through the late 1980s, the United States increasingly viewed Central America through the prism of the Cold War. By the 1950s the US National Security Council document NSC-68 described an aggressive and expanding Communist menace across the hemisphere and urged increasing support for the military across Latin America. Containing the influence of communism became the paramount focus of US policy. The fight against the so-called spread of communism led to placing a premium on stability over democracy, order rather than human rights, and capitalist expansion over social reforms. Popular mobilizations, particularly against friendly governments, were seen as a threat to the stability of the region, and by extension the United States itself. This framework guided US behavior in the early Cold War and spread to Latin America through US training programs for most military establishments of the hemisphere. In Guatemala, the Cold War manifested itself early through a CIA-sponsored coup that toppled an elected government, installed a military dictatorship, and laid the foundations for a thirty-six-year civil conflict that killed over two hundred thousand Guatemalans. In El Salvador, US policy first sought to support the military's hold on power and then through the Alliance for Progress and the Central American Common Market sought to promote limited economic reforms. The latter led to significant economic growth and to the mobilization of middle-class sectors seeking political reforms. However, by the 1970s the success of reform-oriented politicians, such as José Napoleón Duarte, led the military to clamp down on reform, reverse the results of the 1972 national elections, and take power directly. The military then ruled through a series of officers who manipulated elections to remain in power until the early 1980s. In the meantime, sectors of the opposition would take up arms against the military regime through the creation of the FMLN.[51] By the mid-1980s, US military aid to El Salvador had reached more than $500 million, and by the end of the civil war military and economic aid totaled nearly $6 billion.[52]

As observed earlier, US assistance in the 1950s was instrumental to the development of the modern Honduran military. Honduras was important as a strategic location from which to control alleged communist influence in the region. Thus, Honduras served as the launching pad for the CIA-sponsored coup in Guatemala in 1954 and the anti-Sandinista Contra war in the 1980s. Although popular mobilization in Honduras was relatively weak compared to its neighbors, US assistance increased significantly in the 1960s and 1970s. As civil wars raged in Nicaragua and El Salvador, maintaining order in Honduras became paramount. Aid to the country increased in the 1980s reaching more than $55 million per year in 1985–1988.[53]

In Nicaragua, US Cold War strategy meant support for the Somoza regime. Nicaragua was a key ally in Washington's machinations across the region, from the CIA-sponsored invasions of Guatemala (1954) and Cuba (1961), to the US invasion of the Dominican Republic (1965). By the 1970s, the Somoza regime was weakened by corruption, mismanagement, and mishandling of relief efforts after a deadly earthquake hit Managua in 1972. The mobilization of the opposition into an armed rebellion led by the FSLN further challenged the Somoza hold on power. By 1978–1979, the US administration of President Jimmy Carter was pressuring Anastasio "Tachito" Somoza Debayle, son of Anastasio Somoza García, to give up power. Assistance was curtailed and pressure was applied for a negotiated settlement of the revolution. The victory of the FSLN in 1979 ushered in a period of tension and conflict with the United States. While President Carter was initially supportive of the new Nicaraguan government, by the time he left the presidency in 1981 relations had soured and assistance had been curtailed. President Ronald Reagan would intensify the war against the Sandinista-led government. Reagan gave the CIA close to $20 million to support and augment an exile army of anti-Sandinista counterrevolutionaries (the Contras). The Contras were primarily composed of former National Guard officers and soldiers, and political allies of the former dictator. By 1985 the Contras numbered more than fifteen thousand troops. While they had achieved little against the Nicaraguan military, they had managed to sabotage a good part of the country's economy and killed over thirteen thousand people.[54] In the mid-1980s, the US Congress defunded the Contra war and restricted US efforts to overthrow the Sandinista government. However, the Reagan administration responded with covert efforts to assist the Contras that included illegal sales of weapons to Iran,[55] donations of cash by private individuals and friendly foreign governments, and, allegedly, proceeds from drug trafficking.[56] By 1989, US assistance to the Contras had reached nearly $400 million. The Contras did not disband until after the Sandinistas lost the 1990 elections.

THE RETREAT OF THE MILITARY: 1990–PRESENT

By the late 1980s, as armed conflicts intensified in the region, and perhaps because of this intensification, various negotiation processes were initiated to promote a peaceful and regional solution to the conflicts. Together with several national initiatives, the most ambitious international effort was the one led by the *Contadora* Group, comprising the governments of Mexico, Colombia, Venezuela, and Panama. It was a diplomatic initiative that sought to promote peace and democracy in the region between 1983 and 1986. The signing of the Esquipulas Agreement in 1987 by the Central American presidents initiated a process of internal reconciliation sustained by a gradual move toward democracy. From this moment, peace negotiations were linked to processes of democratization, which began in 1982 in El Salvador, in 1985 in Guatemala, and in 1984 in Nicaragua. Geopolitically, the collapse of the USSR, and the impact this had on the Cuban regime, a major supporter of the Central American revolutionary groups, and on US strategic calculations in the region, contributed greatly to the move toward a peaceful settlement of the civil conflicts.

The peace process in Guatemala took nine years, nine accords, and four declarations before the government and the URNG agreed to sign a final agreement of firm and lasting peace in 1996.[57] Demilitarizing the Guatemalan state was a central goal of the accords, given the military's violent past and the role it played in politics and society. The Agreement on Strengthening Civilian Authority and the Role of the Military (AFPC) was designed to reverse the historical power of the armed forces in politics. The accord required reducing the military budget by 33 percent as a proportion of GDP (gross domestic product) from 1995 levels by 2000. Additionally, the agreement called for the elimination of the Estado Mayor Presidencial (EMP), replacing it with two civilian intelligence agencies, one under the interior ministry (Gobernación) and another within the president's office.[58]

President Alvaro Arzú (1996–2000) took significant steps early in his administration to reduce the power of the military. He ousted many of the most reactionary officers and placed in top military positions those favorable to the peace negotiations. A major provision of the accord was the creation of a professional and autonomous Policía Nacional Civil (National Civilian Police, PNC) as the only institution to handle public order and internal security and a clear separation between police and military roles. The new police force, placed under the Ministry of the Interior, was slated to be fully in place by the end of 1999, with at least twenty thousand agents. That figure was reached in early 2003 and by 2005 the number of agents was twenty-two thousand. As of 2017, the PNC numbered thirty-five thousand personnel.[59]

The Peace Accords called for constitutional reforms to eliminate the internal security functions of the military and permit the appointment of a civilian defense minister. Accordingly, the Congress adopted the changes, as well as those relating to other agreements, and they were submitted to a popular vote (referendum) in May 1999. The reforms were rejected by 55 percent to 45 percent of valid votes, with an abstention rate of 81 percent.[60] The failure of the reforms stalled efforts to further change the structure and role of the armed forces.

The administration of Alfonso Portillo (2000–2004) began with high hopes for reviving the reforms. The president led a major shakeup of the military by appointing a colonel, Juan de Dios Estrada Velasquez, as defense minister, thus forcing the retirement of many officers who were passed over for promotion. However, Portillo's changes in Army leadership during the first half of his term had the effect of focusing the attention of the military toward protection of its corporate interests rather than continue the process of democratic reform. In addition, Portillo allowed former military officers, many of whom were members of a shadowy group called *La Cofradia*,[61] to have significant influence in day-to-day operations of the armed forces, including promotions and deployment of troops.[62]

Significant and rapid changes took place after the election of President Oscar Berger in December 2003. The new president embarked on an ambitious program to meet and even exceed the mandates of the Peace Accords. On April 1, 2004, President Berger announced the closing of six military bases and eliminated 4,713 army billets, prompting 6,960 officers and enlisted men to go into retirement.[63] On June 30, 2004, the army was reduced from 27,000 to 15,500 units (troops and officers), and a ceiling of 0.33 percent of GDP (half the amount allowed by the accords) was placed on the military's budget. By 2014, the Guatemalan military had increased to 18,200 troops and the budget 0.39 percent of GDP.

For the FMLN in El Salvador, the collapse of the USSR not only represented the end of an ideological ally but also the end of any possibility of continued material help. In addition to the collapse of the Soviet Union, the defeat of the Nicaraguan Sandinista-led government in the 1990 elections further weakened the international support received by the FMLN. For the United States, pressure to reduce military aid to Central America in general and El Salvador in particular meant an effort toward supporting a way out of the conflict through a negotiated solution. The priority for the US President, George H. W. Bush, was to find an acceptable conclusion to its commitment in El Salvador, one that would end the conflict, allow for a US withdrawal, but nonetheless safeguard the country's democracy. This outcome would require negotiations with the FMLN.

In November 1989, the FMLN launched another offensive in the capital city, proving that it still had significant military capability despite nine years of government counterinsurgency efforts. In 1990 and 1991, the fighting escalated as the FMLN introduced antiaircraft weapons and the Salvadoran Armed Forces attempted to challenge the FMLN's de facto control over the territory. By the beginning of the 1990s, an estimated seventy thousand people had died at the hands of both sides—the majority of them civilians. Because of the geopolitical context and the military stalemate, in April 1990 the Salvadoran combatants embarked on a two-year-long process of negotiations that ended with the signing of the Chapultepec Peace Accords in January 1992.[64] The key reforms from the accords were focused on separating national defense and public security, by establishing a National Civil Police; reduction of up to 50 percent in the armed forces personnel within two years; transformation of intelligence units and their placement under the direct authority of the president; redefining the armed forces doctrine; and reform of the constitutional mission of the armed forces to restrict involvement in domestic security to exceptional circumstances and only under civilian authorization.

The new doctrine emphasized subordination to civilian authority, particularly the elected president; greater accountability with respect to internal institutional mechanisms; and separation of external defense and internal security.[65] The 1992 constitutional reforms redefined the armed forces as "a permanent institution at the service of the nation; obedient, professional, apolitical and non-deliberative."[66]

The budget allocated to the national defense sector went from 20.8 percent of the nation's general budget in 1989 at the time of the armed conflict to 13.7 percent in 1992 at the time of the Peace Accords, followed by a reduction by 1995 (7.4 percent of the national budget), then down to 5.8 percent in 1997, 5.4 percent in 2000, and finally 4.4 percent in 2002.[67] However, the percentage of the national budget made up of defense spending and spending on defense as a percentage of the GDP have been steady since 2008, around 2.5 percent and 0.60 percent respectively. By 2016, El Salvador's armed forces numbered close to twenty-five thousand, the largest force in Central America, and the country was spending 0.60 percent of GDP on the military.[68]

Unlike other Central American countries, where the military and police reforms were the product of peace accords, in Honduras reform resulted from presidential initiatives, institutional circumstances, and changes in the national and international context. Beginning with the election of Carlos Roberto Reina (1994–1998) a process of transformation in civil-military relations and a reduction in the power of the armed forces ensued. In December 1996, the Congress unanimously ratified constitutional reforms that separated internal security from national defense. The former was handed to a new National Civil Police and the latter was left in the hands of the armed forces.

President Carlos Flores Facussé (1998–2002) continued the reforms of President Reina in the demilitarization of public security and subordination of the military to the president. On September 18, 1998, Congress passed constitutional reforms that made the president Commander in Chief of the Armed Forces with the power to appoint a civilian minister of defense. Constitutional changes introduced on January 1999 made substantial reforms that eliminated the office of Chief of the Armed Forces from the

Constitution. Under the new reforms, the President of the Republic would exercise direct command of the armed forces.

It is hard to ascertain the number of troops in the Honduran military prior to the reform period because the exact number was handled as a matter of national security; estimates range from twenty-two thousand to twenty-five thousand troops in the 1980s.[69] By 2012, the institution was reduced to 10,550 troops, and grew to 15,500 by 2014. Despite the reduction in personnel, the military's budget increased from 0.66 percent to 0.76 percent of the GDP between 2000 and 2003. However, between 2003 and 2005, defense spending as a percentage of the GDP was reduced again to 0.65 percent, and increased in dollar terms from $66 million to $116 million between 2006 and 2008. Between 2008 and 2012 the budget increased from 3.8 percent of GDP to 4.6 percent.[70]

Despite significant reforms of Honduras's civil-military relations, including important constitutional reforms, the country's military remains a potent political force. Weak and corrupt institutions, an underdeveloped economy dominated by elites with close ties to illicit activities, and contradictory constitutional norms all contributed to a political crisis in 2009 that saw the first successful coup of an elected president in Central America for decades. The immediate cause of the coup was President Manuel Zelaya's (2006–2009) desire to hold a referendum aimed at changing the constitutional provision that prohibited presidential reelection.[71] The deeper crisis was caused by Zelaya's move toward embracing Venezuela's Hugo Chávez and Bolivia's Evo Morales as well as joining the Bolivarian Alternative for the Americas (Alternativa Bolivariana para las Américas, ALBA).

As the elections of 2009 approached, opposition to President Zelaya mounted among members of Congress and the economic elites. Congress passed a law prohibiting the referendum. Despite the ban, President Zelaya continued with his plans and ordered the military to secure the ballot papers. When the Chief of the Joint Staff General Romeo Vásquez Velasquez refused to abide by this order, President Zelaya tried to fire him. General Vásquez refused the president's orders, calculating that it would be in the interest of the military not to follow the president down a road that would ultimately alienate the armed forces from nearly all established state institutions. In addition, it was clear from the beginning of the crisis that the United States—the military's largest supplier of assistance and equipment—did not support President Zelaya's policies.[72] Without a clear mechanism to impeach and remove a president from office the Constitution virtually guaranteed a political crisis if a president sought to defy the other branches of government. Under these circumstances, military officers concluded that supporting the president would undermine the institutional integrity of the armed forces. Therefore, on the day the referendum was to be held, June 28, 2009, the military forcefully removed President Zelaya from office and exiled him to Costa Rica. The struggle between the president, Congress, the armed forces, the economic elites, and popular sectors allied with Zelaya all collided in a political crisis that undermined civilian control of the military and democratic governance. Post-coup Honduras has seen substantial increases in violence and corruption[73] and a military institution that maintains significant political power.

As indicated above, the Sandinista-led government transformed Nicaragua's National Guard from an arm of the Somoza family into an institution tied to the FSLN party. Throughout the 1980s, the armed forces responded to, and were driven by, party political interests and the revolutionary ethos. The defeat of the Sandinistas in the 1990 presidential elections began the process of transition in Nicaraguan civil-military relations. The basic principles of the transition were contained in the "Protocol of Procedure of the Transfer of Executive Power in Nicaragua," known as the "Transition Accords" of March 27, 1990. The agreement constituted a political pact between the outgoing government (FSLN) and the incoming Chamorro administration (Union Nacional Opositora), emphasizing reductions in the Army's and police's budget, the subordination of both to civilian authorities, the professionalization and apolitical nature of the military and police, and respect for the integrity and professionalism and internal structures of the two institutions. In political terms, the transformation of defense and public security may well be characterized as a process of "de-Sandinization." Some of the key achievements of this early period included the elimination of compulsory military service, reduction in budget and personnel, and effective separation of the police and the military.[74] During the early phase of the transition, however, General Humberto Ortega[75] and the EPS continued to resist effective subordination to civilian authorities. The Sandinista military owed its allegiance primarily to its commanding general, who exercised strong personal control over the institution. By September 1993, President Chamorro sought to move forward with greater changes by replacing General Humberto Ortega as head of the EPS and to increase civilian control by shifting various agencies away from EPS control and by renaming the organization to "reflect more clearly its national character."[76] General Ortega initially resisted, arguing that his removal was against the law and that he would only leave after the adoption of a new military code.

The Chamorro administration came under increasing pressure from the United States to bolster control of the military and to reduce FSLN influence, particularly the removal of General Humberto Ortega as army commander. Ultimately, General Ortega acquiesced to his retirement, which took place in February 1995. General Joaquin Cuadra, chief of the general staff, replaced him and the military changed its name from the Ejercito Popular Sandinista to the Ejercito de Nicaragua, formalizing its break with Sandinista Party control.[77]

Under General Cuadra, the military operated increasingly as a semi-autonomous institution, concerned with institutional interests rather than any partisan political agenda. Relations between the military and the broader civil society improved notably under General Cuadra. Fears of military partisanship had been rampant during the 1990 elections, but these had largely disappeared by the 1996 elections, again won by the opponents of the FSLN.

The army went from 86,810 in 1990 to 14,084 in 1996,[78] and then to 12,187 in 2002,[79] and finally to 10,504 in 2005.[80] The national defense budget was reduced from $94 million (1990) to $35 million in 1999 and went up to $42 million in 2009. Nicaragua's military expenditure for 2011 was $53.2 million, roughly 0.7 percent of GDP. By 2016,

Nicaragua's military counted with 12,790 soldiers, making it the smallest military in the region, and spent 0.56 percent of GDP on the armed forces.[81]

Daniel Ortega, the Sandinista leader who governed the country from 1979 to 1990, returned to the presidency in 2007 after seventeen years out of power. Ortega remains in power today after winning reelection for the second time in 2016. His administration has changed the Constitution to concentrate significant power in the hands of the executive. President Ortega has sought to repoliticize the military by promoting loyal Sandinista officers and continually intervening in internal institutional matters. Initially rebuffed by the armed forces, the president has succeeded by changing the military code in ways that increase presidential authority over the armed forces. The changes approved in 2014 include the addition of a vague reference to "national security" to the army's essential role. Given the lack of explicit definition of the term, including national security to the army's core mission, allows the president the ability to deploy the armed forces in domestic matters as long as "national security" is threatened.

In addition, the reforms further isolated the ministry of defense from the chain of command by giving the president direct management of the armed forces. Active military officers may now hold posts in the executive branch and the Army may recall retired officers to its ranks to create reserve units, without specifying what they will do.[82] Nicaragua's civil-military relations have deteriorated since 2006 in ways that have undermined the military's apolitical nature. While subordination to the elected president remains, the independence of the military has been weakened and many Nicaraguans fear that the institution will return to its pre-1990 condition as the armed wing of the FSLN.

POST-CONFLICT CIVIL MILITARY RELATIONS AND DEMOCRACY

In measuring progress among the four countries that today still have traditional uniformed military institutions, we would contend that El Salvador has led the transformation process, followed by Nicaragua, then Guatemala, and finally Honduras. El Salvador's military has undergone the most significant institutional reforms and has had more success in modernizing its structures. Particularly impressive is the ability of two presidents from the FMLN party (2009–2019) to win and exercise authority over the armed forces for ten years.

Guatemala's military continues to have a constitutionally prescribed role in internal security and exercises considerable political influence. Both Honduras and Nicaragua developed civilian-led ministries of defense, albeit very weak vis-à-vis the armed forces. The recent changes by President Ortega undermine democratic civil-military relations by repoliticizing the armed forces. Honduras had made significant progress in promoting civilian authority through the structure of the civilian-led ministry of defense; however, the military coup that ousted President Zelaya in 2009 represented a significant setback for democratic civil-military relations.

In evaluating the progress of democratic civil-military relations in Central America, one must reflect on the history of the region and the advances relative to that history. By that standard, the region has achieved significant advances. One cannot ignore the changes in military doctrine, the transformation of military education, the separation—at least formally—of police and military functions, and the evident subordination to elected presidents. However, significant problems remain: weak civilian involvement in defense policymaking, underfunded and weak ministries of defense relative to the armed forces, weak or nonexistent legislative oversight, increased involvement in repressive policing, expansion of roles and missions for the military, corruption, dysfunctional institutions, and persistent violence. These problems tend to undermine democratic governance and weaken civilian authority. While the military may not be eager to govern directly again, they have not been reluctant to exercise veto power over defense and security policies, and perhaps other areas such as in the case of Honduras in 2009, and they continue to believe strongly in their constitutional obligation to defend the fatherland from external and internal enemies.

The armed forces continue to exercise significant political influence and are intimately tied to the success or failure of state policies, from defense and security to environmental protection and healthcare. The evidence suggests that citizens of Central America often trust their military more than they do their civilian leaders.[83] The permissive environment, which also includes intractable problems such as crime and economic deprivation, provides opportunities for the armed forces to exercise veto power over civilian authorities. The continued consolidation of democracy and the advances made in that direction over the past thirty years will depend on how well civilian leaders can limit the scope of military activity while strengthening civilian authority by providing effective solutions to national problems.

Notes

1. Max Weber, *Rationalism and Modern Society*, translated and edited by Tony Waters and Dagmar Waters, 129–198 (Palgrave Books, 2015).
2. Miles L. Wortman, "Government Revenue and Economic Trends in Central America, 1787–1819," *Hispanic American Historical Review* 55, no.2 (May 1975): 251–286.
3. Steve C. Ropp and James A. Morris, *Central America: Crisis and Adaptation* (Albuquerque: University of New Mexico Press, 1984), 14–15.
4. Edwin Lieuwen, *Arms and Politics in Latin America* (New York: Praeger, 1961), 18.
5. Thomas L. Pearcy, *The History of Central America* (Westport, CT: Greenwood Press, 2006), 54.
6. Pearcy, *History of Central America*.
7. Mark B. Rosenberg and Luis Guillermo Solis, *The United States and Central America: Geopolitical Realities and Regional Fragility* (New York: Routledge, 2007), 22.

8. Lyle N. McAlister, *The "Fuero Military" in New Spain* (Gainesville: University of Florida Press, 1957), 15.
9. Lieuwen, *Arms and Politics*, 27.
10. Matias H. Funes, *Los Deliberanted: El Poder Militar in Honduras* (Tegucligalpa: Editorial Guaymuras, 1995), 115.
11. Lieuwen, *Arms and Politics*, 20.
12. Ropp and Morris, *Central America*, 126.
13. David McCreery, *Rural Guatemala 1760–1940* (Stanford, CA: Stanford University Press, 1994), 180–181.
14. Ropp and Morris, *Central America*, 130–131.
15. McCreery, *Rural Guatemala*, 180–181.
16. Ropp and Morris, *Central America*, 77.
17. Orlando J. Pérez, *Civil–Military Relations in Post-Conflict Societies* (New York: Routledge, 2015), 51.
18. Orlando J. Pérez and Randy Pestana, *Honduran Military Culture Findings Report* (Miami, FIU–USSOUTHCOM Academic Partnership, 2016). https://gordoninstitute.fiu.edu/pol icy-innovation/military-culture-series/orlando-j-perez-and-randy-pestana-2016-hondu ran-military-culture.pdf.
19. William Stokes, *Honduras: An Area Study in Government* (Madison: University of Wisconsin Press, 1950), 226–227.
20. Steve Ropp, "The Honduran Army in the Sociopolitical Evolution of the Honduran State," *The Americas* 30, no. 4 (April 1974): 505–506.
21. Walter LaFeber, *Inevitable Revolutions: The United States in Central America* (2nd ed.) (New York: W.W. Norton, 1993), 36.
22. William LeoGrande, *Our Own Backyard: The United States and Central America, 1977–1992* (Chapel Hill: University of North Carolina Press, 1998).
23. For more on William Walker's role in Nicaragua, refer to Michel Gobat, *Empire by Invitation: William Walker and Manifest Destiny in Central America* (Cambridge, MA: Harvard University Press, 2018).
24. Randy Pestana and Brian Latell, *Nicaraguan Military Culture Findings Report* (Miami: FIU–USSOUTHCOM Academic Partnership, 2017), 8. https://gordoninstitute. fiu.edu/policy-innovation/military-culture-series/randy-pestana-and-brian-latell-2017-nicaraguan-military-culture.pdf.
25. With the exception of nine months in 1925.
26. John A. Booth, "Representative Constitutional Democracy in Costa Rica: Adaption to Crisis in the Turbulent 1980s," in *Central America: Crisis and Adaption*, edited by Steve Ropp and James Morris, 153-189 (Albuquerque: University of New Mexico Press, 1984).
27. John A. Booth, Christine J. Wade, and Thomas W. Walker, *Understanding Central America: Global Forces, Rebellion, and Change* (6th ed.) (Boulder, CO: Westview Press, 2014), 50.
28. LaFeber, *Inevitable Revolutions*, 57–59.
29. Robert H. Holden, *Armies without Nations: Public Violence and State Formation in Central America, 1821–1960* (New York: Oxford University Press, 2004), 55.
30. Piero Gleijeses, *Shattered Hope: The Guatemalan Revolution and the United States, 1944–1954* (Princeton, NJ: Princeton University Press, 1991).
31. There is little evidence that Colonel Arbenz himself was a communist. Needing domestic political allies for his reform agenda, Arbenz sought the support of local labor and peasant leaders some of whom were associated with the Communist Party.

32. Stephen Schlesinger and Stephen Kinzer, *Bitter Fruit: The Untold Story of the American Coup in Guatemala* (Garden City, NY: Doubleday, 1982); Gleijeses, *Shattered Hope*; Richard H. Immerman, *The CIA in Guatemala: The Foreign Policy of Intervention* (Austin: University of Texas Press, 1982), chs. 2–7.

33. Richard Newbold Adams, *Crucifixion by Power: Essays on the Guatemalan National Social Structure, 1944–1966* (Austin: University of Texas Press, 1970).

34. For an extensive analysis of the nature of the civil war, including the role played by the United States, see Susanne Jonas. *The Battle for Guatemala: Rebels, Death Squads, and U.S. Power* (Boulder, CO: Westview Press, 2000); Gordon L. Bowen, "The Origins and Development of State Terrorism," in *Revolution and Counterrevolution in Central America and the Caribbean*, edited by Donald E. Schulz and Douglas H. Graham, 269-300 (Boulder, CO: Westview Press, 1984).

35. Guatemalan Commission for Historical Clarification, *Guatemala: Memory of Silence: Report of the Commission for Historical Clarifications* (CEH, 1999). http://shr.aaas. org/guatemala/ceh/report/english/toc.html.

36. Carlos Aguirre and Kate Doyle, *From Silence to Memory: Revelations of the AHPN* (Eugene: University of Oregon Libraries, 2013); Robert M. Carmack, ed., *Harvest of Violence: The Maya Indians and the Guatemalan Crisis* (Norman: University of Oklahoma Press, 1988); Victoria Sanford, *Buried Secrets: Truth and Human Rights in Guatemala* (New York: Palgrave Macmillan, 2003); David Stoll, *Between Two Armies in the Ixil Towns of Guatemala* (New York: Columbia University Press, 1993).

37. Paul D. Almeida, *Waves of Protest: Popular Struggle in El Salvador, 1925–2005* (Minneapolis: University of Minnesota Press, 2008); Thomas Anderson, *Matanza: El Salvador's Communist Revolt of 1932* (Lincoln: University of Nebraska Press, 1971); Erik Ching, *Authoritarian El Salvador: Politics and the Origins of the Military Regimes, 1880–1940* (South Bend, IN: University of Notre Dame Press, 2016).

38. For details about the role of the military and their alliance with the landed elites, see Elisabeth J. Wood, *Forging Democracy from Below* (New York: Cambridge University Press, 2001); William D. Stanley, *The Protection Racket State: Elite Politics, Military Extortion and Civil War in El Salvador* (Philadelphia: Temple University Press, 1996); Philip J. Williams and Knut Walter, *Militarization and Demilitarization in El Salvador's Transition to Democracy* (Pittsburgh: University of Pittsburgh Press, 1997); Enrique A. Baloyra, *El Salvador in Transition* (Chapel Hill: University of North Carolina Press, 1982).

39. The first military president in Honduras, General Terencio Sierra, failed to stop the frequent turnover in the officer corps and the increased desertion of cadets from the military academy. For more on the development of the Honduran military, see Pérez and Pestana, *Honduran Military Culture Findings Report*; Stokes, *Honduras*; and Steve Ropp, "The Honduran Army in the Sociopolitical Evolution of the Honduran State," *The Americas* 30, no. 4 (April 1974).

40. James A. Morris, *Honduras: Caudillo Politics and Military Rulers* (Boulder, CO: Westview Press, 1984), 9.

41. Lucas Paredes, "Liberalismo y Nacionalismo," in *Transfuguismo Político*, 371-373 (Tegucigalpa, Honduras: Imprenta Honduras, 1963).

42. J. Mark Ruhl, "Honduras: Militarism and Democratization in Troubled Waters," in *Repression, Resistance, and Democratic Transition in Central America*, edited by Thomas Walker and Ariel Armony, 47-66 (Wilmington, DE: Scholarly Resources, 2000).

43. The roots were issues over land reform in Honduras and immigration and demographic problems in El Salvador. Honduras is more than five times the size of neighboring El Salvador, but in 1969 the population of El Salvador (3.7 million) was some 40 percent higher than that of Honduras (2.6 million). At the beginning of the twentieth century, Salvadorans had begun migrating to Honduras in large numbers. By 1969, more than 300,000 Salvadorans were living in Honduras. Land reform enacted by Honduras in 1962, and fully executed by 1967, stripped many Salvadorians living in Honduras of their lands. Thousands of Salvadorians were forcefully expelled from Honduras creating a migration crisis at the border. The immediate spark to the conflict were a couple of football qualifying matches between Honduras and El Salvador for the 1970 World Cup held in the summer of 1969 in Mexico City in which fans came to blows. After the second match, El Salvador attacked Honduras claiming the need to protect Salvadorian citizens on the border. Mediation by the Organization of American States led to a ceasefire on July 20, 1969. See Thomas P. Anderson, *The War of the Dispossessed: Honduras and El Salvador* (Lincoln: University of Nebraska Press, 1981); Allison Acker, *Honduras: The Making of a Banana Republic* (Toronto: Between the Lines, 1988).

44. For a comprehensive examination of the Somoza regime, see Richard L. Millett, *Guardians of the Dynasty: A History of the U.S. Created Guardia Nacional de Nicaragua and the Somoza Family* (Maryknoll, NY: Orbis Books, 1977). For a review of the downfall of Somoza and the rise of the Sandinista regime, see John A. Booth. *The End and the Beginning: The Nicaraguan Revolution* (2nd ed.) (Boulder, CO: Westview Press, 1985). For an excellent discussion of the Somocista women and their connections to the National Guard and the regime, see Victoria Gonzalez Rivera, *Before the Revolution: Women's Rights and Right-Wing Politics in Nicaragua, 1821–1979* (University Park: Pennsylvania State University Press, 2011).

45. Mercedes Munoz Guillen, *El Estado y La Abolición del Ejercito, 1914–1949* (San Jose, Costa Rica: Editorial Porvenir, 1990).

46. Guillen, *Estado y La Abolición del Ejercito.*

47. John A. Booth, "Democratic Development in Costa Rica," *Democratization* 15, no. 4, 724–725.

48. For more on the elimination of the armed forces in Costa Rica, see Kirk S. Bowman, *Militarization, Democracy, and Development: The Perils of Praeorianism in Latin America* (University Park: Pennsylvania State University Press, 2002).

49. For a day-to-day overview of the Costa Rican Civil War, refer to Juan Diego López, Los cuarenta días de 1948: La Guerra Civil en Costa Rica (San José, Costa Rica: Editorial Costa Rica, 1998).

50. John Coatsworth, *Central America and the United States: The Clients and the Colossus* (New York: Twayne, 1994); Mark B. Rosenberg and Luis G. Solís, *The United States and Central America: Geopolitical Realities and Regional Fragility* (New York: Routledge, 2007).

51. LeoGrande, *Our Own Backyard*, 285–306.

52. James Dunkerley, *The Long War: Dictatorship and Revolution in El Salvador* (London: Verso, 1992).

53. John Booth, Christine Wade, and Thomas Walker, *Understanding Central America: Global Forces, Rebellion, and Change* (6th ed.) (Boulder, CO: Westview Press, 2014), 347.

54. LeoGrande, *Our Own Backyard*, ch. 20.

THE RISE AND RETREAT OF THE ARMED FORCES   399

55. John Tower, Edmund Muskie, and Brent Scowcroft, *The Tower Commission Report: Full Text of the President's Special Review Board*, Introduction by R.W. Apple Jr. (Bantam Press, 1987).
56. Peter Dale Scott and Jonathan Marshall, *Cocaine Politics: Drugs, Armies and the CIA in Central America* (Berkeley: University of California Press, 1991).
57. Miguel Angel Reyes Illescas, "Guatemala: Una Negociación Madura?," Los Complejos Senderos de la Paz: Un analisis comparado de las negociaciones de paz en El Salvador, Guatemala y Mexico, *INCEP, Temasy Documentos de Debate* no. 2/97 (Panorama Centroamericano, Guatemala, Junio de 1997): 47.
58. The agency's main mission was to protect the lives of the president and vice president, but historically it was used as a source of military power within the presidency and as a parallel intelligence agency. Members of the EMP have been accused of responsibility in many of the high-profile human rights abuse cases in Guatemala.
59. RESDAL, *A Comparative Atlas of Defence in Latin America and Caribbean* (Buenos Aires, Argentina: RESDAL, 2016), ch. 19. https://www.resdal.org/ing/atlas-2016.html.
60. For a detailed analysis of the political machinations prior to the referendum and its results, see Susanne Jonas, *Of Centaurs and Doves: Guatemala's Peace Process* (Boulder, CO: Westview Press, 2000), ch. 8.
61. "La Cofradía," or "The Brotherhood," is a clique of current and retired military intelligence officers and a kind of internal army fraternity. It is comprised of various members of the military intelligence community who were associated with common crime and administrative corruption in the period of military dictator Lucas Garcia from July 1978 until March 1982. During the Portillo administration it was led by two retired generals, Manuel Callejas y Callejas, the former head of the Customs agency, and Luis Francisco Ortega Menaldo.
62. Rachel Sieder, Megan Thomas, George Vickers, and Jack Spense, *Who Governs? Guatemala Five Years after the Peace Accords* (Washington, DC: Washington Office on Latin America, 2002).
63. Luisa Rodríguez, "Cancelarán 12 mil 109 plazas en el Ejército," *Prensa Libre* (Guatemala), April 2, 2004. http://www.prensalibre.com/pl/2004/abril/02/85248.html.
64. For a discussion of the peace process, see Terry Lynn Karl, "El Salvador's Negotiated Revolution," *Foreign Affairs* 71, no. 2 (Spring 1992); George Vickers, "A Negotiated Revolution," *NACLA Report on the Americas* 25, no. 5 (May 1992); Tommie Sue Montgomery, *Revolution in El Salvador: From Civil Strife to Civil Peace* (2nd ed.) (Boulder, CO: Westview Press, 1995).
65. A full version of the Chapultepec Peace Accords can be found at http://peacemaker. un.org/sites/peacemaker.un.org/files/SV_920116_ChapultepecAgreement.pdf.
66. El Salvador's Constitution of 1983 with Amendments through 2014, Constituteproject.org. http://extwprlegs1.fao.org/docs/pdf/els127410E.pdf.
67. Ricardo Córdova Macías, *El Salvador: Reforma militar y relaciones cívico-militares* (San Salvador, FUNDAUNGO, 1999); Ricardo Córdova Macías, "El Salvador: los acuerdos de paz y las relaciones cívico-militares," in *Control civil y fuerzas armadas en las nuevas democracias latinoamericanas*, edited by Rut Diamint, 549–574 (Buenos Aires: Universidad Torcuato Di Tella y Grupo Editor Latinoamericano, 1999).
68. RESDAL, *A Comparative Atlas of Defence*, 2016, ch. 18.
69. Kirk S. Bowman, *Militarisation, Democracy and Development: The Perils of Praetorianism in Latin America* (University Park: Pennsylvania State University Press, 2002).

70. RESDAL, *A Comparative Atlas of Defence in Latin America and Caribbean* (Buenos Aires, Argentina: RESDAL, 2014), ch. 20. https://www.resdal.org/ing/atlas-2014.html.

71. "Sin condiciones para romper Constitución," *La Prensa*, March 14, 2009, http://www.lap rensahn.com/Pa%C3%ADs/Ediciones/2009/03/15/Noticias/Sin-condiciones-para-rom per-Constitucion; "Artículos pétreos no pueden reformarse ni con plebiscito ni referendo," *La Prensa*, May 26, 2009, http://www.laprensahn.com/Ediciones/2009/05/26/Noticias/ Articulos-petreos-no-pueden-reformarse-ni-con-plebiscito-ni-referendo.

72. Geoff Thale, "Behind the Honduran Coup," *Foreign Policy in Focus*, July 1, 2009, https:// fpif.org/behind_the_honduran_coup/; Larry Birns, "Caudillismo in Action: Looking Back on Honduras' Plight," Council on Hemispheric Affairs, July 7, 2009, http://www.coha.org/ 2009/07/caudillismo-in-action-looking-back-on-honduras; Secretary of State Hillary Rodham Clinton, "Breakthrough in Honduras," *U.S. Department of State*, October 30, 2009, https://2009-2017.state.gov/secretary/20092013clinton/rm/2009a/10/131078.htm/.

73. Global Witness, "Honduras: The Deadliest Country in the World for Environmental Activism," January 2017, https://www.globalwitness.org/fr/campaigns/environmental-activi sts/honduras-deadliest-country-world-environmental-activism/; Ryan Dube, "Honduran President Is Accused of Drug Conspiracy," *Wall Street Journal*, August 3, 2019, https:// www.wsj.com/articles/honduran-president-is-accused-of-drug-conspiracy-11564876238; Christopher Sherman, Martha Mendoza, and Garance Burke, "Secret Report: Honduras' New Top Cop Helped Move Cocaine," *Associated Press*, January 26, 2018, https://www.apn ews.com/0cc4031c058545fb9247ce5095c644c0.

74. While under separate ministries during the Sandinista era effective command and control over both forces was exercised by the nine-member National Directorate of the *Frente*. These ties ended during the Chamorro administration.

75. General Ortega was a founding member of the FSLN, brother of President Daniel Ortega, and at the time of the 1990 elections served as head of the Sandinista Popular Army (Nicaragua's military).

76. "Chamorro anuncia la próxima destitución de Ortega como jefe del Ejército de Nicaragua," *El País*, September 3, 1993. http://elpais.com/diario/1993/09/03/internacional/747007217_ 850215.html.

77. J. Mark Ruhl, "Civil–Military Relations in Post-Sandinista Nicaragua," *Armed Forces & Society* 30, no. 1 (Fall 2003): 117–139.

78. Roberto J. Cajina, *Transición Política y Reconversión Militar en Nicaragua, 1990–1995* (Managua, CRIES, 1996).

79. Roberto J. Cajina, "Reconversión de la Defensa en Nicaragua: Asimetrías e Incoherencias," *Security and Defense Studies Review* 2 (Summer 2002): 81–101.

80. Roberto J. Cajina, "La reforma del sector seguridad y defensa en Nicaragua," Unpublished paper (2005).

81. RESDAL, *A Comparative Atlas of Defence*, 2016, ch. 22.

82. See Irving Dávila, *Análisis jurídico comparado del Código Militar vigente y la iniciativa de reformas propuestas por la Presidencia de la República a la Asamblea Nacional* (Managua: Instituto de Estudios Estratégicos y Políticas Públicas, 2014). https://www. ieepp.org/media/files/publicacion-4-329.pdf.

83. For an analysis of survey data on levels of trust in the region's military, see Pérez, *Civil– Military Relations in Post-Conflict Societies*, 113–129.

Further Reading

Booth, John A. *The End and the Beginning: The Nicaraguan Revolution*. 2nd ed. Boulder, CO: Westview Press, 1985.

Bowman, Kirk S. *Militarization, Democracy, and Development: The Perils of Praetorianism in Latin America*. University Park: Pennsylvania State University Press, 2002.

Coatsworth, John. *Central America and the United States: The Clients and the Colossus*. New York: Twayne, 1994.

Dunkerley, James. *The Long War: Dictatorship and Revolution in El Salvador*. London: Verso, 1992.

Holden, Robert H. *Armies without Nations: Public Violence and State Formation in Central America, 1821–1960*. New York: Oxford University Press, 2004.

Jonas, Susanne. *The Battle for Guatemala: Rebels, Death Squads, and U.S. Power*. Boulder, CO: Westview Press, 2000.

Jonas, Susanne. *Of Centaurs and Doves: Guatemala's Peace Process*. Boulder, CO: Westview Press, 2000.

LeoGrande, William. *Our Own Backyard: The United States and Central America, 1977–1992*. Chapel Hill: University of North Carolina Press, 1998.

Millett, Richard L. *Guardians of the Dynasty: A History of the U.S. Created Guardia Nacional de Nicaragua and the Somoza Family*. Maryknoll, NY: Orbis Books, 1977.

Pérez, Orlando J. *Civil-Military Relations in Post-Conflict Societies*. New York: Routledge, 2015.

Pérez, Orlando J., and Randy Pestana, "Honduran Military Culture," FIU–USSOUTHCOM Academic Partnership (April 2016). https://gordoninstitute.fiu.edu/policy-innovation/military-culture-series/orlando-j-perez-and-randy-pestana-2016-honduran-military-culture.pdf.

Pestana, Randy, and Brian Latell, "Nicaraguan Military Culture," FIU–USSOUTHCOM Academic Partnership (April 2017). https://gordoninstitute.fiu.edu/policy-innovation/military-culture-series/randy-pestana-and-brian-latell-2017-nicaraguan-military-culture.pdf.

Schlesinger, Stephen, and Stephen Kinzer. *Bitter Fruit: The Untold Story of the American Coup in Guatemala*. Garden City, NY: Doubleday, 1982.

Stanley, William D. *The Protection Racket State: Elite Politics, Military Extortion and Civil War in El Salvador*. Philadelphia: Temple University Press, 1996.

Williams, Philip J., and Knut Walter. *Militarization and Demilitarization in El Salvador's Transition to Democracy*. Pittsburgh: University of Pittsburgh Press, 1997.

CHAPTER 15

···

RELIGION, POLITICS, AND THE STATE

···

BONAR L. HERNÁNDEZ SANDOVAL

What remains with Society when the power and influence of Religion is subtracted from it? It becomes a chaos of confusion, and ungovernable tumult.

— Juan José Aycinena y Piñol[1]

May this body immolated and this blood sacrificed for humans nourish us also, so that we may give our body and our blood to suffering and to pain—like Christ, not for self, but to impart notions of justice and peace to our people.

— Óscar Romero[2]

INTRODUCTION

···

The two pronouncements underscore the enduring influence of religious institutions and sensibilities in Central American societies. While the first statement, issued in 1849 by Guatemalan Bishop Juan José Aycinena y Piñol, speaks to the role of the Catholic Church during the tumultuous era of nation-building, the second one, spoken in March 1980 by Salvadoran Archbishop Óscar Romero just before his assassination, reflects the coalescence of a progressive trajectory during the era of Cold War violence. Each declaration belongs to a different historical milieu, the first one invariably influenced by the heated Liberal-Conservative conflict of nineteenth-century Guatemala and the second one shaped by the Salvadoran civil war and state-sponsored repression against the country's nascent social movement. Certainly, much separates the worldview of

Aycinena from that of Romero, not only temporally but theologically, socially, and even politically. Yet the spoken and written words (and actions) of these religious leaders bespeak of the centrality of Catholicism and more broadly religion in the development of Central American postcolonial societies. Religion, they remind us, cannot be extricated from the major social and political transitions in modern Central America, lest we replicate Eurocentric interpretations that posit that modernization has paved the ground for the inexorable advance of secularism and Marxism at the expense religious traditions.[3]

The scholarship of Central American society helps us parse out the continuing, if changing, role that organized religion and popular religiosity have played during the nineteenth and twentieth centuries. Long gone are the days when scholars predicted the declining influence of religion in Latin America and the inevitable march of secular values and leftist political doctrines almost as a zero-sum game involving the unavoidable deterioration of religious institutions and traditions.[4] Religion, both in its institutional and "popular" manifestations, never ceased to shape the social and political landscape of Central America. The region's civil wars and ensuing political violence of the Cold War only reinforced this reality. Indeed, research on this era resulted in a renewed interest on the history of Catholicism, particularly the progressive Catholic movement that surfaced during the 1970s.[5] Writing on the history of religion in Central America, too, has received impetus from the transformation of the religious landscape in recent decades. The Protestant "explosion" of the postwar years but especially during the 1980s not only challenged scholars to rethink whether Central America was "turning Protestant" but also led them back to the topic of religion and to contextualize its proper place in the history of Central American societies.[6]

This article, which takes a largely chronological and a synthetic approach, should be treated as an entry point into the historiography of religion in modern Central America. It sheds light on interaction, on the one hand, between religion and politics, and, on the other, between clerics and laypeople during three key historical periods: (1) the era of nation-building and anticlericalism during the nineteenth century; (2) the age of liberal dictatorship and the resurgence of Catholicism during the first part of the twentieth century; and (3) the transition from reformism to liberation theology and the concurrent transformation of Central America's religious landscape as a result of the expansion of Protestantism during the Cold War. The article concludes with a brief discussion of avenues for future research. Without any pretensions of comprehensiveness, it analyzes major historical events and themes through a discussion of specific countries, and, as the reader will notice, the history of Guatemala, El Salvador, Nicaragua, Costa Rica, and, to a lesser extent, Honduras, predominates in this article. Research on Central America's religious history suggests that, despite the institutional weakening of the Catholic Church since independence, the rise of leftist political movements, and recent secularizing trends, religion—both at the official and unofficial, or unsanctioned, levels—occupied a central place in the region's social and political history, in many instances serving as a catalyst for change and conflict. Consciously or unconsciously, scholars have moved beyond a purely functionalist approach to the study of religion. They have uncovered the Janus-faced nature of church–state relations (one marked by conflict and cooperation), the reciprocal connection between religion and politics, and the increased agency of the laity within religious institutions. Postcolonial religion, including Pentecostalism, was related to and influenced by political developments, particularly the state, and provided spaces for lay religious and social activism and, in some cases, politicization. A unifying thread in the scholarship, thus, is its attention to the symbiotic—and not always harmonious—relationship between religion, politics, and society.

THE CHURCH, NATION-BUILDING, AND RETRENCHMENT

The Catholic Church was at the heart of nation-building and the formation of national identities. Work on nineteenth-century politics in Central America has stressed the interrelationship between Catholicism and politics, in the process focusing on the central role played by the Church in the construction of the Central American nation-states and the conservative ideological apparatus that guided their creation. In the years immediately after independence, the Catholic Church saw its preeminent position challenged as it become part of the conflict between Liberals and Conservatives. During the 1830s, the liberal governments of the Federal Republic Central America established the separation of Church and state, legalized civil marriage and divorce, proclaimed religious liberty, and, among other anticlerical reforms, confiscated Church properties.[7] The Church, thus, lost key political, institutional, and social spaces it had dominated during colonial times. The force of anticlerical reform was a sign of things to come, for it marked the beginning of conflict between religion and politics and revealed just how inseparable were religious institutions from postcolonial societies.

The Church fought back and recovered most its lost privileges during the middle years of the century, with the consequence that Catholicism played an important role in the creation of the Central American nation-states. It became a central pillar in the conservative coalition—consisting of an alliance of merchants, planters, the officers, and priests—that supported the Guatemalan caudillo Rafael Carrera (1839–1865). A mestizo and political outsider who never completely trusted or relied on the conservative and proclerical elite who dominated Central American society, Carrera nonetheless established close relations with the Church, allowed it to once again become a property owner, and gave clerics the ability to renew their social and political influence. As Ralph Lee Woodward Jr. and Douglass Sullivan-González, among others argue, the Church helped shape nation-building in important ways, to the extent that Carrera's conservatism and national project became imbued with the theological postures embodied by key conservative personages. This was the case of José Milla and the conservative cleric Juan José de Aycinena, who served as the rector of the University of San Carlos from 1825 to 1829 and then from 1840 to 1865. These proclerical figures provided the ideological glue that helped keep together, in the words of Woodward, the "conservative citadel" that partly sustained the Carrera dictatorship.[8] A similar conservative and proclerical arrangement emerged elsewhere in the region. During the middle years of the century, the emerging nation-states of Honduras, Nicaragua, and Costa Rica were generally characterized by Church–state harmony, with the effect that even when religious toleration was enshrined in constitutional law, Catholicism remained the state religion. In the process, the Church provided ideological and theological cohesion to the conservative national project of the mid-nineteenth century.[9]

This functionalist interpretation of religion disappears, however, when examining the history of Church–state relations in the late nineteenth century. The political and ideological consensus of the middle of the century came under attack as a new generation of Liberals came to power. Once in power, Central American Liberals pushed forward a far-reaching and more radical (compared to the 1830s) anticlerical reform campaign that significantly changed Central American politics and society. At the heart of the Church–state conflict of this period was a long-standing debate over the relationship between religion and politics, the supremacy of the secular nation-state, and the nature of the colonial-era concordat, which had given form to the Church–state pact of the colonial period. In most of the region, Liberal governments implemented myriad policies that put an end to the privileged position enjoyed by Catholicism during the Carrera era and colonial times, and eroded, if not completely destroyed, the political and economic clout of the Church. Perhaps the most drastic examples of anticlericalism's impact happened in El Salvador and Guatemala. In the aftermath of the regime of Francisco Dueñas (1863–1871), Salvadoran Liberals put an end to the Church's preeminent position. They did so by legalizing civil marriage, removing education from clerical control, abolishing monastic orders, and proclaiming freedom of religion. Although the Church kept its ability to own property, it entered the twentieth century significantly weakened. The Church faced a similar situation in Guatemala, where Liberal Justo Rufino Barrios (1873–85) enacted a series of anticlerical laws that led, among other reforms, to the confiscation of Church properties, the expulsion of foreign clerics, and the separation of Church and state.[10]

The expulsion of clerics reinforced the Church's weakness. Liberal governments, for instance, further undermined the power of the institutional Church by expelling religious leaders, including the Guatemalan archbishops Bernardo Piñol y Aycinena (sent into exile in 1871) and Ricardo Casanova y Estrada (1886), the Salvadoran bishop Luis Cárcamo y Rodríguez (1875), the Nicaraguan prelate Simeón Pereira y Castellón (1898), and the Costa Rican leaders Anselmo Llorente y La Fuente (1858) and Bernard August Thiel (1884). Together with the other anticlerical reforms, these expulsions, which in some instances were indefinite in nature, left the Central American churches in administrative disarray, without the ability to provide consensus to the nation. The same can be said of the ban on religious orders. The fate of the Society of Jesus provides a good case study for understanding the effects of anticlericalism on the ebb and flow of Church life. Beginning in the 1870s, Liberal administrations expelled the Jesuits, confiscated their properties, and secularized education, which, as already mentioned, meant that these and other religious orders lost their ability to control and direct the region's educational system. Even in Nicaragua, where the exiled Jesuits received asylum, they found themselves unwelcome in 1881. The Society of Jesus was by no means an exception, for Liberal governments banned other regular orders, including the Capuchins, Franciscans, Dominicans, and the Congregation of St. Philip Neri. In the long term, the expulsion of the Jesuits and other religious orders resulted in a chronic scarcity of clerics. In Guatemala alone, of the ninety-nine regular priests, fifty-eight left the country and the remaining forty-one became secular priests. In the late nineteenth century, this situation left a total of 180 priests (all secular) for a population of 1.5 million. The clergy shortage was particularly felt in rural Central America, where the institutional Church continued to project its moral authority but without clerics to oversee the religious life of rural peoples.[11]

A by-product of the clergy shortage was the Church's retrenchment from the countryside and the transformation of Central America's religious landscape. Rural regions, including those with high concentration of Indigenous peoples, became increasingly detached from the institutional or official life of the Church, which gave way to the rise of "folk Catholicism," or what historians of religion have also called "popular religiosity." It is important not to overstate the gulf between "official" and "non-official" practices or to paint a clear-cut boundary between institutional religion and popular religious beliefs and practices, for, as Paul J. Vanderwood and Reinaldo L. Román have reminded us, these supposedly separate religious spheres should be understood as part and parcel of the same cultural matrix.[12] A type of religious syncretism proliferated in Costa Rica. This was the case of the Virgen de los Angeles, popularly known as La Negrita, whose reputed miraculous healing powers made her a national religious icon. Dating back to the colonial era, La Negrita first manifested herself in the form of a small black granite figure and subsequently became a prominent figure among the nonwhite rural population. Her popularity surged in the context of the age of anticlerical reform, the decline of the Catholic Church from national affairs, and the rise of the secular state. By the early twentieth century, Church authorities and elite groups, cognizant of La Negrita's widespread acceptance among the Costa Rican population, had appropriated her cult, in the process making her a patron saint and often depicting her as a source of national unity.[13]

Yet it was often the case that rural regions in the region experienced a palpable separation between the clergy and the laity. In the Guatemalan highlands, rural Maya communities continued to organize local religion around religious brotherhoods, *cofradías*, which, in the context of anticlericalism, functioned without much (if any) clerical supervision. Maya religious leaders, or *chimanes*, and the places of worship and religious practices—combining Indigenous and Catholic religion—they controlled at the local level now took center stage in the life of rural communities.[14] Likewise, El Salvador witnessed the emergence, in the words of Clifford Geertz, of a parallel "cultural system" in the form of a new class of religious figures known as the *hermanos espirituales*. Most prominent among them was Trinidad Huezo, a middle-aged woman who wears a long skirt and a cape on her shoulders and carries a shoulder bag full of pineapples and a basket with fruit on her head. Huezo and other *hermanos espirituales* became well known, among other things, for their ability to cure illnesses, and thus came to occupy important roles in many rural communities.[15] The expansion of these popular religious traditions and figures gave the laity increasing religious autonomy.

The Church's weakness, coupled with the continuing presence of anticlericalism in the region's political landscape, also paved the way for the arrival of new religious institutions and currents and the further erosion of Catholicism's monopoly over society. Liberals, intent on putting an end to Catholicism's influence and bringing "modernity" to the shores of Central America, welcomed various Protestant missionaries from the United States. These new religious actors, imbued with the nineteenth-century religious revival movement and ideas about "progress" in the United States, regarded their work in the region as part of a "civilizing" mission. They might not have seen themselves as part of US imperial objectives, but their presence was a symptom of the expansion of US power and a noteworthy departure from the religious history of Central America. Protestant missionaries contributed, albeit initially in a limited manner, to the erosion of clerical authority and, over time, helped put an end to the Church's control over the religious life of the region. In Nicaragua and Guatemala, where Presbyterians, Adventists, Moravians, and the Central American Mission (CAM) established a presence among rural communities (including among Indigenous peoples), foreign missionaries invariably controlled the local churches. This changed during the second part of the twentieth century, when local Protestant churches expanded their memberships, became increasingly autonomous from US churches, and challenged more forcefully Catholicism's preeminent role in society.[16] Costa Rica experienced not only the decline of Catholicism in the nation's cultural life and the arrival of Protestant missionaries, but also the establishment of new spiritual and intellectual currents. The early twentieth century gave birth to Spiritist circles associated with Freemasonry and theosophy, whose members became known for their devotion to Christ.[17] Although at the time these groups did not gain large number of adherents, they represented the gradual transformation of the religious makeup of the region.

These religious changes or disruptions did not follow the same path or have the same force throughout the region. Church–state relations diverged from the trajectory of conflict seen in Guatemala and El Salvador. This was evident in the early history of Panama, where the Church, while not enjoying any special privileges, did not lose its ability to own property, and in Honduras, where dictator Tiburcio Carías Andino (1924, 1933–1949) expelled two bishops and all foreign clerics. Eventually, however, the government allowed foreign religious orders to return and permitted others, including the Capuchins, Redemptionists, Salesians, and Paulists, to establish a permanent presence. The wealth of the Costa Rican Church was minimal, which meant that Liberals did not have much economic motivation to undermine it. Church–state friction was evident, as when the government expelled Llorente and Thiel. These actions, according to Philip Williams, were the by-product of personal animosities and thus did not represent a breakdown of Church–state relations. In Nicaragua, Liberals, who had been discredited due to their association with and support of the invasion led by filibuster William Walker, did not have the political success of their counterparts in neighboring countries. There, Nicaraguan Conservatives, who remained in power until the early 1890s, generally maintained cordial relations with Church officials. The notable exception occurred in 1881, when the national government expelled the Jesuits, many of whom had recently arrived from Guatemala. Still, stability characterized Church–state relations, with the effect that the struggle between Liberals and Catholic leaders did not always dictate the course of national politics. Of course, this situation changed, at least momentarily under Liberal dictator José Santos Zelaya (1893–1909). Much like his Liberal counterparts, Zelaya promulgated the separation of Church and state, the confiscation of Church property, the establishment of secular education, and, among other anticlerical policies, the expulsion of clerics who opposed his reforms. Harmonious Church–state relations returned after the fall of Zelaya, with the effect that the Church did not suffer from the same long-term institutional weakness seen elsewhere in the region.[18]

New Political Arrangements, Church–State Relations, and Papal Power

If anticlericalism resulted in ruptures and some continuities, the first part of the twentieth century was marked by the resurgence of Catholicism's social and political clout. This is not to say that the Catholic Church recovered its religious monopoly, for the Central American Church was still a frail institution. With a relatively small number of priests, religious leaders left many parishioners, particularly in rural communities, without much formal contact with the sacraments of the Church. This was even the case in Nicaragua, where, as of 1960, there were 4,550 Catholics for each priest.[19] Moreover, anticlericalism did not completely disappear from the region's political landscape. In countries such as Guatemala, the 1920s brought a renewed anticlerical wave, which, although not as sweeping as that of the previous century, reinforced the existing anticlerical regime and served to further cripple the Church's ability to exert social or even political influence.[20] Yet, as the scholarship on Catholicism now reveals, the first part of the twentieth century was also characterized by the expanding power of the Holy See and new political configurations resulting in an era of Church–state conciliation that, in turn, functioned to give legitimacy to the political status quo. These factors helped spark an era of institutional resurgence.

Institutional histories on Church–state relations indicate that, by the 1930s and 1940s, anticlericalism had receded into the background of politics, thus creating opportunities for the Church's resurgence. This "softening" of anticlericalism meant that Liberal dictators, who favored political pragmatism and clung to political power by all means possible, sought to forge new alliances with key conservative sectors, including the Catholic Church. In this changing political environment, Church leaders often emerged as supporters of the status quo. Consequently, the Church of the first part of the century generally avoided confrontation with the state.[21] The history of the Nicaraguan Church is illustrative in this respect. Despite the passage and continuing existence of anticlerical legislation, Nicaraguan Church leaders, on the whole, supported obedience to dictator Anastasio Somoza García (1936–1956), who ruled the country with the support of the US government and Liberal and Conservative sectors and established a political dynasty perpetuated by his two sons, Luis Somoza (1956–1963) and Anastasio Somoza Debayle (1967–1979). There were voices of dissent among the hierarchy, as was the case of Octavio José Calderón y Padilla, bishop of Matagalpa (1946–1970). An opponent of the Somoza dictatorship, he criticized economic inequality, famously skipped Somoza García's funeral in 1956 to visit his parishioners, and once argued that "resistance is a duty and obedience a crime."[22] Nonetheless, the Church adopted a policy of legitimization of the regime. The country's archbishop, José Antonio Lezcano y Ortega (1913–1952), and his successor, Vicente Alejandro Gonzáles y Robledo (1953–1968), distinguished themselves as dependable supporters of the Somozas. Certainly, these prelates were not ignorant of the dynasty's repressiveness, but they viewed it as a way to forestall the advance of communism and as a means to regain certain privileges. The latter materialized in the form of tax exemptions, a role for the Church in the educational system, and the return of the Jesuits and the arrival of new religious groups such as the Capuchins and the brothers of La Salle. In 1959, Gonzáles y Robledo, keenly aware of the beneficial nature of this relationship, famously declared that "our government is not an ungodly one, rather it is a benefactor of the Church." Lezcano y Ortega's decision to "crown" Somoza García's daughter as the "Queen of the Army" in a well-publicized public ceremony held in 1942 at the national stadium captured well the spirit of this era of Church–state conciliation.[23]

Likewise, Guatemalan Catholic leaders became determined to pursue appeasement. Archbishop Luis Durou y Sure (1928–1938) and his successor, Mariano Rossell y Arellano (1939–1964), cultivated close ties with the Liberal state, particularly during the dictatorship of Jorge Ubico (1931–1944). They favored peaceful coexistence—a type of détente—as opposed to conflict. Under their leadership, the Church hierarchy, which considered Ubico a bulwark against what it viewed as the rapid advance of secularism, communism, and Protestantism, sought to regain its public presence. Ubico, who like Somoza, recognized the importance of Church–state conciliation, rewarded the Church in various ways. In contravention of Liberal policy, he allowed for the celebration of several regional- and national-level congresses intended to promote priestly vocations, religious education, and lay participation. More importantly, the dictator adopted a policy similar to his Nicaraguan counterpart by permitting the return of the Jesuits and the arrival of new religious groups, most notably the Salesians, Marists, and the members of the Catholic Foreign Mission Society of America, or Maryknoll.[24] On the whole, therefore, Central American religious leaders proved consistent supporters of the status quo as embodied by the Liberal dictatorships of the first part of the twentieth century.

A transnational focus reveals that this revised Church–state relationship was not only tied to political factors but was the by-product of the Vatican's increasingly interventionist role. Central American Catholicism, after all, was intrinsically tied to the structures of international Catholicism, particularly to the Church of Rome. The Holy

See played an integral, though often understudied, role in spurring an era of Church–state harmony and institutional expansion and renewal. There were precedents for this interventionism. Rome had negotiated a series of concordats with Conservative and Liberal administrations during the nineteenth century. Such accords created a framework for Church–state relations and provided some legal protections for local churches.[25] These arrangements also set the stage for the modern organization of the regional Church, most significantly by mandating the establishment of new administrative sees. Thus, Rome authorized the creation of the archdioceses of San Salvador (1913), Managua (1913), and Tegucigalpa (1916), and the dioceses of Granada (1913), Alajuela (1921), Los Altos (1921), San José de Costa Rica (1921), and Matagalpa (1924). New ecclesiastical jurisdictions helped tie local churches more directly into the structures of the Holy See.[26] In the early twentieth century, the Vatican intervened in more direct and immediate ways, particularly by backing and lobbying in favor of a Church–state *modus vivendi* that, as previously mentioned, set the stage for the restoration of certain privileges. It did so through its expanding network of papal envoys and permanent diplomats based in Central America, first in its Internunciature in Central America (located in San José, Costa Rica) and then in other apostolic missions, or nunciatures, established in each country. During the 1930s, for example, the first papal nuncio in Guatemala, Alberto Levame, played an integral role in bringing about a period of conciliation and cooperation between the local church and Ubico and formalizing diplomatic relations between the Holy See and the state. This also meant that Guatemalan Catholicism, despite the ruptures caused by liberalism, remained connected to the power of Rome.[27]

New Religious Actors and Laypeople during the Age of Development

A focus on papal intervention and the crystallization of cordial Church–state relations gives us a granular perspective of the revival of Central American Catholicism. For one, its sheds new light on the missionary movement that transformed the institutional makeup and direction of Catholicism. Church–state convergence, facilitated by the influence of Rome, contributed to the relaxation of anticlerical legislation. As previously indicated, this shift, in turn, facilitated the return of previously banished religious orders, particularly the Jesuits, and allowed religious leaders to recruit clerics from the United States and Europe. Many of these new religious actors heeded the calls by Pius XI (1922–1929) and Pius XII (1939–1959) to "evangelize" regions in the global South and thus became part of the global missionary movement of the twentieth century. Such undertaking was predicated on the notion that Central American societies (particularly rural Indigenous communities) felt outside the parameters of Catholic orthodoxy. As foreign clerics arrived, the Church witnessed an institutional revival reminiscent of the early colonial era. Missionaries from Maryknoll and the Sacred Heart (from Spain) began their work in Guatemala, El Salvador, Honduras, and Nicaragua. In Guatemala, this missionary movement resulted in a radical remaking of the Church, so that by 1966, as Bruce Calder has pointed out, 1,235 out of the 1,432 clerics in the country were foreign-born.[28] Writing on this period, which focuses on transnational linkages and the Church's growing social presence, reveals that the influx of foreign clergy added much impetus to the institutional expansion and renewal of Catholicism.

The arrival of foreign clerics formed part of a broader resurgence of Catholicism. Such development became reality in the form of renewed clerical presence at the parish level, an assertive Church determined to carve out a public (if not political) face, and the incorporation (albeit in a subordinate position) of the laity into the structures of the Church. Foreign clerics established mission territories to propagate a Romanized vision and practice of Catholicism, one that gave precedence to the sacramental life of the Church, and to expand clerical influence over the laity. They did so partly through new and sometimes existing Church-sanctioned lay associations, which gave Catholic leaders greater control of the religious life of rural populations, and, in certain cases, served to foster divisions at the parish level.[29] Most prominent among these lay associations was Catholic Action, an association of European implant that surfaced in Central America in the early twentieth century. Rural Catholic Action groups appeared in Guatemala during the 1930s, although it was only under the leadership of Archbishop Rossell that this association expanded rapidly in the Diocese of Los Altos, located in the western part of the country. A mostly rural territory populated by the majority of Guatemala's Maya Indigenous population, this ecclesiastical jurisdiction gave rise to one of the most vibrant rural Catholic Action movements in the region. It rested on a network of lay catechists, who, under clerical supervision, sought to advance a hierarchical vision of Catholicism and sacrament-based religious practices among the Maya population. Promoted by Sacred Heart and Maryknoll missionaries, among others, this association and its militant lay members often clashed with Maya *chimanes* and the Indigenous religious beliefs and traditions that had predominated locally particularly since the late nineteenth century. Conflict manifested itself as Catholic Action and Indigenous religious leaders fought over control of church facilities and *cofradías*, as well as over the use of marimba music inside churches, which clerics invariably opposed. Over time, these divisions resulted in a multifaceted religious landscape, one occupied by missionaries and Catholic Action members, on the one hand, and the followers of *costumbre*, on the other. As these groups jockeyed for spaces and positions, they often adopted a policy of mutual coexistence and accommodation.[30]

The rise of Catholic Action was indicative of the rise of a reformist-minded social pastoral. This development was partly the by-product of the diffusion of the social doctrine of the Church in Central America. During the first part of the twentieth century, progressive sectors among the Costa Rican clergy sought to address the "social question." Jorge Volio, a priest-turned politician who was known for resisting the political acquiescence of the rest of the national hierarchy, played a key role in disseminating Catholic social thought as embodied by the so-called social encyclicals. Following Leo XIII's 1893 encyclical, *Rerum Novarum*, Volio contended that charity and justice should guide labor-capital relations. In addition, deeply influenced by his experiences during his residence in Louvain, Belgium, in the early years of the century, Volio became the leading figure within the class-based *Partido Reformista* in the early 1920s. A presidential candidate in 1923 who famously declared that there should "more teachers than soldiers," he personified the rise of an early type of Catholic-based reformist movement that sought to address and provide a response to modernization and the emerging working classes. This type of activism was also evident during the administration of Archbishop Víctor Manuel Sanabria (1940–1952), whose advocacy of the social doctrine of the Church led him to follow in Volio's footsteps, that is, into the path of reformism. Part of the emerging center-of-left social and political alliance led by President Rafael Ángel Calderón (1940–1944), the prelate advocated for a new social contract with the population, formed links with organized labor, and endorsed social legislation favorable to workers during the 1948 revolution.[31]

This reformist Church, the historiography reveals, was propelled forward by greater participation of the laity. Catholic Action and similar lay associations confined laypeople to Catholicism's hierarchical structures and clerical supervision. Church leaders considered Catholic Action a counterweight to "the double threat" of communism and the small yet expanding presence of Protestantism. They officially endorsed it during the *Primera Conferencia del Espiscopado Centroamericano* (the first conference of the Central American bishops), held in San José, Costa Rica, in 1956, and encouraged the organization of Catholic Action groups among university students, young urban workers, and rural communities. This strategy was adopted by the Nicaraguan hierarchy, which sanctioned Catholic Action groups in urban centers in the 1940s.[32] Such development was also evident in Costa Rica, where the former bishop of Alajuela, Archbishop Sanabria, heeded Pius XI's call to promote the "participation of the laity in the apostolate of the hierarchy" and thus proved a great promoter of Catholic Action. Under his direction, this association soon took root among the country's highly politicized working classes. The most important example was the *Confederación Costarricense de Trabajadores* (CCTRN), which by the late 1940s, had become a formidable Catholic labor organization that rose to challenge the *Confederación de Trabajadores de Costa Rica* (CTCR), the powerful communist labor union.[33]

Yet, even when it relegated its members to subservient positions, Catholic Action marks the beginning of increased lay agency and the rise of a new class of lay religious leaders. Catholic Action functioned as a space for the formation of a new generation of religious and social leaders. The laity gained increased visibility amid the proliferation of developmentalist-oriented projects during the early Cold War years. Reformistminded religious sectors, intent on expanding the influence of the Church and providing an alternative to communism and Protestantism, initiated various programs of socioeconomic development. Auxiliary Bishop of Tegucigalpa Evelio Domínguez (1957–1988) instituted a series of "radio schools" to foster a process of *concientización*, or conscious-raising, among rural peoples. This program created the conditions for lay participation in the promotion of land reform as a way to prevent the radicalization of the countryside.[34] Reformism and lay involvement also characterized the Church in the Guatemalan highlands, where a convergence of religious and material prerogatives created the conditions for the formation and expansion of a cooperative movement. By the 1950s, foreign and native-born clerics, supported by laypeople, had established a network of credit and agricultural cooperatives. It was often through their involvement in cooperatives that Maya parishioners associated with Catholic Action gained the knowledge and skills that allowed them to become community and sometimes political leaders. Church-sponsored cooperatives gave Maya peoples access to new (and often less expensive) sources of credit and agricultural methods and technologies (including fertilizers), thus empowering them to interact more directly with regional, national, and even international markets. In the process, cooperatives embodied the development ethos of the Cold War. Clerics and laypeople in the highlands may not have been the tools of the Cold War state (as personified by John F. Kennedy's Alliance for Progress programs), but they certainly became part of an international trend that emphasized development as a bulwark against communism and a solution to the region's socioeconomic problems, including poverty, malnutrition, high mortality rates, and illiteracy. They often used Alliance for Progress funds and resources provided through churches in the United States to jump-start and run not only agricultural but also literacy and health projects.[35] An examination of these initiatives, therefore, highlights the Church's ties to international religious and ideological networks and its ability to impact society and become an engine of socioeconomic change, despite the advance of secularism and the political Left.

FROM REFORMISM TO LIBERATION

The mid-century Church, therefore, was an institution on the move. Certain secular events and trends propelled religious leaders into action. The Cuban Revolution and the fear of communism, for instance, gave impetus to the Church's programs of development. Other factors, including the diffusion of secular values, the advance urbanization, and the growth of Protestantism, further stimulated certain changes and innovations. Within Catholicism, a combination of local and global developments helped spur change. Together with the missionary and Catholic Action movements, the formation of national-level episcopal conferences in Guatemala (1956), El Salvador (1958), and Costa Rica (1963) and new ecclesiastical jurisdictions gave the Church the institutional framework for expansion and transformation, for the dissemination of new pastoral and socioeconomic initiatives, and for greater lay participation. Furthermore, the Second Vatican Council (1962–1965), or Vatican II, further inspired clerics and laypeople to rethink the Church's moral and temporal role in society. The Council, and later the second meeting of the Latin American bishops held at Medellín, Colombia (1968), reinforced local and regional trends. It reaffirmed, for instance, the existing notion that the Church must consider and act upon the material realities of Catholic populations. As we know now, such dynamic fostered the crystallization of a progressive Catholic movement, one that often clashed with state prerogatives that, once again, brought to the forefront the conflict between religion and politics, divided local churches, and created spaces for moments of religious and political radicalization.[36]

Progressive Catholicism helped transform Catholic organizations in important ways. Initially inspired by Cold War developmentalism and Catholic social doctrine, the Church's social programs gained momentum in the late 1960s and early 1970s, so that clerics, Catholic Action catechists, and more broadly laypeople adapted the message of the Gospel to their individual lives and the social environment in which they lived. Encouraged by Vatican II's emphasis on Bible reading, many Catholics, including Catholic Action members, now joined Christian Base Communities (*Comunidades Eclesiales de Base*, CEBs). Contrary to Catholic Action's hierarchical modus operandi, CEBs brought together laypeople who analyzed the relationship between Scripture and their lived experiences. It was in this context that they adopted a critical consciousness that allowed them to put forward a critique of the long-standing history of political exclusion, socioeconomic inequality, and, in areas with large Indigenous populations, institutionalized racism.[37] This shift, which paved the way for the dissemination of liberation theology, did not emerge in a vacuum. It took form in the context of the emergence of revolutionary Marxist groups throughout the region, most notably in Guatemala, El Salvador, and Nicaragua. These two social/religious and political/military movements evolved in parallel fashion, sometimes joining on critical issues such as concern for socioeconomic inequality and racism. Thus, even when the Church did not support the militant Left, in the words of Virginia Garrard, "Central America from the 1960s into the 1980s—more than any other place in Latin America—became the ultimate workshop for liberationist Catholic theology and political action."[38]

Writing on this period reveals that this liberationist trajectory underscores the intrinsic relationship—and continuing conflict—between religion and politics and between Catholicism and the state. Such was the case in Nicaragua, where many members of the post-conciliar Church gradually withdrew their tacit support or passive stance toward the Somoza dynasty. An important shift was palpable during and in the aftermath of the 1969 Pastoral Conference. Given the scarcity of clerics in the countryside, this meeting expanded the role of the laity, thus creating the conditions for the formation of CEBs and *delegados de la palabra* and, equally important, the radicalization of priests. A group of clerics, known as *Los Doce* (most notably Ernesto Cardenal and the Maryknoll priest Miguel d'Escoto), called into question the structures of poverty and repression during the Somoza dictatorship. In addition, in the aftermath of the 1972 earthquake, CEB members responded to increased inequality and state violence by joining the Sandinista National Liberation Front (*Frente Sandinista de Liberación Nacional*, or FSLN), or the Sandinistas. They were often inspired by Fernando Cardenal, who, like other priests (including his brother, Ernesto Cardenal), underwent a "revolution" of their own and formed ties with and became part of the Marxist guerrilla struggle led by the Sandinistas. Cardenal and other Catholics eventually served in the Sandinista-controlled government after 1979. Their actions demonstrated that religion and politics in pre- and revolutionary Nicaragua were (or to be more precise, remained) intrinsically connected to each other.[39]

A similar religious and political turn characterized the Salvadoran Church. Its history during the Cold War showed that there was nothing intrinsically static or conservative when it came to religious institutions. Progressive Catholics, many of whom participated in the CEBs, established links with popular movements that challenged the country's military governments and landowning elite. As they became targets of state repression, many activists abandoned the reformism inherent in programs of development and the centrist political platform of the Christian Democratic Party. Much as in the case of Nicaragua, they contributed to the creation of the Marxist revolutionary movement led by the Farabundo Martí National Liberation Front (*Frente Farabundo Martí para la Liberación Nacional*, FMLN). This radicalization, the historiography tells us, was not simply a by-product of government repression but rather the consequence of a broader alliance between urban and peasant intellectuals who embraced Marxism and liberation theology to create a broad-based revolutionary movement. Archbishop Óscar Romero's transformation from a moderate to a critic of state violence against the popular movement was shaped by escalating repression and the intensification of the country's civil war (1979–1992) and by the conscious-raising process and politicization that affected progressive Catholic groups. His assassination in 1980, as well as that of four churchwomen of Maryknoll in 1981 and the six Jesuits in 1989, all occurred at the hands of the military regime and thus brought to the forefront the complex, if not conflictive, nature of Church–state relations during the Cold War.[40]

Central America's liberationist trajectory also manifested itself in the form of a sociocultural perspective. Guatemala's progressive religious movement encouraged clerics and laypeople to reconsider their support for Cold War development programs. For many Maya Catholics, including those who came of age within the confessional confines of Catholic Action and in the context of military rule after 1954, state repression highlighted the impossibility of eliminating poverty, inequality, and racism through traditional political parties. As in the case of El Salvador, radicalization of Maya and ladino (or non-Indigenous) Catholic groups took place as urban and rural workers and intellectuals came together to forge new popular social organizations in opposition to military dictatorship. These groups gained adherents partly because of the escalation of state-sponsored repression against clerics, catechists and the emerging popular movement, particularly during the military governments of Fernando Romeo Lucas García (1978–1982) and Efraín Ríos Montt (1982–1983). It was in this context that overtly militant organizations such as the Committee of Peasant Unity (*Comité de Unidad Campesina*, CUC) came into existence. Formed largely by former Maya Catholic Action catechists, CUC combined a class-based liberationist perspective found elsewhere in the region and a sociocultural analysis of society to expose the long-standing history of racism against the Indigenous population. The supporters of these two liberationist trajectories—one based on Marxist viewpoint and the other one shaped by inculturation theology—strove to create a class-based revolutionary movement that would bring together poor Maya and ladino workers in the highlands and the Pacific coast and that would join the revolutionary movement of the 1970s and 1980s. Maya communities were often "caught in the middle" between revolutionary groups and the military government, for not all Catholics experienced a process of politicization. Nonetheless, research on the post-conciliar Church in Guatemala (and in Nicaragua and El Salvador) indicates that progressive Catholics actively shaped the social and political landscape of the region. Religious identity, in other words, served as a catalyst for political change.[41]

One should be careful, however, when tracing the shift from the reformist to the liberationist Church. Research on the subject suggests that the path from one era to the other was anything but peaceful or linear in nature. Vatican II, the Medellín conference, and liberation theology created and often exacerbated divisions within the Church. Miguel Obando y Bravo (1970–2005) opposed the Somoza dynasty but was wary of the Left, including the supporters of liberation theology and clerics who joined the Sandinista government after 1979. Likewise, Romero's predecessor, Luis Chávez y González (1938–1977) and the hierarchy emphasized "accompaniment" of the poor but opposed the notion that the Church should be at the forefront of change. In Guatemala, Cardinal Mario Casariego y Acevedo (1964–1983), who often criticized clerics who espoused a liberationist perspective, proved reluctant to condemn state-sponsored violence and became known for his association with military figures. The Vatican reinforced these fractures between progressive and conservative sectors, for it gradually distanced itself from the progressive Church, ostracized key figures within progressive Catholicism, and sided with the opponents of radical politics.[42]

This conservative turn was evident in years leading up to the third meeting of the Latin American Bishops at Puebla, Mexico (1979). It took two forms. In Honduras, the Church had encouraged the politicization of rural communities, as was the case in 1969 when the Prelate of Choluteca, Marcel Gérin y Boulay, sided with peasants who demanded the restitution of their lost lands. In the early 1970s, the Church hierarchy continued to foster this kind of mobilization, which morphed into what became known as the Christian Social Movement, which consisted of students, labor, and progressive Catholic groups. In the aftermath of the 1975 military coup and the massacre at Los Horcones, however, religious leaders gradually distanced themselves from progressive Catholicism. This shift signified abandonment of the developmentalism and reformism of the 1950s and 1960s and the post-conciliar Church. The Costa Rican case demonstrates the tenuous evolution of the progressive Catholic movement. There, with few exceptions, the Catholic hierarchy adopted a timid stance vis-à-vis the country's socioeconomic problems. Their 1979 pastoral letter endorsed many of the central components of liberation theology, including support for the "preferential option for the poor." The strike of the banana workers at Standard Fruit Company's plantations, however, revealed the Church's reluctance to support workers' demands and support for a policy of conciliation and paternalism.[43] As it turned out, it was at the local level, with foreign clerics and progressive lay activists often leading the way, that the theological changes brought about by Vatican II and the Medellín meeting were truly and consistently implemented.

THE PENTECOSTAL EXPANSION

The politicization of Catholicism took place against the backdrop of an evolving religious landscape. In particular, the second part of the twentieth century witnessed the rapid expansion of Protestantism. The Protestant presence in the region was not new, for, as previously mentioned, Protestant churches had had a long history in Central America because of the triumph of Liberalism and the subsequent institutional retrenchment of the Catholic Church. During the second part of twentieth century, the advance of Protestantism in Central America materialized mostly in the form of the expansion of myriad Pentecostal denominations and became tied to political polarization, economic crisis, and civil war. Such was the extent of Protestantism's growth that, according to a Pew Research Center poll, by 2014 approximately 40 percent of the population of Guatemala, Honduras, and Nicaragua identified themselves as Protestant. The same poll revealed that, even though lower, the percentage of the Protestant population in El Salvador (36 percent) and Costa Rica (25 percent) also comprised a significant portion of the population.[44] These figures are in themselves important, for they highlight the transformation of Central Americans' religious identity.

They also underscore the continuing connection between religion and politics. Two case studies help us understand this relationship. In El Salvador, the historic shortage of Catholic clerics, political violence, and displacement during the civil war created the conditions for the erosion, if not disintegration, of community bonds. Pentecostalism allowed many Salvadorans to find answers to the rapidly changing political and economic context in which they lived. It offered a personalistic approach to God, whereby Salvadorans could establish an individual relationship with Jesus, one not mediated by clerics. Likewise, in Guatemala, the 1976 earthquake brought to the forefront a conflagration of political and socioeconomic factors. There, as in the case of El Salvador, Protestantism had had a presence since the late nineteenth century, but its growth had been limited, mainly due to the fact that, in the eyes of many Guatemalans, it was associated with the expansion of US power. The human and physical destruction brought about by the earthquake revealed long-standing conditions of poverty, created the conditions for the revitalization of the fledging guerrilla movement, and opened the way for the arrival of foreign religious aid workers. The intensification of the country's civil war (1960–1996) during the Ríos Montt regime further facilitated the expansion of Pentecostal denominations. His vision for a "New Guatemala" emphasized national unity, anticommunism, and, in stark contrast to liberation theology, a conservative reading of Scripture. For many Guatemalan (and Salvadoran) converts, Pentecostalism stood for a kind of "refuge of the masses" and an opportunity of salvation in time of crisis and violence. This was especially the case during and after the scorched-earth campaign unleashed by the Ríos Montt military government, which resulted in the death of approximately one hundred thousand people. Most of the victims were Indigenous Maya peoples and many had been active socially and politically as part of liberationist-inspired movements.[45] The so-called Protestant boom, therefore, was intrinsically tied to the region's history of political conflict and violence.

Conclusion

Given this discussion, it is safe to conclude that religion—in both its institutional and its popular manifestations—is alive and well in Central America. Nation-building in the nineteenth century inflicted a heavy blow on the power of institutional Catholicism, with the effect that popular and non-Catholic religious forms thrived during the postcolonial era. During the first part of the twentieth century, the Catholic Church, supported by the Vatican, reaffirmed its political presence, underwent a period of institutional resurgence, and, given the polarization brought about by the Cold War and progressive turn of the post-1960s, experienced increased internal politicization and divisions. The growth of Protestantism, which contributed to breaking Catholicism's historic religious monopoly, led to a multifaceted religious environment. Even then, Catholicism has continued to exert much political and social presence. It is perhaps simplistic to conclude that the violence of the Cold War put an end the Church–state modus vivendi of the first part of the twentieth century. In Nicaragua, the stability of the post-Sandinista regime after 1989 owed part of its political base to the conservative sector of the Church led by Cardinal Obando y Bravo. Influenced to varying degrees by the progressive ethos of liberation theology, Central American Catholic leaders have continued to denounce social and political injustice. In Guatemala, Juan José Gerardi, who was assassinated in 1998 by members of the military due to his human rights work, and Álvaro Ramazzini, famous for his work on behalf of the rights of Indigenous communities and recently raised to the rank of cardinal by Pope Francis, point to the continuing role of the Church in social and even political matters. The same can be said of Pentecostal churches, which have played a political role in recent decades. Although they maintained an ostensibly apolitical posture as the Central American civil wars came to an end, Pentecostal leaders have participated in politics, sometimes running for political office.[46]

The analysis provided in this article, thus, emphasizes two themes: religious diversity and conflict and the relationship between religion and politics. Since its inception in Central America, the Catholic Church has been a multifaceted institution consisting of a diversity of institutional and non-institutional voices and actors. The development of postcolonial Central American societies also reminds us of the symbiotic interplay between religion and politics and the necessity of incorporating an analysis of the state into discussions of Catholicism. These two realities—the history of conflict and divisions within Catholicism and the relationship between the religion and politics—are reflected in the two quotes at the beginning of this article. They became palpable during the era of nation-building in the nineteenth century, institutional resurgence and expansion in the first decades of the twentieth century, and religious and political radicalization and revolutionary upheaval during the Cold War.

These trends and themes in the historiography provide a fertile ground for future scholarship. Future research on the history of religion in Central America might benefit, first, from a more in-depth examination of the transnational dimensions of Catholicism. We have relatively few archival-based studies, for instance, that illuminate the international links between local churches and international Catholicism. More studies on the relationship between the Vatican and Central American churches (including during the crucial years of Vatican II) can potentially shed new light on the history of Church–state relations and Catholicism's influence in society. Another fruitful avenue for future research might be a more coherent analysis of the history of popular religious movements. More research on this topic is necessary, particularly covering the nineteenth century and early years of the twentieth century. It was, after all, during this period when the institutional Church lost much influence among the region's population and clerical supervision was superseded by local actors. In doing such research, scholars would do well in incorporating both non-official and institutional sources and voices. Finally, students of religion in Central America might benefit from more comparative approaches, which might allow them to study relations between different religious denominations and, more broadly, the history of religion across national boundaries, including religious traditions among Central Americans in the United States. These topics might give us a better perspective on how Catholicism and Protestantism and more broadly religion shaped local, regional, and national identities during the nineteenth and twentieth centuries.

NOTES

1. Douglass Sullivan-González, *Piety, Power, and Politics: Religion and Nation Formation in Guatemala, 1821-1871* (Pittsburgh, PA: University of Pittsburgh Press, 1998), 70.
2. Óscar Romero, *Voice of the Voiceless: The Four Pastoral Letters and Other Statements* (Maryknoll, NY: Orbis Books, 1985), 193.
3. On Aycinena and his times, see Sullivan-González, *Piety, Power, and Politics*; and David L. Chandler, *Juan José de Aycinena, idealista conservador de la Guatemala del siglo XIX*, translated by Victoria Vázquez, Marina Vázquez, and Lucía Robelo Pereira (Antigua, Guatemala, Guatemala: Centro de Investigaciones Regionales de Mesoamérica, 1988). On the Salvadoran civil war and Romero's role in it, see Michael E. Lee, *Revolutionary Saint: The Theological Legacy of Oscar Romero* (Maryknoll, NY: Orbis Books, 2018).
4. For a discussion of the role of religion in modern Latin America, see Reinaldo L. Román and Pamela Voekel, "Popular Religion in Latin American Historiography," in *The Oxford Handbook of Latin American History*, edited by José C. Moya, 454–455 (Oxford: Oxford University Press, 2010).
5. For this renewed interest on Catholicism and religion more broadly, see particularly Phillip Berryman, *The Religious Roots of Rebellion* (Maryknoll, NY: Orbis, 1984); and Phillip Berryman, *Stubborn Hope: Religion, Politics, and Revolution in Central America* (Maryknoll, NY: Orbis, 1994). Lernoux's powerful and insightful work also helped spark interest on Catholicism. See Penny Lernoux, *Cry of the People: The Struggle for Human Rights in Latin America—The Catholic Church in Conflict with U.S. Policy* (New York: Penguin, 1982).

6. Representative works on this development include Christian Lalive d'Epinay, *Haven of the Masses: A Study of the Pentecostal Movement in Chile* (London: Lutterworth, 1969); Emilio Willems, *Followers of the New Faith: Culture Change and the Rise of Protestantism in Brazil and Chile* (Nashville, TN: Vanderbilt University, 1967); David Stoll, *Is Latin America Turning Protestant? The Politics of Evangelical Growth* (Stanford: University of California Press, 1990); and David Martin, *Tongues of Fire: The Explosion of Protestantism in Latin America* (London: Basil Blackwell, 1990).

7. For this period, see Thomas L. Karnes, *The Failure of Union: Central America, 1824–1960* (Chapel Hill: University of North Carolina Press, 1961); Jordana Dym, *From Sovereign Villages to National States: City, State, and Federation in Central America, 1759–1839* (Albuquerque: University of New Mexico Press, 2006); Mary Wilhelmine Williams, "La política eclesiástica de Francisco Morazán y los demás liberales centroamericanos," *Revista de la Universidad* (Universidad Nacional Autónoma de Honduras) 7, no. 28 (July 1992): 82–93.

8. Ralph Lee Woodward Jr., *Rafael Carrera and the Emergence of the Republic of Guatemala, 1821–1871* (Athens, OH: University of Georgia Press. 1993); and Sullivan-González, *Piety, Power, and Politics*. In his recent work, Sullivan-González has examined the role the Black Christ of Esquipulas in the construction of national identity. See Douglass Sullivan-González, *The Black Christ of Esquipulas: Religion and Identity in Guatemala* (Lincoln: University of Nebraska Press, 2016). To a significant extent, these works have successfully moved beyond Liberal historiography, which for many decades shaped—and distorted—our understanding of the formation of the nation-state. Liberal writings provide a black-and-white historical canvas, which has painted, on the one hand, the nineteenth-century Conservative movement as representing an era of obscurantism and backwardness, and, on the other hand, Liberalism as standing for the diffusion of the political liberties and economic modernization that has become synonymous with modernity. In contrast, Woodward and others have shown that Central American Liberals and Conservative groups such as the Catholic Church shared much, including their support for modernization. See William J. Griffith, "The Historiography of Central America Since 1830," *The Hispanic American Historical Review* 40, no. 4 (1960): 548–569; Ralph Lee Woodward Jr., "The Historiography of Modern Central America since 1960," *The Hispanic American Historical Review* 67, no. 3 (August 1987): 461–496; and Bonar L. Hernández S., "La historia de Guatemala en sus libros," *Istor* 6, no. 24 (Spring 2006): 6–28.

9. J. Lloyd Mecham, *Church and State in Latin America: A History of Politico-Eclesiastical Relations* (2nd ed.) (Chapel Hill: University of North Carolina Press, 1966), 326–327, 329–333.

10. For the Salvadoran case, see Mecham, *Church and State in Latin America*, 324–325; Gary G. Kuhn, "Church and State Conflict in El Salvador as a Cause of the Central American War of 1863," *Journal of Church and State* 27, no. 3 (1985): 455–462; and relevant sections in Rodolfo Cardenal, *El poder eclesiástico en El Salvador, 1871–1931* (San Salvador, El Salvador: UCA Editores, 1980). For Guatemala, see Hubert J. Miller, *La Iglesia y el estado en tiempo de Justo Rufino Barrios*, translated by Jorge Luján Muñoz (Guatemala City, Guatemala: Editorial Universitaria, 1976); relevant sections in Mary P. Holleran, *Church and State in Guatemala* (New York: Columbia University Press, 1949); and relevant sections in Agustín Estrada Monroy, *Datos para la historia de la Iglesia en Guatemala*, Vol. 3 (Guatemala City, Guatemala: Sociedad de Geografía e Historia de Guatemala, 1979).

11. Santiago Malaina, *La Compañia de Jesús en El Salvador, C.A., desde 1864 a 1872* (San Salvador, El Salvador: Imprenta Nacional, 1939); Franco Cerruti, *Los Jesuitas en Nicaragua en el siglo XIX* (San José, Costa Rica: Libro Libre, 1984); Rafael Pérez, *La Compañía de Jesús en Colombia y Centro-América después de su restauración*, 3 Vols. (Valladolid, Mexico: Linde Vaviria, 1896–1898); Hubert J. Miller, "Expulsion of the Jesuits from Guatemala in 1871," *Catholic Historical Review* 54, no. 4 (1969): 636–654; and Buenaventura de Cogollos-Vega, *Los Capuchinos en Guatemala (conmemorado un centenario: 1872–1972)* (Seville, Spain: Talleres Capuchinos, 1972). For the shortage of clergy in Guatemala, see Hubert J. Miller, "The Church and State Question in Guatemala: 1871–1885" (PhD diss., Loyola University, Chicago, 1965), 197–198; and Ricardo Krebs, *La Iglesia de América Latina en el siglo XIX* (Santiago: Ediciones Universidad Católica de Chile, 2002), 210. For anticlericalism in other countries, see Philip Williams, *The Catholic Church and Politics in Nicaragua and Costa Rica* (Pittsburgh, PA: University of Pittsburgh Press, 1989); John M. Kirk, *Politics and the Catholic Church in Nicaragua* (Gainesville: University Press of Florida, 1992); Juan Ramón Martínez B., *Honduras, las fuerzas del desacuerdo: un ensayo histórico sobre las relaciones entre la Iglesia y el Estado (1525–1972)* (Tegucigalpa: Editorial Universitaria, Universidad Nacional Autónoma de Honduras, 1998); Rolando Sierra Fonseca, *Iglesia y liberalismo en Honduras en el siglo XIX* (Tegucigalpa, Honduras: Centro de Publicaciones Obispado Choluteca, 1993); Frederick C. Hopkins, "The Catholic Church in British Honduras (1851–1918)," *The Catholic Historical Review* 4, no. 3 (1918): 304–314; and Ricardo Blanco Segura, *1884: El estado, la iglesia y las reformas liberales* (San José: Editorial Costa Rica, 1984).

12. Paul Vanderwood, "Religion: Official, Popular, and Otherwise," *Mexican Studies/Estudios Mexicanos* 16, no. 2 (Summer 2000): 411–441; and Reinaldo L. Román, *Governing Spirits: Religion, Miracles, and Spectacles in Cuba and Puerto Rico, 1898–1956* (Chapel Hill: University of North Carolina Press. 2007). See also Román and Voekel, "Popular Religion."

13. José Gil Zúñiga, "Un mito de la sociedad costarricense: el culto a la Virgen de los Ángeles (1824–1935)," *Revista de Historia* (Heredia, Costa Rica), no. 11 (July 1985): 47–129.

14. Ricardo Falla, *Quiché rebelde. Estudio de un movimiento de conversión religiosa, rebelde a las creencias tradicionales, en Santiago Ilotenango, Quiché (1948–1970)* (Guatemala City, Guatemala: Editorial Universitaria, 1979); Douglas E. Brintnall, *Revolt against the Dead: The Modernization of a Mayan Community in the Highlands of Guatemala* (New York: Gordon and Breach, 1979); Kay B. Warren, *The Symbolism of Subordination: Indian Identity in a Guatemalan Town* (Austin: University of Texas Press, 1978); E. Micheal Mendelson, *Los escándalos de Maximón: un estudio sobre la religión y la visión del mundo en Santiago de Attilán* (Guatemala City, Guatemala: Tipografía Nacional, 1965); Rubén E. Reina, *The Law of the Saints: A Pokoman Corporate Community and Its Culture* (Indianapolis, IN: Bobbs-Merrill, 1967).

15. Antonio García Estrada, "Historia de los Hermanos Espirituales y otros frutos modernistas de la religiosidad vernácula salvadoreña," *Anuario de Estudios Centroamericanos* (Universidad de Costa Rica) 42 (2016): 261–294. The reference to Geertz comes from *The Interpretation of Cultures* (New York: Basic Books, 1973), ch. 4.

16. For the case of Guatemala, see Virginia Garrard-Burnett, *Protestantism in Guatemala: Living in the New Jerusalem* (Austin: University of Texas Press, 1998). For the arrival of Protestantism in Nicaragua and Honduras, see Kimberly Ann, Fabbri, "In Defiance of Neutrality: A History of the Moravian Church as a Community Leader on the Atlantic Coast of Nicaragua,

1918–1974" (PhD diss., Lehigh University, 2016); Anna Adams, "Moravian Missionaries in Nicaragua: The American Years, 1917–1974," (PhD diss., Temple University, 1994); Karl Mueller, *Among Creoles, Moskitos and Sumos: Eastern Nicaragua and Its Moravian Missions* (Bethlehem, PA: Christian Education Board of the Moravian Church in America, 1932); Jill Breckel, *The Success of the Moravian Missions in Nicaragua and Honduras* (Bethlehem, PA: Provincial Women's Board, North, 1975); and Frank J. Klingberg, "Efforts to Christianize the Mosquito Indians," *Historical Magazine of the Protestant Episcopal Church* 9, no. 4 (1940): 305–321.

17. Ricardo Martínez Esquivel, "Sociability, Religiosity and New Cosmovisions in Costa Rica at the turn of the Nineteenth to Twentieth Centuries," in "UCLA—Grand Lodge of California," special issue, *RHMLAC*, Hors série, no. 1 (October 2013): 156–192. For the history of Protestantism in Costa Rica, see Wilton Nelson, *Historia del protestantismo en Costa Rica* (San José, Costa Rica: Instituto Internacional de Evangelización a Fondo, 1983).

18. For Nicaragua and Costa Rica, see Williams, *Catholic Church and Politics*, 16–18, 99–100, 177; and Arturo Aguilar, *Reseña histórica de la diócesis de Nicaragua* (Léon, Nicaragua: Tipografía Hospicio San Juan de Dios, 1929). For the Honduran case, see Marcos Carías Zapata, *La iglesia católica en Honduras: 1492–1975* (Tegucigalpa, Honduras: Editorial Guaymuras, 1991), 96–94; José María Tojeira, *Panorama histórico de la Iglesia en Honduras* (Tegucigalpa: Centro de Documentación de Honduras, 1990), 207; and Marvin Barahona, *Honduras en el siglo XX: una síntesis histórica* (Tegucigalpa, Honduras: Editorial Guaymuras, 2017), 67–68. Mecham examines, if only briefly, the status of the Panamanian Church. See Mecham, *Church and State in Latin America*, 336.

19. Mecham, *Church and State in Latin America*, 331.

20. Bonar L. Hernández, "Reforming Catholicism: Papal Power in Guatemala during the 1920s and 1930s," *The Americas* 71, no. 2 (2014): 255–280; and Joseph A. Pitti, "Jorge Ubico and Guatemalan politics in the 1920s" (PhD diss., University of New Mexico, 1974).

21. Hubert J. Miller, "Las relaciones entre la Iglesia Católica y el Estado," *Anales de la Sociedad de Geografía e Historia* 71 (1996): 121–152. See also Cardenal, *Poder eclesiástico en El Salvador*.

22. Williams, *Catholic Church and Politics*, 22.

23. The quote comes from Emilio Betances, *The Catholic Church and Power Politics in Latin America: The Dominican Case in Comparative Perspective* (Plymouth, MA: Rowman & Littlefield, 2007), 80. For a detailed discussion of the Church's position toward the Somoza dynasty, see Jeffrey L. Klaiber, *The Church, Dictatorships, and Democracy in Latin America* (Maryknoll, NY: Orbis Books, 1998), 197; Williams, *Catholic Church and Politics*, 19; Manzar Foroohar, *The Catholic Church and Social Change in Nicaragua* (Albany: State University of New York Press, 1989), 38, 42, 17–25; Frederick M. Shepherd, "Church and State in Honduras and Nicaragua Prior to 1979," *Sociology of Religion* 54, no. 3 (Fall 1993): 283; and John M. Kirk, *Politics and the Catholic Church in Nicaragua* (Gainesville: University Press of Florida, 1992).

24. Hernández, "Reforming Catholicism"; Miller, "Relaciones entre la Iglesia Católica y el Estado"; Bruce J. Calder, *Crecimiento y cambio de la iglesia católica guatemalteca, 1944–1966* (Guatemala City, Guatemala: Editorial José de Pineda Ibarra, 1970); José Luis Chea, *Guatemala, la cruz fragmentada* (San José, Costa Rica: DEI, 1988); and Anita Frankel, "Political Development in Guatemala, 1944–1954: The Impact of Foreign, Military, and Religious Elites" (PhD diss., University of Connecticut, 1969); Hubert J. Miller, "Catholic Leaders and Spiritual Socialism during the Arévalo Administration in Guatemala,

1945–1951," in *Central America: Historical Perspectives on the Contemporary Crises*, edited by Ralph Lee Woodward Jr. (New York: Greenwood Press, 1988), 85–105; and Blake D. Pattridge, "The Catholic Church in Revolutionary Guatemala, 1944–1954: A House Divided," *Journal of Church and State* 36, no. 3 (Summer 1994): 27–40. A version of this Church–state *modus vivendi* appeared in El Salvador and Honduras. See Mecham, *Church and State*, ch. 14.

25. Hubert J. Miller, "Conservative and Liberal Concordats in Nineteenth-Century Guatemala: Who Won?" *Journal of Church and State* 33, no. 1 (Winter 1991): 115–130; and Mecham, *Church and State*, ch. 14.

26. Hernández Sandoval, *Guatemala's Catholic Revolution: A History of Religious and Social Reform, 1920–1968* (Notre Dame, IN: University of Notre Dame Press, 2018), ch. 1; Mecham, *Church and State*, 325; Carías Zapata, *Iglesia católica en Honduras*, 84–96; and Williams, *Catholic Church and Politics*, 15–16, 99–101.

27. On Guatemala, see Hernández Sandoval, *Guatemala's Catholic Revolution*, chs. 1 and 2. The Church–state harmonious relationship promoted by Rome was, in many respects, representative of the pacts formalized by the Church with fascist regimes in interwar Europe. For the international context, see Anthony Rhodes, *The Vatican in the Age of the Dictators, 1922–1945* (London: Holt, Rinehart and Winston, 1973); Peter C. Kent and John F. Pollard, eds., *Papal Diplomacy in the Modern Age* (Westport, CT: Praeger, 1994); and Frank J. Coppa, *The Modern Papacy, 1798–1995* (New York: Taylor & Francis, 1998).

28. Calder, *Crecimiento y cambio*, 58–59. See also Chea, *Guatemala*; Frankel, "Political Development in Guatemala"; Miller, "Relaciones entre la Iglesia Católica y el Estado"; Hernández Sandoval, *Guatemala's Catholic Revolution*; Dave C. Kelly, *Maryknoll History, 1943–1969: Guatemala–El Salvador Region* (Guatemala City, Guatemala: n.p., 1969); Susan Fitzpatrick-Behrens, "Maryknoll Sisters, Faith, Healing, and the Maya Construction of Catholic Communities in Guatemala," *Latin American Research Review* 44, no. 3 (2009): 27–49; Fitzpatrick-Behrens, "From Symbols of the Sacred to Symbols of Subversion to Simply Obscure: Maryknoll Women Religious in Guatemala, 1953–1967," *The Americas* 61, no. 2 (2004): 189–216; Jesús Lada Camblor, *Pasaron haciendo el bien. Historia de los Misioneros del Sagrado Corazón en Centroamérica (1954–1995)*, 3 vols. (Guatemala City, Guatemala: Ediciones San Pablo, 2004); and Thomas R. Melville, *Through a Glass Darkly: The U.S. Holocaust in Central America* (Bloomington, IN: Xlibris, 2005). For a more general overview, see Yolanda Bertozzi, "The Church's Mission in Countries under Foreign Domination: A Central American Perspective," *International Review of Mission* 73, no. 292 (1984): 213–238.

29. For examples, see Fitzpatrick-Behrens, "Maryknoll Sisters"; Fitzpatrick-Behrens, "From Symbols of the Sacred to Symbols of Subversion"; Hernández Sandoval, *Guatemala's Catholic Revolution*; and Falla, *Quiché rebelde*.

30. For examples, see Hernández Sandoval, *Guatemala's Catholic Revolution*; Falla, *Quiché rebelde*; Luis Iglesias, *Los misioneros redentoristas y la República de El Salvador, C.A.: apuntes para la historia religiosa de El Salvador* (Mexico City, Mexico: Gerardo Mayela, 1956); Leonard Bacigalupo, *The American Franciscan Missions in Central America: Three Decades of Christian Service* (Andover, MA: Charisma Press, 1980); and John E. Rybolt, *The Vincentians: A General History of the Congregation of the Mission* (New York: New City Press, 2014).

31. Williams, *Catholic Church and Politics*, 106–116. See also Rodrigo Fernández Vásquez, "Costa Rica: Interpretación histórica sobre reforma social y acción eclesiástica: 1940–1982," *Estudios*

Sociales Centroamericanos 33 (September–December 1982): 221–247; Foroohar, *Catholic Church and Social Change*; Ricardo Blanco Segura, *Monseñor Sanabria: apuntes biográficos* (San José: Editorial Costa Rica, 1971); Jávier Solís, *La herencia de Sanabria: análisis politico de la iglesia costarriquense* (San José, Costa Rica: DEI, 1983); James Backer, *La iglesia y el sindicalismo en Costa Rica* (San José: Editorial Costa Rica, 1978); Andrés Opazo Bernales, *Costa Rica: La iglesia católica y el orden social* (San José, Costa Rica: DEI, 1987);. Victoria Ramírez Avendaño, *Jorge Volio y la revolución viviente* (San José, Costa Rica: Guayacán, 1989); and Eugene Miller, *A Holy Alliance? The Church and the Left in Costa Rica, 1933–1948* (London: M. E. Sharpe, 1996).

32. Williams, *Catholic Church and Politics*, 20–21.

33. Williams, *Catholic Church and Politics*, 114–115. See also Fernández Vásquez, "Costa Rica."

34. Shepherd, "Church and State," 283–284. See also Robert A. White, "Structural Factors in Rural Development: The Church and the Peasant in Honduras" (PhD diss., Cornell University, 1977); Rosa Maria Pochet Coronado, "El reformismo estatal y la iglesia en Honduras 1949–1982," *Estudios Sociales Centroamericanos* 33 (September–December 1982): 155–188; and Gustavo Blanco and Jaime Valverde, *Honduras: Iglesia y cambio social* (San José, Costa Rica: DEI, 1987).

35. Hernández Sandoval, *Guatemala's Catholic Revolution*; Falla, *Quiché rebelde*; Falla, "Hacia la Revolución Verde: adopción y dependencia del fertilizante químico en un Municipio del Quiché, Guatemala," *Estudios Sociales* (Instituto de Ciencias Político-Sociales, Universidad Rafael Landívar) 6 (1972): 16–51; Fitzpatrick-Behrens, "The Maya Cooperative Spirit of Capitalism in Guatemala: Civil-Religious Collaborations, 1943–1966," in *Local Church, Global Church Catholic Activism in Latin America from Rerum Novarum to Vatican II*, edited by Stephen J.C. Andes and Julia G. Young, 275–304 (Washington, DC: Catholic University of America Press, 2016). For an urban take on these changes, see also Deborah Levenson-Estrada, *Trade Unionists against Terror: Guatemala City, 1954–1985* (Chapel Hill: University of North Carolina Press, 1994).

36. For these general trends, see, in particular, Berryman *Religious Roots* and *Stubborn Hope*; Berryman *Cry of the People*; William Cook, "Base Ecclesial Communities in Central America," *Mennonite Quarterly Review* 58 (1984): 410–423; Margaret E. Crahan, "International Aspects of the Role of the Catholic Church in Central America," in *Central America: International Dimensions of the Crisis*, edited by R. E. Feinberg, 231–238 (New York: Holmes and Meier, 1982); Calder, *Crecimiento y cambio*, 139–152; relevant sections in Williams, *Catholic Church and Politics*; relevant sections in Scott Mainwaring and Alexander Wilde, eds., *The Progressive Church in Latin America* (Notre Dame, IN: University of Notre Dame Press, 1989); and Tommie Sue Montgomery, "The Church in the Salvadoran Revolution," *Latin American Perspectives* 10, no. 1 (1983): 62–87. For an examination of the rise of liberation theology in Guatemala, see Chea, *Guatemala*, 77–78; Ricardo Bendaña Perdomo, *Ella es lo que nosotros somos y mucho más: síntesis histórica del catolicismo guatemalteco, 1951–2000*, vol. 2 (Guatemala City, Guatemala: Artemis Edinter, 2001), chs. 4–6; and relevant documents in Conferencia Episcopal de Guatemala, *Al servicio de la vida, la justiciar y la paz* (Guatemala City, Guatemala: Ediciones San Pablo, 1997).

37. This theological movement, popularized by the Peruvian priest Gustavo Gutiérrez, spoke to the desire by many Central American Catholics (clerics and laypeople alike) to bridge their spiritual and material conditions and transcend development as a solution to society's problems. See Ivan Petrella, "The Intellectual Roots of Liberation Theology,"

in *The Cambridge History of Religions in Latin America*, edited by Virginia Garrard-Burnett, Paul Freston, and Stephen C. Dove, 359–371 (New York: Cambridge University Press, 2016).

38. Blase Bonpane, *Guerrillas of Peace: Liberation Theology and the Central American Revolution* (Lincoln, NE: toExcel, 1985), 45–47. The quote comes from Virginia Garrard-Burnett, "Religion and Politics in 20th-Century Central America."

39. Philip Zwerling and Connie Martin, *Nicaragua: A New Kind of Revolution* (Westport, CT: Lawrence Hill, 1985), 29; Michael Dodson and Laura Nuzzi O'Shaughnessy, *Nicaragua's Other Revolution: Religious Faith and Political Struggle* (Chapel Hill: University of North Carolina Press, 1990); Williams, *Catholic Church and Politics*; Foroohar, *Catholic Church and Social Change*; Fernando Cardenal, *Sacerdote en la revolución: memorias*, vol. 1 (Managua, Nicaragua: Anamá Ediciones, 2008); and Ernesto Cardenal, *El Evangelio en Solentiname* (Madrid: Editorial Trotta, 2006).

40. Joaquín M. Chávez, *Poets and Prophets of the Resistance: Intellectuals and the Origins of El Salvador's Civil War* (Oxford: Oxford University Press, 2017); Juan Ramón Vega, "La iglesia en El Salvador en 1970," *Estudios Centroamericanos* 268 (January–February 1971): 235–249; Andrés Opazo Bernales, "Las condiciones sociales de surgimiento de una iglesia popular," *Estudios Sociales Centroamericanos* 33 (September–December 1982): 273–310; Jon Sobrino, *Companions of Jesus: The Jesuit Martyrs of El Salvador* (Maryknoll, NY: Orbis, 1990); Theresa Whitfield, *Paying the Price: Ignacio Ellacuría and the Murdered Jesuits of El Salvador* (Philadelphia: Temple University Press, 1994); Judith M. Noone, *The Same Fate as the Poor* (Maryknoll, NY: Maryknoll Sisters, 1984); Anna L. Peterson, *Martyrdom and the Politics of Religion: Progressive Catholicism in El Salvador's Civil War* (Albany: State University of New York, 1996); Rodolfo Cardenal, *Historia de una esperanza: vida de Rutilio Grande* (San Salvador, El Salvador: UCA Editores, 1985); Thomas M. Kelly, "Challenging the Status Quo: How Rutilio Grande, S.J., Used Scripture to Address Socio-Economic Inequality," *Journal of Church and State* (Supplement Series) 16 (2014): 179–189; Tommie Sue Montgomery, *Revolution in El Salvador: From Civil Strife to Civil Peace* (2nd ed.) (Boulder, CO: Westview Press, 1995); Bahman Bakhtiari, "Revolution in the Church in Nicaragua and El Salvador," *Journal of Church and State* 28 (1986): 15–42; Peter Michael Sánchez, *Priest Under Fire: Padre David Rodríguez, the Catholic Church, and El Salvador's Revolutionary Movement* (Gainesville: University Press of Florida, 2015; Santiago Mata, *Monseñor Óscar Romero: Pasión por la Iglesia* (Madrid: Ediciones Palabra, 2015); James R. Brockman, *Romero: A Life* (Maryknoll, NY: Orbis, 1989); Mary Garcia, *The Sufferings, Assassinations, and Martyrdom of the Missionary Church in Olancho, Honduras 1963–1982: The History of a Church That Lived Its Commitment to the Poor*, translated by Winifred Whelan (Lewiston, NY: Edwin Mellen Press, 2011); and María Dolores Albiac, *Los ricos más ricos de El Salvador* (San Salvador, El Salvador: Fundación Heinrich Böll, 1998). See also Oscar Romero's own writings *in Voice of the Voiceless: The Four Pastoral Letters and Other Statements*, translated by Michael J. Walsh (Maryknoll, NY: Orbis, 1985).

41. The anthropologist David Stoll, among others, has advanced the "caught in the middle" argument. See David Stoll, *Between Two Armies in the Ixil Towns of Guatemala* (New York: Columbia University Press, 1993); and Heinrich Schäfer, *Entre dos fuegos: Una historia socio-política de la Iglesia evangélica nacional presbiteriana de Guatemala* (Guatemala City, Guatemala: CEDEPCA, 2002). For in-depth studies on

the post-conciliar Church, see Greg Grandin, "To End with All These Evils: Ethnic Transformation and Community Mobilization in Guatemala's Western Highlands, 1954–1980," *Latin American Perspectives* 24, no. 2 (March 1997): 7–34; Arturo Arias, "Shifts in Indian Identity: Guatemala's Violent Transition to Modernity," in *Guatemalan Indians and the State, 1521–1988*, edited by Carol Smith (Austin: University of Texas Press, 1990), 230–257; Betsy Konefal, *For Every Indio Who Falls: A History of Maya Activism in Guatemala, 1960 1990* (Albuquerque: University of New Mexico Press, 2010). For radicalization among foreign missioners, see Carlos Santos, *Guatemala. El silencio del gallo. Un misionero español en la guerra más cruenta de America* (Barcelona: Debate, 2007); Melville, *Through a Glass Darkly*; and Thomas Melville and Marjorie Melville, *Whose Heaven, Whose Earth?* (New York: Knopf, 1971).

42. Pope John Paul II's visit in 1983 further brought these divisions to the forefront. See Peter Wynn, *Americas: The Changing Face of Latin America and the Caribbean* (Berkeley: University of California Press, 2006), 390; Dodson and O'Shaughnessy, *Nicaragua's Other Revolution*, chs. 9–10; Montgomery, *Revolution in El Salvador*, ch. 3; and Chea, *Cruz fragmentada*, ch. 4.

43. On Costa Rica, see Williams, *Catholic Church and Politics*, 132–145. On the Honduran case, see Shepherd, "Church and State," 287–289; and White, "Structural Factors in Rural Development."

44. Pew Research Center, "Religious Affiliations of Latin American and US Hispanics," in *Religion in Latin America: Widespread Change in a Historically Catholic Region*, as cited in Garrard-Burnett, "Religion and Politics in 20th-Century Central America." On the history of Pentecostalism in El Salvador, see Everett A. Wilson, "Sanguine Saints: Pentecostalism in El Salvador," *Church History* 52, no. 2 (1983): 186–198; Timothy H. Wadkins, *The Rise of Pentecostalism in Modern El Salvador: From the Blood of the Martyrs to the Baptism of the Spirit* (Waco, TX: Baylor University Press, 2017); and Karla Ann Koll, "Struggling for Solidarity: Changing Mission Relationships between the Presbyterian Church (US) and Christian Organizations in Central America during the 1980s" (PhD diss., Princeton University, 2004).

45. Virginia Garrard-Burnett, *Terror in the Land of the Holy Spirit: Guatemala under General Efrain Rios Montt 1982–1983* (Oxford: Oxford University Press, 2010); Garrard-Burnett, *Protestantism in Guatemala*; Manuela Cantón Delgado, *Bautizados en fuego: Protestantes, discursos de conversión y política en Guatemala (1989–1993)* (Woodstock, VT: Plumsock Mesoamerican Studies, 1998); and Virgilio Zapata Arceyuz, *Historia de la obra evangélica en Guatemala* (Guatemala City, Guatemala: Génesis Publicidad, 1982).

46. Irene Selser, *Cardenal Obando* (Mexico City, Mexico: Centro de Estudios Ecuménicos, 1989); Kirk, *Politics and the Catholic Church*; Francisco Goldman, *The Art of Political Murder: Who Killed the Bishop?* (New York: Grove Press, 2007); Mary Jo McConahay, "Cardinal-Designate Has Defended Indigenous People, Migrants for Decades," *National Catholic Reporter*, September 30, 2019. https://www.ncronline.org/news/people/cardinal-designate-has-defended-Indigenous-people-migrants-decades. Gerardi's human rights work culminated in the publication of Oficina de Derechos Humanos del Arzobispado de Guatemala (ODHAG), *Recuperación de la memoria histórica* (Guatemala City, Guatemala: ODHAG, 1999). Harold Caballeros's incursion into politics in Guatemala, exemplifies the continuous links between religion and politics, in this case, between Pentecostalism and politics. See "Caballeros, seguro de triunfo en 2011," *Prensa Libre*, August 26, 2007.

Further Reading

Arias, Arturo. "Shifts in Indian Identity: Guatemala's Violent Transition to Modernity." In *Guatemalan Indians and the State, 1521–1988*, edited by Carol Smith, 230–257. Austin: University of Texas Press, 1990.

Blanco, Gustavo, and Jaime Valverde. *Honduras: Iglesia y cambio social*. San José, Costa Rica: Departamento Ecumenico de Investigaciones, 1987.

Brockman, James R. *Romero: A Life*. Maryknoll, NY: Orbis Books, 2005.

Carías Zapata, Marcos. *La iglesia católica en Honduras: 1492–1975*. Tegucigalpa, Honduras: Editorial Guaymuras, 1991.

Chávez, Joaquín M. *Poets and Prophets of the Resistance: Intellectuals and the Origins of El Salvador's Civil War*. Oxford: Oxford University Press, 2017.

Dodson, Michael, and Laura Nuzzi O'Shaughnessy. *Nicaragua's Other Revolution: Religious Faith and Political Struggle*. Chapel Hill: University of North Carolina Press, 1990.

Falla, Ricardo. *Quiché rebelde. Estudio de un movimiento de conversión religiosa, rebelde a las creencias tradicionales, en Santiago Ilotenango, Quiché (1948–1970)*. Guatemala City, Guatemala: Editorial Universitaria, 1979.

Fitzpatrick-Behrens, Susan. "The Maya Catholic Cooperative Spirit of Capitalism in Guatemala: Civil-Religious Collaborations, 1943–1966." In *Local Church, Global Church: Catholic Activism in Latin America from Rerum Novarum to Vatican II*, edited by Stephen J. C. Andes and Julia G. Young, 275–304. Washington, DC: Catholic University of America Press, 2016.

Foroohar, Manzar. *The Catholic Church and Social Change in Nicaragua*. Albany: State University of New York Press, 1989.

Garrard-Burnett, Virginia. *Protestantism in Guatemala: Living in the New Jerusalem*. Austin: University of Texas Press, 1998.

Garrard-Burnett, Virginia. *Terror in the Land of the Holy Spirit: Guatemala under General Efrain Rios Montt 1982–1983*. Oxford: Oxford University Press, 2010.

Grandin, Greg. "To End with All These Evils: Ethnic Transformation and Community Mobilization in Guatemala's Western Highlands, 1954–1980." *Latin American Perspectives* 24, no. 2 (1997): 7–34.

Hernández Sandoval, Bonar. *Guatemala's Catholic Revolution: A History of Religious and Social Reform, 1920–1968*. Notre Dame, IN: University of Notre Dame Press, 2018.

Kirk, John M. *Politics and the Catholic Church in Nicaragua*. Gainesville: University Press of Florida, 1992.

Miller, Eugene. *A Holy Alliance? The Church and the Left in Costa Rica, 1933–1948*. London: M. E. Sharpe, 1996.

Miller, Hubert J. *La Iglesia y el estado en tiempo de Justo Rufino Barrios*. Translated by Jorge Luján Muñoz. Guatemala City, Guatemala: Universidad de San Carlos de Guatemala, 1976.

Molina Jiménez, Iván. "Catolicismo y comunismo en Costa Rica (1931–1940)." *Revista de Antropología Social* 22 (2006): 157–172.

Montgomery, Tommie Sue. *Revolution in El Salvador: From Civil Strife to Civil Peace*. 2nd ed. Boulder, CO: Westview Press, 1995.

Peterson, Anna L. *Martyrdom and the Politics of Religion: Progressive Catholicism in El Salvador's Civil War*. Albany: State University of New York, 1996.

Shepherd, Frederick M. "Church and State in Honduras and Nicaragua Prior to 1979." *Sociology of Religion* 54, no. 3 (1993): 277–293.

Solís, Jávier. *La herencia de Sanabria: análisis político de la iglesia costarricense*. San José, Costa Rica: DEI, 1983.

Sullivan-González, Douglass. *Piety, Power, and Politics: Religion and Nation Formation in Guatemala, 1821–1871*. Pittsburgh, PA: University of Pittsburgh Press, 1998.

Wadkins, Timothy H. *The Rise of Pentecostalism in Modern El Salvador: From the Blood of the Martyrs to the Baptism of the Spirit*. Waco, TX: Baylor University Press, 2017.

White, Robert A. "Structural Factors in Rural Development: The Church and the Peasant in Honduras." PhD diss., Cornell University, 1977.

Williams, Philip. *The Catholic Church and Politics in Nicaragua and Costa Rica*. Pittsburgh, PA: University of Pittsburgh Press, 1989.

Wilson, Everett A. "Sanguine Saints: Pentecostalism in El Salvador." *Church History* 52, no. 2 (1983): 186–198.

CHAPTER 16

WOMEN IN CENTRAL AMERICA SINCE INDEPENDENCE

EUGENIA RODRÍGUEZ SÁENZ

FROM the moment they gained independence from Spain to the present, the status of Central American women has depended on the prevailing development model in each historical period: the formation and development of the state and agricultural-export economies between 1821 and 1920; the largely unsuccessful efforts to democratize Central American societies between 1921 and 1955; the failed attempts to modernize the region through import-substitution industrialization, culminating in the Sandinista Revolution, the civil wars in Guatemala and El Salvador, and the growing US intervention between 1956 and 1989; and the implementation of peace plans that have proven unable to strengthen democracy, reduce inequalities, and end the violence between 1990 and the present.

During each of these periods, opportunities for change and improvement opened for women, including recognition of their basic rights, the early formation of women's organizations to demand the vote, modernization of their living circumstances, and the passage of laws and the creation of institutions concerned with gender. The entire process has been strongly influenced by class, ethnicity, educational level, geographic (urban or rural) setting, age (with more options open to girls and young women than to their predecessors), and country, given that women in Costa Rica, Panama, and Belize outpaced their counterparts on the rest of the isthmus.

RIGHTS AND EARLY REFORM MOVEMENTS (1821–1920)

On gaining their independence from Spain in 1821, the Central American countries set out on a complex process of transition from the colonial era to the period of nation-building, accompanied by great political and military instability. As a result, the implementation of the liberal political project and its associated reforms was delayed until the 1870s and 1880s, with the partial exception of Costa Rica, which was able to consolidate them early, gradually, and successfully through the nineteenth and early twentieth centuries. These reforms led to a growing separation between the state and the Catholic Church, which saw its control weaken over property; cemeteries; education; and the registration of marriages, births, and deaths.[1]

During the colonial period, the values of honor, race, and class held sway in Central American societies, and women were subjected to labor exploitation, sexual abuse, domestic violence, subjugation, and discrimination.[2] Although women had always found ways to resist these circumstances and continued to do so after independence, the subject of women's rights found its way into public discussion only in the late nineteenth century, before organized feminist movements emerged to defend them, as happened in Argentina, Chile, Uruguay, England, and the United States.[3]

Although late nineteenth-century liberal reforms and the modernization of family law in civil codes perpetuated some gender inequalities that manifested themselves in legal practices and procedures and in customs and daily usage, they also brought about progressive gender changes which, though not based explicitly on women's rights,[4] nevertheless contributed to greater formal equality before the law.[5] Women's rights underwent four major changes in this period: the introduction of civil marriage, separation, and divorce; the elimination of the doctrine of marital power (a husband's unquestioned authority over his wife and her property); the right of married women to exercise parental authority over their children; and greater access by women to education.

As in other Latin American countries, the introduction of civil marriage, separation, and divorce was the subject of intense debate and occurred through a protracted, gradual, and uneven process. The early Central American legal codes did not diverge greatly from those of the colonial period; as the Catholic Church maintained control over marriage and separation, dissolution of the marriage bond was out of the question, and during the separation process, wives were subjected to the destructive process of being "deposited" in an honorable home. Women often had to face physical, verbal, and financial abuse and adultery, abandonment, and lack of child support for their children, but they also resisted these abuses by denouncing them in court.[6]

It should be noted that civil marriage and divorce were first implemented temporarily in Guatemala (1837–1840) and civil divorce in El Salvador (1880–1881). It should also be pointed out that with the exception of Panama (1917), the Central American countries were the first in Latin America to permanently institute civil divorce: Costa Rica in 1888; Guatemala, El Salvador, and Nicaragua in 1894; and Honduras in 1898. Costa Rica was the first Latin American country to successfully consolidate civil divorce in 1888, and Guatemala was the first to decree civil divorce by mutual consent in 1894.[7]

Reforms also eliminated the "marital power" doctrine held over from colonial times, according to which a wife had to request her husband's permission to dispose of her property, enter into a contract, or participate in legal proceedings. The rights of married women were thus strengthened, as their legal rights were recognized to manage, acquire, sell, mortgage, and inherit property freely and to appear in court without their husband's consent. It took almost forty years for this reform to be implemented throughout the region, as it was approved first in Costa Rica (1888), then in El Salvador (1902), Nicaragua (1903), Honduras (1906), Panama (1914), and Guatemala (1926).[8]

Reforms were also introduced to grant women greater power to exercise parental rights and manage the family property. This change was approved first in Guatemala (1877), then in Honduras (1880), El Salvador (1880/1902), Costa Rica (1888), Nicaragua (1904), and Panama (1917). During the colonial period and much of the nineteenth century, parental rights could be exercised by wives only with their husband's authorization, and a husband could even designate another man to exercise his parental rights in case of his death, and if both parents died without designating a guardian, preference was given to the paternal grandfather.[9] However, late nineteenth-century civil codes extended this right to mothers of "illegitimate" children, provided their morality was above reproach; strengthened wives' legal capacity to exercise parental rights jointly with their husbands; and authorized them to be guardians of their children in the absence of a husband.

Nevertheless, women's real ability to exercise parental rights was somewhat limited, as the law allowed a husband to appoint counselors in his will whom his wife would have to obey or risk losing her parental authority. In the event of divorce, parental rights remained with the innocent spouse and were forfeit by the guilty one, although even a guilty mother could exercise parental rights over her children under the age of five. Furthermore, if a mother or widow remarried, she lost the right to manage the minor child's property. In summary, even after death, a father retained control over the property of his children by appointing a male relative (the paternal grandfather) as counselor to ensure that his lands and personal property were transferred to his children, preferably through the male line.[10]

Starting in the mid-nineteenth century, Central American states promoted the expansion of education in general, and instruction for girls and women in particular. This was part of the liberal social policies that aimed to redefine and modernize the role of the family under the conjugal and nuclear model, with the wife as mother and the husband as primary breadwinner.[11] As in other Latin American countries,[12] there was growing debate about the desirability of expanding women's access to education in the context of efforts by reform-minded liberal intellectuals to secularize society and create a citizenry more loyal to the state than to the Catholic Church or other corporatist institutions.[13]

There were many obstacles to the development of female education, but upper- and middle-class girls and young women in the urban centers enjoyed greater access to education in the late nineteenth century. In contrast, Indigenous and Afro-descendent women faced greater discrimination and exclusion. Education had a clear gender bias, as women were educated to be mothers and wives by exalting the ideal of "scientific motherhood" and their virtues in educating and raising healthy children for the country.[14] In the cities, women from the middle class and the highly skilled working class were educated to bring them into the labor force in "gender-appropriate" occupations such as secretaries, telegraph operators, typists, accountants, domestic economists, teachers, and nurses.[15]

Although gender-based educational gaps were narrowed, this was not consistent in all geographical areas, as there were notable differences between urban women (mostly *ladinas*) and peasant and Indigenous women in the countryside.[16] Unlike other countries in the region, however, Costa Rica saw the earliest and most successful expansion of education, as literacy rates in rural areas rose and gender parity in literacy was achieved by the early twentieth century.[17]

The expansion of the coffee-growing sector in Costa Rica, Guatemala, and El Salvador brought more women into the labor market on plantations and in the urban service sector, especially in the artisanal and industrial production of food and beverages, where women were infantilized by the term "little working girls" (*obreritas*).[18] State modernization also boosted the demand for administrative, educational, and health services, promoting the training and employment of women as public servants. The feminization of work was felt most strongly in the educational system, where, since the late nineteenth century, women had been recruited as teachers and could be paid less than male teachers.[19]

With greater access to education, upper- and middle-class mixed-race and White women created a larger audience for women's magazines and participated in groups that discussed literature, current events, culture, and the occult sciences. These activities were carried out in the context of the budding international feminist movement. Teachers and intellectuals also developed a greater awareness of their rights and the gender discrimination to which they were subjected. This process was followed by the early debates about women's rights, political participation, and access to the vote.[20]

In the late nineteenth century, middle- and upper-class women began to join various philanthropic organizations dedicated to caring for abandoned children, building orphanages, and training poor peasant girls, particularly Indigenous women, to work as domestic servants. In contrast, women who worked in urban factories and on coffee and banana plantations faced harsh exploitation and discrimination and were often subjected to sexual abuse and prostitution.[21]

WOMEN'S ORGANIZATIONS AND VOTING RIGHTS (1921–1955)

During this period, primary education continued to expand in the cities. Rural literacy rates increased significantly only in Costa Rica.[22] Gender gaps in education also diminished in urban areas (where most residents were ladinos), but not in the countryside, where peasant and Indigenous women predominated. In 1950, 69 percent of ladina urban women in Guatemala were literate, while only 11 percent of Indigenous women could read.[23] Secondary education also became more accessible to women, especially to young middle- and upper-class urban women, but remained largely out of reach for most Indigenous and Afro-descendant women. This expansion of female secondary education was associated with increasing access to teacher-preparation programs and technical training, which allowed women to enter the labor market in the education and service sectors.[24]

A significant change in this period was that the middle classes gained greater access to public higher education. Although they were admitted on more limited and unequal terms than men, women began to enroll in universities. The first female professional graduates were pharmacists in Costa Rica (1914) and Guatemala (1919), followed by attorneys in Panama (1922), Costa Rica (1925), and Guatemala (1927).[25] Greater access to education led to the growing participation of women in political campaigns and parties (although they could not vote), philanthropic and cultural organizations, unions and teachers' associations, and a variety of social movements.

Strengthened by the emergence of the first generations of female artists, writers, intellectuals, and professionals, this active female participation contributed to the resurgence of the Unionist movement, which sought to reestablish the Federal Republic of Central America during the 1920s. Salvadoran, Guatemalan, and Honduran women played a decisive role in the Unionist movement, which they saw as the best chance to secure lasting peace among their countries and to confront US imperialism, which was already being felt in the Panama Canal region (1903–1979) and Nicaragua (1912–1933).[26] Left-wing Unionist political parties and trade unions encouraged female participation through women's committees, clubs, and branches.[27]

Among the first movements in defense of women's rights, one can highlight the mobilization of female Costa Rican teachers in 1924 and 1928 to protest discriminatory wage increases that privileged male teachers.[28] In Guatemala, more than a hundred Indigenous women went on strike at the La Moderna coffee-processing plant in November 1925. The strike, which garnered the support of various trade union organizations, revealed the exploitative conditions under which these women worked. Although the strike was not harshly suppressed and the company agreed to the workers' demands, it soon retaliated against the female workers by firing them.[29] In El Salvador, women, including Indigenous women, played a significant role in the process that culminated in the uprising of 1932, which was soon brutally suppressed by the Maximiliano Hernández Martínez government.[30]

Although women did not participate in large numbers in the great Costa Rican banana strike of 1934, they played an important role in the great Honduran banana strike of 1954, which was followed by a brief democratic opening that paved the way for development policies under military leadership in the context of the Cold War.[31] The difference between these two cases shows how much women's participation in the labor force and trade unionism had expanded over the course of twenty years. In Costa Rica, women began to organize and mobilize in the 1930s, but they achieved their greatest success after 1940, when they combined their responsibility as mothers with their struggle to ensure their families' livelihoods.[32]

During the 1920s, debates about women's rights intensified as women's organizations were established, feminist and suffragist movements emerged, and demands were raised for women's right to vote. Women's support for the Unionist movement influenced the fact that the short-lived Constitution of the Federal Republic of Central America, promulgated by Guatemala, El Salvador, and Honduras in 1921, first introduced the female vote as a voluntary, personal, confidential, and nontransferable right, but on a limited basis, as it could only be exercised by literate married women or widows over the age of twenty-one, and by single women over the age of twenty-five with a primary school education who had their own income or property. Thus, it seems that Salvadoran women became the first to vote in Latin America, electing Salvadoran representatives to the Federal Republic in 1921, eight years before the Ecuadoran voting reform of 1929.[33]

Although the first attempt at female suffrage in Guatemala was unsuccessful in 1920, the Guatemalan Unión Femenina Guatemalteca Pro Ciudadanía (Women's Union for Citizenship) was formed in 1944 to demand the right to vote. In 1945, the limited and voluntary right to vote was extended to literate women, who voted for the first time in the municipal elections (1947 and 1948), the congressional elections (1948) and the presidential elections (1950) but had to wait until 1965 for universal suffrage.[34] This achievement was brought about, in part, by women's decisive role in the overthrow of the dictatorships of Manuel Estrada Cabrera (1920) and Jorge Ubico (1944) and their active participation in the October Revolution (1944–1954). The limited suffrage divided ladina women from Indigenous women, as only 3 percent of Mayan women could exercise their citizenship rights.[35] Under the leadership of the Alianza de Mujeres Guatemaltecas (Guatemalan Women's Alliance), the Primer Congreso Interamericano de Mujeres (First Inter-American Congress of Women) was held in Guatemala (1947). In the context of the Cold War, women's organizations were formed to oppose the women who supported the revolutionary process; these included the Central Anticomunista Femenina (Women's Anti-Communist Central) in 1952 and the vending-stall operators of the Mercado Central (Central Market) of Guatemala City.[36]

After the establishment of women's voting rights in the short-lived Federal Constitution of 1921, Prudencia Ayala declared her intention to run as the candidate of the Gran Partido Feminista Salvadoreño (Great Salvadoran Feminist Party) in the presidential elections of 1931, but her candidacy was rejected.[37] During the dictatorship of Maximiliano Hernández Martínez (1931–1944), the right to vote was extended to literate women in 1939, making El Salvador the first country in Central America to do so, but the restrictive conditions excluded 80 percent of all women. Following the overthrow of Hernández Martínez, a new democratic space opened, and the La Liga Femenina Salvadoreña (Salvadoran Women's League) in 1948 took advantage of it to push for the enactment of universal female suffrage in 1950, with the first female officeholders being elected in 1952.[38]

Although proposals for female suffrage were put forward in Honduras in 1894, 1924, 1934, 1936, 1948, 1949, and twice in 1952, the reform movement was only able to get underway after the overthrow of the Tiburcio Carías regime (1933–1949).[39] During the subsequent democratic opening, the women's suffrage movement developed, and various women's organizations were established, chief among them the Federación de Asociaciones Femeninas Hondureñas (Federation of Honduran Women's Associations, 1951, or FAFH), which advanced most of the voting rights proposals.[40] In 1955, a reform established the optional vote for single women over the age of twenty-one and for married women over the age of eighteen, provided they were literate. Finally, the constitutional reform of 1957 extended universal voting rights to all Hondurans.[41]

Nicaragua was the first Central American country to see a proposal for women's voting rights in 1893. In 1916, the Partido Liberal Nacional (National Liberal Party, or PLN) supported such a reform, and Juanita Molina de Fromen and María Gamez made similar proposals in 1930, 1932, and 1933.[42] The Somoza family dictatorship (1936–1979) incorporated women's and feminist organizations, which played a key role in supporting the regime. The PLN's Ala Femenina (Women's Branch, 1936) was created under the leadership of the educator Josefa Toledo de Aguerri, who corresponded with feminists in the United States and Latin America.[43] The Ala Femenina presented the first proposal for female suffrage in 1939, then again in 1945, 1948, and the 1950 constituent assembly, but these attempts failed due to antagonisms between feminist organizations and political parties.[44] General Anastasio Somoza and Emiliano Chamorro finally agreed to support women's voting rights in 1955, and women voted for the first time in 1957. The PLN reorganized its Ala Femenina in 1955 under the leadership of Olga Núñez de Saballos, displacing and appropriating independent women's organizations while giving the PLN greater control over the female electorate.[45]

Although women in Costa Rica played a decisive role in overthrowing the regime of Federico Tinoco (1917–1919), the country's brief and final dictatorship, they were unable to gain voting rights then, despite the establishment of the Liga Feminista Costarricense (Costa Rican Feminist League) under the leadership of attorney Ángela Acuña.[46] Following various failed attempts to introduce female suffrage, such a reform was introduced in the 1949 Constitution. After persecuting and outlawing two of the main political forces of the time (the Partido Republicano Nacional and the Partido Comunista—the National Republican Party and the Communist Party), the winners of the 1948 Civil War approved the vote for women because they calculated that, in the absence of any immediate electoral pressure, the expansion of the electorate would play in their favor in the future. Women therefore exercised the vote first in the local elections of 1950 and then in the national elections of 1953.[47]

In Panama, the American occupation of the Canal Zone meant that the earliest feminist organizations were influenced by the experience of the United States. Thus, the Federación de Clubes de Mujeres del Canal (Federation of Canal Women's Clubs, 1907) was supported by the General Federation of Women's Clubs in New York.[48] Under the leadership of the first female attorney, Clara González, the Grupo Feminista Renovación (Feminist Renewal Group) was established in 1922, which became the Partido Nacional Feminista (National Feminist Party) the following year (1923). In turn, educator Esther Neira de Calvo created the Sociedad Nacional para el Progreso de la Mujer (National Society for the Advancement of Women, 1923). As vice president of the Unión Interamericana de Mujeres (Inter-American Union of Women), Neira promoted the organization of the Congreso Interamericano de Mujeres (Inter-American Congress of Women) in Panama (1926), which preceded the one held in Guatemala, 1947).[49] The 1941 Constitution introduced the municipal vote for all literate women, making Panama the second country in Central America to adopt such a reform.[50] Subsequently, during the election of the 1945 Constituent Assembly, women were able to vote and be elected as deputies before universal suffrage was ratified in the 1946 Constitution.[51]

In line with the regional trend toward universal female suffrage, such a reform was adopted in British Honduras (today Belize) in 1954, preceding the experiences of Guatemala, Honduras, and Nicaragua.[52] The colony's head start over these three independent republics was due to two distinct but related processes: women had begun to organize since the early twentieth century in Belize, and this activism combined in the 1930s with a working-class movement that began to demand reformist social policies to meet the needs of the Great Depression. Once these forces were politicized and incorporated national demands, the foundation was laid for the creation of the People's United Party in 1950, which played a key role in Belize's independence (September 21, 1981).[53]

WOMEN AND MODERNIZATION (1955–1989)

In the second half of the twentieth century, Central America experienced a growing urbanization and the implementation of development policies that promoted the expansion of education and health care, the development of infrastructure, and import substitution industrialization. This modernization deepened the differences between the socially unequal and politically authoritarian development style of Guatemala, El Salvador, Honduras, and Nicaragua and the democratic experiences and broader distribution of wealth in Costa Rica, Panama, and British Honduras. In the early 1960s, the overall literacy rate of the population in the first four countries ranged from 37.9 percent in Guatemala to 49.8 percent in Nicaragua. In contrast, the latter three countries all had literacy rates higher than 76.7 percent.[54]

Although the available data do not allow comparison of the female literacy rate in all countries, the existing information shows that the literacy rate in urban areas for women born between 1941 and 1943 was 85.6 percent in Costa Rica, 66.8 percent in El Salvador, and 38.5 percent in Nicaragua. In contrast, the literacy rate among rural women was 60.1 percent in Costa Rica, 29.2 percent in El Salvador, and 7.6 percent in Nicaragua.[55] This persistent lag in rural areas affected especially Indigenous and Afro-descendant women, while greater access to secondary and university education benefited primarily upper- and middle-class urban women. In secondary education, there was a trend toward gender equality in enrollment, as by the mid-1960s women accounted for 50 percent or more of secondary students in Costa Rica and Panama and ranged between 42 percent and 47 percent in Guatemala, El Salvador, Honduras, and Nicaragua.[56]

It was precisely to overcome the low rates of literacy, especially among women, that the Sandinistas began a successful literacy campaign in the 1980s after coming to power in Nicaragua in 1979. This campaign exponentially increased rural literacy. Women were particularly important in this experience, which, despite its achievements, did not result in feminist mobilization as the campaign aimed to reinforce traditional gender roles and sought to perpetuate women's subordination to the nationalist and patriarchal Sandinista project.[57]

As in the previous period, public higher education was expanded but remained most accessible to the urban middle classes, while most Indigenous and Afro-descendant women were still excluded.[58] The process was very uneven throughout the region. In the mid-1960s, girls and women accounted for more than 40 percent of the student population in Costa Rica and Panama, but only between 14 percent and 26 percent in Guatemala and Nicaragua.[59] Despite this disparity, women's career opportunities have expanded in the professions and in sectors of the labor market traditionally dominated by men, such as the medical field, the sciences, and engineering.[60] Growing access to universities has led to greater and more diverse opportunities for female artists, writers, intellectuals, and professionals and the emergence of the first generations of female academics and scientists.

Although women with technical and university degrees became independent professionals (especially as doctors and attorneys) or filled management positions in the public and private sectors, working-class women continued to be employed as agricultural or industrial workers or domestic servants. Although import substitution industrialization expanded industrial employment in the 1960s and 1970s, it did so in a limited way, and companies incorporated labor-saving technology. In the 1980s, this industrialization was displaced by maquiladoras, which meant an expansion in the labor market for women in the textile and clothing industry, but under very exploitative working conditions.[61] Due to the regional crisis of that time, women (mainly Indigenous women) became a larger part of the informal economy: El Salvador (53.4 percent), Honduras (50.4 percent), Nicaragua (46.8 percent), Guatemala (41.7 percent), Costa Rica (32.5 percent), and Panama (25 percent).[62] In turn, the civil wars of the 1970s and 1980s displaced many women, who were forced to migrate in search of better conditions for their families, working primarily in domestic service, agriculture, or maquiladora industries, where their migrant status left them even more vulnerable to exploitation.[63]

In the agricultural sector, most jobs still required little education and consisted of nonskilled, seasonal labor on coffee and banana plantations. In the early twentieth century, Indigenous Guatemalan women working on coffee plantations were designated as "assistants" in agricultural tasks, which condemned them to a subordinate position: their labor was subsumed into the family economy, stripping them of financial independence and turning them into "leverage" that could be used to force their husbands to meet their voluntary or forced labor obligations. This situation had not changed much by the 1970s, despite the revolutionary experience under the governments of Juan José Arévalo (1945–1951) and Jacobo Arbenz (1951–1954) and the subsequent development policies implemented by the military.[64]

During the 1960s, Central American women experienced two fundamental changes, the impacts of which were felt differently according to class, ethnicity, age, and geographical area. The first consisted of the introduction of contraceptive methods, a process that initially reached primarily upper- and middle-class urban women, giving them control over their bodies, sexuality, and reproductive capacity. Subsequently, urban working-class women also began to use these resources, followed by rural non-Indigenous and Indigenous women. As recently as 1987, only 4.5 percent of Indigenous women in Guatemala engaged in family planning, compared to 27.9 percent of non-Indigenous women.[65]

The second change was growing female participation in opposition and revolutionary movements. In the context of the 1960s student rebellion, advanced high school and college students throughout the region mobilized in favor of the democratization of Central American societies (especially in countries dominated by dictatorships or military regimes) and against American imperialism in the region. These student protests included the struggles against Alcoa Corp. in Costa Rica (1970) and Exmibal, the nickel mining subsidiary of the International Nickel Co. in Guatemala (1971).[66] Student radicalism did not spark or feed into insurgent movements in Costa Rica, Panama, and Belize, but it did in the rest of the region, especially in Guatemala, El Salvador, and Nicaragua. So, beginning in the 1960s, the persecution, torture, and murder of students became a common practice in those three countries (state terrorism); an emblematic case was Rogelia Cruz, a student, beauty queen, and leftist activist murdered in Guatemala in 1968.[67]

Although Indigenous Guatemalan women had been joining the guerrilla ranks since 1962,[68] women's participation in these movements intensified in the 1970s and 1980s. In Nicaragua, women made up 25–30 percent of the guerrilla forces of the Sandinista Front for National Liberation (FSLN).[69] Besides armed fighting, new spaces opened for women's participation and struggle, such as the groups of mothers of the disappeared in El Salvador, Guatemala, and Nicaragua.[70] According to Karen Kampwirth, five factors influenced women's participation in the guerrilla movement: land concentration and increased insecurity among the rural poor; ideological factors; organizational changes associated with the rise of liberation theology, and mass mobilization; the brutality of state repression that led to the radicalization of women; family traditions of resistance and participation in student, religious, and union solidarity networks; and the combination of all these factors.[71]

Thus, women's achievement of the right to vote had a differential impact throughout the region. In Guatemala, El Salvador, and Nicaragua, in particular, the space for articulating specifically female and feminist demands diminished or disappeared as women joined the revolutionary fronts. In Costa Rica and Panama, on the other hand, women expanded their sociopolitical spheres of action as they joined community or local organizations, established women's caucuses within the political parties, and later created a wide variety of feminist organizations.[72] All these afforded women greater participation in elections, as some became community leaders and ran for public office on town and city councils, directorships, and mayor's posts.[73] Moreover, in the Costa Rican case, an institutional structure directly related to women and women's rights had begun to take shape in the mid-1970s and led to the creation by the state of the Oficina de Programas para la Mujer y la Familia (Office for Women's Programs, 1974), which formed the basis for the Centro Nacional para el Desarrollo de la Mujer y la Familia (National Center for the Development of Women and the Family, 1986).[74] Despite its traditional perspective, which associated women with the family, this institutional base was crucial to the adoption of the Ley de Promoción de la Igualdad Social de la Mujer (Women's Social Equality Promotion Act) in 1990, the first legislation in Latin America to protect and strengthen women's rights in political representation and other fields, which preceded the first wave of laws establishing gender quotas.[75]

Pro-Woman Laws and Institutions (1990–2021)

Between 1990 and 2021, primary education and, to a lesser extent, secondary education have extended their reach in all the region's countries. There remains a difference between the tier consisting of Costa Rica, Panama, and Belize, where 70 percent or more of the population had access to secondary education between 2015 and 2018, and the tier consisting of Guatemala, El Salvador, Honduras, and Nicaragua, where access is limited to between 44 percent and 60 percent of the population.[76] Access to education also remains deficient in rural areas, where Indigenous and Afro-descendant women are disproportionately affected. Although education has increased, dropout rates remain high after the age of eleven, resulting in a low level of education that limits prospects to low-paid or informal-sector jobs, thereby contributing to the reproduction of poverty.[77]

Although women's access to education has expanded, this increase has been strongly shaped by the regional inequalities mentioned previously. Between 2015 and 2019, women accounted for more than 59 percent of the overall student population in higher education in Costa Rica and Panama, while they made up 31 percent or less of the higher education student body in the rest of the region (including Belize).[78] Despite these gaps, access to higher education has been essential to consolidating women's professionalization in various fields, promoting their artistic, scientific, and literary production; enabling their participation in politics and academia; encouraging study abroad and participation in international activities; and facilitating the creation of feminist networks and organizations. These achievements were accompanied by the increasing use of contraceptive methods, a trend that led to a decline in the fertility rate, particularly in Costa Rica, where it fell below the rate necessary to replenish the population.[79]

Due to their educational lag in the most populous countries of the isthmus, women have been most affected by unemployment and informal employment. Women have a lower rate of participation in the labor force and worse working conditions than do men, as they are paid up to 35 percent less than their male counterparts, with Guatemala having the greatest income gap.[80] In the context of these inequalities, the proportion of female-headed households in the region rose from 25 percent in 2001 to almost 33 percent in 2013. As a result of extreme poverty and unemployment, four million Central Americans (8 percent of the region's population), mainly Guatemalans, Salvadorans, Hondurans, and Nicaraguans, live outside their home countries; of these, 82 percent reside in the United States. The greatest intraregional migration flow is to Costa Rica (64.8 percent), which offers more opportunities for unskilled work (especially in agriculture and domestic service) and better pay.[81]

Women were active participants in the peace process that ended the political and military crisis in Central America in the 1990s. In fact, Guatemalan women were able to incorporate some of their gender demands into the deliberations that gave rise to the Guatemalan peace agreements.[82] Since then, new spaces for women's participation and struggle have opened, resulting in the creation of various types of women's organizations, the strengthening of feminist movements, and the proliferation of nongovernmental organizations that prioritize gender issues.[83] With Costa Rica leading the way since the 1970s, an institutional framework has emerged in all countries, including Belize, to promote and defend women's rights.[84] This process gave rise to institutions dedicated to ensuring the adoption and enforcement of laws promoting workplace, wage, and employment equality; criminalizing gender violence in its various forms; and setting quotas for women's political representation, in terms of both minimum participation and parity.[85] Thus, fifty-three laws on gender policies were adopted in the region between 2000 and 2015 with the aims mentioned previously.[86]

From the perspective of representation and access to elected offices, it is worth mentioning the first women elected to the presidency in Central America. In Nicaragua, Violeta Barrios (1990–1997) became the first female elected president in Latin America. Her experience was followed by Latin America's second female president, Mireya E. Moscoso in Panama (1999–2004), and Laura Chinchilla in Costa Rica (2010–2014), the fifth female president in Latin America.[87] In all three cases, expectations that a woman in the presidency would advance women's rights were frustrated; moreover, these presidential administrations were not only mired in various corruption scandals, they also prioritized the interests of large businesses based on neoliberal policies.[88]

Following the achievement of universal suffrage, the main goal was the implementation of laws that set a minimum quota or equal participation for women in elected public offices to increase women's political representation.[89] These reforms were introduced throughout the region, with the exception of Guatemala and Belize. Costa Rica became the third Latin American country to introduce a minimum quota of 40 percent in 1996, followed by parity in 2009. Panama introduced a 30 percent quota in 1997 and parity in 2012, Honduras approved a 30 percent quota in 2000 and parity in 2012, Nicaragua established parity in 2012, and El Salvador set a 30 percent quota in 2013.[90]

With the implementation of quotas and parities, women increased their representation in the legislative branch. Between 2000 and 2020, the proportion of women in the national legislature grew from 19.3 percent to 46.6 percent in Costa Rica, from 16.7 percent to 33.3 percent in El Salvador, from 9.4 percent to 21.1 percent in Honduras, from 10.8 percent to 47.3 percent in Nicaragua, and from 9.7 percent to 22.5 percent in Panama. Although Guatemala has no quota law, women's participation in the national legislature grew from 7.1 percent to 19.4 percent during the same period. In contrast, Belize reports the smallest gain in female representation in its parliament, from 6.9 percent to 9.4 percent.[91] As with the case of female presidents, women's growing legislative representation did not change the dominant political trends, as most female lawmakers represented the interests of their parties, politically identified with big business, or defended traditional gender values, thereby distancing themselves from the progressive expectations embraced by feminists who were the main drivers of quotas and parity.

The social and cultural conservatism of female legislators was part of a broader process. In response to the advance of women's rights, a bloc of conservative and antifeminist forces began to form in the late twentieth century, including the participation of various sectors of the Catholic Church and evangelical congregations and political parties. The latter used the advantage of the crisis in left-wing organizations, following the peace processes and the collapse of the Soviet Union, to expand, especially among lower-income communities. In fact, even the Frente Sandinista de Liberación Nacional (Sandinista Front for National Liberation, or FSLN) and the Frente Farabundo Martí para la Liberación Nacional (Farabundo Martí Front for National Liberation, or FMLN) succumbed to these conservative trends, which quickly expanded their space in the arena of politics.[92] These forces have dedicated themselves to pursuing and suppressing feminists in Nicaragua, El Salvador, Honduras, and Guatemala, a process that has led to political killings such as that of Honduran environmentalist and feminist Berta Cáceres. This is complemented by an aggressive campaign against women's reproductive rights, embodied in the criminalization of therapeutic abortion (formerly recognized as a legal medical practice to save the life of the mother) in Nicaragua, El Salvador, and Honduras.[93]

Given the prevalence of poverty, political violence, and drug trafficking, violence against women remains a serious regional problem. Its most extreme expression are the murders of women, most notably of victims between twenty and thirty years of age in the northern region. This trend grew during the 2000s, reaching a peak of 12.7 femicides per 100,000 women in El Salvador in 2006, exceeding the rate (10 femicides per 100,000 women) that the World Health Organization deems an epidemic.[94] The trend reversed in the 2010s, and in 2019, the rate of femicide per 100,000 women was 6.2 in Honduras, 3.3 in El Salvador, 1.9 in Nicaragua, 1.8 in Guatemala, 1.0 in Panama, and 0.6 in Costa Rica.[95] In Belize, it was 2.6 in 2018.[96]

In a stable democracy such as Costa Rica, the influence of conservative forces took the form of judicial decisions opposing in vitro fertilization and same-sex marriage. In the face of this institutional blockade, appeals were made to the Inter-American Court of Human Rights to secure decisions favorable to in vitro fertilization (2016) and same-sex marriage (2018). These judicial decisions have not only favored women but have notably strengthened their reproductive and civil rights. In addition, with the implementation of rules regulating therapeutic abortion (2020), Costa Rica went against the prevailing criminalization trend of its northern and central neighbors.[97] Despite these important achievements, the regressive policies promoted by the Carlos Alvarado administration (2018–2022), reducing wages and job security, lengthening the workday, promoting the dissolution of trade unions, and criminalizing social protest, represent a fundamental setback for women, in terms of both their wages and working conditions and their trade union and civic activism.[98]

Women's Rights: Onwards and Backwards

From independence to the present, two development styles can be discerned in the history of Central America: one characterized by greater levels of authoritarianism, violence, poverty, and inequality, prevailing in Guatemala, El Salvador, Honduras, and Nicaragua, and another prevailing in Costa Rica, Panama, and Belize, which combined democracy with improvements in the living and working conditions of the population. This differentiation decisively limited the scope of women's struggles for more opportunities and rights, a process that throughout the region has benefited White and mixed-race women from the urban middle and upper classes more than rural women, especially those of Indigenous and African descent. Class and ethnicity, but also age and geographical origin, have shaped women's access to opportunities and their ability to exercise their rights.

With the establishment of national states over the nineteenth century, women experienced a first step in that they were able to resort to civil authorities rather than ecclesiastical authorities, a change that was consolidated by liberal reforms, which expanded some of their rights in the domestic sphere, promoted their education, and encouraged their inclusion in the labor market, including as public servants. These changes laid the foundation for early twentieth-century women to begin creating their own organizations (including some labor organizations), earn their first professional degrees, emerge as intellectuals, begin to participate in politics, and organize the first campaigns for women's voting rights.

Through the influence of communist parties in the 1930s, women's organizations and movements that had until then been limited to small groups of educated women began to spread to the masses. Reinforced by the Guatemalan Revolution (1944–1954), this process gained strength after 1950 in the midst of the Cold War, as women gained greater access to secondary and university education and women's voting rights were universally recognized throughout the region. While in Costa Rica, Panama, and Belize, women took greater advantage of the opportunities opened by their full-fledged citizenship and the development policies of the period to modernize their living conditions (including birth control), the situation in the rest of the region was very different. Faced with authoritarianism and violence, women tended to postpone their specifically feminist demands as they joined pro-democracy movements, including those that entailed armed struggle.

This resulted in a further gap between Costa Rica, Panama, and, to a lesser extent, Belize, where women expanded their opportunities and rights by institutional routes from the mid-twentieth century on, and Guatemala, El Salvador, Honduras, and Nicaragua, where this process was only revived in the 1990s. From that time to the present day, through activism and the efforts of women's and feminist groups, women have managed to create a legal and institutional infrastructure favorable to women without precedent on the isthmus; however, this has come under increasing siege from conservative religious and neoliberal forces that not only reject therapeutic abortion and same-sex marriage but also seek to undermine women's working conditions and civil rights. These setbacks have been compounded by the differentiated impact of COVID-19, which has had a greater impact on women in terms of rising unemployment and poverty.

NOTES

1. Carmen Diana Deere and Magdalena León, "Liberalism and Married Women's Property Rights in Nineteenth-Century Latin America," *Hispanic American Historical Review* 85, no. 4 (2005): 635; see Patricia Harms, "Imaging a Place for Themselves: The Social and Political Roles of Guatemalan Women, 1871–1954" (PhD diss., Arizona State University, 2007), 637.

2. Catherine Komisaruk, "Women and Men in Guatemala, 1765–1835: Gender, Ethnicity, and Social Relations in the Central American Capital" (PhD diss., University of California Los Angeles, 2000), 28–32, 317–329; María de los Ángeles Acuña, "Mujeres esclavas en la Costa Rica del siglo XVIII: Estrategias frente a la esclavitud," *Diálogos Revista Electrónica de Historia* 5, nos. 1–2 (2005); Eugenia Rodríguez, "Relaciones Ilícitas y Matrimonios Desiguales: Regulating Sexual Mores in Eighteenth-Century Costa Rica," in *The Social and Political Impact of the Bourbon Reforms in Central America, 1759–1808*, ed. Jordana Dym and Christophe Belaubre, 185–210 (Boulder: University Press of Colorado, 2007); Elizabeth Payne, "Vendida desde el vientre de su madre: Josefa Catarina y los esclavos de doña Manuela de Zavaleta (1750–1835)," *Cuadernos Inter.c.a.mbio sobre Centroamérica y el Caribe* 11, no. 1 (2014): 215–232; Brianna Leavitt-Alcántara, *Alone at the Altar: Single Women and Devotion in Guatemala, 1670–1870* (Stanford, CA: Stanford University Press, 2018).

3. Deere and León, "Liberalism and Married Women's Property Rights," 663–666; Asunción Lavrin, *Women, Feminism, and Social Change in Argentina, Chile and Uruguay, 1890–1940* (Lincoln: University of Nebraska Press, 1995), 228–229.

4. Lavrin, *Women, Feminism*, 194.

5. Deere and León, "Liberalism and Married Women's," 628.

6. Ibid., 636; Eugenia Rodríguez, *Hijas, novias y esposas: Familia, matrimonio y violencia doméstica en el Valle Central de Costa Rica (1750–1850)* (Heredia, Costa Rica: Editorial Universidad Nacional, Plumsock Mesoamerican Studies, 2000), 111–153; Eugenia Rodríguez, *Divorcio y violencia de pareja en Costa Rica (1800–1950)* (Heredia, Costa Rica: Editorial Universidad Nacional, 2006), 93–226; Beatriz Palomo, "Vida conyugal de las mujeres de finales de la época colonial e inicios de la vida independiente en Guatemala," in *Mujeres, Género e Historia en América Central durante los Siglos XVIII, XIX y XX*, ed. Eugenia Rodríguez, 25–34 (San José, Costa Rica: UNIFEM, Plumsock Mesoamerican Studies, 2002); Teresa Cobo, *Políticas de género durante el liberalismo: Nicaragua 1893–1909* (Managua, Nicaragua: UCA, Colectivo Gaviota, 2000), 82–108, 123–133.

7. Deere and León, "Liberalism and Married Women's Property Rights," 637–640; Rodríguez, *Divorcio y violencia de pareja*, 45–46.

8. Deere and León, "Liberalism and Married Women's Property Rights," 647–649, 662, 668–669; Eugenia Rodríguez, "Las esposas y sus derechos de acceso a la propiedad en Costa Rica durante el siglo XIX," in *¿Ruptura de la inequidad? Propiedad y género en la América Latina del siglo XIX*, ed. Magdalena León and Eugenia Rodríguez (Bogotá, Colombia: Siglo

del Hombre Editores, 2005), 204–206; *Código Civil de la República de Panamá. Edición conmemorativa del XXV aniversario* (Panamá City: Universidad de Panamá, 1960), Libro IV, Art. 1167.

9. María G. Leret de Matheus, *La mujer: Una incapaz como el demente y el niño (Según las leyes latinoamericanas)* (México City: Costa-Amic Editor, 1975), 239–292; Rodríguez, "Esposas y sus derechos," 216–217; *Código Civil*, Libro I, Arts. 187–192.

10. Rodríguez, "Esposas y sus derechos," 217–218.

11. Harms, "Imaging a Place," 51–56, 69, 244; Rina Villars, *Para la casa más que para el mundo: Sufragismo y feminismo en la historia de Honduras* (Tegucigalpa, Honduras: Editorial Guaymuras, 2001), 64–129; Victoria González, "Josefa Toledo de Aguerri (1866–1962) and the Forgotten History of Nicaraguan Feminism, 1821–1955" (M.A. thesis, University of New Mexico, 1996), 15–37; Cobo, *Políticas de género*, 54–58, 137–151; Yolanda Marco, "Mujeres y política educativa en Panamá a inicios del siglo XX," in Rodríguez, ed., *Mujeres, género e historia en América Central*, 57–64.

12. Asunción Lavrin, "Recuerdos del siglo XX," Revista de Historia Social y de las Mentalidades 8, nos. 1–2 (2004): 11–33; Francesca Miller, *Latin American Women and the Search for Social Justice* (Hanover, NH: University Press of New England, 1991), 35–67.

13. Iván Molina, "La alfabetización popular en El Salvador, Nicaragua y Costa Rica (1885–1950)," in Iván Molina, *La estela de la pluma. Cultura impresa e intelectuales en Centroamérica durante los siglos XIX y XX* (Heredia, Costa Rica: Editorial Universidad Nacional, 2004), 61–62.

14. Rodríguez, *Divorcio y violencia de pareja*, 27–43.

15. Harms, "Imaging a Place," 51–56; Villars, *Para la casa más que para el mundo*, 39–129; Cobo, *Políticas de género*, 32–35, 54–64; Virginia Mora, "Los oficios femeninos urbanos en Costa Rica (1864–1927)," *Mesoamérica* 27, no. 1 (1994): 127–155; Eugenia Rodríguez, "Disciplinar para la maternidad y la acción social en el Colegio Superior de Señoritas (Costa Rica, 1888–1940)," *Descentrada* 4, no. 1 (2020): 8; Eugenia Rodríguez, "Del hogar al colegio y del colegio al hogar y a la calle. Acceso a la educación e identidades de género: El Colegio Superior de Señoritas (Costa Rica, 1888–1940)," in *La educación de las mujeres en Iberoamérica*, ed. Teresa González Pérez, 181–220 (Valencia, Spain: Tirant Humanidades, Gobierno de Canarias, 2019); Yolanda Marco Serra, "Mujeres y política educativa en Panamá a inicios del siglo XX," in Rodríguez, ed., *Mujeres, género e historia en América Central*, 53–70.

16. In Central America, *ladino(a)* is the regional expression for *mestizo*, the standard Latin American word for persons of mixed European and Indigenous descent.

17. Molina, "La alfabetización popular," 70, 73–74.

18. Lorena Carrillo, *Las luchas de las guatemaltecas del siglo XX. Mirada al trabajo y la participación política de las mujeres* (Antigua Guatemala: Ediciones del Pensativo, 2004), 37–47, Virginia Mora, "La mujer obrera en la educación y en el discurso periodístico en Costa Rica (1900–1930)," *Anuario de Estudios Centroamericanos* 19, no. 1 (1993): 67–77; Cobo, *Políticas de género*, 58–64, 154–171.

19. Harms, "Imaging a Place," 53, 55; Steven Palmer ánd Gladys Rojas, "Educating Señorita: Teacher Training, Social Mobility and the Birth of Costa Rican Feminism, 1885–1925," *Hispanic American Historical Review* 78, no. 1 (1998): 45–82; Iván Molina, "Desertores e invasoras. La feminización de la ocupación docente en Costa Rica en 1904," in Iván Molina and Steven Palmer, *Educando a Costa Rica. Alfabetización popular,*

formación docente y género (1880–1950) (San José, Costa Rica: Editorial Porvenir, Plumsock Mesoamerican Studies, 2000), 103–128.

20. Harms, "Imaging a Place."

21. Carrillo, *Luchas de las guatemaltecas,* 53–57; David Mc Creery, "Una vida de miseria y vergüenza: Prostitución en la ciudad de Guatemala, 1880–1920," *Mesoamérica* 8, no. 11 (1986): 35–59; Juan José Marín, "Prostitución y pecado en la bella y próspera ciudad de San José (1850–1930)," in *El paso del cometa: Estado, políticas sociales y culturas populares en Costa Rica, 1800–1950,* ed. Iván Molina and Steven Palmer, 47–80 (San José, Costa Rica: Editorial Porvenir, 1994); Cobo, *Políticas de género,* 118–122.

22. Molina, "Alfabetización popular," 68–69.

23. Harms, "Imaging a Place," 244.

24. Molina, "Desertores e invasoras," 156.

25. Yolanda Marco, *Clara González de Behringer. Biografía* (Panama City: Ministerio de Economía y Finanzas de Panamá, Cooperación Española y UNIFEM, 2007), 72; Ángela Acuña, *La mujer costarricense a través de cuatro siglos,* vol. I (San José, Costa Rica: Imprenta Nacional, 1969), 367; Ana Patricia Borrayo, "Por la equidad de género en la educación superior: Tras las huellas de las precursoras en la educación superior: Universidad de San Carlos de Guatemala 1897–2005" (Guatemala City: UMUSAC, noviembre 2006), 19.

26. Villars, *Para la casa más que para el mundo,* 186–187, 242–245, 248–249; Héctor Pérez, *A Brief History of Central America* (Berkeley: University of California Press, 1989), 66–97; Sonia Ticas, "Avances y retrocesos en el movimiento sufragista femenino salvadoreño en la década de 1920," *Identidades,* 13 (2018): 162–163.

27. Villars, *Para la casa más que para el mundo,* 210, 222–250, 256–280; Carrillo, *Luchas de las guatemaltecas,* 47; Iván Molina, *Demoperfectocracia: La democracia pre-reformada en Costa Rica (1885–1948)* (Heredia, Costa Rica: EUNA, 2005).

28. Eugenia Rodríguez, "Visibilizando las facetas ocultas del movimiento de mujeres, el feminismo y las luchas por la ciudadanía femenina en Costa Rica (1890–1953)," *Diálogos. Revista Electrónica de Historia* 5, nos. 1–2 (2005): 14–15; Marta Solano Arias, "Unidas por sus derechos: Feministas y maestras en 1924," *Anuario del Centro de Investigaciones y Estudios Políticos* (Universidad de Costa Rica) 2 (2011): 218–234.

29. Lorena Carrillo, "Sufridas hijas del pueblo: La huelga de las escogedoras de café de 1925 en Guatemala," *Mesoamérica* 27, no. 1 (1994): 157–173.

30. Jeffrey L. Gould and Aldo A. Lauria-Santiago, *To Rise in Darkness: Revolution, Repression, and Memory in El Salvador, 1920–1932* (Durham, NC: Duke University Press, 2008).

31. Victor Hugo Acuña, *La huelga bananera de 1934* (San José, Costa Rica: CENAP-CEPAS, 1984); Suyapa Portillo, *Roots of Resistance: A Story of Gender, Race, and Labor on the North Coast of Honduras* (Austin: University of Texas Press, 2021).

32. Eugenia Rodríguez, "Madres, reformas sociales y sufragismo: el Partido Comunista de Costa Rica y sus discursos de movilización política de las mujeres (1931–1948)," *Cuadernos Intercambio sobre Centroamérica y el Caribe* 11 (2014): 45–77.

33. Cecilia Mérida, "Mujer y ciudadanía: Un análisis desde la antropología de género" (Licenciatura Dissertation in Anthropology, Universidad de San Carlos de Guatemala, 2000), 38; Héctor Lindo, "Las salvadoreñas fueron las verdaderas pioneras del voto femenino en Latinoamérica," *El Faro.net,* June 26, 2020, https://elfaro.net/es/202006/ef_academico/24586/Las-salvadoreñas-fueron-las-verdaderas-pioneras-del-voto-femenino-en-Latinoamérica.htm; Francesca Miller, "The Suffrage Movement in Latin America,"

448 EUGENIA RODRÍGUEZ SÁENZ

in *Confronting Change, Challenging Tradition. Women in Latin American History*, ed. Gertrude M. Yeager (Wilmington, DE: Scholarly Resources, 1994), 168.

34. Mérida, "Mujeres y ciudadanía," 41–42, 54–55; Carrillo, *Luchas de las guatemaltecas*, 118–119; Harms, "Imaging a Place," 252-254.

35. Harms, "Imaging a Place," 242–243.

36. Ibid., 253; Patricia Harms, "God Doesn't Like the Revolution". The Archbishop, the Market Women, and the Economy of Gender in Guatemala, 1944-1954," *Frontiers: A Journal of Women Studies* 32, no. 2 (2011): 112–113, 116–117, 120.

37. Ticas, "Avances y retrocesos," 166–171.

38. Cristina García, "La Liga Femenina Salvadoreña: Un acercamiento a sus discursos en la década de 1950," *Identidades. Revista de Ciencias Sociales y Humanidades* 9, no. 14: 178–179, 185–186; Sonia Ticas, "Ciudadanía, sufragio y democratización: El feminismo salvadoreño" (Las Vegas, NV: Ponencia LASA Internacional Congress, October 2004, inédito), 2–6.

39. Villars, *Para la casa*, 155, 221, 297, 331, 336.

40. Ibid., 250, 332–335.

41. Ibid., *Para la casa*, 379–387, 393.

42. Victoria González, *Before the Revolution. Women's Rights and Right-Wing Politics in Nicaragua, 1821–1979* (University Park: Pennsylvania State University Press, 2011), 39–41.

43. Ibid., 49.

44. Ibid., 49–51.

45. Ibid., 51–55, 59; Victoria González, "Somocista Women, Right-Wing Politics, and Feminism in Nicaragua," in *Radical Women in Latin America: Left and Right*, ed. Victoria González and Karen Kampwirth, 48–54 (University Park: Pennsylvania State University Press, 2001), 58.

46. Eugenia Rodríguez, "La lucha por el sufragio femenino en Costa Rica (1890–1949)," in *Un siglo de luchas femeninas en América Latina*, ed. Eugenia Rodríguez, 87–110 (San José: Editorial Universidad de Costa Rica, 2002).

47. Ibid., 103–104.

48. Miriam Miranda, "Las organizaciones femeninas en la Zona del Canal, 1907–1930," in *Historia de los movimientos de mujeres en Panamá en el siglo XX*, ed. Fernando Aparicio et al., 19–43 (Panamá City: Instituto de la Mujer de la Universidad de Panamá, Agenda del Centenario, 2002).

49. Yolanda Marco, "El movimiento sufragista en Panamá y la construcción de la mujer moderna," in Aparicio et al., eds., *Historia de los movimientos de mujeres*, 77, 86–87, 100, 103–105.

50. Yolanda Marco, *Mujeres parlamentarias en Panamá, 1945–1995* (Panamá City: Editorial Universidad de Panamá, Congreso de Panamá, 1999), 19–27, 40–43, 49.

51. Marco, "Movimiento sufragista," 120–121, 123–124.

52. Ellen Dubois, "Woman Suffrage: The View from the Pacific," *Pacific Historical Review* 69, no. 4 (2000), 550.

53. Anne S. Macpherson, *From Colony to Nation. Women Activists and the Gendering of Politics in Belize, 1912–1982* (Lincoln: University of Nebraska Press, 2007).

54. George R. Waggoner and Barbara Ashton Waggoner, *Education in Central America* (Lawrence: University Press of Kansas, 1971), 157; AID, *Economic Data Book. Latin America* (Washington, DC: AID, 1971), 99.

55. Molina, "Alfabetización popular," 63–64, 68–69.

WOMEN IN CENTRAL AMERICA SINCE INDEPENDENCE   449

56. UNESCO, *International Yearbook of Education* (Paris: UNESCO, 1970), 190–191, 215.
57. Susy Sánchez, " 'Puño en alto . . . libro abierto': Género y Revolución en la campaña de alfabetización en Nicaragua (1980)," in *Ahora ya sé leer y escribir. Nuevos estudios sobre la historia de la educación en Centroamérica (siglos XVIII al XX)*, ed. Iván Molina (San José, Costa Rica: EUNED, 2016), 296–297; Karen Kampwirth, *Feminism and the Legacy of Revolution: Nicaragua, El Salvador, Chiapas* (Athens, OH: Ohio University Research in International Studies, 2004), 24.
58. Ana Patricia Borrayo, *Experiencias de las mujeres en su acceso a la Universidad de San Carlos de Guatemala Mayas—Xinkas—Garífunas* (Guatemala City: IUMUSAC, Universidad de San Carlos de Guatemala, 2008).
59. UNESCO, *International Yearbook*, 190–191, 215.
60. María Florez-Estrada, *De "ama de casa" a mulier economicus. Sexo, género, subjetividad y economía en Costa Rica contemporáne* (San José, Costa Rica: EUCR, 2011).
61. Wim Dierckxsens, *Mujer y fuerza de trabajo en Centroamérica* (San José: FLACSO Costa Rica, 1991); Ana Lucía Gutiérrez and Carlos Rafael Rodríguez, "La participación de las mujeres en el trabajo remunerado en Costa Rica durante el período 1950–1997," *Revista de Ciencias Sociales* 86–87 (1999): 65–81; Juan Pablo Pérez, *De la finca a la maquila* (San José: FLACSO, Costa Rica, 1996), 164–184; Florence Merienne, "Género y desigualdad laboral en Costa Rica entre 1927 y 1984," in *Historia de las desigualdades sociales en América Central: Una visión interdisciplinaria: siglos XVIII–XXI*, ed. Ronny Viales and David Díaz, 514–539 (San José, Costa Rica: CIHAC-UCR, 2016); Carrillo, *Luchas de las guatemaltecas*, 72–74.
62. J. P. Pérez Sáinz and R. Menjívar Larín, "Central American Men and Women in the Urban Informal Sector," *Journal of Latin American Studies* 26, no. 2 (1994): 436; Saríah Acevedo, "Resistencias de las mujeres indígenas," in Asociación La Cuerda, ed., *Nosotras, las de la historia. Mujeres en Guatemala (siglos XIX–XXI)* (Guatemala: Ediciones La Cuerda, Secretaría Presidencial de la Mujer (SEPREN), Centro Cultural de España en Guatemala, ONU Mujeres, UNFPA, Fondo para el Logro de los ODM, 2011), 230.
63. Roxana Hidalgo, *Mujeres de las fronteras. Subjetividad, migración y trabajo doméstico* (San José, Costa Rica: EUCR, 2016); Carlos Sandoval, Mónica Brenes, and Laura Paniagua, *La dignidad vale mucho: Mujeres nicaragüenses forjan derechos en Costa Rica* (San José, Costa Rica: EUCR, IIS-UCR, 2012).
64. Palomo, "Trabajo al trabajo," 111, 116, 122; David McCreery, *Rural Guatemala (1760–1940)* (Stanford, CA: Stanford University Press, 1994), 279; Arturo Taracena et al., *Etnicidad, estado y nación en Guatemala, 1944–1985* (Guatemala City: CIRMA, 2004), 255–322.
65. Ann Terborgh et al., "Family Planning among Indigenous Populations in Latin America," *International Family Planning Perspectives* 21, no. 4 (1995): 145.
66. Paulino González, "Las luchas estudiantiles en Centroamérica 1970–1983," in *Movimientos populares en Centroamérica*, ed. Daniel Camacho and Rafael Menjívar, 281–284 (San José, Costa Rica: EDUCA, FLACSO, 1985).
67. González, "Luchas estudiantiles," 263, 279, 285; Dora Barrancos, *Historia mínima de los feminismos en América Latina* (Mexico City: El Colegio de México, 2020), 47.
68. Acevedo, "Resistencias," 220; Barrancos, *Historia mínima*, 47.
69. Ilja A. Luciak, *After the Revolution: Gender and Democracy in El Salvador, Nicaragua, and Guatemala* (Baltimore, MD: Johns Hopkins University Press, 2001), 2.
70. Luciak, *After the Revolution*; Lorraine Bayard de Volo, *Mothers of Heroes and Martyrs: Gender Identity, Politics in Nicaragua, 1979–1999* (Baltimore, MD: Johns Hopkins

University Press, 2001), 85; Irina Carlota Silber, *Everyday Revolutionaries: Gender, Violence, and Disillusionment in Postwar El Salvador* (New Brunswick, NJ: Rutgers University Press, 2011).

71. Karen Kampwirth, *Women and Guerrilla Movements: Nicaragua, El Salvador, Chiapas, Cuba* (University Park: Pennsylvania State University Press, 2002), 14.

72. Barrancos, *Historia minima*, 65, 57.

73. Fernando Aparicio and Josefina Zurita, "Vida después del sufragio. Las organizaciones femeninas en el período 1950–1970," in Fernando Aparicio et al., *Historia de los movimientos de mujeres en Panamá en el siglo XX* (Panamá City: Instituto de la Mujer de la Universidad de Panamá, Agenda del Centenario, 2002), 133–212; Mérida, "Mujer y ciudadanía", 41–127; Carrillo, *Luchas de las guatemaltecas*; Victoria González, "Gender, Clientelistic Populism, and Memory: Somocista and Neo-Somocista Women's Narratives in Liberal Nicaragua," in *Gender and Populism in Latin America: Passionate Politics*, ed. Karen Kampwirth, 67–90 (University Park: Pennsylvania State University Press, 2010); Villars, *Para la casa más que para el mundo*, 417–622; María Candelaria Navas and Liza María Dominguez, "Las organizaciones de mujeres en El Salvador y sus aportes a la historia sociopolítica (1957–1999)," in *Mujeres, género e historia en América Central durante los siglos XVIII, XIX y XX*, ed. Eugenia Rodríguez, 135–144 (San José, Costa Rica: UNIFEM, Plumsock Mesoamerican Studies, 2002).

74. Instituto Nacional de las Mujeres, *Nuestra historia* (San José: Inamu, 2021).

75. Adriana Piatti, "The Diffusion of Gender Policy in Latin America from Quotas to Parity," *Journal of International Women's Studies* 20, no. 6 (2019): 44, 53.

76. World Bank data base.

77. Programa Estado de la Nación, *Cuarto Informe Estado de la RegiCst ón Centroamericana en Desarrollo Humano Sostenible: Resumen/PEN* (San José, Costa Rica: Estado de la Nación, 2011), 138–140; Programa Estado de la Nación, *Quinto Informe, Estado de la Región Centroamericana en Desarrollo Humano Sostenible: Resumen/PEN* (San José, Costa Rica: Estado de la Nación, 2016), 151–152.

78. World Bank data base.

79. Programa Estado de la Nación, *Cuarto Informe*, 102, 547; Programa Estado de la Nación, *Quinto Informe*, 87–88, 97; Instituto Nacional de las Mujeres, 77–78, 90–96.

80. Programa Estado de la Nación, *Quinto Informe*, 121, 162.

81. Ibid., 44, 88.

82. Ana Lorena Carrillo and Norma Stoltz, "From Urban Elite to Peasant Organizing: Agendas, Accomplishments, and Challenges of Thirty-Plus Years of Guatemalan Feminism, 1975–2007," in *Women's Activism in Latin America and the Caribbean. Engendering Social Justice, Democratizing Citizenship*, ed. Elizabeth Maier and Nathalie Lebon (New Brunswick, NJ: Rutgers University Press, El Colegio de la Frontera Norte A. C., 2010), 146–147.

83. Ana Leticia Aguilar et. al., *Movimiento de Mujeres en Centroamérica* (Managua, Nicaragua: Programa Regional La Corriente, 1997); Berger, *Guatemaltecas*; Luciak, *After the Revolution*; Silber, *Everyday Revolutionaries*; Ana Isabel García and Enrique Gomáriz, *Mujeres Centroamericanas. Tomo II Efectos del conflicto* (San José, Costa Rica: FLACSO, CSUCA, Universidad para la Paz, 1989), 223–237.

84. OEA-CIM, *Atlas de las luchas de las mujeres 1928–2018 90 años de la Comisión Interamericana de Mujeres. Un camino de luchas, logros y desafíos* (Washington, DC: OEA, CIM, 2018), 19.

85. Ibid., 11–16.

86. Programa Estado de la Nación, *Quinto Informe*, 157.
87. Catherine Reyes-Householder and Gwynn Thomas, "Latin America's *Presidentas*: Overcoming Challenges, Forging New Pathways," in *Gender and Representation in Latin America*, ed. Leslie A. Schmidt-Bayer (New York: Oxford University Press, 2018), 19–20.
88. Reyes-Householder and Thomas, "Latin America's *Presidentas*," 19–20; Karen Kampwirth, "Populism and the Feminist Challenge in Nicaragua: The Return of Daniel Ortega," in Gender and Populism in Latin America: Passionate Politics, ed. Karen Kampwirth, 162–179 (University Park: Pennsylvania State University Press, 2010); Karen Kampwirth, "Gender Politics in Nicaragua: Feminism, Antifeminism, and the Return of Daniel Ortega," in Elizabeth Maier and Nathalie Lebon, eds. *Women's Activism in Latin America and the Caribbean. Engendering Social Justice, Democratizing Citizenship* (New Brunswick, NJ: Rutgers University Press, El Colegio de la Frontera Norte A. C., 2010), 111–112; Jennifer M. Piscopo, "Parity without Equality. Women's Politica Representation in Costa Rica," in *Gender and Representation in Latin America*, ed. Leslie A. Schmidt-Bayer (New York: Oxford University Press, 2018), 172.
89. Beatriz Llanos, *Surcando olas y contra–olas: Una Mirada paritaria a los derechos politicos de las mujeres en América Latina* (Washington, DC: PNUD, ONU Mujeres, IDEA, 2019), 35.
90. Piatti, "Diffusion of Gender Policy," 48–49; Cecilia Schneider, Laura Calvelo, Yanina Welp, and ONU Mujeres, *Estado de los sistemas de información: Estadísticas de los organismos electorales latinoamericanos desde una mirada de género* (Madrid: ONU-Mujeres, Gobierno de España, Ministerio de Asuntos Exteriores y de Cooperación, AECID, 2011), 22; Jacqueline Perchard, "El sistema de cuotas en América Latina," in *La aplicación de cuotas: Experiencias latinoamericanas. Informe del Taller, Lima, febrero del 2003*, ed. International Institute for Democracy and Electoral Assistance (IDEA), Stockholm University (Stockholm, Sweden: Stockholm University, 2003), 23, 27; Ana Isabel García, "Concretando el mandato: reforma judicial en Costa Rica," in International Institute for Democracy and Electoral Assistance (IDEA), Stockholm University, *La aplicación de cuotas: Experiencias latinoamericanas. Informe del Taller, Lima, febrero del 2003* (Stockholm, Sweden: Stockholm University, 2003), 95–109; IDEA, *Global Database of Quotas for Women, Country Overview*, in IDEA, ed., https://www.idea.int/data-tools/data/gender-quotas.
91. Programa Estado de la Nación, *Quinto Informe,* 267; IDEA, *Global Database of Quotas for Women*; https://www.idea.int/data-tools/data/gender-quotas.
92. Maxine Molyneux, "Mobilization Without Emancipation? Women's Interests, the State and Revolution in Nicaragua," in Maxine Molyneux, *Women's Movement's in International Perspective: Latin America and Beyond* (London: Institute of Latin American Studies, University of London, 2001), 38–59; Kampwirth, "Gender Politics in Nicaragua," 111–126; Kampwirth, "Populism and the Feminist Challenge," 162–179; Carrillo and Stoltz, "From Urban Elite," 140–156; María Candelaria Navas and Olga Lucía Rodríguez, *Construcción y ejercicio de la ciudadanía de las mujeres salvadoreñas: Principales obstáculos que la restringen* (San Salvador, El Salvador: FUNDE, 2009); Barrancos, *Historia mínima de los feminismos*, 146–150; Iván Molina, "*Sangri La* en peligro. Las elecciones costarricenses del año 2018," in *¿Cuándo pasará el temblor?: Crisis, violencia y paz en la América Latina Contemporánea*, ed. David Díaz and Christine Hausky, 187–202 (San José: Universidad de Costa Rica, Vicerrectoría de Investigación: Centro de Investigaciones Históricas de América Central, 2019).
93. Barrancos, *Historia mínima de los feminismos,* 142–145; Instituto Interamericano de Derechos Humanos, *Legislación para la igualdad entre mujeres y hombres en América*

Latina (San José, Costa Rica: IIDH, 2010), 9; ONU Mujeres and Gianluca Giuman, *Reporte Anual 2017 ONU Mujeres Guatemala* (Guatemala City: ONU Mujeres Guatemala, 2018), 22–24, 61–69; Guttmacher Institute, *En Resumen: Datos sobre el aborto en América Latina y el Caribe* (New York: Guttmacher Institute, November 2015); Mariana Vargas, "Los países más restrictivos sobre el aborto en Centroamérica," *Revista Level*, February 16, 2019.

94. Asociación Centro Feminista de Información y Acción (CEFEMINA), *No olvidamos ni aceptamos: Femicidio en Centroamérica 2000–2006* (San José,Costa Rica: CEFEMINA, 2010).

95. Gender Equality Observatory for Latin America and the Caribbean, *Femicide or feminicide* (Santiago, Chile: ECLAC, 2020).

96. Economic Commission for Latin America and the Caribbean, *Measuring Femicide: Challenges and Efforts to Bolster the Process in Latin America and the Caribbean* (Santiago, Chile: ECLAC, 2019), 2.

97. Laura Fuentes, "Politización evangélica en Costa Rica en torno a la agenda "provida": ¿Obra y gracia del Espíritu Santo?," *Revista Rupturas* 9, no. 1 (2019): 85–106; Álvaro Murillo, "El 'momento oportuno' llegó: Carlos Alvarado firmó hoy la norma de aborto terapéutico," *Semanario Universidad*, December 12, 2019.

98. Iván Molina, *Costa Rica covidiana: Pandemia politizada y desmantelamiento republicano* (San José, Costa Rica: Del Pasado y del Presente, 2021).

FURTHER READING

Barrancos, Dora. *Historia mínima de los feminismos en América Latina*. Mexico City: El Colegio de México, 2020.

Bayard de Volo, Lorraine. *Mothers of Heroes and Martyrs: Gender Identity, Politics in Nicaragua, 1979–1999*. Baltimore, MD: Johns Hopkins University Press, 2001.

Berger, Susan A. *Guatemaltecas: The Women's Movement 1986-2003*. Austin: University of Texas Press, 2006.

Forster, Cindy. *The Time of Freedom: Campesino Workers in Guatemala's October Revolution*. Pittsburgh, PA: University of Pittsburgh Press, 2001.

González, Victoria. *Before the Revolution: Women's Rights and Right-Wing Politics in Nicaragua, 1821–1979*. University Park: Pennsylvania State University Press, 2011.

González, Victoria, and Karen Kampwirth, eds. *Radical Women in Latin America: Left and Right*. University Park: Pennsylvania State University Press, 2001.

Harms, Patricia. *Ladina Social Activism in Guatemala City 1871–1954*. Albuquerque: University of New Mexico Press, 2020.

Kampwirth, Karen, ed. *Gender and Populism in Latin America: Passionate Politics*. University Park: Pennsylvania State University Press, 2010.

Kampwirth, Karen. *Feminism and the Legacy of Revolution: Nicaragua, El Salvador, Chiapas*. Athens, OH: Ohio University Research in International Studies, Ohio University Press, 2004.

Kampwirth, Karen. *Women and Guerrilla Movements: Nicaragua, El Salvador, Chiapas, Cuba*. University Park: Pennsylvania State University Press, 2002.

Komisaruk, Catherine. *Labor and Love in Guatemala. The Eve of Independence*. Stanford, CA: Stanford University Press, 2013.

Leavitt-Alcántara, Brianna. *Alone at the Altar: Single Women and Devotion in Guatemala, 1670–1870*. Stanford, CA: Stanford University Press, 2018.

Luciak, Ilja A. *After the Revolution: Gender and Democracy in El Salvador, Nicaragua, and Guatemala*. Baltimore, MD: Johns Hopkins University Press, 2001.

Macpherson, Anne S. *From Colony to Nation. Women Activists and the Gendering of Politics in Belize, 1912-1982*. Lincoln: University of Nebraska Press, 2007.

Maier, Elizabeth, and Nathalie Lebon, eds. *Women's Activism in Latin America and the Caribbean. Engendering Social Justice, Democratizing Citizenship*. New Brunswick, NJ: Rutgers University Press, El Colegio de la Frontera Norte A. C., 2010.

Marino, Katherine M. *Feminism for the Americas. The Making of an International Human Rights Movement*. Chapel Hill: University of North Carolina Press, 2019).

Molina, Iván. *La estela de la plumaa; Cultura impresa e intelectuales en Centroamérica durante los siglos XIX y XX*. Heredia, Costa Rica: Editorial Universidad Nacional, 2004.

Molina, Iván, and Steven Palmer. "Popular Literacy in a Tropical Democracy: Costa Rica 1850–1950." *Past & Present: A Journal of Historical Studies* 184 (2004): 169–207.

Molyneux, Maxine. *Women's Movement's in International Perspective: Latin America and Beyond*. London: Institute of Latin American Studies, University of London, 2001.

Portillo, Suyapa. *Roots of Resistance: A Study of Gender, Race and Labor on the North Coast of Honduras*. Austin: University of Texas Press, 2021.

Rodríguez, Eugenia. *Hijas, novias y esposas: Familia, matrimonio y violencia doméstica en el Valle Central de Costa Rica (1750–1850)*. Heredia, Costa Rica: Editorial Universidad Nacional, Plumsock Mesoamerican Studies, 2000.

Rodríguez, Eugenia, ed. *Mujeres, género e historia en América Central durante los siglos XVIII, XIX y XX*. San José, Costa Rica: UNIFEM, Plumsock Mesoamerican Studies, 2002.

Rodríguez, Eugenia, ed. *Un siglo de luchas femeninas en América Latina*. San José, Costa Rica: Editorial Universidad de Costa Rica, 2002.

Rodríguez, Eugenia. *Divorcio y violencia de pareja en Costa Rica (1800–1950)*. Heredia, Costa Rica: Editorial Universidad Nacional, 2006.

Schmidt-Bayer, Leslie A., ed. *Gender and Representation in Latin America*. New York: Oxford University Press, 2018.

Silber, Irina Carlota. *Everyday Revolutionaries: Gender, Violence, and Disillusionment in Postwar El Salvador*. New Brunswick, NJ: Rutgers University Press, 2011.

Villars, Rina. *Para la casa más que para el mundo: sufragismo y feminismo en la historia de Honduras*. Tegucigalpa, Honduras: Editorial Guaymuras, 2001.

CHAPTER 17

···

LITERATURE, SOCIETY, AND POLITICS

···

WERNER MACKENBACH

UNTIL the late twentieth century, and to some extent at the beginning of the twenty-first, Central American literature went largely unnoticed or was relegated to a secondary spot in studies of Latin American literary history. Among scholars of Central American literature and culture, it is commonplace to speak of the region's "marginality within marginality," "periphery of the periphery," and "invisibility" in relation to Latin American literature and culture. Twenty years ago, Guatemalan critic and author Arturo Arias characterized the situation as follows:

> According to the mental map of most Spanish departments in US universities, the southern border of Mexico . . . connects directly with the Andes mountain range; and from Mexico's Lacandon jungle, from which the Paraná, Paraguay and Yaguarón rivers flow, that great literary cornucopia that is the Southern Cone emerges. . . . In this literary map, Central America has no reason to exist because, as we all know, that lost corner of the world only produces revolutions and headaches but no praiseworthy literature.[1]

In 2007, Arias reaffirmed his judgment stated a decade earlier, and spoke of Central America as one of the areas of the world "that [has] been doubly marginalized . . . both by the cosmopolitan center and by countries exercising hegemony in Latin America."[2] This attitude toward Central American literary productions from a North American academy could equally hold true for studies of Latin American literature more generally, especially in Europe and Latin America itself.[3] In the introduction to *La historiografía literaria en América Central (1957–1987)*, dedicated to the place of Central American literature in the Latin American context, Magda Zavala and Seidy Araya also concluded that "there is indeed a forgetfulness, under various guises, of Central American letters."[4]

It is only in recent decades, especially since the mid-1990s, that in Central America itself, in the United States, and partially in Europe, an increasing number of works on Central American literature, individual authors, and singular aspects of its history have been published. Undoubtedly, along with increased international interest in political events in Central America, especially in the 1980s, the literature of the Central American countries has also received greater attention; authors like Ernesto Cardenal, Gioconda Belli, and—but to a lesser degree—Roque Dalton, Manlio Argueta, Sergio Ramírez, Omar Cabezas, Carmen Naranjo, Mario Monteforte Toledo, Augusto Monterroso, Roberto Sosa, Enrique Jaramillo Levi, and others at least are known outside their national borders. At the same time, new national literary histories in these countries were published or existing ones were reworked and republished.[5] Among the compendiums in the history of Spanish American literature, however, Central American literature continues to play—even in the best of cases but with some exceptions such as Rubén Darío and Miguel Ángel Asturias—a subordinate role.[6] In historical-literary studies, the literature of individual Central American countries remained generally unnoticed until the 1990s. Also missing—except for a few exceptions—were compendiums of a general history of Central American literature as well as the literature itself.[7]

Given this situation, how should one approach a critical history of the historiography of Central American literature? From the first half of the nineteenth century, which was when we began to see historiographic-literary records in and from Central America, there was a close relationship between literature, (literary) history, and the political field, especially in the context of projects centered on national construction, whether in its Central American-unionist-federalist variant or in its national-nationalist version. This chapter proposes an approach that analyzes the different periods or moments of change or transition regarding the relations between politics, society, and culture from the perspective of historical change. In other studies, the "macroperiods" of transition have been analyzed—conquest, colonialism, independence, national construction, neo-imperialism, technological revolution.[8] This chapter concentrates on the "microperiods," which are characterized by a paradigm shift with respect to the relationships between literature, history, politics, and society[9]: the nineteenth century (the post-independence moment), the late nineteenth/early twentieth century, the 1930s–1960s, the 1960s–1990s, and the end of the twentieth century/beginning of the twenty-first.

THE NINETEENTH CENTURY: HISTORY, LITERATURE, AND NATION

The beginnings of historiographic-literary writing in Central America—as in Latin America in general—are closely linked to the time of independence and projects of national construction and its development throughout the nineteenth century. In an article published in 1925, Dominican philologist Pedro Henríquez Ureña retrospectively summarized this relationship between nation, history, and literature:

> Since Independence we have aspired to a perfect nationalism, creator of great literatures: our literary history of the last hundred years could be written as the

history of the ebb and flow of aspirations and theories in search of our perfect expression; it should be written as the history of renewed attempts at expression, and above all, of expression achieved.[10]

In her extensive research on the literary historiography of and about Latin America, Venezuelan scholar Beatriz González Stephan points out that literary histories in the nineteenth century played an important ideological role in the construction of a national literature serving the dominant classes to create the necessary images and emblems of the national political and cultural units.[11] Although she maintains that during the colonial period there were precursor forms of historiographic-literary writing *avant la lettre* (i.e., the compilation and sorting of literary works in chronicles, in general and natural histories, as well as in poetic compositions, catalogs, dictionaries, and libraries), she focuses on the formation of literary history proper throughout the nineteenth century, characterized as the century of national literary histories, which started to be elaborated both in Europe and in Latin America in the agitated context of emerging political nationalism.[12] In Hispanic America, this process occurred within the parameters of liberalism and conservatism.

As the dominant ideology of independence aspirations, liberalism sought to build an originality and authenticity typical of Latin or Hispanic American based on miscegenation and a rejection of the Hispanic-colonial, while the "conservative model" was based on the defense of the parameters and values of Hispanic culture and literature and defined by a pronounced Eurocentrism.[13] However, the "liberal model" is not without contradictions and aporia: despite its longing to distance itself from the Spanish metropolis, it did not arrive at a resounding rejection of the Hispanic legacy; rather, historiographic-literary writing was based on European methods, conceptualizations, and periodizations.[14] It tried to incorporate the pre-Hispanic, Indigenous cultures in its project to build an Americanist tradition and a genealogy of the independent Creole nation; however, it only recognized them "as a historically canceled substrate":[15]

> Despite the fact that the liberal model managed to register this type of production—and in some way could have instituted a historiographic tradition in this regard—literary histories . . . would eradicate it and [paradoxically] deepen Enlightenment and Hispanic criteria for elaborating the history of national literature.[16]

Hence the aporia of the historiographic-literary project of liberalism: its attempt to build a literary-cultural tradition of the nation is based on the Indigenous legacy being rendered inferior and invisible and much of the colonial production being liquidated, thus perpetuating the colonialist and Eurocentrist paradigms of Hispanicism.[17] National literature thus lacks a legacy of the past, a corpus based on traditions. It is a national literature that "affirms itself through denial; . . . a hypostasized project, a desideratum . . . a nationality emptied of its own cultural tradition and past, which would have to be realized in the future."[18] Liberal Americanism finds its limitations here and that "perfect nationalism" its imperfection.

In Central America, the first expressions of a historiographic-literary writing occurred in the context of the formation of nation-states and the processes of political and cultural modernization, particularly from the second half of the nineteenth century to the early twentieth century. In that period, states under the political and ideological hegemony of the agro-commercial oligarchy financed the production, publication, and dissemination of history textbooks contributed, through the educational system, to the construction of the nation as an imagined community.[19] This was done in the context of the ideological project of the same dominant class of a national culture and conscience focused on the construction of political, economic, and cultural hegemony in the process of modernization, by controlling the production, significance, and circulation of material and symbolic-cultural goods.[20]

From its first independentist longings, liberalism in Central America oscillated between projects that pointed to the creation of a nation-union (a kind of "small big country"/"pequeña patria grande") and those that advocated the formation of individual nation-states based on the provinces of what was the Appellate Court (Real Audiencia) of Guatemala, the colonial administrative organization of the region. Costa Rican literary scholar Mijail Mondol López differentiates three main areas of historiographic-literary writing about Central American literature throughout the nineteenth and early twentieth centuries: national-local projects that pointed to the creation and institutionalization of a canon and a national literature, projects with Central American regional projection, and supranational projects linked to Spanish publishers.[21] These projects manifested in a variety of forms of writing among which poetry anthologies, panoramas, compilations, notes, reviews, indexes, and *liras* (five-line stanzas) stand out. It was only in the 1920s and early 1930s that the first literary histories were published.[22] Among the first publications with regional/regionalist and unionist purposes are *Galería poética centro-americana* and *El parnaso centroamericano*.[23] Although these anthologies advocate the recognition of Central America as a literary region,[24] Spanish literature remains—as in national/nationalist productions—a norm and model, as emphatically stated by the Nicaraguan-Salvadoran journalist and poet Román Mayorga Rivas:

> Spanish literature, rich in those skills, has been and should be the norm of Central American literature. This forced adhesion, which communicates so much value to the conceptions of our poets, is a natural consequence of origin, customs and language.[25]

Among the Central American elites, whether liberal or conservative, literary Hispanism continued to dominate, and this predominance of Spanish and European models continued until the mid-twentieth century.[26] Regarding Central American historiographic-literary writing of the late nineteenth century and the first half of the twentieth century, Mondol López concludes:

> Linked to the ideological manifestations of a colonized cultural conscience, one of the characteristics detected in the process of the formation of Central American literary historical discourse ... consists of the criteria of legitimacy and modernity that several critical-historiographic productions grant to the Hispanic cultural model. As inferred in some of their respective prologues and dedications, the main argument denoted by

these texts tends to value Hispanic linguistic and cultural criteria as an inherent part of the modernity and national awareness of local literature.[27]

It seems that in the first manifestations of a Central American historiographic-literary writing, something similar happened as in the process of independence in Central America in general. In his essays on Hispanic revolutions, which he presents as "a first approximation to another interpretation of American independence," Spanish-French historian François-Xavier Guerra questions the nature of the total rupture of these movements if analyzed from the transformations of social and economic structures and access to power of a new social class:

> As in America Independence brought with it few substantial modifications of deep economic or social structures, one has lately tended to undervalue its revolutionary character. The Revolution of Independence has come to be considered, by many authors, as a "purely political" phenomenon and therefore of relatively secondary importance with respect to structural permanence. The "purely political" refers here both to the rupture of the link with the metropolis and to the substitution in political power of the mainland Spaniards by the Creoles.[28]

In Central America, this "political rupture" not only did not fundamentally change economic and social structures, but it was carried out without violent confrontations between the Creole class and the defenders of the monarchical *Ancien Régime*. It was the same dominant Creole oligarchy in the colonial system that appropriated independence. This ruling class took the risky way from colonialism to independence without giving up a minimum of its economic, political, and social position.[29]

In relation to the transformations in the cultural sphere, Guerra argues that "the radically new is not the existence of a new global system of references in which are combined ideas, social imaginaries, values and behaviors that have to configure . . . the new society."[30] This is exactly what happened in the incipient Central American cultural-literary field: the independentist aspirations and the search for an identity of the Creole cultural elites were based on a persistent and pronounced Hispanicism/Eurocentrism, particularly in historiographic-literary writings. Here is another imperfect facet of the evoked "perfect nationalism."

MODERNISMO IN THE LATE NINETEENTH AND EARLY TWENTIETH CENTURY: MODERNIZATION, POLITICS, AND LITERATURE

The challenge for Central American writers on the eve of the twentieth century was triple, wrote Costa Rican historian Iván Molina Jiménez, in relation to El Salvador,

Nicaragua, and Costa Rica (a statement that we can also apply to the other countries of the Isthmus):

> To build their own, viable collective identity, which would differentiate them from Europeans and, at the same time, would allow them to be accepted in their countries of origin; legitimize their specific aesthetic and ideological options, a goal whose vital character was evidenced by the rise of *Modernismo*, and diversify and expand the cultural market to ensure the printing, circulation and consumption of its products.[31]

This ambivalent and contradictory nature of the desires of a literary and cultural tradition typical of Central American elites is further exacerbated in the processes of modernization and the positioning of Central American literature in the aesthetic and political debates on modernity:

> The modern project in Central America is based on a fundamental tension between copy and foundation: transplantation of the European model of progress and in turn translation—that is, interpretation—of modernity in the Central American context. Thus, the attempt to "bring progress" to the different Central American nations always implies a search for recognition in the eyes of the European Other, but also an original articulation. . . . In the cultural and literary field, the inscription in modernity passed through the successful practice of the European literary gesture in the Central American context. Thus, intellectual elites assumed European literary culture (academies, newspapers, travels, literary forms) as civilizing discourse, but also used it to prove to themselves and the world the cultural and literary viability of Central America.[32]

For a long time, literary criticism and historiography focused almost exclusively on the renewal of poetry by leading *modernista* authors and its repercussions on Hispanic letters, particularly evoking the importance of Rubén Darío's work.[33] However, the renewal of Hispanic and Hispanic American literature by Central American modernista writers went well beyond a poetic revolution. It had wider aesthetic and cultural repercussions in literary writing in general, which broke with the traditional generic canonization and hierarchy, in the role of the writer, as well as in the institution of literature itself. Forms of writing which had been relegated to a minor role in the dominant classical and romanticist European tradition were emerging as always more important new-old writing practices: the chronicle, the pamphlet, the travel diary.[34]

It is worth highlighting the role beginning to be assumed by women writers, who expressed through literature their questioning of patriarchal societies and created their own identities, despite the pressures and exigencies of their social and family surroundings, which provoked their rejection and contempt by male actors in an incipient cultural-literary field dominated by men and patriarchy.[35] But it was also some of the most prominent male authors who introduced new themes and subjectivities that broke with the secular molds of patriarchy, the novel of Decadentism being a favorite space for this rupture, because "it takes on the pathologizing concept of perversion, which constituted the label which marked and marginalized any erotic manifestation that was not limited to the heterosexual couple."[36] Hence its subversive character, which undermines fixed sexual identities, questions the alleged male–female symmetry, and attacks the prevailing phallocentrism.

With all that, the modernist authors contributed to create a (semi-)autonomous literary field in Central America, for which the growing journalism in the Hispanic and Latin American world played a key role: the technological advances of print culture and the mass delivery of printed products, the increase in a reading public, the transnational places of enunciation (especially important in the Central American case with their societies characterized by high percentages of illiteracy), and the emerging figure of the professional writer-journalist.[37]

However, the increasing autonomy of literature was not limited to these extratextual, more sociological aspects. It was prominent in the aesthetics of modernist writing itself which emphasized the scribal process and insisted on the autonomy of the textual world versus the extratextual, external world—"the core of its aestheticism."[38] With this aestheticism and subjectivism the modernist authors established a new relationship between power/state and culture/literature, a relationship that would remain in conflict throughout the twentieth century. They also broke with Spanish literature as a norm, or at least they renovated it; however, at the same time they reinforced the European and Europeanizing aesthetic paradigm in literature, transforming it from Latin America that means from the "other pole" of artistic and literary modernization.[39]

However, this is not the case in historiographic-literary writing during the last two decades of the nineteenth century and the first two decades of the twentieth century, the era in which modernist aestheticism and subjectivism crystallize. In fact, the works that venture into literary history—unlike literary writing itself—are not characterized by paradigm changes or innovative ruptures. Although the dominant forms in the late nineteenth and early twentieth centuries, such as anthologies and compilations, were combined with other types of text that were more historiographic-literary—"*brief studies, indexes, biographical reviews, historical panoramas, bibliographic compilations and the first attempts to formalize a literary history*"—its parameters and aesthetic patterns did not change.[40] Contrary to the aesthetic practice of modernista literary writing, in historiographic-literary writing there persists "the ideological centrality of the Hispanic *hommes de lettres* model as an ideological horizon of legitimation and cultural recognition of local Central American literature."[41] Nicaraguan Jerónimo Aguilar emphatically proclaimed a modest standpoint for his literary historiography:

> without the pretence of writing a history of Nicaraguan literature, nor the belief that we are possessors of a literature capable of distinguishing itself from that of the rest of the Latin American continent, being only an imitation of the glorious Spanish literature.[42]

This work would always remain institutionally framed and positioned within national-state projects and failed to create a (semi-)autonomous scribal practice as modernismo had done. It is a (literary) historiography serving state power, with a strong didactic character.[43] Modernization processes in Central America did not produce important innovative works of literary historiography.[44]

The 1930s to the 1960s: State, Power, and Literature After *Modernismo*

After the rise and predominance of modernismo development in the Central American literary field—which was still incipient in a sociocultural context marked, among other factors, by a high rate of illiteracy, the lack of important publishers and a reading public, as well as a journalism with wide coverage—the 1930s were characterized by two viewpoints.[45] In their eagerness to distance themselves from the cultural and artistic mediocrity of the dominant Creole classes (i.e., the agricultural and commercial oligarchy), which froze the innovative and revolutionary impulse of modernism, the avant-garde movements—especially the Nicaraguan *Vanguardia*, which came from the self-same social elites—in a first "postmodernist" effort, attacked this cultural environment. They considered the Creole classes "poor and backward, mediated, without cultural structures or a literary tradition, illiterate, heir still to a nineteenth-century rhetoric and elevated by the glitter of Darío's fame."[46] They faced these structures, taking a stand

> against what they call a bourgeoisie, and that is nothing but the same politically and culturally impoverished ruling class: lawyers, apothecaries and surveyor engineers who resist any literary modernization because they resist any modernization at all; they conceive of the country as in the 19th century, as between the cattle ranch and the store, between the cattle prod and the measuring stick.[47]

Against universalist and cosmopolitan modernism domesticated to the service of the state power of the ruling class and the fledgling taste of elites for North American cultural products that began to penetrate the region, the Central American *Vanguard*—in particular, its Nicaraguan variant—evoked the Hispanic-Catholic colonial tradition. As Bernal Herrera points out, Pablo Antonio Cuadra, one of the most prominent poets of the vanguardist literary movement in Nicaragua, proclaimed "to have his heart in the true Nicaragua of the Colony."[48] In its counter- and antimodernist impulse, this group demanded "the rescue of a vernacular national soul, and the repositioning of a national authenticity founded by the colonial and patriarchal nation" as well as the "abolition of the complex of tastes and customs created by a merchant class that embezzled that traditional cultural legacy."[49]

But at the same time, as far as the literary-aesthetic itself was concerned, "it desires cultural renewal" and "wants to replace mediocre taste for a literature located within *modernismo*, and to bring forth a new one," an alternative version of modernization-modernity.[50] The desire for cultural renewal was contradicted by a purported return to the Hispanic colonial tradition.

The second "postmodernist" impetus was characterized—as already mentioned—by the increasing orientation of the Central American elites toward North American cultural-artistic production and its accelerated process of industrialization, massification, and exportation. Along with its political-military interventions and presence (the case of Nicaragua as a symbol) and the economic interventions (the United Fruit Company as the symbol), US cultural-artistic products and patterns also penetrated the societies of the Isthmus, especially since the decade of the 1930s:

> Meanwhile, the refined tastes, habits, fashions, homes, cars, and all possible forms of transplantation from shoes to education, are now taken by these elites from North America, and they no longer have just a distant idea of the metropolis in Paris, but a real and neighboring one in Miami.[51]

This model became even more dominant in the middle of the twentieth century, not only among the elites but also in the customs, tastes, and preferences of large sectors of the Central American populations. It culminated in a gradual process of substitution of the model of cultural dependency imposed during Spanish colonization to dependency on a North American model that began to appear at the end of the nineteenth century.[52]

In this sociocultural context there was no room for innovations in historiographic-literary writing, despite and in contrast to the desire to renew literary writing itself. No doubt, literary historiography experienced greater professionalization because it was now in the academic environment of publishing houses and university institutions where historical-literary studies were carried out and published, especially since the 1950s.[53] Works, among others, by Abelardo Bonilla, Juan Felipe Toruño, Rodrigo Miró, and Jorge Eduardo Arellano stand out.[54]

In all these studies and anthologies, national and nationalist patterns persist in the methodological-interpretative approach:

> As is possible to infer in the prologues and introductions of these texts, literature is conceived in terms of an aesthetic practice in which national and identity values are expressed . . . the historiographic discipline itself is conceived by this group of intellectuals as a genealogical discursive practice from which it is possible to determine the origin, evolution and collective forms and values that characterize and legitimize the existence of a national historical subject and conscience.[55]

In spite of growing North American cultural penetration, the liberal and conservative models on which Latin American literary historiography was founded in the second half of the nineteenth century continued to dominate, with all its legacy of dependence on Hispanic-European patterns.[56] The contradiction persisted between the yearning for the renewal of literary writing that characterized avant-garde literature, and even the realist-regionalist variant, and the pronounced conservatism of literary historiography.[57]

The 1960s to the 1990s: Literature, State, and Counterpower in the Guerrilla Era

In the 1960s, a paradigm shift became apparent, but in a contradictory manner and characterized by elements of rupture and continuity. After the innovative-revolutionary impulse of modernismo in the late nineteenth and early twentieth centuries, the period between the 1960s and 1990s is the second moment that brought fundamental changes and transformations and revolutionized the Central American literary field in several ways: those decades were an agitated and eventful period for literary and cultural production deeply entangled with political and social effervescence.[58] It is the interrelation between the involvement of historical-social and political events in literary processes and texts and the intervention of literature in historical events and processes that reconfigured the literary field and particularly its relationship with the field of political power:

> Literature participated in wide-ranging processes that involved ethical and political positions, performative claims, social and artistic avant-gardes, debates about the nation, about history and the recovery of memory, the emergence of women's voices, of the Indigenous and of the subaltern sectors. Some processes were accompanied by transformations and innovations in languages, expressive resources, textual devices, which affected the different literary genres (poetry, narrative, essay, popular theatre) and were directly connected with others cultural practices that experienced related changes such as crafts, photography, or cinema.[59]

However, although from the 1960s some proliferation of literary-cultural essays and historiographic-literary studies could be noticed, at first there were no changes in their methodological and theoretical bases. Rather, the period was first characterized by the persistence of liberal and conservative paradigms until the second half of the 1980s, despite the transformations in literary writing itself. The triangular relationship literature-identity-nation continued to dominate in literary historiography.[60] Among the historiographic-literary works that follow these patterns are those of Abelardo Bonilla (Costa Rica), Juan Felipe Toruño (El Salvador), Luis Gallegos Valdés (El Salvador), Ismael García (Panama), Jorge Eduardo Arellano (Nicaragua), Rodrigo Miró (Panama), Virginia Sandoval de Fonseca (Costa Rica), Franciscio Albizúrez Palma, and Catalina

Barrios (Guatemala), as well as José Francisco Martínez (Honduras), all published between 1957 and 1987.[61]

It is in literary criticism and cultural-literary essays that the first signs of rupture became manifest under the influence of Marxism, structuralism, sociocriticism, and dependency theory. One of the first works that introduced novel elements into literary studies in this regard is a book of essays by Nicaraguan writer and politician Sergio Ramírez.[62]

What differentiates most of these essays, and the more properly historiographic-literary works that began to be published after the 1980s, is their interest in the complex relationships between literature and society and the critical approach in their analysis of the structures of power between politics and literature.[63]

As Mondol López maintains, this break with the traditional patterns of conservatism and especially liberalism is not total and definitive, rather:

> the vast majority of these studies did not fully overcome the generational and instrumental perspective in which literary practices were conceived. . . . In short, the character of rupture . . . is mainly due to the search for a sociological dimension of the conditions of literary production or the establishment of a thematic and referential link between literary practices and the social political context.[64]

However, many of these works, especially since the pioneering study of Ramón Luis Acevedo, introduced regional and comparative approaches in literary studies that from the mid-nineteenth century to the 1980s were characterized by their strong national orientation and even their nationalist ideology. In the 1970s, a Central American regional cultural-literary space began to be visible, not only in the methodological procedures and theoretical conceptualizations of literary studies but also in the practices and processes in the literary field—for example, through the publication and circulation of regional literary and cultural magazines; the foundation of the publishing house of the public Central American universities, EDUCA (Editorial Universitaria Centroamericana); and the organization of the first Central American meetings and congresses of writers and literary critics.[65]

It should be noted that this process, on the one hand, began to establish a tradition of social historiography of literature that received important impulses and inputs from the sociology of literature, marked by a non-orthodox Marxism.[66] One of the outstanding studies in this area is by Ileana Rodríguez, which was presented as the "first volume of the social history of Nicaraguan literature"; however, there were no subsequent volumes.[67] On the other hand, along with their growing interest in guerrilla movements and utopian projects in the Central American region, the intellectuals in the northern academies (especially in the United States) intensified their concern for cultural, and particularly literary, expressions that were an intrinsic part of political processes. The US cultural-literary-academic influence in the Central American literary field—previously present in works by important authors such as Salomón de la Selva and Ernesto Cardenal—dominated the whole period. The theoretical works and studies on the literary productions of Central America published in this context privilege the writing practices of a "committed" literature, especially political poetry and testimony. For an entire period, the discourse on testimony became dominant not only for writing practice but also for theoretical approaches through which literary productions were analyzed.[68] A consequence of this predominance of the testimonial paradigm is that finally the forms branded "minor" in the secular tradition of Central American literary historiography, such as testimony, journalism, chronicles, and so on, find their entrance not only in the curricula in northern academies but also in the literary history of the region.[69] However, at the same time, in innumerable studies of Central American literature published during that period, other forms of literature that were still being written, but could not be subsumed under the concept of committed or testimonial literature, were ignored. A new canonization, which questioned the traditional Hispanic one, was imposed by North American academies and reinforced by the impact of the Casa de las Américas cultural project from Cuba.[70] So, on the one hand, dependence on North American cultural models and patterns was being questioned.[71] On the other hand, the growing predominance of the North American academy in the analysis and the interpretation of cultural and literary practices in Central America, which managed to impose themes, methods, and conceptualizations, initiated a new form of dependence.

"After the Bombs": Globalization, Market, and Literature in the Late Twentieth and Early Twenty-first Centuries

Since the 1990s, literary studies and historiographic-literary works about the Central American region have experienced a remarkable proliferation for several reasons: the formation of younger generations of Central American academics in universities in Europe and North America who began to work on the literature of the Isthmus systematically and continuously and the growing presence of a significant number of Latin American and Central American academics in universities in the United States who focus on Central American literature and culture.[72] In addition, conferences (national and international) on the literature and culture of the region in the region itself and outside; the creation of research and study programs on Central America in US and Central American universities; and a growing number of publications and editorial projects dedicated to the history, culture, and literature of Central America are periodically being organized.[73]

Among the most outstanding historiographic-literary studies of the period is the pioneering work of Magda Zavala[74] and the studies of Luis Alfredo Arango, Arturo Arias, Claudio Bogantes, Quince Duncan, Kathryn Eileen Kelly, Dante Liano, Juan Antonio

Medina Durón, Lucrecia Méndez de Penedo, Amelia Mondragón, Flora Ovares, Margarita Rojas, Carlos Santander and María Elena Carballo, and Álvaro Quesada Soto.[75] These works mark an important caesura in historiographic-literary research and writing in and about the region that reveals important influences from social history and later from cultural studies. It leaves behind the Hispanic-Eurocentric secular tradition and overcomes the predominance of interpretative models developed by the North American academies of the previous period.[76]

In regard to the processes in the literary field itself since the 1990s, many published studies have been characterized by retrospective approaches in which the paradigm of "committed literature" has remained a model of interpretation. What has dominated has been characterizations of Central American literature as "postwar literature/narrative," "literature of disenchantment," and an "aesthetics of cynicism," among others, and literary periodization has been based on mostly extra-literary criteria.[77] However, the processes that cross and transform the cultural and especially the literary field in Central America, in the current environment of accelerated and generalized globalization, are more complex and cannot be reduced directly to the consequences of armed conflicts in the "postwar" period, although they are present in social relations and also in literary-fiction productions. These literary-fiction productions are characterized by the break with the ideological-political patterns of "committed" literature. In addition, they have experienced deeper changes in relation to the institutions and dimensions of literature: the author's role; the role of literature as an institution; the relationship among literature-politics/state-economy/market, the media, and literary writing itself, under conditions of a growing commercialization of the literary field and the emergence of new technologies in the cultural (and literary) field. These processes have resulted in a vertiginous restructuring and transformation of the cultural field and market, particularly the literary one. The intellectual-writer who traditionally dominated printed culture by exercising his supremacy in the representation and interpretation of realities is confronted with the challenge of redefining his role in a context in which the different forms of communication of the logosphere, graphosphere, videosphere, and cybersphere exist synchronously, and exert strong political and especially economic pressures on literary writing.[78] The demands of the large transnational publishers are becoming more dominant, not only in the dissemination of literary works but even in literary writing itself such that—in order to be successful—the writer has to respond to the commercial criteria of what sells best. Thus, the canon and recognition of writers are already defined much less by the traditional literary-cultural institutions of the state and increasingly by the private enterprise of the large publishers. After the bankruptcy of important Latin American publishers in the Rio de la Plata and Mexico region or their sale to transnationals in the Spanish-speaking world, a predominance and dependence on the peninsular-European-North American publishers has been established once again and what is deemed "Hispanic" has changed due to the strong presence of these large transnational publishers. This reactivates and at the same time renews (in a double sense) the old relations of cultural dependence.[79]

In this situation, academics who deal with the study of Central American literature are confronted with a constellation of new challenges, the starting point for a series of projects and initiatives from the second half of the 1990s. Among those that deal with literary analysis from a historical-historiographic approach, the "Hacia una Historia de las Literaturas Centroamericanas (Towards a History of Central American Literatures)" project[80]; the project of a history of women's literature in Central America; and some other particular works, such as the project and subsequent book, *Literaturas indígenas de Centroamérica*, stand out.[81]

With these projects, the national methodological tradition and the ideological nationalism in the literary studies of Central America were overcome and a regional-comparative approach began to emerge and consolidate in durable, long-lasting research networks between universities and academics in the region itself, and in Latin America, North America, Europe, and Australia, through research projects, congresses, study programs, and collective and shared publications.[82] In regard to theory and method, particularly in "Hacia una Historia de las Literaturas Centroamericanas," a new conceptualization of literary studies was summarized in the introduction to volume III:

> The fundamental axes and nodal points of the project are: the emphasis on Central America as a heterogeneous region; the abandonment of nationalist paradigms; the emergence of new aesthetic paradigms . . .; the commitment to the visibility of the cultural, ethnic and gender diversity that defines the daily life of the Central American context, as well as the transnationalism that characterizes the region.[83]

In this redefinition of literary studies, and especially literary historiography, this innovative project has received important input from previous and parallel projects of Latin American literary historiography, cultural studies, and transareal studies.[84] The project manages to break with national and nationalist traditions and reductionisms; work with a new, expanded, and dynamic concept of literature; and study Central America, its literature, and its culture in its regional, transnational, and transareal interconnections and cross-links, as well as to develop a dialogic relationship between literature and history, literary studies, and historiography and with other disciplines.[85]

Toward New Research Approaches

At the beginning of the second decade of the twenty-first century, what is the situation of Central American and Central Americanist literary historiography? What are the gaps, desiderata, and challenges that arise? One fundamental challenge of literary historiography, which differentiates it from historiography in general, consists of studying the ways in which literary events are implicated in historical events and historical events are implicated in literary processes.[86]

This type of literary historiography requires a set of methodological approaches to investigate the discursive formations in which the texts participate, the networks that connect them, the forms they model, and the symbolic imaginary that they build in the processes of production of meaning in societies. These approaches propose to analyze the textual productions more as facts of social reality than as realizations of individual genius or collections of masterpieces, thus overcoming the standard inventories of (famous) authors (traditionally masculine) and (master) works, of the classification and taxonomy of genres (often in hierarchical form), of styles or groups and literary generations, which assume the author as the protagonist of literary processes or which presume a unilineal and autonomous literary evolution.[87]

Combined with this is another strategic-methodological aspect of equal relevance: to privilege a plural, self-reflective, and dynamic literary historiography that does not silence the controversies within literary criticism itself, thereby constructing a false homogeneity, but insists on the necessity of these debates, polemics, and contradictions for the understanding of literature(s) in its historical evolution.[88]

These multiple challenges persist today to fill the limitations and gaps in literary historiography in and about Central America and to face more challenges at the beginning of the twenty-first century. Among these are the following desiderata:

- investigate further the transformations that the literary field is experiencing in the current environment of accelerated and generalized globalization, in particular in relation to the role and status of the author; the function of literature as an institution and an instance of meaning production; the relationships between literature, state, and market; and changes in writing itself;
- develop extensive and deeper studies of the institutional history of literature, for example, of editorial history and of public and private cultural and literary policies and projects;
- promote studies in the context of literary reception history, that is, the analysis of reading and signifying practices by diverse audiences and in different institutional and cultural contexts (virtually absent in Central American literary historiography);
- encourage Central American literature studies written in languages other than Spanish (in close collaboration with anthropologists and communities that do not have Spanish as their mother tongue);
- deepen the study of the so-called minor, subaltern, anti-hegemonic literature, based on a critical positioning toward the new literary canon construction processes (see the section " 'After the Bombs': Globalization, Market, and Literature in the Late Twentieth and Early Twenty-first Centuries")[89];
- further develop transmedia studies, especially the new relationships between word and image (fixed and mobile) in literary productions;
- expand research on the influences; interrelations; intersections; and transnational, transareal, and intercultural syncretisms in Central American literature;
- conduct historiographic-literary studies within the framework of the history of ideas-concepts, with a global history approach; and
- investigate the influences and repercussions of the new migratory processes on literary productions in a broad sense.

It is obvious that in order to face these challenges successfully it is necessary to develop new forms of work and especially academic collaborations that transgress in many ways the traditional and persistent organization (generation) of knowledge in universities. In particular, it is essential to overcome the "disciplinary" limitations that have dominated the guild of literary scholars and philologists and thus carry out research projects that involve and integrate other fields of knowledge into an interdisciplinary approach. At the same time, it is necessary to leave behind the exaggerated and obsolete individualism so dominant in literary academies that has its roots in the concept of literary "genius" inherited from romanticism and that in Central America until the late twentieth century has been increased by the persistent symbiotic fusion of the *litterateur*/writer and the academic/critic. This requires fostering forms of academic work in teams and networks.[90]

In their introduction to volume IV of *Hacia una Historia de las Literaturas Centroamericanas*, the editors point out that the time-place of enunciation of their work can be understood as a synecdoche of the work of literary historiography:

> The essays represent a kind of cross-section of the academic critique of literary and cultural production in the sense that they offer a view of the state of play, summarize previous contributions, make their own contributions from specific theoretical-political perspectives . . ., from certain geographical-institutional (Central American, Latin American, North American and European universities and research centers) places and in defined temporal coordinates (between the first and second decades of the 21st century). They offer interpretations located and dependent on their moment but in no case are unitary or programmatic.[91]

Hence the main challenge: literary (and not only literary) history has to be permanently rewritten.

ACKNOWLEDGMENT

This work was translated from Spanish by Jeffrey Browitt.

NOTES

1. Arturo Arias, *Gestos ceremoniales. Narrativa centroamericana 1960–1990* (Guatemala City, Guatemala: Artemis & Edinter, 1998), 311–312.
2. Arturo Arias, *Taking Their Word: Literature and the Signs of Central America* (Minneapolis: University of Minnesota Press, 2007), xi–xii. Returning to an argument by Ramón Luis Acevedo in *La novela centroamericana: Desde el Popol-Vuh hasta los umbrales de la novela actual* (Río Piedras: University Editorial, University of Puerto Rico, 1982), one of the pioneering studies of Central American novels, Arías wrote in 1998: "In the Central American context, writing arises from the marginalization of the marginal. The discourse of this particular region of the world is not only marginal in relation to the centres of world power, but even to the small centres of marginal power: Mexico, Buenos Aires, São

LITERATURE, SOCIETY, AND POLITICS   471

Paulo." Arías, *Gestos ceremonials*, 11. Criticizing scholars of the "First World" academy, he states: "The periphery for them is São Paulo, Buenos Aires, Santiago de Chile and Mexico City. San Juan del Sur, Chalatenango, Puerto Limón or Quetzaltenango do not figure, as it is equally evident that the so-called 'periphery' is composed of hybrid cosmopolitan urban centres, but not a periphery where tortillas are eaten with salt and chile, *vigorones* with pork crackling and cassava or snail soup with sliced fruit . . ." Arías, *Gestos ceremonials*, 317–318. In fact, this criterion has been repeated and canonized since the publication of Acevedo's study (see *La novela centroamericana*, 9, 10, 11, 447) and has become a kind of leitmotif of Central American-ist literary criticism with no small dose of self-pity. See Magda Zavala, "La nueva novela centroamericana. Estudio de las tendencias más relevantes del género a la luz de diez novelas del período 1970–1985" (PhD diss., Université Catholique de Louvain, 1990), 5–6, 13; Kathryn Eileen Kelly, "La nueva novela centroamericana" (PhD diss., University of California, Irvine, 1991), 13–14; Carlos Cortés, "Literatura centroamericana del siglo XXI: en los confines de la (des)memoria," in *La tradición del presente. El fin de la literatura universal y la narrativa latinoamericana* (Miami, FL: La Pereza Ediciones, 2015), 104; Werner Mackenbach, *Die unbewohnte Utopie. Der nicaraguanische Roman der achtziger und neunziger Jahre* (Frankfurt am Main: Vervuert Verlag, 2004), 20–23, 27–28.

3. See Mackenbach, *Die unbewohnte Utopie*, 20–28. See Valeria Grinberg Pla, "Estudio crítico de *The Cambridge History of Latin American Literature*," in *Avances de investigación 1: Lecturas críticas de la historia de las literaturas centroamericanas*, ed. Centro de Investigación en Identidad y Cultura Latinoamericanas (San José, Costa Rica: Sección de Impresión del SIEDIN, 2005), 11–28; Werner Mackenbach, "¿El centro vacío de la periferia? Acerca de dos Historias de la Literatura Latinoamericana editadas en Alemania por Michael Rössner y Hans-Otto Dill," in Centro de Investigación en Identidad y Cultura Latinoamericanas, *Avances de investigación 1*, 29–46; Verónica Ríos Quesada, "Reseña de *Anthologie de la littérature hispano-américaine du XX siècle* coeditada por Jean Franco y J.-M. Lemogodeuc," in Centro de Investigación en Identidad y Cultura Latinoamericanas, *Avances de investigación 1*, 47–56: these articles all appeared within the framework of the research program "Hacia una Historia de las Literaturas Centroamericanas." These studies analyze or make reference to more than sixty literary-historiographic texts, including histories, dictionaries, encyclopedias, and Latin and Hispanic American anthologies, as well as studies of specific literary genres (like the novel), published in Spanish, English, French, and German.

4. Magda Zavala and Seidy Araya, *La historiografía literaria en América Central (1957– 1987)* (Heredia, Costa Rica: Editorial Fundación Universidad Nacional, 1995), 15; see also Alexandra Ortiz Wallner, "Historias de la literatura nacional en Centroamérica. Tendencias, continuidades y perspectivas," in Centro de Investigación en Identidad y Cultura Latinoamericanas, *Avances de investigación 1*, 57–73. These works analyze more than twenty texts of historiographic-literary character, including histories, dictionaries, bibliographies, and essays on Central American and Caribbean literatures published in both Spanish and English. See also Bernal Herrera, "Modernidad y modernización literaria en Centroamérica," in *Hacia una Historia de las Literaturas Centroamericanas*, Vol. II, *Tensiones de la modernidad: Del modernismo al realismo*, ed. Valeria Grinberg Pla and Ricardo Roque-Baldovinos (Guatemala City, Guatemala: F&G Editores, 2009), 14–15. Herrera refers also critically to *Historia de la literatura hispanoamericana. Desde 1940 hasta la actualidad*, ed. Claude Cymerman and Claude Fell (Buenos Aires, Argentina: EDICIAL, 2001).

5. Mackenbach, "¿El centro vacío de la periferia?," 46, n. 2. In fact, there has been a notable increase in studies, research projects, university programs, congresses, publications,

etc., on Central American culture and literature inside and outside the region, especially in the last two decades. See Werner Mackenbach, "'El nuevo campo no ofrece sino desafíos': Reflexiones acerca de los estudios literarios centroamericanos a inicios del siglo XXI," in *Voces y silencios de la crítica y la historiografía literaria centroamericana*, ed. Albino Chacón G. and Marjorie Gamboa C. (Heredia Costa Rica: Editorial Universidad Nacional, 2010), 50–53. In a bibliography compiled with Alexandra Ortiz Wallner in 2007, we registered more than 220 publications on Central American literature and cultural processes published in the form of books between the second half of the 1980s and 2007 (without counting articles and essays published in magazines and newspapers), 170 of which were edited in Central America. See Alexandra Ortiz Wallner and Werner Mackenbach, "Publicaciones sobre literatura y procesos culturales centroamericanos contemporaneous: Una selección bibliográfica," *Istmo: Revista virtual de estudios literarios y culturales centroamericanos*, no. 15 (2007): n.p., http://istmo.denison.edu/n15/proyectos/biblio.html. During the past decade this production has witnessed an even more notable proliferation inside and outside the region, but there is no register of these publications—a desideratum for further research.

6. See Mackenbach, "¿El centro vacío de la periferia?," 46, n. 3. This article refers to more than twenty histories of Hispano-American literature as well as introductory or survey studies.

7. For further details on more recent initiatives and projects, see the section "'After the Bombs': Globalization, Market, and Literature in the Late Twentieth and Early Twenty-first Centuries."

8. See Ligia Bolaños, "Discurso histórico e historiografía literaria: ¿Una alternativa en la construcción de un discurso explicativo de las producciones culturales en América Central?," *Káñina: Revista de artes y letras de la Universidad de Costa Rica* 12, no. 1 (1988): 177–184; Ligia Bolaños, "Narraciones y temporalidades en la producción colonial centroamericana," in *Hacia una Historia*, Vol. I, *Intersecciones y transgresiones: Propuestas para una historiografía literaria en Centroamérica*, ed. Werner Mackenbach (2008), 151–182.

9. This study has benefited from Thomas S. Kuhn's methodological approach, especially his concept of "paradigm" in the scientific evolution, and from Reinhart Koselleck, particularly his concept of "saddle time" or "threshold time" ["Sattelzeit"]. See Thomas S. Kuhn, *The Structure of Scientific Revolutions* (Chicago: University of Chicago Press, 1962); Reinhart Koselleck, *Futures Past: On the Semantics of Historical Time* (New York: Columbia University Press, 2004), *Vergangene Zukunft. Zur Semantik geschichtlicher Zeiten* (Frankfurt am Main: Suhrkamp Verlag), 19.

10. Pedro Henríquez Ureña, "Caminos de nuestra historia literaria," in *Historia cultural, historiografía y crítica literaria*, ed. Odalís G. Pérez (Santo Domingo, Dominican Republic: Archivo General de la Nación, 2010), 163–172, here 166. The text was published for the first time in *Valoraciones* (La Plata), no. 6 (1925): 246–252, and subsequently included in Pedro Henríquez Ureña, *Seis ensayos en busca de nuestra expresión* (Buenos Aires, Argentina: Editorial Babel, 1928), 37–51. See Mijail Mondol López, "Historiografía literaria y Sociedad: Una interpretación socio-discursiva del pensamiento histórico literario centroamericano" (PhD diss., Universität Potsdam, 2017), 39.

11. Beatriz González Stephan, *La historiografía literaria del liberalismo hispanoamericano del siglo XIX* (La Habana, Cuba: Casa de las Américas, 1987), 19, v. 10, 15, 97–106, 178. See also Mondol López, "Historiografía literaria y Sociedad," 183, 254–255; Alexandra Ortiz Wallner, "La problemática de la periodización de las literaturas centroamericanas contemporáneas," in Mackenbach, *Intersecciones y transgresiones*, 183–203, here 185. Beatriz

González Stephan's extensive oeuvre on literary historiography also includes *Contribución al estudio de la historiografía literaria hispanoamericana* (Caracas, Venezuela: Academia Nacional de la Historia, 1985); *Escribir la historia literaria: Capital simbólico y monumento cultural* (Barquisimeto-Estado Lara, Venezuela: Universidad Nacional Experimental Politécnica Antonio José de Sucre/Ediciones del Rectorado, 2001); *Fundaciones: canon, historia y cultura nacional. La historiografía literaria del liberalismo hispanoamericano del siglo XIX*, corrected and expanded edition (Madrid: Iberoamericana, 2002).

12. See González Stephan, *La historiografía literaria del liberalismo hispanoamericano*, 14–18.
13. See ibid., especially 210, 219.
14. See ibid., 219, 224.
15. Ibid., 221.
16. Ibid., 224; see 222–223, 227.
17. See ibid., 228.
18. Ibid., 104.
19. In her article, "Escribir la nación en los libros de texto de historia: estado, intelectuales e historia en Costa Rica, Guatemala y El Salvador (1884–1927)," the Costa Rican historian, Patricia Fumero Vargas, analyzes the context in which the official texts of Costa Rican, Salvadoran, and Guatemalan history were written and distributed, financed by the governments of those countries, and published during the period 1884 to 1927. The article will be published in *Hacia una Historia*, Vol. V, *Escribiendo la Nación: Centroamérica en el siglo XIX*, ed. Patricia Fumera Vargas (Guatemala City, Guatemala: F&G Editores, in print). In the "Introducción" to this volume, Fumero Vargas concludes: "The texts studied here show the growing separation between oral and written worlds and state investment in culture and education, which was manifested in the organization and the class structures, the gender roles and the ethnic and age relations. The contribution . . . consists in analysing the operative part of the liberal modernizing and civilizing process through the official history books and the unequal way (based on literacy rates) in which these materials reached the inhabitants of the region." I would like to thank the author for having made available the manuscripts of both texts.
20. Mondol López, "Historiografía literaria y Sociedad," 133; see 254–255.
21. Ibid., 135–137.
22. For an exhaustive account of this production, see ibid., 137–151. Among the first *national* literary histories—properly called as such—are Crispín Ayala Duarte, "Historia de la literatura en Guatemala," *Anales de la Universidad Central de Venezuela* (January–February 1931): 25–53; Crispín Ayala Duarte, "Historia de la literatura en Honduras y San Salvador," *Anales de la Universidad Central de Venezuela* (March–April 1931): 193–224; Crispín Ayala Duarte, "Historia de la literatura en Nicaragua," *Anales de la Universidad Central de Venezuela* (May–June 1931): 259–291. The first Central American literary histories are Leonardo Montalbán, *Historia de la Literatura de la América Central* (San Salvador, El Salvador: Ministerio de Instrucción Pública, 1929); Leonardo Montalbán, *Historia de la Literatura de la América Central. Época colonial* (San Salvador, El Salvador: Ministerio de Instrucción Pública, 1931). It is worth highlighting that Montalbán's work like the national literary histories is organized along national literatures. See Werner Mackenbach, "Introducción," in Mackenbach, *Intersecciones y transgresiones*, ix–xxix, here xvii–xviii.
23. Ramón Uriarte Center, *Galería poética centro-americana: Colección de poesías de los mejores poetas de la América del Centro* (Guatemala City, Guatemala: La Unión

Typograph, 1888); José María García Salas, *El parnaso centroamericano* (Guatemala, 1882; repr. Guatemala City, Guatemala: Ministerio de Educación Pública, 1962).

24. See Mondol López, "Historiografía literaria y Sociedad," 138–140, 152

25. Román Mayorga Rivas, *Guirnalda Salvadoreña: Colección de poesías de los bardos de la República de El Salvador, precedidas de apuntes biográficos y juicios críticos sobre cada uno de sus autores*, Vol. I (San Salvador, El Salvador: Imprenta Nacional del Doctor Francisco Sagrini, 1884), II (cited in Mondol López, "Historiografía literaria y Sociedad," 154).

26. See Mondol López, "Historiografía literaria y Sociedad," 151–155.

27. Ibid. 153.

28. François-Xavier Guerra, *Modernidad e Independencias. Ensayos sobre las revoluciones hispánicas* (Madrid: Editorial MAPFRE, 1992), 17, 12.

29. See Julio César Pinto Soria, "La Independencia y la Federación," in *Historia General de* Centroamérica, bk. III, *De la Ilustración al Liberalismo*, ed. Héctor Pérez Brignoli (Madrid: Sociedad Estatal Quinto Centenario, Facultad Latinoamericana de Ciencias Sociales, 1993), 94 (see also 91, 92, 93–94). See also Sergio Ramírez, "Balcanes y volcanes," in *Balcanes y volcanes y otros ensayos y trabajos* (Managua: Editorial Nueva Nicaragua, 1985), 11–114, here 17–18, 23, 2–31, 32, 38.

30. Guerra, *Modernidad e Independencias*, 13.

31. Iván Molina Jiménez, *La estela de la pluma. Cultura impresa e intelectuales en Centroamérica durante los siglos XIX y XX* (Heredia, Costa Rica: Editorial Universidad Nacional, 2004), 146. See Mondol López, "Historiografía literaria y Sociedad," 137. *Modernismo* as a literary movement had its origins in the 1880s and made a significant impact on Spanish and Hispano-American literature in the last two decades of the nineteenth century and the first two decades of the twentieth century. It is seen as the first literary movement in Latin America, and it contributed in a significant way to the renewal of Spanish and Hispanic letters; at the same time, it had a strong influence on other European literature, especially French literature.

32. Valeria Grinberg Pla and Ricardo Roque-Baldovinos, "Introducción," in Grinberg Pla and Roque-Baldovinos, *Tensiones de la modernidad*, xi, xii. The essays gathered in this volume, especially the sections "Modernidad literaria, modernismo y vanguardia" and "Modernismo: revisiones y márgenes," are attempting to contribute to a new vision of (Central American) *modernismo* and modernity. In his study, Bernal Herrera ("Modernidad y modernización literaria en Centroamérica," in Grinberg Pla and Roque-Baldovinos, *Tensiones de la modernidad*, 3–33) proposes a "bipolar version of modernity" (11) that insists on the differences of literary modernization "at the metropolitan and peripheral poles" (11)—Europe and Central America, where its insertion into local, national, and regional traditions means they acquire their own characteristics. At the same time, he argues: "The bipolar conception also forces us to take into account the asymmetrical relationships of cultural power which permeate the study of the links between European and Hispanic-American literatures" (11, see 30–31).

33. On the particular role of Rubén Darío in the *modernista* and *avant-garde* modernization processes in Central America see Herrera, "Modernidad y modernización literaria en Centroamérica," 5, 16–18.

34. See Grinberg Pla and Roque-Baldovinos, "Introducción," xiv–xvi, and the studies of Jorge Brioso, Julia Medina, Karen Poe, and Ricardo Roque-Baldovinos in the same volume.

35. See Pla and Roque-Baldovinos, "Introducción," xx. See also Maureen Shea, "Del apogeo al desaliento: la audacia de la escritora frente a su comunidad centroamericana entre 1880

y 1950," in Grinberg Pla and Roque-Baldovinos, *Tensiones de la modernidad*ed, 283–313. Shea analyzes the work of ten female writers of the time and argues: "Common to all the authors included here is the female role in their works, often strong women, social and political rebels who reject the subordinate role of women" (284).

36. Karen Poe, "Del vampiro a la lesbiana. El deseo sexual 'femenino' en la novela modernista centroamericana," in Grinberg Pla and Roque-Baldovinos, *Tensiones de la modernidad*, 145–165, here 147; see 146.

37. See Grinberg Pla and Roque-Baldovinos, "Introducción," xx, xiii. See also Jeffrey Browitt and Werner Mackenbach, "Introducción: 'Respirar en el torbellino de su capricho': El cosmopolitismo dariano," in *Rubén Darío: Cosmopolita arraigado*, ed. Jeffrey Browitt and Werner Mackenbach (Managua, Nicaragua: IHNCA-UCA, 2010), 1–16; Jeffrey Browitt, "Rubén Darío ante la crítica literaria en la época del modernismo," in Browitt and Mackenbach, *Rubén Darío*, 238–267; Andrea Ortiz Wallner and Werner Mackenbach, "Escribir en un contexto transareal: Ruben Darío y la invención del modernismo como movimiento," in Browitt and Mackenbach, *Rubén Darío*, 350–382. Jeffrey Browitt points out the pioneering role of the Nicaraguan poet Rubén Darío in this field; see Jeffrey Browitt, "Ruben Darío en Buenos Aires, 1893–1898: La génesis de un campo literario autónomo," in Grinberg Pla and Roque-Baldovinos, *Tensiones de la modernidad: Del modernismo al realismo*, 59–84.

38. Herrera, "Modernidad y modernización literaria en Centroamérica," 9; see 8.

39. See ibid., 11.

40. Mondol López, "Historiografía literaria y Sociedad," 148. See 145–147 for an account of this production between 1873 and 1949 in Nicaragua, Panama, Guatemala, El Salvador, Costa Rica, and Honduras; and 158–161. Also, see some of the works in note 25 of this chapter as well as in Herrera, "Modernidad y modernización literaria en Centroamérica," 3.

41. Mondol López, "Historiografía literaria y Sociedad," 154; see 153 and 154–155: a collection of textual fragments.

42. Jerónimo Aguilar, *Apuntes para una Antología* (Managua, Nicaragua: Tipografía "La Prensa," 1925), 2, cited in Mondol López, "Historiografía literaria y Sociedad," 155.

43. See Mondol López, "Historiografía literaria y Sociedad," 163, 168 and 162–163 as well as 166–167 for an account of works of a didactic nature in relation to their ideological positioning, published between 1878 and 1959. With the exception of the literary history of Leonardo Montalbán, historiographic-literary production is characterized by ignorance of Indigenous, pre-Hispanic, scribal practices and the total absence of traditions of Afro-descendant populations.

44. The historiographic-literary evaluation of *modernismo* is carried out a posteriori, with a lag of several decades, even almost a century, as in the case of non-lyrical writings (e.g., the chronicle); see the pioneering historical-critical edition of the Rubén Darío chronicles in five volumes by Günther Schmigalle, *Rubén Darío: La caravana pasa*, bk. 1 (Managua: Academia Nicaragüense de la Lengua, 2000), bk. 2 (2005), bk. 3 (2001), bks. 4–5 (2004, 2006).

45. See Acevedo, *Novela centroamericana*, 9–14, 447.

46. Sergio Ramírez, "El concepto de burguesía en José Coronel Urtecho," in *Balcanes y volcanes*, 129–137, here 131.

47. Ibid., 131.

48. Cited in Herrera, "Modernidad y modernización literaria en Centroamérica," 26. The manifesto was first published in *Vanguardia* 55 (July 1932).

49. Ramírez, "El concepto de burguesía," 129. Hence, his declaredly reactionary political position which, as Ramírez writes in the same essay, points to the "restoration of the nation through a single and permanent leader, of a dictator who would impose himself on political parties to create a new corporate order" (129); "a unique leader who was none other than Anastasio Somoza" (133), founder of the dynastic dictatorship in Nicaragua, a political position that does not hide its sympathies for European fascisms, especially the Spanish Falange. See Erick Blandón, "Rubén Darío: Mutilación y monumentalización," in Browitt and Mackenbach, *Rubén Darío*, 104–126, here 106–107.

50. Ramírez, "El concepto de burguesía," 132. Bernal Herrera speaks of orthodox and heterodox dimensions in the Latin-American and Central American avant-gardes. While orthodox works followed the path drawn by the canonized European literary *avant-gardes*, the Central American *avant-gardes* are characterized by their heterodoxy, especially the Nicaraguan one as the only articulated movement in the Isthmus, because "although it adopts gestures such as rupturism and the writing of proclamations, its nationalist character and its conservative ideology . . . moves it away from most European models." Herrera, "Modernidad y modernización literaria en Centroamérica," 13; see 12, 24. In relation to the *avant-garde* in Guatemala, El Salvador, and Costa Rica, Herrera argues that "it acts not through an orthodox break with the past and tradition, but through the rescue and the rewriting, often radical, of various traditions and local themes. . . . None of this attenuates the *avant-garde* nature of this production, it simply refers us to different ways of operating, to alternative *avant-garde* models, as valid and modern as those established by metropolitan *avant-gardes*, often seen as the only valid ones" (25, see 27–31).

51. Ramírez, "Balcanes y volcanes," 98; see 91.

52. Ibid., 13.

53. See Mondol López, "Historiografía literaria y Sociedad," 180, 181–182, 255.

54. Abelardo Bonilla, *Historia y Antología de la Literatura Costarricense* (San José, Costa Rica: Editorial Trejos, 1957); Juan Felipe Toruño, *Desarrollo literario de El Salvador. Ensayo cronológico de generaciones y etapas de las letras salvadoreñas* (San Salvador, El Salvador: Ministerio de Cultura, 1958); Rodrigo Miró, *Literatura panameña de la República* (Panamá City, Panama: Impresión de la Academia, 1960); and Jorge Eduardo Arellano, *Panorama de la literatura nicaragüense (De Colón a finales de la colonia)* (Managua, Nicaragua: Editorial Centenario de Rubén Darío, 1966). For a further list of historiographic-literary works published from the 1950s onward, see Mondol López, "Historiografía literaria y Sociedad," 171, 172, 173–174, 178–179. Mondol López also mentions the influence of the *Panorama das Literaturas das Americas* project carried out by the Portuguese diplomat Joaquim de Montezuma Carvalho between 1958 and 1965 that included first versions of the national histories of Panama and El Salvador published later by Rodrigo Miró and Luis Gallegos Valdés (see 180).

55. Mondol López, "Historiografía literaria y Sociedad," 183; see also 168, 184.

56. See ibid., 179.

57. See Herrera, "Modernidad y modernización literaria en Centroamérica," 27–31.

58. See Héctor M. Leyva, Werner Mackenbach, and Claudia Ferman, "Introducción," in Héctor M. Leyva, Werner Mackenbach, and Claudia Ferman, *Literatura y compromiso político. Prácticas político-culturales y estéticas de la revolución*, xi–xli.

59. Ibid., xl.

60. See Mondol López, "Historiografía literaria y Sociedad," 173, 183, 184, 256. This pattern persisted even in the Sandinista Project, which aimed to "create a new culture," as

expressed in 1981 in a speech by the then interior minister of the Sandinista government, Tomás Borge, before a meeting of writers("El arte como herejía," *Ventana* January 24, 1981), especially in the political instrumentalization of Rubén Darío for the construction of the new nation and "as a symbol of nationality." Erick Blandón, *Rubén Darío: Un cisne entre gavilanes* (San José, Costa Rica: URUK Editores, 2016), 41–53, here, 49. See Werner Mackenbach, "Literatura y revolución: La literatura nicaragüense de los años ochenta y noventa entre política y ficción," *Monograma: Revista Iberoamericana de Cultura y Pensamiento* 2, no. 1 (2018): 13–44, here 15–17.

61. Abelardo Bonilla, *Historia y antología de la literatura costarricense*, bk. 1, *Historia* (San José, Costa Rica: Editorial Universitaria, 1957), bk. 2, *Antología*; Juan Felipe Toruño, *Desarrollo literario de El Salvador* (San Salvador, El Salvador: Ministerio de Cultura, 1958); Luis Gallegos Valdés, *Panorama de la literatura salvadoreña. Del periodo precolombino a 1980* (San Salvador, El Salvador: Ministerio de Educación, 1962); Ismael García, *Historia de la literatura panameña* (Mexico City: Editorial de la Universidad Nacional Autónoma de México, 1964); Jorge Eduardo Arellano, *Panorama de la Literatura Nicaragüense: De Colón a los finales de la Colonia* (Managua, Nicaragua: Editorial Centenario de Rubén Darío, 1966); Rodrigo Miró, *La Literatura Panameña de la República* (Panamá City, Panama: Impresión de la Academia, 1970); Virginia Sandoval de Fonseca, *Resumen de la literatura costarricense* (San José: Editorial Costa Rica, 1979); Franciscio Albizúrez Palma y Catalina Barrios, *Historia de la Literatura Guatemalteca*, bks. 1–3 (Guatemala City: Editorial Universitaria de Guatemala, 1981–1987); José Francisco Martínez, *Literatura hondureña y su proceso generacional* (Tegucigalpa: Universidad Nacional Autónoma de Honduras, 1987). For an analysis of these works, see Ligia Bolaños Varela, "Histoire littéraire en Amérique Central et identité nationale" (PhD diss., Université Sorbonne Nouvelle—Paris 3, Paris, 1987); Zavala and Araya, *La historiografía literaria en América Central*; Wallner, "Historias de la literatura nacional en Centroamérica." See also Mondol López, "Historiografía literaria y Sociedad," 173–174, 178–179, 285–286, 292.

62. See Ramírez, "Balcanes y volcanes," 98 (1985 ed.). Mondol López mentions some of the texts that can be placed within this framework: Sergio Ramírez, "Introduction," in *Antología del cuento centroamericano* (San José, Costa Rica: Editorial Universitaria Centroamericana, 1973); Acevedo, *La novela centroamericana*; Esther María Osses, *La novela del imperialismo en Centroamérica* (Maracaibo, Venezuela: Editorial de la Universidad de Zulia, 1986). In the 1980s, the following texts were also published: Seymour Menton, *Historia crítica de la novela guatemalteca* (Guatemala City, Guatemala: Editorial Universitaria, 1985); Helen Umaña, *Literatura hondureña contemporánea* (Tegucigalpa, Honduras: Guaymuras, 1986); Álvaro Quesada Soto, *La formación de la narrativa costarricense* (San José: Editorial de la Universidad de Costa Rica, 1986); Álvaro Quesada Soto, *La voz gesgarrada. La crisis del discurso oligárquico y la narrativa costarricense (1917–1919)* (San José: Editorial de la Universidad de Costa Rica, 1988); Nydia Palacios Vivas, *Antología de la novela nicaragüense* (Managua, Nicaragua: Fondo Editorial INC, 1989). See Mondol López, "Historiografía literaria y Sociedad," 192, 292.

63. See Mondol López, "Historiografía literaria y Sociedad," 189, also 173, 255. Mondol López mentions the following works, among others: Jorge Valdeperas, *Para una nueva interpretación de la literatura costarricense* (San José: Editorial Costa Rica, 1979); Claudio Bogantes Zamora and Ursula Kuhlmann, "El surgimiento del realismo social en Centroamérica: 1930–1970," *Revista de Crítica Literaria Latinoamericana* 9, no. 17 (1983): 39–64; Dante Liano, *La palabra y el sueño. Literatura y sociedad en Guatemala*

(Rome: Bulzoni, 1984); Soto, *La formación de la narrativa costarricense*; Soto, *La voz desgarrada del discurso oligárquico*; Ole Ostergaard, "Esbozo de una historia social de la literatura nicaragüense del siglo XX," in *Diseño social y praxis literaria: Hacia una historia social de la literatura latinoamericana*, Vol. 1, ed. Thomas Bremer and Julio Peñate Rivero (Giessen, Neuchâtel: AELSAL, 1989), 199–219. See Mondol López, "Historiografía literaria y Sociedad," 186–187, 188–189.

64. Mondol López, "Historiografía literaria y Sociedad," 190.

65. See Mondol López, "Historiografía literaria y Sociedad," 191–194. It should be noted that this process of methodological, theoretical, and practical "regionalization" crystallizes first in the social sciences, especially from the history departments of the University of Costa Rica (UCR) and the National University (UNA) of Costa Rica from the 1970s, while consolidating in the literature departments with some lag only in the 1990s. See Mackenbach, "Introducción," vii–xx.

66. It is worth highlighting the influence of the work of the Argentine Alejandro Losada, especially his analysis of Latin American literature based on cultural subregions and his "collective" approach to all cultural production and dissemination. He insisted on not limiting himself to studying literary individual texts as self-sufficient research objects but as formations of social practice from their constitutive operations of production, reception, and transformation. His most important studies are: Alejandro Losada, *La literatura en la sociedad de América Latina*, Vol. 1, *Los modos de producción entre 1750 y 1980* (Odense, Denmark: Universidad de Odense, 1981); Alejandro Losada, *La literatura en la sociedad de América Latina: Perú y el Río de la Plata 1837–1880* (Frankfurt am Main: Vervuert Verlag, 1983).

67. Ileana Rodríguez, *Primer inventario del invasor* (Managua: Editorial Nueva Nicaragua, 1984), 9. See Werner Mackenbach, "Problemas de una historiografía literaria en Nicaragua," *Revista de Historia* (Nicaragua), no. 10 (1997): 5–18.

68. Of great importance in this process are the following studies by US academics: John Beverley, *Del Lazarillo al Sandinismo: Estudios sobre la función ideológica de la literatura española e hispanoamericana* (Minneapolis, MN: Institute for the Study of Ideologies and Literature, 1987); Barbara Harlow, *Resistance Literature* (New York: Methuen, 1987); John Beverley and Marc Zimmerman, *Literature and Politics in the Central American Revolutions* (Austin: University of Texas Press, 1990); Greg Dawes, *Aesthetics and Revolution: Nicaraguan poetry, 1979–1990* (Minneapolis: University of Minnesota Press, 1993).

69. An example is the different editions of *Panorama de la literatura nicaragüense* by Jorge Arellano. In the fifth edition of 1986, he still argues about the testimony: "Heterogeneous in its theme . . . it has been considered by Nicaraguan narrators to be what it is: a secondary genre, although for some it has meant more than a literary exercise." Jorge Eduardo Arellano, *Panorama de la literatura nicaragüense* (Managua: Editorial Nueva Nicaragua, 1986), 106). The 1997 edition includes a short chapter entitled, "Los testimonios cortos de Cabezas y Baltodano," on the testimony writings of militant sandinistas. Jorge Eduardo Arellano, *Literatura nicaragüense* (Managua, Nicaragua: Ediciones Distribuidora Cultural, 1997), 137.

70. For a critical analysis of this process, see Mackenbach, *Die unbewohnte Utopie*, 63–74, 144–150; Werner Mackenbach, "Transmutation in Contemporary Central American Testimony: From Epic to Parody?," in *Violence and Endurance: Representations of War and Peace in Post-War Central American Narratives*, ed. Astvaldur Astvaldsson

LITERATURE, SOCIETY, AND POLITICS   479

(New York: Nova, 2016), 47–66; and the studies on revolutionary narratives and the *testimonio* in Leyva et al., *Literatura y compromiso político*: Héctor M. Leyva, "Narrativa de los procesos revolucionarios centroamericanos (1960–1990)," 37–66; Ana Lorena Carrillo, "Otras palabras de fuego: ensayos centroamericanos 1965–1995," 67–109; Dante Barrientos Tecún, "Discurso político y escritura en la poesía centroamericana contemporánea (1950–2000)," 111–133; Maureen Shea, "Narradoras activistas y guerreras intrépidas de la Centroamérica revolucionaria: discursividades testimoniales de mujeres combatientes," 135–168; Luis Alvarenga, "Vidas de comunistas: pretensiones performativas en los testimonios de Mármol, Fortuny y Padilla Rush," 169–186; María del Carmen Pérez Cuadra, "Una lectura fracturada. Sobre testimonio, memoria y ciudadanía en Nicaragua (1960–1990)," 427–445.

71. It had already been criticized in the 1980s by Ramírez, *Balcanes y volcanes*.

72. "After the Bombs," the first part of this section title, alludes to the novel *Después de las bombas* (Mexico City, Mexico: Joaquín Mortiz, 1979) by the Guatemalan writer Arturo Arias, which narrates the history of dictatorial regimes in Guatemala.

73. See note 5 of this chapter.

74. "The New Central American Novel. A Study of the Most Relevant Trends of the Genre in the Light of Ten Novels from the Period 1970–1985" (PhD diss., Louvain: Université Catholique de Louvain, 1990).

75. Luis Alfredo Arango, *De Francisco a Francisco: 50 años de narrativa guatemalteca* (Guatemala City, Guatemala: Grupo Editorial RIN-78, 1990); Arias, *Gestos*; Arturo Arias, *La identidad de la palabra: Narrativa guatemalteca a la luz del siglo XX* (Guatemala City, Guatemala: Artemis-Edinter, 1998); Claudio Bogantes, *La narrativa social-realista en Costa Rica 1900–1950* (Aarhus, Denmark: Aarhus University Press, 1990); Quince Duncan, *Historia crítica de la narrativa costarricense* (San José: Editorial Costa Rica, 1995; Kathryn Eileen Kelly, "La nueva novela centroamericana" (PhD diss., University of California, Irvine, 1991); Dante Liano, *Visión crítica de la literatura guatemalteca* (Guatemala City, Guatemala: Editorial Universitaria, 1997); Eugenio Martínez Orantes, *32 escritores salvadoreños de Francisco Gavidia a David Escobar Galindo* (San Salvador, El Salvador: Amanecer Editores, 1994); Juan Antonio Medina Durón, *Historia general de la literatura hondureña y glosario de términos literarios* (Tegucigalpa, Honduras: Lithopress, 1995); Lucrecia Méndez de Penedo, *Letras de Guatemala. Del período precolombino a mediados del siglo XX* (Guatemala City, Guatemala: Fundación Paiz, 1993); Amelia Mondragón, ed., *Literatura y literaturas en Centroamérica. Cambios estéticos y nuevos proyectos culturales en Centroamérica* (Washington, DC: Literal Books, 1993); Flora Ovares, Margarita Rojas, Carlos Santander, and María Elena Carballo, *La casa paterna. Escritura y nación en Costa Rica* (San José: Editorial de la Universidad de Costa Rica, 1993); Soto, *La formación de la narrativa nacional costarricense*; Álvaro Quesada Soto, *Breve historia de la literatura costarricense* (San José, Costa Rica: Editorial Porvenir, 2000); Margarita Rojas, *100 años de literatura costarricense* (San José, Costa Rica: Farben Grupo Editorial Norma, 1995). See Mondol López, "Historiografía literaria y Sociedad," 293–306; Mackenbach, *Die unbewohnte Utopie*, 563, 578. See also Carlos Villalobos Villalobos, "De la invención al inventario: el desarrollo de los estudios literarios en Centroamérica" (PhD diss., Universidad Nacional, Costa Rica, 2010).

76. In the same period, a series of dictionaries of literary authors began to be published, works that accompany and support historiographic-literary studies, a practice that continues until today. Among these are Jorge Eduardo Arellano, *Diccionario de autores*

nicaragüenses, 2 vols. (Managua: Instituto Nicaragüense de Cultura, 1994); Jorge Eduardo Arellano, *Diccionario de escritores centroamericanos* (Managua: Instituto Nicaragüense de Cultura, 1997); Mario Argueta, *Diccionario crítico de escritores hondureños* (Tegucigalpa, Honduras: Editorial Universitaria, 1998); Carlos Cañas Dinarte, *Diccionario de autoras y autores de El Salvador* (San Salvador, El Salvador: Dirección de Publicaciones e Impresos, 2002); Albino Chacón Gutiérrez, *Diccionario de la literatura centroamericana* (San José: Editorial Costa Rica, 2007); José González, *Diccionario de autores hondureños* (Tegucigalpa, Honduras: Editores Unidos, 1987); Carlos López, *Diccionario bio-bibliográfico de literatos guatemaltecos* (Mexico City, Mexico: Editorial Praxis, 1993); Aristides Martínez Ortega, *Diccionario de la literatura panameña* (Panama City: Universidad de Panamá, 2002); Alejandro Méndez, *Diccionario de autores y críticos literarios de Guatemala* (Guatemala City, Guatemala: Producción La Tatuana, 2009). See Mondol López, "Historiografía literaria y Sociedad," 293–306; Mackenbach, *Die unbewohnte Utopie*, 537, 550.

77. See Werner Mackenbach, "Más allá de la posguerra: nuevas tendencias en/los estudios sobre/las literaturas centroamericanas: Anotaciones para el debate," in *Más allá del estrecho dudoso: Intercambios y miradas sobre Centroamérica*, ed. Dunia Gras and Tania Pleitez Vela (Granada, Spain: Valparaíso Ediciones, 2018), 41–71, and 43–44, for a critique of these studies, with bibliographic references to the studies and other critical publications. See also Mackenbach, "¿Después de los pos-ismos?", 279–307; and the essays in Beatriz Cortez, Alexandra Ortiz Wallner, and Verónica Ríos, *(Per)Versiones de la modernidad. Literaturas, identidades y desplazamientos*.

78. See Régis Debray, *Loués soient nos seigneurs. Une education politique* (Paris: Gallimard, 1996); Claudia Gilman, *Entre la pluma y el fusil: Debates y dilemas del escritor revolucionario en América Latina* (Buenos Aires, Argentina: Siglo XXI, 2003), 376–379.

79. For a detailed account of these aspects, see Mackenbach, "Más allá de la posguerra," 54–58; Magda Zavala, "Globalización y literatura en América Central: escritores y editoriales," in Mackenbach, *Intersecciones y transgresiones*, 225–245; Dante Liano, "Fuera del canon," *Lejana. Revista crítica de narrativa breve*, no. 6 (2013): 1–13; Dante Liano, "El canon literario hispanoamericano actual," in Cortez et al., *(Per)Versiones de la modernidad*, 141–162; Werner Mackenbach, "¿De la ira al asco? Reflexiones sobre el intelectual-escritor en Centroamérica 'después de las bombas' y sus repercusiones en la literatura," *Centroamericana* 25, no. 2 (2015): 55–77.

80. This project consists of six volumes, the first four of which have been published. The other two will be published in 2020. See section "Further Readings."

81. Magda Zavala and Seidy Araya, *Literaturas indígenas de Centroamérica* (Heredia, Costa Rica: Editorial Universidad Nacional, 2002). Within the framework of the project of the history of women's literature in Central America, the following books stand out: Consuelo Meza, ed., *Aportaciones para una Historia de la Literatura de Mujeres de América Central* (Aguascalientes, Mexico: Universidad Autónoma de Aguascalientes, 2009); Consuelo Meza and Magda Zavala, eds., *Mujeres en las literaturas indígenas y afrodescendientes en América Central* (Aguascalientes, Mexico: Universidad Autónoma de Aguascalientes, 2015); Consuelo Meza, *Narradoras centroamericanas contemporáneas: identidad y crítica socioliteraria seminista* (Aguascalientes: Universidad Autónoma de Aguascalientes, 2007); Consuelo Meza, *Diccionario biobibliográfico de narradoras centroamericanas con obra publicada entre 1890 y 2010* (Aguascalientes, Mexico: Universidad Autónoma de Aguascalientes, 2012).

82. See Mondol López, "Historiografía literaria y Sociedad," 197–199, 256–257, 259, 307–309. For the first time, Belize is included in Central American literary studies. See David Nicolás Ruiz Puga, "Panorama del texto literario en Belice, de tiempos coloniales a tiempos post-coloniales," *Istmo: Revista virtual de estudios literarios y culturales centroamericanos*, no. 1 (2001), http://istmo.denison.edu/no1/articulos/panorama.html.
83. Cortez et al., "Introducción," xi. See Mondol López, "Historiografía literaria y Sociedad," 197.
84. It is important to recognize the influences on the history of Latin American literature project, coordinated by Ana Pizarro in the 1980s; the history of Latin American literary culture project, directed by Mario J. Valdés and Djelal Kadir; as well as the "transarea" studies initiated by Ottmar Ette. See Ana Pizarro, *La literatura latinoamericana como proceso* (Buenos Aires, Argentina: Centro Editor de América Latina, 1985); Ana Pizarro, ed., *Hacia una historia de la literatura latinoamericana* (Mexico City: El Colegio de México, 1987); Ana Pizarro, ed. *América Latina: palavra, literatura e cultura* (São Paulo, Brazil: Memorial de América Latina, 1993–1995); Ana Pizarro, "¿Diseñar la historia literaria hoy?" *Estudios. Revista de investigaciones literarias*, 4, no. 8 (1996): 71–77; Mario J. Valdes and Djelal Kadir, eds., *Literary cultures of Latin America: A comparative history* (Oxford: Oxford University Press, 2004); Ottmar Ette, *Literature on the* Move, trans. Katharina Vester (Amsterdam, NY: Editions Rodopi, 2003); Ottmar Ette, ed., *Caribbean(s) on the Move/Archipiélagos literarios del Caribe* (Frankfurt am Main: Peter Lang, 2008). See Werner Mackenbach, "Tróp(ic)os en movimiento: retos transnacionales/transareales para los estudios de las literaturas caribeñas y centroamericanas," *Cahiers d'études romanes*, no. 28 (2014): 15–32.
85. About the project "Hacia una Historia de las Literaturas Centroamericanas" in general, see Mackenbach, "Introducción," ix–xxix; Mondol López, "Historiografía literaria y Sociedad," 194–252, 208, 307–313.
86. See Leyva et al., "Introducción," xii.
87. See ibid., xii.
88. See Grinberg Pla and Roque-Baldovinos, "Introducción," xxii–xxiii.
89. In his critical study of the authors analyzed in *Istmo: Revista virtual de estudios literarios y culturales centroamericanos*, the magazine linked to the project "Hacia una Historia de las Literaturas Centroamericanas," Mondol López found that most authors would enter the canon defined by the transnational publishing companies mentioned in the previous section, thus reinforcing this canonization. See Mondol López, "Aproximaciones cuantitativas en los estudios literarios centroamericanos: un estudio descriptivo en torno a la revista *Istmo*, 2001–2009," *Istmo. Revista virtual de estudios literarios y culturales centroamericanos*, no. 20 (2010): n.p., http://istmo.denison.edu/n20/proyectos/0-mondol_mijail_aproximaciones_form.pdf.
90. See Mackenbach, "Más allá de la posguerra," 58–59. A challenge—almost utopian in the conditions of the Central American universities—is the creation of registration centers, archiving and documentation of literary productions with regional projection, which currently only exist in the United States and Europe.
91. Leyva et al., "Introducción," xiv.

FURTHER READING

González Stephan, Beatriz. *Fundaciones: Canon, historia y cultura nacional. La historiografía literaria del liberalismo hispanoamericano del siglo XIX*. Madrid: Iberoamericana, 2001.

Hacia una Historia de las Literaturas Centroamericanas. Guatemala City, Guatemala: F&G Editores, 2008–2020.

Vol. I, *Intersecciones y transgresiones: Propuestas para una historiografía literaria en Centroamérica*. Edited by Werner Mackenbach, 2008.

Vol. II, *Tensiones de la modernidad: Del modernismo al realismo*. Edited by Valeria Grinberg Pla and Ricardo Roque-Baldovinos, 2009.

Vol. III, *(Per)Versiones de la modernidad. Literaturas, identidades y desplazamientos*. Edited by Beatriz Cortez, Alexandra Ortiz Wallner, and Verónica Ríos Quesada, 2012.

Vol. IV, *Literatura y compromiso político: Prácticas político-culturales y estéticas de la revolución*. Edited by Héctor M. Leyva, Werner Mackenbach, and Claudia Ferman, 2018.

Vol. V, *Escribiendo la Nación: Centroamérica en el siglo XIX*. Edited by Patricia Fumero Vargas, in print.

Vol. VI, *Textualidades indígenas y escrituras coloniales* Edited by Francisco Rodríguez Cascante, in print.

Jablonka, Ivan. *La historia es una literatura contemporánea: Manifiesto por las ciencias sociales*. Buenos Aires, Argentina: Fondo de Cultura Económica, 2016.

Lyon-Caen, Judith, and Dinah Ribard. *L'historien et la littérature*. París: Éditions La Découverte, 2010.

Meza, Consuelo, ed. *Aportaciones para una historia de la literatura de mujeres de América Central*. Aguascalientes, Mexico: Universidad Autónoma de Aguascalientes, 2009.

Molina Jiménez, Iván. *La estela de la pluma: Cultura impresa e intelectuales en Centroamérica durante los siglos XIX y XX*. Heredia, Costa Rica: Editorial Universidad Nacional, 2004.

Mondol López, Mijail. "Historiografía literaria y Sociedad: Una interpretación socio-discursiva del pensamiento histórico literario centroamericano." PhD diss., Universität Potsdam, Germany, 2017.

Pizarro, Ana, ed. *Hacia una historia de la literatura latinoamericana*. Mexico City: El Colegio de México, 1987.

Pizarro, Ana. "¿Diseñar la historia literaria hoy?" *Estudios: Revista de investigaciones literarias* 4, no. 8 (1996): 71–77.

Valdes, Mario J., and Djelal Kadir, eds. *Literary Cultures of Latin America: A Comparative History*. Oxford: Oxford University Press, 2004.

Zavala, Magda, and Seidy Araya. *La historiografía literaria en América Central (1957–1987)*. Heredia: Editorial Fundación Universidad Nacional, 1995.

Zavala, Magda, and Seidy Araya. *Literaturas indígenas de Centroamérica*. Heredia, Costa Rica: Editorial Universidad Nacional, 2002.

PART IV

CHALLENGES OF MODERNITY SINCE C. 1840: THE NATIONAL FRAME

CHAPTER 18

....

GUATEMALA

....

DAVID CAREY JR.

As Guatemala embarked on nationhood, one of the most pressing challenges was how to address racial and ethnic relations. Throughout the colonial period and particularly by the late eighteenth century, racial classifications varied. Although the precise meaning of these terms shifted over time, the racial distinctions they capture do much to describe the social hierarchy in this nation with Indigenous people (mainly Mayas—of which there were more than twenty different linguistic and ethnic groups including Kaqchikel, K'iche' and Q'eqchi'—and Xinkas), Afro-Guatemalans including Garífunas (an African-Arawak population), ladinos (non-Indigenous people), mestizos (those who recognized their Indigenous and Spanish heritage), and creoles (those who considered themselves pure-blooded Spaniards).[1] After independence, ladinos and mestizos increasingly migrated into the western highlands in search of land and livelihoods. In many ways, that process culminated in the 1871 Liberal revolt whereby the government redistributed land from Indigenous communities to ladino, mestizo, and foreign landowners. Through the censuses, Liberals sought to establish a racial binary of *indígenas* (Indigenous people) and ladinos that betrayed nuanced ethnic realities. Labeled *la raza mejorada* (the improved race) during the first part of the twentieth century, the offspring of German immigrants and Q'eqchi' women reveal the fluidity of racial categories and expose the racial binary as a fiction.[2] Mestizos continued to populate the nation but not the national censuses or discourse. Throughout much of the postcolonial era, *indígenas* comprised the majority of the population.[3] Yet they had little access to wealth and authority. Presiding over some of the most unequal land distribution in Latin America, Guatemalan officials generally neglected the rural poor and Indigenous populations' marginalized living, working, and health conditions. Instead Hispanic elites regularly exploited and abused *indígenas* to maximize their labor and minimize their political and economic power.

As modernization (a set of technological, social, and cultural changes catalyzed by capitalism and science) evolved during the postcolonial period, the Indigenous entrepreneurs, planters, and politicians who thrived contrasted starkly with the majority of *indígenas* who struggled to maintain adequate diets and healthy bodies. Class tensions often marked highland towns and cities when Indigenous elites advanced their own causes to the detriment of their poor and working-class counterparts. Paralleling intracommunal tensions, Indigenous communities often were divided along linguistic and ethnic lines. While K'iche's long maintained animosity toward Kaqchikels because their sixteenth-century ancestors helped Spaniards subdue the K'iche', Ch'orti'speakers in Eastern Guatemala seldom felt any affinity toward *indígenas* in the western highlands.[4] Non-Indigenous Guatemalans often lumped all *indígenas* together, but the latter generally recognized distinctions among themselves that were rooted in local cultural and class understandings.

Independence eradicated some colonial institutions that defined *indígenas*, but Conservatives who overthrew the first Liberal government recognized Indigenous landholdings and afforded Indigenous farmers the opportunity to pursue their *milpa* (corn, bean, and squash) agricultural production.[5] Whereas Conservatives maintained an alliance with the Catholic church, recognized communal landholdings, and emphasized domestic economic development over foreign trade, Liberals largely strove to undercut the power of the church and autonomous Indigenous communities and shift the economy toward agricultural export production. Liberal governments used debt peonage, *mandamientos* (forced labor drafts), vagrancy laws, and other mechanisms to compel poor *indígenas* and other marginalized Guatemalans to work on agricultural estates and public works projects for little or no pay. By the 1860s, Conservative rule similarly encroached on Indigenous land and labor and shifted the economy toward coffee production. After the 1871 Liberal Revolt led by Miguel García Granados (1871–1873) and Justo Rufino Barrios overthrew the conservative government of Vicente Cerna (1865–1871), unfettered abuse and exploitation of *indígenas* increased.[6] Despite that marginalization, Indigenous entrepreneurs and intellectuals enjoyed some success and autonomy throughout the nineteenth and into the twentieth and twenty-first centuries. Except for the 1920s, which saw a string of less authoritarian governments, Liberal rule was dominated by dictators: Justo Rufino Barrios (1873–1885), Manuel Estrada Cabrera (1898–1918), and Jorge Ubico (1931–1944). The 1944 Revolution that ushered in a decade of democratic rule did not buoy the plight of all Guatemalans. Forced labor mechanisms persisted and marginalized populations continued to be exploited. With the support of the US Central Intelligence Agency, military leaders overthrew Jacobo Arbenz to squash his land reform and reestablish oligarchic rule in 1954. By the early 1980s, the military perpetuated genocide against Mayas. Although the 1996 Peace Accords ended the thirty-six-year civil war, violence maintained its tragic grip on Guatemala as criminal organizations and narco-trafficking expanded in the early twenty-first century.

Long dominated by coffee and Conservative and Liberal political machinations,[7] recent Guatemalan historiography has complicated those analyses by focusing on economies beyond export production, interrogating forced labor mechanisms, and highlighting the continuities between Conservative and Liberal rule.[8] The centrality of ethnicity and race in Guatemalan historiography too has shifted in recent years with scholars moving away from a simplified state versus Indian dichotomy (and an earlier journalistic extreme aimed at erasing *indios* from Guatemalan history) to more nuanced understandings of ethnic relations and state power.[9]

Set against a long history of subjugation and violence, Indigenous responses to oppression ranged from resistance to collaboration and capitulation. To advance their agendas, *indígenas* regularly deployed ladino and state discourse in courtrooms and other public forums. They coopted the otherwise derogatory term "*indio*" to identify themselves and to elevate their positions within social hierarchies. Already underway in early twentieth-century courtrooms and municipal offices, such appropriation, which entailed the inversion of the word's meaning, was played out on a national stage by the 1970s. As Q'eqchi' leader Antonio Pop Caal (1941–2002) explained, accepting *indio* as a word that "brings us honor rather than denigration . . . signifies nothing less than a challenge to ladinos."[10] Like ethnic conflict, tensions around class and gender marked the postcolonial era.

From midwives and migrants to activists, intellectuals, and nuns, women shaped postcolonial Guatemala. By founding, operating, and serving in hospitals to treat the poor, religious orders made crucial contributions to public health and health care.[11] Midwives, *curanderas* (female social healers), and nurses enriched the nation's multiplicity of medicines and addressed such trenchant problems as infant mortality.

As much as race, class, and gender compounded the marginalization of many lives, some *indígenas*, Afro-Guatemalans, poor and working-class people, and women deployed those identities to their advantage. In so doing, they influenced the larger political, social, and economic histories in ways that are seldom reflected in Guatemala's *historia patria* or national history.

From Turmoil to Tepid Transformations: Rafael Carrera and Conservative Rule, 1838–1871

By 1840, *indígenas* had already played a significant role in the downfall of the first regime. In his effort to modernize Guatemala, the Liberal governor Mariano Gálvez (1831–1838) passed reforms that undercut Indigenous knowledge, practices, and customs. Angered by Liberal attempts to regularize landownership and alcohol laws that criminalized their moonshine industries, *indígenas* were willing conspirators to a political coup once convinced that government responses to the 1837 cholera epidemic were attempts to poison them. When Rafael Carrera (1844–1848) established conservative rule that would last nearly forty years, he afforded *indígenas* considerable autonomy and protections by reinstituting colonial institutions such as the *Recopilación de las Leyes de Indias* and naming a *Protector de los Indios*.[12] Wedged between two Liberal governments, Conservative rule served as a bridge between the colonial and national era.

For a short time (1838–1840), Los Altos declared itself the sixth independent state of the Federal Republic of Central America (1823–1841) with Quetzaltenango as its capital.

Spearheaded by Liberals who chafed against Carrera's victory and Conservative rule, Los Altos was one of the most productive regions in Central America. By February 1840, Carrera led the Guatemalan army to regain control of Quetzaltenango and most of the departments that comprised Los Altos.[13]

Afforded the right to maintain their land and control their labor, *indígenas* navigated the 1840s and 1850s through negotiation, collaboration, acquiescence, and resistance. Poor and working-class ladinos were as likely to ally with Indigenous laborers as resent *indígenas'* ability to work the legal system to their favor. Struggling to balance their ambiguous position between representing their communities and negotiating with ladino authorities, some Indigenous leaders advanced the cause of ladino elites by selling communal land to them and refusing to hold them accountable for the damage their cattle caused to Indigenous *milpas*.[14] Despite planter abuse and forced labor institutions designed to exploit them, workers could gain the upper hand. Since competition for labor among planters was fierce and laborers were mobile, workers could default on debt peonage agreements when better offers arose.

By the late 1850s, Carrera's second administration (1851–1865) began dispossessing communal landholdings and enlisting Indigenous labor for coffee cultivation. Often at the expense of Indigenous people and communities, coffee revenues increased from constituting less than 1 percent of total exports in 1852 to comprising half of the nation's exports by the end of Conservative rule in 1871.[15] The shift to ideas and policies generally associated with Liberal governments began under Conservative rule and ultimately contributed to its demise.[16] The government's persecution of bootleggers and moonshiners (primarily in Indigenous areas) eroded popular support for the Conservative regime in much the same way it had undermined early nineteenth-century Liberal rule.[17]

Throughout the nineteenth (and twentieth) century, alcohol was a crucial component of the economy.[18] Alcohol lubricated labor systems that funneled workers to agro-export economies as labor brokers used it to lure *indígenas* into signing contracts that entrapped them. For Black laborers on the Gulf of Honduras coast, alcohol and gambling provided temporary escapes from the daily frustrations of plantation labor and racism. Some Black entrepreneurs operated rum shops and juke joints.[19] Even after the 1870s when coffee became the single largest export earner, *aguardiente* (distilled liquor) remained an important source of income for local and national budgets. The structural exclusion of women from most aspects of the economy compelled many to produce and sell alcohol (both legal and illicit).[20]

COFFEE AND CORN: LATE NINETEENTH-CENTURY LIBERAL RULE

During Liberal rule, the coffee economy increasingly came to dominate politics. As part of Liberal legislation that privatized land held communally by Indigenous communities and the Catholic church, President Barrios shepherded a series of decrees that transferred some of the most fertile piedmont to potential coffee planters when local residents could not produce legal land titles.[21] By dispossessing rural *indígenas* of their land and livelihoods, Barrios sought to provide labor for the cash (and more specifically) coffee economy.[22] As part of the nation's forced labor infrastructure, ladino landowners who migrated to Alta Verapaz (where coffee lands regularly overlapped with Indigenous communities) established *fincas de mozos* (rural properties divided among subsistence farmers in exchange for their labor elsewhere) to ensure a steady supply of workers for their agricultural enterprises. Seasonal migrants included Indigenous women who picked coffee, made tortillas, and prepared meals.[23] While the loss of corn cultivation on the piedmont contributed to food shortages, increased agricultural investments during the 1880s and 1890s undergirded the expansion of coffee exports.[24] Liberal policies designed to foment coffee exports combined with population growth (particularly among *indígenas*) and decreased agricultural productivity undermined Indigenous communities.[25] Ranging from adhering to their *milpa* agriculture to embracing coffee production, *indígenas*' responses allowed some communities and individuals to maintain their land and autonomy in diverse ways.[26]

The expansion of export agriculture often undermined domestic-use agriculture (DUA), which comprised subsistence agriculture and foodstuff production for the domestic market. The relationship between corn and coffee production in Guatemala was complicated. Historian David McCreery argues, "Coffee did not so much subtract significant amounts of land from corn production as block the expansion of subsistence cultivation into new areas to help meet the needs of a growing population."[27] Because corn shortages periodically plagued Guatemala, corn sporadically vied for prominence among the nation's commodities.[28] When governments had to import corn, some state authorities developed a heightened (if intermittent) concern for DUA. That attention provided Indigenous small-scale farmers with opportunities to advance their agendas.[29] Instead of embracing capitalist modernization, Guatemala deployed forced labor mechanisms and state mandated prices for certain "articles of daily consumption."[30]

Depending on the region and population, Liberal encroachments on Indigenous land, labor, and autonomy had various effects. In Indigenous regions like Alta Verapaz, Q'eqchi' and other Indigenous leaders lost power to ladinos who increasingly controlled municipalities. The expansion of *mandamientos* eroded their legitimacy as patriarchs and brokers. When advancing such manifestations of modernity as hospitals, new urban plazas, and street lights, they often allied with ladinos.[31] Q'eqchi' patriarchs balanced their roles as defenders of *indígenas* and agents of modernity. Their K'iche' counterparts in Quetzaltenango expanded their power without encroaching upon the Hispanic oligarchy. Embracing modernization, they celebrated the construction of railroads, telecommunication infrastructure, and other public works that facilitated their investments in coffee and other enterprises.[32] Unlike Indigenous elites, however, the vast majority of rural *indígenas* saw their autonomy, livelihoods, and rights diminish during the late nineteenth century as Liberal leaders expropriated *indígenas*' properties to dedicate more fertile land and itinerant labor to agricultural export production.[33]

Beginning with the 1880 census, Liberals sought to solidify a bifurcated nation comprised of two *razas* (races)—*indígenas* and ladinos—whereby the former were depicted as ignorant and inebriated and the latter were associated with Western culture and progress.[34] The 1893 census insisted, "The Ladinos and Indians are two distinct classes; the former march ahead with hope and energy through the paths which have been laid out by progress; the latter, immovable, do not take any part in the political and intellectual life, adhering tenaciously to their old habits and customs. The Indians do not participate actively in the progress of civilization."[35] In reality, Guatemalan society was far more complicated than dichotomous portrayals of *indígenas* and ladinos suggested.[36]

Beneficiaries of the liberal redistribution of land to foment a coffee economy, German planters similarly portrayed *indios* as lazy simpletons who lacked "entrepreneurial spirit."[37] An 1887 trade agreement between the German and Guatemalan government allowed Germans to own land, shops, and warehouses and become citizens (exempt from military service) even as they maintained their German nationality. Armed with those advantages, they bought up fertile land for coffee production and employed *indígenas*. Some Germans in Alta Verapaz deployed philanthropy to buttress their social standing in the region and country and took an ethnographic interest in *indígenas*, learning their language and studying their customs and religion.

Race relations in Guatemala were set against the nation's quest for modernization, which portrayed Western civilization as the triumph of North Atlantic reason and science over Indigenous superstition and fanaticism. Hispanic intellectuals and authorities depicted *indígenas* as primitive drags on Guatemala's development. Unlike racialization in the United States, which operated within a biologized framework, racial typing in Guatemala was closely associated with culture. Elites often distinguished between Hispanics and *indígenas* by such ethnic markers as whether individuals wore Western or hand-woven clothing, wore footwear or walked barefoot, and ate with silverware or tortillas.

Poor and working-class *indígenas*, Afro-Guatemalans, and Garífunas faced significant obstacles to their economic well-being, social mobility, and political freedoms. The Liberal philosophy of equality before the law treated *indígenas* and Afro-Guatemalans as subjects rather than citizens.[38] Armed with positivism, a French social doctrine that emphasized scientific method over metaphysical thinking to achieve civic order, Liberals were unequivocal about casting Guatemala as a ladino nation.[39] Yet *indígenas* never relinquished their sense of citizenship. Even when they cast themselves as indigent members of the "Indian race," their very presence in courtrooms and municipal offices demonstrated their claim to rights as members of the national polity. In 1886, a group of sixty-three Kaqchikel men petitioned the Guatemalan Legislative Assembly to "improve the condition of the citizen . . . because each one, in the orbit of their intellectual and material faculties, can be useful to himself, his fellow citizens and the entire society."[40] As much as they strove for equality, they underscored their reality by identifying themselves as members of "*la raza* that until today [has been] helpless (*desvalida*)." When it served their needs, *indígenas* used rhetoric that reflected racist, sexist, and indigenist discourse. Because it was one of the few institutions that held ladinos, elites, and men accountable, Indigenous women claimed their rights in the legal system even though it tended to be biased against them.[41] Savvy *indígenas* bent the state's institutions to their favor.

Modernity's Manifestations and Maladies

By the end of the nineteenth century, electric lights, telegraph services, wide boulevards, refashioned central plazas, and indoor markets conveyed a sense of modernization and progress in cities like Guatemala City, Quetzaltenango, and Cobán. By the beginning of the twentieth century, photographers were preserving images of middle- and upper-class Guatemalans. Like their liberal counterparts in other areas of Latin America, Guatemalan leaders called upon architects to design grand buildings and other public works that would invite tourism and attract foreign investment.[42]

In a manifestation of Guatemala's long-standing courtship with science, the University of San Carlos in Guatemala City attracted aspiring medical students throughout Central America by the turn of the twentieth century.[43] Sustained by science, medical professionals collaborated with authorities in attempts to craft civilized citizens. *Curanderos* (healers) contested medical racialization and a dearth of doctors undermined the state's ability to sway rural residents from their preference for traditional cures.[44] Because contact was intermittent, *indígenas* shaped the state's foray into rural areas as much as state agents did. Indeed, the Guatemalan state never exercised territorial sovereignty over much of its rural landscape, including coffee plantations.

Despite the state' efforts to establish health care hegemony, a multiplicity of medicines—scientific, Indigenous, Hispanic, and hybrid—characterized health care in Guatemala. Even in urban areas where medical professionals tended to congregate, *curanderos* and *empíricos* (unlicensed practitioners) shaped locally inflected versions of modern medicine. While *curanderos* tacked between spiritual healing and natural remedies, many late nineteenth- and early twentieth-century authorities adhered to the miasma theory and thus feared foul air and odors emanating from putrid water and land; the fields of bacteriology and parasitology only slowly and unevenly shaped Guatemalan health care and public health.[45] Framed as protecting populations from disease, public health initiatives were as much about expanding the state's presence as establishing a hierarchy of scientific medicine over traditional healing practices.

Guatemalan leaders who looked to scientific medicine as a foundation upon which to construct a modern nation were often dependent on foreign expertise and resources. Early twentieth-century public health campaigns by the Rockefeller Foundation, United Fruit Company (UFCO), and Guatemalan government increasingly privileged and demonstrated the efficacy of laboratory-based medicine and the ability of state-sponsored scientific medicine to contain epidemics and cure debilitating diseases. Those efforts improved health care access and public health for many urban Guatemalans, but rural health indicators barely improved.[46]

Like other Latin American countries, Guatemala had alarmingly high infant mortality rates in the late nineteenth and early twentieth centuries. Because Indigenous midwives attended more than 90 percent of births in Indigenous communities, they figured prominently in the state's attempt to reduce infant mortality.[47] When authorities sought to train them in gynecology and other aspects of scientific medicine, Indigenous midwives' responses ranged from compliance to avoidance.[48] As the twentieth century progressed, doctors, nurses, and midwives collaborated with each other to improve natal care, particularly for rural patients, in ways that privileged patriarchy, medicalized childbirth, and maternal health care.[49]

TURN-OF-THE-CENTURY AUTHORITARIANISM

Guatemala had become so dependent on coffee that its market crash in 1897 devastated the economy. Instead of critiquing economic structures or those who championed agricultural exports, president Estrada Cabrera reinforced the notion that Guatemala was a ladino nation hamstrung by Indigenous degeneracy and superstition. Even as he expressed concern about Guatemala's monoculture, Estrada Cabrera facilitated investment in infrastructure that deepened the nation's dependence on agricultural exports. That infrastructure and appeal to foreign capital paved the way for UFCO to establish banana plantations in Caribbean coastal lowlands. Extracting great wealth from Guatemala, UFCO enjoyed significant political and economic influence.

Through an extensive spy network, a draconian police force (funded by the state's coffee export taxes and alcohol revenues), and *mandamientos*, Estrada Cabrera effectively sacrificed liberty and justice for order and progress.[50] Guatemala's mountainous topography and predominantly rural population meant that state power waned quickly beyond the few major urban areas. To project an image of modernization, Estrada Cabrera used any means to prevent social unrest at the same time he obscured such national shortcomings as penury, illiteracy, and racism.[51] Intent on attracting foreign investment, he presided over festivals of Minerva, the Roman goddess of poetry, medicine, wisdom, and commerce to underscore the nation's commitment to education and alignment with Western Europe. Although many *indígenas* looking back on his regime associated it with "disorder, thieves, and delinquency,"[52] his message (if not his actions) resonated with contemporary Kaqchikel and Q'eqchi' elites who promoted education as the means to *superarse* or improve one's lot.[53]

Desperately striving to count itself among the world's modern nations, Guatemala embraced science and positivism to address its self-proclaimed "Indian problem."

Ignoring the diversity of over twenty different linguistic and ethnic groups and expanding on previous associations of *indígenas* with indolence and degeneracy, early twentieth-century intellectuals like Antonio Batres Jáuregui, José Antonio Villacorta Calderón, and Miguel Angel Asturias defined *indios* as obstacles to Guatemala's material progress and social order.[54] Yet Indigenous leaders and entrepreneurs carved out spaces of authority and generated wealth by not infringing upon creoles and ladinos who fiercely clung to power at the national level.[55]

Set against the backdrop of the government's ineptitude, corruption, and exploitation, the 1917 earthquake and 1918–1919 influenza epidemic resulted in a staggering loss of life that catalyzed Indigenous and other Guatemalans to initiate the 1920 Unionist Revolution that overthrew Estrada Cabrera.[56] Revealing the dark side of Estrada Cabrera's courtship with foreigners, influenza most likely originated from US military camps in Guatemala.[57]

ROARING 1920S

The national political conflicts that followed the *coup d'état* allowed some local leaders to reassert control over their communities.[58] Those openings were exceptional however, as political leaders reinforced elite discourse about racial hierarchies that relegated *indígenas* and Afro-Guatemalans to political, economic, and social margins.[59] Impressed by the experiment already underway in Alta Verapaz where German men and Q'eqchi' women were rearing and raising blue-eyed, brown skinned "robust and well endowed" children,[60] the Generation of 20 intellectuals vigorously recycled narratives about *indígenas* who thwarted national development and could be redeemed only through miscegenation with Western Europeans. One intellectual exclaimed, "Redemption for our race should occur through the fertilization of our Indian women with Saxon semen!"[61]

Making good on his promise to restore constitutional democracy and basic political rights, President Carlos Herrera (1920–1921) created the conditions for the revival of the press, political parties, unions, and private interest groups. But his ability to mediate between his Liberal party and Conservatives failed to avert a coup catalyzed partly by his efforts to reduce the size of the army and revive the Central American Federation. After the coup, the nation returned to authoritarian rule under José María Orellana (1922–1926), who quickly restored the power of the military and suspended constitutional guarantees. With coffee prices soaring in the mid-1920s, he turned a blind eye to coffee planters who reinstated *mandamiento* labor as authorities violently suppressed Indigenous organized land invasions and labor strikes.[62]

Even while authorities promoted the domestic production of corn and beans,[63] Orellana's successor Lázaro Chacón (1926–1930) was equally committed to economic growth through coffee exports. In 1928, he established the *Oficina Central de Café* to support coffee planters and promote Guatemalan coffee overseas. Marked by an era of tolerance and corruption, Chacón developed strong relations with some Indigenous communities while others defied his rule. He collaborated with Indigenous communities around Lake Quinzilapa to arrest malaria, but his national police criminalized Indigenous livelihoods and disparaged their lifestyles. Ultimately, the worldwide economic depression doomed his rule. After surviving a 1929 coup, his reign ended when he suffered a cerebral hemorrhage on December 11, 1930.[64]

When major banks recalled loans that set off a solvency crisis in 1931, the Guatemalan economy hits its nadir. Coffee planters insisted paltry wages be reduced; Indigenous laborers parlayed offers to accept credit instead of cash into an opportunity to unfetter themselves from their debts. The national crisis catapulted the career of Jorge Ubico, who had earned a reputation as an astute administrator and powerful leader as governor of Alta Verapaz (1907–1909). With only his name on the ballot, his February 1931 electoral victory was hardly democratic.[65]

UBICO'S REIGN

A decline in export prices that accompanied the depression of the 1930s hit Guatemala particularly hard because it was primarily a commodity-exporting country. With interest payments that threatened to consume nearly all government income, Guatemala had accumulated a debt of more than $5 million. In an effort to combat these challenges, Ubico fostered agricultural diversification, implemented a road and bridge construction program (using conscripted Indigenous labor), imposed new taxes, and gave generous concessions of land and tax exemptions to large-scale landowners and UFCO.[66]

Hailed by many *indígenas* for abolishing debt peonage in 1934, Ubico established the *Ley contra la Vagancia* (Vagrancy Law) in its stead. That change freed poor *indígenas* and ladinos from the servitude of one *finca* (to which they were indebted), but restricted the free movement of labor by requiring 100–150 workdays per year for someone else. By requiring workers to carry *cédulas de vecindad* that verified the number of days they worked, the law made laborers beholden to landowners and foremen (for their signatures) and reinserted the state as a purveyor of labor. That law also required planters to open their plantation to sanitation and school inspections.[67] Ubico's effort to modernize rural areas clipped the autonomy of *indígenas* and planters alike.

To showcase Guatemala as a civilized nation that maintained some of its ethnic charm, Ubico established fairs that celebrated the nation's industry, agriculture, and Indigenous populations. The tension between modernity and tradition was on stark display in health care provision and public health initiatives. Informed by scientific medicine, Ubico's campaign to improve public health through sanitation, vaccination, and disease eradication regularly denigrated Indigenous lifestyles and healing practices and persecuted Indigenous *curanderos*. Yet on at least one occasion he consulted an Indigenous bonesetter.[68] Neither Indigenous healing practitioners nor patients necessarily opposed scientific medicine—often they adapted aspects of it to their own needs—but they maintained the vibrancy of their own healing traditions in the face of attempts to extinguish them in the name of progress.[69]

Famous for traveling to rural communities via motorcycle (see Figure 18.1) and imposing his own brand of justice, Ubico sought to extend his rule of law beyond the

FIGURE 18.1. General President Jorge Ubico on his motorcycle. La Gaceta, November 10, 1940.
Source: Image courtesy of Hemeroteca Nacional de Guatemala.

capital.[70] He employed social justice demagoguery, limited reform, and individualized interventions to secure mass support and strengthen his personal position.[71] In another strategy designed to centralize his control, he instituted the *intendente* (local governor) system to replace mayors and curtail the influence of *indígenas*. Ubico also facilitated the state's extension into rural areas by expanding the role and coverage of the National Police, public health officials, and census takers.[72] The spreading tentacles of the state were facilitated by its massive infrastructure project: by 1943 the nation expanded it road system fivefold with 10,200 kilometers of new roads, bridges, and tunnels.[73]

Rife with ambiguities and contradictions, Ubico's brand of nationalism celebrated Indigenous traditions that served his interests (particularly for tourism) while railing against others—moonshine production, *curanderimso*, and *brujeria*—as inimical to modernization. As evident in the photograph of Kaqchikel officials highlighting their ethnicity (through their clothing) and literacy, many Indigenous elites insisted tradition and modernity were symbiotic (see Figure 18.2).[74]

Ubico's harsh but predictable rule afforded *indígenas* new opportunities to contest their servitude.[75] The government's combination of responding to local concerns and maintaining the rule of law appealed to rural people, despite their loss of civil liberties. While some historians depict his regime as beneficial to *indígenas*, others paint Ubico as one of Latin America's most brutal dictators.[76] Similarly, *indígenas* living in remote regions where Ubico exerted little control generally maintained a certain antipathy toward his rule, whereas many central highland *indígenas* praised him for leveling race

FIGURE 18.2. Indigenous authorities from San Martín Jilotepeque, 1907.

Source: Image courtesy of Colección Fototeca Guatemala, Centro de Investigaciones Regionales de Mesoamérica.

relations and maintaining security.[77] Conducted during the middle of Guatemala's civil war (1960–1996), Guatemalan anthropologist Claudia Dary's 1985 study of Kaqchikel oral histories underscores the government's excessive demands on their time and labor; some informants described his dictatorship as "bitter."[78] In sharp contrast, shortly after the Peace Accords (1991–1996), Kaqchikel elders in the same town lauded Ubico for respecting indigeneity and bringing peace, order, and justice to the region. Compared to late twentieth-century lethal, capricious military rule, Ubico's iron-fisted regime was benign in their view.[79] Although tempting to conclude that such accounts vindicate Ubico's dictatorship, these sources demonstrate the complexity of memory and counter-narratives that challenge hegemonic interpretations about the functioning of authoritarian regimes.

While Ubico adeptly navigated Guatemala through the Great Depression, World War II destabilized his regime. Four days after the December 7, 1941, Pearl Harbor attack, Ubico declared war against Japan and Germany. By December 23, he deported German men who appeared on the US Proclaimed List. For most Guatemalans, their nation's entrance into the war was a strike against fascism that catalyzed a shift toward a more just society. The dictatorship's hold on power was increasingly tenuous as political protests grew in the capital. When Ubico's hand-picked successor General Federico Ponce Vaides nationalized German properties in August 1944, he heightened expectations that the state advance agrarian reform.[80]

In a desperate effort to maintain power, Ponce appealed to *indígenas* by promising to expand their rights and access to resources. On Independence Day (September 15), *indígenas* demonstrated their allegiance to Ponce's administration by protesting in the capital, Chimaltenango, Chichicastenango, and El Quiche.[81]

DEMOCRATIC TRANSITION

Chafing at a dictatorship that allowed little political participation (let alone dissent), a coalition comprised of students, military reformers, teachers, professionals, urban workers, and an emerging middle class toppled Ponce on October 20, 1944. Two days later in Patzicía, about twenty-five Kaqchikel armed with machetes, stones, and axes gathered to support Ponce and protest ladino domination of local resources, particularly land.[82] Ladinos responded with guns. When the civic guard and national army arrived a few days later to restore order, between twelve and fourteen ladinos and between sixty and nine hundred Kaqchikels had been killed.[83] As had happened in the massacre, Kaqchikels were victimized disproportionately in the judicial proceedings: thirty-three were arrested, about a dozen of whom were put to death; the others served out lengthy prison sentences. In contrast, no ladinos were ever tried.[84] The technological advantage in weaponry, the high number of Kaqchikel as opposed to ladino deaths, the anonymity of Kaqchikel victims versus the publicity of ladino victims, and the lopsided legal process were products and proof of political, economic, social, and judicial structures that disadvantaged *indígenas*. The massacre and its reverberations cast a dark hue over the first democratic government of Juan José Arévalo Bermejo (1945–1950), which won free and fair elections shortly after the October Revolution.

As recent scholarship has demonstrated, the new democratic government regularly undermined the well-being of marginalized populations.[85] From 1946 to 1948, the Ministry of Health collaborated with the US Public Health Service to infect Guatemalan prisoners, mental hospital inmates, orphans, and Indigenous military recruits with syphilis, gonorrhea, and chancroid.[86] As abhorrent as the experiments were, abuse and inequality in the health care and public health systems were not an aberration.[87] Privileging ladinos, the democratic government offered few benefits to *indígenas* or Afro-Guatemalans.[88]

Despite denigrating discourse, depictions, and deprivations, Arévalo had lofty goals. He sought to increase workers' economic and political power, expand education, modernize health care around a social security model, and extend other social services.[89] The 1946 Social Security Law established the Guatemalan Institute of Social Security, which provided workers' compensation, maternity benefits, and child care, among other provisions. Passed in 1947 and amended in 1948, the Labor Code allowed collective bargaining and the right to strike (except during harvest), set minimum wages, and restricted child and female labor. With an eye toward Indigenous rights, the government also created the *Instituto Indigenista Nacional* (National Indigenist Institute).[90] Arévalo extended suffrage to all literate and illiterate men so more *indígenas* could vote, but only literate women could vote so most of their Indigenous counterparts remained disenfranchised; by the end of Arévalo's rule only 4.8 percent of Indigenous women could vote.[91] Gender-based violence and sexism further marginalized women.[92]

More than Arévalo's initiatives, the 1952 Agrarian Reform Law defined the democratic movement. Faced with land ownership that was among the most unequal in Latin America, President Jacobo Arbenz (1951–1954) broke up large landholdings that were not used efficiently and redistributed them to people who worked the land.[93] Two percent of the farming units controlled 72 percent of the land, while half of the farming units (165,850 families) owned less than two *manzanas* (barely enough to subsist), and many rural families were landless. The ethnic disparities were as stark as the class differences: ladino farmers averaged 35 *manzanas*, while Indigenous farmers averaged 4.4 *manzanas*.[94] In correcting these disparities, Arbenz sought to augment agricultural production and improve rural residents' realities. By June 1954, the government had expropriated more than two million acres and redistributed land to over one hundred thousand *campesinos*. Thousands of beneficiaries received credit.[95] In some areas, favorable living conditions ensued.[96]

Arbenz pursued economic and political policies that were pragmatic and capitalist in nature, but staunch anticommunists—particularly those in the Dwight D. Eisenhower administration (1953–1961) with close ties to UFCO—portrayed Arbenz as communist and agrarian reform as anti-capitalist. With much of its landholdings laying fallow, UFCO stood to lose considerable wealth to expropriation. In the context of the Cold War, the Eisenhower administration heeded anticommunist fear mongering. Supported by the US Central Intelligence Agency, Colonel Carlos Castillo Armas led a group of some 150 to 200 Guatemalan exiles to overthrow Arbenz. Although he was assassinated three years later, Castillo Armas (1954–1957) established a military government that dominated politics even after the 1986 democratic elections.

Thanks largely to US funding, the economic development groundwork laid by Arévalo and Arbenz came to fruition during authoritarian rule that succeeded them. The nation's economy expanded as Guatemala embraced industrialization and joined the Central American Common Market in 1960. As part of Guatemala's globalization, the capital increasingly attracted rural peoples, particularly *indígenas*, with the promise of jobs and improved living standards.[97]

MILITARY RULE AND *LA VIOLENCIA*

Orchestrated by the Guatemalan military with US aid during the height of the Cold War, the thirty-six year civil war (1960–1996) devastated Guatemala, claiming more than two hundred thousand (mostly Indigenous) lives and displacing over one million more. During the 1960s, political violence escalated as the military government terrorized insurgents. As rural organizations adapted to these threats, ideologies became more radical, resilient, and Indigenous; dissident organizations became more democratic, flexible, and participatory; and mobilization strategies became more concerned with protecting, educating, and empowering members.[98] Some organizations like the Committee for Peasant Unity worked hard not to appear too Indigenous as it strove to bring ladinos and *indígenas* together under one banner.[99] Even groups that welcomed Indigenous perspectives and concerns were reluctant to create opportunities for *indígenas* to assume leadership roles.

Myriad economic, social, and political forces catalyzed and shaped the civil war. Exacerbated by the country's economic crisis in the 1970s and 1980s, the vastly unequal distribution of resources motivated revolutionary groups. Indigenous leaders were acutely aware of how class and other divisions cut across ethnic solidarity.[100] In 1974, one K'iche' *reina indígena* (Indigenous queen) called for "the well-being of our *campesino* brothers who are vilely exploited, not only by foreigners but also by our own race."[101] Some Indigenous activists advocated dismantling racial and class barriers in tandem. As Nobel Prize Laureate K'iche-Maya activist Rigoberta Menchú and Kaqchikel Maya Congresswoman Rosalina Tuyuc demonstrated, women were outspoken leaders in the struggle against the military regime.[102]

Further polarizing the country, the 1976 earthquake devastated much of the central highlands where the Indigenous population predominated. When military officials associated international outreach with communism, accepting aid could be lethal.[103]

United Nations and Guatemalan Catholic Church truth and reconciliation commission reports identify genocide during the early 1980s, mainly under the regime of José Efraín Ríos Montt (1980–1981).[104] Relying almost exclusively on oral testimony from participants and survivors, the reports concluded that the military perpetrated more than 90 percent of human rights crimes and Indigenous people comprised the vast majority of victims.[105] In some instances, age-old conflicts among individuals and between communities precipitated state terror.[106] Soldiers raped women and razed hundreds of Indigenous communities; many never reconstituted themselves.[107] Developing a close friendship with Ríos Montt, President Ronald Reagan (1980–1988) ensured US military aid continued during the Guatemalan military's most violent rule.[108]

President Jorge Serrano Elias' 1993 attempt to concentrate power in the presidency catalyzed the peace process by aligning powerful factions of the elite and consolidating popular sectors such as unions, students, and Indigenous leaders who convinced the military that Serrano Elias' regime would lack legitimacy. Ironically envisioning themselves as protectors of democracy, military leaders rejected Serrano Elias's power grab even as they repressed dissent. The experience grassroots organizations gained by opposing the *Serranazo* emboldened them to demand participation in the peace process that culminated in the 1996 Peace Accords. At that point, the popular left and Indigenous organizations were among the best organized groups in Guatemala. Despite being excluded from peace negotiations, Indigenous leaders developed strategies for implementing the Peace Accords even before they were signed.[109]

Local, national, and international actors comprised a multilateral coalition that facilitated the 1996 Peace Accords. The United Nations ensured that human rights were paramount in the negotiations. Learning from El Salvador's mistake of excluding civil sector input from the 1992 Peace Accords, Guatemala—largely thanks to the Catholic church's efforts—solicited feedback from popular organizations. Realizing their investments would suffer if the Peace Accords failed because rural areas would remain unstable and Guatemala would continue to be an international pariah, economic elites endorsed the Peace Accords.[110]

POST-PEACE IN GUATEMALA, 1996–PRESENT

Throughout and after the civil war, Guatemala remained wedded to neoliberal economic strategies of embracing agricultural exports. By the 1960s, agrochemicals were a crucial component of agricultural production. At first reluctant to employ agrochemicals because of concerns about public health, many Indigenous farmers ultimately became dependent on them. When the 1973 international oil crisis sent agrochemical prices soaring, pressure to migrate to agro-export plantations resurged. Instead of alleviating migrant labor, agrochemicals deepened that dependent relationship.[111]

After the war, foreign capital and war refugees returned and shaped the economy and civil society.[112] Like their early twentieth-century forebears who cultivated coffee, some Indigenous farmers embraced the new agricultural export markets of broccoli, strawberries, and blackberries. Whereas Ch'orti' farmers from eastern Guatemala largely abandoned broccoli and other nontraditional agricultural exports because plagues, envious neighbors, and the greed of private export companies undermined those USAID projects, some Kaqchikel farmers thrived as broccoli growers and exporters. Despite the vagaries of volatile markets, unscrupulous middlemen, and fickle US consumers, these Kaqchikel entrepreneurs improved their standard of living and retained ownership of their land.[113] Agricultural export economies could both undermine and sustain Indigenous people and communities. For many Indigenous people straddling local subsistence lifestyles and neoliberal economic currents, economic modernization and international development projects often exacerbated rather than alleviated poverty.[114] The increasing privatization of health care did little to improve public health as Guatemala continued to struggle to reduce infant mortality and increase life expectancy.[115]

Because neoliberal economic reforms exacerbated structural poverty but also opened up new opportunities, Guatemalans experienced them in dramatically different ways.[116] In sharp contrast to female employees in foreign-owned factories or *maquiladoras* who became trapped in cycles of poverty, dependency, and violence, many Indigenous women who worked in tourist markets enjoyed increased prestige and privilege vis-à-vis their male kin. In a radical shift from their communities' division of labor, Indigenous men cleaned, cooked, and took care of children while their wives labored in tourist markets![117] Modernization could help people preserve such mutable traditions as wearing *traje* (hand-woven clothing), which, incidentally, labeled Indigenous women as inferior in Guatemalan society.

Part of a late twentieth-century intellectual and social effervescence, Indigenous intellectuals guided cultural and linguistic movements as part of the Movimiento Maya (Maya Movement).[118] As international nongovernmental organizations and the state embraced notions of multiculturalism, ladinos increasingly felt marginalized by the attention and resources afforded Mayas. Many ladinos felt they lacked an authentic identity or culture when set against Maya ethnic revitalization.[119] Supported by the United Nations, students and teachers throughout the highlands painted public murals portraying Indigenous histories, cultures, and realities—including the brutality of the civil war and their hopes for productive peace thereafter where everyone would have sustainable access to education, technology, water, and other resources (see Figure 18.3).[120]

Although understudied, Afro-Guatemalans long have been crucial contributors to the complex tapestry of race relations in Guatemala. In the Gulf of Honduras coastal city of Livingston, Garífunas portray their Q'eqchi' neighbors as dirty, smelly, and stupid, but diligent when compelled to be so. Similarly echoing ladino attempts to denigrate and exclude non-Hispanics, Q'eqchi's do not consider Garífunas Guatemalans. That mutual disdain notwithstanding, Garífunas see ladinos, not Q'eqchi's, as their oppressors. Such rancor toward ladinos speaks to the irony of Q'eqchi'-Garífuna discord: they share marginalized positions based on colonial and capitalist exploitation. Recognizing themselves as hybrids rather than *indígenas*, Livingston Q'eqchi's trace their roots to Indigenous, Spanish, and German influences. When Maya Movement organizations went to Livingston in the 1990s, they considered Garífunas more Indigenous than Q'eqchi's.[121]

FIGURE 18.3. Youths Building Peaceful Future. Image from San Juan Comalapa mural.
Source: Photograph courtesy of Walter Little.

In the civil war's wake, truth and reconciliation commissions provided survivors and witnesses forums to recount gruesome details of torture and murder. "[We] collectively and responsibly took on the task of breaking the silence that thousands of war victims have kept for years. We opened up the possibility for them to speak and have their say, to tell their stories of suffering and pain, so they might feel liberated from the burden that has weighed them down for so many years," explained Guatemalan Bishop Juan José Gerardi Conedera when he released the Catholic Church's study of human rights abuses on April 24, 1998.[122] Two days later, he was bludgeoned to death in his garage.

While the Catholic Church's report pointed to the war's broader historical and structural conditions such as racism and poverty that dated to the colonial era, Gerardi's assassination demonstrated that history is regularly (and often violently) contested in Guatemala. Guatemalan authorities had denied the existence of the Archivo Histórico de la Policía Nacional (AHPH, Guatemalan National Police Archive) until investigators from the Human Rights Ombudsman Office stumbled upon it on July 5, 2005.[123] Official denial of those secret state documents fueled Guatemalan conservatives' criticisms that the nation's human rights reports were baseless because their findings were grounded in oral testimony rather than documentary evidence. AHPH documentation has provided crucial evidence in the convictions of high-level officials for crimes against humanity. In 2013, Guatemala became the first nation to try to convict (albeit briefly) one of its own former heads of state for crimes against humanity in its own territory.[124]

As postbellum Guatemala reduced its military forces and pursued such neoliberal economic reforms as promoting free trade and slashing government subsidies and employment, violence became more insidious and less selective than during the civil war. What threatened democracy was good for capitalism: one of the economy's fastest growing areas was private security. Often attributed to corruption and the vestiges of civil war and fueled by narco-trafficking violence and neoliberal reforms that dispropor-tionately disadvantaged the poor and working classes, Guatemala's per capita murder rate increased from 52/100,000 people to 68/100,000 from 2010 to 2013—more than ten times that of the United States.[125] Those extremes speak to the terrifying phenomena of feminicide (killing of women because they are women) and *juvencidio* (killing of youths because they are young) that plague Guatemala. The Policía Nacional Civil (National Civil Police) estimated that more than 7,200 women were killed between 2000 and 2013.[126] Impunity compounded violence. Of the 5,027 femicides in Guatemala from 2000 to 2009, only eleven perpetrators were convicted.[127] Legal leniency provided pow-erful state and private actors impunity.[128]

Faced with the government's inability to address such threats as increased gang ac-tivity and competition over scarce resources (mainly farm and forest land), rural leaders developed legal procedures grounded in traditional justice systems to regain control of their communities. Indigenous-informed and locally determined approaches to law and punishment created extralegal venues that were more adept at addressing community concerns than the state-sanctioned legal system.[129] Bankrupt judicial and police systems also catalyzed vigilantism and lynchings.

Another response to Guatemala's increasing instability and insecurity was em-igration. During the civil war and in response to grinding poverty, Guatemalans fled to North America for safety and prosperity. As the number of Guatemalans abroad increased, so did remittances. In 2011, Guatemalan immigrants sent nearly $4.4 billion home to their families. By 2018, that number more than doubled when they remitted more than $9 billion—a 13 percent increase from 2017.[130] Concurrently, escalating law-less violence and gang persecution compelled Guatemalan parents to send their chil-dren to the United States unaccompanied.

CONCLUSION

The process of identity formation among historic and contemporary Guatemalans—male and female *indígenas*, ladinos, mestizos, Africans and their descendants, Garífunas, Xinkas, and creoles—has long been embedded in the complex interplay of economic, political, social, and cultural relations. More so than other ethnic groups, *indígenas* were emboldened and belittled by national identities. A number of Guatemalan scholars, most famously Severo Martínez Peláez, argued that *indio* was an invented colonial category and that the Indigenous culture was imposed upon them rather than being autochthonous.[131] To promote the nation, many leaders hailed ancient *indígenas* as fervently as they denigrated contemporary *indios*. Although such characterizations hindered their socioeconomic positions, few *indígenas* internalized that debasement; many rose above it.[132] When he wrote directly to Estrada Cabrera in 1918, for example, German Medina identified himself as a member of the "Indigenous race and citizen of the nation."[133]

As a Maya from Jacaltenango who survived the civil war, earned a doctorate in anthropology (while in exile), became a University of California professor, and later returned to Guatemala as an elected member of congress, Victor Montejo embodies the complex combination of talents that Mayas possess but that so few Guatemalans afford them the opportunity to develop. Like many other marginalized Guatemalans, Mayas committed to contributing to national development are not bent on revenge or excluding those who have enriched themselves on the backs of poor and working-class Guatemalans. Rather, Maya intellectuals like Montejo, Irma A. Velásquez Nimatuj, Luis Enrique Sam Colop, Demetrio Cojtí Cuxil, and Edgar Esquit have demanded full participation in the nation with equal access to its resources. With historical writings that reassess and include Indigenous contributions and actors in Guatemala's nation-building, Indigenous intellectuals challenge Hispanocentric national histories.[134]

The tension between celebrating an Indigenous past and suppressing an Indigenous present is palpable in Guatemala. Since the 1870s, liberal governments sought to assimilate *indígenas*. But in the 1930s, the state marketed *indígenas* to attract international tourists and investors. Images of colorful Mayas in tourist marketplaces and statues of the sixteenth-century Indigenous warrior Tekún Umán form a perplexing backdrop in a nation where racism morphed into genocide and continues to preclude access to power and resources. That many Guatemalans refused to celebrate Menchú's 1992 Nobel Peace Prize even as their country's civil war was winding down is emblematic of a nation struggling to reconcile its multiple and contradictory pasts.

ACKNOWLEDGMENTS

I wish to express my deep gratitude to Julie Gibbings, Bob Holden, and J. T. Way whose comments and critiques on earlier versions of this essay have greatly improved it.

NOTES

1. Generally, ladinos do not identify themselves as Indigenous but rather in opposition to *indígenas* (Indigenous people). The term "ladino" dates to the late seventeenth century and was first used to describe persons of mixed descent (mestizos, mulattos, *castas*). Some Indigenous "Mexicanos" in Guatemala identified themselves as ladino to distinguish themselves as more civilized (and thus more deserving of privileges) than other

Indigenous groups. After Guatemalan independence in 1821, ladinos were increasingly disassociated from *mestizos* (people of mixed Indigenous and Spanish descent). Instead, they took pains to identify themselves with European or Spanish culture. Although culture is paramount in identifying ladinos, blood stricture is still important on a personal level, at least ideologically if not biologically. Most ladinos have some Indigenous blood but choose not to recognize or represent these cultural, social, or historical aspects of their identity. They are the minority in Guatemala but enjoy political and economic power. Even poor ladinos often hold themselves to be superior to Mayas. Thus political, economic, social, and cultural structures are predicated on racist views that are at best paternalistic and at worst ethnocidal. The Maya-ladino binary reveals the construction of socioracial categories in Guatemala but belies the complex concatenations of ethnic, gender, racial, and class identities. See Marta Casaús Arzú, *Guatemala: Linaje y racismo* (Guatemala City, Guatemala: Facultad Latinoamericana de Ciencias Sociales, 1994), 119–126; Christopher Lutz, *Santiago de Guatemala, 1541–1773* (Norman: University of Oklahoma Press, 1994); Greg Grandin, *The Blood of Guatemala: A History of Race and Nation* (Durham, NC: Duke University Press, 2000), 83–85, 239; Laura E. Matthew, *Memories of Conquest: Becoming Mexicano in Colonial Guatemala* (Chapel Hill: University of North Carolina Press, 2012); Carol Smith, "Origins of the National Question in Guatemala: A Hypothesis," in *Guatemalan Indians and the State: 1540–1988*, edited by Carol Smith, 86–87 (Austin: University of Texas Press, 1990); Carol Smith, "Race-Class-Gender Ideology in Guatemala: Modern and Anti-Modern Forms," *Comparative Studies in Society and History* 37 (1995): 734–735; Kay Warren, *Symbolism of Subordination: Indian Identity in a Guatemalan Town* (Austin: University of Texas Press, 1978).

2. Julie Gibbings, "Mestizaje in the Age of Fascism: German and Q'echi' Maya Interracial Unions in Alta Verapaz, Guatemala," *German History* 34, no. 2 (2016): 214–236.

3. According to two Guatemalan intellectuals who bookended the twentieth century, *indígenas* comprise more than 70 percent of the population. See Jorge García Salas, "Comentarios a la Iniciativa del Club 'Freedom of the Indian,'" *Diario de Centro-América*, May 1, 1920; Leopoldo Tzian, *Kajab'aliil Maya'iib' Xuq Mu'siib': Ri Ub'antajiik Iximulew/ Mayas y ladinos en cifras: El caso de Guatemala* (Guatemala City, Guatemala: Cholsamaj, 1994). Keeping in mind the political (and at times corrupted) nature of census data in Guatemala, the 2002 census reported that 41.03 percent of Guatemalans identified as Indigenous. See Instituto Nacional de Estadística, *Censos nacionalies XI de población y VI de habitaciones: características de la población y de los locales de habitación censados* (Guatemala City, Guatemala: Instituto Nacional de Estadística, 2003), 30–31.

4. Brent Metz, *Chorti-Maya Survival in Eastern Guatemala: Indigeneity in Transition* (Albuquerque: University of New Mexico Press, 2006),

5. Ralph Lee Woodward Jr., *Rafael Carrera and the Emergence of the Republic of Guatemala, 1821–1871* (Athens, GA: University of Georgia Press, 1993); Arturo Taracena Arriola, *Invención criolla, sueño ladino, pesadilla indígena: Los Altos de Guatemala, de región a Estado, 1740–1850* (Antigua, Guatemala: Centro de Investigaciones Regionales de Mesoamérica, 1997).

6. Jim Handy, *Gift of the Devil: A History of Guatemala* (Boston: South End, 1984), 60–61, 67; Ralph Lee Woodward Jr., *Central America: A Nation Divided* (3rd ed.) (New York: Oxford University Press, 1999), 154; Bonar L. Hernández Sandoval, *Guatemala's Catholic Revolution: A History of Religious and Social Reform, 1920-1968* (Notre Dame, IN: University of Notre Dame Press, 2019), 23–26.

7. Julio Castellanos Cambranes, *Café y campesinos en Guatemala, 1853–1897* (Guatemala City, Guatemala: Editorial Universitaria, 1985); David McCreery, "Coffee and Class: The Structure of Development in Liberal Guatemala," *Hispanic American Historical Review* 56, no. 3 (1976): 457; David McCreery, "Coffee and Indigenous Labor in Guatemala, 1871–1980," in *The Global Coffee Economy in Africa, Asia, and Latin America, 1500-1989*, edited by William Gervase Clarence-Smith and Steven Topik, 206–231 (Cambridge, U.K.: Cambridge University Press, 2003); Handy, *Gift of the Devil*, 68; Robert Carmack, *Historia social de los quichés* (Guatemala City, Guatemala: Editorial José de Pineda Ibarra, Ministerio de Educación, 1979), 248; David McCreery, *Rural Guatemala, 1760–1940* (Stanford, CA: Stanford University Press, 1994), 214, 236–254, 301; David McCreery, "State Power, Indigenous Communities, and Land in Nineteenth-Century Guatemala, 1820–1920," in *The Indian in Latin American History: Resistance, Resilience, and Acculturation*, edited by John E. Kicza, 191–212 (Wilmington, DE: Scholarly Resources, 2000); David McCreery, "Debt Servitude in Rural Guatemala, 1876–1936," *Hispanic American Historical Review*,63 (Nov. 1983): 735–759; Robert G. Williams, *Export Agriculture and the Crisis in Central America* (Chapel Hill: University of North Carolina Press, 1986).
8. René Reeves, *Ladinos with Ladinos, Indians with Indians: Land, Labor, and Regional Ethnic Conflict in the Making of Guatemala* (Stanford, CA: Stanford University Press, 2006); Lowell Gudmundson and Héctor Lindo-Fuentes, *Central America, 1821–1871: Liberalism before Liberal Reform* (Tuscaloosa: University of Alabama Press, 1995); Julie Gibbings, *Our Time Is Now: Race and Modernity in Postcolonial Guatemala* (Cambridge, U.K.: Cambridge University Press, 2020); David Carey Jr., "'The Heart of the Country': The Primacy of Peasants and Maize in Modern Guatemala," *Journal of Latin American Studies* 51, no. 2 (2019): 273–306.
9. Grandin, *Blood of Guatemala*; Reeves, *Ladinos with Ladinos*; Taracena Arriola, *Invención criolla, sueño ladino, pesadilla indígena*; Marta Elena Casaús Arzú, "El gran debate historiográfico de 1937 en Guatemala: 'Los indios fuera de la historia y de la civilización'. Dos formas de hacer historia," *Revista Complutense de Historia de América* 34 (2008): 209–231; Casaús Arzú, *Guatemala*; Marta Elena Casaús Arzú, "La Generación del 20 en Guatemala y sus imaginarios de nación (1920–1940)," in *Las redes intelectuales centroamericanas: un siglo de imaginarios nacionales (1820–1920)*, edited by Marta Elena Casaús Arzú and Teresa García Giráldez, 253–290 (Guatemala City, Guatemala: F&G Editores, 2005). More nuanced and incisive analysis about the role of ethnicity in charting the past has been evident in recent colonial historiography too. See Laura E. Matthew and Michel R. Oudijk, eds., *Indian Conquistadors: Indigenous Allies in the Conquest of Mesoamerica* (Norman: University of Oklahoma Press, 2007); Matthew, *Memories of Conquest*.
10. Betsy Konefal, *For Every Indio Who Falls: A History of Maya Activism in Guatemala, 1960-1990* (Albuquerque: University of New Mexico Press, 2010).
11. Brianna Leavitt-Alcántara, *Alone at the Altar: Single Women and Devotion in Guatemala, 1670-1870* (Stanford, CA: Stanford University Press, 2018).
12. Woodward, *Rafael Carrera*, 54, 60–83; McCreery, *Rural Guatemala*, 23, 56, 148–149; Woodward, *Central America*, 103, 108; Grandin, *Blood of Guatemala*, 101; Mario Rodríguez, "The Livingston Codes in the Guatemalan Crisis of 1837–1838," in *Applied Enlightenment: Nineteenth-Century Liberalism, 1830-1839*, edited by Mario Rodríguez et al., 1–32 (New Orleans, LA: Middle American Research Institute Tulane University, 1972); Jorge Luján Muñoz, "Del derecho colonial al derecho nacional: el caso de Guatemala,"

Jahrbuch für Geschichte Lateinameikas 38 (2001): 85–107; Reeves, *Ladinos with Ladinos*, 1, 2, 45, 149, 173–174; Rachel Sieder, "Customary Law and Local Power in Guatemala," in *Guatemala After the Peace Accords*, edited by Rachel Sieder, 99 (London: Institute of Latin American Studies, 1998); Arturo Taracena Arriola, "Nación y Republica en Centroamérica (1821-65)," in *Identidades nacionales y estado moderno en Centroamérica*, edited by Arturo Taracena Arriola y Jean Piel, 47 (San José, Costa Rica: EDUCA, 1995).

13. Taracena Arriola, *Invención criolla, sueño ladino, pesadilla indígena*. Mexico annexed the department of Soconusco, which was part of Los Altos.

14. Reeves, *Ladinos with Ladinos*; Grandin, *Blood of Guatemala*.

15. Woodward, *Rafael Carrera*, 383.

16. Gudmundson and Lindo-Fuentes, *Central America*; Reeves, *Ladinos with Ladinos*; Grandin, *Blood of Guatemala*, 167; Douglass Sullivan-González, *Piety, Power, and Politics: Religion and Nation Formation in Guatemala, 1821–1871* (Pittsburgh, PA: University of Pittsburgh Press, 1998).

17. Reeves, *Ladinos with ladinos*; Taracena *Invención criolla, sueño ladino, pesadilla indígena*.

18. Stacey Schartzkopf, "Consumption, Custom, and Control: Aguardiente in Nineteenth-Century Maya Guatemala," in *Distilling the Influence of Alcohol: Aguardiente in Guatemalan History*, edited by David Carey Jr., 17–41 (Gainesville: University Press of Florida, 2012).

19. Frederick Douglass Opie, "Alcohol and Lowdown Culture in Caribbean Guatemala and Honduras, 1898–1922," in *Distilling the Influence of Alcohol: Aguardiente in Guatemalan History*, edited by David Carey Jr., 96-119 (Gainesville: University Press of Florida, 2012).

20. Reeves, *Ladinos with Ladinos*,

21. Handy, *Gift of the Devil*, 68.

22. *Recopilación de las leyes de la República de Guatemala*, vol. 1 (Guatemala City, Guatemala: Tipografía Nacional, 1881), 457; J. C. Méndez Montenegro, "444 años de legislación agraria, 1520-1957," *Revista de la Facultad de Ciencias Jurídicas y Sociales de Guatemala* 6 (1960): 123–164, 234–238; Handy, *Gift of the Devil*, 60–61, 68–69; McCreery, "State Power, Indigenous Communities, and Land," 106; Woodward, *Central America*, 154, 174; Carmack, *Historia Social de los Quiches*, 248; Robert Carmack, "Barrios y los indígenas: el caso de Santiago, Momostenango," *Estudios Sociales* 6 (1974): 52–73.

23. David Carey Jr., "Empowered through Labor and Buttressing Their Communities: Mayan Women and Coastal Migration, 1875-1965," *Hispanic American Historical Review* 86, no. 3 (August 2006): 501–534.

24. *Recopilación de leyes agrarias* (Guatemala City, Guatemala: Tipografía El Progreso, 1881); David McCreery, "Coffee and Class," 457; Handy, *Gift of the Devil*, 68; Carmack, *Historia Social de los Quiches*, 248; McCreery, *Rural Guatemala*, 214, 236–254, 301.

25. McCreery, *Rural Guatemala*, 1–3, 148, 294, 308, 326–333; Oliver LaFarge, "Maya Ethnology: The Sequence of Cultures," in *The Maya and Their Neighbors*, edited by C. L. Hay (New York: 1940); Guillermo Náñez Falcón, "Erwin Paul Dieseldorff, German Entrepreneur in the Alta Verapaz of Guatemala, 1889–1937" (PhD diss., Tulane University, 1970), 323; Richard Adams, "La población indígena en el estado liberal," in *Historia General de Guatemala*, Vol. 5, edited by Jorge Luján Muñoz, 176 (Guatemala City, Guatemala: Asociación de amigos del país, fundación para la cultura y desarrollo, 1995); John Early, "Population Increase and Family Planning in Guatemala," *Human Organization* 34, no. 3 (1975): 276; Robert Carmack, John Early, and Christopher Lutz,

eds., *The Historical Demography of Highland Guatemala* (Albany: State University of New York, Institute for Mesoamerican Studies, 1982); James D. Sexton and Clyde M. Woods, "Demography, Development, and Modernization in Fourteen Highland Guatemalan Towns," in *The Historical Demography of Highland Guatemala*, edited by Robert Carmack, John Early, and Christopher Lutz, 199 (Albany: State University of New York, Institute for Mesoamerican Studies, 1982).

26. David Carey Jr., *Our Elders Teach Us: Maya-Kaqchikel Historical Perspectives. Xkib'ij kan qate' qatata'* (Tuscaloosa: University of Alabama Press, 2001), 67; Reeves, *Ladinos with Ladinos*; Jim Handy, "The Violence of Dispossession: Guatemala in the Nineteenth and Twentieth Centuries," in *Politics and History of Violence and Crime in Central America*, edited by Sebastian Huhn and Hannes Warnecke-Berger, 287 (New York: Palgrave Macmillan, 2017); Gibbings, *Our Time Is Now*.

27. McCreery, *Rural Guatemala*, 311.

28. *Diario de Centro América*, February 1, 1933, July18, 20, and 22, 1933, August 19, 1933, and September 3, 1936; McCreery, *Rural Guatemala*, 308; Woodward, *Rafael Carrera*, 191.

29. Carey, "'The Heart of the Country.'"

30. *Memoria de los trabajos realizados por la dirección general de la Policía Nacional durante el año de 1933*, (Guatemala City, Guatemala: Tipografía Nacional, 1935), 81–82; *Memoria de los trabajos realizados por la dirección general de la Policía Nacional durante al año de 1937* (Guatemala City, Guatemala: Tipografía Nacional, 1938), 22; David Carey Jr., *Engendering Mayan History: Kaqchikel Women as Agents and Conduits of the Past, 1875–1970* (New York: Routledge, 2006), 93–94; David McCreery, "Wage Labor, Free Labor, and Vagrancy Laws: The Transition to Capitalism in Guatemala, 1920–1945," in *Coffee, Society and Power in Latin America*, edited by William Roseberry, Lowell Gudmundson, and Mario Samper Kutschabach, 206–231 (Baltimore: John Hopkins University Press, 1995); McCreery, *Rural Guatemala*, 161–193, 301–322; Carey, "Empowered through Labor," 510; Steve J. Stern, "Feudalism, Capitalism, and the World-System in the Perspective of Latin America and the Caribbean," in *Confronting Historical Paradigms: Peasants, Labor, and the Capitalist World System in Africa and Latin America*, edited by Frederick Cooper et al., 23–83 (Madison: University of Wisconsin Press, 1993); Robert Carmack, "State and Community in Nineteenth-Century Guatemala" in *Guatemalan Indians and the State*, edited by Carol Smith, 123 (Austin: University of Texas Press, 1990).

31. Gibbings, *Our Time Is Now*.

32. Grandin, *Blood of Guatemala*; Reeves, *Ladinos with Ladinos*; Gibbings, *Our Time Is Now*.

33. Arturo Taracena Arriola, *Etnicidad, estado y nación en Guatemala, 1808–1944* (Antigua, Guatemala: Centro de Investigaciones Regionales de Centroamérica, 2002).

34. Dirección General de Estadística, *Censo General de la República de Guatemala, levantado en el año de 1880 26* (Guatemala City, Guatemala: Establecimiento Tipografíco de *El Progreso*, 1881), 69–73.

35. Dirección General de Estadística, *Censo General de la República de Guatemala. Levantado en 26 de Febrero de 1893* (Guatemala City, Guatemala: Tipografía y Encuadernación "Nacional," 1894), 40.

36. Grandin, *Blood of Guatemala*.

37. Gibbings, *Our Time Is Now*.

38. *Código Civil de la República de Guatemala. 1877* (Guatemala City, Guatemala: Imprenta de "El Progreso 1877), 1.

39. Reeves, *Ladinos with Ladinos*, 156.

40. Archivo General de Centroamérica (hereafter AGCA), Jefe Político de Sacatepéquez 1886, Carta al Honorable Asamblea Legislativa de San Antonio Augascalientes, May 10, 1886.

41. David Carey Jr., *I Ask for Justice: Maya Women, Dictators, and Crime in Guatemala, 1898–1944* (Austin: University of Texas Press, 2013).

42. Grandin, *Blood of Guatemala*, 162–164; Greg Grandin, "Can the Subaltern Be Seen? Photography and the Effects of Nationalism," *Hispanic American Historical Review* 84, no. 1 (2004): 83–111; McCreery, *Rural Guatemala*; Walter E. Little, "A Visual Political Economy of Maya Representations in Guatemala, 1931-1944," *Ethnohistory* 55, no. 4 (Fall 2008): 633–663; Gibbings, *Our Time Is Now*.

43. David Carey Jr., "The Politics and Culture of Medicine and Disease in Central America," *The Oxford Research Encyclopedia of Latin American History* (New York: Oxford University Press, 2019).

44. James H. Tenzel, "Shamanism and Concepts of Disease in a Mayan Indian Community," *Psychiatry: Journal for the Study of Interpersonal Processes* 33, no. 3 (1971): 372–380.

45. David McCreery "'This Life of Misery and Shame': Female Prostitution in Guatemala City," *Journal of Latin American Studies* 18, no. 2 (Nov. 1986), 333–353.

46. Marcos Cueto, "Introduction," in *Missionaries of Science: The Rockefeller Foundation and Latin America*, edited by Marcos Cueto, xi–xiv (Bloomington: University of Indiana Press, 1994); Marcos Cueto and Stephen Palmer, *Medicine and Public Health: A History* (Cambridge, U.K.: Cambridge University Press, 2015), 141.

47. Elena Hurtado and Eugenia Sáenz de Tejada, "Relations between Government Health Workers and Traditional Midwives," in *Mesoamerican Healers*, edited by Brad R. Huber and Alan R. Sandstrom, 214–216 (Austin: University of Texas Press, 2001).

48. David Carey Jr., "Heroines of Healthcare: Germana Catu and Maya Midwives," in *Faces of Resistance: Maya Heroes, Power, & Identity*, edited by Ashley Kistler, 137–156 (Tuscaloosa: University of Alabama Press, 2018).

49. Brad Huber, "Introduction," in *Mesoamerican Healers*, edited by Brad R. Huber and Alan R. Sandstrom, 17 (Austin: University of Texas Press, 2001).

50. Catherine Rendon, "El Gobierno de Manuel Estrada Cabrera," in *Historia General de Guatemala, Tomo V Epoca Contemporánea: 1898-1944*, edited by Jorge Luján Muñoz (director general) and J. Daniel Contreras R. (director del tomo), 19 (Guatemala City, Guatemala: Asociación de Amigos del País, Fundación para la Cultura y el Desarrollo, 1996).

51. Carmack, "State and Community in Nineteenth-Century Guatemala," 122; Woodward, *Central America*, 166, 208; McCreery, *Rural Guatemala*, 290, 297; Handy, *Gift of the Devil*, 57; Paul Dosal, *Power in Transition: The Rise of Guatemala's Industrial Oligarchy, 1871–1994* (Westport, CT: Praeger, 1995), 42

52. Ixjo'q, November 6, 1997, San Juan Comalapa, oral history interview with Mam Maya woman conducted by author.

53. Edgar Esquit, *La superación del indígena: la política de la modernización entre las élites indígenas de Comalapa, Siglo XX* (Guatemala City, Guatemala: Universidad de San Carlos, 2010); Gibbings, *Our Time Is Now*; Frederick Douglass Opie, "Adios Jim Crow: Afro-North American Workers and the Guatemalan Railroad Workers' League, 1884-1921" (PhD diss., Syracuse University, 1999), 141–143.

54. Antonio Batres Jáuregui, *Los Indios, su historia y su civilización* (Guatemala City, Guatemala: La Unión, 1894), III–XII, 173–196; José Antonio Villacorta Calderón, *Curso de Geografía de la América Central para uso de los Institutos y Escuelas Normales*

510 DAVID CAREY JR.

(Guatemala City, Guatemala: Tipografía Sánchez y de Guise, 1928), 73–74; José Antonio Villacorta Calderón, *Prehistoria e historia antigua de Guatemala* (Guatemala City, Guatemala: Impreso en la Tipografía Nacional, 1938), 7–8; Miguel Angel Asturias, *El problema social del indio y otros textos* (Paris: Centre de recherches de l'institut d'etudes hispaniques, 1971), 72, 101–113; David Carey Jr., "*Indigenísmo* and Guatemalan History in the Twentieth Century," *Revista Interamericana de Bibliografía* 47, no. 2 (1998): 379–408; Grandin, *Blood of Guatemala*, 84–85, 239, 265–266 n.9; Taracena Arriola, *Invención criolla, sueño ladino, pesadilla indígena*; Casaus Arzú, *Guatemala*, 119–126; Marta Elena Casaús Arzú and Teresa García Giráldez, *Las redes intelectuales centroamericanas: un siglo de imaginarios nacionales (1820-1920)* (Guatemala City, Guatemala: F & G Editors, 2009).

55. Edgar Esquit, *Otros poderes, nuevos desafíos: Relaciones interétnicas en Tecpán y su entorno departamental (1871-1935)* (Guatemala City, Guatemala: Magna Terra Editores, 2002); Esquit, *La superación del indígena*; Grandin, *Blood of Guatemala*.

56. *Recopilación de las Leyes 1917-1918* (Guatemala City,Guatemala: Tipografía Nacional, 1924) ("10 de Septiembre"); "Grippe," *La República*, December 2, 1918; "Salubridad," *Díario de Centro América*, January 9, 1919; *Memoria de la Secretaría de Gobernación y Justicia presentada a la Asamblea Nacional Legislativa en sus sesiones ordinarias* (Guatemala City, Guatemala: Minerva Centro Editorial, 1919), 20; Luis Gaitan and Julio Roberto Herrera, "II día PanAméricano de la Salud en Guatemala," *Boletín Sanitario de Guatemala, órgano de la Dirección General de Sanidad Pública de Guatemala* 12, no. 49 (1941): 7–10; McCreery, *Rural Guatemala*, 277–278; David McCreery, "Guatemala City," in *The 1918–1919 Pandemic Influenza: The Urban Impact in the Western World*, edited by Fred R. van Hartesveldt, 161–183 (New York: Edwin Mellen Press, 1992); Richard N. Adams, "Estado e Indígenas durante la epidemia de influenza de 1918–1919 en Guatemala," *Mesoamérica* 34 (1997): 484–485, 495, 547–548; Alfred Crosby, *Epidemic and Peace, 1918* (Westport, CT: Greenwood Press, 1977); Carey, *Our Elders Teach Us*, 118–129, 139–140.

57. Steven Palmer, *Launching Global Health: The Caribbean Odyssey of the Rockefeller Foundation* (Ann Arbor: University of Michigan Press, 2010).

58. Esquit, *Otros poderes*, 350; Jim Handy, "Chicken Thieves, Witches, and Judges: Vigilante Justice and Customary Law in Guatemala," *Journal of Latin American Studies* 36 (2004): 555.

59. Florencia E. Mallon, "Indian Communities, Political Cultures, and the State in Latin America, 1780–1990," *Journal of Latin American Studies* 24, no. Quincentenary Supplement: The Colonial and Post Colonial Experience (1992): 35–53.

60. Asturias, *El problema social del indio y otros textos* 101–103; Gibbings, *Our Time Is Now*.

61. Cited in Joseph A. Pitti, "Jorge Ubico and Guatemalan Politics in the 1920s" (PhD diss., University of New Mexico, Albuquerque, 1975), 217.

62. Paul Dosal, *Power in Transition: The Rise of Guatemala's Industrial Oligarchy, 1871–1994* (Westport, CN: Praeger, 1995), 54; Guillermo Diaz Romeu, "Del Régimen de Carlos Herrera a la Elección de Jorge Ubico," in *Historia General de Guatemala, Tomo V Epoca Contemporánea: 1898–1944*, edited by Jorge Luján Muñoz (director general) and J. Daniel Contreras R. (director del tomo) (Guatemala City, Guatemala: Asociación de Amigos del País, Fundación para la Cultura y el Desarrollo, 1996), 39; Gibbings, *Our Time Is Now*.

63. Carey " 'The Heart of the Country.' "

64. Carey, *Our Elders Teach Us*, 132–137, 183; Diaz Romeu, "Del Régimen de Carlos Herrera," 39–40; Dosal, *Power in Transition*, 55, 58, 63–64; Gibbings, *Our Time Is Now*.

65. Pitti, "Jorge Ubico and Guatemalan Politics"; Gibbings, *Our Time Is Now*.

66. Handy, *Gift of the Devil*, 93; James Dunkerley, "Guatemala Since 1930," in *Cambridge History of Latin America*, vol. 7, edited by Leslie Bethell, 214–216 (Cambridge, U.K.: Cambridge University Press, 1984); Nathan Whetten, *Guatemala: The Land and the People* (New Haven, CT: Yale University Press, 1961), 333.

67. Kenneth Grieb, *Guatemalan Caudillo: The Regime of Jorge Ubico, Guatemala 1931–1944* (Athens, OH: Ohio University Press, 1979), 34. Carey, *Our Elders Teach Us*, 203–206.

68. Benjamin D. Paul and Clancy McMahon "Mesoamerican Bonesetters," in *Mesoamerican Healers*, edited by Brad R. Huber and Alan R. Sandstrom, 243–69 (Austin: University of Texas Press, 2001).

69. Gibbings, *Our Time Is Now*.

70. Archivo Municipal de Sololá (AMS), "Libro de actas de sesiones municipales del 1-10-35 al 10-6-43," January 23, 1937, February 9, 1938; Carey, *Our Elders Teach Us*, 211–212.

71. Federíco Hernández de León, *Viajes presidenciales; breves relatos de algunas expediciones administrativos del General D. Jorge Ubico, presidente de la República*, vols. I and II (Guatemala City, Guatemala: Tipografía Nacional, 1940); Grieb, *Guatemalan Caudillo*, 35–37.

72. Gibbings, *Our Time Is Now*.

73. Grieb, *Guatemalan Caudillo*, 35.

74. Esquit, *La superación del indígena*; Kenneth Grieb, "El Gobierno de Jorge Ubico," in *Historia General de Guatemala, Tomo V Epoca Contemporánea: 1898–1944*, edited by Jorge Luján Muñoz and J. Daniel Contreras R., 45 (Guatemala City, Guatemala: Asociación de Amigos del País, Fundación para la Cultura y el Desarrollo, 1996); David Carey Jr., "Mayan Soldier-Citizens: Ethnic Pride in the Guatemalan Military 1925–1945," in *Military Struggle and Identity Formation in Latin America: Race, Nation and Community 1850–1950*, edited by Nicola Foote and René D. Harder Horst, 136–156 (Gainesville: University Press of Florida, 2010).

75. Warren, *Symbolism of Subordination*, 149; Rachel Sieder, " 'Paz, progreso, justicia y honradez': Law and Citizenship in Alta Verapaz during the Regime of Jorge Ubico," *Bulletin of Latin American Research* 19, no. 3 (2000): 301; Metz, *Chorti-Maya Survival*, 113; Carey, *I Ask for Justice*.

76. See, for example, Cindy Forster, *In the Time of Freedom: Campesino Workers in Guatemala's October Revolution* (Pittsburgh, PA: University of Pittsburgh Press, 2001); Carey, *Our Elders Teach Us*; Grieb, *Guatemalan Caudillo*; Jones, *Guatemala Past and Present* (Minneapolis: University of Minnesota Press, 1940), 74, 351; Vera Kelsey and Lilly de Jongh Osborne, *The Four Keys to Guatemala* (New York: Funk & Wagnalls, 1939), 60. For praise for Ubico from a contemporary Latin American author, see Santiago Arguello, *Barrios y Ubico: la obra creadora de dos constructores de naciones* (Havana, Cuba: Cia Tipografía, S.A., 1937), 33–34.

77. Compare, for example, Grieb, *Guatemalan Caudillo*; Forster, *Time of Freedom*; and Carey, *Our Elders Teach Us*.

78. Claudia Dary, *Relatos de los antiguos: estudios de la tradición oral de Comalapa, Chimaltenango* (Guatemala City: Universidad de San Carlos de Guatemala, 1992), 61.

79. Carey, *Our Elders Teach Us*, 195–219.

80. Regina Wagner, "Los alemanes en Guatemala" (PhD diss., Tulane University, New Orleans, 1992), 763–765; Gibbings, *Our Time Is Now*.

81. Piero Gleijeses, *Shattered Hope: The United States and the Guatemalan Revolution, 1944–1954* (Princeton, NJ: Princeton University Press, 1991), 28; Richard Adams,

512   DAVID CAREY JR.

"Ethnic Images and Strategies in 1944," in *Guatemalan Indians and the State*, edited by Carol Smith, 144–145 (Austin: University of Texas Press, 1990); Jim Handy, "A Sea of Indians": Ethnic Conflict and the Guatemalan Revolution, 1944–1952," *The Americas* 46, no. 2 (1989): 189–204.

82. Oscar de León Aragón, *Caída de un Régimen: Jorge Ubico-Federico Ponce, 20 de Octubre 1944* (Guatemala City, Guatemala: Facultad Latinoamerica de Ciencias Sociales, 1995); Jim Handy, *Revolution in the Countryside* (Chapel Hill: University of North Carolina Press, 1994), 23; Forster, *Time of Freedom*, 33–34; David Carey Jr. "A Democracy Born in Violence: Maya Perceptions of the 1944 Patzicía Massacre and the 1954 Coup," in *After the Coup: An Ethnographic Reframing of Guatemala 1954*, edited by Timothy J. Smith and Abigail E. Adams, 73–98 (Champaign: University of Illinois Press, 2011).

83. The estimates of Indigenous deaths vary greatly, but two independent studies indicate that somewhere between four and nine hundred Kaqchikel were killed during the three-day massacre, see Isabel Rodas and Edgar Esquit, *Élite Ladina-vanguardia indígena: de tolerancia a la violencia, Patzicia 1944* (Guatemala City, Guatemala: CAUDAL, 1997), 195; and Richard Adams, "Las masacres de Patzicía de 1944," *Revista Winak Boletín Intercultural* 7, nos. 1–4 (1992): 16–18, 23.

84. *Imparcial*, November 18 and 25, 1944; *Nuestro Diario*, October 30, 1944, 12; Esquit, *Otros poderes, nuevos desafíos*, 356 n.24; Forster, *Time of Freedom*, 93–94.

85. Julie Gibbings and Heather Vrana, *Out from the Shadow: Revisiting the Revolution from Post-Peace Guatemala* (Austin: University of Texas Press, 2020).

86. Lydia Crafts, "Mining Bodies: U.S. Medical Experimentation in Guatemala during the Twentieth Century" (PhD diss., University of Illinois, 2019); Susan M. Reverby, " 'Normal Exposure' and Inoculation Syphilis: A PHS 'Tuskegee' Doctor in Guatemala, 1946–1948," *Journal of Policy History* 23, no. 1 (2011): 7–28; Steven Palmer, "Caminos transnacionales de la Ciencia Aplicada en Guatemala," *Mesoamérica* 32, no. 53 (2011): 1–6; Cueto and Palmer, *Medicine and Public Health*, 127.

87. Gibbings, *Our Time Is Now*; Miguel Angel Asturias, *Sociologia Guatemalteca: el problema social del indio*, translated by Maureen Ahern, 99 (Tempe: Arizona State University, 1977).

88. Tarcena Arriola, *Etnicidad, estado y nación en Guatemala*; Casaús Arzú, *Guatemala*.

89. Anita Chary and Peter Rohloff, *Privatization and the New Medical Pluralism: Shifting Healthcare and Landscapes in Maya Guatemala* (New York: Lexington Books, 2015), xiii

90. *Diario de Centro América*, May 18, 1945.

91. Sieder, " 'Paz, progreso, justicia y honradez,' " 292; Susanne Jonas, *The Battle for Guatemala: Rebels, Death Squads, and U.S. Power* (Boulder, CO: Westview Press, 1991), 23; Forster, *In the Time of Freedom*, 2.

92. Forster, *In the Time of Freedom*, 7, 35–36, 46.

93. Handy, *Revolution in the Countryside*, 66, 72, 153, 202–204; Jim Handy, "National Policy, Agrarian Reform, and the Corporate Community during the Guatemalan Revolution, 1944–54," *Comparative Studies in Society and History*, 30 (October 1988): 705; Handy, *Gift of the Devil*, 110, 116; Richard Adams, *Crucifixion by Power* (Austin: University of Texas Press, 1970), 185; Grandin, *The Blood of Guatemala*, 198–219.

94. Jorge Skinner-Klee, ed., *Legislación indigenísta de Guatemala* (México, D.F.: Instituto Indigenísta Interamericano, 1954), 134–135; Handy, *Revolution in the Countryside*, 82–83, 93, 146; Handy, "Corporate Community, Campesino Organizations, and Agrarian Reform: 1950–1954," 165–169; Robert Wasserstrom, "Revolution in Guatemala: Peasants and Politics under the Arbenz

Government," *Comparative Studies in Society and History* 17 (1975): 474; Adams *Crucifixion by Power*, 396; Handy, "National Policy, Agrarian Reform, and the Corporate Community," 708.

95. Wasserstrom, "Revolution in Guatemala," 478; Handy "National Policy, Agrarian Reform, and the Corporate Community," 723; Handy, *Revolution in the Countryside*, 69–71, 205; Handy, *Gift of the Devil*, 129; Adams *Crucifixion by Power*, 444–446.

96. Handy, *Revolution in the Countryside*, 66, 72, 153, 202–204; Handy, "National Policy, Agrarian Reform, and the Corporate Community during the Guatemalan Revolution," 705; Handy, *Gift of the Devil*, 110, 116; Adams, *Crucifixion by Power*, 185; Grandin, *The Blood of Guatemala*, 198–219.

97. J. T. Way, *The Mayan in the Mall: Globalization, Development, and the Making of Modern Guatemala* (Durham, NC: Duke University Press, 2012), 67–123; Stephen M. Streeter, *Managing the Counterrevolution: The United States and Guatemala, 1954–1961* (Athens, OH: Ohio University Press, 2000); Dosal, *Power in Transition*; Manuela Camus, *La colonia Primero de Julio y la "clase media emergent"* (Guatemala City, Guatemala: FLACSO, 2005).

98. Rachel May, *Terror in the Countryside: Campesino Responses to Political Violence in Guatemala, 1954–1985* (Athens, OH: Ohio University Press, 2001).

99. Ibid.

100. Esquit, *Otros poderes*; Esquit, *La superación del indígena*; Grandin, *Blood of Guatemala*.

101. Konefal, *For Every Indio Who Falls*, 92.

102. Ibid., 168.

103. Alcohol too became a powerful trope during the civil war. Even as rural peoples feigned or embraced inebriation to avoid being conscripted into the military or recruited into insurgent groups, the Guatemalan National Police used "drunkenness" as a euphemism for suspected subversive activity; many alleged drunks who were arrested were never seen again. See Kirsten Weld, *Paper Cadavers: The Archives of Dictatorship in Guatemala* (Durham, NC: Duke University Press, 2014), 169.

104. Comisión para el Esclarecimiento Histórico (CEH), *Guatemala: Memoria del Silencio Tz'inil Na'tab'al* (Guatemala City: CEH, 1999); Oficina de Derechos Humanos del Arzobispado de Guatemala (ODHAG)— Proyecto Interdiocesano de Recuperación de la Memoria Histórica (REMHI), *Guatemala, Nunca más: Impactos de la violencia*, 4 vols. (Guatemala City, Guatemala: ODHAG, 1998).

105. ODHAG, *Nunca más*; CEH, *Guatemala, memoria del silencio*, conclusion, part 2, nn. 108–123.

106. Matilde González, "The Man Who Brought Danger to the Village: Representations of the Armed Conflict in Guatemala from a Local Perspective," *Journal of Southern African Studies* 26, no. 2 (2000): 321.

107. González, "Man Who Brought Danger to the Village," 335.

108. Amidst this horrific violence, Ríos Montt deployed long-winded evangelical sermons—informed by his church *El Verbo*—to legitimize his reign of terror. Dating to the late nineteenth-century, evangelical religions played an increasingly influential political role and ultimately challenged the hegemony of the Catholic Church. Protestant evangelical sects that preached abstinence and sobriety as paths to increased wealth and improved domestic relations caught on in the second half of the twentieth century. In turn, many Guatemalans became evangelicals during Ríos Montt's regime to shield themselves from his bloodthirsty regime.

109. Susan Burgerman, *Moral Victories: How Activists Provoke Multilateral Action* (Ithaca, NY: Cornell University Press, 2001); Jennifer Schirmer, *The Guatemalan Military Project: A Violence Called Democracy* (Philadelphia: University of Pennsylvania

Press, 1998); Rachel McCleary, *Dictating Democracy: The End of Violent Revolution* (Gainesville: University of Florida Press, 1999); Susanne Jonas, *Of Centaurs and Doves: Guatemala's Peace Process* (Boulder, CO: Westview Press, 2000).

110. Burgerman, *Moral Victories*; Schirmer, *Guatemalan Military Project*; McCleary, *Dictating Democracy*; Jonas, *Of Centaurs and Doves*.

111. David Carey Jr., "Guatemala's Green Revolution: Synthetic Fertilizer, Public Health, and Economic Autonomy in the Mayan Highlands," *Agricultural History* 83, no. 3 (Summer 2009): 283–322; Luisa Frank and Philip Wheaton, *Indian Guatemala: The Path to Liberation* (Washington, DC: EPICA Task Force, 1984), 39; Handy, *Gift of the Devil*, 221–224; Marilyn M. Moors, "Indian Labor and the Guatemalan Crisis: Evidence from History and Anthropology," in *Central America: Historical Perspectives on the Contemporary Crisis*, edited by Ralph Lee Woodward Jr., 75–76 (New York: Greenwood Press, 1988); Adams, "Población indígena en el estado liberal," 176.

112. Lisa North and Alan B. Simmons, eds., *Journeys of Fear: Refugee Return and National Transformation in Guatemala* (Montreal: McGill University Press, 1999); Clark Taylor, *Return of Guatemala's Refugees: Reweaving the Torn* (Philadelphia: Temple University Press, 1998); Beatriz Manz's *Paradise in Ashes: A Guatemalan Journey of Courage, Terror, and Hope* (Berkeley: University of California Press, 2004)

113. Metz, *Ch'orti'-Maya Survival in Eastern Guatemala*, 133, 243–245; Claudia Dary Fuentes, *Mujeres tradicionales y nuevos cultivos* (Guatemala City, Guatemala: FLACSO, 1991); Edward F. Fischer and Peter Benson, *Broccoli and Desire: Global Connections and Maya Struggles in Postwar Guatemala* (Stanford, CA: Stanford University Press, 2006); Carey, *Our Elders Teach Us*.

114. Metz, *Ch'orti'-Maya Survival in Eastern Guatemala*, 228; Walter Little, *Mayas in the Marketplace: Tourism, Globalization, and Cultural Identity* (Austin: University of Texas Press, 2004).

115. Chary and Rohloff, *Privatization and the New Medical Pluralism*.

116. Robert Williams, *Export Agriculture and the Crisis in Central America* (Chapel Hill: University of North Carolina Press, 1986); Christopher Chase-Dunn, Susanne Jonas, and Nelson Amaro, eds., *Globalization on the Ground: Postbellum Guatemalan Democracy and Development* (New York: Rowman & Littlefield, 2001); Thomas W. Walker and Ariel C. Armony, eds., *Repression, Resistance, and Democratic Transition in Central America* (Wilmington, DE: Scholarly Resources, 2000).

117. Little, *Mayas in Marketplace*.

118. Kay Warren in *Indigenous Movements and Their Critics: Pan-Maya Activism in Guatemala* (Princeton, NJ: Princeton University Press, 1998).

119. Charles Hale, *Más que un indio: Racial Ambivalence and Neoliberal Multiculturalism in Guatemala* (Santa Fe: University of New Mexico Press, 2006).

120. David Carey Jr. and Walter Little, "Reclaiming the Nation through Public Murals: Maya Resistance and the Reinterpretation of History," *Radical History Review* 106 (Winter 2010): 5–26.

121. Hilary E. Kahn, *Seeing and Being Seen: The Q'eqchi' Maya of Livingston, Guatemala, and Beyond* (Austin: University of Texas Press, 2006).

122. REMHI, *Guatemala Never Again!*

123. Weld, *Paper Cadavers*.

124. The oral testimonies of 103 K'iche' Maya survivors were crucial contributors to Judge Yassmín Barrios's 2013 verdict that found Ríos Montt guilty of genocide. Compelling and

consequential, oral testimonies and the literary genre in Latin America that emerged from them known as *testimonios* were subject to scrutiny. Partly because its powerful story and production have been so hotly contested, *I Rigoberta Menchú* is among the best-known volumes of the *testimonio* tradition. Although the Venezuelan anthropologist and journalist Elizabeth Burgos-Debray collaborated with Menchú to produce *I Rigoberta Menchú*, Burgos-Debray claimed authorship and royalties. As tension between Burgos-Debray and Menchú festered, anthropologist David Stoll insisted that Menchú lied about some aspects of her account, though he recognized the veracity of the broader outlines of her story—particularly that a military dictatorship massacred thousands of *indígenas* and forced many others into exile. Drawing upon the UN and Catholic Church reports and other sources, many scholars responded by pointing to the accuracy of her larger narrative and highlighting the nuances of Maya storytelling that has a long tradition of departing from full disclosure and accurate portrayals in native texts. See George W. Lovell and Christopher H. Lutz, "The Primacy of Larger Truths: Rigoberta Menchú and the Tradition of Native Testimony in Guatemala," in *The Rigoberta Menchú Controversy*, edited by Arturo Arias, 171–197 (Minneapolis: University of Minnesota Press, 2001). Menchú and others also pointed to the necessity to obscure details that might allow authorities to identify dissidents as the as civil war raged on. See Greg Grandin, *Who Is Rigoberta Menchú?* (New York: Verso Books, 2011), viii, 16–18; CEH, *Guatemala, memoria del silencio*. Many marginalized Guatemalans have an acute sense of how important history is to forging a more just future. See Juan Yool Gómez and Juan Kaqjay, *Tzijonik kan qate' qatata'* (Guatemala City, Guatemala: Universidad Rafael Landivar, 1990); Rainer Hostnig and Luis Vásquez Vicente, eds. *Nab'ab'l Qtanam: La memoria colectiva del pueblo Mam de Quetzaltenango* (Quetzaltenango, Guatemala: Centro de Capacitación e Investigación Campesina, 1994), x.

125. Pamela Engel and Christina Sterbenz, "The 50 Most Violent Cities In The World," *Business Insider*, Nov. 10, 2014. http://www.businessinsider.com/the-most-violent-cities-in-the-world-2014-11.

126. David Carey Jr. and Gabriela E. Torres, "Precursors to Femicide: Guatemalan Women in a Vortex of Violence," *Latin American Research Review* 45, no. 3 (2010): 142–164; Godoy-Paiz, "Not Just 'Another Woman,'" 90–91. Like bootlegging and moonshining, femicide is difficult to quantify since many perpetrators are never caught, let alone tried. Impunity makes legal records unreliable sources. To compile statistics, many groups depend on media reports, but those do not necessarily capture all the incidents. Programa de las Naciones para el Desarrollo, *Informe regional de desarrollo humano, 2013-2104. Seguridad ciudadana con rostro humano: diagnóstico y propuestas para América Latina* (New York: PNUD, 2013). Government reports tend to underestimate the number of femicides, see Instituto Nacional de Estadística, *Violencia contra la mujer, 2008-2013* (Guatemala City, Guatemala: Instituto Nacional de Estadística, 2014), 8. http://www.ine.gob.gt/sistema/uploads/2014/11/05/T1xrqTC3FToq96nhaAtLolQKfCKpeA3n.pdf. In 2011, Guatemala had the second highest femicide rate in the world. See Anna Alvazzi del Frate, "When the Victim Is a Woman," in *Geneva Declaration Secretariat* (2001): 113–144.

127. *Prensa Libre* June 4, 2010; James McKinley, "In Guatemala, Officers' Killings Echo Dirty War," *New York Times*, March 5, 2007, p. A1; William Fisher, "House Tackles 'Femicide' in Latin America," *Truthout*, July 4, 2007; NISGUA, "Guatemalan Congress Passes Femicide Law," April 18, 2008. http://www.nisgua.org/themes_campaigns/index.asp?id=3114.

128. Carlos Mendoza and Edelberto Torres-Rivas, *Linchamientos: barbarie o justiciar popular?* (Guatemala City, Guatemala: Facultad Latinoamericana de Ciencias Sociales, 2003); Daniel Núñez, "'There Are No Lynchings Here': The Invisibility of Crime and Extralegal Violence in an Eastern Guatemalan Town," in *Violence and Crime in Latin America: Representations and Politics*, edited by Gema Santamaría and David Carey Jr., 181–197 (Norman: University of Oklahoma Press, 2017).

129. John P. Hawkins, James H. McDonald, and Walter Randolph Adams, eds., *Crisis of Governance in Maya Guatemala: Indigenous Responses to a Failing State* (Norman: University of Oklahoma Press, 2013).

130. "Remittances in Guatemala, Record Figure in 2018," *CentralAmericaData.com*, January 10, 2019. https://www.centralamericadata.com/en/article/home/Remittances_in_Guatemala_Record_figure_in_2018.

131. Severo Martínez, *La patria del criollo: Ensayo de interpretación de la realidad colonial guatemalteca* (Guatemala City, Guatemala: Editorial Universitaria Centroamericana, 1973), 567–570, 599–600, 612, 617; Metz, *Ch'orti'-Maya Survival in Eastern Guatemala*, 56; Jean Piel, *Sajcabajá: muerte y resurrección de un pueblo de Guatemala, 1500-1970*, translated by Eliana Castro Ponslen (Mexico City, Mexico: Centre d'Études Mexicaines et Centraméricaines and Seminario de Integración Social, 1989); Luis Fernando Granados, "Everything Must Change So that Everything Can Stay the Same: Miscegenation, Racialization, and Culture in Modern Mesoamerica," in *Hemispheric Indigeneities: Native Identity and Agency in Mesoamerica, the Andes, and Canada*, edited by Miléna Santoro and Erick D. Langer (Lincoln: University of Nebraska Press, 2018).

132. Esquit, *Superación del indígena*.

133. AGCA, Indice 116, Chimaltenango, legajo 19a, expediente 42.

134. Irma A. Velásquez Nimatuj, *Pueblos Indígenas, estado y lucha por tierra en Guatemala* (Guatemala City, Guatemala: AVANCSO, 2008); Irma A. Velásquez Nimatuj, *La pequeña burguesía indígena comercial de Guatemala:desigualdades de clase, raza y género* (Guatemala City, Guatemala: AVANCSO-SERJUS, 2002); Demetrio Cojtí Cuxil, *Politicas para la reivindicacion de los Mayas de hoy: (Fundamentos de los derechos específicos del Pueblo Maya)* (Guatemala City, Guatemala: Cholsamaj, 1994), 60; Luis Enrique Sam Colop, "The Discourse of Concealment and 1992," in *Maya Cultural Activism in Guatemala*, edited by Edward F. Fischer and R. McKenna Brown, 109–112 (Austin: University of Texas Press, 1996); Warren, *Indigenous Movements and Their Critics*, 132–147.

FURTHER READING

Carey, David, Jr. *I Ask for Justice: Maya Women, Dictators, and Crime in Guatemala, 1898–1944*. Austin: University of Texas Press, 2013.

Casaus Arzú, Marta Elena. *Guatemala: Linaje y racism*. Guatemala City, Guatemala: Facultad Latinoamericana de Ciencias Sociales, 1995.

Esquit, Edgar. *La superación del indígena: la política de la modernización entre las élites indígenas de Comalapa, Siglo XX*. Guatemala City, Guatemala: Universidad de San Carlos, 2010.

Gibbings, Julie. *Our Time Is Now: Race and Modernity in Postcolonial Guatemala*. Cambridge, U.K.: Cambridge University Press, 2020.

GUATEMALA 517

Grandin, Greg. *The Blood of Guatemala: A History of Race and Nation.* Durham, NC: Duke University Press, 2000.

Handy, Jim. *Revolution in the Countryside: Rural Conflict and Agrarian Reform in Guatemala, 1944–1954.* Chapel Hill: University of North Carolina Press, 1994.

Konefal, Betsy. *For Every Indio Who Falls: A History of Maya Activism in Guatemala, 1960–1990.* Albuquerque: University of New Mexico Press, 2010.

Luján Muñoz, Jorge, ed. *Historia General de Guatemala.* 6 vols. Guatemala City, Guatemala: Asociación de Amigos del País, Fundación para la Cultura y el Desarrollo, 1996.

McCreery, David. *Rural Guatemala, 1760–1940.* Stanford, CA: Stanford University Press, 1994.

Oficina de Derechos Humanos del Arzobispado de Guatemala—Proyecto Interdiocesano de Recuperación de la Memoria Histórica (REMHI). *Guatemala, Nunca más: Impactos de la violencia.* 4 vols. Guatemala City, Guatemala: ODHAG, 1998.

Reeves, René. *Ladinos with Ladinos, Indians with Indians: Land, Labor, and Regional Ethnic Conflict in the Making of Guatemala.* Stanford, CA: Stanford University Press, 2006.

Taracena Arriola, Arturo. *Etnicidad, estado y nación en Guatemala, 1808–1944.* Antigua, Guatemala: Centro de Investigaciones Regionales de Mesoamérica, 2002.

Velásquez Nimatuj, Irma A. *Pueblos Indígenas, estado y lucha por tierra en Guatemala.* Guatemala City, Guatemala: AVANCSO, 2008.

Way, J. T. *The Mayan in the Mall: Globalization, Development, and the Making of Modern Guatemala.* Durham, NC: Duke University Press, 2012.

Weld, Kirsten. *Paper Cadavers: The Archives of Dictatorship in Guatemala.* Durham, NC: Duke University Press, 2014.

Woodward, Ralph Lee Jr. *Rafael Carrera and the Emergence of the Republic of Guatemala, 1821–1871.* Athens, GA: University of Georgia Press, 1993.

CHAPTER 19

....

HONDURAS

....

DARIO A. EURAQUE

BEYOND its borders, Honduras's long, complicated, and tragic history is often reduced to caricature, the so-called classic Banana Republic.[1] Bananas as the main exports from Honduras consolidated only during the latter 1910s. By 1929, Honduras was the main exporter of bananas in the world via two US corporations: United Fruit Company, created in 1899, and Standard Fruit Company, whose predecessors dated to the later nineteenth century. These companies often financed wars among political elites to secure privileged access to land, infrastructure concessions, and tax benefits detrimental to national interests. By the late 1920s, Honduras's banana agro-export economy became the main motor of a tragic modernity whose structural legacies remain with the country to this day. After the 1930s, United Fruit, headed then by Sam "the Banana Man" Zemurray, enjoyed close relations with the US State Department, and later the CIA. In 1954, Zemurray, drawing on decades of experiences in Honduras, helped elites engineer a military coup against one of the few democratically elected presidents of Guatemala, Jacobo Arbenz. He had challenged United Fruit's privileged concessions there.[2]

Banana Republic tropes often frame US assessments of resistance to its hegemony in Central America. Between 2006 and 2009, Manuel Zelaya Rosales became the first president of Honduras to consistently and publicly question US intervention in the country's policy and political priorities and affairs. He searched for an independent foreign policy, among other novel policies, including more inclusive economic and social programs. His populism appealed to deep-rooted Honduran resentment of being reduced by US diplomats and corporations to "the classic Banana Republic." In doing so, Zelaya often aligned himself with Latin America's historic anti-US nationalism and contemporary Leftist leaders, even though he is descendant of elite families from eighteenth-century Spanish colonialism. He was violently ousted in a coup in 2009 led by his former Minister of Defense, General Romeo Vasquez Velasquez. By June 2009 President Zelaya had often clashed with US foreign policies.[3] In her memoirs published in 2014, Hillary Clinton, President Barak Obama's former Secretary of State, characterized Zelaya as "a throwback to the caricature of a Central American strongman, with his white cowboy hat, dark mustache, and fondness for Hugo Chavez and Fidel Castro."[4]

There is little doubt that Clinton's caricature is grounded in the clichés and stereotypes of US-generated myths about Banana Republics, including those deployed by Clinton as she and others in her inner circle colluded to overthrow President Zelaya, and then keep him from returning to power late in 2009.[5] On June 28, 2019, the Honduran people witnessed the tenth anniversary of the coup that destroyed almost thirty years of civil, nominally democratic government, a unique period since independence from Spain in the 1820s.

With President's Zelaya's violent removal from power, one expert observer noted early on that

> the concept of coup underwent a new innovation in the Honduran context. The events of 28 June 2009 constituted neither a classic coup nor a self-coup. Yet they did equate to a coup in the sense that an elected head of state was involuntarily, forcefully, and physically removed, not only from office and the presidential palace but also from the country, by elements of the military. The coup was not classic in that the military never seized power through its actions; rather, it carried out orders from the Supreme Court. To some extent, the coup was clouded by the actions of the supreme court and congress. Whereas the former issued a formal arrest warrant against Zelaya, the latter quickly appointed Micheletti, the closest in the constitutional line of succession as the president of congress, to succeed Zelaya as president.[6]

The military repression unleashed against the varied and deep resistance to the coup was not clouded. It was violent and widespread, and it drew on a deep and long history of state practices that went back to the establishment of the Honduran nation after independence from Spanish colonialism.

THE LEGACIES OF SPANISH COLONIALISM AND THE NEW NATION-STATE, 1820S–1840S

"Nations," Eric Hobsbawm argued some time ago, "do not make states and nationalisms but the other way around."[7] In Honduras, the process of modern state formation as the basis of nation-building began in the 1820s after formal independence from Spain. However, the process did not assume strength until well after the 1870s. Numerous problems confronted nation builders who undertook that task after independence in 1821, and after becoming a member of the United Provinces of Central America. These problems ranged from virtually nonexistent transportation infrastructure, and a geographical topography of mountains that divided production centers from integrating in Honduras, and actually connected the territory's western and eastern regions in opposite directions, toward Guatemala and El Salvador west and southwest, and toward Nicaragua east and southeast. Most of the early nation's problems originated in the colonial period, intensified between the 1820s and 1870s, and especially after the 1880s when the period known as *La Reforma* (The Reform), which took hold in the latter 1870s, became effective. After the 1880s and 1890s, Honduras emerged as a country with a very specific economic structure whose connections to the world economy affected the country's different geographic regions rather distinctively. The Honduran North Coast slowly accumulated a social and political prominence intimately connected to the peculiarities of the region's class structure, and with a specific relation to the rest of the nation's territory. The North Coast of Honduras, a Caribbean coast, lacked the rigid *hacienda*-peasant hierarchy of land ownership on the interior's larger population centers. In many ways it was a frontier area with comparatively more fluid class identities, and more mobile racial and ethnic sensibilities that allowed for a political culture less controlled by the weak state almost five hundred miles away.[8]

In the 1820s, the Honduran population amounted to about 130,000 people, of which an estimated 60,000+ consisted of many Indigenous ethnicities recovering from their demographic collapse in the sixteenth century. Then, the Indigenous population amounted to about eight hundred thousand, very roughly divided into the following categories: Indians, *mestizos* or *ladinos* (mixture of indian and white Spanish), *mulato* (mixture of white and black), and *pardo* (mixture of indian and black). (The latter, in the vast northeastern region bordering with Nicaragua, the pardos were often referred to as *zambo*). The census of 1804 added another category to this complicated colonial heritage, the *Garifuna*, a Black population of more recognizably African descent which the Spaniards had introduced as slaves and servants beginning in the sixteenth century, probably no more than two thousand. In 1804, the Garifuna amounted to about five thousand people, most of whom lived on the country's Caribbean coast. Most of this Black population on the Caribbean coast lived in colonies of escaped slaves from the interior, or consisted of Garifuna recently deported there by the British from St. Vincent. Honduras eventually was officialized as a "mestizo" nation, bereft of the complex colonial and postcolonial racial and ethnic identities lived in everyday life. By the mid-twentieth century, its ancient Indigenous past was largely reduced to its Maya monuments and tourism in western Honduras, a process I have called the "Mayanization" of Honduras.[9] The African-descendant populations of the Caribbean coast represented only a tiny minority of the Honduran population of the nineteenth century. By 1900, Honduras's population was about 543,841, and by 1950 it had almost doubled to 1,368,605.

Between the 1770s and the 1820s, Honduran elites enjoyed three basic sources of wealth: a tobacco factory near the provincial capital of Comayagua, exploitation of silver ores near Tegucigalpa, and the domestic cattle market. In the late eighteenth century, all three enjoyed substantial profits. Unfortunately, these exports collapsed early in the nineteenth century, shortly after independence from Spain.[10] Civil wars in the 1820s further aggravated the collapse.[11] Before the 1870s, a few exports alternated as the country's most profitable exports: hardwoods, and mineral products, mahogany and silver and gold to England and the United States.[12] While coffee plants were known in Honduras by the 1840s and 1850s, unlike elsewhere in Central America, coffee commercialization and exports from Honduras only became important in the mid-twentieth century.

The Unique Political Economy
of Bananas in Honduras, 1880s–1950s

Unlike the pre-1990s scholarship on nation-state formation in Central America, a consensus has since emerged among historians regarding the following propositions: Central American elites—Liberals and Conservatives—deployed liberalizing policies toward the Catholic Church, state, land, and people long before the Liberal Reform period of the 1870s. These policies promoted the "coffee and banana republics" established thereafter. Second, this occurred by the 1850s and 1860s, not because of a unified commitment to Liberalism but, rather, because of local responses to new incentives offered to export agriculture unavailable before: political stability and the stimulus and cost savings offered by maritime transportation on the Pacific coast of the region, itself a process linked to the demands of the California Gold Rush of the late 1840s.[13] This was most often done via legislative concessions for import duties for railroad construction, and generous tax exemptions on land purchase or rental, most often without local input.

Consistent fiscal revenues never energized the Honduran state before the 1870s, from lumber, cattle, or silver mining exports. This happened only with bananas, especially after the 1890s, when coffee was already important elsewhere in Central America. Honduran coffee exports only assumed national importance after the 1960s. More importantly, coffee in Honduras did not become a key source of financial capital. In Honduras bananas became the main exports, albeit controlled by US capital. Thus, popular lore and even scholarship in the United States often reduced the country's complexities to the trope of a "Banana Republic," in social science terms of dependency theory pioneered by Edelberto Torres-Rivas, the so-called banana enclave.[14]

The work of Robert G. Williams is important for framing nation-state formation and political regimes in Honduras after 1870, particularly when comparing and contrasting coffee's role in that the process.[15] According to Williams, the different intraregional political cultures and government structures existent in Central America after the 1850s exhibited "patterns of governance" founded during the "moment of construction of Central American states"—that is, when "coffee townships" emerged politically dominant (1840s–1900). He also argues that local elites and patriarchs within the coffee township boundaries eventually coordinated cross-regional politics against the pre-coffee national governments, largely legacies of the late colonial period, including descendants of colonial creoles. He notes that an element key to this process involved using police and military forces to enforce labor discipline as well as institutionalizing violent, elitist, and exclusivist "patterns of governance," especially in Guatemala, El Salvador, and Nicaragua.[16] Therefore, political cultures and government structures that emerged between the 1840s and 1900 persisted despite agro-export diversification and even limited industrialization in the twentieth century.[17] In stark contrast to the other countries in Central America, "Honduras did not develop a national class of coffee growers capable of building a national state."[18] Instead, "Honduras retained a state that lived of concessions, [and] the government was run by a succession of generals and lawyers."[19] This is what made Honduras radically different from its counterparts in Central America. In this context, it is best to understand Honduras as a "concessionary state," that is, a state whose capacity to generate revenues for administration and the exercise of bureaucratic power originated not in taxes and tariff regimes but in marketing and selling concessionary privileges to national resources. This created a corresponding political culture among its elites that remained a core business model and policy strategy among successive generations into the twenty-first century.[20] It has representatives among the descendant elite generations today, some involved in the coup of 2009.

In Honduras, other processes were relevant, including the problem of the old foreign debt, associated with railroad construction as it intensified in the 1860s and 1870s, *before* the Liberal Reform period (1877–1883), when agro-exports were fomented with greater consistency than ever before. That is, after the 1840s, when Honduran governments tried to float bonds in British financial markets for more infrastructure developments like railroads, the debt assumed in the 1830s originating in the federation period had to either be totally paid or have a great percentage canceled. This left little for actual investments prioritized by the states at the time, especially given that exports did not produce much revenue on which to draw or that could be offered as collateral.[21]

According to the most detailed study of Honduran debt in the nineteenth century, "by 1888, one observer calculated the debt at £12 million. This sum equaled approximately £55 per inhabitant or about £210,000 per mile of railroad constructed. The same observer estimated that, at prevailing land values, Honduras could not repay such a debt by selling its entire national territory."[22] In short, between the 1870s and 1900 elites from coffee townships in the Departments of Santa Barbara and Comayagua, where coffee was relatively important, never seemed to have considered regional alliances for insurrections against the concessionary state. Something different happened in Honduras.

The fact is that by 1900, Washington S. Valentine, a New York-based capitalist, had purchased the main silver mines near Tegucigalpa once owned by Honduran elites who promoted Liberal-era reforms deepening nation-state formation since the mid-1870s via export agriculture. Valentine's family was favored with concessions for duty imports for building the mines by the only coffee plantation president of Honduras, Luis Bogran. He died in 1895 in exile in Guatemala. His children moved to San Pedro Sula in the 1910s, abandoned serious coffee investments in Santa Barbara, and became banana planters. By the 1920s they became banana planters in co-investments with Samuel Zemurray when he owned the Cuyamel Fruit Company. By 1929 when Zemurray sold the Cuyamel Fruit Company to the United Fruit Company, old Luis Bogran's children became small shareholders in United Fruit.[23] Finally, Valentine also secured control of Honduras's so-called Interoceanic Railroad, which exported bananas, not coffee or silver, a railroad that itself had a sordid financial history.[24] Between 1869 and the early 1870s the Honduran state had assumed even more loans in London and Paris than those inherited from the 1820s and 1830s, mostly to finance only about sixty miles of railroad in the Sula Valley and a port on the Caribbean Coast called Puerto Cortes. It was supposed to reach the Pacific shores of the country, but large percentages of the funds were either stolen or ill-spent, and many efforts in the nineteenth century to complete the project failed. The debt accumulated and interests were not canceled until 1953, and during its long history was yet another extraordinary drain of economic and political capital on Honduran state formation.[25] In fact, the mechanisms for the corruption associated with the interoceanic debacle became a model for other concessionary fiascoes in the twentieth century.[26]

As to the issue of how bananas came to dominate Honduran exports and not coffee, Washington S. Valentine's control of the North Coast Interoceanic Railroad between the 1890s and 1912 is critical. What was this mining tycoon based in Tegucigalpa transporting during almost two decades? He was transporting mostly bananas, bananas providing a small export tax to a state deeply indebted to the British bondholders associated with the debt incurred for financing that railroad since the 1870s. Regional elites, nonetheless, began migrating toward the Caribbean coast and focused capital and political energies. By 1900, coffee investments were not a priority or even on the agenda. By the end of the nineteenth century, most Honduran elites saw banana exports as the key to "national" progress, not coffee or silver.[27] By the 1920s the old Interoceanic Railroad continued carrying bananas when it was controlled by Zemurray via a state-sanctioned contract signed in 1920.

In 1940, the British ambassador in Tegucigalpa characterized United Fruit's general manager as the second most influential person in Honduras—second only to President Tiburcio Carias (1933–1949). The ambassador could have added that the general manager of Standard Fruit Company, the other key banana company on the North Coast, was then the third most influential person in Honduras. On the other hand, the British Ambassador's 1940 comments should be considered given the character of General Carias's relations with the banana companies especially beginning in 1933.[28]

Social and Political Context of the Political Economy of Bananas, 1880s–1954

One of the central implications of the lack of social and political cohesion among Honduran elites and their commitment to a national development project,[29] besides their collective subservience to US capital, was their commitment to organizing violence for political ends, either among themselves and/or by involving subaltern populations in their confrontations, especially before the 1950s. The use of electoral violence was even more common during the supposedly more "stable" *Reforma* and post*Reforma* era, that is, between the 1870s and 1890s.

US officials recognized this very well. Late in 1914, John Ewing, the US Minister in Tegucigalpa, recognized recent State Department instructions that he "write fully and frankly concerning all matters that enter into or tend to control the internal political situation and conditions here, and I would not be reporting unreservedly if I failed to direct the attention of the Department to a source which is an ever present factor. I speak of the United Fruit Company and its subsidiaries and its railroad connections."[30] After recognizing United Fruit's economic system and its relationship to concessions, Ewing admitted that the company, "in order to obtain these concessions and privileges and to secure their undisturbed enjoyment, it has seen fit to enter actively into the internal politics of these countries, and it has pursued this course so systematically and regularly until it now has its ramifications in every department of the government and is a most important factor in all political movements and actions."[31]

Ewing also remarked that "government officials throughout the whole of the North Coast are subject to its influence and it is openly asserted that even in the Cabinet it has its friends and advocates."[32] Finally, "President [Francisco Bertrand] and some of his Cabinet are chafing under its domination but feel themselves too weak to act contrary to its demands unless assured of the support of our Government."[33] As US Minister John Ewing put it from Tegucigalpa in 1914, "the higher classes are composed of wealth, education, and refinement and these classes really constitute the governing element and dominate all public action. There is, however, no unity of purpose or action amongst them. They are divided into numberless factions, each faction representing some individual of dominant intellectual ability, or qualities of leadership, or possession of such personal charms as attract or draw other men unto them."[34]

After the 1950s, repressing subalterns became much more important as organized segments of these populations mobilized in defense of themselves and for their social, economic, and political rights and hopes, especially when unionization was legalized after the 1950s. What is striking in the social and political history of Honduras until the 1950s is the degree of lethal violence that elite Hondurans wrought on themselves, including generating a political culture of profound authoritarianism and practices of governance, involving, of course, mostly males as active and sanctioned agents of such practices. Between the 1840s and the late 1960s, formal politics in Honduras was, as Rina Villars has documented it, a patriarchal practice. As Honduran feminist Graciela Bogran put it in 1952, until that time "citizenship was a privilege accorded to one sex only."[35]

After the 1840s, albeit rarely researched systematically, a key problem has been the depth of Honduras's postcolonial national "political anarchy," in its extreme version civil wars, beginning of course with the wars over the Central American Federation from 1824 to 1839. According to rough calculations, about seven thousand Central Americans died in military engagements between 1821 and 1842. This amounted to about 0.6 percent of Central America's population in 1821 and 0.4 percent of the population in the 1840s. During this period some seven hundred Hondurans were killed in twenty-seven battles. These deaths represented about 0.39 percent of the country's population in the 1840s, and about 0.51 percent of the population in the 1820s. Military engagements during this period rarely produced more than fifty to one hundred deaths. This was probably true for most conflicts between 1827 and 1879 in Honduras.[36] During almost

526   DARIO A. EURAQUE

any twenty-year period between 1840 and 1900, except for the 1860–1880 decades, the number of battles that occurred was roughly equal to the thirty-odd conflicts reported for the 1820–1840 period. The number of casualties did increase, probably due to more deadly firepower, about which we know very little. It was the beginnings of what Robert H. Holden has characterized as a time of "caudillos in search of an army."[37]

Between 1870 and 1949, Hondurans killed themselves in 146 military engagements, probably involving mobilizations of no more than five thousand troops in any war. Few researchers have offered data on casualties sustained in the battles. In 1928, the US Embassy in Tegucigalpa offered rough estimates on the major civil wars between the 1890s and 1924, and offered data on casualties for the following civil wars: five thousand dead for the 1892–1894 battles, the most bloody war of the nineteenth century; fifteen hundred dead for the 1906–1907 war; "only" five hundred dead during the 1910–1911 battle; twice that number in the 1919 conflict; and, for the most macabre battle of this century, the 1924 civil war, again, about five thousand dead.[38] Therefore, the other military engagements recorded during this period probably rarely produced more than fifty or one hundred deaths, like numbers registered for conflicts recorded between 1827 and 1879.[39] When General López Gutierrez assumed office in 1920, his government contracted a US State Department financial expert who in 1921 filed an extensive report on government finances. He began his report thus: "The history of Honduras shows clearly the grave effects of civil wars upon public finances. The expenditures of the Department of War completely dominate the financial situation during a revolution and for many succeeding months."[40]

Between 1839 and 1939 government organization and administration was grounded in nine different constitutions. Robert Holden has compiled other data that illustrate these tragic processes. According to Holden,

> from 1824 to 1900, Honduras passed through 98 changes of government, an average of 1.3 per year. Although the rate of governmental change fell to almost one every two years between 1900 and 1933, the annual rate of lethal civil conflict rose 66 percent in the second period, compared to the nineteenth century. From 1824–1950, the executive branch changed hands 116 times; only thirteen presidents held office for four or more years and most presidents gained office using violence. Of the eighteen heads of state between 1883 and 1948, nine identified themselves as professional soldiers (with the rank of general) who governed the country for 60 percent of the period. Of the ten administrations that governed from 1892 to 1919, only one was initially elected to office and only one retired at the end of his term; the heads of all but two called themselves generals.[41]

Of course, the bloody battles over the concessionary state represented a consistent drain on the little revenues available for basic bureaucratic state administration and formation, to say nothing of investments in education and health and "development." Between the late nineteenth century and the late 1910s, the structural problem linked to the concessionary system became enmeshed in the drain on revenues and loans promoted by the incessant insurrections promoted by virtually every political leader of either of the country's two main political parties, the Liberal Party and the National Party. The major political figures associated with these parties since the 1870s paid lip service to a nineteenth-century Liberalism that in economic and political terms can be summarized thus: it was a Liberalism that promoted an intensification of the export agricultural trade by means of the following incentives: stimulating the easy purchase of public lands, the commercialization of common lands via rental or open sale, and tax-free importation of agricultural tools and seeds for export crops; politically, both parties, in many constitutions and laws promoted freedom of religion, assembly, and press and expanding the suffrage for males. Only the latter principle was respected by both parties into the 1950s. By the 1920s these parties consolidated into a bipartisan system of spoils and job patronage. In Honduras, noted a detailed study written in the 1940s, "personal and partisan factors dominate all phases of administration at every level in government. The merit system is as foreign to the thinking of the typical Honduran politico as it was to the supporters of Jackson in the 1830s in the US."[42]

The Honduran political system before the 1960s never represented a form of general popular and participatory electoral democracy, especially one that engendered a culture of civic participation. There are various issues relevant here besides incessant "lethal" political and military violence. First, formal exclusionary constitutional restrictions on political citizenship and electoral participation as candidates and voters remained in force until the 1890s, including literacy and property requirements and age-based exclusions. As late as 1877, only 7.25 percent of the population could vote, all male, and mostly propertied and literate. Women did not secure the right to vote in presidential elections until 1955.

This period saw the emergence in Honduras of political groupings resembling modern political parties, the Liberal and National parties. Known as "electoral clubs," they developed within the elite groupings that could participate formally in the political system. When given the chance, parties used almost any means, including force or fraud, to impose overwhelming electoral victories, in large part, as William S. Stokes astutely asserted in a classic study long ago, because all Honduran constitutions since 1824 insisted "that a presidential candidate receive an absolute majority for election."[43] In the case of pluralities, Congress was charged with selecting a winner among the candidates. When candidates winning pluralities did not receive a favorable vote in Congress, they almost invariably revolted, although not always successfully, but nonetheless exacting terrible material, civic, and human costs well into the 1930s.

A very real and only recently studied cost of the old civil wars and governing political culture for the prospects of democratic modernization in Honduras in the twentieth century has been researched by Kevin C. Coleman.[44] According to Coleman, during all kinds of political contexts in Honduras between the 1890s and the mid-1950s, from civil wars to violent electoral strife and campaigning and/or the threat thereof, Honduran political leaders, perhaps like no other country in Central America, suspended "the rule of law" as the way to hold on to "power, divvied up resources, and kept uppity citizens in check, all while feigning adherence to the country's constitution."[45] Coleman characterizes the 1890s to 1950s political history as peppered with governments he calls "constitutional dictatorships" when Honduran's political life was mostly experienced during states of siege and similar states of suspended civic rights.

BEYOND THE CONCESSIONARY STATE, 1954–1982

After the 1950s, the economic legacies of the postcolonial period and the social and political implications of Honduras's agro-export modernization witnessed certain critical changes that distanced the late twentieth-century generations from the more notorious tragedies of the first 150 years of independence. The changes are best illustrated by the emergence of powerful labor and peasant movements whose organizational capacities finally forced the old parties and governing but divided elites to address inequality, educational, health, and social security needs that were becoming part of modern societies and even prescribed in the constitutions since 1924.[46]

In May and June 1954, the US banana corporations in Honduras faced the largest and most far-reaching labor strike they ever confronted, what Ramon Amaya Amador, a communist intellectual of the period and founder of the country's Communist Party called, Honduras's "Paris Commune." At the time, US Ambassador William Willauer was involved in coordinating the overthrow of Jacobo Arbenz, the Guatemalan government's president with his diplomatic counterparts in Guatemala and elsewhere in Central America.[47] Samuel Zemurray's managers in United Fruit Company in Honduras were helping the process. But surprisingly to most Hondurans, the workers won the strike, leading to securing the right to strike and union organization. It involved about thirty-five thousand workers on the Caribbean Coast, and it was led by communists, left-wing liberals, and laborers radicalized in the process of the struggles. For sixty days, workers paralyzed not only banana company operations but all other economic sectors associated with the export economy. Virtually all Hondurans supported the strike, including, albeit quietly, most elites customarily subservient to the US economic and political interests generally, and especially to the banana companies.

During the latter years of the Carias dictatorship, in 1947, John D. Erwin, the US Ambassador to Honduras, reported that only six millionaire families lived in the country, and not one family possessed $2 million or more.[48] An International Monetary Fund (IMF) study from 1949 noted that "few fortunes exceed more than 500,000 dollars" and "a man whom Hondurans call rich could scarcely be characterized as such in any other Latin American country." More importantly, the IMF study concluded that "none of the national fortunes have been amassed through agriculture."[49] That is, agricultural capitalism beyond the banana agro-export economy was not the basis of great individual wealth and economic power well into the 1950s. A confidential report generated by informants to the US Embassy in 1949 that listed shareholders of the country's only two banks, the Banco de Honduras and the Banco Atlántida, when compared to lists of Honduran banana planters between 1900 and the 1940s, has allowed us to confirm that none of the major shareholders in the financial system originated with capital from Honduran banana growers. This means that the few banana growers who did not succumb to the foreign banana companies were not among the few wealthy capitalists in Honduras well into the 1950s.[50] It is not surprising, then, that William S. Stokes in the latter 1940s felt comfortable arguing that Honduras's structure of land tenure could "in time be the basis for the development of a kind of rural, agrarian democracy."[51] In short, Stokes inferred that the lack of great wealth concentrated in land, especially for export to the world market, translated into the existence of a large class of independent yeomen farmers with democratic aspirations, presumably capable at some point of wrestling power away from the Liberal and National parties. That did not happen.

Along with labor legislation passed after 1949, the negotiations consequent to the 1954 strike finally opened the way for legal unionization in Honduras, including unionization of the banana plantation workers. In February 1955, the state legalized fifty unions, including the union of greatest importance, namely, the thousands of workers of United Fruit Company. Some of these dissolved, and others fused with others, but legal unionization nonetheless continued after 1955. By the 1960s, Honduran workers had achieved the highest level of labor unionization in Central America. In 1961, union membership in Central America amounted to 109,000 workers, with Honduran labor representing about 16 percent of the total, some eighteen thousand laborers, and already greater than labor union membership in Nicaragua and Guatemala, and second to Costa Rica and El Salvador. In 1967, Honduran union membership amounted to 22,377 workers. Between 1967 and 1970, union membership jumped from 22,377 to 30,779. By this point Honduran labor was well on its way to becoming the most organized working class in Central America.[52]

This also allowed for significant organization of rural peoples, mostly peasants in the south and north of the country, whose leaders often received material and logistical support from the banana plantation unions, and largely from the Liberal Party. Personalities and segments of this party not only supported unionization but an Agrarian Reform Law in 1962 that distributed thousands of acres of land and provided credit via development banks. Thousands of peasants also organized rural cooperatives even for banana production, especially by the 1970s, often in old banana plantation lands abandoned by the US corporations. An Industrial Development Law in 1958 promoted the elimination of the old concessionary state, and promoted industrialization with other incentives, mainly state investments in public–private enterprises, and mainly in the country's two main cities, San Pedro Sula and Tegucigalpa.

By the mid-1970s, about 15 percent of the country's gross domestic product (GDP) originated in the manufacturing sector, often in enterprises in joint ventures with foreign capital subsidized by the Honduran post-concessionary state. Another Agrarian Reform Law in 1973, more far reaching than its counterpart from 1962, led to a backlash spearheaded by new rural capitalists who invested in agro-export opportunities virtually nonexistent in the late 1950s: processed beef exports, sugar, and even some cotton. While these new economic sectors generated new opportunities in the late 1970s, the income distribution remained limited, and even regressed under explosive demographic growth rates. By 1980, the Honduran population reached 3.5 million, double the population in 1950.

Paradoxically, during these rather important social and economic changes in Honduran society after the 1950s, the political system and culture did not experience profound structural changes, as many expected after General Carias left power early in 1949. The government of Juan Manuel Galvez between 1949 and 1954 might be characterized as a period of "transition" similar to the end of the years of dictatorship of Francisco Franco in Spain in the early 1970s, with the great difference that there the transition from the 1970s to the 1980s led to a flowering of democracy and a wide-open political culture. Something different occurred in Honduras, yet distinct from what happened elsewhere in Central America. Other than the democratic regime of Juan Manuel Galvez, a United Fruit Company lawyer since the 1920s, the decades between 1933 and 1957 are best characterized as decades of dictatorships and patriarchal coup plotting, violence, and intrigue among the leaders of the Liberal and National parties, including Galvez and his enemies in the National Party and beyond.[53]

In the 1957 elections, the first in which a new generation of women could vote in Honduras, Dr. Ramon Villeda Morales, a Liberal Party upstart who benefited from the liberalization generated by the banana strike of 1954, received labor support and was elected president, the first Liberal Party head of state elected since 1929. General Carias had kept a tight grip on the military, and during the Villeda Morales government the Liberal Party's alliance with labor and peasant activism managed to survive constant characterizations of communist policies and commitments attributed to the Cuban Revolution's influence and even to Soviet communism. Besides Agrarian Reform Legislation, Villeda Morales signed Honduras's first Labor Code, as well as Social Security legislation. By late 1963, National Party militants of the newer generations allied themselves with the ambitious young military leaders beyond the control of old Carias and his followers, and organized a bloody military coup that, on October 3, 1963, ousted Villeda Morales from office and sent him into exile to Costa Rica almost in the same way that Manuel Zelaya Rosales suffered ousting on June 28, 2009.[54]

The 1963 coup was led by Villeda Morales's Minister of Defense, Col. Oswaldo Lopez Arellano, who remained the military head of state until he was ousted by the military in 1975 after receiving a $1 million bribe from the successor to United Fruit, United Brands. The scandal came to be called, "Banana-Gate."[55] While General Lopez Arellano allowed elections in 1971, in December 1972 he ousted the National Party winner of the 1971 elections. After 1972, generals and colonels governed as heads of state, and they also served as ministers and directors of key state agencies until 1982. Political culture and the security forces became militarized in a "modern" way different from decades earlier in the century yet grounded in the legacies that Kevin C. Coleman documented for the 1890–1950s period. During the 1970s, most members of the Liberal and National parties served the military governments while simultaneously conspiring to return to power, as their grandfathers had, and as their children do today.[56] The military governments that ruled Honduras until early 1982, when Liberal Party traditionalist Roberto Suazo Cordova assumed the presidency for four years, tolerated a degree of controlled agricultural and industrial reformism. Pressured by US foreign policymakers, who feared a revolution in Honduras like the one achieved by the Sandinistas in Nicaragua in July 1979, General Policarpo Paz Garcia (1978–1981) called for National Constituent Assembly elections in 1980.[57] A transition away from the military reformism of the 1970s to democracy resulted in the Constitution existent today, the twelfth since 1839. Depending on how one counts, in Latin America only Bolivia has had more constitutions than Honduras.

THE RISE AND FALL OF HONDURAN DEMOCRACY, 1982–2019

In Honduras, the military governments of the 1970s—now largely equipped and financed with US government funds, with their chief officers trained in US military academies—faced social and political dynamics in countries with which the nation shares borders in Central America: Guatemala, El Salvador, and Nicaragua. In some ways these dynamics were similar to those that marked the first fifty years of the twentieth century. In the latter 1970s and into the 1980s, when tens of thousands of civilians were killed in insurrections against military dictatorships elsewhere in the region, mostly at the hand of the region's armed forces and specially created "death squads," Honduras largely escaped that bloodbath of the Cold War that ended with the fall of the Soviet Union in 1989. The 1990s opened with a degree of hope for the prospects of the benefits of democracy, albeit dim again by the beginning of the next decade.[58] This is largely the problem to analyze here.

Two decades ago, Marta Elena Casaus Arzu argued that the transitions to civilian rule in Central America between 1979 and 1990, including via the National Party of Rafael Leonardo Callejas in Honduras (1990–1994), represented a generalized tendency in the entire region: the return to power of the traditional Central American oligarchies through a social and economic "metamorphosis" that the descendants of these elites promoted.[59] What did Casaus Arzu mean by a socioeconomic metamorphosis? The landed elites of Central America, including those with colonial heritage, in the 1960s and 1970s diversified their landed holdings, especially from coffee, into industrial and financial capitalism, and even into newer forms of agricultural capitalism. Business organizations, namely, "economic groups" or holding companies, associated with certain families and associates and more intimately connected to international capital.[60]

This oligarchical metamorphosis, argued Casaus Arzu, drew on local capital, but especially on shared investments with multinational capital, mainly from the United States, and in the process became associated with segments of capitalist elites averse to old military dictatorships and repression as the primary solution to political problems. Finally, the new investments also drew on new financial institutions sanctioned by state intervention supportive of industrial capitalism in Central America and the Americas as a whole—in Central America, the Central Bank for Economic Integration (BCIE) is a good example; and in Latin America, the Inter-American Bank for Economic Development (IDB) is an excellent example. These institutions were also staffed with technocratic elites averse to anti-democratic regimes and politics, and often the children of old oligarchic elites as well.

Years ago, my analysis of Honduran economic elites, the legacies of the concessionary state, and its social and political implications, led me to very different conclusions from Casaus Arzu's hypothesis. I believe that it remains valid today. While I agreed with the general character of a metamorphosis of old oligarchical interests, I instead argued that the metamorphosis began in the 1880–1940s period, intensified during the 1960s and 1970s, and failed to include the most prominent colonial families in Honduras. The latter means that Honduran landed elites who did diversify into agro-exporting did not appeal to colonial familial ties as a mechanism for ensuring economic solidarity, especially via marriages. More importantly, the new economic power in the commercial and industrial sectors in Honduras in the 1960s and 1970s, and today, lay with the immigrant families of Arab descent, mostly Palestinians, and even with some of the Jewish families who arrived in Honduras mostly after the 1920s, who only became naturalized citizens in the late 1940s and 1950s. Most emblematic in contemporary history is Jaime Rosenthal Oliva (1936–2019), who passed away in 2019.[61] Paradoxically, however, as younger generations of these powerful families, even when often intermarried with elite Honduran mestizo families, they lacked the cultural political capital necessary for engagement with the vast majority of the impoverished Honduran population, particularly in electoral campaigns.[62] That is, these generations did not have mentors in the old Liberal and National parties to socialize them in the "arts" of campaign politics, particularly in rural Honduras, that generations of mestizo politicians had enjoyed since the latter nineteenth century. This has largely not changed outside major urban areas even in 2020.

Despite laws promoting foreign immigration to Honduras since the latter nineteenth century, especially European and US immigrants given that postcolonial Honduran leaders were largely of Spanish descent, few Europeans had arrived by 1900. Probably less than one hundred, European or otherwise, settled in Honduras between the 1830s and 1860s or even during the 1870s. A trickle began in the 1880s, and 1890s. A significant inflow began in the 1910s, attracted to the emerging boom in the banana export economy. The censuses of the 1920s, 1930s, and 1940s indicate that most European, North American, and Middle Eastern immigration settled on the North Coast, and fewer in Tegucigalpa. The Arab-descendant population, while small, grew substantially between the 1910s and the 1930s. The 1910 census registered 200 Arabs, while the 1926 census counted 1,066, and 868 were noted in the 1935 census.[63]

There were greater opportunities on the Caribbean coast because of the larger market associated with larger concentration of plantations workers and their buying power. On the Caribbean coast they were also attracted, very early on, by the railroad system that the country's capital, Tegucigalpa, lacked, since it meant easier and cheaper access to the seaports on the Caribbean. Arab-Palestinians and other Middle Eastern surnames were prominent in commerce in Tegucigalpa by the mid-1920s.

During the critical period of Honduran history from the 1880s to the 1930s, when foreign banana companies achieved control of the country's only relevant export product to the world market, Honduran families that could trace their ancestry to the colonial period lost control of the commercial and industrial sector of the economy, and it served to differentiate modern Honduran history from the history of its counterparts in Central America, especially on issues of political power and state formation. What is more, this situation proved critically significant for issues of class formation and the country's political system during and after the 1960s, when a new wave of industrialization finally positioned the commercial and industrial bourgeoisie to at least challenge the post-depression political system. For example, in the 1960s, more Atalas of Arab descent arrived, including from Cuba, to complement earlier immigrants, as well as Zablahs also from Cuba and from elsewhere in Latin America. Also, Zablahs began taking Honduran citizenship in the 1950s and 1960s.

During the 1970s, the old, largely locally financed industrialization referenced in the last paragraph was connected to a state-promoted effort to finance industrialization, particularly via the establishment in 1974 of the Corporacion Nacional de Desarrollo Industrial, or the National Corporation of Industrial Development (CONADI). CONADI became a "piñata" of corruption; by the 1980s, when it was abolished, CONADI nonetheless had made fortunes for many of the old commercial groups and their descendants who came of age in the 1990s and after. According to experts on this process,

> set up under the Lopez Arellano government in 1974 for the purpose of fostering a national industrial sector, the CONADI provided low-cost loans to private investors. Between 1975 and 1980, it authorized 102 million lempiras (U5$51 million) in direct loans and 208 million (U5$104 million) in loan guarantees to industrialists at a ratio of 8.08 lempiras for every lempira of private capital invested. To finance its operations, it borrowed heavily on international capital markets, where its dealings were underwritten by the Honduran government. Unfortunately, many of the recipients found it more profitable to convert their lempiras into dollars and deposit the money in foreign banks. There was also an abundance of poor investments and incompetent or corrupt administration.[64]

At any rate, the fact is that non-European immigrants achieved control of the country's elite commerce and industry by the 1980s, even if the process did not get the scholarly attention it merited. Even in the early 1990s it seemed few understood that, and unlike the general Latin American experience, that Arab-Palestinian immigrant families or groups became the predominant immigrant interests in Honduran elite commerce, and industry, and later finance.[65]

On the other hand, even in the early 1990s, the Zablahs and Atalas, critical promoters of the 2009 coup, were not among the most significant of the capitalist groups in Honduras. Members of the Atala-Zablah clan were minor shareholders in the establishment of the Banco Comercial S.A. in 1980. However, it no doubt was eventually the basis of their rise to financial capital stardom twenty years later during the National Party government of Ricardo Maduro Joest (2002–2006). This government's Finance Minister was Camilo Atala Faraj (b. 1963), principal shareholder in Financiera

Table 19.1. Most Important Economic Groups in Honduras, 1980s (By Percentage of Financial Capital of the Country)

Economic Group	Percentage
1. Multinational Enterprises	22.51
2. SOGERIN	9.82
3. Inversiones Facussé, S.A.	8.27
4. Inversiones Continental	6.29
5. BANCATLAN, S.A.	5.00
6. Grupo Goldstein	4.49
7. Inversiones Andonie Fernández	3.94
8. Inversiones Williams	3.70
9. El Ahorro Hondureño, S.A.	3.60
10. Inversiones Honduras, S.A.	2.98
11. Inversiones Bendeck S.A.	2.90
12. Inversiones Fasquelle	2.69
13. Inversiones Kafati, S.A.	2.58
14. Inversiones Kattan	2.57
15. Intereses Militares	2.18
16. Inversiones Bamer, S.A.	2.13
17. Inversiones Larach, S.A.	1.94
18. Inversiones Canahuati	1.88
19. Inversiones Maduro	1.68
20. Grupo Hasbun	1.60
21. Inversiones Flores Rodil	0.94
22. Inversiones Callejas	0.79
23. Inversiones Occidente	0.61
24. Inversiones Sikafy	0.58
25. Inversiones Handal, S.A.	0.15
26. Inversiones Kafie	0.06
Other	1.84
Independent Businesses	2.54

Source: Mario Flores G., "El Capital Financiero en Honduras" (master's thesis, Universidad Nacional Autónoma de Honduras, 1990), 81–82.

Comercial Hondureña S.A. (FICOHSA), established in 1991, which itself transformed into Banco Financiera Comercial Hondureña, S.A. in 1994. In 2014, its directors and presumably main shareholders were President Jorge A. Faraj Rishmagui, Vice President, Camilo A. Atala Faraj, and others.[66]

By the middle of the last decade, members of the Atala-Faraj clan were visible representatives of the new neoliberal economy connected to the globalized economy in ways much more complicated than those of their parents and grandparents. They were very open leaders and supporters of the coup against President Manuel Zelaya Rosales in June 2009, including lobbying stints in Washington. Moreover, by 2012, FICOHSA's leaders were identified in lending projects that might have involved narco money laundering, as well as loans to agricultural and food processing conglomerates based in Honduras. The ownership of these conglomoratres originated in the older economy from the 1960s and 1970s but also controlled by Hondurans of Arab-Palestinian descent, namely, Corporación Dinant, owned primarily by Miguel Facusse Barjum. Facusse was president of Dinant until his death in 2015. Unlike the Atala-Zablah clan, the Facusse-Barjums had been prominent in Tegucigalpa's economy since the 1920s, and they were Honduras's top economic business group as of the 1980s.

During the 1980s, when some descendants from the early Palestinian families appeared as major presidential candidates, their "ethnicity" and Arab "race" became public and controversial issues in Honduras, and these became connected to their economic power. At that time, Carlos Flores Facusse, thirty years old, at the suggestion of his uncle, Miguel Facusse, became private secretary to the new Liberal Party president of the country until 1986.[67] Interestingly, the political ascendancy of certain families of Jewish descent never seemed to draw the same public fire that the Arab-descendant families did. The same was not true in the late 1980s, when finally Carlos Flores Facusse, of Palestinian descent on his mother's side (his mother was a sister to Miguel Facusse), became the presidential candidate of the Liberal Party in the elections of November 1989. He lost to Callejas, but he won in 1997. When Flores Facusse won the 1997 elections as the candidate of the Liberal Party, Honduras was in its fifteenth consecutive year of democratic, civilian rule, a unique moment in the country's tumultuous political history. By the coup of 2009, the Facusses and newer generations of Arab-descendant Honduran families became the focus of narrow interpretations of the main actors of the country's breakdown of democracy. In fact, two months after the 2009 coup interpretations of its key events profiled Arab-descendant Honduran elites as central protagonists in the coup and high-profile members of the country's so-called capitalist oligarchy composed of ten to twelve families. The Facusses, Atalas, and Zablahs were frequently featured in mostly polemical denunciations of the coup. Honduras's Consejo Hondureño de la Empresa Privada, the country's peak business association, as early as August 2009 took note of the racialized xenophobia in graffiti in many streets in San Pedro Sula and Tegucigalpa.[68]

So, to summarize, between 1963 and 1981, open, democratic political party competition ceased in Honduras, with the exception of elections in 1971 that ended with a coup in 1972. What is more, other than the democratic regime of Juan Manuel Galvez between 1949 and 1954, the decades between 1933 and 1957 are best characterized as transitions between dictatorships and coup plotting, and intrigue among the old leaders of the Liberal and National parties. That ceased between 1973 and 1981, when CONADI became the vehicle of capital accumulation now globalized beyond the old banana economy. This is the time when the young Carlos Flores Facusse came of political age, with his father marginalized from active politics, but with Honduras undergoing socioeconomic transitions that nonetheless set the stage for the young Flores Facusse's own political ascendancy, and later the ascendance the Atalas and Zablahs, now in a very different Honduras, but grounded in decades of historical legacies summarized here. It is with this historical background that the Atalas and Zablahs became key actors sustaining the 2009 coup.

In the 1990s, when Carlos Flores Facusse's presidency was defying the old myths of a homogenous *mestizaje*, Indigenous and Black leaders in Honduras made race and ethnicity central to national politics in ways that had never occurred in Honduras. Between 2009 and 2019, leaders from the Lenca to the Garifuna ethnic groups, the dominant non-mestizo subjects excluded from the national pantheon since the 1930s, often deployed narratives of various historic figures deemed representative of past struggles that could serve as examples of inspiration for current battles. Garifuna intellectuals and leaders, representing the largest Black population in Honduras, recovered Satuye as the last great Garifuna leader to lead their ancestors' resistance to British imperialism in St. Vincent before their fateful deportation to Honduras in 1797. By 1997, in the midst of the two-hundred-year celebration and commemoration of the Garifuna's arrival in Honduras, Satuye emerged as a powerful symbol of continuing resistance to the marginalization of the Garifuna by the majority mixed-race population, the mestizos.

On July 20, 1995, thousands of Honduran Indigenous and Garifuna groups arrived in Tegucigalpa to protest then President Carlos Roberto Reina's failure to comply with political agreements reached a year earlier. Indeed, in 1994 the protests marked the first time that Lenca, Garifuna, and other ethnic groups managed to arrive in Tegucigalpa to insist on their rights in a major urban center grounded in collective ethnic organization. What happened here, one could argue, was a form of subaltern "nationalism against the state," a radically new phenomenon in the long history of Honduras and unique to the last thirty years. Starting in the 1990s, younger generations of Honduras negotiated a much greater degree of ethnic and racial sensibilities than their parents and grandparents. Besides a redefined mestizaje at home, meaning a mestizaje not exclusive to an Indian-Spanish mixture, thousands of Hondurans at this same time migrated to the United States and there encountered a racial and ethnic context radically different than their own. Many began to think of themselves as "Latinos" and "Latinas," or "Latinx."

Immigration from Honduras to the United States increased dramatically after 1982. Since 1998, three moments have spurred three different flows of immigration: first, in the 1980s, a small number of Hondurans fled the war-like conditions consequent to the wars in Guatemala, El Salvador, and Nicaragua; second, hurricane Mitch late in 1998 provoked a much larger immigration after the destruction wrought, and because of the economy's slow recovery. In January 1999, the US government designated Honduras as meriting "Temporary Protective Status," or TPS. This meant the country's condition "temporarily prevent[ed] the country's nationals from returning safely, or in certain circumstances, where the country is unable to handle the return of its nationals adequately." Between the late 1990s and 2010, Hondurans in the United States have been estimated to have increased from about one hundred thousand in 1990, to close to half a million almost ten years ago. A third flow of Hondurans now complements the previous larger waves: those fleeing persecution and death at the hands of the criminal gangs connected to narco-trafficking, more tragically caught in the so-called Caravans that departed from San Pedro Sula late in 2018.[69] Simultaneous to this fact is another: the degree to which Honduras's GDP during the last fifteen years has come to depend on dollar remittances from immigrants in the United States, documented and otherwise. Their dollars annually amount to between 15 and 19 percent of the country's GDP.

Ten years after the 2009 coup, Honduras is more mired than ever in the tragic legacies of a long history of pernicious structural problems inherited from the early postcolonial period and reproduced and made even more complex during the twentieth century. Almost at the time of the 2009 coup, many studies produced compact characterizations of Honduras's contemporary history and its relationship to the structural origins of the coup.

One of these, published in 2007, was prophetic and precise, and merits citation at length:

> The last 25 years of Honduran history have been characterized by limited political and economic transitions. The current political process ostensibly seeks to consolidate a more participatory democracy that goes beyond the electoral system which replaced military rule in 1982. However, progress towards eliminating obstacles in key political processes has been limited. Although the influence of the military undoubtedly declined during the 1980s and new civil society networks and actors emerged, clientelism and partisanship persisted within the traditional political parties that continued to dominate policymaking in Honduras (the Liberal Party [PL] and National Party [PN]). The electoral system contributed to a weak sense of accountability on the part of congressional deputies as until the 2000 elections ballots for President, Congress and municipalities were not separated. Presidents have tended to lack strong congressional majorities and are barred from running for re-election, making it difficult for the Executive to secure legislative support for major reform initiatives. This translates into a perverse dynamic in which the Executive is effectively prevented from challenging the status quo of traditional policy making. When proposed reform measures touch on issues such as social protection or rural development, which channel funds essential to maintaining clientelist networks or are linked to special privileges for specific interest groups represented in Congress, the logic of the political process becomes an obstacle to pro-poor growth."[70]

The deep historical roots of the "the logic of the political process" that has been "an obstacle to pro-poor growth" policies, to say nothing of a fundamental obstacle to World Bank and International Monetary Fund conceptualized "Poverty Reduction Strategies" during the last two decades,[71] should be traced to the legacies of the concessionary state that originated in the mid-nineteenth century and its transition to the corrupt politics and policies that established the banana agro-export economy in the first half of the twentieth century.[72] While various laws from the 1950s onward tried to abolish the concessionary state and its economic and political culture, a study completed in 2013 on tax exemptions and other privileges awarded by many legislatures and presidents showed that these amounted to about 7 percent of the GDP. The value of these concessionary privileges, the 2013 study reported, represented almost 50 percent of the taxes collected by the state.[73]

Foreign "development workers" that international aid agencies have deployed to Honduras to help remedy this situation during the last thirty years seem oblivious to the country's history.[74] Knowing the social and political implications of the concessionary state for policy conceptualization and implementation in Honduras may have guarded against the degree to which governments, local and national, remain sinecures for securing wealth and status, and not a civil service. The coup of 2009 unleashed a varied resistance movement that today grapples with the history their forefathers and mothers forged.[75]

NOTES

1. Dario A. Euraque, "Banana Republic," in *America in the World, 1776 to the Present: A Supplement to the Dictionary of American History*, edited by Edward J. Blum et al., 115–116 (New York: Charles Scribner & Sons, 2016).
2. Richard Cohen, *The Fish That Ate the Whale: The Life and Times of America's Banana King* (New York: Picador, 2013), 173–211. Roberto García Ferreira, *Operaciones en contra: La CIA y el exilio de Jacobo Árbenz* (Guatemala City, Guatemala: FLACSO, 2014), 63–65.
3. Clayton Filho Cunha, André Luiz Coelho, and Fidel I. Pérez Flores, "A right-to-left policy switch? An analysis of the Honduran case under Manuel Zelaya," *International Political Science Review/Revue internationale de science politique* 34, no. 5 (November 2013): 519–542; Rene Pedraja, "Honduras: The Coup of June 2009," in Rene Pedraja, *The United States and the Armed Forces of Mexico, Central America, and the Caribbean, 2000–2014* (Jefferson, NC: McFarland, 2014), 144–164; Dana Frank, *The Long Honduran Night: Resistance, Terror, and the United States in the Aftermath of the Coup* (Chicago: Haymarket Books, 2018).
4. Hillary Clinton, "Honduras, 2008–2009," in Hillary Clinton, *Hard Choices: A Memoir* (New York: Simon & Schuster, 2014), 257.
5. Alexander Main, "The Hillary Clinton Emails and the Honduras Coup," Center for Economic and Policy Research Blog, September 24, 2015. http://cepr.net/blogs/the-americas-blog/the-hillary-clinton-emails-and-honduras.
6. Thomas Legler, "Learning the Hard Way: Defending Democracy in Honduras," *International Journal*, 65, no. 3 (Summer 2010): 612.
7. Eric Hobsbawm, *Nations and Nationalism since 1780: Programme, Myth, Reality* (Cambridge, U.K.: Cambridge University Press, 1990), 9.
8. Dario A. Euraque, *Reinterpreting the Banana Republic: Region and State in Honduras, 1870–1972* (Chapel Hill: University of North Carolina Press, 1996), xix–xxi, 12–13, 158–159.

9. I discuss Honduras's racial and ethnic history in the context of Central America in Dario A. Euraque, "Political Economy, Race, and National Identity in Central America, 1500–2000," in *Oxford Research Encyclopedia of Latin American History* (Oxford University Press, 2018). A more detailed look is available in, Dario A. Euraque, *Conversaciones históricas con el mestizaje en Honduras y su identidad nacional* (San Pedro Sula, Honduras: Centro Editorial, 2004).

10. Darío A. Euraque, "Los recursos económicos del Estado Hondureño, 1830–1970," in *Identidades nacionales y Estado moderno en Centroamérica*, edited by Arturo Taracena and Jean Piel, 134–136 (San José, Costa Rica: EDUCA, 1995).

11. Dario A. Euraque, "On the Origins of Civil War in Nineteenth-Century Honduras," in *Rumours of Wars: Civil Conflict in Nineteenth-Century Latin America*, edited by Rebecca Earle, 87–102 (London: Institute of Latin American Studies, 2000).

12. Dario A. Euraque, "La 'Reforma Liberal' en Honduras y la hipótesis de la 'oligarquía ausente': 1870s–1930s," *Revista de Historia* (San José, Costa Rica) 23 (January–June 1991): 7–56.

13. Lowell Gudmundson and Héctor Lindo-Fuentes, *Central America, 1821–1871: Liberalism before Liberal Reform* (Tuscaloosa: University of Alabama Press, 1995).

14. Vilma Laínez and Victor Meza, "El Enclave Bananero Hondureño," *Economía Política* (Tegucigalpa) 5 (May–August 1973): 115–149.

15. Robert G. Williams, *States and Social Evolution: Coffee and the Rise of National Governments in Central America* (Chapel Hill: University of North Carolina Press, 1994). For an extensive review of Williams's book, see Dario A. Euraque, *International Labor and Working-Class History* 50 (Fall 1996): 188–190.

16. For a path-dependence perspective on Honduras in Central America, see James Mahoney, *The Legacies of Liberalism: Path Dependence and Political Regimes in Central America* (Baltimore: Johns Hopkins University Press, 2001).

17. Robert G. Williams, *States and Social Evolution: Coffee and the Rise of National Governments in Central America* (Chapel Hill: University of North Carolina Press, 1994), 204–226.

18. Williams, *States and Social Evolution*, 210.

19. Williams, *States and Social Evolution*, 91–98, 210.

20. Maaria Seppanen, "Transforming the Concessional State? The Politics of Honduras's Poverty Reduction Strategy," Institute of Development Studies, University of Helsinki, Policy Paper 3, 2002.

21. Gene S. Yeager, "The Honduran Foreign Debt, 1825–1953" (PhD diss., Tulane University, 1975), 96.

22. Yeager, "Honduran Foreign Debt," 293.

23. On the history of Honduran banana planters, see Dario A. Euraque, *Un hondureño ante la Modernidad de su país: Rafael Lopez Padilla (1875–1963)* (Tegucigalpa, Honduras: Editorial Guaymuras, forthcoming). I am currently completing a long biography of Rafael Lopez Padilla (1875–1963). Lopez Padilla was a Honduran banana plantation cultivator and exporter, and a critic of the monopolistic stranglehold of the United Fruit Co. over the Honduran economy between the 1930s and his death. In Lopez Padilla's private and legal archive, one finds a rich variety of personal and legal documents that uniquely illustrate his relations with Samuel Zemurray and most of the United Fruit Company executives in Honduras in the 1930s, 1940s, and early 1950s. I inherited Lopez Padilla's extraordinary archive in the early 1990s from Mr. Pompeyo Melara, who in turn had purchased the

archives from one of Lopez Padilla's sons. Lopez Padilla's grandchildren have collaborated with me on this project for years.

24. Kenneth V. Finney, "Our Man in Honduras: Washington S. Valentine," *Dependency Unbends: Case Studies in Inter American Relations* 17 (1978): 13–20.

25. Yeager, "Honduran Foreign Debt, 309.

26. Maria de los Angeles Chaverri and Vicente Zavala Pavón, "Los empréstitos ferrocarrileros como modelos de la corrupción en Honduras durante el siglo XIX," in *Sobre la Historia de la Corrupción en Honduras*, edited by Chaverri and Vicente Zavala Pavón, 65–87 (Tegucigalpa, Honduras: Consejo Nacional de Anticorrupción, 2004).

27. Dario A. Euraque, "Policarpo Bonilla (1858–1926) luego de ejercer la presidencia de Honduras ¿Se convirtió el Dr. Bonilla en el principal abanderado del capitalismo bananero norteamericano en su época?" *Ponencia, XIV Congreso Centroamericano de Historia, Guatemala*, August 6–10, 2018.

28. Dario A. Euraque, "The Social, Economic & Political Aspects of the Carías Dictatorship in Honduras: The Historiography," *Latin American Research Review* 29, no. 1 (1994): 238–248; Mario A. Argueta, *Tiburcio Carías: anatomía de una época, 1923–1948* (Tegucigalpa, Honduras: Editorial Guaymuras, 1989); and Thomas J. Dodd, *Tiburcio Carías: Portrait of a Honduran Political Leader* (Baton Rouge: Louisiana State University Press, 2005).

29. This theme is developed in Cesar Indiano, *Los hijos del infortunio: Historia de un país, al revés* (Tegucigalpa, Honduras: Litografía López, 2009).

30. Dario A. Euraque, "Los Políticos Hondureños y la Costa Norte (1876–1950)," *Revista Política de Honduras* (Tegucigalpa, Honduras) 24 (December 2000): 135–137. I detail and develop this argument at length in my forthcoming biography of Rafael Lopez Padilla.

31. Dispatch 84, U.S. Minister John Erwing, Tegucigalpa, to U.S. Secretary of State, 19 September 1914, U.S. national Archives, Record Group 59, 815.00/1547 in *Records of the Department of State Relating to Internal Affairs of Honduras, 1910–29* (Washington: U.S. National Archives, 1967).

32. Ibid.

33. Ibid.

34. Ibid.

35. Rina Villars, *Para la casa más que para el mundo: Sufragismo y feminismo en la historia de Honduras* (Tegucigalpa, Honduras: Editorial Guaymuras, 2001), 335. On masculinity, violence, and political culture and sexism in Honduras before the 1950s, see Rocio Tabora, *Masculinidad y violencia en la cultura política hondureña* (Tegucigalpa, Honduras: CEDOD, 1995).

36. Dario A. Euraque, "On the Origins of Civil War in Nineteenth-Century Honduras," in *Rumours of Wars: Civil Conflict in Nineteenth-Century Latin America*, edited by Rebecca Earle, 89–90 (London: Institute of Latin American Studies, 2000).

37. Robert H. Holden, *Armies without Nations: Public Violence and State Formation in Central America, 1821–1960* (Oxford: Oxford University Press, 2004), 68.

38. Dario A. Euraque, "Los políticos hondureños y la Costa Norte (1876–1950)," *Revista Política de Honduras* (Tegucigalpa, Honduras) 24 (December 2000): 118.

39. Dario A. Euraque, "On the Origins of Civil War in Nineteenth-Century Honduras," in *Rumours of Wars: Civil Conflict in Nineteenth-Century Latin America*, edited by Rebecca Earle, 89 (London: Institute of Latin American Studies, 2000).

40. Dario A. Euraque, *Reinterpreting the "Banana Republic": Region and State in Honduras, 1870s–1972* (Chapel Hill: University of North Carolina Press, 1996), 48–49.

41. Robert H. Holden, *Armies without Nations: Public Violence and State Formation in Central America, 1821–1960* (Oxford: Oxford University Press, 2004), 69–70.
42. William S. Stokes, *Honduras: An Area Study in Government* (Madison: University of Wiscons in Press, 1950), 191.
43. Stokes, *Honduras*, 104.
44. Kevin C. Coleman, "'En uso de las facultades de que está investido': El estado de sitio en Honduras, 1890–1956," in *Historia de las desigualdades sociales en América Central*, edited by Ronny J. Viales Hurtado and David Díaz Arias, 275–304 (San José, Costa Rica: Colección Nueva Historia Contemporánea de Centroamérica, 2016).
45. Coleman, "'En uso de las facultades de que está investido,'" 277.
46. Yesenia Martinez Garcia, *La seguridad social en Honduras: actores sociopolíticos, institucionalidad y raíces históricas de su crisis* (Tegucigalpa, Honduras: Editorial Guaymuras, 2015), 69.
47. Roberto García Ferreira, "'Usted bien sabe que los militares, gente práctica, hacen las cosas más rápidamente que los diplomáticos': notas acerca del rol de Honduras como actor regional anticomunista," in *Guerra Fría y anticomunismo en Centroamérica*, edited by Roberto García Ferreira y Arturo Taracena Arriola, 143–162 (Guatemala City, Guatemala: FLACSO, 2017).
48. Thomas L. Leonard, *The United States and Central America* (Mobile: University of Alabama Press, 1984), 194.
49. Javier Márquez et al., *Estudio sobre la economía de Honduras* (Tegucigalpa: Banco Central de Honduras, 1951), 6.
50. Dario A. Euraque, "Estructura económica, formación de capital industrial, relaciones familiares y poder político en San Pedro Sula: 1870s–1958," *Revista Polémica* (San José, Costa Rica) 18 (September–December 1992): 44.
51. Stokes, *Honduras*, 24.
52. Euraque, *Reinterpreting the "Banana Republic,"* 97–98.
53. Euraque, *Reinterpreting the "Banana Republic,"* 41–75.
54. Dario A. Euraque, *Reinterpreting the "Banana Republic,"* 107–120. The historiography of the 1963 coup is extremely poor, especially regarding the violence unleashed in its aftermath.
55. Thomas C. McCann, *An American Company: The Tragedy of United Fruit Co.* (New York: Crown, 1976).
56. A good introduction and overview of the reformist period is Rachel Seider, "Honduras: The Politics of Exception and Military Reformism (1972–1978)," *Journal of Latin American Studies* 27, no. 1 (Feb. 1995): 99–127.
57. Jack R. Binns, *The United Status in Honduras, 1980–1981: An Ambassador's Memoir* (Jefferson, NC: McFarland, 2000), 24–91.
58. The best overview of the transition from 1979 to the late 1980s remains Marvin A. Barahona, *Honduras en el siglo XX: una síntesis histórica* (Tegucigalpa, Honduras: Editorial Guaymuras, 2005), 227–305. The situation before the 2009 coup is detailed in important essays in Diego Achard and Luís E. González, eds., *Política y desarrollo en Honduras, 2006–2009: los escenarios posibles* (Tegucigalpa, Honduras: PNUD, 2006). Early assessments of the origins of the coup are Thomas Legler, "Learning the Hard Way: Defending Democracy in Honduras," *International Journal* 65, no. 3 (Summer 2010): 601–618; and Kevin Casas-Zamora, "The Honduran Crisis and the Obama Administration," in *Shifting the Balance: Obama and the Americas*, edited by Abraham F. Lowenthal, Theodore

J. Piccone, and Laurecen Whitehead, 114–130 (Washington, DC: Brookings Institution Press, 2011).

59. Marta Elena Casaus Arzú, "La metamorfosis de las oligarquías centroamericanas," in *Centroamérica: Balance de la década de los 80*, edited by Marta Casaus Arzú y R. Castillo Quintana, 59–83 (Madrid: Fundación CEDEAL, 1993).

60. William I. Robinson, *Transnational Conflicts: Central America, Social Change and Globalization* (London: Verso, 2003); Benedicte Bull, "Honduras: Privatization in the Ritual Aid Dance," in Benedicte Bull, *Aid, Power, and Privatization: The Politics of Telecommunications Reform in Central America* (Cheltenham, U.K.: Edward Elgar, 2005); Víctor Meza et al., *Honduras: poderes facticos y sistema político* (Tegucigalpa, Honduras: CEDOH, 2007); and Eugenio Sosa, "Transformaciones en las elites económicas, estado y el proceso de democratización: el caso de Honduras, 1990–2017," *Anuario de Estudios Centroamericanos* 43 (2017): 125–148.

61. Jaime was the son of Yankel Rosenthal and Ester Oliva Berganza. "Yankel Rosenthal (1903–1979), El ahorro, inversión y educación de un inmigrante judío del siglo XX en Honduras" (Unpublished manuscript, 2018). Thanks to Dr. Pastor Fasquelle for sharing this manuscript, part of a biography of Jaime Rosenthal that he is currently writing.

62. Dario A. Euraque, "Los árabes de Honduras: entre la inmigración, la acumulación y la política," in *Contribuciones árabes a las identidades iberoamericanas*, edited by Karim Hauser and Daniel Gil, 233–284 (Madrid: Casa Árabe-IEAM, 2009).

63. Dario A. Euraque, "Nacionalidad, mestizaje, y la inmigración árabe, palestina y judía a Honduras, 1880–1930," in *Conversaciones históricas con el mestizaje en Honduras y su identidad nacional* (San Pedro Sula, Honduras: Centro Editorial, 2004), 102.

64. Donald Schulz and Deborah Sundloff Schulz, *The United States, Honduras, and the Crisis in Central America* (Boulder, CO: Westview Press, 1994), 204.

65. Allan Discua et al., "Las grandes empresas familiares de Honduras: la influencia del estado y la inmigración del siglo XX," *Familias empresarias y grandes empresas familiares en América Latina y España, una visión de largo plazo*, edited by Allan Discua, P. Fernández Pérez, and A. Luch, 319–343 (Bilbao, Spain: Fundación BBVA, 2015).

66. Ismael Jiménez et al., "Los 12 millonarios más importantes de Centroamérica," *Forbes Magazine* (December 27, 2014).

67. Jack R. Binns, *The United States in Honduras, 1980–1981: An Ambassador's Memoir* (Jefferson, NC: McFarland, 2000), 34.

68. Consejo Hondureño de la Empresa Privada, Position Paper, August 19, 2009. http://www.cohep.com/pdf/Documento%20Juridico%20COHEP%2019%20Agosto%202009.pdf; Cordelia Frewen. "Las paredes hablan cuando los medios callan: grafiti & memoria histórica en Honduras pos-golpe" (Final Project, SOWK 570, University of British Columbia, Canada, April 2014). A detailed analysis of this and related issues will soon be available in Dario A. Euraque, "La configuración histórica de las élites de Honduras ante el golpe de Estado del 2009," in *Anuario de Estudios Centroamericanos* (San José: Universidad de Costa Rica, forthcoming).

69. In November 2018, many press reports in the United States noted that Tony Hernandez, brother of Honduras's President Juan Orlando Hernandez, had been apprehended in Miami and accused of international drug-trafficking and other crimes. See US Drug Enforcement Association, "DEA announces arrest of former Honduran congressman and brother of current President of Honduras for drug trafficking and weapons charges," November 26, 2018. https://www.dea.gov/press-releases/2018/11/26/dea-announces-arr

est-former-honduran-congressman-and-brother-current. In short, the current Honduran state is now practically a "narco-state," possibly a variant of the concessionary state.

70. Jose Cuesta, "Political Space, Pro-Poor Growth and Poverty Reduction Strategy in Honduras: A Story of Missed Opportunities," *Journal of Latin American Studies* 39, no. 2 (2007): 334.

71. Carlos Villalobos Barrias, "The Dynamics of Inequality Change in a Highly Dualistic Economy: Honduras, 1991–2007," in *Economic Inequality in Latin America: Migration, Education and Structural Change* (New York: Peter Lang, 2013), 25–64.

72. A historical look at Honduran poverty is to be found in the classic by Marvin A. Barahona, *Evolución histórica de la identidad nacional* (Tegucigalpa, Honduras: Editorial Guaymuras, 1991), 193–222.

73. "Informe de la Comisión Especial para el Análisis y Control de las Exoneraciones, Exenciones y Franquicias Aduaneras" (2013). I thank Honduran sociologist Eugenio Sosa for sharing this important official document. Sosa analyzes this and other excellent sources on the contemporary version of the Honduran concessionary state. See Eugenio Sosa, "Transformaciones en las elites económicas, estado y el proceso de democratización: el caso de honduras, 1990–2017," *Anuario de Estudios Centroamericanos* 43 (2017): 125–148.

74. Jeffrey T. Jackson, *The Globalizers: Development Workers in Action* (Baltimore: Johns Hopkins University Press, 2005).

75. Excellent reviews of the social and political situation in Honduras between the 1990s and 2018 are available in Eugenio Sosa, *Democracia y movimientos sociales en Honduras: de la transición política la ciudadanía indignada* (Tegucigalpa, Honduras: Editorial Guaymuras, 2016); Victor Meza et al., *El blindaje de la corrupción en Honduras* (Tegucigalpa, Honduras: CEDOH, 2018); Ernesto Paz Aguilar, *Honduras: crónicas de un Estado degradado* (Tegucigalpa: Docucentro, 2019).

FURTHER READING

Achard, Diego, and Luís E. González, eds. *Política y desarrollo en Honduras, 2006–2009: los escenarios posibles.* Tegucigalpa, Honduras: PNUD, 2006.

Argueta, Mario R. *Tiburcio Carías: anatomía de un época.* 2nd ed. Tegucigalpa, Honduras: Editorial Guaymuras, 2008.

Barahona, Marvin A. *Honduras en el siglo XX: una síntesis histórica.* Tegucigalpa, Honduras: Editorial Guaymuras, 2005.

Carias, Marcos. *De la patria del criollo a la patria compartida: una historia de Honduras.* Tegucigalpa, Honduras: Ediciones Subirana, 2006.

Cohen, Rich. *The Fish That Ate the Whale: The Life and Times of America's Banana King.* New York: Picador, 2013.

Coleman, Kevin. *A Camera in the Garden of Eden: The Self-Forging of a Banana Republic.* Austin: Texas University Press, 2016.

Dodd, Thomas. *Tiburcio Carías: Portrait of a Honduran Political Leader.* Baton Rouge: Louisiana State University Press, 2005.

Euraque, Dario A. *Conversaciones históricas con el mestizaje y su identidad nacional en Honduras.* San Pedro Sula, Honduras: Centro Editorial, 2004.

Euraque, Dario A. *Reinterpreting the "Banana Republic": Region and State in Honduras, 1870–1972.* Chapel Hill: University of North Carolina Press, 1996.

Frank, Dana. *The Long Honduran Night: Resistance, Terror, and the United States in the Aftermath of the Coup.* Chicago: Haymarket Books, 2018.

Meza, Victor, ed. *El blindaje de la corrupción en Honduras: contexto, dimensiones, formas y mecanismos.* Tegucigalpa, Honduras: CEDOH, 2018.

Meza, Victor, ed. *Manejo, percepción e impacto de la impunidad, corrupción e inseguridad en Honduras.* Tegucigalpa, Honduras: CEDOH, 2019.

Pastor Fasquelle, Rodolfo. *Biografía de San Pedro Sula, 1536–1954.* San Pedro Sula, Honduras: Centro Editorial, 1990.

Schulz, Donald, and Deborah Sundloff Schulz. *The United States, Honduras, and the Crisis in Central America.* Boulder, CO: Westview Press, 1994.

Soluri, John. *Banana Cultures: Agriculture, Consumption, and Environmental Change in Honduras and the United States.* Austin: University of Texas Press, 2005.

Sosa, Eugenio. *Democracia y movimientos sociales en Honduras: de la transición política a la ciudadanía indignada.* Tegucigalpa, Honduras: Editorial Guaymuras, 2016.

CHAPTER 20

EL SALVADOR

ERIK CHING

In 1910, Enrique Córdova, the Salvadoran lawyer and recurrent government official, traveled to Costa Rica where he had the chance to meet Ricardo Jiménez, eventual President of the Republic, who was then serving as a deputy in the National Assembly. As Córdova described the meeting in his memoir, Jiménez asked him how much the Salvadoran government had budgeted that year for public education versus national defense. When Córdova told him 800,000 Colones for education and 4,500,000 Colones for defense, Jiménez said that El Salvador would be better off reversing those figures, as Costa Rica had done.[1]

Salvadorans reading that anecdote might feel a tinge of nationalist antipathy toward Jiménez, as their nation is often compared unfavorably to Costa Rica in achievements in national development. Nonetheless, Jiménez had a point; Costa Rica invested in public education and other common goods, while El Salvador spent money on the military and the policing of its citizenry. Scholars naturally debate the reasons for Costa Rica's and El Salvador's alternative approaches to development, but some consensus has emerged around the relationship between racialist ideologies and notions of the public good. Costa Rica's population was more ethnically homogenous than El Salvador's, and thus it avoided much of the racially charged competition for resources that typically defined more ethnically diverse nations. Subsequently, as the argument goes, Costa Rica found it easier to create a sense of common purpose and collective identity, and therein to commit to things like public education. In contrast, El Salvador has suffered from what can be called the "zero-sum game of ethnic politics," whereby a dominant minority sees any loss to its privilege and power as a benefit to its racial/class adversaries and thus as a threat to its survival. In El Salvador, these lines of contest were drawn between a wealthy, non-Indigenous elite, and a mass of rural peasants and laborers, many of whom were Indigenous. Even after ethnicity became less of a central issue in the mid-twentieth century, the lines of division between haves and have-nots had become firmly entrenched. Subsequently, those who had wealth and power spent money on guns rather than on schools.[2]

Ethnicity is not singularly determinant of national development, and predilection is not destiny; peoples' decisions matter. But the underlying premise of the comparative-development scholarship is that if a country like El Salvador was going to follow a different developmental path, then its peoples needed to have acted with purposeful intentionality to overcome the negative endowments of racial hierarchy and the corresponding divisive ideologies. Unfortunately, that intentionality failed to take hold, despite the efforts, and even the fleeting victories, of many Salvadorans who tried to chart a more egalitarian route.

INDEPENDENCE AND THE EARLY REPUBLIC

Scholarship of the independence era was defined initially by a liberal-nationalist historiography that portrayed the leaders of the independence movement in hagiographic terms as patriotic Founding Fathers. A leftist revisionist scholarship emerged in the 1960s that used class analysis to tell a more cynical story of elite leaders controlling the process for their own benefit, although it tended to leave the issue of ethnicity aside. Recent scholarship has emerged that relies on original evidence from Guatemalan and Spanish archives to reveal a more nuanced, complicated story that shows the relevance of ethnicity and mass-based social movements to the process.[3]

At risk of oversimplification, the new scholarship suggests that El Salvador's independence can be understood through the lens of ethnicity, and that El Salvador's experience was more akin to Mexico's and Guatemala's than other less ethnically diverse areas, like Argentina or Chile. It is ironic to make El Salvador analogous to Guatemala because so much of Salvadoran identity, especially in its earliest manifestations, was rooted in antipathy toward Guatemala. As the traditional center of colonial governance on the isthmus, Guatemala was seen by many Salvadorans as a bullying bastion of conservative governance and economic suffocation. Hence, a liberalist bent settled into the Salvadoran consciousness, such that throughout the nineteenth century Salvadorans were not torn apart by the Liberal-Conservative divide that often defined politics in, say, Mexico and Guatemala.[4] That liberal inclination perhaps explains why Salvadorans were first on the isthmus to break out in open rebellion for independence in 1811, and then again in 1814.

However, the new scholarship suggests that El Salvador was more akin to Guatemala then we previously appreciated. In both countries a handful of Creole elites (i.e., people of Spanish descent who had been born in the Americas) were anxious to break ties with Spain and what they considered to be its oppressive rule over them. The problem was that most Creole elites in both El Salvador and Guatemala were more afraid of their Indigenous neighbors than they were of the Spanish Crown. Indications of mass support for independence, especially among Indigenous communities, only exacerbated Creole fears of rebellious, uncontrollable, ethnically diverse masses rising up in autonomous action. As a result, most Creoles, when faced with the choice, chose continued

Spanish colonialism over the option of shared governance in an independent republic. Recent evidence reveals that even the earliest and most ardent advocates of independence in El Salvador, such as Manuel José Arce, the priest José Matias Delgado, Juan Manuel Rodríguez, and Domingo Antonio de Lara, had threads of conservatism running throughout their ideological worldview. Subsequently, independence in El Salvador occurred slowly, concurrent with Guatemala and Mexico, in 1821.[5]

The two decades after 1821 were not conducive to economic stability and political centralization. Three years of Mexican/Guatemalan occupation, followed by more than a decade of failed experimentation in Federation (1824–1838) left El Salvador finally independent in 1841 atop what historian Héctor Lindo dubbed "Weak Foundations."[6] The economy was at least better off than some places in the Americas thanks to indigo. But the national government was frequently insolvent, and the defining characteristic of governance was the inability of the central state to exert control over its regional peripheries, even in the small geographical space that was El Salvador. National-level political leaders were little more than regional players who had somehow managed to ascend to the national stage and who remained heavily reliant on regional networks for political survival; those networks were prone to constant breakdown and realignment, resulting in ongoing political destabilization.[7]

Throughout most of the nineteenth century, as much as one-third of Salvadoran national territory was owned communally, either by municipalities, in the form of *ejidos*, or by groups of Indigenous people as part of their formal Indigenous communities, or *comunidades*. In either case, communal land could not be bought or sold, because its purpose was to benefit the residents of the entity that held it. The existence of these communal lands, combined with the weakness of central government, resulted in peasants, Indigenous and non-Indigenous (*Ladino*) alike, enjoying some autonomy and possessing the ability to exert political influence. Sometimes this influence came in the form of rural insurrections, a classic example being the Indigenous uprising in 1833 in the Nonualcos region to the south of San Salvador. In the face of abusive practices by local landowners, and the ineffectiveness of the central government to do anything about them, Indigenous peoples rose up in insurrection and eventually crowned as king a local Indigenous leader, Anastasio Aquino. The rebellion was eventually put down, but the specter of Indigenous peoples rising up and using violence to create autonomous space for themselves highlighted all the fears local elites felt throughout the independence period (*c.* 1810–1841). Scholarship is revealing the degree to which such insurrectionary movements, if not quite as large or sustained as the Aquino rebellion, occurred repeatedly throughout the nineteenth century across the Salvadoran countryside.[8]

Another way peasant communities exerted political influence was by forming alliances with local elites, or political bosses, to create political patronage networks that bargained with rival networks throughout the country for influence and position. A prototypical example is the vast political network built up by General Rafael Rivas atop a base of Indigenous people in the Cojutepeque Department. Rivas and his supporters were a force to be reckoned with by any political aspirant throughout the latter half of the nineteenth century.[9]

COFFEE

Salvadorans began cultivating coffee a little later than some of their neighbors, in part because indigo remained a viable export commodity into the latter half of the nineteenth century. But once the transition to coffee began, it took off in earnest, and soon El Salvador became one of the world's leading producers. By the eve of the Great Depression, 90 percent of El Salvador's export earnings derived from coffee.

The main coffee-growing area in El Salvador was the western highlands around Sonsonate, Ahuachapán, Santa Ana, and La Libertad Departments. Much of the viable coffee land in that region was owned communally, so any policies relating to land tenure were going to have serious consequences. Salvadoran political leaders at the time believed that the communal lands had to be subjected to market forces in order for coffee cultivation to take off. Thus, they chose to address the issue of communally owned land by passing a series of privatization decrees in the early 1880s that ordered the partition and distribution of all communal properties. Every scholar of nineteenth-century El Salvador has recognized the importance of the privatization decrees. The debate is over the pace and method by which land alienation occurred. The original argument, shared ironically by liberal apologists and Marxist critics alike, was that alienation was sudden and widespread, and that it caused the proletarianization of the former communal holders who had no choice but to work for low wages on the spreading coffee plantations.[10]

A subsequent generation of scholarship, based on newly available land records in El Salvador's National Archives reveals the alienation process to have been slower and more complicated, even if the end result was largely the same. The historian Aldo Lauria, in particular, has shown that the overwhelming majority of former communal landholders received plots of land during the privatization process. The consequence was not the sudden creation of a vast rural proletariat but rather the emergence of a vast, small-holding peasantry, which in the western highlands remained disproportionately Indigenous. Lauria agrees that the eventual consequence of privatization was proletarianization, economic inequality, and the increasing demise of Indigenous identity, but he shows that these processes took decades not years, and that the slow pace of change helps to explain why privatization did not immediately produce widespread rural insurrections. Communal landholders were not inherently opposed to private property, but what they needed was enough land to sustain themselves over multiple generations, as their former communal properties had done.[11]

The so-called original sin of privatization in El Salvador was the size of the private plots. Most of them were just large enough to sustain one family for one generation. As soon as a family had a financial emergency, or a second generation was in line to receive its inheritance, the original plot was sold off or divided and thereby became too small to sustain a family. In this way, speculators and entrepreneurs with political connections and access to capital bought up the properties, resulting in time in widespread proletarianization and economic inequality. But those issues didn't reach a boiling point until the onset of the Great Depression in the early 1930s.[12]

The emergent coffee economy resulted in the creation of a vast internal security apparatus. One of the more notorious units to come into existence at this time was the National Guard in 1912. Its roughly three hundred members patrolled the countryside and enforced laws designed to benefit coffee growers, such as property rights, vagrancy laws, and labor contracts. Guardsmen became notorious for their brutality, and scholars have long described them as the storm troopers of the coffee oligarchy.[13]

Recent scholarship, inspired once again by new archival sources, reveals some complexities around the story of the Guardia. In addition to being the enforcers of the coffee economy, National Guardsmen often got into armed conflagrations with local landowning elites and their network of supporters. The centralization of the national state meant that some elites benefited more than others from their access to state power, and the new national elites wanted to curtail the autonomy that local and regional elites had enjoyed for decades, which had produced the destabilizing, internecine political conflicts of the past. And so, at times, the armed enforcers of the national state (e.g., the National Guard) got into armed conflicts with local elites who did not want to surrender their traditional autonomy.[14]

The transition to coffee in El Salvador had significant economic and political consequences. It required the creation of new capital markets, the reorganization of labor relations, and the transference of ownership over large quantities of land. It also allowed for the consolidation of the national state and the centralization of the military. The manner in which El Salvador went about creating its coffee economy produced clear winners and losers. The former was a small handful of non-Indigenous (Ladino) families, the so-called Salvadoran oligarchy, who came to control the overwhelming majority of coffee-growing land, as well as the processing facilities and the lending institutions that bankrolled the process. The losers were, for the most part, everyone else, but especially the rural peasantry, and in particular the Indigenous communities that once controlled large amounts of land and enjoyed a relative degree of autonomy. El Salvador's coffee economy could have been constructed differently, in a more egalitarian manner, but it wasn't, and thus it became a major contributor to El Salvador's zero-sum game of ethnic politics—that is, the intense division between social groups over economic opportunity and political power.[15]

THE EVENTS OF 1932

The social pressures that had built up during the making of the coffee economy exploded in a tragic fashion in 1932, and El Salvador was never the same thereafter. Over a roughly three-day span between January 22 and January 25, a few hundred, or perhaps as many as a couple of thousand, peasant rebels attacked approximately one dozen municipalities across western El Salvador. The rebels gained control over one-half of the targeted municipalities and held them for as many as three days. The rebels focused their attacks on institutions of state power, for example, military posts, police stations, and municipal offices, as well as the homes and businesses of local elites. In all, the rebels killed approximately one hundred people during the three days of insurrection, including the soldiers and police who engaged them in combat. While the rebels committed a few acts of violence upon some civilians, mostly members of local elite families, for the most part their activities were limited to looting and destroying property. Local military units recovered and ousted the rebels relatively easily from the occupied towns in no more than three days' time.[16]

While shocking, the insurrection of 1932 was not an unprecedented event in Salvadoran history. Peasant mobilization had been a recurrent feature of nineteenth-century life, and thus the only surprise is how few such rebellions had taken place in the roughly fifty years prior to 1932. The insurrection of 1932 could have gone down in Salvadoran history as a notable but unremarkable event. What transpired in the roughly two weeks after the insurrection made the events of 1932 wholly transformative. Whereas in the past, the typical government reaction to rural destabilization was to kill or castigate a few leaders and get everyone back to their homes and the status quo as quickly as possible, for whatever reason, and we still don't know exactly why, the government in 1932 took a wholly different approach.

The government at the time was under the leadership of General Maximiliano Martínez, who had come to power in a coup in December 1931. We still don't know the precise chain of command, or how or when orders were sent down. What we do know is that over the next two weeks, fast-moving and heavily armed military units rampaged throughout the western countryside, killing peasants indiscriminately, without either a trial or evidence that they had been involved in the insurrectionary events. When the smoke cleared at the end of the second week, the numbers of victims were impossible to determine. Estimates range from a low of ten thousand to a high of thirty thousand. Regardless, the massacre of 1932, known locally as La Matanza, is one of the single worst episodes of state violence against a citizenry in modern Latin American history.

We have many questions about the events of 1932: Who were the rebels? How did they organize? What were their goals? Why did the government perpetrate the Matanza? In seeking answers to these questions, we know a great deal more today than we did even twenty years ago. Sadly, there are still gaps in our knowledge that may never be filled.

As to the origins of the rebellion, we can say with confidence that it was caused by the long-standing pressures bearing down on the western peasantry, and especially on Indigenous communities by the coffee economy. Those pressures became acute in 1929/1930 with the onset of the Great Depression. The western countryside was the region most intensely affected by the privatization of communal lands, and most of the municipalities at the heart of the rebellion were heavily Indigenous; some of them, like Nahuizalco, were upwards of 90 percent Indigenous. So even though we don't know the specific names of the rebels, it is safe to say that many, if not most, of them were Indigenous, and therein the insurrection took on a fundamentally Indigenous overtone.

We have strong evidence of long-standing conflicts between Ladinos and Indigenous communities over local political power coming to a head in late 1931. We also have evidence that gender issues were coming to a conflictive boil as well, as Ladino men were taking advantage of Indigenous women sexually, giving Indigenous men a strong incentive to respond.[17]

Emphasizing the ethnic component of the 1932 rebellion raises a historiographic debate over the role of communism. Most of the original interpretations of the rebellion identified it as "communist" and attributed its origins to the formal leftist organizations at the time, particularly the Partido Comunista Salvadoreño (PCS, Salvadoran Communist Party), as well as subsidiary organizations like the Socorro Rojo Internacional (SRI, International Red Aid), and individual leftist activists, like Farabundo Martí. This argument of "communist causality," as it was later dubbed, held sway until the 1990s when scholars working with new archival evidence questioned the role of the radical organizations and their capacity to have organized something on the scale of the 1932 insurrection, especially among heavily Indigenous populations when their known members were almost entirely Ladino and living in urban centers. This new scholarship pushed the impetus for the rebellion toward the autonomous actions and decisions of the peasantry, and especially its Indigenous members. A "third wave" of scholarship reemphasized the role of the radical organizations, noting large membership numbers in the SRI across the western countryside. This third wave of scholarship acknowledges that even if western peasants nominally joined formal leftist organizations like the SRI, they made them their own in the process and thus they were not at the organizational mercy of outside radical leaders. As will be shown in the section "The Civil War, 1980–1992," a similar debate will play out in regard to the mass mobilization in the 1970s leading into the civil war of the 1980s.[18]

There has also been some debate over the consequences of the Matanza. Assuming many if not most of the victims were Indigenous, some scholars and spokespersons have begun to identify the Matanza as a genocide or an ethnocide—that is, a purposeful attempt to eradicate Indigenous people from El Salvador. The evidence for that is somewhat debatable. Nevertheless, the Matanza was one component of a long-standing assault upon Indigenous culture, wherein over time fewer and fewer Indigenous children learned the language and customs of their parents, and subsequently they became part of a homogenous non-Indigenous "mestizo" majority. By the middle of the twentieth century, it was common to hear Salvadorans describe themselves as "the most mestizo people in the Americas."[19]

Collectively, the events of 1932 solidified El Salvador's zero-sum game of ethnic politics. Its government murdered thousands, perhaps tens of thousands, of its own citizens, many, if not most of whom belonged to an Indigenous minority. From that point forward, Salvadoran society would be defined by a series of binaries—us/them, rich/poor, Indigenous/mestizo, rural/urban, haves/have-nots, communist/anticommunist. Amidst these binaries, elite Salvadorans constructed a self-serving narrative to justify their privilege and the use of unmitigated violence to defend it. They portrayed themselves as a disaffected minority under constant threat from traitorous laborers, heathen

Indians, and/or communist terrorists, all of whom wanted to steal their hard-earned wealth. This mythic narrative hardened elite resolve and set the battle lines that would play out in longer and even more destructive fashion in the 1980s.[20]

THE MILITARY GOVERNMENTS, 1931–1979

El Salvador has the ignominious distinction of having had the longest run of uninterrupted military rule in modern Latin American history, nearly five decades between 1931 and 1979. Even after 1979, the military's influence over governance did not fundamentally change until the end of the civil war in 1992. Parallel to its long run of military rule, El Salvador had almost no experience with genuinely democratic elections prior to 1992. Furthermore, El Salvador stands out for its utter lack of reformist/progressive governments—that is, leaders or parties that sought to balance the distribution of wealth, implement social reform programs, and expand opportunities to a broader swathe of the population. Whereas most every other country in Latin America had at least some period of sustained progressive governance, El Salvador had next to none.[21]

The lone exception to this drought of democracy and social reform was the short-lived presidency of Arturo Araujo (March 1931–December 1931), a civilian coffee planter with reformist tendencies who came to power in an unprecedented free and fair election. His presidency came crashing down in December 1931 with a coup that brought General Maximiliano Martínez to power. That failure of democracy and reform in 1931 began a recurrent cycle in Salvadoran political life, whereby mass support for democracy and reform surged up, only to be crushed by authoritarian reactionaries. After 1931, El Salvador experienced five main episodes that established the pattern: the fall of Martínez in 1944; the civil-military coup of October 1960; the presidential election of 1972; the presidential election of 1977; and the civil-military coup of 1979. Each of these episodes was a mostly non-violent, mass-based, pro-democracy, pro-reform movement that was suppressed by a combination of military officials and intransigent civilian elites, who eventually resorted to bankrolling paramilitary death squads to defend their interests. Without being overly simplistic, the onset of the civil war in 1980/1981 reflects the truism that when nonviolent demands for change are repeatedly forestalled, support for violent alternatives is likely to grow.[22]

No one knew that the military would be in power for fifty years when a group of young officers ousted Araujo in 1931, so there was no playbook for how military governance would unfold. The standard storyline of military rule in El Salvador is that it was an alliance between coffee oligarchs and officers, with the former allowing the latter to hold government office as long as they protected elites' interests. To an extent, that interpretation is correct. But if military rule was analogous to a marriage, then it was a rocky one, because despite some common goals officers and elites had distinct and competing interests. They united around anticommunism and maintaining the status quo, which meant forestalling mass mobilization and tamping down any popular demands for change. However, officers and elites were from two different worlds. Most officers came from humble backgrounds and they often felt that elites looked down on them. Most elites wanted El Salvador structured in a way that ran contrary to some officers' views. They wanted a society divided between haves and have-nots such that a pool of proletarian labor was available to work on their plantations for minimal wages without government protections. Many officers were more nationalist in their views, and they were willing to countenance reform programs. Consequently, elites distrusted the officers and guarded against any reforms that they believed had the potential to affect their economic freedoms.

The era of military governance can be divided into three periods: the "Martinato," or the rule of General Maximilano Marínez and the four-year continuation after his demise, 1931–1948; the Partido Revolucionario de Unificación Democrática (PRUD, Revolutionary Party of Democratic Unification), 1948–1961; and the Partido de Conciliación Nacional (PCN, National Conciliation Party), 1961–1979. A fourth period of military rule can be defined as 1979–1982, when three different military-civilian juntas governed prior to a national election in 1982 when the civilian Álvaro Alfredo Magaña became president.

Even though military governance in El Salvador unfolded ad hoc without set guidelines, it came to follow a distinct pattern; junior officers accusing their senior counterparts of failing to live up to their promises of modernizing reform and then using those accusations to justify regime change. Each of the three transitions in military rule—1948, 1961, and 1979—were coups led by junior officers against senior officials who they defined as recalcitrant bureaucrats adhering to policies that failed to benefit common Salvadorans. Numerous other failed coups and plots by junior officers followed the same pattern. This pattern came to exist for two main reasons. First, even though the military governments in El Salvador were brutal, authoritarian regimes, their leaders sought popular support. They understood the basic truism of governance, authoritarian or otherwise, that it is easier to rule if the governed lend consent. One of the ways military rulers sought to gain consent was to portray themselves as nationalistic defenders of common people, protecting them from enemies abroad, namely, Communists, and enemies at home, namely greedy economic elites whose only concern was making money. The government of General Martínez set the precedent. No sooner had it murdered thousands of poor Salvadorans in 1932, it turned around and began portraying itself as the reformist defender of working people.[23]

The second reason this pattern of military governance existed is because of the internal structure of the Salvadoran officer corp. Every Salvadoran military officer attended the military academy and graduated in groups of roughly one to two dozen individuals every three years. These graduating classes were called *tandas*, and the members of each tanda were fiercely loyal to one another. Military rule was basically defined by inter-tanda rivalries. When members of a senior tanda occupied the ranking positions in government, then members of junior tandas had nowhere to go. So they employed a highly reformist, populist-sounding rhetoric to justify the overthrow of their superiors. And if they managed to succeed in doing so, which, once again, occurred three times (1948, 1961, and 1979), then when in office they had to at least pretend to live up to their reformist credentials, until the next tanda came along and accused them of being entrenched, selfish bureaucrats.[24]

There was an inherent schizophrenia to military rule in El Salvador. On the one hand, it was a series of non-democratic, authoritarian dictatorships designed to violently maintain the status quo against any form of autonomous, mass-based social change. To achieve these goals, the military had its regular troops, as well as special branches, such as the National Guard, the Hacienda Police, and the Judicial Police, all of which rightfully earned their reputation for brutality. In addition, in 1960, the military founded ORDEN, a massive paramilitary organization that recruited as many as one hundred thousand poor, rural people into its ranks and tasked them with monitoring their neighbors for any signs of "communism."[25]

On the other hand, military rule revolved around this notion of reform. With each passing year, and with each successive administration, the language of reform became more strident, the scapegoating of economic elites became more explicit, and the types and scale of reform initiatives grew. By 1976, the government of Colonel Arturo Molina (1972–1977) even proposed a land reform in the eastern cotton-growing region. He famously said that he would "not take one step back" (*Ni un paso atrás*) from seeing the land reform to fruition, but then he reneged amidst fierce elite opposition.[26]

THE CIVIL WAR, 1980–1992

A civil war occurred in El Salvador because a militant opposition emerged that took up arms against the authoritarian state. The origins of that opposition are complex, and scholarship is beginning to deepen our understanding of its dynamics. Broadly speaking, it resides in the conjoining of an urban guerrilla and urban workers with a vast mobilization of the peasantry in the countryside.[27]

The urban guerrillas emerged out of factional disputes within the leftists over the proper timing for revolution. Between 1932 and 1970, the Salvadoran Communist Party was the sole leftist organization and its ideological line was that El Salvador was not ready for revolution. In 1970, dissidents from within the party who disagreed with that interpretation broke away under the leadership of a former party leader, Salvador Cayetano Carpio, and founded the first autonomous guerrilla organization, the Fuerzas Populares de Liberación Farabundo Martí (FPL, Popular Liberation Forces).

Over the next decade, a half dozen or more distinct guerrilla organizations emerged, with four of them surviving into the civil war along with the FPL. They were: the Ejército Revolucionario del Pueblo (ERP, Peoples' Revolutionary Army), 1972; the Resistencia Nacional (RN, National Resistance), 1975; the Partido Revolucionario de los Trabajadores Centroamericanos (PRTC, Revolutionary Party of the Central American Workers), 1977; and the Fuerzas Armadas de Liberación (FAL, Armed Liberation Forces), 1980. The internecine fighting between these five organizations is not worth going into at the present time, but suffice it to say it was at once personal, ideological, and strategic, and that they competed with one another for resources, members, and international sponsors. It was not until October 1980 that they managed to unite under the banner of the Frente Farabundo Martí para la Liberación Nacional (FMLN, Farabundo Martí National Liberation Front), which became the guerrilla army that waged war against the Salvadoran state until 1992. The "formal" start to the war is often cited as January 1981, when the FMLN, just three months after officially forming, launched its first "Final Offensive," hoping to deliver a quick and lethal blow to the Salvadoran state before Ronald Reagan was sworn in on January 20. The offensive failed, and eventually the war turned into a protracted twelve-year stalemate.[28]

Throughout much of the 1970s, the guerrilla organizations were heavily oriented toward urban areas; most of their members were urbanites, and many of their leaders had college degrees. Each guerrilla organization had an affiliated civilian-front group, which tended to be comprised disproportionately of urban poor and urban-based labor activists. This urban bias characterized even the FPL, despite its Maoist orientation that emphasized protracted peasant mobilization in the countryside. Throughout the 1970s, guerrilla leaders recognized the need to extend their influence into the countryside, not only to expand their support but also to enhance their survivability, because the military's counterinsurgency tactics were most effective in urban areas. A prototypical example of this outreach effort was Rafael Arce Zablah, a leader of the ERP who ventured into the rural areas of Morazán Department, in El Salvador's far northeastern corner, and began building ties with peasant communities. The compelling question for scholarship is what did guerrilla leaders like Arce Zablah find when they arrived at the rural areas. A traditional argument, one naturally supported by the guerrilla leaders and their intellectual allies, was to credit the guerrillas with fomenting a militant consciousness among the peasantry and then subsequently leading the peasants in insurrection throughout the 1980s. The newer scholarship shows the extent to which guerrilla leaders found organized, even militant masses who were ready to fight, or at least to form alliances with the guerrillas, but who didn't necessary need to be awakened to their lived reality by outsiders.[29]

The newer scholarship shows that the popular wing of the Catholic Church, inspired by the emergent theology of liberation and its "preferential option for the poor," nurtured much of this rural consciousness raising. Heeding the call of Vatican II and the Second General Conference of the Latin American and Caribbean Bishops at Medellín, Colombia in 1968, liberationist-oriented parish priests and layworkers established various outreach programs, like peasant training centers to train laypeople to serve as catechists in their communities amidst an extreme shortage of clergymen. The trainees were encouraged to think for themselves and to apply the teachings of the Bible to their everyday reality. Many of the peasants who went through the training centers became grass-roots leaders in their communities, or "peasant intellectuals," in the words of one historian. The training centers did not encourage violence or militancy. But when the peasants began to question the conditions in which they lived, and then faced subsequent repression for doing so, some of them formed self-defense groups and began to consider militancy as a necessary option. This milieu is what the guerrilla leaders entered into in the 1970s. What emerged thereafter would be an evolving relationship between urban guerrillas and rural masses over mobilizing against the authoritarian state.[30]

The failure of the 1981 offensive forced the guerrillas to transfer their entire command structures to the countryside. The ties that each organization had established in the rural areas in the 1970s determined the location of their respective rearguard strongholds and set the geographic pattern for the remainder of the war. The two largest organizations that did the bulk of the fighting, the ERP and the FPL, were based out of Morazán and Chalatenango, respectively, with a strong presence in the San Vicente region. Over the next twelve years, the FMLN functioned as a single army comprised of five distinct, somewhat autonomous "branches" waging war from their respective rural bases atop a peasant army.

In a region of the world that is infamous for violent civil conflicts, El Salvador holds yet another ignominious distinction as having had the most violent conflict per capita between 1980 and 1983. In that period, in a nation of roughly five million people, approximately thirty thousand Salvadorans died, mostly noncombatants, either at the hands of paramilitary death squads or combat units of the Salvadoran military. Many of the victims were killed in large-scale army massacres, including, but hardly limited to, the Sumpul River (May 1980), El Mozote (December 1981), El Calabozo (August 1982), and Copapayo (November 1983). During this phase, the military employed the notorious counterinsurgency tactic of "draining the sea to get to the fish"—that is, eliminating all possible bases of support for the guerrillas, including livestock, agriculture, housing, and people.[31]

By late 1983, the war was at a tipping point. The guerrillas controlled approximately 25 percent of Salvadoran territory and were still confronting the military head on with battalion-sized units. The brutality of the Salvadoran army was putting US funding at risk due to opposition in the US Congress, so the Reagan administration struck a deal. The Salvadoran military would limit the mass killings, curtail the death squads, and purge some of the officers who were most notorious for committing human rights abuses and in exchange the United States would dramatically ramp up its support.[32]

In response to this infusion of material and financial aid to its adversary, the FMLN had to shift its strategy, from a war of position to a war of attrition. Its leaders had to acknowledge that their enemy was stronger than ever, and decided to scale down their combat units into smaller cells and disperse them throughout the countryside. The new strategy was to slowly bleed the Salvadoran state to death through numerous small strikes rather than one decisive blow.[33]

By 1989, it was common to hear Salvadoran government officials and ranking officers in the military say that the FMLN was more or less defeated and the war was effectively over. But those claims proved fantastical, because in November 1989, the guerrillas launched a second final offensive that included nothing less than hundreds of guerrillas occupying portions of the capital city for up to three weeks. The Salvadoran military resorted to carpet bombing poor neighborhoods to dislodge the guerrillas and, infamously, assassinating six Jesuit priests who had been intellectual critics of the government. The offensive was a remarkable tactical achievement, and it exposed the fallacy that the war was near an end. Now the war was truly at a stalemate, and three years later, after protracted negotiations, the opposing sides signed a treaty to end the war.[34]

Women comprised roughly 25 percent of the guerrillas' combatant and leadership ranks, and an even higher percentage of women made up its affiliated support crews. An interesting scholarly dialogue is emerging over the extent to which this female involvement during the war represented a high tide of feminist activism that then retracted after the war, or whether the guerrillas remained patriarchal throughout the war, focusing on class liberation over gender emancipation, thereby setting the stage for a postwar feminist surge.[35]

Regardless of one's views of the Salvadoran guerrillas, their accomplishments were remarkable. Comparative sociological research shows us that their failure to gain power probably extended from a combination of their internal divisions and their adversary's unity, as well as unwavering financial support from the United States.[36] By the time it was over, the war cost some seventy-five thousand lives and displaced nearly one million Salvadorans from their homes. Many Salvadorans are asking themselves if the cost was worth it.

Postwar El Salvador, 1992–2019

To understand postwar El Salvador, one needs look no further than the 1992 Peace Accords. Two sides met at the negotiating table, the Salvadoran government and the FMLN. The FMLN failed to achieve its primary objective in the war, assuming power, but it fought the Salvadoran military to a draw and so it came to the negotiations from a position of relative strength. The Salvadoran government was represented by officials from the conservative Alianza Republicana Nacionalista (ARENA, Nationalist Republican Alliance) party, which had won presidential elections in 1989 that the FMLN had boycotted. Representatives from the Salvadoran military were ostensibly on the government's side, but they found themselves at times negotiating independently.

Since the government's position was to more or less maintain the status quo, its primary demand was that the FMLN disarm and disband. The FMLN refused to do so unless the government addressed the issues that ignited the war in the first place: a reformation of the political system to allow for democratic elections, reforms to the economy to allow for a more equitable distribution of wealth, and reforms to the military. In fact, the FMLN initially demanded that the military be disbanded all together, a la Costa Rica.[37]

It was on the issue of the future of the military that its representatives found themselves negotiating alone. The main representative for the military was General Mauricio Vargas. He is often maligned by military hardliners for giving away too much at the negotiating table, but he insists that ARENA initially joined with the FMLN on disbanding the military, seeing an opportunity to eliminate a historic power rival, so his line of defense is that the military's mere survival was a victory.[38]

Of the FMLN's demands, indeed the military was downsized, which included the elimination of the various units and combat battalions, like the notorious Atlactl Battlion, that had been responsible for so many human rights violations. Still, the military was left with tens of thousands of troops and it retained significant budgetary priority in the postwar era. Economic reforms were a non-starter for ARENA, and so postwar El Salvador remains structurally much the same. The FMLN was most successful in the political realm. It set in place conditions for democratic elections and it transitioned itself into a political party that emerged as the main rival to ARENA. However, much to the surprise and chagrin of many onlookers, to say nothing of the FMLN's supporters, ARENA won the first three presidential elections after the war, in 1994, 1999, and 2004. The FMLN won the next two in 2009 and 2014, and then a third party, Gran Alianza por la Unidad Nacional (GANA, Grand Alliance for National Unity), with a young breakaway candidate from the FMLN, won in 2019. Six elections with a peaceful transition of power between three distinct political parties is a remarkable achievement for a country ravaged by civil war and lacking historic precedent in democracy.[39]

An additional agreement coming out of the negotiations was that the United Nations would form a Truth Commission to investigate human rights abuses during the war. Critics of the Truth Commission claim that its investigators failed to scrutinize the guerrillas with the same intensity as the military. They have a modest leg to stand on.[40] But the overarching findings of the Truth Commission have stood the test of time and confirm what any reasonable-minded person knew throughout the war, that is, that the military and its various affiliates, including the paramilitary death squads, were responsible for the overwhelming majority of human rights violations, no less than 85 percent. By comparison, the Truth Commission found the FMLN responsible for 5 percent, and deemed the other 10 percent indeterminable. One of the most decisive policies coming out of the civil war was the Amnesty Law put through by the ruling ARENA party in 1993. The law made it impossible, with very few exceptions, for anyone to be prosecuted for their actions during the civil war.[41]

Scholars of postwar El Salvador have found a deep sense of malaise among poor Salvadorans, and it is to them that we should turn for the most authentic assessment of the war's aftermath. Sociologists and anthropologists conducting interview-based research find poor Salvadorans asking questions like "Was the war worth it?" and "Democracy is good, but if it doesn't change my life, what difference does it make?" One anthropologist even found people claiming that conditions before the war were better than after the war. These interviews provide qualitative evidence that corresponds to some hard quantitative realities.[42]

In economic terms, postwar El Salvador has shown little ability to generate viable economic productivity. The coffee economy collapsed during the war. Tourism is hampered by violence and gangs. And manufacturing, one of El Salvador's strengths relative to its neighbors prior to the war, is now dominated by *maquila*-like enterprises that provide low-paying jobs but little else in terms of sustained economic growth. As a consequence, nearly 40 percent of Salvadorans live below the poverty line, and the richest 10 percent of the population receives approximately fifteen times the income of the poorest 40 percent.[43]

One of the largest single contributors to GDP (gross domestic product) is remittances from Salvadorans living abroad. In 2019, El Salvador had approximately 6.5 million citizens, with as many as 3 million citizens and/or people of Salvadoran descent living outside the country, mostly in the United States. According to El Salvador's Central Reserve Bank, in 2018 those migrants and expats sent back $5.47 billion in remittances, which accounted for nearly 20 percent of El Salvador's GDP. In short, one of El Salvador's main exports after the war is its people.

In light of these economic constraints, there is not much any Salvadoran government can do, regardless of which political party holds the reins. Nonetheless, the distinct policies pursued by the four ARENA governments between 1989 and 2009 have compounded the problems. ARENA ruled as expected and as promised. Its leaders adopted all the prototypical policies of a rigid neoliberal agenda—a massive privatization of public assets, a downsizing of government resources and capacities, a reduction in taxes for the wealthy, and a reliance on trickle-down economics to address poverty and working-class wages. In the words of a former minister of the economy, ARENA's policies "achieved macroeconomic stability at the price of poverty and unemployment."[44] The privatization policies generated wide-scale social protests, which security forces tamped down. Some analysts contend that El Salvador's disproportionate access to remittances compared to many other countries in the region is the only thing that kept the social pressure from exploding, especially after the global economic downturn in 2008.[45]

By the time the FMLN came to power in 2009, it had little capacity for an alternative economic agenda. Between the path set down by ARENA and neoliberal pressure from the international community, FMLN officials could do little more than reprioritize some spending to implement such policies as free uniforms and lunches to schoolchildren. One political scientist uses the term "captured peace" to describe the extent to which wealthy elites successfully set the parameters for postwar El Salvador.[46] However, a notable exception to this seemingly dire state of affairs is the fact that in 2017 El Salvador became the first nation in the world to prohibit the mining of gold and other metals. This outcome was the product of a conjoining of FMLN governance with a vigorous social/environmental movement.[47]

Government corruption is another topic that sparks the ire of everyday Salvadorans, and also reveals similarities between ARENA and FMLN governments. It is widely believed that ARENA officials and their friends and family members manipulated the system to reap the rewards of the sale of public assets starting in the early 1990s, and similarly to benefit from the decision to make the US dollar the official currency in 2001. ARENA President Francisco Flores (1999–2004) passed away before he could face the accusation that he pocketed $15 million from Taiwan intended for earthquake relief. His successor, Tony Saca, was sentenced in 2018 to ten years in prison for money laundering and improprieties with public funds. And the first FMLN president, Mauricio Funes, fled into exile in Nicaragua in 2016 ahead of accusations of impropriety relating to $300 million in government money. Research indicates that these cases of corruption at the highest level are tips of the iceberg for what was occurring down below.[48]

The issues that most define life for everyday Salvadorans are gangs, gang violence, and the accompanying insecurities. Gangs have become a ubiquitous presence in almost every community and neighborhood throughout El Salvador. One of their primary activities is extortion, charging protection fees to businesses and individuals with the threat of violence for failure to comply. It is common to hear that when a boy becomes a teenager in El Salvador he has two choices, join a gang or leave the country. Young women are targeted for either affiliation with a gang or sexual predation. Rivalries between the two main gangs, Mara Salvatrucha (MS-13) and Calle 18, and the violence associated with their extortionist activities have contributed to El Salvador consistently having one of the highest murder rates in the world outside active warzones.[49]

In their response to the gangs, ARENA and the FMLN have pursued a similarly hard-line approach, which an ARENA government in the mid-2000s dubbed *La Mano Dura* (the Iron Fist). It refers to militarizing gang-ridden neighborhoods and giving security forces carte blanche to deal with suspected gang members. Paramilitary death squads also reemerged that may be responsible for untold numbers of suspected gang members' deaths. The result has been a massive escalation in violence and human rights violations and prisons overflowing with gang members, without any attendant reduction in gang activity or gang membership. One consequence of these hard-line policies is to return the military to a position of prominence within the government.[50]

The combination of economic deprivation, gang violence, and insecurity has resulted in outmigration becoming the defining element of postwar El Salvador. The images of tens of thousands of unaccompanied children arriving at the US border in the mid- to late-2010s only highlighted in extreme form what many Salvadorans believe, that is, that their only hope for a quality, secure life resides outside the country. As many as one thousand Salvadorans leave the country every day. It is a sad testimony about a country that successfully negotiated an end to its civil war and experienced six democratic presidential elections thereafter. And yet, hope endures. Social movements continue to flourish, the second generation of the liberationist church is alive and well, and the winner of the 2019 presidential election, Nayib Bukele, won behind a huge surge in young voters who demanded change. Regardless of whether Bukele can deliver on his promises, clearly his young supporters have not given up hope in El Salvador.[51]

CONCLUSION

The political scientists Scott Mainaring and Anibel Pérez Líñan insist that El Salvador's civil war was not the inevitable consequence of poor economic conditions.[52] In fact, they reveal that many of El Salvador's neighboring countries had worse economic indicators but did not fall into civil war. They insist that the difference lay in politics and the corresponding decisions made by human actors. In other words, the same priorities that caused El Salvador to have the skewed budgetary priorities in 1910 were those that sent the country hurtling down the path to war in the 1970s. The present chapter began with the notion that these decisions were rooted in a zero-sum game of "ethnic politics," a term meant to indicate that Salvadorans have been hopelessly divided throughout their modern history and thus incapable of embracing shared notions of the public good. This division had a distinctly ethnic component in the nineteenth and early twentieth centuries, which was then transformed into a more ethnically homogenous class divide by the mid- to late-twentieth century. Regardless, the result was the same. There were key moments when alternative paths could have followed, but in each of them a less communitarian choice was made. And thus the story of El Salvador has been that of recurrent attempts to create a more egalitarian society, only to see those attempts repeatedly forestalled by intransigent authoritarians, who want to defend their privilege against all comers.

NOTES

1. Enrique Córdova, *Miradas retrospectivas por el Dr. Enrique Córdova, 1881–1966* (San Salvador: n.p., 1993), 86.
2. Robert Williams, *States and Social Evolution: Coffee and the Rise of National Governments in Central America* (Chapel Hill: University of North Carolina Press, 1994); James Mahoney, *The Legacies of Liberalism: Path Dependence and Political Regimes in Central America* (Baltimore, MD: Johns Hopkins University Press, 2001); Robert Holden, *Armies without Nations: Public Violence and State Formation in Central America, 1821–1960* (New York: Oxford University Press, 2004); and Paul Drake, *Between Tyranny and Anarchy: A History of Democracy in Latin America* (Stanford, CA: University of Stanford Press, 2009).
3. Josefa Viegas Guillem, "Historiografía salvadoreña de 1950 a 2000," *Revista La Universidad* 21 (2013): 77–158; Sajid Alfredo Herrera Mena, "Versiones y usos de la historia desde el estado salvadoreño: a propósito del bicentenario, 1811–2011," *Revista de Historia* 70 (julio-diciembre, 2014): 143–158.
4. Lowell Gudmundson and Héctor Lindo-Fuentes, *Central America, 1821–1871: Liberalism before Liberal Reform* (Tuscaloosa: University of Alabama Press, 1995).
5. Sajid Alfredo Herrera Mena, "Luchas de poder, prácticas políticas y lenguaje constitucional: San Salvador a fines de 1821," *Hacer Historia en El Salvador: Revista Electrónica de Estudios Históricos* 1, no. 1 (2007): 1–15; María Eugenia López Velásquez, "Pueblos de indios, de ladinos y de mulatos de San Salvador y Sonsonate en tiempos de reformas y transiciones políticas, 1737–1841," PhD diss., El Colegio de Michoacán, 2017. The classic comparative study of the independence process in Latin America remains. John Lynch, *The Spanish American Revolutions: 1808–1826* (New York: W.W. Norton, 1973).
6. Héctor Lindo Fuentes, *Weak Foundations: The Economy of El Salvador in the Nineteenth Century* (Berkeley: University of California Press, 1990).
7. Erik Ching, *Authoritarian El Salvador: Politics and the Making of the Military Regimes, 1880–1940* (South Bend, IN: University of Notre Dame Press, 2014).

8. Carlos Gregorio López Bernal," Historiografía y movimientos sociales en El Salvador, 1811–1932: un balance preliminar," *Revista de Historia* 67 (Enero–Junio 2013): 89–119; Jorge Alberto Domínguez Sosa, *Ensayo histórico sobre las tribus nonualcas y su caudillo Anastasio Aquino* (San Salvador: Ministerio de Educación, 1964); Alfredo Ramírez, "Anastacio Aquino: ícono histórico de los Nonualcos," *Revista de Humanidades y Ciencias Sociales* 2, no. 8 (Julio-Diciembre, 2016): 87–122.

9. Aldo Lauria, "Los indígenas de Cojutepeque: la política faccional y el estado en El Salvador, 1830–1890," in *Identidades nacionales y estado moderno en Centroamérica*, edited by Arturo Taracena and Jean Piel, 237–252 (San José: FLACSO/EDUCA, 1995); Aldo Lauria, *An Agrarian Republic: Commercial Agriculture and the Politics of Peasant Communities in El Salvador, 1823–1914* (Pittsburgh: University of Pittsburgh Press, 1999); Carlos Gregorio López Bernal, *Tradiciones inventadas y discursos nacionalistas: El imaginario nacional de la época liberal en El Salvador, 1876–1932* (San Salvador: Imprenta Universitaria, 2007); Ching, *Authoritarian El Salvador*.

10. David Browning, *El Salvador: Landscape and Society* (Oxford: Clarendon Press, 1971). For a full sense of the historiography, see Lauria, *Agrarian Republic*.

11. As a notable exception on the absence of rural insurrection vis-à-vis the privatization decrees, see Aldo Lauria, "Land, Community, and Revolt in Late-Nineteenth Century Indian Izalco, El Salvador," *Hispanic American Historical Review* 79, no. 3 (1999): 495–534. On the issue of the privatization decrees, see Lauria, *Agrarian Republic*; and Geraldina Portillo, *La tenencia de la tierra en El Salvador: La Libertad, 1897–1901, Santa Ana, 1882–1884, 1897–1898* (San Salvador: Universidad de El Salvador, 2006).

12. Lauria, *Agrarian Republic*.

13. Carlos Pérez Pineda, *La Guardia Nacional y le república cafetalera, 1912–1932* (San Salvador: Ministerio de Cultura/Universidad Gerardo Barrios, 2018).

14. Ching, *Authoritarian El Salvador*, 164–171.

15. Héctor Lindo is shedding new light on subaltern activism and social movements around the issue of anti-imperialism in the 1910s and their influence on national politics. Héctor Lindo Fuentes, El Alborotador de Centroamérica. San Salvador: UCA Editores, 2019.

16. Thomas Anderson, *Matanza: El Salvador's Communist Revolt of 1932* (Lincoln: University of Nebraska Press, 1971); Jeff Gould and Aldo Lauria, *To Rise in Darkness: Revolution, Repression, and Memory in El Salvador, 1920–1932* (Durham, NC: Duke University Press, 2008); Ching, *Authoritarian El Salavdor*, ch. 8; Patricia Alvarenga, *Cultura y ética de la violencia: El Salvador, 1880–1932* (San José: EDUCA, 1996); and Héctor Pérez Brignoli, "Indians, Communists, and Peasants: The 1932 Rebellion in El Salvador," in *Coffee, Society, and Power in Latin America*, edited by William Roseberry, Lowell Gudmundson, and Mario Samper Kutschbach, 232–261 (Baltimore, MD: Johns Hopkins University Press, 1995).

17. On the political battles, see Ching, *Authoritarian El Salvador*. On both politics and sexuality, see Gould and Lauria, *To Rise in Darkness*.

18. The outlines of the debate can be found in Ching, *Authoritarian El Salvador*, 295–304.

19. Virginia Tilley, *Seeing Indians: A Study of Race, Nation, and Power in El Salvador* (Albuquerque: University of New Mexico Press, 2005). On the issue of ethnicity and government conduct relating to Indians in the immediate aftermath of the Matanza, see Ching, *Authoritarian El Salvador*, ch. 8.

20. Héctor Lindo-Fuentes, Erik Ching, and Rafael Lara-Martínez, *Remembering a Massacre in El Salvador: The Insurrection of 1932, Roque Dalton, and the Politics of Historical Memory*

(Albuquerque: University of New Mexico Press, 2007); and Erik Ching, *Stories of Civil War in El Salvador: A Battle over Memory* (Chapel Hill: University of North Carolina Press, 2016), ch. 2.

21. On military rule, see Roberto Turcios, *Autoritarismo y modernización: El Salvador, 1950–1960* (San Salvador: Ediciones Tendencias, 1993); William Stanley, *The Protection Racket State: Elite Politics, Military Extortion and Civil War in El Salvador* (Philadelphia: Temple University Press, 1996); Philip Williams and Knut Walter, *Militarization and Demilitarization in El Salvador's Transition to Democracy* (Pittsburgh: University of Pittsburgh Press, 1997); Jorge Cáceres Prendes, "Discourses of Reformism: El Salvador, 1944–1960," PhD diss., University of Texas, 1995; and Héctor Lindo Fuentes and Erik Ching, *Modernizing Minds in El Salvador: Education Reform and the Cold War, 1960–1980* (Albuquerque: University of New Mexico Press, 2012).

22. The range of relevant titles is quite vast, but as a preliminary sampling, see Patricia Parkman, *Nonviolent Insurrection in El Salvador: The Fall of Maximiliano Hernández Martínez* (Tucson: University of Arizona Press, 1988); Roberto Turcios, *Rebelión: San Salvador, 1960* (San Salvador: MINED/CENICSH, 2018); José Inocencio Alas, *Iglesia, tierra y lucha campesina: Suchitoto, El Salvador, 1968–1977* (El Salvador: Asociación de Frailes Franciscanos, 2003); and Jeff Gould, "Ignacio Ellacuría and the Salvadorean Revolution," *Journal of Latin American Studies* 47, no. 2 (May 2015): 285–315.

23. See Ching, *Authoritarian El Salvador*, ch. 8.

24. On the tanda system, see Brian Bosch, *The Salvadoran Officer Corps & the Final Offensive of 1981* (Jefferson, NC: McFarland, 1999).

25. US Bureau of Citizenship and Immigration Services, "El Salvador: The role of ORDEN in the El Salvadoran civil war," October 16, 2000, SLV01001.ZAR. https://www.refworld.org/docid/3dee04524.html.

26. The 1968 education reform is another prototypical example of this schizophrenia. See Lindo Fuentes and Ching, *Modernizing Minds*.

27. The two standard surveys of the war are Hugh Byrne, *El Salvador's Civil War: A Study of Revolution* (Boulder, CO: Lynne Rienner, 1996); and Tommie Sue Montgomery, *Revolution in El Salvador: From Civil Strife to Civil Peace* (2nd ed.) (Boulder, CO: Westview Press, 1995). It is difficult to find an academic analysis that accuses the guerrilla leadership of starting the war unnecessarily, but the rare exception is Yvon Grenier, *Emergence of Insurgency in El Salvador: Ideology and Political Will* (Pittsburgh: University of Pittsburgh Press, 1999). For a good window into the growing body of postwar scholarship on the war and its origins, see Jorge Juárez, ed., *Historia y debates sobre el conflicto armado salvadoreño y sus secuelas* (San Salvador: Fundación Friedrich Ebert, 2014); Mauricio Menjívar Ochoas and Ralph Sprenkels, *La revolución revisitada: nuevas perspectivas sobre la insurrección y la guerra en El Salvador* (San Salvador: UCA Editores, 2017); Joaquín Chávez, *Poets and Prophets of the Resistance: Intellectuals and the Origins of El Salvador's Civil War* (New York: Oxford University Press, 2017); Jeff Gould, *Solidarity under Siege: The Salvadoran Labor Movement, 1970–1990* (New York: Cambridge University Press, 2019); and Luis Huezo Mixco, *Desafiando los poderes: acción colectiva y frentes de masas en El Salvador, 1948–1980* (San Salvador: Secretaría de Cultura de la Presidencia, Dirección Nacional de Investigaciones en Cultura y Arte, Universidad Gerardo Barrios, 2017).

28. Charles Brockett, *Political Movements and Violence in Central America* (New York: Cambridge University Press, 2005); and Alberto Martín Álvarez and Eudald Cortina Orero, "The Genesis and Internal Dynamics of El Salvador's People's Revolutionary Army, 1970–1976," *Journal of Latin American Studies* 46, no. 4 (November 2014): 663–689.

29. Joaquín Villalobos, "Homenaje a Rafael Antonio Arce Zablah," *El Diario de Hoy*, September 28, 2005; Martín Álvarez and Cortina Orero, "The Genesis"; and Chávez, *Poets and Prophets*, 10.

30. Leigh Binford, "Peasants, Catechists and Revolutionaries: Organic Intellectuals in the Salvadoran Revolution, 1980–1992," in *Landscapes of Struggle: Politics, Society and Community in El Salvador*, edited by Aldo Lauria and Leigh Binford, 105–125 (Pittsburgh: University of Pittsburgh Press, 2004); and Peter Sánchez, *Priest under Fire: Padre David Rodríguez, the Catholic Church, and El Salvador's Revolutionary Movement* (Gainesville: University Press of Florida, 2015). Chávez, *Poets and Prophets*, employed the term "peasant intellectuals." In a review of Chávez and other related books, I suggested that the relationship between urban guerrillas and rural peasants is best understood in dialectical terms. See Erik Ching, "The Popular Church and Revolutionary Insurgency in El Salvador," *Latin American Research Review* 53, no. 4 (December 2018): 876–885.

31. Leigh Binford, *The El Mozote Massacre: Human Rights and Global Implications* (2nd ed.) (Tuscon: University of Arizona Press, 2016); Mark Danner, *The Massacre at El Mozote* (New York: Vintage, 1994).

32. On the US role in the civil war, from competing perspectives, see Russell Crandall, *The Salvador Option: The United States in El Salvador, 1977–1992* (New York: Cambridge University Press, 2016); and Brian D'Haeseleer, *The Salvadoran Crucible: The Failure of U.S. Counterinsurgency in El Salvador, 1979–1992* (Lawrence: University Press of Kansas, 2017).

33. John Waghelstein, "El Salvador: Observations and Experiences in Counterinsurgency, an Individual Study Project," Carlisle Barracks, PA, Army War College, Senior Officers Oral History Program, 1985.

34. On the Jesuits, see Theresa Whitfield, *Paying the Price: Ignacio Ellacuría and the Murdered Jesuits of El Salvador* (Philadelphia: Temple University Press, 1994); and Philip Bennett, "Burying the Jesuits," *Vanity Fair*, November 1990, 110–123.

35. Diana Sierra Becerra, "Insurgent Butterflies: Gender and Revolution in El Salvador, 1965–2015," PhD diss., University of Michigan, 2017; Jocelyn Viterna, *Women in War: The Micro-processes of Mobilization in El Salvador* (New York: Oxford University Press, 2013); Ilja Luciak, *After the Revolution: Gender and Democracy in El Salvador, Nicaragua, and Guatemala* (Baltimore, MD: Johns Hopkins University Press, 2001); Karen Kampwirth, *Women & Guerrilla Movements: Nicaragua, El Salvador, Chiapas, Cuba* (University Park: Pennsylvania State University Press, 2003); Karen Kampwirth, *Feminism and the Legacy of Revolution: Nicaragua, El Salvador, Chiapas* (Athens: Ohio University Press, 2004); and Julie Shayne, *The Revolution Question: Feminisms in El Salvador, Chile, and Cuba* (New Brunswick, NJ: Rutgers University Press, 2004).

36. Timothy Wickham-Crowley, *Guerrillas and Revolution in Latin America: A Comparative Study of Insurgents and Regimes since 1956* (Princeton, NJ: Princeton University Press, 1991).

37. On the negotiations, see Christine Wade, *Captured Peace: Elites and Peacebuilding in El Salvador* (Athens: Ohio University Press, 2016); and Diana Negroponte, *Seeking Peace in El Salvador: The Struggle to Reconstruct a Nation at the End of the Cold War* (New York: Palgrave Macmillan, 2012).

38. Mauricio Vargas and Jean Krasno, "Yale-UN Oral History Project: Central American Peace Process," San Salvador, El Salvador, June 27, 1997; and Ricardo Vaquerano et al., "Plática con general Mauricio Vargas," *El Faro*, January 24, 2010. http://www.elfaro.net/es/201001/el_agora/977/.

39. Wade, *Captured Peace*; Ralph Sprenkels, *After Insurgency: Revolution and Electoral Politics in El Salvador* (South Bend, IN: University of Notre Dame Press, 2018); Ruben Zamora, *La izquierda salvadoreña: partidaria salvadoreña: entre la identidad y el poder* (San Salvador: FLACSO, 2003); and Ainhoa Montoya, *The Violence of Democracy: Political Life in Postwar El Salvador* (New York: Palgrave Macmillan, 2018).

40. Geovani Galeas and Edwin Ernesto Ayala, *Grandeza y miseria en una guerrilla* (2nd ed.) (San Salvador: Centroamérica 21, 2008).

41. UN Commission on the Truth for El Salvador, *From Madness to Hope: The Twelve-Year War in El Salvador* (New York: United Nations Security Council, 1993).

42. Irina Carlota Silber, *Everyday Revolutionaries: Gender, Violence and Disillusionment in Postwar El Salvador* (New Brunswick, NJ: Rutgers University Press, 2011); Ellen Moodie, *El Salvador in the Aftermath of Peace: Crime, Uncertainty and the Transition to Democracy* (Philadelphia: University of Pennsylvania Press, 2010); Michael Gorkin and Marta Evelyn Pineda, *From Beneath the Volcano: The Story of a Salvadoran Campesino and His Family* (Tucson: University of Arizona Press, 2011); and Sprenkels, *After Insurgency*.

43. Alexander Segovia, *Transformación estructural y reforma económica en El Salvador* (Guatemala: F&G Editores, 2002); Wade, *Captured Peace*; and Alexander Segovia, *Economía y poder: recomposición de las élites económicas salvadoreñas* (Guatemala: F&G Editores/INCIDE, 2018).

44. Wade, *Captured Peace*, 121.

45. Paul Almeida, *Waves of Protest: Popular Struggle in El Salvador, 1925–2005* (Minneapolis: University of Minnesota Press, 2008). On remittances, see Wade, *Captured Peace*, 133–142.

46. Wade, *Captured Peace*.

47. Gene Palumbo and Elisabeth Malkin, "El Salvador, Prizing Water over Gold, Bans All Metal Mining," *New York Times*, March 29, 2017; and Rose Spalding, *Contesting Trade in Central America: Market Reform and Resistance* (Austin: University of Texas Press, 2015).

48. Wade, *Captured Peace*, 142–146; and Bryan Avelar, "A Former El Salvador President Tells How He Robbed the State," *Insight Crime*, August 14, 2018. https://www.insightcrime.org/news/analysis/former-el-salvador-president-story-how-he-stole/.

49. Óscar Martínez et al., "Killers on a Shoestring: Inside the Gangs of El Salvador," *New York Times*, November 16, 2016; and T. W. Ward, *Gangsters without Borders: An Ethnography of a Salvadoran Street Gang* (New York: Oxford University Press, 2012).

50. Sonja Wolf, *Mano Dura: The Politics of Gang Control in El Salvador* (Austin: University of Texas Press, 2017); and Spring Miller and James Cavallaro, eds., *No Place to Hide: Gang, State and Clandestine Violence in El Salvador* (Cambridge, MA: Harvard Law School, 2009).

51. Carlos Sandoval Garcia, ed., *Migraciones en América Central Políticas, territorios y actores* (San José, CR: Editorial UCR, 2016).

52. Scott Manwairing and Aníbel Pérez Liñán, *Democracies and Dictatorships in Latin America: Emergence, Survival, and Fall* (New York: Cambridge University Press, 2014).

FURTHER READING

Binford, Leigh. *The El Mozote Massacre: Human Rights and Global Implications*. 2nd ed. Tuscon: University of Arizona Press, 2016.

Chávez, Joaquín. *Poets and Prophets of the Resistance: Intellectuals and the Origins of El Salvador's Civil War*. New York: Oxford University Press, 2017.

D'Haeseleer, Brian. *The Salvadoran Crucible: The Failure of U.S. Counterinsurgency in El Salvador, 1979-1992*. Lawrence: University Press of Kansas, 2017.

Gould, Jeff, and Aldo Lauria. *To Rise in Darkness: Revolution, Repression, and Memory in El Salvador, 1920–1932*. Durham, NC: Duke University Press, 2008.

Lauria, Aldo. *An Agrarian Republic: Commercial Agriculture and the Politics of Peasant Communities in El Salvador, 1823–1914*. Pittsburgh: University of Pittsburgh Press, 1999.

Lindo Fuentes, Héctor. *Weak Foundations: The Economy of El Salvador in the Nineteenth Century*. Berkeley: University of California Press, 1990.

Lindo Fuentes, Héctor, and Erik Ching. *Modernizing Minds in El Salvador: Education Reform and the Cold War, 1960-1980*. Albuquerque: University of New Mexico Press, 2012.

Montgomery, Tommie Sue. *Revolution in El Salvador: From Civil Strife to Civil Peace*. 2nd ed. Boulder, CO: Westview Press, 1995.

Moodie, Ellen. *El Salvador in the Aftermath of Peace: Crime, Uncertainty and the Transition to Democracy*. Philadelphia: University of Pennsylvania Press, 2010.

Silber, Irina Carlota. *Everyday Revolutionaries: Gender, Violence and Disillusionment in Postwar El Salvador*. New Brunswick, NJ: Rutgers University Press, 2011.

Sprenkels, Ralph. *After Insurgency: Revolution and Electoral Politics in El Salvador*. South Bend, IN: University of Notre Dame Press, 2018.

Viterna, Jocelyn. *Women in War: The Micro-processes of Mobilization in El Salvador*. New York: Oxford University Press, 2013.

Wade, Christine. *Captured Peace: Elites and Peacebuilding in El Salvador*. Athens: Ohio University Press, 2016.

Whitfield, Theresa. *Paying the Price: Ignacio Ellacuría and the Murdered Jesuits of El Salvador*. Philadelphia: Temple University Press, 1994.

Wolf, Sonja. *Mano Dura: The Politics of Gang Control in El Salvador*. Austin: University of Texas Press, 2017.

CHAPTER 21

NICARAGUA

JULIE A. CHARLIP

LEÓN VS. GRANADA, OR LIBERALS VS. CONSERVATIVES

The collapse of the Central American Federation in 1838 should have set the stage for the emergence of a Nicaraguan nation-state. But Nicaragua was little more than a region of city-states. The dominant areas were long-time rivals: León, the traditional colonial administrative center, and Granada, the commercial hub located on Lake Nicaragua. Nicaragua's elites organized into two main parties: Liberals, based in León, and Conservatives, in Granada. Although in some areas of Latin America the two parties professed different political beliefs, in Nicaragua ideology was not what divided them. As Arturo J. Cruz Jr. put it, "in their great majority the gentry of the epoch were imbued by the ethos of positivism, progress and world trade. In this context all considered themselves 'Liberals' in spirit, if not in name, regardless of their political affiliation. By the same token, when it came to the subject of order all were 'Conservatives,' and following the trauma of independence they shared a common horror of anarchy and the mob."[1] Yet they fought each other and among themselves in groups that Enrique Guzmán called "tiny, idealess clusters."[2] Their often violent political struggles were centered in regional networks of ambitious elites, dominated by wealthy landowning families.[3]

Because the would-be state builders feared a strong, centralized power, they wrote a constitution in 1838 that gave the supreme director a two-year term with no reelection. The controversial constitution remained in effect until 1854, not because of its strength but because elites could not agree on its revision. A proposed draft in 1848 was deemed by the Liberals to give the executive too much authority. A similar proposal in 1854 sparked the civil war that would lead to the infamous intervention of filibuster William Walker.

Meanwhile, most Nicaraguans continued to live their lives independently in scattered villages. The very weakness of the Nicaraguan state enabled them to live much as they had in the colonial era in a mixture of subsistence and market economy. Struggling national governments, both Conservative and Liberal, tried to incorporate these communities as sources of taxes, labor, and land, sparking countrywide rebellions in the late 1840s.[4] What elites feared most was that scattered rebellions of Indigenous and ladinos might unite, a specter raised by the popularity of charismatic leader Bernabé Somoza. With elite dominance at stake, Conservatives and Liberals found rare unity to capture and execute the "bandit" Somoza.[5] The bandit epithet would be employed to discredit any lower-class challengers, including Augusto C. Sandino in the twentieth century.

While weakness at the top gave freedom to the communities, elites were also carefully building a power structure in the countryside. They sought links with regional and local caudillos, who provided people with leadership, patronage, and protection. "Caudillo power, in turn, derived from . . . private ownership of large tracts of land; dense webs of personalistic, patrimonial relationships in city and countryside; personal control of local and regional state offices; and personal control of the means of organised violence."[6] Their relationship with elites at the national level was one of mutual need—the caudillo could mobilize people in support of Liberal and Conservative leaders, who could provide the caudillo with resources. That is not to imply that caudillos had a monopoly of power in town and countryside, where Indigenous communities jockeyed with ladino *campesinos* to protect their spaces.

The William Walker intervention, the conflict that most marked the nineteenth century, was sparked by a dispute over the election of Fruto Chamorro as president under the new 1854 Constitution. Chamorro was already supreme director, and the new constitution doubled the executive term to four years. The new charter also attempted to curtail the León-Granada rivalry by moving the capital to Managua.[7] León objected and set siege to Granada for eight months. The Liberals were virtually defeated in February 1855, but peace negotiations failed. Instead, the Liberals decided to seek foreign help and hired filibuster William Walker, a Tennessee mercenary.[8] Although Walker arrived with only fifty-seven men, he quickly gained control of the struggle. Rather than a head-on attack on Granada, he spent three months securing the San Juan del Sur-La Virgen transit road—the final overland section of the transisthmian route—establishing a route for additional men and supplies. With about one hundred filibusters and three hundred Nicaragüenses, he waged a surprise attack on Granada, winning the war in a mere five months.

Walker had dreams of leading Nicaragua and populating it with US colonists, and a surprising number of Nicaraguans supported his idea. Both Liberals and Conservatives admired Yankee know-how and sought a civilizing influence over the Indigenous and lower-class ladinos. Walker's influence strengthened more radical Liberals, who supported a more inclusive political system with direct elections, largely because they sought popular support to offset the power of the Conservative Granada elites.[9] Walker, too, made promises of an anti-elite revolution. He gained the support of regional caudillos who struggled against nationalizing elites, and Indigenous who wanted to keep their lands and autonomy. They supported his presidency in 1856 but were appalled by the obviously fraudulent election.[10] He then betrayed the popular classes by enforcing anti-vagrancy laws, sentencing violators to forced labor, and, finally, decreeing slavery and decrying "mongrel" mestizos. He then alienated elites by confiscating their land and political power.[11]

Walker's actions led Liberals and Conservatives to set aside their differences and fight the North American usurper. On September 12, 1856, leaders from León and Granada signed the *Pacto Providencial*, and their unity encouraged support from Guatemala, El Salvador, and Costa Rica in the "National War." The final blow was struck by US Commodore Cornelius Vanderbilt, founder of the Accessory Transit Company, which provided steamship service across Nicaragua. Walker had supported Vanderbilt's rivals, and Vanderbilt returned the favor. Without the transit company steamships, Walker could not replenish his forces.[12] Walker fled, after burning down Granada, and was executed in Honduras when he attempted a return in 1860. But the transit route, Nicaragua's hope for prosperity, was gone too.

THE CONSERVATIVE REPUBLIC

Because they had recruited him, the Liberals were blamed for Walker. The elite unity of the *Pacto Providencial*, an agreement that transcended narrow political party interests, proved ephemeral. In June 1857, a joint government was formed by Liberal Máximo Jerez and Conservative General Tomás Martínez. But the Constitutional Assembly overlooked the Liberal and elected Martínez as supreme director, initiating thirty years of Conservative rule.[13]

The Conservative Republic has been idealized as "a 'golden age' of conservative administration, national identity and unified policy."[14] It has been disparaged as stagnant, especially in contrast to the dynamism of the Liberal period that would follow.[15] Neither view fully captures the thirty years. Conservatives as much as Liberals wanted to modernize Nicaragua's economy; they built infrastructure for an export economy and incentivized the new production of coffee.[16] Before the introduction of coffee, Nicaragua produced indigo and cochineal, but due to competition from neighboring countries it did not earn enough from these exports to fund the infrastructure desired for modernization. Most Nicaraguans had access to land for subsistence, and elites turned to cattle ranching due to the paucity of labor. While the Conservatives succeeded in creating a functional state, establishing a property registry in 1877 to regularize and commercialize property, attempts at forcing campesinos to work on large estates were much more difficult to enforce.[17]

The Conservatives also hoped that a transisthmian canal would bring prosperity. The canal was an old dream: Spanish colonial authorities studied the idea, Thomas Jefferson expressed US interest in 1788,[18] and the Central American Federation surveyed the region in the 1830s. Cornelius Vanderbilt hoped to replace his transit route across Nicaragua with a canal. The United States and Great Britain agreed in the 1850

Clayton-Bulwer Treaty that neither country would pursue a canal without the acquiescence of the other. Characteristically, neither saw a need to include Nicaraguans in the discussion. But Nicaraguans had their own discussions about the canal. Conservative President José Laureano Pineda (1851–1853) promoted the canal's ability to "transform Nicaragua into a 'cosmopolitan nation' by making it the world's greatest emporium and a center of foreign immigration."[19] As a result, the canal "determined foreign policy during the Conservative Thirty Years."[20]

In the 1870s, President Ulysses S. Grant authorized a survey of Nicaragua. As a young captain and quartermaster in 1852 he had been tasked with leading the Fourth Infantry regiment to the Pacific Coast from Sackets Harbor, New York. He had crossed via Panama, and the miserable experience convinced him that Nicaragua was the better path; his appointed commission agreed. But in 1876, as Grant left office, the French were already digging a canal in Panama directed by Ferdinand de Lesseps, of Suez Canal fame.[21] By the late 1880s, the French had failed, and both the United States and Nicaragua were back in the game. The US Congress granted a corporate charter to the Maritime Canal Company, authorizing the privately held company to build the canal with no US government fiscal responsibilities,[22] and reached agreement with Nicaragua to build the canal in 1887.[23] In 1890, the company began dredging the San Juan River, but the 1893 depression halted work after more than $5 million had been spent.[24]

The "golden age" peaceful, democratic image of the Conservative Republic ignores the era's political intrigue and violent uprisings. Martínez wanted to serve a second term, and when rejected by his own Conservative party, he turned to the Liberals he had once fought. Ambition trumped party loyalty. Violent revolt was still an acceptable alternative to democratic transitions: when Martínez could not control his successor, Fernando Guzmán, he recruited his former enemy, Jerez, to overthrow the government. The four-month 1863 uprising posed enough of a threat for Guzmán to step down as president to lead troops to defeat the coup attempt.[25]

Guzmán could be credited with beginning the short-lived tradition of respecting the constitutional prohibition on reelection. He did, however, handpick his successor, Vicente Cuadra, the first of five Granadans to serve as president. "All were wealthy hacendados and merchants, all were descended from Spanish families established in Nicaragua in the eighteenth century; all had attained maturity in the years of . . . anarchy of the first half of the nineteenth century and were haunted by the memory of vainglorious caudillos and their foreign entanglements."[26]

Although Liberal–Conservative rivalry was still the primary political struggle, there were divisions within each group and a willingness to cross party lines when convenient. The Conservatives divided into the Catholic Conservative Party (Iglesieros), the Progressives, and the Genuines, in constant conflict throughout the 1880s.[27] The last president of the Conservative Republic, Roberto Sacasa, found both his support and challenge from these fractured groupings. He appointed Liberals from León and Managua and Conservative Iglesieros, repressing the rest of the Conservative Party.[28] The old Conservative leadership in turn joined forces with Liberals to overthrow Sacasa. But a coalition junta ruled a mere ninety days before León revolted and Granada formed its own government. The tide turned when José Santos Zelaya, a Managua coffee grower, joined the Liberals of León. His forces quickly took Managua and Granada, and a new Liberal junta was formed. In September 1893, a constituent assembly wrote a new, Liberal constitution and elected Zelaya president.[29]

José Santos Zelaya and the Canal Redux

Zelaya would rule for sixteen years. His presidency coincided with the growth of international trade, as newly industrialized countries provided growing markets for Nicaragua's agricultural and mineral products. The Conservatives had provided the groundwork for economic growth, but Zelaya accelerated modernization with increased trade and foreign investment. While coffee dominated, Nicaragua also produced sugar, rubber, and gold. Modernization was not just economic; it included expanding education, secularization, and limited military professionalization. Sometimes considered a sharp break from the Conservative Republic, both regimes had bipartisan support.[30]

Zelaya has been vilified as a dictator, lauded as a modernizer, and idealized for standing up to the United States. There is truth in elements of all three descriptions. Much of the earlier historiography about Zelaya repeated the negative attitudes of contemporary US officials, such as President William Howard Taft's famous description of him as "a blot on the history of Nicaragua." That assessment prevailed until Zelaya's reputation was reconsidered and rehabilitated in 1977 by Charles L. Stansifer, who described him as Nicaragua's great modernizer. "Business, education, the military, transportation, church-state relations—all witnessed a rapid transformation in the Zelaya years, so much so that we are entitled to equate the onset of modernization with the years of the Zelaya government."[31] Stansifer's reevaluation of Zelaya also promoted the idea that, in contrast, the Conservative era did little to develop Nicaragua, a view reinforced by Sandinista historians.[32]

Zelaya did rule as a dictator, reelected by the Assembly with no opposition between his frequent states of siege.[33] He repressed his Conservative opponents with detention, expulsion, and expropriation.[34] Frequent revolts prompted the militarization of society. Nonetheless, Conservatives maintained control of their local bases of support. They positioned themselves as defenders of the popular classes, particularly the Indigenous, against Liberal land and labor laws designed to commercialize *ejidos* and require labor on private coffee fincas, even though "Zelaya did little more than intensify the policies of his Conservative predecessors."[35] That the Conservatives would foster Indigenous support by defending their land rights shows their deep opposition to Liberal Party leadership, given their earlier support for similar policies.[36]

The regime's greatest achievement was to be the incorporation of the Atlantic Coast within Nicaragua's national boundaries. The area had never been conquered by the Spanish and was isolated from the rest of the country, divided by mountains and forests. The region was originally populated by three Indigenous groups—Miskitu, Sumu, and Rama; they were later joined by creoles, a Black population of freed or escaped slaves and Jamaican immigrants. The British developed relationships with the Indigenous groups during the seventeenth century as they competed with the Spanish in the Caribbean. In 1631, Britain crowned a Moskitu king and gave him a royal commission. Recognizing competing groups among the Moskitu, the British gave out a few commissions, though not kingships, from 1730 to 1740. These leaders carried out trade with both the British and Spanish and levied taxes, even on British colonists. The British left after they ceded the territory to Spain in the 1783 Treaty of Versailles ending the American Revolution. The Spanish independence wars and subsequent Central American conflicts left the Kingdom of Mosquitia on its own until 1844, when the British returned, supposedly at the king's request, and established a protectorate.[37] Great Britain recognized Nicaraguan sovereignty in the 1860 Treaty of Managua, with a guarantee of self-governance in the newly designated Moskito Reserve; arbitration in 1881 confirmed Mosquitia autonomy.[38]

Zelaya dispatched soldiers to the Mosquitia in February 1894, shortly after taking power. The government saw the Mosquitia, which became half of Nicaragua's territory, as a region of great wealth that unfortunately was occupied by people who had no interest in becoming part of Nicaragua. "The government wanted to conquer territory and riches, but it had to integrate men and women."[39] The Miskitu responded by petitioning Queen Victoria for protection.[40] But this time, Great Britain left the region to the Nicaraguan government.[41] The Miskitu were pressured into the Convención Mosquita of 1894; the government conceded communal autonomy and exemption from taxes and military service and pledged to invest income from Mosquitia production back into the region. In subsequent agreements, however, the Indigenous "voluntarily" gave up rights guaranteed in the 1894 accord.[42]

Zelaya's 1894 conquest of the Mosquitia left no doubt about Nicaragua's right to negotiate with the United States for a canal. And the United States was still interested. When they intervened in the Cuban War of Independence in 1898, the Pacific-based battleship Oregon had to travel twelve thousand miles from San Francisco around Cape Horn; a route through Central America would be four thousand miles.[43] Two separate US canal commissions recommended Nicaragua as the canal site.[44] In 1900, the United States offered Nicaragua $11 million for canal rights, an offer Zelaya rejected because it required US control over Nicaraguan territory.[45] The Panamanians were more cooperative, and the French dropped their price from $109 million to $40 million for all of their works—excavations, equipment, surveys, maps, and the Panama Railroad. Nicaragua was abandoned. A disappointed Zelaya tried, without success, to interest German, Japanese, and French investors in building a competing canal.

Zelaya was also eager to profit from the $2 million that US business had invested in gold mines, banana plantations, mahogany logging, import houses, docks, and warehouses through concessions from Conservative administrations. But Zelaya paired concessions with required investments in roads, railways, shipping, and ports, resulting in tension with US businesses.[46] After 1903 and the canal loss, Zelaya's attitude toward Atlantic Coast businessmen hardened. They claimed that he made arbitrary changes in contracts and concessions, while Zelaya complained they did not meet their commitments. In 1909, Zelaya raised tariffs on the coast by 30 percent and threatened to cancel the mining concession for the US & Nicaragua Company.[47]

The 1909 revolt that overthrew Zelaya clearly had US support. US Consul Thomas Moffat cabled Secretary of State Philander Knox that Juan José Estrada would rebel the next day and would respect US property. But the coup had Nicaraguan roots: Estrada, Zelaya's Atlantic Coast governor, acted on his own ambitions. His fellow conspirators were from the Conservative Party, including Adolfo Díaz, an employee of the La Luz y Los Angeles mining company, and Emiliano Chamorro, who had led numerous revolts against Zelaya. US businessmen contributed $1 million, and the US government found the perfect excuse to support them. Two US citizens, Leonard Groce, a mining supervisor, and Lee Roy Cannon, a rubber planter, attempted to mine the San Juan River in an admitted attempt to sink a Nicaraguan troop transport. Under Zelaya's orders, the two were court martialed and executed. Supposedly in retaliation, the United States sent seven hundred Marines to support the anti-Zelaya forces.

In December 1909, Zelaya stepped down and turned the presidency over to Vice President José Madriz. The United States objected to Madriz and now had the influence to insist on appointment of Estrada as president and Díaz as his vice president.

Liberals vs. Conservatives and the United States

The overthrow of Zelaya reinvigorated the Liberal–Conservative conflict. As in the nineteenth century, there was little ideological difference between the parties. Both sought power, and they quickly learned that US support was needed. Liberals in the nineteenth century had reached out to individuals, such as Walker and Vanderbilt. Conservatives of the twentieth century reached out to the US government.

Both Estrada and Díaz were amenable to US demands. Estrada agreed to the Dawson Pact, making Nicaragua a financial protectorate of the United States; resistance to the plan forced him out in 1911.[48] Díaz took over and signed the Knox-Castrillo Treaty, providing a $1.5 million loan from Brown Brothers Bank and W. & J. Seligman guaranteed by a customs receivership, control over the Bank of Nicaragua and Pacific Railways.[49] Secretary of War General Luis Mena, a co-conspirator in the Zelaya coup, revolted in July 1912, accusing Díaz of selling Nicaragua to New York bankers. At Díaz's request, the United States sent in the Marines, which would remain for thirteen years.[50] In return, Díaz signed the Bryan-Chamorro Treaty, giving the United States perpetual rights to a canal route, an option for a naval base on the Gulf of Fonseca, and the use of the Corn Islands.[51]

From 1913 to 1923, the United States propped up Conservative governments, yet unrest continued with at least ten civil wars and almost continuous martial law.[52] In 1916, Emiliano Chamorro won his long-sought presidency in an uncontested election guarded by the Marines. Continued disputes over presidential succession appeared to briefly end with the 1924 "reconciliation ticket" of Conservative Carlos José Solórzano and Liberal Juan Bautista Sacasa. Nicaragua momentarily seemed stable, prompting the United States to withdraw the Marines. But stability was a mirage—the Solórzano–Sacasa presidency lasted little more than a year before another Emiliano Chamorro uprising. Solórzano resigned, but rather than pass the presidency to Vice President Sacasa, he turned to the usurper Chamorro. Sacasa fled to exile, but his Liberal ally, José Maria Moncada, launched a revolt.

As Nicaragua descended into war, the United States sent the Marines to back up the Conservatives. The war lasted until 1927, when the United States brokered a peace plan satisfying both Conservatives and most Liberals: Díaz, who had been elected president by the Nicaraguan Congress in 1926, would remain president until 1928, when the United States would supervise elections guaranteeing Moncada the presidency. The ambitious Moncada agreed.

One Liberal general, however, refused to put down his arms: Augusto C. Sandino.

SANDINO AND HIS CRAZY LITTLE ARMY

Sandino was not an elite Liberal or Conservative politician. He was from the lower-class majority, the illegitimate son of a landowner, Gregorio Sandino, and his maid, Margarita Calderón. Like many landless Nicaraguans, he followed an itinerant path—warehouseman at the Monte Cristo sugar mill in Honduras, banana plantation worker for United Fruit Company in Guatemala, oil field worker in Mexico. He returned to Nicaragua in 1926 and organized a battalion to fight with the Liberals.

He gathered men from the mines, banana plantations, and logging operations in the Atlantic area, along with campesinos from the Segovias. The workers were veterans of the 1920s strikes ending in violent repression at Cuyamel Fruit Company and Cukra Development Company. With Moncada's recognition, Sandino led his own column against the Conservatives and their US backers. But when Moncada settled in favor of his own political ambitions, Sandino refused to put down his arms. His battalion became the Army in Defense of the National Sovereignty of Nicaragua.

In some ways, Sandino could be seen as the regional leader of yet another Nicaraguan rebellion. There was no shortage of Nicaraguan popular resistance, from the 1881 Matagalpa Indigenous uprising to ongoing revolts against regional caudillos and national government impositions. The mass of Nicaraguans had a mixed relationship with the national government. They participated when necessary in structures such as land registration but often successfully evaded labor laws designed to force them to work on coffee haciendas. If eligible, they voted in municipal elections when officials weren't appointed by the government. To some extent, they adopted the language of the nation-state. But their political allegiances were as weak as Nicaragua's political system.[53]

Sandino was different, however, because he targeted the real power in Nicaragua—the US Marines and their creation, the Nicaraguan National Guard (Guardia Nacional). He viewed Nicaraguan leaders as *vendepatrias* who sold out to the United States. Rather than fighting for the victory of a political party or faction, he elevated the struggle to a fight for national sovereignty, Nicaraguan nationalism versus US domination. He brought a class dimension to the struggle by recruiting both workers from Atlantic Coast enclaves and poor campesinos. And from 1927 to 1933, his "crazy little Army," as Chilean poet Gabriel Mistral dubbed his Army in Defense of the National Sovereignty of Nicaragua, led the Marines and National Guard on a fruitless chase through the rugged Segovias.

The Sandinistas, the revolutionaries who adopted his name, would claim that Sandino had driven the United States out. But while the United States could not defeat Sandino's guerrilla war, their withdrawal had much more to do with the pressing concerns of the Great Depression, the rise of fascism in Europe, and President Franklin Delano Roosevelt's desire to promote the Good Neighbor policy.

Before the United States pulled out, it named the ambitious Anastasio Somoza García to head the National Guard. It was an odd appointment—Somoza had no military training. He led one battle—and lost—in the Liberal–Conservative conflict. But he had deftly won the confidence of US Minister Matthew Hanna while serving as Moncada's interpreter during peace negotiations.

Somoza was well positioned to launch his own bid for power.

DICTATORSHIP AS DYNASTY

Nicaragua's dynastic dictatorship is unique in Latin America. The Somozas ruled from 1936 until the overthrow of the last scion in 1979, a dictatorship notable for greed and brutality. The attitude of the founder, Anastasio Somoza García, was illustrated by two famous quotes. Asked by US reporters how many *fincas* he owned, he said "only one"—all of Nicaragua. Asked about the value of an educated populace, he replied, "I don't want educated people; I want oxen." The first of his sons to succeed him, Luis Somoza Debayle, led what the United States viewed as a "relatively mild authoritarian regime."[54] The last, Anastasio Somoza Debayle, was the most brutal and corrupt of the three, and he would fall to the Sandinistas.

Anastasio Somoza García came from wealth but not prestige. His family was the seventh largest landowner in Carazo, owning substantial coffee estates.[55] His father, Anastasio Somoza Reyes, was a Conservative Party senator and a signer of the Bryan-Chamorro Treaty. But the Somozas were not among Nicaragua's old families.[56] He was sent to study at the Pierce School of Business Administration in Philadelphia, where he met Salvadora Debayle Sacasa, daughter of an old, prominent family. In 1919 they were wed over her parents' objections. Nothing in his background presaged his climb to power: he worked as a bookkeeper, a meter reader, a toilet inspector. But the English he learned served him well.

During the Moncada presidency (1929–1933), Somoza rose from governor of León, to consul to Costa Rica, Minister of Foreign Affairs, and aide to Moncada. In 1932, Juan Bautista Sacasa—for whom Moncada had launched his revolt—was elected president, and planning began to withdraw the Marines. The United States counted on order bestowed by the National Guard, a supposedly apolitical force it had created in 1927. General Calvin B. Matthews was to be succeeded by a Nicaraguan, and Matthews, Moncada, and Hanna wanted Somoza. The National Guard would become Somoza's base of power.[57]

Because US withdrawal was Sandino's goal, he was willing to negotiate peace. Sacasa, eager to end the war, did not see him as a threat. Sandino was guaranteed an area for farm cooperatives and relinquished most of his weapons. Somoza, however, was not as sanguine about Sandino as Sacasa. Skirmishes continued even after the peace agreement was signed in February 1933. More importantly, when Sandino arrived in Managua to sign the agreement, Somoza escorted him from the airport to the presidential palace. Along the way thousands cheered the rebel leader. In February 1934, Sacasa invited Sandino to Managua to resolve the ongoing conflicts. Afterward, as Sandino headed to the airport, he was executed by Guardia, undoubtedly under Somoza's orders.[58] The only remaining obstacle to power was Sacasa, and Somoza used the Guardia and civilian supporters to force the president's resignation.

The Conservative era had ended with President Roberto Sacasa; the traditional Liberal era ended with his son, Juan Bautista Sacasa. Since independence, Nicaraguan politics had been based on the rivalry between Liberals and Conservatives. But a new political era dawned based on whether they supported Somoza. Both the Liberal and Conservative parties were divided by Somoza's candidacy in 1936. Somoza belonged to the Liberal Party, but an anti-Somoza faction formed, which in 1944 would break away and become the Partido Liberal Independiente (PLI). The Conservatives also split: Somoza supporters formed the Nationalist Conservative Party (PCN); the Traditional Conservative Party (PCT) followed Emiliano Chamorro. The entire political content of the parties was their position on Somoza.[59]

Somoza based his power on four elements: corruption, coercion, cooptation, and US support. He "won" his first election in 1936 by 107,201 to 169.[60] He solidified the victory with the new 1939 Constitution, giving him control over the electoral and legislative machinery, broad powers to declare a state of siege, and extending the presidency from four to six years; his term was extended to 1947.

In 1941, Somoza declared war on the Axis powers, providing US naval and air bases in exchange for military equipment. He confiscated German-owned farms, which helped build his empire: By 1944 he was Nicaragua's largest landowner, with fifty-one cattle ranches, forty-six coffee fincas, and eight sugar mills. He controlled meat exports, mining concessions, import-export licenses, transportation, and communications.

Somoza also controlled gambling, brothels, and illegal alcohol. His wealth was estimated at $10 million.[61]

By 1944, some Nicaraguans began to contest Somoza's seemingly unassailable position. Student protests against his intention to run for reelection rippled through society. Dissident Liberals formed the PLI, and when PLI leader Carlos Pasos spoke, twenty thousand gathered.[62] But Somoza had cultivated a good working relationship with labor, which did not participate in the 1944 protests. He was even able to win the limited support of the *Partido Socialista de Nicaragua* (PSN), which had begun to openly organize.[63]

Somoza intended to run for reelection in 1948 but acquiesced to domestic and US pressure. He chose as his successor Leonardo Argüello, his 1936 opponent, expecting the now elderly man to be easily manipulated. Instead, Argüello ordered Somoza into exile; Somoza responded by fomenting unrest. Argüello lasted twenty-five days before Congress removed him as ineffectual and ratified his acting replacement, Benjamín Lacayo Sacasa. A few months later, Lacayo was replaced by Somoza's uncle, Victor Roman y Reyes, whose term was extended to 1952 by a new constitution.

Somoza's control over the political process was complete, and his Conservative opponents saw that the only way to carve out a political space was to make a deal. The pacts they made would become a notorious example of opposition moral bankruptcy. First came the Pact of 1948 with moderate leader Carlos Cuadra Pasos to guarantee minority representation in the National Assembly, the courts, and the municipal government and, most importantly, on the board of directors of state banks and institutions.[64] The exiled, radical General Emiliano Chamorro excoriated the pact and then agreed to his own pact in 1950. The Pact of the Generals agreed to guarantee Conservatives twenty seats in the Constituent Assembly and to appoint Conservative ministers of finance and education.[65] The Conservatives sold out for a voice but no power. They did not object when Somoza became provisional president on the death of Roman y Reyes and was reelected in 1950. Somoza expanded the state bureaucracy and drew business groups into his economic plans.[66] New agencies developed infrastructure that benefited business, with little for social programs.[67]

The PLI and the Conservatives had no platform other than opposing Somoza. They were middle-class parties with no outreach to campesinos or labor.[68] Labor remained divided; the Socialist Party outlawed. The press was censored, though some reporters were bribed by Somoza.[69] Nicaraguan exiles formed the Partido Revolucionario Nicaragüense (PRN) and the Unión Revolucionaria Democrática (URD), but they could not organize within the country. Exiles also launched doomed invasions in 1947 and 1954, leading to a state of siege.[70]

Somoza's reelection in 1956 seemed inevitable. But at the celebration of his nomination in León on September 21, he was shot by an uninvited guest, poet Rigoberto López Pérez. The young student was immediately shot to death by the Guardia. Somoza was flown to the Panama Canal Zone, where he died a week later. The Guardia rounded up political activists suspected or at least accused of conspiring with López, but he had not worked with the traditional opposition. As a result, there was no organization to continue after his death.[71]

Somoza García's older son, Luis Somoza Debayle, succeeded his father, first because of his position as head of the National Assembly and then by election. His younger brother, Anastasio, continued as head of the National Guard, a position he held since graduation from West Point in 1946. Little is written about Luis, partly because his term of office was short, and partly because he was viewed as relatively reformist. But have no doubt: Luis, too, was a dictator.

Luis undertook economic modernization and attracted increased foreign investment. He opened the political system to more participation and became a mentor to a generation of educated women who had won the vote in 1955.[72] He gave the press more freedom. But he also had no problem declaring martial law, especially in response to armed attacks in 1959 and 1960. The 1959 attack included two future foes: *La Prensa* editor Pedro Joaquín Chamorro and Carlos Fonseca, who would cofound the Frente Sandinista de Liberación Nacional (FSLN) in 1961.

The FSLN members were inspired by the success of the Cuban Revolution in 1959. US President John Fitzgerald Kennedy reacted to the Cuban revolution in two ways. First was the disastrous Bay of Pigs invasion in 1961, which set sail from Nicaragua's Puerto Cabezas. Luis was on hand to wish them well and ask them to bring him a hair from Fidel Castro's beard. After the invasion failed, JFK turned to economic development programs, proclaiming: "Those who make peaceful revolution impossible will make armed revolution inevitable." Programs included the Alliance for Progress and the Peace Corps in 1961 and the US Agency for International Development (USAID) in 1962. Those programs appealed to Luis, who was eager for aid to develop the Nicaraguan economy. But the Alliance for Progress, a woefully underfunded and poorly planned Marshall Plan for Latin America, also had a darker unpublicized side providing counterinsurgency training, which appealed to Anastasio, as did increased US military aid and the 1964 creation of the Central American Defense Council.

Like his father, Luis would allow puppets to hold the presidency, giving a veneer of democracy. Rene Schick was elected in 1963 and replaced upon his death in 1966 by Lorenzo Guerrerro. But there was no doubt who was really in control. Luis's reforms were foundering when he died of a massive heart attack in 1966. His death opened the door for his younger brother.

Anastasio Somoza Debayle was notorious for his use of National Guard brutality. In 1967 he campaigned for the presidency against Fernando Agüero, whose call for a demonstration against the regime drew sixty thousand. The Conservatives had promised to arm the protesters if attacked, but they were unarmed when the Guardia opened fire with machine guns and tanks. Officially, 201 were killed; the Guardia later admitted to 600. In May, Somoza won the election. He would hold power until overthrown by the Sandinistas in 1979.

Somoza used the Guardia against dissidents, while he appointed cronies to government positions and expanded his economic empire. He monopolized cement and textile production and milk pasteurizing and owned a merchant shipping line, the state airline LANICA, and Puerto Somoza. USAID funds bought him paper mills, fisheries, and meat processing plants. Throughout the decades of Somoza rule, Nicaragua's poor majority were further impoverished. While many had held onto their land as coffee growing spread—indeed, there were many small and medium coffee producers—many more would lose their landholdings to the spread of cotton and cattle starting in the 1950s for an expanding US market. Nicaragua jockeyed with Haiti and Honduras as the poorest countries in the hemisphere.

Like his father, Somoza handled politics by making deals. In 1970, he made a pact with Agüero to allow Somoza's reelection through 1981. In exchange, in 1972 Somoza stepped down and ruled behind puppets while still heading the Guardia and counter-intelligence.[73] Somoza's position seemed unshakable until the 1972 earthquake. At 12:30 A.M. on December 23, Managua was struck by a massive earthquake leveling much of the city, killing at least six thousand, injuring twenty thousand, and leaving three hundred thousand homeless in a city of four hundred thousand. Somoza imposed a dawn-to-dusk curfew to prevent looting, giving the Guardia orders to "shoot to kill." The looting, however, was carried out by the Guardia, even stripping jewelry from dead bodies. Some $250 million in international aid was stolen by Somoza, while material aid was sold on the black market. To Somoza, the destruction offered a "revolution of possibilities." He controlled reconstruction: demolition, construction, concrete, building materials, roofing, asbestos, plastics. They built shoddy housing sold at exorbitant prices. Land speculation created fortunes: Assembly President Cornelio Hueck bought land for $17,000 and resold to the state for $1.2 million.[74]

But the earthquake also sowed the seeds of Somoza's downfall. Elites who did not share in the reconstruction bonanza resented Somoza's unfair competition. The earthquake also came during a drought, which drove campesinos to Managua. They helped fill the numbers of an urban proletariat needed in construction and related trades. The workers were underpaid and worked long hours, leading to a 1973 strike. And although Somoza "won" reelection in 1974 by a large margin, the Sandinistas were beginning to inspire Nicaraguans.

Borrowing Cuba's tactics, from 1961 to 1963 the FSLN fought a guerrilla war in northern mountains near the border, where they were captured and jailed by the Honduran army.

From 1963 to 1967, they mostly agitated on university campuses. In 1967 they returned to the mountains, building relationships with campesinos. A Guardia massacre drove the FSLN underground from 1967 to 1974, a time they later labeled the period of accumulation of forces in silence. Sporadic actions included armed attacks on banks and businesses to raise funds, with urban revolutionaries hiding in safe houses.

In 1974, desperate to draw attention to the struggle, the Sandinistas attacked and took hostage guests at a Christmas party at the home of Somoza associate José María "Chema" Castillo. They demanded the release of eighteen prisoners, including future president Daniel Ortega, $2 million in ransom, publication and airing of FSLN communiques, raises and bonuses for state employees—including the National Guard—and passage to Cuba, where they were able to train and regroup. While they met their immediate goals, Somoza responded with a vicious state of siege that lasted until 1977.

Somoza's repression was savage. It was a dangerous time to be young, as all were suspect. Prisoners were tortured brutally in his jails, radicalizing their friends and families. Civil opposition developed, and in 1977, twelve prominent Nicaraguans, including renowned poet Ernesto Cardenal and novelist Sergio Ramírez, formed *Los Doce* and called for negotiations. The dialog ended when on January 10, 1978, *La Prensa* editor Pedro Joaquín Chamorro was gunned down. Chamorro was beloved for the newspaper's brave criticism of Somoza. His murder sparked an outpouring in the streets and a two-week strike by businessmen. Somoza laughed that the businessmen depended on his control of the masses for their wealth. After two weeks, the businesses reopened, leaving only the Sandinistas with the ability to lead the struggle.

Conflict escalated in 1978. In February, Guardia attacked a commemoration of Sandino's assassination in the largely Indigenous Masaya community of Monimbó. Residents were attacked by tanks, machine guns, and helicopters as they closed off streets and launched open rebellion, sparking increased resistance. Events moved quickly: September uprisings in Masaya, Estelí, Managua, León, Chinandega, and Matagalpa led to open warfare. From October 1978 to January 1979, the United States and the Organization of American States tried fruitlessly to convince Somoza to resign. By June, towns were falling to the Sandinistas. On July 17, Somoza fled, taking with him the bodies of his father and brother and $1.5 billion in Central Bank reserves, after ordering the bombing of Nicaragua's five largest cities. On July 19, the Sandinistas took over Managua.

THE REVOLUTION IN POWER

With fifty thousand dead, one hundred thousand injured, and one hundred thousand orphaned, the Junta of National Reconstruction faced a daunting task. The United Nations estimated direct damage at $481 million. Nicaragua was saddled with $1.65 billion in foreign debts and an empty treasury. They needed to dig out from the damage, provide for basic needs, and reactivate the economy. And they were doing this in the context of the 1979 oil crisis, which led to an international recession.

Because the revolution had popular support, people could be mobilized: Sandinista Defense Committees cleared rubble; Worker Reactivation Assemblies revived businesses and agricultural production. International support provided donations of food, and the Sandinistas offered food for work. Loans were renegotiated and new loans acquired.

FSLN ideology combined Marxism, Sandino's nationalism, and liberation theology, which reread the Bible as a revolutionary document emphasizing Jesus's commitment to the poor and oppressed. Recognizing support from "the patriotic bourgeoisie," the Sandinistas committed to political pluralism and a mixed economy. Banks and foreign trade were nationalized to control hard currency and prevent capital flight, but 60 percent of the economy remained private. Somoza's estate became state property: 20 percent of the arable land, 50 percent of farms over five hundred hectares, and 25 percent of industry. The Sandinistas used the property to create state farms and cooperatives and carry out agrarian reform. The first five years were a success: Cumulative growth was 22.5 percent, and GDP per capita rose 7 percent.[75]

In 1984, using a voting system designed with assistance from Sweden, Nicaragua had its first free and fair elections, observed by international organizations. All candidates received public funding for their campaigns and uncensored equal access to the media. The Sandinistas were challenged by three parties to their left and three to their right.[76] Voter turnout was 75 percent; 67 percent of voters chose Daniel Ortega as president and Sergio Ramírez as vice president.

The achievements of the revolution were remarkable: a 1979 literacy campaign that reduced illiteracy from 50 percent to 12 percent; adult education; elimination of public school fees; a vaccination campaign recognized by the World Health Organization for eradicating polio and malaria; free health clinics in urban and rural areas; construction of low-cost housing; installation of electricity and potable water. The Ministry of Culture under Ernesto Cardenal sponsored poetry and dance workshops. Murals painted by local and foreign artists adorned buildings. It is even more remarkable that these accomplishments were achieved during a new war.

Shortly after the Sandinista victory, 141 former Guardia gathered in Honduras to discuss waging war against the new government. They turned to Colonel Enrique Bermúdez, Somoza's former attaché in Washington, who was already on the CIA payroll. They were trained by Argentine generals, who had counted Somoza as a strong supporter, and paid with initial funding from President Jimmy Carter's administration. In 1980, President Ronald Reagan was elected promising to restore US power after losing the Vietnam War and control of client states in Iran and Nicaragua. In 1981, the Reagan administration poured funds into the enterprise, and numbers of the counterrevolutionaries, or Contras, grew to three hundred by October 1981, five hundred by January 1982.[77] By January 1988, their numbers were estimated to be as high as fifteen thousand in the largest Contra group, the Nicaraguan Democratic Front (FDN). Many were forcibly recruited or kidnapped by the Contras; others were volunteers who felt that the revolution had not done enough for poor campesinos in the northern highlands.[78] The FDN targeted the new Sandinista clinics and schools; they were particularly known for their brutality, destroying entire villages and torturing their victims. The CIA also paid two additional Contra groups: the Democratic Revolutionary Alliance (ARDE), formed by former Sandinista commander Eden Pastora, and MISURASATA, an Atlantic Coast grouping of Miskitu, Sumu, and Rama people. The Contra groups were never strong enough to hold any Nicaraguan territory. But they were able to cause a great deal of damage and terrorize the countryside. Furthermore, in 1983 the Sandinistas instituted highly unpopular obligatory military service to fight them.

As the war and embargo wore on, an increasing amount of the national budget was spent on military defense instead of social programs, and there were no funds to replace what the Contras destroyed. The Reagan administration waged economic warfare by imposing a trade embargo in 1985, crippling the economy. By 1989, due to the Contra war, Nicaragua had suffered more than thirty thousand deaths, property destruction estimated at $221 million, and production losses of $984 million. The trade embargo alone had cost $254 million. The ongoing economic hardship and war deaths led the Sandinistas to become more hierarchical in their relationship with supporters in the mass organizations.

In 1990, new elections were held, and the United States supported a fourteen-party coalition, the United Nicaraguan Opposition, and encouraged them to nominate Violeta Chamorro, widow of the martyred Pedro Joaquin. If the Sandinistas won, the United States made it clear that it would assume the elections were fraudulent, and the waning Contra war would be revived. Chamorro won 55 percent of the vote, while Ortega, the FSLN nominee, received 41 percent.[79]

The Sandinistas had presented a united front because of the war, but electoral defeat opened the door to airing differences within the party. At party congresses in 1991 and 1994, Ortega was elected general secretary. His firm grip on the party led to conflict: in 1994, Sergio Ramírez left to form the Sandinista Renovation Movement (MRS), and many Sandinista leaders joined him. Ortega became the perpetual FSLN presidential candidate, losing the next two elections before returning to power in 2006.

From Sandinistas to Danielistas

The three presidents who succeeded Ortega—Chamorro, Arnoldo Alemán, and Enrique Bolaños—all governed as neoliberals, emphasizing privatization of public activity and deregulation of private activity. They encouraged market solutions to social problems and cuts in government spending on social needs. It was a repudiation of government responsibility to provide for basic needs, and a repudiation of the Sandinistas. Chamorro rolled back most Sandinista programs, cutting health and education spending. Polio and malaria reappeared. She expected increased US aid but was disappointed. The United States had primarily been concerned with defeating the Sandinistas.

Chamorro's successor, Alemán, was a former Somocista. As mayor of Managua he was infamous for painting over Sandinista murals, as if to wipe out the legacy of the Revolution. The legitimacy of Alemán's election was questioned; a Costa Rican observer said such irregularities would demand new elections in his country. Alemán won the 1996 election with 51 percent of the vote, while Ortega polled 38 percent. When his term ended, Alemán was convicted of corruption and sentenced to twenty years in prison; the sentence was later drastically reduced and then commuted to house arrest.

After two defeats, Ortega decided to make a deal, the 1999 Ortega-Alemán Pact; the convicted Alemán was still the undisputed boss of his Constitutionalist Liberal Party. While the old Somoza pacts guaranteed only the appearance of competing parties, power in the Ortega-Aleman pact was more evenly divided. The pact guaranteed representation on the Electoral Council, giving both parties representation at voting tables to oversee the tally, lacking when the Sandinistas lost to Alemán. Most significant for Ortega, the percentage to win the presidency dropped from 45 percent to 40 percent, or even 35 percent if he polled at least 5 percent more than the next candidate.[80]

Two elements of the pact were particularly controversial: the outgoing president and runner-up were eligible for two consecutive National Assembly terms. With parliamentary immunity, Alemán was protected from further corruption charges and Ortega from accusations of sexual abuse by his stepdaughter. And, second, both parties were guaranteed seats on an expanded Supreme Court.

The pact did not help Ortega in 2001, although he had been the projected frontrunner. As the United States bombed Afghanistan after the 9/11 attack on the World Trade Center, the press took to running old photos of Ortega in military uniform with Yassar Arafat, implying that an Ortega presidency would bring the return of war and US opposition. Alemán's vice president, Enrique Bolaños, convincingly distanced himself from the corruption, winning with 56 percent of the vote to Ortega's 42 percent.

Finally, in the 2006 election, Ortega benefited from the pact and won the presidency with 38.7 percent of the vote. The new government eliminated school fees, opened free health clinics, built housing for the poor, provided food subsidies, and instituted microloans for small businesses. The social programs were funded in part by $580 million a year, 34 percent of state revenue, that Nicaragua received by joining ALBA, the Bolivarian Alliance for the Peoples of Our America, established by Venezuela's Hugo Chavez. Some hailed the return of the revolution. Opponents, including Ramírez's MRS, were more skeptical, suggesting the government was not Sandinista but Danielista.

In 2010, the Supreme Court lifted the ban on consecutive presidential election and in 2014 eliminated term limits completely. In 2011, Ortega won reelection with 62.5 percent of the vote, and in 2016, he won the presidency with 72 percent, with his wife, Rosario Murillo, as his vice president. His approval rating in 2016 was 64 percent, undoubtedly linked to reduction of poverty from 49.8 percent in 2005 to 24.9 percent in 2016.[81]

Corruption, the Canal, and Orteguismo

In 2012, Ortega revived the dream of a canal. The idea had never gone away. Somoza García gave FDR a mahogany and ebony gold-inlaid coffee table adorned with a map of Nicaragua with a canal, which he pitched as "Key to US Security."[82] Although larger ships had outgrown Panama, US military engineers found a Nicaraguan canal too costly.[83] In the 1990s, Nicaragua considered a dry canal, a railway moving containers between deep-water ports on each coast. The plan prompted concerns about impact on the environment, Indigenous communities, and Atlantic Coast autonomy and never moved beyond the planning stages.[84] There have been numerous proposals to build a Nicaraguan canal, but none has come to fruition.

Ortega urged the National Assembly to authorize a commission to research canal construction. Then he announced unilaterally, without open bidding, that the Great Interoceanic Canal of Nicaragua would be built by Hong Kong Nicaragua Canal Development Investment Co. (HKND).[85] In June 2013, the National Assembly approved controversial Law 840, giving HKND a sweeping array of benefits: tax exemption for all activities, exclusive rights to "finance, build and operate the Canal, the harbors, railway, airports, pipelines for 50 years," renewable for another fifty. The canal area was not specified, giving HKND access to the entire country, with the canal zone exempt from Nicaraguan laws.[86]

The project sparked widespread opposition, particularly because of inadequate environmental impact studies.[87] Amnesty International voiced concerns about the irregular way Law 840 was approved, without public discussion.[88] The canal would run directly through Lake Nicaragua, the main source of drinking water, and plow through four hundred thousand hectares of rain forest, including biosphere reserves, and bisect the Mesoamerican Biological Corridor. The canal also would damage or destroy Indigenous and Afro-Caribbean communities.[89]

Ortega had already been accused of massive corruption, primarily through Albanisa, the conduit for Venezuelan investment. There was no public accounting for Albanisa, which reportedly invested in "shadowy private businesses controlled by the Ortega family, including a wind energy project, an oil refinery, an airline, a cell phone company, a hotel, gas stations, luxury condominiums, and a fish farm."[90] Albanisa was run by Ortega's son Rafael, while son Laureano served as "Investment Promotion Advisor" for ProNicaragua, a government agency. The canal has been decried as Ortega's "personal family project."[91]

Suspicions of corruption were intensified by government repression of the *No al Canal* movement.[92] The government violently attacked marches, protest leaders, and their families and used roadblocks, rubber bullets, and tear gas to disperse protesters.[93] The demonstrations were the harbingers of a wave of protests that would be met with unprecedented violence.

The canal protests were followed in April 2018 by demonstrations against the government's poor handling of a fire that destroyed more than 5,400 hectares of tropical rain forest in the Indio Maíz biological reserve. Protesters, mostly students, took to the streets in peaceful demonstrations that were blocked and dispersed by riot police.[94]

On the heels of the fire, the government announced that taxes would increase to pay for pensions, which would be decreased, by the Nicaraguan Social Security Institute (Instituto Nicaragüense de Seguridad Social). Ortega could argue that Nicaragua was feeling the effects of the region-wide economic downturn, exacerbated by the decline of Venezuela and its aid. Many Nicaraguans, however, contended that the economic problems would not have been as severe if not for Ortega's corruption and theft of millions.

On April 18, protesters flooded the streets. They were violently attacked by pro-government supporters and the police. The protests spread across the country the next day, and police and paramilitary forces shot into the crowds, using live ammunition. Dissidents were killed in the streets or in jail, where hundreds were detained. Although the government abandoned the Social Security increase within days, protests continued, demanding Ortega's resignation. By the end of the first week, forty-three people had been killed and hundreds wounded.[95] By August, an estimated three hundred were dead and two thousand injured, and twenty-three thousand had fled to Costa Rica and sought refugee status.[96] In September, public demonstrations were banned.[97] One year later, the number of exiles had risen to sixty thousand as persecution continued.[98]

Throughout most of Nicaragua's national history, a handful of elites battled for control over a political system that would bring them wealth and power. Elite political parties were largely devoid of ideological content, with Liberals and Conservatives fighting for power and profit. The Liberal–Conservative rivalry splintered over the Somoza candidacy in 1936, replaced by a struggle between Somocistas and anti-Somocistas. The unexpected victory of the Sandinista Revolution sparked genuine popular participation and a distinctive political ideology of inclusion. The Revolution was a time of hope, killed in the Contra war, which was organized and financed by the United States and its right-wing Nicaraguan allies. The transformations of the ten years were rolled back by subsequent neoliberal alliances. Like most Nicaraguan political parties, the Sandinistas splintered, facilitating the party's transformation into a vehicle for the political ambitions of one man. But the FSLN is confronting its own legacy: the transformation of Nicaraguans into political actors who would struggle for national change.

Notes

1. Arturo J. Cruz, Jr., *Nicaragua's Conservative Republic, 1858–93* (Houndsmills, U.K.: Palgrave, 2002), 11.
2. Cruz, *Nicaragua's Conservative Republic*, 60–61.
3. Miles Wortman, *Government and Society in Central America, 1860–1840* (New York: Columbia University Press, 1982), 271.
4. E. Bradford Burns, *Patriarch and Folk: The Emergence of* Nicaragua, *1798–1858* (Cambridge, MA: Harvard University Press, 1991), 147.
5. Burns, *Patriarch and Folk*, 153–159.
6. Michael J. Schroeder, "Horse Thieves to Rebels to Dogs: Political Gang Violence and the State in the Western Segovias, Nicaragua, in the Time of Sandino, 1926–1934," *Journal of Latin American Studies* 28, no. 2. (May 1996): 383–434, 391.
7. Cruz, *Nicaragua's Conservative Republic*, 37.
8. Michel Gobat, *Confronting the American Dream: Nicaragua under U.S. Imperial Rule* (Durham, NC: Duke University Press, 2005), 29–30.
9. Gobat, *Empire by Invitation: William Walker and Manifest Destiny in Central America* (Cambridge, MA: Harvard University Press, 2018), 188.
10. Gobat, *Empire by Invitation*, 228–229.
11. Gobat, *Empire by Invitation*, 243; and Gobat, *Confronting the American Dream*, 30–37.

12. Cruz, *Nicaragua's Conservative Republic*, 44.
13. Cruz, *Nicaragua's Conservative Republic*, 48.
14. Edmond G. Konrad, "Nicaragua durante los 30 años de gobierno conservador (1857–1893): la familia Zavala," *Mesoamerica* 30 (December 1995): 287–308, 287.
15. See Jaime Biderman, "El Desarollo del Capitalismo en Nicaragua: Una Historia Político-Económica," *Estudios Sociales Centroamericanos* 12, No. 36 (September–December 1983): 77. See also Jaime Wheelock Román, *Imperialismo y Dictadura* (Managua: Editorial Nueva Nicaragua, 1985).
16. See Maria del Carmen Collado H., "Liberales y conservadores de Nicaragua: ¿falsos estereotipos?" *Secuencia* 11 (May–August 1988): 65–76; Frances Kinloch Tijerino, "Identidad Nacional e Intervención Estranjera. Nicaragua, 1840–1930," *Revista Historia* 45 (January–June 2002): 163–189.
17. See Julie A. Charlip, *Cultivating Coffee: The Farmers of Carazo, Nicaragua, 1880–1930* (Athens, OH: Ohio University Press, 2003), 146–169.
18. Gobat, *Confronting the American Dream*, 1.
19. Gobat, *Confronting the American Dream*, 46.
20. Kinloch, "Nicaragua durante los 30 años de gobierno conservador," 184.
21. Lawrence A. Clayton, "The Nicaragua Canal in the Nineteenth Century: Prelude to American Empire in the Caribbean. *Journal of Latin American Studies* 19, No. 2 (Nov. 1987): 327.
22. An act to incorporate the Maritime Canal Company of Nicaragua, 50th Cong., ch. 176, February 20, 1889, 673–675. https://www.loc.gov/law/help/statutes-at-large/50th-congress/session-2/c50s2ch176.pdf.
23. Clayton, "The Nicaragua Canal in the Nineteenth Century," 328.
24. Clayton, "The Nicaragua Canal in the Nineteenth Century," 323, 328.
25. Cruz, *Nicaragua's Conservative Republic*, 61.
26. Cruz, *Nicaragua's Conservative Republic*, 62.
27. Cruz, *Nicaragua's Conservative Republic*, 97–98, 107–108.
28. Cruz, *Nicaragua's Conservative Republic*, 123–124, 127.
29. Cruz, *Nicaragua's Conservative Republic*, 131–134.
30. Gobat, *Confronting the American Dream*, 42.
31. Charles L. Stansifer, "José Santos Zelaya: A New Look at Nicaragua's 'Liberal' Dictator," *Revista/review interamericana* 7, no. 3 (1977): 468–485, 469.
32. Biderman, "El Desarollo del Capitalismo en Nicaragua: Una Historia Político-Económica," and Wheelock, *Imperialismo y Dictadura*.
33. Stansifer, "José Santos Zelaya," 474.
34. Volker Wünderich, "La unificación Nacional que Dejó una Nación Dividida: el Gobierno del Presidente Zelaya y la 'Reincorporación' de la Mosquitia a Nicaragua en 1894," *Revista de Historia* (Costa Rica) 34 (July–Dec. 1996): 13.
35. Jeffrey Gould, "'¡Vana Ilusión!' The Highlands Indians and the Myth of Nicaragua Mestiza, 1880–1925," *Hispanic American Historical Review* 73, no. 3 (August 1993): 403.
36. Wünderich, "Unificación Nacional que Dejó una Nación Dividida," 13–14. Also see Jeffrey Gould, "'¡Vana Ilusión!' The Highlands Indians and the Myth of Nicaragua Mestiza, 1880–1925," *Hispanic American Historical Review* 73, No. 3 (August 1993): 39–429.
37. See Luciano Baracco, "The Historical Roots of Autonomy in Nicaragua's Caribbean Coast: From British Colonialism to Indigenous Autonomy," *Bulletin of Latin American Research* 35, no. 3 (2016): 291–305.

NICARAGUA   587

38. "Award as to the interpretation of the Treaty of Managua between the United Kingdom and Nicaragua," *Reports of International Arbitral Awards* 28 (July 2, 1881): 167–184 (reprinted by the United Nations, 2007), 175.

39. Wünderich, "Unificación Nacional que Dejó una Nación Dividida," 32.

40. Wünderich, "Unificación Nacional que Dejó una Nación Dividida," 19.

41. Wünderich, "Unificación Nacional que Dejó una Nación Dividida," 19–20.

42. Wünderich, "Unificación Nacional que Dejó una Nación Dividida," 25–26.

43. Clayton, "The Nicaragua Canal in the Nineteenth Century," 332.

44. Clayton, "The Nicaragua Canal in the Nineteenth Century," n. 60, 347.

45. Michael Gismondi and Jeremy Mouat, "Merchants, Mining and Concessions on Nicaragua's Mosquito Coast: Reassessing the American Presence, 1893–1912," *Journal of Latin American Studies* 34 (2002): 856.

46. Gismondi and Mouat, "Merchants, Mining and Concessions," 851–852.

47. Gismondi and Mouat, "Merchants, Mining and Concessions," 862–863.

48. Career diplomat Thomas C. Dawson negotiated for the Taft administration. Dan La Botz, *What Went Wrong? The Nicaraguan Revolution: a Marxist Analysis* (Chicago: Haymarket Books, 2016), 47; Gismondi and Mouat, "Merchants, Mining and Concessions," 872.

49. La Botz, *What Went Wrong?*, 48; Edward S. Kaplan, *U.S. Imperialism in Latin America: Bryan's Challenges and Contributions* (Westport, CT: Greenwood Press, 1998), 39–40.

50. George Black, *Triumph of the People* (London: Zed Books Ltd, 1984), 17.

51. Adam Burns, *American Imperialism: The Territorial Expansion of the United States, 1783–2013* (Edinburgh: Edinburgh University Press, 2017), 141.

52. James Mahoney, *The Legacies of Liberalism: Path Dependence and Political Regimes in Central America* (Baltimore: Johns Hopkins University Press, 2001), 230.

53. See Schroeder, "Horse Thieves to Rebels to Dogs"; Justin Wolfe, *The Everyday Nation-State: Community and Ethnicity in Nineteenth-Century Nicaragua*, Lincoln: University of Nebraska Press, 2007); Charlip, *Cultivating Coffee*.

54. Foreign Relations of the United States, 1958–1960, Memorandum of Discussion at the 410th Meeting of the National Security Council, Washington, June 18, 1959. https://history.state.gov/historicaldocuments/frus1958-60v16/d36.

55. Charlip, *Cultivating Coffee*, 73.

56. According to Samuel Z. Stone, "Somoza's first ancestor in the New World, Francisco Somoza y Gámez Ballesteros, settled in Guatemala toward the end of the seventeenth century. A distinction has been made between 'old' aristocratic families, who can trace their roots to the early colonial period (the Sacasas, the Chamorros, and the Cuadras), and 'new' ones who arrived later (the Reyes, the Somozas, and the Ortegas, among others). In the case of the Somozas, their family tree leads back to both 'old' and 'new' blood." *The Heritage of the Conquistadors: Ruling Classes in Central America from the Conquest to the Sandinistas* (Lincoln: University of Nebraska Press, 1990), 38.

57. Knut Walter, *The Regime of Anastasio Somoza, 1936–1956* (Chapel Hill: University of North Carolina Press, 1993), 29.

58. Walter, *Regime of Anastasio Somoza*, 33; "Nicaragua: Death at the Cross Roads (Cont'd)," *Time Magazine*, April 16, 1934.

59. Walter, *Regime of Anastasio Somoza*, 91 and 134.

60. Andrew Crawley, *Somoza and Roosevelt: Good Neighbour Diplomacy in Nicaragua, 1933–1945* (Oxford: Oxford University Press, 2007), 119.

61. Walter, *Regime of Anastasio Somoza*, 135.

62. Walter, *Regime of Anastasio Somoza*, 130–133.
63. Walter, *Regime of Anastasio Somoza*, 137–138.
64. Walter, *Regime of Anastasio Somoza*, 172–173.
65. Walter, *Regime of Anastasio Somoza*, 175–176.
66. Walter, *Regime of Anastasio Somoza*, 186–187.
67. Walter, *Regime of Anastasio Somoza*, 193.
68. Walter, *Regime of Anastasio Somoza*, 217–218.
69. Walter, *Regime of Anastasio Somoza*, 221–222, 226–227.
70. Walter, *Regime of Anastasio Somoza*, 229–233.
71. Walter, *Regime of Anastasio Somoza*, 234.
72. Victoria González-Rivera, *Before the Revolution: Women's Rights and Right-Wing Politics in Nicaragua, 1821–1979* (University Park, PA: Penn State University Press, 2012), 85.
73. The triumvirate of Alfonso Lovo Cordero, Roberto Martinez Lacayo, and Agüero Rocha.
74. Black, *Triumph of the People*, 56–62.
75. See Thomas W. Walker, ed., *Nicaragua: The First Five Years* (New York: Praeger, 1985).
76. On the left, Communist Party of Nicaragua, Nicaraguan Socialist Party, and Marxist-Leninist Popular Action Movement. On the right, Democratic Conservative Party, Independent Liberal Party, and Popular Social Christians.
77. René De La Pedraja, *Wars of Latin America, 1982–2013: The Path to Peace* (Jefferson, NC: McFarland, 2013), 4–6.
78. De la Pedraja, *Wars of Latin America,* 112.
79. Social Christian Party, Revolutionary Unity Movement, Workers' Revolutionary Party, Marxist-Leninist Popular Action Movement, Social Conservative Party, Central American Unionist Party, Democratic Conservative Party of Nicaragua, Independent Liberal Party for National Unity.
80. While the lowering of the necessary percentage sparked some outrage, it is not unusual in multiparty countries for candidates to be elected by a relatively low plurality. In 1970 in Chile, Salvador Allende won the presidency with Allende 36.3 percent, to Jorge Allessandri's 34.9 and Radimiro Tomic's 27.8 percent. The vote was confirmed by Chile's National Congress. In the past, the candidate with the plurality polled even lower: Jorge Allesandri won with 31.6 percent of the vote in 1958.
81. *Mactrotrends*, "Nicaragua Poverty Rate 1993–2019," https://www.macrotrends.net/countr ies/NIC/nicaragua/poverty-rate; The World Bank, "The World Bank in Nicaragua," https://www.worldbank.org/en/country/nicaragua/overview; David C. Adams, "Daniel Inc: How Nicaragua's Ortega financed a political dynasty," *Univision News*, May 5, 2018, https://www.univision.com/univision-news/latin-america/daniel-inc-how-nicaraguas-ortega-financed-a-political-dynasty.
82. Christian Brannstrom, "Almost a Canal: Visions of Interoceanic Communication across Southern Nicaragua," *Ecumene* 2, no. 1 (January 1995): 65–87, 77.
83. J. David Rogers, "70 years of schemes to improve and enlarge the Panama Canal," Paper presented at the World Environmental and Water Resources Congress, May 2012, 1; and Brannstrom, "Almost a Canal," 78.
84. Nicaragua Network, "Nicaragua's Proposed Dry Canal," August 31, 2004, http://www.nica net.org/news/images//?page=blog&id=23771; Estuardo Robles, "The Great Dry Canal Race," *Site Selection Magazine* (March 2013), https://siteselection.com/issues/2013/mar/central-america.cfm.
85. Anne Tittor, "Conflicts about Nicaragua's Interoceanic Canal Project: Framing, Counterframing and Government Strategies," *Cahiers des América Latines* 87 (2018): 117–140. https://journals.openedition.org/cal/8561, 13.

86. Tittor, "Conflicts about Nicaragua's Interoceanic Canal Project," 14.
87. Sarah McCall and Matthew J. Taylor, "Qué Diría Carlos? The 'No al Canal' Movement and the Rhetoric of Resistance to Nicaragua's 'Grand Canal,'" in *Civil Resistance and Violent Conflict in Latin America*, Studies of the Americas, edited by C. Mouly and E. Hernández Delgado, 193 (Cham, Switzerland: Palgrave Macmillan).
88. McCall and Taylor, "Nicaragua's 'Grand' Canal," 202.
89. Carter Hunt, "The Land of Lakes and Volcanoes . . . and a Canal," *Anthropology News*, 9/22/16, http://www.anthropology-news.org/index.php/2016/05/17/the-land-of-lakes-and-volcanoes-and-a-canal/
90. Benjamin Waddell, "Examining the Embattled Nicaraguan President's Deep Ties with Venezuelan Oil Money," *Pacific Standard*, August 21, 2018. https://psmag.com/economics/the-oil-money-behind-daniel-ortega.
91. McCall and Taylor, "Nicaragua's 'Grand Canal,'" 70.
92. *No al Canal* had organized ninety-three peaceful marches as of September 2017 and petitioned the National Assembly to repeal Law 840. The movement also brought their case to the Inter-American Commission on Human Rights and the Latin American Tribunal for Water. McCall and Taylor, "Nicaragua's 'Grand Canal,'" 203.
93. McCall and Taylor, "Nicaragua's 'Grand Canal,'" 66.
94. Josh Mayer, "Behind the Fire that Propelled Nicaragua's Uprising," NACLA, December 12, 2018. https://nacla.org/news/2018/12/12/behind-fire-propelled-nicaragua%E2%80%99s-uprising.
95. Courtney Desiree Morris, "Unexpected Uprising: The Crisis of Democracy in Nicaragua," *NACLA*, May 14, 2018. https://nacla.org/news/2018/07/11/unexpected-uprising-crisis-democracy-nicaragua.
96. Office of the United Nations High Commissioner for Human Rights, *Human rights violations and abuses in the context of protests in Nicaragua* April 19–August 18, 2018, 7. https://www.ohchr.org/Documents/Countries/NI/HumanRightsViolationsNicaraguaApr_Aug2018_EN.pdf.
97. Washington Office on Latin America, "In Banning Demonstrations, Nicaragua's Government Makes Clear its Disdain for Basic Human Rights and Closes All Space for Peaceful Dissent," October 2, 2018. https://www.wola.org/2018/10/nicaragua-ortega-government-bans-public-protests/.
98. UN News, "Nicaragua crisis: One year in, more than 60,000 have fled, seeking refuge." https://news.un.org/en/story/2019/04/1036711.

FURTHER READING

Overviews of Nicaraguan History

Baracco, Luciano. *Nicaragua: The Imagining of a Nation: From Nineteenth-Century Liberals to Twentieth-Century Sandinistas*. New York: Algora, 2005.
Radell, David Richard. "Historical Geography of Western Nicaragua: The Spheres of Influence of León, Granada, and Managua, 1519–1965." PhD diss., University of California, Berkeley, 1969.

Nineteenth-Century Nicaragua

Kinloch Tijerino, Frances. *Nicaragua: Identidad y Cultura Política (1821–1858)*. Managua: Fondo Editorial Banco Central de Nicaragua, 1999.
Wheelock Román, Jaime. *Raices indigenas de la Lucha Anticolonialista en Nicaragua*. Managua: Editorial Nueva Nicaragua, 1985.

Turn-of-the-Century Nicaragua

Gould, Jeffrey L. *To Lead as Equals: Rural Protest and Political Consciousness in Chinandega, Nicaragua, 1912–1979*. Chapel Hill: University of North Carolina Press, 1990.

Gould, Jeffrey L. *To Die in This Way: Nicaraguan Indians and the Myth of Mestizaje, 1880–1965*. Durham, NC: Duke University Press, 1998.

Hale, Charles R. *Resistance and Contradiction: Miskitu Indians and the Nicaraguan State, 1894–1987*. Stanford, CA: Stanford University Press, 1994.

Vargas, Oscar-Rene. *La Intervencion norteamericana y sus consecuencias, Nicaragua 1910–1925*. Managua, Nicaragua: Fondo Editorial CIRA, 1989.

Augusto C. Sandino and the Somozas

Macaulay, Neill. *The Sandino Affair*. Chicago: Quadrangle Books, 1967.

Millett, Richard. *Guardians of the Dynasty: A History of the U.S. Created Guardia Nacional de Nicaragua and the Somoza Family*. Maryknoll, NY: Orbis Books, 1977.

Selser, Gregorio. *Sandino*. New York: Monthly Review Press, 1981.

The Sandinistas

Dodson, Michael, and Laura Nuzzi O'Shaughnessy. *Nicaragua's Other Revolution: Religious Faith and Political Struggle*. Chapel Hill: University of North Carolina Press, 1990.

Gilbert, Dennis. *Sandinistas: The Party and the Revolution*. New York: Basil Blackwell, 1988.

Hoyt, Katherine. *The Many Faces of Sandinista Democracy*. Athens, OH: Ohio University Press, 1997.

Ortega Saavedra, Humberto. *50 años de la lucha Sandinista*. Havana, Cuba: Editorial de Ciencias Sociales, 1980.

Walker, Thomas W., ed. *Nicaragua: The First Five Years*. New York: Praeger, 1985.

Walker, Thomas W., ed. *Nicaragua without Illusions: Regime Transition and Structural Adjustment in the 1990s*. Wilmington, DE: Scholarly Resources Books, 1997.

Walker, Thomas W., ed. *Nicaragua in Revolution*. New York: Praeger, 1982.

Walker, Thomas W., ed. *Reagan versus the Sandinistas: The Undeclared War on Nicaragua*. Boulder, CO: Westview Press, 1987.

Walker, Thomas W., ed. *Revolution and Counterrevolution in Nicaragua*. Boulder, CO: Westview Press, 1991.

Wright, Bruce E. *Theory in the Practice of the Nicaraguan Revolution*. Athens, OH: Ohio University Press, 1995.

Zimmerman, Matilde. *Sandinista: Carlos Fonseca and the Nicaraguan Revolution*. Durham, NC: Duke University Press, 2000.

Postrevolutionary Nicaragua

Anderson, Leslie E., and Lawrence C. Dodd. *Learning Democracy: Citizen Engagement and Electoral Choice in Nicaragua, 1990–2001*. Chicago: University of Chicago Press, 2005.

Close, David, and Kalowatie Deonandan, eds. *Undoing Democracy: The Politics of Electoral Caudillismo*. Lanham, MD: Lexington Books, 2004.

Close, David, Salvador Martí i Puig, and Shelley A. McConnell, eds. *The Sandinistas and Nicaragua since 1979*. Boulder, CO: Lynne Rienner, 2011.

CHAPTER 22

COSTA RICA

IVÁN MOLINA

Since the beginning of the nineteenth century, travelers, journalists, and diplomats have pointed out that Costa Rica differed from the rest of Central America. Later, this trend spread to the academic world. However, being different in some aspects does not mean that it is exceptional. In fact, Costa Rica was not exempt from the poverty, rurality of the population, inequalities, and political instability that characterized other Central American countries. After independence from Spain (1821), it also shared with its neighbors an export-oriented economy based on coffee and bananas, an import substitution industrialization process since 1950 and the rise of policies favorable to corporate capitalism—known as neoliberalism—from 1980 onward.

This chapter proposes an interpretation of the history of Costa Rica based on a perspective that considers common trends and divergent results: while distancing itself from approaches that celebrate its exceptionalism, it seeks to explain the origin of its specificities. Throughout the nineteenth and twentieth centuries, three main myths have been associated with these particularities: Costa Rican society is different because of its racial condition (a white population), because of its land ownership regime (a country of owners), and because of its extended educational system, which made civil governance and democracy possible (a nation with more teachers than soldiers).

In contrast to these myths, this chapter argues that Costa Rica's difference is the outcome of a specific balance of social forces. The groups that dominated the economy and the state after independence never had the resources or means to subjugate the rest of society. Therefore, the demands of the middle classes and popular sectors for public policies that satisfied their needs gave shape, since the nineteenth century, to a socially reformist institutionality and to a culture more prone to inclusion than social exclusion. In the long run, this modernizing trend played in favor of population integration, reduction of inequalities, and political system legitimacy.

Agrarian Capitalism and State Formation

By 1840, Costa Rica barely had over eighty thousand people and was divided into two main regions: the Central Valley, which comprises approximately 6 percent of the country's territory and concentrated more than 80 percent of the population at that time, and the central and northern Pacific, where extensive ranching prevailed and was usually practiced in large haciendas. In addition, border areas near Nicaragua and Panama were inhabited by Indigenous communities not dominated by the Spaniards. Ethnically, 58 percent of the population was mestizo, 17 percent Afro-descendant, 16 percent Indigenous, and 9 percent white. In the Central Valley, mestizos and whites predominated, many of whom were peasants with broad—though unequal—access to land ownership.[1]

After independence from Spain in 1821, society settled in the Central Valley became the basis of the national experience of Costa Rica (see Map 22.1). The expansion of coffee,

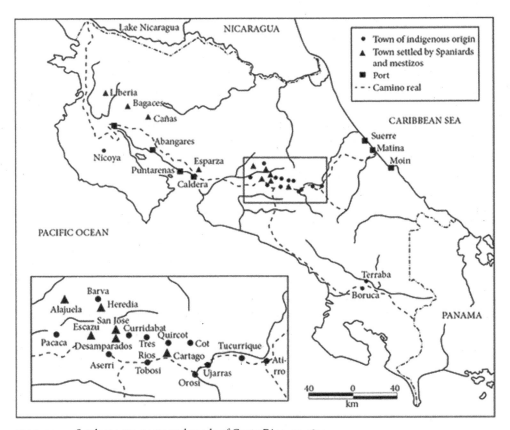

MAP 22.1. Settlements, ports and roads of Costa Rica, *ca.* 1821.
Source: Courtesy of Editorial de la Universidad de Costa Rica. Molina and Palmer, *History of Costa Rica*, 46.

which gained momentum after 1830, reinforced this process, consolidating the insertion in the world market. Furthermore, coffee cultivation implied a decisive transformation: the rise of agrarian capitalism, which encouraged privatization of communal lands and a growing demand for wage labor. The winners of this change were those merchants who dedicated themselves to coffee activity and a sector of small and medium producers who had enough resources to develop coffee plantations, build platforms to process coffee (dry process), and make other investments.[2] The main losers were the Indigenous communities that survived in the Central Valley, which were soon displaced from their settlements by mestizo and white peasants.[3]

Unlike what happened in other Latin American areas, the Costa Rican transition to capitalism did not involve the massive expropriation of peasantry or the constitution of a labor market based on very low wages. The agricultural colonization initiated by the Central Valley peasantry in the eighteenth century expanded during the nineteenth century: thanks to the combination of abundant uncultivated lands and sparse population, the peasant farms were able to multiply in the west of Alajuela, east of Cartago, and south of San José.[4] The possibility of occupying virgin lands by large sectors of the rural world, contributed—in a context of labor shortage due to the low population—to systematically raise wages, which increased from 3 to 5 pesos per month in the 1820s to 7 and 11 pesos per month in the 1840s (there is no inflation data available for this period).[5]

With the development of coffee agriculture, inequalities between merchants and peasants, originated during the colonial era, adopted new forms. The large coffee exporters and processors, thanks to their control of the annual funding of the harvests and hiring salaried labor, could secure considerable profits in their dealings with the small and medium coffee growers, and with the laborers. Despite this, prosperity generated by the coffee expansion was shared by all social sectors, albeit unevenly. Peasants improved their income by specializing in profitable coffee cultivation, by colonizing new lands for agriculture, and by providing transportation services, and workers benefited from the increase in wages.[6]

From 1821 to 1849, the internal political conflicts that occurred in Costa Rica were brief and sporadic, in contrast to the prolonged civil wars that tore apart the rest of the Federal Republic of Central America, constituted in 1824. San José, in the course of these disputes, was consolidated as the new capital of the country after the civil war of 1823. In turn, the state, which depended on customs taxes and resources provided by tobacco and liquor monopolies (all income of colonial origin), prevailed, little by little, over municipalities. The state authorities promoted the constitution of a network of civil courts, which began to limit the role played by the Catholic Church and peasant communities in the resolution of diverse conflicts. Likewise, authorities promoted land privatization, vacant land occupation, and the construction of the necessary infrastructure for the coffee activity.[7]

During the three decades after independence, access to power depended on a combination of periodical elections and interventions by the military; however, the only dictatorship in those first decades of independent life was short-lived: that of Braulio Carrillo (1838–1842). Its regime, institutionally modernizing, strengthened the central power over municipalities and political localisms. The electoral legislation, influenced by the Constitution of Cádiz (1812), was characterized in its early years by an almost universal exercise of male suffrage. This tendency was modified in the 1840s, when the right to vote was limited according to economic and cultural criteria: to have a certain level of income and be able to read and write. The Constitution of 1848, which definitively separated Costa Rica from the rest of Central America by declaring it a "sovereign, free and independent" republic, strengthened these restrictions. The outcome was a considerable proportion of adult Costa Ricans excluded from the polls.[8]

Identities originated during the colonial era were reconfigured by the new economic and social differences arising with agrarian capitalism, by the institutional incentives linked to the process of state formation, and by divisions produced by the competition for political power. Artisans, peasants, and day laborers remained attached to worldviews dominated by the Catholic religion and local politics. In contrast, middle and affluent sectors tended to become Europeanized and secularized rapidly. This process was more intense in San José, where a small circle of immigrants from diverse countries of America and Europe settled.[9] The cultural tension that resulted from this differentiation deepened after 1850.

FILIBUSTERISM, MILITARISM, AND LIBERAL REFORMS

Politically, the decade after the declaration of the republic was characterized by the predominance of the group of large coffee producers led by Juan Rafael Mora (1849–1859). His government, which further promoted the privatization of land, faced an unprecedented threat in the short term. The struggle between Liberals and Conservatives in Nicaragua helped the US mercenary William Walker to reach an extraordinary position of power in 1855. By then, the Nicaraguan southern border had a geostrategic importance: besides being significant as the route for a future interoceanic canal, it was the base of operations for the Accessory Transit Company. This company took advantage of the San Juan River and the Lake Nicaragua to move through passengers from the East Coast to the West Coast of the United States.[10]

Understanding the danger that Walker and his forces posed for the territorial integrity of the country, Mora called his compatriots to arms. Initially, Costa Rica waged the battles alone. Later, the other Central American countries armies joined. However, it was only after Costa Ricans took control of the San Juan River in December 1856 that the filibusters, lacking reinforcements and supplies, began to lose the war. Walker surrendered on May 1, 1857.[11] This conflict had a high cost for Costa Rica, due to an epidemic of cholera, which wiped out approximately 10 percent of the population, and started a short but deep economic crisis, which was overcome only in 1859. The demographic fall and the losses of properties to pay debts affected unequally social sectors, and dissatisfaction with the government of Mora intensified.[12]

Exacerbated by this unrest, the political crisis culminated in August 1859, when Mora, who had just been reelected for the third consecutive time in April, was overthrown, accused of using power for his own benefit and expelled from the country. The new administration, led by coffee magnate José María Montealegre, promoted the approval, in December of that year, of a new constitution, which practically established universal male suffrage. In addition, the government secured support from the Catholic Church and won the sympathy of the majority of the population when allowing the return to Costa Rica of Bishop Anselmo Llorente, who had been exiled by Mora in 1858.[13]

The pronounced cycle of corruption, which characterized the last years of Mora's government, did not disappear after he was overthrown. Authorities and main collaborators of the Montealegre administration took advantage of their positions or their influence to compensate for the losses they experienced when they were out of power, at the expense of public funds. Although Mora tried to regain the presidency, he did not succeed: after disembarking in Puntarenas and rising up in arms, he was captured and executed on September 30, 1860.[14] Periodic and increasingly competitive electoral practices, which took place in the following years, led to the formation, still very incipient, of the first political parties. However, the process was interrupted by the increasing involvement of the military in politics. From 1870 onward, they directly assumed the administration of the state.[15]

Politically strengthened after the war of 1856–1857, the military consolidated its influence during the 1860s, when they actively participated in the struggles between different factions formed by the powerful coffee-growing families. In this context, President Jesús Jiménez, despite coming to power as a consequence of a coup d'état in 1868, sought to reinforce the position of civil authorities: at the beginning of 1869, he forced the resignation of two main military authorities of the country: generals Máximo Blanco and Lorenzo Salazar. This presidential initiative was successful in the short term, but in April 1870 Colonel Tomás Guardia overthrew the government and initiated a dictatorship that lasted for more than twelve years.[16]

Characterized by a modernizing authoritarianism, Guardia's regime transformed Costa Rican politics by making it independent from direct control of the coffee magnates, and encouraged the formation of specialized cadres mainly of lawyers, who assumed the management of public affairs. The dictatorship, apart from promoting a new political Constitution (1871) that consolidated universal male suffrage, maintained the free compulsory nature of primary education for children of both sexes, decreed by the government of Jiménez in 1869. In addition, it abolished the death penalty in 1877, and to achieve a cheaper and direct trade with Europe, the building of the Caribbean coast railway became its main public works project.[17]

Many factors—especially corruption and technical difficulties due natural obstacles—contributed to the failure of this railroad initiative. Its potential to promote a national identity disappeared once the project was taken over by foreign capital. The businessman in charge of it, US citizen Minor C. Keith, was authorized to bring thousands of West Indians to build the railway, and received huge land grants on the Caribbean coast, where he started to grow bananas. The success of this product in the United States favored, from the 1880s onward, a new agricultural activity developed in the current province of Limón. As a result, the agro-export model, based on coffee, experienced a decisive diversification.[18]

Próspero Fernández (1882–1885) and Bernardo Soto (1885–1889), successors of the Guardia dictatorship, made it easier for intellectuals and professionals, who emerged during the 1870s, to reinforce their political position and begin the so-called Liberal reforms. Their main purposes were to strengthen the central government, update current legislation, reform education in a secular and positivist sense, modernize public administration, promote capitalism, and disseminate the ideology of progress, in its capitalist version, among popular sectors. Although the Catholic Church agreed with some of these changes, it opposed those that weakened its influence. This originated a growing conflict with the executive branch, which culminated in mid-1884, when a bishop of German origin, Bernardo Augusto Thiel, and the Jesuits were expelled from the country.[19]

Shortly after, the government of Fernandez had to face a serious conflict of an external nature. On February 28, 1885, Guatemalan President Justo Rufino Barrios decreed the union of Central America and declared that his intention was to carry it out by force, in case his area neighbors did not voluntarily join such an initiative. Faced with the prospect of a new war, the confrontation with the Catholic Church was momentarily deactivated and the discontent of the majority of Costa Ricans with the government decreased. Immediately, authorities called the population to arms; but the mobilization of troops was of short duration, since Barrios died in El Salvador on April 2, 1885. The threat posed by Guatemala, although it was ephemeral, had a decisive cultural impact in Costa Rica. Liberal politicians and intellectuals, who were concerned that confrontation with the Church affected popular support for the struggle against Guatemalans, proceeded to raise the memory of the war of 1856–1857 and turned soldier Juan Santamaría (who died in the Battle of Rivas on April 11, 1856) into a national hero.[20]

Before 1885, the cultural construction of a national identity was a process that lacked a basic structure. Certainly, since 1821, some high-ranking police officers began to elaborate a discourse that tried to differentiate Costa Ricans from their Central American neighbors. Previous to 1870, the characteristics emphasized to support this differentiation were the peaceful and laborious nature of the inhabitants and their status as small landowners. From the dictatorship of Guardia on and in response to the growing immigration of West Indian workers for the construction of the railroad first and for the banana activity later, a racial component was increasingly emphasized: the population of Costa Rica was white.[21]

The Liberals of the 1880s recovered previous contents of identity construction and, based on the war of 1856–1857, elaborated a coherent discourse on national identity. Initially, the outcome of this process was a masculine, military, and white patriotism, which was used to promote the popular sectors to recognize themselves as Costa Ricans and to appropriate the positivist and capitalist values. Of course, the model for peasants, artisans and workers was Santamaría, who had died in foreign territory to defend the existing order—peace, work, institutionality, and property—in Costa Rica. In contrast to the male and military hero, the Catholic Church began to nationalize the cult of the Virgin of the Angels.[22]

In the long term, the success of this nationalism, developed from the historical experience of the Central Valley, was favored by the concentration of West Indians in Limón, of the majority of Indigenous people in the border areas with Nicaragua and Panama, and of the ethnically more diverse population in Guanacaste and Puntarenas. Forged since the 1880s, national identity soon had a literary dimension (the *costumbrista* narrative with its emphasis on peasant manners and characters) and later an artistic one (paintings of the adobe houses).[23] Such a nationalist construction was strategic to face the deep cultural gap between the increasingly secularized urban middle and upper classes and the rest of society—especially rural dwellers– still heavily influenced by worldviews based on religion.

Nationalism was also decisive because the imagined community that it invoked made it possible to counterbalance, in terms of appealing to a common identity, the growing social inequality, manifested in the decrease in the percentage of artisanal and agricultural owners and in the increase in the proportion of salaried workers. The differences between capitalists and workers were especially visible in the main cities. After 1870, the industrial sector grew and diversified: along with small and medium workshops, factories were opened, while proletarianization deepened.[24] The first response to this trend was the formation, starting in 1874, of mutual aid societies of workers. This process, initially led by employer craftsmen, intensified during the 1880s and 1890s. As a result of this first organizational experience, a specifically workers' press soon emerged and workers began to organize politically.[25]

Still under construction, national identity was not enough to stop popular dissatisfaction, exacerbated by the Liberal reforms, and by the conflict with the Catholic Church. The unexpected death of Fernandez on March 12, 1885, opened a space for opposition groups to begin to organize, led by Víctor Guardia. However, this attempt to dispute the control of the executive branch was quickly dismantled by those politicians and intellectuals who supported Bernardo Soto. In the end, Soto participated as a sole candidate in the elections of February 1886 and, after being elected, assured his predominance for almost the rest of the 1880s.[26]

Containing dissatisfaction in an increasingly literate society proved impossible during the electoral campaign of 1889. At that time, a public sphere was in the process of being constituted, with the participation of diverse social and cultural organizations (including those formed by artisans and workers) and articulated by a press that circulated on a daily basis. In this context, the candidate backed by Soto, Ascensión Esquivel, had to face opposition led by José Joaquín Rodríguez and Rafael Iglesias, and strongly supported by the Catholic Church, which had the expectation of repealing the Liberal reforms. The adversaries of the government triumphed in the polls and, faced with a potential fraud attempt, promoted a popular uprising on November 7 to remove Soto and his group from power.[27]

Soon the new administration deceived many of its supporters by demonstrating that it did not intend to revoke liberal reforms, and by assuming an authoritarian character. However, this authoritarianism did not prevent Costa Rican politics from undergoing fundamental changes. Between 1889 and 1902, the main political innovations were the foundation of permanent political parties, holding of periodic elections with varying degrees of competitiveness, and the constitution of legitimate institutional spaces for opposition.[28] In this initial phase in the transition to democracy, a decisive connection between the growing exercise of electoral rights by the majority of the adult male population and the appropriation of national identity was established, all of which resulted in a sustained process of construction of citizenship.

AGRO-EXPORT MODEL AND DEMOCRACY

From the beginning of the 1890s to late 1930s, the economy of Costa Rica diversified, first based on the cultivation of bananas in the Caribbean and then on the basis of other export products, such as sugar, cocoa, and precious metals. Extensive cattle ranching was consolidated in the central and northern Pacific,[29] and peasant agricultural colonization went beyond the limits of the Central Valley. In main cities, especially in San José, commercial, industrial, and service activities expanded. At the same time, the public sector increased its influence in strategic areas (in transportation with the construction of a new railway toward the Pacific coast between 1895 and 1910), and raised its participation in the economy as a consumer as well as an employer (in particular, for professionals, technicians, and intellectuals).[30]

During those years, the economic growth depended on the incorporation of more land and more labor force. Technological innovation was limited and concentrated on urban production processes (factories and workshops) and in the processing phases of agricultural activities such as coffee (coffee processing plants) and sugar (sugar mills), transportation (railways), and, in the case of banana cultivation, the control of plant diseases.[31] The main crises faced by this agro-export model was at the end of the nineteenth century, due to the fall of the international coffee prices caused by the impact of the Brazilian harvests; the closure of the European markets caused by World War I (1914–1918); and the collapse of the New York Stock Exchange Market in 1929, which marked the beginning of the Great Depression, during which United Fruit Company (founded in 1899) moved its operations from the Caribbean coast to the South Pacific coast of Costa Rica.[32]

Economic diversification was particularly beneficial for an influential circle of entrepreneurs with investments in agriculture, industry, commerce, banking, and services. The professionals, technicians, and intellectuals also achieved an advantageous insertion in the economy, either as self-employed or as employees of the state, as did the small and medium-sized urban and rural employers. Agricultural producers who depended on family labor force were in a more vulnerable position (especially those who were engaged in staple crops for the domestic market); and workers of various kinds—with the partial exception of those specialized artisans—experienced a stagnation or deterioration of their income. This was due to the growth of the population (more than six hundred thousand inhabitants in 1936) and a proletarianization process: by increasing the labor supply, wages decreased.[33]

Due to increasing social differentiation, conflicts intensified in cities and in the countryside, as artisans and workers moved from mutual societies to workers unions, a change that was consolidated in the 1920s. Also, small and medium coffee growers organized themselves to deal with big coffee exporters and producers. In addition, in 1923 the Costa Rican Feminist League was founded to fight for the approval of the female vote and against salary discrimination based on gender. These processes were complemented by the radicalization of groups of intellectuals concerned with the poverty generated by the expansion and diversification of agro-export capitalism. Such interest soon contributed to the opening of a decisive space in the public sphere and in the political agenda for the so-called social question.[34]

The attention given to social problems occurred at an essential moment of the country's political and institutional development. Initiated since 1889, the transition toward electoral democracy was consolidated after 1902. Thereafter, and except for the brief dictatorship of Federico Tinoco Granados (1917–1919), periodic and competitive elections, based on direct voting (1913) and secret ballot (1925–1927), became a key way for popular demands to be institutionally channeled. To comply with the commitments to the voters, governments systematically decreased administrative, police, and military expenses and increased investment in education, health, pensions, and public works (which included school and health infrastructure). This trend intensified after the fall of the Tinoquista dictatorship, since the Reformist (1923) and Communist (1931) parties denounced poverty and the exploitation of workers as the basis of their strategies to win votes, militants, and supporters.[35]

Led by Manuel Mora, communists were more effective than the reformists since their party was a permanent one; they had their own union organizations and a weekly newspaper called *Trabajo*. Quickly, the communists' electoral success forced their political opponents to promote socially reformist initiatives. The banana strike of 1934, which paralyzed the activities of United Fruit Company in the Caribbean, did not lead to an indiscriminate repression of the workers and their leaders. Rather, this conflict strengthened those sectors that considered that unemployment and poverty should be faced with measures similar to those of the New Deal, promoted by the Franklin D. Roosevelt administration in the United States.[36]

Founded by Ricardo Jiménez in 1931 to compete in the presidential elections of 1932, the National Republican Party became a majority political organization during the rest of the 1930s. Its favorable performance at the polls was precisely a consequence of promoting a socially reformist anticommunism. As electoral support grew for the National Republican Party, a division began to emerge between a Liberal wing and a trend dominated by Catholic politicians. The leader of the first group ("Cortesistas") was León Cortés, the lawyer who became president in 1936 and implemented an active public works construction program. His opponents ("Calderonistas") supported Dr. Rafael Ángel Calderón Guardia, who reached the presidency in 1940.[37]

SOCIAL REFORMS, CIVIL WAR, AND DEVELOPMENTALISM

A group of Catholic politicians and intellectuals who aspired to repeal Liberal legislation emerged in Costa Rica in the late nineteenth century. By 1940, their candidate, Calderón Guardia, won the elections held in February with more than 80 percent of the votes. The Calderonistas got the support of the Cortesistas by promising to endorse Cortés return to the presidency in 1944. Simultaneously, they reached an agreement with the future archbishop of Costa Rica, Víctor Manuel Sanabria, so the Catholic Church would favor a social reform project. In exchange, the pro-government congressmen would revoke Liberal laws that limited the ecclesiastical influence in the educational system and prevented the establishment of monastic orders.[38]

According to the Calderonistas, the social doctrine of the Church was what inspired the reform that created the University of Costa Rica (1940) and the Costa Rican Social Security Fund (1941), enacted the Labor Code, and introduced a chapter of Social Guarantees in the Constitution (1943). This initiative followed the interventionist tradition of the Costa Rican State, which was developed by late nineteenth century and intensified from the 1920s on. However, its main purpose was, in the short term, to electorally weaken the communists, whose party became the key competitor of the National Republican Party in the cities and in the banana provinces of Puntarenas and Limón.[39]

The strategy of the Calderonistas was quickly complicated due to a conflict with the Cortesistas that broke out in 1941 and led the supporters of Cortés to leave the National Republican Party, to establish their own political parties, and to undertake a systematic campaign to discredit the government. In this context, the communists began to approach the executive branch and decidedly supported the establishment of the Costa Rican Social Security Fund, the introduction of the chapter on Social Guarantees in the Constitution, and the approval of the Labor Code. In addition, they dissolved their political party to found a new one in June 1943, called Popular Vanguard Party. In September of that same year, an electoral alliance between Calderón Guardia and Mora originated the "Victory Bloc," whose candidate, Teodoro Picado, won the presidential elections of February 1944. The opposition compared that triumph with a *coup d'état*.[40]

After the Cold War began between the United States and the Soviet Union, Costa Rican politics became increasingly polarized, a process that ended in an armed conflict in 1948. The main winners of this confrontation were two politically marginal groups: the young intellectuals and professionals who founded the Center for the Study of National Problems in 1940 and the small and medium entrepreneurs who formed the Democratic Action Group in 1943, whose leader was José Figueres. Both organizations merged into the Social Democratic Party in 1945, but because their electoral support was very limited, the only way they could reach power was through a break in the constitutional order.[41]

Constituted as a hard-line sector, the Social Democrats elaborated a discourse in which they presented the Costa Rica of the 1940s as totally corrupt and urged for a comprehensive transformation. At the same time, they condemned any initiative of negotiation with the pro-government forces—an option that was acceptable to the opposition moderates—and began to prepare the armed struggle. The presidential election of February 1948, controversially won by Otilio Ulate, was revoked by a Congress dominated by Calderonistas and communists on March 1 of that year. This decision provided the necessary excuse for the group headed by Figueres, without considering the efforts undertaken to peacefully resolve the political crisis, began a civil war that lasted for five weeks and left a balance of some four thousand people dead.[42]

After the conflict, Figueres and Ulate signed a pact that allowed the so-called Founding Junta of the Second Republic, led by Figueres, to govern for eighteen months, starting in May 1948, without a congress. The new regime, although it soon faced growing unrest, nationalized the banking system, abolished the army, and managed to pass a new Constitution (1949), which favored state modernization and extended the right to vote to women and Afro-Costa Ricans. The "Figueristas," in addition, initiated a systematic persecution of Calderonistas and communists. Such repression, by dismantling two of the main electoral forces, prepared the conditions to create, in 1951, the National Liberation Party, which dominated Costa Rican politics from 1953 to 1979.[43]

Identified with the development policies of the 1950s, the Liberationist project aimed to diversify the economy by supporting small and medium entrepreneurs and strengthen the domestic market by increasing wages. The state was the responsible for the promotion and regulation of both processes, whose implementation benefited from the boom experienced by the capitalist system after 1945 and the Alliance for Progress promoted by the United States during the administration of John F. Kennedy (1960–1963). With the emergence of new sources of capital accumulation supported by the state, Costa Rica experienced the main diversification of the business groups in the twentieth century.[44]

The decisive redistribution of income that happened in this context favored upward social mobility (poor households decreased from 51 to 25 percent between 1961 and 1977), the increasing insertion of women in the labor market (see Figure 22.1), and the consolidation of new middle strata, decisively linked to the expansion of the public sector, which employed two of ten workers by the end of the 1970s. At that time, the population had already surpassed two million inhabitants and urbanization had intensified as a consequence of migration from the countryside to the cities.[45]

With the increasing urbanization, the popular mobilizations in the cities acquired more and more importance, as much to protest against specific policies (increases in public service rates) as to demand that the state immediately attend to problems related to housing, public transport, and the water and energy supply. In the 1920s, 1930s, and

FIGURE 22.1. Processing lard at the Numar plant (then a subsidiary of United Fruit Company), *ca.* 1960s.
Source: Courtesy of Archivo Nacional de Costa Rica. Molina and Palmer, *History of Costa Rica*, 121.

1940s, protests of this kind were carried out mainly by students, workers, and women; from 1950, the neighborhoods became the main protagonists of these movements. In this change, the communists played a central role, as they sought to compensate for the loss of their influence at the union level through the organization of urban communities.[46]

Since the Liberationist project financed the economic diversification with nationalized banking resources, from 1970 onward it faced three basic imbalances related to the import substitution industrialization, the increase in state spending, and the rise in external debt. The first of these processes, which encouraged the industrial development of the region, was initially promoted by the Economic Commission for Latin America; but, in the late 1950s, that process was decisively led by the United States, which contributed financial and technical resources to support industrialization. The final outcome was that the corporations of that country opened subsidiaries in Central America under exceptionally favorable conditions in regard to tax exemption, profit repatriation, and other incentives.[47]

Although Costa Rica did not join this strategy initially, its resistance was brief and, once it disappeared, the Costa Rican industry experienced a sudden penetration of foreign capital. The growing purchases abroad of equipment and raw materials were the basis of an upward deficit in the trade balance: from 1966 to 1972, the value of industrial imports exceeded that of exports by $250 million. The decapitalization of the economy, which resulted from this imbalance, was reinforced by the transfer to the parent companies of the profits obtained by placing more than 80 percent of the manufacturing production in the domestic market.[48]

To try to compensate for the unfavorable effects of this type of industrialization, the Liberationist governments of the 1970s founded the Costa Rican Development Corporation (1972), whose purpose was to start companies that would later be transferred to the private sector. However, this entity, which inaugurated the stage of the entrepreneurial state, promoted megaprojects that concentrated an increasing proportion of the state credit and produced substantial losses.[49] The resultant fiscal deficit increased even more because, at the same time, health services became universal and the Joint Social Welfare Institute and the Family Allowances program were created.[50]

Without being able to reform a regressive tax system or properly tax the higher-income sectors or control tax evasion, the Costa Rican State in need of resources chose to borrow to face its financial problems. External public debt rose from 164 to 1,061 million dollarsfrom 1970 to 1978. During this period, with the rapid increase in international interest rates and oil prices, the exhaustion of the Liberationist model was imminent. The collapse, which was only moderate in the years 1973–1975, was delayed by a brief bonanza in the value of coffee exports from 1976 to 1977 due to the frosts that affected Brazil, but the economic crisis finally broke out in 1980.[51]

ECONOMIC CRISIS AND NEOLIBERALISM

Although severe, the economic crisis of the early 1980s (which entailed a drop in production and rise in unemployment, inflation, and poverty) was short term. The quick recovery was possible because, in the context of political and military conflicts that prevailed in the other Central American countries after the triumph of the Sandinista Revolution in Nicaragua (1979), Costa Rica became a key ally of the United States, demonstrating that capitalist democracy was possible in Central America. The Agency for International Development provided the necessary funds so that the Costa Rican economy could be reoriented to exports to third markets, while the project of the entrepreneurial state was liquidated and state regulations and controls diminished. Some activities were partially privatized and the expansion of corporate capitalism was favored.[52]

Politicians, professionals, intellectuals, and businessmen, belonging to the political parties National Liberation and Christian Social Unity (1983), identified with these reforms. Known as "Neoliberals," these groups assumed the Reagan administration objectives as their own and were backed by the Agency for International Development, the International Monetary Fund, and the World Bank. The middle classes and urban and rural popular sectors, deeply affected by the crisis and by the divisions and conflicts that tore apart leftist organizations and unions after 1982, failed to stop changes; but they did manage, through several forms of protest and resistance (see Figure 22.2), to reduce the impact of the reforms that were gradually implemented.[53]

FIGURE 22.2. Peasants and farmers demonstrate against the economic policies of the Óscar Arias government, San José, September 1986.
Source: Courtesy of Archivo Nacional de Costa Rica.Molina and Palmer, *History of Costa Rica*, 152.

In exchange for the resources provided by the Agency for International Development, the government of Luis Alberto Monge (1982–1986) partially cooperated with the military strategy endorsed by the United States (the Contra war), and at the same time promoted the neutrality of Costa Rica and sponsored public demonstrations for peace. In contrast, his successor, Óscar Arias (1986–1990), challenged Washington's official policy toward Nicaragua and proposed a peace plan. Its success earned him the Nobel Peace Prize in 1987. This initiative made possible a negotiated resolution of the political crisis and favored a fragile and limited democratization process in the rest of Central America. To the pronounced social differences, the deep cultural gaps, and the extended institutional weaknesses that characterized the region, the foreign intervention left behind a legacy of trafficking of arms, drugs, and people.[54]

By the end of the 1980s, the magnitude of the changes experienced by Costa Rica was evident: as Agency for International Development support decreased, foreign direct investment rose, and unionism, especially strong among state employees, began to lose its place in the face of solidarist associations, a form of labor organization based on cooperation between employers and employees. In addition, for the first time in over a century, coffee and bananas ceased to be the main sources of foreign exchange. These goods were displaced by tourism and nontraditional exports, such as textiles produced in customs-free zones, pineapple, seafood, and ornamental plants. The increase in the arrival of tourists was based on the exceptional biodiversity of Costa Rica and the structure of national parks and natural reserves, developed since the 1950s.[55]

Starting in 1990, the economic and social trends of the 1980s were accentuated, although with a basic difference: the proximity to the US market, political stability, and the specialized labor force favored the development of a high-tech sector, associated with direct foreign investment in Costa Rica. This process was led by the transnational Intel, which established a process plant in 1996. The new activities, however, were not the basis of a strategic integration with other productive sectors, so their contribution to the country tended to be limited to wages—sometimes for very significant amounts—and few taxes.[56]

The lack of productive linkages is mainly explained by the fact that a considerable proportion of the Costa Rican industry remained composed by small and medium-sized companies, which are not technologically advanced and are characterized by low levels of productivity and wages.[57] In 2019, the manufacturing and construction occupied 18 percent of the total workforce, while the agriculture and extractive industries concentrated 13 percent and the service sector 69 percent.[58] The participation of peasants in the economy has declined steadily since the 1980s, displaced by an agricultural production increasingly dominated by capitalist employers, which hired foreign wage-earners, especially Nicaraguan immigrants.[59]

With the transition into a service economy, social unrest consolidated the characteristics acquired after the 1980 crisis. The initiatives of businessmen and politicians, who sought the privatization of public activities and institutions, were strongly resisted by large sectors of the population, whose protests were led by state unions. Of these mobilizations, the main ones were those that opposed the reform of the teachers' pension system (1995), the privatization of the Costa Rican Electricity Institute (2000), and the Free Trade Agreement between the United States, Central America, and the Dominican Republic (2006–2007).[60]

Although they had unequal success, the popular mobilizations once again achieved gradual implementation of reforms. After the Free Trade Agreement was approved through a plebiscite (2007), some state monopolies were opened up to private-sector competition, but public institutions were not privatized.[61] Due to this, the economy of Costa Rica remains a mixed model by the end of the second decade of the twenty-first century: in 2019, the state concentrated 13 percent of the country's labor force (in 1980 its participation was 20 percent) and its various institutions maintained a decisive influence in different areas, especially in health, education, finance, insurance, water and power supply, and telecommunications.[62]

From 1995 onward, citizens' dissatisfaction with the bipartisan political system dominated by National Liberation and Christian Social Unity parties intensified due to the growing denunciations of corruption against politicians and businessmen of those political organizations. Precisely, that year teachers (many of them women) were attacked by the police, while mobilizing in defense of their pensions. The deep cultural rupture that supposed such repression became manifest in the presidential elections of 1998, when the voter turnout was of 70 percent (in 1994 participation was 80 percent). In the 2000s, the elections were characterized by the opening of spaces for new political organizations, in the context of decreasing attendance at the polls. Of these, the most important was the Citizen Action Party, founded by former liberationist leaders who dreamed of returning to the social democratic policies before 1980.[63]

The end of the Cold War also contributed to the crisis of the political parties. From the beginning of the 1930s, Costa Rican politics was strongly dominated by anticommunism. After that agglutinating factor disappeared at the beginning of the 1990s, increasingly diverse social demands, coming from environmental organizations, feminist movements, LGBTQ communities, and others, reconfigured the political agenda. As a result of this change, from the 2000s onward matters related to the environment, family, sexuality, gender equity, and religion expanded their spaces in the public sphere.[64] In contrast, rising unemployment and growing social inequality have lost relevance in politics and in the media, although these processes have deeply affected the living conditions of the popular sectors and the lower middle class. It remains to be seen what will be the impact of demographic change on the labor market and the concentration of income in the near future. In 2019, the population reached five million inhabitants and tends rapidly to aging, due to the reduction in the fertility rate (1.7 child per woman) and the rise in expectancy of life (eighty years).[65]

In the 2014 elections, the triumph of the Citizen Action Party demonstrated the growing electoral deterioration of the National Liberation and Christian Social Unity parties.[66] This weakening deepened in the immediate future and contributed to growing uncertainty and high electoral volatility in the 2017–2018 campaign. In the end, the tiny National Restoration Party, dominated by evangelical Christians, achieved the highest number of votes in the February 2018 elections. This outcome was favored by various initiatives undertaken by the Catholic Church in defense of the traditional family values and against sex education, and by a ruling of the Inter-American Court of Human Rights, which forced Costa Rica to legalize same-sex marriage.[67]

Although the National Restoration Party was in first place, it couldn't secure the necessary proportion of votes (40 percent) to reach the presidency, so it had to go to a new ballot with the Citizen Action Party. Elections were scheduled for April 1, 2018. Between February and March of that year, for the first time since the nineteenth century, Costa Rican politics was once again decisively dominated by religion. During those months, an intense and polarized confrontation, which will be remembered as one of the key cultural conflicts experienced in the twenty-first century, deeply divided the country. Secularized sectors of the population experienced the process as a struggle between civilization and religious fanaticism, but Catholics experienced it as a battle between the nationalist cult of the Virgin of the Angels and an evangelism that they identified as of foreign origin and close to sorcery.[68]

Faced with the threat of an evangelical party assuming control of the executive branch, Costa Ricans voted massively in favor of the Citizen Action Party, which partnered for the election with a sector of the Christian Social Unity Party. Once the new administration took office (May 8, 2018), neoliberals assumed strategic positions in the management of the economic policy and devoted themselves to promote socially regressive initiatives, like those implemented in the 1990s. After an intense social conflict between public workers and the government, motivated by a tax reform that affected popular sectors and middle classes, the division of the Costa Rican society deepened and the disenchantment of citizens with politics intensified.[69] In these circumstances, the call to national unity made by the authorities in its early days quickly lost all credibility and legitimacy.

CONCLUSION

Today in Central America, Costa Rica is the country with the lowest proportion of Indigenous population, the widest access to real estate property, and the highest level of education. None of these specificities, by themselves, explain the Costa Rican difference. Overestimating any of these specificities leads to mythologizing them and losing sight of the key process that originated such difference. After the Indigenous communities were decimated by exploitation and diseases, the Central Valley was populated in the eighteenth century by free peasants, who organized themselves to obtain property rights. This solid foundation of popular power was strengthened in three historical moments after independence.

The first one happened throughout the 1840s and the 1850s, when peasants, who had unequal access to land ownership, managed to maintain their rights over land despite the rapid advance of agrarian capitalism. Small and medium agricultural producers, artisans of tiny villages and emerging cities, and urban and rural wage laborers became the decisive social forces of the future republic. Since they were not subject to forced labor and couldn't be quickly proletarianized, the early republican institutions incorporated them in various ways, a process that was consolidated with the establishment of universal male suffrage in 1859.

During a second moment (1889–1902), the country managed to consolidate a stable system of political parties, civil governments, legitimate institutional spaces for the opposition, and a strategic connection between popular demands and public policies, especially in the areas of education and health. Although rarely recognized, Costa Rica was part of what Samuel P. Huntington called the first democratic wave in the world.[70] In addition, Costa Rican democratization had the peculiarity that, from very early on, it acquired a socially reformist dimension. Although this development was briefly interrupted by the Tinoco dictatorship, it continued to strengthen in the 1920s, under pressure from the middle classes and popular-sector struggles.

In a third moment (1930–1949), while in the context of the Great Depression democratic governments gave in throughout the planet and were replaced by military dictatorships, Costa Rica not only preserved its democracy but deepened its socially reformist tendency. This was first done by implementing policies similar to those of Roosevelt's New Deal, and then by pushing forward the great social reforms of the 1940s. Such achievements, instead of being abolished were extraordinarily reinforced after the 1948 civil war, when the country combined capitalist modernization with broad processes of upward social mobility and unprecedented reduction of poverty.

This decisive institutional legacy has preserved its foundations thanks to the resistance of the middle classes and popular sectors, despite repeated attempts made by neoliberal politicians and businessmen to dismantle it after the 1980 economic crisis. Since the Costa Rican state maintains control over some of the most profitable activities in a service economy (banking, insurance, telecommunications, energy, water), the main social conflict is between governments and business groups that promote the privatization of those activities, and public-sector unions that oppose privatization. In this context, the business groups and their political allies in Congress, with the purpose of weakening their rivals, were promoting legislation in 2019 to prohibit strikes in the public sector and to outlaw unions of government employees.

From 1990 to 2017, Costa Rica's Human Development Index value increased from 0.653 to 0.794, but in that same time frame the Gini coefficient (which measures inequality on a scale of zero to one) rose from 0.374 to 0.5114.[71] Thus, a general improvement in the standard of living has been combined with increasing inequality, especially outside the Central Valley. The social unrest generated by this process is being politically exploited by evangelical Christian parties, not by the leftist parties (consisting now of people with university studies or degree), which have detached themselves from the popular sectors' claims and instead are prioritizing gender equity and the rights of sexually diverse communities. By 2019, public-sector unions and evangelical Christian parties were converging in opposition to the governing party. On the eve of the commemoration of the bicentennial of Central America independence in 2021, different groups that make up Costa Rican society were preparing to fight new battles in defense of their own interests.

NOTES

1. Héctor Pérez, *La población de Costa Rica 1750-2000. Una historia experimental* (San José: Editorial de la Universidad de Costa Rica, 2010), 3–22, 191; Bernardo A. Thiel, "Monografía de la población de la República de Costa Rica en el siglo XIX," in *Población de Costa Rica y orígenes de los costarricenses* (San José: Editorial Costa Rica, 1977), 20–23.
2. Lowell Gudmundson, *Costa Rica antes del café: sociedad y economía en vísperas del boom exportador* (2nd ed.) (San José, Costa Rica: EUNED, 2010), 81–126.
3. Margarita Bolaños, "La lucha de los pueblos indígenas del Valle Central por su tierra comunal: siglo XIX" (master's thesis, University of Costa Rica, 1986).
4. Mario Samper, *Generations of Settlers. Rural Households and Markets on the Costa Rican Frontier, 1850–1935* (Boulder, CO: Westview Press, 1990); Brunilda Hilje, *La colonización agrícola de Costa Rica (1840–1940)* (San José, Costa Rica: EUNED, 1991).
5. Ciro Cardoso, "La formación de la hacienda cafetalera en Costa Rica (siglo XIX)," *Proyecto de Historia Económica y Social de Costa Rica 1821–1945*, 4 (1976): 21; Lowell Gudmundson, *Estratificación socio-racial y económica de Costa Rica: 1700–1850* (San José, Costa Rica: EUNED, 1978), 98–102.
6. Carolyn Hall, *El café y el desarrollo histórico geográfico de Costa Rica* (San José: Editorial Costa Rica, 1986); Patricia Alvarenga, *Los productores en la Costa Rica precafetalera*

(1750–1840) (San José, Costa Rica: EUNED, 1991); Mario Samper, *El trabajo en la sociedad rural costarricense (1840–1940)* (San José, Costa Rica: EUNED, 1991).

7. David Díaz, *Construcción de un Estado moderno. Política, Estado e identidad nacional en Costa Rica 1821–1914* (San José: Editorial de la Universidad de Costa Rica, 2005), 6–34; Pablo Augusto Rodríguez, *La cuestión fiscal y la formación del Estado de Costa Rica 1821–1859* (San José: Editorial de la Universidad de Costa Rica, 2017).

8. Hugo Vargas, *El sistema electoral en Costa Rica durante el siglo XIX* (San José: Editorial de la Universidad de Costa Rica, 2005), 1–18.

9. Florencia Quesada, *La modernización entre cafetales. San José, Costa Rica, 1880–1930* (Helsinki: Publicaciones del Instituto Renvall, 2007), 31–59.

10. Rafael Obregón, *Costa Rica y la guerra contra los filibusteros* (Alajuela, Costa Rica: Museo Histórico Juan Santamaría, 1991); Michel Gobat, *Empire by Invitation. William Walker and the Manifest Destiny in Central America* (Cambridge, MA: Harvard University Press, 2018).

11. Rafael Obregón, *Costa Rica y la guerra del 56 (la Campaña del Tránsito) 1856-1857* (San José: Editorial Costa Rica, 1976).

12. Eugenia Rodríguez, *Campaña Nacional, crisis económica y capitalismo. Costa Rica en la época de Juan Rafael Mora (1850–1860)* (San José: Editorial Costa Rica, 2014).

13. Carlos Meléndez, *Dr. José María Montealegre. Contribución al estudio de un hombre y una época poco conocida de nuestra historia* (San José: Editorial Costa Rica, 1968); Vargas, *El sistema electoral*, 24–26.

14. Carmen María Fallas, *Elite, negocios y política en Costa Rica 1849–1859* (Alajuela, Costa Rica: Museo Histórico Cultural Juan Santamaría, 2004).

15. Esteban Corella, *Las fuerzas armadas y la formación del Estado costarricense 1821–1870* (Alajuela, Costa Rica: Museo Histórico Cultural Juan Santamaría, 2018).

16. Rafael Obregón, *Hechos militares y políticos*, 2nd ed. (Alajuela, Costa Rica: Museo Histórico Cultural Juan Santamaría, 1981), 150–163.

17. Dona Lilliam Cotton, "Costa Rica and the Era of Tomas Guardia, 1870–1882" (PhD diss., George Washington University, 1972); Ileana Muñoz, *Educación y régimen municipal en Costa Rica 1821–1882* (San José: Editorial de la Universidad de Costa Rica, 2002), 201–228; Efraín Pérez, *El control y la dominación política en el régimen de Tomás Guardia* (San José, Costa Rica: EUNED, 2013).

18. Jeffrey Casey, *Limón 1880–1940. Un estudio de la industria bananera en Costa Rica* (San José: Editorial Costa Rica, 1979); Carmen Murillo, *Identidades de hierro y humo. La construcción del Ferrocarril al Atlántico 1870–1890)* (San José, Costa Rica: Editorial Porvenir, 1995); Lara Putnam, *The Company They Kept: Migrants and the Politics of Gender in Caribbean Costa Rica 1870–1960* (Chapel Hill: University of North Carolina Press, 2002).

19. Claudio Vargas, *El liberalismo, la Iglesia y el Estado en Costa Rica* (San José, Costa Rica: Ediciones Guayacán, 1991); Ástrid Fischel, *El uso ingenioso de la ideología en Costa Rica* (San José, Costa Rica: EUNED, 1992), 39–76.

20. Steven Paul Palmer, "A Liberal Discipline: Inventing Nations in Guatemala and Costa Rica" (PhD diss., Columbia University, 1990), 156–171.

21. Víctor Hugo Acuña, "La invención de la diferencia costarricense," *Revista de Historia* 45 (2002): 191–228; Ronald Soto and David Díaz, "Mestizaje, indígenas e identidad nacional en Centroamérica: de la colonia a las repúblicas liberales," *Cuaderno de Ciencias Sociales* 143 (2006): 40–77; Marco Antonio Cabrera-Geserick, "The Legacy of the Filibuster War: National Identity, Collective Memory, and Cultural Anti-Imperialism" (PhD diss., Arizona State University, 2013), 210–221.

22. Palmer, "A Liberal Discipline," 156–171; José Daniel Gil, *El culto a la Virgen de los Ángeles (1824–1935)*. *Una aproximación a la mentalidad religiosa en Costa Rica* (Alajuela, Costa Rica: Museo Histórico Cultural Juan Santamaría, 2004), 89–95.

23. Álvaro Quesada, *La formación de la narrativa nacional costarricense (1890–1910)*. *Enfoque histórico social* (San José: Editorial de la Universidad de Costa Rica, 1986); Eugenia Zavaleta, *Las Exposiciones de Artes Plásticas en Costa Rica (1928–1937)* (San José: Editorial de la Universidad de Costa Rica, 2004), 132–151.

24. Mario Samper, "Los productores directos en el siglo del café," *Revista de Historia* 7 (1978): 123–217; Lowell Gudmundson, "Peasant, Farmer, Proletarian: Class Formation in a Smallholder Coffee Economy, 1850–1950," *Hispanic American Historical Review* 69, no. 2 (1989): 221–257.

25. Mario Oliva, *Artesanos y obreros costarricenses 1880–1914* (San José: Editorial Costa Rica, 1985).

26. Vargas, *El sistema electoral*, 46–52.

27. Orlando Salazar, *El apogeo de la república liberal en Costa Rica 1870–1914* (San José: Editorial de la Universidad de Costa Rica, 1990), 177–183.

28. Salazar, *El apogeo*, 183–211.

29. Marc Edelman, *The Logic of the Latifundio: The Large Estates of Northwestern Costa Rica Since the Late Nineteenth Century* (Stanford, CA Stanford University Press, 1992).

30. Carlos Araya, *Historia económica de Costa Rica 1821–1971* (4th ed.) (San José, Costa Rica: Editorial Fernández Arce, 1982), 43–87; Ólger González, *El fenómeno bucrocrático en el sector de instrucción pública en Costa Rica: 1871–1919* (San José, Costa Rica: Librería Alma Máter, 2007), 37–52.

31. Héctor Pérez, "Economía política del café en Costa Rica (1850–1950)," in *Tierra, café y sociedad*, edited by Héctor Pérez and Mario Samper, 83–116 (San José, Costa Rica: FLACSO, 1994).

32. Cardoso, "La formación," 42–45; Ana María Botey, *Costa Rica entre guerras: 1914–1940* (San José: Editorial de la Universidad de Costa Rica, 2005), 2–66.

33. Mario Ramírez and Manuel Solís, "El desarrollo capitalista en la industria costarricense" (licenciatura's thesis, Universidad de Costa Rica, 1979); José Manuel Cerdas, "Condiciones de vida de los trabajadores manufactureros de San José 1930–1960" (master's thesis, University of Costa Rica, 1994); Pérez, *Población de Costa Rica*, 128.

34. Víctor Hugo Acuña, "Patrones del conflicto social en la economía cafetalera costarricense (1900–1948," *Revista de Ciencias Sociales* 31 (1986): 113–122; Gerardo Morales, *Cultura oligárquica y nueva intelectualidad en Costa Rica: 1880–1914* (Heredia, Costa Rica: Editorial Universidad Nacional, 1993); Carlos Hernández, "De la represión a las fórmulas de consenso: contribución al estudio de la conflictividad huelguística costarricense (1900–1943)" (licenciatura's thesis, Universidad Nacional, 1994); Eugenia Rodríguez, *Dotar de voto político a la mujer. ¿Por qué no se aprobó el sufragio femenino en Costa Rica hasta 1949?* (San José: Editorial de la Universidad de Costa Rica, 2003).

35. Salazar, *El apogeo*, 173–243; Mercedes Muñoz, *El Estado y la abolición del ejército 1914–1949* (San José, Costa Rica: Editorial Porvenir, 1990), 97–101; Jorge Mario Salazar, *Crisis liberal y Estado reformista. Análisis político electoral 1914–1949* (San José: Editorial de la Universidad de Costa Rica, 1995); Ana Cecilia Román, "Las finanzas públicas de Costa Rica: metodología y fuentes (1870–1948)," *Trabajos de Metodología* 3 (1995): 5–96.

36. Ana María Botey, *Los orígenes del Estado de bienestar en Costa Rica: salud y protección social (1850–1940)* (San José: Editorial de la Universidad de Costa Rica, 2019), 512–615.

37. Theodore S. Creedman, *El gran cambio. De León Cortés a Calderón Guardia* (San José: Editorial Costa Rica, 1994).
38. Gustavo Adolfo Soto, *La Iglesia costarricense y la cuestión social: antecedentes, análisis y proyecciones de la reforma social costarricense de 1940-1943* (San José, Costa Rica: EUNED, 1985); Fabrice Edouard Lehoucq, "The Origins of Democracy in Comparative Perspective" (PhD diss., Duke University, 1992), 164-167.
39. Botey, *Los orígenes del Estado de bienestar*, 613-614.
40. David Díaz, *Crisis social y memorias en lucha: guerra civil en Costa Rica, 1940-1948* (San José: Editorial de la Universidad de Costa Rica, 2015), 5-157.
41. John Patrick Bell, *Crisis in Costa Rica: The 1948 Revolution* (Austin: University of Texas Press, 1971).
42. Díaz, *Crisis social y memorias en lucha*, 161-278; Juan Diego López, *Los cuarenta días de 1948. La guerra civil en Costa Rica* (San José: Editorial Costa Rica, 1998).
43. Jorge Rovira, *Estado y política económica en Costa Rica 1948-1970* (San José: Editorial Porvenir, 1982), 39-63; Marielos Aguilar, *Clase trabajadora y organización sindical en Costa Rica 1943-1971* (San José: Editorial Porvenir, 1987), 71-91; Muñoz, *Estado y la abolición*, 148-163; Rodríguez, *Dotar de voto político*.
44. Rovira, *Estado y política económica*, 63-176.
45. Carolyn Hall, *Costa Rica, a Geographical Interpretation in Historical Perspective* (Boulder, CO: Westview Press, 1985); Víctor Hugo Céspedes and Ronulfo Jiménez, *La pobreza en Costa Rica. Concepto, medición, evolución* (San José, Costa Rica: Academia de Centroamérica, 1995), 47-55; Pérez, *La Población de Costa Rica*, 113.
46. Patricia Alvarenga, *De vecinos a ciudadanos: movimientos comunales y luchas cívicas en la historia contemporánea de Costa Rica* (San José: Editorial Universidad de Costa Rica and Editorial Universidad Nacional, 2005).
47. Francisco Esquivel, *El desarrollo del capital en la industria de Costa Rica, 1950-1970* (Heredia, Costa Rica: Editorial Universidad Nacional, 1985); Jorge León, Nelson Arroyo and Andrea Montero, *La industria en Costa Rica en el siglo XX* (San José: Editorial de la Universidad de Costa Rica, 2016), 112-256.
48. Carlos Izurieta, "Empresas extranjeras, producción bajo licencia y formas oligopólicas en la industria manufacturera en Costa Rica," *Revista de Ciencias Sociales* 24 (1982): 33-46.
49. Ana Sojo, *Estado empresario y lucha política en Costa Rica* (San José, Costa Rica: EDUCA, 1984).
50. Carmelo Mesa-Lago, *Market, Socialist, and Mixed Economies: Comparative Policy and Performance. Chile, Cuba and Costa Rica* (Baltimore: Johns Hopkins University Press, 2000), 444-445.
51. Eugenio Rivera, *El Fondo Monetario Internacional y Costa Rica 1978-1982* (San José, Costa Rica: DEI, 1982): 48-158; Jorge Rovira, *Costa Rica en los años' 80* (San José, Costa Rica: Editorial Porvenir, 1987), 26-42.
52. Rovira, *Costa Rica en los años' 80*, 43-141.
53. Roberto Salom, *La crisis de la izquierda en Costa Rica* (San José, Costa Rica: Editorial Porvenir, 1987); Elisa Donato and Manuel Rojas, *Sindicatos, política y economía 1972-1986* (San José, Costa Rica: Editorial Alma Mater, 1987); Mary A. Clark, *Gradual Economic Reform in Latin America. The Costa Rican Experience* (Albany: State University of New York Press, 2001); Marc Edelman, *Peasants Against Globalization. Rural Social Movements in Costa Rica* (Stanford, CA: Stanford University Press, 1999); Alvarenga, *De vecinos a ciudadanos*.

54. Martha Honey, *Hostile Acts: U.S. Policy in Costa Rica in the 1980s* (Gainesville: University Press of Florida, 1994); Edward A. Lynch, *The Cold War's Last Battlefield: Reagan, the Soviets, and Central America* (Albany: State University of New York Press, 2011); Fabrice Lehoucq, *The Politics of Modern Central America. Civil War, Democratization, and Underdevelopment* (New York: Cambridge University Press, 2012).

55. Antonio Luis Hidalgo, *Costa Rica en evolución. Política económica, desarrollo y cambio estructural del sistema socioeconómico costarricense (1980–2002)* (San José: Editorial de la Universidad de Costa Rica and Servicio de Publicaciones de la Universidad de Huelva, 2003).

56. Eva Paus, *Foreign Investment, Development, and Globalization: Can Costa Rica Become Ireland?* (New York: Palgrave Macmillan, 2005).

57. Leonardo Garnier and Laura Cristina Blanco, *Costa Rica: un país subdesarrollado casi exitoso* (San José, Costa Rica: Uruk Editores, 2010).

58. Instituto Nacional de Estadística y Censos, *Costa Rica: población ocupada según características del empleo, I trimestre 2019* (San José, Costa Rica: Instituto Nacional de Estadística y Censos, 2019).

59. OCDE/OIT, *Cómo los inmigrantes contribuyen a la economía de Costa Rica* (París: Éditions OCDE, 2018).

60. Sindy Mora, *La política de la calle. Organización y autonomía en la Costa Rica contemporánea* (San José: Editorial de la Universidad de Costa Rica, 2016).

61. Ciska Raventós, *Mi corazón dice no. El movimiento de oposición al TLC en Costa Rica* (San José: Editorial de la Universidad de Costa Rica, 2018).

62. Instituto Nacional de Estadística y Censos, *Costa Rica: población ocupada*; Donato and Rojas, *Sindicatos, política y economía*, 18.

63. Mora, *Política de la calle*, 74–98; Fernando Sánchez, *Partidos políticos, elecciones y lealtades partidarias en Costa Rica: erosión y cambio* (Salamanca, Spain: Ediciones Universidad de Salamanca, 2007).

64. Patricia Alvarenga, "Identidades y política en la era de los fundamentalismos," *Praxis. Revista de Filosofía* 78 (2018): 1–10; Herrera, Bernal, "Panorama sociopolítico en Costa Rica (2018): una lectura ciudadana," *Praxis. Revista de Filosofía* 78 (2018): 1–24.

65. Programa Estado de la Nación, *Estado de la nación en desarrollo humano* (San José, Costa Rica: Programa Estado de la Nación y Consejo Nacional de Rectores, 2018), 48, 118; Instituto Costarricense de Estadística y Censos, *Costa Rica: Población nacional según indicadores generales de la condición de actividad I trimestre 2019* (San José, Costa Rica: Instituto Costarricense de Estadística y Censos, 2019).

66. Rotsay Rosales, "Elecciones Costa Rica 2014: el aparente giro hacia el progresismo de izquierda mediante el triunfo del Partido Acción Ciudadana y el ascenso del Frente Amplio," *Anuario CIEP* 6 (2015): 155–175; Ilka Treminio, "El PAC al poder: elecciones 2014 y los principales cambios en el sistema político costarricense," *Península* 11, no. 1 (2016): 103–126.

67. José Andrés Díaz, "El gobierno del bicentenario en Costa Rica. De elecciones complejas a régimen complicado," *Foreign Affairs Latinoamérica* 18, no. 4 (2018): 37–44.

68. Uriel Quesada, ed., *El mundo era otro. Cartas sobre el proceso electoral del 2018* (San José, Costa Rica: Uruk Editores, 2018); Florisabel Rodríguez, Fernando Herrero, and Wendy Chacón, *Anatomía de una fractura. Desintegración social y elecciones del 2018 en Costa Rica* (San José, Costa Rica: FLACSO, 2019).

69. Abelardo Morales, "Fracturas sociales y claroscuros ideológicos: Costa Rica en el segundo Gobierno de Acción Ciudadana," *Praxis. Revista de Filosofía* 78 (2018): 1–17.

70. Samuel P. Huntington, "Democracy's Third Wave," *Journal of Democracy* 2, no. 2 (1991): 12.
71. Programa Estado de la Nación en Desarrollo Humano Sostenible, *Vigésimo informe estado de la nación en desarrollo humano sostenible* (San José, Costa Rica: Programa Estado de la Nación en Desarrollo Humano Sostenible, 2014), 286; Instituto Nacional de Estadística y Censos, *Costa Rica: coeficiente de Gini por zona según año, julio 2010–2017* (San José, Costa Rica: Instituto Nacional de Estadística y Censos, 2019); United Nations Development Programme, "Human Development Indices and Indicators: 2018 Statistical Update. Costa Rica." http://hdr.undp.org/sites/all/themes/hdr_theme/country-notes/CRI.pdf.

FURTHER READING

Bourgois, Philippe I. *Ethnicity at Work: Divided Labor on a Central American Banana Plantation*. Baltimore: Johns Hopkins University Press, 1989.

Edelman, Marc, and Joanne Kenen, eds. *The Costa Rica Reader*. New York: Grove Weidenfeld, 1989.

Fuentes Belgrave, Laura. *La tibieza de quien peca y reza: cambios en las creencias religiosas en Costa Rica*. Heredia, Costa Rica: Escuela Ecuménica de Ciencias de la Religión, 2015.

Lehoucq, Fabrice, and Iván Molina. *Stuffing the Ballot Box. Fraud, Electoral Reform, and Democratization in Costa Rica*. Cambridge, U.K.: Cambridge University Press, 2002.

Leitinger, Ilse Abshagen, ed. and trans. *The Costa Rican Women's Movement: A Reader*. Pittsburgh, PA: University of Pittsburgh Press, 1997.

Molina, Iván, and Steven Palmer. *The History of Costa Rica. Brief, Up-to-Date and Illustrated*. 3rd ed. San José: Editorial de la Universidad de Costa Rica, 2018.

Palmer, Steven. *From Popular Medicine to Medical Populism. Doctors, Healers, and Public Power in Costa Rica, 1800–1940*. Durham, NC: Duke University Press, 2003.

Palmer, Steven, and Iván Molina, eds. *The Costa Rica Reader. History, Culture, Politics*. Durham, NC: Duke University Press, 2004.

Ras, Barbara, ed. *Costa Rica: A Traveler's Literary Companion*. San Francisco: Whereabouts Press, 1994.

Rojas, Margarita, and Flora Ovares. *100 años de literatura costarricense*. San José: Editorial Costa Rica, Editorial de la Universidad de Costa Rica, 2018.

Zavaleta, Eugenia. *La construcción del mercado de arte en Costa Rica: políticas culturales, acciones estatales y colecciones públicas (1950–2005)*. San José: Editorial de la Universidad de Costa Rica, 2019.

CHAPTER 23

PANAMA

MICHAEL E. DONOGHUE

PANAMA alone among the nations of Central America celebrates four independence days—and some say should even consider a fifth. November 10, 1821 commemorates the day when the rural town of Los Santos proclaimed independence from Spain at the height of the revolution against Madrid as the movement for independence among the colonies of Spain and Portugal was cresting across the Americas. On November 28 that year the provincial capital of Panama City made a similar announcement. On November 3, 1903, Panama declared its independence from Colombia, the successor state to New Granada under which the province had been subordinated since 1821. Panama received considerable and controversial US help for this secession. Two days later in the Caribbean port of Colón, local officials persuaded the Colombian forces near the Caribbean not to oppose the revolution, completing the four independence days that so crowd the republic's November calendar. Still others claim December 31 should be the most appropriate independence day since on that date in 1999 full control of the US-run canal was transferred to the republic. This unique array of independence events speaks to the complexities of Panama's long struggle for sovereignty first from Spain, then from Gran Colombia, then from New Granada, then from Colombia, and finally from the United States. Few countries have endured such a twisted path to freedom over a one-and-three-quarter-century struggle. And few Latin American nations have had such a close relationship with the United States since the 1840s that influenced its domestic affairs and fight for sovereignty so profoundly.[1]

EARLY BIRTHING PAINS

Numerous geographers and historians still claim Panama is not a Central American nation but belongs to South America. This status arises from the fact that Panama is split roughly in half by the Continental Divide and was assigned initially to the Viceroyalty of Peru and later New Granada—not to New Spain (Mexico). Panama was never a member of the United Provinces of Central America, a political union that held from 1823 to 1840. Another factor in this jurisdictional dispute is what one might call Panamanian exceptionalism. The isthmus has long regarded itself as unique among all the territories of the Americas, the "Center of the World," the "Door of the Seas," or the "Keystone of the Spanish Empire," all deriving from its narrow, strategic isthmus, a little over forty miles at its slimmest point from Pacific to Atlantic which served as the Spanish silver route for its Andean mines from the 1540s to the year 1739 when the Bourbon dynasty's reforms stripped Panama of its trade monopoly.[2]

Spain's efforts to hold onto Panama in the revolutionary tumult of the early 1800s failed by the fall of 1821 when along with its neighbors in the viceroyalties of New Granada and New Spain, the isthmus vanquished Madrid's authority and won independence. After the Great Liberator Simón Bolívar crushed the remnants of Spanish power in Bolivia in 1825, he focused on shoring up his new super state of Gran Colombia (which included present-day Panama, Ecuador, Colombia, and Venezuela) as the foundation for what he hoped would be the United States of Latin America. To further his vision in 1826 Bolívar convened a hemispheric congress in Panama City. But various South American nations refused to send delegates, arguments wracked the deliberations, and Bolívar's brave new vision foundered. On the home front, centrifugal forces tore Gran Colombia apart, driving Bolívar from office and to an early death. In Panama, equally disillusioned patriots saw their province reduced to a mere appendage of New Granada dominated by its capital Bogotá. Frustration over this subservience led to an early rebellion by General Tomás Herrera who established the Free State of the Isthmus during a brief period of independence in 1841 before reincorporation into New Granada proceeded.[3]

ENTER THE UNITED STATES

The prospects for a canal across the isthmus to revitalize Panama's post-1739 trade had been discussed long before the Panama Congress where it was briefly broached. Canal dreams in the region harkened back to Emperor Charles V in the early sixteenth century. But British imperial expansion in Belize and along Nicaragua's Miskito coast in the 1830s–1840s aroused concerns in Bogotá of a new imperial predator. The US *chargé d'affaires* in New Granada, Benjamin Bidlack, took advantage of these fears during an era of renewed Anglo-American hostility over claims to Oregon. In 1846, Bidlack negotiated a treaty that granted the United States transit rights across the isthmus with New Granada's commissioner Manuel María Mallarino. The treaty also conferred military powers on Washington to suppress any independence revolts on the isthmus. Bogotá saw advantages to this pact that would employ the United States, a rising power after its Mexican War victory, as a counterweight to British ambitions in the region and a gendarme to protect Granadan interests. For Washington, the treaty awarded important rights to expand its power and trade via an isthmian railroad or even a canal in the future. US interests rose exponentially two years later when huge gold deposits were discovered in California touching off a massive gold rush. Before the 1869 completion of the Transcontinental Railroad, crossing the Great Plains and Rockies presented formidable challenges to settlers from the East. Might not a US railroad across Panama solve that problem? Fearing British opposition to its larger goals on the isthmus, Washington accommodated London in the 1850 Clayton-Bulwer Treaty that granted both Great Britain and the United States joint rights to build a canal across Panama in the future.[4]

Cognizant of these new opportunities in 1851, US businessman William H. Aspinwall's investor group created the Panama Railway Company. By 1855, it completed construction on what became the world's first transcontinental line though it stretched only forty-seven miles from the new Caribbean port of Colón to the Pacific. As many as ten thousand West Indian workers died from tropical diseases during the difficult and expensive construction. But the railroad soon earned high profits for its investors, charging premium rates for those determined to get to the gold fields quickly. The strong American presence along the rail line included ex-Texas Rangers as private armed guards, and transiting US soldiers on their way to garrison California helped form the "Yankee Strip" across Panama, a precursor to the later Canal Zone. This presence also fomented deep cultural conflicts, among them the infamous "Watermelon War" of 1856 when a racist US citizen's refusal to pay for a slice of watermelon from an Afro-Panamanian in the capital's railroad station touched off a riot that claimed fifteen American and two Panamanian lives. The incident spoke to the anger built up in Panama City for years over so many haughty US travelers and their general contempt for the local "greasers." Rumors also swirled about the isthmus at the time that the notorious US filibuster William Walker, already the conqueror of Nicaragua, might be targeting Panama for his next invasion. The US Navy bombarded Panama City and landed troops there a few months later in retaliation for the US deaths. Though the watermelon incident was not an independence movement, the attack marked the first of thirteen separate US interventions in Panama from 1856 to 1903 to maintain order along the transit line and prevent future secessionist efforts against Bogotá. Attempting to dampen such separatist sentiments, New Granada morphed into the United States of Colombia in 1863 and granted Panama considerable autonomy as an associated state. These developments proved significant as they recognized the growing sense of Panamanian identity in contrast to later claims that the United States "created Panama."[5]

THE FRENCH CHALLENGE AND PANAMANIAN FRUSTRATIONS

In 1879 Ferdinand de Lesseps, builder of the Suez Canal, shocked Washington by announcing plans to excavate a waterway across the isthmus. The Colombian government granted de Lesseps's company a concession and the digging began in 1881. Americans expressed outrage at what they regarded as a violation of the Monroe

618   MICHAEL E. DONOGHUE

Doctrine, the Mallarino-Bidlack Treaty, and the Clayton-Bulwer Treaty. But Colombia saw benefits in using another great power to offset US influence and the entire project was more of a business than an imperial intervention. In any event, US worries over the French effort proved exaggerated. After nine years of costly work in lives and money plagued by torrential rains and mudslides, a yellow fever epidemic, and huge cost overruns, the French project collapsed amidst a financial scandal that ruined thousands of investors and led to the imprisonment of company officials. A central error of de Lesseps was his attempt to construct a sea-level canal and not a multileveled lock canal.[6]

Despite its concerns over the French efforts, Washington continued to exercise police powers on the isthmus to the frustration of local nationalists. In 1885, the US Navy bombarded Colón and landed troops there to put down Pedro Prestan's rebellion. The hanging of this Afro-Panamanian rebel reinforced the racial animus that strongly influenced US policy. A year later in 1886, a new constitution sharply centralized Bogotá's control over Panama, intensifying local resentment and the desire for independence.[7]

In 1894, the New Panama Canal Company emerged from the ruins of de Lesseps's bankruptcy. The old company's chief engineer, Frenchman Philippe Bunau-Varilla, put together a consortium and began the process of selling its concession to the United States then flexing its muscles in the Caribbean versus Great Britain in a dispute over British Guiana's Orinoco boundary with Venezuela. This more aggressive US policy in the region culminated in Washington's 1898 victory in the Spanish-American War which established Washington's dominance in the Caribbean Basin. As the company's rights only lasted ten years, the clock was ticking for anxious investors and US players hoping to build a canal. Still the competing Nicaraguan route obsessed many US legislators. A combination river and stagecoach transit line had already existed there since the late 1850s. Initially, a majority of US senators preferred the Nicaraguan route until Bunau-Varilla shrewdly sent them all a local stamp featuring that nation's smoldering Momotombo volcano which lay astride the proposed route, suggesting the territory there was seismically unstable. US officials also fretted over British rights in Panama established in the Clayton-Bulwer accord. Panamanians now confronted a familiar problem in their history, the reduction of their region to a prize fought over by powerful outsiders with little regard for native aspirations. Hoping to forge their own destiny, Panamanian liberals fought in the 1899–1902 Thousand Days' War against Colombian conservatives' centralized state, hoping for greater autonomy though not independence at this stage. When the war ended in liberal defeat, however, it further galvanized Panamanian national identity and the belief that local citizens must finally chart their own path to sovereignty. By this time, the machinations of Bunau-Varilla and his Wall Street lawyer William Nelson Cromwell helped eliminate Nicaragua as a competitor to the Panama route. Two diplomatic agreements in 1901–1902 between Secretary of State John Hay and the British ambassador, Lord Pauncefote, ended Britain's canal claims on the isthmus, clearing the field for unilateral US action. London virtually ceded the Caribbean to the United States and concentrated its naval resources in the region to the North Sea and English Channel to confront the growing German naval threat. With the 1902 Spooner Act, Congress set aside $40 million to purchase the rights of Bunau-Varilla's syndicate.[8]

BETRAYAL AND PROTECTORATE

Negotiations with Colombia for US rights to a canal were finalized in the January 1903 Hay-Herrán Treaty. But the Colombian Senate refused to ratify the accord demanding more financial and political concessions. This "ingratitude" in President Theodore Roosevelt's eyes sparked his decision to support a secessionist revolution in Panama, something Washington had opposed for over half a century. The carefully planned revolution included several elements: sincere Panamanian nationalists such as Manuel Amador Guerrero, Federico Boyd, and José Agustín Arango; powerful US players on the scene such as James Shaler, superintendent of the Panama Railroad; vital financial interests coordinated by Cromwell and Bunau-Varilla; and an expansionist White House determined for empire. On November 3, 1903, key Panamanians in the capital declared their independence. US railroad officials separated the Colombian garrison from its officers and bribed both not to fight with funds from Cromwell and Bunau-Varilla. US warships arrived right on time to forestall Colombian intervention and land a marine battalion. Forty-eight hours later, the State Department recognized Panama's independence in a flagrant example of "the Big Stick" that outraged Colombia and other Latin American states. Bunau-Varilla, acting as special envoy for the new republic, quickly penned a very lopsided, pro-US treaty with Secretary Hay. The accord granted US rights as "if sovereign" in perpetuity over a fifty-mile-long, ten-mile-wide canal zone in exchange for a $250,000 annuity and $10 million payment upon the waterway's completion. Bunau-Varilla's company received $40 million for its rights, equipment, and diggings. The unjust deal infuriated Panamanian nationalists but faced with rejoining Colombia and mass executions for treason, they reluctantly ratified it. Here emerged the "black legend" of Panama's birth not as an authentic nation but rather as a Potemkin one created by the United States and not local efforts, betrayed not only by Frenchman Bunau-Varilla but also by its own elites who treacherously "sold" their patrimony to the gringos.[9]

THE US PROJECT AND RESTRICTIONS ON PANAMA

In 1904, canal construction began. The same disease problems that dogged the French effort resurfaced, but chief engineer John Stevens wisely acceded to the advice of his top medical officer, Dr. William Gorgas, for a comprehensive sanitary program. This "war on mosquitos" (the Americans, unlike the French, knew they carried yellow fever) delayed the excavation in the short term but proved to be the turning point for success. Stevens also opted for a lock canal—not a sea-level one like the French—and the creation of two artificial lakes to harness Panama's prodigious rainfall and rivers to lift ships over the mountainous central region so workable transits could be forged. Though less publicized than the excavation, the 1912–1916 eviction of Panamanians and their towns from the transit zone caused enormous social and environmental damage and the destruction of a commercial and republican way of life for thousands of mixed-race citizens.[10]

In the construction of the canal and its later operation, Americans also imposed a controversial racial pay system. US officials brought with them the same Social Darwinist beliefs then prevalent in the Western world. Following the pay practices of the Panama Railroad, US workers received higher wages in gold while West Indian, Panamanians, and other foreign workers earned lower salaries in silver. This "gold-silver roll" unequal pay system was based initially on nationality—not race—as even Spanish, Greek, and Italian canal workers were relegated to the silver roll. But the overwhelming number of non-US imported laborers (some 85 percent of the labor force) were the forty thousand Black West Indian workers, so the system quickly morphed into a racial one. The US isthmian canal commission segregated all non-US workers using this same gold-silver demarcation in housing, schools, and transportation, reducing West Indian and Panamanian workers to second-class citizens in the Zone.[11]

In 1907, chief engineer John Stevens, who mobilized the international labor force for the vital early work, resigned unexpectedly, frustrated with constant pressure from Washington and perhaps bored with the project now that his final plan for completing the work was in place. His decision infuriated Theodore Roosevelt who saw Stevens as shirking his duty to his nation and to a world-historical mission. Roosevelt replaced him with army engineer Colonel George W. Goethals who also served as Canal Zone governor. Goethals pushed the workers hard, outlawed strikes, fired anarchist laborers, and finally completed the excavation. The epic effort cost nearly $400 million in 1914 currency and included unearthing a million cubic yards of rock and soil, and the pouring of giant 110-foot-wide, 41-foot-deep, 1,000-foot-long concrete locks hinged with colossal steel gates. Construction ended in August 1914 with the first transit of the canal.[12]

All during construction the strong US presence impeded the creation of a fully independent Panama which languished as an American protectorate. In 1910, Washington helped force the resignation of mulatto President Carlos Mendoza due to his "unsuitability," illustrating Washington's domination and the racial attitudes that informed it. Elite liberal presidents mostly from the merchant oligarchy ruled the political scene in these early years with dreams of a "Hanseatic Republic" patterned after the fourteenth- to seventeenth-century German trade league. They supported republican values dating back to nineteenth-century Colombia but feared popular democracy. In 1912, however, Belisario Porras, something of a populist *caudillo* (strongman) won the presidency, a post he would hold for ten of the next twelve years. Porras appealed openly to the poorer mixed-race Panamanian majority angering the lighter-complexioned Spanish-heritage elites—the *rabiblancos* or "white tails." Porras and his successors took the first steps toward state formation by founding scores of secondary schools, a national theater and institute, and art and music academies. A key contradiction of the oligarchy was its fascination with European models and their "modernity and civilization," while in reality the most "progressive" force on the isthmus was the United States, a segregationist imperial power which obstructed local state development.[13]

The completion of the canal confirmed the rise of the United States to the first rank of world powers, allowing Washington to transfer its warships rapidly from one ocean to another. The canal also increased global and hemispheric trade. But after the 1912–1916 eviction of Panamanian towns and populations from the Zone, the republic failed to profit much from the commerce of the canal except to a limited degree in the transit cities. The long-awaited prosperity and positive impact of internationalization did little for most impoverished, working-class, and even many well-to-do, Panamanians.[14]

IN THE SHADOW OF THE YANKEES

Friction between Panama and the United States erupted from the earliest days of construction, when Washington ran a state-within-a-state in the Zone with functions beyond the treaty's parameters. US officials operated a government, police force, fire department, post offices, court system, prison, schools, commissaries, and clubhouses that made the enclave nearly self-sufficient and separate from Panama. Such actions affronted Panamanian businessmen as the canal administration soon imported most food and consumer goods from the United States, selling them in commissaries and clubhouses to workers at subsidized prices. All the best jobs, housing, schools, and facilities in the Zone were reserved for white US officials, workers, and their families, the so-called Zonians. Non-US workers, especially the majority West Indians, lived in austere quarters with inferior wages, rations, and healthcare. These Black Protestant English-speaking immigrants also aroused the ire of Catholic Panamanians who saw them as cultural aliens, stealing what should be their jobs. Majority mixed-race Panamanians could only view Zone prosperity after 1916 as outsiders looking in.[15]

The US military in the Zone also challenged Panama's constricted sovereignty. US troops intervened nine times from 1904 to 1925 to quell rebellions, strikes, disputed elections, and border conflicts, using their rights under the 1903 treaty and Article 136 of the Panamanian Constitution which granted Washington broad powers of intervention. Zone-based troops also reinforced US occupations in Nicaragua, the Dominican Republic, Haiti, and Cuba justified in part "to protect the Panama Canal." A US judicial system in the Zone meanwhile enforced extraterritoriality on the isthmus subjecting all foreign nationals, including Panamanians in the enclave, to US law and punishment. And the Zone proved a font for Americanization in Panama as US influence, culture, and technology spread into the republic competing with local customs and practices.[16]

Construction and World War I brought something of a boom to the overall economy. But Panamanian leaders and merchants grew increasingly frustrated with the high-handed manner in which Zonians and their military treated their nation as a mere annex to the US-run canal. When General Pershing, famed leader of the US World War I expeditionary force, toured Panama in 1920, locals pelted him with fruit forcing his motorcade to retreat to the enclave. A massive strike in 1920 by West Indian and Panamanian canal workers trying to establish a union led to hundreds of firings and blacklisting by the Zone governor.[17]

POLITICAL REVOLUTION ON THE ISTHMUS

In 1926 the Panamanian government began a policy it would follow throughout the century of trying to revise or amend the 1903 accord that was known to many frustrated Panamanians as the "black treaty" due to its one-sided nature. But this first attempt failed when the National Assembly rejected the agreement's inadequate changes. By 1930 the decline in global trade from the Great Depression devastated business in and around the canal. The next year, a political revolution exploded partly in response, and the *Acción Comunal* nationalist movement overthrew liberal President Florencio H. Arosemena. This new political party of middle-class professionals, students, and activists led by the rural-born Arias brothers, Harmodio and Arnulfo, elected the former to the presidency in 1932. In 1936, Harmodio negotiated a revision of the 1903 treaty with the new Franklin D. Roosevelt administration. Cognizant of gathering war clouds in Europe and the Pacific, FDR viewed the canal and better relations with the republic as essential for US defense. In accordance with his Good Neighbor Policy toward Latin America, he compromised on Washington's hegemony. The Hull-Alfaro Treaty renounced the US right of intervention and eminent domain, limited purchases of commissary goods to canal workers only, and raised the annuity from \$250,000 to \$430,000. The accord also called for equal treatment of all canal employees while citing few specifics. Still, the treaty proved the turning point in ending the US protectorate and allowing Panama to intensify its state formation, creating a national university, expanding government jobs, and strengthening the republic's diplomatic corps and international standing.[18]

PANAMA AND WORLD WAR II

Harmodio Arias's more radical younger brother, Arnulfo, won the presidency in 1940, brandishing a fiercer anti-Americanism than his brother. He personified the *Panameñismo* movement ("Panama for the Panamanians") that decried Americanization and national passivity in the face of US power. Striking a populist pose, Arnulfo expanded the vote to women and called for cultural regeneration. But his obsession with *hispanidad* would alienate Panama's minorities and fashion a nativist, at times racist, national identity. Arnulfo enacted a xenophobic 1941 Constitution that stripped West Indians, Chinese, Arabs, and Jews of their Panamanian citizenship and barred their further immigration to the republic. Arnulfo also displayed a troubling admiration for fascist Germany and Italy that alarmed the US military given the canal's strategic paramountcy.[19]

US concerns over Arnulfo's threat to the waterway, combined with the oligarchy's worries over his populist appeal, provoked an October 1941 coup that ousted him from power. In his place, the moderate Adolfo de la Guardia occupied the presidential palace. The US operation of the canal proved vital for the two-ocean war in Europe and the Pacific which started that December. From 1939 to 1942, Washington began work on the Third Locks project to add a set of wider canal locks, but wartime labor demands forced its cancellation. The Zone's thirteen-thousand-man garrison grew to sixty-seven thousand by 1942 stationed in the furthest reaches of the interior at runways, radar stations, and sonar stations to deter any Axis threats. The 1942 US–Panamanian Defense Treaty granted this expansion, though embittered Panamanians called the 134 new US bases "little Canal Zones," due to their restrictive fences and adjoining bars, brothels, and casinos. Still, from 1939 to 1945, Panama's GDP nearly tripled from the wartime bonanza of construction and spending. The 1942 treaty called for Washington to give up all its bases outside the Zone one year after the war's end. But the Pentagon delayed the shutdowns and even requested a dozen new bases in the republic to defend the canal in the postwar era.[20]

POSTWAR BLUES

Anti-American riots and the opposition of Foreign Minister Ricardo J. Alfaro in late 1947 forced Washington to renounce these plans and abandon all bases outside the enclave. The following year, Tocumen International Airport opened in Panama, ending reliance on Albrook Airforce Base in the Zone as the isthmus's only air hub and furthering local sovereignty. Panamanians celebrated the 1946 US grant of independence to the Philippines, and India and Indonesia's independence that followed, hoping a decolonizing world was moving in their favor. President Harry S. Truman made positive gestures, sanctioning the 1947 McSherry Report that criticized labor and race discrimination in the Zone. But it soon became apparent that Washington had no intention of transferring the canal to Panama, given its military significance in the newly emerging Cold War. On the contrary in 1946, the Pentagon established the US Army Caribbean School at Fort Amador in the Zone. This facility trained Latin American militaries to defeat leftist subversion through enhanced interrogations, crowd control, and psychological warfare. The installation moved to Fort Gulick in 1949 and later became known as the School of the Americas—or "School of Assassins" to its detractors.[21]

On the domestic front, the key leader who emerged from the byzantine politics of this era was Colonel José Antonio Remón, commander of the Panamanian National Guard, 1947–1952, and later president of the republic, 1952–1955. Remón rose through the ranks of another US-fostered instrument of control, though he led his institution in a political direction for his own aggrandizement. While he initially persecuted anti-American students, communists, and agitators, Remón expanded his political outreach to become something of a populist *caudillo* in Panamanian politics. He even helped bring an earlier populist strongman, Arnulfo Arias, back to power briefly in 1949–1951 before Arias's authoritarian measures provoked his second overthrow. While a reliable US ally, Remón felt compelled to demand changes in US-Panamanian relations once he himself was elected president in 1952. He surprised his US mentors when he proclaimed before his 1953 visit to the White House to negotiate a new treaty: "Neither alms nor millions, we want justice!"[22]

The deal that Remón garnered in 1955 contained elements of all three but not enough to satisfy all his citizens. In 1951 the US-run canal underwent a major fiscal and bureaucratic reorganization that led to fewer Panamanian hires and less money for the already struggling postwar economy. After a long negotiation, both sides signed the 1955 Eisenhower-Remón accord. The treaty increased the canal annuity to Panama from $430,000 to $1.93 million, limited commissary purchases only to canal employees who lived in the Zone, and made all West Indians in the enclave subject to the Panamanian income tax for the first time and to a Spanish not English curriculum in the Zone's "colored schools."[23]

The treaty also conceded some small territories to Panama and a US pledge to build a $20 million suspension bridge across the Pacific entrance of the canal to facilitate traffic across the Zone and into the interior which the Zone had long impeded. The treaty finally put some teeth in generalities about greater employee equality via an apprentice program to train more Panamanians for higher-paid "US-rate" jobs. President Remón did not live to see the fruits of his diplomacy since in January 1955 he was assassinated at the Juan Franco Racetrack, possibly by the US mafia due to his narcotics trafficking, in one of the still great unsolved mysteries of Panamanian history. His violent exit also damaged his populist program of greater aid for Panama's poor. The oligarchy regained political control with the 1956 election of President Ernesto de la Guardia, which had longer-term consequences due to the *rabiblancos'* failure to address the gross income inequality of the nation. With Remón's expansion of its power, the National Guard also emerged as a growing political force with portentous ambitions.[24]

A year after ratification of Remón's treaty, President Gamal Abdel Nasser of Egypt nationalized the Suez Canal. This act galvanized Panamanian nationalists, students, and activists who dreamed of a similar patriotic redemption by taking over "their canal." In 1958, groups of students dashed into the Zone and planted scores of small Panamanian flags during "Operation Sovereignty," infuriating US authorities. In November 1959 during the celebration of the republic's independence, a group of activists entered the Zone with their flag and proclaimed that it should fly over all national territory. One Panamanian died and scores were injured as the US military confronted the protest. In reaction to this first "flag riot," Zone authorities added additional fencing on their side of the Fourth of July Avenue border, walling off the Zone from Panama City and revealing US myopia regarding the growing local nationalism.

The contrast between the impoverished barrios of El Chorrillo and Curundu on the other side of the fence from the prosperous Zone accentuated local resentments toward its US inhabitants, many of whom rarely visited Panama or spoke Spanish despite having lived on the isthmus for decades.[25]

Nationalist Explosion and Legacy

In 1960, attempting to mollify this rising nationalism, President Eisenhower ordered the flying of the Panamanian flag in the Shaler Triangle near the entrance to the Zone. This was, the first time a Panamanian flag had flown in the US enclave since construction days. In a further concession in 1963, President John F. Kennedy signed an accord with President Roberto Chiari to allow the republic's banner to fly alongside the US flag at fifteen chosen sites in the Zone. The agreement called for the removal of the US flag from numerous sites first to shorten the list to fifteen. One such locale was Balboa High School, a shrine of historical memory for generations of Zonians. Over Christmas break in early January 1964, US students from the school raised the Stars and Stripes on their empty flagpole in violation of the Kennedy-Chiari accords as the school was not one of the fifteen designated sites and both flags were prohibited there. Hearing of this, angry Panamanian students from the highly nationalistic *Instituto Nacional* nearby marched into the enclave to hoist their colors on the same pole. A violent scuffle erupted between the two groups in which the Panamanian flag was allegedly torn.[26]

News of this outrage quickly touched off a cross-border uprising. Thousands of impoverished Panamanians from the capital and Colón tore down border fencing, burned US cars, and hurled rocks and Molotov cocktails at symbols of US power and at the Canal Zone police after a Panamanian student was shot dead by them early in the conflict. US Southern Command declared martial law in the Zone, deployed its fourteen thousand troops, and began targeting local snipers. When the violence subsided four days later, twenty-one Panamanians had died along with four US soldiers killed in combat. For the first time in history, Panama's government broke relations with Washington. This horrific event provoked a long negotiating process of thirteen years that finally resulted in the 1977 Carter-Torrijos treaties. But in the meantime, radical government changes in Panama reset the political stage for a generation.[27]

Military Dictatorship

In October 1968 a military coup ousted the established political system sometimes referred to as a "protected oligarchic democracy." Arnulfo Arias won the presidency for the third time that year after coming to an agreement with Panama's military not to tamper with their independence. When he reneged, a group of colonels overthrew him. By late

1969 General Omar Torrijos emerged as the leading figure of the National Guard junta that now ruled Panama. Besides seizing political control, Torrijos deliberately pursued a populist program to build support for his extraconstitutional regime. Washington recognized and tolerated the coup since during the Cold War, the United States often preferred military regimes to the threat of communism from "unstable" democracies.[28]

After consolidating power during his first years in office, Torrijos turned to negotiating an end to the US presence and the final transfer of the canal to Panama. At the 1973 UN Security Council meeting in Panama City, Torrijos shrewdly linked Panama's struggle with the decolonization movement in the larger developing world to gain greater leverage versus Washington. In 1975, Panama joined the Non-Aligned Movement, alarming the United States with its apparent rejection of their long-standing alliance. Torrijos also deliberately rejected the *hispanidad* project of the oligarchy and championed a more inclusive multiracial identity attractive to the majority of mestizo and mulatto workers and campesinos.[29]

THE CARTER-TORRIJOS TREATIES

In January 1977 newly elected President Jimmy Carter placed the resolution of the canal conflict at the top of his foreign policy agenda. Carter felt that fair play toward small nations and better relations with Latin America superseded the privileges of a few thousand US canal workers. He also saw the canal as strategically obsolete due to its too narrow locks for aircraft carriers and oil tankers—and the US deployment of a vast two-ocean navy for many years. Airlift had replaced sealift at this juncture of military development and Carter calculated that Washington could still use the canal for many years without the stain of colonialism through a negotiated settlement that called for a gradual transfer to Panama. By September 1977 diplomatic teams from both nations produced a new set of accords. The first, called the Panama Canal Treaty, focused on the operation and management of the canal from ratification through December 31, 1999, when Panama would assume full control. The second agreement, known as the Neutrality Treaty, guaranteed the permanent neutrality of the canal from external or internal intervention. Under the terms of the treaties on October 1, 1979, the old Canal Zone with its separate government, commissaries, and schools ended. A new joint administration called the Panama Canal Commission replaced it with nine commissioners (five US commissioners and four Panamanians). Also, on October 1, 1979, nearly 60 percent of the Canal Zone's territory was transferred to the republic, the remaining 40 percent reserved for US military bases and the operation of the canal. Payments from canal tolls to Panama rose substantially to $40–$50 million annually by the end of the twenty-year transition as more and more Panamanians were trained to run the waterway. Sixty-seven percent of Panamanian voters approved the treaty in an October 1977 plebiscite.[30]

But an epic showdown over ratification in the US Senate soon unfolded involving massive lobbying from conservative and "patriotic" groups opposed to any US "giveaway" or "surrender" in the wake of recent US defeat in Vietnam. Prior to the debate, Republican presidential hopeful Ronald Reagan claimed that the Canal Zone was as much US territory "as Louisiana or Alaska," a ludicrous assertion since the original 1903 treaty and subsequent revisions recognized the Zone as Panamanian territory for which Washington had merely leased rights "as if sovereign." Congressional opponents of the treaties such as Daniel Flood, Strom Thurmond, and Jesse Helms marshaled resistance. But Carter deployed a domestic education campaign and successfully recruited Republican moderates to his cause. Still, Republican Senator Dennis DeConcini of Arizona nearly torpedoed the treaties attaching a clause granting Washington the right to intervene militarily in Panama if any force threatened the waterway. Torrijos vowed to rip up the treaty if the DeConcini amendment passed. But persuaded by Carter, the general relented, and on April 18, 1978, the treaties passed sixty-eight to thirty-two, one vote more than the required two-thirds majority.[31]

TORRIJOS'S EXIT AND THE NORIEGA CRISIS

General Torrijos did not live long to savor his triumph. He made a major effort while negotiating the treaties to diversify the Panamanian economy, emphasizing rural development and creating an international banking center in the capital. The general enacted several pro-worker labor laws and increased hiring in the state sector to build a popular base for the return of democracy via the military's new political party, the Revolutionary Democratic Party (PRD). Still, Torrijos maintained a strict dictatorship and by the late seventies numerous Panamanians wearied of his repression of free speech and elections. The steam had run out of Torrijos's "revolution" by the time the 1979–1982 global recession hit right after the treaty first went into force on October 1, 1979. During the downturn, energy, interest rates, and debt soared—and the long-promised prosperity from the canal treaties failed to materialize.[32]

The debate over Torrijos's role in Panama continues to this day, viewed as a hero by the popular classes, and a betrayer of democracy and murderer of Father Jesús Gallego, a popular critic of the regime tortured and killed by the military in 1971. Torrijos reached out to the West Indian community, incorporating them into the national family from which they had long been excluded. He also strived to include the impoverished Indigenous communities: the Kunas, Guaymis, Ngöbes, and Emberas. But while *El Comandante* employed more working-class citizens of color in his burgeoning public sector and injected an undeniable *machismo* into Panamanian nationalism, he also left an ambiguous legacy of corruption, repression, and narcotics trafficking worsened by his mentorship of top aide General Manuel Noriega. Various theories over the plane crash that took Torrijos's life in July 1981 blame the CIA, the Medellin cartel, Noriega, or pilot/mechanical failure.[33]

By 1983 Torrijos's intelligence chief and his main enforcer, Noriega, rose to command the Panamanian Defense Forces (PDF). Once in charge, Noriega tightened his grip on drug and weapons smuggling, money laundering, and domestic politics, continuing Torrijos's policy of appointing ceremonial civilian presidents and ousting them at the first sign of independence. Noriega's excesses included the arrests, torture, and assassinations of political opponents, especially the 1985 murder and decapitation of Dr. Hugo Spadafora. As a paid CIA agent of many years, Noriega enjoyed virtual impunity throughout the early to mid-1980s due to his support for the Contras whom the Reagan administration backed against the Nicaraguan Sandinistas.[34]

Noriega gradually became more of a US liability than an asset, though he remained fairly popular in his early years among working-class Panamanians due to a strong economy. After efforts to persuade Noriega to resign failed, the US Senate in 1987 passed a resolution demanding his regime return to civilian rule or face a cut-off in aid. In February 1988, federal grand juries in Tampa and Miami indicted Noriega for drug trafficking and money laundering. The following month the Reagan administration enforced major economic sanctions. Trying to put a good face on his rule, Noriega permitted the May 1989 elections but quickly annulled the results owing to the election of his Arnulfista enemy, Guillermo Endara, over his hand-picked candidate Carlos Duque. Noriega turned loose his thugs, the "dignity battalions," on those who demonstrated against the rigged election, beating hundreds and killing several.[35]

Such atrocities pushed the Bush administration to ramp up sanctions and reinforce the canal garrison. Domestic resistance on a variety of levels also increased. In October 1989, Noriega barely survived a military coup by Major Moisés Giroldi which Washington bungled by its failure to support it rapidly. By December 1989 violent incidents and stand-offs between the US military and the Panamanian Defense Forces mounted. On December 15, 1989, the rubber-stamp National Assembly declared Noriega official leader of Panama after which he announced while waving a machete that "a state of war existed between Panama and the United States!"[36]

On December 20, 1989, President Bush ordered the invasion of Panama by a force of twenty-seven thousand troops. Bush gave four justifications: safeguarding the forty thousand US citizens in the republic, defending democracy and human rights, interdicting the drug trade, and protecting the integrity of the Carter-Torrijos treaties. Controversy still swirls over the real reasons for the US invasion. These include possible revelations from Noriega over President Bush's collaboration with him while Bush was CIA chief in the 1970s, continued US domination over Panama and the hemisphere through a resort to force, and erasing the "wimp image" that tainted Bush in comparison to Ronald Reagan's "heroic" leadership. Latin American skeptics were certain that Washington would tear up the Carter-Torrijos Treaty in the wake of the invasion—but it did not. US commanders nonetheless unleashed their forces ruthlessly and overwhelmed the outgunned and outnumbered PDF. Several hundred Panamanian civilians caught in the crossfire tragically lost their lives. An estimated 215 Panamanian military were also killed along with twenty-four US soldiers.[37]

A few days after the attack, Noriega surrendered at the Papal Nunciature and was flown to Tampa to face drug charges for which he received a twenty-five-year sentence. Panama suffered enormous destruction from the invasion, which while popular in unscathed upper- and middle-class districts, caused extreme damage in the poorer sectors of the capital and Colón. Reconstruction of both the infrastructure and the economy, ruined by US sanctions, proceeded slowly, in part due to underfunding by Washington. Observers viewed the leadership of a restored President Endara compromised by his swearing in on the night of the invasion at a US military base, reinforcing the view of Panamanian elites as US puppets. The Organization of American States and the United Nations condemned the invasion as a violation of the non-intervention principle. A key accomplishment from the US perspective was the destruction of the Panamanian military and its replacement with a police force that could never challenge the United States or threaten the canal.[38]

SOVEREIGNTY AT LAST?

US military bases remained in the "Panama Canal Area," which comprised the remaining 40 percent of the old Canal Zone still in US hands after the initial transfer of 60 percent of the enclave on October 1, 1979, as stipulated by the 1978 treaties. The final transfer of all territory to the republic remained slated for the end of 1999. In stages during the 1980s–1990s, US military bases were gradually shut down. An attempt in the mid-1990s by President Ernesto Pérez Balladares to keep some US bases in Panama for drug interdiction faced rejection and protests from most Panamanians. The US imperial era in Panama ended officially with the final canal transfer at noon on December 31, 1999. Amid the celebrations, local activists complained that the Pentagon failed to clean up live munitions and environmental damage on abandoned bases and firing ranges.[39]

The Panamanian economy slumped immediately after the transfer, given the global recession and the loss of nearly $300 million in annual US military spending. But Panama soon recovered and business in the waterway flourished with increased transits and a lower accident rate than under US control. Panama especially emphasized ship repairs, container rail shipping, and ancillary industries to increase canal revenues. The nation diversified its economy with shrimp exports, construction, banking, services, and tourism. While Panama was criticized by some for its overly Americanized and capitalist society, these very qualities encouraged thousands of North American, European, and recently Venezuelan expatriates to retire in Panama and bring their capital with them.[40]

In the wake of the US invasion, democracy of a sort returned to Panama which some critics viewed negatively as the restoration of the oligarchy. Two major parties emerged: the Arnulfistas associated with their namesake, three-time president Arnulfo Arias, and the Democratic Revolutionary Party (PRD)—a more populist, leftist organization formed initially by Torrijos's military. The two groupings tended to alternate in office every five years with Endara (1989–1994) preplaced by Balladares of the PRD (1994–1999) replaced by Mireya Moscoso, former wife of Arnulfo (1999–2004) replaced by Martín Torrijos (2004–2009), Omar's son. Complaints over continued corruption ensued in all these administrations to the frustration of local reformers who advocated clean government and more social programs for the poor. But accomplishments were forged in rebuilding Panama's economy from its post-invasion and postcolonial hard times. To some degree, the political scene suffered from a sense of anticlimax by the early 2000s. Having finally ejected the United States from the isthmus after a century-long struggle, the question arose: what was the new national mission?[41]

In a 2006 referendum, the Panamanian people voted overwhelmingly to build a larger set of locks to expand the canal's capacity. Two new complexes measuring 180 feet wide, 1,400 feet long, and 60 feet deep for larger container ships were soon constructed. They cost $7 billion and opened in June 2016. Panamanians took pride in the fact that this was now truly *their* canal devoid of any imperial association. But a 2011 US-Panama Free Trade Agreement highlighted still important economic ties. The United States remains the canal's number-one customer and the waterway still operates under an informal US security umbrella. Though it should be noted that the canal now comprises less than 10 percent of Panama's GDP down from the 50 percent after construction or the still significant 25 percent during the 1960s.[42]

The ascension of wealthy businessman Ricardo Martinelli to the presidency in 2009 first brought a strong construction and investment boom, 9 percent annual growth, and 4 percent unemployment—followed by the depths of presidential corruption. Martinelli was the founder of a new coalition, the Democratic Change Party. A charismatic authoritarian, Martinelli was elected on a wave of popular revulsion over scandals under President Martín Torrijos and the PRD. By 2013 Martinelli held the highest popular approval ratings of any world leader at 91 percent. Then came a series of revelations over his illegal bugging of political enemies, allegations of $56 million in kickbacks from the Brazilian construction firm Odebrecht, and the apparent theft of $45 million from a school meals program among other charges that led to his incarceration in a Miami jail after he fled prosecution in Panama. In 2018, Panama extradited him back to the republic where he awaited trial until his 2019 vindication due to the prosecution's failure to provide evidence beyond a "reasonable doubt" against him according to the judges. While in office in 2011, Martinelli oversaw the return of Manuel Noriega to Panama to face indictments on human rights violations after his long US incarceration and a brief French prison stay for money laundering. In 2017 Noriega died in custody before his potentially embarrassing trial began. Soon afterward, Martinelli followed Noriega as the second Panamanian leader to be locked up in a US jail.[43]

Troubled by a wave of immigration to build the canal early in the twentieth century, Panama faced similar challenges in the 1990s and early 2000s, first from a surge in Colombian immigration to escape the narco and civil wars there—and in recent years, a sharp spike in Venezuelan immigration sparked by the collapse of *Chavismo*. More onerous is the nearly 20 percent poverty rate linked to race in a nominally prosperous nation especially in urban slums, Afro-Panamanian Colón, and *comarcas* (rural

Indigenous regions). The strong cultural and ideological bonds with the United States in Panama, a country where commerce remains an obsession and "Spanglish" functions in some sectors as a *lingua franca*, still form a lasting postcolonial association. But with the successful, nonviolent transfer of the waterway and the new set of strictly Panamanian locks, resentments have eased with greater appreciation for the contributions made by both sides to this once highly conflicted relationship. The future of Panama in any case is no longer predicated solely on the canal and relations with the Northern Colossus, as it was throughout most of the twentieth century. Freed from such constraints, Panama appears ready to chart its own course as a truly independent state in the new century.[44]

NOTES

1. Alex Pérez-Venero, *Before the Five Frontiers: Panama from 1821 to 1903* (New York: AMS Press, 1978), 2–23; Berthold Seemann, *Historia del Istmo de Panama* (Panamá: Imprenta de la Revista Loteria, 1959), 84–91.
2. Clifford Kraus, *Inside Central: Its People Politics, and History* (New York: Summit Books, 1991), 248; John A. Booth et al., *Understanding Central America: Global Forces, Rebellion, and Change* (Boulder, CO: Westview Press, 2006), 4; Ignacio J. Gallup-Diaz, *The Door of the Seas: Indian Politics and Imperial Rivalry in the Darién, 1640–1750* (New York: Colombia University Press, 2005); and Walter LaFeber, *The Panama Canal: The Crisis in Historical Perspective* (New York: Oxford University Press, 1989), 3.
3. Peter M. Sánchez, *Panama Lost?: U.S. Hegemony, Democracy, and the Canal* (Gainesville: University of Florida Press, 2007), 41–42.
4. LaFeber, *Panama Canal*, 8–10.
5. Aims McGuinness, *Path of Empire: Panama and the California Gold Rush* (Ithaca, NY: Cornell University Press, 2008), 123–163, 171–183.
6. John Major, *Prize Possession: The United States and the Panama Canal: 1903–1979* (New York: Cambridge University Press, 1993), 20–24.
7. John Lindsay-Poland, *Emperors in the Jungle: The Hidden History of the U.S. in Panama* (Durham, NC: Duke University Press, 2003), 18–21.
8. David McCullough, *The Path between the Seas: The Creation of the Panama Canal, 1870–1914* (New York: Simon and Schuster, 1977), 256–291.
9. Robert C. Harding, *The History of Panama* (Westport, CT: Greenwood Press, 2006), 30–37; For Panamanian refutations of the "black legend," see Justo Arosemena, *Fundacion de la nacionalidad panameña* (Caracas, Venezuela: Biblioteca Ayacucho, [1855] 1982); and Ricaurte Soler, *Formas ideologicas de la nación panameña* (Panamá: Ediciones de la Revista Tareas, 1985). For an affirmation of the legend, see Ovidio Diaz Espino, *How Wall Street Created a Nation: J. P. Morgan, Teddy Roosevelt, and the Panama Canal* (New York: Four Walls Eight Windows, 2001).
10. Marixa Lasso, *Erased: The Untold Story of the Panama Canal* (Cambridge, MA: Harvard University Press, 2019).
11. Michael L. Conniff, *Black Labor on a White Canal: Panama, 1904–1981* (Pittsburgh: University of Pittsburgh Press, 1985), 31–36.
12. Julie Greene, *The Canal Builders: Making America's Empire at the Panama Canal* (New York: Penguin, 2010).

13. Major, *Prize Possession*, 125–126; Peter A. Szok, *"La ultima gaviota": Liberalism and Nostalgia in Early Twentieth-Century Panama* (Westport, CT: Greenwood, 2001), 61–62; and Celestino Andrés Arauz, *Belisario Porras y las Relaciones de Panama con los Estados Unidos* (Panamá: Ediciones Formato Dieciséis, 1988).

14. Thomas M. Leonard, *Panama, The Canal, and the United States: A Guide to Issues and References* (Clairemont, CA: Regina Books, 1993), 18–22; Szok, "La ultima gaviota," 67–77; and Lasso, *Erased*.

15. Lancelot Lewis, *The West Indian in Panama: Black Labor in Panama, 1850–1914* (Washington, DC: University Press of America, 1980); John Biesanz, "Race Relations in the Canal Zone," *Phylon* 11 (1950): 23–30; John Biesanz, "Race Relations in Panama and the Canal Zone," *American Journal of Sociology* 57 (March 1952): 7–24; Velma Newton, *The Silver Men: West Indian Labour Migration to Panama, 1850–1914* (Kingston, Jamaica: Ian Randle, 1984); Conniff, *Black Labor*, 4–6.

16. LaFeber, 54–60; Lawrence Ealy, "The Development of an Anglo-American System of Law in the Panama Canal Zone," *American Journal of Legal History* 2 (1958): 283–303; and Wayne D. Bray, *The Common Law Zone in Panama: A Case Study in Reception* (San Juan, Puerto Rico: Inter-American University Press, 1977).

17. Conniff, *Black Labor*, 64–78; Augustín Jurado, *John Peter Williams: El Robin Hood Panameño* (Panama City: Impresora Nacional, 1974); Michael E. Donoghue, *Borderland on the Isthmus: Race, Culture, and the Struggle for the Canal Zone* (Durham, NC: Duke University Press, 2014), 107–114.

18. Victor Manuel Pérez and Rodrigo Oscar de Leon, *El Movimiento de Acción Comunal en Panamá* (Panamá: Arte Tipografico, 1964); Jorge Conte- Porras, *Arnulfo Arias Madrid* (Panama City: Litho Impresora Panamá, 1980); Demostenes Vega Mendez, *El Panameñismo y su doctrina* (Panama City: Estrella de Panama, 1963).

19. Felipe Juan Escobar, "Arnulfo y las razas minoritarias (1940–41)," in *Panamá: Un Aporte A Su Historia*, edited by Carlos Alberto Mendoza, 300-303 (Panama City: Corporación La Prensa, 2005); William Francis Robinson, "Panama for the Panamanians: The Populism of Arnulfo Arias Madrid," in *Populism in Latin America*, edited by Michael L. Conniff, 184-200 (Tuscaloosa: University of Alabama Press, 1999); Manuel Cambra, *Arnulfo Arias: El Hombre* (Panamá: Editorial Fundación Museo Arias Madrid, 2018).

20. David Vergara, *Acuerdos militares entre Panamá y los Estados Unidos* (Chitré, Panama: Impresora Rios, 1995), 83–89; Ramón Carillo and Richard Boyd. "Some Aspects of the Social Relations between Latin and Anglo Americans on the Isthmus of Panama," *Boletín de la Universidad Interamericana de Panamá* 2 (1945): 703–784; Reymundo Gurdian Guerra, ed., *La presencía militar de los Estados Unidos en Panamá* (Panama City: Instituto del Canal de la Universidad de Panama, Editorial Universitaria, 1999), 59–71.

21. Thomas Pearcy, *We Answer Only to God: Politics and the Military in Panama, 1903–1947* (Albuquerque: University of New Mexico Press, 1998) 109–137; David Acosta, *La influencia de la opinión pública en el rechazo del convenio Filos- Hines de 1947* (Panama City: Editorial Universitaria, 1993); Leslie Gill, *The School of the Americas: Military Training and Political Violence in the Americas* (Durham, NC: Duke University Press, 2004).

22. Larry LaRae Pippin, *The Remón Era: An Analysis of the Decade of Events in Panama, 1947–1957* (Stanford, CA: Stanford University Press, 1964).

23. Robert C. Harding II, *Military Foundations of Panamanian Politics* (Somerset, NJ: Transaction, 2001), 33–42.

24. Michael L. Conniff, *Panama and the United States: The Forced Alliance* (Athens: University of Georgia Press, 2012), 107–110; Conniff, *Black Labor*, 145–153.

PANAMA   633

25. Daniel Goldrich, *Radical Nationalism: The Political Orientations of Panamanian Law Students* (East Lansing: Michigan State University Press, 1962); Miguel J. Moreno, *La politica exterior de Panama 1958–1960* (Panamá: Imprenta Nacional, 1960); Donoghue, *Borderland on the Isthmus*, 60.

26. Alan L. McPherson, *Yankee No! Anti- Americanism in U.S.- Latin American Relations* (Cambridge, MA: Harvard University Press, 2003), 77–116; Eugene H. Methvin, "Anatomy of a Riot: Panama 1964," *Orbis* 14 (Summer 1970): 463–489.

27. "Panama Crisis, 1964," National Security File, NSC Histories, Lyndon Baines Johnson Library; "Los Sucesos de Enero 1964," Ministerio de Relaciones Extraneros: Memoria 1964, vol. 1, Archivo de Ministerio de Relaciones Exteriores, Panamá, República de Panamá; Major, *Prize Possession*, 336–340.

28. Paul W. Drake, *Between Tyranny and Anarchy: A History of Democracy in Latin America: 1800–2006* (Stanford, CA: Stanford University Press, 2009), 127; Sánchez, *Panama Lost?*, 142–153.

29. For critical views of the military government, see R. M. Koster and Guillermo Sánchez, *In the Time of the Tyrants: Panama: 1968–1990* (New York: W.W. Norton, 1990); Carlos Guevara Mann, *Panamanian Militarism: An Historical Interpretation* (Athens: Ohio University Center for International Studies, 1996). For a more sympathetic take on Torrijos, see George Priestley, *Military Government and Popular Participation in Panama: The Torrijos Regime, 1968–1975* (Boulder, CO: Westview Press, 1986).

30. For an overview of treaty and ratification fight, see LaFeber, *Panama Canal*, 158–192; Moffett, *The Limits of Victory: The Ratification of the Panama Canal Treaties, 1977–1978* (Ithaca, NY: Cornell University Press, 1985); William Jorden, *Panama Odyssey* (Austin: University of Texas Press, 1984). For more negative Panamanian views, see Miguel Antonio Bernal, *Los tratados Carter-Torrijos: Una traición histórica* (2nd ed.) (Panama City: Ediciones Revistas, 1985). For a plebiscite, see Nohlen Dieter, *Elections in the Americas: A Data Handbook*, vol. 1 (New York: Oxford University Press, 2005), 524.

31. J. Michael Hogan, *The Panama Canal in American Politics: Domestic Advocacy and the Evolution of Policy* (Carbondale: Southern Illinois University Press, 1986); Adam Clymer, *Drawing the Line at the Big Ditch: The Panama Canal Treaties and the Rise of the New Right* (Lawrence: University Press of Kansas, 2008), 50–51, 103–105.

32. Harding II, *Military Foundations*, 137–152; Marco A. Gandásegui, "The Military Regimes of Panama," *Journal of InterAmerican Studies and World Affairs* 37, no. 3 (Fall 1993): 3–26.

33. For Torrijos's own take on his "revolution," see Omar Torrijos Herrera, *La Batalla de Panamá* (Buenos Aires: Eudeba, 1973). For a more critical view of Torrijos and Noriega, see John Dinges, *Our Man in Panama: How General Noriega Used the United States and Made Millions in Drugs and Arms* (New York: Random House, 1990), 120–121; and Harding II, *Military Foundations*, 71–152; John Otis, "Noriega Downfall Also Tarnishes Torrijos Image," *UPI*, January 28, 1990; "3 in Panama Guilty in '71 Priest Killing," *Chicago Sun-Times*, November 22, 1993.

34. Koster and Sánchez, *In the Time of the Tyrants*, 26–31: Gloria Rudolf, *Panama's Poor: Victims, Agents, and Historymakers* (Gainesville: University of Florida Press, 1999).

35. Margaret E. Scranton, *The Noriega Years: U.S.–Panamanian Relations, 1981–1990* (Boulder, CO: Lynne Rienner, 1991); Luis Murillo. *The Noriega Mess: The Drugs, the Canal and Why America Invaded* (Berkeley, CA: Video Books, 1995).

36. Malcolm McConnell, *Just Cause: The Real Story of America's High-Tech Invasion of Panama* (New York: St. Martin's Press, 1991); Margaret Roth and Caleb Baker, *Operation Just Cause: The Storming of Panama* (Lanham, MD: Lexington Books, 1991).

634 MICHAEL E. DONOGHUE

37. Giancarlo Soler Torrijos, *La invasión de Panamá: Estrategias y tácticas para el nuevo orden mundial* (Panama City: Cela, 1993); Cynthia Weber, "Something's Missing: Male Hysteria and the U.S. Invasion of Panama," in *The "Man" Question in International Relations*, edited by Marysia Zalewski and Jane Parpart, 150–168 (Boulder, CO: Westview Press, 1998).

38. *Independent Commission of Inquiry on the U.S. Invasion of Panama. The U.S. Invasion of Panama: The Truth behind Operation "Just Cause"* (Boston: South End Press, 1999); Cristina Jacqueline Johns and P. Ward Johnson. *State Crime, the Media, and the Invasion of Panama* (Westport, CT: Praeger, 1994).

39. "Closing of U.S. Army Headquarters in Panama an End of an Era," *Associated Press* (AP), July 31, 1999; Lindsay-Poland, *Emperors in the Jungle*, 138–162.

40. Shannon K. O'Neil, "Panama Twenty-Five Years Later," *Council on Foreign Relations*, December 19, 2014.

41. Michael L. Conniff and George E. Bigler, *Modern Panama: From Occupation to Crossroads of the Americas* (Cambridge: Cambridge University Press, 2019); Orlando J. Pérez, ed., *Post-Invasion Panama: The Challenges of Democratization in the New World Order* (Lanham, MD: Lexington Books, 2000); Orlando J. Pérez, ed., *Political Culture in Panama: Democracy after Invasion* (New York: Palgrave Macmillan, 2010).

42. "Panama's Economic Outlook," *Focus Economics*, June 11, 2019, https://www.focus-economics.com/countries/panama; Christena Appleyard, "Why Panama Is Far More Than Just a Famous Canal," *Independent*, November 13, 2011, https://www.independent.co.uk/news/business/analysis-and-features/why-panama-is-far-more-than-just-a-famous-canal-6261297.html.

43. La Interpol pide la captura de Ricardo Martinelli por un caso de espionaje" *El País*, May 24, 2017; Álvaro Pulido, "Odebrecht Corruption Scandal Has Left Traces In Panama," *Panamá Today*, July 7, 2017, https://www.panamatoday.com/special-report/odebrecht-corruption-scandal-has-left-traces-panama-4624; Randall C. Archibold, "Manuel Noriega, Dictator Ousted by U.S. in Panama, Dies at 83," *New York Times*, May 30, 2017; "Former Panamanian President Ricardo Martinelli Arrested in Coral Gables," *Miami Herald*, June 12, 2017; Elida Moreno, "Panama Court Finds Ex-President Martinelli Not Guilty of Spying Charges," *Reuters*, August 9, 2019.

44. "Debating Disparity: Panama Poverty Rate Declining," *The Borgen Project*, September 16, 2017, https://borgenproject.org/panama-poverty-rate/; "The World Bank in Panama: Overview," *The World Bank*, April 4, 2019, http://www.worldbank.org/en/country/panama/overview; for poverty in Colón, see Randall C. Archibold, "A Once-Vibrant City Struggles as Panama Races Ahead on a Wave of Prosperity," *New York Times*, March 23, 2013; Conniff and Bigler, *Modern Panama*.

Further Reading

Castillero R., Ernesto J. *Historia de Panamá*. Panamá: Editorial Universitaria, 1989.

Conniff, Michael L. *Panama and the United States: The Forced Alliance*. Athens: University of Georgia Press, 2012.

Conniff, Michael L., and Gene E. Bigler. *Modern Panama: From Occupation to Crossroads of the Americas*. Cambridge, UK: Cambridge University Press, 2019.

Donoghue, Michael E. *Borderland on the Isthmus: Race, Culture and the Struggle for the Canal Zone*. Durham, NC: Duke University Press, 2014.

Gasteazoro, Carlos Manuel, Celestino Andrés Araúz, and Armando Muñoz Pinzón. *La Historía de Panamá en sus textos 1501–1903*. Panamá: Editorial Universitaria, 1980.

Gasteazoro, Carlos Manuel, Celestino Andrés Araúz, and Armando Muñoz Pinzón. *La Historía de Panamá en sus textos Tomo II 1903–1968*. Panamá: Editorial Universitaria, 1999.

Greene, Julie. *The Canal Builders: Making America's Empire at the Panama Canal*. New York: Penguin, 2010.

Harding II, Robert C. *Military Foundations of Panamanian Politics*. Somerset, NJ: Transaction, 2001.

LaFeber, Walter. *The Panama Canal: The Crisis in Historical Perspective*. New York: Oxford University Press, 1989.

Lasso, Marixa. *Erased: The Untold Story of the Panama Canal*. Cambridge, MA: Harvard University Press, 2019.

Lindsay-Poland, John. *Emperors in the Jungle: The Hidden History of the U.S. in Panama*. Durham, NC: Duke University Press, 2003.

Major, John. *Prize Possession: The United States and the Panama Canal, 1903–1979*. New York and London: Cambridge University Press, 1993.

Murillo, Luis. *The Noriega Mess: The Drugs, the Canal and Why America Invaded*. Berkeley, CA: Video Books, 1995.

Sánchez, Peter M. *Panama Lost? U.S. Hegemony, Democracy, and the Canal*. Gainesville: University of Florida Press, 2007.

Seemann, Berthold. *Historia del Istmo de Panamá*. Panamá: Imprenta de la Revista Loteria, 1959.

CHAPTER 24

···

BELIZE

···

MARK MOBERG

INTRODUCTION

···

In its history, culture, and politics, Belize is often regarded as the most atypical nation of Central America. Formerly a Crown Colony of Great Britain, the country was officially known as British Honduras until 1973. Belize became an independent state in 1981, long after the rest of the region, and it is the only officially English-speaking Central American country. It belongs to the Commonwealth of fifty-three associated states, most of them former British territories, and maintains extensive political and economic ties to the Anglophone Caribbean.

Facing the Caribbean Sea to the east, Belize borders Mexico to the north and Guatemala to the west and south (Figure 24.1). With a land area of 8,867 square miles (22,965 square kilometers), Belize claims the smallest national territory in Central America after El Salvador, whose 6.35 million people occupy 8,292 square miles. Yet it is by far the most sparsely populated country in the region, with only 322,453 residents recorded in its 2010 census. For administrative purposes Belize is divided into six districts. The largest share of the population (60,184) is concentrated in the original colonial settlement and port town of Belize City. Following the extensive destruction of coastal areas during Hurricane Hattie in 1961, most government operations were transferred to a new inland capital at Belmopan (population 18,326). Five decades after its founding, Belmopan remains a distant second to Belize City as a center for most of the country's commercial, cultural, and educational institutions.

The small size of Belize's workforce and domestic markets have long been recognized as barriers to sustainable economic growth, particularly with respect to agricultural self-sufficiency. Marshy coastal terrain precludes settlement over much of the national territory, but Belize's sparse population is more the result of historical than natural factors. Well into the twentieth century, the country's contested sovereignty, narrow reliance on forest products, and land monopolies among a handful of economic elites inhibited agricultural development. Historically, most of the working population was restricted to

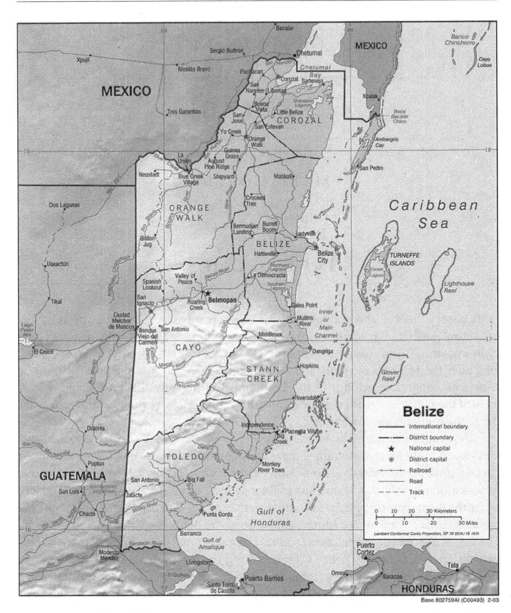

FIGURE 24.1. Map of Belize.
Source: U.S. Central Intelligence Agency, 2003. Available at https://www.cia.gov/library/publications/resources/cia-maps-publications/Belize.html.

seasonal employment (first as slaves, later as heavily indebted wage workers) in the colonial timber industry. Only since the 1950s have sustained efforts been made to diversify the economy from a narrow array of forest products. In the decades since Belizean independence, the distribution and ethnic composition of the population have been dramatically altered by an immigrant influx from other Central American countries. Yet Belize's colonial legacy persists in a Westminster-based parliamentary political system dominated by the descendants of the original settler and slave populations.

COLONIAL PATTERNS OF LAND AND LABOR CONTROL

Until the Kingdom of Guatemala gained independence in the early nineteenth century, Spain claimed Belize among its possessions on the isthmus. Through the 1640s, Spanish military forces and missionary priests launched forays into the interior of Belize. The Indigenous Maya resisted Spanish demands for tribute, burning several outposts established through the Spanish policy of *reducción*, or resettlement.[1] Maya recalcitrance led Spain to shift its attentions elsewhere, creating an opportunity for rival powers to establish a foothold. Colonial-era historians maintained that by 1640 English buccaneers had occupied a marshy site near the mouth of the Belize River, at the location of present-day Belize City.[2] Such claims are more likely legendary than factual: the settlement does not appear on contemporary maps and in records until the 1710s.[3] By the mid-eighteenth century it was known as the "British Settlement in the Bay of Honduras," although Britain long deigned to officially claim it as a colony.[4] In later centuries, the "Baymen," as the settlers called themselves, were to become mythical progenitors of the Belizean nation and even immortalized in the country's national anthem. A contemporary account rendered them less heroically as "ungovernable wretches . . . a rude and drunken Crew, some of which have been Pirates, and most of them Sailors."[5] The English were drawn by the presence of logwood (*Haematoxlylum campechianum L.*), a low-growing tree found only on the Yucatán peninsula and the Caribbean coast of Central America. As a source of fixing compounds for clothing dyes, logwood was in great demand by Britain's expanding textile industry, which regarded it as "absolutely essential to our Woolen Manufactures."[6] British seamen along the Caribbean littoral sought to circumvent Spanish monopolies, either by seizing Spanish logwood shipments through piracy or cutting the wood outright. Earliest records note that the Baymen brought with them enslaved Africans and Indigenous Miskito from Lower Central America to work in timber harvesting. By 1779, slaves accounted for 86 percent of the settlement's population of 3,500.[7]

The status of the settlement varied with the state of English–Spanish relations in Europe. Throughout the eighteenth century, the Baymen were periodically routed by Spanish forces, but after the Spanish withdrew, they inevitably returned to resume woodcutting. Under the Treaty of Paris in 1763, Spain granted settlers the right to harvest logwood in exchange for their acknowledgment of Spanish sovereignty. The Treaty also prohibited them from engaging in agriculture or establishing "fortifications and permanent settlements."[8] Subsequent conventions required England to surrender its settlements in Mosquitia and Roatan, most of whose residents were evacuated to Belize.[9]

In 1786, an English-appointed superintendent arrived to enforce Treaty provisions and parliamentary mandates over British subjects. Britain's reluctance to antagonize Spain lest it lose access to logwood precluded any formal territorial claim. After a renewed outbreak of war between the two powers, Spain mounted a final (unsuccessful) effort to expel the settlers during the Battle of St. George's Caye in 1798. Despite Spain's waning control over Central America, Britain did not recognize the territory as a Crown Colony until 1862.

Prior to the assignment of British superintendents, the Baymen governed themselves with laws of their own devising (known as Burnaby's Code) and direct representation in a regularly convened public meeting. The small minority of residents who controlled the timber trade and importation of basic goods came to dominate local governance. Participation in the public meeting was limited to white male British subjects possessing at least £100 in property or "free colored" men with £200 or more.[10] Whites alone could serve as magistrates who enforced local laws and contracts. As an instrument of elite governance, the public meeting defied the superintendents charged to end the slave trade and expand rights for free colored British subjects. Local elites had privately appropriated most of the territory by the time Britain established a formal colonial government. Their near-monopoly on land was exercised largely to *prevent* its use for agriculture, ensuring that the resident labor force remained dependent on timber employment following Britain's abolition of slavery in 1838.[11] By then, the colony's economic fortunes had shifted from logwood to mahogany, a resource that demanded considerably more labor for harvesting, transport, and processing. Well into the twentieth century, an elite "forestocracy"[12] of timber companies and import merchants repeatedly clashed with colonial governors who sought to promote agriculture. Given their limited terms of office and the threat of ostracism by local whites, most appointees from the Colonial Office either refused to challenge elite prerogatives or gave up trying.[13] A prolonged slump in mahogany prices after 1850 led to further political and economic consolidation, with a few English firms acquiring the lands of most local timber companies. By century's end, the London-based Belize Estate and Produce Company had amassed half of the land in the colony.[14]

Following the abolition of slavery, an "advance-truck" system of debt peonage deepened the dependence of the colony's now nominally freed workers on the timber industry.[15] During their off-season in Belize City, workers were recruited with an advance in wages and supplies, committing them to a work contract for the remainder of the year. While laboring in isolated logging camps, workers obtained the balance of their needs on credit. Timber workers were charged prices that greatly exceeded their earnings, keeping them "virtually enslaved for life," according to the resident Colonial Secretary in 1890.[16] By the late 1800s, nearly 40 percent of all criminal convictions were of laborers who failed to return to employers to whom they were indebted. Reforms instituted elsewhere in the British Caribbean during the 1890s, which established a "reconstituted peasantry" on former estate lands as a source of political stability,[17] were strenuously resisted by employers and merchants who relied on an indebted work force.

By the 1920s, mahogany and chicle (for chewing gum) constituted 85 percent of all exports, subjecting the colony to a narrow and volatile niche in the world market.[18] Laborers and returning veterans had rioted in 1894 and 1919 over persistent economic and racial inequities, prompting the dispatch of British warships and Marines.[19] Most of the working population was left destitute when timber exports collapsed during the Great Depression. Their desperation was compounded by a 1931 hurricane that destroyed Belize City and killed over one thousand of its sixteen thousand residents. In the face of government inaction, idled workers organized the Labourers and Unemployed Association (LUA) to press for relief work, an expanded electoral franchise, and labor reforms, including the right to strike. Although British Honduras differed in key respects from the sugar-producing islands of the British Caribbean, labor leaders such as LUA's Antonio Soberanis drew inspiration from the waves of labor protest then sweeping the West Indies.[20] Soberanis recruited working-class women into the LUA, unleashing women's participation in a wave of strikes from which their partners were legally barred.[21] The colonial government responded with modest constitutional changes in 1935. These opened five of the twelve seats on the Legislative Council to election but imposed such severe property restrictions that only 822 of the colony's 50,000 residents were entitled to vote.[22] In the face of continued protests, the government conceded the right to join trade unions in 1941 and abolished the advance-truck system two years later.

NATIONHOOD AND INDEPENDENCE

During World War II, many Belizean men emigrated to contribute to the British war effort or work at the Panama Canal. The colony's moribund timber industry failed to revive, however, and unemployment rose sharply with their return at the end of the war. Under the General Workers Union (GWU), a newly invigorated labor movement struck for higher wages for waterfront, sawmill, and sugar workers. When the governor devalued the British Honduras currency against the US dollar in 1949, labor's demands turned from a narrow economic agenda to national independence. Devaluation prompted a steep rise in the cost of living for most workers, who depended on imported food from the United States. Massive protests followed, culminating in a ten-thousand-strong march organized by a "People's Committee" of union and middle-class activists. The Committee's successor, the People's United Party (PUP), adopted a pro-independence platform and demanded universal adult suffrage. The government responded with repression (arresting some PUP leaders for "disloyalty") and attempted co-optation, including an invitation to party moderates to serve in quasi-ministerial roles. The PUP split in 1956 over the question of collaboration, with the charismatic and staunchly anticolonial George C. Price (1919–2011) emerging as the party's leader. In a bid to strengthen Price's more conservative opponents, the government charged him with sedition in 1958 for an allegedly uncomplimentary joke about the British royal family.[23] The move backfired badly: Price's popularity soared when he was acquitted by a local jury in a highly publicized trial. In elections held under an expanded franchise in 1961, the PUP swept all eighteen seats in a newly created Legislative Assembly. The outcome forced Britain to accept the eventual goal of national independence with Price as the First Minister of an interim government. British Honduras achieved self-governance over its internal affairs in 1964, while Britain retained control of its defense and foreign relations. The colony was officially renamed Belize in 1973, but it did not become fully independent of Britain until 1981.

The broad outlines of Belize's modern political system were established at the time of self-governance, and they resemble other Westminster-based arrangements throughout the Commonwealth Caribbean. Executive power is held by a prime minister and cabinet of ministers, who are drawn from elected members of the majority party in the National Assembly. The Assembly currently consists of a House of Representatives of twenty-nine elected members representing local districts for terms of up to five years, and a Senate of twelve members, all appointed with a largely advisory role. The ceremonial head of state remains the British monarch, whose local interests are represented by an appointed governor general. Since the mid-1950s, there have been two main political parties and a few smaller transitory parties that have at times given critical support to either of the main political groupings. The PUP held power continuously from 1961 until 1984. Under Price and his "peaceful, constructive Belizean revolution," the PUP established itself as an anticolonial, center-left party that identified with the Non-Aligned Movement of nations. A famously ascetic man who had once studied for the priesthood, Price invoked the social justice teachings of the Catholic Church (particularly the encyclical Rerum Novarum, *On the Rights of Labor*) as a political compass.[24] At its outset, the PUP was closely aligned with the country's largest labor union, the GWU. When the PUP split in 1956, the GWU leadership followed Price's opponents out of the party, but most of the rank-and-file remained in the PUP to form the Christian Democratic Union (CDU). Since then, the country's unions have retained a partisan identity that diminishes their ability to act cohesively across political lines.

When Leigh Richardson and Philip Goldson defected from the PUP in 1956, they formed the more conservative National Independence Party, becoming the United Democratic Party (UDP) in 1973. The NIP/UDP long claimed that Price, in his zeal to rid the country of the British, would offer territorial concessions to Guatemala or seek some political association with it. These accusations were first leveled by the colonial government to discredit Price but were taken up by the UDP throughout its years in the opposition.[25] Belize experienced its first change of power at the national level in 1984, when the PUP was defeated in national elections. The ensuing UDP government professed greater affinity for the Reagan administration's aims in Central America. Since then, power at the national level has alternated between the two parties. Said Musa, once regarded as a leader of the PUP's "socialist" wing, succeeded Price as party leader and served as prime minister from 1998 until 2008. Despite Musa's leftist reputation, his government embraced a neoliberal economic program focused on tourism, foreign investment, offshore banking, and privatization of state-run utilities. Once ideologically distinct on a left-to-right continuum, the two parties have converged in economic policy in recent decades. Amid accusations of corruption within Musa's government, the UDP swept to power in the 2008 elections. Since then Belize has been governed under Prime Minister Dean Barrow.

THE GUATEMALAN CLAIM

Belize's path to independence was complicated by a long-standing Guatemalan territorial claim that it was said to have inherited from Spain. The border between British Honduras and Guatemala had been settled by an Anglo-Guatemalan treaty in 1859, which acknowledged English control while committing both parties to "establish the easiest communication . . . either by cart-road, or employing the rivers" from Belize to Guatemala City.[26] The road was never built, but Britain subsequently offered a monetary settlement and proposed joint alternatives such as a railway. No agreement was finalized on these terms, and the issue was essentially forgotten for decades. In 1940, Guatemalan President Jorge Ubico abruptly revived his country's claim to "Belice," arguing that Britain had failed to fulfill its obligations under the 1859 treaty. The territorial claim has been asserted ever since by a succession of military-dominated governments, whose periodic threats and massing of troops at the border seem calculated to rally domestic political support. A threatened invasion by the Guatemalan army in 1948 prompted Britain to post combat forces in the colony. Britain entered negotiations with Guatemala in 1961, but Price and other elected Belizeans—who were excluded from the talks—strenuously rejected Britain's proposed concessions. A later US-directed mediation effort by Bethuel Webster, a lawyer appointed by President Lyndon Johnson, was also rejected when he proposed that Belize surrender most of its internal governance and foreign policy to Guatemala. Washington's position was a reward to a government that it then regarded as a key Cold War ally. In 1961, Guatemala had helped train Cuban exiles for the failed Bay of Pigs invasion in the hope that the United States would pressure Britain to give up Belize.[27]

Guatemalan threats to invade in 1972 and 1975 were met by the dispatch of more British forces, including naval frigates and Harrier jet fighters. Frustrated at dealing with Guatemala directly, the Price government instead took its case to the United Nations and the countries of the Commonwealth and Non-aligned Movement. After the United States finally signaled its assent in 1980, the UN overwhelmingly voted to recognize Belizean independence, with Guatemala offering the only dissent. A final round of negotiations in 1981 produced a proposed "Heads of Agreement" by which Guatemala would accept Belizean independence and territorial integrity in exchange for continued discussions over maritime access. Within Belize, the opposition UDP and its affiliated Public Service Union (PSU) mounted public protests against the proposal that escalated into violence. Rioting culminated in four deaths, many more injuries, and considerable property damage, leading the governor general to declare a state of emergency in April 1981. With the Guatemalan claim still unresolved but with firm backing from the UN and regional allies (especially Panama, Cuba, and the new Sandinista government in Nicaragua), Belize proceeded to independence under Price on September 21, 1981.

In 1991, Jorge Serrano, Guatemala's civilian president, surprised many by accepting Belizean independence without preconditions, leading the governments to establish full diplomatic relations for the first time. Two years later, the Guatemalan presidency was assumed by Ramiro de Leon Carpio, who had earlier criticized Serrano's recognition of Belize. While not renouncing diplomatic relations outright, he challenged the territorial waters proposed under Belize's recently passed Maritime Areas Act. Tensions increased as Belize sought to evict the growing numbers of Guatemalans who established slash-and-burn farms, hunted, and engaged in illegal logging within Belizean boundaries, much of it inside protected conservation areas. Confrontations between squatters and the Belize Defense Force in turn escalated domestic political pressures on the Guatemalan government to take a harder line on Belize. In 1999, Guatemala reasserted most of its territorial demands, this time invoking Spain's eighteenth-century treaties limiting British settlement to areas north of the Sibun River. In effect, Guatemala claimed the right to 12,272 square kilometers of Belize, or approximately 53 percent of the country's territory as established in the 1859 treaty. The Guatemalan claims include the entirety of the southern districts of Stann Creek and Toledo, and most of the western district of Cayo. School textbooks approved by Guatemala's Ministry of Education now depict the disputed territory as a part of Guatemala.

In 2007, the Organization of American States (OAS) proposed that the countries resolve their territorial disputes through adjudication by the International Court of Justice (ICJ) in The Hague. Under this plan, Guatemala would have a year to present written and oral arguments in its case, with equal time granted to a Belizean rebuttal. The adjudication process, from opening arguments to deliberations and final decision by the ICJ, was projected to last six years. The Court's determination was to be binding, with no appeal permitted to either party, and would be implemented by a binational commission selected within three months of the verdict. After protracted negotiation and internal debate, both governments agreed to identical national referenda asking their voters whether to accept the proposal. Only 26 percent of eligible voters cast ballots in Guatemala's referendum, held in April 2018, but those who did so supported ICJ adjudication by a vast (96 percent) margin. Public opinion within Belize remained divided as that country's referendum approached in 2019. In an unusual gesture of unity, Prime Minister Barrow assembled a press conference with former Prime Minister Musa and past PUP and UDP foreign ministers to jointly urge voters to support the proposal. Approximately 66 percent of eligible voters participated in the May 8, 2019, Belizean referendum, with over 55 percent voting in favor. In June 2019, the ICJ accepted both governments' formal requests for adjudication, and asked Guatemala to submit its first supporting documents by June 7, 2020.[28]

ETHNICITY AND NATIONAL IDENTITY

Belize exhibits extraordinary diversity in identity and language, reflecting its long history of slavery and forced or voluntary immigration. Until the 1980s, the largest share of the population was of mixed African ancestry. Creoles, the descendants of African slaves and British settlers, are native speakers of English and/or a related patois (known locally as Kriol). The Garifuna first arrived from Honduras during the early nineteenth century as a "free coloured" population originating in the Eastern Caribbean. Often phenotypically indistinguishable from creoles, they are culturally distinctive for their mixed African and Island Carib heritage and use of a language of Arawakan origin.[29] The country's Amerindian groups comprise Yucatecan Mayas in the north, and Mopan and Q'eqchi' Mayas in the south.[30] Spanish-speaking mestizos currently make up the largest share of the national population. Smaller minorities of East Indian, Asian, and Middle Eastern descent predominate in the commercial sectors of Belize City and the country's towns. The Chinese population has grown measurably in recent years with the arrival of immigrants from Hong Kong and Taiwan. Since their settlement in rural Belize during the 1950s, white Mennonite farmers have come to dominate the country's domestic agricultural markets. Belize has also become home to growing numbers of North American and European expatriates, most of whom are white. Nearly 90 percent of Belizeans identify as Christian, with considerable variation in affiliation and practice by ethnicity. As the largest faith community, Roman Catholicism claims the adherence of most mestizos, Maya, and Garifuna, as well as many Creoles, although its practices have been extensively reworked into local or folk idioms. Catholicism is frequently combined with pre-Columbian belief systems in Maya communities, while many Garifuna fuse it with African spiritism.[31] As in much of Central America, evangelical Protestantism has also made recent inroads into Indigenous communities. Many creoles also practice Catholicism, but the majority are Methodists, Anglicans, evangelicals, or other Protestants.

Reflecting the country's ethnic diversity, patterns of language use are complex, with extensive code switching according to context and locale. English is the official language of education, the mass media, and government, but its related lexifier Kriol predominates in social and home interactions among English-speakers. Kriol and English are the primary languages in Belize City and other areas with a majority creole population. In 2010, about 63 percent of the population reported English fluency, with 57 percent reporting fluency in Spanish.[32] Hence, many Belizeans are comfortably multilingual, but Spanish predominates to the north and west of Belize City and its surrounding district. At home many Belizean mestizos employ a "Kitchen Spanish" utilizing both Spanish and (English) Kriol lexical items and syntax. Garifuna, Mopan, and Q'eqchi' are still spoken in their respective communities of the south, although Yucatecan Maya has been largely supplanted by Spanish in the northern districts. In general, however, Indigenous languages have become less widely used in recent decades as their speakers acculturate to either Kriol or Spanish home use. A German dialect (*Plattdeutsch*) predominates in Mennonite settlements, which have retained a high degree of social separation from other communities.

This complex ethnic mosaic plays out against a history of British colonialism and contested Guatemalan territorial claims. The demographic makeup of Belize changed dramatically in the 1980s and 1990s as people fled political repression and economic hardship in the neighboring Central American countries. The 1991 census revealed that the mestizo share of the population increased by more than 70 percent over the previous decade, replacing creoles as the single largest ethnic group. These changes were accelerated by the emigration of an estimated eighty thousand Afro-Belizeans (creoles and Garifuna) for the United States, where large Belizean immigrant neighborhoods are found in New York, Chicago, Los Angeles, and New Orleans. The creole segment of the population fell from about 40 percent in 1980 to about 22 percent in 2010, and continues to decline (Table 24.1). For many remaining Afro-Belizeans, these demographic changes portend a "Latinization" of the country that challenges a long-standing conception of national identity rooted in the British colonial past.

Throughout the colonial period, territorial claims by Spain and later Guatemala intensified British efforts, notable throughout its Caribbean colonies, to cultivate an affinity with the Empire. British Honduran identity became implicitly associated with the creole culture and Anglophone orientation of Belize City. By the late nineteenth century, a status hierarchy had emerged in which creoles were accorded particular privilege based on their command of English and association with mahogany cutting.[33] Colonial authorities justified creoles' higher status in the social order,

Table 24.1. Ethnic Groups in Belize (percentage of national population)

	1980	2010
Creole	39.7	22.2
Mestizo	33.1	49.7
Garifuna	7.6	4.7
Maya	9.3	9.9
White	3.8	5.8
Mennonite	3.1	3.6
East Indian	2.2	2.2
Asian	.1	.9
Syrian/Lebanese	.2	.1
Other/unknown	.8	.7

Note: Totals may not sum to 100 due to rounding.

Sources: *Population Census 1980.* Government of Belize Central Statistical Unit; *Belize Population and Housing Census 2010.* Government of Belize Statistical Institute.

including their assignment to minor civil service and constabulary posts, in terms of their putative "attachment" to the British. As evidence of this, colonial commentators regularly invoked the territory's "creation myth" of the 1798 Battle of St. George's Caye, which marked the last Spanish effort to seize the settlement by force.[34] In later official accounts of the battle, slaves were reputed to have stood "shoulder to shoulder" with their English masters to repel the attackers.[35] September 10, the date of the battle, became a major colonial-era and then national holiday, and was celebrated most ardently in Belize City and other creole communities as a triumph over Spanish "treachery." During the colonial era, non-creoles were deemed members of the polity to the extent that they exhibited fidelity to Anglo norms. Because of their association with the Spanish and Guatemalans who challenged British sovereignty, mestizos—especially newly arrived, non–English-speaking immigrants—were often seen to be of dubious loyalty.[36]

These attitudes were affirmed in official policies until the very end of the colonial period, as evidenced by an influential 1959 government report on development. In reference to the colony's creole population, the study noted with satisfaction that a "race of 'British Central Americans' seems to be in the making."[37] Its authors were less complimentary in their depiction of non-English speakers, who were thought to resist this emerging national identity. They described the "Spanish" (mestizos) as a "volatile" group "in closest affinity with that often inscrutable, rather reserved individual, the Maya Indian." To the colony's Amerindians the report attributed a child-like rationality common to stereotypical characterizations of "primitives": "on a sudden impulse they may throw away the labour of weeks on something which has no use or meaning in their home life."[38] These prejudices reflected and rationalized tangible differences in the rights accorded to each of the colony's ethnic groups. In contemplating universal adult suffrage in 1951, a colonial commission recommended that English literacy tests be maintained as a precondition for voting to prevent "a premature extension of political responsibility" to non-creoles.[39]

Despite such stereotypes, until the 1980s ethnic strife was less pronounced than in many colonial and postcolonial societies. While the British established a status hierarchy based on race and language, these demarcations were not always uniform in practice. As English speakers and (mostly) Protestants, creoles were often favored over mestizos for positions in the civil service, but officials' color prejudices could also advantage light-skinned mestizos who acquired English fluency and a secondary education. At a more general level, patterns of ethnic interaction in the colonial economy conspired against overt antagonism within the work force: "free Creole and Garifuna labourers worked alongside slaves in the mahogany camps, and in the early sugar plantations Creole, Garifuna, Mestizo, and Maya workers were subject to the same system of labour control, through a system of advance payments and truck practices at the company stores."[40] Such practices inclined workers to a sense "of being in the same rotten boat" rather than open rivalry.[41] Similarities of lived experience facilitated wide acceptance of the multicultural nationalism promoted by Price and the PUP in the years following self-government. In 1982, the newly independent government outlined its policy on national identity in a history textbook commissioned for high school use:

> For much of our history, the natural interaction of cultures which co-exist within one community was inhibited by the colonial policy of divide and rule, which ensured that our various cultures remained largely isolated from, and suspicious of, each other, and that the colonizer's culture remained dominant. An essential part of the decolonization process must therefore be the elimination of all colonially inherited prejudices about each other's cultures.[42]

For these reasons, as well as the fact that all of Belize's ethnic groups were numerical minorities, decolonization was accompanied by little overt strife. While the state has historically been dominated by Creoles, neither political party could attain power without multiethnic support. At the local level, the parties recruited voters through patronage, jobs, or other rewards rather than ethnic appeals.[43] This stands in notable contrast to other plural Commonwealth Caribbean societies, such as Trinidad or Guyana, where party identification and ethnicity closely correspond. Programmatically, the PUP favored somewhat closer relations with the rest of Central America, while the UDP oriented itself toward the Anglophone Caribbean. Polarization increased dramatically with the surge in immigration from other Central American countries during the 1980s and 1990s, even leading to predictions of an impending "ethnic war."[44] Some employers exacerbated this antagonism by displacing unionized Afro-Belizean workers with low-paid Central Americans in the country's banana industry and other labor markets.[45] Anti-immigrant rhetoric proved decisive in the UDP's electoral campaigns to garner the lion's share of creole votes.[46] Many creoles and Garifuna, who historically regarded each other with some suspicion, increasingly identified a common cause against the country's Hispanics. An editorial in the country's most widely read newspaper, for example, warned that "there is a common adversity now being faced by both [Creoles and Garifuna]. Blacks, and it does not matter to which tribe they belong, will be marginalized in Belize in the next ten years unless they develop conscious, common strategies for survival here"[47] Another editorialist called for racial "balance" in immigration policy, demanding that the government admit one Garifuna from Honduras to. every Hispanic Central American.[48]

Some thirty years later, these anxieties about national identity have lessened somewhat, at least to the extent that they play out in political campaigns and media commentary. While the complexion of the Belizean population has changed since the 1980s, fears that immigrants would comprise an internal fifth column to advance Guatemalan interests have not materialized. Mestizos currently comprise nearly half of the national population, but reported levels of English fluency are now actually slightly higher than before the immigrant wave of the 1980s. Much as has been documented for Latino communities in the United States,[49] most children of earlier immigrants have assimilated the language and norms of their adopted country. To a large extent, this reflects a conscious effort on the part of both PUP and UDP governments to establish primary schools in the communities that have sprung up in areas of migrant settlement. Although access to secondary schooling is problematic in rural areas, education is compulsory throughout the country for children between the ages of six and fourteen. Given that status mobility within government, banking and commerce, and tourism remain wedded to a command of English, there is little evidence that the country's primary political or economic institutions have been fundamentally altered (or "Latinized") by these demographic changes.

ECONOMY AND ENVIRONMENT

For most of the country's history, Belize was subject to volatile world demand for its products and a deep dependence on imported goods. Few sustained efforts were made to diversify a "boom and bust" economy that benefited forest product firms and importers. Some governors did attempt, with varying success, to challenge the juggernaut of the colony's "forestocracy" over its land and labor. Their efforts were usually short-lived, succumbing to officials' limited terms of office, stiff local resistance to diversification, and the scant attractiveness of the labor-scarce colony to foreign capital. Yet even those officials most eager to trim the power of timber barons and merchants rarely took the interests of the working class or small-scale farmers into major consideration. Nor were their initiatives always sustained by their successors in office. Several governors at the outset of the twentieth century aggressively courted investment by the US-based United Fruit Company, offering a 12,500-acre land concession in the Stann Creek valley and constructing a railroad at public expense to assist in its export of bananas.[50] By 1920, United Fruit had withdrawn from the colony after its plantation was devastated by Panama Disease, a virulent soil-borne fungus. Some years later a government less sympathetic to agriculture ordered the railroad dismantled, stranding hundreds of independent farmers who had settled along its right of way. These fitful and intermittent efforts to promote export agriculture did contribute, if indirectly, to the rise of a nascent class of commercial farmers. After United Fruit's departure, several of Stann Creek's larger growers replanted their banana farms in grapefruit and oranges. In 1936, a canning factory was opened to export segmented fruit to England, encouraging others to grow fruit in order to supply the cannery. Citrus cultivation and processing remain Stann Creek's primary agricultural activity to the present day.

As the forest sector lurched toward extinction after World War II and the colony became chronically reliant on British financial aid, the government finally embraced agricultural diversification as both economically imperative and politically feasible.[51] These efforts built upon earlier agricultural traditions. Mestizo and Maya farmers had cultivated sugar in northern Belize since the mid-nineteenth century, but it remained a minor export until the late 1960s, when the British multinational Tate and Lyle opened two factories to supply Commonwealth markets. Aided by high world prices during the 1970s, government subsidies, and Commonwealth tariff and quota protection, production soared on medium- and small-scale farms in the northern districts. State support and export preferences were also extended to citrus farmers, whose fruit is processed for export as juice concentrate. In 1969, the Price government reestablished a banana industry under state ownership as a source of revenue and employment in the economically depressed South. Yet, all three commercial agricultural sectors have, like forestry before them, proven subject to volatile world prices and a long-term trend toward market liberalization.

Sugar exports fell sharply during the 1980s because of declining world demand, due in part—ironically—to Tate and Lyle's own development of sugar substitutes such as sucralose. The British firm closed its largest processing plant in Belize and sold its remaining operation in 1985. The Belizean government privatized its banana industry around the same time, with its farms at Cowpen acquired by some of the country's largest landowners. Drawing upon a growing pool of low-wage (and often highly insecure) Central American immigrants, the industry witnessed an expansion of banana exports to Britain through the multinational Fyffes. Since 1998, however, the banana industry has experienced significant attrition and a decline in prices due to a World Trade Organization (WTO) ruling that struck down its preferential quotas in the European market. It has also drawn international criticism for its violation of labor rights, including the employment of children. Citrus has been similarly affected by market deregulation, as well as disease outbreaks that forced many smaller farms out of production. Since 1990, sugar, citrus, and bananas have declined from about 60 percent of the country's official (legal) exports to 44 percent today. About 11 percent of its official exports are derived from fish and shellfish, mostly for the US market. The remainder comprises other agricultural products, manufactured goods, forest products, and petroleum.[52]

The fastest growing sector of the economy is tourism, which now represents the largest official source of foreign exchange. Despite wide expanses of pristine wilderness and the world's second largest barrier reef, tourism had long been discounted as a contributor to national development. During the 1960s and 1970s, Price himself famously dismissed tourism as a renewed form of colonial subservience to foreign masters,[53] arguing that independence must be accompanied by economic sovereignty under state oversight. Such policies helped Belize attain self-sufficiency by the late 1970s in the major agricultural staples of rice, maize, and beans.[54] Yet government price supports for small farmers soon confronted a balance of payments crisis due to depressed prices for agricultural exports and rising costs of imported goods and petroleum. As a condition of debt financing from the International Monetary Fund (IMF), the government deregulated the staple crop market in 1984 and initiated a privatization of state sectors. The country has since resumed a heavy reliance on imported basic foods.

Under the aegis of neoliberal economic planning, Belize now emphasizes its global comparative advantage as a destination for eco- and cultural heritage tourism, much of it in the formerly neglected South. It has undertaken extensive road improvement to enhance the region's accessibility, while awarding duty-free concessions to investors who import supplies for hotels and restaurants. Largely to encourage eco-tourism, approximately 26 percent of the country's land and sea area has been set aside as conservation areas in ninety-five reserves, a larger proportion of national territory than any other Central American country.[55] Between 1992 and 2017, annual tourist arrivals rose from about 247,000 to 1.3 million, with the largest share of visitors coming from the United States on cruise ships.[56] In the latter year, tourism revenues directly and indirectly accounted for more than 38 percent of the official gross domestic product (GDP), considerably exceeding any single agricultural sector. Belize's eco-tourism model has generated impressive growth and may mitigate some adverse environmental effects of traditional resort tourism. Yet it has also raised tensions between conservation nongovernmental organizations (NGOs) and nearby communities whose access to natural resources has been sharply curtailed.[57] In at least two recent instances, members of nearby communities have attempted sabotage against conservation sanctuaries that they believe responsible for such restrictions.[58] The country's increasing demands for energy, in part attributable to an expanding tourism sector, have also conflicted with its ambitious conservation goals. Over the protests of local and international conservationists, in 2005 the newly privatized electric utility completed a hydroelectric dam on the Chalillo River that flooded habitats of several endangered species, including Central America's largest remaining Red Macaw population.[59] The dam's environmental impacts also rendered downriver water sources unhealthful for fishing and drinking.

Omitted from official statistics, the international drug trade has loomed large in the economy and society at large. By 1985, illegally grown marijuana was thought to be the country's largest de facto source of foreign earnings, and Belize was identified as the fourth largest supplier of the drug to the United States. US-sponsored eradication programs reduced much of this production. The void was filled by narcotics trafficking as Belize emerged as a major transit point for South American cocaine, with its unregulated offshore banking sector identified as a site of money laundering.[60] Sparsely populated rural areas contain clandestine airstrips where planes refuel while en route to the United States, an arrangement abetted by the lack of air defense or nighttime monitoring. The US State Department has also cited government corruption as a factor in unimpeded drug traffic across the country's airspace and territorial waters. Because local workers in the narcotics trade are often paid with cocaine, surrounding areas have experienced epidemics of drug abuse and associated crime. Areas of Belize City have witnessed a surge in gang violence, with many perpetrators having returned to the country as criminal deportees from the United States. Ironically, the country's homicide rate now exceeds that of Guatemala, which many Belizeans have long viewed as a far more violent society than their own.

FUTURE DIRECTIONS IN SCHOLARSHIP

Belize's history and politics reflect its anomalous position between the English-speaking Caribbean and Hispanic Central America. In official historical narratives that predominated until the 1970s, its British affinities were presented as foils to the "Black Legend" of Spanish colonialism, which was held responsible for all manner of political and cultural iniquity in the rest of Central America. If the politics of the neighboring countries were dominated by *caudillismo* and random violence, the British, in the words of the country's national anthem, planted in Belize a "tranquil haven of democracy." Belize has certainly averted the traumatic human rights abuses suffered by neighboring countries under military rule. But official narratives of benign colonialism were belied by the squalor and open sewers of Belize City, the country's extremely inequitable land distribution, and severe material deprivation of most residents. And they were definitively swept away by revisionist historians who revealed the complicity, or at least ambivalence, of colonial authorities with the forces that created such disparities. The scholarship of Assad Shoman and Nigel Bolland, in particular, documented the profound inequities that Belize shared with its culturally and politically distinct neighbors, demonstrating that the path to national independence was hard-won by generations of working people rather than a beneficent gift from enlightened colonialists. The most recent iteration of this history, by Anne Macpherson, reveals working-class women to be political actors, sustaining popular movements when male leadership was divided or timid.

In recent years, Belize has charted a distinctive course through a neoliberal world system that undermined many of the economic and institutional safeguards it enjoyed in its first decades of self-government. Its membership in the Commonwealth as an ACP (African, Caribbean, Pacific) member state once secured the same protected export markets as other vulnerable "high cost" agricultural producers in the Caribbean. Although more economically diversified than its banana-exporting counterparts of the Windward Islands, Belize has suffered a similar fate with the WTO-mandated deregulation of European markets. Like the Windwards, as well, the Belizean government has turned to tourism as an alternative. But unlike the Caribbean, whose all-inclusive resorts compete in an already saturated tourist market, Belize has tied its economic future to marketing its eco-diversity and Maya heritage. As such, it might be considered an exemplar of the neoliberal model of development through comparative advantage. Future scholarship on Belize might explore the political and environmental contradictions that arise from this strategy. The designation of much of the country's territory as conservation areas under NGO control has surrendered sovereignty in a way that make George Price's warnings about tourism eerily prescient.[61] The privatization of public utilities and growing energy demands of tourism combined to create the environmental disaster of the Chalillo dam, as well as other planned projects that threaten the very resources on which tourism depends.[62] The global threat of climate change imperils the country's major settlements (most of which are near sea level) and its prime natural attractions (such as its coral reefs), posing long-term challenges to the sustainability of tourism. Finally, cultural heritage can be both diminished by tourism (likely a factor in the decline of spoken Garifuna in many locales)[63] as well as selectively revitalized (as in the Garifuna musical genre of *punta* rock, which has gained international prominence). Much as formal political sovereignty has been reshaped in neoliberal Belize, so too has the country's view of nationhood. Large, active diasporic communities in

North America sustain Belizean communities of origin through remittances and the occasional return of educated professionals, while deterritorializing national identity and politics.[64] Transnational ties cut both ways, however, as gang affiliations forged in urban America assume murderous proportions in Belize City and elsewhere. In this feature, the country shares in a common trajectory of migrant, economic, and disruptive cultural flows that characterize contemporary Central America and the Caribbean.

NOTES

1. Elizabeth Graham, David M. Pendergast, and Grant D. Jones, "On the Fringes of Conquest: Maya-Spanish Contact in Colonial Belize," *Science* 246, no. 4935 (1989): 1254–1259. The Spanish presence in Belize clearly provoked mixed responses from the Maya. Grave goods and other evidence from burials suggest that they continued many introduced Catholic practices after the Spanish withdrew. See Elizabeth Graham, *Maya Christians and Their Churches in Sixteenth-Century Belize* (Gainesville: University Press of Florida, 2011).
2. Colonial governor and historian John Burdon placed the date of English settlement at 1603. John Burdon, *Archives of British Honduras* (London: Sifton, Prae, and Company, 1931), 31. During the 1940s, historian Calderón Quijano assigned a date of 1638. O. Nigel Bolland, *Colonialism and Resistance in Belize: Essays in Historical Sociology* (Belize City, Belize: Cubola, 1988), 15. Both identified the settlement's founder as an English buccaneer named Wallace or Willis, but such claims, originating in the early 1800s, are almost certainly apocryphal. Matthew Restall, "Creating 'Belize': The Mapping and Naming History of a Liminal Locale," *Terrae Incognitae* 51, no. 1 (2019): 5–35.
3. Restall, "Creating 'Belize,'" 13.
4. O. Nigel Bolland, *The Formation of a Colonial Society: Belize, From Conquest to Crown Colony* (Baltimore: Johns Hopkins University Press, 1977), 32–40.
5. Nathaniel Uring, *A History of the Voyages and Travels of Capt. Nathaniel Uring with New Draughts of the Bay of Honduras and the Caribbee Islands*, 1726, cited in Bolland, *Formation of a Colonial Society*, 355.
6. Quoted in Burdon, *Archives of British Honduras*, 77.
7. Assad Shoman, *Thirteen Chapters in a History of Belize* (Belize City, Belize: Angelus Press, 1994), 46.
8. Cedric H. Grant, *The Making of Modern Belize: Politics, Society and British Colonialism in Central America* (New York: Cambridge University Press, 1976).
9. Michael D. Olien, "General, Governor, and Admiral: Three Miskito Lines of Succession," *Ethnohistory* 45, no. 2 (1998): 277–318, 283.
10. Shoman, *Thirteen Chapters*, 69.
11. Land had been freely available to timber cutters without charge until 1838. After abolition, they could be accessed only for a fee "high enough to be out of the reach of the average freedman." O. Nigel Bolland and Assad Shoman, *Land in Belize: 1765–1871* (Mona, Jamaica: University of the West Indies Press, 1977), 59.
12. Grant, *Making of Modern Belize*, 35.
13. Peter D. Ashdown, "Sweet-Escott, Swayne, and the Unofficial Majority in the Legislative Council of British Honduras, 1904–1911," *Journal of Imperial and Commonwealth History* 9 (1980): 57–75. As observed elsewhere in the West Indies, British colonial governors

"discovered a local white society whose members were eager to welcome [them] as their ceremonial head . . . To join with them meant a pleasant tour of duty, to fight them meant . . . political conflict and social ostracism." Gordon K. Lewis, *The Making of the Modern West Indies* (New York: Monthly Review, 1969), 104.

14. Norman Ashcraft, *Colonialism and Underdevelopment: Processes of Political Economic Change in British Honduras* (New York: Teachers' College Press, 1973), 39.

15. Bolland, *Formation of a Colonial Society*; O. Nigel Bolland, *Colonialism and Resistance in Belize: Essays in Historical Sociology* (Belize City, Belize: Cubola, 1988).

16. Ashcraft, *Colonialism and Underdevelopment*, 36.

17. Sidney Mintz, *Caribbean Transformations* (Chicago: Aldine, 1974); Bonham Richardson, *Economy and Environment in the Caribbean: Barbados and the Windwards in the late 1800s* (Gainesville: University of Florida Press, 1997).

18. Bolland, *Colonialism and Resistance in Belize*, 169.

19. British forces were joined by a US gunboat during the government's efforts to suppress the 1919 riot. Shoman, *Thirteen Chapters*, 175–180.

20. O. Nigel Bolland, *On the March: Labour Rebellions in the British Caribbean, 1934–1939* (Kingston, Jamaica: Ian Randle, 1995), 51.

21. Anne S. Macpherson, *From Colony to Nation: Women Activists and the Gendering of Politics in Belize, 1912–1982* (Lincoln: University of Nebraska Press, 2007).

22. Bolland, *Colonialism and Resistance in Belize*, 176.

23. Assad Shoman, *Party Politics in Belize, 1950–1986* (Belize City, Belize: Cubola, 1987).

24. Price, like most leaders of the independence movement, had been educated by American Jesuits at St. John's College in Belize City. After graduation, he attended seminaries in Mississippi and Guatemala before entering politics. Shoman, *Party Politics in Belize*, 20; see also the interview with Price in Andrew Gordon, *Agents of Change in Bullet Tree Falls: How a Village in Belize Responded to the Influences of Globalization* (Boston: Cengage, 2017), 128–129.

25. The British publicly excoriated Price with this accusation even while they themselves were secretly exploring a formal association of Belize with Guatemala. See Godfrey P. Smith, *George Price: A Life Revealed* (Kingston, Jamaica: Ian Randle, 2011), 140.

26. Quoted in Shoman, *Thirteen Chapters*, 261.

27. Tony Thorndike, "The Conundrum of Belize: Anatomy of a Dispute," *Social and Economic Studies* 32, no. 2 (1983): 65–102, esp. 97.

28. Later extended to December 8, 2020 at the request of the Guatemalan government, which requested additional time due to the Covid-19 pandemic.

29. Nancie L. González, *Sojourners of the Caribbean: Ethnogenesis and Ethnohistory of the Garífuna* (Urbana: University of Illinois Press, 1988).

30. Although legally and socially identified as Indigenous, many Maya are themselves immigrants or descendants of immigrants to Belize. Thousands of Yucatecan Maya fled to northern Belize from the Caste Wars that convulsed neighboring areas of Mexico after 1847. Much of the Q'eqchi' and Mopan population first arrived in the southern district of Toledo from Guatemala following liberal "reforms" during the 1870s that alienated their traditional lands. See Richard Wilk, "The Kekchi and the Settlement of Toledo District," *Belizean Studies* 15 (1987): 33–50. These immigrant streams intensified a century later as a result of the Guatemalan military's scorched-earth policies against Maya communities. Further complicating the question of indigeneity in Belize is that fact that the Garifuna, who were deported by the British from St. Vincent to Central America in 1797, now identify

as Indigenous in order to better leverage land and legal rights. See Joseph Palacio, "How Did the Garifuna Become an Indigenous People?: Reconstructing the Cultural Persona of an African-Native American People in Central America," *Revista Pueblos y Fronteras* 4 (2008). http://www.pueblosyfronteras.unam.mx.

31. Byron Foster, "Heart Drum: Spirit Possession in the Garifuna Communities of Belize," in *The Garifuna: A Nation Across Borders,* edited by Joseph O. Palacio, 159–175 (Belize City, Belize: Cubola, 2005).

32. Statistical Institute of Belize. *Belize Population and Housing Census 2010* (Belmopan: Government of Belize, 2013). http://sib.org.bz/wp-content/uploads/2017/05/Census_Report_2010.pdf.

33. Melissa A. Johnson, "The Making of Race and Place in Nineteenth Century British Honduras," *Environmental History* 8, no. 4 (2003): 598–617, 602.

34. For slave owners and colonial officials, the legendary battle served dual ideological purposes. While emphasizing the creoles' loyalty to Empire, it also framed a long-standing myth that slavery in the colony was "much less oppressive" than elsewhere. See Bolland, *Colonialism and Resistance,* 20. Within a year of the battle, slave owners were congratulating themselves that "We have rendered the galling yoke of Slavery so light and easy as to animate our Negroes to a gallant defence of their Masters." Quoted in Burdon, *Archives of Belize,* 272. Such assertions—all of which originate in the claims of slave owners themselves—have been refuted by more recent scholarship that documents the extreme sanctions, even by West Indian standards, used to control scarce labor in the colony. Spain sought to economically undermine the British settlement by promising to free slaves entering its territory "under pretence of embracing the Holy Catholic Religion." Burdon, *Archives of Belize,* 79. Thousands fled to Guatemala or the Yucatán to seek such "enticements," while others established maroon colonies in the interior. A major slave rebellion convulsed the colony in 1820, involving the cooperation and support of fugitives. In addition to recruiting "free colored" populations, such as the Garifuna, to replace escaping slaves, owners publicly flogged and mutilated captured fugitives to deter others from fleeing. Early nineteenth-century superintendents who attempted to introduce the minimal protections accorded slaves in the West Indies were regularly overruled by local magistrates who acquitted their slave-owning peers on charges of torture and abuse. See Shoman, *Thirteen Chapters,* 48–50.

35. Burdon, *Archives of Belize,* 272.

36. Michael C. Stone, *Caribbean Nation, Central American State: Ethnicity, Race, and National Formation in Belize, 1978–1990* (PhD diss., Department of Anthropology, University of Texas, 1994); Mark Moberg, *Myths of Ethnicity and Nation: Immigration, Work, and Identity in the Belize Banana Industry* (Knoxville: University of Tennessee Press, 1997); Laurie Kroshus Medina, *Negotiating Economic Development: Identity Formation and Collective Action in Belize* (Tucson: University of Arizona Press, 2004); Melissa A. Johnson, *Becoming Creole: Nature and Race in Belize* (New Brunswick, NJ: Rutgers University Press, 2018).

37. A. C. S. Wright, D. H. Romney, R. H. Arbuckle, and V. E. Vial, *Land in British Honduras: Report of the British Honduras Land Use Survey Team* (London: Her Majesty's Stationer's Office, 1959), 35.

38. Wright et al., *Land in British Honduras,* 38.

39. Shoman, *Thirteen Chapters,* 207.

40. Bolland, *Colonialism and Resistance in Belize,* 200.

41. Bolland, *Colonialism and Resistance in Belize*, 201. Stone, *Caribbean Nation*, 269, interprets pay rates on two nineteenth-century sugar plantations as evidence of differential job assignment and payment by ethnicity in colonial agriculture. While the handful of Chinese laborers employed on the farms were paid significantly less than other ethnic groups, Stone's quantitative data indicate that creoles, Garifuna, and "Spanish" employed on the farms were paid and employed in nearly identical fashions. *Caribbean Nation*, 227.

42. Ministry of Education, Government of Belize, *A History of Belize* (Belize City, Belize: Cubola, 1983), 73. The textbook was withdrawn from use in schools by the subsequent United Democratic Party government.

43. Mark Moberg, "Citrus and the State: Factions and Rural Class Formation in Belize," *American Ethnologist* 18, no. 2 (1991): 21–39.

44. Harriot Topsey, "The Ethnic War in Belize," in *Belize: Ethnicity and Development* (Belize City, Belize: Society for the Promotion of Education and Research, 1987).

45. Moberg, *Myths of Ethnicity and Nation*, 82–103.

46. O. Nigel Bolland and Mark Moberg, "Development and National Identity: Creolisation and Ethnic Conflict in Belize," *International Journal of Comparative Race and Ethnic Studies* 2, no. 2 (1995): 1–18.

47. "A Message to the Garinagu," *Amandala* (Belize City), November 15, 1991, 2.

48. "Between the Lines," *Amandala* (Belize City), November 22, 1991, 5.

49. Leo R. Chavez, *The Latino Threat: Constructing Immigrants, Citizens, and the Nation* (2nd ed.) (Palo Alto, CA: Stanford University Press, 2013).

50. Mark Moberg, "Responsible Men and Sharp Yankees: The United Fruit Company, Resident Elites, and Colonial State in British Honduras," in *Banana Wars: Power, Production, and History in the Americas,* edited by Steve Striffler and Mark Moberg, 141–170 (Durham, NC: Duke University Press, 2003).

51. By the 1950s, the timber companies that had once ruled the colony by fiat had ceased to operate profitably due to overexploitation of mahogany and declining demand for the wood abroad. Acquired as a minor subsidiary of a transnational corporation, Belize Estate and Produce surrendered most of its lands in lieu of taxes. O. Nigel Bolland, *Belize: A New Nation in Central America* (Boulder, CO: Westview, 1986), 77.

52. OEC Belize Exports, Imports, and Trade Partners, 2017. https://oec.world/en/profile/country/blz/.

53. Ian Munt and Egbert Higinio, "Eco-Tourism Waves in Belize," in *Globalization and Development* (Belize City, Belize: Society for Promotion of Education and Research, 1993), 61.

54. Mark Moberg, "Marketing Policy and the Loss of Food Self-Sufficiency in Rural Belize," *Human Organization* 50, no. 1 (1991): 16–25.

55. Adele Ramos, "Belize Protected Areas: 26%, Not 40-Odd Percent," *Amandala*. http://amandala.com.bz/news/belize-protected-areas-26-not-40-odd-percent/.

56. Belize Tourism Board, *Travel and Tourism Statistics Digest 2017* (Belize City, Belize: Belize Tourism Board). https://belizetourismboard.org/wp-content/uploads/2018/07/TravelTourismDigest2017v2.pdf.

57. Laurie Kroshus Medina, "Governing through the Market: Neoliberal Environmental Government in Belize," *American Anthropologist* 117, no. 2 (2015): 272–284.

58. Janelle Chanona, "Out of the Ashes," *Audubon* (Winter 2017), 12.

59. Bruce Barcott, *The Last Flight of the Scarlet Macaw* (New York: Random House, 2008).

60. Rosaleen Duffy, "Shadow Players: Ecotourism Development, Corruption and State Politics in Belize," *Third World Quarterly* 21, no. 3 (2000): 549–565.

61. See, for example, Laurie Kroshus Medina "When Government Targets 'The State': Transnational NGO Government and the State in Belize," *Political and Legal Anthropology Review* 33, no. 2 (2010): 245–263.
62. In 2017, the government canceled long-standing plans for offshore oil drilling after ferocious opposition by the tourist industry, although onshore exploration and extraction continue.
63. Donna M. Bonner, "Garifuna Children's Language Shame: Ethnic Stereotypes, National Affiliation, and Transnational Immigration as Factors in Language Choice in Southern Belize," *Language in Society* 30, no. 1 (2001): 81–96.
64. See, for example, Sara England, *Afro-Central Americans in New York City: Garifuna Tales of Transnational Movements in Racialized Space* (Gainesville: University Press of Florida, 2006).

FURTHER READING

Bolland, O. Nigel. *Colonialism and Resistance in Belize: Essays in Historical Sociology*. Belize city, Belize: Cubola Books, 1988.
Bolland, O. Nigel. *The Formation of a Colonial Society: Belize, from Conquest to Crown Colony*. Baltimore: Johns Hopkins University Press, 1977.
Graham, Elizabeth. *Maya Christians and Their Churches in Sixteenth-Century Belize*. Gainesville: University Press of Florida, 2011.
Grant, Cedric H. *The Making of Modern Belize: Politics, Society and British Colonialism in Central America*. London: Cambridge University Press, 1976.
Johnson, Melissa A. *Becoming Creole: Nature and Race in Belize*. New Brunswick, NJ: Rutgers University Press, 2018.
Macpherson, Anne S. *From Colony to Nation: Women Activists and the Gendering of Politics in Belize, 1912–1982*. Lincoln: University of Nebraska Press, 2007.
Medina, Laurie Kroshus. "Governing through the Market: Neoliberal Environmental Government in Belize." *American Anthropologist* 117, no. 2 (2015): 272–284.
Medina, Laurie Kroshus. *Negotiating Economic Development: Identity Formation and Collective Action in Belize*. Tucson: University of Arizona Press, 2004.
Moberg, Mark. *Myths of Ethnicity and Nation: Immigration, Work, and Identity in the Belize Banana Industry*. Knoxville: University of Tennessee Press, 1997.
Moberg, Mark. "Responsible Men and Sharp Yankees: The United Fruit Company, Resident Elites, and Colonial State in British Honduras." In *Banana Wars: Power, Production, and History in the Americas,* edited by Steve Striffler and Mark Moberg, 145–170. Durham, NC: Duke University Press, 2003.
Palacio, Joseph, ed. *The Garifuna, A Nation across Borders: Essays in Social Anthropology*. Belize City, Belize: Cubola Books, 2008.
Restall, Matthew. "Creating 'Belize': The Mapping and Naming History of a Liminal Locale." *Terrae Incognitae* 51, no. 1 (2019): 5–35.
Shoman, Assad. *Thirteen Chapters of a History of Belize*. Belize City, Belize: Angelus Press, 1994.
Smith, Godfrey P. *George Price: A Life Revealed. The Authorized Biography*. Kingston, Jamaica: Ian Randle, 2011.
Wilk, Richard. "Learning to Be Local in Belize: Global Systems of Common Difference." In *Worlds Apart: Modernity through the Prism of the Local,* edited by Daniel Miller, 110–133. New York: Routledge, 1995.

INDEX

Figures are indicated by *f* following the page number

A

Abangares Gold Mining, 42
Academia de las Lenguas Mayas, 123, 157
Accessory Transit Company, 594
Acción Católica. See Catholic Action
Acción Comunal (Panama), 622
Acevedo, Ramón Luis, 465
Acuña, Ángela, 437
Afro-Central Americans
  in Belize, 645
  cofradías and, 200
  as conquistadors, 197
  in Costa Rica, 198, 296
  discrimination against, 170
  European imperial rivalries and, 153
  in Guatemala, 199–200, 485, 487, 490, 493, 498, 501
  in Honduras and, 521, 536
  Indigenous populations and, 198
  Mosquitia and, 153–54
  mulatos and, 169–70, 208, 521
  in Panama, 617
  slavery and, 152, 197–98
  Spanish colonial era and, 196–97, 200
  territorial rights of, 124
Agüero, Fernando, 578–79
Aguilar Moran, Jose David, 369
Aguilar, Jerónimo, 461–62
Aj Itz, 145
Ala Femenina, 437
Albanisa, 584
Albizúrez Palma, Francisco, 464
Alcoa Corporation, 440
Alemán, Arnoldo, 582–83
Alfaro, Ricardo J., 622–23

Alianza de Mujeres Guatemaltecas, 436
Alliance for Progress
  Cold War and, 318–19, 341
  counterinsurgency training and, 319, 578
  democratic reform and, 262
  educational programs and, 414
  Kissinger Report and, 266
  market-oriented economic policies and, 274, 319, 601
  military aid and, 262, 388
  trade policies and, 263–64
Alta Verapaz (Guatemala), 489–90, 493–94
Alvarado, Carlos, 443
Alvarado, Jorge de, 144, 149, 152
Alvarado, Pedro de
  death of, 146
  global expeditions of, 144
  gold and, 143
  as governor of Guatemala, 144, 176
  Guatemalan nationhood and, 144–46
  invasion of Central America (1524) by, 141–43
  Maya territories conquered by, 142
  Pipil settlements conquered by, 94
  Santiago de Guatemala founded (1524) by, 62, 171
  slaves of, 197
  Tekum and, 145
Amador Guerrero, Manuel, 619
Amaya Amador, Ramon, 528
American Federation of Labor and Congress of Industrial Organizations (AFL-CIO), 261
Anguiciano de Gamboa, Alonso, 148
Antigua Guatemala (UNESCO site), 171, 201
Aquino, Anastasio, 232, 547

660 INDEX

Arana, Carlos, 264
Arana, Francisco, 336
Arango, José Agustín, 619
Araujo, Arturo, 552
Arbenz, Jacobo
  coup (1954) overthrowing, 261, 295, 317–18,
    337, 340, 384, 486, 499, 519, 528
  democratic revolution (1944-54) and, 336,
    338–39
  election (1950) of, 337, 384
  land reform and, 260–61, 337–38, 439, 498
  United Fruit Company and, 384
Arce Zablah, Rafael, 555
Arce, Manuel José, 229–31, 235, 547
Archaic period (8000-2000 BCE), 83–85
Arellano, Jorge Eduardo, 410, 463–64
Arévalo Bermejo, Juan José, 260, 336–37, 383,
    439, 498–99
Argüello, Leonardo, 577
Argueta, Manlio, 456
Arias, Arnulfo, 622–25, 629
Arias, Arturo, 455, 466
Arias, Harmodio, 622
Arias, Óscar, 322, 349, 604
Arosemena, Florencio H., 622
Arzú, Alvaro, 389
Aspinwall, William H., 617
Asselbergs, Florine, 144, 149
Asturias, Miguel Ángel, 295, 456, 493
Atala Faraj, Camilo, 534–35
Atlacatl, 120, 293
Atlacatl Battalion, 558
avant-garde literature in Central America, 462
Ayala, Prudencia, 436
Aycinena y Piñol, Juan José, 403–5
Aztecs, 62, 141–42

B

Bajo Aguán Valley (Honduras), 273
Balboa, Vasco Núñez de, 61, 145
Baldetti, Roxana, 370
Balladares, Ernesto Pérez, 629–30
bananas
  Belize and, 649–50
  Costa Rica and, 596, 598
  environmental consequences associated
    with cultivation of, 39–40

Great Depression and, 259
in Honduras, 259, 312, 519, 522–29
Panama disease and, 40, 259–60, 313,
    315, 649
railroad development and, 38–39
Sigatoka disease and, 40, 260
United Fruit Company's control over
    cultivation of, 38–39
Baratta, María de, 293
Barillas, Manuel, 255
Barrios, Catalina, 464–65
Barrios, Gerardo, 290
Barrios, Justo Rufino
  authoritarian rule of, 486
  Catholic Church and, 381, 406
  death of, 596
  labor drafts under, 255
  land use under, 112, 254, 381, 489
  union of Central America as aspiration of,
    585
Barrow, Dean, 643–44
Barrundia, José Francisco, 224, 237
Barrundia, Juan, 230
Batres Jáuregui, Antonio, 493
Belén Conspiracy, 224–25
Belize. *See also* British Honduras
  Afro-Central Americans in, 645
  agricultural diversification in, 648–49
  anti-immigrant sentiment in, 648
  banana economy and, 649–50
  British Commonwealth and, 637, 643, 652
  Catholic Church in, 645
  creoles in, 646–48
  emigration from, 646
  English as official language in, 645
  ethnic identity in, 645–48
  Hurricane Hattie (1961) and, 637
  immigration to, 638
  independence (1981) of, 637, 642–44
  Indigenous populations in, 64f, 66, 157,
    645, 647
  International Monetary Fund and, 650
  Maritime Areas Act in, 644
  Maya in, 154, 645
  mestizos in, 646–47
  narcotics trade and, 651
  neoliberal economic policies in, 650–52

INDEX 661

Non-Aligned Movement and, 642–43
parliamentary system in, 642
Spanish colonial presence and, 145, 191
textiles and, 234
tourism in, 650–51
women's status in, 440–44
Belize City (Belize), 637, 641, 645, 651–53
Belli, Gioconda, 456
Belmopan (Belize), 637
Berger, Oscar, 367, 390
Bermúdez, Enrique, 581
Bertrand, Francisco, 525
Bidlack, Benjamin, 616
Black Christ of Esquipulas, 204–5
Blanco, Máximo, 595
Bográn, Luis, 523, 525
Bolaños Geyer, Enrique, 279, 582–83
Bolívar, Símon, 616
Bolivarian Alternative for the Americas
    (ALBA), 273, 392, 583
Bonaparte, José, 221
Bonaparte, Napoleon, 184, 288
Bonilla, Abelardo, 463–64
Borge, Tomás, 297
Bourbon Dynasty
    absolutism and, 9, 182–83
    Catholic Church and, 8–10, 183, 220
    estancos (state monopolies) under, 183
    intendancy system and, 183
    Kingdom of Guatemala and, 286
    municipal reform in Central America
        under, 220
    reforms by, 8, 36, 182–84, 205–6, 236, 286,
        288, 616
Boyd, Federico, 619
British Honduras. *See also* Belize
    Burnaby's Code in, 640
    debt peonage in, 640
    Great Depression and, 641
    Guatemala's claims to, 643–44
    independence movement in, 641–42
    Indigenous populations in, 72
    logwood and, 639–40
    mahogany and, 640–41
    Maya population in, 639
    Paris Treaty (1763) and, 639–40
    Spanish claims before 1640 to, 639

United Fruit Company and, 314, 649
    women's status in, 438
    World War II and, 641
Bryan-Chamorro Treaty, 573
Bukele, Nayib, 351, 560
Bunau-Varilla, Philippe, 618–19
Bush, George H.W., 350, 353, 390, 628
Bush, George W., 268
Bustamante, José de, 222, 224–26
Bustillo, José, 232–33
Butler, Smedley, 314

C

Cabrillo, Juan Rodríguez de, 147
cacao, 198
Cáceres, Berta, 157, 274, 443
Cádiz constitution (1812)
    Catholic Church and, 8
    citizenship laws and, 224
    colonial governing class in Central America
        and, 6–7
    elections and popular sovereignty under,
        223, 235
    Ferdinand VII's abolition of, 225
    Kingdom of Guatemala and, 224–25
    liberal nationalism and, 12
Calakmul, 91
Calderón Guardia, Rafael Angel, 262, 292, 337,
    386, 413, 600
Calderón y Padilla, Octavio José, 410
California, 235, 310, 323, 522, 585, 617
Calle 18 gang (Eighteenth Street Gang, El
    Salvador), 323, 361, 368, 560
Callejas, Rafael Leonardo, 531, 535
Canal Zone. *See* Panama Canal
Candelaria, María de, 196
Cannon, Lee Roy, 573
Cantel (Guatemala), 115
Cantón Corralito, 86
Capuchins, 407–8, 410
Caracol, 91
Carazo, Rodrigo, 296
Cárcamo y Rodríguez, Luis, 406
Cardenal, Ernesto, 343–44, 415, 456, 465,
    580–81
Cardenal, Fernando, 415
Cardona, Edgar, 387

Carías Andino, Tiburcio, 259, 261, 337, 385, 408, 436
Caribbean Basin Initiative, 41
Carlos IV (king of Spain), 221
Carrera, Rafael
  authoritarian rule and consolidation of power by, 291, 301
  Catholic Church and, 11, 236, 238, 254, 291, 405–6
  caudillo politics and, 380
  concordat of 1852 and, 11
  Conservative faction and, 254, 380–81, 487–88
  Guatemalan unity under, 12
  Indigenous populations and, 11, 112, 117, 294–95, 487
  land use policies and, 112, 488
  Rebelión de la Montaña (1837) and, 236–37
  Second Federal War and, 232
Carrillo, Braulio, 231, 238, 593–94
Cartago (Costa Rica), 31–32
Carter, Jimmy
  human rights policies and, 319–20
  Nicaragua and, 319, 345, 388, 581
  Panama and, 625–28
Casa de las Américas, 466
Casanova y Estrada, Ricardo, 406
Casariego y Acevedo, Mario, 417
Casaus y Torres, Ramón, 7, 222, 226
Castillo Armas, Carlos, 261, 317–18, 340, 384, 499
Castillo, Bernal Díaz del, 144
Castillo, José María "Chema," 579
Castro, Fidel, 341–42, 578
Catholic Action, 115, 412–16
Catholic Church
  administrative structure of, 178, 411
  Belize and, 645
  Bourbon Dynasty and, 8–10, 183, 220
  Cádiz constitution and, 8
  Central American Federation and, 236, 405
  Cold War and, 403, 419
  Conservatives and, 253, 409, 486
  Costa Rica and, 292, 407, 413–14, 417, 593, 595–97, 600, 606
  El Salvador and, 341, 343, 406, 412, 414–16, 418, 555–56

elite creole families and, 179–80
  folk Catholicism and, 407
  Guatemala and, 11, 236, 238, 254, 291, 337, 340–41, 343, 381, 405–7, 409–12, 414–18, 500
  Honduras and, 342, 408, 412
  Indigenous populations and, 115, 416
  lay associations and, 412–16
  Liberals and, 253, 406–10, 486
  Liberation Theology and, 297, 343–44, 415–19, 440, 580
  marriage laws and, 432
  Medellín Conference and, 414, 417, 555
  nation-building and, 405–9, 419
  Nicaragua and, 341, 343, 407, 409–10, 412, 415–17
  Panama and, 408
  progressive movements in, 341, 343, 403–4, 412–19, 555–56
  religious orders' roles in, 178–79
  Second Vatican Council and, 335, 341, 414–15, 417, 555
  Spanish colonialism in Central America and, 7, 141, 145, 158, 173, 177–79, 194–96
  The Enlightenment and, 7
  Vatican concordats with Central American governments and, 11, 411
  wealth of, 179–80, 183
  women in Central America and, 443
Catholic Conservative Party (Nicaragua), 570
Catholic Foreign Mission Society of America, 410
Cavendish, Thomas, 153
Cayetano Carpio, Salvador, 554
Central American Common Market (CACM), 262–63, 388, 499
Central American Federation
  ayuntamientos (municipal councils) in, 236
  canal proposals and, 235, 569
  Catholic Church and, 236, 405
  challenges to establishing authority in, 10–11
  Colombia and, 228, 235, 288
  constitution (1825) of, 225, 228–29, 234, 288–89, 300, 436
  Costa Rica and, 229, 231, 289, 593
  dissolution (1840s) of, 208

efforts to re-establish, 493
El Salvador and, 229–34, 289–90, 547
end (1838) of, 567
epidemic disease outbreaks in, 33–34, 237
establishment (1821) of, 227–28
federal district of, 230
finance and economy in, 233–34
First Federal War (1826-29) and, 228–31, 235, 289, 380, 525
Great Britain and, 228
Guatemala and, 228–32, 234, 289–90
Honduras and, 229, 231–34, 289–90, 520
land expropriation in, 234–35
Mexico and, 228, 235, 288
Nicaragua and, 229, 231, 289–90
Nonualco Indian rebellion (1833) and, 232–33
Ochomogo War (1823) and, 231
Rebelión de la Montaña (1837) and, 232–33, 236–38
Second Federal War (1832-39) and, 231–32, 525
state-building efforts in, 286, 290
territorial divisions in, 229–30
Central American Free Trade Agreement (CAFTA), 268, 270–72, 302, 322
Central American Mission (CAM), 408
Central Anticomunista Femenina, 436
Central Bank for Economic Integration (BCIE), 532
Central Intelligence Agency (CIA)
Bay of Pigs invasion in Cuba (1961) and, 342, 388, 643
El Salvador and, 349
Guatemala coup (1954) engineered by, 261, 274, 295, 301, 316–18, 337–38, 340–41, 384, 388, 486, 499
Honduras and, 261, 388, 519
Nicaragua and, 266, 581
Panama and, 627–28
Central Valley (Costa Rica)
climate variability in, 30
coffee and, 254, 592–93
epidemic disease outbreaks in, 34
information technology firms in, 269
land ownership in, 607
railroads in, 257

Spanish colonial settlement and administration of, 148, 173
Cerezo, Vinicio, 298, 385
Cerna, Vicente, 486
Ch'orti', 57, 64, 66, 157, 204, 500
Chacón, Lázaro, 383, 493–94
Chalchuapa, 60, 87–88, 90, 93
Chamorro, Emiliano, 437, 573–74, 576–77
Chamorro, Fruto, 568
Chamorro, Pedro Joaquín, 112, 353, 578, 580
Chamorro, Violeta, 267, 298, 350, 393, 442, 582
Charles II (king of Spain), 182
Charles III (king of Spain), 182, 219, 223
Charles IV (king of Spain), 223
Charles V (king of Spain), 616
Chatfield, Frederick, 290
Chávez y González, Luis, 417
Chávez, Hernando de, 143
Chávez, Hugo, 392, 583, 630
Chávez, Joaquin M., 16
Chiapas region (Mexico)
Maya population in, 157
mining in, 147
prehistoric sites in, 82–84, 88, 91
Spanish colonial settlement and administration in, 171, 181, 183, 191
Spanish conquest of territories in, 142, 148
Zapatista uprising (1994) in, 157
Chiari, Roberto, 625
Chibchan, 35, 60, 91, 93
Chichen Itza, 93
Chinchilla, Laura, 442
Chocoan, 60
cholera, 33–34, 232, 237, 311, 487, 594
Cholsamaj publishing house, 157
Chontal, 152
Chorotega, 61–62, 93–94, 157
Christian Democratic Party, 416
Christian Democratic Union (CDU), 642
Christian Social Movement, 417
Christian Social Unity Party (Costa Rica), 603, 605–6
Cicimba, 146
Cihuatan, 93
Citizen Action Party (Costa Rica), 606
Ciudad Real (Chiapas), 171, 178, 201, 220–21
Clayton-Bulwer Treaty (1850), 570, 617–18

664 INDEX

Clinton, Hillary, 519–20
Clovis, 82
Coba, 91
Coclé, 61–62, 84
coffee
  Costa Rica and, 254, 259, 592–93, 598
  El Salvador and, 256, 548–50
  environmental consequences associated
    with cultivation of, 37–38
  Great Depression and, 258–59
  Guatemala and, 254–55, 489, 492–94
  Honduras and, 256, 521–23
  introduction to Central American
    agriculture of, 36–37, 111
  labor demands associated with cultivation
    of, 113–14
  land privatization and, 112–13
  Nicaragua and, 256, 259
cofradías (religious brotherhoods), 174, 195–96
Cojtí Cuxil, Demetro, 158
Colindres, Fabio, 368
Colombia
  canal plans and, 617–19
  Central American Federation and, 228, 235,
    288
  drug trafficking and, 361
  Panama's establishment of independence
    (1903) from, 18, 312, 615
colonialism. See Spanish colonialism in
    Central America
Columbus, Christopher, 145, 168
Comarca de San Blas (Panama), 122, 126
Comarca Emberá-Wounaan, 73
Comarca Guna Yala, 72–73
Comarca Ngäbe-Buglé, 73
Comayagua (Honduras)
  Catholic Church and, 178
  Central American Federation and, 229
  establishment (1537) of, 171
  intendancy established in 1780s in, 220, 224,
    288
  Kingdom of Guatemala and, 223
  Mexico and, 226
Committee for Peasant Unity (CUC,
    Guatemala), 265, 416
Communist Party (Costa Rica), 437, 599–600
Communist Party of El Salvador, 343

Company of Scotland, 154
Concejos Territoriales, 73
Confederación Costarricense de Trabajadores
    (CCTRN), 413
Confederación de Trabajadores de Costa Rica
    (CTCR), 413
Congregation of St. Philip Neri, 407
Congreso Interamericano de Mujeres, 436–37
Consejo de Organizaciones Mayas de
    Guatemala, 157
Conservatives
  Catholic Church and, 253, 409, 486
  economic policy and, 253
  Indigenous populations and, 118
  land privatization and, 111–12
  in Nicaragua, 569–71
Contadora Group, 348–49, 389
Contras (Nicaragua)
  ceasefire (1988) and, 267
  Central Intelligence Agency and, 266, 581
  Congressional ban on funding for, 266, 321,
    389
  demobilization of, 350
  El Salvador and, 349–50
  Indigenous populations and, 347
  Iran-Contra scandal and, 266–67, 389
  Reagan and, 320
  Sandinistas' civil war against, 266, 301,
    581–82
  US support for, 320, 347, 388, 581
Contreras, Rodrigo de, 176
Convención Mosquita of 1894, 572
Cooke, Richard, 59–60
Coordinating Committee of the Agricultural,
    Commercial, Industrial and Financial
    Associations of Guatemala (CACIF), 261,
    266, 272
Corbette, 154–55
Córdoba, Francisco Hernández de, 62, 146
Córdova, Enrique, 545
corn, 113, 489
Corregimiento del Valle de Guatemala, 177
Cortés y Larraz, Pedro, 207
Cortés, Hernán, 62, 144, 146, 149–50
Cortés, León, 599–600
Costa Rica
  Afro-Central Americans in, 198, 296

agricultural practices in, 36–40, 111, 198, 287
anti-communism in, 262, 296, 337–38, 606
banana economy and, 596, 598
Cartago earthquake (1910) in, 31–32
Catholic Church and, 292, 407, 413–14, 417, 593, 595–97, 600, 606
Central American Federation and, 229, 231, 289, 593
Central American Free Trade Agreement and, 302
civil war (1948) in, 262, 317, 386–87, 600
climate variability in, 30
coffee economy in, 254, 259, 592–93, 598
constitution (1848) in, 594
constitution (1871) and, 595
corruption in, 595
declaration of independence (1847) in, 238
democratization in, 335, 337, 370–71, 599, 607
economic crisis (1980-82) in, 296–97, 301, 603
education in, 591, 607
epidemic disease outbreaks in, 33–34
ethnic and racial identity and, 545, 591–92
foreign investment in, 602–3
forest exploitation in, 43
Great Depression and, 259–60
Guatemala's potential war (1885) with, 596
independence (1848) of, 289
Indigenous populations in, 64f, 67, 71–72, 110, 112, 124, 156–57, 253, 294, 592–93, 607
industrialization in, 602
international financial institutions and, 603–4
Junta Fundadora (1948-49) in, 296, 601
Labor Code in, 262, 600
land use issues in, 112, 265, 591, 607
Liberal Reforms (1884) in, 292
liberal reforms in, 593–98
livestock production in, 44, 46, 598
macroeconomic successes in, 18, 269, 275
marriage and divorce law in, 432
mestizos in, 592
military forces in, 257, 382, 386–87, 595
mining in, 42
neoliberal economic policies and, 301, 603–8

Nicaraguan civil war (1980s) and, 604
Protestantism in, 408, 418
protests against privatization in, 604–5
railroads in, 257–58
remittances and, 272
slavery in, 170, 198
Social Security Fund in, 600
Spanish colonial settlement and administration in, 176, 181, 183, 191–92, 220
Spanish conquest of territories in, 145, 148
state-building and national identity in, 254, 291–92, 300–301, 596–97
strike (1909-10) in, 313
strike (1934) in, 260, 599
United Fruit Company and, 257, 260, 298, 598–99
violence and violent crime (1990-2020) in, 270, 359–60, 362–66, 443
Walker's wars in Central America (1850s) and, 289–90, 292, 311, 594
welfare state in, 337
women's status in, 433–44
Costa Rican Feminist League, 437, 599
cotton, 40–41, 262–63
Cristiani, Alfredo F., 349–50, 352
Cromwell, William Nelson, 618–19
Cruz, Rogelia, 440
Cuadra Pasos, Carlos, 577
Cuadra, Joaquín, 353, 393
Cuadra, Pablo Antonio, 462
Cuadra, Vicente, 570
Cuba
    Bay of Pigs invasion (1961) in, 342, 388, 643
    Central American revolutions (1980s) and, 320, 346, 578–80
    immigration to Honduras from, 533
    mining in, 42
    missile crisis (1962) in, 342
    Reagan and, 347
    revolution (1959) in, 262–63, 295, 318, 335, 341–42, 414, 530, 578
    Soviet Union and, 389
    Spanish-American War (1898) and, 572
Cucul, Alfredo, 339
Cueva, 61–62
Cukra Development Company, 574
Cuyamel Fruit Company, 39, 523, 574

D

d'Escoto, Miguel, 415
Dalton, Roque, 456
Darién-San Blas-Bayano area, 67–68
Darío, Rubén, 456, 460, 462
Davidson, William, 72
Dávila, Pedrarias, 61–62, 145–46, 176
Dawson Pact, 573
DDT (dichlorodiphenyltrichloroethane), 40
de Bastidas, Rodrigo, 145
de la Guardia, Adolfo, 623
de la Guardia, Ernesto, 624
de la Selva, Salomón, 465
de Lara, Domingo Antonio, 547
de Leon Carpio, Ramiro, 644
Debayle Sacasa, Salvadora, 575–76
DeConcini, Dennis, 627
Delgado, José Matias, 547
Del Valle, José Cecilio, 226, 230
Democratic Action Group (Costa Rica), 600–601
Democratic Revolutionary Alliance (ARDE), 464, 581
Díaz del Castillo, Bernal, 144
Díaz, Adolfo, 573–74
Dinant Corporation, 273–74, 535
Diriomo Indians, 108
dollar diplomacy, 314–15
Domínguez, Evelio, 413
Dominican priests, 193–94, 200, 407
Dominican Republic
    Central American Free Trade Agreement and, 268, 302, 605
    dollar diplomacy and, 314
    mining in, 42
    US occupations during twentieth century of, 318, 388, 621
Dos Erres massacre (Guatemala, 1982), 384
Drake, Francis, 153
Duarte, José Napoleón, 388
Dueñas, Francisco, 290, 406
Dulles, John Foster, 260–61
Duque, Carlos, 628
Durou y Sure, Luis, 410

E

Early Classic period (250-600 CE), 89–90
Early to Middle Formative Period (1200-300 BCE), 87–88

Economic Commission for Latin America (ECLA), 263, 602
Editorial Universitaria Centroamericana (EDUCA), 465
Eighteenth Street Gang, 323, 361, 368, 560
Eisenhower, Dwight D., 340, 498, 624–25
El Gigante Rockshelter, 84
El Niño Southern Oscillation, 29–30
El Perú (Mayan Classic Era settlement), 90
El Rayo site, 93
El Salvador
    agricultural practices in, 36–37, 40, 111
    anti-communism in, 345
    Aquino uprising (1833) in, 547
    authoritarian and military governments in, 295, 301, 336, 552–54
    Catholic Church and, 341, 343, 406, 412, 414–16, 418, 555–56
    Central American Common Market and, 263
    Central American Federation and, 229–34, 289–90, 547
    Central American Free Trade Agreement and, 302
    Central Intelligence Agency and, 349
    civil war and death squads (1980s) in, 2, 116, 267, 297, 320–21, 344–45, 348, 359, 385, 403, 416, 554–57
    coffee economy and, 256, 548–50
    corruption in, 559–60
    cotton economy and, 263
    coup (1960) in, 552
    coup (1977) in, 552
    declaration of independence (1854) by, 238
    democratization in, 298–300, 370–71
    earthquakes in, 30
    emigration from, 3, 300, 321, 323, 372, 560
    ethnic and racial identity and, 545–46
    forest exploitation in, 42
    Great Depression and, 258, 385
    guerrilla movements in, 345–47
    independence of, 546
    Indigenous populations in, 63, 64f, 109–10, 112, 114–18, 157, 253, 256, 293–94, 297, 301, 344, 545, 547, 549–51
    indigo and, 36, 234, 287, 547
    land use issues in, 112, 261, 267, 547–49
    leftist movements of 1960s in, 342–43

livestock production in, 265
Mano Dura policies in, 367–68, 371, 560
marriage and divorce law in, 432
Matanza (1932) in, 158, 385, 550–51
mestizo identity in, 294
military forces in, 257, 301, 381, 385–86, 388, 390–91, 394, 553
mining and, 559
National Guard and, 549
neoliberal economic policies and, 271–72, 274, 352, 559
Peace Accords (1992) in, 267, 298, 349–51, 364–65, 368, 390–91, 500, 557–58
peasant uprising (1932) in, 549–50
poverty in, 558–59
prehistoric sites in, 88
Protestantism in, 418
remittances and, 272
Spanish colonial settlement and administration in, 168, 171, 183, 191
Spanish conquest of territories in, 142–44
state-building and national identity in, 293–94, 301
uprising (1932) in, 118
US military aid to, 321
violence and violent crime (1990-2020) in, 3, 270, 360–64, 367–68, 372–73, 443, 560
Walker's wars in Central America (1850s) and, 311
women's status in, 433–44, 557
World War II and, 261
Emberá, 68, 72–73, 157
encomienda system, 174–76
Endara, Guillermo, 628–30
England, 153–54. *See also* Great Britain
Erwin, John D., 528
Esaiasz, Pieter, 153
Espino, Miguel Ángel, 293
Espinoza, Nicolás, 232
Esquipulas II Agreements (1987-89), 349–50, 389
Esquivel, Ascensión, 597
Estrada Cabrera, Manuel, 436, 486, 492–93
Estrada Velasquez, Juan de Dios, 390
Estrada, José Dolores, 292
Estrada, Juan José, 573
Ewing, John, 524–25

Eximbal (Exploraciones Y Exploitaciones Mineral Izabal S. A.), 440

F
Facultad Latinoamericana de Ciencias Sociales (FLACSO), 2–3
Farabundo Martí National Liberation Front (FMLN, El Salvador)
    Catholic Church and, 416
    civil war (1980s) and, 267, 321, 555
    establishment of, 297, 346, 385
    military offensive (1989) by, 349, 391
    peace process (1989-92) and, 349–50, 364
    as political party after civil war, 351, 353, 443, 559–60
    protests (1931) organized by, 258
    Sandinistas and, 347
Farabundo Martí, Agustín, 258
Faraj Rishmagui, Jorge A., 535
Federación de Asociaciones Femeninas Hondureñas, 436
Federación de Clubes de Mujeres del Canal, 437
Federación Regional de Trabajadores Salvadoreños, 293
Federal Republic of Central America. *See* Central American Federation
Ferdinand VI (king of Spain), 207
Ferdinand VII (king of Spain), 6, 221, 225
Fernández, Próspero, 596
Figueres, José
    anti-communism and, 337–38
    on banana republics, 313
    civil war (1948) and, 317, 386–87, 601
    Democratic Action Group and, 600
    Junta Fundadora and, 601
    presidential ascension (1948) of, 262
    social democratic policies of, 296
Filisola, Vicente, 227
Financiera Comercial Hondureña S.A. (FICOHSA), 534–35
Finn, John E., 13–14
Flores Facussé, Carlos, 391, 535–36
Flores, Francisco, 367, 559
Flores, José, 205–6
Fonseca Amador, Carlos, 297, 342–43, 578
forest exploitation, 42–46, 69
Fort Amador (Panama), 623

Fort Gulick (School of the Americas), 623
Fort Matamoros uprising (Guatemala, 1960), 342
Fortuny, José Manuel, 339
Foundation for Social and Economic Development (FUSADES), 351–52
France, 153–54, 570, 572, 618–20
Franciscans, 68, 178, 407
Frente Morazanista para la Liberación de Honduras (FMLH), 297
FSLN. *See* Sandinistas (Sandinista National Liberation Front, FSLN)
Fuerza Democrática Nicaraguense (FDN), 347, 581
Fuerzas Armadas de Liberación (FAL), 554
Fuerzas Armadas de Resistencia Nacional, 297
Fuerzas Armadas Rebeldes (FAR), 342, 345
Fuerzas Populares de Liberación "Farabundo Martí" (FPL), 297, 343, 345, 554–56
Funes, Mauricio, 351, 368, 559–60
Funes, Reinaldo, 42

G
Gage, Thomas, 179
Gaínza, Gabino, 226–27, 288
Gallego, Jesús, 627
Gallegos Valdés, Luis, 464
Gálvez Durón, Juan Manuel, 337
Gálvez, Juan Manuel, 530, 535–36
Gálvez, Mariano, 231–32, 236–37, 487
Gamez, María, 437
García Granados, Miguel, 486
García-Pelayo, Manuel, 10
García, Ismael, 464
García, Virginia, 30
Garífuna
  in Belize, 645
  modernization in Guatemala and, 490
  political activism in contemporary Honduras among, 536
  race relations in Guatemala and, 501–2
General Confederation of Workers of Guatemala (CGTG), 339
General Workers Union (GWU), 641–42
Generation of 1920 intellectuals, 493
Gerardi, Juan José, 247, 419, 502
Gérin y Boulay, Marcel, 417

germ theory, 33
Giroldi, Moíses, 628
Goethals, George W., 620
Goldson, Philip, 642
Gonzáles y Robledo, Vicente Alejandro, 410
González de Ávila, Gil, 146
González Nájera, Pedro, 143
González Saravia, Antonio, 221
González, Clara, 437
Good Neighbor policy, 315–16, 383, 575, 622
Gorbachev, Mikhail, 350
Gorgas, William, 619
Gran Alianza por la Unidad Nacional (GANA, El Salvador), 558
Gran Colombia, 615–16
Granada (Nicaragua), 62, 145, 223, 226, 290, 567
Grant, Ulysses S., 292, 570
Great Britain. *See also* England
  abolition of slavery (1838) by, 640
  Atlantic lowlands of Central America and, 121
  canal plans in Central America and, 290, 569–70, 616–17
  Central American Federation and, 228
  Honduras and, 523–24
  Mosquito kingdom and, 122, 572, 616
  Panama Canal and, 618–19
  Spain's trade with, 182
  treaties with postindependence governments in Central America and, 71
Great Depression
  banana economy and, 259
  coffee economy and, 258–59
  in Costa Rica, 259–60
  dollar diplomacy and, 315
  in El Salvador, 258, 385
  Good Neighbor Policy and, 315
  in Guatemala, 258, 494
  in Nicaragua, 258–59
  Panama Canal and, 622
Great Salvadoran Feminist Party, 436
Grijalva, Juan de, 146
Groce, Leonard, 573
Grupo Feminista Renovación, 437
Guanacaste (Costa Rica), 46
guano, 37–38
Guardia, Tomás, 291–92, 595

Guardia, Victor, 597

Guatemala. *See also* Kingdom of Guatemala
Afro-Central Americans in, 199–200, 485, 487, 490, 493, 498, 501
Agrarian Reform Law (1952) in, 498
Agreement on Strengthening Civilian Authority and the Role of the Military in, 389
agricultural practices in, 35–40, 111, 489, 500–501
authoritarian governments in, 295–96, 301, 336, 492–93
British Honduras claims by, 643–44
Catholic Church in, 11, 236, 238, 254, 291, 337, 340–41, 343, 381, 405–7, 409–12, 414–18, 500
Central American Common Market and, 263, 499
Central American Federation and, 228–32, 234, 289–90
Central American Free Trade Agreement and, 272, 302
civil war (1962-96) in, 66, 116, 119, 123, 297, 320–21, 344, 348, 350–51, 359, 388, 418, 499–500, 502
coffee economy in, 254–55, 489, 492–94
concordat of 1852 and, 11
cotton economy and, 263
coup (1954) in, 261, 274, 295, 301, 316–18, 337–38, 340–41, 499, 528
declaration of independence (1821) by, 226
declaration of independence (1847) by, 238
democratic revolution (1944-54) in, 295, 318, 336–40, 383–84, 436, 498
democratization in, 299–300, 370–71
earthquakes in, 31
emigration from, 3, 300, 321, 372, 503
forced labor in, 113–14
Fort Matamoros uprising (1960) in, 342
German planters in, 490
Great Depression in, 258, 494
guerrilla movements in, 345–46
Indigenous populations in, 63–66, 71–72, 108, 110, 112, 115–20, 123–25, 155, 157, 207, 253, 258, 291, 294–97, 344, 351, 485–99, 501, 503–4
Labor Code in, 337, 498

ladino identity in, 490, 493
land use issues in, 112, 260–61, 339–40, 485, 498
Liberal Revolt (1871) in, 485–86
livestock development in, 264–65
Livingston Code in, 291
marriage and divorce law in, 432
medicine in, 205–7
military forces in, 257, 301, 381, 383–84, 389–90, 394
military governments in, 2, 383–84
mining in, 124, 147
modernization and science in, 491–92
neoliberal economic policies and, 274, 500–501, 503
Northern Transversal Strip in, 264–67
Peace Accords (1996) in, 120, 267, 365, 389–90, 442, 486, 500
Plan Escoba (2004) in, 367–68
prehistoric sites in, 88
Protestantism in, 408, 418
racial identity and race relations in, 485, 490, 501–2
railroads in, 257–58
remittances and, 272
slavery in, 198–200
Spanish colonial settlement and administration in, 62, 168, 171, 176–77, 191–92
Spanish conquest of territories in, 142–44, 148
state-building and national identity in, 255
strike (1909-10) in, 313
United Fruit Company and, 257, 338–40, 384, 492, 494, 519
violence and violent crime (1990-2020) in, 3, 270, 360–67, 372–73, 443, 503
Walker's wars in Central America (1850s) and, 311
women's status in, 433–36, 439–44, 499, 501, 503
World War II and, 260, 497

Guatemalan National Revolutionary Unity (URNG), 346, 351, 353, 384, 389

Guaymí, 72, 121

Guerra, François-Xavier, 459

Guerrerro, Lorenzo, 578

670 INDEX

Guerrilla Army of the Poor (EGP), 345, 384
Guevara, Che, 340–41
Gulf of Mexico, 29, 32, 84
Guna, 61, 67–68, 70, 72–73
Guzmán, Fernando, 570

H

Habermas, Jürgen, 13
Hanna, Matthew, 575–76
Hay, John, 618–19
Helms, Jesse, 350, 627
Henríquez Ureña, Pedro, 456–57
Herrera, Bernal, 462
Herrera, Carlos, 493
Herrera, Thomas, 616
Hidalgo, Miguel, 222
Holocene period, 29, 34, 82–83
Honduran Private Enterprise Council, 273
Honduran Solidarity Network, 322
Honduras
  Afro-Central Americans in, 521, 536
  agrarian reform laws in, 273, 529
  agricultural practices in, 36–37, 40, 111–12
  authoritarian regimes in, 296, 337, 525, 531
  banana economy and, 259, 312, 519, 522–29
  Banana-Gate scandal (1975) in, 530
  Catholic Church in, 342, 408, 412
  Central American Common Market and, 263
  Central American Federation and, 229, 231–34, 289–90, 520
  Central American Free Trade Agreement and, 302
  Central Intelligence Agency and, 261, 388, 519
  coffee economy and, 256, 521–23
  constitution (1957) of, 385
  coup (1963) in, 530
  coup (1972) in, 296, 298
  coup (2009) in, 273, 299, 302, 322, 362, 392, 395, 520, 535, 538
  declaration of independence (1862) by, 238
  democratization in, 298, 370–71
  emigration from, 3, 273, 300, 372, 536–37
  forest exploitation in, 42
  Great Britain and, 523–24
  Hurricane Mitch (1998) and, 31–32
  Indigenous populations in, 63–64, 66–67, 71–73, 110, 112, 124, 155, 157, 253, 273–74, 294, 521, 536
  industrialization and, 529, 533
  international financial institutions and, 531–32
  La Reforma period (1880s) in, 521
  labor code in, 261, 530
  labor unions in, 261, 529
  land use and land reform in, 265, 296
  Liberal Reform period in, 522–23
  livestock production in, 44, 264, 287, 521
  marriage and divorce law in, 432
  mestizo identity in, 294, 521
  Middle Eastern merchant families in, 532–34
  military forces in, 257, 381–82, 385, 388, 391–92, 394
  mining in, 41–42, 147, 180, 256, 287, 521, 523
  National Police in, 365, 369
  neoliberal economic policies and, 274, 531–32
  North Coast region of, 521, 532–33
  Operacion Guerra Contra la Delincuencia in, 367
  police reform in, 370
  Protestantism in, 418
  railroads in, 257–58, 523–24
  remittances and, 272–73
  Spanish colonial settlement and administration in, 171, 176, 183, 191–92, 224
  Spanish conquest of territories in, 144–46, 148
  state-building and national identity in, 294, 300–301, 520
  strike (1954) in, 528
  United Fruit Company and, 259, 337, 519, 523–25, 528–29
  US military and, 266–67, 273, 388, 531, 537
  violence and violent crime (1990-2020) in, 3, 270, 273, 360–68, 373, 443
  women's status in, 433, 435, 437–39, 441–44, 525
Hong Kong Nicaragua Canal Development Investment Co. (HKND), 584
Hueck, Cornelio, 579
Huetar, 61–62, 157

Huezo, Trinidad, 407
Hull-Alfaro Treaty, 622
Hurricane Mitch (1998), 31–32, 323, 536

I

Ice Age, 29–30, 34
Iglesias, Rafael, 597
Ilopango volcanic eruption, 90–91
Indigenous populations. *See also specific*
  groups
  Afro-Central Americans and, 198
  as agricultural laborers, 112–14, 174–75
  agricultural practices among, 60, 67, 115
  assimilation and, 108–9, 120, 157–58
  Atlantic lowlands and, 121–22
  in Belize, 64f, 157, 645, 647
  Catholic Church and, 115, 416
  censuses of, 63–64, 110
  Conservatives and, 118
  in Costa Rica, 64f, 67, 71–72, 110, 112, 124,
    156–57, 253, 294, 592–93, 607
  definition of, 57–58, 107–8
  discrimination against, 64, 120
  in El Salvador, 63, 64f, 109–10, 112, 114–18,
    157, 253, 256, 293–94, 297, 301, 344, 545,
    547, 549–51
  electoral politics and, 116–17, 121
  epidemic disease among, 32–33, 62, 73, 147,
    155–56, 169
  extractive industries' impact on, 124
  forced labor and, 147
  forest exploitation in ancestral lands of, 69
  growth in size since 1940 of, 64–65
  in Guatemala, 63–66, 71–72, 108, 110, 112,
    115–20, 123–25, 155, 157, 207, 253, 258, 291,
    294–97, 344, 351, 485–99, 501, 503–4
  in Honduras, 63–64, 66–67, 71–73, 110, 112,
    124, 155, 157, 253, 273–74, 294, 521, 536
  international organizations and, 120
  land privatization's impact on, 111–15
  Liberals and, 119, 253
  mestizaje (mixing) with settler populations
    and, 108, 119–20
  national identities and, 12, 119–20
  in Nicaragua, 64f, 66–67, 71, 73, 108, 110, 115,
    117–18, 120, 124, 155–58, 253, 256, 292–93,
    347

in Panama, 64f, 67, 70, 72, 110, 124–25, 154–55,
  157, 627
pre-Columbian era and, 59–61
resistance among, 117–19
slavery and, 148, 169, 175
social stratification among, 114–16
territorial rights of, 58–59, 64, 70–74, 124–26
twentieth-century demographic resurgence
  of, 58, 73, 109
indigo
  El Salvador and, 36, 234, 287, 547
  environmental consequences associated
    with cultivation of, 36
  global trade networks and, 44, 147, 182–83,
    192, 208, 286–87
  Kingdom of Guatemala and, 36, 221, 286–87
  slavery and, 197
Initial Formative period (2000-1200 BCE),
  85–86
Inkas, 141
Inter-American Congress of Women, 436–37
Inter-American Development Bank (IDB),
  264, 532
International Commission against Impunity
  in Guatemala (CICIG), 272, 369–70, 372
International Labour Organization
  Convention on Indigenous and Tribal
    Peoples (1989), 71
International Monetary Fund (IMF), 267–68,
  603, 650
International Nickel Co., 440
Intertropical Convergence Zone (ITCZ), 29
Iran-Contra Affair (1985-86), 266–67, 321–22,
  347
Iturbide, Agustín de, 226–28, 288
Iximché, 142–43, 171
Izapa, 88–89

J

Jefferson, Thomas, 309, 569
Jerez, Máximo, 569–70
Jesuits
  assassination in El Salvador (1989) of, 416
  Liberal regimes' expulsion of, 406–7, 409,
    596
  readmission to Central America of, 410–11
Jicaque, 72, 147, 152, 157

672 INDEX

Jiménez, Jesús, 595
Jiménez, Ricardo, 545, 599
Juventud Patriótica del Trabajo (JPT), 342

K

K'iche'
 Christian missionaries and, 193–94
 Indigenous identity and, 108
 modernization in Guatemala and, 489
 size of contemporary population in
  Gutamela of, 65
 Spanish conquest and, 142–43
 Titulos (land dispute resolutions) and, 194
Kaji' Imox, 144
Kaminaljuyu (Guatemala), 88, 90
Kaqchikel
 epidemic disease among, 155–56
 Guatemalan state and exploitation of the
  labor of, 497
 modern farming by, 501
 size of contemporary population in
  Guatemala of, 65
 Spanish conquest and, 62, 142–44, 171, 486
 uprising (1944) by, 497–98
Keith, Minor, 257, 595–96
Kennedy, John F.
 Alliance for Progress policies and, 262, 266,
  318, 341, 414, 578, 601
 Bay of Pigs invasion (1961) and, 578
 Costa Rica and, 295
 Panama and, 625
Kingdom of Guatemala
 boundaries of, 6, 286
 Bourbon Dynasty and, 286
 Cadíz Constitution (1812) and, 224–25
 economic relations in, 220–21
 indigo cultivation in, 36, 221, 286–87
 intendancies in, 220
 Mexico and, 226
 Napoleonic Wars and, 221
 New Spain revolt (1810) and, 222
 population size of, 6
 Regency Council and, 222, 225
 separation from Spain (1808-21) by, 6–7
 Supreme Central Junta and, 221–22
Kissinger Report, 266
Kiyawit Kawoq, 144

Krakatoa volcano eruption (1883), 30
Kuna, 121–22, 126, 157

L

La Liga Femenina Salvadoreña, 436
La Venta, 88
Labourers and Unemployed Association
  (LUA), 641
Lacayo Sacasa, Benjamín, 577
Lacayo, Antonio, 350, 353
ladinos (Spanish-speakers)
 as agricultural laborers, 113
 Atlantic lowlands and, 121
 definition of, 169
 Guatemalan national identity and, 490, 493
 mulattos and, 198
 social differentiation among, 108, 115
Lake Nicaragua, 180, 310, 567, 584, 594
Las Casas, Bartolomé de, 144, 148, 171, 173, 175,
  178
Las Palmas group, 350
Late Formative Period (300-250 CE), 89
Late Postclassic Era settlements (1200-1500
  CE), 93–94
Laureano Pineda, José, 570
Lempira, 120, 146, 294
Lenca
 in contemporary Central America, 65, 157,
  536
 displacement of, 274
 Ilopango volcanic eruption and, 90
 recovery of cultural practices by, 68
 Spanish conquest and, 146–47, 152
Leo XIII (pope), 412
León (Nicaragua)
 Catholic Church and, 178
 Central American Federation and, 229, 290
 foundry at, 148
 intendancy established in 1780s in, 220
 Kingdom of Guatemala and, 222–23
 Liberals and, 567
 Mexico and, 226
 Spain's establishment (1524) of, 62, 145, 171
Lesseps, Ferdinand de, 570, 617–18
Levame, Alberto, 411
Lezcano y Ortega, José Antonio, 410
Liberal Party (Guatemala), 493

INDEX 673

Liberal Party (Honduras), 527, 529–30, 535, 537
Liberals
  Catholic Church and, 253, 406–10, 486
  economic policy and, 253
  Indigenous populations and, 119, 253
  land privatization and, 111–12
  Protestant missionaries and, 408
Liberation Theology, 297, 343–44, 415–19, 440, 580
Lienzo de Quauhquechollan, 144, 149–52
Liga Feminista Costarricense, 437
Lira, Bravo, 13
Little Ice Age, 29–30
livestock
  Central American Common Market and, 262
  Costa Rica and, 44, 46, 598
  El Salvador and, 265
  environmental consequences of raising, 264
  Guatemala and, 264–65
  Honduras and, 44, 264, 287, 521
  international financial institutions and, 264
  Nicaragua and, 44, 264–65, 287
  population displacement related to production of, 264–65
  Spanish colonization of Central America and, 169
Llorente y La Fuente, Anselmo, 406, 408, 595
López Arellano, Osvaldo, 296, 386, 530, 533
López de Salcedo, Diego, 176
López Gutierrez, Rafael, 526
López Pérez, Rigoberto, 577–78
Los Altos
  Carrera's conquest of, 487–88
  Catholic Church and, 411–12
  Central American Federation and, 229–30, 237–38
  secessionist efforts by, 290
Los Doce clerics, 415, 580
Lucas García, Fernando Romeo, 416
Lunaldi, Federico, 294

M
MacLeod, Murdo J., 181
Madriz, José, 573
Maduro, Ricardo, 367, 534–35
Magaña, Álvaro Alfredo, 553

Mallarino-Bidlack Treaty, 618
Mallarino, Manuel María, 616
Mam, 65, 143
Managua earthquake (Nicaragua, 1972), 30, 388, 579
Mangue, 61–62, 93–94
Manifest Destiny doctrine (United States), 309–12
Mano Dura policies (El Salvador), 367–68, 371, 560
Mara Salvatrucha gang (MS-13), 323, 361, 368, 560
Marists, 410
Marroquín, Francisco, 173
Martí, Farabundo, 551
Martinelli, Ricardo, 630
Martínez Peláez, Severo, 144, 173–74
Martínez, José Francisco, 465
Martínez, Maximiliano Hernández
  coup (1931) installing, 258, 552
  Matanza (1932) and, 258, 336, 550
  military dictatorship of, 385, 553
  resignation (1944) by, 261, 336, 436
  uprising (1932) against, 109, 435
Martínez, Thomás, 569–70
Maryknoll missionaries, 410–12, 416
Matagalpa (Nicaragua)
  epidemic disease outbreaks among, 62
  Indian revolt (1881) in, 117, 256, 574
  livestock production in, 264
  relations between Indigenous people and ladinos in, 115
  uprising (1990s) in, 256
Matanza (El Salvador, 1932), 158, 258–59, 385, 550–51
Matthews, Calvin B., 576
Maximón (Saint Simon), 196
Maya
  agricultural practices of, 34–35, 60
  Belize and, 154, 645
  in British Honduras, 639
  calendars of, 90
  Catholicism and, 145
  in Chiapas, 157
  Christian missionaries and, 193–96
  Classic Era settlements (250-600 CE), 89–91

674   INDEX

Maya (*cont.*)
   cofradías and, 195
   in contemporary Guatemalan society, 65–66,
      120–21, 157, 266–67, 272–73, 339, 346, 351,
      384, 417, 504
   Dance of the Conquest and, 145
   displacement of, 255
   Early Postclassic settlements (800-1200
      CE) and, 92–93
   Ilopango volcanic eruption and, 90–91
   Late Classic Era settlements (600-900 CE)
      and, 91–92
   leftist movements in twentieth-century
      Guatemala and, 119
   linguistic unification among, 123
   massacres (1982-83) of, 266–67
   medicine and, 206
   millenarianism among, 196
   modern linguistic movement among, 501
   religious practices among, 407
   Spanish colonial era and, 62, 191
   Spanish conquest and, 142, 144–45, 147–51, 171
   Teotihuacan intrusion (378 CE) and, 90
   in the United States, 157
   urban centers during pre-Columbian era
      of, 60
Mayangna, 66–67, 122, 124, 157
Mayapan, 93
Mayorga Rivas, Román, 458
McSherry Report (1947), 623
measles, 32–33
Medellín Conference, 414, 417, 555
Mejía Victores, Óscar Humberto, 384
Meléndez Obando, Mauricio, 170
Meléndez, Douglas, 368
Mena, Luis, 573
Menchú, Rigoberta, 499, 504, 514–15n124
Mendieta, Salvador, 5–6, 11–12
Mendoza, Carlos, 620
Mexico. *See also* Chiapas region (Mexico)
   Central American Federation and, 228,
      235, 288
   climate variability in, 29–30
   drug trafficking and, 361
   independence (1821) of, 288
   Kingdom of Guatemala and, 226
   Olmec civilization and, 60

Mexico City (Mexico), 179, 192
miasmatic theory, 33
Mijango, Raul, 368
Milicias Populares Anti-Sandinistas
   (MILPAS), 347
Milla, José, 405
Miró, Rodrigo, 463–64
Miskitu
   Atlantic lowlands and, 121–22
   Contras and, 122
   England's alliances with, 153–54
   linguistic unification among, 123
   Nicaraguan civil war and, 581, 585
   Sandinistas and, 122
   slavery and, 148
   in Tegucigalpa, 68
   territorial rights of, 73
Mistral, Gabriel, 575
Misumalpan, 60–61
MISURASATA (Contra group), 581
modernist literature in Central America,
   459–62
Moffat, Thomas, 573
Molina de Fromen, Juanita, 437
Molina Jiménez, Iván, 459–60
Molina, Arturo, 554
Monagrillo pottery, 84
Moncada, José Maria, 574–76
Mondol López, Mijail, 458, 465
Monge, Luis Alberto, 604
Monimbó attack (Nicaragua,
   1978), 580
Monroe Doctrine, 617
Monte Verde (Chile), 59, 82
Montealegre, José María, 595
Montejo, Francisco de, 146, 152, 176
Montejo, Victor, 157, 504
Montúfar y Coronado, Manuel, 291
Montúfar, Lorenzo, 5–6, 11
Mopan, 66, 72, 645
Mora, Juan Rafael, 594–95
Mora, Manuel, 599–600
Morales, Evo, 392
Morales, Jimmy, 299, 370
Morazán, Francisco
   Carrera's defeat of, 291
   caudillo politics and, 380

Central American Federation state-
building and, 290
First Federal War and, 231
Rebelión de la Montaña (1837) and, 237–38
Second Federal War and, 231–32
Moscoso, Mireya, 442, 630
Mosquitia, 61, 66–67, 69
Afro-Central Americans and, 153–54
geography of, 29
Great Britain and, 229, 235, 290
protected areas of, 122, 124
Mosquito Kingdom, 122, 192, 199
Mosquito Shore, 180, 286
Movimiento Popular de Liberación
Cinchonero, 297
MS-13 gang (Mara Salvatrucha), 323, 361, 368,
560
mulatos, 169–70, 198, 200, 521
Munguía Payés, David, 368
Munro, Dana Gardner, 289
Musa, Said, 642–44
Myers, Norman, 46

N

Nahua
in complementary Honduras, 157
Indigenous identity and, 108
initial settlement in Central America of,
60, 194
Spanish colonists' alliances with, 142–43,
149–53
Nasser, Gamal Abdel, 624
National Association of Private Enterprise
(ANEP, El Salvador), 272
National Center for the Development of
Women and the Family, 440
National Conservative Party (PCN,
Nicaragua), 576
National Corporation of Industrial
Development (CONADI, Honduras),
533, 536
National Endowment for Democracy (NED),
322
National Independence Party (NIP), 642
National Liberation Party (Costa Rica), 601,
603, 605–6
National Party (Honduras), 385, 527, 530–31, 537

National Peasant Confederation of Guatemala
(CNCG), 339
National Republican Alliance Party (ARENA,
El Salvador), 271–72, 353, 557–60
National Republican Party (Costa Rica), 437,
599–600
National Resistance (RN, El Salvador), 345,
554
National Restoration Party
(Costa Rica), 606
Nationalist Conservative Party (PCN, El
Salvador), 385, 553
Neira de Calvo, Esther, 437
Netherlands, 153–54, 235
New Granada, 615–17
New Spain. *See also* Mexico
agricultural labor system in, 175
Chiapas and, 181
independence (1821) of, 226
Kingdom of Guatemala and, 286
land distribution in, 174
revolt (1810) in, 222
Ngäbe, 67–68, 72–73
Nicaragua
agricultural practices in, 36–37, 40, 111–12
Atlantic lowlands and, 122
California gold rush and, 310
canal plans in, 290, 292, 310, 312, 569–70,
572–73, 583–84
Catholic Church and, 341, 343, 407, 409–10,
412, 415–17
Central American Federation and, 229, 231,
289–90
Central American Free Trade Agreement
and, 270, 302
civil war (1980s) in, 266, 297, 301, 359,
581–82, 604
coffee economy and, 256, 259
Conservatives in, 569–71
Constitution of 1858 and, 112
cotton economy and, 263
declaration of independence (1854) in, 238
democratization in, 299–300, 370–71
dollar diplomacy and, 314–15
draft of soldiers (1980s) in, 347–48
emigration from, 321, 323
epidemic disease outbreaks in, 33–34

INDEX

Nicaragua (*cont.*)
  forced labor in, 113–14
  forest exploitation in, 42
  Great Depression and, 258–59
  Indigenous populations in, 64f, 66–67, 71,
    73, 108, 110, 115, 117–18, 120, 124, 155–58,
    253, 256, 292–93, 347
  land use in, 112, 261
  livestock production in, 44, 264–65, 287
  macroeconomic successes in, 275
  Managua earthquake (1972) in, 30, 388, 579
  Managua Protocol (1990) and, 350
  marriage and divorce law in, 432
  mestizo identity in, 294
  military forces in, 257, 382, 386, 393–94
  mining in, 42
  Miskito Coast annexed by, 293, 572
  National Guard in, 262, 301, 316, 320, 337,
    382, 386, 393, 575–81
  neoliberal economic policies and, 269–70,
    582
  peace agreement (1988) and, 298, 322, 349
  Protestantism in, 408, 418
  protests (2018) in, 584–85
  remittances and, 272
  revolution (1979) in, 2, 265, 297, 319–20, 335,
    338, 345–46, 386, 388, 580
  Sandino uprising (1927-33) in, 315, 574–76
  sovereignty declaration (1838) by, 237
  Spanish colonial settlement and
    administration in, 62, 171, 176, 183, 191–92
  Spanish conquest of territories in, 144–45,
    148, 155
  state-building and national identity in,
    292–93, 300
  US occupation (1912-33) of, 257, 314, 382,
    386–87, 621
  US sanctions against Ortega regime in, 271
  violence and violent crime (1990-2020) in,
    270, 323, 360, 362–63, 365–66, 443
  Walker's control (1850s) over, 238, 289–90,
    292, 300, 311, 387, 567–69
  women's status in, 433, 437–44
  World War II and, 261, 576–77
Nicarao, 61–62, 94, 120
Nicoya (Costa Rica), 229
Nonualco Indian rebellion (1833), 232–33

Noriega, Manuel, 322, 627–30
Norman, Edward, 7
North Pacific Oscillation, 29
Northern Transversal Strip (Guatemala), 264–67
Northern Triangle, 269–71, 275, 323, 364. *See
    also* El Salvador; Guatemala; Honduras
Nueva Guatemala de la Asunción, 31, 171
Núñez de Saballos, Olga, 437

O

Obando y Bravo, Miguel, 417, 419
Ochomogo War (1823), 231
Oduber, Daniel, 296
Olancho (Honduras), 146–47, 264, 291
Olid, Cristobal de, 146
Olman, 87
Olmec, 60, 86–88, 91, 94
Order of Mercy, 178
Orellana, José Maria, 383, 493
Organization of American States (OAS), 296,
    298, 580, 629, 644
Orlich, Francisco J., 296
Ortega, Daniel
  authoritarian rule and consolidation of
    power by, 302, 370, 373, 394
  canal plans and, 583–84
  election (1984) and, 581
  election (1990) and, 267
  election (1996) and, 582
  peace negotiations and, 349
  presidency (2007-) of, 270, 299, 583–85
  release from prison (1974) of, 579
  US sanctions against regime of, 271
Ortega, Humberto, 353, 393
Our Lady of Peace of San Miguel shrine, 205

P

Panama. *See also* Panama Canal
  Afro-Central Americans in, 617
  agricultural practices in, 36
  anti-US protests in, 623
  California gold rush and, 310
  canal plans in, 310, 312, 616 (*see also* Panama
    Canal)
  Catholic Church in, 408
  Central Intelligence Agency and, 627–28
  Constitution of, 621

corruption in, 630
coup (1941) in, 623
coup (1968) in, 625
economic downturn (1979-82) in, 627
Gran Colombia and, 616
independence from Colombia (1903) and,
18, 312, 615
Indigenous populations in, 64f, 67, 70, 72,
110, 124–25, 154–55, 157, 627
McSherry Report (1947) and, 623
military governments in, 626
mining in, 124
Non-Aligned Movement and, 626
Operation Sovereignty (1958) in, 624
railroads in, 617
Republic of Tule and, 121–22
slavery in, 169
Spanish colonial settlement and
administration in, 171, 181
Spanish conquest of territories in, 145–48,
154
Thousand Days' War (1899-1902) in, 618
US bombing (1885) of, 618
US invasion (1989) of, 322, 628–29
US-Panama Free Trade Agreement (2011)
and, 630
US-Panamanian Defense Treaty (1942)
and, 623
violence and violent crime (1990-2020)
in, 443
Watermelon War (1856) and, 310–11, 617
women's status in, 433, 435, 437–44
World War I and, 621–22
World War II and, 622–23
Panama Canal
construction of, 619–20
Eisenhower-Remón Accord (1955) and, 624
foreign labor and, 620–21
Great Britain and, 618–19
Great Depression and, 622
Hay-Pauncefote Treaty and, 618
Panama Canal Treaty (1977) and, 626
Panama's assumption of control (1999) over,
18, 615, 629
protests at, 624–25
United Fruit Company and, 314
US control (1904-99) over, 312, 621

Partido Guatemalteco del Trabajo (PGT),
339–40, 342–43, 345, 384
Partido Liberación Nacional (PLN), 296, 301,
437
Partido Liberal Independiente (Independent
Liberal Party, PLI), 299, 576–77, 582
Partido Nacional Feminista, 437
Partido Restauración Nacional, 299
Partido Revolucionario de Unificación
Democrática (PRUD), 553
Partido Revolucionario Nicaragüense (PRN),
577
Partido Socialista de Nicaragua (PSN), 343, 577
Paso de la Amada, 86–87
Pasos, Carlos, 577
Pastora, Eden, 581
Paulists, 408
Pauncefote, Lord, 618
Paya, 60–61, 72, 157
Paz García, Policarpo, 531
Peace Corps, 578
Pech, 61, 66–67, 147, 157
Penados del Barrio, Próspero, 4, 9–12, 14
peninsulars (Spanish-born residents of
Central America), 170, 183
Pentecostalism, 405, 418–19
People's Revolutionary Army (Ejército
Revolucionario del Pueblo, ERP), 297,
345, 554–56
People's United Party (PUP, Belize), 438, 641–
42, 644, 647–48
Pereira y Castellón, Simeón, 406
Pérez Brignoli, Héctor, 3, 5–6, 11, 28
Pérez de Cuellar, Javier, 349–50
Pérez Molina, Otto, 299, 370
Pershing, John J., 622
Petén (Guatemala), 148, 180
Philip V (king of Spain), 182
Picado Michalski, Teodoro, 337–38, 600
Pickering, Thomas, 350
Piñol y Aycinena, Bernardo, 406
Pipil
in contemporary El Salvador, 157–58
epidemic disease outbreaks among, 62
initial settlements in Central America of,
60–61
Late Postclassic city-states of, 94

678 INDEX

Pipil (*cont.*)
  Matanza (1932) and, 158
  settlement in Central American during
    Early Postclassic Era by, 93
  Spanish conquest and, 144, 147
Pius XI (pope), 411, 413
Pius XII (pope), 411
plague, 33
Ponce Vaides, Federico, 336, 383, 497
Pop Caal, Antonio, 487
Popol Vuh, 194
Popular Sandinista Army (EPS), 348, 350, 353,
  386, 393
Popular Vanguard Party, 600
Porras, Belisario, 620
Portillo Valdés, José, 8
Portillo, Alfonso, 390
postmodern literature in Central America,
  462–63
Prado, Mariano, 230–31
Prestan, Pedro, 618
Price, George C., 641–43, 647
Primer Congreso Interamericano de Mujeres, 436
Primera Conferencia del Espiscopado
    Centroamericano (1956), 413
Protestantism
  growth in Central America since 1950 of,
    17, 404
  Liberal regimes and, 408
  missionaries in Central America and, 123,
    315, 408
  North America and, 8–9
  Pentecostalism and, 405, 418–19
Providence Island, 153
Public Service Union (PSU, Belize), 643

Q

Q'eqchi'
  in Belize, 645
  in British Honduras, 72
  modernization in Guatemala and, 489
  race relations in Guatemala and, 501
  Spanish conquest and, 486
Quauhquecholteca, 149–50, 152
Quelepa, 90, 93
Quetzaltenango, 226–27, 255
Qumarkaj, 142

R

Rama, 66–67, 122, 145, 157, 572, 581
Ramazzini, Álvaro, 419
Ramírez, Bernardo, 200
Ramírez, Sergio, 456, 465, 580–83
Reagan, Ronald
  Costa Rica and, 603
  El Salvador and, 320, 353, 556
  Guatemala and, 500
  Honduras and, 320
  Iran-Contra scandal (1986) and, 266, 321,
    347, 389
  Nicaragua and, 266, 297, 320, 322, 347, 353,
    388, 581–82
  Panama and, 627–28
  Vietnam Syndrome and, 320
Rebelión de la Montaña (1837), 232–33, 236–38
Redemptionists, 408
Reformist Party (Costa Rica), 599
Reina, Carlos Roberto, 391, 536
Remón, José Antonio, 623–24
Republic of Tule, 121–22
Revolutionary Democratic Party (PRD,
    Panama), 627, 629–30
Revolutionary Organization of the People in
    Arms (ORPA), 345, 384
Revolutionary Party of Central American
    Workers (PRTC), 345, 554
Reyes Maaz, Efraín, 339
Richardson, Leigh, 642
Riego, Rafael, 225
Ríos Montt, Efraím, 266, 384, 416, 418,
    499–500
Rivas, Rafael, 547
Rivera, Diego, 340
Rockefeller Foundation, 491
Rodas Alvarado, Modesto, 386
Rodríguez, José Joaquin, 597
Rodríguez, Juan Manuel, 547
Román y Reyes, Victor, 577
Romero, Carlos, 346
Romero, Óscar, 403–4, 416
Roosevelt Corollary, 312
Roosevelt, Franklin D., 315–16, 383, 575, 599, 622
Roosevelt, Theodore, 619–20
Rosenswig, Robert M., 84–85
Rosenthal Oliva, Jaime, 532

Rossell y Arellano, Mariano, 410
Rpyal Economic Society, 205
Royal Tobacco Monopoly, 287

S

Saavedra, Hernando de, 146
Saca, Antonio, 367, 559
Sacasa, Juan Bautista, 574, 576
Sacasa, Roberto, 570
Sacred Heart missionaries, 411–12
Salazar, Lorenzo, 595
Salesians, 408, 410
Salinas, Francisco, 368
Salvadoran Catholic University Action
    (ACUS), 343
Salvadoran Communist Party (PCS), 118, 258,
    343, 551, 554
Sam Colop, Luis Enrique, 144, 158, 504
San Antonio volcanic eruption (1st century
    BCE), 89
San Isidro Coronado Declaration (1989),
    349–50
San Juan del Norte (Nicaragua), 310–11
San Juan Ostuncalco protests, 233
San Juan River, 180, 290, 310, 570, 573, 594
San Lorenzo Tenochtitlan, 87–88
San Miguel (El Salvador), 171, 232, 287
San Pedro Sula (Honduras), 171, 256, 261, 337,
    529
San Salvador (El Salvador)
    Central American Federation and, 227, 229
    earthquakes in, 30
    establishment (1525) of, 144, 171
    intendancy established in 1780s in, 220, 288
    Kingdom of Guatemala and, 222
    uprising (1811) in, 223
    uprising (1814) in, 225
Sanabria, Víctor Manuel, 413, 600
Sánchez Cerén, Salvador, 351, 368
Sandinistas (Sandinista National Liberation
    Front, FSLN)
    Atlantic lowlands and, 122
    business enterprises of, 269
    Catholic Church and, 415–16
    ceasefire (1988) and, 267
    Contras' war against, 266, 301, 581–82
    Cuban Revolution and, 342, 578–80

demobilization of, 350
education and public health campaigns by,
    438–39, 581
establishment of, 578
Farabundo Martí National Liberation Front
    and, 347
guerrilla tactics of, 579
land reform and, 266
Marxism and, 580
Matagalpa region in, 264
Miskitu and, 122
peace process and, 390
as political party after civil war, 350, 352, 365,
    393, 443, 582, 585
revolution (1979) and ascent to power of,
    265, 297, 319–20, 335, 338, 345–46, 386,
    388, 580
Sandinista Renovation Movement (MRS)
    and, 582–83
Tercerista faction in, 346
women activists among, 440
Sandino, Augusto Cesar
    Americanization opposed by, 315
    assassination of, 259, 338, 386, 576
    biographical background of, 574
    Indigenous supporters of, 293
    protests (1944) against, 577
    uprising (1927-33) led by, 315, 574–76
Sandoval de Fonseca, Virginia, 464
Santa María la Antigua, 61, 145, 148
Santa Marta cave (Chiapas), 82–83
Santa Marta earthquakes (1770s), 31
Santamaría, Juan, 292, 596–97
Santiago Atitlan (Guatemala), 196
Santiago de Guatemala
    Afro-Central Americans and, 152, 199
    Catholic Church and, 178, 201
    Corregimiento del Valle de Guatemala
        jurisdiction and, 177
    earthquake (1773) and, 200–201
    establishment (1524) of, 62, 144, 171
    Kingdom of Guatemala and, 192, 286
    landslide (1541) in, 171
    slavery in, 198–200
    Spanish colonial administration in, 172,
        177–78, 181, 201–2
    women in, 202–4

680   INDEX

Santiago de los Caballeros, 31, 62
Schick, Rene, 578
School of the Americas (Fort Gulick), 623
Sebastian, Fernández, 7
Second Vatican Council (Vatican II), 335, 341,
    414–15, 417, 555
Serrano, Jorge, 298, 500, 644
Shaler, James, 619
Sihyaj Chan K'awil II, 90
slavery
    Afro-Central Americans and, 152, 197–98
    Caribbean and, 148
    European imperial rivalries and, 153
    Indigenous populations and, 148, 169, 175
    Montejo expedition and, 152
    New Laws of 1542 and, 148, 175
    in Panama, 169
    Peru and, 148, 169
    Spanish law and, 199–200
smallpox, 32–33, 155, 205–6
Soberanis, Antonio, 641
Social Democratic Party (Costa Rica), 601
Socialist Party of Nicaragua (PSN), 343
Sociedad Nacional para el Progreso de la
    Mujer, 437
Soconusco (Chiapas)
    Alvarado's conquest of, 62, 142
    Central American Federation and, 229–30,
    235
    independence era (1820s) and, 227
    prehistoric sites in, 84, 86, 88, 91
    trade corridor of, 153
Socorro Rojo Internacional (SRI), 551
Solentiname community, 343
Solórzano, Carlos José, 574
Somoza Debayle, Anastaio
    authoritarian regime of, 296, 580
    Catholic Church and, 410
    corruption of, 388, 579
    Managua earthquake (1972) and, 579
    National Guard and, 296, 578
    overthrow (1979) of, 262, 265, 338, 345, 386,
    388, 575, 578, 580
Somoza Debayle, Luis, 296, 410, 575, 578
Somoza García, Anastasio
    agrarian reform and, 319
    assassination of, 296, 577

authoritarian regime of, 295–96, 338, 575
biographical background of, 575–76
Catholic Church and, 410
Matagalpa region and, 264
National Guard and, 257, 301, 386, 575–76
personal fortune of, 261–62
populist support for, 316
presidential ascension (1937) of, 259
Sandino assassination (1934) by, 259, 338,
    386, 576
United States and, 261–62, 316
women's suffrage and, 437
World War II and, 576–77
Somoza Reyes, Anastasio, 575
Somoza, Bernate, 568
Sonsonate (Guatemala), 180, 220, 229
Soto, Bernardo, 596–97
Soviet Union
    Cold War and, 340
    collapse (1991) of, 350, 389–90, 443, 531
    Cuba and, 389
    Nicaragua and, 267, 343, 349
Spadafora, Hugo, 628
Spain. *See also* Cádiz constitution (1812);
        Spanish colonialism in Central America
    The Enlightenment and, 9
    Catholic Church's preeminent role in, 8
    crisis of 1808 in, 16
    Great Britain's trade with, 182
    Napoleonic Wars and, 184, 221
    Spanish-American War (1898) and, 312
Spanish colonialism in Central America
    administrative institutions of, 174–77
    Afro-Central Americans and, 196–97, 200
    agriculture and, 35, 172–75
    Atlantic lowlands and, 121
    audiencias (tribunals) in, 176–77
    Bourbon reforms and, 182–83
    Catholic Church and, 7, 141, 145, 158, 173,
        177–79, 194–96
    city settlements as characteristic
        of, 170–72
    in El Salvador, 142–44, 168, 171, 183, 191
    encomienda system and, 174–76
    end (1821) of, 1, 7
    epidemic disease during early period of, 33,
        62, 155–56, 169

INDEX 681

establishment of a single Central American
 jurisdiction (1543) and, 15
gold and, 143, 147, 181
in Guatemala, 62, 142–44, 148, 168, 171, 176–
 77, 191–92
in Honduras, 144–46, 148, 171, 176, 183, 191–
 92, 224
intendancy system and, 183
mining and, 41, 62, 144, 147
municipal councils and, 172
Napoleonic Wars and, 221
Nicaragua and, 62, 144–45, 148, 155, 171, 176,
 183, 191–92
Panama and, 145–48, 154, 171, 181
pillage economy in early stages of, 181
rural life in, 172–75
slavery and, 62, 144, 152, 181, 197–98
tributary revenue and, 147, 220, 225
women's status under, 201–4, 208, 432
Spice Islands (Maluku Islands), 144, 147
St. George's Cove, battle (1798) of, 647
Standard Fruit Company, 39, 259, 417, 519, 524
Stein, Eduardo, 368
Stephens, John L., 289
Stevens, John, 619–20
Suazo Córdoba, Roberto, 298, 530–31
Subtiaba, 61–62
sugar cane, 40, 169
Sumu, 60, 66, 572, 581
Superior Council of Private Enterprise
 (COSEP, Nicaragua), 265–66, 269

T

Taft, William Howard, 570
Tah Itzá (Tayasal), 148
Talamanca, 62, 67, 72, 124, 180
Tate and Lyle, 649–50
Tawahka, 66, 148, 157
Tecún-Umán, 120, 504
Tegucigalpa (Honduras)
 industrialization in, 529
 Kingdom of Guatemala and, 223, 226
 mining industry and, 180, 256, 287, 521, 523
Tekum (Tecum Umán), 142, 145
Tenochca, 142, 149, 151–52
Tenochtitlan, 142, 153
Teotihuacan, 60, 90, 193

Tepetate, 93
Thiel, Bernard August, 406, 408, 596
Thousand Days' War (Panama, 1899-1902), 618
Tikal, 60, 90, 148
Tilley, Virginia, 109, 118
Tinoco Granados, Federico, 382, 437, 599, 607
Tinoco, José Joaquín, 382
Tlacuachero, 84
Tlaxcalteca, 142, 149
tobacco, 220, 287, 521
Toledo de Aguerri, Josefa, 437
Torres-Riva, Edelberto, 3–6, 11–12, 14, 522
Torrijos, Martín, 630
Torrijos, Omar, 626–29
Toruño, Juan Felipe, 463–64
Traditional Conservative Party (PCT), 576
Treaty of Managua (1860), 572
Tronadora complex, 85
Tronadora Vieja, 85
Trujillo (Honduras), 145, 178, 180, 192
Truman, Harry S., 623
Tulum, 93–94
Turcios Lima, Luis Augusto, 342
Tuyuc, Rosalina, 499
typhus, 31–33, 206–7

U

Uaxactun, 90
Ubico, Jorge
 British Honduras claimed by, 643
 Catholic Church and, 410–11
 debt peonage abolished by, 117
 Great Depression and, 258
 Indigenous populations and, 494–97
 international fruit companies and, 259
 labor drafts and, 258
 land expropriation by, 260
 military dictatorship of, 383
 overthrow (1944) of, 295, 336, 383, 436
 public health campaigns and, 494–95
 United Fruit Company and, 494
 World War II and, 497
Ulate, Otilio, 337–38, 601
Unión Femenina Guatemalteca Pro
 Ciudadanía, 436
Unión Interamericana de Mujeres, 437
Unión Nacional Opositora (UNO), 350

Unión Revolucionaria Democrática (URD), 577
United Democratic Party (UDP, Belize), 642–44, 648
United Fruit Company (UFCO)
  "civilizing mission" of, 313
  in British Honduras, 314, 649
  in Costa Rica, 257, 260, 298, 598–99
  establishment (1899) of, 38–39, 257
  Great Depression and, 315
  in Guatemala, 257, 338–40, 384, 492, 494, 519
  in Honduras, 259, 337, 519, 523–25, 528–29
  monopolistic control of Central American banana crop held by, 38–39
  national sovereignty in Central America undermined by, 313
  Panama Canal and, 314
  public health campaigns and, 491
  railroad development and, 257–58
  strikes (1909) against, 313
United Nicaraguan Opposition, 582
United States
  Agency for International Development (USAID) in, 263–64, 266–67, 319, 351, 501, 578–79
  Alliance for Progress policies and, 262–63, 266, 274, 295, 318–19, 341, 388, 414, 578, 601
  canal plans in Central America and, 292, 309–10, 569–70, 573, 616–17 (see also Panama Canal)
  Department of Agriculture (USDA) in, 44–45, 264
  dollar diplomacy and, 314–15
  Good Neighbor Policy and, 315–16, 383, 575, 622
  gunboat diplomacy and, 312–15
  immigration from Central America to, 3, 300, 321, 323, 361, 536–37
  Iran-Contra Affair (1985-86) and, 266–67, 321–22, 347
  Manifest Destiny doctrine in, 309–12
  Marines and, 293, 316, 338, 382, 386, 575
  meat and livestock exports to, 45–46
  mining companies in, 42
  National Security Council in, 387
  National Security Doctrine and, 295, 319, 321
  naval forces of, 18, 310, 617–18

Nicaragua occupied (1912-33) by, 257, 314, 382, 386–87, 621
Panama Canal and, 312, 621
Panama invaded (1989) by, 322, 628–29
Roosevelt Corollary and, 312
Spanish-American War (1898) and, 312, 572, 618
Spooner Act (1902) and, 619
State Department in, 43, 264, 297, 519, 526
transcontinental railroad in, 310, 617
World War II and, 260
University of Costa Rica, 600
University of San Carlos, 201, 205, 491
Urquía, Lesbía Yaneth, 157
Urrutia, Carlos, 225–26

V

Valentine, Washington S., 523–24
Valero, José Mariano, 221
Vampiros-1 rock shelter, 59–60
Vanderbilt, Cornelius, 312, 569, 573
Vanguardia Popular, 337
Vargas, Mauricio, 557–58
Vásquez Velasquez, Romeo, 392, 519
Vatican II (Second Vatican Council), 335, 341, 414–15, 417, 555
Vázquez de Coronado, Juan, 148, 176
Villacorta Calderón, José Antonio, 493
Villeda Morales, Ramón, 296, 530
violence in Central America
  Costa Rica and, 270, 359–60, 362–66, 443
  democratization efforts hampered by, 370–72
  drug trafficking and, 361, 364–66
  efforts to combat, 366–70
  in El Salvador, 3, 270, 360–64, 367–68, 372–73, 443, 560
  gangs and, 361, 366–68, 560
  gender-based violence and, 362, 443
  in Guatemala, 3, 270, 360–67, 372–73, 443, 503
  in Honduras, 3, 270, 273, 360–68, 373, 443
  immigration to the United States and, 372
  interpersonal violence and, 361–62
  journalists as target of, 363, 373
  LGBT community as target of, 363
  low levels of trust in police and, 372
  in Nicaragua, 270, 323, 360, 362–63, 365–66, 443

INDEX   683

in Panama, 443
police reform in, 370
political activists as target of, 362–63, 373
security vacuum in postwar societies and, 364–65
state security agencies and, 369
Virgen de los Angeles ("La Negrita"), 407, 597, 606
Volio, Jorge, 412–13

W

Walker, William
  Costa Rica and, 289–90, 292, 311, 594
  Liberals (Nicaragua) and, 290, 311, 382, 408, 568, 573
  memoir of, 312
  Nicaragua controlled (1850s) by, 238, 289–90, 292, 300, 311, 387, 567–69
  Panama and, 617
  slavery and, 311
  surrender (1856) by, 290
  Vanderbilt and, 569
Watermelon War (Panama, 1856), 310–11, 617
Weber, Max, 379
Webster, Bethuel, 643
Willauer, William, 528
Wisconsin Glacial Episode, 82
women in Central America
  abortion and, 443, 445
  Belize and, 440–44
  British Honduras and, 438
  contraception and, 439–41
  Costa Rica and, 433–44
  education and, 433–35, 438–39
  El Salvador and, 433–44, 557
  in elected office, 442–43
  employment conditions among, 441
  Guatemala and, 433–36, 439–44, 499, 501, 503
  Honduras and, 433, 435, 437–39, 441–44, 525
  informal economy and, 439
  liberal reforms of the nineteenth century and, 432
  marriage and divorce laws and, 432
  modernization and, 438–41

Nicaragua and, 433, 437–44
Panama and, 433, 435, 437–44
parental rights and, 433
political mobilization by, 435, 499
property rights and, 432–33
in Spanish colonial era, 201–4, 208, 432
voting rights and, 434–38
Word Bank
  Costa Rica and, 301
  cotton export economy and, 263
  Indigenous populations and, 120
  livestock trade and, 264
  neoliberal economic policies and, 267–68, 603
Wounaan, 68, 73, 157

X

Xinka, 66, 144, 147, 157

Y

Yax Nuun Ayiin I, 90
Ydígoras, Miguel, 342
Yon Sosa, Marco Antonio, 342
Yucatan Peninsula, 89, 92–94

Z

Zapatista uprising (Chiapas, 1994), 157
Zelaya, José Santos
  authoritarian regime of, 571
  canal plans and, 572
  Catholic Church and, 409
  Indigenous populations and, 292
  land privatization and, 112
  Matagalpa uprising (1890s) and, 256
  Miskito Coast annexation and, 293, 572
  modernization efforts under, 571
  overthrow (1909) of, 257, 573
Zelaya, Manuel
  anti-gang law and, 368
  business leaders in Honduras and, 535
  coup (2009) against, 273, 299, 302, 322, 362, 392, 395, 520, 535
  economic policies of, 273
  Honduran military and, 392
  United States and, 519
Zemurray, Sam, 519, 523–24, 528